Psychosocial Treatments for
CHILD AND ADOLESCENT DISORDERS

*Empirically Based Strategies
for Clinical Practice*

SECOND EDITION

Edited by
EUTHYMIA D. HIBBS &
PETER S. JENSEN

AMERICAN PSYCHOLOGICAL ASSOCIATION • WASHINGTON, DC

RJ
504
.P75
2005

Copyright © 2005 by the American Psychological Association. All rights reserved. Except as permitted under the United States Copyright Act of 1976, no part of this publication may be reproduced or distributed in any form or by any means, or stored in a database or retrieval system, without the prior written permission of the publisher.

Chapters 1 and 29 were coauthored by an employee of the United States government as part of official duty and are considered to be in the public domain.

Published by
American Psychological Association
750 First Street, NE
Washington, DC 20002
www.apa.org

To order
APA Order Department
P.O. Box 92984
Washington, DC 20090-2984

Tel: (800) 374-2721; Direct: (202) 336-5510
Fax: (202) 336-5502; TDD/TTY: (202) 336-6123
Online: www.apa.org/books/
E-mail: order@apa.org

In the U.K., Europe, Africa, and the Middle East, copies may be ordered from
American Psychological Association
3 Henrietta Street
Covent Garden, London
WC2E 8LU England

Typeset in Goudy by Argosy, Newton, MA

Printer: United Book Press, Inc., Baltimore, MD
Cover Designer: Mercury Publishing Services, Rockville, MD
Project Manager: Argosy, Newton, MA

The opinions and statements published are the responsibility of the authors, and such opinions and statements do not necessarily represent the policies of the American Psychological Association. Any views expressed in chapter 1 do not necessarily represent the views of the United States government, and the author's participation in the work is not meant to serve as an official endorsement.

Library of Congress Cataloging-in-Publication Data

Psychosocial treatments for child and adolescent disorders : empirically based strategies for clinical practice / edited by Euthymia D. Hibbs and Peter S. Jensen.—2nd ed.
    p. cm.
Includes bibliographical references and index.
ISBN 1-59147-092-7
1. Child psychotherapy. 2. Adolescent psychotherapy. I. Hibbs, Euthymia D.
II. Jensen, Peter S.

RJ504.P75 2005
618.92'8914—dc22

2004014282

British Library Cataloguing-in-Publication Data

A CIP record is available from the British Library.

Printed in the United States of America
Second Edition

55679952

CONTENTS

CONTRIBUTORS

Howard B. Abikoff, PhD, Child Study Center, New York University Medical Center, New York

Fredrik Almqvist, MD, Department of Child Psychiatry, University of Helsinki, Helsinki, Finland

Dimitris Anastasopoulos, MD, Child Psychiatry, Athens, Greece

Arthur D. Anastopoulos, PhD, Department of Psychology, University of North Carolina, Greensboro

Melanie Ballatore, Department of Educational Psychology, University of Texas at Austin

Russell A. Barkley, PhD, Medical Center, University of Massachusetts, Worcester

Deborah C. Beidel, PhD, ABPP, Department of Psychology, University of Maryland, College Park

Guillermo Bernal, PhD, University Center for Psychological Services and Research, University of Puerto Rico, Rio Piedras

Christina Bostrom, MA, Department of Child Psychiatry, University of Helsinki, Helsinki, Finland

Lauren I. Brookman, MA, Autism Research and Training Center, University of California, Santa Barbara

Elsa Cardalda, PhD, Clinical Program, Carlos Albizu University, San Juan, Puerto Rico

Patricia Chamberlain, PhD, Oregon Social Learning Center, Eugene

Irene Chatoor, MD, Infant and Toddler Mental Health Center, Children's National Medical Center, Washington, DC

Muniya Choudhury, MA, Child and Adolescent Anxiety Disorders Clinic, Temple University, Philadelphia, PA

Gregory N. Clarke, PhD, Kaiser Permanente Center for Health Research, Portland, OR

Judith A. Cohen, MD, Center for Traumatic Stress in Children and Adolescents, Allegheny General Hospital, Pittsburgh, PA

Arin M. Connell, MA, Child and Family Center, University of Oregon, Eugene

Giuseppe Costantino, PhD, Sunset Park Mental Health Center, Brooklyn, NY

Esther Deblinger, PhD, College of Public Health and Health Professions, University of Florida, Gainesville

Kristen Pollack Dorta, PhD, College of Physicians and Surgeons, Columbia University, New York

Sheila M. Eyberg, PhD, Department of Psychology, University of Florida, Gainesville

Gregory A. Fabiano, MA, Department of Psychology, State University of New York at Buffalo

Edna Foa, PhD, Center for the Treatment and Study of Anxiety, University of Pennsylvania School of Medicine, Philadelphia

Frederick D. Frankel, PhD, Department of Psychiatry, University of California, Los Angeles

Martin Franklin, PhD, Center for the Treatment and Study of Anxiety, University of Pennsylvania, Philadelphia

Elizabeth M. Gnagy, Center for Children and Families, State University of New York at Buffalo

Howard Goldstein, PhD, Professor of Speech and Language Pathology, Florida State University, Tallahassee

Andrew R. Greiner, Western Psychiatric Institute and Clinic, University of Pittsburgh Medical Center, Pittsburgh, PA

Julie Griffin, Department of Educational Psychology, University of Texas at Austin

Jeana R. Griffith, PhD, Department of Psychiatry and Behavioral Sciences, Emory University School of Medicine, Atlanta, GA

Lily Hechtman, MD, FRCP, Division of Child Psychiatry, Montreal Children's Hospital, Montreal, Quebec, Canada

Euthymia D. Hibbs, PhD, private practice, Bethesda, MD

Stephen P. Hinshaw, PhD, Institute of Human Development, University of California, Berkeley

Julia Hoke, Department of Psychology, University of Texas at Austin

Hyman Hops, PhD, Oregon Learning Center, Oregon Research Institute, Eugene

Betsy Hoza, PhD, Department of Psychological Sciences, Purdue University, West Lafayette, IN

Jennifer L. Hudson, PhD, Child and Adolescent Anxiety Disorders Clinic, Temple University, Philadelphia, PA

Amanda L. Jensen, Department of Psychology, University of California, Los Angeles

Peter S. Jensen, MD, Center for the Advancement of Children's Mental Health, Columbia University, New York

Nadine J. Kaslow, PhD, Department of Psychiatry and Behavioral Sciences, Emory University School of Medicine, Atlanta, GA

Alan E. Kazdin, PhD, Child Study Center, Yale University School of Medicine, New Haven, CT

Philip C. Kendall, PhD, ABPP, Child and Adolescent Anxiety Disorders Clinic, Temple University, Philadelphia, PA

Lynn Kern Koegel, PhD, Autism Research and Training Center, University of California, Santa Barbara

Robert L. Koegel, PhD, Autism Research and Training Center, University of California, Santa Barbara

Frank W. Kohler, PhD, Department of Special Education, University of Northern Iowa, Cedar Falls

David J. Kolko, PhD, School of Medicine, University of Pittsburgh, Pittsburgh, PA

Israel Kolvin, MD, (deceased), Child and Family Department, Tavistock Center, London, England

William M. Kurtines, PhD, Child and Family Psychosocial Research Center, Florida International University, Miami

Peter M. Lewinsohn, PhD, Oregon Learning Center, Oregon Research Institute, Eugene

Robert G. Malgady, PhD, Program in Quantitative Studies, New York University, New York

Anthony P. Mannarino, PhD, Department of Psychiatry, Allegheny General Hospital, Pittsburgh, PA

John S. March, MD, MPH, Departments of Psychiatry and Psychology, Duke University Medical Center, Durham, NC

Erin B. McClure, PhD, Mood and Anxiety Disorders Program, National Institute of Mental Health, Bethesda, MD

Bryce D. McLeod, Department of Psychology, University of California, Los Angeles

Gillian Miles, SSW, Child and Family Department, Tavistock Clinic, London, England

Donna Moreau, MD, College of Physicians and Surgeons, Columbia University, New York

Laura Mufson, PhD, College of Physicians and Surgeons, Columbia University, New York

Renos Papadopoulos, PhD, Child and Family Department, Tavistock Clinic, London, England

William E. Pelham Jr., PhD, Center for Children and Families, State University of New York at Buffalo

Sandra Pimentel, Child and Adolescent Anxiety Disorders Clinic, Temple University, Philadelphia, PA

Jane G. Querido, Department of Psychiatry and Behavioral Sciences, University of Miami, Miami

Roxann Roberson-Nay, PhD, Department of Psychology, University of Maryland, College Park

Paul Rohde, PhD, Oregon Learning Center, Oregon Research Institute, Eugene

Jeannette Rosselló, PhD, Department of Psychology, University of Puerto Rico, Rio Piedras

Nancy Scammaca, Department of Educational Psychology, University of Texas at Austin

Laura Schreibman, PhD, Department of Psychology, University of California, San Diego, La Jolla, CA

John R. Seeley, MS, Oregon Learning Center, Oregon Research Institute, Eugene

Terri L. Shelton, PhD, Center for the Study of Social Issues, University of North Carolina, Greensboro

Wendy K. Silverman, PhD, Child and Family Psychosocial Research Center, Florida International University, Miami

Dana K. Smith, MS, Oregon Learning Center, Oregon Research Institute, Eugene

Mika Soininen, MD, Department of Child Psychiatry, University of Helsinki, Helsinki, Finland

Kevin D. Stark, PhD, Department of Educational Psychology, University of Texas at Austin

Phillip S. Strain, PhD, Department of Education and Psychology, University of Colorado, Denver

Vlassis Tomaras, MD, School of Medicine, Athens University, Athens, Greece

Judith Trowell, MD, DPM, FRC Psych, Child and Family Department, Tavistock Clinic, London, England

John Tsiantis, MD, DPM, FRC Psych, School of Medicine, University of Athens, Athens, Greece

Carmen Valdez, Department of Educational Psychology, University of Texas at Austin

Alicia Webb, Child and Adolescent Anxiety Disorders Clinic, Temple University, Philadelphia, PA

Carolyn Webster-Stratton, PhD, FAAN, Parenting Clinic, University of Washington, Seattle

Myrna M. Weissman, PhD, College of Physicians and Surgeons, Columbia University, New York

John R. Weisz, PhD, Department of Psychology, University of California, Los Angeles

Marla Zucker, PhD, The Trauma Center, Allston, MA

I

INTRODUCTION

1

ANALYZING THE RESEARCH: WHAT THIS BOOK IS ABOUT

EUTHYMIA D. HIBBS AND PETER S. JENSEN

The majority of youth who experience mental disorders and seek help receive some form of psychosocial intervention. About 4 million children and adolescents (5%) in the United States experience various types of mental illnesses that cause serious problems at home, at school, and with peers. Helping youth to overcome such difficulties early in life offers the possibility of alleviating their suffering, promoting healthy development, encouraging them to reach their full potential in life, reducing stress and conflict in their families, and as a consequence, diminishing the nation's overall health care costs.

This chapter was coauthored by an employee of the United States government as part of official duty and is considered to be in the public domain. Any views expressed herein do not necessarily represent the views of the United States government, and the author's participation in the work is not meant to serve as an official endorsement.

We wish to thank our contributors for their willingness to share their work with colleagues and for surviving the editors' push for meeting the deadlines. We want to thank the National Institute of Mental Health for encouraging and supporting our endeavor. And lastly, we gratefully acknowledge the support and love of our families, which allow us to spend some evenings and weekends on such worthy pursuits.

Since the first volume of this book was published in 1996, psychosocial treatments for children and adolescents have received great attention. This topic has been on the political agenda during the year 2000 elections, was considered at a White House meeting in March of the same year, was further reviewed by a Surgeon General's Listening Session, and then considered at a large-scale Surgeon's General's Conference on Children's Mental Health. The latter provided several recommendations to improve the identification and care of youth (Weisz, 2000).

The issue that still remains in debate is which treatments are proven to be efficacious with which disorders. The *Journal of Clinical Child Psychology* (1998) devoted a volume on the topic of empirically validated treatments as reviewed by the American Psychological Association (APA) Child Task Force. The overall review indicated that although not all treatments were empirically supported because of the strict criteria used, there was in fact good empirical support for the efficacy of both cognitive–behavioral therapy (CBT) and behavioral therapy (BT) techniques in eliminating core aspects of children's psychopathologic symptoms. For example, good evidence now exists that CBT is an effective treatment for adolescent depression, anxiety disorders, various phobias, and other anxiety spectrum disorders. Parent training and problem-solving skills for youth and their families are appearing useful for the treatment of externalizing disorders. Evidence also shows that videotape modeling and parent training are effective modalities for the treatment of very young children with oppositional defiant disorders. Behavior training and behavioral interventions in the classroom are also well-established treatments for attention deficit hyperactivity disorders.

In spite of this rather extensive knowledge, hundreds of treatments continue to be used on children without scientific verification of their efficacy. One example is that of psychodynamic treatments (including play therapy), which are still used extensively. Clinicians using this modality undergo rigorous training, but no rigorous scientific studies attest to its efficacy, other than various case reports. To address such gaps, the authors wholeheartedly encourage scientists to engage in new research programs that will develop the appropriate methodologies to examine such commonly practiced treatment modalities.

OBJECTIVES OF THIS VOLUME

This volume was written for several audiences: practitioners, treatment researchers, professors and students, health care administrators, and others who make decisions about treatment services provided to the nation's youth. Thus, a key objective of this volume is to address the troublesome issue of the lack of communication that has been occurring between clinical investigators in the child and adolescent treatment field and the practitioners who are the front line of service for most children and adolescents.

As was the case in the previous volume, it continues to be the authors' view that these two fields remain largely separate. Clinicians continue to see efficacy researchers as focusing only on highly specific disorders, unlike the comorbid conditions seen in day-to-day practice. They wonder how findings from treatment studies of pure disorders conducted in university settings relate to their clinic settings, which serve multiproblem children and families weighed down with comorbid conditions aggravated by economic survival issues, family violence, parental psychopathology, and poor neighborhoods and school environments. In their view, jargon-filled journal articles focusing on design questions and multivariate statistical methods seem to have too little to offer clinicians in the scant time that is left for their professional development at the end of the work day.

Efficacy researchers continue to be rightfully concerned with verifying basic facts about treatment efficacy. Understandably, they focus tightly on research methods, starting with simpler cases first and attempting to have enough participants to secure the statistical power needed to test for clinically meaningful results. In fairness, this is not because they do not understand the complexity of problems presented in community settings but because they are testing new hypotheses, methodologies, and measurements. Nonetheless, the need is now more urgent than ever to understand what types of treatments are most appropriate for which conditions; which psychosocial treatments are effective; how developmental, family, school, and contextual factors influence treatment outcomes; and which effective treatments actually work in the real world. Moreover, if efficacy studies are to prove useful, there is a great need to disseminate existing research findings from the field of psychosocial treatments to real-world clinical health care providers and to academic institutions devoted to the training of future professionals.

We suggest that there has never been a time when these two groups of professionals—efficacy researchers and real-world clinicians—were so dependent on one another for survival. We are somewhat heartened that in the last 5 years, a significant increase in efforts includes, within the research designs, real-world variables such as complex social environments and comorbid conditions. Based on the solid foundation of results from existing efficacy studies, effectiveness studies are in fact beginning to come into their own, and their results may eventually be more helpful to practitioners in translating interventions into day-to-day practice contexts.

In reporting their research, chapter authors in this book have tried to bridge the gap between researchers and practitioners by (a) describing their treatment strategies more fully than usually occurs in journal articles on treatment research, (b) presenting these treatments in their environmental contexts, and (c) making available source information on the manuals, and (d) including more real-world variables.

Psychosocial treatment investigators, practitioners, and graduate students aspiring to work with children must all be aware that conducting psychosocial treatment research with children and adolescents requires making choices among methodologies that may be more complicated than those used in research with the adult populations. For example, the research reported in this volume indicates that the child and adolescent treatment researcher must choose which comorbid conditions to include in the treatment protocol, whom to exclude, and why. They must consider the level of the child's developmental abilities. They must consider the implications of their choices on the generalizability of results, the applicability of the interventions for community populations, and whether the same treatment methods could be applied to a wider range of ages. For example, would CBT be appropriate for a 6-year-old, or would parent training only be more effective? To what extent, if any, should parents be involved in the treatment? Should parents of adolescents be as involved as parents of prepubertal children? Should future methodologies attempt treatment of parents as one component of a holistic approach to the treatment of children, given that it is now widely accepted that psychopathology often has a genetic basis? All the above-mentioned methodologic issues may be scientifically important but may also restrict the generalizability of the treatment and treatment results.

How can treatment research address the mosaic of diverse ethnic and cultural backgrounds of the United States? Recruitment strategies for studies may have to be adjusted to take into account cultural norms about seeking and accepting treatment. Unfortunately, very little research has been done thus far to understand how individuals from various cultures experience psychopathology, much less how investigators should measure and treat mental illness across various cultural groups. The need for culturally sensitive psychosocial treatment research, tailored to address specific groups, looms very large indeed. How can innovative treatments and research designs be developed to address these thorny issues? To address this issue in part, this volume presents a sample of treatments tailored for Hispanic and African American populations that might serve as a catalyst for the development of other culturally sensitive treatment approaches.

Dissemination of research findings is even more critical at this juncture in health care system reform, because questions concerning the utility, validity, intensity, and especially the length of psychosocial treatments are common. Therefore, additional research is urgently needed to examine the utility of these treatments and to inform clinicians, educators, other investigators, policy makers, and insurance companies of the benefits, limitations, and transferability of psychosocial treatments.

Our final audience includes health care administrators (e.g., in health maintenance organizations [HMOs], hospital and community clinics, and health insurance companies) who make decisions about which services are offered, for whom, and for how long. For example, we know that most childhood mental disorders recur throughout life and that most so-called adult disorders have their roots in childhood. Thus, one aim of psychosocial treatment research is to provide answers to cost-benefit questions that grow more pressing as funds available for health care continue to decline. For example, most of the treatments documented in this book show significant efficacy after 12 to 20 sessions delivered in consecutive weeks. However, some managed care guidelines for certain disorders allow only 8 to 10 sessions for treatment, and providers are often advised to budget these sessions so that youth are seen over a longer period. Is this really the wisest and most fiscally sound way to proceed? If a treatment has been shown to work under certain conditions, it may in fact be highly wasteful over the long run to deliver it in a different manner. Yet research on such questions has just begun. Investigations such as those reported in this volume must be followed up to see how much effectiveness is or is not compromised when treatments are altered. Health care administrators who want to make the most intelligent managed care decisions, based in part on the most effective dose and duration of treatment of children, adolescents, and families struggling with specific psychological disorders, need to follow the treatment research field carefully. This book may serve this purpose.

ORGANIZATION OF THIS VOLUME

First, some changes from the first volume should be highlighted. Several chapters were replaced either because the authors did not have any recent results to report or because new, state-of-the-art, ongoing research needed to be included.

Alan E. Kazdin's introductory chapter, "Developing Effective Treatments for Children and Adolescents," was replaced with a chapter by John R. Weisz et al., "Development and Dissemination of Child and Adolescent Psychotherapies: Milestones, Methods, and a New Deployment-Focused Model." In Part II, the chapter by Anne Marie Albano and David H. Barlow, "Cognitive Behavioral Group Treatment for Socially Anxious Youth," was replaced with a chapter by Deborah C. Beidel and Roxann Roberson-Nay, "Treating Childhood Social Phobia: Social Effectiveness Therapy for Children." In Part III, the chapter by David Brent et al., "Psychosocial Interventions for Treating Adolescent Suicidal Depression," was replaced with a chapter by Erin B. McLure et al., "The Adolescent Depression Empowerment Project (ADEPT): A Culturally Sensitive Family Treatment for Depressed African American Girls." The chapter by Arthur Robin et al., "Therapy for Anorexia Nervosa," was replaced with Irene Chatoor's "Evaluation and Treatment of Infantile Anorexia." Peter Fonagy and Mary Target's chapter, "A Contemporary Psychoanalytical Perspective," was replaced with a chapter by John Tsiantis et al., "Psychotherapy for Early Adolescent Depression: A Comparison of Two

Psychotherapeutic Interventions in Three European Countries." In Part V, the chapter by Samuel Vuchini et al., "Coalitions and Family Problem Solving in Psychosocial Treatment of Preadolescents," was replaced with a chapter by Jane G. Querido and Sheila M. Eyberg, "Parent–Child Interaction Therapy: Maintaining Treatment Gains of Preschoolers With Disruptive Behavior Disorders." In Part VII, William Kurtines and Jose Szapocznik's chapter was replaced with a chapter by Judith A. Cohen et al., "Trauma-Focused Cognitive–Behavioral Therapy for Sexually Abused Children."

Chapter 2 focuses on treatment development, testing processes, and outcome evidence. It provides a review and commentary on traditional treatment research approaches, followed by a critique of the model and a proposal for an alternative model. The remainder of the book is arranged into six parts: Each of the first five parts represents a major disorder commonly seen in practice with children and adolescents: anxiety disorders, affective disorders, attention deficit hyperactivity disorder, conduct disorders, and autism. Part VI describes treatments that are not specific to a particular disorder.

In each chapter, the authors describe the nature and characteristics of the disorder, their program of research, their research intervention strategies, the manual used, and their results. The research strategies include such issues as definition of target populations, sampling procedures, assessment instruments, follow-up methods, and other salient methodological issues. Descriptions of interventions include theory, technique, timing, and order of interventions, and, depending on the particular chapter, session outlines, case examples, session dialogue, checklists, and other information of particular interest to the therapists who want to integrate into their practices all or part of the treatment described. Many of the chapters contain additional sources of information for treatment manuals, assessment instruments, and the like. Updated outcome data, some more preliminary than others, are provided by most authors. In each chapter the authors discuss the limitations, issues of generalizability, and future directions of research and practice in their area of expertise.

In closing, the goals for this edition are to disseminate the emerging findings on child and adolescent treatment research to investigators and practitioners alike, to demystify the research milieu, to generate increased linkages among specialists working in different areas of the field, and to kindle the motivation of students who would consider venturing into the new world of psychosocial treatment research and empirically based practice for child and adolescent disorders. We invite you to join us.

REFERENCE

Weisz, J. R. (2000). Lab-clinic differences and what we can do about them: III. National policy matters. *Clinical Child Psychology Newsletter, 15*(3), 1.

2

DEVELOPMENT AND DISSEMINATION OF CHILD AND ADOLESCENT PSYCHOTHERAPIES: MILESTONES, METHODS, AND A NEW DEPLOYMENT-FOCUSED MODEL

JOHN R. WEISZ, AMANDA L. JENSEN, AND BRYCE D. MCLEOD

How well are we doing, as a field, in generating youth treatments that work and in getting those treatments to the youngsters who need them? In this chapter, we address this two-part question and present a model for treatment development and testing that is closely linked to the question.

The work reported here was facilitated by support to the authors through a grant from the John D. and Catherine T. MacArthur Foundation ("Research Network on Youth Mental Health Care"), National Institute of Mental Health (NIMH) Research Grants (R01 MH49522 and R01 MH57347), a NIMH Senior Research Scientist Award (K05 MH01161), and two NIMH National Research Service Awards (F31 MH64993 to Bryce McLeod and F31 MH72901 to Amanda Jensen). We thank members of the Research Network and visiting consultants to the Network for thoughtful discussions that contributed to ideas presented in this chapter.

OVERALL MAGNITUDE OF TREATMENT IMPACT: FINDINGS OF META-ANALYSES

One way to gauge our success in generating beneficial treatments is to carry out meta-analyses, syntheses of the evidence, with multiple studies pooled to generate an overall picture of average treatment impact. The hard currency of meta-analysis is the effect size (ES; for group comparison studies, ES = [$M_{\text{treatment group}} - M_{\text{control group}}$]/$SD_{\text{outcome measure}}$), an index of the size and direction of treatment effects. As an aid to interpretation, many in the field follow Cohen's (1988) guidelines suggesting that an ES of 0.20 may be considered a "small" effect, 0.50 a "medium" effect, and 0.80 a "large" effect. By averaging across the various outcome measures used, meta-analysts can compute a mean ES for each study, or each treatment-control comparison, and in turn an overall mean ES for an entire collection of studies (Mann, 1990). Mean ES may also be compared across groups of studies that differ in potentially important ways—for example, in the types of therapy used or the ages of the youngsters treated.

To date, there have been four broad-based youth psychotherapy meta-analyses (i.e., meta-analyses in which few limits were imposed on the kinds of treated problems or types of intervention to be included). In the first of these, Casey and Berman (1985) surveyed outcome studies published between 1952 and 1983 involving children 12 years of age and younger. Mean ES was 0.71 for the studies that included treatment-control comparisons; in percentile terms, the average treated child was doing better after treatment than 76% of the children in the control group, averaging across outcome measures. In a second meta-analysis, Weisz, Weiss, Alicke, and Klotz (1987) included outcome studies published between 1952 and 1983, with ages 4 through 18. Mean ES was 0.79; after treatment, the average treated child was better off than 79% of control group peers. In a third meta-analysis, Kazdin, Bass, Ayers, and Rodgers (1990) included studies published between 1970 and 1988, with ages 4 through 18. For studies comparing treatment groups with no-treatment control groups, mean ES was 0.88, with the average treated child better after treatment than 81% of the no-treatment comparison group. For the subset of studies comparing treatment groups with active control groups, mean ES was 0.77, with the average treated child functioning better after treatment than 78% of the control group. In the fourth meta-analysis, Weisz, Weiss, Han, Granger, and Morton (1995) included studies published between 1967 and 1993, with subjects ranging in age from 2 through 18; mean ES was 0.71; after treatment, the average treated child was functioning better than 76% of the control group. These four meta-analyses, shown in Figure 2.1, indicate consistently beneficial treatment effects. ES values ranged from 0.71 to 0.84 (estimated overall mean for Kazdin et al., 1990), with an average just below Cohen's (1988) threshold for a "large" effect and (as shown in Figure 2.1) within the

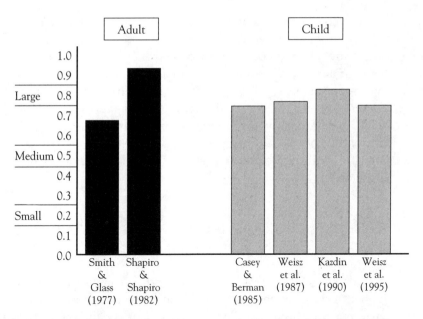

Figure 2.1. Mean effect sizes found in meta-analyses of psychotherapy outcome studies in the predominantly adult meta-analysis by Smith and Glass (1977), in the exclusively adult meta-analysis by Shapiro and Shapiro (1982), and in four broad-based meta-analyses of psychotherapy outcome studies with children and adolescents. From "Bridging the Gap Between Laboratory and Clinic in Child and Adolescent Psychotherapy," by J. R. Weisz, G. R. Donenberg, S. S. Han, and B. Weiss, 1995, *Journal of Consulting and Clinical Psychology, 63,* pp. 688–701. Copyright 1995 by the American Psychological Association.

range of what has been found in two widely cited meta-analyses with older groups—Smith and Glass's (1977) analysis of mostly adult outcome studies and Shapiro and Shapiro's (1982) analysis of exclusively adult outcome studies. Note, though, that (a) analyses in Weisz et al. (1995) suggest that, with weighting to adjust for sample size and heterogeneity of variance, ES means may be closer to "medium" effects than to "large" effects; and (b) findings by McLeod and Weisz (2004) support the notion that publication bias may have inflated our picture of the mean impact of treatment.

Two other meta-analytical findings warrant attention here. First, we have found (in Weisz et al., 1987, 1995) that effects measured immediately after treatment are quite similar to effects measured at follow-up assessments (which on average take place 5 to 6 months after treatment termination), suggesting that benefit is fairly durable. Second, we have found (Weisz et al., 1995) evidence for the "specificity" of treatment effects. Frank (1973) and others have proposed that psychotherapy has general, "nonspecific" effects on diverse problems—for example, by making people feel understood. An alternative view is that therapies help in specific, focused ways, doing the most good with the specific problems they are designed to address. We have found evidence for the latter view; our analyses (in Weisz et al., 1995) showed effect sizes about twice as large for the specific problem domains targeted by a treatment than for other, more incidental domains (e.g., anxiety treatments produced bigger effects on anxiety than on depression). Encouraging findings have also come from diverse other meta-analyses (discussed in Weisz, 2004) focused only on specific types of therapies (e.g., cognitive–behavioral), individual therapeutic techniques (e.g., self-statement modification), types of problems (e.g., impulsivity), and types of disorders (e.g., depression).

IDENTIFYING SPECIFIC EVIDENCE-BASED TREATMENTS: TASK FORCE FINDINGS

Meta-analyses can characterize mean treatment impact across groups of studies, but they do not ordinarily tell us much about the individual treatments that generate the mean effects. Therefore, a useful complement to meta-analysis is focused evidence review designed to identify specific beneficial treatments. Various mental health disciplines have taken differing approaches. The American Psychiatric Association (APA; 1995), for example, has developed practice guidelines constructed partly from evidence on treatment outcome. Groups within the APA (e.g., Chambless et al., 1998; Task Force, 1995) have approached the topic by focusing exclusively on the outcome evidence to identify specific empirically supported psychotherapies—treatments we refer to here as *evidence-based treatments* (EBTs). The most widely used set of criteria for these EBTs was originally developed by a Task Force within Division 12 (Society of Clinical Psychology) of the APA (see Task Force, 1995) to classify treatments as either *well-established* or *probably efficacious*. Treatments in both categories are empirically supported, but the *well-established treatments* were judged to have stronger support than the *probably efficacious* treatments on such criteria as number and quality of studies and independent replication of effects. Using the Task Force criteria, a child specialist task force (Lonigan et al., 1998) sought to identify *well-established* and *probably efficacious* treatments for childhood autism, depression, fears and anxiety, attention-deficit/hyperactivity disorder (ADHD), and conduct problems–conduct disorder.

Autism and Internalizing Conditions

Rogers (1998), in her task force report on autism, concluded that "the field does not yet have a treatment that meets the present criteria for well-established or probably efficacious treatment" (p. 168). Kaslow and Thompson (1998), in their task force review of depression studies, found that no treatment qualified as well-established but that specific cognitive–behavioral treatments for children and adolescents were probably efficacious. In their task force review on treatments for youth anxiety, Ollendick and King (1998) identified several empirically supported interventions. Two probably efficacious treatments, *imaginal desensitization* and *in vivo desensitization*, were variants of systematic desensitization therapy. Both *live modeling* and *filmed modeling* were also rated probably efficacious, as were *cognitive–behavioral therapies for fears* and for full anxiety disorders. Two anxiety treatments qualified as well established: *participant modeling* (model and treated child engage in the feared activities together) and an operant procedure called *reinforced practice* (rewarding or praising progressive, voluntary exposure to feared objects or situations—sometimes called *exposure*).

Attention-Deficit/Hyperactivity Disorder

The task force review by Pelham, Wheeler, and Chronis (1998) identified two broad classes of intervention for ADHD as well-established: *behavioral parent training* and *behavioral classroom intervention*. Although such interventions can be beneficial, their acute effects tend to be more modest than effects of stimulant medication such as methylphenidate (MTA Cooperative Group, 1999; Pelham et al., 1998). Because 10% to 30% of youngsters with ADHD do not respond well to stimulants (Swanson, McBurnett, Christian, & Wigal, 1995) and because some parents object to drug treatment of children, task force efforts to identify effective psychosocial approaches are valuable.

Conduct Problems and Conduct Disorder

Brestan and Eyberg (1998), applying the Task Force criteria to 82 studies of psychosocial treatments for conduct problems, identified two treatments as well established and 10 as probably efficacious. The well-established category included (a) a family of treatments involving *behavioral parent training*, all based at least partly on Patterson and Gullion's 1968 book, *Living with Children*; and (b) a *video-guided behavioral parent-training* program, developed by Webster-Stratton (e.g., 1984). The probably efficacious treatments included (a) two programs that teach youngsters *anger management*; (b) two programs that teach parents behavioral skills for addressing conduct problems in young children; (c) one program that teaches children to solve interpersonal problems instead of resorting to aggression; (d) a program designed to prevent delinquency by combining behavioral parent training with exposure of at-risk kindergarteners to prosocial peer models; (e) programs involving assertiveness training and *rational emotive therapy*; (f) improved methods of monitoring time out; and (g) *multisystemic therapy*, in which therapists intervene in multiple social systems (e.g., family, school, peer group) to address serious delinquent behavior.

THE EVIDENCE BASE ON YOUTH TREATMENT:
STRENGTHS AND GAPS

Although the evidence base on youth treatments offers much to appreciate, some gaps remain. On the plus side, meta-analytic reviews point to mean
effects of tested treatments that (a) fall within the "medium-"to"-large" range
(as per Cohen, 1988); (b) are relatively specific to the problems and disorders
targeted in treatment, not just general improvements in overall adjustment;
and (c) show substantial holding power, at least over the 5- to 6-month period
characteristic of most follow-up assessments. Task force reviews by child specialist teams (Brestan & Eyberg, 1998; Kaslow & Thompson, 1998; Ollendick
& King, 1998; Pelham et al., 1998) have identified 27 specific treatments as
either "well-established" or "probably efficacious." Because some problems and
disorders have not yet been addressed by task force review and because new
evidence has accumulated since the review was published in 1998, additional
treatments that would meet task force criteria are now likely to exist.

Another strength is the creative array of treatment delivery models
used. The traditional weekly-office-visit model still predominates in the
research base, but investigators have pushed the boundaries, with tests of
more intensive approaches geared to school breaks and summer camp programs (e.g., see chap. 16, this volume), treatments in which core skills
training is embedded in videotaped vignettes (see chap. 20, this volume),
interventions providing behavioral training and support for foster parents
(see chap. 21, this volume), treatment supplements in the form of postt.her-
apy booster sessions (see chap. 10, this volume), and a peripatetic model in
which therapists navigate the youth's environment (see Henggeler, Schoenwald, Borduin, Rowland, & Cunningham, 1998). Researchers in the field
are increasingly concerned not only about what to do in treatment but also
about how best to package and deliver interventions.

Gap 1: Limits in Coverage of Problems and Disorders

On the downside, some limitations in the evidence base warrant attention. First, there are significant gaps in coverage of youth problems. As one
example, eating disorders pose sinister risks: The annual mortality rate in 15-
to 24-year-old female individuals diagnosed with anorexia is more than 12
times the rate for this age × gender group from all other causes (Sullivan,
1995). Yet treatment testing has moved slowly, with only a few investigators
focusing on anorexia or bulimia in youth (e.g., Robin, Bedway, Siegel, & Gilroy, 1996). In addition, with few exceptions (e.g., Azrin, Donohue, Besalel,
Kogan, & Acierno, 1994), potent treatments for substance-abusing youth are
rare, particularly for users of harder drugs such as cocaine. Also with few exceptions (e.g., Borduin, Henggeler, Blaske, & Stein, 1990), the literature lacks
successes in the treatment of youthful sex offenders. Moreover, despite

attempts by several research teams, the field still lacks interventions for suicidal youth that clearly reduce the risk of further attempts (see Miller & Glinski, 2000; Weisz & Hawley, 2002). Finally, most of the psychosocial treatment success with ADHD has been with preadolescents, and some of the behavioral treatments that work within that age range may not travel so well up the developmental ramp into adolescence. Indeed, a major figure in ADHD research who has authored a widely used behavioral program for parents argues that adolescents should not be considered candidates for the program, that they often do not respond well, and that their reaction may exacerbate family conflict (Barkley, 1997). The limited success of psychosocial treatments among teens with ADHD could make stimulant medication the EBT of choice for this age group by default (Weisz & Jensen, 1999). To put the coverage issue more starkly, at least 150 disorders in the fourth edition of the *Diagnostic and Statistical Manual of Mental Disorders* (*DSM–IV*; American Psychiatric Association, 1994) can be applied to children and adolescents, as well as many more problems of living (not diagnoses) for which youngsters need help; our list of EBTs to date encompasses only a modest percentage of these.

Gap 2: Limited Attention to Covariation and Comorbidity

The problem of limited coverage is even more pronounced if we consider covariation and comorbidity. Some treatment research relevant to children and teens has focused on relatively homogeneous problem clusters or diagnoses, with youths who have comorbidities that might undermine treatment success often excluded from study samples. Extensive evidence (e.g., Angold, Costello, & Erkanli, 1999) shows that co-occurrence of disorders and problems is quite characteristic of the youngsters seen in everyday clinical care. Rates of comorbidity, striking even in community samples, are markedly higher in clinical samples (Angold et al., 1999). We need to understand the extent to which comorbidities of various kinds moderate the effects of treatments. Indeed, more than a decade ago, Kendall and Clarkin (1992) referred to comorbidity as the "premier challenge facing mental health professionals in the 1990s" (p. 833). The 1990s have now come and gone, and the challenge remains largely unaddressed by youth treatment researchers.

Gap 3: Limited Range of Treatment Models Examined

Meta-analyses that encompass both children and adolescents (Kazdin et al., 1990; Weisz et al., 1987, 1995) have found a heavy emphasis on tests of behavioral and cognitive–behavioral treatments, with nonbehavioral approaches (e.g., psychodynamic, client-centered, psychoanalytic, existential–humanistic) constituting 18% to 26% of the studies sampled. Yet these nonbehavioral approaches are actually much more representative of the treatment models used in everyday clinical practice. Thus, it seems appropriate for researchers to broaden the array of models tested, working to include more of the approaches service providers use and trust. Failure to expand in this way may deepen practitioners' concern that treatment research lacks relevance to their work (e.g., see Cohen, Sargent, & Sechrest, 1986; Havik & VandenBos, 1996; Morrow-Bradley & Elliott, 1986).

Gap 4: Omnibus Treatments With Limited Evidence on Necessary and Sufficient Components

A fourth concern is that many of our treatments are omnibus in style— comprising a variety of intervention procedures but without a clear picture of which procedures really matter. Despite a long tradition of "dismantling" research, we have only begun the process of identifying the specific components of our multisession, multiconcept, multiskill treatments that are actually necessary for good outcomes. The comprehensive multicomponent nature of so many manualized treatments makes them rather lengthy and often a poor fit to the current emphasis in real-world clinical care on session limits and maximal efficiency. Some of the treatments almost certainly contain excess baggage (i.e., elements that do not actually contribute much to the outcomes achieved). Making treatment programs leaner and more efficient could enhance their attractiveness to practitioners, render the procedures more teachable, increase treatment viability in the marketplace of clinical care, and thus perhaps reach more of the children who need their benefits.

Gap 5: Limited Understanding of the Effective Range or Moderators of Outcome

For each treatment in the armamentarium, we need to understand the range of clinical and demographic characteristics within which the treatments produce benefit and outside of which benefit diminishes. Even the best-supported EBTs are good for some conditions but not others, with benefit potentially constrained by comorbid conditions, age, socioeconomic status (SES), ethnicity, family configuration, or other clinical and demographic factors. With relatively few exceptions (e.g., Brent et al., 1998; Kazdin & Crowley, 1997), research to date has left us rather poorly informed about such constraints. Racial, ethnic, and cultural factors, for example, are embedded but unexamined in most of our treatment outcome research (Weisz, Huey, & Weersing, 1998), and this makes it difficult to know how robust most treatment effects are across various population groups. At this early stage in youth treatment development research, it is understandable that most tested treatments have not been designed to take into account broad variations in language, values, customs, child-rearing traditions, beliefs and expectancies about child and parent behavior, and distinctive stressors and resources associated with different cultural traditions. But many would agree that the interplay between such factors and treatment characteristics may influence the relationships between child, family, and therapist; the likelihood of treatment completion; and the outcome of the treatment process (Weisz et al., 1998). Understanding this interplay and its impact can enrich efforts to produce treatments that can be applied across a broad spectrum of individuals and groups.

Gap 6: Limited Understanding of Change Processes That Mediate Treatment Outcome

Sustained attention to the change processes that actually account for observed outcomes in treatment is also necessary. At present, we know much more about what outcomes our treatments produce than about what actually causes the outcomes (Kazdin, 2000a; Shirk & Russell, 1996). If we fail to identify core causal processes, we risk a proliferation of treatments administered only because studies show they work, with little understanding of the change processes therapists must actually set in motion to produce results. To understand how the treatments work, we need a generation of research testing hypothesized mediators of outcome. Mediation testing procedures have been amply described (Baron & Kenney, 1986; Holmbeck, 1997; Judd & Kenney, 1981), and a few treatment researchers have applied the procedures to good effect. Huey, Henggeler, Brondino, and Pickrel (2000), for example, found that decreased affiliation with delinquent peers mediated reductions in delinquent behavior in youths treated with multisystemic therapy. Eddy and Chamberlain (2000) found that improved family management skills and reduced deviant peer associations mediated the effects of their behaviorally oriented foster-care treatment program on adolescent antisocial behavior. Other investigators have probed change processes associated with other treatments (see Weersing & Weisz, 2002), though not always with complete mediation test methods. We need more studies in which proposed mediators are identified a priori, measured repeatedly, and tested with care (see Kazdin, 2000a, 2000b). Failure to rigorously test for mediation leaves an information vacuum that may be filled by faulty assumptions about the nature and causes of treatment benefit. Increased understanding of the actual processes underlying therapeutic improvement will improve prospects for (a) understanding and addressing impediments, stalls, and failures in treatment; (b) training therapists by teaching them what change processes they need to effect rather than simply what techniques to use; and (c) identifying crosscutting principles that can be used in designing, refining, and perhaps combining interventions.

Gap 7: Limited Attention to Therapeutic Relationship and Alliance Building

The current array of EBTs is strong in describing principles and procedures to apply in treatment but weak in helping therapists build a warm, empathic relationship and a strong working alliance with children and families. This gap is striking in light of the widespread belief that the quality of the therapeutic relationship or alliance is important to success in most treatment encounters. Indeed, many child therapists rate the therapeutic relationship as more important than the specific techniques used in treatment (Kazdin et al., 1990; Motta & Lynch, 1990; Shirk & Saiz, 1992), and some treated children may agree, even those treated by EBTs. Kendall and Southam-Gerow (1996), for example, found that children treated for anxiety disorders using the Coping Cat program rated their relationship with the therapist as the most important aspect of treatment. What we lack thus far is a strong body of evidence that (a) clearly defines a positive therapeutic relationship, (b) establishes how best to measure it, (c) identifies therapist characteristics and behaviors that foster it, and (d) tests the extent to which it actually predicts outcome when EBTs are used.

Gap 8: Lack of Evidence on Evidence-Based Treatments in Real-World Practice Contexts

In the treatment literature, both psychotherapeutic and medical, a distinction is drawn between two very different forms of outcome research. In efficacy designs, experimental control is used to test treatment impact under carefully arranged idealized conditions (e.g., with just the right kind of clients selected; with potentially troubling comorbidities excluded; with treatment done by the best possible therapists, who were selected and paid by the researcher and trained to deliver the target treatment as perfectly as possible; and with arrangements designed to keep therapists functioning at their best and treated clients engaged). In effectiveness designs, intervention effects are assessed under ordinary clinical conditions, with treatment delivered to "average" or representative patients or clients, by "average" or representative practitioners working under conditions that reflect typical practice realities (e.g., large caseloads, clinic productivity pressures). Given the nature of the data collected up to this point, researchers know a good deal about the efficacy of EBTs but relatively little is known about their effectiveness. This is a problem in its own right, but it also contributes to a number of other problems, including the limited dissemination our EBTs have enjoyed to date. We will return to this issue in a later section.

Gap 9: Heavy Reliance on a Biologically Derived Model of Treatment Development and Testing

The dearth of effectiveness testing may reflect a more general limitation in the field: We have relied heavily on a model of intervention development and testing that may not be ideally suited to the realities of treatment in a psychosocial context. This possibility is examined later.

Looking to the Future

The gaps identified here may help us lay out an itinerary for the journey from present to future in evidence-based care. Exhibit 2.1 summarizes some tasks for future research suggested by the list of gaps. These include diversifying coverage to encompass problems and disorders for which research and EBTs are scarce, extending treatment research beyond its current emphasis on single problems and single disorders, broadening the range of treatment models tested, expanding the "dismantling" research agenda, intensifying research on moderators and mediators of outcome, expanding our understanding of the therapeutic relationship and its impact, complementing our large efficacy research base with evidence on effectiveness in typical practice conditions, and considering an alternative to the biologically derived model that now drives, but may not be very well suited to, much of the treatment development and testing in our field. When we return to this topic, we will consider a specific alternative model in some detail.

CLINICALLY DERIVED TREATMENTS IN PRACTICE SETTINGS: WHAT WE KNOW

Although the EBTs we have discussed thus far are important in many ways, they reflect only a very modest component of mental health care for

EXHIBIT 2.1
Steps Toward Strengthening Research on Child and Adolescent Psychotherapy

Diversify coverage to encompass understudied problems and disorders (e.g., substance use, sex offending, suicidality)

Extend focus of research beyond single-problem and single-disorder youth to include treatments for youth with co-occurring problems and comorbid disorders

Broaden range of treatment models tested, emphasizing nonbehavioral approaches thus far unstudied or understudied

Expand "dismantling research" to identify necessary and sufficient elements, enhance treatment efficiency, and strengthen competitiveness of EBTs in the real-world marketplace

Intensify research on moderators of outcome (e.g., comorbid conditions, age, SES, race and ethnicity, family configuration) to define the effective range of treatments

Strengthen research on mediators of outcome to identify the change process (e.g., improved parenting skills, altered cognitions) that explain how treatments work

Expand understanding of the therapeutic relationship—how best to measure it, what characteristics and behaviors of the therapist foster it, and what elements of it predict outcome of EBTs

Generate evidence on effectiveness of EBTs with referred youth treated by representative practitioners under typical clinical practice conditions

Re-examine the prevailing model of treatment development and testing; consider alternatives to a biologically derived approach children and adolescents—modest in the number of settings in which the EBTs are practiced and modest in the number of young lives actually touched by the treatments. Of the millions of children treated in service settings each year, the vast majority receive treatments that have never been tested in any outcome study. Of the more than 550 named treatments used with children and adolescents (see Kazdin, 2000b), only a tiny proportion have been tested in any research. Moreover, although each named treatment has adherents, most youth clinical practice involves not strict adherence to one named treatment but rather an eclectic mixture of goals and methods that therapists have fashioned from their own previous training, supervision, and clinical experience. We will call this array of approaches *clinically derived treatment*.

Frequently, clinically derived treatment includes the following elements: (a) talking or playing with the child and talking with the parent; (b) establishing a warm, accepting relationship in which the child is encouraged to express thoughts and feelings; (c) listening reflectively and being empathic; (d) responding to the issues the child brings to each session, rather than imposing an agenda; and (e) flexibly applying an eclectic mix of techniques and procedures. Of course, any list of content and procedural examples will miss what many therapists do in their practice because the range is potentially infinite. But a common denominator of all clinically derived treatments is that they are fashioned by individual therapists based on their clinical training, supervision, and experience, not primarily on research.

The general clinically derived treatment approach and the five illustrative features noted here have considerable intuitive appeal. Indeed, they are quite close to what many of us were taught to do during graduate training and internships, and some of the features may contribute in important ways to a strong working alliance with children and parents. But a key question is whether clinically derived treatment alone is sufficient to generate genuine significant measurable benefit, on average, when applied by a variety of clinicians with a variety of youths and families in a variety of settings. Answering that question is difficult because of the dearth of research on clinically derived usual care as provided in clinical service settings and programs. Our own research team found only 14 comparisons (in 13 published articles) of clinically derived treatment, in various forms, to some form of control condition in mental health service programs with representative referred youth. The 14 comparisons, shown in Figure 2.2, differed from one another in methodological rigor; some, for example, did not use random assignment of youths to conditions. ES estimates shown in the figure range rather widely, but the overall mean was about 0, even when we restricted analyses to the better designed random assignment studies. Certainly, more favorable evidence may emerge in the future.[1] But the findings thus far provide little evidence of benefit in the forms and contexts in which clinically derived treatment has been tested.

Does it help to link individual clinically derived treatments together into "systems of care," providing a menu of mental health services and perhaps a case manager to help children obtain the services (Stroul & Friedman, 1986)? The evidence to date is generally no more encouraging on this front than for clinically derived treatments provided one at a time. In one assessment (Bickman, 1996; Bickman et al., 1995), the U.S. Army spent $80 million to provide an extensive continuum of care for children in the Fort Bragg (North Carolina) area, and to test its cost effectiveness relative

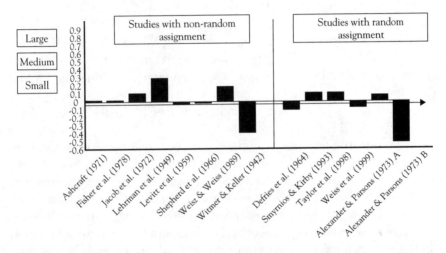

Figure 2.2. Estimated effect sizes for 14 comparisons of clinically derived child and adolescent treatment with control conditions. Horizontal arrow shows mean effect size averaging across the comparisons. From *Psychotherapy for Children and Adolescents: Evidence-Based Treatments and Case Examples* (p. 14), by J. R. Weisz, 2004, Cambridge, England: Cambridge University Press. Copyright Cambridge University Press. Reprinted with permission.

---

[1]As one possible example, a recent article by Angold, Costello, Burns, Erkanli, and Farmer (2000) reported that naturally occurring outpatient mental health care in one region of North Carolina showed a dose–effect relationship (more sessions associated with greater symptom reduction) and apparently greater symptom reduction overall than a control group. However, the finding is difficult to interpret with confidence because (a) the interventions used included medication; (b) the control group consisted of youths from the community who had not been identified as needing treatment, had not been referred, and showed significantly lower symptom and impairment levels at Time 1 than treated youth; and (c) real improvement was not seen in the treated youth who had fewer than eight sessions—our experience suggests that this tends to be the majority of treated youth in most outpatient settings. Moreover, the dose–effect finding reported by Angold et al. conflicts with findings of other research (e.g., Salzer, Bickman, & Lambert, 1999) indicating a null relationship between dose and effect with children, and some of this other research may have done a more thorough job of controlling for factors that could produce a spurious dose–effect association.

to the more fragmented services in a matched comparison site. The Fort Bragg program did produce well-integrated services (see Roberts, 1994), and the data showed that it generated better access to treatment and higher levels of client satisfaction, at higher cost, than the comparison site (Bickman et al., 1995); however, children's clinical and functional outcomes were no better at Fort Bragg than at the comparison site. In a study with stronger experimental design (including random assignment of children to system-of-care services versus control group), Bickman, Noser, and Summerfelt (1999) found a pattern very similar to the Fort Bragg results. Studying a mature system of care in Stark County, Ohio, Bickman et al. found that the system produced more intervention than did assignment to control group but not better clinical or functional outcomes.

Rather similar findings have emerged from other studies designed to combine, modify, or improve delivery of conventional clinically derived services (Evans, Armstrong, Dollard, Kuppinger, & Wood, 1994; Lehman, Postrado, Toth, McNary, & Goldman, 1994; Weisz, Walter, Weisz, Fernandez, & Mikow, 1990). Certainly, alternative interpretations of these null findings may be plausible, but one possible interpretation is that the various treatments that are linked and coordinated within these continua of care may simply not be very effective, individually or in combination (Weisz, Han, & Valeri, 1997).

To summarize findings on clinically derived treatments with children, (a) the evidence on individual treatments does not show beneficial effects, on average, and (b) studies on effects of integrating these treatments into systems of care also shows little evidence of benefit. To be clear, it seems quite possible that many individual therapists use their own clinically derived approaches to good effect and that treatment settings or programs where the prevailing forms of clinically derived care produce benefit may well exist. Moreover, the "system-of-care" concept may be workable, but the impact of any given system may be limited by the component services it provides; a system composed of empirically tested and supported services might generate a more positive picture. But the question addressed here concerns the mean impact of clinically derived treatments when averaging across practitioners and settings. The outcome evidence regarding this question is limited, and the picture may change in the future, given additional evidence. But in the studies to date, clinically derived treatments have not shown very positive effects.

EVIDENCE-BASED TREATMENTS, CLINICALLY DERIVED TREATMENTS, AND CLINICAL PRACTICE REALITIES

Although the findings for clinically derived treatments have not been encouraging and the findings for EBTs have been generally positive, general practice patterns continue to emphasize clinically derived procedures used eclectically by individual therapists. Child and adolescent clinicians, for the most part, have not incorporated evidence-based procedures into their practice. Indeed, clinical training programs seeking to emphasize such treatments tend to have major difficulty even identifying local practitioners who can supervise trainees in EBTs. Research has produced beneficial treatments for the main mental health problems that bring most children into clinics (e.g., conduct problems, oppositional behavior, ADHD, depression, fears and anxiety), but when youngsters do go to these clinics, they are not likely to find EBTs there. Instead, most EBTs continue to be used primarily in universities and research programs. Widespread dissemination, training, and deployment to practice settings has not happened. Why not?

Why Such Limited Dissemination and Deployment of Evidence-Based Treatments?

Natural Time Course

There are many possible reasons that the dissemination and deployment of EBTs have been limited, but a few warrant attention here. One of the most innocuous explanations is that there is a natural time course for the movement of treatments from research to practice. The time required to develop a good idea for a treatment program, pilot the program, develop and refine a detailed protocol, write grant applications and secure funding for a clinical trial, carry out the trial, complete analyses, traverse the journal review process, and wait for the study to appear in print may occupy most of a decade. Many more years are required for researchers to complete additional trials and build a body of evidence and for practitioners to learn about the program and the evidence. Some of the gap between science and practice is certainly due to this natural time course.

Evidence Is Not a Requirement

A second explanation is that, unlike medications, which cannot be legally prescribed without FDA approval, psychosocial treatments are not required to be supported by scientific evidence. Therefore, no sanction against the use of untested treatments exists, and they now proliferate.

No Consensus Criteria or List

Third, despite the abundance of practice guidelines, parameters, and lists of empirically supported treatments from the various mental health disciplines, the field lacks interdisciplinary consensus as to which provides the most appropriate standard; in the absence of consensus, even practitioners who would like their work to reflect the scientific evidence and parents who seek the best-supported treatment for their child will find it difficult to know which treatments warrant emphasis.

Differing Disciplinary Traditions

Another cross-disciplinary issue is that most EBTs grow out of research done by psychologists and psychiatrists, whereas the majority of mental health visits in North America involve social workers and specialists trained in professions that have not generally emphasized research as the path to effective treatment.

Limited Practitioner and Public Awareness and No Dissemination Engine

The fifth and sixth factors are closely related. Practitioners and parents have only limited awareness of EBTs, in part because large-scale dissemination efforts have not been central to the agenda for treatment developers. Those of us who do the research have little training and skill in dissemination, promotion, or advertising. Furthermore, because psychotherapy does not result in massive industry profits, we lack a potent dissemination engine (with drug representatives, academic detailing, television advertising, etc.) such as that used by the pharmaceutical industry in marketing new drugs to practitioners and the public.

Training and Supervision Requirements

Seventh, for practitioners who want to adopt EBTs, training and supervision requirements are substantial (compared, for example, with the physician's task of learning to prescribe a new medication) and may simply be unavailable for some of the treatments.

Few Incentives to Change, With Many Not to Change

Eighth, there are few incentives for practitioners to change their current practice patterns and numerous disincentives—including the discomfort of giving up familiar and trusted procedures, the cost of training and supervision in new approaches, and the lost income from suspending or reducing current practice to accommodate new learning.

Practitioner Concerns About the Relevance of Evidence-Based Treatments

Finally, many practitioners are concerned about the clinical relevance of EBTs. Some see the manualized treatments as neither relevant to their work nor appropriate for their clients. The specific concerns are diverse, but among those frequently mentioned are that (a) manualized treatments limit the therapist's creativity and innovation; (b) manual use interferes with the development of a good therapeutic relationship and makes it hard to individualize treatment; (c) the treatments have been tested with simple cases and may not work with severe cases; (d) the treatments focus on single problems or disorders and may not work with comorbid cases; and (e) the complexity and volatility of clinically referred individuals and families make each week unpredictable, rendering a predetermined series of session plans unworkable (see other clinician views in Addis, Wade, & Hatgis, 1999; Addis & Krasnow, 2000; Garfield, 1996; Havik & VandenBos, 1996; Strupp & Anderson, 1997).

Some of these concerns may be exaggerated, and certainly not all of them fit all EBTs equally well. But simply dismissing the clinicians' points would be a mistake. If researchers are to succeed in getting these treatments into practice settings, they must understand the concerns that make practitioners reluctant to use EBTs. Moreover, researchers must attend to these concerns because some might contain elements of truth. This is our impression on the basis of work we have done in practice contexts.

Our Current Research: Putting Science Into Practice and Learning From the Process

Much of our research team's work involves taking empirically tested treatments into community clinics in Los Angeles and training and supervising clinic therapists in the use of these treatments with children referred through normal community pathways. In general, the therapists do find it challenging to fit manualized treatments into their clinic routines, their demanding workloads, and the complex array of life circumstances that their clients present. The referred youngsters are often rather different from those treated in a number of the university trials, with frequent comorbidity and mingling of internalizing and externalizing conditions. Moreover, the parents are often different from the middle-class volunteers who are most likely to enroll in efficacy trials. Financial and social stresses may limit clinic parents' participation in their child's treatment, and the parents often have serious problems of their own, sometimes diagnosable disorders.

What do all these differences mean for the success of lab-tested treatments when they are exported to practice settings? It is difficult to say at this point because so little research testing such exporting efforts exists. But one thing is clear already: Treatment protocols developed through laboratory research can present challenges when used in typical practice. We strongly believe that empirical testing is critical to the development of beneficial treatments. But the critical question, in our view, is what approach to empirical testing will give us the best treatments for the youngsters who need them? And the challenge of fitting lab-tested treatments into real-world practice raises a question as to whether the primary model that has guided psychosocial treatment development and testing for decades is appropriate to the task.

The Medical–Pharmaceutical Model

Most of the research leading to our current collection of EBTs for youth has implicitly followed the strategy that has guided medical and pharmaceutical research for decades (see descriptions in Greenwald & Cullen, 1984; National Institutes of Health, 1994). That strategy, which we will refer to as the *medical–pharmaceutical (MP) model*, involves a sequence in which treatments are first developed in the laboratory, then tested via a series of *efficacy* experiments; in this model, it is only at the later stages of testing, after extensive efficacy research, that the intervention is brought into community settings "to measure the public health impact" (Greenwald & Cullen, 1984).

The MP model may work reasonably well for interventions that operate directly on the biological system (e.g., psychoactive drugs and medical procedures for cancer treatment) or other targets of impact in which lab and clinic conditions do not differ widely. In such cases, relegating effectiveness tests to the last stages of treatment research may be reasonable because the intervention may need relatively little adaptation to be downloaded and brought to scale successfully in real-world clinical contexts. (Recent evidence on stimulant treatment of ADHD in community settings, however, suggests that the "bringing to scale" process may not be simple even for some medications [MTA Cooperative Group, 1999].)

But the gap between lab and clinic appears to be quite broad in the case of psychosocial treatments, much broader than with biologically focused treatments. In the psychosocial case, the gap includes characteristics of the treated individuals (e.g., more severe problems, more likely to meet criteria for a diagnosis, more likely to have comorbidities, and more likely to drop out of treatment), their families (e.g., more parental psychopathology, family life-event stressors, and perhaps even child maltreatment), reasons for seeking treatment (e.g., not recruited from schools or through ads but referred by caregivers because of unusually serious problems or family crisis, or even court-ordered), the settings in which treatment is done (e.g., more financial forms to complete, more bureaucracy, and sometimes a less welcoming approach in the clinic), the therapists who provide the treatment (e.g., not grad students or research assistants hired by the developer and committed to his or her EBT program but rather clinic staff who barely know the treatment developer or the EBT and who may prefer different treatment methods), the incentive system (e.g., not paid by the treatment developer to deliver the EBT with close adherence to the manual but paid by the clinic to see many cases, with no method prescribed), and the conditions under which therapists deliver the treatment (not grad students' flexible time but strict productivity requirements, paperwork to complete, and little time to learn a manual or adhere closely to it).

Perhaps these many differences between therapy in lab research and therapy in actual clinical practice are too pronounced to be bridged as simply the final step at the end of a long series of efficacy experiments. Perhaps the number of dimensions along which treatment would need to be changed to bridge the lab-to-clinic gap makes the task of moving from lab-based efficacy trials to clinic-based effectiveness tests so complex that the task needs to be made an integral part of the treatment development process. Indeed, the very real-world factors that experimentalists might view as impediments (e.g., child comorbidity, parent pathology, life stresses that produce no-shows and dropouts, therapists with heavy caseloads) and thus attempt to control or prevent (e.g., by recruiting and screening cases, applying exclusion criteria, hiring their own therapists) may in fact be precisely what we need to include, understand, and address if researchers are to develop psychosocial treatment protocols that work well in practice. Treatments that cannot cope with these real-world factors may not fare so well in practice, no matter how efficacious they are in carefully controlled efficacy trials.

A Deployment-Focused Model of Intervention Development and Testing

If researchers value the development of treatments that are robust in real-life clinical care, they may need to consider a shift from the traditional MP model to a new model of treatment development research. The model we have in mind is one that would bring treatments into the crucible of clinical practice early in their development and then treat testing in the practice setting as a sequential process, not as a single final phase. This proposed deployment-focused model (DFM) of intervention development and testing[2] is intended in part to break down the long-standing distinction between clinical trials research and mental health services research, a distinction that may have discouraged the movement of clinical trials into service settings. Indeed, despite a general adherence to the MP model described above, clinical trials researchers have generally not made it to the final step in the MP sequence. That is, even mature EBTs that have undergone rather extensive efficacy testing have generally not reached the stage of full effectiveness tests in community settings, even late in the process—as evidenced by the fact that our field is largely devoid of such tests.

The proposed DFM is designed to address this lapse. The model is geared to ensuring that tests in practice and service settings do occur and thus to the production of interventions that work well in those settings. The model, as applied to psychotherapies, reflects three primary aims: (a) producing treatments that can fit smoothly into everyday practice, working

---

[2]The model can be applied to interventions across a broad spectrum (e.g., treatment, prevention, and mental health promotion programs) and to diverse population groups (e.g, children, adolescents, and adults). In the context of this chapter, we focus specifically on the model as applied to psychotherapies for children and adolescents.

well with clinic-referred individuals treated in clinic settings by practicing clinicians; (b) generating evidence on treatment outcome in actual clinical practice, the kind of evidence clinicians need to assess the likely utility of the treatments for their settings; and (c) producing a body of evidence on the treatment's nature, necessary and sufficient components, boundary conditions (i.e., moderators), and change processes (i.e., mediators) associated with treatment impact that is externally valid and relevant to the treatment in genuine practice conditions. The model entails six steps of intervention development and testing, as shown in Figure 2.3 and discussed in greater detail in Weisz (2004).

Step 1: Theoretically and Clinically Guided Construction, Refinement, and Manualizing of the Intervention Protocol

The initial step is the development, refinement, pilot testing, and manualizing of the treatment protocol. The theory and evidence on the nature and treatment of the target condition, the clinical literature, and input from clinicians who treat youngsters with that condition are used to guide the design of treatment components and plan clinically sensitive ways to present those components. Ideally, feedback from experienced clinicians who treat the condition is used to refine procedures, language, and supporting materials. The goal is a treatment protocol that (a) is well grounded in the theoretical and empirical literature on the target condition (e.g., depression); (b) conveys treatment components clearly to the therapist and includes clinically appropriate ways to present those components to clients; and (c) uses engaging and clinically appropriate supporting materials (e.g., youth practice book) to convey key ideas. The treatment protocol should grow out of a clearly articulated model of the condition being treated and of the mechanism(s) by which change in that condition is brought about through the treatment protocol.

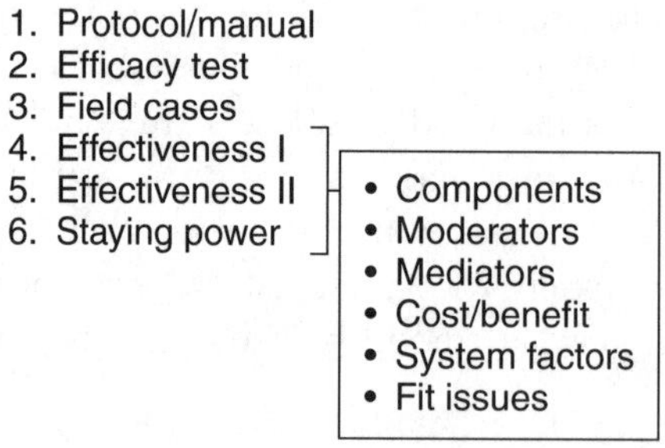

Figure 2.3. Steps and procedures in the Deployment Focused Model (DFM) of treatment development and testing. From *Psychotherapy for Children and Adolescents: Evidence-Based Treatments and Case Examples* (p. 465), by J. R. Weisz, 2004, Cambridge, England: Cambridge University Press. Copyright Cambridge University Press. Reprinted with permission.

Step 2: Initial Efficacy Trial Under Controlled Conditions to Establish Evidence of Benefit

Next, an initial efficacy trial is used to assess whether the treatment (compared with a control group) can produce beneficial effects with recruited symptomatic youth who are treated under controlled conditions. The focus here is on symptomatic study volunteers, not clinically referred cases, because it is important in the initial test to avoid exposing severely disordered individuals who seek clinical care to a totally untested intervention. Step 2 research addresses this ethical issue, helping to determine whether the program is sufficiently promising when delivered under optimal experimental conditions to warrant further development and testing in clinical practice settings with referred youth.

Step 3: Single-Case Applications in Practice Settings, With Progressive Adaptations to the Protocol

The third step is a series of single-case[3] pilot tests (e.g., see Kazdin, 2003) with clinic-referred individuals treated in clinical settings by research-affiliated therapists who know the protocol well. The setting(s) should be representative of those in which the developer intends for the treatment ultimately to be used. Ideally, dual supervision takes place, with one individual from the research team who is an expert in the treatment protocol and a second who is an experienced clinic staff member; this is to help ensure (a) faithfulness to the core principles and the model of change guiding the treatment protocol and (b) appropriateness of the treatment for the clinical setting and the community of the child and family. As problems of fit are identified, successive modifications are made in the specifics of the treatment protocol and procedures, to satisfy b, while adhering to a. Changes are anticipated in the nature of the treatment elements, the ways the elements are presented to the clients and their family members, and the materials used to guide therapists and clients through the treatment, but not in the core principles of the treatment model. In this regard, Step 3 can guide an important decision as to the type of manualizing best suited to real-life practice, with choices ranging from highly structured, session-by-session instructions (e.g., Clarke, Lewinsohn, & Hops, 1990) to broad treatment principles with illustrations of how to apply them (Henggeler et al., 1998), and with various manual formats as viable candidates for "best fit" with the treatment setting. Step 3 will be most informative to the extent that it encompasses a range of client factors such as age, gender, ethnicity, culture, and pattern of comorbidity.

---

[3] The term *single-case* refers most often to designs in which treatment is alternately applied and withdrawn and treatment effects are inferred from associated changes in client behavior; despite the name, these designs may be applied to either a single individual or to a group.

Step 4: Partial Effectiveness Tests

The fourth step involves a series of group-design studies testing the newly adapted treatment protocol in ways that entail selected elements of representative clinical care. The idea is to explore, in stepwise fashion, the extent to which the protocol works (a) with referred youngsters, (b) when used in clinical care settings, (c) when used by representative practitioners, and (d) when compared with usual care in the practice settings of interest. Tests that encompass all these elements concurrently would risk a loss of inferential power because if such tests showed that the target treatment did not outperform usual care it would be difficult to discern the reason; such findings might reflect the inappropriateness of the protocol for referred youths, a mismatch between protocol and constraints of the treatment setting, or clinicians' difficulties in using the procedures. To maximize learning in regard to prospects and problems of the protocol, tests in Step 4 will need to focus on the various elements of effectiveness testing, considered separately and eventually in strategically selected combinations. The specific structure of the tests in Step 4 and their sequential order would depend, of course, on the nature of the protocol, the nature of the context for which it is ultimately intended, and the goals of the developer of the intervention. A common goal across these variations, however, would be sequential testing that examines the protocol in relation to key elements of representative clinical practice and eventually positions the protocol for a full test of effectiveness and disseminability in Step 5.

Step 5: Full Tests of Effectiveness and Dissemination

Step 5 entails a series of group-design clinical trials, with the treatment provided to referred clients in the practice setting by practitioners who have been trained in the protocol and with the target treatment compared to usual care. As in Step 4, clients are randomly assigned to either the target treatment or usual care. A key goal is to assess the *effectiveness and disseminability* of the treatment program under the most representative clinic conditions possible. "Success" is assessed by asking at least two questions: (a) Do trained staff practitioners actually adhere to the manual in their treatment sessions, and (b) Do clients treated by the manual-trained staff practitioners show greater treatment gains than clients receiving usual care?

Step 6: Tests of Sustainability in Practice Contexts

The final step involves a genre of research focused on the relation between the treatment program and the practice contexts in which it is used. One aim is to assess the protocol's staying power (i.e., its continued use, with treatment fidelity and maintenance of outcomes) after the researchers have left the scene. Such staying power, according to the model, will increase to the extent that the treatment program has been designed to mesh well with the clients, families, therapists, settings, and conditions of real-world clinical practice.

Additional Foci Throughout Steps 4, 5, and 6: Components, Moderators, Mediators, Cost-Benefit, System Factors, and Fit Issues

Steps 4 through 6 offer many opportunities for additional learning. As shown in Exhibit 2.1, an important goal is to use variations in the design and measurement of the studies to (a) ascertain the necessary and sufficient components of our complex treatment packages; (b) identify moderators of outcome that set boundaries around treatment impact; (c) assess whether proposed mediators of treatment outcome do in fact mediate; (d) assess treatment costs in relation to benefits; (e) investigate which organizational factors in the systems and settings where the treatments are used (e.g., community mental health clinics, inpatient psychiatric units, primary care clinics, schools, social service agencies) relate to effectiveness of use; and (f) test variations in treatment procedures, packaging, training, and delivery designed to improve fit between the treatment and the various settings in which it is deployed. The aim is to generate a rich mosaic of information about the target treatment, its most essential ingredients, the factors that enhance or undermine its success, the demographic and clinical boundary conditions within which the treatment works, the change processes that account for its effects, and procedural modifications (e.g., booster sessions) that can magnify effects or extend their duration.

Of course, current efficacy research already includes numerous dismantling studies and has begun to include tests for potential moderators and mediators. Some might argue that controlled lab studies are the most appropriate context for such work. A counterargument, though, is that what we learn through dismantling studies and through moderator and mediator tests in efficacy trials may not apply so well to a treatment when it is used in real-world service settings (see Weisz, 2004). Because the clients, therapists, and conditions of treatment in those settings differ in so many ways from those of the lab tests, the degree to which separate components of the treatment package can produce effects in practice may be quite different from what was found in the lab. Similarly, the impact of various moderators and the processes that mediate treatment effects may be different for real-world clinical cases and settings than for an experimental sample tested in a university lab clinic. For example, a treatment may work well across the range of SES tested in a lab clinic with clients who are all study volunteers, paid or treated free of charge, but when the treatment is tested in community clinics with clients who are neither paid nor given free treatment, SES is linked to both attendance and treatment outcome. In general, we suspect that the most valid answers to questions about treatment outcome, component contributions, moderators, and mediators are less likely to come from research with recruited samples seen under controlled conditions than from referred samples seen under representative clinical practice conditions.

Questions and Answers About the Deployment Focused Model

Three questions about the model and its application warrant attention here.

1. How Does the Model Relate to Untested, Clinically Derived Treatments?

From the perspective of the model, clinically derived treatments can be put on track for testing but with a somewhat different emphasis than for EBTs. The fact that clinically derived treatments are already in clinical use may mean that much of the work of fitting treatment to setting has already been done. However, there is likely to be a need to develop and refine a treatment manual and supporting materials and to generate outcome evidence. For these treatments, Step 1 may be less a matter of creating a manual from scratch than of describing in detail treatment procedures already in use. The individual field tests of Step 3 may lead to less modification than in the case of treatments not derived from practice. Still, the full range of empirical testing described in the model, from Steps 2 through 6, should apply to clinically derived treatments.

2. How Does the Model Relate to Current Evidence-Based Treatments?

Most current EBTs already have a manualized protocol, and most have had the benefit of multiple efficacy trials (a kind of extended version of Step 2 in the DFM). In some cases, some of the trials may have elements of clinical representativeness. They may have, for example, involved clinically referred youths with severe problems. What may remain are opportunities to bring the treatments more fully into the effectiveness domain, perhaps beginning with field cases (Step 3), then proceeding to effectiveness and dissemination tests (Steps 4 and 5) with referred youth treated by practicing clinicians in service settings and under practice conditions. In brief, the DFM is relevant to most current EBTs, to the extent that treatment developers agree with the goals of the model.

3. How Does the Model Relate to Evidence-Based Treatments That Use Alternate Models of Delivery?

An especially interesting question surrounds treatments using models of delivery that bypass conventional service settings. As an example, consider the ADHD Summer Treatment Program described in this volume by Pelham et al. In all research on this program, the intervention has been carried out by supervised bachelors-level counselors in day camp settings. Although this is not conventional "clinical practice," the key question from the perspective of the DFM is, How does the treatment developer intend for the treatment to be used ultimately—that is, with which kinds of youth, treated in which settings, by what kinds of providers? To the extent that the approach used in the research of Pelham et al. matches the way the authors intend their program to be delivered in every practice, their work may already be consistent with the core values of the DFM. As another example, consider multisystemic therapy (MST; Henggeler et al., 1998). Critical tests of MST have involved therapists who are not a part of the conventional mental health or juvenile justice systems but who are hired and trained by MST researchers. The therapists' role—visiting the youth's life settings, working with individuals in multiple systems, being on call at all hours—goes well beyond what most therapists do in conventional clinical practice. To the extent that MST developers believe that the way they deliver treatment in their research resembles the way it should be delivered in everyday practice outside of research, their research may already be consistent with DFM goals. A basic premise of the DFM is that the treatment developer's goal regarding ultimate deployment of his or her program should be reflected in the way treatment development, refinement, and testing are done.

SUMMARY

The evidence on treatments for children and adolescents includes more than 1,500 treatment outcome studies. Several hundred have qualified for inclusion in meta-analyses, and these have generated medium-to-large effect sizes; the effects have shown specificity to targeted problems and holding power over the 5- to 6-month follow-up periods that are characteristic of the field. Task force reviews have identified more than two dozen specific beneficial treatments for problems and disorders that are common in clinically referred children and teens. The treatment evidence shows genuine strengths as well as gaps, suggesting directions for future research. A particularly worrisome gap is the failure of most EBTs to make their way into everyday practice. Several possible reasons for this failure are identified, including the possibility that the medically derived model that has guided so much of psychosocial treatment development and research may not be ideally suited to the task. As an alternative, a deployment-focused model of intervention development and testing is proposed. Its basic premise is this: If we want our treatments to be used effectively in real-world clinical care, we should design and test them with that end in mind.

REFERENCES

Addis, M. E., & Krasnow, A. D. (2000). A national survey of practicing psychologists' attitudes toward psychotherapy treatment manuals. *Journal of Consulting and Clinical Psychology, 68,* 331–339.

Addis, M. E., Wade, W. A., & Hatgis, C. (1999). Barriers to dissemination of evidence-based practices: Addressing practitioners' concerns about manual-based psychotherapies. *Clinical Psychology: Science and Practice, 6*, 430–441.

American Psychiatric Association. (1994). *Diagnostic and statistical manual of mental disorders* (4th ed.). Washington, DC: Author.

American Psychiatric Association. (1995). Practice guidelines for the treatment of patients with substance use disorders: Alcohol, cocaine, opioids. *American Journal of Psychiatry, 152*(Suppl. 11), 1–59.

Angold, A., Costello, E. J., Burns, B. J., Erkanli, A., & Farmer, E. M. Z. (2000). Effectiveness of nonresidential specialty mental health services for children and adolescents in the "real world." *Journal of the American Academy of Child and Adolescent Psychiatry, 39*, 154–160.

Angold, A., Costello, E. J., & Erkanli, A. (1999). Comorbidity. *Journal of Child Psychology and Psychiatry, 40*, 57–87.

Ashcraft, C. W. (1971). The later school achievement of treated and untreated emotionally handicapped children. *Journal of School Psychology, 9*, 338–342.

Azrin, N. H., Donohue, B., Besalel, V. A., Kogan, E. S., & Acierno, R. (1994). Youth drug abuse treatment: A controlled outcome study. *Journal of Child and Adolescent Substance Abuse, 3*, 1–16.

Barkley, R. A. (1997). *Defiant children: A clinician's manual for assessment and parent training.* New York: Guilford Press.

Baron, R. M., & Kenny, D. A. (1986). The moderator–mediator variable distinction in social psychological research: Conceptual, strategic, and statistical considerations. *Journal of Personality and Social Psychology, 51*, 1173–1182.

Bickman, L., (1996). A continuum of care: More is not always better. *American Psychologist, 51*, 689–701.

Bickman, L., Guthrie, P. R., Foster, E. M., Lambert, E. W., Summerfelt, W. T., Breda, C. S., et al. (1995). *Evaluating managed mental health services: The Fort Bragg Experiment.* New York: Plenum Press.

Bickman, L., Noser, K., & Summerfelt, W. T. (1999). Long-term effects of a system of care on children and adolescents. *Journal of Behavioral Health Services Research, 26*, 185–202.

Brent, D. A., Kolko, D. J., Birmaher, B., Baugher, M., Bridge, J., Roth, C., et al. (1998). Predictors of treatment efficacy in a clinical trial of three psychosocial treatments for adolescent depression. *Journal of the American Academy of Child and Adolescent Psychiatry, 37*, 906–914.

Brestan, E. V., & Eyberg, S. M. (1998). Effective psychosocial treatments of conduct-disordered children and adolescents: 29 years, 82 studies, 5,272 kids. *Journal of Clinical Child Psychology, 27*, 180–189.

Borduin, C. M., Mann, B. J., Cone, L. T., Henggeler, S. W., Fucci, B. R., Blaske, D. M., & Williams, R. A. (1995). Multisystemic treatment of serious juvenile offenders: Long-term prevention of criminality and violence. *Journal of Consulting and Clinical Psychology, 63*, 569–578.

Casey, R. J., & Berman, J. S. (1985). The outcome of psychotherapy with children. *Psychological Bulletin, 98*, 388–400.

Chambless, D. L., Baker, M. J., Baucom, D. H., Beutler, L. E., Calhoun, K. S., Crits-Christoph, P., et al. (1998). Update on empirically validated therapies II. *The Clinical Psychologist, 51*, 3–16.

Clarke, G., Lewinsohn, P., & Hops, H. (1990). *Leader's manual for adolescent groups: Adolescent Coping with Depression Course*. Eugene, OR: Castalia Publishing Company.

Cohen, J. (1988). *Statistical power analysis for the behavioral sciences* (2nd ed.), Hillsdale, NJ: Erlbaum.

Cohen, L., Sargent, M., & Sechrest, L. (1986). Use of psychotherapy research by professional psychologists. *American Psychologist, 41*, 198–206.

DeFries, Z., Jenkins, S., & Williams, E. C. (1964). Treatment of disturbed children in foster care. *American Journal of Orthopsychiatry, 34*, 615–624.

Eddy, J. M., & Chamberlain, P. (2000). Family management and deviant peer association as mediators of the impact of treatment condition on youth antisocial behavior. *Journal of Consulting and Clinical Psychology, 68*, 857–863.

Evans, M. E., Armstrong, M. I., Dollard, N., Kuppinger, A. D., & Wood, V. M. (1994). Development and evaluation of treatment foster care and family-centered intensive case management in New York. *Journal of Emotional and Behavioral Disorders, 2*, 228–239.

Frank, J. D. (1973). *Persuasion and healing: A comparative study of psychotherapy*. Baltimore: Johns Hopkins University Press.

Garfield, S. L. (1996). Some problems associated with "validated" forms of psychotherapy. *Clinical Psychology: Science and Practice, 3*, 218–229.

Greenwald, P., & Cullen, J. W. (1984). The scientific approach to cancer control. *CA: A Cancer Journal for Clinicians, 34*, 328–332.

Havik, O. E., & VandenBos, G. R. (1996). Limitations of manualized psychotherapy for everyday clinical practice. *Clinical Psychology: Science and Practice, 3*, 264–267.

Henggeler, S. W., Schoenwald, S. K., Borduin, C. M., Rowland, M. D., & Cunningham, P. B. (1998). *Multisystemic treatment of antisocial behavior in children and adolescents*. New York: Guilford Press.

Holmbeck, G. N. (1997). Toward terminological, conceptual, and statistical clarity in the study of mediators and moderators: Examples from the child-clinical and pediatric psychology literatures. *Journal of Consulting and Clinical Psychology, 65*, 599–610.

Huey, S. J., Jr., Henggeler, S. W., Brondino, M. J., & Pickrel, S. G. (2000). Mechanisms of change in multisystemic therapy: Reducing delinquent behavior through therapist adherence and improved family and peer functioning. *Journal of Consulting and Clinical Psychology, 68*, 451–467.

Jacob, T., Magnussen, M. G., & Kemler, W. M. (1972). A follow-up of treatment terminators and remainers with long-term and short-term symptom duration. *Psychotherapy: Theory, Research, and Practice, 9*, 139–142.

Judd, C. M., & Kenney, D. A. (1981). Process analysis: Estimating mediation in treatment evaluations. *Evaluation Review, 5*, 602–619.

Kaslow, N. J., & Thompson, M. P. (1998). Applying the criteria for empirically supported treatments to studies of psychosocial interventions for child and adolescent depression. *Journal of Clinical Child Psychology, 27*, 146–155.

Kazdin, A. E. (2000a). Developing a research agenda for child and adolescent psychotherapy. *Archives of General Psychiatry, 57*, 829–835.

Kazdin, A. E. (2000b). *Psychotherapy for children and adolescents: Directions for research and practice.* New York: Oxford University Press.

Kazdin, A. E. (2003). Drawing valid inferences from case studies. In A. E. Kazdin (Ed.), *Methodological issues and strategies in clinical research* (3rd ed., pp. 655–669). Washington, DC, American Psychological Association.

Kazdin, A. E., Bass, D., Ayers, W. A., & Rodgers, A. (1990). Empirical and clinical focus of child and adolescent psychotherapy research. *Journal of Consulting and Clinical Psychology, 58*, 729–740.

Kazdin, A. E., & Crowley, M. J. (1997). Moderators of treatment outcome in cognitively based treatment of antisocial children. *Cognitive Therapy and Research, 21*, 185–207.

Kendall, P. C., & Clarkin, J. F. (1992). Introduction to special section: Comorbidity and treatment implications. *Journal of Consulting and Clinical Psychology, 60*, 833–834.

Kendall, P. C., & Southam-Gerow, M. A. (1996). Long-term follow-up of a cognitive-behavioral therapy for anxiety-disordered youth. *Journal of Consulting and Clinical Psychology, 64*, 724–730.

Lehman, A. E., Postrado, L. T., Roth, D., McNary, S. W., & Goldman, H. H. (1994). Continuity of care and client outcomes in the Robert Johnson Wood Foundation program on chronic mental illness. *Milbank Quarterly, 72*, 105–122.

Lehrman, L. J., Sirluck, H., Black, B. J., & Glick, S. J. (1949). Success and failure of treatment of children in the child guidance clinics of the Jewish Board of Guardians: Analysis and follow-up of cases closed between April 1, 1941, and March 31, 1942. *Research Monograph No. 1*, 1–87.

Levitt, E. E., Beiser, H. R., & Robertson, R. E. (1959). A follow-up evaluation of cases treated at a community child guidance clinic. *American Journal of Orthopsychiatry, 29*, 337–349.

Lonigan, C. J., Elbert, J. C., & Johnson, S. B. (1998). Empirically supported psychosocial interventions for children: An overview. *Journal of Clinical Child Psychology, 27*, 138–145.

Mann, C. (1990). Meta-analysis in the breech. *Science, 249*, 476–480.

McLeod, B. D., & Weisz, J. R. (2004). Increasing the accuracy of treatment effect estimates in using dissertations to examine potential bias in child and adolescent clinical trials. *Journal of Consulting and Clinical Psychology, 72*, 235–251.

Miller, A. L., & Glinski, J. (2000). Youth suicidal behavior: Assessment and intervention. *Journal of Clinical Psychology, 56*, 1131–1152.

Morrow-Bradley, C., & Elliott, R. (1986). Utilization of psychotherapy research by practicing psychotherapists. *American Psychologist, 41*, 188–197.

Motta, R. W., & Lynch, C. (1990). Therapeutic techniques vs. therapeutic relationships in child behavior therapy. *Psychological Reports, 67*, 315–322.

MTA Cooperative Group. (1999). A 14-month randomized clinical trial of treatment strategies for attention-deficit/hyperactivity disorder. *Archives of General Psychiatry, 56*, 1073–1086.

National Institutes Health. (1994). Behavioral therapies development program. *NIH Guide, 22*, No. 26.

Ollendick, T. H., & King, N. J. (1998). Empirically supported treatments for children with phobic and anxiety disorders. *Journal of Clinical Child Psychology, 27*, 156–167.

Pelham, W. E., Wheeler, T., & Chronis, A. (1998). Empirically supported psychosocial treatments for attention deficit hyperactivity disorder. *Journal of Clinical Child Psychology, 27*, 190–205.

Roberts, M. C. (1994). Models for service delivery in children's mental health: Common characteristics. *Journal of Clinical Child Psychology, 23*, 212–219.

Robin, A. L., Bedway, M., Siegel, P. T., & Gilroy, M. (1996). Therapy for adolescent anorexia nervosa: Addressing cognitions, feelings, and the family's role. In E. D. Hibbs & P. S. Jensen (Eds.), *Psychosocial treatments for child and adolescent disorders: Empirically based strategies for clinical practice* (pp. 239–262). Washington, DC: American Psychological Association.

Rogers, S. J. (1998). Empirically supported comprehensive treatments for young children with autism. *Journal of Clinical Child Psychology, 27*, 168–179.

Salzer, M. S., Bickman, L., & Lambert, E. W. (1999). Dose-effect relationship in children's psychotherapy services. *Journal of Consulting and Clinical Psychology, 67*, 228–238.

Shapiro, D. A., & Shapiro, D. (1982). Meta-analysis of comparative therapy outcome studies: A replication and refinement. *Psychological Bulletin, 92*, 581–604.

Shepherd, M., Oppenheim, A. N., & Mitchell, S. (1966). Childhood behavior disorders and the child-guidance clinic: An epidemiological study. *Journal of Child Psychology and Psychiatry, 7*, 39–52.

Shirk, S. R., & Russell, R. L. (1996). *Change processes in child psychotherapy: Revitalizing treatment and research.* New York: Guilford Press.

Shirk, S. R., & Saiz, C. C. (1992). Clinical, empirical, and developmental perspectives on the therapeutic relationship in child psychotherapy. Special Issue: Developmental approaches to prevention and intervention. *Development and Psychopathology, 4*, 713–728.

Smith, M. L., & Glass, G. V. (1977). Meta-analysis of psychotherapy outcome studies. *American Psychologist, 32*, 752–760.

Smyrnios, K. X., & Kirkby, R. J. (1993). Long-term comparison of brief versus unlimited psychodynamic treatments with children and their parents. *Journal of Consulting and Clinical Psychology, 61*, 1020–1027.

Stroul, B. A., & Friedman, R. (1986). *A system of care for children and youth with severe emotional disturbances* (Rev. ed.). Washington, DC: Georgetown University Child Development Center, CASSP Technical Assistance Center.

Strupp, H. H., & Anderson, T. (1997). On the limitations of therapy manuals. *Clinical Psychology: Science and Practice, 4*, 76–82.

Sullivan, P. F. (1995). Mortality in anorexia nervosa. *American Journal of Psychiatry, 152*, 1073–1074.

Swanson, J. M., McBurnett, K., Christian, D. L., & Wigal, T. (1995). Stimulant medication and treatment of children with ADHD. In T. H. Ollendick & R. J. Prinz (Eds.), *Advances in clinical child psychology* (Vol. 17, pp. 265–322). New York: Plenum Press.

Task Force on Promotion and Dissemination of Psychological Procedures, Division of Clinical Psychology, American Psychological Association. (1995). Training in and dissemination of empirically validated psychological treatments: Report and recommendations. *The Clinical Psychologist, 48*, 3–23.

Webster-Stratton, C. (1984). Randomized trial of two parent-training programs for families with conduct-disordered children. *Journal of Consulting and Clinical Psychology, 52*, 666–678.

Weersing, V. R., & Weisz, J. R. (2002). Mechanisms of action in youth psychotherapy. *Journal of Child Psychology and Psychiatry, 43*, 3–29.

Weiss, B., Catron, T., Harris, V., & Phung, T. M. (1999). The effectiveness of traditional child psychotherapy. *Journal of Consulting and Clinical Psychology, 67*, 82–94.

Weisz, J. R. (2004). *Psychotherapy for children and adolescents: Evidence-based treatments and case examples*. Cambridge, England: Cambridge University Press.

Weisz, J. R., Han, S. S., & Valeri, S. M. (1997). More of what? Issues raised by Fort Bragg. *American Psychologist, 52*, 541–545.

Weisz, J. R., & Hawley, K. M. (2002). Developmental factors in the treatment of adolescents. *Journal of Consulting and Clinical Psychology, 70*, 21–43.

Weisz, J. R., Huey, S. J., & Weersing, V. R. (1998). Psychotherapy outcome research with children and adolescents: The state of the art. In T. H. Ollendick & R. J. Prinz (Eds.), *Advances in clinical child psychology* (Vol. 20, pp. 49–91). New York: Plenum Press.

Weisz, J. R., & Jensen, P. S. (1999). Efficacy and effectiveness of child and adolescent psychotherapy and pharmacotherapy. *Mental Health Services Research, 1*, 125–157.

Weisz, J. R., Walter, B. R., Weiss, B., Fernandez, G. A., & Mikow, V. A. (1990). Arrests of emotionally disturbed violent and assaultive individuals following minimal versus lengthy intervention through North Carolina's Willie M. Program. *Journal of Consulting and Clinical Psychology, 58*, 720–728.

Weisz, J. R., Weiss, B., Alicke, M. D., & Klotz, M. L. (1987). Effectiveness of psychotherapy with children and adolescents: A meta-analysis for clinicians. *Journal of Consulting and Clinical Psychology, 55*, 542–549.

Weisz, J. R., Weiss, B., & Donenberg, G. R. (1992). The lab versus the clinic: Effects of child and adolescent psychotherapy. *American Psychologist, 47,* 1578–1585.

Weisz, J. R., Weiss, B., Han, S. S., Granger, D. A., & Morton, T. (1995). Effects of psychotherapy with children and adolescents revisited: A meta-analysis of treatment outcome studies. *Psychological Bulletin, 117,* 450–468.

Witmer, H. L., & Keller, J. (1942). Outgrowing childhood problems: A study of the value of child guidance treatment. *Smith College Studies in Social Work, 13,* 74–90.

II

ANXIETY DISORDERS

INTRODUCTION: ANXIETY DISORDERS

Anxiety disorders are pervasive in young children and adolescents and tend to impair them at a time in their lives when they need all their faculties for academic achievement and acquisition of the social skills necessary to function in the community. Developing research has shown that anxiety disorders are persistent and are not inconsequential, as once thought. It is estimated that 8% to 10% of the child population suffer from some form of anxiety. Yet children do not always recognize when their anxieties and fears are excessive, and they may not report distress about it. Instead, very young children may express their disquietude by crying, clinging, and so forth. It is important, therefore, for parents, teachers, and health care providers to recognize anxiety early and refer the children for treatment.

The term *anxiety disorders* encompasses a wide variety of conditions, such as generalized anxiety, panic, obsessive compulsive disorder, separation anxiety, social phobia, and specific phobias such as animal or situational phobias. Promising work has been done in recent years on the treatment of anxiety disorders. Of the few types of treatments studied empirically, cognitive–behavioral therapy (CBT) and behavioral treatments (BT) have been shown to be especially promising, offering reasonable hope for respectable outcomes. This section discusses studies conducted using these techniques in treating children and adolescents with anxiety disorders.

Using CBT, Kendall and colleagues present an impressive research program that tests the efficacy of treatments for children with generalized anxiety disorder, separation anxiety, and social phobia. The recent research reveals the effort they made to bridge efficacy and real-world research by including comorbid conditions such as coprimary anxiety, mood, and behavior and developmental disorders, as well as the use of parents in supportive roles. The aim of the treatment is to equip children with skills that will help them manage anxious distress in the future. The authors discuss their assessment and treatment methods, including relapse prevention, work with the families, and outcomes of various studies on the treatment of anxiety. In addition, they present long-term follow-up results indicating that treatment gains are maintained greatly beyond 1 year. In these authors' hands, CBT has also been beneficial to some comorbid conditions. Highlighting future directions, the authors recommend that research next examine the active components of CBT, its influence on the sequelae of the disorder, its impact on parental psychopathology, the role of process variables (i.e., therapeutic alliance) in determining the CBT outcomes, and its effectiveness when provided by practicing clinicians in mental health settings.

Deborah C. Beidel and Roxann Roberson-Nay discuss their work on the treatment of social phobia with young children. They use a cognitive behavioral model called Social Effectiveness Therapy for Children (SET-C) that aims to address competence across various dimensions such as increased social skills, decreased social fear and avoidance, and increased self-concept. The treatment components include social skills training, peer generalization, and exposure. The authors describe in detail their assessment and outcome measures. The results indicate that SET-C is an effective treatment for social phobia in children. Likewise, a 6-month follow-up revealed a significant improvement in social performance. The authors suggest that a 5-year follow-up of children involved in the original study should be completed to determine the long-term efficacy of the SET-C; that an adolescent version, SET-A, be developed; and that this approach be compared to medication treatment.

Wendy K. Silverman and William M. Kurtines summarize the progress that has been done on the development and evaluation of interventions used with anxious children. They discuss their CBT/BT model's exposure-based "transfer of control" that they use to treat children with phobic and anxiety disorders. This model has a pragmatic and contextual orientation and can be of use to practitioners. The authors discuss their assessment methods and treatment procedures in detail. They also propose techniques to bridge university-based research and real-world or clinic settings. The evidence of their work suggests that the transfer-of-control model is efficacious for the treatment of childhood anxiety and phobias. In highlighting future directions, the authors propose to examine empirically the mediational effects of the treatment to allow therapists to have maximal clinical flexibility in the therapeutic procedures, strategies, formats, and potential stances.

John S. March, Martin Franklin, and Edna Foa review the current status of the principles underlining the cognitive behavioral treatments for obsessive–compulsive disorder (OCD), discuss empirical studies supporting the use of CBT as a treatment for OCD, and present their CBT treatment for children with OCD used in both research and clinical settings. The protocol used by the authors follows the typical gradual exposure regimen. The 12 weeks of treatment is conducted in five phases: psychoeducation, cognitive training, mapping of OCD, exposure, and response prevention. Results indicated that treatment gains were maintained at the 6-month follow-up, and the researchers concluded that psychotherapy alone or in combination with pharmacotherapy is the treatment of choice for children and adolescents with OCD. The authors recommend several areas for future research, including the comparison of CBT/BT and medication, comparison of individual- and family-based treatments, and follow-up studies to evaluate relapse rates and the utility of booster sessions.

It should be noted that in all of the research programs described in this section, parents are involved as an essential part of the treatment protocol. Also, male, female, and minority children are included in all programs presented. The studies indicate that CBT treatments may be effective in alleviating anxiety spectrum disorders in children and adolescents. All authors recommend that parental involvement in the treatment of children with anxiety disorders should be more vigorous, even in treating concurrent parental psychopathology. They also present ideas on how to make efficacy research more real-world friendly. Although other therapies currently used by clinicians may or may not be efficacious, empirical data are lacking. In addition to further refining CBT, future research should examine other treatment modalities that may be useful for the anxiety disorders.

3

COGNITIVE–BEHAVIORAL TREATMENT FOR CHILDHOOD ANXIETY DISORDERS

PHILIP C. KENDALL, JENNIFER L. HUDSON, MUNIYA CHOUDHURY, ALICIA WEBB, AND SANDRA PIMENTEL

Knowledge of childhood anxiety disorders has expanded over the last 15 years. Advancement has occurred not only in understanding the nature of these disorders but also in assessment, treatment, and, more recently, prevention and etiology. It has become increasingly clear that anxiety in youth is not necessarily transient, minor, and inconsequential. Rather, anxiety can be associated with a negative impact on social, academic, and family functioning. The disorders are common forms of psychopathology in children and adolescents (Anderson, Williams, McGee, & Silva, 1987; Fergusson, Horwood, & Lynskey, 1993; Verhulst, van der Ende, Ferdinand, & Kasius, 1997), and they have high rates of comorbidity (Anderson et al., 1987; Kendall, Brady, & Verduin, 2001; Last, Hersen, Kazdin, Finkelstein, & Strauss, 1987; Last, Strauss, & Francis, 1987). Left untreated, anxiety disorders can persist, leading to other difficulties such as substance use and depression (Brady & Kendall, 1992; Beidel, Fink, & Turner, 1996; Strauss, Lease, Last, & Francis, 1988; Keller et al., 1992).

Treatment of these disorders has seen significant and promising developments. According to the American Psychological Association guidelines for determining whether a treatment meets the criteria for being designated "empirically supported" cognitive–behavioral therapy (CBT) for youth diagnosed with anxiety disorders has been established as a "probably efficacious" treatment (Kazdin & Weisz, 1998; Ollendick & King, 1998). This conclusion is based on multiple reported outcomes from several randomized clinical trials. Researchers at the Child and Adolescent Anxiety Disorders Clinic (CAADC) at Temple University have completed two randomized clinical trials (Kendall, 1994; Kendall, Flannery-Schroeder, Panichelli-Mindel, et al., 1997) of the "Coping Cat" program (Kendall, 2000), a manual-based CBT for children with anxiety disorders. Both statistically and clinically significant improvements have been found on parent-, child- and teacher-reported measures at posttreatment. A number of independent treatment outcome studies show further support for the efficacy of CBT for childhood anxiety disorders (e.g., Barrett, Dadds, & Rapee, 1996; Spence, Donovan, & Brechman-Toussaint, 2000; Cobham, Dadds, & Spence, 1998; Silverman, Kurtines, Ginsburg, Weems, Rabian, et al., 1999). Some results suggest benefits from adding a family anxiety management component to the child's treatment. Follow-up visits 1 year after treatment and two long-term follow-up studies have shown that the gains achieved by CBT for childhood anxiety have been maintained at these 1-, 3-, 6-, and 7.4-year follow-ups (Barrett, Duffy, Dadds, & Rapee, 2001; Kendall, 1994; Kendall & Southam-Gerow, 1996; Kendall, Safford, Flannery-Schroeder, & Webb, 2004).

The primary aims of the CAADC are to continue to develop and evaluate efficacious and effective interventions for youth with anxiety disorders. The CAADC provides assessment and treatment for these children and their families in the Philadelphia tri-state region. Services are provided for children between 7 and 16 years of age who currently meet *Diagnostic and Statistical Manual of Mental Disorders, Fourth Edition* (*DSM–IV*; American Psychiatric Association, 1994) criteria for a primary diagnosis of social phobia, generalized anxiety disorder, or separation anxiety disorder. Referrals to the clinic come from word of mouth, community practitioners and school counselors, media releases about the services provided by the clinic, and occasional workshops and seminars for mental health professionals.

Established in 1986, the clinic has undertaken numerous studies examining the nature and assessment of anxiety disorders in youth, in addition to outcome trials already mentioned (e.g., Chansky & Kendall, 1997; Kendall & Chu, 2000; Kortlander, Kendall, & Panicchelli, 1997; Krain & Kendall, 2000; Ronan & Kendall, 1997; Siqueland, Kendall, & Steinberg, 1996; Southam-Gerow & Kendall, 2000). The clinic has also facilitated the dissemination of manual-based CBT programs through cooperative translations in a number of countries, including Australia, Canada, Italy, Hungary, the Netherlands, and Japan.

The purpose of this chapter is to provide a description of the procedures used at the CAADC. A potential criticism of university-affiliated research is the perceived gap between a research setting and a so-called real-world setting. We have strived to operate a clinic not unlike real-world clinics while conducting research on the services that are provided. It is also our hope to bridge this gap by offering service-providing clinicians with clearer descriptions of our treatment program and more detailed information about our methodology. First, this chapter outlines the current assessment procedures used at the CAADC. Second, the manual-based cognitive–behavioral treatment is reviewed along with the results of treatment outcome studies. Finally, directions for future research are discussed.

METHOD

Participants and Selection

Referred from multiple community sources, youth between the ages of 7 and 17 years who receive a diagnosis of primary childhood anxiety disorder, based on structured diagnostic interviews, and their families are accepted into the program. Our target diagnoses, as described in DSM–IV (American Psychiatric Association, 1994), include generalized anxiety disorder (GAD), separation anxiety disorder (SAD), and social phobia (SoP). Children with a primary diagnosis of simple phobia (SP), obsessive compulsive disorder (OCD), or panic disorder (PD) are not included as principal diagnoses, though those youth with any of these as a coprincipal or additional diagnosis are included. Children with comorbid diagnoses (either coprincipal or additional) of anxiety, mood, behavior, or pervasive developmental disorders are included in the program. Thus far, children with mental retardation or psychotic symptoms or those being treated with antianxiety or antidepressant medication have not been included in the program.

Procedure

After receiving a referral to CAADC, parents schedule an intake evaluation with staff diagnosticians. At intake, the parent(s) and child sign informed-consent forms. To assess DSM–IV childhood disorders, structured diagnostic interviews are administered separately to both parents and the child. If the child meets diagnostic criteria (using a composite of parent and child interview data), the family is asked to return for an additional assessment that includes family observations, behavioral observations of the child, and structured interviews with each parent to diagnose current or past adult anxiety disorders. Self-report measures for the child and parents, as well as reports of child functioning from the parents and teachers, are also completed before treatment begins. These measures assess the nature of the child's symptoms and the role of family factors in the child's anxiety and enable the evaluation of therapeutic change. Additionally, parents complete questionnaires to assess their own levels of depression and anxiety and marital adjustment. Parents and child also complete questionnaires regarding parenting characteristics to evaluate changes in parenting over the course of treatment and follow-up. The measures are administered before and after treatment and at 1-year follow-up visits.

Assessments

Structured Diagnostic Interviews and Diagnostic Ratings

Anxiety Disorders Interview Schedule for Children. The Anxiety Disorders Interview Schedule for Children (ADIS-C/P; Silverman & Albano, 1997) is a semistructured diagnostic interview. It has favorable psychometric properties (March & Albano, 1998) and first-rate sections for diagnosing anxiety disorders. The ADIS-C/P also permits diagnosis of other disorders such as major depression, dysthymia, attention-deficit/hyperactivity disorder (ADHD), and oppositional defiant disorder and is used to assess comorbid conditions. Interrater reliability has been established (Kappa >.85) at the CAADC. As recommended in the ADIS-C/P (Silverman & Albano, 1997) an integration of child and parent report can be used to determine primary (and secondary) diagnoses.

Children's Global Assessment Scale. The Children's Global Assessment Scale (CGAS; Shaffer, Gould, Brasic, Ambrosini, Fisher, Bird, & Aluwahlia, 1983) reflects the level of the child's functioning during a specified time period. Clinicians rate the child's functioning over the last month using a 1-to-100 scale (with behavioral anchors).

Anxiety Disorders Interview Schedule for DSM–IV, Lifetime Version.
The Anxiety Disorders Interview Schedule for DSM–IV, Lifetime Version (ADIS–IV-L; DiNardo, Brown, & Barlow, 1994) is a structured interview to diagnose current and past episodes of adult anxiety disorders. In addition, the instrument includes assessments of current and past mood, somatoform, and substance use disorders.

Children's Self-Report Measures

Multidimensional Anxiety Scale for Children. The Multidimensional Anxiety Scale for Children (MASC; March, Parker, Sullivan, Stallings, & Conners, 1997) is a 39-item self-report inventory containing four major factors: physical symptoms (e.g., tension), social anxiety (e.g., rejection), harm avoidance (e.g., perfectionism), and separation anxiety.

Social Phobia and Anxiety Inventory for Children. The Social Phobia and Anxiety Inventory for Children (SPAI-C; Beidel, Turner, & Morris, 1995) is a 26-item self-report instrument assessing social anxiety in children. Items tap anxiety-arousing situations, cognitive and physical symptoms, and avoidance behavior.

Children's Depression Inventory. The Children's Depression Inventory (CDI; Kovacs, 1981) includes 27 items regarding the cognitive, affective, and behavioral signs of depression. The scale correlates with measures related to constructs such as self-esteem, negative cognitive attributions, and hopelessness (Kazdin, French, Unis, Esveldt-Dawson, & Sherick, 1983; Kovacs, 1981).

Coping Questionnaire—Child. The Coping Questionnaire—Child (CQ–C; Kendall & Marrs-Garcia, 1999) is a measure that assesses the child's ability to cope with anxious distress in challenging situations. The three most difficult areas for the child are identified, and the instrument provides a situation-based and individualized assessment of the child's ability to cope in them.

Parent Measures of Child

Child Behavior Checklist. The 118-item Child Behavior Checklist (CBCL) assesses a broad range of behavioral problems and social competencies. The measure has been analyzed for both narrow-band and broad-band scales as well as profiles of different disorders (Achenbach, 1991a).

Coping Questionnaire—Parent. The Coping Questionnaire—Parent (CQ–P; Kendall & Marrs-Garcia, 1999) parallels the child version (CQ–C) described earlier. The parent rates the child's ability to cope with the three most anxiety-provoking situations identified in the CQ–C.

Parent's Self-Report Measures

State–Trait Anxiety Inventory. The State–Trait Anxiety Inventory (STAI; Speilberger, Gorsuch, & Lushene, 1970). On the Form Y, 20 items assess how respondents generally feel (A-Trait), and 20 items assess respondents' feelings at the moment (A-State).

Beck Depression Inventory. The Beck Depression Inventory (BDI; Beck, Rush, Shaw, & Emery, 1979) is a 21-item instrument that broadly assesses the symptoms of depression, including the affective, cognitive, behavioral, and somatic components of depression as well as suicidal thoughts.

Dyadic Adjustment Scale. The 32-item Dyadic Adjustment Scale (DAS; Spanier, 1976) taps dyadic satisfaction, dyadic cohesion, dyadic consensus, and affectional expression and provides a global marital adjustment (conflict) score.

Teacher Report of Child

Teacher's Report Form. Using the Teacher's Report Form (TRF; Achenbach, 1991b), the primary teacher rates the child's classroom functioning, behavior, and social and academic performance. The TRF assesses the child's anxious behavior in the school setting and may be especially relevant for children whose fears involve social and evaluative situations.

Parent and Child Reports

Children's Report of Parenting Behavior Inventory. The Children's Report of Parenting Behavior Inventory (CRPBI; Schluderman & Schluderman, 1970 revision) is a 30-item questionnaire that assesses children's perception of their parents' behavior toward them along three dimensions: Psychological Control (PC), Acceptance (AC), and Firm Control (FC). Children complete separate inventories for mother and father. In addition to the child's report, the items on the CRPBI have been adapted to allow each parent to rate perceptions of their parenting.

Behavioral Observations

Direct behavioral observations are crucial but often overlooked as indices of outcome. As part of our assessment procedures, we include videotaped observation tasks, which involve the child alone, the parent alone, and, most important, the parents interacting with the child. These taped observations are later coded to evaluate the ways in which treatment may have affected both the child's anxiety and family interactions.

Treatment

Once the child has been accepted and all measures have been completed, he or she is randomly assigned to a treatment condition and to a therapist. All therapists have previously served as diagnosticians for other cases and have studied written treatment manuals and participated in training workshops before initiating supervised pilot experience. Workshops include didactic presentations, role-playing exercises, trainee demonstration, videotape playback, and discussion. After training and continuing throughout the treatment, all therapists participate in weekly supervision.

A primary goal of CBT for anxious youth is to help children learn to recognize their signs of anxious arousal and to use these signs as cues to implement anxiety-management strategies. At the CAADC, anxious children participate in a structured 16-week treatment program that is divided into two segments: education and practice. During the first half of treatment, the therapist helps the child to recognize signs of anxiety, to acquire relaxation skills, and to identify and modify anxious self-talk and cognitive processing. Through self-monitoring homework assignments and in-session role-playing exercises, the child learns about anxiety and, more important, the cognitive, somatic, emotional, and behavioral aspects of his or her own personal anxious experience. To address this experience, the therapist and child work together to create a personalized FEAR plan that is used by the child to cope when anxiety-provoking situations arise. The steps of the FEAR plan reflect the components of the treatment and include the following: Feeling frightened?; Expecting bad things to happen?; Attitudes and actions that help; Results and rewards (Figure 3.1). The child learns these four steps, symbolized memorably by the acronym FEAR, and becomes armed with a coping plan that he or she can then practice during the second half of treatment. Exhibit 3.1 provides an example of a FEAR plan for a socially anxious child giving a class presentation.

During initial sessions, the anxious child learns to distinguish between various bodily reactions to feelings as well as the more specific somatic reactions characteristic of his or her anxiety. First, the child learns to ask "Am I *Feeling frightened?*" as an important first signal for managing unwanted anxiety. With this awareness, children are taught progressive muscular relaxation to help develop further awareness of, and control over, physiological and muscular reactions to anxiety (see King, Hamilton, & Ollendick, 1988). These exercises are audiotaped so that the child may listen and practice at home. Children learn that physiological responses to anxiety-provoking situations can be early warning signals to initiate relaxation procedures.

F	Feeling frightened?	"Well, I have butterflies in my stomach and my palms are kind of sweaty."
E	Expecting bad things to happen?	"I will mess up." "The other kids make fun of me." "I'm going to look stupid and they'll laugh at me."
A	Attitudes and actions that help	"I can practice before and make sure I know what I'm going to say." "I didn't mess up the last time I gave a report and the teacher said I did a good job." "Even if I mess up, it's not a big deal anyway because everybody messes up sometime." "I can laugh too."
R	Results and rewards	"I was nervous in the beginning, but I felt okay by the end." "Nobody laughed." "I think I did a pretty good job, and I tried really hard." "My reward is to go to the movies with Mom and Dad this weekend."

Figure 3.1. Sample FEAR plan for a socially anxious child giving a class presentation.

In the second step of the FEAR plan, the child asks, "*Am I Expecting bad things to happen?*" Children identify and modify anxious self-talk (cognition) in their internal dialogues. Figure 3.2 provides an example of a cartoon from the *Coping Cat Workbook* used to illustrate how different self-talk can lead to different feelings about the same situation. With strategies such as cognitive modeling, rehearsal, social reinforcement, and role-playing, the therapist encourages the child to challenge anxious thoughts and consider the many possibilities that may occur in a given situation. With the theorized link among cognition, emotion, and behavior, it is believed that helping a child to challenge his or her distorted or unrealistic self-talk will promote more constructive ways of thinking and less dysfunctional emotional and behavioral responses. The goal is for the anxious child to examine, test out, and reduce his or her negative self-talk; modify unrealistic expectations; and generate more realistic and less negative self-statements. Note: The aim is not to fill the child with positive self-talk. The ameliorative power rests in the reduction of negative self-talk, or the "power of nonnegative thinking" (Kendall, 1984). This phenomenon is supported by recent evidence indicating that changing children's anxious and negative self-talk—but not positive self-talk—mediates the changes in anxiety that are associated with treatment-produced gains (Treadwell & Kendall, 1996).

Next, children learn active problem-solving skills that assist in the development of a behavioral plan to cope with their anxiety. With "*Atti-*

Figure 3.2. Sample page from *Coping Cat Workbook* illustrating how some different thoughts in our thought bubbles (or self-talk) can lead to different feelings about the same situation. Reprinted from Kendall (1992) *Coping Cat Workbook.* Copyright (1992) Workbook Publishing, Ardmore, PA. (www.workbookpublishing.com) Reprinted by permission.

tudes and actions that help," they learn that after recognizing the problem, they can brainstorm and generate alternatives to managing their anxiety, weigh the consequences of each alternative, and then choose and follow through with the plan (see D'Zurilla & Goldfried, 1971; D'Zurilla & Nezu, 1999). The therapist models problem-solving skills by helping to brainstorm ideas without judgment, for example.

The fourth and final step in the FEAR plan, *"Results and rewards,"* allows children to judge the effectiveness of their efforts and reward themselves for these efforts. Children identify the favorable aspects of how they handled a situation as well as those things that they may want to do differently in the future. Anxious children place high standards for achievement on themselves and are critical of themselves if they fail to meet these standards, so the child is encouraged to reward both complete and partial successes. The therapist emphasizes and encourages self-reward and does not endorse self-perceived imperfections.

Homework assignments are key in the program. Throughout, the child completes "Show That I Can," or STIC, tasks in a personal notebook, which allows him or her to practice the skills outside the session. Rewards (e.g., stickers) are provided upon completion of STIC assignments to encourage the child to work on these tasks throughout the week. After the completion of 3 or 4 STIC tasks the child earns a more substantial reward (e.g., baseball cards, stickers).

Practice, Practice, Practice

During the second half of treatment, the child focuses practicing the newly acquired skills. In these sessions, the child is prepared for and exposed to various situations intended to induce anxiety. At first, the child is exposed to imaginary- and low-anxiety situations and gradually is exposed to moderate- and then high-anxiety situations. With graded exposure, children not only can habituate themselves to these anxiety-provoking situations but can apply their coping strategies in actual situations, thereby experiencing a sense of mastery that is incompatible with previous expectations.

Throughout the imaginal and in vivo exposures, the child provides a Subjective Unit of Distress (SUDS) rating before and after the exposure as well as every minute during the exposure. The therapist records the child's SUDS rating and also rates how anxious he or she feels the child is, using the same scale before, during (every minute), and after exposure. Armed with this information, therapist and child can discover patterns to the child's anxiety, determine trouble spots, and, most important, note areas of improvement. After each exposure, the therapist facilitates the child's processing of the experience, helping the child to evaluate and reward his or her performance. The exposure experience is framed and evaluated in terms of a pattern for future coping.

Clinical Vignette

The following example demonstrates a representative exchange between a child and therapist as they prepare for an in vivo exposure. The child is afraid to visit new places for fear of getting lost. The following plan was developed to prepare for a trip to a shopping mall:

Therapist: So, are you feeling nervous now?

Child: I don't know. Not really.

Therapist: How would you know when you were starting to get nervous?

Child: My heart would start beating faster.

Therapist (recalling a common somatic complaint for this child): What about your breathing?

Child: I might start breathing faster.

Therapist: And what would you be thinking to yourself?

Child: I might get lost, or I don't know where I am.

Therapist: And what are some things you could do if you start getting nervous?

Child: I could take deep breaths and say everything is going to be okay.

Therapist: That's good, but what if you were unsure where you were or got lost?

Child: I could ask somebody.

Therapist: Yes, you could ask somebody. Would it be a good idea to ask one of the guards or policemen? How are you feeling? Do you think you are ready to give it a try?

The therapist and child agree on a number of trips to make within the mall, varying in distance and degree of familiarity. During the trip, the child was to ask the guard for directions so that he could feel comfortable doing this in the future. Although conducted in a supportive environment, exposure tasks are intended to be challenging and anxiety provoking.

Going "Hollywood"

Approximately 4 weeks before the end of the program, the therapist and child begin to discuss how the child will create and produce a "commercial" about his or her experiences in the program during the last session of the treatment. Imagination and creativity are encouraged. The child can create a videotape, audiotape, or booklet describing the experience (e.g., with the FEAR plan) to help tell other children about coping with anxiety. The commercial is intended to help children organize their experiences, to provide an opportunity to share their newly acquired skills, and to recognize their accomplishments. The commercial serves as a tangible reward that children can take home with them, and although it may not be described as such, it is an in vivo exposure task with emotional, social, creative, and organizational features.

Developmental Considerations

The treatment manual for CBT was designed for children between the ages of 7 and 13 years. Also designed for this age range, the *Coping Cat Workbook* (Kendall, 1992) contains exercises that parallel treatment sessions in an effort to facilitate the child's involvement in the program and the acquisition of skills. Although some manual-based treatments have acquired the reputation of being somewhat rigid, the therapist working with this program uses flexibility to breathe life into the manual and to better fit the needs of the child (Kendall, Chu, Gifford, Nauta, & Hayes, 1998). Although adaptations can be made when working with older children (see the *C.A.T. Project*; Kendall, Choudhury, Hudson, & Webb, 2002), very young children (under age 7 years) may not have the cognitive skills necessary for full participation in or maximal benefit from this intervention.

Relapse Prevention

The goal of treatment is not to cure anxiety (see Kendall, 1989). The ultimate goal is to equip children with skills that will help them manage anxious distress. Therapeutic intervention is a first step. Once treatment is completed, the guiding principle is for children to continue to practice and learn. There are several strategies that help to guide children toward consolidation of treatment-produced gains. First, the therapist shapes and encourages effort attributions regarding the management of anxiety. Children are encouraged to reward their hard work and coping efforts always, even if the successes are only partial.

A second principle for continued posttreatment functioning includes introducing children to the concept of lapses in efforts, rather than relapses (see also Brownell, Marlatt, Lichtenstein, & Wilson, 1986; Marlatt & Gordon, 1985). Mistakes and partial successes are not viewed as incompetence or inability; rather, they are constructively framed as vital to and inextricably linked to the learning process. Within this framework, children label and accept inevitable setbacks as temporary. Mistakes are viewed as an acceptable part of the learning process and not as excuses for giving up or returning to anxious self-talk.

Working With Families

Parental involvement can be paramount in assessing and addressing anxiety in children. Although the treatment program discussed is focused on helping the child think and behave differently, parents participate in supportive roles. The therapist meets with the parents in the beginning and after the third session to collaborate with them on treatment plans. Parents are routinely given the opportunity to discuss any concerns they may have and are encouraged to provide any information that may be useful for treatment. When appropriate, they are encouraged to help their children practice relaxation skills and participate in some of the in vivo exposures; parents can also be integral to the reward process.

Given the clinical and empirical attention highlighting the potential contributing role of the family in the genesis and maintenance of childhood anxiety (Hudson & Rapee, in press; Kendall, MacDonald, & Treadwell, 1995; Rapee, 1997; Sanders, 1996; Siqueland et al., 1996) and the positive outcomes of initial research that has introduced family-focused CBT (Barrett et al., 1996; Howard & Kendall, 1996), we have adapted the individual CBT and developed a family CBT intervention (FCBT). The principles and strategies discussed already are used, but parents attend and are directly involved in each session.

More specifically, FCBT pays added attention to the family's (i.e., parents') role in the maintenance of a child's anxiety. Consistent with the individual program, FCBT is also divided into two segments—education and practice. However, parental beliefs about and responses to the child's anxious behavior are also targeted in session. During the education component, the child and family together learn the steps of the FEAR plan as a strategy to cope with anxiety. Therapists help to train family members in communication patterns that allow them to better discuss the child's anxious experience (e.g., "Expecting bad things to happen?"), as well as parents' expectations of their child's anxious behavior. Family members learn active problem-solving skills that they can take home with them to change the child's and parents' ways of reacting when the child becomes anxious. The therapist serves as a coping model for the child and parents, and throughout the treatment, parents are encouraged to become coping models themselves. Parent involvement during the practice segment is highly valued. As the child participates in imaginal and in vivo exposures to anxiety-provoking situations, problematic parental expectations about and responses to the child's anxious experience are addressed. At first, the therapist plays a more active and direct role as an in vivo coach, reminding the child to use the FEAR plan and modeling appropriate responses to parents. However, as exposures become more challenging, the therapist becomes less involved and parents become the in vivo coaches for their child. After practice, parents are encouraged to become less involved in order to allow the child to cope independently. Thus, FCBT aims to teach the anxious child active coping strategies and the parents more constructive responses to their anxious child's experience.

A manual describing this program is available (Howard, Chu, Krain, Marrs-Garcia, & Kendall, 1999). Although we support and encourage the input of parents during child treatment as well as the development of family-focused programs, we recognize the need for continued research and empirical evaluation regarding when it is most therapeutically beneficial to include, or to not include, parents in the treatment of their child's anxiety disorder.

Treatment Outcome

Following a number of promising single-case design studies (e.g., Eisen & Silverman, 1993; Kane & Kendall, 1989; Ollendick, 1985), CBT for childhood anxiety disorder underwent a series of randomized clinical trials. Conducted by independent research teams in several parts of the United States and in Australia and Canada (Barrett et al., 1996; Cobham et al., 1998; Kendall, 1994; Kendall et al., 1997; Silverman et al. 1999; Spence et al., 2000), the clinical trials investigated the efficacy of both child-focused CBT and CBT including parental involvement.

Child-Focused CBT

The first of the randomized clinical trials (Kendall, 1994) examined the efficacy of CBT for 47 youth (ages 9–13 years) with overanxious, separation anxiety, or avoidant disorders. Compared with a wait-list control, children who received the 16-session CBT displayed significant improvement on self-report, parent-report, and behavioral observation measures. In addition, 64% of treated children no longer received their principal anxiety disorder diagnosis at posttreatment, and, at 1-year follow-up, treatment gains were maintained (Kendall, 1994).

Kendall and colleagues (1997) reported a second randomized trial of CBT versus wait-list with 9- to 13-year-olds (n = 94) diagnosed with a primary anxiety disorder. At posttreatment and at 1-year follow-up, treated children revealed positive outcomes on a variety of measures when compared to the control group. In a project in Australia, Barrett and colleagues (1996) reported that, a year after the child-focused CBT (based on Kendall, 1992), 72% of children (ages 7–14 years) with primary diagnoses of SAD, overanxious disorder (OAD) or social phobia no longer met diagnostic criteria for an anxiety disorder.

To investigate the effect of child CBT held in group format, Flannery-Schroeder and Kendall (2000) compared a group CBT condition, an individual CBT condition, and a wait-list control condition using 37 subjects (ages 8–14 years) with anxiety disorders. Analysis of diagnostic status indicated that at posttreatment significantly more treated youth (73% individual, 50% group) than wait-list youth (8%) no longer met criteria for their principal anxiety disorder. The superiority of the treatment conditions to the wait-list condition was also demonstrated through other measures. However, in terms of child-report of anxious distress, only the individual treatment yielded significant improvement. Furthermore, there were no notable differences between the three conditions on measures of social functioning. Treatment gains were maintained at a 3-month follow-up. Other studies have also demonstrated that the group CBT for children with anxiety disorders produces significant improvements compared with a wait-list condition (e.g., Hayward et al., 2000; Silverman, Kurtines, Ginsburg, Weems, Lumpkin, & Carmichael, 1999).

Family Involvement in CBT

Researchers have recognized the potential benefits of greater parental involvement in the treatment of childhood anxiety disorders (e.g., Dadds, 1995; Kendall, MacDonald, & Treadwell, 1995; Rapee, Wignall, Hudson, & Schniering, 2000; Siqueland & Diamond, 1998). For instance, adding family management for parents to the individual child's CBT has yielded promising results in single-case designs and in clinical trials. Howard and Kendall (1996) used a multiple baseline, across-cases design to evaluate a family-based CBT program with six children (ages 9–13 years) who met criteria for an anxiety disorder. They reported gains at posttreatment on diagnostic and questionnaire measures for four of the children, and with the exception of one child, these gains were maintained at 4-month follow-up.

Barrett and colleagues (1996) compared several versions of CBT (based on Kendall, 1992); a child-only program, a combined program of child CBT plus family anxiety-management training (CBT+FAM), and a wait-list control. Seventy-nine children (ages 7–14 years) with a primary diagnosis of overanxious disorder, separation anxiety disorder, or social phobia were randomly assigned to the three 12-week conditions: CBT, CBT+FAM, or wait-list control. The FAM component added parental training in contingency management strategies, communication and problem-solving skills, and recognition and management of parents' own emotional and anxious responses to stimuli. Seventy percent of children participating in either the CBT or the CBT+FAM treatment, versus less than 30% of the wait-list controls, no longer met diagnoses. The clients that received CBT+FAM showed greater improvement than the CBT-only group on some measures. Furthermore, at the 1-year follow-up, 70% of the CBT group versus 95% of the CBT+FAM group no longer met the diagnostic criteria for any anxiety disorder.

Cobham and colleagues (1998) studied the effectiveness of one component of the family management program: parental anxiety management

(PAM). Sixty-seven children (ages 7–14 years) with anxiety disorders were assigned to conditions based on their parents' anxiety level, measured via the State Trait Anxiety Inventory (STAI; Speilberger, Gorsuch, & Lushene, 1970). Of these, 32 youth made up the child-anxiety-only group, wherein parents were classified as nonanxious, and 35 formed the child + parental anxiety group, because one or both parent(s) reported high levels of anxiety. Children from both of these groups were then randomly assigned either to child-focused CBT or to the child-focused CBT and parental-anxiety management (CBT+PAM). At posttreatment, results indicated that within the child-anxiety-only condition, 82% of the CBT youth versus 80% of the CBT+PAM youth no longer met criteria for an anxiety disorder. Within the child + parental anxiety condition, 39% in the CBT versus 77% in CBT+PAM condition no longer met anxiety disorder criteria. These results indicated that children with two nonanxious parents responded more favorably to child-focused CBT than did children who had one or more anxious parents. Moreover, the inclusion of the PAM increased the efficacy of child-focused CBT for children but only for children who had at least one anxious parent. However, at 6- and 12-month follow-ups, these differential effects became less evident.

Spence et al. (2000) investigated the effectiveness of a social-skills training-based CBT for the treatment of childhood social phobia. The authors randomly assigned 50 children (ages 7–14 years) with a primary diagnosis of social phobia to child-focused CBT, CBT plus parent involvement, or a wait-list control. At posttreatment, significantly more children in the treatment conditions (87.5% CBT plus parental involvement; 58% child-only CBT) versus control condition (7%) were free of the clinical diagnosis of social phobia. Although more children in the parent involvement versus the child-only condition were diagnosis-free at posttreatment, this difference was not statistically significant. In comparison with the wait-list control, children in both treatments also demonstrated significant improvements on other dependent measures, including measures of child social and general anxiety and parental ratings of social skills performance. At 12-month follow-up, both treatment conditions retained their improvement.

Other studies have examined the effectiveness of family treatments held in a group format (Mendlowitz et al., 1999; Toren et al., 2000). The results suggest that group family CBT produces significant changes from pretreatment to posttreatment compared with the wait-list control group. For example, Mendlowitz et al. (1999) examined the effect of a group CBT intervention on anxiety, depression, and coping strategies among children with anxiety disorders, as well as the role of parental involvement. Sixty-eight children (ages 7–12 years) and their parents were randomly assigned to three 12-week treatment conditions: parent + child intervention, child-only intervention, and parent-only intervention. All treatment groups reported fewer anxious and depressive symptoms as well as changes in their use of coping strategies posttreatment. Compared with the singular conditions (e.g., parent-only, child-only), youth in the combined parent + child intervention demonstrated notable improvements posttreatment, employing more active coping strategies and showing greater gains in parental reports of emotional well-being. Although all modes of the group CBT were effective in reducing symptoms of anxiety and depression, in this study, it was the concurrent parental involvement that conferred the additional benefit on the child's coping strategies.

Longer-Term Follow-Up

Although the reported results point to the effectiveness of CBT in treating children with anxiety disorders and to the maintenance of effects at 1-year follow-up, longer-term follow-up of clients is warranted (Kendall, 1998; Weisz & Hawley, 1998). At present, three long-term follow-up studies have been reported. Kendall and Southam-Gerow (1996) reassessed 36 of the 47 children treated in the 1994 clinical trial. The length of time from completion of the treatment program to reassessment ranged from 2 to 5 years, with an average of 3.35 years. On both self-report and parent-report measures and in terms of diagnostic status, the treatment gains seen at 1-year follow-up were maintained at longer-term follow-up. An average of 6 years after treatment in Barrett et al.'s 1996 study, 52 of the 79 original clients (ages 14–21 years) were reassessed with diagnostic interviews, clinician ratings, and self- and parent-report measures (Barrett et al., 2001). Analyses of diagnostic status revealed that 86% no longer met criteria for any anxiety disorder. Consistent with Kendall and Southam-Gerow's (1996) findings, treatment gains noted at the 12-month follow-up were maintained on a majority of the measures. However, contrary to Barrett et al.'s predictions, CBT and CBT+FAM were no longer discernibly different at long-term follow-up, suggesting that both treatments are effective in treating childhood anxiety disorders. At an average of 7.4 years after treatment, Kendall et al. (2004) studied 86 of the original 94 cases reported in Kendall et al. (1997) and the results of diagnostic evaluations and self- and parent-reports support the maintenance of gains.

Clinical Significance

Several randomized clinical trials provide evidence supporting the merits of CBT for child anxiety. A caveat is worth noting. Randomized clinical trials document efficacy by testing the statistical significance of its outcomes (changes are beyond that expected by chance); however, these analyses do not indicate the clinical significance or meaningfulness of the magnitude of change attributed to the treatment (Kendall, Flannery-

Schroeder, & Ford, 1999). Researchers have posed the following question: Does the treated individual's level of functioning fall within normal limits? To address this question, the use of normative comparisons has been developed (Kendall, Marrs-Garcia, et al., 1999; Kendall & Sheldrick, 2000) and applied to the evaluation of treatment outcomes. For example, Kendall, Marrs-Garcia, et al. (1999) evaluated the clinical significance of the findings in the Barrett et al. study (1996) by comparing the posttreatment data (i.e., CBCL internalizing scale T scores; Achenbach, 1991a) on treated individuals with the data on normative (nondisordered) individuals. Before treatment, the CBT+FAM group averaged above the clinical cutoff point on the CBCL ($M = 66.3$, $SD = 7.3$; clinical cutoff = 63; Achenbach, 1991a), suggesting that the group was indeed in the clinical range. In contrast, 6 months after treatment, this group was well below the normative range ($M = 45.8$, $SD = 7.6$, borderline clinical cutoff = 60; Achenbach, 1991a). This analysis determined that the treated group was statistically indistinguishable from a normative sample, whereas the mean of the control condition remained outside the normative range. These results indicate that the once deviant cases were successfully treated and returned to within a normative range. Several of the evaluations of CBT (e.g., Kendall et al., 1997) included documentation regarding the clinical significance of the outcomes.

Variables Affecting Treatment Outcome

In addition to the progress made in evaluating the effectiveness of CBT for anxious children, steps have been taken to examine potential factors that may moderate treatment outcome. Factors such as gender, ethnicity, and comorbidity have been considered. Very few of these factors have been found to predict treatment outcome. For example, Treadwell, Flannery-Schroeder, and Kendall (1995) examined gender and ethnic differences in the levels of anxious symptomatology experienced by 178 children (ages 9–13 years) referred to the CAADC. In addition, the study examined treatment sensitivity across gender and ethnicity in 81 children diagnosed with a *DSM–III–R* childhood anxiety disorder. The study examined child, parent, teacher, and clinical diagnostician ratings of clinically anxious youth and found no differences in the prevalence or intensity of fears as a function of gender or ethnicity. Similarly, content of the children's fears did not differ significantly across gender or ethnicity. Furthermore, pertaining to treatment outcomes, reductions in symptoms of anxiety and the presence of an anxiety disorder diagnosis were consistent across gender and ethnicity.

Correlates of good versus poor treatment response (Southam-Gerow, Kendall, & Weersing, 2001) were investigated in 135 youth (ages 7–15 yeras) receiving CBT for a primary anxiety disorder diagnosis. Results indicated that, in general, although the participants as reported in earlier work had improved, higher levels of maternal- and teacher-reported internalizing psychopathology reported before the child was treated, higher levels of maternal self-reported depressive symptoms, and older child age were all correlated with less favorable treatment response. However, other factors such as child ethnicity, child gender, family income, family composition (i.e., dual- versus single-parent household), child-reported symptomatology, and maternal-reported level of child externalizing problems did not predict treatment response.

Kendall, Brady, and Verduin (2001) investigated the impact of comorbidity on treatment outcome among children with *DSM–III–R/DSM–IV* primary anxiety disorder diagnoses (ages 9–13 years) who had been treated at the CAADC. Seventy-nine percent of the 173 participants had at least one comorbid diagnoses. At posttreatment, 68% of noncomorbid versus 71% of comorbid participants were free of their primary diagnosis. The CBT program was similarly effective with comorbid and noncomorbid anxious children, with both showing significant reductions in pretreatment diagnoses and parent–child self-reported symptomatology.

Treadwell and Kendall (1996) examined the relationship between childhood anxiety disorders and the valence (i.e., positive or negative) and content of self-statements, as well as the impact of treatment on self-statements. Of the 151 (ages 8–13 years) participants, 71 had anxiety disorders and 80 were control participants. Positive and negative self-statements and a states-of-mind (SOM) ratio were examined. Results indicated that the negative (but not the positive) self-statements and the SOM ratio of anxiety-disordered children significantly predicted anxiety and posttreatment anxiety improvements as well as mediated treatment gains. Gains were mediated by reductions in the children's negative self-talk.

Berman, Weems, Silverman, and Kurtines (2000) examined predictors of treatment outcome in an exposure-based CBT for phobic and anxiety disordered youth. A number of child, parent, and treatment variables were explored: children's sociodemographics, diagnostic characteristics (e.g., number of diagnoses), treatment format (i.e., individual, group), parent and child reports of child symptoms, parent symptoms, and marital adjustment. Analyses determined the best predictors to be depression and trait anxiety in the child and symptoms such as depression, hostility, and paranoia in the parent, although these parental symptoms were less effective predictors among older children and group treatment.

Although few variables differentiate treatment responders from less favorable treatment responders, one study reported differences between treatment completers and treatment noncompleters. Kendall and Sugarman (1997) examined the differences between 190 CBT completers (*n* = 146) and terminators (*n* = 44; including both refusers and dropouts), finding that terminators were more likely to live in a single-parent household, be ethnic minorities, and self-report fewer anxious symptoms than completers. Follow-up interviews suggested that these factors were influential in the terminators' decisions to discontinue treatment. Importantly, SES and parent education were not predictors of termination.

FUTURE CONSIDERATIONS

Although the treatment of childhood anxiety disorders has advanced significantly, important questions remain to be examined. What are the active components of CBT of childhood anxiety disorders? Can CBT for anxious children have long-term effects, and will these effects, if present, also influence the sequelae of the disorder? What impact does CBT for youth, either child- or family-focused, have on parental psychopathology? What role do process variables (e.g., therapeutic alliance) play in determining the outcomes of CBT? How effective will CBT be found to be when it is provided by practicing clinicians working in community mental health settings?

Active Components of Treatment

Reviewers of the literature (Kazdin & Weisz, 1998; Ollendick & King, 1998) find reasonable support for the efficacy of CBT for childhood anxiety disorders, yet the treatment is multifaceted and we know little about the types of features that contribute most to the observed gains. Are the exposure experiences, the changes in cognitive processing, or the learning of coping skills key to success? Studying a different sample (phobic youth), Silverman, Kurtines, Ginsburg, Weems, Rabian, and Serafini (1999) reported that a treatment involving education about anxiety and therapeutic support (ES) produced results akin to those produced by CBT. Eighty-one children (ages 6–16 years) with phobic disorders and their parents completed a 10-week program in which children and parents participated in separate treatment sessions. On all outcome measures, both CBT-treated youth demonstrated significant improvements and maintained these gains at 3-, 6-, and 12-month follow-ups. Children receiving ES also showed similar improvements at posttreatment and at 3-, 6-, and 12-month follow-ups, suggesting that attending a treatment for 10 weeks may reduce anxiety symptoms in children. However, an inspection of the ES condition finds that it included some of the cognitive and educational features seen in CBT. Future research must evaluate the efficacy and effectiveness of CBT by making comparisons to conditions other than wait-list but that do not include some of the features thought to be active within CBT. For instance, a randomized clinical trial being conducted at the CAADC is comparing individual CBT and family CBT to an active control condition in which participants receive family treatment involving education about anxiety, support for dealing with an anxious child, and therapeutic attention. The outcomes will provide useful information about the differential merits of family inclusion in CBT and about relative efficacy when compared to a non-CBT treatment condition.

Long-Term Follow-Up

Does successful treatment of an anxiety disorder in childhood have long-term benefits? In a 7.4-year follow-up, Kendall and colleagues (2004) evaluated not only the long-term maintenance of treatment gains but also the potential impact that treatment had on subsequent depressive symptoms and substance use problems. Of the 94 youth who had completed treatment an average of 7 to 8 years prior (Kendall et al., 1997) 88 were evaluated using structured diagnostic interviews (completed by both youth and parent [about the youth]) and multiple self-report measures to assess anxiety levels, depressive symptoms, substance use, and other comorbid disorders. Results indicated that not only did a meaningful percentage of participants maintain significant improvements in anxiety at 7.4-year follow-up, but also those positive responders to treatment had a reduced amount of substance use involvement and related problems at the 7.4-year follow-up. These findings suggest that the amelioration of anxiety in children can have positive effects on the sequelae of anxiety as well.

Parental Psychopathology

Does the treatment of an anxious child have beneficial spillover for the parents? What is the impact of child CBT on parental psychopathology? Rates of anxiety disorders in parents of anxious children have been found to be high. Last, Hersen, Kazdin, Francis, and Grubb (1987) reported that up to 87% of mothers of children with anxiety disorders from a clinic sample also exhibited an anxiety disorder, and parental anxiety has been hypothesized as an important factor in the development and maintenance of childhood anxiety disorders (e.g., Cobham et al., 1998; Rapee, 2001). It is interesting to speculate that a reduction in parental anxiety may be a concurrent effect of a reduction in the child's anxiety. Using structured interviews before and after treatment to assess parental psychopathology (current and lifetime), an ongoing project at CAADC will be examining the comparative effectiveness of individual and family treatments in reducing symptoms of parental anxiety.

Process Variables

With good reason, researchers have discussed both the process of therapy and the outcomes associated with therapy. Although reports of outcomes associated with CBT of childhood anxiety are fairly numerous, less attention has been paid to the association between outcome and treatment process variables such as therapeutic alliance. Traditionally, the study of process has been considered secondary to the evaluation of outcome (Russell & Shirk, 1998); one first needs to show that a treatment produces beneficial gains before one examines the factors that may be associated with the gains (Chambless & Hollon, 1998; Kazdin & Kendall, 1998; Kendall, Flannery-Schroeder, & Ford, 1999; Kiesler, 1966). Now that CBT for youth with anxiety disorders has been shown to have promise with respect to efficacy, exploration of the therapy process is warranted because such results will provide valuable information about the specific therapeutic mechanisms that contribute to psychological change. In addition, process research may assist in bridging the gap between treatments that have empirical support and their application in clinical settings (Russell & Shirk, 1998). Both clinicians and researchers have earmarked the examination of process variables within empirically supported treatments as a priority for research. Research being conducted at the CAADC is examining therapy process within manual-based treatment, focusing on the therapeutic alliance, therapist flexibility, and child involvement.

The Transportability of Cognitive–Behavioral Treatment

Efficacy studies support the usefulness of CBT, and the treatment has been provided to real-world cases. But the field has yet to fully examine the effectiveness of CBT for anxious children provided in typical community mental health settings. The study of the transportability of treatments with demonstrated efficacy is a much-needed area of research. Children with coprimary mood or behavior disorders (comorbid diagnoses that are as interfering or distressing to the child or family as the anxiety diagnosis) are included in our randomized clinical trials, but it would also be informative to know if research-clinic samples and mental health center samples respond comparably. These are beginning steps toward examining effectiveness, and we welcome further research that provides relevant data.

REFERENCES

Achenbach, T. M. (1991a). *Manual for the child behavior checklists/4–18 and 1991 profile*. Burlington: University of Vermont.

Achenbach, T. M. (1991b). *Manual for the teacher's report form and 1991 profile*, Burlington: University of Vermont.

American Psychiatric Association. (1994). *Diagnostic and statistical manual of mental disorders* (4th ed., rev.). Washington, DC: Author.

American Psychological Association Task Force on Promotion and Dissemination of Psychological Procedures. (1995). Training in and dissemination of empirically validated psychological treatments: Report and recommendations. *Clinical Psychologist, 48*, 3–24.

Anderson, J. C., Williams, S., McGee, R., & Silva, P. A. (1987). *DSM–III* disorders in preadolescent children. Prevalence in a large sample from a general population. *Archives of General Psychiatry, 44*, 69–76.

Barrett, P. M., Dadds, M. R., & Rapee, R. M. (1996). Family treatment of childhood anxiety: A controlled trial. *Journal of Consulting and Clinical Psychology, 64*, 333–342.

Barrett, P. M., Duffy, A. L., Dadds, M. R., & Rapee, R. M. (2001). Cognitive–behavioral treatment of anxiety disorders in children: Long-term (6-year) follow-up. *Journal of Consulting and Clinical Psychology, 69*, 1–7.

Beck, A., Rush, A., Shaw, B., & Emery, G. (1979). *Cognitive therapy of depression.* New York: Guilford Press.

Beidel, D. C., Fink, C. M., & Turner, S. M. (1996). Stability of anxious symptomatology in children. *Journal of Abnormal Child Psychology, 24*, 257–269.

Beidel, D. C., Turner, S. M., & Morris, T. (1995). A new inventory to assess childhood social anxiety and phobia: The Social Phobia and Anxiety Inventory for Children. *Psychological Assessment, 7*, 73–79.

Berman, S. L., Weems, C. F., Silverman, W. K., & Kurtines, W. M. (2000). Predictors of outcome in exposure-based cognitive and behavioral treatments for phobic and anxiety disorders in children. *Behavior Therapy, 31*, 713–731.

Brady, E., & Kendall, P. C. (1992). Comorbidity of anxiety and depression in children and adolescents. *Psychological Bulletin, 111*, 244–255.

Brownell, K. D., Marlatt, G. A., Lichtenstein, E., & Wilson, G. T. (1986). Understanding and preventing relapse. *American Psychologist, 41*, 765–782.

Chambless, D., & Hollon, S. (1998). Defining empirically supported treatments. *Journal of Consulting and Clinical Psychology, 66*, 5–17.

Chansky, T. E., & Kendall, P. C. (1997). Social expectancies and self-perceptions in anxiety-disordered children. *Journal of Anxiety Disorders, 11*, 347–363.

Cobham, V. E., Dadds, M. R., & Spence, S. H. (1998). The role of parental anxiety in the treatment of childhood anxiety. *Journal of Consulting and Clinical Psychology, 66*, 893–905.

Dadds, M. (1995). *Families, children, and the development of dysfunction.* London: Sage.

DiNardo, P., Brown, T., & Barlow, D. (1994). *The Anxiety Disorders Interview Schedule for DSM–Lifetime version (ADIS–IV-L).* Albany, NY: Graywind.

D'Zurilla, T. J., & Goldfried, M. R. (1971). Problem-solving and behavior modification. *Journal of Abnormal Psychology, 78*, 107–126.

D'Zurilla, T. J., & Nezu, A. M. (1999). *Problem-solving therapy: A social competence approach to clinical intervention* (2nd ed.). New York: Springer.

Eisen, A. R., & Silverman, W. K. (1993). Should I relax or change my thoughts? A preliminary examination of cognitive therapy, relaxation training, and their combination with overanxious children. *Journal of Cognitive Psychotherapy: An International Quarterly, 7*, 265–279.

Fergusson, D. M., Horwood, L. J., & Lynskey, M. T. (1993). Prevalence and comorbidity of *DSM–III–R* diagnoses in a birth cohort of 15 year olds. *Journal of the American Academy of Child and Adolescent Psychiatry, 32,* 1127–1134.

Flannery-Schroeder, E. C., & Kendall, P. C. (2000). Group and individual cognitive–behavioral treatments for youth with anxiety disorders: A randomized clinical trial. *Cognitive Therapy and Research, 24,* 251–278.

Hayward, C., Varady, S., Albano, A. M., Thienemann, M., Henderson, L., & Schatzberg, A. F. (2000). Cognitive–behavioral group therapy for social phobia in female adolescents: Results of a pilot study. *Journal of the American Academy of Child and Adolescent Psychiatry, 39,* 721–726.

Howard, B. L., & Kendall, P. C. (1996). Cognitive–behavioral family therapy for anxiety disordered children: A multiple baseline evaluation. *Cognitive Therapy and Research, 20,* 423–443.

Howard, B. L., Chu, B., Krain, A., Marrs-Garcia, A., & Kendall, P. C. (1999). *Cognitive–behavioral family therapy for anxious children: Therapist manual* (2nd ed.). Ardmore, PA: Workbook Publishing.

Hudson, J. L., & Rapee, R. M. (in press). Parent-child interactions and the anxiety disorders: An observational study. *Behaviour Research and Therapy.*

Kane, M., & Kendall, P. C. (1989). Anxiety disorders in children: A multiple baseline evaluation of cognitive–behavioral treatment. *Behavior Therapy, 20,* 499–308.

Kazdin, A. E., & Kendall, P. C. (1998). Current progress and future plans for developing effective treatments: comments and perspectives. *Journal of Consulting and Clinical Psychology, 27,* 217–226.

Kazdin, A., & Weisz, J. (1998). Identifying and developing empirically supported child and adolescent treatments. *Journal of Consulting and Clinical Psychology, 66,* 100–110.

Kazdin, A., French, N., Unis, A., Esveldt-Dawson, K., & Sherick, R. (1983). Hopelessness, depression, and suicidal intent among inpatient children. *Journal of Consulting and Clinical Psychology, 51,* 504–510.

Keller, M. B., Lavori, P. W., Wunder, J., Beardslee, W. R., Schwartz, R., & Roth, J. (1992). Chronic course of anxiety disorders in children and adolescents. *Journal of the American Academy of Child and Adolescent Psychiatry, 31,* 595–599.

Kendall, P. C. (1984). Behavioral assessment and methodology. In G. T. Wilson, C. M. Franks, K. D. Brownell, & P. C. Kendall (Eds.), *Annual review of behavior therapy: Theory and practice* (Vol. 9). New York: Guilford Press.

Kendall, P. C. (1989). The generalization and maintenance of behavior change: Comments, considerations and the "no-cure" criticism. *Behavior Therapy, 20,* 357–364.

Kendall, P. C. (1992). *Coping cat workbook.* Ardmore, PA: Workbook Publishing.

Kendall, P. C. (1994). Treating anxiety disorders in children: Results of a randomized clinical trial. *Journal of Consulting and Clinical Psychology, 62,* 100–110.

Kendall, P. C. (1998). Empirically supported psychological therapies. *Journal of Consulting and Clinical Psychology, 66*, 3–8.

Kendall, P. C. (2000). *Cognitive–behavioral therapy for anxious children: Therapist manual* (2nd ed.). Ardmore, PA: Workbook Publishing.

Kendall, P. C., Brady, E. U., & Verduin, T. V. (2001). Comorbidity in childhood anxiety disorders and treatment outcome. *Journal of the American Academy of Child and Adolescent Psychiatry, 40*, 787–794.

Kendall, P. C., Choudhury, M., Hudson, J., & Webb, A. (2002). *The C.A.T. Project manual for the cognitive–behavioral treatment of anxious adolescents*. Ardmore, PA: Workbook Publishing.

Kendall, P. C., & Chu, B. C. (2000). Retrospective self-reports of therapist flexibility in a manual-based treatment for youths with anxiety disorders. *Journal of Clinical Child Psychology, 29*, 209–220.

Kendall, P. C., Chu, B., Gifford, A., Hayes, C., & Nauta, M. (1998). Breathing life into a manual: Flexibility and creativity with manual-based treatments. *Cognitive and Behavioral Practice, 5*, 177–198.

Kendall, P. C., Flannery-Schroeder, E. C., & Ford, J. D. (1999). Therapy outcome research methods. In P. C. Kendall, J. N. Butcher, & G. N. Holmbeck (Eds.), *Handbook of research methods in clinical psychology* (pp. 330–363). New York: Wiley.

Kendall, P. C., Flannery-Schroeder, E., Panichelli-Mindel, S., Southam-Gerow, M., Henin, A., & Warman, M. (1997). Therapy for youth with anxiety disorders: A second randomized clinical trial. *Journal of Consulting and Clinical Psychology, 65*, 366–380.

Kendall, P. C., MacDonald, J. P., & Treadwell, K. R. H. (1995). The treatment of anxiety disorders in youth. In A. R. Eisen, C. A. Kearney, et al. (Eds.), *Clinical handbook of anxiety disorders in children and adolescents* (pp. 573–597). Northvale, NJ: Jason Aronson.

Kendall, P. C., & Marrs-Garcia, A. (1999). *Psychometric analyses of a therapy-sensitive measure: The Coping Questionnaire (CQ)*. Manuscript submitted for publication.

Kendall, P. C., Marrs-Garcia, A., Nath, S. R., & Sheldrick, R. C. (1999). Normative comparisons for the evaluation of clinical significance. *Journal of Consulting and Clinical Psychology, 67*, 285–299.

Kendall, P. C., Safford, S., Flannery-Schroeder, E., & Webb, A. (2004). Child anxiety treatment: Outcomes in adolescence and impact on substance use and depression at 7.4-year follow-up. *Journal of Consulting and Clinical Psychology, 72*, 276–287.

Kendall, P. C., & Sheldrick, R. C. (2000). Normative data for normative comparisons. *Journal of Consulting and Clinical Psychology, 68*, 767–773.

Kendall, P. C., & Southam-Gerow, M. (1996). Long-term follow-up of treatment for anxiety disordered youth. *Journal of Consulting and Clinical Psychology, 65*, 883–888.

Kendall, P. C., & Sugarman, A. (1997). Attrition in the treatment of childhood anxiety disorders. *Journal of Consulting and Clinical Psychology, 65*, 883–888.

Kiesler, D. J. (1966). Some myths of psychotherapy research and the search for a paradigm. *Psychological Bulletin, 65*, 110–136.

King, N. J., Hamilton, D. I., & Ollendick, T. H. (1988). *Children's phobias: A behavioral perspective.* London: Wiley.

Kortlander, E., Kendall, P. C., & Panicchelli-Mindel, S. M. (1997). Maternal expectations and attributions about coping in anxious children. *Journal of Anxiety Disorders, 11*, 297–315.

Kovacs, M. (1981). Rating scales to assess depression in school-aged children. *Acta Paedopsychiatrica, 46*, 305–315.

Krain, A. L., & Kendall, P. C. (2000). The role of parental emotional distress in parent report of child anxiety. *Journal of Clinical Child Psychology, 29*, 328–335.

Last, C. G., Hersen, M., Kazdin, A. E., Finkelstein, R., & Strauss, C. C. (1987). Comparison of *DSM–III* separation anxiety and overanxious disorders: Demographic characteristics and patterns of comorbidity. *Journal of the American Academy of Child and Adolescent Psychiatry, 26*, 527–531.

Last, C. G., Hersen, M., Kazdin, A., Francis, G., & Grubb, H. J. (1987). Psychiatric illness in the mothers of anxious children. *American Journal of Psychiatry, 144*, 1580–1583.

Last, C. G., Strauss, C. C., & Francis, G. (1987). Comorbidity among childhood anxiety disorders. *The Journal of Nervous and Mental Disease, 175*, 726–730.

March, J. S., & Albano, A. M. (1998). New developments in assessing pediatric anxiety disorders. In T. Ollendick & R. Prinz (Eds.), *Advances in clinical child psychology: Vol. 20.* New York: Plenum Press.

March, J. S., Parker, J., Sullivan, K., Stallings, P., & Conners, C. (1997). The Multidimensional Anxiety Scale for Children (MASC): Factor structure, reliability & validity. *Journal of the American Academy of Child and Adolescent Psychiatry, 36*, 554–565.

Marlatt, G. A., & Gordon, J. J. (1985). *Relapse prevention.* New York: Guilford Press.

Mendlowitz, S. L., Manassis, K., Bradley, S., Scapillato, D., Miezitis, S., & Shaw, B. F. (1999). Cognitive–behavioral group treatments in childhood anxiety disorders: The role of parental involvement. *Journal of the American Academy of Child and Adolescent Psychiatry, 38*, 1223–1229.

Ollendick, T. H. (1995). Cognitive–behavioral treatment of panic disorder with agoraphobia in adolescents: A multiple baseline design analysis. *Behavior Therapy, 26*, 517–531.

Ollendick, T. H., & King, N. J. (1998). Empirically supported treatments for children with phobic and anxiety disorders: Current status. *Journal of Clinical Child Psychology, 27*, 156–167.

Rapee, R. M. (1997). The potential role of childrearing practices in the development of anxiety and depression. *Clinical Psychology Review, 17*, 47–67.

Rapee, R. M. (2001). The development of generalized anxiety. In M. W. Vasey & R. Dadds (Eds.), *The developmental psychopathology of anxiety* (pp. 481–503). New York: Oxford University Press.

Rapee, R. M., Wignall, A., Hudson, J. L., & Schniering, C. A. (2000). *Evidence-based treatment of child and adolescent anxiety disorders*. Oakland, CA: New Harbinger Publications.

Ronan, K. R., & Kendall, P. C. (1997). Self-talk in distressed youth: States-of-mind and content specificity. *Journal of Clinical Child Psychology, 26*, 330–337.

Russell, R. L., & Shirk, S. R. (1998). Child psychotherapy process research. In T. H. Ollendick & R. Prinz (Eds.), *Advances in clinical child psychology: Vol. 20*. New York: Plenum Press.

Sanders, M. (1996). New directions in behavioral family intervention with children. In T. Ollendick & R. Prinz (Eds.), *Advances in clinical child psychology: Vol. 18*. New York: Plenum Press.

Schluderman, E., & Schluderman, S. (1970). Replicability of factors in children's report of parent behavior (CRPBI). *Journal of Psychology, 76*, 239–249.

Shaffer, D., Gould, M., Brasic, J., Ambrosini, P., Fisher, P., Bird, H., & Aluwahlia, S. (1983). A children's Global Assessment Scale. *Archives of General Psychiatry, 40*, 1228–1231.

Silverman, E., & Albano, A. M. (1997). *The Anxiety Disorders Interview Schedule for Children (DSM–IV)*. San Antonio, TX: Psychological Corporation.

Silverman, W. K., Kurtines, W. M., Ginsburg, G. S., Weems, C. F., Lumpkin, P. W., & Carmichael, D. H. (1999). Treating anxiety disorders in children with group cognitive–behavioral therapy: A randomized clinical trial. *Journal of Consulting and Clinical Psychology, 67*, 995–1003.

Silverman, W. K., Kurtines, W., Ginsburg, G. S., Weems, C. F., Rabian, B., & Serafini, L. (1999). Contingency management, self-control, and education support in the treatment of childhood phobic disorders: A randomized clinical trial. *Journal of Consulting and Clinical Psychology, 67*, 675–687.

Siqueland, L., & Diamond, G. (1998). Engaging parents in cognitive behavioral treatment for children with anxiety disorders. *Cognitive Behavioral Practice, 5*, 81–102.

Siqueland, L., Kendall, P. C., & Steinberg, L. (1996). Anxiety in children: Perceived family environments and observed family interaction style. *Journal of Clinical Child Psychology, 25*, 225–237.

Southam-Gerow, M. A., & Kendall, P. C. (2000). A preliminary study of the emotion understanding of youths referred for treatment of anxiety disorders. *Journal of Clinical Child Psychology, 29*, 319–327.

Southam-Gerow, M. A., Kendall, P. C., & Weersing, V. R. (2001). Examining outcome variability: Correlates of treatment response in a child and adolescent anxiety clinic. *Journal of Clinical Child Psychology, 30*, 422–436.

Spanier, G. (1976). Measuring dyadic adjustment: Scales for assessing the quality of marriage and similar dyads. *Journal of Marriage and the Family, 38*, 15–28.

Speilberger, C. D., Gorsuch, R. L., & Lushene, R. E. (1970). *Manual for the state-trait anxiety inventory*. Palo Alto, CA: Consulting Psychologists Press.

Spence, S. H., Donovan, C., & Brechman-Toussaint, M. (2000). The treatment of childhood social phobia: The effectiveness of a social skills training-based, cognitive–behavioural intervention, with and without parental involvement. *Journal of Child Psychology and Psychiatry, 41*, 713–726.

Strauss, C., Lease, C., Last, C., & Francis, G. (1988). Overanxious disorder: An examination of developmental differences. *Journal of Abnormal Child Psychology, 11*, 433–443.

Toren, P., Wolmer, L., Rosental, B., Eldar, S., Koren, S., Lask, M., et al. (2000). Case series: Brief parent-child group therapy for childhood anxiety disorders using a manual-based cognitive–behavioral technique. *Journal of the American Academy of Child and Adolescent Psychiatry, 39*, 1309–1312.

Treadwell, K. R. H., Flannery-Schroeder, E. C., & Kendall, P. C. (1995). Ethnicity and gender in relation to adaptive functioning, diagnostic status, and treatment outcome in children from an anxiety clinic. *Journal of Anxiety Disorders, 9*, 373–384.

Treadwell, K. H., & Kendall, P. C. (1996). Self-talk in anxiety-disordered youth: States-of-mind, content specificity, and treatment outcome. *Journal of Consulting and Clinical Psychology, 64*, 941–950.

Verhulst, F. C., van der Ende, J., Ferdinand, R. F., & Kasius, M. C. (1997). The prevalence of *DSM–III–R* diagnoses in a national sample of Dutch adolescents. *Archives of General Psychiatry, 54*, 329–336.

Weisz, J. R., & Hawley, K. M. (1988). Finding, evaluating, refining, and applying empirically supported treatments for children and adolescents. *Journal of Clinical Child Psychology, 27*, 206–216.

4

TREATING CHILDHOOD SOCIAL PHOBIA: SOCIAL EFFECTIVENESS THERAPY FOR CHILDREN

DEBORAH C. BEIDEL AND ROXANN ROBERSON-NAY

Social phobia is a marked and persistent fear of social situations, characterized by pervasive social inhibition and timidity (American Psychiatric Association, 1994). Although the average age of onset is mid to late adolescence, the disorder can appear much earlier (Beidel, 1991; Schneier, Johnson, Hornig, Liebowitz, & Weissman, 1992). Youth with the disorder fear speaking, reading, eating, or writing in public; going to parties; using public restrooms; speaking to authority figures; and participating in informal social interactions (Beidel, Turner, & Morris, 1999). Unstructured peer interactions (e.g., playing games with other children) are the most frequent distressing events (Beidel, 1991), occurring as often as every other day

This chapter was supported in part by National Institute of Mental Health Grants 53703 and 60332 to the first author.

75

(Beidel, Turner, & Morris, 1999). Emotional reactions include headaches or stomach aches, occasional panic attacks, crying, and behavioral avoidance. About 30% of one sample of children who refused to go to school for anxiety-based reasons had social fears (Last, Perrin, Hersen, & Kazdin, 1992), and 10% of children with social phobia refused to go to school (Beidel, Turner, & Morris, 1999). Additionally, children often use subtle avoidance strategies to minimize distress, including getting someone else to do the feared task or pretending to be sick (Beidel, Turner, & Morris, 1999).

In addition to social fears and avoidance, these youth also suffer from higher trait anxiety, dysphoria and depression, loneliness, a very restricted range of social relationships, and deficient social skills (Beidel, Turner, & Morris, 1999). Oppositional behaviors sometimes result, and abuse of alcohol and other substances have been reported in adolescents (Clark, 1993). In one study (Beidel, Turner, & Morris, 1999), approximately 60% of children with social phobia met criteria for a comorbid disorder, including generalized anxiety disorder (10%), attention deficit hyperactivity disorder (10%), specific phobia (10%), selective mutism (8%), obsessive–compulsive disorder (6%), panic disorder (2%), adjustment disorder with depressed mood (2%), and major depression (2%).

Before the *Diagnostic and Statistical Manual of Mental Disorders, Fourth Edition (DSM–IV)*, prevalence data indicated that social phobia affected about 1% of the general child population (Anderson, Williams, McGee, & Silva, 1987; Benjamin, Costello, & Warren, 1990; Costello, 1989; Kashani & Orvaschel, 1990). However, in light of changes in *DSM–IV* (i.e., removal of social fears from the criteria for overanxious disorder and the deletion of avoidant disorder of childhood), the prevalence rate no doubt is higher. For example, whereas only 18% of children in one clinic sample were diagnosed with the *Third Edition, Revised (DSM–III–R)* social phobia, 40% of the same sample was diagnosed with social phobia when *DSM–IV* criteria were used (Kendall & Warman, 1997), primarily because of the deletion of avoidant disorder of childhood. Furthermore, the incidence of social phobia rises with increasing age (e.g., Kashani & Orvaschel, 1990); thus, more adolescents than preadolescents are affected. Recently reported prevalences rates were 3.7% based on adolescent self-report and 6.3% based on parental report. The gender distribution is approximately equal and both Caucasian and African American children have a similar clinical presentation (Beidel, Turner, & Morris, 1999).

The sequelae of childhood social phobia include depression (Perrin & Last, 1993) and social isolation (Beidel, Turner, & Morris, 1999). Clark (1993) reported that among some adolescent social phobias, conduct problems, oppositional behaviors, and alcohol and substance abuse problems were detected. When distress reaches a certain level, children sometimes refuse to engage in social activities and are therefore perceived as oppositional. Davidson (1993) noted that conduct problems and truancy were part of the childhood history of adults with social phobia and that onset of social phobia before age 11 predicted nonrecovery in adulthood. Although some data are preliminary and retrospective data reported by Davidson (1993) must be regarded cautiously, these consistent findings document the pervasive negative outcomes when childhood social phobia is unrecognized and untreated.

Severe social anxiety hinders the development of adequate social abilities, interfering in the ability to establish friendships and increasing negative self-evaluation (Rubin, LeMare, & Lollis, 1990). Although it is accepted that children with social phobia experience significant social impairment compared with nonanxious peers, few empirical data exist. However, in comparison with controls, these children were rated by independent observers as having significantly poorer social and performance skills as well as higher social anxiety when engaged in social and performance tasks (Beidel, Turner, & Morris, 1999); Spence, Donovan, & Brechman-Toussaint, 1999). Furthermore, preliminary data from our clinic indicate that socially anxious children are less likely than their nonanxious peers to engage in activities such as conversing with others, attending social events, and participating in class (Ferrell, Beidel, & Turner, 2001). Moreover, these differences become more pronounced between the ages of 11 and 12.

In summary, studies of childhood social phobia reveal a pattern of pervasive fear and anxiety, typically beginning at a very early age. This pervasive pattern, in turn, often prevents engagement in social activities, interfering with the establishment of normal social relationships and social development (Rubin et al., 1990). Thus, social isolation in social phobic children appears to prevent the development of appropriate social skills, thereby increasing social isolation, dysphoria, and loneliness. These data suggest that an intervention program for preadolescent children with social phobia would have to be multidimensional, addressing the children's deficient social skills as well as reducing their social distress and social avoidance.

THE MARYLAND CENTER FOR ANXIETY DISORDERS

The Maryland Center for Anxiety Disorders (MCAD) was established in 1998 at the Department of Psychology, University of Maryland-College Park, under the codirection of Samuel M. Turner and Deborah C. Beidel. MCAD is a clinical research center that offers behavioral treatment to children, adolescents, and adults with anxiety disorders. Disorders treated include social phobia, obsessive-compulsive disorder, panic disorder, agoraphobia, specific phobia, generalized anxiety disorder, and posttraumatic stress disorder. Clinical research activities at MCAD include projects sponsored by the National Institute of Mental Health. In addition, MCAD conducts various studies of clinical psychopathology, etiology, treatment development, and treatment evaluation. Research in social phobia is international in scope, with ongoing collaborative studies in Brazil and Spain. In addition to the clinical research program, MCAD is a specialty treatment clinic, providing outpatient services for adults, adolescents, and children with anxiety disorders. Finally, MCAD serves as a training site for graduate students, postdoctoral fellows, and professionals interested in training in empirically supported treatments for anxiety disorders.

SOCIAL EFFECTIVENESS THERAPY FOR CHILDREN

Social Effectiveness Therapy for Children[1] (SET-C; Beidel, Turner, & Morris, 2004) was developed based on research addressing the psychopathology of social phobia in general and childhood social phobia (and related conditions such as shyness) in particular. The program was originally developed for preadolescent children between the ages of 8 and 12. More recently, the treatment has been adapted for adolescents between the ages of 13 and 17 (see the Future Directions section later in this chapter). The intervention is short-term but intensive, with 24 therapy sessions over a 12-week period. SET-C includes both once-weekly group training in social skills and once-weekly individualized exposure sessions. In addition, the program includes a unique treatment component, peer generalization sessions, designed to ensure opportunities for transfer of training to situations outside the clinic. Finally, the program includes homework assignments, also designed to extend the intervention and promote generalization. Although parents are not directly included in the treatment sessions, SET-C includes a parent–child educational component. Furthermore, because parents play an important role in carrying out the homework assignments, their cooperation is essential to the success of the program.

Goals of SET-C and Overview of Treatment Components

As previously noted, SET-C (Beidel et al., 2004) was designed to specifically address the psychopathology of childhood social phobia, based on empirical studies of the clinical syndrome as it exists in preadolescent children. As such, it uses a multidimensional treatment approach designed to increase social skills, decrease social fear and avoidance, and increase self-concept. In short, SET-C addresses social competence across various behavioral dimensions. The first component, **Education,** was designed to educate parents and children about the nature of social fears and anxiety and therapeutic expectations. We firmly believe that understanding the psychopa-

---

[1]The SET-C manual is available from Multi-Health Systems, Inc., Toronto, Canada or at www.mhs.com.

thology of this disorder is important for both the clinicians who implement the treatment as well as the parents and children who participate in the intervention.

The second phase of SET-C is **Social Skills Training.** As noted, because of the history of social isolation among children with social phobia, many have not had the opportunity to acquire social skills through so-called normal social interactions. Therefore, social skills training remediates these deficiencies by teaching necessary social skills. Furthermore, group sessions provide an opportunity for intensive practice in interpersonal discourse. These sessions are cumulative, and a new skill is introduced each week. An important element of the social skills training program is a structured **Peer Generalization Program.** Following the group sessions, children with social phobia join a group of nonanxious same-age peers for participation in various social activities. Practice sessions with same-age peers are crucial and allow the accomplishment of two very important goals. First, the sessions guarantee that children with social phobia participate in group activities and practice their social skills with non-shy children in natural settings, such as roller skating rinks and basketball courts. Second, peer generalization sessions harness the positive effects of peer-pairing procedures, such as by providing positive peer role models and positive reinforcement. Peer generalization occurs weekly, and specific activities are tailored to the particular group (e.g., an all-boys group may play basketball one week) but include activities such as roller skating, video arcades, and children's museums.

Concurrent with and complementary to social skills training is **Exposure.** All SET-C components include some degree of exposure (because the social skills training sessions and the peer generalization group sessions involve interactions with others); it is formalized in this component. Individual exposure sessions are therapist assisted and may occur in the clinic or in naturalistic settings or both, depending on the specific nature of the child's fears.

Patient Considerations

As noted in the treatment outcome section later in this chapter, SET-C appears to be effective for children between the ages of 8 and 12 with social phobia. Some preliminary clinical evidence suggests that it also might be effective for children with selective mutism. Although the specific relationship between these two disorders is not known, most children with selective mutism appear to meet diagnostic criteria for social phobia. Children with selective mutism tell their parents that they are too scared to speak. However, unique components of selective mutism (e.g., oppositional behaviors, operant behaviors) appear to exist; these traits may differentiate them from children with social phobia (see Beidel & Turner, 1998). Children with selective mutism are not appropriate for inclusion in SET-C as long as they refuse to speak in group settings. Initially, we included children with selective mutism in SET-C program, but they had a negative effect on the social skills group process. As expected, they refused to participate verbally, answer the therapist's questions, or engage in role-playing activities. Compounding the problem, their refusal served as a model for behavior among the other children in the group. After observing the selectively mute children's refusals to speak, they also began to refuse to speak in the group. Our current treatment recommendation is that children with selective mutism first require individual treatment using exposure until they are comfortable at least talking softly in a group setting. At that point, they can participate in the SET-C protocol.

Most children with comorbid disorders appear to benefit from SET-C treatment as long as social phobia is the primary disorder. However, children with conduct disorders, primary oppositional defiant disorder, psychotic disorders, mental retardation, or pervasive developmental disorders are not appropriate for the SET-C program. Although they may benefit from social skills training, the specific skills needed by children with these disorders are often different from those offered in the SET-C program. Children with primary attention-deficit/hyperactivity disorder (ADHD) also fall into this category. On occasion, children with ADHD are referred to the SET-C program because they have difficulty in social interactions, lack friends, and admit being anxious in social interactions. However, unlike children with social phobia who are neglected by their peers, those with true ADHD behave in a manner that invites *rejection* by other children. They refuse to wait their turn, interrupt conversations, and generally behave inappropriately. Again, although they are in need of social skills training, their skill deficits are different from those addressed by the SET-C program.

Another consideration is comorbid major depression. Children with suicidal ideation, for example, must first be treated for depression. Those without suicidal ideation who still suffer from substantial depressive symptoms may need antidepressants to alleviate their irritability and low energy, both of which could interfere with their ability to participate in an intensive behavioral program. However, once these symptoms are under control, the social phobia should be reassessed; if social phobia is still present after the depressive symptoms have been treated, the child can participate in and benefit from the SET-C program.

The combination of group social skills training and individualized exposure allows SET-C to deal economically with basic social skills deficits found in most children with social phobia and also address each child's unique fear pattern. Thus, group social skills training teaches basic skills needed for effective social interaction and allows practice with various interpersonal partners in a safe clinical setting. In contrast, individual sessions are tailored to the child's specific needs. As part of treatment planning, each child helps to generate a fear hierarchy, which forms the basis of the exposure sessions. It is therefore common for the exposure sessions to be different for all the children, even while they are participating in the same social skills training group.

Assessment

It cannot be overemphasized that a thorough understanding of the psychopathology of childhood social phobia in general and of each child's unique fear pattern is necessary for successful SET-C treatment outcome. It is not sufficient to assume that each child has a fear of negative evaluation. Through diagnostic interviews, self-report data, and behavioral assessment, the specific characteristics (e.g., gender, size of the audience, age of the audience) and the specific fear (of being embarrassed, of looking foolish, of looking unintelligent, of not knowing what to say) will be elucidated. We refer to this as the *core fear*, and it is the primary focus of the individual SET-C sessions. In addition to diagnostic interviews and self-report data, self-monitoring data (daily diaries) can provide a finer-grain analysis of social interaction and avoidance, thereby avoiding the overgeneralization that is common with global self-report measures. All of these assessment methods are part of our standard clinical assessment procedures and used when conducting treatment outcome trials.

Additionally, unlike pharmacological trials, it is not possible to "blind" the SET-C treatment from children, parents, or therapists; therefore, our clinical research trials include evaluation by an independent evaluator who is blinded to treatment condition. Our assessment strategy always includes a comprehensive pre- and posttreatment assessment. If the children are participating in a research protocol, follow-up assessments usually occur 3, 6, and 12 months posttreatment.

Diagnostic Interview

Assessment begins with the Anxiety Disorders Interview Schedule for Children (ADIS–IV-C/P; Silverman & Albano, 1996). As the name implies, this semistructured interview focuses most specifically on childhood anxiety disorders but also allows for assessment of affective disorders, conduct problems, and screening for other disorders (e.g., psychosis, eating disorders, somatoform disorders). Children and parents are interviewed separately, and initial diagnoses are based on independent interviews, which then are combined to derive a final composite diagnosis. Although this protocol works well for adolescents and some older preadolescent children, we have found that 8- to 10-year-old children with social phobia often are reluctant to speak outside the presence of their parents. Furthermore, young boys with social phobia often deny the extent, and sometimes even the existence, of their social fears. The practice of the SET-C program is to interview young children and their parents simultaneously, which increases the efficiency of the interviewing process and allows assessment of the child's perception of (or denial of) phobic symptoms. This denial may play an important factor in the child's cooperation in the treatment program.

Self-Report Measures

Because of the young age of the SET-C participants, we keep self-report measures to a minimum. First and foremost, we use the Social Phobia and Anxiety Inventory for Children (SPAI-C; Beidel, Turner, & Morris, 1995). The SPAI-C has excellent psychometric properties and is one of the few anxiety measures capable of differentiating children with social phobia from children with externalizing disorders (Beidel, Turner, & Fink, 1996) and other types of anxiety disorders (Beidel, Turner, & Hamlin, 2000). The SPAI-C assesses the severity of children's social fears across a range of social situations and with different social partners: familiar children, unfamiliar children, and adults. The SPAI-C is useful to help establish the diagnosis of social phobia (children must endorse social fears with peers as well as with adults), and because it assesses social anxiety across situations and across interpersonal partners, the information provided on the SPAI-C can assist the clinician in identifying the child's specific fear pattern.

In addition to the SPAI-C, the self-report battery includes the Junior Eysenck Personality Inventory (JEPI; Eysenck & Eysenck, 1968), which assesses temperament (introversion–extroversion and neuroticism) hypothesized to be related to social phobia. General anxiety and depression are assessed using the State–Trait Anxiety Inventory for Children (STAIC; Spielberger, 1973) and the Children's Depression Inventory (CDI; Kovacs, 1985). Finally, because our earlier studies suggested that children with social phobia suffer from loneliness (Beidel, Turner, & Morris, 1999), the assessment battery includes the Loneliness Scale (Asher & Wheeler, 1985), which assesses friendships and isolation. Unlike the other self-report instruments that assess clinical symptoms, the Loneliness Scale allows us to assess effects of the SET-C program on social functioning, a measure of treatment effectiveness as opposed to treatment efficacy.

Parent and Teacher Ratings

Parents complete the Child Behavior Checklist (CBCL; Achenbach, 1991). Although not a measure of social phobia, the two broad-band scales (Internalizing and Externalizing) allow a determination of parental perception of problem behaviors. Furthermore, the pattern of change that we have observed to date as a function of SET-C treatment (decreased problems associated with the Internalizing Scale but no change on Externalizing

Scale) suggests that parents are reporting behavioral change consistent with the goals of the intervention.

For those participating in SET-C treatment outcome trials, we request that the child's teacher complete the Child Behavior Checklist—Teacher's Report Form (TRF; Edelbrock & Achenbach, 1980). Teacher reports are valuable inasmuch as teachers are usually unaware that the child is participating in a treatment program. The letter requesting completion of the form states only that the child is involved in a study of child development at the University of Maryland. Thus, teacher data are unbiased by knowledge of treatment status.

Behavioral Assessment Test

The behavioral assessment test (BAT) allows direct observation of the child's social interaction anxiety and performance anxiety. There are two behavioral tasks. The first is a social skills assessment wherein children engage in five role-plays with a same-age peer. Specific skills assessed through the role-play vignettes include the ability to carry on a conversation, to give help, to receive help, to give a compliment, to receive a compliment, and to act assertively. To assess performance anxiety, the second task requires the children to read aloud in front of three people (at least one of whom is a same-age peer) for 10 minutes using material appropriate to the child's reading level. In our paradigm, children between the ages of 8 and 12 read the story of Jack and the Beanstalk, but any story with an appropriate reading level could be used. After each task, children rate their anxiety using a 5-point rating scale. Raters blind to time of the assessment and sometimes to group membership rate skill and anxiety using 4-point rating scales of skill and anxiety.

Daily Diary

Children are asked to record (a) distressful social situations, (b) distress using the 5-point rating scale described above, and (c) behaviors used to cope with the events. Based on the age of the child, a pictorial or written version of the diary may be used (see Beidel, Neal, & Lederer, 1991). Particularly with preadolescent children, compliance with the daily diary assessment is often sporadic at best. Reinforcers in the form of stickers or fast-food certificates can enhance cooperation, but 100% compliance is rarely achieved. Because of this reality, we use the daily diary in a pulsed fashion: Rather than requiring children to record their experiences throughout the duration of the 12-week intervention, we administer the diary assignments for a 2-week period at pretreatment, posttreatment, and for 2 weeks before each follow-up assessment.

This comprehensive battery is not inordinately time consuming and does not pose a hardship for the children. The interview with the child requires about an hour. The self-report instruments can be completed in 30 minutes, as with the behavioral assessment. The daily diary requires only a few minutes per day. Children participate fully for the duration of the assessment.

Treatment Components and Procedures

An overview of the intervention with an outline of the content of each SET-C session is presented in Exhibit 4.1.

Psychoeducation

The psychoeducation phase consists of one group session, with all parents and children participating in the SET-C group. It provides an opportunity for parents and children to meet the group leaders and the other participants. The format of the group is didactic, followed by a question-and-answer period. The didactic presentation includes a descriptive overview of the nature and etiology of social phobia, followed by a discussion of individual differences in the expression and experience of social phobia. An overview of the treatment package and its specific elements is provided in this initial session.

Social Skills Training

Social skills groups usually consist of four to six children within the same age range (e.g., ages 8–10 or 10–12). Groups can be conducted by one or two group leaders, and each session is usually 60 minutes in length. The 12 SET-C social skills training sessions include two components that together address a specific set of common problems (Beidel et al., 2004). **Social Environment Awareness** teaches children when, where, and why to initiate and terminate interpersonal interactions. Interpersonal Skills Enhancement teaches the verbal and nonverbal mechanics of successful social encounters, focusing on areas problematic for children with social phobia (e.g., joining a group of children, establishing and maintaining friendships, being assertive). SET-C uses traditional social skills training strategies: instruction, modeling, behavior rehearsal, corrective feedback, and positive reinforcement. Behavior rehearsal (behavioral practice) appears crucial for the acquisition of social skills, and thus the majority of group time is devoted to this component. Children role play with the therapist and one another until all have acquired the skill. For each skill, the procedures are incorporated into a social skills training model that is elaborated as follows: instruction in the identified skill, modeling the appropriate behavioral components, behavioral rehearsal until group members reach the behavioral criterion, constructive feedback, and positive reinforcement.

EXHIBIT 4.1
Format and Content of the SET-C Program

Week number	Session number	Content
Session 1	1 - Social skills training	Recognition of social cues, greetings and introduction
	2 - In vivo exposure	Content based on child's unique fear
Session 2	1 - Social skills training	Initiating conversations and appropriate conversation topics
	2 - In vivo exposure	Content based on child's unique fear
Session 3	1 - Social skills training	Maintaining conversations and topic transitions
	2 - In vivo exposure	Content based on child's unique fear
Session 4	1 - Social skills training	Attending and remembering
	2 - In vivo exposure	Content based on child's unique fear
Session 5	1 - Social skills training	Skills for joining groups
	2 - In vivo exposure	Content based on child's unique fear
Session 6	1 - Social skills training	Establishing and maintaining friendships
	2 - In vivo exposure	Content based on child's unique fear
Session 7	1 - Social skills training	Giving and receiving compliments
	2 - In vivo exposure	Content based on child's unique fear
Session 8	1 - Social skills training	Refusing unreasonable requests
	2 - In vivo exposure	Content based on child's unique fear
Session 9	1 - Social skills training	Asking for a change in behavior
	2 - In vivo exposure	Content based on child's unique fear
Session 10	1 - Social skills training	Assertion with authority figures
	2 - In vivo exposure	Content based on child's unique fear
Session 11	1 - Social skills training	Telephone skills
	2 - In vivo exposure	Content based on child's unique fear
Session 12	1 - Social skills training	Review and wrap-up
	2 - In vivo exposure	Content based on child's unique fear

(The topical content areas that are covered in the social skills component of SET-C are presented in Exhibit 4.1.) As depicted, social skills training sessions are cumulative, with each skill building upon those previously acquired. Furthermore, in addition to verbal content, nonverbal and para-linguistic social skills such as eye contact, voice volume, and vocal tone are addressed as necessary.

Peer Generalization

The SET-C peer generalization session immediately follows the social skills training session. Generalization experiences take advantage of the particular age and interests of the children in the group. The settings vary each week and across the various groups, but the structure and the goals are identical: to ensure that socially phobic children have the opportunity to practice newly acquired skills with age-appropriate, socially competent peers in appropriate, real-life settings. For example, an activity may occur at a Children's Museum, where a new dinosaur exhibit attracts many other children. The museum provides the setting, and the goal of the outing is to practice the newly acquired skill of greeting new people. The task in the peer generalization session may be for the socially phobic child to greet five people. Peer facilitators help the child with social phobia to complete the task, either by serving as someone the child may greet or by modeling appropriate greetings to others. All peer generalization sessions are directed and supervised by the social skills therapist.

Peer generalization sessions are 90 minutes in length and always include lunch or a snack. Because children with social phobia often report being too nervous to eat at school, including lunch provides them the opportunity to engage in this activity in a group setting. Note, however, that some children still find ways to avoid participating in the activity. At the bowling alley, for example, extremely anxious children sometimes spend an inordinate amount of time tying their bowling shoes or looking for the perfect bowling ball. Even if they are successful in isolating themselves through part of the activity, having to sit down with peers to eat eliminates this avoidance and encourages social engagement. Peers are specifically instructed not to allow children to isolate themselves during the activity, particularly during lunch time.

Successful implementation of the peer generalization component depends on recruitment of appropriate peer facilitators who are within the same age range as the children participating in the treatment program. Inclusion of both boys and girls is advantageous, and peers must be good role models of age-appropriate social behavior, exhibit reasonably outgoing (but not overbearing) behavior, and adapt well to new social situations. Peers are trained about their role in the activities and in confidentiality.

In Vivo Exposure

SET-C uses in vivo exposure procedures based on a model of fear reduction and extensive scientific data noting that repeated exposure to an anxiety-provoking stimulus results in new learning. With multiple pairings of sufficient duration, the stimulus gradually loses its ability to elicit the fear response. Repeated pairings across sessions and of progressively more fearful stimuli also is necessary for the learning process. In addition to habituation within each session, the goal of exposure is to achieve between-session habituation. In other words, across exposure sessions peak distress should be lower and the time to return to baseline should become shorter.

In vivo exposure can be accomplished using a graduated hierarchy or a flooding paradigm. In the latter case, the individual is exposed immediately to the situation that elicits the most intense distress. In the SET-C program, a graduated in vivo approach is used. Particularly with preadolescent children, a graduated approach appears to be better accepted by the children, allowing for greater compliance. Therefore, an in vivo hierarchy is constructed and each task is presented until habituation is achieved. Exhibit 4.2 presents examples of potential *in vivo* exposure activities. The list is by no means exhaustive, and the tasks are not necessarily appropriate for every child. Because exposure activities must tap each child's specific fear pattern, certain activities (such as reading aloud in front of a group) may be appropriate for a number of children but cannot be applied indiscriminately. The therapist supervises all activities. The context, location, and duration of the activities are modified weekly as treatment progresses (i.e., when between-session habituation to one item is achieved). With a little creativity, individual

EXHIBIT 4.2
Examples of SET-C Exposure Assignments

Fearful situation	Potential exposure situation
Reading aloud in front of a class	Child reads aloud in public (in the clinic or in a public place).
Asking a teacher a question or for help	Child asks store clerk to help find an item.
	Child takes a "survey for school" in a public place (e.g., "Why are you here at the Smithsonian Museum today?").
Taking tests	Child takes an oral spelling test using some words that are far above grade level (so the child will make errors).
Starting or joining in on a conversation	Child goes to a child-friendly place (e.g., pizza parlors, children's museums). Child's task is to invite another child to engage in an activity together (e.g., a video game, a hands-on exhibit).
Eating in front of others	Child visits fast-food restaurant or food court at the mall. Child must sit in view of others and eat.
Answering or talking on the telephone	Child calls pet stores and asks questions such as "Do you sell yellow parakeets?"
Musical or athletic performances	Child plays a musical instrument in a public place (such as a park).

exposure activities can be generated that do not tax the resources and constraints inherent in clinical settings. Activities do not necessarily require significant financial or personnel resources. Public areas (e.g., parks, restaurants, office corridors) are located within walking distance of most clinics, allowing easy implementation of a vast array of exposure activities.

SET-C in vivo exposure is conducted once weekly, concurrently with the social skills training–peer generalization program. Thus, the child receives treatment twice per week. The length of the in vivo exposure sessions varies depending on the time necessary for habituation, but these sessions usually average 60 to 90 minutes.

Homework Assignments

Both social skills training sessions and in vivo exposure sessions are concluded with homework assignments, each directly relevant to the content of the particular session. Therefore, if the social skills session is focused on initiating conversations, the homework assignment might be for the child to start a conversation with two children to whom they usually do not speak (e.g., classmates, children at the bus stop, children in the neighborhood). Similarly, if the in vivo exposure session was directed at talking to adults, the assignment might be for the child to interact with adults on as many occasions as possible over the next week (e.g, ordering their own food at a fast-food restaurant, paying for gas, asking for something in a store). As illustrated, completion of homework assignments requires cooperation on the part of the parent. To increase compliance, reinforcers such as stickers, later bedtimes, or other rewards may be used.

Why No Cognitive Component?

SET-C does not include a direct cognitive intervention. There are two reasons for this exclusion. First, recent meta-analyses, substantive reviews, and treatment dismantling studies in adult populations indicate that exposure is the crucial ingredient in effective treatment outcome (see Feske & Chambless, 1995; Taylor, 1996; Wenzel, Statler-Cowen, Patton, & Holt, 1998). In a dismantling study, cognitive restructuring did not enhance the intervention's effectiveness over exposure therapy alone (Hope, Heimberg, & Bruch, 1995). In a study with socially phobic children (Spence, Donovan, & Brechman-Toussaint, 2000), younger children had difficulty with the cognitive restructuring component of their multicomponent intervention, and in some cases, this element was eliminated. Second, as noted, SET-C was developed based on several years of empirical study of the psychopathology of childhood social phobia. The initial study (Beidel, 1991) did not find evidence of negative cognitions among a sample of children with social phobia, and a recent review of the literature of cognitions in childhood anxiety disorders (Alfano, Beidel, & Turner, 2002) found only equivocal evidence for the existence of negative cognitions in children with anxiety disorders in general. Furthermore, this review concluded that specifically targeting cognitive content is not necessary for positive treatment outcome (e.g., Beidel, Turner, & Morris, 2000; Silverman et al., 1999; Spence et al., 2000). See Alfano et al. (2001) for a comprehensive review of this literature.

TREATMENT MEASURES

The treatment outcome measures for SET-C randomized controlled trials use the same measures that are used in our standard outpatient assessment. In addition, we include independent evaluator ratings of the child's current level of functioning. To allow for cross-study comparisons of outcome, the SET-C program uses the Children's Global Assessment Scale (CGAS; Shaffer et al., 1983) to assess children's academic, social, and occupational functioning and the Clinical Global Impressions Scale (CGI; Guy, 1976) to assess symptom severity and improvement. Both scales are completed by an independent evaluator unaware of group assignment.

Clinical Vignette

Jessica is a 9-year-old girl referred to MCAD because of severe social fears. Although she will speak very softly in small groups and in one-on-one conversations, she refuses to read aloud in front of the class. Outside of school she interacts only with her immediate family and her cousins. Using a 5-point rating scale in which 5 represents extreme fear and 1 complete relaxation, the results of the clinical assessment indicated that Jessica experienced moderate to severe anxiety in the following situations: reading aloud in front of a group, speaking to adults, joining in with a group of children, performing in front of others, ordering food in a restaurant, and writing on the blackboard. With help from her parents, her core fear was conceptualized as a fear of making a mistake and becoming embarrassed. Her pretreatment SPAI-C score was 29, her ADIS-C clinical severity rating was 6, and her CGAS rating was 6. The results of the behavioral assessment of Jessica's social skills revealed the following deficits: one-word answers, barely audible voice volume, flat vocal tone, minimal eye contact, and tearful responses to social interactions.

A decision was made to treat Jessica through the SET-C protocol. In addition to the standard verbal content taught in the group social skills training program, the group leaders targeted improvements in her vocal tone and voice volume as part of her social skills training. Her individual hierarchy, established using a 4-point rating scale (0, representing complete relaxation, to 4, representing extreme fear) was as follows: taking a spelling test on the blackboard (2), reading aloud in front of people (3), inviting a peer to join her in an activity (3), learning a dance and performing it in a public place (4). To illustrate the in vivo component, the following situation was used to address Jessica's fear of inviting a peer to join her in an activity. Jessica met her therapist at a pizza parlor, which also contained a video arcade. Her mother purchased some tokens, and Jessica's task was to approach another child and ask him or her to play a game. Jessica rated her anxiety using the 0–4 scale and repeated the task until her self-report and the therapist's observation indicated that her anxiety returned to baseline. Figure 4.1 illustrates within- and between-session habituation over three sessions.

Jessica's homework assignments were as follows: answer the telephone (to practice talking to adults), invite a classmate over to play (to address inviting peers to join an activity), go to Sunday school (where she would have to read aloud), interact with adults in stores and order food in a restaurant (to practice talking to adults), and have two friends sleep over (to invite peers to an activity and provide an opportunity for extended interactions with other children). At posttreatment, Jessica's SPAI-C score decreased to 15, her ADIS-C severity rating decreased to 3, and her CGAS increased to 8. In addition, her posttreatment BAT ratings indicated improved social skill and decreased observed anxiety.

TREATMENT OUTCOME

In the first study to examine the effectiveness of SET-C (Beidel, Turner, & Morris, 2000), 67 children between the ages 8 and 12 diagnosed with social phobia were randomly assigned to either a SET-C or an active but nonspecific intervention (i.e., Testbusters). Testbusters is a study-skills and test-taking strategies skills program designed specifically for children ages 8 to 12. The program is effective in decreasing test anxiety and increasing academic achievement (Beidel, Turner, & Tayler-Ferreira, 1999), inasmuch as test anxiety is a common complaint among children with social phobia. Of the children receiving SET-C, 67% did not qualify for a diagnosis at the posttreatment assessment compared with 5% of those treated with Testbusters. Responder status, a more conservative measure of clinical significance, indicated that 53% of the SET-C children met responder criteria compared with 5% of the Testbusters children. Statistically significant decreases in symptoms also were observed across a range of other domains, with the SET-C group demonstrating less overall anxiety, social avoidance, and depressed mood compared with those receiving Testbusters. The BAT conducted at posttreatment also revealed a significant improvement in subjective anxiety, independent evaluator's rating of anxiety, and social performance in general for the SET-C group. All treatment gains were maintained at the 6-month follow-up visit.

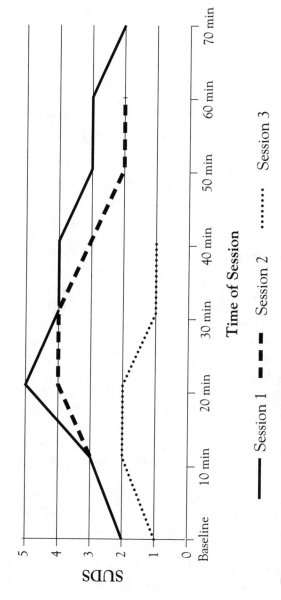

Figure 4.1. Between-session habituation for one exposure task for a child with social phobia. SUDs = subjective units of distress.

FUTURE DIRECTIONS

At the time our program was initiated, well-controlled behavioral treatment studies for socially phobic youth were lacking. Currently, three published studies (Beidel, Turner, & Morris, 2000; Hayward, Varady, Albano, Thienemann, Henderson, & Schatzberg, 2000; Spence et al., 2000) represent randomized controlled trials using adequate sample sizes of socially phobic children and rigorous methodology. Overall, these studies indicated statistically significant improvement across various dimensions of functioning. However, the extant literature still is quite small, and further studies are needed.

We are presently engaged in several trials to further examine the efficacy of SET-C. First, we are undertaking a 5-year follow-up study of the children who participated in the Beidel, Turner, and Morris (2000) treatment trial. The goal of this project, funded by the National Institute of Mental Health, is to determine the long-term efficacy of SET-C treatment over a 5-year follow-up period. This project will provide some of the most extensive follow-up data on preadolescent children with social phobia treated with behavior therapy. Given that these children were treated during preadolescence (ages 8–12), the follow-up period covers adolescence, a particularly crucial time frame, inasmuch as youth of this age group are considered to be at greatest risk for the onset of social phobia. In addition to following this sample for a 5-year period, this study has two additional specific aims: to determine factors that predict improvement or relapse from posttreatment to follow-up and to examine the clinical significance of the SET-C outcome by comparing the social functioning of this treated sample to age-matched adolescents who never suffered from social phobia. Thus, we not only will be able to determine whether the improvement of our sample is statistically significant; we will be able to determine the clinical significance of our intervention through comparison with a group of children who never had the disorder.

In a related research initiative, we are developing an adolescent version of SET-C (called Social Effectiveness Therapy for Adolescents, or SET-A) and comparing the effects of both interventions to fluoxetine and a pill placebo. This research program also is funded by the National Institute of Mental Health. With respect to the development of SET-A, we first examined the original treatment with an emphasis on changing components to be relevant for an adolescent sample. To date, it appears that the skill deficits and distressing situations identified for preadolescent children are also relevant for adolescents. In other words, the basic skill deficits of youth with social phobia are the same whether the child is a preadolescent or an adolescent. However, adolescents with social phobia may have additional areas of concern, such as heterosocial interactions. What is different, however, is the age-appropriateness of the specific role-playing scenes developed for the SET-C manual. Therefore, manual revisions are addressing changing situations and role-play scenes to make them relevant for adolescents. Similarly, the goal of peer generalization sessions (to provide opportunities to practice newly acquired skills with same-age peers who do not experience social anxiety) also is appropriate for adolescents. However, many of the specific activities appropriate for children are likely not appropriate for adolescents (e.g., adolescents are not likely to enjoy going to pizza arcades designed for preadolescent children). Therefore, different and age-appropriate peer generalization activities must be developed. Finally, there is the issue of in vivo exposure, in which the procedures for implementing the intervention remain the same as for children (or for adults, for that matter).

As noted, this particular research initiative also has a second component. We are conducting a randomized controlled trial of SET-C and SET-A compared to fluoxetine and pill placebo among children and adolescents with social phobia. To date, no randomized controlled trials of selective serotonin reuptake inhibitors in children with social phobia only exist, although there are some controlled trials using samples of children with various anxiety disorders. Thus, even though clinically many children currently are prescribed these medications, this study will provide initial empirical data on the efficacy of a pharmacological treatment. Another reason for conducting this trial is that SET-C is an efficacious treatment but an intensive and time-consuming intervention. Because many families may not be able or willing to commit to such an intensive intervention, less time-consuming alternatives should be investigated. In addition, this will be the first such trial comparing pharmacological and psychosocial interventions for children and adolescents with social phobia. The results of this comparative trial, as well as the results of the long-term follow-up study, undoubtedly will provide the basis for further investigations in this area.

SUMMARY

In this chapter, we reviewed the current literature on the psychopathology of social phobia in youth and demonstrated how our endeavors in that area formed the basis for our multicomponent behavioral intervention, Social Effectiveness Therapy for Children. The initial randomized controlled trial indicates that this intervention has very positive effects for preadolescent children with social phobia. Further research is necessary to examine the generalizability of this intervention for adolescent youth, comparative trials with other efficacious interventions, its long-term outcome, and the applicability of this intervention for minority youth.

REFERENCES

Achenbach, T. M. (1991). *Manual for the child behavior checklists/4–18 and 1991 profile.* Burlington: University of Vermont.

Alfano, C., Beidel, D. C., & Turner, S. M. (2002). Considering cognition in childhood anxiety disorders. *Clinical Psychiatry Review, 22,* 1209–1238.

American Psychiatric Association. (1994). *Diagnostic and statistical manual of mental disorders* (4th ed. Rev. ed.). Washington, DC: Author.

Anderson, J. C., Williams, S. M., McGee, R., & Silva, P. A. (1987). *DSM–III* disorders in preadolescent children: Prevalence in a large sample from the general population. *Archives of General Psychiatry, 44,* 69–76.

Asher, S. R., & Wheeler, V. A. (1985). Children's loneliness: A comparison of rejected and neglected peer status. *Journal of Consulting and Clinical Psychology, 53,* 500–505.

Beidel, D. C. (1991). Social phobia and overanxious disorder in school-age children. *Journal of the American Academy of Child and Adolescent Psychiatry, 30,* 545–552.

Beidel, D. C., Neal, A. M., & Lederer, A. S. (1991). The feasibility and validity of a daily diary for the assessment of anxiety in children. *Behavior Therapy, 22,* 505–517.

Beidel, D. C., & Turner, S. M. (1998). *Shy children, phobic adults: The nature and treatment of social phobia.* Washington, DC: American Psychological Association.

Beidel, D. C., Turner, S. M., & Fink, C. M. (1996). The assessment of childhood social phobia: Construct, convergent and discriminative validity of the Social Phobia and Anxiety Inventory for Children (SPAI-C). *Psychological Assessment, 8,* 235–240.

Beidel, D. C., Turner, S. M., & Hamlin, K. L. (2000). The Social Phobia and Anxiety Inventory for Children: External and discriminant validity. *Behavior Therapy, 31,* 75–67.

Beidel, D. C., Turner, S. M., & Morris, T. L. (1995). A new instrument to assess childhood social anxiety and phobia: The Social Phobia and Anxiety Inventory for Children. *Psychological Assessment, 1,* 73–79.

Beidel, D. C., Turner, S. M., & Morris, T. L. (1999). Psychopathology of childhood social phobia. *Journal of the American Academy of Child and Adolescent Psychiatry, 38,* 643–650.

Beidel, D. C., Turner, S. M., & Morris, T. L. (2000). Behavioral treatment of childhood social phobia. *Journal of Consulting and Clinical Psychology, 68,* 1072–1080.

Beidel, D. C., Turner, S. M., & Morris, T. L. (in press). *Social effectiveness therapy for Children: A treatment manual.* Toronto, Canada: Multi-Health Systems, Inc.

Beidel, D. C., Turner, S. M., & Taylor-Ferreira, J. C. (1999). Teaching study-skills and test-taking strategies to elementary school children: The Testbusters program. *Behavior Modification, 23,* 643–650.

Benjamin, R. S., Costello, E. J., & Warren, M. (1990). Anxiety disorders in a pediatric sample. *Journal of Anxiety Disorders, 4,* 293–316.

Clark, D. B. (1993, March). *Assessment of social anxiety in adolescents.* Paper presented at the Anxiety Disorders Association of America Annual Convention, Charleston, SC.

Costello, E. (1989). Child psychiatric disorders and their correlates: A primary care pediatric sample. *Journal of the American Academy of Child and Adolescent Psychiatry, 28*, 851–855.

Davidson, J. (1993, March). *Childhood histories of adult social phobics.* Paper presented at the Anxiety Disorders Association Annual Convention, Charleston, SC.

Edelbrock, C., & Achenbach, T. M. (1980). A typology of child behavior profile patterns: Distribution and correlates for disturbed children aged 6–16. *Journal of Abnormal Child Psychology, 8*, 441–470.

Eysenck, H. J., & Eysenck, S. B. G. (1968). *Manual for the Junior Eysenck Personality Inventory.* San Diego, CA: Educational and Industrial Testing Service.

Ferrell, C., Beidel, D. S., & Turner, S. M. (2001). *An instrument to assess social functioning in children with social phobia.* Manuscript in preparation, University of Maryland at College Park.

Feske, U., & Chambless, D. L. (1995). Cognitive–behavioral versus exposure only treatment for social phobia: A meta-analysis. *Behavior Therapy, 26*, 695–720.

Guy, W. (Ed.). (1976). *ECDEU assessment manual for psychopharmacology.* Washington, DC: DHEW.

Hayward, C., Varady, S., Albano, A. M., Thienemann, M., Henderson, L., & Schatzberg, A. F. (2000). Cognitive–behavioral group therapy for social phobia in female adolescents: Results of a pilot study. *Journal of the American Academy of Child and Adolescent Psychiatry, 39*, 721–726.

Hope, D. A., Heimberg, R. G., & Bruch, M. A. (1995). Dismantling cognitive–behavioral therapy for social phobia. *Behaviour Research and Therapy, 33*, 637–650.

Kashani, J. H., & Orvaschel, H. (1990). A community study of anxiety in children and adolescents. *American Journal of Psychiatry, 147*, 313–318.

Kendall, P. C., & Warman, M. J. (1997). Anxiety disorders in youth: Diagnostic consistency across *DSM–III–R* and *DSM–IV. Journal of Anxiety Disorders, 10*, 453–463.

Kovacs, M. (1985). The Children's Depression Inventory (CDI). *Psychopharmacology, 21*, 995–998.

Last, C. G., Perrin, S., Hersen, M., & Kazdin, A. E. (1992). DSM–III–R anxiety disorders in children: Sociodemographic and clinical characteristics. *Journal of the American Academy of Child and Adolescent Psychiatry, 31*, 1070–1076.

Perrin, S., & Last, C. G. (1993, March). *Comorbidity of social phobia and other anxiety disorders in children.* Paper presented at the Association for Advancement of Behavior Therapy Annual Convention, Charleston, SC.

Rubin, K. H., LeMare, L. J., & Lollis, S. (1990). Social withdrawal in childhood: Developmental pathways to peer rejection. In S. R. Asher & J. D. Coie (Eds.), *Peer rejection in childhood* (pp. 217–249). Cambridge, England: Cambridge University Press.

Schneier, F. R., Johnson, J., Hornig, C., Liebowitz, M., & Weissman, M. (1992). Social phobia: Comorbidity and morbidity in an epidemiological sample. *Archives of General Psychiatry, 49,* 282–287.

Shaffer, D., Gould, M. S., Brasic, J., Abrosini, P., Fisher, P., Bird, H., & Aluwahlia, S. (1983). A Children's Global Assessment Scale (K-GAS). *Archives of General Psychiatry, 40,* 1228–1231.

Silverman, W. K., & Albano, A. M. (1996). *The Anxiety Disorders Interview Schedule for DSM–IV, child and parent versions.* San Antonio, TX: Psychological Corporation.

Silverman, W. K., Kurtines, W. M., Ginsburg, G. S., Weems, C. F., Rabian, B., & Serafini, L. T. (1999). Contingency management, self-control, and education support in the treatment of childhood phobic disorders: A randomized clinical trial. *Journal of Consulting and Clinical Psychology, 67,* 675–687.

Spence, S. H., Donovan, C., & Brechman-Toussaint, M. (1999). Social skills, social outcomes, and cognitive features of childhood social phobia. *Journal of Abnormal Psychology, 108,* 211–221

Spence, S. H., Donovan, C., & Brechman-Toussaint, M. (2000). The treatment of childhood social phobia: The effectiveness of a social skills training-based, cognitive–behavioral intervention with and without parental involvement. *Journal of Child Psychology and Psychiatry and Allied Disciplines, 41,* 713–726.

Spielberger, C. (1973). *Manual for the State-Trait Anxiety Inventory for Children.* Palo Alto, CA: Consulting Psychologists Press.

Taylor, S. (1996). Meta-analysis of cognitive–behavioral treatment for social phobia. *Journal of Behavior Therapy and Experimental Psychiatry, 27,* 1–9.

Wenzel, A., Statler-Cowen, T., Patton, G. K., & Holt, C. S. (1998). *A comprehensive meta-analysis of psychosocial and pharmacological interventions for social phobia and social anxiety.* Paper presented at the 19th Annual Conference of the Anxiety Disorders Association of America, San Diego.

5

PROGRESS IN DEVELOPING AN EXPOSURE-BASED TRANSFER-OF-CONTROL APPROACH TO TREATING INTERNALIZING DISORDERS IN YOUTH

WENDY K. SILVERMAN AND WILLIAM M. KURTINES

Internalizing disorders, such as excessive fear and anxiety, are pervasive in a large segment of children and adolescents (hereon referred to as "*children*" or "*youth*") (see Silverman & Ginsburg, 1998). Although psychosocial treatment research on child internalizing disorders has lagged behind research on child externalizing disorders since the appearance of this volume's first edition, considerable progress has been made in the development of empirically based interventions for internalizing disorders in children. The purpose of the present chapter is to summarize the progress that has been made on the development and evaluation of psychosocial interventions for use with children with phobic and anxiety disorders. In keeping with the exposure-based "transfer of control" approach that we outlined in our previous version of this

The writing of this chapter was supported in part by NIMH grant # 63997.

chapter (Silverman & Kurtines, 1996a), we discuss how an essential component of efficacious anxiety treatments involves gradual exposure of the child to fearful objects or situations and how the therapist may facilitate exposure by "transferring" to agents of change (e.g., child, parent, peers) knowledge about therapeutic procedures and strategies. The therapeutic procedures and strategies that have been used and evaluated have generally emanated from the behavioral and cognitive therapy traditions. Before we describe these therapeutic procedures and strategies and discuss their application for private practice, we provide a brief description of our program, followed by a brief review of the treatment research literature in the area.

PROGRAM DESCRIPTION

The work summarized in this chapter has been conducted under the auspices of the Childhood Anxiety and Phobia Program (CAPP), which is housed within the Child and Family Psychosocial Research Center at Florida International University, Miami, and is codirected by Drs. Silverman and Kurtines. The center comprises a number of programs and laboratories and provides multifaceted child and family interventions that include both clinic- and school-based services. Within the center, CAPP has the distinctive mission of developing and evaluating approaches to assessment and intervention specific to the phobic and anxiety disorders of youth. In terms of assessment, the focus of CAPP's work has been on developing, testing, and refining methods of assessment, particularly diagnostic interview schedules (e.g., the Anxiety Disorders Interview Schedule for Children; Silverman & Albano, 1996; Silverman & Eisen, 1992; Silverman & Nelles, 1988; Silverman & Rabian, 1995; Silverman, Saavedra, & Pina, 2001). These interviews have been used in all the childhood anxiety clinical trials (e.g., Barrett, Dadds, & Rapee, 1996; Beidel, Turner, & Morris, 2000; Kendall, 1994; Kendall, Flannery-Schroeder, Panichelli-Mindell, Southam-Gerow, Henin, & Warman, 1997), including those at the Center (Silverman, Kurtines, Ginsburg, Weems, Lumpkin, & Carmichael, 1999; Silverman, Kurtines, Ginsburg, Weems, Rabian, & Serafini, 1999). In addition, a considerable part of the CAPP's efforts has been devoted to developing and evaluating measures for assessing constructs relevant to childhood anxiety disorders, such as anxiety sensitivity (e.g., Silverman, Fleisig, Rabian, & Peterson, 1991; Silverman, Ginsburg, & Goedhart, 1999; Silverman, Goedhart, Barrett, & Turner, 2003), school refusal behavior (e.g., Kearney & Silverman, 1993), and worry (e.g., Silverman, La Greca, & Wasserstein, 1995; Weems, Silverman, & La Greca, 2000). The instruments that have emerged from this work also have been adopted by investigators and practitioners.

A pragmatic orientation of the center guides our clinical and research activities as well as our efforts to bridge the gap between these activities.

Our pragmatic orientation grew out of the recognition that effective interventions can draw on many traditions (see Silverman & Kurtines, 1996a, 1996b, 1997). Thus, the center's efforts in developing interventions seek to integrate and combine in useful ways the most efficacious procedures previously identified by research and to modify and adapt these procedures for use with particular populations in particular contexts. Further, we seek to evaluate various formats of interventions as a way to provide evidence that these interventions can be applied in a flexible manner, thereby rendering them usable in diverse contexts (e.g., clinics, schools). Our overall interest in developing "user- and clinician-friendly" procedures developed in response to the hiatus between clinical research and practice and reflects a recognition of the need to close this hiatus (e.g.,Weisz, Weiss, & Donenberg, 1992).

REVIEW OF THE LITERATURE

The pioneering work of Philip Kendall is the foundation for most of the existing psychosocial treatment research studies on anxiety disorders in children. Kendall showed in a series of single case studies and clinical trials that *child-focused individual cognitive–behavioral therapy* reduces anxiety disorders in youth (Kane & Kendall, 1989; Kendall, 1994; Kendall et al., 1997). The efficacy of child-focused cognitive–behavioral treatment has been replicated and extended to a range of child anxiety disorders (e.g., phobias, panic disorder, obsessive compulsive disorder) via case studies (e.g., Eisen & Silverman, 1991) and single case study designs (Eisen & Silverman, 1993; Kearney & Silverman, 1990a; Lumpkin, Silverman, Weems, Markham, & Kurtines, 2002; Ollendick, 1995).

In addition, randomized clinical trials have produced evidence that cognitive–behavioral therapy can be efficaciously delivered in a *group* format to reduce child phobic and anxiety disorders (e.g., Barrett, 1998; Hayward, Varady, Albano, Thienemann, Henderson, & Schatzberg, 2000; Silverman, Kurtines, Ginsburg, Weems, Lumpkin, & Carmichael, 1999) as well as in a format that involves increased *peer* (Beidel et al., 2000) and *parental* (e.g., Barrett et al., 1996; Cobham, Dadds, & Spence, 1998) involvement. Further, a literature has begun to form suggesting that the components of the cognitive–behavioral "package" are similarly efficacious (i.e., the "behavioral" part of the package is as efficacious as the "cognitive" part), suggesting clinical flexibility with respect to application (Silverman, Kurtines, Ginsburg, Weems, Lumpkin, & Carmichael, 1999). A literature also has begun to form suggesting that the various components of the package may be "prescribed" to children as a function of predominant child response classes (e.g., cognitive therapy for children who worry excessively; Eisen & Silverman, 1998) and predominant "motivating conditions" or functional aspects of the child's anxiety problem (e.g., contingency management for families in which the child's avoidant behavior is maintained by inappropriate parental contingencies; e.g., Kearney & Silverman, 1999).

In consideration of the aforementioned literature and consistent with the need for conceptual models of child treatment in child psychotherapy research if the field is to move forward with respect to theory, research, and practice (e.g., Kazdin, 1999), we believe that one can frame the research literature as support (albeit indirect support) for the exposure-based transfer-of-control approach that we outlined in the previous version of this chapter (Silverman & Kurtines, 1996a). In accordance with the transfer of control, the therapist is viewed as a consultant or collaborator who shares with or "transfers" to agents of child change (e.g., child, parents, peers) knowledge of behavioral and cognitive therapeutic strategies that can be used to facilitate the child's exposure to fearful or anxiety-provoking situations, thereby producing child treatment response (e.g., anxiety reduction).

Accordingly, in child-focused individual cognitive–behavioral therapy (e.g., Kane & Kendall, 1989; Kendall, 1994; Kendall et al., 1997) the transfer of control occurs directly from the therapist to the child. In peer-based group cognitive–behavioral therapy (e.g., Barrett, 1998; Beidel et al., 2000; Hayward et al., 2000; Silverman et al., 1999), a transfer of control from therapist to child through peers occurs. In family-based cognitive–behavioral therapy (Barrett et al., 1996), a transfer of control from therapist to child through parents and family members occurs, and for families in which parents have high anxiety, the transfer of control can be facilitated by the simultaneous targeting of parental anxiety (along with child anxiety; Cobham et al., 1998), thereby "unblocking" the lines of transfer (Ginsburg, Silverman, & Kurtines, 1995).

Similarly, providing "prescriptive treatment" to children as a function of particular characteristics (e.g., response classes, motivating conditions; Eisen & Silverman, 1993, 1998; Kearney & Silverman, 1990b, 1999) is another way to help facilitate a transfer of control that may be "blocked." Finally, we would argue that even a nondirective, psychoeducational intervention that is delivered within a therapeutic context is a potential way to facilitate a transfer of control that can lead to positive child treatment response (Silverman, Kurtines, Ginsburg, Weems, Rabian, & Serafini, 1999).

METHODS USED AT THE CHILDHOOD
ANXIETY AND PHOBIA PROGRAM

Procedure for Screening Participants

Parents who make initial contact with CAPP are administered a brief telephone screen by a staff member. The telephone screen elicits information about the child's sociodemographic characteristics, presenting problem, and treatment history (psychosocial and medication). The telephone screen is a useful way to determine initially whether the child presents with the main inclusion criteria that have been used in our treatment studies—namely, a primary *Diagnostic and Statistical Manual of Mental Disorders, Fourth Edition* (DSM) anxiety disorder diagnosis (American Psychiatric Association, 1994) as well the main exclusion criteria (i.e., primary diagnoses other than anxiety, the presence of a developmental disorder, or both).

Procedure for Assessing Participants

The initial administration of the assessment measures (interviews and questionnaires) is conducted in two separate sessions within a 2-week period. During the first session, all children and parents are administered the Anxiety Disorders Interview Schedule for DSM–IV; child and parent versions, ADIS-C/P; Silverman & Albano, 1996). The interviews are administered to the children and parents in a randomly determined order. While one source is interviewed, the other is completing a series of questionnaires, with assistance by a staff member, as needed. During the second session, questionnaires not completed at the first session are completed, and any additional assessment procedures that are needed are administered. The assessment procedure is conducted at baseline (before the first treatment session), after treatment, and at two follow-up points (6- and 12-months following treatment).

Measures Administered to Participants

The first section describes the main measures administered to all children and parents who come to CAPP for treatment. These measures are primarily designed to assess child treatment response (i.e., anxiety reduction) and from a research perspective, comprise the main set of outcome measures. Child treatment response is assessed on two main levels. The first is on a *global level* via severity–interference ratings by clinician, child, and parents. The second is on a *specific symptom level* as rated by children and parents. The second section describes additional measures administered to assess other variables relevant to advancing understanding regarding factors that influence child treatment response. In our treatment research studies, assessors who are blind to participants' treatment conditions conduct all assessments at each assessment point.

Child Treatment Response–Global Level

Severity–Interference Rating Scales

Child treatment response is assessed on a global level by obtaining clinician, child, and parent ratings regarding the extent to which the child's anxiety symptoms interfere with or impair functioning. To obtain each of these sources' severity–interference ratings, the clinician asks respondents to consider, overall, how the child's anxiety symptoms interfere with respect to school (e.g., deteriorating academic performance), peer relations (e.g., little or no social interactions), family life (e.g., leads to family disruption), and internal distress (e.g., child is upset or distraught about symptoms). The overall impairment ratings are made using the rating scales contained on the ADIS-C/P, which involves a 9-point scale ranging from 0 to 8, with adverb qualifiers underneath selected points (e.g., "no severity–disruption of functioning"). In making their ratings, respondents use a "Feelings Thermometer," which is contained in the interview packet. The Feelings Thermometer is a visual prompt (i.e., a picture of a thermometer) that serves to simplify the rating task and remove some of the variability attributed to language skills. All clinicians, children, and parents receive practice in using the scale before the assessment takes place to establish common scale anchors and ensure familiarity with the task. We have found in our ADIS-C/P research studies that interrater agreement on these rating scales is moderate to high (Silverman & Eisen, 1992; Silverman & Nelles, 1988; Silverman et al., 2001).

Child Treatment Response–Specific Symptom Level

Children's Manifest Anxiety Scale, Revised

Child treatment response is assessed on a specific symptom (anxiety) level from the child's perspective using the Children's Manifest Anxiety Scale, Revised (RCMAS; Reynolds & Richmond, 1978). The RCMAS has been used as a primary outcome measure in almost all previous childhood anxiety clinical trials and has been found to be a sensitive measure of change in these studies (e.g., Kendall, 1994; Kendall et al., 1997; Silverman, Kurtines, Ginsburg, Weems, Lumpkin, & Carmichael, 1999; Silverman, Kurtines, Ginsburg, Weems, Rabian, & Serafini, 1999). The RCMAS consists of 37 items that describe anxious symptoms to which children respond either "yes" or "no." Extensive work supports the RCMAS's reliability and validity (see Reynolds & Richmond, 1985).

Revised Fear Survey Schedule for Children

Child treatment response also is assessed in terms of reductions in the number and intensity of fear-provoking objects and events using the Revised Fear Survey Schedule for Children (FSSC-R; Ollendick, 1983). The FSSC-R consists of 80 items to which the child rates his or her level of fear (i.e., "none," "some," "a lot"), yielding a total fear score. Ollendick (1983) reported satisfactory reliability and validity, and normative data are available.

Child Behavior Checklist

Child treatment response is assessed on a specific symptom level from parents' perspectives using the Child Behavior Checklist (CBCL; Achenbach, 1991). The CBCL has been the primary parent-completed specific symptom measure in past childhood anxiety clinical trials and has been found to be sensitive to statistical and clinical change. The CBCL is a 113-item measure that assesses children's behavior problems and competencies. The CBCL provides scores on a total behavior problem scale, as well as internalizing and externalizing subscales. For child treatment response in anxiety clinical trials, the internalizing subscale of the CBCL is typically used. CBCL items, scaled scores, and clinical cut-points have been found to discriminate between clinic-referred and nonreferred children, and normative data are available (Achenbach, 1991).

The internalizing subscale of the CBCL also is used for evaluating child treatment response in terms of clinically significant change using normative comparison. Consistent with Kendall and Grove (1988), clinically significant improvement is defined as changes that return deviant participants to within nondeviant limits. To be considered clinically significant and consistent with previous research (e.g., Kendall, 1994), improvement is a minimum criterion T-score of less than 70, adjusted according to age norms.

Revised Children's Manifest Anxiety Scale—Parent Completed

Like other investigators working in the area of child fear and anxiety (Kendall, 1994), we also ask parents to rate the occurrence of anxious symptoms in their children using a parent-completed anxiety-rating scale. For this measure, the stem of the Revised Children's Manifest Anxiety Scale has been changed from "I" to "My child...." Like the child version, the parent version has been shown to be sensitive to treatment outcome (Silverman, Kurtines, Ginsburg, Weems, Lumpkin, & Carmicheal, 1999; Silverman, Kurtines, Ginsburg, Weems, Rabian, & Serafini, 1999).

Revised Fear Survey Schedule for Children—Parent Completed

A modified version of the Revised Fear Survey Schedule for Children also is administered to parents to obtain an index of parental perceptions about their child's fears, as used in past research (e.g., Bondy, Sheslow, & Garcia, 1985; Silverman & Nelles, 1989). The FSSC-R/P has been shown to have acceptable internal consistency and validity estimates (Weems, Silverman, Saavedra, Pina, & Lumpkin, 1999).

Additional Measures

Children's Depression Inventory

The 27-item Children's Depression Inventory (CDI; Kovacs, 1981) assesses the cognitive, affective, and behavioral symptoms of childhood depression. For each item, children select one of three choices that best describes themselves over the past 2 weeks. The CDI has high internal consistency and moderate test–retest reliability, which amounts to acceptable validity. In a recent investigation (Berman, Weems, Silverman, & Kurtines, 2000) of predictors of success in our exposure-based cognitive–behavioral treatment programs for children (Silverman, Kurtines, Ginsburg, Weems, Lumpkin, & Carmichael, 1999; Silverman, Kurtines, Ginsburg, Weems, Rabian, & Serafini, 1999), levels of depression were important predictors of treatment success. Specifically, higher levels of depression in children were linked to treatment failure. This finding highlights the importance of assessing for childhood depression and examining its role in treatment response. From the perspective of our exposure-based transfer-of-control approach, depression may block a transfer of control to the child and thus might require "unblocking" (i.e., decreasing symptoms of depression) for positive treatment response.

Symptom Check List

The Symptom Check List (SCL-90-R; Derogatis & Melisaratos, 1983) is a 90-item scale designed to assess current psychological symptom status in adults. The SCL-90-R contains nine primary symptom dimensions and a global index of distress. The scale has adequate test–retest reliability, internal consistency, and construct validity (Derogatis & Melisaratos, 1983). In Berman et al. (2000) several symptom scales of the SCL-90-R (e.g., fear) were linked to child success and failure. As with the CDI, these findings highlight the importance of assessing for parental psychopathology and symptoms and examining their role in these factors as a moderator of child treatment response. From our perspective, as noted, parental symptoms may potentially block a transfer of control to the child and thus might require "unblocking" (i.e., decreasing parental symptoms) for positive child treatment response.

Treatment Integrity and Distinctiveness

A necessary condition for making valid conclusions on the basis of the results of treatment outcome research is evidence that the treatment procedures were administered appropriately (Kazdin, 1994). The purpose of the treatment integrity and distinctiveness checks is to ensure that the delivery of the treatment protocols by therapists is standardized and that the distinctive features of the various interventions being tested are in fact being delivered to clients. We have assessed treatment integrity and distinctiveness by means of judges' ratings of the content of periodic videotaped spot checks of therapy sessions

Therapist Training

All therapists involved in our treatment study receive training in the proper administration of the interventions. Wendy Silverman conducts this training, which involves the following training steps: Therapists first familiarize themselves with the treatment protocols, followed by both didactic and clinical training via extensive role-playing exercises related to the interventions' procedures. Therapists also study videotapes of interventions used by Dr. Silverman, and therapists are required to treat successfully at least one case using the particular intervention under investigation, under the observation and supervision of Dr. Silverman, before admittance as a therapist in any CAPP project. During the projects themselves, Dr. Silverman conducts weekly on-site supervision meetings with therapists to prepare for upcoming sessions and process sessions just completed.

Treatment Procedures

The treatment is divided into the following three phases: education, application, and relapse prevention. Each of these areas, as administered in our "basic program," is summarized below. By "basic program," we are referring to an exposure-based transfer-of-control approach in which control is transferred from the therapist to parent to child. Exhibit 5.1 shows the sequence for the administration of the treatment procedures. As noted, our view is that the alternative formats or "programs" (e.g., group cognitive–behavioral therapy) used to treat childhood anxiety disorders can be conceptualized within the frame of our exposure-based transfer-of-control approach with the main variant as follows: To whom is transfer given—the child, parents, or peers?

EXHIBIT 5.1
Sequence for Administration of the Behavioral and Cognitive Strategies in the "Basic" Exposure-Based Transfer of Control Approach

Education Phase A	Parent training in contingency management
Application Phase A	Parental application of contingency management to facilitate child exposure
Education Phase B	Child training in self-control
	Gradual fading of contingency management–parental control
Application Phase B	Child application of self-control to facilitate child exposure

The various strategies thus employed within the different formats and programs thereby serve, in our view, mainly to facilitate child exposure by the various agent(s) of change (i.e., child, parents, peers).

Education Phase

In the first phase, the therapist provides information about the strategies that facilitate child exposures. Families must understand the importance of child approach behaviors. Therapists explain that when children stay away from (or avoid) things that frighten them, the anxiety is maintained because they do not have the opportunity to learn that "there is nothing to lead them to feel afraid or anxious." We emphasize that to learn this, children must approach what they fear or do what they avoid. We give the family numerous examples, such as "getting back on a bicycle after falling off," which are readily understood. We explain that the family will learn several *facilitative strategies* in treatment to encourage child approach or exposures, including *contingency management* and *self-control*.

In teaching contingency management, we explain to children and parents the concept of reinforcement and the proper delivery of reinforcement. We differentiate the types of rewards (social, tangible, activity) and highlight the use of social and activity rewards. We also explain that rewards are provided contingent on completion of desired behaviors—specifically, approach or exposure to fearful objects and situations. The importance of consistency and follow-through is explained as well as potential difficulties parents might encounter that could prevent effective follow-through. The advantages in using contingency contracts that explicate the specific rewards to be given contingent on specific behaviors are described.

In teaching self-control, we explain to children and parents the concepts of self-observation, self-evaluation, and self-reward. We differentiate positive and negative self-statements, stress the "power of nonnegative thinking" in light of current research findings (Kendall & Chansky, 1991), and explain that, like the rewards given by the parents, the child's positive, self-rewarding statements also should be contingent on approach or exposure to fearful objects or situations. The importance of parental support and encouragement for the child's use of cognitive self-control procedures is highlighted for parents, as well as the difficulties they may encounter in providing support.

Application Phase

In the application phase, the parents and children practice the principles and procedures they were taught in the education phase. The therapist serves as a coach as they perform graduated exposure tasks that begin with the lowest, or easiest, steps on a fear or anxiety hierarchy. For example, children with a social phobia might begin by saying "hello" to another child, then asking the child a question, then holding a conversation, and finally calling the child on the telephone to ask a question. The importance of "staying with the feeling of fear or anxiety" for "as long as they can" until the fear or anxiety abates is underscored.

Contingency management also is implemented in the treatment sessions to help parents decrease their children's avoidant behaviors. The therapist helps the parent and child to generate a *contingency contract*, which is a detailed written agreement about the specific exposure task that the child will try (e.g., what to do, when to do it, how long to do it) and the specific reward the parent will provide to the child for his or her attempt to complete the task or successful completion thereof.

Once parents have some control of their children's exposure behavior, we begin teaching the children to control their own behavior with self-control strategies. Treatment concentrates on the children's thoughts and *self-statements* (statements children make silently to themselves) and how these statements potentially inhibit their attempts to complete exposure tasks. To gain self-control, children learn to use the mnemonic STOP: Scared, Thoughts, Other thoughts or Other things I can do to handle my fear, and Praise myself for successful handling of my fear and exposure (e.g., "I'm really proud of myself," and "I am a brave boy/girl").

Relapse Prevention Phase

In the final phase of treatment, the children and parents learn the importance of continued exposures. That is, we explain that the more children continue to engage in exposure, the less likely it is they will have a relapse. We explain that much of what the children have accomplished is due to the exposure exercises, and, like any accomplishment, "if you don't use it, you lose it." They also learn how to interpret "relapses." We explain that no matter how much children may continue to practice exposure, a relapse, or slip, is likely. We use the analogy of a person on a diet who successfully loses 20 pounds but then eats a piece of cake at a party, and we explore the different ways that the person could interpret the slip. This case is analyzed with the children and parents until they recognize that the most adaptive interpretation of the slip is as a single event: "It does not mean that everything is blown or ruined. I need to pick myself back up and get back on the positive track I was on." The parents' roles in handling a slip also are stressed, and we point out that children look to their parents for cues in interpreting slips.

Clinical Vignette

Presenting Problem

Henry, an 11-year-old Caucasian boy, was brought to CAPP by his mother because of extreme distress reactions pertaining to parental separation. According to Henry's mother, almost all events that entailed his separation from her would lead to severe protest and anxious reactions. The only exception to this, fortunately, was separation that surrounded school attendance: Henry could apparently manage going to school because he was a good student and enjoyed attending school. Events other than going to school, however, such as the mother leaving the house to run errands, were "impossible." Her son would repeatedly ask questions about her plans for the day and whether she was planning to go out somewhere; if so, he wanted to know where and whether he could go with her. If he knew in advance that his mother was intending to go out somewhere, Henry would report that his "stomach hurt," and he generally appeared tense and nervous. Upon her leaving the house, Henry fussed and pleaded with her not to go or to take him along.

In addition, Henry refused to participate in other activities if his mother did not go with him. Although he played with other children his age, he preferred that they play in his house; he refused to camp out with his Boy Scout troop, unless either his mother or father accompanied them. Similarly, although Henry enjoyed playing soccer, he would play only in the local soccer sports organization and only when his father served as the coach. His father consequently did coach for several years, but now he wanted "a break" from coaching for at least a couple of seasons. Henry therefore was currently not playing soccer.

Henry's mother reported that her son "never liked to be alone" and that even as a toddler his protests about separation appeared to her to be much worse than what she recalled experiencing with her other two children. Her other two children, she noted, were 10 and 12 years older than Henry. She wondered whether having Henry relatively "late in life" led her to treat him "differently than the others" because he was, in her words, "the baby in the family." She noted how she found that she "worried" much more about Henry than she had with her other two children because he was "the baby" and because he seemed "to need her" more than the others. Mother acknowledged, however, that her perceptions were somewhat tainted because while she was raising her other children she also worked full-time and thus "did not have the time to worry." With Henry, however, she was now home full-time and could spend more of her time worrying.

Assessment and Diagnosis

Henry and his mother were administered respective child and parent versions of the ADIS (Silverman & Albano, 1996). Henry and his mother also completed several questionnaires. As noted, Henry's mother reported that his anxiety about separation from her was interfering in various aspects of his and the family's life, and she provided several examples (e.g., making it difficult for her to leave the house, limitations placed on where he played with friends, participation in sports unless father coached, father not wanting to coach). Based on Henry's and his mother's responses to the interviews, Henry was assigned a diagnosis of separation anxiety disorder. On the ADIS-C/P, both Henry and his mother reported that his concerns about separation translated to a "7" on the 9-point fear thermometer rating scale. His scores on the questionnaires also were elevated.

Treatment

Henry and his mother participated in CAPP's exposure-based transfer-of-control treatment approach, in which parent and child are seen individually and then briefly together. More specifically, Henry's mother first was taught the strategies of contingency management, and then both Henry and his mother were taught child self-control strategies. They then applied these strategies in graduated exposure tasks that involved Henry gradually participating in events that required him to separate from his mother.

Exposure tasks were both imaginal and in vivo and were based on a hierarchy that varied the duration of time that Henry needed to be away from his mother. Initial in vivo steps on the hierarchy ranged in duration from 1 to 5 minutes. They completed these exposures successfully. As the duration of time for the exposures became longer, however, Henry did not complete the exposures. In examining the reasons for the failure to complete the exposures, the therapist learned that Henry's mother was ambivalent about Henry moving up the hierarchy. Mother reported concern that "maybe something could happen" while she was away from her son and noted the high incidence of burglary in her neighborhood.

To deal with these concerns, subsequent treatment sessions addressed the common obstacles encountered in treating children with anxiety disorders. For instance, emphasis was placed on reviewing with Henry's mother the importance of parental modeling of courageous behavior. In part, this was accomplished by discussing common parental "protective behaviors" and her concerns about child–parent separation. In addition, treatment focused on helping Henry and his mother think of alternative ways to handle their anxieties, including specific steps they could take to help ease the burden of separation. This included arranging for "telephone checks," which would gradually decrease over time, and giving Henry advanced warning about subsequent maternal leave so that he could be more prepared. This approach helped to empower the family, enabling them to have an action plan for handling Henry's (and his mother's) anxieties. All of these methods were helpful, and subsequent contracts were successfully carried out, including the one that required Henry to sleep over at a friend's house—a task on the hierarchy that Henry had initially considered impossible.

In the final phase of the transfer of control, wherein self-control strategies were used (using self-reward and fading out parental rewards) Henry practiced using STOP. He examined the specific cognitions that played a role in maintaining his fears (e.g., "my mother will leave and never come back"). He learned to recognize when he was afraid or worried, to employ more adaptive coping thoughts and behaviors, and to praise himself for doing so.

Posttreatment and Follow-Up

At posttreatment assessment, readministration of the ADIS-C and ADIS-P revealed that Henry no longer met diagnostic criteria for separation anxiety disorder and there was no longer any interference in his daily functioning. In addition, his scores on the questionnaires decreased markedly. These gains were maintained at 6- and 12-month follow-up assessments.

Application to "Real-World" Settings

The issue of efficacy versus effectiveness has come to the foreground in the treatment literature (e.g., Weisz et al., 1992). Overall, we believe that research in university-based settings should strive to "seem" as much as possible like "real-world" clinic settings. This serves to enhance the generalizability of research findings to clinic settings. By the same token, we also believe that clinic settings should strive to seem as much as possible like university-based clinic settings. This similarity seems particularly important in light of evidence suggesting that psychological services as presently received in community clinics are *not* effective (e.g., Weiss, Catron, Harris, & Phung, 1999). The following section illustrates ways in which research clinics might maximize the generalizability of their findings to "real-world" settings *and* ways in which clinic settings might improve the likelihood of positive outcomes among the children and families with whom they work.

What Research Clinics Might Do

Although the use of *DSM* primary diagnoses of anxiety disorders as the main inclusionary criteria for children seeking to participate in the anxiety clinical trials (e.g., Barrett et al., 1996; Kendall, 1994; Silverman, Kurtines, Ginsburg, Weems, Lumpkin, & Carmichael, 1999; Silverman, Kurtines, Ginsburg, Weems, Rabian, & Serafini, 1999) made a great deal of sense more than a decade ago, during the early period of efficacy trials, we believe it is important to move beyond primary anxiety diagnoses. This is because most children do *not* receive treatment from child anxiety specialty clinics, and most do not receive treatment for single disorders. Rather, most children are treated at general outpatient mental health clinics (e.g., community mental health centers, private practice), and when they seek treatment at these places, it is usually because they are showing disturbing or severe deterioration or impairment in functioning in multiple areas, such as at school and with peers and family members; they also may show increased signs of distress about their functioning or lack thereof (Angold, Costello, Farmer, Burns, & Erkanli, 1999). Moreover, although children's deterioration in some cases may be due entirely to anxiety and its disorders, it is more commonly due to myriad factors (e.g., other comorbid disorders, upsetting life events).

Consequently, we believe that it is important for childhood anxiety research clinics to improve their ways of assessing clinical impairment among children *and* begin to develop and evaluate interventions that are geared not just toward reducing primary anxiety diagnoses but also toward reducing clinical impairment *and* associated disorders and symptoms. Refocusing on children's impairment and comorbid or associated disorders and symptoms will go a long way, in our view, toward improving the relevance of clinical research findings to "real-world" settings.

Developing and evaluating treatment programs of specified lengths or duration (e.g., 10-week sessions, 14-week sessions) similarly made a great deal of sense in the early treatment efficacy stage in childhood anxiety disorders. It made sense from both a research and practical perspective. From a research perspective, evaluating a treatment of a specified length that was administered to all participants in an identical manner (e.g., weekly, 60 minutes) provided for systematic and direct control of these important variables. From a practical perspective, evaluating a short-term, time-limited treatment program further provided evidence for the type of therapy that was particularly needed during the health care climate of the 1990s, in which third-party payers and health maintenance organizations had become much more financially restrictive with respect to reimbursement for medical care in general and mental health care in particular.

Despite the research and practical rationale for evaluating treatments of specified lengths, the reality is that therapy is rarely so specific in terms of duration. In fact, the average length of treatment received by most children and families in a mental health setting is not even as high as what is being evaluated in the efficacy trials but instead hovers at approximately 3 to 5 sessions (Weisz et al., 1992). On the other hand, other children and families stay in therapy for long periods of time (even indefinitely) as they continue to require support for or help with a wide array of issues that crop up in their daily lives. Other families attend therapy on a sporadic basis, receiving "booster" sessions as needed, and so forth. We believe an important future direction for research clinics lies in developing and evaluating interventions that reflect these varying lengths and patterns of therapy attendance. Although this type of research poses many methodological challenges, some of the methods and analytical strategies used by Howard and colleagues in the adult psychotherapy area (e.g., Howard, Moras, Brill, Martinovich, & Lutz, 1996) and developments in other analytical areas (e.g., growth curve analyses; Duncan, Duncan, Strycker, Li, & Alpert; 1999) would seem to be important tools that could be used to help conduct child anxiety treatment research that more closely resembles therapy in "real-world" settings.

What Clinic Settings Might Do

In the preceding section, we mentioned our belief that research settings should move beyond *DSM* diagnoses and begin using other important information about children and families (e.g., impairment, comorbid disorders) for inclusionary criteria in research studies. By the same token, we believe clinic settings should move toward gathering information about their clients (e.g., children, parents) in ways that more closely mirror the ways that information is gathered in research clinics. More specifically, although all types of information-gathering procedures are used in research clinics, some type of structured data-gathering procedure (i.e., a structured or semistructured interview schedule) is *always* used. The reason that diagnostic information is obtained with structured or semistructured interview schedules is that they have been found to yield more reliable and valid information than do unstructured, clinical interviews.

Indeed, one could make the case that it is this characteristic of research settings (i.e., the use of interview schedules) that contributes, in large part, to the positive findings obtained in research clinics. For example, given the high rates of comorbid, or co-occurring, disorders in youth, determining and prioritizing all the various problems children display are not simple tasks. Interview schedules can assist with making reliable and accurate determination and prioritization decisions. In addition, because effective child anxiety treatments, as previously noted, depend heavily on the child's exposure to fearful or anxious objects and situations, accurate differential diagnoses (e.g., knowing that a child has a social phobia, not separation anxiety disorder) simplifies the process of designing appropriate and effective exposure tasks. Further, some of the interview schedules are useful in obtaining information about the functional relations, or motivating conditions, with respect to anxiety problems, which might be important for prescriptive treatment approaches.

In light of these considerations, this characteristic of the research setting should be an important part of the clinic setting as well. At a minimum, doing so would mean the administration of a semistructured interview schedule on intake. As noted, the ADIS–IV-C/P (Silverman & Albano, 1996; Silverman & Nelles, 1988; Silverman et al., 2001) is the most widely used interview in childhood anxiety treatment studies. Semistructured in nature, the ADIS–IV-C/P contains specific questions that cover the diagnostic criteria for the anxiety disorders as well as other internalizing and externalizing childhood disorders described in the *DSM–IV*. The ADIS–IV-C/P also contains screening questions for other, less prevalent childhood disorders (e.g., sleep terror disorder).

Because of its extensive coverage, the ADIS–IV-C/P assists in determining primary, secondary, tertiary, and other diagnoses. Specifically, multiple or comorbid problems are prioritized by obtaining child and parent ratings of severity or interference via the ADIS–IV-C/P. These ratings are then used to determine a ranking of the symptoms that might be targeted in treatment. To the extent that the primary target symptoms are those other than anxiety, such as depression or attention deficit hyperactivity disorder, the therapist may need to ascertain how these other symptoms might be incorporated in a given treatment formulation and plan, as discussed previously. The ADIS–IV-C/P also contains questions that can assist in providing a functional analysis (e.g., antecedents and consequence of various problems). Additional questions on the ADIS–IV-C/P pertain to the history of the problems, family members' reactions to the problems, and family history with respect to medical and psychological problems. All of this information is helpful not only in ascertaining diagnoses but also in case conceptualization and formulation. Overall, the interview schedules should be regarded as templates that can guide clinicians' questioning, not as rigid, inflexible scripts (Silverman & Kurtines, 1996a, 1996b).

FUTURE CONSIDERATIONS

Consistent with the need for conceptual models of child treatment in child psychotherapy research, which are necessary if the field is to move forward with respect to theory, research, and practice (e.g., Jensen, 1999; Kazdin, 1999), we outlined in this chapter our exposure-based transfer-of-control approach for treating anxiety disorders in children and adolescents. We described in detail the "basic" treatment approach, which largely rests on the use of behavioral (e.g., contingency management) and cognitive (e.g., self-control) therapeutic procedures as a way to facilitate exposure to fearful or anxiety-provoking situations, thereby producing treatment response (e.g., anxiety reduction) in children. As we noted earlier, however, the research literature currently contains only *indirect*, empirical support for the transfer of control approach. It contains indirect support in that ample evidence now suggests that the various formats and programs (e.g., individual, family, peer group) are *all* efficacious in reducing childhood anxiety disorders, with no evidence to suggest differential efficacy (e.g., Barrett, Duffy, Dadds, & Rapee, 2001; Flannery-Schroeder & Kendall, 2000). Although this does *not* mean that the mechanisms, or mediators, of change are, in fact, what we have proposed in this chapter (i.e., in accordance with our exposure-based transfer-of-control treatment approach), we do believe it provides considerable support for the importance of continuing to push forward the frontiers of knowledge with respect to what works in therapy.

This will require empirical research to fully and adequately evaluate the mechanisms, or mediators, of therapeutic change in childhood anxiety psychosocial interventions. For example, when implementing a family-based cognitive–behavioral treatment program, do the specific therapeutic strategies used in that program (e.g., parent–child problem solving, parent–child management training) actually lead to changes on the specific targeted variables (e.g., parent–child problem-solving skills, improved parent management)? More important, is it the specific changes in these variables that actually lead to (i.e., mediate) positive child treatment response? We would predict that they do. However, at present, this prediction is not based on systematic, direct empirical support. We are currently conducting an NIMH-funded clinical trial aimed at investigating these types of specific therapy and mediational effects analyses.

Empirical evaluation of the mediators of child anxiety treatment response (i.e., child anxiety reduction) will not just serve to advance "theoretical understanding" of why and how therapeutic change occurs in cognitive–behavioral treatment programs; it also would have significant clinical or practical significance. That is, if evidence becomes available that the various treatment formats and programs (e.g., group, family) all "work" by allowing for a transfer of control from therapist to various agents of change to facilitate child exposure to anxiety-producing objects and situations (e.g., peers, parents) or, in other words, that child treatment response and exposure is *mediated* by the procedures used in these various treatment formats and programs (e.g., social skills training in group, parent training in family), then this would provide private practitioners with increased flexibility regarding effective therapeutic procedures that they can use with children and families in different settings.

This flexibility is important, given that in some settings, such as school settings, parents are not readily available to participate in child interventions. Or in other settings, such as psychiatric or community-health facilities, parents may be too impaired themselves to be actively engaged in the child's treatment. Alternatively, children sometimes are unable to grasp the cognitive or self-control aspects of the intervention, perhaps because of developmental factors. Clinicians may select to work in such instances with parents only, facilitating child exposures via contingency management procedures (Silverman, Kurtines, Ginsburg, Weems, Rabian, & Serafini, 1999). Along similar lines, a group approach offers many clinical advantages (e.g., opportunities for peer support, peer comparison, intrinsic "social" exposures that may be particularly useful for youth with social phobias) and also is time- and cost-effective, thereby offering many additional practical advantages for use in a number of different institutions or settings. Further, if empirical data show that what might occur in psychoeducational-support programs is yet another transfer of control from therapists to the recipients of the program, then this would suggest another therapeutic approach for delivering effective anxiety treatment procedures to children and families (Silverman, Kurtines, Ginsburg, Weems, Rabian, & Serafini, 1999).

Empirical evidence for the mediators of child anxiety treatment response also can be helpful in terms of leading to improved "prescriptive "treatment approaches to child anxiety (Eisen & Silverman, 1998; Kearney & Silverman, 1999). For example, if the transfer of control from therapist to child can be even further facilitated by "matching" aspects of the exposure-based cognitive–behavioral program to characteristics of a given child, then, for example, those aspects of the treatment that are particularly applicable to that child's "response class" of anxious behaviors (e.g., self-control strategies for a child who worries excessively) or "functional condition" (e.g., rearranging parental contingencies for the child who is obtaining positive consequences) might be "prescribed" to that particular child.

In sum, systematic and direct evidence for the specific therapy and mediational effects of cognitive–behavioral therapies for anxiety disorders in youth, or from our perspective, of exposure-based transfer-of-control treatment approaches, would allow therapists to have maximal clinical flexibility in therapeutic procedures, strategies, formats, and even potential stances (e.g., directive, nondirective) that they might use or adapt when working with anxious children and their families. This is good news in light of the multitude of settings in which therapists work, as well as the heterogeneity that exists among children and families.

REFERENCES

Achenbach, T. M. (1991). *Manual for the child behavior checklists/4–18 and 1991 profile*. Burlington: University of Vermont.

American Psychiatric Association. (1994). *Diagnostic and statistical manual of mental disorders* (4th ed., rev.). Washington, DC: Author.

Angold, A., Costello, E. J., Farmer, E. M. Z., Burns, B. J., & Erkanli, A. (1999). Impaired but undiagnosed. *Journal of the American Academy of Child and Adolescent Psychiatry, 38*, 129–137.

Barrett, P. M. (1998). Evaluation of cognitive–behavioral group treatments for childhood anxiety disorders. *Journal of Clinical Child Psychology, 27*, 459–468.

Barrett, P. M., Dadds, M. R., & Rapee, R. M. (1996). Family treatment of childhood anxiety: A controlled trial. *Journal of Consulting and Clinical Psychology, 64*, 333–342.

Barrett, P. M., Duffy, A. L., Dadds, M. R., & Rapee, R. M. (2001). Cognitive–behavioral treatment of anxiety disorders in children: Long-term (6-year) follow-up. *Journal of Consulting and Clinical Psychology, 69*, 135–141.

Beidel, D. C., Turner, S. M., & Morris, T. L. (2000). Behavioral treatment of childhood social phobia. *Journal of Consulting and Clinical Psychology, 68*, 1072–1080.

Berman, S. L., Weems, C. F., Silverman, W. K., & Kurtines, W. M. (2000). Predictors of outcome in exposure-based cognitive and behavioral treatments for phobic and anxiety disorders in children. *Behavior Therapy, 31*, 713–731.

Bondy, A., Sheslow, D., & Garcia, L. T. (1985). An investigation of children's fears and their mothers' fears. *Journal of Psychopathology and Behavioral Assessment, 7*, 1–12.

Cobham, V. E., Dadds, M. R., & Spence, S. H. (1998). The role of parental anxiety in the treatment of childhood anxiety. *Journal of Consulting and Clinical Psychology, 66*, 893–905.

Derogatis, L. R., & Melisaratos, N. (1983). The brief symptom inventory: An introductory report. *Psychological Medicine, 13*, 595–605.

Duncan, T., Duncan, S., Strycker, L., Li, F., & Alpert, A. (1999). *An introduction to latent variable growth curve modeling: Concepts, issues and applications.* Mawah, NJ: Erlbaum.

Eisen, A. R., & Silverman, W. K. (1991). Treatment of an adolescent with bowel movement phobia using self-control therapy. *Journal of Behavior Therapy and Experimental Psychiatry, 22*, 45–51.

Eisen, A. R., & Silverman, W. K. (1993). Should I relax or change my thoughts?: A preliminary study of the treatment of overanxious disorder in children. *Journal of Cognitive Psychotherapy, 7*, 265–280.

Eisen, A. R., & Silverman, W. K. (1998). Prescriptive treatment for generalized anxiety disorder in children. *Behavior Therapy, 29*, 105–121.

Flannery-Schroeder, E. C., & Kendall, P. C. (2000). Group and individual cognitive–behavioral treatments for youth with anxiety disorders: A randomized clinical trial. *Cognitive Therapy and Research, 24*, 251–278.

Ginsburg, G. S., Silverman, W. K., & Kurtines, W. M. (1995). Family involvement in treating children with phobic and anxiety disorders: A look ahead. *Clinical Psychology Review, 15*, 457–473.

Hayward, C., Varady, S., Albano, A. M., Thienemann, M., Henderson, L., & Schatzberg, A. F. (2000). Cognitive–behavioral group therapy for social phobia in female adolescents: Results of a pilot study. *Journal of the American Academy of Child and Adolescent Psychiatry, 39*, 721–734.

Howard, K. I., Moras, K., Brill, P. L., Martinovich, Z., & Lutz, W. (1996). Evaluation of psychotherapy: Efficacy, effectiveness, and patient progress. *American Psychologist, 51*, 1059–1064.

Jensen, P. S. (1999). Links among theory, research, and practice: Cornerstones of clinical scientific progress. *Journal of Clinical Child Psychology, 28*, 553–557.

Kane, M. T., & Kendall, P. C. (1989). Anxiety disorders in children: A multiple-baseline evaluation of a cognitive–behavioral treatment. *Behavior Therapy, 20,* 499–508.

Kazdin, A. E. (1994). Methodology, design, and evaluation in psychotherapy research. In A. E. Bergin & S. L. Garfield (Eds.), *Handbook of psychotherapy and behavior change* (4th ed.). New York: Wiley.

Kazdin, A. E. (1999). Current (lack of) status of theory in child and adolescent psychotherapy research. *Journal of Clinical Child Psychology, 28,* 533–543.

Kearney, C. A., & Silverman, W. K. (1990a). Treatment of an adolescent with obsessive-compulsive disorder by alternating response prevention and cognitive therapy. *Journal of Behavior Therapy and Experimental Psychiatry, 21,* 39–49.

Kearney, C. A., & Silverman, W. K. (1990b). A preliminary analysis of a functional model of assessment and treatment for school refusal behavior. *Behavior Modification, 14,* 340–366.

Kearney, C. A., & Silverman, W. K. (1993). Measuring the function of school refusal behavior: The School Refusal Assessment Scale. *Journal of Clinical Child Psychology, 22,* 85–96.

Kearney, C. A., & Silverman, W. K. (1999). Functionally based prescriptive and nonprescriptive treatment for children and adolescents with school refusal behavior. *Behavior Therapy, 30,* 673–695.

Kendall, P. C. (1994). Treating anxiety disorders in children: Results of a randomized clinical trial. *Journal of Consulting and Clinical Psychology, 62,* 100–110.

Kendall, P. C., & Chansky, T. E. (1991). Considering cognition in anxiety-disordered children. *Journal of Anxiety Disorders, 5,* 167–185.

Kendall, P. C., Flannery-Schroeder, E., Panichelli-Mindel, S. M., Southam-Gerow, M., Henin, A., & Warman, M. (1997). Therapy for youths with anxiety disorders: A second randomized clinical trial. *Journal of Consulting and Clinical Psychology, 65,* 366–380.

Kendall, P. C., & Grove, W. (1988). Normative comparisons in therapy outcome. *Behavioral Assessment, 10,* 147–158.

Kovacs, M. (1981). Rating scales to assess depression in school-aged children. *Acta Paedopsychiatrica: International Journal of Child and Adolescent Psychiatry, 46,* 305–315.

Lumpkin, P. W., Silverman, W. K., Weems, C. F., Markham, M. R., & Kurtines, W. M. (2002). Treating a heterogenous set of anxiety disorders in youth with group cognitive behavior therapy: A partially nonconcurrent multiple baseline evaluation. *Behavior Therapy, 33,* 163–177.

Ollendick, T. H. (1983). Reliability and validity of the Revised Fear Survey Schedule for Children (FSSC-R). *Behaviour Research and Therapy, 21,* 685–692.

Ollendick, T. H. (1995). Cognitive–behavioral treatment of panic disorder with agoraphobia in adolescents: A multiple baseline design analysis. *Behavior Therapy, 26,* 517–531.

Reynolds, C. R., & Richmond, B. O. (1985). *Revised Children's Manifest Anxiety Scale (RCMAS) manual*. Los Angeles, CA: Western Psychological Services.

Reynolds, C. R., & Richmond, B. O. (1978). What I think and feel: A revised measure of children's manifest anxiety. *Journal of Abnormal Child Psychology, 6,* 271–280.

Silverman, W. K., & Albano, A. M. (1996). *The Anxiety Disorders Interview Schedule for DSM–IV: child and parent versions*. San Antonio, TX: Psychological Corporation.

Silverman, W. K., & Eisen, A. R. (1992). Age differences in the reliability of parent and child reports of child anxious symptomatology using a structured interview. *Journal of the American Academy of Child and Adolescent Psychiatry, 32,* 117–124.

Silverman, W. K., Fleisig, W., Rabian, B., & Peterson, R. A. (1991). Childhood anxiety sensitivity index. *Journal of Clinical Child Psychology, 20,* 162–168.

Silverman, W. K., & Ginsburg, G. S. (1998). Anxiety disorders. In T. H. Ollendick & M. Hersen (Eds.), *Handbook of child psychopathology*. New York: Plenum Press.

Silverman, W. K., Ginsburg, G. S., & Goedhart, A. W. (1999). Factor structure of the childhood anxiety sensitivity index. *Behaviour Research and Therapy, 37,* 903–917.

Silverman, W. K., Goedhart, A. W., Barrett, P., & Turner, C. (2003). The facets of anxiety sensitivity represented in the childhood anxiety sensitivity index: Confirmatory analyses of factor models from past studies. *Journal of Abnormal Psychology, 112,* 365–374.

Silverman, W. K., & Kurtines, W. M. (1996a). Transfer of control: A psychosocial intervention model for internalizing disorders in youth. In E. D. Hibbs & P. S. Jensen (Eds.), *Psychosocial treatment of child and adolescent disorders: Empirically based strategies for clinical practice* (pp. 63–82). Washington, DC: American Psychological Association.

Silverman, W. K., & Kurtines, W. M. (1996b). *Anxiety and phobic disorders: A pragmatic approach*. New York: Plenum Press.

Silverman, W. K., & Kurtines, W. M. (1997). Theory in child psychosocial treatment research: Have it or had it? A pragmatic alternative. *Journal of Abnormal Child Psychology, 25,* 359–367.

Silverman, W. K., Kurtines, W. M., Ginsburg, G. S., Weems, C. F., Lumpkin, P. W., & Carmichael, D. H. (1999). Treating anxiety disorders in children with group cognitive–behavioral therapy: A randomized clinical trial. *Journal of Consulting and Clinical Psychology, 67,* 995–1003.

Silverman, W. K., Kurtines, W. M., Ginsburg, G. S., Weems, C. F., Rabian, B., & Serafini, L. T. (1999). Contingency management, self-control, and education support in the treatment of childhood phobic disorders: a randomized clinical trial. *Journal of Consulting and Clinical Psychology, 67,* 675–687.

Silverman, W. K., La Greca, A. M., & Wasserstein, S. B. (1995). What do children worry about? Worry and its relation to anxiety. *Child Development, 66,* 671–684.

Silverman, W. K., & Nelles, W. B. (1988). The Anxiety Disorders Interview Schedule for Children. *Journal of the American Academy of Child and Adolescent Psychiatry, 27*, 772–778.

Silverman, W. K., & Nelles, W. B. (1989). The stability of mothers' ratings of child fearfulness. *Journal of Anxiety Disorders, 3*, 1–5.

Silverman, W. K., & Rabian, B. (1995). Test-retest reliability of the DSM–III–R childhood anxiety disorders symptoms using the Anxiety Disorders Interview Schedule for Children. *Journal of Anxiety Disorders, 9*, 1–12.

Silverman, W. K., Saavedra, L. M., & Pina, A. A. (2001). Test-retest reliability of anxiety symptoms and disorders with the Anxiety Disorders Interview Schedule for DSM–IV: child and parent versions. *Journal of the American Academy of Child and Adolescent Psychiatry, 40*, 937–943.

Spence, S. H., Donovan, C., & Brechman-Toussaint, M. (2000). The treatment of childhood social phobia: The effectiveness of a social skills training-based, cognitive–behavioural intervention, with and without parent involvement. *Journal of Child Psychology and Psychiatry and Allied Disciplines, 41*, 713–726.

Weems, C. F., Silverman, W. K., & La Greca, A. M. (2000). What do youth referred for anxiety problems worry about? Worry and its relation to anxiety and anxiety disorders in children and adolescents. *Journal of Abnormal Child Psychology, 28*, 63–72.

Weems, C. F., Silverman, W. K., Saavedra, L. S., Pina, A. A., & Lumpkin, P. W. (1999). The discrimination of children's phobias using the Revised Fear Survey for Children. *Journal of Child Psychology and Psychiatry and Allied Disciplines, 40*, 941–952.

Weiss, B., Catron, T., Harris, V., & Phung, T. M. (1999). The effectiveness of traditional child psychotherapy. *Journal of Consulting and Clinical Psychology, 67*, 82–94.

Weisz, J. R., Weiss, B., & Donenberg, G. R. (1992). The lab versus the clinic: Effects of child and adolescent psychotherapy. *American Psychologist, 47*, 1578–1585.

6

COGNITIVE–BEHAVIORAL PSYCHOTHERAPY FOR PEDIATRIC OBSESSIVE–COMPULSIVE DISORDER

JOHN S. MARCH, MARTIN FRANKLIN, AND EDNA FOA

At any given time, one in 200 children and adolescents suffers from obsessive–compulsive disorder (OCD, which in many cases severely disrupts academic, social, and vocational functioning (Adams, Waas, March, & Smith, 1994; Leonard et al., 1993). Among adults with OCD, one third to one half develop the disorder during childhood or adolescence (Rasmussen & Eisen, 1990). Hence, besides reducing the suffering of youth with OCD, improvements in treating pediatric OCD have the potential to reduce adult morbidity. Over the past 15 years, cognitive–behavioral therapy (CBT) has emerged as the initial treatment of choice for OCD across the life span

This manuscript was adapted from "Cognitive–behavioral psychotherapy for pediatric obsessive–compulsive disorder," by J. S. March, M. Franklin, A. Nelson, and E. Foa, 2001, *Journal of Clinical and Child Psychology, 30*, pp. 8–18. Copyright 2001 by Erlbaum. Adapted with permission. It also appeared, under the same name, in the previous edition of this volume. It was supported in part by NIMH Grants 1 R10 MH55121 (Drs. March and Foa) and 1 K24 MHO1557 (Dr. March) and by the Robert and Sarah Gorrell family.

(March, Frances, Kahn, & Carpenter, 1997). Unlike other psychotherapies that have been generally unsuccessful when applied to OCD (March & Leonard, 1996), CBT presents a logically consistent and compelling relationship between the disorder, the treatment, and the specified outcome (Foa & Kozak, 1991; March & Leonard, 1998). Nevertheless, despite a consensus that CBT is usually helpful, clinicians routinely complain that patients will not comply with behavioral treatments, and parents routinely complain that clinicians are poorly trained in CBT, with the result that many, if not most, children and adolescents are denied access to effective CBT. This unfortunate situation may be avoidable, given the increased understanding of the use of CBT in children and adolescents with OCD. To this end, this chapter reviews the current status of cognitive–behavioral treatment of OCD in children and adolescents. We begin by reviewing the principles that underlie the cognitive–behavioral treatment of OCD, then provide a brief review of our CBT protocol as used in both clinical and research settings (March & Mulle, 1998), move on to discuss empirical studies supporting the use of CBT and directions for future research, and conclude with a set of clinical recommendations. Readers wishing to follow the protocol are advised to purchase and use the treatment manual itself (March & Mulle, 1998).

CONCEPTUAL FRAMEWORK

Overview

A wide variety of dynamic, family, and supportive psychotherapies not systematically applied or even conceptually linked have been brought to bear on children and adolescents with OCD. For the most part, insight-oriented psychotherapy, whether delivered individually or in the family setting, has proved disappointing in both youth (Hollingsworth, Tanguay, & Grossman, 1980) and adults (Esman, 1989). Conversely, effective, flexible, and empirically supported cognitive–behavioral treatments are now available for many childhood mental illnesses (March, 2000), including OCD (March & Mulle, 1995). In adults the cognitive–behavioral treatment of OCD generally involves a three-stage approach consisting of information gathering; therapist-assisted exposure and response prevention (EX/RP), including homework assignments; and generalization training and relapse prevention. Both graded exposure and flooding procedures have garnered strong empirical and clinical support (Foa & Kozak, in press). Component analyses suggest that both exposure and response prevention are active ingredients of treatment, with exposure reducing phobic anxiety and response prevention reducing rituals (Foa & Kozak, in press; Foa, Steketee, Grayson, Turner, & Latimer, 1984; Foa, Steketee, & Milby, 1980). Relaxation has been shown to be an inert component of behavioral treatment for OCD and has been used as an active placebo in brief (4–6 weeks) studies in adults (Marks, 1987). Similarly, cognitive interventions seem less potent than EX/RP in reducing OCD symptoms (van Oppen et al., 1995).

Cognitive–Behavioral Therapy in Children and Adolescents

While CBT is routinely described as the psychotherapeutic treatment of choice for children and adolescents with OCD (March & Leonard, 1998), robust empirical support is only now emerging (King, Leonard, & March, 1998). In practice, the following treatment components, which generally parallel the identical interventions in adults, make up the typical CBT treatment package (Franklin et al., 1998; March & Mulle, 1998).

Exposure and Response Prevention

As applied to OCD, the exposure principle relies on the fact that anxiety usually attenuates after sufficient duration of contact with a feared stimulus (Foa & Kozak, 1985). Thus, a child with fear of germs must confront relevant feared situations until his or her anxiety decreases. Repeated exposure is associated with decreased anxiety across exposure trials, with anxiety reduction largely specific to the domain of exposure, until the child no longer fears contact with specifically targeted phobic stimuli (March & Mulle, 1995; March, Mulle, & Herbel, 1994). Adequate exposure depends on blocking the negative reinforcement effect by rituals or avoidance behavior, a process termed *response prevention*. For example, a child who worries about germs must not only touch "germy things" but must refrain from ritualized washing until his or her anxiety diminishes substantially. EX/RP is typically implemented in a gradual fashion (sometimes termed *graded exposure*), with exposure targets under the patient's or, less desirably, the therapist's control (March & Mulle, 1996; March et al., 1994). However, intensive prescriptive approaches work equally well for children who subscribe in advance to this approach (Franklin et al., 1998). Intensive approaches may be especially useful for treatment-resistant OCD or for patients who desire a very rapid response.

Cognitive Therapy

A wide variety of cognitive interventions have been used to provide the child with the necessary tools to facilitate compliance with EX/RP. The goals of cognitive therapy (CT) typically include increasing a sense of personal efficacy, predictability, controllability and self-attributed likelihood of a positive outcome within EX/RP tasks. Specific interventions include the following: (a) constructive self-talk (Kendall, Howard, & Epps, 1988), (b) cognitive restructuring (March et al., 1994; van Oppen & Arntz, 1994), and (c) cultivating nonattachment (Schwartz, 1996) or, stated somewhat differently, minimizing thought suppression (Salkovskis, Westbrook, Davis, Jeavons, & Gledhill, 1997). Each must be individualized to match the specific OCD symptoms that afflict the child and must mesh with the child's cognitive abilities, developmental stage, and individual differences in preference among the three techniques.

Extinction

Because blocking rituals or avoidance behaviors removes the negative reinforcement effect of the rituals or avoidance, response prevention technically is an extinction procedure. By convention, however, *extinction* is usually defined as the elimination of OCD-related behaviors through removal of parental positive reinforcement for rituals. For example, a child with reassurance-seeking rituals may ask parents to refrain from gratifying the child's reassurance seeking. Extinction frequently produces rapid effects but can be hard to implement when the child's behavior is bizarre or very frequent. In addition, nonconsensual extinction procedures often lead to unmanageable distress on the part of the child, disrupt the therapeutic alliance, miss important EX/RP targets that are not amenable to extinction procedures, and, most important, fail to help the child internalize a strategy for resisting OCD. Hence, as with EX/RP, placing the extinction program under the child's control leads to increased compliance and improved outcomes (March & Mulle, 1998).

Modeling and Shaping

Modeling—whether overt (i.e., the child understands that the therapist is demonstrating more appropriate or adaptive coping behaviors) or covert (i.e., the therapist informally models a behavior)—may help improve compliance with in-session EX/RP and generalization to between-session EX/RP homework. Intended to increase motivation to comply with EX/RP, shaping involves positively reinforcing successive approximations to a desired target behavior. Modeling and shaping reduce anticipatory anxiety and provide an opportunity for practicing constructive self-talk before and during EX/RP (Thyer, 1991). Because EX/RP has not proved particularly helpful with obsessional slowness, modeling and shaping procedures are currently the behavioral treatment of choice for children with this OCD subtype (Ratnasuriya, Marks, Forshaw, & Hymas, 1991), although deterioration often occurs when therapist-assisted shaping, limit setting, and temporal speeding procedures are withdrawn (Wolff & Rapoport, 1988).

Operant Procedures

Clinically, positive reinforcement seems not to directly alter OCD symptoms but rather to help encourage compliance with EX/RP, thereby producing a noticeable if indirect clinical benefit. In contrast, punishment (defined as imposition of an aversive event) and response–cost (defined as removal of a positive event) procedures have shown themselves to be unhelpful in the treatment of OCD (Harris & Wiebe, 1992). Most CBT programs use liberal positive reinforcement for EX/RP and proscribe aversive contingency management procedures unless targeting disruptive behavior outside the domain of OCD (March & Mulle, 1996). Because OCD itself is a powerful tonic aversive stimulus, successful EX/RP breeds willingness to engage in further EX/RP via negative reinforcement (e.g., elimination of OCD symptoms boosts compliance with EX/RP) as manifested by unscheduled generalization to new EX/RP targets as treatment proceeds (March et al., 1994).

Individual Versus Family Treatment

Family psychopathology is neither necessary nor sufficient for the onset of OCD; nonetheless, families affect and are affected by the disorder (Amir, Freshman, & Foa, 2000; Lenane, 1989). Hence, although empirical data are lacking, clinical observations suggest that a combination of individual and family sessions is best for most patients (March & Mulle, 1996; March, Leonard, & Swedo, 1995a).

A Typical Cognitive–Behavioral Therapy Protocol

The protocol used by March and Foa in their NIMH study (discussed below), which is fairly typical of a gradual exposure regimen (March & Mulle, 1998), consists of 14 visits over 12 weeks spread across five phases: (a) psychoeducation, (b) cognitive training, (c) mapping OCD, (d) exposure and response prevention, and (e) relapse prevention and generalization training. As shown in Table 6.1, except for Weeks 1 and 2, during which

TABLE 6.1
CBT Treatment Protocol

Visit number	Goals	Targets
Weeks 1 and 2	Psychoeducation	Neurobehavioral model
	Cognitive training	Labeling OCD as OCD
Week 2	Mapping OCD	Set up stimulus hierarchy
	Cognitive training	Cognitive restructuring
Weeks 3–12	Exposure and response prevention	Imaginal and in vivo EX/RP
Weeks 11 and 12	Relapse prevention	Targets, relapse, follow-up plans
Visits 1, 7, and 9	Parent sessions	Decrease reinforcement of OCD
		Enlist parents as cotherapists

patients come twice weekly, all visits are administered once a week, last 1 hour, and include one between-visit 10-minute telephone contact scheduled during Weeks 3 through 12. Psychoeducation, definition of OCD as the identified problem, cognitive training, and development of a stimulus hierarchy (mapping OCD) take place during Visits 1 and 4; EX/RP takes up visits 5 and 12, with the last two sessions incorporating generalization training and relapse prevention. Each session includes a statement of goals, review of the previous week, provision of new information, therapist-assisted practice, homework for the coming week, and monitoring procedures.

Parents are centrally involved during Sessions 1, 7, and 11, with the latter two sessions devoted to advising the parents about their central role in assisting their child to accomplish the homework assignments. Sessions 13 and 14 also require significant parental input. Parents check in with the therapist at each session, and the therapist provides feedback describing the goals of each session and the child's progress in treatment. The therapist works with parents to assist them in refraining from insisting on inappropriate EX/RP tasks, which is a common problem in pediatric OCD treatment. The therapist also encourages parents to praise the child for resisting OCD, while at the same time refocusing their attention on positive elements in the child's life, an intervention technically termed *differential reinforcement of other behavior (DRO)*. In some cases, extensive family involvement in rituals or the developmental level of the child (or both) require that family members play a more central role in treatment, and the CBT. The CBT protocol provides sufficient flexibility to accommodate variations in family involvement dictated by the OCD symptom picture.

In this regard, clinical lore strongly suggests the importance of flexibility in delivering protocol-driven treatments as a function of developmental factors (Clarke, 1995). In our hands, CBT has been shown effective in children as young as 5 years old. We promote developmental appropriateness by allowing flexibility in CBT within the constraints of fixed session goals. More specifically, the therapist adjusts the level of discourse to each patient's cognitive functioning, social maturity, and capacity for sustained attention. Younger patients require more redirection and activities to sustain attention and motivation. Adolescents are generally more sensitive to the effects of OCD on peer interactions, which in turn require more discussion. Cognitive interventions in particular require adjustment to the developmental level of the patient; adolescents, for example, are less likely to appreciate giving OCD a "nasty nickname" than younger children. Developmentally appropriate metaphors relevant to the child's areas of interest and knowledge are also used to promote active involvement in the treatment process. For instance, an adolescent male football player treated with CBT was better able to grasp treatment concepts when they were cast in terms of offensive and defensive strategies used during football games (e.g., blitzing). Patients whose OCD symptoms entangle family members require more attention to family involvement in treatment planning and implementation than those without as much family involvement. On the other hand, although the CBT manual (March & Mulle, 1998) includes a section on developmental sensitivity that is specific to each treatment session, the general format and goals of the treatment sessions will be the same for all children.

Course of Initial Treatment

Nicely illustrating a typical course of initial treatment, March and Mulle (1995) used a within-subject multiple baseline design plus global ratings across treatment weeks to treat an 8-year-old girl with OCD with CBT alone. Eleven weeks of treatment produced complete resolution in OCD symptoms in this patient with uncomplicated OCD; treatment gains were maintained at 6-month follow-up. Figure 6.1 illustrates the progress of treatment at each week for each symptom baseline. Initially, symptom reduction

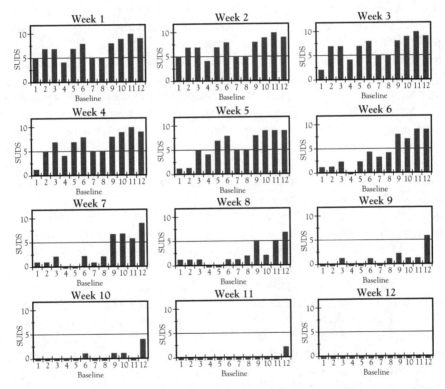

Figure 6.1. Multiple baselines over time. Each box represents a treatment week. The Y (vertical) axis represents SUDS (fear thermometer) scores for each symptom present at baseline on the symptom hierarchy, depicted as bars on the X (horizontal) axis. (Symptom Key: Week 1: touching mouth; week 2: snack after touching plants; week 3: not washing for meals; week 4: wearing turtlenecks again; week 5: touching something sticky; week 6: touching dish liquid; week 7: use towel again; week 8: touch cat; week 9: use abrasive cleanser; week 10: use ammonia-based glass cleaner; week 11: toxic paint; week 12: touching sick people.)

within each baseline was specific to the exposure or response prevention targets for that baseline. As is often the case, however, once a child got the idea, generalization across baselines appeared with some slowing down again as she reaches the most difficult symptoms at the top of the symptom hierarchy. Improvement slows down at the high end of the hierarchy, but progress continues until most, if not all, OCD symptoms remit, whereupon relapse and generalization training are appropriate.

TREATMENT OUTCOME STUDIES

Assessing Obsessive–Compulsive Disorder Outcomes

The primary efficacy measure in virtually all adult or pediatric OCD studies is the Children's Yale–Brown Obsessive–Compulsive Scale (CY-BOCS; Goodman & Price, 1992); secondary measures typically include the NIMH Global OCD Scale (NIMH OCS) and the Clinical Global Impression of Severity (CGI-S) and Improvement (CGI-I) scales. The children's version of the Y-BOCS, the CY-BOCS, is identical in form and scoring to the widely used adult scale, but the questions are slightly modified for age appropriateness (Scahill et al., 1997). The CY-BOCS score ranges from 0 to 40, with a score of 20 indicating moderate severity of obsessive and compulsive symptoms. Based on extensive adult and pediatric treatment literature, a 6-point difference between groups on the Y-BOCS is typically thought of as a meaningful clinical difference either between pre- and posttreatment or between treatment groups. Six points reflect a 35% to 50% Y-BOCS change in studies of medication and engenders a 1 or 2 point CGI-Impairment scale decrease (Goodman & Price, 1992). The NIMH OCS has been extensively used in both adult (Goodman & Price, 1992) and pediatric (Leonard et al., 1989; March & Mulle, 1998) OCD trials. It assesses severity of OCD symptoms in relation to their functional impact (Murphy, Pickar, & Alterman, 1982). Scores of 1 to 3 indicate minimal impairment, scores of 7 indicate clinically meaningful OCD symptoms, and scores of 13 to 15 indicate very severe obsessive and compulsive behaviors. The two CGI scales provide a clinician-rated overall summary: the Clinical Global Severity scale, which ranges from 1 (normal, not at all ill) to 7 (extremely ill), and the Clinical Global Improvement scale, which ranges from 1 (very much improved) to 7 (very much worse) judgments (Guy, 1976). Responders are defined as patients rated much improved (CGI = 2) or very much improved (CGI = 1) on the CGI. Considered with reference to the CY-BOCS, a CGI of 2 corresponds to a 33% to 66% decrease in Y-BOCS score from baseline, and a CGI of 1 represents a greater than 66% score. Lastly, illness burden and functional impairment are of critical importance with respect to demonstrating the public health impact of treatment on outcome.

Empirical Studies

Although the empirical literature still awaits the results of several currently running randomized controlled trials of CBT against control and active comparison treatments, existing literature is sufficiently robust to have resulted in widespread acceptance of CBT as the initial treatment of choice for OCD in children and adolescents (Franklin et al., 1998; March & Mulle, 1996; King et al., 1998; March & Leonard, 1998).

Efficacy

Uncontrolled evaluations published to date (Franklin et al., 1998; March, 1998) have yielded remarkably similar findings: After treatment, the vast majority of patients were responders, with mean CY-BOCS reductions ranging from 50% to 67%. Although strong conclusions require a randomized controlled study, these reported CY-BOCS reductions associated with CBT are impressive. However, complicating interpretation of the findings is the fact that many, if not most, patients were on selective serotonin reuptake inhibitors (SSRIs) before or during the course of CBT, and therefore the separate effects of CBT cannot be determined.

Dose and Time-Response

Most of the published studies of CBT outcome in pediatric OCD have employed a weekly therapy regimen. In contrast, Wever and Rey (1997) used an intensive CBT protocol that included two information-gathering sessions followed by 10 daily sessions of CBT over 2 weeks. Franklin et al. (1998) found no differences between 14 weekly sessions over 12 weeks and 18 sessions over 4 weeks, but interpretation of this finding is hampered by the lack of random assignment. Taken together, the available studies suggest that patients respond well to CBT delivered either weekly or intensively. Given the greater acceptability of weekly treatment for patients and providers, most providers likely will use the widely available 14-session, 12-week protocol (March & Mulle, 1998) that we use in our collaborative R01 study.

Durability

Epidemiological studies suggest that OCD is a chronic condition (Rasmussen & Eisen, 1990). On the other hand, clinical research in adults shows that long-term outcomes for patients successfully treated with CBT alone or CBT plus medication are generally favorable. Hembree et al. (2003) concluded that gains achieved with behavior therapy persist without continuing treatment, whereas those achieved with medication alone require continuing medication for maintenance. As in adults, OCD in children and adolescents is often a chronic mental illness. For example, in the first NIMH follow-up study, 68% of patients had clinical OCD at follow-up (Flament et al., 1990). In a subsequent, more systematic 2- to 7-year follow-up study (Leonard et al., 1993), 43% still met diagnostic criteria for OCD; only 11% were totally asymptomatic. Seventy percent continued to take medication at the time of follow-up, plainly illustrating the limitations of the treatments received by these patients. The three pediatric OCD pilot studies that have included a follow-up evaluation (Franklin et al., 1998; March et al., 1994; Wever, 1994) support the durability of CBT, with therapeutic gains maintained up to 9 months after treatment. Moreover, since relapse commonly follows medication discontinuation, the finding of March et al. (1994) that improvement persisted in six of nine responders after the withdrawal of medication provides limited support for the hypothesis that behavior therapy inhibits relapse when medications are discontinued.

Direct Comparison of Cognitive–Behavioral Therapy and Pharmacotherapy

Results from a single small n randomized comparison of CBT and clomipramine indicated benefit for both CBT and clomipramine relative to baseline and superiority of CBT compared with clomipramine (de Haan, Hoogduin, Buitelaar, & Keijsers, 1998). In the study by Franklin et al. (1998), which compared CBT outcomes in patients who were provided medication naturalistically and those who were not, 12 of the 14 patients were at least 50% improved over pretreatment Y-BOCS severity, and the vast majority remained improved at follow-up; mean reduction in Y-BOCS was 67% at posttreatment and 62% at follow-up (mean time to follow-up = 9 months). No differences were apparent between those who received gradual exposure and those who received intensive exposure or in those who received medication and those who did not. Thus, a definitive answer to the question of whether CBT and medication alone differ in outcome or whether the combination is equivalent or better than either monotherapy awaits the results of the Duke–Penn randomized controlled trial currently under way.

Availability, Acceptability, and Tolerability

Experts have recommended CBT with a strong emphasis on EX/RP as a first-line treatment for OCD in children and adolescents (March et al., 1997), yet several barriers may limit its widespread use. First, few therapists have extensive experience with CBT for pediatric OCD; thus, CBT typically is available only in areas associated with major medical centers, if at all. Second, even when the treatment is available, some patients and families reject it as too difficult. Once involved in CBT, some patients find their initial distress when confronting feared thoughts and situations while simultaneously refraining from rituals so aversive that they drop out of treatment. In our protocol we use hierarchy-driven EX/RP, actively involve the patient in choosing exposure exercises, and include anxiety-management techniques for the few who need them. As a result, the drop-out rates in our pilot studies and in our ongoing comparative treatment trial (unpublished data) are quite low, which in turn suggests that the vast majority of children and adolescents can tolerate and will benefit from CBT when delivered in a clinically savvy and developmentally sensitive fashion.

Modifiers of Treatment Outcome

The question of paramount interest to clinicians and to researchers attempting to refine and improve treatment outcome is as follows: "Which treatment for which child with what characteristics?"

Conventional wisdom holds that patients with OCD who benefit from CBT and medication differ in important if ill-understood ways. However, other than comorbid schizotypy (Baer et al., 1992) and tic disorders (McDougle et al., 1993), which may represent treatment impediments and possible indications for neuroleptic augmentation, the meager empirical literature on moderators of treatment outcome in adults provides no clear support for any of the putative predictors proposed by Goodman, Rasumussen, Foa, & Price (1994) in their review of pharmacotherapy trials' methodology in OCD. Conversely, predictors of a successful response to behavior therapy include the presence of rituals, the desire to eliminate symptoms, ability to monitor and report symptoms, absence of complicating comorbidities, willingness to cooperate with treatment, and psychophysiological indicators (Foa & Emmelkamp, 1983; Steketee, 1994).

Although many researchers have suggested that the presence of comorbidity, especially with the tic disorders; lack of motivation or insight; and the presence of family psychopathology might predict a poor outcome in children undergoing CBT, little or no empirical data have yet emerged by which to predict treatment outcome in children undergoing psychosocial treatment. In contrast, a rather extensive literature on prediction of outcome for drug treatment has failed to identify any predictor variables (March & Leonard, 1996). For example, in a recently published multicenter trial of sertraline and pill placebo in children and adolescents with OCD (March & Mulle, 1998), neither age, race, gender, body weight, baseline OCD score, baseline depression score, comorbidity, socioeconomic status, or plasma sertraline or desmethylsertraline level predicted the outcome of treatment.

In research studies, the answer to the question of which treatment is best for which child focuses on moderation and mediation of treatment response (March & Curry, 1998). In general, moderators are variables that change the size or direction of relationships between independent and dependent variables (Holmbeck, 1997). In clinical trials, moderators comprise those individual, familial, or wider systemic variables existing before treatment assignment that may be associated with differential response to intervention (Kraemer, 2000). Thus, moderator analyses afford an understanding of which types of participants respond optimally to assigned interventions and under what circumstances treatments yield optimal effects. In pediatric studies, six groups of moderator variables corresponding to outcome domains prespecified by the NIMH Consensus panel are typically evaluated: demographics, baseline OCD score, comorbidity, secondary adversities, family status (e.g., single parent), and functioning (e.g., family or academic functioning) (Jensen, Hoagwood, & Petti, 1996). In contrast to moderator variables, which predate randomization, a mediator variable helps explain the relationship between an independent and dependent variable in such a manner that, when the mediator is accounted for, the relationship between the independent and dependent variables is attenuated or eliminated (Holmbeck, 1997). In other words, inclusion of the mediator explains the relationship. For clinical trials, Kraemer, Wilson, Fairburn, and Agras (2002) define a mediator as a variable that follows random assignment and that may help to explain a particular pattern of treatment results. With respect to mediational effects, two mediating variables are often examined: (a) compliance with treatment defined as attendance at a prespecified percentage of the manualized treatment sessions and (b) compliance with treatment defined as compliance with EX/RP homework.

Given that the research literature is as yet undecided on which treatments—CBT, pharmacotherapy with an SSRI, or a combination—are best for which children with OCD, the candidate predictors summarized in Table 6.2, which we will test as potential moderators of treatment outcome in our currently funded NIMH comparative treatment trial of CBT and medication alone and in combination, should be evaluated at least by history when structuring treatment plans for children and adolescents with OCD.

TABLE 6.2
Sets of Predictor Variables

Set	Variables evaluated
Demographics	Age, gender, race, socioeconomic status
Neurocognitive profile	Full-scale, verbal, and performance IQ
Medical history	PANDAS; weight and height; obstetrical history
OCD-specific factors	Symptom profile; initial severity; impact on functioning; insight; treatment history
Treatment expectancy	Treatment expectancy
Comorbidity	Internalizing and externalizing disorders and symptoms; tic disorders
Parental psychopathology	General symptoms, depression, anxiety, OCD
Family functioning	Parental stress, expressed emotion, marital distress

Demographics

Patient age, gender, and socioeconomic status (SES) failed to predict response to treatment in pharmacological cases (see for example, March et al., 1998) or to predict relapse on desipramine for clomipramine substitution (Leonard et al., 1991). However, symptom presentation for OCD varies by age and gender (Last & Strauss, 1989; Swedo, Rapoport, Leonard, Lenane, & Cheslow, 1989), and it is not unreasonable to assume that younger children, for example, might have more difficulty with CBT or that boys, with more ticlike symptoms, might fare more poorly with medication.

Neurocognitive Profile

Several lines of evidence suggest that specific impairments in neurocognitive functioning—especially nonverbal learning disorders (Thompson, 1997)—may be present in children and adults with OCD (reviewed in Hooper & March, 1995; see also Cox, Fedio, & Rapoport, 1989; Denckla, 1989). Some authors posit a negative relationship between cognitive deficits and treatment outcome in adults (Hollander, Neville, DeCaria, & Mullen, 1990) and children (March et al., 1990); others do not (Leonard et al., 1989; Swedo, Leonard, & Rapoport, 1990). WISC–III full scale IQ (general cognitive capacity), verbal IQ (verbal skills), and performance IQ (visual–spatial skills) scores serve as very rough indicators of neurocognitive processes that might predict treatment outcome.

PANDAS

The term *pediatric autoimmune neuropsychiatric disorder associated with streptococcal infection (PANDAS)* has been used to identify a subset of children with infection-related obsessive–compulsive or tic disorders that meet the following five criteria: (a) presence of OCD or a tic disorder, or both; (b) prepubertal symptom onset; (c) episodic course of symptom severity; (d) association with group A β-hemolytic streptococcal (GABHS) infection; and (e) association with neurological abnormalities (Swedo et al., 1998). A mechanism similar to Sydenham's chorea has been proposed for PANDAS, where, in susceptible individuals, GABHS infection triggers an antineuronal autoimmune response that negatively affects striatal circuitry responsible for mediating OCD and tic symptoms (Swedo, 1994). Thus, PANDAS by definition assumes that symptom onset or exacerbation is etiopathogenically associated with GABHS (Trifiletti & Packard, 1999). Because an accurate diagnosis of PANDAS implies the need for acute and possibly prophylactic antibiotic treatment or even riskier immunomodulatory treatments, such as plasmapheresis, either alone or in addition to conventional treatments for OCD, it is critical to accurately establish the presence of PANDAS to prevent inappropriate application of immunomodulatory therapies (Singer, 1999; see also National Institute of Mental Health, 2004).

Obsessive–Compulsive Disorder—Specific Factors

Neither initial severity, duration of symptoms, or symptom pattern predicted response to treatment in the NIMH (Leonard & Rapoport, 1989) or industry studies of medication management for pediatric OCD (March, Leonard, & Swedo, 1995b). However, children who acknowledge that their obsessions are senseless and their rituals distressing may be better candidates for CBT than those who do not, although lack of insight does not necessarily render CBT ineffective (Kettl & Marks, 1986).

Treatment Expectancy

While there is no literature on this topic in youth with OCD, clinical experience clearly suggests that some patients find CBT and medication with sertraline (MED) different in acceptability and expectation regarding the potential for a beneficial outcome. Willingness to engage in treatment and premature discontinuation of treatment may be related not only to efficacy and side effects but to expectancy effects. Thus, assessment of treatment expectancy by patients, parent(s), and treatment providers is important because this information may well inform readiness-for-change interventions applied to CBT or medication management (or both).

Comorbidity

Because the diagnosis of OCD is for the most part nonexclusionary, more than one disorder may be diagnosed in a single patient. Of 70 children and adolescents in the NIMH sample, which excluded children with mental retardation, eating disorders, and Tourette's Syndrome, only 26% of the study patients had OCD as the sole disorder at baseline (Swedo et al., 1989). Clinically, comorbidity, especially with the oppositional and tic disorders, appears to predict nonresponse or partial response to both pharmacotherapy and CBT, but the hypothesis remains untested in pediatric patients, and these comorbid conditions do not present a contraindication to CBT or to pharmacotherapy. Hence, it is important to examine categorical and scalar indices of internalizing and externalizing psychopathology, including specific assessment of tic symptoms, when structuring a treatment plan for youth with OCD.

Parental Psychopathology

Despite the fact that OCD appears familial in many cases (Lenane et al., 1990) and likely shares a genetic diathesis with Tourette's syndrome in some cases (Pauls, Towbin, Leckman, Zahner, & Cohen, 1986; Riddle et al., 1990), parental psychopathology remains unexplored as a predictor of outcome. However, in clinical contexts, referral of a mentally ill parent for treatment when desired and indicated often helps to move treatment forward.

Family Dysfunction

Although family dysfunction doesn't cause onset of OCD, it certainly complicates its treatment (Hibbs et al., 1991). Thus, the extent to which family dysfunction, if present, is predicated on or independent of OCD must be established as part of the routine clinical evaluation of the patient with OCD.

FUTURE DIRECTIONS

Overview

Current research efforts are now (or shortly will be) focused on eight areas: (a) controlled trials comparing medications, behavior therapy, and combination treatment to controls to determine whether medications and behavior therapy are synergistic or additive in their effects on symptom reduction; (b) follow-up studies to evaluate relapse rates, including examination of the utility of booster CBT in reducing relapse rates in patients treated with medications, alone or in combination with CBT; (c) component analyses, such as a comparison of EX/RP, cognitive therapy, and their combination, to evaluate the relative contributions of specific treatment components to symptom reduction and treatment acceptability; (d) comparisons of individual- and family-based treatments to determine which is more effective in which children; (e) development of innovative treatment for OCD subtypes, such as obsessional slowness, primary obsessional OCD, and ticlike OCD, that do not respond well to EX/RP; (f) treatment innovations targeted to factors, such as family dysfunction, that constrain the application of CBT to patients with OCD; (g) research treatments exported to divergent clinical settings and patient populations in order to judge the acceptability and effectiveness of CBT as a treatment for child and adolescent OCD in real-world settings; and (h) once past initial treatment, the management of partial response, treatment resistance, and treatment maintenance and discontinuation.

Comparative Treatment Trial

Despite the by-now-routine recommendation of CBT alone or the combination of CBT and an SSRI as the treatment of choice for OCD in the pediatric population (March et al., 1997), the relative efficacy of CBT and medication, alone and in combination, remains uncertain. Thus, as Kendall and Lipman (1991) have clearly stated, well-designed comparative treatment outcome studies are necessary in both adults and children. We will shortly complete an NIMH-funded comparative treatment outcome study of initial treatments in OCD. Using a volunteer sample of 120 (60 per site) youth ages 8 to 16 with a *Diagnostic and Statistical Manual of Mental Disorders, Fourth Edition (DSM–IV)* diagnosis of OCD, this 5-year treatment outcome study contrasts the degree and durability of improvement obtained across four treatment conditions: MED, OCD-specific cognitive behavior therapy, both MED and CBT (COMB), and two control conditions, pill placebo (PBO) and educational support (ES). The experimental design covers two phases. Phase I compares the outcome of MED, CBT, COMB, and control conditions. In Phase II, responders advance to a 16-week discontinuation study to assess treatment durability. The primary outcome measure is the Y-BOCS. Assessments blind to treatment status take place at week 0 (pretreatment); weeks 1, 4, 8, and 12 (Phase I treatment); and weeks 16, 20, 24, and 28 (Phase II discontinuation). Besides addressing comparative efficacy and durability of the specified treatments, this study also examines time-action effects; differential effects of treatment on specific aspects of OCD, including functional impairment; and predictors of response to treatment. Once completed, this study will be followed by an augmentation trial of CBT versus an atypical neuroleptic in SSRI partial responders.

SUMMARY

Despite limitations in the research literature, CBT, alone or in combination with pharmacotherapy, is the psychotherapeutic treatment of choice for children and adolescents with OCD. Ideally, young persons with OCD should first receive CBT that has been optimized for treating childhood-onset OCD; if they are not rapidly responsive, either intensive CBT or concurrent pharmacotherapy with a SSRI may be effective (Franklin et al., 1998; March et al., 1997). Moreover, because CBT, including booster treatments during medication discontinuation, may improve both short- and long-term outcome in drug-treated patients, all patients who receive medication also should receive concomitant CBT. In this regard, arguments advanced against CBT for OCD, such as symptom substitution, danger of interrupting rituals, uniformity of learned symptoms, and incompatibility with pharmacotherapy, have all proved unfounded. Perhaps the most insidious myth is that CBT is a simplistic treatment that ignores real problems. We believe that the opposite is true. Helping patients make rapid and difficult behavior change over short time intervals takes both clinical savvy and focused treatment. Currently, state-of-the-art treatments for pediatric OCD are best delivered by a multidisciplinary team, usually but not always located in a subspecialty clinic setting (March, Mulle, Stallings, Erhardt, & Conners, 1995). Translation of specialty practice to community settings is essential if demonstrably effective treatments, such as CBT for OCD, are to be made available to the children and adolescents suffering from this disorder (Kendall & Southam-Gerow, 1995).

REFERENCES

Adams, G. B., Waas, G. A., March, J. S., & Smith, M. C. (1994). Obsessive–compulsive disorder in children and adolescents: the role of the school psychologist in identification, assessment, and treatment. *School Psychology Quarterly, 94*, 274–294.

Amir, N., Freshman, M., & Foa, E. B. (2000). Family distress and involvement in relatives of obsessive–compulsive disorder patients. *Journal of Anxiety Disorders, 14*, 209–217.

Baer, L., Jenike, M. A., Black, D. W., Treece, C., Rosenfeld, R., & Greist, J. (1992). Effect of axis II diagnoses on treatment outcome with clomipramine in 55 patients with obsessive–compulsive disorder. *Archives of General Psychiatry, 49*, 862–866.

Clarke, G. N. (1995). Improving the transition from basic efficacy research to effectiveness studies: Methodological issues and procedures. *Journal of Consulting and Clinical Psychology, 63*, 718–725.

Cox, C., Fedio, P., & Rapoport, J. (1989). Neuropsychological testing of obsessive–compulsive adolescents. In J. Rapoport (Ed.), *Obsessive–compulsive disorder in children and adolescents* (pp. 73–86). Washington, DC: American Psychiatric Press.

de Haan, E., Hoogduin, K. A., Buitelaar, J. K., & Keijsers, G. P. (1998). Behavior therapy versus clomipramine for the treatment of obsessive–compulsive disorder in children and adolescents. *Journal of the American Academy of Child and Adolescent Psychiatry, 37*, 1022–1029.

Denckla, M. (1989). Neurological examination. In J. Rapoport (Ed.), *Obsessive–compulsive disorder in children and adolescents* (pp. 107–118). Washington, DC: American Psychiatric Press.

Esman, A. (1989). Psychoanalysis in general psychiatry: Obsessive–compulsive disorder as a paradigm. *Journal of the American Psychoanalytical Association, 37*, 319–336.

Flament, M. F., Koby, E., Rapoport, J. L., Berg, C. J., Zahn, T., Cox, C., et al. (1990). Childhood obsessive–compulsive disorder: A prospective follow-up study. *Journal of Child Psychology and Psychiatry and Allied Disciplines, 31*, 363–380.

Flament, M. F., Whitaker, A., Rapoport, J. L., Davies, M., Berg, C. Z., Kalikow, K., et al. (1988). Obsessive compulsive disorder in adolescence: An epidemiological study. *Journal of the American Academy of Child and Adolescent Psychiatry, 27*, 764–771.

Foa, E., & Emmelkamp, P. (1983). *Failures in behavior therapy.* New York: Wiley and Sons.

Foa, E., & Kozak, M. (1985). Emotional processing of fear: Exposure to corrective information. *Psychological Bulletin, 90*, 20–35.

Foa, E., & Kozak, M. (in press). Obsessive–compulsive disorder: Long-term outcome of psychological treatment. In M. Mavissakalian & R. Prien (Eds.),

Long-term treatments of anxiety disorders: Psychological and pharmacological approaches. Washington, DC: American Psychiatric Press.

Foa, E. B., & Kozak, M. J. (1991). Emotional processing: Theory, research, and clinical implications for anxiety disorders. In J. Safran & L. Greenberg (Eds.), *Emotion, psychotherapy and change* (Vol. 372, pp. 21–49). New York: Guilford Press.

Foa, E. B., Steketee, G., Grayson, B., Turner, M., & Latimer, P. (1984). Deliberate exposure and blocking of obsessive–compulsive rituals: Immediate and long-term effects. *Behavior Therapy, 15,* 450–472.

Foa, E. B., Steketee, G., & Milby, J. B. (1980). Differential effects of exposure and response prevention in obsessive–compulsive washers. *Journal of Consulting and Clinical Psychology, 48,* 71–79.

Franklin, M. E., Kozak, M. J., Cashman, L. A., Coles, M. E., Rheingold, A. A., & Foa, E. B. (1998). Cognitive–behavioral treatment of pediatric obsessive–compulsive disorder: An open clinical trial. *Journal of the Academy of Child and Adolescent Psychiatry, 37,* 412–419.

Goodman, W., Rasmussen, S., Foa, E., & Price, L. (1994). Obsessive–compulsive disorder. In R. Prien & D. Robinson (Eds.), *Clinical evaluation of psychotropic drugs: Principles and guidelines* (pp. 431–466). New York: Raven Press.

Goodman, W. K., & Price, L. H. (1992). Assessment of severity and change in obsessive compulsive disorder. *Psychiatric Clinics of North America, 15,* 861–869.

Guy, W. (1976). *ECDEU assessment manual for psychopharmacology* (2nd ed., Vol. DHEW Publication No. [ABM] 76-388). Washington, DC: U.S. Government Printing Office.

Harris, C. V., & Wiebe, D. J. (1992). An analysis of response prevention and flooding procedures in the treatment of adolescent obsessive compulsive disorder. *Journal of Behavior Therapy and Experimental Psychiatry, 23,* 107–115.

Hembree, E. A., Riggs, D. S., Kozak, M. J., Franklin, M. E., & Foa, E. B. (2003). Long-term efficacy of exposure and ritual prevention therapy and serotonergic medications for obsessive–compulsive disorder. *CNS Spectrum, 8,* 363–371, 381.

Hibbs, E. D., Hamburger, S. D., Lenane, M., Rapoport, J. L., Kruesi, M. J., Keysor, C. S., et al. (1991). Determinants of expressed emotion in families of disturbed and normal children. *Journal of Child Psychology and Psychiatry and Allied Disciplines, 32,* 757–770.

Hollander, E., Neville, D., DeCaria, C. M., & Mullen, L. (1990). Neurological and structural involvement in OCD. *Neuropsychiatry, Neuropsychology, and Behavioral Neurology, 3,* 314–315.

Hollingsworth, C., Tanguay, P., & Grossman, L. (1980). Long-term outcome of obsessive compulsive disorder in childhood. *Journal of the American Academy of Child Psychiatry, 19,* 134–144.

Holmbeck, G. N. (1997). Toward terminological, conceptual, and statistical clarity in the study of mediators and moderators: Examples from the child–clinical and pediatric psychology literatures. *Journal of Consulting and Clinical Psychology, 65,* 599–610.

Hooper, S. R., & March, J. S. (1995). Neuropsychology. In J. March (Ed.), *Anxiety disorders in children and adolescents* (pp. 35–60). New York: Guilford Press.

Jensen, P. S., Hoagwood, K., & Petti, T. (1996). Outcomes of mental health care for children and adolescents: II. Literature review and application of a comprehensive model. *Journal of the American Academy of Child and Adolescent Psychiatry, 35,* 1064–1077.

Kendall, P. C., Howard, B. L., & Epps, J. (1988). The anxious child. Cognitive–behavioral treatment strategies. *Behavior Modification, 12,* 281–310.

Kendall, P. C., & Lipman, A. J. (1991). Psychological and pharmacological therapy: Methods and modes for comparative outcome research. *Journal of Consulting and Clinical Psychology, 59,* 78–87.

Kendall, P. C., & Southam-Gerow, M. A. (1995). Issues in the transportability of treatment: The case of anxiety disorders in youths. *Journal of Consulting and Clinical Psychology, 63,* 702–708.

Kettl, P., & Marks, I. (1986). Neurological factors in obsessive–compulsive disorder. *British Journal of Psychiatry, 149,* 315–319.

King, R. A., Leonard, H., & March, J. (1998). Practice parameters for the assessment and treatment of children and adolescents with obsessive–compulsive disorder. *Journal of the American Academy of Child and Adolescent Psychiatry, 37* (Suppl. 10).

Kraemer, H. C. (2000). Pitfalls of multisite randomized clinical trials of efficacy and effectiveness. *Schizophrenia Bulletin, 26,* 533–541.

Kraemer, H. C., Wilson, G. T., Fairburn, C. G., Agras, W. S. (2002). Mediators and moderators of treatment effects in randomized clinical trials. *Archives of General Psychiatry, 59,* 877–883.

Last, C. G., & Strauss, C. C. (1989). Obsessive–compulsive disorder in childhood. *Journal of Anxiety Disorders, 3,* 295–302.

Lenane, M. (1989). Families in obsessive–compulsive disorder. In J. Rapoport (Ed.), *Obsessive–compulsive disorder in children and adolescents* (pp. 237–249). Washington, DC: American Psychiatric Press.

Lenane, M. C., Swedo, S. E., Leonard, H., Pauls, D. L., Sceery, W., & Rapoport, J. L. (1990). Psychiatric disorders in first-degree relatives of children and adolescents with obsessive compulsive disorder. *Journal of the American Academy of Child and Adolescent Psychiatry, 29,* 407–412.

Leonard, H. L., & Rapoport, J. L. (1989). Pharmacotherapy of childhood obsessive–compulsive disorder. *Psychiatric Clinics of North America, 12,* 963–970.

Leonard, H. L., Swedo, S. E., Lenane, M. C., Rettew, D. C., Cheslow, D. L., Hamburger, S. D., et al. (1991). A double-blind desipramine substitution during long-term clomipramine treatment in children and adolescents with obsessive–compulsive disorder. *Archives of General Psychiatry, 48,* 922–927.

Leonard, H. L., Swedo, S. E., Lenane, M. C., Rettew, D. C., Hamburger, S. D., Bartko, J. J., et al. (1993). A 2- to 7-year follow-up study of 54 obsessive–compulsive children and adolescents. *Archives of General Psychiatry, 50,* 429–439.

Leonard, H. L., Swedo, S. E., Rapoport, J. L., Koby, E. V., Lenane, M. C., Cheslow, D. L., et al. (1989). Treatment of obsessive–compulsive disorder with clomipramine and desipramine in children and adolescents. A double-blind crossover comparison. *Archives of General Psychiatry, 46*, 1088–1092.

March, J. (1998). Cognitive behavioral psychotherapy for pediatric OCD. In M. Jenike, L. Baer, & W. E. Minichiello (Eds.), *Obsessive–compulsive disorders* (3rd ed., pp. 400–420). Philadelphia: Mosby.

March, J. (2000). Child psychiatry: Cognitive and behavior therapies. In B. Saddock & V. Saddock (Eds.), *Comprehensive textbook of psychiatry* (Vol. 7, pp. 2806–2812). New York: Williams & Wilkins.

March, J., & Curry, J. (1998). The prediction of treatment outcome. *Journal of Abnormal Child Psychology, 26,* 39–52.

March, J., Frances, A., Kahn, D., & Carpenter, D. (1997). Expert consensus guidelines: Treatment of obsessive–compulsive disorder. *Journal of Clinical Psychiatry, 58*(Suppl. 4), 1–72.

March, J., Johnston, H., Jefferson, J., Greist, J., Kobak, K., & Mazza, J. (1990). Do subtle neurological impairments predict treatment resistance in children and adolescents with obsessive–compulsive disorder. *Journal of Child and Adolescent Psychopharmacology, 1,* 133–140.

March, J., & Leonard, H. (1996). Obsessive–compulsive disorder in children and adolescents: A review of the past 10 years. *Journal of the American Academy of Child and Adolescent Psychiatry, 35,* 1265–1273.

March, J., & Leonard, H. (1998). Obsessive–compulsive disorder in children and adolescents. In R. Swinson, M. Antony, J. Rachman, & M. Richter (Eds.), *Obsessive compulsive disorder: Theory, research and treatment* (pp. 367–397). New York: Guilford Press.

March, J., & Mulle, K. (1995). Manualized cognitive–behavioral psychotherapy for obsessive–compulsive disorder in childhood: A preliminary single case study. *Journal of Anxiety Disorders, 9,* 175–184.

March, J., & Mulle, K. (1996). Banishing obsessive–compulsive disorder. In E. Hibbs & P. Jensen (Eds.), *Psychosocial treatments for child and adolescent disorders* (pp. 82–103). Washington, DC: American Psychological Association.

March, J., & Mulle, K. (1998). *OCD in children and adolescents: A cognitive–behavioral treatment manual.* New York: Guilford Press.

March, J., Mulle, K., Stallings, P., Erhardt, D., & Conners, C. (1995). Organizing an anxiety disorders clinic. In J. March (Ed.), *Anxiety disorders in children and adolesents* (pp. 420–435). New York: Guilford Press.

March, J. S., Biederman, J., Wolkow, R., Safferman, A., Mardekian, J., Cook, E. H., et al. (1998). Sertraline in children and adolescents with obsessive–compulsive disorder: A multicenter randomized controlled trial [see comments]. *Journal of the American Medical Association, 280,* 1752–1756.

March, J. S., Leonard, H. L., & Swedo, S. E. (1995a). Obsessive–compulsive disorder. In J. March (Ed.), *Anxiety disorders in children and adolescents* (pp. 251–275). New York: Guilford Press.

March, J. S., Leonard, H. L., & Swedo, S. E. (1995b). Pharmacotherapy of obsessive–compulsive disorder. *Child and Adolescent Psychiatric Clinics of North America, 4,* 217–236.

March, J. S., & Mulle, K. (1998). *OCD in children and adolescents: A cognitive–behavioral treatment manual.* New York: Guilford Press.

March, J. S., Mulle, K., & Herbel, B. (1994). Behavioral psychotherapy for children and adolescents with obsessive–compulsive disorder: An open trial of a new protocol-driven treatment package. *Journal of the American Academy of Child and Adolescent Psychiatry, 33,* 333–341.

Marks, I. (1987). *Fears, phobias, and rituals.* New York: Oxford Unversity Press.

McDougle, C. J., Goodman, W. K., Leckman, J. F., Barr, L. C., Heninger, G. R., & Price, L. H. (1993). The efficacy of fluvoxamine in obsessive–compulsive disorder: Effects of comorbid chronic tic disorder. *Journal of Clinical Psychopharmacology, 13,* 354–358.

Murphy, D., Pickar, D., & Alterman, I. (1982). Methods for the quantitative assessment of depressive and manic behavior. In E. Burdock, A. Sudilovsky, & S. Gershon (Eds.), *The behavior of psychiatric subjects* (pp. 355–391). New York: Marcel Dekker.

National Institute of Mental Health. (2004). *Official P.A.N.D.A.S. web page.* Retrieved August, 6, 2004, from http://intramural.nimh.nih.gov/research/pdn/web.htm

Pauls, D., Towbin, K., Leckman, J., Zahner, G., & Cohen, D. (1986). Gilles de la Tourette syndrome and obsessive–compulsive disorder: Evidence supporting a genetic relationship. *Archives of General Psychiatry, 43,* 1180–1182.

Rasmussen, S. A., & Eisen, J. L. (1990). Epidemiology of obsessive–compulsive disorder. *Journal of Clinical Psychiatry, 53*(Suppl.), 10–13; discussion 14.

Ratnasuriya, R. H., Marks, I. M., Forshaw, D. M., & Hymas, N. F. (1991). Obsessive slowness revisited [see comments]. *British Journal of Psychiatry, 159,* 273–274.

Riddle, M. A., Scahill, L., King, R., Hardin, M. T., Towbin, K. E., Ort, S. I., et al. (1990). Obsessive–compulsive disorder in children and adolescents: Phenomenology and family history. *Journal of the American Academy of Child and Adolescent Psychiatry, 29,* 766–772.

Salkovskis, P. M., Westbrook, D., Davis, J., Jeavons, A., & Gledhill, A. (1997). Effects of neutralizing on intrusive thoughts: An experiment investigating the etiology of obsessive–compulsive disorder. *Behavior Research and Therapy, 35,* 211–219.

Scahill, L., Riddle, M., McSwiggin-Hardin, M., Ort, S., King, R., Goodman, W., et al. (1997). Children's Yale-Brown Obsessive–Compulsive Scale: Reliability and validity. *Journal of the American Academy of Child and Adolescent Psychiatry, 36,* 844–852.

Schwartz, J. (1996). *Brain lock.* New York: HarperCollins.

Steketee, G. (1994). Behavioral assessment and treatment planning with obsessive–compulsive disorder: A review emphasizing clinical application. *Behavior Therapy, 25,* 613–633.

Swedo, S., Leonard, H., & Rapoport, J. (1990). Childhood-onset obsessive–compulsive disorder. In M. Jenike, L. Baer, & W. E. Minichello (Eds.), *Obsessive–compulsive disorder*. Littleton, MA: PSG.

Swedo, S. E. (1994). Sydenham's chorea. A model for childhood autoimmune neuropsychiatric disorders [clinical conference] [see comments]. *Journal of the American Medical Association, 272,* 1788–1791.

Swedo, S. E., Leonard, H. L., Garvey, M., Mittleman, B., Allen, A. J., Perlmutter, S., et al. (1998). Pediatric autoimmune neuropsychiatric disorders associated with streptococcal infections: Clinical description of the first 50 cases. *American Journal of Psychiatry, 155,* 264–271.

Swedo, S. E., Rapoport, J. L., Leonard, H., Lenane, M., & Cheslow, D. (1989). Obsessive–compulsive disorder in children and adolescents. Clinical phenomenology of 70 consecutive cases. *Archives of General Psychiatry, 46,* 335–341.

Thompson, S. (1997). *The sourcebook for non-verbal learning disorders*. East Moline, IL: LinguiSystems.

Thyer, B. A. (1991). Diagnosis and treatment of child and adolescent anxiety disorders. *Behavior Modification, 15,* 310–325.

Trifiletti, R. R., & Packard, A. M. (1999). Immune mechanisms in pediatric neuropsychiatric disorders. Tourette's syndrome, OCD, and PANDAS. *Child and Adolescent Clinics of North America, 8,* 767–775.

van Oppen, P., & Arntz, A. (1994). Cognitive therapy for obsessive–compulsive disorder. *Behavior Research and Therapy, 32,* 79–87.

van Oppen, P., de Haan, E., van Balkom, A. J., Spinhoven, P., Hoogduin, K., & van Dyck, R. (1995). Cognitive therapy and exposure in vivo in the treatment of obsessive–compulsive disorder. *Behavior Research and Therapy, 33,* 379–390.

Wever, C. (1994). Combined medication and behavioral treatment of OCD in adolescents. *Proceedings of the Second Annual Australian Conference on OCD, Sydney, Australia.*

Wever C., & Rey, J. M. (1997). Juvenile obsessive–compulsive disorder. *Australia and New Zealand Journal of Psychiatry, 31,* 105–113.

Wolff, R., & Rapoport, J. (1988). Behavioral treatment of childhood obsessive–compulsive disorder. *Behavior Modification, 12,* 252–266.

III

AFFECTIVE AND RELATED DISORDERS

INTRODUCTION: AFFECTIVE
AND RELATED DISORDERS

Depression in youth is a severely disabling illness. Because of chronicity and associated impairments, it may result in life long struggles; in some cases, it may even be lethal. It is estimated that 0.4% to 5.9% of children suffer from some form of depression. Rates may increase two- or threefold during adolescence to approximate those of adults, with estimates suggesting 1-year prevalence rates as high as 13%. Depression in children and adolescents can be a somewhat elusive condition, however. Children and some adolescents may not verbalize their distress and may express it only through somatic symptoms, such as irritability and withdrawal. As a consequence, the child or adolescent with depressive symptoms may be dismissed simply as being quiet or irritable. Many children and youth with depression will not necessarily be troublesome to parents and teachers, and because adults may not recognize any overt symptoms, such a child or adolescent can easily fall through the cracks. In fact, the best informants in reporting depressive symptoms are usually the children and adolescents themselves.

Depression in children and adolescents is commonly comorbid with other childhood disorders and, as such, is a destructive disorder, by virtue of both its own symptoms and its associated conditions. Fortunately, the last few years have seen an increasing effort to emphasize research on childhood and adolescent depression. In this section we present seven studies using various modes of treatment for childhood and adolescent depression, including cognitive–behavior therapy (CBT), systemic behavior family therapy, interpersonal psychotherapy for adolescents (IPT-A), as well as psychodynamic treatments. Also in this section we have included the treatment of a different but related disorder, infantile anorexia nervosa.

Erin B. McClure and her colleagues outline a review of empirically supported interventions for depressed children and adolescents and then present their work focused on the treatment of depressed African American adolescent girls with a history of physical abuse. The goals of their adolescent depression empowerment psychosocial treatment (ADEPT) are to develop, implement, and evaluate a manualized family intervention program for low-income girls. ADEPT is a culturally competent model of a psychoeducationally oriented family empowerment intervention. It includes components of CBT, ITP-A, and culturally competent family systems interventions. The authors also discuss the procedures of their treatment. Although this is an ongoing study, the preliminary results appear promising for the treatment of depressed minority adolescents. In highlighting future directions, the authors suggest studies with larger samples, including control groups, in order to allow the examination of the relative impact of the treatment.

Laura Mufson and her colleagues present a brief review of current research findings on the nature and treatment of adolescent depression, an overview of the theory and principles of IPT-A, the results of the completed efficacy trial of ITP-A, and a discussion of the ongoing effectiveness trial being conducted in school-based health clinics. The treatment goals, phases of treatment, problem areas, and limitations are discussed in this chapter. Their final results indicate that patients reported a significant decrease in depressive symptoms and improvement in functioning. The authors highlight the need for further studies comparing IPT-A with medication, study of relapse prevention, and replication of the IPT-A treatment to ensure reliability of the findings.

Jeannette Rosselló and Guillermo Bernal present a comparative study of CBT and IPT, adapted for the treatment of depressed Puerto Rican adolescents. They discuss the adaptation of CBT and IPT-A for depression to ensure ecological validity and cultural sensitivity, and they describe the cultural developmental and practical and technical issues that guided them in the adaptation of the treatments. Results indicate that both CBT and IPT-A are efficacious treatments for depressed Puerto Rican adolescents. In outlining future directions, the authors recommend that more studies be done to determine IPT-A and CBT interventions' sustainability in real-world settings (e.g., clinics and hospitals) and with other Latino populations and in light of process variables.

Paul Rohde and his colleagues have a long history of studying CBT in adolescents with depression. They have developed a group-administered Adolescents Coping With Depression (CWD-A) course, based on a cognitive model of depression, and they provide good evidence of the effectiveness of the treatment. In this chapter they present a brief overview of psychosocial treatments for adolescent depression and the rationale of their treatment approach and summarize the results of two clinical trials after a 24-month follow-up. The results indicate that CWD-A is a beneficial treatment for adolescent depression and that the treatment gains were maintained at follow-up. In highlighting future directions, the authors propose that their treatment needs be evaluated and modified to use with racial and cultural minorities and incorporate booster sessions.

Kevin D. Stark and his colleagues present their work—a large-scale school based intervention—using group-format CBT in depressed children. They also present a brief review of the research done on disturbances of emotion regulation, cognition, and interpersonal and family functioning. Assessment measures and treatment procedures are discussed. This is an ongoing study, but previous research with earlier CBT versions has demonstrated the efficacy of the intervention, with gains sustained at follow-up. In highlighting future directions, the authors call for additional studies to determine the interventions' feasibility in real-world settings and in the hands of other investigators.

John Tsiantis and colleagues present a European multisite study of the treatment of childhood depression conducted by the University of Athens, Greece; the Tavistock Clinic, London, England; and the University of Helsinki, Finland. Their work is based on psychodynamic theory, which incorporates psychoanalytic concepts and techniques in the treatment of depressed children. The study compares brief individual psychodynamic psychotherapy (BIPP) with systems integrative family therapy (SIFT). The authors delineate the assessment instruments and treatment procedures and offer clinical vignettes to provide preliminary evidence that BIPP and SIFT are promising treatments for peripubertal children with major depression. Because this is an ongoing study, results are not available at this time. The authors hope that this study will prepare the way for more treatment studies on childhood depression based on psychodynamic theory.

Irene Chatoor is well known for her efforts in classifying and treating infants and toddlers with feeding disorders. In this chapter she presents in detail the diagnostic criteria for the disorder, offers a brief review of the research done on the topic, and describes the assessment measures and the treatment procedures of her study on infantile anorexia. The treatment is based on a transactional model, with the goal to facilitate infants' internal regulation of eating by helping parents disengage from conflict and by changing their interactions with the infant. The results indicate that the treatment is beneficial for infants and toddlers with anorexia nervosa. In discussing future considerations, the author mentions that although the treatment is short-term and easy for practitioners to apply, the challenge remains: how to help parents who are unable to break the cycle of maladaptive interactions with their anorexic children.

The authors in this section use a variety of treatment modalities and combination techniques for the treatment of depression in children and adolescents. They unanimously note the need for more research pertaining to the treatment of depression and its comorbid conditions, the need to evaluate studies and their use for racial and cultural minorities, the need to compare psychosocial treatments to medication, and the importance of studies on relapse prevention. They note the need for the replication of the treatments to ensure generalizability of findings and transferability to real-world settings. In addition, the authors note the need for more refined tools to detect and differentiate aspects of and risks for the disorder, because it is often difficult to diagnose depression in young children, and differentiate adolescent moodiness from full-blown disorder. We note that future research must examine differences in treatment effectiveness as a function of the severity of the condition, as well as the setting in which it is identified and treated (e.g., school versus clinic versus inpatient setting). Although parents were involved to a varying extent in the treatment protocols of the studies presented in this section, future research must include more systematically parents as clients because affective disorders seem to be familial. Although minority and female subjects were included in all studies, no separate sex or cultural differences were reported here.

7

THE ADOLESCENT DEPRESSION EMPOWERMENT PROJECT (ADEPT): A CULTURALLY SENSITIVE FAMILY TREATMENT FOR DEPRESSED AFRICAN AMERICAN GIRLS

ERIN B. MCCLURE, ARIN M. CONNELL, MARLA ZUCKER,
JEANA R. GRIFFITH, AND NADINE J. KASLOW

This chapter outlines an ongoing clinical-research program focused on treatment of depressed African American adolescent girls, in particular those with a history of physical and sexual abuse. This program has emerged in response to the dearth of information regarding culturally competent and developmentally informed psychosocial treatments for depressed minority youth. In addition, the focus on physically and sexually abused depressed youth reflects the need to attend to this high-risk group of young people and their families.

Research suggests that until recently many depressed youth did not receive treatment (Keller, Lavori, Beardslee, Wunder, & Ryan, 1991). As consensus has emerged regarding the existence, diagnosis, and public health significance of depression in children and adolescents, researchers and clinicians have developed and implemented a variety of psychosocial interventions, and treatment rates have improved (Hamilton & Bridge, 1999). How effective current standard practice is at alleviating depression or preventing its recurrence remains unclear; psychosocial interventions have only recently undergone empirical evaluation, and rigorously designed treatment studies are scarce.

Results from the small existing pool of treatment studies indicate that a variety of therapies, including cognitive–behavioral therapy (CBT; e.g., Stark, Reynolds, & Kaslow, 1987; Stark, Rouse, & Livingston, 1991), interpersonal therapy (e.g., IPT-A; Mufson, Weissman, Moreau, & Garfinkel, 1999; Rosselló & Bernal, 1999), and systemic behavioral family therapy (SBFT; Brent et al., 1997), show promise for helping depressed adolescents. Shortcomings of the existing literature regarding these treatments, however, limit the extent to which they can be generalized and applied. Among these shortcomings are the lack of a developmental framework informing treatment formulation, the relatively restricted range of treatment approaches examined (especially for children), the scarcity of data regarding the relative efficacy of various treatments, the near absence of long-term follow-up data, and the unknown impact of comorbid diagnoses on treatment outcome (for review, see Kaslow, McClure, & Connell, 2002). One problem is more pertinent to the present chapter, however; the influences of sex and ethnicity on treatment outcome have not been adequately examined. No treatment protocols have been designed with gender in mind, and little research has examined how well interventions apply across cultural boundaries. Although preliminary findings indicate that CBT and IPT-A effects may generalize to varied cultural groups (Rosselló & Bernal, 1999), more study is needed in traditionally underserved populations, such as African American, Asian American, Latino, and Native American youth.

For depressed adolescents within these underserved groups, family-oriented approaches may be particularly useful because of the high value placed on family and extended family and the preference for educational and skills-based interventions. Family interventions in general are important because children are embedded within a family context, and a mutual interplay occurs between family interactional processes and a child's depression (Kaslow, Deering, & Racusin, 1994).

ADOLESCENT DEPRESSION EMPOWERMENT PSYCHOSOCIAL TREATMENT PROGRAM

The goals of adolescent depression empowerment psychosocial treatment (ADEPT) are to develop, implement, and evaluate a manualized family intervention for low-income, depressed 12- to 16-year-old African American girls who have been physically or sexually abused. Funded by the Turner Foundation, which has demonstrated a commitment to underserved populations through its support of programs for minority girls and women, ADEPT is conducted at Grady Health System (GHS), an Emory University School of Medicine–affiliated public hospital that serves a primarily low-income, minority, urban population. The project team also collaborates with various community organizations. ADEPT consists of multiple steps, beginning with referral, eligibility screening, and pretreatment assessment for adolescents who meet study criteria. Eligible adolescents and their families are then assigned to a culturally competent, developmentally informed, psychoeducationally oriented family empowerment intervention. Family therapy was chosen because depression runs in families, because many depressed youth are embedded in family environments characterized by problems in interactions that may serve to maintain the child's depression, and because family interventions have been found effective for other childhood disorders (e.g., Kaslow et al., 1994). This integrative family intervention program includes elements of CBT, IPT-A, and culturally competent family systems interventions. After completing their assigned treatment, adolescents and their families return for three follow-up assessments (after treatment and during 3-month and 6-month follow-up visits).

Method

Procedures

Potential participants are recruited from GHS clinics, churches, community mental health centers, local programs for teens and abused youth, and the juvenile court system. All potential participants first take part in a 2-hour screening assessment to determine eligibility. Youth are enrolled in ADEPT if they (a) meet diagnostic criteria for depression or have elevated levels of depressive symptoms, or both; (b) have a history of sexual or physical abuse before the onset of puberty according to self-, guardian-, or Child Protective Services reports; and (c) score greater than 65 on an intelligence test. Youth are excluded and referred elsewhere if they are receiving special education services for mental retardation, are actively suicidal or psychotic, have a significant legal or substance abuse history, or have an imminently life-threatening medical condition. All family members, including parents or guardians, siblings, grandparents, and other relatives, are encouraged to participate in the ADEPT program by taking part in all family intervention sessions and completing assessments before and after treatment.

Youth who meet study inclusion criteria, along with their participating family members, then complete an additional 1-hour preintervention assessment. After completing treatment, all participants complete a postintervention assessment comparable to that administered at the screening and preassessment (Table 7.1). Participants also complete a treatment satisfaction survey. This postassessment lasts approximately 2 hours. Similar assessments are conducted 3 and 6 months after the completion of the postassessment.

Assessments

Table 7.1 presents the screening, pre-intervention, post-intervention, and follow-up assessment measures for all family members. Self-report, informant report, and semistructured clinical interviews are used to gather background information and assess intelligence, psychiatric disorders and symptoms, trauma, cognitions, family relatedness, parent and peer attachment, and social support. The primary outcome variables are changes in depressive symptoms and disorders. The other measures of psychological and psychosocial functioning listed in Table 7.1 serve as secondary outcome variables.

Treatment Procedures

During the 12-session family intervention, each family is assigned cotherapists (one of whom is African American), who meet with the entire

TABLE 7.1
Screening and Follow-Up Assessment Measures

Construct	Measure	Participant			
		Teen	Adult	Sibling	Other relative
Background information	Demographic data sheet	*x	*x	*x	*x
Intelligence	Kaufman Brief Intelligence Test (Kaufman & Kaufman 1990)	*			
Psychiatric disorders	Children's Interview for Psychiatric Symptoms (ChIPS-C) (Weller, Weller, Fristad, & Rooney, 1999a)	*x			
	Children's Interview for Psychiatric Symptoms—Parent (ChIPS-P) (Weller, Weller, Fristad, & Rooney, 1999b)		*x		
	Symptom Checklist-90-Revised (SCL-90-R) (Derogatis, 1975)		x		*x

TABLE 7.1 (Continued)
Screening and Follow-Up Assessment Measures

Construct	Measure	Participant			
		Teen	Adult	Sibling	Other relative
Depressive symptoms	Children's Depressive Inventory (CDI) (Kovacs, 1992)	*x		*x	*x
Trauma	Adolescent Trauma Screening Questionnaire	*	*		
	Trauma Symptom Checklist (Briere, 1996)	*	*		
Cognitions	Children's Attributional Style Questionnaire (Thompson, Kaslow, Weiss, & Nolen-Hoeksema, 1998)	x			
	Cognitive Triad Inventory –Child (Kaslow, Stark, Printz, Livingston, & Tsai, 1992)	x	x		
Family relatedness	McMaster Family Assessment Device (Epstein, Baldwin, & Bishop, 1983)	x	x	x	x
Parent and peer attachment	Inventory of Parent and Peer Attachment (Armsden & Greenberg, 1987)	x			
Social support	Social Support Appraisal Scale (Dubow & Ullman, 1989)	x			
	Medical Outcomes Survey Measure of Social Support (Sherborne & Stewart, 1991)		x		

Note. * = Screening measure; x = measure given at preintervention, postintervention, and follow-up.

family weekly. Before beginning to work with families, all therapists undergo several hours of training, during which a doctoral-level clinical psychologist reviews the rationale for the family-based treatment, discusses issues related to culturally competent therapy, and provides instruction regarding the treatment manual. Weekly ongoing supervision is also provided.

The family intervention integrates didactic and discussion segments in an effort to provide families with information about and skills for coping with depression and abuse, as well as a time and place to address current concerns and questions. Although one session also provides education about posttraumatic stress disorder (PTSD) and other potential sequelae of abuse, depressive symptoms serve as the primary target of the intervention. Therapists use a variety of tactics, such as games, role-playing exercises, group discussion, and handouts, to facilitate discussion and keep families engaged. Family members earn points toward prizes for attendance, timeliness, and participation. With the exception of Meetings 1 and 12, which serve as orientation and soft termination meetings, respectively, the meetings follow a standard format including week in review, home practice review, mood rating, didactics, break, role-playing activities and games, summary and questions, and home practice assignment. All participants, including the depressed adolescent, attend all 12 sessions (see Exhibit 7.1 for a summary of the sessions).

The first meeting focuses on getting acquainted, introducing the intervention, and formulating family goals. After breaking the ice, the family members and therapists use preassessment results collaboratively to identify treatment goals that build upon family strengths. The therapists then explain the overarching goals of the intervention and explore the family's beliefs and concerns about counseling. The focus then shifts to the topic of

EXHIBIT 7.1
Summary of ADEPT Sessions

Session	Topics covered
1	Getting acquainted, introducing the intervention, formulating family goals
2	Continued bond with the family, adolescent development, African American identity development
3	The symptoms of depression, its causes, and treatment
4	Depression management, the effects of physical activity on mood, relaxation
5	Child abuse and neglect and their prevention
6	Identifying, labeling, and appropriately expressing emotions
7	Associations among thought processes/cognitions, feelings, and behavior
8	Problem-solving (five-step model)
9	Family communication (six steps)
10	Understanding and improving family interactions
11	Social skills
12	Termination

depression, which the therapists introduce from a family perspective. To further promote discussion and education about depression, the family plays a "Wheel of Fortune"-type game that tests their knowledge about depression and teaches them new information. Finally, each family member is asked to write out his or her project goals as a home practice assignment.

The second meeting revolves around furthering the bond with the family, educating them about adolescent development, and discussing African American identity development. The therapists and family discuss each participant's individual goals and review the general intervention goals. Therapists collaborate with the family to establish meeting rules. The didactic portion focuses on adolescent development, with particular attention paid to African American identity development; a role-playing activity facilitates group discussion. Family members also learn to use mood-rating sheets, sheets rating the quality of family and peer relationships, and methods of event recording. These assessments are completed weekly.

During the third meeting, the therapists educate the family about the symptoms of depression, its causes, and its treatment (Mufson, Moreau, Weissman, & Klerman, 1993). Rather than lecture, therapists ask open-ended questions to encourage family members to think about, suggest, and discuss possible manifestations and roots of depression. They play the "Depression Detective Game," in which therapists read brief vignettes aloud and ask family members to identify depressive symptoms in the main characters. This activity not only reinforces participants' learning, but also allows the therapists to identify and address misconceptions about depression. The therapists then provide the family with an introduction to basic mechanisms for coping with depression, including seeking social support, using stress management techniques, and engaging in pleasant activities. Family members identify individuals with whom they can talk when they are under stress and receive information about community support resources. Additionally, they learn about how pleasant activities can improve mood (Clarke et al., 1995; Clarke et al., 1992; Clarke & Lewinsohn, 1986; Clarke, Rhode, Lewinsohn, Hops, & Seeley, 1999). The therapists end the session by asking the family members to engage in a pleasant activity in the coming week; this home practice assignment is repeated at each of the remaining sessions.

The fourth meeting addresses depression management in greater depth. The therapists provide education about the effects of physical activity on mood, teach relaxation exercises (Feindler & Guttman, 1994), and ask the family to rehearse these exercises as home practice. Family members also are encouraged to increase the number of pleasant activities they engage in together and individually. At the end of the session, family members play a short game to identify pleasant activities and increase family cohesion.

At the fifth meeting, the therapists educate the family about different forms of child abuse and neglect, including their manifestations and sequelae.

A substantial portion of the session is devoted to processing the family's feelings about child abuse and neglect. The therapists encourage all members to participate and validate each individual's responses. Further discussion focuses on enhancing the family's ability to cope with the effects of child maltreatment and to prevent future occurrences. For home practice, families are instructed to design a home safety plan to prevent further abuse. We acknowledge that dealing with child maltreatment often requires more ongoing individual, family, and group intervention and make appropriate referrals.

In Meeting 6, family discussions, games, and activities focus on identifying, labeling, and appropriately expressing emotions. Using demonstrations and role-playing exercises, the therapists teach the family active listening skills (Stark, Swearer, Kurowski, Sommer, & Bowen, 1996) to facilitate and reinforce appropriate communication, especially with regard to emotional topics. Family members are asked to practice their active listening skills together for home practice.

The seventh meeting teaches family members about associations among thought processes and cognitions, feelings, and behavior. The therapists provide information on automatic thoughts and the negative cognitive triad and teach the family attributional retraining (Stark, Reynolds, & Kaslow, 1987). Activities include a game in which family members monitor negative statements and practice positive statements. Participants receive a handout on thought processes and a worksheet on which to practice labeling their thoughts and feelings.

In Meeting 8, therapists introduce a five-step problem-solving model (Stark, Raffaelle, & Reysa, 1994) and provide opportunities to practice this approach during the meeting with vignettes and a family tower-building activity. Families learn to identify a problem, generate possible solutions, name probable consequences for each solution, select a solution, and anticipate likely outcomes for the chosen solution. They are then encouraged to apply this five-step model to challenging family issues. For home practice, family members identify a problem and try to solve it using the skills they learned in the meeting.

Meeting 9 focuses on improving family communication. Different games during the session help the family learn ways to express themselves directly and clearly. In the first game, family members give instructions for making a peanut-butter-and-jelly sandwich to one of the therapists. The therapist follows the instructions literally (e.g., if a family member says "put the peanut butter on the bread," the therapist might place the jar of peanut butter on top of the loaf of bread). This exercise illustrates the ease with which miscommunication can occur and helps participants to formulate clear, precise statements. Family members then learn six steps to good communication (Lewinsohn, Clarke, Rhode, Hops, & Seeley, 1996): (a) Maintain good eye contact, (b) monitor speech volume, (c) speak clearly and succinctly, (d) use "I" statements to communicate emotion, (e) talk with others rather than at them, and (f) ask others to paraphrase to be sure that they have understood you. To help participants master these steps, the therapists engage the family in a second communication game. For home practice, family members gather at least once to rehearse both their communication and active listening skills.

The tenth meeting helps the family better understand their interaction patterns and increase positive interactions among family members (Schwartz, Kaslow, Racusin, & Carton, 1998). After practicing the communication skills introduced in Session 9, the family constructs a family sculpture (Duhl, Kantor, & Duhl, 1973; Papp, 1976) to depict family interaction patterns. This activity facilitates discussion of how family members currently view their family and how they would like family members to relate to each other. The therapists teach family members different ways that families interact and encourage family members to discuss ways they can achieve their desired patterns of interaction, reflecting on the roles they play, the strengths they exhibit, and their needs as a family. The family is instructed to participate in a joint activity and to write or draw pictures about their feelings afterwards.

The eleventh meeting revolves around social skills and ways in which family members can improve their peer interactions. Therapists identify the difficulties depressed individuals often experience making friends as normal and explain how being more assertive can improve their relationships. With help from the therapists, the family members discuss differences among passivity, assertiveness, and aggression and practice appropriately assertive behavior through role-playing activities (Stark, Brookman, & Frazier, 1990; Stark et al., 1994). Family members are encouraged to discuss places they can go to make friends, ways to start conversations, and ways to build and maintain friendships (LeCroy, 1994). For home practice, the family is asked to select a situation and generate ideas about ways to handle it assertively.

During the final meeting, the therapists and family review previous meetings, progress that has been made, current functioning, and potential referrals. The therapists and family also discuss stressors that may arise in the future and ways to plan for and cope with these stressors and prevent future depressive episodes. Although earlier sessions deal with termination, this session emphasizes separation and loss and their relation to depression. Family members discuss their feelings regarding the end of the family meetings and provide positive and negative feedback about ADEPT. Therapists also share their feelings and insights that they have gained from the family. Family members receive certificates of completion.

Treatment Measures

Several approaches to documenting the treatment process were used. First, therapists kept detailed progress notes regarding material discussed, status of family members, and any notable events discussed in each session. Second, after each session, therapists completed two brief rating scales: (a) a session evaluation form, on which therapists rate the family's engagement with and understanding of materials covered during the completed session; and (b) a documentation form, on which therapists note which family members attended the session and rate the therapeutic relationship, as well as general family engagement and progress in therapy, on a 7-point scale.

Clinical Vignette

Kamila S. is a 15-year-old African American female who was sexually abused at the age of 14 by an adult male neighbor. Her mother, who read about the treatment project in a newspaper advertisement, brought her in for treatment. Though initially reluctant, Kamila agreed to come to the screening after speaking with the project coordinator. Kamila, her mother (Ms. S.), and her 12-year-old sister (Monica) completed the initial assessment. Her father, with whom Kamila has no contact, did not take part. By her own and Ms. S.'s report, Kamila met diagnostic criteria for major depressive disorder (MDD), PTSD, and oppositional defiant disorder (ODD). All family members reported high levels of conflict and poor communication at home. According to Ms. S., no one had reported the abuse to authorities. After discussing the need to file a report, the therapist contacted Child Protective Services at the conclusion of the assessment with the support of the interviewers and the on-call licensed psychologist.

The family began sessions the following week. They were late to the first session because of public transportation delays. Through discussion with their therapists, family members generated a plan that enabled them to arrive on time for most of the remaining sessions. The prospect of earning rewards provided a powerful incentive for attendance and participation, particularly for the children. In the first session, the family identified several goals, including "spending more time together as a family," "building more communication and trust in the family," and "fighting less." They agreed that it was important to decrease Kamila's depression and her acting-out behavior.

The family was receptive when the therapists reframed Kamila's depression as a problem that they all could solve. Ms. S. and her daughters caught on quickly to several new concepts: use of relaxation techniques to decrease tension and stress, active listening and communication skills for improving family interactions, and problem-solving methods for preventing and resolving conflict. Although they applied these concepts effectively during sessions, they had difficulty translating them to their lives outside of therapy. As they brought in examples of their struggles, however, the therapists were able to help them identify ways to use their new skills in their daily lives. Homework assignments also provided a way for the S. family to practice these skills.

The family members found most appealing sessions that included games or other fun activities illustrating new ideas. They were less engaged when sessions were primarily didactic or when concepts did not seem directly applicable to their current concerns. At these times, the therapists drew on their rapport with the family members and their sense of humor to maintain their interest. During the course of therapy, crises often arose that required deviation from the manual. For example, Monica was suspended from school for fighting, and the family was evicted from their apartment. When such problems occurred, the therapists supported family members in discussing their feelings and assisted them in formulating plans for action. It was usually possible to resume the manualized sequence after one or two crisis sessions. In addition, family members applied strategies from the manual to these crises.

Throughout treatment, the therapists encouraged the family to reflect on termination. Such discussion intensified during the last few weeks of therapy, and family members raised concerns about ending treatment before their problems had been fully resolved. To address these concerns, the therapists reviewed the progress the family had made and reminded them of their newly acquired skills and the ways in which they had successfully applied them. The therapists also worked with the family in the final session to develop a crisis plan to implement if a family member were to become depressed. Finally, because Kamila continued to struggle with mild depressive symptoms, she was referred to a community mental health center for individual counseling.

At the close of treatment, the family members completed evaluations of the project and a postassessment interview. They reported meeting some of their goals: improved communication, reduced conflict, and increased family cohesiveness. They also reported that Kamila's acting-out behavior had decreased. They all indicated satisfaction with the project and the therapists and expressed appreciation for the culturally sensitive context in which concepts were introduced.

At 3- and 6-month follow-up assessments, the S. family reported improvement both individually and as a family. Kamila had continued in individual therapy, where she had received support in applying the skills she learned during the program; her depression remitted 6 months after treatment.

Outcomes

Of the 60 families that were contacted or referred to ADEPT, eight have enrolled in the program. Although 45 families were identified as eligible to participate, 37 chose not to enroll in ADEPT, citing various reasons, including the substantial time commitment required, transportation difficulties, and reluctance to focus attention on or to discuss the abused teen's traumatic experiences.

To date, six families, consisting predominantly of depressed teens, their mothers or grandmothers (or both), and their siblings, have completed ADEPT. Only three fathers or grandfathers have taken part in the program. The participating depressed teens (n = 6) have ranged in age from 13 to 16 (M = 14.67, SD = 1.21). Although the small number of families limits potential analyses of changes in functioning as a result of the low power available, means and standard deviations of child and parent measures from the preintervention and postintervention assessments are presented in Table 7.2. The change in children's reports of family functioning approached significance ($F(1,5) = 4.24, p < .10$); although changes on most measures were in the predicted direction, none was statistically significant as a result of low power.

Children's reports of their depressive symptoms generally improved across the intervention, moving into the nonclinical range by the end of treatment and indicating that the family-based intervention is generally associated with decreases in adolescents' depressive symptoms. Indeed, by the end of treatment, five of the six teens no longer met diagnostic criteria for depression on the basis of their responses to a structured clinical interview. Comparable improvement was also found on parents' reports of their teens' functioning on the diagnostic interview. Such improvements in depressive symptoms were mirrored by slight improvements in depressive cognitions and attributions. Taken together, such improvements are consistent with the notion that ADEPT is beneficial for teens, associated with

TABLE 7.2
Change in Child and Parent Ratings Before and After Intervention

Rater	Variable	Preintervention mean (SD)	Postintervention mean (SD)
Child	Depressive symptoms (CDI)	15.83 (8.57)	9.00 (6.88)
	Depressive cognitions (CTI: Total score)*	55.50 (15.98)	59.67 (7.00)
	Depressive attributions (CASQ: Overall Composite)*	4.17 (3.48)	5.80 (2.59)
	Peer support (SSAS)	76.00 (9.21)	79.5 (13.81)
	Parent support (SSAS)	50.00 (7.77)	53.67 (6.53)
	Teacher support (SSAS)	39.33 (6.41)	32.83 (7.57)
	General family functioning (FAD)	2.07 (.41)	1.63 (.62)
Parent	General psychological distress (SCL-90: Global Severity Index)	46.17 (22.94)	43.00 (21.56)
	General family functioning (FAD)	1.49 (.34)	1.63 (.34)

*Higher scores indicate better functioning.

changes in their depressogenic cognitions and attributional styles and, ultimately, improvements in their levels of depression.

Like participating teens, parents reported decreased levels of psychological distress following treatment. As such, it appears that parents and other family members may benefit from ADEPT as well, as evidenced by their lower posttreatment levels of symptoms associated with a range of psychological problems.

Self-reports of the support available to adolescents from peers and parents show slight improvements. Similarly, their reports of family functioning improved from the problematic range to the nonproblematic range after treatment. Parents reported that family functioning was nonproblematic both before and after the family-based intervention. Thus, although parents appeared to view family functioning as less problematic in general, teens reported improved family functioning following treatment.

It should be emphasized that, with only six families having completed treatment thus far, these conclusions are preliminary. In light of the low power available, none of these changes from preintervention to postintervention is statistically significant, and they are generally small to moderate in magnitude. However, because the changes are generally in the predicted direction, we are encouraged by these preliminary results, particularly in light of the fact that the families who have participated in our treatment are generally exposed to multiple stresses associated with living in economically underprivileged neighborhoods. Despite these multiple stresses, families who have completed our manualized family-based intervention are generally showing improvements both in the adolescent's depression and in the level of family functioning.

FUTURE CONSIDERATIONS

These results mark one of the first attempts to examine the outcome of a manualized family therapy treatment specifically designed to address the needs of adolescent African American girls who have experienced either physical or sexual abuse. As such, these preliminary results extend our knowledge of the generalizability of the effects of treatments for adolescent depression across cultural boundaries. We are still collecting data and do not yet know whether the changes in teen and family functioning will be found in a larger sample. Such findings would extend our confidence in the effects of our treatment approach. Even with a larger sample, however, the results of this preliminary investigation must be augmented by studies using control groups to allow us to examine the relative impact of approach to treatment relative to either no-treatment or alternative-treatment control groups.

REFERENCES

Armsden, G. C., & Greenberg, M. T. (1987). The Inventory of Parent and Peer Attachment: Individual differences and their relationship to psychological well-being. *Journal of Youth and Adolescence, 16,* 427–454.

Brent, D., Holder, D., Kolko, D., Birmaher, B., Baugher, M., Roth, C., Iyengar, S., & Johnson, B. (1997). A clinical psychotherapy trial for adolescent depression comparing cognitive, family, and supportive therapy. *Archives of General Psychiatry, 54,* 877–885.

Briere, J. (1996). *Trauma Symptom Checklist for Children (TCSC): Professional manual.* Odessa, FL: Psychological Assessment Resources.

Clarke, G., Hawkins, W., Murphy, M., Sheeber, L., Lewinsohn, P., & Seeley, J. (1995). Targeted prevention of unipolar depressive disorder in an at-risk sample of high school adolescents: A randomized trial of a group cognitive intervention. *Journal of the American Academy of Child and Adolescent Psychiatry, 34,* 312–321.

Clarke, G., Hops, H., Lewinsohn, P. M., Andrews, J., Seeley, J. R., & Williams, J. (1992). Cognitive–behavioral group treatment of adolescent depression: Prediction of outcome. *Behavior Therapy, 23,* 341–352.

Clarke, G., & Lewinsohn, P. (1986). *The coping with depression course: Adolescent version.* Eugene, OR: Oregon Research Institute.

Clarke, G., Rhode, P., Lewinsohn, P., Hops, H., & Seeley, J. (1999). Cognitive–behavioral treatment of adolescent depression: Efficacy of acute group treatment and booster sessions. *Journal of the American Academy of Child and Adolescent Psychiatry, 38,* 272–279.

Derogatis, L. (1975). *SCL-90-R: Administration, scoring, and procedures manual: II.* Baltimore, MD: Clinical Psychometric Research.

Dubow, E. F., & Ullman, D. (1989). Assessing social support in elementary school children: The survey of children's social support. *Journal of Clinical Child Psychology, 18,* 52–64.

Duhl, K., Kantor, D., & Duhl, B. (1973). Learning, space and action in family therapy: A primer of sculpture. In D. Bloch (Ed.), *Techniques of family psychotherapy* (pp. 47–63). New York: Grune & Stratton.

Epstein, M. B., Baldwin, C. M., & Bishop, D. S. (1983). The McMaster Family Assessment Device. *Journal of Marital and Family Therapy, 9,* 171–180.

Feindler, E. L., & Guttman, J. (1994). Cognitive–behavioral anger control training. In C. W. LeCroy (Ed.), *Handbook of child and adolescent treatment manuals* (pp. 170–199). New York: Lexington Books.

Hamilton, J. D., & Bridge, J. (1999). Outcome at 6 months for 50 adolescents with major depression treated in a health maintenance organization. *Journal of the American Academy of Child and Adolescent Psychiatry, 37,* 35–39.

Kaslow, N. J., Deering, C. G., & Racusin, G. R. (1994). Depressed children and their families. *Clinical Psychology Review, 14,* 39–59.

Kaslow, N. J., McClure, E., & Connell, A. (2002). Treatment of depression in children and adolescents. In I. H. Gotlib & C. L. Hammen (Eds.), *Handbook of depression* (pp. 441–464). New York: Guilford Press.

Kaslow, N. J., Stark, K., Printz, B., Livingston, R., & Tsai, S. (1992). Cognitive Triad Inventory for Children: Development and relation to depression and anxiety. *Journal of Clinical Child Psychology, 21*, 339–347.

Kaufman, A. S., & Kaufman, N. L. (1990). *Kaufman brief intelligence test manual.* Circle Pines, MN: American Guidance Service.

Keller, M. B., Lavori, P. W., Beardslee, W. R., Wunder, J., & Ryan, N. (1991). Depression in children and adolescents: New data on "undertreatment" and a literature review on the efficacy of available treatments. *Journal of Affective Disorders, 21*, 163–171.

Kovacs, M. (1992). *Children's Depression Inventory.* North Tonawanda, NY: Multi-Health Systems.

LeCroy, C. W. (1994). Social skills training. In C. W. LeCroy (Ed.), *Handbook of child and adolescent treatment manuals* (pp. 126–169). New York: Lexington Books.

Lewinsohn, P., Clarke, G., Rhode, P., Hops, H., & Seeley, J. (1996). A course in coping: A cognitive–behavioral approach to the treatment of adolescent depression. In E. D. Hibbs & P. S. Jensen (Eds.), *Psychosocial treatments for child and adolescent disorders: Empirically based strategies for clinical practice* (pp. 109–135). Washington, DC: American Psychological Association.

Mufson, L., Moreau, D., Weissman, M., & Klerman, G. (1993). *Interpersonal psychotherapy for depressed adolescents.* New York: Guilford Press.

Mufson, L., Weissman, M. M., Moreau, D., & Garfinkel, R. (1999). Efficacy of interpersonal psychotherapy for depressed adolescents. *Archives of General Psychiatry, 56*, 573–579.

Papp, P. (1976). Family choreography. In P. Guerin (Ed.), *Family therapy: Theory and practice* (pp. 465–479). New York: Gardner Press.

Rosselló, J., & Bernal, G. (1999). The efficacy of cognitive–behavioral and interpersonal treatments for depression in Puerto Rican adolescents. *Journal of Consulting and Clinical Psychology, 67*, 734–745.

Schwartz, J. A., Kaslow, N. J., Racusin, G. R., & Carton, E. R. (1998). Interpersonal family therapy for childhood depression. In V. B. V. Hasselt & M. Hersen (Eds.), *Handbook of psychological treatment protocols for children and adolescents* (pp. 109–151). Mahwah, NJ: Erlbaum.

Sherborne, C. D., & Stewart, A. C. (1991). The MOS Social Support Survey. *Social Science Medicine, 32*, 705–714.

Stark, K. D., Brookman, C. S., & Frazier, R. (1990). A comprehensive school-based treatment program for depressed children. *School Psychology Quarterly, 5*, 111–140.

Stark, K. D., Raffaelle, L., & Reysa, A. (1994). The treatment of depressed children: A skills training approach to working with children and families. In C.

W. LeCroy (Ed.), *Handbook of child and adolescent treatment manuals* (pp. 343–397). New York: Lexington Books.

Stark, K. D., Reynolds, W. M., & Kaslow, N. J. (1987). A comparison of the relative efficacy of self-control therapy and behavior problem-solving therapy for depression in children. *Journal of Abnormal Child Psychology, 15*, 91–113.

Stark, K. D., Rouse, L., & Livingston, R. (1991). Treatment of depression during childhood and adolescence: Cognitive behavioral procedures for the individual and family. In P. Kendall (Ed.), *Child and adolescent therapy* (pp. 165–206). New York: Guilford Press.

Stark, K. D., Swearer, S., Kurowski, C., Sommer, D., & Bowen, B. (1996). Targeting the child and the family: A holistic approach to treating child and adolescent depressive disorders. In E. D. Hibbs & P. S. Jensen (Eds.), *Psychosocial treatments for child and adolescent disorders: Empirically based strategies for clinical practice* (pp. 207–238). Washington, DC: American Psychological Association.

Thompson, M., Kaslow, N. J., Weiss, B., & Nolen-Hoeksema, S. (1998). Children's Attributional Style Questionnaire—Revised: Psychometric examination. *Psychological Assessment, 10*, 166–170.

Weller, E. B., Weller, R. A., Fristad, M. A., & Rooney, M. T. (1999a). *Children's Interview for Psychiatric Syndromes*. Washington, DC: American Psychiatric Press.

Weller, E. B., Weller, R. A., Fristad, M. A., & Rooney, M. T. (1999b). *Children's Interview for Psychiatric Syndromes: Parent version*. Washington, DC: American Psychiatric Press.

8

EFFICACY TO EFFECTIVENESS: ADAPTATIONS OF INTERPERSONAL PSYCHOTHERAPY FOR ADOLESCENT DEPRESSION

LAURA MUFSON, KRISTEN POLLACK DORTA,
DONNA MOREAU, AND MYRNA M. WEISSMAN

Myriad psychotherapies are used to treat adolescent depression, but only a handful of them have been demonstrated to be efficacious in clinical trials (Kaslow & Thompson, 1998). With the advance of managed care and the establishment of standards of care, increased emphasis has been placed on the use of empirically based, or evidence-based, therapies both for research purposes as well as general clinical practice. Because most of these therapies have been examined in efficacy trials, in which homogeneous samples are treated in tightly controlled settings, critics contend that these studies do not help practitioners, who see a more heterogeneous sample in

Excerpts of this chapter were reprinted from Mufson, L., & Pollack, D. K. (2000). Interpersonal psychotherapy for depressed adolescents: Theory, practice, and research. In A. H. Essman (Ed.), *Adolescent psychiatry: The annals of the American Society for Adolescent Psychiatry* (Vol. 25, pp. 139–168). Hillsdale, NJ: The Analytic Press. Reprinted with permission.

less controlled settings. Therefore, the field has seen a push to bring evidence-based treatment into real-world settings and assess their efficacy with more heterogeneous samples and a wider array of outcome measures. Researchers cannot assume that efficacy in a controlled setting will necessarily translate to effectiveness in the real world but instead must test this hypothesis in a variety of community settings. Consistent with the movement from efficacy to effectiveness, the research program on interpersonal psychotherapy (IPT) has expanded to include both efficacy as well as effectiveness research. This chapter provides a brief review of current research findings on the treatment of adolescent depression, an overview of the theory and principles of interpersonal therapy for adolescents (IPT-A), the results of a completed efficacy trial of IPT-A, and a discussion of an ongoing effectiveness trial being conducted in school-based health clinics.

CURRENT PSYCHOTHERAPIES FOR DEPRESSION

Despite the high prevalence and social morbidity of early onset depression, relatively little research has been conducted on the efficacy of treatments for depressed adolescents compared with the research done on treatment for depressed adults. Several randomized clinical trials of selective serotonin reuptake inhibitors (SSRIs; Emslie et al., 1997, 2000; Keller et al., 2001) demonstrate efficacy in the treatment of adolescent depression. In addition, several clinical trials of individual psychotherapies (cognitive–behavioral therapy [CBT]: Brent et al., 1997; IPT-A: Mufson, Weissman, Moreau, & Garfinkel, 1999; Rosselló & Bernal, 1999) and group CBT (Clarke et al., 1995; Lewinsohn, Clarke, Hops, & Andrews, 1990) have demonstrated efficacy of CBT and IPT-A therapies for adolescent depression. Nonetheless, given the substantial rates of depressive disorders in adolescents and the concomitant negative developmental trajectory, the development of new treatments and further establishment of the efficacy of these and other treatments for adolescent depression are critical. This is the context in which the studies of IPT-A have developed.

THEORETICAL UNDERPINNINGS OF INTERPERSONAL
PSYCHOTHERAPY

IPT for depressed adolescents, or IPT-A, is an adaptation of IPT, a brief treatment originally developed for the treatment of depressed, non-bipolar adults (Klerman, Weissman, Rounsaville, & Chevron, 1984; Weissman, Markowitz, & Klerman, 2000). IPT places the depressive episode in the context of interpersonal relationships and focuses on current interpersonal conflicts. The goals of IPT are (a) to decrease depressive symptoms and (b) to improve interpersonal functioning. The theoretical roots of this treatment can be found in the interpersonal schools of thought and, more specifically, in the teachings of Harry Stack Sullivan and Adolf Meyer. Research amply supports an interpersonal approach to the conceptualization and treatment of depression (Hammen, 1999; Joiner, Coyne, & Blalock, 1999). Data suggest that depression, even at subclinical levels, is related to significant interpersonal problems and interpersonal stress (Aseltine, Gore, & Colten, 1994; Puig-Antich et al., 1985, 1993; Stader & Hokason, 1998). In addition, researchers have documented that interpersonal experiences often precipitate the onset of depression (Hammen, 1999). Clinical research conducted in the 1970s and 1980s clearly established the efficacy of IPT for the treatment of depression in adults (DiMascio et al., 1979; Elkin et al., 1989; Weissman et al., 1979).

ADAPTATION FOR DEPRESSED ADOLESCENTS

Given the success of IPT in clinical trials with adult outpatients as well as the documented similarities between adult and adolescent depressive symptoms, IPT has been adapted to treat outpatient adolescents who are suffering from a nonbipolar, nonpsychotic depressive episode. IPT also was selected for use with adolescents as a result of its developmental relevance to the adolescent population. IPT-A focuses largely on current interpersonal issues that are likely to be of greatest concern to adolescents. The treatment has been adapted to address developmental issues most common to adolescents, including separation from parents; development of dyadic, romantic interpersonal relationships; initial experiences with the death of a relative or friend; and peer pressures. Strategies were developed to include family members in various phases of the treatment and to address special issues that arise in the treatment of adolescents, such as school refusal, physical or sexual abuse, suicidal ideation, aggression, and involvement of a child protective service agency. As with IPT, the general goals of IPT-A are to decrease depressive symptoms and to improve interpersonal functioning. Although IPT-A's goals are not necessarily different from the goals of other treatments for depression, the techniques employed to attain them are uniquely combined within a short-term structured treatment program. The adolescent treatment program is specifically defined in a treatment manual (Mufson, Pollack Dorta, Moreau, & Weissman, 2004).

MANUAL DEVELOPMENT

Standardization of the treatment in a manual was necessary to ensure that different therapists adhere to the same structure and techniques, a consistency that allows for future efficacy studies and dissemination of the treatment to clinicians in a variety of settings. The development of the manual for IPT-A began with the application of the revised techniques to depressed adolescents seeking treatment at the outpatient clinic of a university hospital. Therapy sessions, conducted by an experienced child clinical psychologist under the supervision of the developer of IPT, were videotaped and discussed regarding the application of the general IPT principles and the modifications needed for its use with adolescents. The final manual (Mufson et al., 2004) is intended to be used to train experienced child and adolescent therapists in the specific IPT-A principles. The modified manual for adolescents should be read in conjunction with the manual for adults (Weissman et al., 2000). The IPT-A manual balances the need for structure and the need for flexibility, with the assumption that clinicians already have a certain level of training and expertise in the conduct of psychotherapy.

PATIENT SELECTION

On the basis of clinical experience, we have ascertained several patient conditions associated with the optimal likelihood of success of IPT-A. Adolescents whose families are supportive of and willing to participate in the treatment are more likely to benefit from IPT-A. This benefit appears to be due to a combination of improved treatment compliance and increased receptivity of the family members to the changes in interpersonal communication strategies. IPT-A is not recommended for patients who have a long-standing history of severe interpersonal problems; rather, it is most suited to patients who have experienced an identifiable interpersonal event that precipitated or exacerbated a depressive episode, patients who are motivated to be in treatment or to feel better, and patients who are willing to receive time-limited treatment. IPT-A, as an outpatient treatment, is not appropriate for the treatment of adolescents who are currently actively suicidal, homicidal, psychotic, or bipolar or who are abusing substances.

COURSE OF TREATMENT

IPT-A is designed as a once-a-week, 12-week treatment. If a crisis occurs, the therapist and patient may meet for an additional session if they feel that the crisis is short-term and manageable on an outpatient basis. The two main approaches for achieving IPT-A's goals are to identify one or two problem areas as the focus of treatment and to emphasize the interpersonal nature of the problem as it occurs in current relationships. The treatment is divided into three phases: (a) the initial phase, (b) the middle phase, and (c) the termination phase. Across each of these phases, several general treatment factors remain consistent, and we believe they are integral aspects of the intervention.

General Factors

The general factors underlying IPT-A are the organization and predictability of the treatment, the defined therapist and patient roles, and the use of a collaborative approach. Although the content of each IPT-A session varies somewhat, the structure and organization of the sessions remain generally consistent. The predictability that this structure creates helps the adolescent play a more active role in guiding treatment and in gaining a framework through which to address the depression.

In IPT-A the therapist assumes an active role by conducting directed assessments of depressive symptoms and interpersonal functioning. The therapist continually relates the adolescent's symptoms to his or her interpersonal functioning and interpersonal problem areas and employs directive techniques for clarifying conflicts, aiding in the generation of alternative solutions, and improving communication skills. In contrast to other types of therapists, the IPT-A therapist is responsible for the direction of the session and does not simply discuss issues raised by the adolescent. The IPT-A therapist must ensure that the treatment focuses on issues related to the identified problem area and doesn't get off target.

The patient's role in IPT-A also is active insofar as the patient is expected to be involved in the therapeutic process by working with the therapist in finding solutions to interpersonal dilemmas, in exploring feelings, and in practicing new techniques for managing interpersonal situations and relationships. The patient is encouraged to take an increasingly active role over the course of treatment, resulting in the development of a "collaborative team approach" wherein the therapist serves as a coach for the teen while the teen tries out new interpersonal problem-solving skills and communication strategies.

Ideally in IPT-A, the team extends beyond the therapist and patient to include people collateral to the treatment, including family and personnel at school and in outside agencies. Although IPT-A is largely an individual treatment, it offers considerable flexibility by involving significant people in aspects of the treatment. In addition, the relationship with the therapist serves as a context in which patients can practice strategies that they eventually may use with significant people in their lives.

Initial Phase

In the initial phase, during Sessions 1 through 4, the therapist reviews the depressive symptoms and confirms the diagnosis, identifies the problem areas, and establishes the treatment contract. Six specific tasks need to be accomplished: (a) conduct a diagnostic assessment, which includes reviewing the symptoms with the patient, giving the syndrome a name, explaining depression and its treatment, giving the patient the sick role, and evaluating the need for medication; (b) conduct an interpersonal assessment, referred to as an *interpersonal inventory*, that includes identifying the type and nature of the patient's social and familial relationships and relating the patient's depression to the interpersonal context; (c) identify the problem area(s); (d) explain the rationale and intent of the treatment; (e) draft a treatment contract with the patient; and (f) explain the patient's expected role in the treatment.

We recommend that the patients' parents and guardians participate in at least some portions of the first session of the treatment. If joint participation is not possible or recommended in this session, the therapist should conduct a separate session with the parent(s) to obtain information that will aid in confirming the patient's diagnosis and establishing the patient's interpersonal functioning. The parent, along with the adolescent, is educated about depression: its nature, its course, and its treatment options. Both the parent and the adolescent are involved in discussing the various treatment options as part of the education about depression. The initial phase is also an important time for the therapist to develop an alliance with the school system (see Mufson et al., 2004, for a more detailed explanation).

As part of the psychoeducation component, adolescents are encouraged to think of themselves as in treatment and are given a limited sick role. Because adolescents tend to withdraw socially or avoid usual social expectations when depressed, they are encouraged to maintain their usual social roles in the family, at school, and with friends. In addition, adolescents and parents are encouraged to view symptoms such as diminished school performance and the inability to complete chores to previous standards as symptoms of depression that should improve over the course of treatment. Parents are advised to be supportive, to encourage adolescents to engage in as many normal activities as possible, and to focus on encouraging the effort, with the belief that the performance will improve as the depression remits. Together, the assignment of the limited sick role and psychoeducation can reverse the negative behavior among family members that sometimes accompanies the depressed patient's decreased social and academic performance.

During much of Sessions 2 through 4, the focus is on conducting the interpersonal inventory. The therapist reviews current and past interpersonal relationships as they relate to current depressive symptoms. The therapist clarifies the nature of interactions with significant others, the expectations of the adolescent and significant others for the relationships, the satisfying and unsatisfying aspects of the relationships, and the changes the patient wants in the relationships. During the review, the therapist should be looking for patterns of communication problems—maladaptive communication strategies as well as communication and interpersonal strengths. In addressing the areas of weakness, a brief treatment needs to build upon the patient's strengths. Although the primary informant for the inventory is the adolescent, other significant people in the adolescent's life, including parents and teachers, also may serve as informants if their involvement is acceptable to the adolescent. While conducting the interpersonal inventory, the therapist also should probe for any significant interpersonal life events that may be related to the depression, including changes in family structure; death, illness, accident, or trauma; changes in school or living situation; and the onset of sexual relationships.

At the end of the initial phase, the therapist and patient collaborate in making an explicit treatment contract. The contract specifies which of the five problem areas they will focus on in the treatment, as well as confidentiality, frequency of sessions, rules regarding missed appointments, level of parental involvement in treatment, and the patient's role in the treatment. The therapist discusses the hope that the adolescent will be feeling better at the end of the 12 weeks but also reminds the patient that if this does not occur, further treatment will be arranged. The middle phase begins once an agreement is reached on the treatment plan.

Middle Phase

During the middle phase, Sessions 5 through 8, the therapist and patient begin to work directly on one or two of the designated problem areas. The tasks associated with the middle phase are to (a) alleviate the symptoms, (b) clarify the problem, (c) identify effective strategies to attack the problem, (d) implement the interventions, and (e) improve interpersonal functioning. The therapist encourages the patient to bring in feelings, monitors the depressive symptoms, and continues to work with the family to support the treatment. Techniques vary depending on the problem area being addressed but may include exploratory questioning, encouragement of affect, linkage of affect with events, clarification of conflicts, communication analysis, and behavior change techniques such as role-playing exercises. The therapist gives continuous feedback about the use of strategies and any observed changes in the patient's functioning.

Throughout the middle phase, the therapist and patient work as a team. Together they assess the accuracy of the initial formulation of the problem area and shift the focus of the treatment to events occurring outside of the session that appear related to the patient's depressive symptoms. The therapist and patient discuss interpersonal style as it relates to interactions that may be occurring outside of the session. The role that family and key school personnel play in this phase of treatment is specific to each case. As a rule, however, the more collaboration, the more likely the adolescent will generalize any treatment gains to settings outside of treatment. Education about depression and interpersonal relationships continues throughout this phase.

Termination Phase

The termination phase takes place approximately between Sessions 9 and 12. The subject of termination is broached at the beginning of treatment and periodically during the course of therapy to remind the adolescent of the time-limited nature of the treatment. The adolescent's two main tasks during termination are (a) to give up the relationship with the therapist and (b) to establish a sense of competence to deal with future problems. Patients and families are advised that a slight recurrence of symptoms is common as termination approaches and that feelings of apprehension, anger, or sadness are not unusual and do not necessarily portend a relapse. To support the patient's ability to cope with problems, the therapist highlights the patient's skills and external supports. Specifically, therapist and adolescent try to generate strategies to use in anticipated future situations to demonstrate the adolescent's acquisition of new skills that will remain after treatment concludes.

The IPT-A therapist conducts a final termination session with the adolescent alone and then with any family members who have been involved in the treatment, which usually includes at least one parent. The sessions include explicit discussion of feelings engendered by the end of treatment, a review of strategies learned and goals accomplished, recognition of the adolescent's areas of competence, and goal-directed anticipation of possible future episodes. Termination with family members addresses the same issues. In addition, the therapist and family discuss any changes that occurred in the family as a result of the treatment. The therapist helps family members anticipate future episodes of depression and educates them about the warning signs of possible recurrence and appropriate management of recurrent episodes.

Problem Areas

In IPT-A four interpersonal problem areas contain one or more specific goals with respect to improving interpersonal functioning. For each problem area an array of strategies can be used to accomplish the goals associated with that specific problem area as well as the more general treatment goals of IPT-A. Throughout work on any of the problem areas, the therapist weaves together the interpersonal issues and the adolescent depressive symptoms and helps the adolescent understand how these factors interact with and serve to potentiate the others. Below we briefly discuss each problem area; for a more detailed discussion of each area, see the IPT-A manual (Mufson et al., 2004a).

Grief

Grief is identified as a problem if it is abnormal (distorted grief, delayed grief, or chronic grief) either in its duration or its severity of response

(Raphael, 1983). For many adolescents, grief often represents a first experience with death and the loss of a significant relationship. Grief reactions can include withdrawal and depressed feelings, a display of pseudomaturity, identification with the deceased, or regression to earlier developmental stages (Krupnick, 1984). Because these difficulties may manifest themselves in behavioral problems rather than affective symptoms, the therapist must be alert to problems of drug or alcohol abuse, sexual promiscuity, or truancy (Raphael, 1983).

The specific interpersonal goal for this problem area is to help the adolescent appropriately mourn a significant loss and then to re-establish relationships and interests that can help compensate for it. In treating a grief reaction, one must consider the adolescent's role in the family system, the nature of the relationship lost, the remaining social support network, and the adolescent's psychological maturity in addressing the impact of the loss. The therapist helps the patient discuss the loss and identify the associated feelings. As the patient begins to grieve appropriately and the symptoms dissipate, the patient should better understand and accept the loss and feel free to pursue new relationships.

Interpersonal Role Disputes

An *interpersonal dispute* is defined as a situation in which an individual and at least one significant other person have nonreciprocal expectations about their relationship. Adolescents' role disputes commonly occur with parents over issues of sexuality, authority, money, autonomy, and life values (Miller, 1974). A common interpersonal role dispute is the conflict between a parent with traditional values and an adolescent responding to peer pressure. Often these conflicting values lead to different expectations for the adolescent's behavior. This conflict is frequently seen in the normal adolescent rebellion against parental authority that accompanies the developmental task of individuation and separation.

The specific interpersonal goals for this problem area are to identify the dispute, develop a plan of action for addressing the dispute, and modify communication and expectations to help bring about some resolution to the dispute. What differs in treating adolescents' role disputes is the nature of the problems and the involvement of the parents. The therapist needs to explain to the adolescent and the parents how the disputes contribute to depressive symptoms and how resolution of these disputes can alleviate the symptoms. A useful approach is for the therapist to involve the parent (or parents) with whom there is a dispute and to facilitate the negotiations of the relationship in the session. Often it is necessary and helpful to coach the parents in the use of more constructive communication strategies with their adolescent, either in a joint or separate session. Improvements may take the form of a change in the expectations and behavior of the patient, the other person, or both. The goal of IPT-A is to help the adolescent clarify his or her expectations for the relationship, evaluate which expectations are realistic, and find strategies for coping with the immutable expectations.

Role Transitions

Role transitions are defined as changes that occur as a result of progression from one social role to another. People may develop depression when they experience difficulty coping with the life changes associated with a role change. The transition may result in impaired social functioning if it occurs too rapidly or is experienced by the individual as a loss. Adolescents and their families recognize normal role transitions as rites of passage and typically handle them successfully (Miller, 1974). Normal role transitions for adolescents include (a) passage into puberty; (b) shift from group to dyadic relationships; (c) initiation of sexual relationships or desires; (d) separation from parents and family; and (e) work, college, or career planning. Problems arise when parents are unable to accept the transition or when adolescents are unable to cope with the changes. Role transitions also can be thrust upon adolescents as a result of unanticipated circumstances such as parenthood, parental divorce or remarriage, death, illness, and parental impairment or separation. Problems that occur with expected and unexpected role transitions include loss of self-esteem, failure to meet one's own and others' expectations, increased pressures and responsibilities, and inability to separate from family or family's inability to allow that separation (Erikson, 1968).

An adolescent's ability to cope with unforeseen circumstances rests on prior psychological functioning and social supports. Role transitions can be perceived as a loss to adolescents, particularly if they felt more competent in their old role and are uncertain about their ability to fulfill the expectations associated with the new role. Consequently, the psychological reaction to the transition can resemble that of mourning.

The specific interpersonal goals for this problem area are to help adolescents understand what the specific role transition means to them, the demands of the new situation, and what has been gained and lost in the transition. The therapist then helps adolescents learn new skills to facilitate acceptance of and success in their new roles. If the role transition problem involves changes in family roles, the therapist may include the parents in several sessions to help support the adolescent or, if necessary, help family members adjust to the normative role transition so that they do not restrict the adolescent's development and impair his or her functioning. If the family is adjusting more easily to the transition, this will likely facilitate an easier transition for the adolescent.

Interpersonal Deficits

Interpersonal deficits are identified when an individual appears to lack the requisite social skills to establish and maintain appropriate relationships within and outside the family. Interpersonal deficits can impede an adolescent's achievement of developmental tasks, which are primarily social and include making same-age friends, participating in extracurricular activities, becoming part of a peer group, beginning to date, and learning to make choices regarding exclusive relations, career, and sexuality (Hersen & Van Hasselt, 1987). As a result of interpersonal deficits, the adolescent may be socially isolated from peer groups and relationships, which can lead to feelings of depression and inadequacy. These feelings of depression can in turn lead to increased social withdrawal and a lag in interpersonal skills when the depressive symptoms abate.

Treatment focuses on interpersonal deficits that are more a consequence of the depression than long-standing personality traits. The specific interpersonal goals for this problem area are to help adolescents reduce their sense of social isolation by improving their social skills, including communication and relationship-building skills; increasing self-confidence; strengthening current relationships; and building new relationships.

The strategies for treating adolescents with interpersonal deficits include reviewing past significant relationships and exploring repetitive or parallel interpersonal problems. Therapists identify and discuss new strategies for approaching situations and encourage patients to apply these strategies to current issues. The therapist may incorporate role-playing exercises that involve problematic interpersonal situations, enabling adolescents to explore and practice new communication skills and interpersonal behaviors and engendering a sense of social competence that they can generalize to other situations.

Clinical Vignette

Psychosocial Background

The patient is a 16-year-old African American female adolescent who is currently living with her maternal aunt. Lacey had lived with her father and paternal grandmother until the age of 11, when she was removed from the home following several years of abuse by a paternal uncle who lived in the home with the father and grandmother as well as the uncle's fiancée and 2-year-old child. Lacey finally reported the abuse to a school counselor, who contacted the authorities. Her father and grandmother refused to believe her, and the uncle continued to reside in the home. The uncle's fiancée left, and Lacey's father and grandmother reportedly blamed her for the disruption she supposedly caused in the family. Lacey spent several years in foster care until her mother, who had been incarcerated, was released and able to obtain custody. For several years, Lacey lived with her mother and maternal aunt. Several months before presenting at the clinic, her mother moved out of the aunt's home to live with her new boyfriend of 1 year. Her mother also became pregnant around this time. Lacey reported that, despite all that had happened, she still saw her father occasionally in the neighborhood, although they did not have formal visits. She also reported significant anger toward her father, feeling that he blamed her for all the family trouble that ensued after the report of the abuse.

Symptom Presentation

Lacey presented to the clinic with the following symptoms: depressed mood; early insomnia (taking 2 to 3 hours to fall asleep at night); middle insomnia; occasional late insomnia; anhedonia; increased social isolation; feelings of fatigue, irritability, and low self-esteem; and some thoughts about being dead but with no plan or intent. She reported that as far back as she can remember she has felt sad but that it worsened when her mother moved out of the apartment without her.

Initial Phase of Interpersonal Psychotherapy for Depressed Adolescents

The therapist presented the educational material to Lacey and reviewed the concept of the limited sick role, focusing particularly on trying to get her to attend school more regularly despite her feelings of apathy and fatigue. A comprehensive interpersonal inventory was conducted, reviewing all aspects of her relationships with her mother, mother's boyfriend, father, paternal grandmother, and maternal aunt. Lacey reported that she and her mother had become close during the past several years and that she was devastated by the abrupt way in which her mother told her she was moving out of the aunt's home and by the fact that she never even discussed the possibility of Lacey's coming with her. Although Lacey could describe these angry and painful feelings in the session, she reported that she never expressed these feelings to her mother. In discussing her other relationships, a recurrent theme appeared: Lacey felt that everyone in her family blamed her for all the things that go wrong at home. As a result, she withdrew from these relationships, never sharing her feelings about how her family life was affecting her.

Given the involvement of several family members in Lacey's life, the therapist had a telephone session with the maternal aunt, with whom Lacey was living, to get her perspective on the situation and educate her regarding the methods and goals of the treatment. In addition, the therapist invited Lacey's mother to come for an individual session to gain her perspective on the situation and prep her for the type of therapeutic work Lacey would be engaging in during the treatment.

After completion of the interpersonal inventory, the therapist made an explicit treatment contract with Lacey emphasizing that her primary problem area seemed to be one of *role transition*, with a secondary problem area of *role dispute* in dealing with her mother's departure from the home and initiation of a new life with her boyfriend; the different expectations Lacey and her mother appear to have for their relationship; and Lacey's struggle to deal with the new family structures and to find a new role for herself in her father's new family constellation. This transition was made more difficult for Lacey because of her difficulties in communicating her feelings to others for fear of their reactions and responses.

Middle Phase of Interpersonal Psychotherapy for Depressed Adolescents

During the middle phase of treatment, the therapist actively worked with Lacey to examine what it had been like living with her mother and her aunt; what she was missing now, given the recent changes; and what she was concerned about in the new constellation. Together they explored what she still needed and wanted to have in her relationship with her mother, and how she could communicate these things to her mother and mother's boyfriend. Therapeutic techniques that were used included (a) clarifying what Lacey wanted from her relationship with her mother and her boyfriend; (b) examining whether this desire was reasonable; (c) examining Lacey's communications with her mother and, through role-playing exercises, developing more effective ways of expressing her feelings and needs; and (d) examining Lacey's mother's possible perspective on the situation and what, if anything, Lacey might be doing or saying that may be contributing to the perceptions. To facilitate improved communication and negotiation between Lacey and her mother, the therapist held a joint session with them during which they practiced communicating and listening to each other. The therapist modeled for them how to start a conversation about the effects of the move on their relationship and helped them identify the conflicts they were having and more constructive ways to approach their difficult situation. The mother reported at the end of the session that she had learned a great deal about Lacey's feelings and expectations. In the session, Lacey's mother was able to express very positive and loving feelings toward Lacey, including how much she missed her and wanted her in her life.

After the joint session, Lacey reported that it had been a positive experience, despite her difficulties in expressing her feelings. Her mother had responded to the session by immediately increasing their time together. Interestingly, Lacey also generalized her new ability to express herself by reaching out to her father and paternal grandmother to start working on ways to improve those relationships. Her reported depressive symptoms began to decrease and continued to do so throughout the remainder of treatment.

Termination Phase of Interpersonal Psychotherapy for Depressed Adolescents

Termination focused on reviewing the warning symptoms of Lacey's depression; highlighting the accomplishments Lacey and her family had made over the course of treatment; discussing the potential for relapse in the future and steps she could take to manage such a relapse; and examining her experience ending the relationship with her therapist.

Interpersonal Psychotherapy for Depressed Adolescents Research: Efficacy

Preliminary Study

Before conducting a controlled clinical trial, the researchers established the acceptability and feasibility of IPT-A through an open clinical trial. The sample for the open trial consisted of fourteen 12- to 18-year-old subjects with depression. The results of this trial provided preliminary support for the use of IPT-A with depressed adolescents (Mufson et al., 1994).

Therapist Training

A therapist training program was created in preparation to conduct a randomized controlled clinical trial. This program consisted of two components: a didactic seminar using the training manual (Mufson et al., 2004) and a clinical practicum. Training was designed to modify the practices of fully trained child and adolescent clinicians to conform to IPT-A, not to train participants to become therapists. After completing the didactic program, the therapists entered the clinical practicum. Each therapist consecutively treated two cases for 12 weeks each. All sessions were videotaped and discussed in supervision that occurred weekly for 1 hour. Therapists' videotapes also were reviewed by clinical IPT experts who decided whether they were competent to be certified as IPT-A therapists. Rating forms designed for the National Institute of Mental Health (NIMH) Collaborative Study of the Treatment of Depression (Elkin et al., 1989; Weissman, Rounsaville, & Chevron, 1982) were used to document the competency criteria.

Design and Methodology

Researchers conducted a randomized, controlled clinical trial comparing IPT-A with clinical monitoring in a sample of clinic-referred depressed adolescents (Mufson, et al., 1999). Adolescents were identified using a clinician-rated scale (Hamilton Rating Scale for Depression [HRSD]; Williams, 1988) and a self-report measure (Beck Depression Inventory [BDI]; Beck, Steer, & Garbin, 1988), as well as two clinical interviews (Schedule for Affective Disorders and Schizophrenia for School Aged Children [K-SADS-E]; Chambers et al., 1985) and the Diagnostic Interview Schedule for Children Version 2.3 [DISC 2.3]; Shaffer et al., 1996). Adolescents with a diagnosis of major depressive disorder who were not currently suicidal or psychotic and were not diagnosed with a chronic medical illness, Bipolar I or II, conduct disorder, substance abuse disorder, eating disorder, or obsessive–compulsive disorder were included in the study. Of the 57 adolescents who were determined to be eligible for the study, 48 agreed to be randomized.

Adolescents were randomized to IPT-A or clinical monitoring. Treatment was provided for 12 weeks in both conditions. Clinical monitoring consisted of once monthly 30-minute sessions with a therapist, with the option for a second session each month and a phone call the third week of each month. Adolescents enrolled in the study, in either treatment condition, were assessed at Weeks 0, 2, 4, 6, 8, 10, and 12. Therefore, those adolescents who received clinical monitoring had a face-to-face clinical encounter 3 out of 4 weeks of the month, plus a monthly phone call. The outcomes assessed included diagnosis and symptoms levels (HRSD, BDI, and the Clinical Global Impression Form [CGI]), as well as global and social function (Children's Global Assessment Scale and the Social Adjustment Scale—Self Report Version, respectively) and social problem-solving skills (Social Problem-Solving Inventory—Revised).

Results

The results of this controlled trial were promising with respect to the efficacy of IPT-A in comparison with clinical monitoring. Treatment outcome was assessed in several ways. Firstly, with respect to rates of treatment completion, significantly more IPT-A patients (88%) completed treatment than did the control patients (46%). Given the rates of noncompletion, particularly in the control group, all subsequent analyses were conducted using both a completer sample (N = 32 adolescents) and an intent-to-treat sample (N = 48 adolescents). In addition, all analyses were conducted on outcome measures at termination while controlling for the baseline measurements.

With respect to depressive symptoms, for both the completer and the intent-to-treat samples, IPT-A patients reported fewer depressive symptoms. Using standards for recovery set forth by the National Collaborative Study for the Treatment of Depression (Elkins et al., 1989), significantly more IPT-A patients than control patients met the recovery criteria for major depression. The results of this study showed that treatment with IPT-A led to improved social functioning compared with treatment in the control condition. More specifically, IPT-A patients demonstrated a better overall level of functioning, functioning with peers, and functioning in dating relationships. Finally, although these results were somewhat tentative as a result of missing data and small sample size, IPT-A patients demonstrated better skills than control patients in certain areas of social problem-solving skills, including positive problem-solving orientation and rational problem solving. With respect to the latter, IPT-A patients exhibited better performance in the generation of alternatives and the implementation and verification of solutions. Although further research with different comparison groups and across different adolescent populations are needed, the results of this randomized controlled trial suggest that IPT-A is an efficacious treatment for adolescent depression.

Limitations

Although the results from the controlled clinical trial are extremely promising, the sample size is relatively small. In addition, these results do not establish the generalizability of the treatment to real-world settings, wherein clinical services are often delivered in less than optimal conditions, patient populations are more complex, and therapists' backgrounds and training are more varied.

Interpersonal Psychotherapy for Depressed Adolescents Research: Effectiveness

Throughout the past decade, researchers have increasingly emphasized the importance of establishing not only the efficacy but also the effectiveness of treatments (Hoagwood, Hibbs, Brent, & Jensen, 1995; Goldfried & Wolfe, 1998). Effectiveness research is thought to better capture the impact of treatments on individuals who may have comorbid conditions and situations that might otherwise exclude them from more traditional efficacy studies, thereby more closely approximating the treatment's efficacy for the more general population.

We recently completed an effectiveness study of IPT-A in school-based health clinics in the New York metropolitan area. The study is a randomized, controlled trial comparing the outcome of IPT-A with that of mental health treatment as it is usually provided at the school-based health clinics. We selected school-based health clinics as the setting for the study because they provide an alternative and uniquely available setting to provide care to adolescents, particularly in the current health care climate, in which services are increasingly costly and difficult to obtain. The Methods for Epidemiology of Child and Adolescent Mental Disorders (MECA) study demonstrated that schools were the most common setting in which adolescents received mental health services (Leaf et al., 1996). Recently published results of a multisite epidemiological study indicate that school-based health clinics differ from more traditional mental health centers with respect to adolescent utilization in several relevant and important ways (Wu et al., 1999). Firstly, children with depressive disorders are as likely as children with disruptive disorders to receive school-based mental health services. This is not the case for treatment utilization in mental health treatment settings outside of the school, where children with disruptive disorders are more likely to receive treatment. Secondly, demographic and parental factors are less likely to affect children's use of school-based mental health services than their use of mental health services in settings outside the school. Through this study we are hoping to gain further support for not only the effectiveness but also the generalizability, feasibility, and cost-effectiveness of delivering IPT-A in a real-world setting.

Therapist Training

With respect to training in IPT-A, half of the therapists (social workers or psychologists) at each school site were randomized to deliver IPT-A. The other therapists served as the "treatment as usual" clinicians. Because most participating sites have only two therapists, typically one therapist from each site is trained in IPT-A. The IPT-A training is a scaled-down version of the training used in the controlled clinical trial in light of the time constraints imposed by working in a community setting. Although the didactic component remained the same, the practicum was eliminated. At the completion of this training, each therapist began to receive weekly supervision on actual study cases; there were therefore no real training cases. Supervision was provided in both group and individual formats depending on the school site. During supervision, actual cases were reviewed in great detail and techniques were introduced through role-playing exercises. Given that the study was conducted in a community setting, taping of sessions was not permitted; thus, supervision was based upon therapist session notes.

Design and Methodology

Subjects

Adolescents from five urban schools (three middle schools and two high schools) were recruited for the project. Adolescents were between the ages of 12 and 18. Given the population served by the school sites for the projects, the majority of adolescents were of minority descent, with over 70% Latino and over 20% African American participation. The majority of adolescents' family would be characterized as having low socioeconomic status.

Procedures

Adolescents who were referred to the mental health clinicians in their school's clinic for any reason were screened for the project by one of the school-based clinicians who received training in the administration of a semistructured interview for depression (HRSD) and a measure of global functioning (CGAS). All clinicians in each of the schools received training in the administration of these measures. Adolescents who received a HRSD score of 10 or above and a CGAS score of 65 or below were eligible for further evaluation for the study. These evaluations included assessments of clinical diagnosis, symptomatology, clinical status, functioning, problem-solving skills, parent–child relationships, treatment utilization, and school performance.

Once clinicians determined that the adolescents were eligible for the project and had, along with their parents, consented to treatment, the subjects were randomized to one of two treatment modalities—IPT-A or treatment as usual—and were assigned to the relevant school-based clinician. IPT-A consists of 12 individual sessions. The first eight sessions are delivered weekly, and the final four sessions are delivered over the course of the next 8 weeks at the most appropriate frequency for the particular adolescent. This provides the therapist with the option of tapering from an acute treatment to more of a maintenance model toward the end of treatment. Treatment as usual consists of whatever the typical treatment at that clinic is: It could be treatment delivered in the clinic at any frequency and in any modality, including triage, crisis management, or referral to an outside community agency.

Objectives and Hypotheses

The primary objectives of this study were (a) to train school-based social workers in IPT-A and (b) to test the effectiveness of IPT-A as compared with usual care in school-based health clinics in addressing clinical symptoms, social functioning, and school performance. The secondary objectives of this particular study were (a) to improve student satisfaction with clinical services offered at the school-based clinic and (b) to create an effective treatment that would be continued in the school-based clinics at the conclusion of the study and would serve as a model for other schools.

Results

The results demonstrate the efficacy of IPT-A as compared with TAU for the treatment of adolescent depression in school-based health clinics in impoverished urban communities in New York City. Adolescents treated with IPT-A showed significant reductions in depression symptoms by both clinician and self-report, as well as significant improvement in overall functioning and in specific domains of social functioning. Depressed adolescents treated with IPT-A as compared with TAU improved faster and were significantly better by Week 8. These findings were consistent in self-ratings, independent evaluations, and clinican ratings (Mufson, Pollack Dorta, Wickramaratne, Nomura, Olfson, & Weissman, 2004).

While there were initial obstacles and protocol modifications made before implementation of the project into the schools, IPT-A as a treatment modality appears to be easily integrated into the clinic setting. Therapists were able to conduct weekly sessions for the length of an academic class with their IPT-A patients, and their session attendance was significantly better as was treatment outcome than for those students receiving usual care.

FUTURE CONSIDERATIONS

Although these initial studies of IPT-A are promising, further studies are needed to confirm the efficacy data and ensure its generalizability to other populations and settings. Examples of needed studies include (a) a comparison of interpersonal psychotherapy with medication and other active treatments for depressed adolescents (or both) and (b) a study of relapse prevention for depressed teens through the conduct of a maintenance therapy study. Currently, the treatment has been adapted for a group setting (IPT-AG; Mufson, Gallagher, Pollack Dorta, & Young, in press) and is being examined in a preliminary clinical trial. The group treatment could fill many niches both as a cost-effective treatment for an underserved population and also as a possible continuation treatment for adolescents who have made a partial recovery in the acute individual treatment but who could benefit from further interpersonal work in a group setting with peers. Lastly, to ensure the replicability of the findings, more investigations of IPT-A must be conducted by research teams other than those that developed the treatment.

REFERENCES

Aseltine, R., Gore, S., & Colten, M. (1994). Depression and the social developmental context of adolescence. *Journal of Personality and Social Psychology, 67*, 252–263.

Beck, A. T., Steer, R. A., & Garbin, M. G. (1988). Psychometric properties of the Beck Depression Inventory: Twenty-five years of evaluation. *Clinical Psychology Review, 8*, 77–100.

Brent, D. A., Holder, D., Kolko, D., Birmaher, B., Baugher, M., Roth, C., et al. (1997). A clinical psychotherapy trial for adolescent depression comparing cognitive, family, and supportive therapy. *Archives of General Psychiatry, 54*, 877–885.

Chambers, W. J., Puig-Antich, J., Hirsch, M., Paez, P., Ambrosini, P. J., Tabrizi, M. A., et al. The assessment of affective disorders in children and adolescents by semi-structured interview. *Archives of General Psychiatry, 42*, 696–702.

Clarke, G. N., Hawkins, W., Murphy, M., Sheeber, L. B., Lewinsohn, P. M., & Seeley, J. R. (1995). Targeted prevention of unipolar depressive disorder in an at-risk sample of high school adolescents: A randomized trial of a group cognitive intervention. *Journal of the American Academy of Child and Adolescent Psychiatry, 34*, 312–321.

DiMascio, A., Klerman, G. L., Weissman, M. M., Prusoff, B. A., Neu, C., & Moore, P. (1979). A control group for psychotherapy research in acute depression: One solution to ethical and methodological issues. *Journal of Psychiatric Research, 15*, 189–197.

Elkin, I., Shea, M. T., Watkins, J. T., Imber, S. D., Sotsky, S. M., Collins, J. F., et al. (1989). National Institute of Mental Health Treatment of Depression Collaborative Research Program: General effectiveness of treatments. *Archives of General Psychiatry, 45*, 971–983.

Emslie, G. J., Rush, A. J., Weinburg, W. A., Kowatch, R. A., Hughes, C. W., Carmody, T., et al. (1997). A double-blind randomized, placebo-controlled trial of fluoxetine in children and adolescents with depression. *Archives of General Psychiatry, 54*, 1031–1037.

Erikson, E. H. (1968). *Identity, youth, and crisis.* New York: Norton.

Goldfried, M., & Wolfe, B. (1998). Toward a more clinically valid approach to therapy research. *Journal of Consulting and Clinical Psychology, 66*, 143–150.

Hammen, C. (1999). The emergence of an interpersonal approach to depression. In T. Joiner & J. Coyne (Eds.), *The interactional nature of depression: Advances in interpersonal approaches* (pp. 22–36). Washington, DC: American Psychological Association.

Hersen, M., & Van Hasselt, V. B. (1987). *Behavior therapy with children and adolescents: A clinical approach.* New York: Wiley.

Hoagwood, K., Hibbs, E., Brent, D., & Jensen, P. (1995). Introduction to the special section: Efficacy and effectiveness in studies of child and adolescent psychotherapy. *Journal of Consulting and Clinical Psychology, 63*, 683–687.

Jacobson, G., & Jacobson, D. S. (1987). Impact of marital dissolution on adults and children: The significance of loss and continuity. In J. Bloom-Feshbach & S. Bloom-Feshbach (Eds.), *The psychology of separation and loss: Perspective on development, life transitions, and clinical practice* (pp. 316–344). San Francisco: Jossey-Bass.

Joiner, T., Coyne, J., & Blalock, J. (1999). On the interpersonal nature of depression: Overview and synthesis. In T. Joiner & J. Coyne (Eds.), *The interactional nature of depression: Advances in interpersonal approaches* (pp. 3–20). Washington, DC: American Psychological Association.

Kaslow, N. J., & Thompson, M. P. (1998). Applying the criteria for empirically supported treatments to studies of psychosocial interventions for child and adolescent depression. *Journal of Clinical Child Psychology, 27*(2), 146–155.

Keller, M. B., Ryan, N. D., Strober, M., Klein, R. G., Kutcher, S. P., Birmaher, B., et al. (2001). Efficacy of paroxetine in the treatment of adolescent major depression: A randomized, controlled study. *Journal of the American Academy of Child and Adolescent Psychiatry, 40*, 762–772.

Klerman, G., Weissman, M. M., Rounsaville, B., & Chevron, E. (1984). *Interpersonal psychotherapy of depression.* New York: Basic Books.

Krupnick, J. (1984). Bereavement during childhood and adolescence. In M. Osterweis, F. Solomon, & M. Green (Eds.), *Bereavement: Reactions, consequences, and care* (pp. 99–141). Washington, DC: National Academy Press.

Leaf, P. J., Alegria, M., Cohen, P., Goodman, S. H., Horwitz, S. M., Hoven, C. W., et al. (1996). Mental health service use in the community and schools: Results from the four-community MECA study. *Journal of the American Academy of Child and Adolescent Psychiatry, 35,* 889–897.

Lewinsohn, P. M., Clarke, G. N., Hops, H., & Andrews, J. (1990). Cognitive-behavioral treatment for depressed adolescents. *Behavioral Therapy, 21,* 385–401.

Miller, D. (1974). *Adolescence: Psychology, psychopathology, psychotherapy.* Northvale, NJ: Jason Aronson.

Mufson, L., Gallagher, T., Pollack Dorta, K., & Young, J. F. (in press). Interpersonal psychotherapy for adolescent depression: Adaptation for group therapy. *American Journal of Psychotherapy.*

Mufson, L., Moreau, D., Weissman, M. M., & Klerman, G. L. (1993). *Interpersonal psychotherapy for depressed adolescents.* New York: Guilford Press.

Mufson, L., Moreau, D., Weissman, M. M., Wickramaratne, P., Martin, J., & Samoilov, A. (1994). The modification of interpersonal psychotherapy with depressed adolescents IPT-A: Phase I and Phase II studies. *Journal of the American Academy of Child and Adolescent Psychiatry, 33,* 695–705.

Mufson, L., Pollack Dorta, K., Moreau D., Weissman, M. M. (2004a). Interpersonal psychotherapy for depressed adolescents. *Archives of General Psychiatry, 61,* 577–584.

Mufson, L., Pollack Dorta, K., Wickramaratne, P., Nomura, Y., Olfson, M., & Weissman, M. M. (2004b). The effectiveness of interpersonal psychotherapy for depressed adolescents. *Archives of General Psychiatry, 45,* 742–747.

Mufson, L., Weissman, M. M., Moreau, D., & Garfinkel, R. (1999). Efficacy of interpersonal psychotherapy for depressed adolescents. *Archives of General Psychiatry, 56,* 573–579.

Puig-Antich, J., Lukens, E., Davies, M., Goetz, D., Brennan-Quattrock, J., & Todak, G. (1985). The psychological functioning and family environment of depressed adolescents. *Archives of General Psychiatry, 42,* 500–507.

Puig-Antich, J., Kaufman, J., Ryan, N. D., Williamson, D. E., Dahl, R. E., Lukens, E., et al. (1993). The psychosocial functioning and family environment of depressed adolescents. *Journal of the American Academy of Child and Adolescent Psychiatry 32,* 244–253.

Raphael, B. (1983). *The anatomy of bereavement.* New York: Basic Books.

Rossello, J., & Bernal, G. (1999). The efficacy of cognitive–behavioral and international treatments of depression in Puerto Rican adolescents. *Journal of Consulting and Clinical Psychology, 67* (5), 734–745.

Stader, S., & Hokanson, J. (1998). Psychological antecedents of depressive symptoms: An evaluation using daily experiences methodology. *Journal of Abnormal Psychology, 107,* 17–26.

Weissman, M. M., Prusoff, B. A., DiMascio, A., Neu, C., Goklaney, M., & Klerman, G. L. (1979). The efficacy of drug and psychotherapy in the treatment of acute depressive episodes. *American Journal of Psychiatry, 136,* 555–558.

Weissman, M. M., Markowitz, J. C., & Klerman, G. L. (2000). *Comprehensive guide to interpersonal psychotherapy*. Albany, NY: Basic Books.

Weissman, M. M., Rounsaville, B. J., & Chevron, E. (1982). Training psychotherapists to participate in psychotherapy outcome studies: Identifying and dealing with the research requirements. *American Journal of Psychiatry, 139,* 1442–1446.

Williams, J. B. (1988). A structured interview guide for the Hamilton Depression Rating Scales. *Archives of General Psychiatry, 45,* 742–747.

Wu, P., Hoven, C., Bird, H., Cohen, P., Alegria, M., Dulcan, M., et al. (1999). Depressive and disruptive disorders and mental health service utilization in children and adolescents. *Journal of the American Academy of Child and Adolescent Psychiatry, 38,* 1081–1092.

9

NEW DEVELOPMENTS IN COGNITIVE–BEHAVIORAL AND INTERPERSONAL TREATMENTS FOR DEPRESSED PUERTO RICAN ADOLESCENTS

JEANNETTE ROSSELLÓ AND GUILLERMO BERNAL

Latinos now number 38.8 million in the United States (excluding another 3.8 million in Puerto Rico). Latinos in the continental United States are estimated to represent 13% of the population (U.S. Census Bureau, 2002). Between 1989 and 1990, the Latino population grew eight times faster than the non-Latino White population. Latinos are now the largest minority group in the United States. But despite advances in understanding and treating youth with mental disorders in recent years, little is known about the effect of such interventions on Latinos. Overall, ethnic minorities have grown in number over the last decade. Racial minorities make up more

Preparation of this chapter was supported in part by the National Institute of Mental Health Grant (MH 49368) and Fondos Institucionales para la Investigación (FIPI) from the University of Puerto Rico, Río Piedras Campus. Correspondence concerning this chapter may be addressed to Jeannette Rosselló: Department of Psychology, Centro Universitario de Servicios y Estudios Psicológicos (CUSEP), PO Box 23174, San Juan, PR 00931.

than 25% of the population (U.S. Census Bureau, 2001). By the year 2050, minority youth between 5 and 17 years of age will constitute over 80% of the nation's youth population (U.S. Census Bureau, 1999). Minority youth is a population at risk for mental health problems because of low socioeconomic conditions, stressful life events associated with poverty, and the lack of accessible mental health services (Casas, 1995; Ho, 1992). When minorities do have access to services, they seem to be inappropriate (Acosta, Yamamoto, & Evans, 1982; Aponte, Rivers, & Wahl, 1995; Dana, 1993; Ghali, 1977; Smith, Burlew, Mosley, & Whitney, 1978). Sue (1977) found that Asians and Hispanics were underrepresented in mental health centers. Ethnic minority clients had a higher drop out rate (50%) than White clients (30%).

The underrepresentation of minorities in mental health services may be explained by a failure on the therapist's part to provide culturally appropriate forms of treatment (Sue & Zane, 1987). These authors report that the most frequent reason minority patients drop out of treatment is a negative reaction to the therapist. To simply apply therapeutic interventions created for White, middle-class Anglo Americans to minorities without considering language, cultural, and socioeconomic issues is not effective (American Psychological Association [APA], 1990; Aponte, 1990; Canino & Spurlock, 1994; Dana, 1993; Ho, 1992; Szapocznik, Scopetta, & Aranalde, 1978; Sue & Zane, 1987). Researchers have identified an increasing demand for efficient treatment for ethnic minorities (Cross, Bazron, Dennis, & Isaacs, 1989).

The role of culture and ethnicity has been an important consideration of clinicians from different theoretical positions (Mays & Albee, 1992; Tharp, 1991). A variety of cultural models for individual psychotherapy (Comas-Díaz & Griffith, 1988; Jones & Korchin, 1982) and family therapies (McGoldrick, Pearce, & Giordano, 1982) have been proposed. Other writers have developed culturally sensitive frameworks (Bernal, Bonilla, & Bellido, 1995; Lopez et al., 1989) to inform clinicians of cultural and minority issues in conducting psychotherapy.

Despite important clinical advances in the consideration of cultural and ethnic minority issues for a wide range of psychotherapies, treatment research has not kept pace with these developments. Most treatment outcome research concerning adults and children is not generalizable to ethnic minority populations. In fact, treatment outcome research concerning minority populations is almost absent. The literature shows few studies that include minority participants (Mays & Albee, 1992) and even fewer studies that include Hispanics (Bernal & Scharrón del Río, 2001). Researchers need to adapt, develop, and test treatment approaches that show empirical promise with the inclusion of minority populations.

This chapter offers clinical guidelines for the treatment of Puerto Rican adolescents with depression through the presentation of work aimed at adapting and testing two promising treatments. The adaptations of cognitive–behavioral therapy (CBT) and interpersonal psychotherapy treatment (IPT) for depression followed ecological validity and culturally sensitive criteria (Bernal et al., 1995). In the following pages, we present a brief description of the problem of depression in Puerto Rico, followed by the guidelines and process used in the adaptation of the two treatments. Next, we present the basic steps employed in both CBT and IPT. Finally, the chapter closes with a description of our research findings about the efficacy of the two treatment interventions.

DEPRESSION IN PUERTO RICAN CHILDREN AND ADOLESCENTS

Nationally representative epidemiological studies of depression in the U.S. adolescent population have not been reported in the literature (Petersen et al., 1993). Therefore, no reference exists on the incidence of depression among adolescents that compares ethnic groups and social classes.

However, epidemiological data have revealed that depression among children and adolescents is not as rare as previously thought by investigators (Kanner, 1972; Rie, 1966). Given the different definitions of depression in youth, measurement instruments (self-report, interview), and samples studied (clinical, community, age ranges, sex, special education groups), prevalence figures vary widely. The prevalence rates of depression range from between 1% and 2% among children and adolescents when the *Diagnostic and Statistical Manual of Mental Disorders, Third Edition* (DSM–III) criteria are used to 1.3% to 52.4% when self-report depression scales are used (Albert & Beck, 1975; Chien & Change, 1985; Fleming, Offord, & Boyle, 1989; Gibbs, 1985; Kandel & Davies, 1982; Kaplan, Hong, & Weenhold, 1984; Kashani, Holcomb, & Orvaschel, 1986; Kashani & Simonds, 1979; Reynolds, 1983; Schoenback, Kaplan, Grimson, & Wagner, 1982; Siegel & Griffin, 1984; Sullivan & Elgin, 1986; Teri, 1982; Weinberg & Emslie, 1988; Wells, Klerman, & Deykin, 1987).

An epidemiological study in Puerto Rico estimated a prevalence of 5.9% of depression and dysthymia among children 4- to 16-years-old, using DSM–III criteria in combination with the Children's Global Assessment Scale (Bird et al., 1988). Depression was found to be the third most frequent disorder in Puerto Rican children (after oppositional and attention deficit disorders). Bird's study also revealed that 15% of the Puerto Rican population in this age group manifests moderate to severe psychopathology. In numerical terms, this means that between 125,000 and 150,000 children need professional services. Because fewer than 10,000 individual children received mental health services as reported by the Puerto Rican Division of Mental Health (during the time the study was conducted), the authors concluded that there is a "major public health problem in the treatment of mental disorders for children in Puerto Rico" (Bird et al., 1988, p. 1126).

Because oppositional and attention deficit disorders may mask or coexist with depressive characteristics (Carlson & Cantwell, 1980), the importance of the study of depression and its treatment in the Puerto Rican youth population becomes even more significant. As we mentioned earlier, the need to adapt, develop, and test treatments that show positive empirical results with other populations and hold promise as therapeutic interventions is critical.

ADAPTATIONS OF THE TREATMENTS TO THE PUERTO RICAN CONTEXT

The present project is an attempt to contribute to the development of effective interventions for depression in Puerto Rican adolescents. Drawing upon the adult treatment outcome literature for depression as a starting point, the authors selected two psychosocial treatment approaches. For theoretical and practical reasons CBT and IPT, which have shown to be effective with adults, were adapted to the Puerto Rican adolescent population. Developmental, cognitive, linguistic, and cultural factors were considered in the translation and adaptation of these therapeutic modalities.

One question in developing cultural sensitivity is when to apply specific norms versus universal norms for a particular cultural group. This issue is known as the *etic–emic conflict*. Draguns (1981) has defined *etic* as the universal norms and *emic* as the group-specific norms. Lopez et al. (1989) have proposed that cultural sensitivity is the "ability to entertain both etic and emic views within the context of the individual" (p. 375). According to our experience, some dimensions must be culturally adapted in a way that is specific to Puerto Rican adolescents whereas others are more universal or generic and could therefore apply to other adolescents as well.

In the treatment of culturally diverse populations, ecological validity is an important aspect to consider (Bernal et al., 1995). This phrase refers to the congruence between the client's experience, embedded in his or her ethnic context, and the properties of that treatment assumed by the clinician or investigator. Therefore, the ecological validity of a therapeutic intervention is related to its cultural sensitivity: What is implicit for one normative group must be explicit for another. This understanding has motivated the development of culturally sensitive treatments (McGoldrick et al, 1982; Rogler, Malgady, Rodríguez, & Bumenthal, 1987; Tharp, 1991).

Using the framework of cultural sensitivity developed by Bernal et al. (1995), the authors adapted the treatment manuals for Puerto Rican adolescents. This framework identifies the following eight elements or dimensions, which must be considered to guarantee ecological validity: language, persons, metaphors, content, concepts, goals, methods, and context. In addition, developmental, technical, and theoretical issues were considered in the adaptation process.

Language

The language used in therapy must be culturally appropriate and syntonic. Because language is often the carrier of the culture, a treatment delivered in the language of the target population assumes an integration of culture. The matching of ethnic backgrounds increases the therapist's cultural knowledge of the client and thus augments his or her credibility (Sue & Zane, 1987), which in turn may contribute to treatment effectiveness. In our project, since treatment was carried out in Spanish by native Spanish-speaking therapists to native Spanish-speaking patients, the criterion of a language appropriate intervention was met.

Although the CBT manual was originally in Spanish, adaptations were made in the Spanish language itself to make it syntonic with the Puerto Rican manner of speech. Through case studies (Rosselló, 1993), language was evaluated and adapted to the populations. Words, phrases, or concepts that were not understood by test cases were changed. School personnel, graduate and undergraduate students, and expert translators were consulted. Language more appropriate to adolescents was introduced. For example, throughout the manual, the informal (*tú*) rather than the formal (*usted*) manner of speech is used in reference to the adolescents. The informal form of language serves to reduce interpersonal distance and is more characteristic of Caribbean Spanish. Alternatively, when parents are addressed, the formal form is replaced as a means of acknowledgment of parental authority and respect for the parents' position. Also, words in the original manual were simplified to clarify concepts. For example: "*Porque rompí este vaso soy una* nulidad" ("Because I broke this glass I am worthless"). The word *nulidad*, although conceptually equivalent to "worthless," is too sophisticated to be understood by the average adolescent. It was changed to: "*Porque rompí este vaso no sirvo para nada*" ("Because I broke this glass I am not worth anything"), which is the conceptual equivalent of *nulidad* and a simpler version of the same idea.

The IPT manual was originally in English and was first translated into Spanish. The manual reminds therapists to keep the language simple in the sessions so that adolescents will be able to understand the concepts presented in therapy. We substituted examples and illustrative cases appropriate to our population and context (Rosselló, 1993; Rosselló, Guisasola, Ralat, Martínez, & Nieves, 1992). These examples and case studies were used in the therapists' training.

Persons

Persons refers to the role that racial and ethnic similarities play in the shaping of the therapy relationship. Research supports the notion of culturally matching therapist–client psychotherapy dyads (Tyler, Brome, &

Williams, 1991). In our project, therapists were sensitized during training and supervision to socioeconomic, racial, and cultural aspects and encouraged to accept different ways of living as valid. Puerto Rican therapists delivered treatment to Puerto Rican adolescents. However, socioeconomic and racial differences were likely to surface in certain dyads, and these differences were to be discussed and accepted. In the adaptation of the intervention models, flexibility was allowed to accommodate different solutions, alternatives, and examples of the contents to be presented.

Metaphors

Metaphors refers to the use of symbols and concepts shared by the cultural group. The manual incorporates suggestions made by Muñoz and Miranda (1982) and Zuñiga (1992). On entering the waiting room and office, adolescents and their parents were greeted by objects and symbols of Puerto Rican adolescent culture. Posters with positive Puerto Rican role models and messages are also recommended. In addition, culturally consonant ideas, sayings, and images served as metaphors in the therapy to communicate ideas more effectively (Muñoz & Miranda, 1982; Zuñiga, 1992).

Content

Content refers to cultural knowledge and information about values, customs, and traditions. The literature has identified some of these values and traditions, such as familism, *respeto*, *simpatía*, personal space, parental authority, and present-time orientation, among others.

We considered these content issues equally for both CBT and IPT. For example, familism is one of the strongest cultural values held by Puerto Ricans and Hispanics in general (Rogler et al., 1987; Sabogal, Marín, & Otero-Sabogal, 1987). It refers to a strong identification with and attachment to the family, with strong feelings of solidarity, loyalty, and reciprocity. The family is considered the most important unit for meeting psychological needs and enhancing the identity and emotional security of its members. Even in the midst of poverty, discrimination, racism, and isolation, minority families survive and handle problems (Smith et al., 1978). Familism promotes psychological adjustment by protecting against stressors and providing a natural support system (Mannino & Shore, 1976). Therefore, familism is a dimension that has to be evaluated. Issues of family obligation, support, and self-esteem also must be evaluated. The therapist should be sensitive to the values of familism and try to strengthen its positive aspects. Conflicts and aggression within the family receive priority as a content issue to be dealt with in therapy. Because Puerto Rican adolescents depend on their parents for solutions, alternatives, and even transportation to attend therapy sessions, parents are interviewed before and after the therapy in a climate of utmost respect. If needed, therapists are allowed to discuss issues related to treatment with parents individually or together with the adolescent. The adolescent's confidentiality must be guaranteed and explained to both parents and adolescents.

Because Puerto Rican parents often adopt cultural values of absolute parental authority and respect, the period of dependence on parents is somewhat longer in the Puerto Rican culture (as compared to mainstream Anglo American culture). Therapists need to be aware of these values and address such issues in ancillary meetings with parents. The issues of family dependence and interdependence have to be understood.

In one case, the mother of an adolescent male told us she was withdrawing her son from therapy as a punishment for a drop in his grades. A meeting with the mother helped clarify the reasons for the lower grades and the objectives of the therapy. This subject was discussed in an atmosphere of respect so that the mother did not feel that her authority was being threatened or questioned.

In another case, parents of an adolescent boy were extremely overprotective of their son because an older son had drug-related problems. The younger son was permitted to go only to school and could not attend any activities or have any friends. Without affecting the family unit, the therapist respectfully explored alternatives with the parents and the adolescent. After-school karate classes seemed to be acceptable to all.

Therapists meet with parents and the adolescent before the first session begins. This gives the therapist one open session to explore in detail the adolescent's condition within the family context and initiate the building of rapport with the adolescent and parents.

Concepts

Concepts refers to a consonance with the culture and context and the ways that constructs are used within the intervention model. The underlying concepts of CBT and IPT were examined within the concepts and belief systems of the Puerto Rican culture. Congruence was established, with a focus on present orientation and in the interpersonal components of both therapeutic models. These two factors make these constructs consonant to Puerto Rican cultural concepts. Family dependence and interdependence also were considered and integrated in both therapies.

Goals

The therapist and client must agree to the goals of treatment; the establishment of such goals is an important dimension of the framework. In our adaptation of the models, these goals must be defined within the first session for CBT and within the first four sessions for IPT. Parents' goals are also considered and evaluated.

Methods

The procedures for achieving the goals defined in the treatment are another dimension of the framework. Creating culturally sensitive methods requires incorporating cultural knowledge into the treatment procedures. As previously explained, the family unit is a very important component of Puerto Rican culture, one that can be incorporated into both treatment models as needed. We have found that depression in Puerto Rican teens tends to manifest itself as a struggle to find an acceptable balance among dependence, interdependence, and independence. Defining this balance is part of the therapy and may involve the participation of parents or other family members before and after the 12 sessions and during some of the sessions if necessary. The short-term nature and present-time orientation of both the CBT and the IPT models are also consonant with the Puerto Rican culture, wherein long-term commitments to therapy are difficult to achieve.

Context

Context includes elements such as daily stress, developmental stages, and availability of social support. The social, economic, and political context of the presenting problem is considered. A very large percentage of the Puerto Rican population meets the criteria for poverty level. This economic reality must be considered in both treatment models. Therapists are trained to identify available resources in the community, such as free after-school programs or classes, organizations that support youth employment, and health services.

Developmental Issues

In our adaptation of the CBT model, examples of the different types of thoughts—specifically misguided or pessimistic thinking—were selected from actual thoughts of Puerto Rican adolescents identified in a pilot study (Rosselló, 1993). Therapists were encouraged to use examples from the intake interview to tailor the material to each adolescent. Exercise materials were revised to make homework assignments more relevant to adolescents. One such assignment entails making a list of negative thoughts and another list of enjoyable activities. Some examples of thoughts taken from these assignments are as follows: "If I don't do well in school, I'm a failure"; "I can't concentrate, so I'm stupid." Some pleasant activities that our adolescents identified include going to the shopping mall or to the movies, cooking, and playing with their pets.

Some teens resist doing the homework or assigned exercises. To deal with this reluctance, the therapist can choose between two alternatives:

Either explore with the client the negative thoughts related to the home-work (e.g., "This is not going to help me."), or do the homework with the adolescent at the beginning of the session. We found that Puerto Rican adolescents reacted positively to role-playing exercises.

For the IPT model the manual was revised to present situations that would be relevant and typical of adolescents. The original manual included examples that applied mostly to adults. We replaced these with examples gathered from the Puerto Rican adolescent population. For example, cases from our population were used in the adaptation of the manual to illustrate the following four problem areas: grief, interpersonal disputes, role transitions, and interpersonal deficits. The following is an example of how we used a case story to illustrate the problem areas grief and interpersonal problems:

> A 15-year-old female came to us after having been adopted by her aunt and uncle because her mother couldn't raise her. Her adoptive mother was sick with terminal brain cancer and had deteriorated rapidly, to the point that she could no longer identify the people around her. For the client this represented a loss of her relationship with her adoptive mother, an obviously meaningful bond that seemed related to the client's depressive symptoms. During the course of therapy, the adoptive mother died, and a process of mourning as well as role transition were addressed in the subsequent sessions.

For both models, therapists were trained to speak in terms that the adolescent could understand and give concrete examples of the principles and ideas communicated in the sessions. Some adolescents may have more limited skills in abstract thinking, verbal knowledge, psychological awareness, and capacity to form a therapeutic relationship.

As a result of their age and dependence on their parents, some adolescents are brought into therapy without their consent. This fact is evaluated and addressed in both therapies.

Both models permit one session before the start of therapy for the adolescent or parents (or both) to work on motivational issues and establish a rapport with the therapist.

Practical–Technical Issues

Because the CBT model is based on a group format, we had to adapt it to an individual treatment modality. Such an individual modality concentrates more on the adolescent's particular problems and on his or her experiences, thoughts, actions, and relationships as examples for the material that is to be taught and presented. Because adolescents usually do not like to be lectured or treated as though they were in school, we designed the model to be more interactive between the therapist and the adolescent. At the beginning of each session, the therapist may devote time to the adolescent's free expression of feelings or reports of what has changed or happened since the last session.

The IPT manual establishes a hypothetical 16-session schedule. We adapted the number of sessions to 12, making both IPT and CBT treatments equivalent in length of sessions.

Theoretical Issues

The IPT manual utilizes the concept of the "sick role" as part of its interpersonal conceptualization of depression. The medical model's definition of the sick role did not seem compatible with the psychosocial nature of IPT. We eliminated this notion from the IPT manual to help adolescents assume more responsibility for their interpersonal relationships and the therapy itself. The sick-role concept had negative implications for the adolescent's self-esteem and evaluations.

DESCRIPTION OF THE PSYCHOTHERAPEUTIC APPROACHES

The two psychotherapeutic approaches adapted for the treatment of depression in Puerto Rican adolescents are summarized in the subsequent pages. For a more detailed description of the treatments and case studies, refer to the original manuals (Muñoz & Miranda, 1982) or the revised manuals in Spanish (Rosselló, 1993, 1994).

Cognitive–Behavioral Therapy

The CBT model is based on the cognitive–behavioral model developed by Muñoz and Miranda (1982). This model is a group intervention for depressed adults and has been used with an adult Hispanic population in the San Francisco area. It is based on concepts of CBT (Lewinsohn & Libet, 1972; Lewinsohn, 1975, 1976; Lewinsohn, Antonuccio, Steinmetz, & Teri, 1984), cognitive therapy (Beck, Rush, Shaw, & Emery, 1979), and rational–emotive therapy (Ellis, 1962, 1983). CBT is based on the relationship between thoughts, actions, and feelings. To work with depressive feelings, this model attempts to identify those thoughts and actions that influence these feelings. The primary goals of this therapy are to diminish depressive feelings, shorten the time that the person feels depressed, teach alternative ways of preventing depression, and increase the person's sense of control over his or her life.

CBT is a short-term intervention consisting of 12 weekly sessions. The sessions are divided into the following three major themes: How thoughts influence mood (Sessions 1–4); how daily activities influence mood

(Sessions 5–8); and how interactions with other people affect mood (Sessions 9–12).

Working With Cognitions (Sessions 1–4)

The structure and purpose of the therapy are established in the initial session. The therapist discusses scheduling weekly appointments and maintaining confidentiality. The therapist asks the adolescent about his or her problems and emotions, explaining that the teen will learn alternative ways to control feelings and deal with depression. The specific goals in treatment are made explicit: to reduce feelings of depression, to shorten the periods of depression, to learn new ways of preventing depression, and to develop more control over one's life. The therapist reviews the definition of depression and describes its symptoms, which should lead to a discussion of how the adolescent has been feeling and which symptoms apply to his or her experience. The teen is asked to elaborate on his or her feelings about depression. The therapist facilitates a discussion of how thoughts can affect mood. The therapist may define *thoughts* as "things we tell ourselves" and give examples of how thoughts affect body, actions, and mood. The adolescent may provide his or her own examples, or the therapist may provide them on the basis of what he or she already knows about the adolescent. This session ends with the introduction of "The Daily Mood Scale," which provides a scale to select the mood that characterizes each day of the week (best, very good, good, better than average, average, worse than average, low, very low, worst). The adolescent is asked to fill out the scale every day of the following week and to bring it to the next session. The purpose of this exercise is to help the adolescent identify his or her mood and its fluctuations throughout the week.

During the next three sessions, the focus of treatment is on cognitions. Depressed thinking is defined as inflexible and judgmental, whereas nondepressed thinking is changeable, specific, and hopeful.

The adolescent is also taught to identify types of thinking:

1. Constructive versus destructive thinking
2. Necessary versus unnecessary thinking
3. Positive versus negative thinking

Positive thoughts reflect optimism and hope, making the person feel better (e.g., "Although I'm the youngest and least experienced member of the team, I will try to do my best in the game."). Negative thinking makes the person feel worse (e.g., "All the other players are better than me. I will never be able to make it."). To convey the importance of positive thinking, a Puerto Rican saying is used: *"Todo se ve a través del cristal con que se mira."*

The therapist explains to the adolescent the ways in which negative or pessimistic thinking exacerbates depressive feelings. Definitions and examples of 10 thinking errors are given and discussed: "All or none" thinking (e.g., seeing one example of something bad and concluding that everything will be bad); mental filters; discounting the positive; jumping to conclusions (e.g., mind-reading and fortune-telling); making more or less of a situation than is appropriate; taking feelings too seriously; labeling; and self-blame. To help the adolescent identify errors in thinking, the therapist assigns exercises to be carried out during the week.

By the third session, the therapist introduces techniques to increase healthy thinking and decrease unhealthy thinking. Teens are encouraged to increase the number of good thoughts they have about themselves, to recognize and take credit for the good things they do, to take time for relaxation, and to make projections to a time when things will be better. To decrease negative thoughts, the therapist suggests the following activities: practice thought-stopping exercises, set up a specific time to worry that lasts no longer than 30 minutes a day, make fun of problems by exaggerating them, consider the worst that could happen, and be your own coach. The therapist then makes a connection between these activities and the adolescent's own thoughts.

Pleasant Activities (Sessions 5–8)

In Sessions 5 through 8, the adolescent is introduced to the following concept: The fewer pleasant activities people do, the more depressed they feel. The vicious cycle that ensues between depression and activities is explained as follows: The less you do, the more depressed you feel; the more depressed you feel, the less you do. To break this cycle, the depressed person must increase pleasant activities. To this end, the therapist and teen compile a list of activities that the teen finds pleasant, rewarding, or inspiring.

The therapist then asks the adolescent to consider different activities in his or her community that do not necessarily involve spending money and identify obstacles to these activities. The therapist explains two ways to deal with obstacles: making a contract and "pleasure predicting." The therapist tells the adolescent that it isn't necessary to wait until he or she feels like doing something; the teen can choose to do something and then do it. Activities can be enjoyable even when a person does not think they will be.

Another aspect of pleasant activities entails creating a plan to overcome depression: setting reasonable goals, noticing positive accomplishments, and planning rewards. Goals should be clear, concrete, and realistic. The therapist presents examples of goals. For instance, an unclear goal is "to be less bored on weekends." A clear goal is "to go to the movies on Sunday afternoon."

The adolescent is asked to define his or her goals and the obstacles blocking them. The therapist explains the concept of short-term, long-term, and life goals and introduces an exercise on time management: The teen makes a list of what he or she wants to accomplish the following week and assigns priorities to each goal. The adolescent learns to schedule the high-priority goals and pleasant activities into his or her weekly plans.

Contacts With People (Sessions 9–12)

The last four sessions focus on the ways in which human contact affects mood. The therapist discusses whether depression causes people to be less sociable or whether being less sociable causes depression in people. Both statements are likely to be true because each element affects the other. The therapist also discusses the importance of social support. A support system is defined as the network of people a person has available; it could include family, friends, neighbors, teachers, teammates, and acquaintances. The stronger the social support system, the better and easier it is to face tough situations.

The therapist then asks the adolescent to describe his or her support system. The therapist suggests that if the support system is weak, strengthening or enlarging it will help. If the support system is adequate, finding a way to maintain its strength is important.

The therapist encourages the adolescent to reflect on his or her thoughts, expectations, behavior, and feelings when in the company of other people. Expectations may also facilitate or impede positive relationships. If expectations are too high, disappointment and frustration will probably follow. If expectations are too low, the relationship may not be getting a fair chance.

The therapist examines the actions of the adolescent in his or her personal relationships. The therapist then explores how the adolescent feels when interacting with others, emphasizing the importance of recognizing one's feelings and learning to communicate these feelings appropriately. The therapist teaches ways to be more assertive by leading the teen through a visualization exercise in which he or she imagines the scene as though it were a photograph, imagines the action starting as if it were a movie, imagines himself or herself saying something assertively, and imagines the response.

In the closing session, concepts from previous sessions are reviewed. The therapist explains the importance of social contacts, such as how they can help increase rewarding experiences, support one's personal values, provide companionship and a sense of stability, and serve as a reflection of one's own image. Finally, the therapist evaluates the adolescent's progress over the course of the 12-session treatment and shares his or her recommendations with the adolescent.

Clinical Vignette

Angela is a 14-year-old girl. She and her two younger sisters live with both of their parents, who work full time. When we met her, Angela had recently been moved to a new, more demanding school. She was referred to our project by the social worker at this new school, who had observed a marked decrease in her academic performance and her participation in school activities.

Upon initial evaluation, Angela presented a depressed affect and expressed feelings of unworthiness and hopelessness. She also spoke of a recurrent desire to end her life. These symptoms seemed to result from a stressful school transition and difficulty communicating with her parents, especially her father.

Angela was randomly assigned to the CBT method, and she attended all 12 therapy sessions. During the first four sessions, Angela and her therapist identified the following thoughts that related to Angela's depression: "I will never be anything in the future"; "I used to be intelligent, now I am not"; "I'm stupid"; "Nothing is going right." Angela became aware of the multiple thoughts that were affecting her mood and deterring her from improving her performance. She also worked with the following thought: "When I feel a lot of pressure from my parents about my academic work, I have considered that I would be better off dead." Through the use of the mood thermometer and the ABCD (Activating event, Beliefs, Consequence, Debate) method, Angela was able to relate her thoughts to her depression and analyze her errors and inflexible thinking, thus creating alternative, more positive thoughts.

Over the course of the following four sessions, Angela continued working with her thoughts. During that time she learned that her best friends were leaving the island. Her thoughts about losing her friends were as follows: "I will always be alone…. I will never have friends again." Angela was able to understand that she could stay in contact with her friends and that she had the ability to make new friends or get closer to other teens at school and in her neighborhood. She also continued working with the thoughts that she was no good and that her sister was more intelligent than she was. After analysis of her activities during the week, she realized that, apart from school, she was not involved in any other activities. The therapist discussed the importance of pleasant activities, and Angela said that she enjoyed playing volleyball and spending time with her pet. Angela started to incorporate these activities into her weekly schedule. She also identified her goals. Her immediate goal was to graduate from intermediate school and start high school. Her long-term goals included earning a degree from a university.

During the last four sessions, Angela was able to understand the connection between her depressed mood and her relationships with people. She talked about ways to make her family relationships better and create a larger and stronger social support system. The therapist explained assertive behavior to Angela, who was able to assume an active role in strengthening her relationships.

In the last session Angela was able to identify changes in her life and feelings. Postevaluations revealed elimination of depressive symptoms and a more positive self-concept.

Interpersonal Psychotherapy

The IPT intervention is based on the Klerman, Weissman, Rounsaville, and Chevron (1984) model, which was developed for the treatment of depressed adults. Mufson (1991) and Mufson, Moreau, Weissman, and Klerman (1993) adapted IPT to an Anglo American adolescent population based on the original model. For the purpose of this study, an adaptation and translation of the same original model was made for Puerto Rican adolescents suffering from depression. The present study began in 1991. At that time the original IPT manual (Klerman et al., 1984) and a draft of Mufson's (1991) and Mufson et al.'s (1993) adapted versions were available. We decided, however, to base our adaptation and translation solely on the original model to maintain a stronger theoretical and practical fidelity.

The IPT approach maintains that difficulties in interpersonal relationships are a strong factor in depression, so this issue is the main focus of this intervention. IPT alleviates depressive feelings by facilitating the development of healthier, more satisfying relationships. Together, the therapist and the patient (or client) evaluate and try to solve the client's current problems in his or her relationships.

IPT is a short-term psychotherapy adapted to 12 weekly sessions. Sessions are divided into three groups of four sessions each. The objectives of the initial four sessions are as follows: to obtain information about the depression and its development, to explain what IPT is, to evaluate the patient's interpersonal relationships, to identify main problems, to establish a treatment plan, and to explain what is expected of the patient in therapy. During the intermediate sessions (Sessions 5–8), the therapist helps the patient work on his or her problematic interpersonal relationships; monitors the patient's depressive feelings; facilitates a positive therapeutic relationship so that communication is maximized; and prevents the patient's parents from sabotaging treatment. The last four sessions (Sessions 9–12), oriented toward termination of treatment, address the following issues: feelings of separation upon termination of treatment, a review of the course of treatment and the patient's symptoms, and recognition of the patient's competence and new ways of coping in interpersonal contexts.

Primary Interpersonal Problem Areas

Because IPT is a short-term treatment, the therapist must identify and focus on one or two problem areas. The problem areas are categorized as grief, interpersonal disputes, role transitions, and interpersonal deficits. The problem areas identified for a given individual do not exclude each other and are usually present in combinations. The therapist may use the precipitating events (e.g., loss of a relationship, current conflicts, death of a family member) as a guide by which to define the main problem areas. The problem to be focused on may change as therapy progresses. The four main problem areas follow.

1. *Grief:* The feelings that follow the death or loss of a loved one are considered grief. If the depression is associated with grief reactions resulting from the loss of a loved one, this will be the focus of the interventions. The therapy facilitates the mourning process and helps the adolescent establish new interests and relationships to compensate for the lost one. IPT uses the following strategies to deal with grief reactions: elicitation of feelings, nonjudgmental exploration, reassurance, reconstruction of the adolescent's relationship with the lost person, development of awareness, and behavioral change.

2. *Interpersonal disputes:* These are situations in which the adolescent and at least one important person in his or her life have nonreciprocal expectations about their relationship. Although interpersonal disputes can happen with almost anyone in the adolescent's life, only those that seem related to the depression will be considered in depth. Disputes that are recurrent and continuous and seem to increase in frequency lead to loss of self-esteem, lack of control, and a threat of losing the relationship. The adolescent may feel helpless and hopeless, sensing that nothing can be done to change the situation. Generally, the most frequent role disputes in an adolescent's life occur with one or both of the parents. The treatment goals with regard to interpersonal disputes are to identify the dispute, elaborate a plan of action, encourage better communication patterns, and reassess expectations. The satisfactory resolution of an interpersonal dispute may involve a change in the expectations and behavior of the adolescent or the significant other, a more accepting attitude of the adolescent with or without attempts to satisfy needs outside the relationship, or a satisfactory dissolution of the relationship. The therapist may use the following strategies to achieve these goals: analysis and exploration of role disputes and their stages (renegotiations, impasse, and dissolution), discussion of how nonreciprocal role expectations relate to disputes and lead to or augment depression, and exploration of the adolescent's expectations, values, options, and resources. Parallels between the present problematic relationship and other

relationships may also be explored. Communication patterns and problems should be identified, and more adequate communication styles encouraged.

3. *Role transitions:* Sometimes depression in adolescents is related to life changes of some kind, which can be perceived as losses. Some examples of life changes an adolescent is likely to experience are divorce of parents, the birth of a sibling, a change in schools, parental unemployment and subsequent change in social status, immigration, and physical changes associated with puberty. Some of the issues that make it difficult to cope with role transitions are loss of familiar social support or other support systems, management of new emotions such as anger or fear, demands for new social skills, and loss of self-esteem or sense of belonging. The therapist should explore the adolescent's lifestyle and pay special attention to any recent life changes, illuminating for the patient any possible connections between these changes and his or her depression. The goals for the treatment of depression associated with role transitions are to increase self esteem and encourage a new sense of competence in the adolescent, enabling him or her to deal with the demands created by the new role. The adolescent is encouraged to perceive the new role as a positive opportunity to grow and restore self-esteem. The therapist may use any of the following strategies: encourage an examination of positive and negative aspects of the old and new roles; facilitate a realistic evaluation of what has been lost; encourage the release of affect related to the change; and explore with the adolescent the development of new social support systems and additional social skills to deal with the new role.

4. *Interpersonal deficits:* These become evident when an adolescent presents a history of poor interpersonal relationships. The adolescent may describe feelings of loneliness and severe social isolation. An interpersonal deficit may involve the absence of lasting, intimate, and satisfying relationships. IPT describes three types of interpersonal deficits: those in which patients are socially isolated, those in which patients are socially unfulfilled with the relationships they have, and those in which patients are chronically depressed. The goal of the treatment of interpersonal deficits is to reduce social isolation. The strategies are to explore past relationships and the patient–therapist relationship and to encourage the development of new relationships. The therapist may analyze communication styles and may use role-playing exercises.

Initial Phase (Sessions 1–4)

During the first four sessions, the therapist obtains a history of the depressive condition, explains the nature and objectives of IPT, makes an evaluation of the patient's interpersonal relationships and problems, identifies the main problem areas, sets a treatment contract, and informs the adolescent about the expectations of therapy. In the first session the therapist elicits from the adolescent a description of what brought him or her to therapy, a history of his or her depressive condition within an interpersonal context, and an enumeration and elaboration of the depressive symptoms. Suicidal ideation and intent are assessed. The therapist explains the relationship between the depressive phenomena and the adolescent's interpersonal functioning. The therapist offers information about IPT, explaining that most of the work will center on present events and relationships and that the focus will be on significant current relationships and relevant past ones. The emphasis of treatment is to clarify problems and search for solutions. The adolescent is told that the therapy will consist of 12 sessions that will be held once a week and is given other practical information about appointment time and cancellations. The therapist also discusses confidentiality issues. The therapist identifies the primary problem area, which can usually be categorized as a combination of the four areas previously discussed (grief, role dispute, role transition, and interpersonal deficit).

After the primary problem areas have been defined, the therapist establishes therapeutic goals. The main goal is improvement of the patient's interpersonal relationships. Symptom reduction and emotional well-being are other goals that can be accomplished as consequences of the first. The therapist and the adolescent should collaborate in setting goals and evaluating outcomes. The therapist works on developing a therapeutic alliance with the adolescent during these four sessions. The initial phase is complete when the treatment goals and the problem area or areas have been defined.

Intermediate Phase (Sessions 5–8)

The next four sessions concentrate on the assessment and resolution of each particular case: grief, role dispute, role transition, or interpersonal deficit. The therapist has five tasks to accomplish in each of these sessions: (a) to help the adolescent open up and discuss topics relevant to the problem area; (b) to stimulate the adolescent's self-disclosure by creating a climate of trust; (c) to attend to the adolescent's feelings; (d) to strengthen the therapeutic relationship; and (e) to prevent the adolescent or his or her parents from sabotaging the treatment.

In each of these intermediate sessions, the adolescent is encouraged to speak freely and present topics spontaneously. This allows new material to be introduced, which could suggest unrecognized or suppressed problems that have not yet been discussed. Sometimes, as a result of mistrust or genuine misunderstanding, the adolescent does not present the most important problem during the first four sessions. It will probably emerge in the following four sessions. The therapist needs to bring the focus of the session back to the problem area or treatment goals. Each problem area is addressed in the following sequence: general exploration of the problem, definition of the maladaptive behavior or demands, analysis of options to solve the problem, and encouragement of new behavior.

The therapist must be aware of signs of negative and countertherapeutic feelings to prevent the adolescent or his or her parents from sabotaging treatment. Behaviors such as lateness, missed appointments, silence, evasion of significant material, uncooperativeness, acting out, and suicidal attempts should be discussed. The therapist should try to curb the behavior and relate it to the patient's problems of interpersonal relationships outside of therapy. Resolving problems within the therapeutic session can help the adolescent handle problems in other relationships.

Termination Phase (Sessions 9–12)

To the adolescent, termination means giving up a valued relationship and developing a sense of competence to solve further problems alone. If the adolescent is not able to successfully address these issues, depressive symptoms and maladaptive behavior could reappear at the end of treatment or later. The resurgence of feelings of hopelessness should be avoided.

To help the adolescent deal with termination, the therapist must allow for an open discussion about the end of therapy. Openly discussing the end of treatment by acknowledging the adolescent's feelings and acknowledging the possibility of grief while recognizing the adolescent's newfound competence in solving interpersonal difficulties is an important aspect of these last four sessions. The therapist and the adolescent review the course of treatment and new options discovered through therapy. If a need for further treatment should be identified, the therapist discusses the options with the adolescent and his or her parents. A session with parents upon termination summarizing the accomplishments of therapy is helpful.

Clinical Vignette

Elena is a 13-year-old girl who was referred to our project by her school's psychologist. He had observed her depressed affect and its negative impact on her academic performance.

Elena came from a family riddled with drug abuse. As a result of her mother's heroin addiction, she had moved in with her aunt and uncle at the age of 7. Her father, also an addict, had been completely absent from her life. Elena's only sibling, an 8-year-old brother who was born with a chronic illness, had stayed with their mother and was being raised primarily by their grandmother.

Elena expressed sadness about her separation from her mother and her brother. Her aunt, in an attempt to protect her from the potential negative influence of her mother's addiction, strictly limited her visits to her grandmother's house. Elena felt sorry for her mother and brother and longed for more frequent visits with them. She talked about how much better her life was than theirs in terms of economic resources.

Family visits were not the only thing Elena's aunt and uncle denied her. They also forbade her to participate in after-school activities or spend time with friends. Elena expressed worry that her aunt and uncle were planning to legally adopt her, which she feared would increase their power over her actions. She was conflicted about her relationship to them, appreciating what they had done for her but resenting the lack of freedom they allowed her. Her relationship with her aunt was especially problematic. Elena felt that her uncle was more flexible than her aunt, and she spoke of conflicts in which he had at first shown understanding of Elena's side only to take his wife's side later. Elena often felt that she had to lie to her aunt to avoid conflicts. This issue arose in an especially troublesome way when Elena found out that her mother was HIV positive. Elena did not want her aunt to find out because this would mean even greater restrictions on her visits home.

Elena did not want to hurt her aunt and uncle's feelings. She still wished to live with them and didn't want them to abandon her. Elena appreciated what they had done for her but felt that she would be happier if she could have the liberty to spend more time with her mother, brother, and grandmother.

In interpersonal terms, Elena had two areas of difficulties: grief over the psychological loss of her biological family and her mother's and brother's illnesses and interpersonal disputes with her aunt. These issues were linked to her depression. During the course of treatment, Elena was able to express her feelings of sadness, anger, and guilt related to the situations in her biological family. She was also able to develop better communication with her aunt and became better at expressing her feelings and fears. They were able to agree on the postponement of the adoption, a more acceptable visitation schedule with her mother and brother, and more freedom to attend activities with her friends. This helped Elena to feel better and to perform better in school. After the 12 sessions of interpersonal psychotherapy, Elena's depressive symptoms were markedly reduced.

Efficacy and Outcome of Cognitive–Behavioral Therapy and Interpersonal Psychotherapy Treatment With Puerto Rican Adolescents

The efficacy of the CBT and IPT models with Puerto Rican adolescents has been described in two case studies (Rosselló, 1993) and the first controlled clinical trial completed that includes this population (Rosselló

& Bernal, 1999). A second controlled clinical trial was conducted in which the two treatments were tested in group and individual formats. Results of the first trial and preliminary findings of the second trial are presented in the following sections.

First Controlled Clinical Trial

The purpose of the first clinical trial was to adapt and test the efficacy of the CBT and IPT models with Puerto Rican adolescents suffering from depression.

Referrals with parental consent were received from seven schools. Referred adolescents were then interviewed and evaluated by a clinical psychologist. Their parents also were interviewed and asked to fill out the Child Behavior Checklist. Subjects who scored over 11 on the Children's Depression Inventory (CDI; Kovacs, 1983) and who met DSM–III–R criteria for depression (DISC-2, parent or adolescent versions) were invited to participate in the study. Exclusionary criteria included (a) serious imminent suicidal risk; (b) psychotic features; (c) organic brain syndrome; (d) marked hyperaggression; (e) current use of psychopharmacological medication or psychotherapy; and (f) legal or court proceedings.

The authors used a pretreatment, posttreatment, and follow-up design with three groups. Participants were randomly assigned to either the CBT model or the IPT model or to a wait-list control group. Adolescents and their parents were evaluated in interviews and tested at intake, posttreatment, and at a 3-month follow-up using the following instruments: (a) CDI (Kovacs, 1992; Rosselló et al., 1992); (b) Piers–Harris Children's Self-Concept Scale (Piers, 1972); (c) Social Adjustment Measure (Beiser, 1990); (d) Child Behavior Checklist (Achenbach, 1983); and (e) Family Emotional Involvement and Criticism Scale (Shields, Franks, Harp, McDaniel, & Campbell, 1992).

A total of 161 adolescents were referred and evaluated. Of these, 71 met the criteria for the study. The reasons for exclusion were as follows: 30% met the above-mentioned exclusion criteria, 21% were not interested in participating, 18% did not meet inclusion criteria, 14% did not show up for the initial appointment, and 3% moved from Puerto Rico. The 71 participants ranged in age from 13 to 17 years (M = 14.70, SD = 1.40) and were 54% female and 46% male. All participants were in school from 5th to 12th grades.

To ensure treatment integrity, the following measures were taken: (a) detailed treatment manuals were used for both CBT and IPT; (b) for both treatments, the content of each session or group of sessions was detailed in a checklist of therapist actions; (c) therapists received training in one of the treatment models to which they were assigned; and (d) weekly supervisions were held separately for each CBT and IPT team in which sessions were reviewed and planned using the manual's indications. As a manipulation check, all sessions were videotaped and evaluated by an independent coder (who was trained in each of the treatment models) using an integrity checklist. These checklists were created using the treatment manuals. All therapy sessions were videotaped and rated for therapy fidelity, which revealed a compliance rate of 85% for IPT therapists and a compliance rate of 91% for CBT therapists.

The results showed a significant change from prettreatment to posttreatment in all outcome measures across treatment conditions. Planned orthogonal comparisons between the two treatment conditions and the wait-list control condition revealed that participants in IPT ($f[1,33] = 11.62$, $p < .002$) and CBT ($F[1,37] = 2.58$, $p < .015$) showed significantly lower depression scores when compared with participants in the wait-list control condition. No significant differences were found between IPT and CBT on the CDI at pretesting. Self-esteem, $F(1,33) = 12.73$, $p < .001$, significantly increased for the IPT group when compared with the wait-list control group. No differences were found between IPT and CBT groups or between CBT and wait-list control groups for self-esteem or social adaptation.

Mean scores on the CDI decreased from 21.21 to 10.79 in the IPT group (effect size = .73) and from 20.12 to 13.28 in the CBT group (effect size = .43). At posttreatment 77% of the treated adolescents in IPT and 67% of the treated adolescents in CBT were better off than the adolescents in the control group.

Upon follow-up, attrition was high (52% for IPT, 44% for CBT) because some of the adolescents still needed additional treatment and were referred, some had moved, and others did not attend their follow-up appointments. In light of ethical considerations, we discontinued the wait-list control group after the postevaluation and offered treatment to participants in this condition. Thus, we do not have data on follow-up for the wait-list control. No significant differences between IPT and CBT groups were found at follow-up. Although not statistically significant, the CBT group appeared to continue to make gains in reduced symptoms of depression at follow-up.

Second Controlled Clinical Trial

The purpose of the second trial was to test the efficacy of CBT and IPT in group and individual formats for the treatment of depression in Puerto Rican adolescents with a larger sample size. The CBT and IPT interventions were adapted to a group format. The same procedure, criteria for inclusion, evaluations, and design were used. This time 322 referrals were received. Of these, 210 did not meet the requirements to participate in the study and 112 met the criteria. The reasons for exclusion from the study were as follows: 20% did not meet inclusion diagnostic criteria, 33% did not want to receive treatment, 7% needed family therapy, 6% were referred to psychiatric evaluation for psychotic symptoms, 2% of the parents refused participation, 8% were receiving either medication or psychotherapy elsewhere, 10% did not meet age criteria, 11% did not show up for the initial appointment, and 3% were highly suicidal and were referred for immediate attention.

Participants were 112 adolescents ranging from 12 to 18 years of age (M = 14.52, SD = 1.85). The sample was 55.4% female and 44.6% male. All participants were in school from sixth to 12th grades. Participants were randomly assigned to one of four treatment conditions: individual CBT, group CBT, individual IPT, and group IPT.

All therapy sessions were videotaped and rated for therapy fidelity, revealing a compliance rate of 92% for CBT, 90% for group CBT, 78.2% for individual IPT, and 88.3% for group IPT. Our preliminary analysis of this second trial suggests that in general both group and individual formats were efficacious in reducing depressive symptoms. Although we found no differences in efficacy between treatment formats, both formats showed significant reductions in symptoms of depression at posttreatment. The effect size for individual therapy (for both IPT and CBT) was .407 and for group therapy (including both IPT and CBT) was .358. The results suggest that both IPT and CBT were efficacious in reducing depression symptoms from pretreatment to posttreatment. However, there was a significant effect for treatment modality, with CBT (group and individual) showing a more significant effect than IPT (group and individual) in reducing depression at posttreatment.

We are currently in the process of conducting further analyses to understand and interpret the data. Again, both IPT and CBT were found to significantly reduce depression symptoms at posttreatment, with CBT showing a significantly more powerful effect than IPT. Group and individual formats were equally beneficial in reducing depression symptoms. Thus, a group format, particularly a CBT-based group format, should be considered as a viable and cost-effective means of providing efficacious treatments to adolescents.

SUMMARY

With regard to efficacy, the results of our first study (Rosselló & Bernal, 1999) provided preliminary evidence that ITP and CBT are efficacious for the treatment of depressed Puerto Rican adolescents. Participants in the treatment groups significantly improved at posttreatment, with marked reductions in depressive symptoms in comparison with the wait-list control group. Moderate effect sizes were obtained for the groups receiving either IPT or CBT. These effect sizes compare favorably with the reported average effect size (.58) in the literature on child and adolescent therapy. In our second clinical trial, in which treatment type (CBT versus IPT) was crossed with format (group versus individual), the effect sizes ranged from .358 to .401. It should be noted, however, that the literature reports on effect sizes are based largely on comparisons with a wait-list control group. In our second study, the effect size was produced in comparison with an active psychosocial condition. Nevertheless, these findings are also favorable when compared with the effect size established by two meta-analytic studies—.79 (Weisz, Weiss, Alicke, & Klotz, 1987) and .71 (Casey & Berman, 1985). Thus, the average treated participant in our two trials compares favorably with other participants from studies reported in the literature, suggesting a significant advantage of treatment.

Important progress has been made in the treatment of child and adolescent depression thanks to a variety of studies conducted over the past 20 years (Birmaher & Brent, 1998; Birmaher et al., 2000; Brent et al., 1997; Butler, Miezitis, Friedman, & Cole, 1980; Jaycox, Reivich, Gillham, & Seligman, 1994; Kahn, Kehle, Jenson, & Clark, 1990; Lewinsohn, Clarke, Rhode, Hops, & Seely, 1996; Lewinsohn, Clarke, Hops, & Andrews, 1990; Liddle & Diamond, 1991; Mufson, 1991; Mufson, Moreau, Weissman, Wickramaratne, Martin, & Samoilov, 1994; Reynolds & Coats, 1986; Stark, 1990; Stark, Reynold, & Kaslow, 1987; Weisz, Thurber, Sweeney, Proffit, & La Gagnoux, 1997; Wood, Harrington, & Moore, 1996). These studies should be used as a starting point for future research with ethnic minority youth. Our studies represent an important step in the process of demonstrating that adaptations of empirically supported treatments can be successfully performed.

Additional studies are needed to determine the sustainability of IPT and CBT interventions in real-world scenarios. Further research and development is necessary to test the efficacy of these interventions in clinics and hospital settings. Also, clinicians must be informed of, and trained in, the use of empirically supported treatments, the manuals themselves, and treatment efficacy. We also recommend using these interventions with other Latino populations to test efficacy with culturally consonant groups.

Another avenue of development lies in the use of crossover designs using IPT and CBT or in the integration of these two treatments. This is a promising possibility; given that both treatments are effective, a combination could be superior for patients who do not respond to one of these treatments individually. Additional studies are needed with regard to process variables such as the reason that these treatments work and the types of people for whom the treatments seem to work. Addressing these variables might help in the tailoring of treatments to individual needs. Clinicians would find it useful to know which patients are likely to benefit more from IPT or CBT before starting treatment.

In conclusion, our findings support the results obtained in other outcome studies with adolescents (Carey, 1993; Fine, Forth, Gilbert, & Haley, 1991; Kahn et al., 1990; Lewinsohn et al., 1990; Reynolds & Coats, 1986;

Schrodt, 1992; Stark, Swearer, Kurowski, Sommer, & Bowen, 1996), in which psychosocial interventions proved effective in the treatment of depressive symptoms. The present clinical trial for the treatment of depressive symptoms used an adolescent sample of Puerto Ricans. In this regard, our study contributes to the small but growing literature of the treatment of ethnic minorities and nonmainstream groups. In fact, the positive findings of the present studies suggest that the adequate adaptation of therapeutic models with demonstrated empirical support (Bernal, Padilla, Pérez-Prado, & Bonilla, 1999) is a promising avenue to explore in the treatment of ethnic minorities and other diverse populations. It also provides a model that clinicians can use in their therapeutic work with Hispanic populations. This can help bridge the gap between researchers and clinicians, making available empirically supported treatments to real-world settings.

REFERENCES

Achenbach, T. M. (1983). *Manual for the Child Behavior Checklist and Revised Child Behavior profile*. Burlington: Department of Psychiatry, University of Vermont.

Acosta, F. X., Yamamoto, J., & Evans, L. A. (1982). *Effective psychotherapy for low-income and minority patients*. New York: Plenum Press.

American Psychological Association. (1990). *Guidelines for providers of psychological services to ethnic, linguistic and culturally diverse populations*. Washington, DC: Author.

Albert, N., & Beck, A. T. (1975). Incidence of depression in early adolescence: A preliminary study. *Journal of Youth and Adolescence, 4*, 301–305.

Aponte, H. (1990). Ethnicity dynamics important in therapeutic relationships. *Family Therapy News, 21*, 3.

Aponte, H., Rivers, R. Y., & Wahl, J. (1995). *Psychological interventions and cultural diversity*. Boston: Allyn & Bacon.

Beck, A. T., Rush, A. J., Shaw, B. F., & Emery, G. (1979). *Cognitive therapy of depression*. New York: Guilford Press.

Beiser, M. (1990). Final report submitted in fulfillment of requirements for the grants of the United States National Institute of Mental Health (5-R01-MH36678-04) and the Canada Health and Welfare National Health Research Directorate Program (NHRDP 6610-132-04). Unpublished manuscript.

Bernal, G., Bonilla, J., & Bellido, C. (1995). Ecological validity and cultural sensitivity for outcome research: Issues for the cultural adaptation and development of psychosocial treatments with Hispanics. *Journal of Abnormal Child Psychology, 23*, 67–82.

Bernal, G., Padilla, L., Pérez-Prado, E., & Bonilla, J. (1999). La alianza terapéutica: Evaluación y desarrollo de instrumentos [The therapeutic alliance: Evaluation and development of techniques]. *Revista Argentina de Clínica Psicológica, 8*, 69–80.

Bernal, G., & Scharrón del Río, M. R. (2001). Are empirically supported treatments valid for ethnic minorities? Toward an alternative approach for treatment research. *Cultural Diversity and Ethnic Minority Psychology, 7,* 328–342.

Bird, H. R., Canino, G., Rubio-Stipec, M., Gould, M. S., Ribera, J., Sesman, M., et al. (1988). Estimates of the prevalence of childhood maladjustment in a community survey in Puerto Rico. *Archives of General Psychiatry, 45,* 1120–1126.

Birmaher, B., & Brent, D. (1998). Practice parameters for the assessment and treatment of children and adolescents with depressive disorders. *Journal of the American Academy of Child and Adolescent Psychiatry, 37,* 63S–83S.

Birmaher, B., Brent, D. A., Kolko, D., Baugher, M., Bridge, J., Holder, D., et al. (2000). Clinical outcome after short-term psychotherapy for adolescents with major depressive disorder. *Archives of General Psychiatry, 57,* 29–36.

Brent, D. A., Holder, D., Kolko, D., Birmaher, B., Baugher, M., Roth, C., et al. (1997). A clinical psychotherapy trial for adolescent depression comparing cognitive, family, and supportive treatments. *Archives of General Psychiatry, 54,* 877–885.

Butler, L., Miezitis, S., Friedman, R., & Cole, E. (1980). The effect of two school-based intervention programs on depressive symptoms in preadolescents. *American Educational Research Journal, 17,* 111–119.

Canino, I. A., & Spurlock, J. (1994). *Culturally diverse children and adolescents: Assessment, diagnosis, and treatment.* New York: Guildford Press.

Carey, M. (1993). Child and adolescent depression: Cognitive–behavioral strategies and interventions. In A. J. Finch (Ed.), *Cognitive–behavioral procedures with children and adolescents* (pp. 289–314). Boston: Allyn & Bacon.

Carlson, G. A., & Cantwell, D. P. (1980). Unmasking masked depression in children and adolescents. *American Journal of Psychiatry, 137,* 445–449.

Casas, M. (1995). Counseling and psychotherapy with racial/ethnic minority groups in theory and practice. In V. Bongar & L. E. Buetler (Eds.), *Comprehensive textbook of psychotherapy: Theory and practice* (pp. 311–335). New York: Oxford University Press.

Casey, R. J., & Berman, S. (1985). The outcome of psychotherapy with children. *Psychological Bulletin, 98,* 388–400.

Chien, C., & Change, T. (1985). Depression in Taiwan: Epidemiological survey utilizing the CEOs-D. *Sunshine Shank Gaku Zasshi, 87,* 355–338.

Comas-Díaz, L., & Griffith, E. E. H. (Eds.). (1988). *Clinical guidelines in cross-cultural mental health.* New York: Wiley.

Cross, T., Bazron, B., Dennis, K., & Isaacs, M. (1989). *Towards a culturally competent system of care.* Washington, DC: Georgetown University Child Development Center.

Dana, R. H. (1993). *Multicultural assessment perspectives for professional psychology.* Boston: Allyn & Bacon.

Draguns, J. G. (1981). Counseling across cultures: Common themes and distinct approaches. In P. B. Pedersen, W. J. Lonner, & S. E. Trimble (Eds.), *Counseling across cultures* (pp. 3–21). Honolulu: University of Hawaii Press.

Ellis, A. (1962). *Reason and emotion in psychotherapy.* New York: Lyle Stuart.

Ellis, A. B. M., (1983). *Rational–emotive approaches to the problems of childhood*. New York: Plenum Press.

Fine, S., Forth, A., Gilbert, M., & Haley, G. (1991). Group therapy for adolescent depressive disorder: A comparison of social skills and therapeutic support. *Journal of the American Academy of Child and Adolescent Psychiatry, 30*, 79–85.

Fleming, J. E., Offord, S. R., & Boyle, H. M. (1989). Prevalence of childhood and adolescent depression in the community: Ontario Child Health Study. *British Journal of Psychiatry, 155*, 647–654.

Ghali, B. (1977). *Ethnic America*. New York: Basic Books.

Gibbs, J. T. (1985). Psychological factors associated with depression in urban adolescent females: Implications for treatment. *Journal of Youth and Adolescence, 14*, 47–60.

Ho, M. K. (1992). *Minority children and adolescents in therapy*. Newbury Park, MA: Sage Publications.

Jaycox, L. M., Reivich, K. J., Gillham, J., & Seligman, M. E. P. (1994). Prevention of depressive symptoms in school children. *Behavior Research and Therapy, 32*(2), 801–816.

Jones, E. E., & Korchin, S. J. (Eds.). (1982). *Minority mental health*. New York: Praeger.

Kahn, J., Kehle, T., Jenson, W., & Clark, E. (1990). Comparison of cognitive–behavioral, relaxation, and self-modeling interventions for depression among middle-school students. *School Psychology Review, 19*, 196–211.

Kandel, D. B., & Davies, M. (1982). Epidemiology of depressive mood in adolescents. *Archives of General Psychiatry, 39*, 1205–1212.

Kanner, L. (1972). *Child psychiatry*. Springfield, IL: Charles C Thomas.

Kaplan, N. J., Hong, G. H., & Weenhold, C. (1984). Epidemiology of depressive symptomatology in adolescents. *Journal of the American Academy of Child Psychiatry, 23*, 91–98.

Kashani, J. H., Holcomb, W. R., & Orvaschel, H. (1986). Depression and depressive symptoms in preschool children from the general population. *American Journal of Psychiatry, 143*, 1138–1143.

Kashani, J. H., & Simonds, J. F. (1979). The incidence of depression in children. *American Journal of Psychiatry, 136*, 1203–1205.

Klerman, G. L., Weissman, M. M., Rounsaville, B. J., & Chevron, E. S. (1984). *Interpersonal psychotherapy of depression*. New York: Basic Books.

Kovacs, M. (1983). *The Children's Depression Inventory: A self-report depression scale for school-aged youngsters*. Pittsburgh, PA: University of Pittsburgh School of Medicine.

Kovacs, M. (1992). *Children's Depression Inventory (CDI) manual*. New York: Multi-Health Systems.

Lewinsohn, P. M. (1975). The behavioral study and treatment of depression. In M. Hersen & P. Miller (Eds.), *Progress in behavior modification* (Vol. 1). New York: Academic Press.

Lewinsohn, P. M. (1976). Activity schedules in treatment of depression. In J. Krumboltz & C. Thorensen (Eds.), *Counseling methods*. New York: Holt, Rinehart & Winston.

Lewinsohn, P. M., Antonuccio, D. O., Steinmetz, J., & Teri, L. (1984). *The coping with depression course*. Eugene, OR: Castalia Press.

Lewinsohn, P. M., Clarke, G. N., Hops, H., & Andrews, J. (1990). Cognitive-behavioral treatments for depressed adolescents. *Behavior Therapy, 21*, 385–401.

Lewinsohn, P. M., Clarke, G. N., Rhode, P., Hops, H., & Seely, J. (1996). A course in coping: A cognitive–behavioral approach to the treatment of depression. In E. D. Hibbs & P. S. Jensen (Eds.), *Psychosocial treatments for child and adolescent disorders: Empirically based strategies for clinical practice* (pp. 109–135). Washington, DC: American Psychological Association.

Lewinsohn, P. M., & Libet, J. (1972). Pleasant events, activity schedules, and depression. *Journal of Abnormal Psychology, 79*, 291–295.

Liddle, H. L., & Diamond, G. (1991). Adolescent substance abusers in family therapy: The critical initial phase of treatment. *Family Dynamics of Addictions Quarterly, 1*, 63–75.

Lopez, S. R., Grover, K. P., Holland, D., Johnson, M. J., Kain, C. D., Kanel, K., et al. (1989). Development of culturally sensitive psychotherapists. *Professional Psychology: Research and Practice, 20*, 369–376.

Mannino, F. V., & Shore, M. F. (1976). Perceptions of social support by Spanish-speaking youth with implications for program development. *The Journal of School Health, 46*, 471–474.

Mays, V. M., & Albee, G. W. (1992). Psychotherapy and ethnic minorities. In D. K. Freedheim & H. J. Freudenberger (Eds.), *History of psychotherapy: A century of change* (pp. 552–570). Washington, DC: American Psychological Association.

McGoldrick, N., Pearce, J. K., & Giordano, J. (1982). *Ethnicity and family therapy*. New York: Guilford Press.

Mufson, L. (1991). Interpersonal psychotherapy for depressed adolescents (IPT-A): Description of modification and preliminary application. *Journal of the American Academy of Child and Adolescent Psychiatry, 30*, 624–651.

Mufson, L., Moreau, D., Weissman, M. M., & Klerman, G. L. (1993). *Interpersonal psychotherapy for depressed adolescents*. New York: Guilford Press.

Mufson, L., Moreau, D., Weissman, M. M., Wickramaratne, P., Martin, J., & Samoilov, A. (1994). Modification of interpersonal psychotherapy with depressed adolescents (IPT-A): Phase I and II studies. *Journal of the American Academy of Child and Adolescent Psychiatry, 33*, 695–705.

Muñoz, R. F., & Miranda, J. (1982). The Spanish speaking consumer and the community mental health center. In E. E. Jones & S. Korchin (Eds.), *Minority mental health* (pp. 362–398). New York: Praeger Publishers.

Muñoz, R. F., & Miranda, J. (19686). *Group therapy for cognitive–behavioral treatment of depression. San Francisco General Hospital Depression Clinic*. San Francisco: University of California Press.

Petersen, A. C., Compas, B. E., Brooks-Gunn, J., Stemmler, M., Ey, S., & Grant, K. E. (1993). Depression in adolescence. *American Psychologist, 48*, 155–168.

Piers, E. V. (1972). Prediction of children's self-concepts. *Journal of Consulting and Clinical Psychology, 38*, 428–433.

Reivich, K. J. (1993). *Cognitive behavioral skills training for the prevention of depression in inner city, African American children.* Unpublished manuscript.

Reynolds, W. M. (1983). *Depression in adolescents: Measurement, epidemiology, and correlates.* Paper presented at the annual meeting of the National Association of School Psychologists, Detroit, MI.

Reynolds, W. M., & Coats, K. I. (1986). A comparison of cognitive–behavioral therapy and relaxation training for the treatment of depression in adolescents. *Journal of Consulting and Clinical Psychology, 54*, 653–660.

Rie, H. E. (1966). Depression in childhood: A survey of pertinent contributions. *Journal of the American Academy of Child Psychiatry, 4*, 653–686.

Rogler, L. H., Malgady, R. G., Rodríguez, O., & Bumenthal, R. (1987). What do culturally sensitive mental health services mean? The case of Hispanics. *American Psychologist, 42*, 565–570.

Rosselló, J. (1993). Treatment approaches for depression in Puerto Rican adolescents: Two case studies. [Special issue: Latin American contributions to treatment outcome research.] *Revista Interamericana de Psicología, 27*, 163–180.

Rosselló, J. (1994). Manuales para las terapias interpersonal y cognoscitiva–conductual para el tratamiento de la depresión en adolescentes puertorriqueños/as [Manuals of interpersonal and cognitive–behavioral depression in Puerto Rican adolescents]. Río Piedras, Universidad de Puerto Rico. Unpublished manuscript.

Rosselló, J., & Bernal, G. (1999). The efficacy of cognitive–behavioral and interpersonal treatments for depression in Puerto Rican adolescents. *Journal of Consulting & Clinical Psychology, 67*, 734–745.

Rosselló, J., Guisasola, E., Ralat, S., Martínez, S., & Nieves, A. (1992). La evaluación de la depresión en niños/as y adolescentes puertorriqueños [The evaluation of depression in Puerto Rican children and adolescents]. *Revista Puertorriqueña de Psicología, 8*, 155–162.

Sabogal, F., Marín, G., & Otero-Sabogal, R. (1987). Hispanic familism and acculturation: What changes and what doesn't? *Hispanic Journal of Behavioral Sciences, 9*, 397–412.

Schoenback, V. J., Kaplan, B. H., Grimson, R. C., & Wagner, E. H. (1982). Use of a symptom scale to study the prevalence of a depressive syndrome in young adolescents. *American Journal of Epidemiology, 116*, 791–800.

Schrodt, G. R. (1992). Cognitive therapy of depression. In M. Shafii & S. L. Shafii (Eds.), *Clinical guide to depression in children and adolescents* (pp. 197–219). Washington, DC: American Psychiatric Press.

Shields, C., Franks, P., Harp, J., McDaniel, S., & Campbell, T. (1992). Development of the Family Emotional Involvement and Criticism Scale (FEICS): A self-report scale to measure expressed emotion. *Journal of Marital and Family Therapy, 18*, 395–407.

Siegel, L., & Griffin, N. J. (1984). Correlates of depressive symptoms in adolescents. *Journal of Youth and Adolescence, 10*, 475–487.

Smith, W. D., Burlew, A. K., Mosley, M. H., & Whitney, W. M. (1978). *Minority issues in mental health*. Boston: Addison-Wesley.

Stark, K. (1990). *Childhood depression and school-based intervention*. New York: Guilford Press.

Stark, K. D., Reynold, W., & Kaslow, N. J. (1987). A comparison of the relative efficacy of self-control therapy and behavioral problem solving therapy for depression in children. *Journal of Abnormal Child Psychology, 15*, 91–113.

Stark, K. D., Swearer, S., Kurowski, C., Sommer, D., & Bowen, B. (1996). Targeting the child and the family: A holistic approach to treatment of child and adolescent depressive disorders. In E. Hibbs & P. Jensen (Eds.), *Psychosocial treatments for child and adolescent disorders: Empirically based strategies for clinical practice* (pp. 207–238). Washington, DC: American Psychological Association.

Sue, S. (1977). Community mental health services to minority groups. *American Psychologist, 32*, 616–624.

Sue, S., & Zane, N. (1987). The role of culture and cultural techniques in psychotherapy: A critique and reformulation. *American Psychologist, 42*, 37–45.

Sullivan, H. S., & Elgin, A. W. (1986). Adolescent depression: Its prevalence in high school students. *Journal of School Psychology, 24*, 103–109.

Szapocznik, J., Scopetta, M. A., & Aranalde, M. A. (1978). Cuban value structure: Treatment implications. *Journal of Consulting and Clinical Psychology, 46*, 961–970.

Teri, L. (1982). Depression in adolescence: Its relationship to assertion and various aspects of self-image. *Journal of Clinical Child Psychology, 11*, 101–106.

Tharp, R. G. (1991). Cultural diversity and treatment of children. *Journal of Consulting and Clinical Psychology, 59*, 799–812.

U. S. Census Bureau. (1999). *Resident population estimates of the United States by sex, race, and Hispanic origin: April 1, 1990 to November 1, 1999*. U.S. Census Bureau, Population Division, Statistical Information Staff. Retrieved April 4, 2000, from http://www.census.gov/population/www/estimates/nation3.html

U.S. Census Bureau. (2001). *Resident population estimates of the United States by sex, race, and Hispanic origin: April 1, 1990 to November 1, 1999*. U.S. Census Bureau, Statistical Information Staff. Retrieved January 29, 2001 from http://www.census.gov/population/estimates/nation/intfile3-1.txt

U.S. Census Bureau. (2002). *Hispanic population in the United States: March 2002*. U.S. Census Bureau, Population Division. Retrieved June 24, 2003, from http://www.census.gov/prod/2003pubs/p20-545.pdf

Weinberg, W. A., & Emslie, G. J. (1988). Weinberg Screening Affective Scales (WSAS and WSAS-SF). *Journal of Child Neurology, 3*, 294–296.

Weisz, J. R., Thurber, C. A., Sweeney, L., Proffit, V. D., & La Gagnoux, G. L. (1997). Brief treatment of mild to moderate child depression using primary and secondary control enhancement training. *Journal of Consulting and Clinical Psychology, 65,* 703–707.

Weisz, J. R., Weiss, B., Alicke, M. D., & Klotz, M. L. (1987). Effectiveness of psychotherapy with children and adolescents: A meta-analysis for clinicians. *Journal of Consulting and Clinical Psychology, 53,* 542–549.

Wells, V., Klerman, G. L., & Deykin, E. Y. (1987). The prevalence of depressive symptoms in college students. *Social Psychology, 22,* 20–28.

Wood, A., Harrington, R., & Moore, A. (1996). Controlled trial of a brief cognitive–behavioral intervention in adolescent patients. *Journal of Child Psychology and Psychiatry, 37,* 737–746.

Zuñiga, M. E. (1992). Using metaphors in therapy: Dichos and Latino clients. *Social Work, 37,* 55–60

10

THE ADOLESCENT COPING WITH DEPRESSION COURSE: A COGNITIVE–BEHAVIORAL APPROACH TO THE TREATMENT OF ADOLESCENT DEPRESSION

PAUL ROHDE, PETER M. LEWINSOHN, GREGORY N. CLARKE, HYMAN HOPS, AND JOHN R. SEELEY

The goal of this chapter is to describe our program of research evaluating a cognitive–behavioral group treatment approach for adolescent depression. Since 1982, our group has been involved in a major research effort to develop and test the efficacy and effectiveness of the Adolescent Coping With Depression Course (CWD-A; Clarke, Lewinsohn, & Hops, 1990). We initially conducted two randomized, controlled clinical trials evaluating the efficacy of this cognitive–behavioral group intervention with depressed adolescents who lived in the community. Since then, we have developed and evaluated modifications of the CWD-A as a prevention intervention

This research was supported by National Institute of Mental Health Grants MH41278, MH40501, and MH56238. Correspondence concerning this article should be addressed to Paul Rohde, Oregon Research Institute, 1715 Franklin Boulevard, Eugene, OR 97403-1983, U.S.A.

for high-risk youth and for use as a group and individual treatment intervention with various adolescent populations.

We begin this chapter by briefly reviewing psychosocial treatments for adolescent depression. Next, we review the rationale and theoretical background for our treatment approach, describe the CWD-A course and its companion course for the parents of depressed adolescents, and summarize results from two randomized clinical trials with 24-month follow-up. A clinical vignette is provided to illustrate the changes that have occurred with this intervention. To better understand the mechanisms of therapeutic change in depressed adolescents, we next address several issues related to treatment response. We conclude by describing more recent research with the CWD-A intervention and future directions.

COGNITIVE–BEHAVIORAL TREATMENT FOR ADOLESCENT DEPRESSION

The study of psychosocial treatments for depression in adolescents has become an active area of research and clinical attention, with over a dozen treatment studies generally indicating positive results (reviewed by Curry, 2001; Kaslow & Thompson, 1998; Reinecke, Ryan, & DuBois, 1998). Cognitive–behavioral therapy (CBT) has been shown to be superior to wait-list control and often is more efficacious than alternative treatments, including relaxation training, supportive therapy, and traditional counseling (e.g., Brent et al., 1997; Kahn, Kehle, Jenson, & Clark, 1990; Stark, Reynolds, & Kaslow, 1987; Vostanis, Feehan, Grattan, & Bickerton, 1996; Wood, Harrington, & Moore, 1996). Individual CBT was found to be comparable to interpersonal psychotherapy for adolescents and superior to wait-list control in a sample of 71 depressed Puerto Rican adolescents (Rosselló & Bernal, 1999). Brent et al. (1997) contrasted individual CBT, systemic behavior family therapy, and individual nondirective supportive therapy in 107 clinically referred depressed adolescents. CBT showed a lower rate of major depressive disorder (MDD) posttreatment compared with supportive therapy and higher remission (defined as no MDD and consecutively low Beck Depression Inventory [BDI; Beck, Ward, Mendelson, Mock, & Erbaugh, 1961] scores) compared with both of the other two treatments. However, by the end of a 2-year follow-up period, no differential effects for the three treatment conditions were evident (Birmaher et al., 2000), with 80% of adolescents in all treatments recovering and 30% experiencing a recurrence of their depression. CBT in the form of bibliotherapy also has been shown to be effective, compared with wait-list, for adolescents with mild and moderate depressive symptoms (Ackerson, Scogin, McKendree-Smith, & Lyman, 1998). As summarized in this chapter, our own program of research has shown the CWD-A course to be efficacious in treating depression in older (ages 14 to 18) adolescents in the community.

RATIONALE FOR THE ADOLESCENT COPING WITH DEPRESSION COURSE

Our treatment approach is rooted in behavioral (Ferster, 1966; Lewinsohn, Weinstein, & Shaw, 1969) as well as cognitive formulations of depression (Beck, 1967; Ellis & Harper, 1961; Seligman, 1975). The primary goal of cognitive therapy is to help the depressed client become aware of pessimistic and negative thoughts, depressotypic beliefs, and causal attributions in which the person blames himself or herself for failures but does not take credit for successes. Once these depressotypic patterns are recognized, the client is taught ways to substitute more constructive cognitions for these destructive ones. The primary goal of behavior therapy for depression is to increase engagement in behaviors that either elicit positive reinforcement or avoid negative reinforcement from the environment. The CWD-A course combines cognitive and behavioral strategies aimed at ameliorating the types of problems that commonly characterize depressed individuals (e.g., pessimism; internal, global, and stable attributions for failure; low self-esteem; infrequent engagement in pleasant activities; social withdrawal; anxiety and tension; low social support and increased conflict). The treatment incorporates other elements shared by cognitive–behavioral treatments, such as the focus on specific and current actions and cognitions as targets for change, structured intervention sessions, repeated practice of skills, use of rewards and contracts, homework assignments, and a relatively small (typically under 20) number of therapy sessions.

Our approach rests on an underlying theoretical model of depression (Lewinsohn, Hoberman, Teri, & Hautzinger, 1985), which assumes that multiple risk factors contribute to the outcome of depression, none of which by themselves is necessary or sufficient. The CWD-A course is based on the premise that teaching adolescents a variety of coping skills and strategies allows them to counteract the diverse putative causal factors that contribute to their depressive episodes and deal more effectively with the problems posed by their environment.

THE COPING WITH DEPRESSION COURSE, ADULT VERSION

The CWD-A course was originally adapted from the adult version of the Coping With Depression (CWD) course (Lewinsohn, Antonuccio, Steinmetz-Breckenridge, & Teri, 1984). In modifying the course for use with adolescents, in-session material and homework assignments were simplified, experiential learning opportunities (e.g., role-playing exercises) were enhanced, and problem-solving skills were added to the curriculum.

The CWD-A course consists of 16 two-hour sessions conducted over an 8-week period for mixed-gender groups of up to 10 adolescents. Each participant receives a workbook that provides structured learning tasks, short quizzes, and homework forms. To encourage generalization of skills to everyday situations, adolescents are given homework assignments, which are reviewed at the beginning of the subsequent session.

Parent Participation

Given that parents are an integral part of the adolescent's social system and may contribute to the onset and maintenance of depression, a parallel group intervention for the parents of depressed adolescents was developed (Lewinsohn, Rohde, Hops, & Clarke, 1991). The parent course has two primary goals: (a) to inform parents of the CWD-A material to encourage support and reinforcement of the adolescent's use of skills, and (b) to teach parents the communication and problem-solving skills that are being taught to their son or daughter. Parents meet with a separate therapist weekly for 2-hour sessions conducted at the same time as the teen group's sessions. Two joint sessions are held in the seventh week during which the adolescents and the parents practice these skills on issues that are salient to each family. Specially designed workbooks guide parents through these sessions.

Components of the Coping With Depression Course, Adult Version

In the first session therapists present guidelines for the group, the rationale for treatment, and the social-learning concept of depression (Lewinsohn et al., 1985). From the very beginning, participants learn to monitor their mood to provide baseline data and a method for demonstrating changes in mood as a result of learning new skills and engaging in activities. As shown in Figure 10.1, the remaining sessions focus on teaching the various skills.

Increasing Social Skills

Depressed individuals are often deficient in social skills (Libet & Lewinsohn, 1973). To remedy this issue, training in basic conversational techniques, the planning of social activities, and strategies for making friends is spread throughout the course and provides a foundation upon which to build other essential skills (e.g., communication).

Increasing Pleasant Activities

Sessions designed to increase pleasant activities are based on the assumption that relatively low rates of positive reinforcement are critical antecedents of depressive episodes (Lewinsohn, Biglan, & Zeiss, 1976). To increase pleasant activities, adolescents are taught basic self-change skills: (a) self-monitoring to establish a baseline, (b) setting realistic goals,

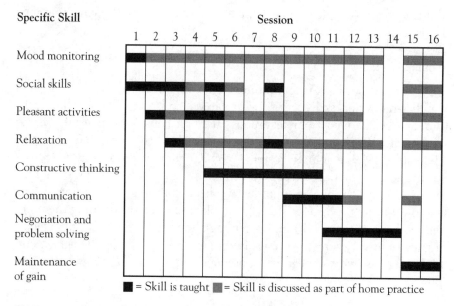

Specific Skill	Session

Figure 10.1. Overview of the Adolescent Coping With Depression course.

(c) developing a plan for behavior change, and (d) self-reinforcement for achieving the goals of their plan. The Pleasant Events Schedule (PES) (MacPhillamy & Lewinsohn, 1982), a comprehensive list of potentially pleasant activities that has been adapted for use with adolescents, provides each participant with an individualized list of activities to be targeted for increase.

Decreasing Anxiety

Adolescents learn relaxation training through the Jacobson (1929) progressive muscle relaxation procedure. A less conspicuous deep-breathing method (Benson, 1975) is also taught for use in public settings. Relaxation training is necessary because many depressed individuals are also anxious (Maser & Cloninger, 1990), which may reduce their potential enjoyment of many pleasant activities, especially social ones.

Reducing Depressogenic Cognitions

Elements of interventions developed by Beck and his colleagues (Beck, Rush, Shaw, & Emery, 1979), Ellis and Harper (1961), and Kranzler (1974) for identifying, challenging, and changing negative thoughts and irrational beliefs have been adapted and simplified. Cartoon strips with popular characters that appeal to adolescents (e.g., Garfield the cat) are used to illustrate depressotypic thoughts and alternative positive thoughts that may be used to counter them.

Communication and Problem Solving

Six sessions provide training in communication, negotiation, and conflict-resolution skills for use with parents and peers. The specific techniques were derived from techniques used in behavioral marital therapy (Gottman, 1979) and their adaptations for use with parents and children (Forgatch, 1989; Robin & Foster, 1989). Communication training focuses on the acquisition of positive behaviors (e.g., active listening) and the inhibition or correction of nonproductive behaviors (e.g., accusations). The adolescents are taught four steps for problem solving: (a) defining the problem without criticism; (b) brainstorming alternative solutions; (c) evaluating and mutually agreeing on a solution; and (d) specifying the agreement, including positive and negative consequences for compliance and noncompliance, respectively.

Planning for the Future

The final two sessions focus on the integration of skills, anticipation of future problems, and development of a life plan and goals. Aided by the group leader, each adolescent develops a written personalized emergency plan, which details the steps he or she will take to counteract renewed feelings of depression, should they occur in the future.

Therapist Compliance

In our research projects, all CWD-A sessions are videotaped for supervision and reliability purposes. An experienced group leader randomly selected and rated for protocol compliance is given three tapes from each adolescent group and two tapes from each parent group. Our protocol compliance scales were shown in the first clinical trial to be reliably completed and have good psychometric properties (Clarke, 1998). In the second trial, mean therapist compliance was 90% (SD = 9.0; range 67%–100%) across 72 rated sessions, indicating excellent compliance.

Booster Sessions

Recurrence following treatment-mediated recovery occurs in up to 50% of depressed adults within 2 years after initial recovery (Belsher & Costello, 1988; Thase, 1990). We initially assumed that the high rate of relapse noted in adults would also occur among depressed adolescents. Therefore, for the second clinical trial we adapted relapse prevention procedures from the addictive disorder treatment literature (Marlatt & Gordon,

1985) to develop a protocol in which individualized booster sessions were offered at 4-month intervals for a 2-year period after treatment. The manual for the booster sessions is designed to address the specific concerns of individual adolescents. After the follow-up assessment, the therapist works with the family and adolescent or the adolescent alone to determine which of the six booster protocols (pleasant events, social skills and communication, relaxation, cognitions, negotiation and problem-solving, and maintaining gains and setting goals) would be most appropriate. The booster sessions (one or two meetings) focus on ways that specific skills previously learned in the CWD-A course might be used to cope with the specific problems that have emerged since the group ended. Because of staff turnover, booster sessions were generally not conducted by the same therapist who led the CWD-A group.

Treatment Efficacy

The First Clinical Trial

Our first controlled clinical trial (Lewinsohn, Clarke, Hops, & Andrews, 1990) involved 59 adolescents meeting the *Diagnostic and Statistical Manual of Mental Disorders, Third Edition* (DSM–III; American Psychiatric Association, 1980) criteria for MDD or dysthymia who were randomly assigned to one of three treatment conditions: (a) a group for adolescents only (Condition A; $n = 21$); (b) an identical group for adolescents but with their parents enrolled in a separate parent group (Condition A+P; $n = 19$); or (c) a wait-list condition (WL; $n = 19$). Participants and their parents completed extensive diagnostic and psychosocial measures at intake and posttreatment and 1, 6, 12, and 24 months after treatment. Multivariate analyses demonstrated significant change from prettreatment to posttreatment on all dependent variables across treatment conditions. Planned comparisons indicated that all significant improvement was accounted for by the two active treatment conditions (e.g., mean scores on the BDI for the two active treatments dropped from 21.5 to 8.3; Cohen's d = 1.18, which represents a large effect size). Contrary to expectation and with only one exception, differences between Conditions A and A+P on diagnostic and other outcome variables failed to attain statistical significance. The one exception was that parents assigned to Condition A+P reported fewer problems on the Child Behavior Checklist (Achenbach & Edelbrock, 1983) at the end of therapy. By the end of treatment 46% of the treated adolescents no longer met DSM–III criteria for depression (compared with 5% in the wait-list condition). By 6 months after treatment, the rate of recovery for treated adolescents increased to 83%. Data collected at 2-year follow-up indicated that treatment gains were maintained for the adolescents in the two active interventions, with very few teenagers experiencing recurrence.

The Second Clinical Trial

Our second clinical trial (Clarke, Rohde, Lewinsohn, Hops, & Seeley, 1999) involved 96 adolescents meeting *DSM–III–R* (American Psychiatric Association, 1987) criteria for MDD or dysthymia who were randomly assigned to one of the following treatment conditions: (a) adolescents only group (Condition A; $n = 37$); (b) adolescent plus parent groups (Condition A+P; $n = 32$); or (c) wait-list control (WL; $n = 27$). Our primary purpose in this study was to replicate our initial findings with a larger sample.

Our second purpose was to evaluate the previously described booster protocol in the maintenance of treatment gains. At the end of treatment, clients in the two active treatment conditions were randomly assigned to one of three 24-month follow-up conditions: (a) "booster," consisting of booster sessions and independent assessments every 4 months ($n = 24$); (b) "frequent assessment," consisting of assessments (but no booster sessions) every 4 months ($n = 16$); or (c) "annual assessment," consisting of assessments every 12 months ($n = 24$). The latter two assessment-only conditions evaluated whether more frequent posttreatment assessment contacts had a therapeutic effect independent of booster therapy.

As in the first clinical trial, diagnostic recovery rates at posttreatment in the two treatments were superior to the wait-list control (67% versus 48%; Cohen's d = .38, a small-to-medium effect size). Likewise, recovery in the two active treatments did not differ significantly (65% in Condition A versus 69% in Condition A+P). Regarding continuous measures, the two active treatments (which did not differ) were associated with significantly greater reductions in both BDI scores (change score effect size = .61) and Global Assessment of Functioning scores (change score effect size = .54). The two active treatments also did not significantly differ in recovery rates across the 2-year follow-up.

This replication study confirmed our previous finding that parent involvement in the CWD-A course was not associated with significantly enhanced improvement. These results are contrary to widely held clinical beliefs and our own initial hypotheses concerning the importance of parental involvement in adolescent treatment. Parental attendance (especially for fathers) in these trials was not perfect, and both of our studies examined only one method of involving parents in treatment. Other modalities, such as an integrated family therapy approach, may yield better outcomes. Our results, however, are consistent with the findings of Brent et al. (1997), who also found no advantage in family therapy relative to individual CBT for the treatment of adolescent depression.

The primary impact of the booster condition was to significantly accelerate recovery among adolescents who were still depressed at the end of acute treatment. By 12-month follow-up, 100% (5 of 5) of depressed adolescents randomized to the booster condition had recovered, versus 50%

(6 of 12) of participants in the two assessment-only conditions, a significant ($p < .05$) difference. However, by 24-month follow-up, these rates had converged, with 90% (9 of 10) of participants in the two assessment-only conditions achieving remission. The mean time for recovery for adolescents in the booster condition who were still depressed at the end of the CWD-A course was 23.5 weeks ($SE = 3.8$), compared with 67.0 weeks ($SE = 8.4$) for adolescents in the two assessment-only conditions ($p < .001$). Although comparable proportions of adolescents eventually recovered in the two assessment-only conditions, the shorter time to recovery in the booster condition (a mean reduction of almost 44 weeks) is clinically meaningful. In light of the present findings, our booster intervention may be better described as a continuation treatment aimed at improving on the gains of the acute intervention, rather than a prophylactic treatment focused on prevention of future depressive episodes. Regarding depression recurrence, at 2-year follow-up, differences in recurrence rates among participants in the three follow-up conditions were minimal (overall depression recurrence rate was 22%).

Several possible explanations for the negative findings for the booster protocol can be offered. First of all, many adolescents assigned to the booster condition completed the assessment interviews but not the actual booster sessions. Complete booster session attendance data were not collected, but attendance was estimated at less than 50%. Given the high recovery rates obtained during acute treatment, many adolescents may have had no motivation to continue with treatment. The participants who were still depressed or were having other difficulties after treatment may have been uncomfortable or unwilling to wait 4 months for the first scheduled booster session and therefore may have sought another form of treatment. Based on our experience, we propose that the provision of individual booster sessions be limited to adolescents who are still experiencing depressive symptoms at the end of group therapy and that boosters occur at more frequent intervals at the beginning and diminish in frequency as the adolescent improves. An alternative approach that capitalizes on the positive group relationships that generally form during the CWD-A course sessions is to conduct group boosters with the original group members and therapist.

Clinical Vignette

Jane (not her real name), an attractive and neatly dressed 15-year-old female, appeared sullen and unhappy at her intake interview. Her speech was notably slow, although she had no difficult answering the questions. She lived with her biological mother, father, and two older sisters. She reported her relationship with her mother and sisters as average but noted that she argued several times a week with her father. In 10th grade, she reported boredom and discomfort with the social aspects of school and often lost her temper with teachers. She was skipping approximately seven classes per month. Her grades were down, and she had recently received two Ds, much to the concern of her mother, who felt that Jane just didn't care. Jane did not belong to any clubs but had played on the soccer team. She reported having no close friends for the past year; she talked to one girl but saw her only at school. Her spare-time activities were doing homework, reading, babysitting, and watching television.

Jane reported being in a depressed mood for the previous 6 months. In addition to depressed mood, anhedonia, guilt, and concentration and indecision problems, she reported wanting to be dead but loving her family too much to actually hurt herself. Indications of functional impairment included withdrawal from and conflict with her family, an inability to make and maintain friends, isolation, and academic problems. Jane had a previous MDD episode that occurred at age 12 and lasted 3 months. Her mother felt that Jane had been depressed for several years. They had taken her to counseling at their church and to a personal growth seminar, but neither was viewed as helpful. In addition to MDD, Jane had some weight loss, a fear of becoming obese, and a preoccupation with food; however, she did not meet the criteria for a diagnosis of anorexia nervosa.

Jane attended all 16 sessions of the CWD-A groups and actively participated in group. She completed all of her homework for 40% of the sessions and partial or no homework for the remaining 60% of sessions. On a 7-point scale of skill mastery (7 = complete mastery; 4 = average), she was rated by her therapist as achieving 6 on relaxation skills; 5 on pleasant activities, cognitions, and communication; and 4 on problem solving. Her BDI score in the first session was 35. At the last session, her BDI score was 18.

At the posttreatment interview, the MDD episode was considered to be in remission. Her affect and speech were normal, and her BDI score was 2. Jane could not recall any difficult times since intake interview, although she said that some situations at school still "bring me down." Her grades had improved considerably, and she was very satisfied about the academic aspect of school. She no longer skipped classes. She reported having three new friends, in whom she could confide and count on. Relationships with family members were relatively unchanged, but she felt that she was more open and confiding with her parents and less likely to withdraw from family activities. About halfway through the group, she reported no longer having daily thoughts of death or the desire to be dead. Her mother was not as aware of changes or improvements, although she stated that Jane's eating behavior was no longer a concern.

During the 2-year follow-up, Jane remained free of depression (BDI scores ranged from 0 to 15). Her school grades improved (GPA = 3.8 at 16 months posttreatment) and she made the cheerleading squad, which she very much enjoyed. She also worked for the school newspaper. She lost the three friendships she had developed at the end of group but developed new ones, stating that she had "lots" of close friends. She enjoyed a 2-month relationship with her first boyfriend. At the last follow-up interview, Jane reported periods of mild depression lasting approximately 1 hour per week. She was taking advanced college preparation classes, which she found very challenging. She also was working 20 hours per week but no longer participating in extracurricular school activities. When asked about spare-time activities, she said she never has much spare time.

Better Understanding Response to the Coping With Depression Course, Adult Version

Predictors of Recovery

Using data from the first clinical trial (Clarke et al., 1992), we found that a greater change in BDI from pretreatment to posttreatment had significant univariate associations with a greater number of past diagnoses, a younger onset age of first depression, parent involvement in treatment, female gender, fewer dysfunctional attitudes, and residence in a single-parent or blended-family home. A simultaneous multivariate regression analysis predicting BDI change retained the first three variables; multiple $R = .84$, $p < .001$. The significance of parental involvement in treatment seems to contradict the earlier findings that outcome for Condition A+P did not differ from Condition A. This discrepancy may be due to the fact that multivariate analyses were conducted in the original report, whereas only the BDI was used for predicting change.

In a discriminant function analysis with posttreatment recovery as per diagnosis as the dependent variable, the overall canonical correlation was $R = .63$ ($p < .005$). Diagnostic recovery at posttreatment was associated with lower initial levels of self-reported depression, lower initial state anxiety, higher initial enjoyment and frequency of pleasant activities, and more rational thoughts at intake.

In the second clinical trial, the dependent variable was represented by an aggregate of scores on the BDI and Hamilton Depression Rating Scale (Hamilton, 1960). Pretreatment variables with significant univariate associations with lower scores on the depression aggregate posttreatment included higher enjoyment and frequency of pleasant activities, younger age, male gender, no past history of suicide attempt, lower intake depression levels, and more rational thoughts. A simultaneous multiple regression analysis predicting the depression measure at posttreatment retained the first three variables; multiple $R = .57$, $p < .001$. A lower initial level of depression, greater enjoyment and frequency of pleasant activities, and more frequent endorsement of rational thoughts predicted positive treatment response in both samples. Unfortunately, the lack of crossvalidation for the remaining variables is not uncommon in treatment outcome research.

Impact of Initial Severity

We also evaluated whether predicted treatment differences would be greater among more severely depressed adolescents (Rohde, Lewinsohn, & Seeley, 1994). In the second clinical trial, improvement for the two active treatment conditions in comparison with the control condition was greater in the more severely depressed group than in the less severely depressed group. This finding, however, was not replicated in the first clinical trial. In addition, our prediction that the relative effectiveness of the A+P condition over the A-only condition would be accentuated in the more severely depressed group was not supported in either clinical trial. Overall, both forms of the CWD-A treatment appeared effective for mild and more severely depressed adolescents.

Impact of Comorbidity

We examined several hypotheses concerning the potentially negative impact of lifetime psychiatric comorbidity on participation in, and benefit from, the CWD-A course (Rohde, Clarke, Lewinsohn, Seeley, & Kaufman, 2001). Combining data from the first two clinical trials, we examined 151 depressed adolescents, 40% of whom had one or more lifetime comorbid diagnoses at intake. Comorbid anxiety disorders were associated with higher depression measure scores at intake and with greater decrease in depression scores by posttreatment. Although total lifetime comorbidity was unrelated to recovery from depression, the presence of lifetime substance abuse or dependence was associated with slower recovery time. Participants with a lifetime history of attention-deficit and disruptive behavior disorders at intake were more likely to experience depression recurrence during follow-up. The presence of comorbidity was unrelated to therapy participation or group process measures. In conclusion, although some outcomes were worse for some comorbidities, the reassuring overall conclusion is that the presence of psychiatric comorbidity was generally not a contraindication for the use of the CWD-A intervention with depressed adolescents.

Subsequent Research With the Coping With Depression Course, Adult Version

School-Based Prevention

On the basis of our successful tertiary treatment outcome research, we initiated a randomized trial to examine the efficacy of a school-based, group cognitive therapy prevention program in reducing the incidence of unipolar affective disorders in high-school adolescents at risk for future depression (Clarke et al., 1995). Ninth-grade adolescents in three high schools were identified as potentially at risk for depression through school-wide administration ($N = 1,652$) of the Center for Epidemiologic Studies Depression

Scale (CES-D; Radloff, 1977), followed by a structured diagnostic interview (Schedule for Affective Disorder and Schizophrenia for School-Age Children; Orvaschel & Puig-Antich, 1986) for the 222 adolescents with CES-D scores of 24 or greater. The 172 adolescents identified as not currently depressed but with elevated CES-D scores were invited to participate in the prevention study; 150 accepted and were randomly assigned to either (a) a 15-session, after-school, cognitive–behavioral preventive intervention (n = 76); or (b) a usual-care control condition (n = 74). The intervention, titled the Adolescent Coping With Stress course (CWS-A; Clarke & Lewinsohn, 1990) consisted of fifteen 45-minute sessions in which participants learned cognitive therapy techniques to identify and challenge negative or irrational thoughts that may contribute to the development of future affective disorder. Survival analysis results indicated significantly fewer cases of either MDD or dysthymia in the experimental group (Mantel-Cox χ^2 = 2.72, $p < .05$) at 12-month follow-up, with affective disorder total incidence rates of 14% for the active intervention versus 26% for the control condition.

Health Maintenance Organization–Based Prevention

Clarke et al. (2001) conducted a randomized trial of a cognitive–behavioral prevention program for adolescents with subsyndromal levels of depressive symptoms whose parents were receiving treatment for depression in a health maintenance organization (HMO). Adults in treatment for depression who had children between the ages of 13 and 18 received letters from their health care providers inviting them to participate in the study. Interested parents were interviewed to confirm their diagnosis of a mood disorder, and the children were evaluated with regard to their history and current level of depressive symptoms and disorders. A "demoralized" group was identified that had current subdiagnostic levels of depressive symptoms (i.e., a CES-D score >24) or a previous episode of MDD. These adolescents were randomly assigned to either a usual-care control condition (n = 49) or the CWS-A course (n = 45). Survival analyses revealed significantly fewer new episodes of affective disorder in the CWS-A group (9%) versus the treatment-as-usual group (29%) at the 15-month follow-up ($p < .005$). The odds ratio of depression at 12 months was 5.6 (95% CI = 1.6–20.4) when adjusted for gender, age, CES-D score, and previous depression history (the latter two were the criteria for inclusion). In conclusion, the CWS-A course appears to be a brief group cognitive therapy prevention program that can reduce the risk for depression among high-risk adolescents.

Health Maintenance Organization–Based Treatment

As part of the previously mentioned case-finding procedure, some adolescents with depressed parents were currently experiencing a depressive episode at the time of assessment. These adolescents participated in a separate randomized controlled effectiveness trial to evaluate the CWD-A relative to treatment as usual in an HMO setting (Clarke et al., 2002). Eligible offspring (ages 13 to 18) who met current *DSM–III–R* criteria for MDD or dysthymia were randomly assigned to either usual HMO care (*n* = 47) or usual care plus the CWD-A course (*n* = 41). Participants were assessed up to 24 months after treatment. Using intent-to-treat analyses, we were unable to detect any significant advantage of the CBT program over usual care, either for depression diagnoses, continuous depression measures, nonaffective measures, or functioning outcomes. Thus, the group cognitive–behavioral treatment did not appear to incrementally benefit depressed adolescents who were also allowed to receive the usual amounts of care provided in this HMO setting.

Use of the Coping With Depression Course, Adult Version, With Comorbid Depressed Adolescents

Given the high rate of psychiatric comorbidity with depression in adolescents (e.g., Rohde, Lewinsohn, & Seeley, 1991) and the fact that most efficacy trials have excluded depressed youth with current comorbidity, our next trial evaluated the effectiveness of the CWD-A intervention for depressed adolescents with comorbid conduct disorder (Rohde, Clarke, Mace, Jorgensen, & Seeley, 2004). Between 1998 and 2001, 93 adolescents (ages 13 to 17) meeting criteria for MDD and conduct disorder were recruited from a county juvenile justice department and randomly assigned to CWD-A or a life-skills and tutoring (LS) control. Participants were assessed posttreatment and at 6- and 12-month follow-up. MDD recovery rates posttreatment were greater in the CWD-A group (39%) compared with the LS (19%) control; odds ratio = 2.66 (95% CI = 1.03–6.85). In addition, CWD-A participants reported greater reductions in BDI and Hamilton Depression Rating Scale scores. Group differences in MDD recovery rates at 6- and 12-month follow-up were nonsignificant, however, as were differences in conduct disorder both posttreatment and during follow-up. To our knowledge, this study is the first randomized controlled trial of a psychosocial intervention with depressed adolescents with conduct disorders. In a related study (Rohde, Jorgensen, Seeley, & Mace, 2004), the CWD-A intervention was modified to serve as a more general prosocial copings skills group beneficial to youth incarcerated in state youth correctional facilities.

Individual Cognitive–Behavioral Therapy Augmenting Pharmacotherapy

Clarke and his colleagues are currently evaluating the effectiveness of a short-term, collaborative care model of CBT as an adjunct to antidepressant medication treatment for adolescents with MDD in primary care. This 4-year randomized controlled trial is being conducted at four major primary care clinics in a large HMO. A total of 150 adolescents will be randomly assigned to either (a) usual-care depression pharmacotherapy, or (b) usual-care pharmacotherapy plus six to eight individual sessions of CBT delivered by a trained mental health therapist. The aim is to examine whether adjunctive CBT improves medication adherence and duration reducing overall depression.

Individual Cognitive–Behavioral Therapy: Treatment for Adolescents With Depression Study

The National Institute of Mental Health has funded a large multisite clinical trial to study adolescents (ages 12 to 17) with MDD. The Treatment for Adolescents With Depression Study (TADS) compares the immediate and long-term effectiveness of different treatments and combinations of treatments for depression. A total of 439 adolescents with MDD were randomly assigned across four treatment conditions: (a) fluoxetine alone, (b) pill placebo, (c) individual CBT, and (d) combination fluoxetine and CBT. The CWD-A program was one of the two source CBT interventions on which the TADS CBT program was based. Comparison of the four conditions at the end of the 12-week acute phase of treatment (The TADS Team, 2004) indicated that combined treatment resulted in the highest rate of diagnostic remission (71%). Contrary to expectation, CBT monotherapy had a lower remission rate (43%) compared with fluoxetine monotherapy (61%) and was not statistically superior to clinical management with a pill placebo (35%) at the end of 12 weeks. Longer-term comparisons of the three active treatments to each other will be available in 2005.

FUTURE DIRECTIONS

Although results for the CWD-A intervention are highly encouraging, several issues still need to be addressed. The treatment approach must be evaluated and modified for use with racial and cultural minorities. Researchers must also evaluate whether the CWD-A intervention can be used in conjunction with other modes of therapy (e.g., family therapy, pharmacotherapy). Additional research might examine alternative approaches for prophylactic treatment, including reunion meetings of the acute treatment groups. Our experience indicates that many adolescents are very enthusiastic about seeing their former group members and the group leader. Other possible recurrence prevention interventions include telephone boosters or boosters only for those adolescents with the highest risk for recurrence (e.g., those with past history of multiple episodes or chronicity, those with high rates of depression in family members; Thase, 1990).

SUMMARY

Although adolescent depression is common and has a serious impact on functioning, it is often unrecognized and untreated. Our CBT group intervention, CWD-A, has been shown to be an effective, nonstigmatizing, and cost-efficient treatment for depression. We believe that with relatively minor modifications, this form of therapy can be successfully implemented in clinical practice. We are very interested in hearing about the efforts of clinical psychologists and other mental health providers to incorporate the intervention in clinics, private practice, and schools.

REFERENCES

Achenbach, T. M., & Edelbrock, C. S. (1983). *Manual for the Child Behavior Checklist and Revised Child Behavior Profile*. Burlington: University of Vermont Department of Psychiatry.

Ackerson, J., Scogin, F., McKendree-Smith, N., & Lyman, R. D. (1998). Cognitive bibliotherapy for mild and moderate adolescent depressive symptomatology. *Journal of Consulting and Clinical Psychology, 66*, 685–690.

American Psychiatric Association. (1980). *Diagnostic and statistical manual of mental disorders* (3rd ed.). Washington, DC: Author.

American Psychiatric Association. (1987). *Diagnostic and statistical manual of mental disorders* (3rd ed., rev.). Washington, DC: Author.

Beck, A. T. (1967). *Depression: Clinical, experimental, and theoretical aspects*. New York: Harper & Row.

Beck, A. T., Rush, A. J., Shaw, B. F., & Emery, G. (1979). *Cognitive therapy of depression*. New York: Guilford Press.

Beck, A. T., Ward, C. H., Mendelson, M., Mock, J. E., & Erbaugh, J. K. (1961). An inventory for measuring depression. *Archives of General Psychiatry, 4*, 561–571.

Belsher, G., & Costello, C. G. (1988). Relapse after recovery from unipolar depression: A critical review. *Psychological Bulletin, 104*, 84–96.

Benson, H. (1975). *The relaxation response*. New York: William Morrow.

Birmaher B., Brent, D. A., Kolko D., Baugher, M., Bridge, J., Holder, D., et al. (2000). Clinical outcome after short-term psychotherapy for adolescents with major depressive disorder. *Archives of General Psychiatry, 57*, 29–36.

Brent, D. A., Holder, D., Kolko, D., Birmaher, B., Baugher, M., Roth, C., et al. (1997). A clinical psychotherapy trial for adolescent depression comparing cognitive, family, and supportive therapy. *Archives of General Psychiatry, 54*, 877–885.

Clarke, G. N. (1998). Intervention fidelity in the psychosocial prevention treatment of adolescent depression. *Journal of Prevention and Intervention in the Community, 17*, 19–33.

Clarke, G. N., Hawkins, W., Murphy, M., Sheeber, L. B., Lewinsohn, P. M., & Seeley, J. R. (1995). Targeted prevention of unipolar depressive disorder in an at-risk sample of high school adolescents: A randomized trial of a group cognitive interview. *Journal of American Academy of Child and Adolescent Psychiatry, 34,* 312–321.

Clarke, G. N., Hops, H., Lewinsohn, P. M., Andrews, J. A., Seeley, J. R., & Williams, J. A. (1992). Cognitive–behavioral group treatment of adolescent depression: Prediction of outcome. *Behavior Therapy, 23,* 341–354.

Clarke, G. N., Hornbrook, M. C., Lynch, F. L., Polen, M. R., Gale, J., Beardslee, W., et al. (2001). A randomized trial of a group cognitive intervention for preventing depression in adolescent offspring of depressed parents. *Archives of General Psychiatry, 58,* 27–1134.

Clarke, G. N., Hornbrook, M. C., Lynch, F. L., Polen, M. R., Gale, J., O'Connor, E., et al. (2002). Group cognitive behavioral treatment for depressed adolescent offspring of depressed parents in an HMO. *Journal of the American Academy of Child and Adolescent Psychiatry, 41,* 305–13.

Clarke, G. N., & Lewinsohn, P. M. (1990). *Instructor's manual for the Adolescent Coping with Stress Course for the secondary prevention of depression.* Retrieved August 14, 2004, from http://www.kpchr.org/public/acwd/acwd.html

Clarke, G. N., Lewinsohn, P. M., & Hops, H. (1990). *Instructor's manual for the Adolescent Coping with Depression Course.* Retrieved August 14, 2004, from http://www.kpchr.org/public/acwd/acwd.html

Clarke, G. N., Rohde, P., Lewinsohn, P. M., Hops, H., & Seeley, J. R. (1999). Cognitive–behavioral treatment of adolescent depression: Efficacy of acute group treatment and booster sessions. *Journal of the American Academy of Child and Adolescent Psychiatry, 38,* 272–279.

Curry, J. (2001). Specific psychotherapies for childhood and adolescent depression. *Biological Psychiatry, 49,* 1091–1100.

Ellis, A., & Harper, R. A. (1961). *A guide to rational living.* Hollywood, CA: Wilshire Book.

Ferster, C. B. (1966). Animal behavior and mental illness. *Psychological Record, 16,* 345–356.

Forgatch, M. S. (1989). Patterns and outcome with family problem solving: The disrupting effect of negative emotions. *Journal of Marriage and the Family, 51,* 115–124.

Gottman, J. M. (1979). *Marital interaction: Empirical investigations.* New York: Academic Press.

Hamilton, M. A. (1960). A rating scale for depression. *Journal of Neurology and Neurosurgical Psychiatry, 23,* 56–62.

Jacobson, E. (1929). *Progressive relaxation.* Chicago: University of Chicago Press.

Kahn, J., Kehle, T., Jenson, W., & Clark, E. (1990). Comparison of cognitive–behavioral, relaxation, and self-modeling interventions for depression among middle-school students. *School Psychology Review, 19,* 196–211.

Kaslow, N. J., & Thompson, M. P. (1998). Applying the criteria for empirically supported treatments to studies of psychosocial interventions for child and adolescent depression. *Journal of Clinical Child Psychology, 27*, 146–55.

Kranzler, G. (1974). *You can change how you feel.* Eugene, OR: RETC Press.

Lewinsohn, P. M., Antonuccio, D. O., Steinmetz-Breckenridge, J., & Teri, L. (1984). *The coping with depression course: A psychoeducational intervention for unipolar depression.* Eugene, OR: Castalia Press.

Lewinsohn, P. M., Biglan, A., & Zeiss, A. (1976). Behavioral treatment of depression. In P. Davidson (Ed.), *Behavioral management of anxiety, depression, and pain* (pp. 91–146). New York: Brunner/Mazel.

Lewinsohn, P. M., Clarke, G. N., Hops, H., & Andrews, J. (1990). Cognitive–behavioral group treatment of depression in adolescents. *Behavior Therapy, 21*, 385–401.

Lewinsohn, P. M., Hoberman, H., Teri, L., & Hautzinger, M. (1985). An integrative theory of depression. In S. Reiss & R. Bootzin (Eds.), *Theoretical issues in behavior therapy* (pp. 331–359). New York: Academic Press.

Lewinsohn, P. M., Rohde, P., Hops, H., & Clarke, G. (1991). *Leader's manual for parent groups: Adolescent coping with depression course.* Retrieved August 14, 2004, from http://www.kpchr.org/public/acwd/acwd.html

Lewinsohn, P. M., Weinstein, M., & Shaw, D. (1969). Depression: A clinical research approach. In R. D. Rubin & C. M. Frank (Eds.), *Advances in behavior therapy* (pp. 231–241). New York: Academic Press.

Libet, J., & Lewinsohn, P. M. (1973). Concept of social skill with special reference to the behavior of depressed person. *Journal of Consulting and Clinical Psychology, 40*, 304–312.

MacPhillamy, D. J., & Lewinsohn, P. M. (1982). The pleasant events schedule: Studies on reliability, validity, and scale intercorrelations. *Journal of Consulting and Clinical Psychology, 50*, 363–380.

Marlatt, G. A., & Gordon, J. R. (1985). *Relapse prevention: Maintenance strategies in the treatment of addictive behaviors.* New York: Guilford Press.

Maser, J. D., & Cloninger, C. R. (1990). *Comorbidity in anxiety and mood disorders.* Washington, DC: American Psychiatric Press.

Orvaschel, H., & Puig-Antich, J. (1986). *Schedule for affective disorder and schizophrenia for school-age children. Epidemiologic version: Kiddie-SADS-E (K-SADS-E)* (4th ed.). [Technical report.]. Pittsburgh, PA: Western Psychiatric Institute and Clinic.

Radloff, L. S. (1977). The CES-D Scale: A self-report depression scale for research in the general population. *Applied Psychological Measurement, 1*, 385–401.

Reinecke, M. A., Ryan, N. E., & DuBois, D. L. (1998). Cognitive–behavioral therapy of depression and depressive symptoms during adolescence: A review and meta-analysis. *Journal of the American Academy of Child and Adolescent Psychiatry, 37*, 26–34.

Robin, A. L., & Foster, S. L. (1989). *Negotiating parent-adolescent conflict: A behavioral family systems approach.* New York: Guilford Press.

Rohde, P., Clarke, G. N., Lewinsohn, P. M., Seeley, J. R., & Kaufman, N. K. (2001). Impact of comorbidity on a cognitive–behavioral group treatment for adolescent depression. *Journal of the American Academy of Child and Adolescent Psychiatry, 40*, 795–802.

Rohde, P., Clarke, G. N., Mace, D. E., Jorgensen, J. S., & Seeley, J. R. (2004). An efficacy/effectiveness study of cognitive-behavioral treatment for adolescents with comorbid major depression and conduct disorder. *Journal of the American Academy of Child and Adolescent Psychiatry, 43*, 660–668.

Rohde, P., Jorgensen, J. S., Seeley, J. R., & Mace, D. E. (2004). Pilot evaluation of the coping course: A CBT intervention to enhance coping skills in incarcerated youth. *Journal of the American Academy of Child and Adolescent Psychiatry, 43*, 669–676.

Rohde, P., Lewinsohn, P. M., & Seeley, J. R. (1991). Comorbidity with unipolar depression II: Comorbidity with other mental disorders in adolescents and adults. *Journal of Abnormal Psychology, 100*, 214–222.

Rohde, P., Lewinsohn, P. M., & Seeley, J. R. (1994). Response of depressed adolescents to cognitive–behavioral treatment: Do differences in initial severity clarify the comparison of treatment? *Journal of Consulting and Clinical Psychology, 62*, 851–854.

Rosselló, J., & Bernal, G. (1999). The efficacy of cognitive–behavioral and interpersonal treatments for depression in Puerto Rican adolescents. *Journal of Consulting and Clinical Psychology, 67*, 734–745.

Seligman, M. E. P. (1975). *Helplessness: On depression, development, and death.* San Francisco: Freeman.

Stark, K., Reynolds, W., & Kaslow, N. (1987). A comparison of the relative efficacy of self-control therapy and a behavioral problem-solving therapy for depression in children. *Journal of Abnormal Child Psychology, 15*, 91–113.

Thase, E. (1990). Relapse and recurrence in unipolar major depression: Short-term and long-term approaches. *Journal of Clinical Psychiatry, 51*, 51–57.

The Treatment for Adolescents with Depression Study (TADS) Team (2004). The Treatment for Adolescents with Depression Study (TADS): Short-term effectiveness and safety outcomes. *Journal of the American Medical Association 292*, 807–820.

Vostanis, P., Feehan, C., Grattan, E., & Bickerton, W. (1996). A randomized controlled outpatient trial of cognitive–behavioral treatment for children and adolescents with depression: Nine-month follow-up. *Journal of Affective Disorders, 40*, 105–116.

Wood, A., Harrington, R., & Moore, A. (1996). Controlled trial of brief cognitive–behavioural intervention in adolescent patients with depressive disorders, *Journal of Child Psychology and Psychiatry, 37*, 737–746.

11

TREATMENT OF CHILD AND ADOLESCENT DEPRESSIVE DISORDERS

KEVIN D. STARK, JULIA HOKE, MELANIE BALLATORE,
CARMEN VALDEZ, NANCY SCAMMACA, AND JULIE GRIFFIN

BRIEF REVIEW OF LITERATURE

The number of youngsters who are experiencing depressive disorders is increasing at the same time that the age of onset is decreasing (Klerman & Weissman, 1989). An estimated 20% of children and adolescents will have experienced an episode of major depression before completing high school (Seligman, 1998). Depressive disorders during childhood also appear to be more virulent and of longer duration than depressive disorders in adults (Jensen, Ryan, & Prien, 1992), and they are a risk factor for the development of additional psychological disturbances (Kovacs, Feinberg, Crouse-Novak, Paulauskas, & Finkelstein, 1984) as well as for the development of depressive disorders later in life (Pine, Cohen, Gurley, Brook, & Yuju, 1998).

Given the scope and the severity of the problem, effective treatment of depressed children and adolescents is of paramount concern.

Research Into the Nature of Depressive Disorders

Guiding our treatment outcome research has been the belief that a treatment program should be designed to address the disturbances in emotional, cognitive, interpersonal, and family functioning that are identified through basic research. Since the previous edition of this book, we have been conducting a series of studies into the possible contribution of cognitive, emotional, interpersonal, and family variables in depressive disorders. One possible pathway to the development of a depressive disorder is a disturbance in cognition that serves as a diathesis in the presence of stress to produce the disorder (see Stark, Boswell Sander, Yancy, Bronik, & Hoke, 2000, for a review). In a series of investigations, we have evaluated the relationship between attributional style, self-schema, and depressive disorders in youngsters. Our research found partial support for the attributional model of depression (Abramson, Metalsky, & Alloy, 1989), with the youngsters' attributions for positive events but not negative events predicting severity of depression (Sommer Reinemann, Stark, Swearer, & Kaslow, 2001). In addition, their sense of self, world, and future (depressive–cognitive triad), their automatic thoughts, and severity of sexual abuse independently predicted severity of depression.

Given the importance of self-schema in depression, our follow-up research has focused on more clearly understanding the nature and origin of the depressive youth's self-schema. In the aforementioned study (Sommer et al., 2001), a self-report measure was used to assess self-schema. To address concerns about the validity of paper-and-pencil measures of self-schema, a thematic coding system for youngster's Thematic Apperception Test stories was used with youngsters who received diagnoses of major depression, conduct disorder, or both disorders, and a group of matched controls. An undesirability self-schema (Young & Lindemann, 1992) was coded as present if the predominant theme in the story was one in which the characters were defective, socially undesirable or alienated, or failed to achieve a successful outcome. An impaired limits self-schema (Young & Lindemann, 1992) was coded if a theme was present in which the characters expressed a sense of entitlement, insufficient self-control or self-discipline, or dehumanization. As expected, stories of depressed youngsters were characterized by themes of undesirability, and stories of youngsters with a conduct disorder were characterized by themes of impaired limits. Stories of comorbid youngsters were characterized by both undesirability and impaired limits. Thus, the information processing of depressed youngsters appears to be guided by an undesirability self-schema. These results add to a growing body of research that indicates the importance of intervening at the level of the self-schema when treating depressed children and adolescents. However, whether the objective of treatment should be to build a more positive self-schema or whether it is necessary to change a negative self-schema remains unclear.

We have hypothesized that the self-schema of some depressed young-sters develops as a result of repeated learning experiences that convey negative messages from their parents about the child himself or herself, the world, and the future. Studies of nonhospitalized youngsters with depressive disorders relative to those with anxiety disorders or attention-deficit/hyper-activity disorder (ADHD) suggest a relationship between negative messages from the parents and the depressive self-schema, a relationship unique to depressive disorders (Schmidt, Stark, Carlson, & Anthony, 1998; Stark, Schmidt, & Joiner, 1996). These studies indicate the importance of designing treatments that address the family interactions leading to and supporting the development of these negative beliefs.

Depression in children and adolescents is also characterized by a difficulty regulating emotion and coping with stress. Depressed children tend to generate more passive, less effective methods for regulating mood relative to nondepressed children and hold lower expectations for the efficacy of strategies generated by others (Garber, Braafladt, & Weiss, 1995; Garber, Braafladt, & Zeman, 1991). Depressed children are also more likely to report using strategies that may exacerbate distress (Garber et al., 1991, 1995). Depressed girls tend to avoid direct problem-solving in interpersonal situations, and depressed boys tend to act in aggressive ways that further interpersonal conflict. In general, children and adolescents with depression are more likely to choose avoidant means for coping with stressors (c.f. Chan, 1995). In contrast, the use of more adaptive strategies for coping with stressors and related affect is associated with fewer depressive symptoms (Jeney-Gammon, Daugherty, Finch, Belter, & Foster, 1993).

The acquisition of coping and emotion regulation strategies over the course of development progresses naturally. Infants, children, and adolescents use different coping strategies (see Stark et al., 2000, for a description of this developmental process). During cognitive–behavioral training for depression, youngsters learn coping, emotion regulation, and cognitive strategies that are designed to help them manage stress and their depressive symptoms and to modify their depressive thinking. Typically, depressed children are taught the same strategies as depressed adults. We have been conducting another line of research that addresses these issues, and data collection is being completed as this chapter is being written. Students deemed to be effective at coping with stress by their teachers were asked to complete measures and participate in focus groups about the stressors they face, the skills they use to cope with these stressors, and the strategies they use to manage sadness, anger, and anxiety. Data were also collected from both youngsters and parents regarding the role parents may have played in the development of these coping skills.

The youngsters reported using a variety of behavioral, cognitive, and social support strategies for managing their moods and stress. For example, both fifth- and sixth-grade boys reported hitting their stuffed animals as a means of reducing anger. They also reported talking to older friends about what to do. Sometimes they would think about it and come to the conclusion that it was "no big deal," which would reduce their anger. When feeling sad, they reported talking to their stuffed animals, talking to their parents or friends, and trying to think about happier times. They reported using distraction as a means of managing both emotions. They would do things like play a video game, get on the Internet, watch television, or do something else engaging and distracting. The paper-and-pencil measures have not yet been analyzed. In pilot data, the boys reported that their mothers encouraged them to engage in problem-solving and to think about the problem more often than mothers of girls. These preliminary findings suggest that children use developmentally equivalent strategies for managing their emotions and that it is important for therapists to teach the youngsters strategies that are developmentally appropriate.

Treatment Outcome Research

Treatment outcome research with depressed children is scarce. A few clinical case studies suggest that a cognitive–behavioral therapy (CBT) may be effective in improving depressive symptoms (Frame, Johnstone, & Giblin, 1988; Frame, Matson, Sonis, Fialkov, & Kazdin, 1982; Petti, Bornstein, Delamater, & Conner, 1980). In general, control group comparison studies of 10 to 12 sessions with depressed schoolchildren have shown CBT to be more effective than no treatment (Butler, Miezitis, Friedman, & Cole, 1980; Stark, Reynolds, & Kaslow, 1987; Weisz, Thurber, Sweeney, Proffitt, & LeGagnoux, 1997) and an attention placebo condition (Butler et al., 1980). However, results have been mixed when CBT has been compared with another active treatment. CBT was not superior to a social-skills training program (Butler et al., 1980) or a behavioral problem-solving treatment (Stark et al., 1987), although it was more effective than a traditional nondirective counseling condition in another study (Stark, 1990). The improvements in treatment effects were maintained at 5-week (Stark et al., 1987), 7-month (Stark, 1990), and 9-month (Weisz et al., 1997) follow-up assessments.

The effectiveness of CBT when administered in a less time-intensive format seems to be even less clear. In a study in which social competence training (CBT-based) was completed in eight sessions with children between the ages of 7 and 12, CBT was not found to be superior to an attention placebo (drama training) nor to a no-treatment control condition (Liddle & Spence, 1990). These results may be due to the small sample size (10 or 11 children per condition) that limited the investigators' power to find between-group differences. An examination of their results reveals that participants in the active treatment reported almost a standard deviation reduction in depressive symptoms at posttreatment, placing their scores in the normal range, whereas participants in the control conditions reported about half as much improvement and continued to report levels of depressive symptoms that exceeded the normal range of functioning.

Two recent investigations have evaluated the effectiveness of CBT for a mixed population of children and adolescents with depressive disorders. In a study of youth outpatients (Vostanis, Feehan, Grattan, & Birkenton, 1996a), a brief (average of six sessions) CBT intervention was compared with an inactive treatment that controlled for time with therapist. Both interventions were effective in reducing depressive symptoms at posttreatment, and the gains were maintained at 9-month follow-up (Vostanis, Feehan, Grattan, & Birkenton, 1996b). Somewhat surprisingly, CBT was not superior to the inactive treatment. The investigators noted that the brief number of sessions over an extended period of time (3.5 months) may have contributed to the nonsignificant findings. Youth outpatients typically forget what they have discussed during treatment sessions when they are 1 week apart and are much less likely to employ the strategies that they are learning during extended between-session intervals. Thus, it is questionable as to whether these youngsters learned and used the problem-solving strategies they were taught. The improvements that were accrued could be due to the nonspecifics of psychotherapy.

In a similar brief intervention that included six sessions of CBT administered in an individual format, CBT was more effective at posttreatment than relaxation training (Wood, Harrington, & Moore, 1996). However, the improvements were not maintained at 3- and 6-month follow-up assessments. Again, the investigators attributed this result to the brevity of the treatment and the fact that it was designed to treat acute symptoms. In a follow-up study, Kroll, Harrington, Jayson, Fraser, and Gowers (1996) provided youngsters who had been successfully treated with CBT (Wood et al., 1996) an additional 6 months of CBT. Results indicated that youngsters who received the additional treatment were significantly less likely to relapse.

There have been a number of studies that have evaluated the effectiveness of CBT for the treatment of depressive disorders in adolescents. CBT has been shown to be superior to a wait-list control condition (Kahn, Kehle, Jenson, & Clark, 1990; Reynolds & Coats, 1986), but not relaxation training in the treatment of depressed adolescents. Improvements were maintained at 1-month (Kahn et al., 1990) and 5-week (Reynolds & Coats, 1986) follow-up assessments. In both of these investigations, a more comprehensive CBT intervention was used that was heavily based on behavioral and self-control treatments for depressive disorders in adults.

Parental variables affect the nature and severity of child impairment, the degree of therapeutic change among children who complete treatment, and the extent to which therapeutic changes are maintained at follow-up (Kazdin & Weisz, 1998). To maximize treatment effects, addressing parent and family issues may be necessary (Kazdin & Weisz, 1998). Sanford and colleagues (1995) came to a similar conclusion and stated "a program to educate both the adolescent and parent about depressive disorders, combined with specific strategies to foster positive parent–adolescent emotional involvement, improve discipline practices, and decrease levels of conflict could prove an effective primary intervention for major depressive disorders" (p. 1627). For the most part, previous treatment programs for depressed children have not involved the family. Thus, the child may remain in an unhealthy environment that may contribute to the development and maintenance of the depressive disorder (Birmaher, Ryan, Williamson, Brent, & Kaufman, 1996).

Surprisingly, the existing treatment outcome research suggests that parent training does not add to the efficacy of CBT in reducing depressive symptoms (Lewinsohn, Clark, Hops, & Andrews, 1990). However, parents who participated in the training, relative to parents whose children were the only participants and to parents whose children were in the wait-list control group, reported significantly fewer behavior problems in their children at posttreatment. At the 24-month follow-up, participants in both active treatments reported continued improvement. In an evaluation of the effectiveness of CBT relative to systemic behavior family therapy (SBFT), or nondirective supportive therapy (NST) (Brent et al., 1997), CBT resulted in a higher rate of remission and more rapid relief from depression. Given background research that suggests the importance of family variables for youth depression and the limited amount of treatment research that exists, future outcome research should address the effectiveness of including parents in intervention.

Implications of Gender for the Treatment of Depression

Gender is an important but often overlooked variable in conceptualizing, assessing, and treating depression (Culbertson, 1997). A consistent finding in the literature is that significantly more females than males experience depressive disorders (Hankin et al., 1998), females experience more severe symptoms (Kandel & Davies, 1982), and they experience a different pattern of symptoms (Ostrov, Offer, & Howard, 1989). This gender difference is a true difference that is not due to response style (Nolen-Hoeksema, Girgus, & Seligman, 1992). Before adolescence, the gender difference in the rate and expression of depressive disorders does not exist, or it may be reversed given that a number of investigators have reported that more boys than girls experience depressive disorders (Anderson, Williams, McGee, & Silva, 1989). Between the ages of 13 and 15, girls appear to experience depressive disorders and depressive symptoms at a greater rate than do boys of the same age (Hankin et al., 1998), and the rate continues to increase through high school (Allgood-Merten, Lewinsohn, & Hops, 1990). In fact, researchers are consistently finding that these gender differences emerge during early adolescence (Nolen-Hoeksema, 1995; Petersen et al., 1993). A vulnerability factor to the development of depression is the concurrent experience of multiple changes that occur in girls during early adolescence. Female children experience more concurrent changes and stressors during early adolescence and are more vulnerable to developing depressive disorders as a result of their tendency to use a ruminative, internally focused style of coping with stress rather than an active coping style that enables them to obtain relief through distractions and active problem-solving (Nolen-Hoeksema, 1991). The gender differences in the prevalence and expression of depression have led investigators to call for gender-specific treatment programs (Allgood-Merten et al., 1990; Avison & Mcalpine, 1992; Kavanagh & Hops, 1994; Petersen, Sarigiani, & Kennedy, 1991).

Summary

In general, results of these investigations suggest that CBT is effective in reducing the severity of depressive symptoms and disorders among children and adolescents. In some of the studies, CBT was found to be superior to control conditions; in others, it was not. In general, treatment, regardless of its specific nature, appears to be superior to no treatment. However, this was not found across studies. The improvements appear to be maintained over the short-term, but the long-term benefits are not well established. One of the major limitations of the existing outcome research is that the interventions are very short. Although this brevity is consistent with the short-term nature of children's involvement in real-world therapy, it does not give the youngsters enough time to actually acquire and use the problem-solving, interpersonal, cognitive-restructuring, emotion-regulation, coping, and self-control skills. As Kroll and colleagues' (1996) results suggest, extending the intervention specifically to program for the acquisition and application of the skills across environments and stressors may be more useful. It is evident from our clinical experience that we, like most other investigators in the field, have not adequately addressed the disturbance in family functioning that often appears to support youngsters' depressive symptoms and pessimistic style of thinking. Research consistently finds excessive conflict and lack of support in the families of depressed children and adolescents. Consequently, conflict-resolution skills and relationship-enhancement skills should be taught to parents and their children. Some have expressed concern about the long-term efficacy of the intervention program when the youngster is returned to an unhealthy environment. Even if the family environment is healthy and the parents effectively manage their children's behavior, the therapeutic skills that the children are taught during therapy are difficult to implement outside of sessions. Thus, parents learn how to systematically reinforce their children's use of the therapeutic skills. However, although research and clinical practice suggest that parent training is a necessary component for producing long-term, meaningful change, it is costly and time consuming. To be maximally effective, the specific skills that the youngsters are being taught also may have to vary depending on the child's developmental level and gender.

BRIEF DESCRIPTION OF PROGRAM METHOD

Procedures

Per the recommendations in the literature, developmentally sensitive and gender-specific treatment programs have been developed. The treatment for depressed girls is currently being empirically evaluated. Thus this intervention and the methods used for evaluating it will be described in the following sections.

Screening

Because our treatment outcome research has been based in the schools, a multiple-gate screening and identification procedure has been used to identify depressed girls (Kendall, Cantwell, & Kazdin, 1989). Parental permission for participation in the study is obtained at each step of the screening, identification, and treatment procedure. After parental permission and child assent is secured, the participants complete the Children's Depression Inventory (CDI; Kovacs, 1983) in large groups. Girls who score at least the clinical cut-off (19 or greater) complete a second administration in small groups within 1 week. Girls who once again score at least the clinical cut-off and their primary caregiver are individually interviewed with a hybrid version of the epidemiolocal form of the Schedule for Affective Disorders and Schizophrenia for School-Aged Children (K-SADS-EP; Orvaschel & Puig-Antich, 1994), and a Children's Global Assessment Scale rating is made.

Pretreatment and Posttreatment Assessments

The second administration of the CDI that is used in the screening procedure, the Last Week ratings from the Present Episode section of the child and parent K-SADS-EP interviews, and the CGAS serve as pretreatment measures of symptom severity. In addition, the children complete the CTI-C, Automatic Thoughts Questionnaire for Children (Stark, Humphrey, Laurent, Livingston, & Christopher, 1993), KASTAN CASQ-R (Kaslow, Tanenbaum, & Seligman, 1978), Hopelessness Scale for Children (HSC; Kazdin, Rodgers, & Colbus, 1986), Matson Evaluation of Social Skills for Youths (MESSY; Matson, Rotatori, & Helsel, 1983), Self-Report Measure of Family Functioning for Children (SRMFF-C; Stark, Humphrey, Crook, & Lewis, 1990), Family Messages Measure (FMM; Stark et al., 1996), and Life Events Checklist (LEC), and they individually complete the Thematic Apperception Test

246   STARK ET AL.

(TAT). Concurrently, each primary caregiver completes the Symptom Check-list 90–R (SCL-90-R; Derogatis, 1983), Cognitive Triad Inventory (CTI; Beckham, Leber, Watkins, Boyer, & Cook, 1986), Child Behavior Checklist (CBCL; Achenbach & Edelbrock, 1983), and Self-Report Measure of Family Functioning (SRMFF; Stark et al., 1990). The girls' school records for the 2 weeks preceding the pretreatment assessments are reviewed, and attendance, percentage of assignments completed per class, frequency and severity of discipline referrals, and grade averages in each class are documented. The day after treatment is completed, the child and her primary caregiver complete the same assessment battery, including the interview and the self-report measures. The girls' school records for the 2 weeks following treatment are assessed, and attendance, percentage of assignments completed, frequency and severity of discipline referrals, and grade average in each class are recorded. In addition to outcome measures, the girls and their primary caregivers complete measures of the acceptability and credibility of the treatment (Acceptability and Credibil-ity Questionnaire [ACQ]), as well as their satisfaction with the treatment pro-gram (Satisfaction Questionnaire [SQ]). In addition, the girls and their parents are asked to complete a measure of their understanding and applica-tion of the therapeutic concepts and skills that were taught during treatment (Treatment Check). The Patient Therapist Rating (PTR) is completed as a means of assessing the therapeutic relationship.

Ongoing Assessment

At the beginning of every other meeting, the girls complete the CDI to assess treatment effectiveness and to map the time frame and course of change. After participants have completed the fourth treatment meeting, they are asked to complete the Expectancies for Change Questionnaire (ECQ). They complete this measure again during the final meeting. Parents also complete the ECQ measure after the second parent-training meeting and again during the final meeting.

Follow-Up Assessments

The girls and their primary caregivers complete the posttreatment assess-ment battery annually. School records are reviewed for the preceding 2 weeks, and attendance, percentage of assignments completed, frequency and severity of discipline referrals, and grade average in each class are documented.

Treatment Procedures

Child Treatment

The treatment (Stark, Simpson, Schnoebelen, Hargrave, Glenn, & Molnar, 2004a) is a modification of the program that Stark and Kendall

(1996) developed. It has been modified to reflect the emotion-regulation skills that preadolescent girls naturally use. It is a coping-skills training program in which the youngsters learn a variety of affective, problem-solving, coping, mood-regulation, and cognitive interventions. The child treatment is conducted in the schools in groups of 4 to 6 girls. Each of the 20 group meetings lasts for 50 to 60 minutes and is conducted twice a week for 10 weeks. The therapists consult with teachers to ensure that the girls do not get behind in their class work. The treatment is designed to be fun and engaging while teaching the girls a variety of skills that can be applied to their depressive symptoms, interpersonal difficulties, and other stressors. The skills are taught to the girls through didactic presentations and activities, rehearsed during in-session activities, and applied through therapeutic homework. Skill application is monitored and recorded through completion of workbook activities (Stark et al., 2004b), and completion of the activities is encouraged through an in-session reward program and through an in-home reward system that the parents are taught to implement.

Overall, the intervention targets five major areas: (a) affective education, (b) problem-solving training, (c) coping-skills training, (d) cognitive restructuring, and (e) sense of self. A fuller description of each of the rationale and activities for each of these target areas is outlined below. In general, the first five sessions of the treatment program focus primarily on affective education, teaching coping skills, and introducing a problem-solving philosophy. In Sessions 6 through 10, a greater emphasis is placed on teaching and using the problem-solving steps as a means to manage their depressive symptoms, their interpersonal conflicts, and their daily hassles. Beginning with Session 7 and continuing throughout the remaining sessions, intervention includes activities aimed at enhancing the youth's sense of self. During Session 10, cognitive restructuring is introduced, and Sessions 11 through 15 focus primarily on learning and applying cognitive-restructuring techniques, as well as the continued use of strategies learned previously. This intervention appears later in the program, when the participants have developed a set of skills for coping with their depressive symptoms, because focusing on depressive thoughts heightens distress. Beginning with Session 14, independent application of the skills learned becomes paramount, and the remaining sessions are focused largely on supporting the adolescents as they work toward self-improvement.

The ability to recognize, identify, and understand emotion is critical to overcoming depression and is therefore an important aspect of intervention. Depressed children and adolescents tend not to have an adequate set of labels for their range of affective experiences and tend to label themselves as either happy or depressed, with nothing in between. Initial stages of the intervention use games such as emotional vocabulary, emotion charades, and emotion statues to teach participants the names of various emotions and the fact that emotions vary in intensity. These games also help participants identify the internal and cognitive cues that signal various emotions and to identify the situations and thoughts that are typically associated with their emotions. The foundation for cognitive restructuring is established through recognition of the link between thoughts and feelings.

Problem-Solving Training

Treatment also focuses on teaching an overarching problem-solving philosophy of life in which depressive symptoms, unpleasant situations, interpersonal conflicts, and so forth are viewed as problems to be solved. This approach combats the rigidity and hopelessness common in depression and builds self-efficacy as the girls experience some success and mastery over their problems. First, participants are taught problem identification and definition. Second, they are taught to "psych-up," a step that is designed to counter the pessimism inherent in depressive thinking. Third, girls are taught to generate as many possible solutions to the problem as possible. Next, they are taught to evaluate each possible solution and choose to implement the best plan. Lastly, they are taught to evaluate the effectiveness of their plan and either congratulate themselves on an effective outcome or select another plan. The problem-solving steps are taught informally, at first through modeling and then formally through a series of board games, such as checkers and Jenga. Each move in the game can be seen as a miniproblem to be solved. As participants learn the steps and become successful in applying them to gain mastery in games, the therapist begins to shift away from playing games to teaching the girls to apply the process to hypothetical problems, interpersonal problems, and then to problems in daily life.

Coping Skills

Coping skills are also an important aspect of intervention. Participants are taught a variety of coping strategies for managing their depressive symptoms, including dysphoric and angry mood. One of the primary ways that girls learn to manage their mood is through the purposeful scheduling of pleasant events, or enjoyable and goal-directed daily activities. To combat the withdrawal and passivity associated with depression, participants are taught always to do something to make themselves feel better. They are encouraged to both schedule and monitor their engagement in pleasant events in conjunction with their mood and are taught to use problem-solving skills to confront barriers to engaging in pleasant events. They are also taught to cope with the negative thoughts by countering them with more realistic positive thoughts and actively holding on to more positive ways of thinking. Girls also learn what their nondepressed same-age peers do when they are feeling down and are encouraged to use these strategies, as well as strategies that have worked for them in the past.

Cognitive Restructuring

From the first day of treatment through the last day of treatment, a variety of cognitive-restructuring procedures are also used, with the primary objective being to improve the girls' sense of self and thoughts about interpersonal relationships and to teach them to identify and subsequently counter depressogenic thinking as well as other thoughts that interfere with successful, rewarding, interpersonal relationships. "What's the evidence?" is one cognitive restructuring strategy in which participants learn to examine the evidence that supports or refutes their depressive thoughts. With the help of the therapist, they are taught to establish the evidence that is believed necessary to support or refute their beliefs and then to evaluate the existing evidence and establish a procedure for collecting additional evidence. Finally, the evidence is evaluated, and the girls are helped to construct a more realistic, adaptive belief. "Alternative interpretations" is another cognitive restructuring technique that can be used to counter negative thoughts and broaden the participants' thinking. The girls learn to generate a number of plausible, more adaptive, and realistic interpretations for something that has happened or for a particular belief. Next, they evaluate the evidence for these alternative interpretations and choose the most plausible. The third major restructuring technique taught in therapy is "What if?" Given that depressed children and adolescents often exaggerate the significance of a situation and predict unrealistically dire outcomes, "What if?" can be used to help them see that the probable outcome is not going to be as bad as expected. Through this strategy, they are taught to examine the evidence for their catastrophic and pessimistic thinking and to consider more realistic outcomes. They are also helped to see that even if the worst outcome occurred, it would likely not be as bad as predicted. Initially, the therapists help the girls identify depressogenic thoughts and model and coach these strategies. As treatment progresses, they are encouraged to begin practicing and applying these strategies independently within the context of their individual lives.

Sense of Self

Consistent with our earlier treatment outcome research, participants are taught more adaptive self-control skills, including self-monitoring, self-evaluation, and self-reinforcement. Initially, the girls learn to self-monitor positive events, thoughts, and activities and pleasant emotions. As treatment progresses, they learn to monitor interpersonal conflicts, unpleasant emotions, and depressogenic thoughts, as well as their attempts to cope with them. Through all these activities and their effort to obtain self-improvement, the girls learn a more adaptive and realistic means of evaluating themselves and gain self-efficacy. Therapists model self-reinforcement, and the girls learn how to use this technique while working toward symptom relief. By gaining a sense that they can effect a change in their lives and symptoms, they gain an enhanced sense of self. Activities throughout the intervention are also aimed at helping participants recognize and remember their successes and the things they like about themselves.

Parent Training

Parents learn how to support their daughter's efforts to manage depression by learning the skills themselves, and they also learn a variety of parenting strategies designed to remediate disturbances in the family milieu that have been associated with depressive disorders during childhood and early adolescence. Parent training sessions are conducted in groups during the evening at their daughter's school. The parent training consists of eight 60- to 90-minute sessions.

One unique aspect of the combination of the child and parent training is its focus on changing the depressogenic cognitive style and interpersonal relationships of depressed girls while concurrently changing the family and school environments that may lead to, and maintain, these disturbances. The parent intervention component is designed to teach parents to identify and change maladaptive interactions and verbalizations as well as family beliefs that contribute to the development and maintenance of a depressogenic cognitive style and ineffective interpersonal behaviors in their daughters. To combat the negative affective tone and often punitive, conflictual, and coercive pattern of interactions in the family, parents learn a positive style of managing their daughters' behavior. Parents are taught to set realistic limits and appropriate expectations, to allow their daughters to succeed at meeting them, and to involve their daughters in activities that build competence. Thus, the girls build a positive, efficacious sense of self. Parents are taught problem solving and conflict resolution skills as a means of reducing the conflict that is commonly reported in the homes of depressed youngsters (Stark et al., 1990). Parents are also taught how to be supportive and to express positive feelings and affection. An overarching objective of the intervention is to reduce conflict and improve relationships between the child and her parents.

To encourage girls to apply the skills that they are learning, parents learn to reinforce their daughter's acquisition and use of the cognitive, interpersonal, and emotion-regulation skills. During this process, the parents learn how to apply these skills to their own emotional distress and how to cope with their own stress. They are encouraged to apply positive parenting procedures to manage the behavior of all of their children. On the basis of recommendations from Lewinsohn and colleagues (Lewinsohn et al., 1990), children and parents meet together during a number of the meetings.

Review and Application or Booster Sessions

After completing treatment, the girls participate in three booster sessions each semester. The objective of these sessions is to review the skills the girls' have learned and, more importantly, to discuss the application of the skills to current stressors and negative thinking. Evidence that supports a positive sense of self is identified and integrated into the girls' sense of self. Participants also discuss skills for continuing positive interpersonal relationships and establishing new ones. Primary caregivers also meet three times. The first meeting involves a review of what was learned during treatment. Conflict resolution skills, communication skills, and family problem solving are applied to the new situations that have arisen during the intervening period.

Treatment Measures

Assessment of Treatment Integrity

Audiotapes of therapy sessions are reviewed and rated for the degree to which the therapists implemented the treatment program as designed and their ability to incorporate the participant's life experiences into the session. In addition, the degree to which each therapeutic objective was achieved is rated on a 10-point scale. Furthermore, the level of each participant's involvement in the session is rated on a 10-point scale. At the end of every third meeting, the girls and their parents are asked to complete a measure of their understanding and application of the therapeutic concepts and skills that had been discussed during the previous three meetings. In addition, each girl's therapeutic homework is collected and rated for the extent that it was completed and for the degree of application. At the end of each meeting, the therapist completes a 33-item, 5-point rating scale (Session Summary Sheet) measuring participation, compliance, understanding of concepts, and overall improvement of each participant. Attendance at the session and the session duration are recorded.

Therapist Training

Training consists of a combination of structured experiences and specific instruction about the way to conduct the treatment program. The graduate student therapists are in at least their third year of doctoral training in a professional training program and have completed a year of prior practicum experience in CBT with children and families and graduate-level seminars on depressive disorders during childhood and child psychopathology. Therapists participate in 1 year of training in how to implement the treatment manuals. The art and science of implementing each session are discussed and illustrated. Extensive use of videotaped role-playing exercises is used. After the didactic training, therapists conduct a trial run of the child and parent treatment program with a group of children who have been identified as depressed through the special education process. Sessions are videotaped, and the trainees are provided with supervision and feedback. In some instances therapists cannot complete a trial run of the treatment. In these cases, the trainees observe one group being conducted from start to completion before co-facilitating any groups.

Clinical Vignette

Case Description

We designed this treatment program to be implemented in a group format. However, it may be easily adapted for use with individuals. The case that follows suggests one way that the intervention may be adapted for individuals.

Amanda Phillips is a 12-year-old girl who is in the seventh grade. Amanda's school counselor contacted her parents because her grades were slipping and she had been making frequent trips to the nurse's office, where she complained of stomachaches. The counselor also noted that she often appeared sleepy in class. Amanda's parents had begun sending her to bed at an earlier hour because they too had noticed that she looked tired. Despite this change in sleep schedule, Amanda reported that she still wakes up feeling tired. In addition, her parents have noticed that Amanda has become increasingly "cranky" and "mopey." Amanda's parents noted that the family moved to this city 6 months ago and that Amanda's behavior and mood have changed dramatically since then.

Since the move, Amanda has become withdrawn and developed a "negative attitude" toward her parents and new school. They described Amanda before the move as being very sweet, easygoing, and fun-loving. She had been active in sports and spent a lot of time with her friends. Amanda's negative mood seems to have persisted beyond the expected adjustment period. As a result of her irritable mood, tension in the home has increased. She has been fighting with her 8-year-old brother, and her parents have been arguing about how they can best help her. Both parents report that Amanda seems very angry at them about the move. In an attempt to ease her transition to the new school, they tried to sign her up for soccer, but she refused to go. They encourage her to invite friends over, but she refuses. She is easily upset, often to the point of tears. Mrs. Phillips believes that she needs to be patient with Amanda and provide her with emotional support. Mr. Phillips thinks that this view is too indulgent and believes that his wife is encouraging Amanda's moodiness.

Amanda attributes her difficulties to the move. She misses feeling accepted, understood, and successful. She reports feeling different because her classmates are older and "cool." She once took pride in her academic success, and her slipping grades have compounded her sense of failure. Amanda complains that she feels tired in class, can't concentrate on her schoolwork, and that her subjects are harder than they were in her old school. She also says that her new teachers are mean and boring. Amanda believes that she will "never adjust to her new school." She doesn't play soccer anymore because she's tired and doesn't know anybody on the team. Amanda says that she doesn't want to invite friends over because "they wouldn't want to come anyway."

Case Conceptualization

As with most depressed children, Amanda's depression appears to stem from, and reciprocally interact with, disturbances in cognitive, interpersonal, and family functioning. The move that Amanda experienced with her family was a major stressor. She lost her support system, stopped participating in activities that defined her and provided her with success (e.g., "I am an athlete. I am a good student."), and moved into a more academically demanding school district, which also affected her sense of self. In addition, the high-status students in the new school do not value academic performance; being disruptive, not participating in classroom activities, and not doing homework partially define the "popular" group. Thus, the means by which Amanda gained a sense of worth have been removed. The ways that she defined herself are not valued by peers. In fact, they are rejected as too juvenile. She believes that she is different from the other seventh-grade girls. She is not developing a new social support system because she doesn't believe that the other students will like her. Such beliefs reflect the cognitive error of overgeneralization. She attends too much to the students who are different from her and generalizes from their behavior. She is failing to perceive the other girls who hold similar values. She is engaging in all-or-nothing thinking when she believes that because the "popular girls" don't like her, none of the girls likes her. Her expectations are that nothing will improve and that she will remain alone and isolated. Amanda's primary mode of coping, seeking social support, no longer exists as a result of the move, and because she is angry with her parents, she doesn't go to them instead. Her primary coping strategy is avoidance. She avoids finding a new soccer team and new friends that would help her to feel accepted and valued. Rather than try to solve the problem of her lower grades, she persuades herself that she is not smart enough and avoids doing homework, talking to her teachers, or getting a tutor.

In her previous school, the teachers knew Amanda as a good student and treated her with respect and the expectation that she would be a high achiever. In the new school, the teachers assume that she will try to become popular by misbehaving and therefore do not give her any special attention; this leads her to feel that the teachers do not like her. Because the new school is more academically advanced and demanding than her previous school, she wasn't performing as well as she had expected, which led to an internal dialog dominated by two themes: "I am not smart enough" and "This whole mess is my parents' fault for moving us here." She attributes her dislike of the new school to two reasons: (a) her parents' failure to consider her when making the decision to move and (b) her personality, which, she says, "will never change to fit in to the new school."

Treatment

The first step in treating Amanda was establishing a therapeutic relationship. This was not easy because Amanda had lost trust in others and saw the therapist as yet another person from this new city who wouldn't understand her. Her interpersonal schema was as follows: "Getting close to others means getting hurt, either because I leave them or they leave me or because they cut me down and reject me." Thus, Amanda was distant and somewhat evasive, with an angry edge that made her somewhat difficult to work with. However, her company was also enjoyable because her feistiness seemed to be masking a sensitive and vulnerable person. While establishing rapport, the therapist tried to help Amanda learn how to become a good client (i.e., to be introspective, complete therapeutic homework, become self-observant). In addition, Amanda and the therapist collaborated to gain an understanding of how Amanda's depressive symptoms were tied to her thinking, interpersonal relationships, and family functioning. Initially, Amanda's affect and behavior during sessions were the focus of treatment, and the therapist used these reactions to demonstrate that the way Amanda thinks about things affects her emotions and interpersonal behavior. The honesty, intensity, and shared emotions of these exchanges contributed to the establishment of rapport and the dismantling of Amanda's interpersonal schema, at least as it related to the therapist.

Amanda was withdrawn and failed to engage in pleasant activities. In part this was due to the move and Amanda's lack of social partners, but it also was due to her belief that there wasn't anything good about the new city. She appeared to be determined to be miserable to retaliate against her parents for the move. She could see that her behavior really hurt them, but this realization didn't lessen her anger. Therefore, three interventions were implemented concurrently. First, the therapist and Amanda identified the thoughts about others that led her to believe that she could not find any friends at the new school. Underlying this belief was the intermediate belief that making new friends would be tantamount to forsaking her old friends, a sign that she wanted to forget about them. In addition, because of her tendency to overgeneralize, she believed that none of the other girls in her school would like her. Secondly, because Amanda could see that a relationship exists between doing fun things and feeling good, she was able to understand her problem: She isn't doing anything fun. She was therefore encouraged to identify fun things that she could do. The third intervention strategy was scheduling pleasant events—scheduling things that Amanda was going to do for fun and when she would do them. Over time, she discovered that doing fun things made her feel good and distracted her from the things that upset her. In addition, these activities helped her to build new friendships. Monitoring engagement in pleasant events and scheduling such activities were ongoing components of her treatment.

Amanda believed that making new friends would represent a betrayal of her old friends. To restructure this belief, the therapist helped Amanda to understand that a person can have an unlimited number of friends and an unlimited amount of friendship. During these discussions, Amanda identified a problem. She wanted to have contact with her old friends, but she wasn't communicating with them. This was used as an opportunity to improve Amanda's problem-solving skills. One possible solution was requesting her parents' permission to use their free evening and weekend long-distance minutes to call her friends on her parents' cell phone. Then, with the therapist's encouragement, her parents obtained an Internet service provider so that Amanda could e-mail her friends whenever she wanted. These solutions also helped her to feel reconnected and gave her a source of social support. She saw that she could maintain her friendships and also that her friends were able to move on and do things with other girls even though they still missed her and continued to value her as a friend.

Another problem was identified: Amanda wanted to have friends but hadn't made any yet because of the aforementioned intermediate beliefs. Through a series of Socratic questions, Amanda could see that not "all of the girls" rejected her. Rather, it just was the "popular" girls. The therapist asked Amanda to identify behaviors that a girl her age might enact as a means of reaching out to befriend her. Then they reviewed each class and tried to identify girls who have reached out to her. To restructure the belief that "all of the girls at the school are mean," the therapist and Amanda reviewed each class and identified girls that had similar values and were nice to her. Then Amanda and the therapist developed a plan for making friends with these girls. The plan started with identifying the girls who had been the nicest and seemed most approachable. Amanda agreed to try to engage these girls in conversation and to try to pass through the halls and eat lunch with them. She was encouraged to try to guide the conversation to common recreational activities to see whether any of the girls would invite her to participate. At the same time, the therapist and Amanda talked with her parents about the importance of making friends and engaging in pleasant activities. The parents agreed to provide transportation and to cover the costs of asking a friend to go to the movies, rent movies, go to a theme park, go swimming at the lake or local public pool, go to a minor-league baseball game, and any other reasonable activities. It was decided that Amanda would start small, inviting a friend to the movies, a baseball game, or the local swimming pool. With encouragement and some goal setting, Amanda found a group of girls to join for lunch every day. This helped counter her belief that she would never fit in or find any friends and started to foster the belief that the school had a niche for her.

Another important activity for Amanda was playing soccer. She was a good player and had become quite close to her former teammates. She didn't believe that she could be as good as the girls at her new school because they were from a bigger city with many more players and a good system of training camps. To help counter this belief, she was encouraged (with her parents' support) to go to the city fields on Saturday and watch some of the games and determine how she played relative to the other girls. Secondarily, Amanda and the therapist restructured the belief that she wouldn't play well enough and that the other girls would make fun of her. Playing soccer was reframed as an activity that she could use to make friends and get some exercise. If she was good and received the accolades that she was used to, this was just "frosting on the cake."

Amanda's grades were not as good as they had been in the past, which represented another problem to be solved. Her attribution "I'm not smart enough" was restructured to "This is a different city with a different curriculum, so it is going to take some time to get caught up." Secondarily, she had been bullied into acting as if she didn't care by the "popular" girls, who made fun of her for asking questions in class, doing her homework, and getting upset about her lower grades. Through some discussion, she was able to see that what had happened was not due to a lack of intelligence. In addition, as she developed her own network of friends and regained a sense of her own values, she was able to dismiss the "popular girls'" cutting comments with the following statements: "It's their problem if they don't want to learn and prepare for college" and "I'm not going to get bullied into their ignorance and immaturity." Although her thoughts about her grades had changed, a practical problem remained: She was academically behind the average student in her new school. Through problem solving and consultation with her parents and school counselor, Amanda and her therapist developed a plan. Amanda and her parents enrolled Amanda in a local tutoring center for help in math and reading. For other subjects, Amanda would come to school a half-hour early for tutoring. She arrived before the buses arrived and received tutoring with other students who valued learning. The tutoring had multiple benefits: She made some new friends, and her teachers began to see her as a student who wanted to learn, one whose poor performance in the past was due to inadequate preparation by a less demanding school district. Thus, the teachers' interactions with Amanda changed, as did the subtle interpersonal aspects of their interactions. This led Amanda to see herself as more accepted and valued by her teachers. Amanda and the therapist addressed Amanda's concern that she would be seen as the "teacher's pet" if the teachers mentioned anything in front of the class about her tutoring sessions. Amanda and the therapist engaged in role-playing exercises in which Amanda respectfully asked her teachers not to say anything in front of class about her efforts to improve her grades. Her grades did improve.

Amanda and her parents were in conflict over the move and Amanda's coercive behavior, which in turn led to more conflict regarding the best way to handle the situation. The therapist initially met with the parents alone to discuss their perceptions of what was going on with Amanda and the conflict that they were experiencing. The parents' conflict was resolved relatively easily through a compromise position. They agreed to try the following approach: When Amanda was upset, they would be empathic at first; if her behavior escalated, they would follow this response by telling her that she was behaving rudely and asking her to stop; then, if she continued to be rude or disrespectful, they would apply consequences in a calm and reasonable way. The therapist met with Amanda and her parents to discuss and practice the use of conflict-resolution skills. They created a hierarchy of conflicts arranged from least provocative to most provocative (the move). They next began applying the skills to solve the least provocative conflict and then worked up the hierarchy in later meetings. The parents learned problem-solving techniques to handle everyday problems. Amanda's parents were encouraged to reinforce her efforts to cope, build friendships, and look at things more optimistically by giving her more privileges for these behaviors.

Amanda's progress in treatment was monitored through completion of the CDI every other week. After 4 meetings, improvement was evident; by the end of 14 meetings, Amanda's CDI score (7) was within the nonde-pressed range of functioning. This improvement was verified through an interview of Amanda and her mother using the K-SADS-P. Improvement was noted on the measures of cognitive functioning because she reported feeling good about herself, life in general, and her future. Her attributions for negative events became more external, specific, and unstable, and her attributions for positive events became more internal. The frequency of depressive cognitions decreased. The TAT showed a reduction of the codes for defective self-schema. We are currently developing a coding system for positive self-schema, but it has not been empirically tested, so there was no way to determine with empirical certainty that Amanda's sense of self had become more positive on the TAT. However, the themes were noticeably more positive. Amanda and both of her parents completed the SRMFF at the beginning of treatment and again during the last session. All three reported a significant reduction in conflict within the family and significant improvements in family cohesion, expression, and active recreational orientation. At the beginning of each meeting, Amanda was asked to discuss her therapeutic homework. During these discussions, Amanda's ability to understand and apply the therapeutic skills was obvious, so she was not asked to complete the treatment check measure. Both Amanda and her parents rated the treatment as very acceptable and credible and said they would recommend it to a friend or another family member.

Because Amanda was no longer experiencing a depressive disorder, treatment was terminated and a plan was made to meet again in 6 months.

During the initial follow-up visit, Amanda's CDI score continued to improve and she did not report any new difficulties. She also was able to describe a number of times when she successfully applied problem-solving skills. She noticed some negative thinking when she had a falling-out with a new friend, but she was able to counter it by seeking out social support. Her parents reported that the level of conflict in the family remained low and they felt that their experiences were typical ones for parents of a teenage daughter. The therapist, Amanda, and her parents agreed to meet again in 6 months. In 6 months, Amanda will be back in school, which is a more stressful time for her and her family.

OUTCOMES

As noted earlier, the intervention study outlined in this chapter is part of an ongoing study that is currently under way. Thus, no new outcome data are available at this writing. Previous research with earlier versions of the treatment have demonstrated its efficacy (Stark et al., 1987; Stark, 1990).

FUTURE CONSIDERATIONS

A great deal of research in the treatment of childhood depression is necessary, including basic effectiveness research using a comprehensive treatment program with a population of youngsters who have diagnosed depressive disorders. To date, when a comprehensive treatment program has been used, the participants have not been diagnosed with depressive disorders; rather, a severity index was used to identify the participants. In contrast, when diagnosed cases participated in the treatment, the treatment was unrealistically circumscribed in length. It is not realistic to expect children to learn to self-monitor their mood, cognitions, and specific behaviors and to learn problem-solving, emotion-regulation, and coping skills; cognitive restructuring; and methods for enhancing their sense of self in six sessions. Understanding how and when to apply the skills and experiencing the results both require time. In addition, clients typically need the therapist's feedback to see what they have done, what it means, and how it has helped them. Although we are arguing for more comprehensive treatments, this is itself an empirical question that needs to be addressed. What is the optimal length of treatment, and what are variables that can help the therapist make such determinations for their clients? Do longer treatments produce greater maintenance of treatment effects? Is it necessary or beneficial to schedule regular booster sessions for maintenance purposes? As our pediatric clients enter adolescence, they go through myriad changes and experience new stressors that pose a very real challenge for them and their families. Is it realistic to assume that these children are going to be able to remember and apply the skills they have acquired during childhood when they are in the midst of adolescence?

What are the necessary and sufficient components of treatment? A comparison of the various CBT interventions reveals that they comprise similar components, although they vary in the extent to which cognitive restructuring is taught to the youngsters. Is the efficacy of the interventions due to these shared components or is it due to the nonspecifics of psychotherapy? Some of the interventions are so short that the nonspecifics might be the source of the treatment effects. To date, the addition of a parent-training or family-therapy component has not increased the efficacy of the treatment for adolescents. Is it possible that this is a developmental phenomenon and that children would benefit from the addition of this component? To be maximally effective in our intervention efforts, do we need to create more developmentally sensitive treatments as well as treatments that are gender and culturally sensitive? How well does CBT work for depressed youngsters from different socioeconomic classes? Research clearly points to the 13- to 15-year-old age range as critical for the appearance of depressive disorders among young women. Can we inoculate girls by providing them with preventive interventions?

NIMH is funding a multisite study of the treatment of depressed adolescents. By looking at the efficacy of the interventions, CBT and fluoxetine, alone and together in treating the youngest participants in the study, the efficacy of CBT for younger adolescents and older children might become more clear. However, similar research conducted with a wider age range of children remains important. This research is being conducted in university hospitals that represent unique treatment settings insofar as the therapists often are unusually well qualified, have helped to develop the treatment program, and have participated in other clinical trials as therapists. How effective will the interventions be when they are applied by practitioners who have never had a course in CBT or whose training in CBT was limited to a one-semester course? In previous sections we argued that children who participate in CBT are expected to learn many skills. Similarly, contrary to popular belief, the effective delivery of CBT to pediatric clients is an art, not a science. To artfully and thus effectively implement the intervention requires a good deal of training.

The one place that children can be found daily is the schools. Thus, the schools represent a potentially ideal setting for providing depressed youngsters with treatment. The environment is relatively structured, and teachers can help the children apply the skills they are being taught in therapy. However, the mental health professionals that practice in the schools typically practice at the master's-degree-plus level of certification and rarely have training in CBT. Can these practitioners successfully implement such interventions? What about therapists in other high-volume settings, such as community mental health agencies? The majority of the interventions have been delivered in a group format. Can the interventions be effectively implemented in an individual format? Is the ideal format one in which the youngsters participate in both group and individual meetings? Is one format more effective than the other? As is evident from the questions that we have raised, there is much more that we do not know about the effective treatment of depressed children than we do know.

REFERENCES

Abramson, L. Y., Metalsky, G. I., & Alloy, L. B. (1989). Hopelessness depression: A theory-based subtype of depression. *Psychological Review, 96,* 358–372.

Achenbach, T. M., & Edelbrock, C. (1983). *Manual for the Child Behavior Checklist and Child Behavior Profile.* Burlington: University of Vermont, Department of Child Psychiatry.

Allgood-Merten, B., Lewinsohn, P. M., & Hops, H. (1990). Sex differences and adolescent depression. *Journal of Abnormal Psychology, 99,* 55–63.

Anderson, J. C., Williams, S., McGee, R., & Silva, P. (1989). Cognitive and social correlates of *DSM–III* disorders in preadolescent children. *Journal of the American Academy of Child and Adolescent Psychiatry, 28,* 842–846.

Avison, W. R., & McAlpine, D. D. (1992). Gender differences in symptoms of depression among adolescents. *Journal of Health and Social Behavior, 33,* 77–96.

Beckham, E. E., Leber, W. R., Watkins, J. R., Boyer, J. L., & Cook, J. B. (1986). Development of an instrument to measure Beck's cognitive triad: The Cognitive Triad Inventory. *Journal of Consulting and Clinical Psychology, 42,* 861–865.

Birmaher, B., Ryan, N. D., Williamson, D. E., Brent, C. A., & Kaufman, J. (1996). Childhood and adolescent depression: A review of the past 10 years: Part II. *Journal of the American Academy of Child and Adolescent Psychiatry, 35,* 1575–1583.

Brent, D., Holder, D., Kolko, D., Birmaher, B., Baugher, M., Roth, C., et al. (1997). A clinical psychotherapy trial for adolescent depression comparing cognitive, family, and supportive therapy. *Archives of General Psychiatry, 54,* 877–885.

Butler, L., Miezitis, S., Friedman, R., & Cole, E. (1980). The effect of two school-based intervention programs on depressive symptoms in preadolescents. *American Educational Research Journal, 17,* 111–119.

Chan, D. (1995). Depressive symptoms and coping strategies among Chinese adolescents in Hong Kong. *Journal of Youth and Adolescence, 24,* 267–279.

Culbertson, F. M. (1997). Depression and gender. *American Psychologist, 52,* 25–31.

Derogatis, L. R. (1983). *SCL-90-R: Administration, scoring, and procedures manual. II.* Baltimore: Clinical Psychometric Research.

Frame, C. L., Johnstone, B., & Giblin, M. S. (1988). Dysthymia. In M. Hersen & C. G. Last (Eds.), *Child behavior therapy casebook* (pp. 71–83). New York: Plenum Press.

Frame, C., Matson, J. L., Sonis, W. A., Fialkov, M. J., & Kazdin, A. E. (1982). Behavioral treatment of depression in a prepubertal child. *Journal of Behavior Therapy and Experimental Psychiatry, 3*, 239–243.

Garber, J., Braafladt, N., & Weiss, B. (1995). Affect regulation in depressed and nondepressed children and young adolescents. *Development and Psychopathology, 7*, 93–115.

Garber, J., Braafladt, N., & Zeman, J. (1991). The regulation of sad affect: An information-processing perspective. In J. Garber & K. Dodge (Eds.), *The development of emotion regulation and dysregulation* (pp. 208–237). New York: Cambridge University Press.

Hankin, B. L., Abramson, L. Y., Silva, P. A., McGee, R., Moffitt, T. E., & Angell, K. E. (1998). Development of depression from preadolescence to young adulthood: Emerging gender differences in a 10-year longitudinal study. *Journal of Abnormal Psychology, 107*, 128–140.

Jeney-Gammon, P., Daugherty, T. K., Finch, A. J., Belter, R. W., & Foster, K. Y. (1993). Children's coping styles and report of depressive symptoms following a natural disaster. *Journal of Genetic Psychology, 154*, 259–266.

Jensen, P. S., Ryan, N. D., & Prien, R. (1992). Psychopharmacology of child and adolescent major depression: Present status and future directions. *Journal of Child and Adolescent Psychopharmacology, 2*, 31–45.

Kahn, J. S., Kehle, T. J., Jenson, W. R., & Clark, E. (1990). Comparison of cognitive–behavioral, relaxation, and self-modeling interventions for depression among middle-school students. *School Psychology Review, 19*, 196–208.

Kandel, D. B., & Davies, M. (1982). Epidemiology of depressive mood in adolescents. *Archives of General Psychiatry, 39*, 1205–1212.

Kaslow, N. J., Tanenbaum, R. L., & Seligman, M. E. P. (1978). *The KASTAN-R: A Children's Attributional Style Questionnaire (KASTAN-R-CASQ).* Unpublished manuscript. University of Pennsylvania, Philadelphia.

Kavanagh, K., & Hops, H. (1994). Good girls? Bad boys? Gender and development as contexts for diagnosis and treatment. In T. H. Ollendick & R. J. Prinz (Eds.), *Advances in clinical child psychology* (pp. 45–79). New York: Plenum Press.

Kazdin, A. E., Rodgers, A., & Colbus, D. (1986). The Hopelessness Scale for Children: Psychometric characteristics and concurrent validity. *Journal of Consulting and Clinical Psychology, 54*, 241–245.

Kazdin, A. E., & Weisz, J. R. (1998). Identifying and developing empirically supported child and adolescent treatments. *Journal of Consulting and Clinical Psychology, 66*, 19–36.

Kendall, P. C., Cantwell, D. P., & Kazdin, A. E. (1989). Depression in children and adolescents: Assessment issues and recommendations. *Cognitive Therapy and Research, 13*, 109–146.

Klerman, G. K., & Weissman, M. M. (1989). Increasing rates of depression. *Journal of the American Medical Association, 261*, 2229–2235.

Kovacs, M. (1983). *The Children's Depression Inventory: A self-rated depression scale for school-aged youngsters.* Unpublished manuscript. University of Pittsburgh, Pittsburgh, PA.

Kovacs, M., Feinberg, T. L., Crouse-Novak, M. A., Paulauskas, S. L., & Finkelstein, R. (1984). Depressive disorders in childhood. I. A longitudinal prospective study of characteristics and recovery. *Archives of General Psychiatry, 41,* 229–237.

Kroll, L., Harrington, R., Jayson, D., Fraser, J., & Gowers, S. (1996). Pilot study of continuation cognitive–behavioral therapy for major depression in adolescent psychiatric patients. *Journal of the American Academy of Child and Adolescent Psychiatry, 35,* 1156–1161.

Lewinshohn, P. M., Clarke, G. N., Hops, H., & Andrews, J. (1990). Cognitive–behavioral treatment for depressed adolescents. *Behavior Therapy, 21,* 385–401.

Liddle, B., & Spence, S. H. (1990). Cognitive behaviour therapy with depressed primary school children: A cautionary note. *Behavioural Psychotherapy, 18,* 85–102.

Matson, J. L., Rotatori, A. F., & Helsel, W. J. (1983). Development of a rating scale to measure social skills in children: The Matson Evaluation of Social Skills with Youngsters (MESSY). *Behavioral Research and Therapy, 41,* 335–340.

Nolen-Hoeksema, S. (1991). Responses to depression and their effects on the duration of depressive episodes. *Journal of Abnormal Psychology, 100,* 569–582.

Nolen-Hoeksema, S. (1995). Epidemiology and theories of gender differences in unipolar depression. In M. V. Seeman (Ed.), *Gender and psychopathology* (pp. 63–87). Washington, DC: American Psychiatric Press.

Nolen-Hoeksema, S., Girgus, J. S., & Seligman, M. E. P. (1992). Learned helplessness in children: A longitudinal study of depression, achievement, and explanatory style. *Journal of Personality and Social Psychology, 51,* 435–442.

Orvaschel, H., & Puig-Antich, J. H. (1994). *Schedule for affective disorders and schizophrenia for school-age children* (epidemiologic version, 5th ed.). Pittsburgh, PA: Western Psychiatric Institute and Clinic.

Ostrov, E., Offer, D., & Howard, K. I. (1989). Gender differences in adolescent symptomatology: A normative study. *Journal of the American Academy of Child and Adolescent Psychiatry, 28,* 394–398.

Petersen, A. C., Compas, B. E., Brooks-Gunn, J., Stemmler, M., Ey, S., & Grant, K. E. (1993). Depression in adolescence. *American Psychologist, 48,* 155–168.

Petersen, A. C., Sarigiani, P. A., & Kennedy, R. E. (1991). Adolescent depression: Why more girls? *Journal of Youth and Adolescence, 20,* 247–271.

Petti, T. A., Bornstein, M., Delamater, A., & Conner, C. K. (1980). Evaluation and multimodality treatment of a depressed prepubertal girl. *Journal of the American Academy of Child Psychiatry, 19,* 690–702.

Pine, D. S., Cohen, J. D., Gurley, D., Brook, J., & Yuju, M. (1998). The risk for early-adulthood anxiety and depressive disorders in adolescents with anxiety and depressive disorders. *Archives of General Psychiatry, 55,* 56–64.

Reynolds, W. M., & Coats, K. I. (1986). A comparison of cognitive–behavioral therapy and relaxation training for the treatment of depression in adolescents. *Journal of Consulting and Clinical Psychology, 54,* 653–660.

Sanford, M., Szatmari, P., Spinner, M., Monroe-Blum, H., Jamieson, E., Walsh, C., et al. (1995). Predicting the one-year course of adolescent major depression. *Journal of the American Academy of Child and Adolescent Psychiatry, 34,* 1618–1628.

Schmidt, K. L., Stark, K. D., Carlson, C. L., & Anthony, B. J. (1998). Cognitive factors differentiating attention-deficit-hyperactivity disorder with and without a comorbid mood disorder. *Journal of Consulting and Clinical Psychology, 66,* 673–679.

Seligman, M. E. P. (1998, December). *Ending the epidemic of depression.* Paper presented at the John Templeton Foundation's Research Symposium on the Science of Optimism and Hope, Philadelphia.

Sommer Reinemann, D., Stark, K. D., Swearer, S. M., & Kaslow, N. D. (2001). *Relationships among sexual abuse, cognitive factors, and depression in adolescent psychiatric inpatients.* Manuscript submitted for publication.

Stark, K. D. (1990). *The treatment of depression during childhood: A school-based program.* New York: Guilford Press.

Stark, K. D., Boswell Sander, J., Yancy, M. G., Bronik, M. D., & Hoke, J. A. (2000). Treatment of depression in childhood and adolescence: Cognitive–behavioral procedures for the individual and family. In P. C. Kendall (Ed.), *Child and adolescent therapy: Cognitive behavioral procedures* (pp. 173–234). New York: Guilford Press.

Stark, K. D., Humphrey, L. L., Crook, K., & Lewis, K. (1990). Perceived family environments of depressed and anxious children: Child's and maternal figure's perspectives. *Journal of Abnormal Child Psychology, 18,* 527–547.

Stark, K. D., Humphrey, L. L., Laurent, J., Livingston, R., & Christopher, J. (1993). Cognitive, behavioral, and family factors in the differentiation of depressive and anxiety disorders during childhood. *Journal of Consulting and Clinical Psychology, 61,* 878–886.

Stark, K. D., & Kendall, P. C. (1996). *Treating depressed children: Therapist manual for "Action."* Ardmore, PA: Workbook Publishing.

Stark, K. D., Reynolds, W. M., & Kaslow, N. J. (1987). A comparison of the relative efficacy of self-control therapy and a behavioral problem-solving therapy for depression in children. *Journal of Abnormal Child Psychology, 15,* 91–113.

Stark, K. D., Schmidt, K., & Joiner, T. E. (1996). Depressive cognitive triad: Relationship to severity of depressive symptoms in children, parents' cognitive triad, and perceived parental messages about the child him- or herself, the world, and the future. *Journal of Abnormal Child Psychology, 24,* 615–625.

Stark, K. D., Schnoebelen, S., Simpson, J., Hargrave, J., Glenn, R., & Molnar, J. (2004a). *Treating depressed children: Therapist manual for ACTION.* Ardmore, PA: Workbook Publishing.

Stark, K. D., Schnoebelen, S., Simpson, J., Hargrave, J., Glenn, R., & Molnar, J. (2004b). *ACTION Workbook.* Ardmore, PA: Workbook Publishing.

Vostanis, P., Feehan, C., Grattan, E., & Bickerton, W. (1996a). Treatment for children and adolescents with depression: Lessons from a controlled trial. *Clinical Child Psychology and Psychiatry, 1*, 199–212.

Vostanis, P., Feehan, C., Grattan, E., & Bickerton, W. (1996b). A randomized controlled out-patient trial of cognitive–behavioural treatment for children and adolescents with depression: 9-month follow-up. *Journal of Affective Disorders, 40*, 105–116.

Weisz, J. R., Thurber, C. A., Sweeney, L., Proffitt, V. D., & LeGagnoux, G. L. (1997). Brief treatment of mild-to-moderate child depression using primary and secondary control enhancement training. *Journal of Consulting and Clinical Psychology, 65*, 703–707.

Wood, A., Harrington, R., & Moore, A. (1996). Controlled trial of a brief cognitive–behavioural intervention in adolescent patients with depressive disorders. *Journal of Child Psychology and Psychiatry, 37*, 737–746.

Young, J. E., & Lindemann, M. D. (1992). An integrative schema-focused model for personality disorders. *Journal of Cognitive Psychotherapy: An International Quarterly, 6*, 11–23.

12

PSYCHOTHERAPY FOR EARLY ADOLESCENT DEPRESSION: A COMPARISON OF TWO PSYCHOTHERAPEUTIC INTERVENTIONS IN THREE EUROPEAN COUNTRIES

JOHN TSIANTIS, ISRAEL KOLVIN,[1] DIMITRIS ANASTASOPOULOS, JUDITH TROWELL, VLASSIS TOMARAS, GILLIAN MILES, RENOS PAPADOPOULOS, MIKA SOININEN, CHRISTINA BOSTROM, AND FREDRIK ALMQVIST

This study was partly supported by the European Community: Concerted action contract No. BMH4-CT98-3231 DG12–SSMI. Central coordination of the project is by the Tavistock Clinic in London. The following centers participated: *Greece*—Department of Child Psychiatry, Athens University Medical School; John Tsiantis, Dimitris Anastasopoulos, Effie Lignos, Olga Maratos, Vlassis Tomaras, Valeria Pomini, Evi Athanassiadou, Makis Kolaitis, Vasso Moula, Irene Tsanira. *U.K.*—Child and Family Department, Tavistock Center, London; Issy Kolvin, Judith Trowell, Maria Rhode, Anne Alvarez, Margaret Rustin, Gillian Miles, David Campbell, Emilia Dowling, Sarah Barratt, Renos Papadopoulos, Carmen Clemente, Kate Grayson. *Finland*—Department of Child Psychiatry, University of Helsinki; Fredrik Almqvist, Mika Soininen, Christina Bostrom, Eija Korpinen, Ulla Koskenranta-Aalto, Annu Kuikka, Helena Lounavaara-Rintala, Kaija Mankinen, Pirkko Pingoud, Liisa Pirhonen, Anjaleena Rissanen, Marja Schulman, Esko Varilo, Leena Varilo, Jan-Christer Wahlbeck, Sheila Weintraub, Reija Graeffe. Each center has a national principal investigator.

[1]Deceased during the implementation of the study.

This chapter describes the background, methodology, and observations of an ongoing clinical trial of the treatment of children and early adolescents with depressive disorder diagnosed according to the *Diagnostic and Statistical Manual of Mental Disorders, Fourth Edition (DSM–IV)* criteria. Two established forms of psychotherapeutic interventions are used: a manualized brief individual psychodynamic psychotherapy (BIPP) and systems integrative, family therapy (SIFT). The trial is a crossnational European study implemented in three clinical settings: the Tavistock Clinic, London, England; the University Department of Child Psychiatry, Children's Hospital, Athens, Greece; and the University Department of Child Psychiatry, Helsinki, Finland.

The need for empirically based psychological treatment research has been emphasized over the last two decades (Chambless & Hollon, 1998; Fonagy & Roth, 1998; Hibbs & Jensen, 1996; Hoagwood, Hibbs, Brent, & Jensen, 1995; Kazdin, 1996; Kazdin, Siegel, & Bass, 1990; Kolvin et al., 1981). Kovacs and Sherrill (2001) did an excellent review of the literature of existing controlled trials of the treatment of youth with depression, including studies up to 1999, that seem to approximate the American Psychological Assocation (APA) criteria for the empirically supported psychosocial treatments. In general, more research is needed on child psychotherapy using representative clinical conditions involving cases of psychopathology commonly seen in clinical practice (Kazdin et al., 1990). Efficacy studies that include comorbid conditions can be the foundation on which to build much-needed effectiveness studies (Burns, Hoagwood, & Maultsby, 1998; Hoagwood, Hibbs, Brent, & Jensen, 1995; Kazdin, 1996; Weisz, Donenberg, Han, & Weiss, 1995).

PARENTAL FAMILY AND INTRAPSYCHIC ETIOLOGICAL FACTORS IN DEPRESSION

Evidence suggests that parental and family factors are involved in the depression of children and adolescents (Harrington et al., 1997; Kovacs & Bastiaens, 1995; Newman et al., 1996; Weissmann et al., 1987). In addition, researchers have not yet paid sufficient attention to deep-seated psychological and intrapsychic etiological factors regarding the development of depression. Some of the etiological factors found to be linked to childhood depression are as follows: (a) unresolved conflicts and unmet needs in early childhood, such as emotional, social, and economic stresses (Bemporal, 1994; Brown, Harris, & Bifulco, 1986; Kolvin et al., 1991); (b) early losses of childhood attachments and loss of significant others (Bowlby, 1981) as well as adverse experiences (parental death or separations) during childhood and adolescence (Birmaher, Ryan, Williamson, Brent, & Kaufman, 1996); (c) early environmental frustration and disappointments or abuse beyond the child's control; (d) exposure to traumatic or negative life events (e.g., intrafamily violence) as well as disturbed family relationships either through interactions with other risk factors (e.g., parental depression, alcoholism) or because of a lack of parental support and communication problems between the parent and adolescent; (e) insecure attachments giving rise to negative perceptions of the self and thus increasing the risk of depression (Armsden, McCauley, Greenberg, Burke, & Mitchell, 1990). All of these factors may contribute to the elements of superego or ego ideal that can foster unrealistic expectations, shame, and low self-esteem or a harsh, punitive superego leading to self-blame, self-punishment, and guilt. In addition to the aforementioned etiological factors, there is an extensive psychoanalytic theory on the contribution of internal factors to the development of psychopathology and depression. Systematic exploration of these issues may provide a greater depth of understanding of their complexity and may guide the treatment of specific subgroups. Seligman, Peterson, and Kaslow (1984) also emphasize the attribution of problems to the child, which in psychoanalytic terms denotes the projection of unwanted or unbearable thoughts and feelings of significant others (e.g., parents) toward the child.

Evidence From Preliminary or Pilot Studies on the Usefulness of Individual Psychodynamic Psychotherapy

In 1995, Wrate and colleagues studied, using a quasi-experimental design, 72 clinical cases who attended as outpatients or inpatients a university child psychiatry department in London. Approximately 31% of the sample was diagnosed as having clinical depression at intake. Cases were evaluated systematically approximately 15 and 27 months after the intake. Eight of 10 children received individual psychodynamic psychotherapy with social casework services for the family. Of those diagnosed as depressed at intake, over 50% showed comorbidity with conduct disorder. At the first follow-up the depression was reduced by 91%; at the second follow-up, it was reduced by 95.5%. These findings offer support of the effectiveness of individual psychodynamic psychotherapy combined with multimodal approaches for depressed children. Tebbutt, Swanston, Oates, and O'Toole (1997) reported a disquieting continuity of depression in sexually abused children over a long time span (5 years) and stated that treatment appeared to have little effect on depression. However, a study by Trowell, Kolvin, Weeramanthri, Berelowitz, and Leitch (1998) of sexually abused girls using brief individual psychodynamic psychotherapy once a week for 1 year found that from 59% of the subjects entering therapy who were diagnosed as having major depression at the intake, only 17% presented with a depressive disorder at the end of treatment and at follow-up, indicating that the treatment effects were maintained (Trowell et al., 1998; Trowell & Kolvin, 1999). They also found that the extent of additional psychiatric disturbance in this female cohort was considerable. Abused girls who came from disturbed family backgrounds exhibited substantial chronic psychiatric impairment and comorbidity. Families often had complex psychopathology, giving rise to negative self-perceptions in the child and therefore increasing the risk of depression. These preliminary studies support the utility of psychodynamic psychotherapy (Kolvin, Trowell, Tsiantis, Almqvist, & Sadowski, 1999). Although progress has been made in psychotherapeutic approaches for the treatment of depression, more research is needed. First, there is a dearth of studies in individual psychodynamic psychotherapy, especially as there are indications that its effects can persist longer. Second, a substantial proportion of depressed children come from dysfunctional families, but insufficient attention has been paid thus far to treatment approaches that incorporate family and contextual variables. Specific interventions should be provided to parents and other caregivers during the acute treatment phase to help them effectively manage the child's irritability, anxiety, isolation, and other behavior problems. Parental mental health issues should be addressed, and, if indicated, parents should be offered treatment (Brent et al., 1997; Kovacs & Bastiaens, 1995; Lewinsohn, Clarke, Hops, & Andrews, 1990).

One worthwhile treatment approach for depressed children is brief psychodynamic psychotherapy based on psychoanalytic thinking, in combination with parental intervention. The existing literature indicates that this approach may prevent relapse, at least in some cases, because it can provide children with a better understanding of the self and existing internal conflicts by enhancing their capacity, and that of their parents, to cope with the family conflict during the developmental milestones. Many clinicians have found psychodynamic psychotherapy useful for the treatment of depressed youth. Many believe that psychodynamic psychotherapy can help youth understand themselves, identify feelings, improve self-esteem, change maladaptive patterns of behavior, interact more effectively with others, and cope with ongoing and past conflicts (Bemporal, 1988, 1994). Shirk (2001) noted the dearth of research on nonbehavioral therapies for children, especially those with specific disorders. Controlled studies using psychodynamic psychotherapy for the treatment of depressed children and adolescents are particularly difficult to design and expensive to conduct, but they are greatly needed.

OBJECTIVES

Our aim was to compare two well-established forms of psychotherapeutic interventions, BIPP and SIFT, for the treatment of depressed children. We hypothesized that individual therapy (BIPP) will (a) lead to a substantial reduction in symptoms in the short term and a greater sense of stability by the end of therapy, relieving any associated distress and promoting children's emotional development; (b) improve the child's self-esteem and enhance attachments with primary caregivers; (c) improve social functioning; (d) improve academic functioning.

We hypothesized that family therapy (SIFT) will (a) reduce family overinvolvement; (b) reduce the extent of criticism within the family; (c) reduce any conflict in relationships between parents; (d) reduce distress in psychologically fragile youths; (e) alleviate depressive symptoms in parents by the end of the treatment.

Differential predictors of response will be identified in the two different therapy programs.

METHOD OVERVIEW

We intended to recruit 96 youngsters, ages 10 to 14 years, from three countries. For referral purposes, each center identified ways of gaining access to local clinical populations, such as through community clinics, general practitioners, and other mental health professionals. It was not possible in the time frame required by the study grant to recruit 96 subjects, as originally planned. The subjects finally recruited totaled 71 (Figure 12.1): 23 from Greece (11 individual and 12 family therapy) and 24 each from England and Finland (12 in each treatment modality).

Case identification occurred at three levels: (a) an initial assessment using the Child Depression Inventory (CDI; Kovacs, 1992); (b) a clinical

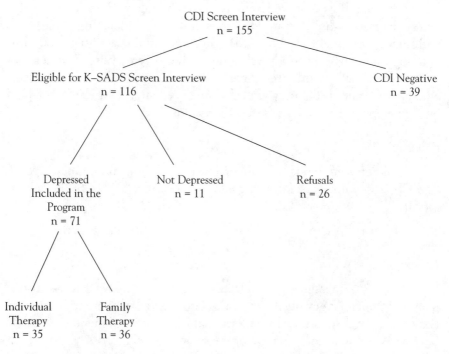

Figure 12.1. Depression study draft consort diagram.

interview of those whose scores exceed a standard deviation on the CDI or who were reported as depressed by mental health professionals; (c) an interview using the Kiddie-SADS, present and lifetime versions (K-SADS-PL; Kaufman et al., 1997). Primary caretakers and children were interviewed separately. Using this information, a best-estimated diagnosis was decided, and children who meet criteria for major depressive disorder (MDD) are randomly assigned to one of the two treatment arms.

Methods

Inclusion and Exclusion Criteria

All subjects who met MDD criteria were included irrespective of gender or race. An age range was stipulated that would ensure the availability of continuing information about educational progress and school behavior while the children were still at school. The age range also would ensure that the children were old enough to cope with the self-completion instruments. We included children of normal intelligence with a CDI score greater or equal to 15 and fulfilling the diagnostic criteria of major depression according to DSM–IV diagnostic criteria. Only subjects living with at least one biological parent were accepted to ensure reasonable comparability of families in the trial. Subjects on prescribed antidepressants or other psychotropic agents were expected to stop these with a reasonable period (2–3 weeks) before entering the program. Excluded were children and adolescents with severe depressive disorders meriting hospitalization, including adolescents with bipolar disorders, children with developmental disabilities, and children of parents who have a psychotic or other severe Axis I disorder or a severe personality disorder (e.g., borderline personality disorder). Subjects who dropped out of the study after the screening interviews were contacted by phone up to three times to assess their status.

Randomization

Children were randomly assigned to one of the two treatment groups (BIPP or SIFT) using the following allocation design: "A" for BIPP, and "B" for SIFT:

ABBA,   BAAB,   AABB,   BBAA,   ABAB,   BABA

Measures

A series of measures were selected (see Table 12.1). For those instruments not immediately available in the language of the potential subjects, the standard translation technique was applied. All instruments eventually became available in the language of the subject populations.

TABLE 12.1
Summary of Research Instruments Used
Common to Both Intervention Groups

Instruments	Self-rating/ interview	Baseline	During therapy	End of therapy	Follow-up
CHILD					
CDI (Kovacs, 1992)	SR	X		X	X
K-SADS (Kaufman et al., 1997; Chambers et al., 1985; Puig-Antich & Chambers, 1978)	I	X		X	X
Moods/feelings (Angold et al., 1987)	SR	X	Every 4 weeks	X	X
Screen for Child Anxiety Related Emotional Disorders (SCARED) (Birmaher, 1998)	SR	X		X	X
Social Adjustment (Weissman, 1975; Weissman, Sholomskas, & John, 1981)	I	X		X	X
Battle Self Esteem (Battle, 1981)	SR	X		X	X
Attachment (Armsden & Greenberg, 1987)	SR	X		X	X
PARENTS re. Child					
5MSS (Magana-Amato, 1993)	I	X		X	X
K-SADS (Kaufman et al., 1997; Chambers et al., 1985; Puig-Antich & Chambers, 1978)	I	X		X	X
Moods/feelings (Angold et al., 1987)	SR	X	Every 4 weeks	X	X
PARENTS re. Family					
BDI (Beck & Weissman, 1974)	SR	X		X	X
Social Adjustment (Weissman, 1975; Weissman et al., 1981)	SR	X		X	X
Self-Esteem (Battle, 1981)	SR	X		X	X
Demography (Kolvin et al., 1991)	I	X		X	X

SR = Self-rating; I = Interview.

continues

TABLE 12.1 (Continued)
Summary of Research Instruments Used
Common to Both Intervention Groups

Instruments	Self-rating/ interview	Baseline	During therapy	End of therapy	Follow-up
PARENTS re. Family (continued)					
Life Events (Goodyer, Kolvin, & Gatzanis, 1985; Berney et al., 1991)	SR	X		X	X
Family Assessment Devide (FAD) (Epstein, Baldwin, & Bishop 1983)	SR	X		X	X
Dyadic Adjustment Scale (Spanier, 1976)	SR	X		X	X
SCHOOL					
Educational Achievement Questionnaire (EAQ) (Fundudis et al., 1991)	Teacher	X		X	X
Child Behavior Checklist (CBCL) (Achenbach, 1991)	Teacher	X		X	X
OTHERS					
Kernberg (Kernberg, 1991) brief form Individual Therapy	SR		Every session		
Kernberg (Kernberg, 1991) extended form Individual Therapy	SR		Every 4th session		
Beaver A (Lewis, Beavers, Gosset, & Philips, 1976; Beavers & Hampson, 1990) Family Therapy	SR		4th, 12th session		
Beaver B (Lewis et al., 1976; Beavers & Hampson, 1990) Family Therapy	SR		4th, 12th session		
Beaver E (Lewis et al., 1976; Beavers & Hampson, 1990) Individual and Family Therapy	SR		4th, 12th session		
TASC-r (Shirk & Saiz, 1992) Individual Therapy	SR		4th, 12th session		

SR = Self-rating; I = Interview.

TABLE 12.1
Summary of Research Instruments Used
Common to Both Intervention Groups

Instruments	Self-rating/ interview	Baseline	During therapy	End of therapy	Follow-up
OTHERS (continued)					
TASC-r (Shirk & Saiz, 1992) Family Therapy	I		3rd, 8th session		
Improvement Scale by clinician (Almqvist)	SR			X	X
Improvement Scale with mother (Almqvist)	I			X	X
Improvement Scale by therapist (Almqvist)	SR			X	X

SR = Self-rating; I = Interview.

Statistical Analysis

The effects of treatment and change over time were compared using basic outcome measures and also appropriate multivariate analyses. The treatment groups were compared at baseline, using suitable between-subject techniques to test for equivalence of groups (e.g., age, gender, severity of depression). The analysis of outcome included measurement at the different time periods, so Repeated Measures Multivariate Analysis of Variance (MANOVA) was used to analyze both within-subject and between-subject measures. Analysis of Covariance also was used to control for the effects of individual baseline differences in some of the clinical measures. If the sample size allows, multiple regression or logistic regression may be used to try and establish which independent variables or combinations of independent variables best predict outcome. Improvements in psychopathology were analyzed using survival analysis, possibly including a comparison of independent factors. The categorical data were investigated using suitable procedures, such as loglinear analysis or related techniques. However, it must be noted that in all the preceding examples, sample size may well have limited the number and range of statistical tests that could be used.

Multilevel Meetings: Electronic Communication Between the Three Sites

The principal investigators have been meeting at regular intervals since 1995 to plan and monitor the progress of Psychotherapy Early Adolescent Depression (PEAD) and also for training purposes. These meetings have been hosted in each of the participating countries in turn. An e-mail link was established, and a PEAD standard database was created. Each center has been coordinating and organizing basic data collection and has been transmitting it to the coordinating center in London during the study. This link also has allowed members of the research team in the various countries to maintain close and regular contact, which is useful for the rapid solution of both clinical and statistical problems.

Staff Training

The training of research staff was organized both within the host country and cross-country. The initial meeting took place in London and alternated each year to each of the participating countries. Key diagnostic interviewers were trained in the principles of assessment of the referred cases. Therapists and their supervisors were not involved in the screening exercises and the assessment of cases. The manual was circulated among the therapists, who then discussed it during workshop sessions until they felt comfortable using it. The workshop discussions were based on a number of sessions or in one or two psychotherapy pilot cases. The purpose was training in the use of manuals, therapists' rating of process, and, to the extent possible, standardization of procedures, adherence to treatment techniques and principles outlined in the manual, discussion of therapy vignettes, observation of videotapes (family therapy), and audiotape review (individual therapy). Joined crosscenter training among the supervisors and the principal investigations of each center took place in workshops organized between the three centers. Crosscenter consultation also took place.

Therapeutic Procedures

After diagnosis, the child and parents were informed by the assessor as to the type of therapy the child would be receiving. Before the last assessment interview with the parents, the research coordinator gave the assessor the random treatment allocation in a closed envelope so the assessor would be blind to the type of therapy being used.

Individual Therapy. The patient was offered thirty 45-minute sessions of brief individual psychodynamic psychotherapy, with complementary sessions for the parents every other week. The framework of the project was explained at the onset. The audiotaping of every session was also clarified and accepted (no written consent forms are necessary in Europe) before the beginning of treatment. The sessions with the parents, as well as the supervision sessions, were also audiotaped. Detailed notes of the therapy and supervision process notes were also kept in order to study in detail both the material of the session and the supervision process. Children attending only one to seven sessions were considered drop-outs and were replaced; children attending between 8 and 14 sessions were considered early completers; and children attending 15 to 30 sessions were considered completers. Early completers were included in the statistical analysis.

Family Therapy. The treatment was designed to last 9 to 12 months, with 90-minute sessions conducted every 2 or 3 weeks. Families who attended only one to three sessions were considered drop-outs and were replaced. Those who attended four to seven sessions fell into the category of early completers. To complete treatment, the participants must attend 8 to 14 sessions. Early completers were included in the statistical analysis. According to the guidelines of the manual, parents were invited to participate after the second session and at that time the family was seen as a whole. The work with the parents focuses on their coparenting rather than on marital issues. The manual proposes an ideal ratio of two or three sessions with the whole family to one with the parents. Occasionally, other family members (notably grandparents) participated in the sessions. All family sessions were also videotaped with prior consent of the family.

Supervision. BIPP therapists received individual supervision twice a month by a senior therapist or supervisor. This arrangement was regarded as necessary for the reliable monitoring and reflection of the interactive therapeutic processes. Supervision was based on the audiotapes and the process notes that the therapist kept for every session, where the details of the session (verbal and nonverbal) were included with the therapists' countertransference feelings. Through this process, therapists were able to better understand patients' communication, work through the different obstacles in the treatment, and adhere to the manual. As with the regular meetings with the child psychotherapist, the parent workers were also included in the discussions to support the parents in difficult management situations and help them learn when to offer support in a crisis. The supervision of the parent workers by a senior therapist or supervisor took place once a month. The built-in requirement for supervision and discussion of the work was very important, particularly given the vulnerable nature of most of the families and the powerful projections that take place within the work.

Family Therapists. The supervision style for family therapists varied among the three centers. In London, four experienced family therapists worked in pairs, one interviewing the family while the other offered live supervision from behind the screen. The four therapists met monthly with the four supervisors to look at tapes and discuss them. In London, therefore, supervision took place at three levels: (a) by the cotherapist behind a one-way mirror, (b) by a supervisor of the pair of therapists at other times, (c) at a group meeting where all therapists and supervisors discussed their work. In Athens, six junior family therapists worked in pairs seeing the family as cotherapists. Each dyad was supervised by one of the two supervisors. Live supervision was offered every second session and video supervision every fourth session. In Helsinki, four senior family therapists worked in pairs, one with the family and the other behind the screen offering on-the-spot supervision.

The Application of Brief Individual Psychodynamic Psychotherapy

BIPP is a dynamic therapeutic process based on psychoanalytic principles of development, object relations theory, the role of defensive mechanisms, the unconscious drives, and the transference phenomena. Brief therapy uses the same tools as the traditional psychodynamic psychotherapy. It uses the same tools as in psychoanalytic psychotherapy but adapts them to the needs of brief therapy (Davanloo, 1980; Malan, 1976; Sifneos, 1972). The time limit plays a crucial role, diminishing regression and dependence of the patient (Mann, 1973; Mander, 2000). The time constraints also leave less time for the patient to work through the issues during treatment, but this is a process that starts in the therapy and continues indefinitely, depending on patients' ability to continue their insightful experiences. This approach aims to develop the capacity of the patient to tolerate frustration; to face anxiety and loss; and to transform unbearable, incapacitating feelings into thoughts that encourage the patient to trust his or her own psychic recourses. The technique is based on understanding the patient's communications (verbal and behavioral) as they are revealed in the transference situation by bringing them into consciousness, putting them into words, and making the child more able to deal with them. Alongside the gaining of insight, an important therapeutic aspect is the patient's emotional experience that there is someone (the therapist) who can tolerate the unbearable thoughts and feelings of the patient (which the child has been considering intolerable). Such an emotional experience can facilitate the assimilation of painful experiences that the child had previously avoided. The therapist provides and maintains a reliable holding environment for the patient within a secure therapeutic frame. The therapist's ability to bear the patient's pain and anger, the patient's experience of the therapeutic relationship as helpful, the management of crises, and a working-through of separation and loss all promote an internalization of a good corrective emotional experience (Alexander & French, 1946). This leads the patient from weakness and dependence to autonomy and promotes the capacity for self-reflection and the ability to cope with anxiety and uncertainty. The therapists are neither directive nor suggestive, and they are not exclusively supportive; they utilize the main psychoanalytic technique (e.g., interpretation, clarification, and confrontation of the patient's defenses, anxieties, and impulses in connection with current, past, present, and transference relationships). The therapists use the focus as a guideline to understand patients' conflicts and anxieties and through interpretation give meaning to their emotional upheaval. This is usually done by transference interpretations, which reveal the patient's repetitive patterns of relating and deal with his or her problems in the current therapeutic relationship. At the same time, therapists are more confrontational and more active in asking questions, avoiding long silences and general comments. The time limit sets boundaries and pushes young patients to face their dependence and move toward a more mature and realistic stance. In most cases of depressed adolescents, the focus fell into the following categories:

- unresolved mourning of an important loss;
- low self-esteem;
- maladaptive modes of coping with anxiety or aggressive impulses;
- inability to cope with the emotional demands of everyday life; and
- poor object relationships.

Careful monitoring and reflection on the interactive therapeutic processes and the patient's material help the therapist understand and process the patient's communication, leading to the formulation and implementation of a therapy manual.

Work With Parents

The manual describes the main issues for therapists working with the parents. It outlines the topics that must be addressed in each phase of the intervention and the particular difficulties that may arise during the work with parents of children with MDD. Moreover, it ensures a common basis for the approach the therapists follow in their work. Regular contact between the parent and child workers is an important aspect of this brief focused work. Both therapists need to respect the confidentiality of the parents and the child, but they need to share the general themes and preoccupations of the sessions to enable their own work to proceed.

Phases of Treatment of Individual Psychotherapy

Introduction to Therapy (5 Sessions). The framework by now established, the therapist defines the frame and the treatment arrangements, explains that this is brief focused work, and defines the duration and frequency of sessions, indicating that the aim is to help young people handle their worries and concerns. The client is encouraged to discuss and explore the arrangements. The therapist explains to children and parents the need for regular attendance, the issues of confidentiality, and treatment goals. The children are informed that if the concerns that emerge during treatment are acute, they will need to be shared with their parents. The child is clearly informed of the parallel work with the parents. The reasons for the referral (i.e., what was the particular issue and why it must be addressed now) are also reviewed during the initial phase. The therapist also explains that not all problems, conflicts, and concerns can be resolved during the treatment. Significant life events are also explored. Possible issues might include bereavement; separation from significant others; serious illness of family members or close friends; and serious disputes with parents, family members, teachers, or peer group; and transitions, such as the birth of a sibling, a sibling's departure from home, parental divorce, new partner for parent, and change of school.

Treatment Work (Sessions 6–20). During the middle phase, all the issues raised by the young person at the beginning of the therapy are explored, examined, and addressed. The therapist makes connections of what happens in the therapy as concerns the relationship of the child with the therapist and the relevant material identified during the session in the introductory phase. In particular the tasks of the treatment work (middle phase) are as follows: (a) to encourage the therapeutic alliance to develop to the point at which both child and therapist are able to face negative feelings; (b) to allow the child to acknowledge all these negatives—pain, rage, destructiveness, self-destructiveness—to put them into words and to be able to tolerate them without the need to "look only on the bright side"; (c) to keep the communication open between the parent worker and the child therapist (throughout the treatment) and check whether any serious problems have occurred; (d) to monitor the young person's symptoms to detect deterioration. It is important during treatment to deal with crises and, if possible, to anticipate them. Some of the problems that usually arise are as follows: (a) marital and family conflict; (b) transitions, such as change of school, birth of sibling, parental divorce, which can arouse fear, rage, betrayal, and rivalry; (c) difficulties in interpersonal relationships, such as problems in expressing feelings, initiating relationships, maintaining relationships, and poor communication; (d) friendships, peer group pressures, and social isolation

Termination (Sessions 21–30). Previous separation and loss are likely to emerge during the therapy sessions. Sadness and anxiety are common. The termination phase addresses the process of the treatment, reviewing what has been worked on and achieved. Again, the link with the parents is the most important feature of the last sessions. Termination review meetings are held with caregivers, and an end of treatment meeting with the therapist is essential. If further treatment is needed, children are referred to outside mental health clinics. Whenever possible, time to permit the full impact of the therapy to emerge is helpful for the young person and his or her family.

Clinical Vignette

Natasha, a 14-year-old girl and the firstborn child of divorced parents, lived with her mother, her younger sister, and her mother's new husband, by whom Natasha's mother was pregnant at the commencement of therapy (she gave birth during Natasha's treatment). Natasha made regular visits to her father and his new family from his second marriage. Natasha was referred to treatment because of learning difficulties. During the diagnostic assessment Natasha showed significant depression in addition to her learning difficulties. It was also revealed that Natasha's paternal uncle made sexual advances to her when she was 9 years of age, immediately after her parents' divorce. Her uncle's behavior filled her with guilt, particularly because her father did not believe her allegations. Natasha also blamed herself for her parents' divorce. Her relationship with her mother was highly conflictual. Her symptoms included low self-esteem; poor school performance, despite her high intellectual ability; hopelessness; and a sense of isolation, both at school and within the family. She entertained suicidal thoughts, although not in an organized way.

Initial Phase: Introduction to Therapy (First 5 Sessions)

From the initial meeting, Natasha seemed quite burdened. Without much faith in therapy, she was suspicious of her therapist. The discussion about the brief therapy exemplified further her difficulty in trusting and communicating with her therapist. The therapist acknowledged these difficulties, which enabled them to start forming a therapeutic alliance. Natasha was able to express her difficulty in relating with others, her conflictual relationship with the rest of the family, and her feelings of guilt about her parents' divorce. On the basis of her previous traumatic life experiences, Natasha expected her therapist to be harsh and judgmental like her father. The interpretations on such transference phenomena reinforced her hope and revealed her hidden strength and healthy desire to unload some of her burden. As a consequence, she proceeded to test the resilience of the therapist, revealing some hidden aggression by missing a session without explanation. Natasha's communication of her experience of rejection and her need to keep a safe distance after having experienced a closer contact with the therapist became clear. Her unconscious communication was then addressed and acknowledged. This initial deep understanding enabled Natasha to proceed with her therapy despite her original ambivalence.

Middle Phase: Treatment (Sessions 6–20)

This phase is a consolidation of trust and the most difficult part of the treatment. External factors such as her new step-sibling and her grandmother's illness gave rise to feelings of loss and the anxiety of being rejected and replaced. Her therapist's acknowledgment and containment of Natasha's mixed feelings were, although hard and painful, a source of comfort to Natasha. The therapist enabled her to talk about her mixed feelings toward her mother's new baby. As more primitive defenses came to the front, such as splitting and denial, the therapist began to regard the continuation of therapy as unlikely. The therapist, having personally experienced feelings of hopelessness and being able to reflect on them, could empathize with Natasha's feelings. Her empathic stance, with the acknowledgment of the negative feelings involved in the therapeutic relationship, helped Natasha maintain a secure link with a reliable and supportive therapist who could survive attacks without retaliating or losing interest in her. Natasha was helped to understand that her aggressive feelings were of limited destructiveness, leaving room for reparation. Transferring this experience to her relationship with her mother, Natasha was able to see that expressing negative feelings does not lead to catastrophe. During this phase Natasha's appearances started to change: She became more attractive and lively, taking an interest in her looks and dressing up according to her age. Her school performance improved, and she developed some friendships at school. Furthermore, Natasha's mother, who had a similar therapeutic experience with her own parent-worker, was better able to see Natasha's needs and make reparative efforts. A reparation process comes naturally out of a tolerable guilt and concern; both mother and daughter were enabled to set such a process in motion.

Termination (Sessions 21–30)

After having acknowledged the positive aspects of her relationship with her therapist, Natasha seemed to find it difficult to accept the termination of the treatment, looking surprised when she realized how few sessions were left. Natasha's existing anger became more obvious during the termination phase when Natasha missed another session. This behavior gave the the therapist another opportunity to address the negative feelings triggered by termination. The missed sessions played an important role in the therapeutic process. They became a useful demonstration of appropriate ways to express anger and deal with loss rather than merely unused session time. Natasha did not attack the relationship with her therapist, but she expressed anger about losing the contact.

Outcome

The significant outcome of Natasha's therapy, besides symptom relief, was that she learned how to express negative feelings without being destructive externally or internally. The therapy revealed her hidden, healthy strengths and helped reinforce her hope.

Systems Integrative Family Therapy

Overall, a systemic approach to any psychological difficulty in the family is understood in terms of a temporary imbalance that is (a) a product of a variety of factors at several domains (i.e., individual, family, social, cultural) and (b) supposed to have some meaning, purpose, or function in the family ecology. In other words, the fact that a family comes to the attention of professionals through symptoms manifested by a family member or members constitutes information that must be included in the investigation.

Ultimately, systemic approaches attempt to explore difficulties in terms of their impact at several contextual domains.

SIFT represents a form of family therapy that can be used in a wide variety of contexts. The main feature of SIFT is its focus on the central tenets of systemic approach, away from sectarian adherence to specific theories and techniques of the various schools of family therapy. Consequently, according to SIFT, depression must be understood as an expression of the family systems' functioning at that particular time. The integrative approach is developed on a shared common ground in the field of family therapy (Byng-Hall & Campbell, 1981; Lebow, 1984), and the underpinning theory is systems theory. Attuned to the design of the study, SIFT has been manualized by J. Byng-Hall, D. Campbell, and R. Papadopoulos, all family systems psychotherapists at the Tavistock Clinic, London. The main considerations in constructing the manual were as follows: (a) to be an appropriate research tool; (b) to provide clear, coherent, specific, and systemic guidance for therapists without restricting their individual styles; (c) to be based on the broad systemic principles that are common to most schools across the spectrum of family therapy; (d) to be exportable and flexible. Given that the manual is used by therapists in three countries in the treatment of families from widely varying socioeconomic backgrounds, it should allow for cultural and social variations.

In an explicit way, the manual includes techniques from the following approaches: structural (Minuchin & Fishman, 1981), problem solving and solution-focused (de Shazer, 1988), Milan Systemic (Palazzoli-Selvini, Boscolo, Cecchin, & Prata, 1980), narrative (White & Epston, 1989), and historical–life cycle and transgenerational (McGolddrick & Gerson, 1985). Other techniques that are widely used but not necessarily attributable to specific schools of thought have also been included to match the study's population needs. For ethical and therapeutic reasons the techniques known as "paradoxical injunctions" were excluded. The manual outlines in a systematic way the various contexts within which index patients (children) exhibit depressive symptoms. These cover the areas of the referring network, as well as sociocultural and family contexts. In addition, attention is drawn to the factors that maintain these symptoms, and the hereditary racial or ethnic component is also considered. From the technical side of therapy, the manual offers guidelines on the following: (a) number and frequency of sessions and length of treatment; (b) phases of therapy (initial, middle, ending); and (c) recommendations on specific aspects of family therapy with children and family subsystems. The techniques described in the manual are as follows: joining, exploring family history, constructing a geneogram, exploring gender and cultural issues, examining the family life cycle, circular interviewing, enacting, challenging, reframing, externalizing, problem solving, focusing on strengths and positives, and assigning tasks. In addition, the family therapists tend to investigate issues such as the following:

- developmental changes in the family, such as births and deaths, onset of puberty, transferring to another school, and changing residences or careers;
- the various dominant (as well as subjugated) belief systems in the family with particular reference to dysfunction and, more specifically, to sadness and depression;
- ways of relating within the family with particular emphasis on subsystems and alliances and their respective distance and proximity;
- transgenerational themes relevant to the presenting symptoms; and
- common themes across the interrelated systems of individuals, family, and wider sociocultural contexts.

In terms of interventions, therapists work on the following:

- to improve the security of the family base;
- to improve the security of the child's attachments (Byng-Hall, 1995); and
- to assist with the creation of a more coherent and relevant perspective (story) within which the crucial elements, phenomena, and circumstances of the family are accounted in a more appropriate way.

In the following vignette the modes of intervention in SIFT are illustrated.

Clinical Vignette

The M. family consists of the mother, age 35 and a hard-working employee, and Angela, her 11-year-old daughter. Angela's father abandoned his wife when she was pregnant with Angela. They were not married. Angela seldom sees him. He is married and has two other children, who ignore their stepsister's existence. For the time being, Angela lives with her mother, grandfather, and uncle. Angela was diagnosed with depression and referred to the study; after undergoing the initial assessment, she was randomized into the SIFT arm of the study. Her symptoms were thoughts of dying, sad feelings, withdrawal from friends, feelings of inadequacy, tearfulness, weight loss, threats of running away, and school difficulties over the last year. The family was assigned to a couple of therapists, a male child psychiatrist and a female psychologist. The following issues characterized the therapeutic process:

- The onset of Angela's depression coincided with her maternal grandmother's death, 2 years ago. Angela had been reared mainly by her.
- Angela's mother displays bulimic behavior (the nonpurging type). She is obese and almost always on an unsuccessful diet, frequently involving Angela by controlling her food intake and shopping.
- The mother–daughter relationship is very conflictual: Mother often reacts to escalations of arguments with physical violence, and Angela expresses fear of being killed during these outbursts.
- Angela is trapped in a triangulated position within the mother–father system. On behalf of her mother, she expresses hate toward her father and a desire to exact revenge because he abandoned them. On the other hand, if she expressed a wish to approach her father and stepsiblings, she would feel as if she were betraying her mother.
- In the four-member household, Angela's grandfather plays a paternal role for Angela, who loves him. Her uncle, age 30, is a drug addict, a fact that is concealed from Angela.

The 14-session treatment was carried out in 11 months. The family missed only one session. All but two sessions involved Angela and her mother; in one session, her grandfather participated, too, and in another session, her mother was seen alone. Frequently used techniques included the following: sympathetic listening, enactment of conflictual interactions between mother and daughter, communication training, problem solving, hypothetical questioning (mainly oriented to the future), a focus on strengths and positives, and use of humor. The therapists offered understanding and support to both women by which (a) they developed a more secure attachment, (b) the mother gained assertiveness within the family, (c) the mother allowed her daughter to approach her father and his new family, (d) instead of parenting her mother, Angela encouraged her to take care of herself and not count on Angela for support. By the end of treatment, mother and daughter moved to a new house, Angela successfully completed her grade, and Angela's mother decided to take care of her obesity and scheduled a relevant plastic surgery. According to the therapists' and supervisor's impressions, the mother–daughter relationship was considerably improved. On the completion of treatment the therapists felt the need for at least one booster session about 6 weeks after the termination of the study. Nevertheless, they had to adhere to the protocol, which did not permit booster sessions. They became aware of the significant role of the male therapist, who probably represented the absent father during the therapeutic process.

DISCUSSION

In our experience, the parents of the children seen up to this point in the project, whether in individual or family therapy, are contending with very severe issues in their own right. The following issues may be relevant:

1. Many are single parents (whether by death or divorce). Many of the couples had very severe marital conflicts. In some families, early parenting had been primarily carried out by the father, who might no longer live with the child but who had significant importance in the beginning. Therefore, both parents must be engaged in the work, either together or separately.

2. The child's depression is usually of long standing and brought to a professional's attention at a point of crisis by doctors, school, or the parents themselves. Seriously depressed children create extremely difficult management problems for parents who end up having to cope with their children's suicidal threats, school attendance problems, and other behavioral issues. Some referred children were out of school in London, whereas some children in Athens were referred for learning problems at school. The situation can be further complicated by the conscious or unconscious guilt of parents, who are questioning why their child should be ill. They are often only too aware of the importance of events early in the child's life.

3. Within the individual treatment program a key issue has been the provision of a separate space for both parents and child. This process has facilitated the separation of the different issues for the parents and the child; over time, it has enabled the parents to begin to see the child as an individual, with a separate world and identity. Childhood depression engenders understandable parental anxiety, particularly when the illness disrupts the child's life or when of the child threatens suicide. When appropriate, parents need permission not to be controlled by the child's illness and support in their difficult parenting task.

4. Often the parents of children in psychotherapy for depression have many emotional difficulties themselves. It is often difficult to say whether their difficulties occur because of their child's disorder or whether they were preexisting triggering factors. Often parents feel frustrated in their expectations for their child and find it difficult to fulfill their parenting role. In most cases we have found very difficult family histories; many of the parents had gone on from unhappy childhoods to unsatisfactory relationships or marriages, which sometimes led to traumatic family breakdowns.

Issues in Work With the Parents

Generally the main parental difficulties that we face during the project involve parents who are burdened by elements of their personal history. Their own severe difficulties may include unresolved mourning or losses; immaturity and preoccupation with their own issues, which decrease their ability to function adequately as parents; marital problems; and difficulties in being able to see their children as separate individuals in their own right.

Because this has been short-term, focused work, the therapist must focus on key issues for the family. Therapists must be aware of the time limits to set priorities for treatment and address central or urgent subjects. These might include parental problems, traumatic life events, child neglect or maltreatment, and difficulties in parenting. The families include divorced parents, one-parent families, and reconstituted families. The parent-worker might need to consider referring a parent for individual psychotherapy or psychiatric help. The parent-worker may also find it helpful to involve other agencies in the community to help with the child's difficulties (e.g., in going to school). In a few cases the team may consider appropriate interventions for major crises, such as suicidal thoughts or actions or family violence. Sometimes this time-limited focused work is advantageous. Many of the families we studied would have been unwilling to engage in long-term therapeutic work despite considerable difficulties. This focused intervention has often felt very powerful in freeing family members to get on with their individual lives. Some have clearly needed long-term help, and this intervention has allowed them to see that this way of working can be beneficial.

Limitations

One of the limitations of our study was our decision to exlude severely depressed children and adolescents meriting hospitalization, including adolescents with a bipolar disorder. Although our referrals came to our university clinics and from outside sources such as community clinics, we indicated to the possible referral sources at the outset that we were not accepting these cases. However, only three cases, one in Athens and two in Helsinki, were excluded because the children were seriously depressed and had to be admitted. This decision limits our ability to generalize our findings for the treatment of more seriously depressed and suicidal patients. Referred children who were depressed and on antidepressant medication had to stop their medication for 3 weeks before entering the program. Although the number of subjects was originally planned to be 96, we ended up with only 71 cases in the three centers. Recruiting the required number of subjects according to the inclusion and exclusion criteria proved difficult in the three centers, although a major effort was made. Fortunately the number of drop-outs was rather small—four in Athens and two in London. Moreover, because of the time constraints imposed by the protocol, we were obliged to finish the study within 36 months, which did not allow us to replace drop-outs. The intent-to-treat design was introduced during the implementation of the project, after we realized that the recruitment was slow and we would not be able to replace the drop-outs.

In London, Helsinki, and Athens the supervision styles are different regarding family therapy, which may influence the outcome. Moreover, it seems that in London and Helsinki the family therapists are more experienced. Some research suggests that therapist characteristics such as experience may affect the outcome (Lambert & Okishi, 1997). Another limitation concerns what modifications, if any, were required for interventions to be applied across the different cultures and sites. One wonders whether this variability may have affected the intervention in the three different countries. On the other hand, this study provides an opportunity to detect differences that are due to cultural factors.

SUMMARY

It is too soon to draw conclusions from a psychotherapy research project in progress. However, these are the main impressions from the experience we have had up to this point. The project was a long, difficult, and complex one. Across all three centers we encountered the same types of parental problems. Many parents, mainly mothers, are depressed, and some are involved in treatment. Serious marital conflict is common. Differences in the study population among the different centers indicated that although many of the young people have had problems with school attendance in London, there were fewer school attendance problems in Athens and Helsinki. In Athens many of the young people were labeled during referral as "learning disabled," as depression was believed to be a result of the stigma of the diagnosis. All three centers responded quite well to the implementation of the project, and the therapies were delivered reliably and according to the manuals and the agreed-upon process.

Although we have not yet analyzed the data, we are under the impression that these children have improved and will probably continue to improve during the 6-month follow-up in some of the cases. This has been also the feeling of the vast majority of children in individual therapy. Our colleagues on the family therapy teams are noting that, regardless of the fact that the children exhibited clear depressive symptoms and the families were worried about them, the families easily became engaged in family therapy and were willing to work together with the therapists as a family, rather than insisting that the index patient had the problem and the focus should remain exclusively on him or her. As treatment approaches its end, both individual and family therapists share the impression that the depressed children have improved. Many children seem to be back in school and learning. However, in cases complicated by comorbidity, the improvement might not be quite clear. Nevertheless, quite a few parents of children who have so far completed either treatment report improvement in their offsprings' affect and intrafamilial and peer relationships, as well as school behavior and achievement. In some instances, the family situation is still seriously problematic and the parents remain very troubled. These families apparently need to continue therapy, although the children have maintained their improvement. The extent of the parental problems can be seen as an obstacle to further improvement for the children. On the other hand, this study includes two therapy approaches, psychodynamic and family, which are characteristic of clinical child practice. Because many interventions in use in a majority of clinical settings lack strong empirical support, we hope that this study, despite its limitations, may shed some light on the two nonbehavioral interventions and prepare the way for more targeted research. However, the empirical findings of the intervention in the various areas explored, as well as the results in the follow-up, remain to be seen.

REFERENCES

Achenbach, T. M. (1991). *Manual for the teacher's report form and 1991 profile*. Burlington: University of Vermont, Department of Psychiatry.

Alexander, F., & French, T. (1946). *Psychoanalytic therapy*. New York: Ronald Press.

Altman D. G. (1991). *Practical statistics for medical research*. London: Chapman & Hall.

Angold, A., Costello, E. J., Pickles, A., Winder, F., & Silver, A. (1987). *The development of a questionnaire for use in epidemiological studies of depression in children and adolescents*. London: Institute of Psychiatry, London University.

Armsden, G., & Greenberg, M. (1987). The inventory of parent and peer attachment. *Journal of Youth and Adolescence 16*, 427–454.

Armsden, G., McCauley, E., Greenberg, M., Burke, P., & Mitchell, J. (1990). Parent and peer attachment in early adolescent depression. *Journal of Abnormal Child Psychology 18*, 683–697.

Battle, J. (1981). *The culture-free self-esteem inventory, Form B*. Washington, DC: Special Child Publications.

Beavers, W., & Hampson, R. (1990). *Successful families: Assessment and intervention*. New York: Norton.

Beck, A., & Weissman, A. (1974). The measurement of pessimism: The hopelessness scale. *Journal of Consulting and Clinical Psychology 42*, 861–865.

Bemporal, J. R. (1994). Dynamic and interpersonal theories of depression. In W. M. Reynolds & H. F. Johnson (Eds.), *Handbook of depression in children and adolescents* (pp. 81–95). New York: Plenum Press.

Berney, T. P., Bhate, S. R., Kolvin, I., Famuyiwa, O. O., Barett, M. L., Fundudis, T., et al. (1991). The context of childhood depression project. *British Journal of Psychiatry 159*(Suppl. 2), 28–35.

Birmaher, B. (1998). Psychometric properties of the Screen for Child Anxiety Related Emotional Disorders (SCARED): A replication study. *Journal of the American Academy of Child and Adolescent Psychiatry, 38*, 1230–1236.

Birmaher, B., Ryan, N. D., Williamson, D. E., Brent, D. A., & Kaufman, J. (1996). Childhood and adolescent depression: A review of the past 10 years. *Journal of the American Academy of Child and Adolescent Psychiatry, 35*, 1575–1583.

Bowlby, J. (1981). *Attachment and loss. Vol. III. Loss: Sadness and depression.* Middlesex, England: Penguin Education.

Brent, D. A., Holder, D., Kolko, D. J., Birmaher, B., Baugher, M., Roth, C., et al. (1997). A clinical psychotherapy trial for adolescent depression comparing cognitive, family and supportive therapy. *Archives of General Psychiatry, 54*, 877–885.

Brown, G. W., Harris, T. O., & Bifulco, A. (1986). Long-term effects of early loss of parent. In M. Rutter, C. E. Izard, & P. B. Read (Eds.), *Depression in young people: Developmental and clinical perspectives* (pp. 251–296). New York: Guilford Press.

Burns, B., Hoagwood, K., & Maultsby, L. T. (1998). Improving outcomes for children and adolescents with serious emotional and behavioral disorders: Current and future directions. In M. Epstein, K. Kutash, & A. G. Duchnowski (Eds.), *Outcomes for children and youth with emotional and behavioral disorders and their families: Programs and evaluation best practices* (pp. 686–707). Austin, TX: PRO-ED.

Byng-Hall, J. (1995). Creating a secure family base. Some implications of attachment theory for family therapy. *Family Process, 34*(1), 45–58.

Byng-Hall, J., & Campbell, D. C. (1981). Resolving conflicts in distance regulation: An integrative approach. *Journal of Marital and Family Therapy, 7*, 321–330.

Chambers, W., Puig-Antich, J., Hirsch, M., Paez, P., Ambrosini, P. J., Tabrizi, M. A., & Davies, M. (1985). The assessment of affective disorders in children and adolescents by semi-structured interview: Test–retest reliability of the Schedule for Affective Disorders and Schizophrenia for School-Age Children, Present Episode version. *Archives of General Psychiatry, 42*, 696–702.

Chambless, D. L., & Hollon, S. D. (1998). Defining empirically supported therapies. *Journal of Consulting and Clinical Psychology, 66*, 7–18.

Davanloo, H. (1980). *Short-term dynamic psychotherapy and emotional crisis.* New York: Jason Aronson.

de Shazer, S. (1988). *Clues. Investigating solutions in brief therapy.* New York: W. W. Norton.

Epstein, N. B., Baldwin, L. M., & Bishop, D. S. (1983). The McMaster Family Assessment Device. *Journal of Marital and Family Therapy, 9*, 171–180.

Fonagy, P., & Roth, T. (1998). Therapy with children. In A. Roth & P. Fonagy (Eds.), *What works for whom?: A critical review of psychotherapy research.* London: Guilford Press.

Fundudis, T., Berney, T. P., Kolvin, I., Famuyiwa, O. O., Barrett, L., Bhate, S., et al. (1991). Reliability and validity of two self-rating scales in the assessment of childhood depression. *British Journal of Psychiatry, 159* (Suppl. 11), 36–40.

Goodyer, I., Kolvin, I., & Gatzanis, S. (1985). Recent undesirable life events and psychiatric disorder in childhood and adolescence. *British Journal of Psychiatry, 147,* 517–523.

Harrington, R., Rutter, M., Weissman, M., Fudge, H., Groothues, C., Bredenkamp, D., et al. (1997). Psychiatric disorders in the relatives of depressed probands. I. Comparison of prepubertal, adolescent and early adult-onset cases. *Journal of Affective Disorders, 42,* 9–22.

Hibbs, E., & Jensen, P. (Eds.). (1996). *Psychosocial treatments for child and adolescent disorders: Empirically based strategies for clinical practice.* Washington, DC: American Psychological Association.

Hoagwood, K., Hibbs, E., Brent, D., & Jensen, P. (1995). Introduction to the special section: Efficacy and effectiveness in studies of child and adolescent psychotherapy. *Journal of Consulting and Clinical Psychology, 63,* 683–687.

Kaufman, J., Birmaher, B., Brent, D., Rao, U., Flynn, C., Moreci, P., et al. (1997). Schedule for Affective Disorders and Schizophrenia for School-Age Children —Present and Lifetime Version (K-SADS-PL): Initial reliability and validity data. *Journal of the American Academy of Child and Adolescent Psychiatry, 36,* 980–988.

Kazdin, A. (1996). Developing effective treatments for children and adolescents. In E. Hibbs & P. Jensen (Eds.), *Psychosocial treatments for child and adolescent disorders: Empirically based strategies for clinical practice.* Washington, DC: American Psychological Association.

Kazdin, A., Siegel, T., & Bass, D. (1990). Drawing upon clinical practice to inform research on child and adolescent psychotherapy. *Professional Psychology: Research and Practice, 21,* 189–198.

Kernberg, P. F. (1991). *Therapist verbal interventions: A reliability study.* Proceedings on research in psychoanalysis at the International Psychoanalytic Association's First Scientific Research Meeting, London.

Kolvin, I., Garside, R. F., Nicol, A. R., Macmillan, A., Wolstenholme, F., & Leitch, I. M. (1981). *Help starts here: The maladjusted child in the ordinary school.* New York: Tavistock Publications.

Kolvin, I., Barrett, L. M., Bhate, S. R., et al. (1991). Issues in the diagnosis and classification of childhood depression. *British Journal of Psychiatry, 159*(Suppl. 11), 9–11.

Kolvin, I., Trowell, J., Tsiantis, J., Almqvist, F., & Sadowski, H. (1999). Psychotherapy for childhood depression. In M. Maj & N. Sactorius (Eds.), *WPA Series, Depressive Disorders* (pp. 304–306). Chichester, England: Wiley.

Kovacs, M. (1992). *Children's Depression Inventory (CDI) manual.* North Tonawanda, NY: Multi-Health Systems.

Kovacs, M., & Bastiaens, L. J. (1995). The psychotherapeutic management of major depressive and dysthymic disorders in childhood and adolescence: Issues and prospects. In I. M. Goodyer (Ed.), *The depressed child and adolescent: Developmental and clinical perspectives* (pp. 281–310). New York: Cambridge University Press.

Kovacs, M., & Sherrill, T. (2001). The psychotherapeutic management of major depressive and dysthymic disorders in childhood and adolescence: Issues and prospects. In I. M. Goodyer (Ed.), *The Depressed Child and Adolescent* (pp. 325–352). Cambridge, England: Cambridge University Press.

Lambert, M. J., & Okishi, C. J. (1997). The effects of the individual psychotherapist and implications for future research. *Clinical Psychology: Science and Practice*, 4(1), 66–75.

Lebow, J. L. (1984). On the value of integrating approaches to family therapy. *Journal of Marital and Family Therapy*, 10(2), 127–138.

Lewinsohn, P. M., Clarke, G. N., Hops, H., & Andrews, J. (1990). Cognitive–behavioral treatment for depressed adolescents. *Behavior Therapy*, 21, 385–401.

Lewis, J., Beavers, W. R., Gosset, J. T., & Philips, V. A. (1976). *No single thread: Psychological health and family systems*. New York: Brunnert Mazel.

Magana-Amato, A. B. (1993). *Manual for coding expressed emotion from the 5-minute speech sample*. Los Angeles: UCLA Family Project.

Malan, D. (1976). *The frontier of brief psychotherapy*. New York: Plenum.

Mander, G. (2000). *A psychodynamic approach to brief therapy*. London: Sage Publications.

Mann, J. (1973). *Time limited psychotherapy*. Cambridge, MA: Harvard University Press.

McGoldrick, M., & Gerson, R. (1985). *Genograms in family assessment*. New York: Norton.

Minuchin, S., & Fishman, H. C. (1981). *Family therapy techniques*. Cambridge, MA: Harvard University Press.

Newman, D. L., Moffitt, T. E., Caspi, A., Magdol, L., Silva, P. A., & Stanton, W. R. (1996). Psychiatric disorder in a birth cohort of young adults: Prevalence, comorbidity, clinical significance and new case incidence from ages 11 to 21. *Journal of Consulting and Clinical Psychology*, 33, 695–705.

Palazzoli-Selvini, M., Boscolo, L., Cecchin, G., & Prata, G. (1980). Hypothesising-circularity-neutrality. Three guidelines for the conductor of the session. *Family Process*, 19(1), 3–12.

Puig-Antich, J., & Chambers, W. J. (1978). *The schedule for affective disorders and schizophrenia for school aged children*. New York: New York State Psychiatric Institute.

Seligman, M., Peterson, C., & Kaslow, N. (1984). Attributional style and depressive symptoms among children. *Journal of Abnormal Psychology*, 93, 235–238.

Shirk, S., & Saiz, C. (1992). Clinical, empirical and developmental perspectives on the therapeutic relationship in child psychotherapy. *Development and Psychopathology. Special Issue: Developmental approaches to prevention and intervention*, 4, 713–728.

Shirk, S. (2001). The road to effective child psychological services. In J. Hughes, A. La Greca, & J. C. Conoley (Eds.), *Handbook of psychological services for children and adolescents*. Oxford, England: Oxford University Press.

Sifneos, P. (1972). *Short-term psychotherapy and emotional crisis*. Cambridge, MA: Harvard University Press.

Spanier, G. (1976). Measuring dyadic adjustment. *Journal of Marriage and the Family, 58*, 5–28.

Tebbutt, J., Swanston, R. K., Oates, R., & O'Toole, B. J. (1997). Five years after child sexual abuse: Persisting dysfunction and problems of prediction. *Journal of the Academy of Child and Adolescent Psychiatry, 36*, 330–339.

Trowell, J., & Kolvin, I. (1999). Lessons from a psychotherapy outcome study with sexually abused girls. *Clinical Child Psychololgy and Psychiatry, 4*, 79–89.

Trowell, J., Kolvin, I., Weeramanthri, T., Berelowitz, M., & Leitch, I. (1998). *Treating girls who have been sexually abused*. Report presented to the Department of Health, United Kingdom.

Weissman, M. M. (1975). Assessment of social adjustment. *Archives of General Psychiatry, 32*, 357–365.

Weissman, M. M., Gammon, G. D., John, K., Merikangas, K. R., Warner, V., Prusoff, B. A., et al. (1987). Children of depressed parents: Increased psychopathology and early onset of major depression. *Archives of General Psychiatry, 44*, 847–853.

Weissman, M. M., Sholomskas, P., & John, K. (1981). The assessment of social adjustment. An update. *Archives of General Psychiatry, 38*, 1250–1258.

Weisz, J. R., Donenberg, G. R., Han, S. S., & Weiss, B. (1995). Bridging the gap between laboratory and clinic in child and adolescent psychotherapy. *Journal of Consulting and Clinical Psychology, 63*, 688–701.

White, M., & Epston, D. (1989). *Literate means to therapeutic ends*. Adelaide, Australia: Dulwich Center Publications.

Wrate, R., Kolvin, I., Garside, R., Wolstenholme, F., Humbert C. M., & Leitch, I. (1995). Helping seriously disturbed children. In R. Nichol (Ed.), *Longitudinal studies in child psychology and psychiatry* (pp. 265–318). Chichester, England: Wiley.

13

EVALUATION AND TREATMENT OF INFANTILE ANOREXIA

IRENE CHATOOR

REVIEW OF THE LITERATURE

Feeding difficulties represent one of the most common pediatric problems. An estimated 25% of otherwise normally developing infants and young children have feeding problems (Chatoor, Hamburger, Fullard, & Rivera, 1994; Lindberg, Bohlin, & Hagekull, 1991). Feeding disorders can disrupt the infant's early development and are linked to later behavioral problems (Galler, Ramsey, Solimano, Lowell, & Mason, 1988), anxiety disorders (Timimi, Douglas, & Tsiftsopoulou, 1997), and eating disorders (Marchi & Cohen, 1990). Consequently, it is very important to understand and treat early feeding problems. As Emde, Bingham, and Harmon (1993) have pointed out, classification schemes are crucial tools for determining the etiology and the course of specific disorders and evaluating the efficacy of treatment. However, research on early feeding problems has been hampered by the lack of a standard classification system.

Before the inclusion of the diagnostic category of feeding disorder of infancy or early childhood in the *Diagnostic and Statistical Manual of Mental Disorders, Fourth Edition* (DSM–IV; American Psychiatric Association,

1994), nationally defined criteria for the diagnosis of feeding disorders in young children did not exist. In the absence of a recognized standard, several labels have been assigned by different authors to describe various feeding problems. Some authors have used descriptive terms, including *food refusal* (Lindberg, Bohlin, Hagekull, & Palmerus, 1996), *problem eaters* (Sanders, Patel, LeGrice, & Shepherd, 1993), *picky eaters* (Marchi & Cohen, 1990), *choosy eaters* (Rydell, Dahl, & Sundelin, 1995), and *food selectivity* (Shore, Babbitt, Williams, Coe, & Snyder, 1998; Timimi et al., 1997). Others have chosen terms that refer to an underlying etiology, such as *food aversion* (Siegel, 1988; Archer & Szatmari, 1990), *food phobia* (Singer, Ambuel, Wade, & Jaffe, 1992), *food neophobia* (Pliner & Lowen, 1997), or *phagophobia* (Culbert, Kajander, Kohen, & Reaney, 1996). However, these terms were applied without clear definitions of what diagnostic criteria were used and how these feeding disorders can be differentiated from other feeding disorders. Consequently, comparing these studies and case reports is very difficult.

The field of feeding disorders is further complicated because feeding disorder and failure to thrive (FTT) have been used as synonyms, although not all infants with feeding disorders fail to thrive and not all infants who do not thrive have feeding disorders (Benoit, 1993). The term *FTT* has been applied as a diagnostic label for individuals who are younger than 3 years of age and who are judged to gain weight inadequately (Fosson & Wilson, 1993; Frank, Silva, & Needlman, 1993). Historically, the etiology of FTT has been divided into organic FTT and nonorganic FTT (NOFTT). Defined as growth failure without a diagnosable medical illness, NOFTT was considered to be caused by maternal deprivation (Patton & Gardner, 1962). Homer and Ludwig (1981) described a third category of FTT that represents a mixture of organic and environmental components in the etiology of the growth failure. Several authors have expressed concern about the usefulness of the term *FTT* as a diagnostic label. Goldbloom (1987) pointed out that the term is purely descriptive and tells nothing about the process that caused the infant to grow inadequately. Bithoney and colleagues (1992) suggested abandoning *FTT* as a diagnostic label in favor of *growth deficiency* as a purely descriptive term for infants and young children who, for whatever reason, do not grow adequately.

In summary, numerous diagnostic labels for feeding disorders exist. However, there are no operational criteria for specific feeding disorders. As a result, researchers continue to use different terminology to describe similar disorders or use the same name when referring to very different disorders. This confusion continues in spite of the fact that the *DSM–IV* (American Psychiatric Association, 1994) introduced Feeding Disorder of Infancy or Early Childhood with the following diagnostic criteria: persistent failure to eat adequately with significant failure to gain weight or significant loss of weight over at least 1 month; the disturbance is not due to an associated medical condition; the disturbance is not accounted for by another mental disorder or by lack of available food; the onset is before 6 years of age. Although the *DSM–IV* operationalizes diagnostic criteria for feeding disorders, these criteria are at once nonspecific and too narrow. They exclude feeding disorders that are not associated with growth failure and feeding disorders that are associated with medical conditions.

To address these issues, Chatoor, Dickson, Schaefer, and Egan (1985) first proposed a classification system of three developmental feeding disorders: feeding disorder of homeostasis, feeding disorder of attachment, and infantile anorexia. Later, Chatoor (1991) added posttraumatic feeding disorder as a fourth feeding disorder. More recently, Chatoor (2002) published operational diagnostic criteria for the aforementioned and two additional feeding disorders (sensory food aversions and feeding disorder associated with a medical condition). This chapter will address the evaluation and treatment of one specific feeding disorder *infantile anorexia*.

INFANTILE ANOREXIA

Clinical Description

Infants[1] with infantile anorexia usually elicit concern because of their food refusal and growth failure. Some parents report that even during the first few months of life, their infants became disinterested in feeding if someone entered the room or if they were otherwise distracted while feeding. By the end of the first year, most infants begin to show a lack of interest in feeding, a curiosity in exploration, and an interest in play and interaction with the caretakers. Typically, during the transition to spoon- and self-feeding, these infants take only a few bites of food and then refuse to eat any more. They may refuse to open their mouths for feeding, throw food and feeding utensils, and frequently try to climb out of the high chair or leave the table to play. Usually, parents become increasingly concerned about their infants' poor food intake. They may try coaxing, distracting, offering different food, feeding during play, feeding at night, and even force-feeding to get their infants to eat more. However, most parents report that their infants simply do not seem to feel hungry and that these methods worked only temporarily, if at all.

Diagnostic Criteria

1. The child refuses to eat adequate amounts of food for at least 1 month.

---

[1]The term *infant* is used for children under 3 years of age. To differentiate between parent and infant, the parent is referred to as *she* and the infant is referred to as *he*.

2. Onset of food refusal occurs when subject is under age 3 years of age, usually between 9 and 18 months of age, during the transition to spoon- and self-feeding.
3. Hunger is not communicated, lacks interest in food, but shows strong interest in exploration and interaction across caregiver contacts; shows acute and/or chronic growth deficiency.
4. The onset of food refusal is not linked to a traumatic event.
5. Food refusal is not caused by an underlying medical illness.

Summary of Research

Chatoor and Egan (1983) first described a group of toddlers who displayed food refusal and FTT and who did not fit the description of NOFTT. The toddlers showed no signs of maternal deprivation. Quite the contrary, their parents were extremely concerned about their toddlers' poor food intake and growth failure. Initially, the authors called this feeding disorder *a separation disorder* because of its onset during the developmental period of separation and individuation. Later, Chatoor, Egan, Getson, Menvielle, and O'Donnell (1988) and Chatoor (1989) referred to it as *infantile anorexia nervosa* because of its similarities to anorexia nervosa in the child's struggle for autonomy and control. However, distinguishing this feeding disorder from anorexia nervosa is important because of its onset during infancy rather than adolescence. To emphasize the child's lack of appetite in this particular feeding disorder, Chatoor and colleagues (1992) decided to describe it as *infantile anorexia*.

More recently, Chatoor, Ganiban, Hirsch, Spurrell, and Reiss (2000) developed a transactional model for infantile anorexia. Specifically, they postulated that infantile anorexia will emerge when a toddler who has a difficult temperament (i.e., emotionally reactive, demanding, and willful) is raised by a parent who has difficulty setting effective limits upon the toddler's challenging behaviors. This combination leads to poorly structured, conflictual feeding interactions that further interfere with the toddler's awareness of hunger and desire to eat. In support of this hypothesis, Chatoor et al. (2000) reported that toddlers with infantile anorexia are rated by their parents as more emotionally intense, negative, dependent, unstoppable, and difficult than healthy eaters. Difficult temperament was also associated with lower percent ideal weight, suggesting that the most difficult infants demonstrated the highest levels of growth failure. (*Percent ideal weight* is a specific description of how children's weight for height is compared with the fiftieth percentile of children of that age.) In regard to associated parent characteristics, mothers of infantile anorexics were more likely to describe insecure attachment to their own parents than mothers whose infants did not have a feeding disorder (Chatoor et al., 2000). Moreover, the insecure attachment of the mothers, as well as their own drive for thinness, correlated significantly with mother–infant conflict during feeding. In turn, mother–infant conflict during feeding was positively associated with low percent ideal weight in the infantile anorexic toddlers and in the two control groups of nonclinical infants, a group of healthy eaters, and a second group of picky eaters. In two studies, Chatoor and colleagues also explored the mother–infant interactional patterns associated with infantile anorexia. In the first study, Chatoor et al. (1988) found that toddlers with infantile anorexia and their mothers demonstrated less dyadic reciprocity, less maternal contingency (the mother's ability to read the infant's cues and to respond appropriately), more dyadic conflict, and more struggle for control than toddlers who were healthy eaters and their mothers. These findings were recently replicated within a different sample (Chatoor, Hirsch, Ganiban, Persinger, & Hamburger, 1998). An additional study by Chatoor et al. (1997) demonstrated that high mother–infant conflict during feeding differentiates toddlers with infantile anorexia not only from healthy well-feeding toddlers but also from infants with a feeding disorder of attachment, which has been described in the early literature as maternal deprivation (Patton & Gardner, 1963).

As these studies demonstrate, high mother–infant conflict during feeding appears to be central to this feeding disorder. The conflict centers on the infant's lack of interest and refusal to eat and the mother's disappointment and negative affect because of her failed efforts to get the infant to accept her food. Interestingly, Chatoor et al. (2000) found that the intensity of the dyadic conflict and the degree of the infant's insecure attachment (Chatoor et al., 1998) correlated significantly with the infant's degree of malnutrition. The more insecurely the infants were attached and the more conflict that existed between the infants and their mothers during feeding, the more malnourished were the infants.

The findings of these diagnostic studies support the previously described transactional model for infantile anorexia and led to the development of a psychotherapeutic intervention. This intervention addresses the three components of the model: (a) It serves to help the parents understand and deal with the anorectic infant's temperament; (b) it explores the difficulties the parents may have in setting limits to the infant's provocative behaviors that interfere with feeding; and (c) it provides parents with recommendations on structuring mealtimes and dealing with the infant's provocative behaviors to facilitate the infant's internal regulation of eating. This treatment model was tested in a pilot project that involved 20 infants with infantile anorexia. The author diagnosed and treated all infants in the study. This chapter summarizes the findings from this pilot project (Chatoor, Hirsch, & Persinger, 1997) and the ongoing randomized treatment study of infantile anorexia.

Program Description

The Multidisciplinary Feeding Disorders Clinic is one of the specialty clinics of the Infant and Toddler Mental Health Program at Children's

National Medical Center, in Washington, DC. Because many feeding disorders are associated with nutritional problems, medical illnesses, and impairment of oral motor or general development, a multidisciplinary team is required to assess the various aspects of feeding disorders and to differentiate infantile anorexia from other feeding disorders that may accompany food refusal.

The following assessments are carried out by a Multidisciplinary Feeding Disorders Team:

- *psychiatric assessment of feeding disorder and psychiatric comorbidity* through parental history and observation of mother and infant during feeding;
- *assessment of infant temperament and parental characteristics* through parent questionnaires and direct observation of infant and mother during play;
- *medical evaluation* through medical history and physical examination;
- *nutritional assessment* through anthropometric measurements and 3-day record of what the child ate;
- *oral motor assessment* through parental history and direct observation; and
- *developmental assessment* if any specific concern exists.

The team performs the assessments on the same day (except for the developmental assessment), and the family receives feedback and diagnostic information with all team members in the room. In our clinic, the individual team members present the findings and recommendations of their discipline, and at the end, the child psychiatrist or gastroenterologist integrates the diagnostic assessments of all the team members, presents the parents with a specific diagnosis, and develops an integrated treatment plan for the child. If the child is diagnosed with infantile anorexia and meets criteria for the ongoing treatment study, the study is explained to the parents and the parents are invited to participate in the study. For all other feeding disorders, the family is assigned a primary therapist or case manager who helps to coordinate the personnel involved in the child's treatment plan.

Method

Procedures

Under the supervision of a pediatric gastroenterologist, an experienced nurse practitioner interviews the parents and performs the physical examination of the infant. The nurse practitioner uses a semistructured interview for feeding disorders, which was developed by Chatoor, McWade Paez, Simenson, & Ganiban (1998). This interview gathers information about the infant's feeding behavior and medical health. In addition, the parents are asked to fill out questionnaries about demographic data and the infant's developmental and health history. The nurse practitioner and the gastroenterologist address the possibility of organic causes of food refusal, such as gastroesophageal reflux, celiac disease, intercurrent infections, and allergic gastritis. If indicated by the history and physical examination, screening procedures include serological tests, microscopic examination of the stool, and depending on the symptoms of the child, X-ray assessments, scans of various organs, ph-probes, and endoscopic visualization of the stomach and esophagus. This examination rules out organic conditions that would exclude infants from participation in the treatment study for infantile anorexia.

A nutritionist conducts a nutritional assessment consisting of anthropometric measurements of the infant and a review of the infant's 3-day food record. The nutritionist determines the infant's ideal weight according to height and whether the infant meets criteria for acute or chronic malnutrition or both (Waterlow, 1972).

A psychiatrist then reviews the general developmental and feeding history; the data from the interview; and the evaluation by the nurse practitioner, gastroenterologist, and nutritionist. The psychiatrist observes mother–infant interactions during feeding and play to assess the amount of conflict in the dyad and then meets with the parents to address any questions that were not fully answered by the previous evaluations. If the history or the observation of the mother–infant dyad indicates that an additional psychopathological condition exists, the psychiatrist explores comorbid conditions through further questioning of the parents. In our experience, infantile anorexia is frequently associated with separation anxiety, sleep disorders, and sensory food aversions. These conditions should be clearly explored because they complicate the treatment.

We assess the parents' possible psychopathological conditions only through questionnaires and direct observation. We have refrained from conducting structured psychiatric interviews with the mothers because most mothers feel very guilty about the difficulties in feeding their infants. We are concerned that an interview focusing on the mother's emotions would intensify these feelings. Additionally, in past studies of infantile anorexia, we found a very low rate of overt psychopathology among the mothers. However, the mothers showed a high degree of anxiety about their infants' health.

An occupational therapist and the psychiatrist simultaneously observe the infant and mother during feeding. The occupational therapist focuses on the oral motor development of the infant to rule out any neurological dysfunction or oral motor delay secondary to lack of experience with age appropriate food. This assessment is particularly helpful for infants who have sensory food aversions and therefore avoid several foods.

The mother–infant interactions during feeding and the psychiatric interview are videotaped. This videotape, the questionnaires filled out by the parents, the feeding history interview, and the evaluations by the nurse practitioner or gastroenterologist, nutritionist, and occupational therapist are made available to a second psychiatrist, who independently performs a diagnostic evaluation of all infants. Throughout the study, the two psychiatrists confer with each other to ensure diagnostic agreement, and only children who are diagnosed with infantile anorexia by both psychiatrists are enrolled in the study. (The various diagnostic assessments are summarized in Table 13.1.)

Assessments

The same measures that will be used for treatment outcome are given at baseline. These measures address the functioning of the infant; the mother; the mother–infant relationship; and the marital relationship, with special emphasis on parental child-rearing disagreements.

The baseline and treatment outcome measures are summarized in Table 13.2 and described below.

Assessment of Infant's Feeding Behavior. The Infant Feeding Behavior Questionnaire (Benoit, 1992, 1996) is a Likert instrument that asks the parent to rate the infant's behavior according to a 6-point system that ranges from "never" to "almost always." All the behaviors listed in this questionnaire relate to the infant's food refusal and are summarized in one total score. We measure whether the infant's food refusal behaviors decrease after the treatment.

Assessment of Infant's Food Intake. The mother is asked to keep a 3-day record of everything the infant ate. The nutritionist adds the calories and analyzes the nutritional content of the food that the mother reports that the infant ate. The nutritionist compares the daily average of the child's food intake with the required daily allowance for a child of that age. Although this method suffers from several biases, it allows us to monitor whether the child's food intake improves with treatment.

Assessment of Infant's Growth. Standardized growth charts (Kuczmarski et al., 2000) are used to compare the infant's weight and height measurement with those of other infants of the same age. Weight per height reflects current or "acute" nutritional status. The reference "normal" represents 50th percentile weight for height. The current weight divided by this number yields the percentage of ideal body weight. This measure is sensitive to small increments in growth.

The Waterlow criteria (1977) for acute and chronic malnutrition were used for the diagnostic assessment of the toddlers' nutritional status. To meet diagnostic criteria for infantile anorexia, the toddlers had to meet the following Waterlow criteria for acute and/or chronic malnutrition.

TABLE 13.1
Diagnostic Procedures

Measure	Description of measure	Purpose
Diagnostic Evaluation of Infant		
Feeding history	Semistructured interview (Chatoor et al., unpublished) (NP) Clinical interview (P)	Determine nature and onset of feeding problems and rule out other feeding disorders
Developmental history	Child history questionnaire (M) Clinical interview (P)	Rule out neurological impairment and/or psychiatric disorder
Medical history	Child history questionnaire (M) Semistructured Interview (NP) Clinical interview (G) if indicated	Rule out organic causes of feeding problems
Physical status	Physical examination (NP and/or G)	Rule out organic causes of feeding problems
Weight, height, and weight for height	Nutritional assessment (N)	Determine degree of malnutrition
Infant's oral movements during feeding	Observation of feeding (OT)	Rule out oral motor delay
Diagnostic Evaluation of Mother		
Demographic data	Child history questionnaire (M)	Determine marital, educational, socioeconomic, and employment status
Psychopathology	Clinical interview (P)	Rule out current major depression, bipolar disorder, alcohol or substance abuse, psychotic disorder
Diagnostic Evaluation of Mother–Infant Relationship		
Mother–infant interactions during feeding and play	Observation of 20 minutes of feeding and 10 minutes of play from behind a one-way mirror (P)	Assess infant's feeding and play behavior and mother's responses, the degree of reciprocity or conflict in the relationship
Mother's Perception of Infant's Temperament		
Mother's perception of infant's temperament	Infant Characteristics Questionnaire (Bates et al., 1979) (M)	Assess mother's perception of infant's special characteristics

Mother's report (M); gastroenterologist (G); nurse practitioner (NP); nutritionist (N); occupational therapist (OT); psychiatrist (P).

TABLE 13.2

Baseline and Treatment Outcome Assessments

Variable	Assessment tool	Assessment times			
		BA	TOA #1	TOA #2	TOA #3
Assessment of Mother–Infant Relationship					
Conflict	Feeding Scale (Chatoor et al., 1997) (O)	X	X	X	X
Assessment of Infant's Growth					
Percent ideal weight for height	Measurement of weight, height, and percent of ideal weight for height (N)	X	X	X	X
Assessment of Infant's Feeding Behavior					
Infant feeding behavior	Feeding Behavior Checklist (Benoit, 1992) (M)	X	X	X	X
Assessment of Mother's Feeding Behavior					
Maternal feeding behavior	Subset of items from the Feeding Scale (Chatoor et al., 1997) (O)	X	X	X	X
Assessment of Mother's Self-Perception, Stress, and Functioning					
Parent domain subscales of stress and total stress index	Parenting Stress Index (Abidin, 1983) (M) (F)	X	X	X	X
Assessment of Mother's Symptoms of Depression and Anxiety					
Symptoms of depression	Depression Inventory (Beck, Steer, & Garbin, 1988) (M)	X	X		X
Symptoms of anxiety	State-Trait Anxiety Inventory (Spielberger, 1973) (M)	X	X		X
Assessment of Mother's Perception of Infant					
Infant's temperament	Infant Characteristics Questionnaire (Bates et al., 1979) (CM)	X			X
Child domain subscales	Parenting Stress Index (Abidin, 1983) (M)	X	X	X	X
Assessment of Marital Relationship					
Marital satisfaction	Snyder, Wills, & Keiser, 1981 (M) (F)	X	X		X
Child-rearing disagreements	Snyder et al., 1981, and Jouriles et al., 1991 (M) (F)	X	X		X

Baseline assessment (BA); mother's report (M); nutritionist (N); observer (O); psychiatrist or psychologist (P); treatment outcome assessment (TOA) #1, #2, and #3 = at end of treatment, 2, 4, 6, and 8 months thereafter.

Acute malnutrition is an index of muscle depletion or wasting. It is determined by dividing the child's current weight by his or her weight for height at the 50th percentile and multiplied by 100. The remaining value represents the percentage of ideal body weight. Mild, moderate, and severe malnutrition corresponds with 80% to 89%, 70% to 79%, and less than 70% of ideal body weight, respectively (Waterlow, Buzina, Keller, Lan, & Tanner, 1977).

Chronic malnutrition, an index of faltering linear growth or stunting, is determined using the 50th percentile for height for age, or ideal length or height. The child's current length or height is divided by his or her ideal height and multiplied by 100. Mild, moderate, and severe chronic malnutrition corresponds with 90% to 95%, 85% to 89%, and less than 85% of ideal height, respectively (Waterlow et al., 1977).

Assessment of Mother–Infant Relationship During Feeding. The Feeding Scale (Chatoor et al., 1997) contains 46 items relating to the mother's and the infant's behaviors and affective expressions. After the observation of 20 minutes of videotaped feeding, the items are rated according to a 4-point scale ranging from "none" to "very much." The items are grouped in five subscales as follows: dyadic reciprocity, dyadic conflict, talk and distraction, struggle for control, and maternal noncontingency. Through a series of studies, scale reliability, discriminant validity, and age-specific descriptors from 1 month to 3 years have been established. All feedings are independently rated by two observers who are blind to the infant's treatment status. The average score of the two observers will be used in the final analysis. In our pilot study (Chatoor et al., 1997), dyadic conflict was significantly reduced after treatment in the majority of cases and was comparable to that of the control group.

Assessment of Mother's Feeding Behavior. The mother's behavior while feeding the infant is assessed through seven assorted items from the Feeding Scale (Chatoor et al., 1997). The Feeding Behavior Score summarizes four items reflecting the mother's maladaptive behaviors and three items reflecting her adaptive behaviors while feeding the infant. This use of the Feeding Scale is new and has not yet been validated.

Assessment of Mother's Perception of the Infant and Her Self-Perception. The Parenting Stress Index (PSI; Abidin, 1983) is a 120-item parent questionnaire that yields subscales for the Child Domain (adaptability, acceptability, demandingness, mood, distractibility or hyperactivity, reinforces parent); subclass for Parental Domain (depression, attachment, sense of competence, social isolation, relationship with spouse, parent health); a life-stress subscale; and a total stress score. The PSI has been shown to have content validity (Burke, 1978) and concurrent and discriminant validity (Loyd, 1983). It is appropriate for parents who have children under 10 years of age, and it identifies parent–child systems under stress. We hypothesize that the mother will experience the child as less difficult, report a significantly higher sense of competence and less depression, and demonstrate a significantly reduced total stress score after treatment.

Assessment of Mother's Anxiety. The State–Trait Inventory (Spielberger, 1973) self-rating scale consists of two separate 20-item scales for measuring state and trait anxiety. The anxiety-state scale requires people to describe how they feel at a particular moment in time; the anxiety-trait scale asks people to describe how they generally feel. Internal consistency and test–retest reliability across no-stress situations have been demonstrated (Kendall, Finch, Auerback, Hooker, & Mikula, 1976). We hypothesize that the mothers' anxiety will be high at baseline and significantly reduced after treatment.

Assessment of Mother's Depression. The Beck Depression Inventory (BDI; Beck & Beamesderfer, 1974) questionnaire consists of 21 symptoms and attitudes that are frequently displayed by depressed patients and infrequently by nondepressed individuals. The Center for Cognitive Therapy has distributed the following guidelines for BDI cut-off scores for patients diagnosed as having an affective disorder: None or minimal depression is < 10; mild to moderate depression is 10 to 18; moderate to severe depression is 19 to 29; and severe depression is 30 to 63. The BDI has high internal consistency in psychiatric and nonpsychiatric samples, and it distinguishes psychiatric and nonpsychiatric patients (Beck, Stree, & Garbin, 1988).

Assessment of Marital Relationship. The 61-item Marital Satisfaction Inventory (Snyder, 1979) includes a measure of social desirability, global distress, affective communication, problem-solving communication, quality and quantity of leisure time together, disagreement about finances, sexual dissatisfaction, dissatisfaction with children, and spousal conflict over child rearing. Snyder, Wills, and Keiser (1981) have reported reliability and validity of the scale. We use this instrument to explore any indirect effect of fathers on their infants' feeding difficulties. We are especially interested in the subscale on spousal child-rearing disagreements.

Treatment Procedures

The treatment is based on a transactional model for infantile anorexia. This model has three components that we believe interact with and maintain the feeding disorder:

1. The infant's temperament characteristics of strong reactivity to external stimuli, emotional intensity, arrhythmic eating and sleeping patterns, and willfulness
2. The mother's uncertainty in balancing nurturance and limit-setting

3. The ensuing conflict in the mother–infant relationship, especially during feeding

The infant's difficult temperament and persistent food refusal evoke feelings of insecurity and anxiety in the mother. The mother's anxiety propels her to engage in inappropriate feeding behaviors (distracting, bargaining, feeding the infant day and night, threatening or even force-feeding). The infant responds with increasingly oppositional behaviors and food refusal. This leads to a cycle of mother and infant behaviors that maintain the feeding disorder. Mother and infant become engaged in struggles of control and autonomy, in the same way as has been described in adolescents with anorexia nervosa (Chatoor, 1989). The infant's eating or refusing to eat occurs in response to the interactions with the parent instead of being internally regulated by hunger and fullness. The goal of treatment is to facilitate the infant's internal regulation of eating by helping the parents disengage from conflict and change their interactions with the infant.

The intervention addresses all three components of the transactional model:

1. The parents are offered positive ways to reframe the infant's difficult temperament characteristics.
2. The parents are helped to understand the difficulties they have in setting limits to the infant's provocative behaviors.
3. The parents are offered concrete information on how to structure mealtime and how to deal more effectively with the infant's behaviors that interfere with feeding.

If possible, this treatment is carried out with both parents in six sessions. The first three sessions last up to 2 hours and are scheduled weekly to foster more intensity and a deeper therapeutic alliance. The last three sessions last on average 1 hour. The fourth session follows a week after the previous session. The last two sessions are scheduled at monthly intervals.

Treatment is most effective when both parents participate in the therapy sessions and agree on the treatment plan. In situations wherein the parents are divorced or not living together and grandparents or other caretakers assume an important role in daily child care (including feeding), the mother is encouraged to bring these other important family members or caretakers to the therapy sessions.

Session 1. The therapist summarizes the mother's description of the infant's temperament from the parent questionnaire and, with the parents, looks at the videotape of the feeding that was made during the diagnostic session. The therapist highlights certain behaviors that are characteristic of the infant. She discusses the infant's interpersonal sensitivity as an asset and also as a vulnerability. She points out the ways in which infants can become so caught up in interpersonal interactions that they have trouble focusing on their internal state of hunger or fullness. The therapist highlights segments of the videotape of the feeding, most especially episodes when the infant becomes distracted and allows the parent to put food in the infant's mouth without becoming aware of eating. The therapist explains that the infant's acceptance of food when distracted may obviously encourage the parents to engage in more distractions in the hope of getting the infant to eat more. However, it is important that the therapist help the parents see that this ploy is only a short-term solution because as soon as the infant becomes bored with the distraction and aware of eating, he or she will refuse the food. As infants grow older, the parents experience increasing difficulty in finding new distractions; more important, if infants eat only in response to external events, they will not learn to recognize internal signals of hunger and fullness and their eating will be externally controlled, which further weakens the infant's poor awareness of hunger.

The infant's willfulness is discussed in a similar way—as an asset and also as a challenge to the parents because the infant wants to be in control at all times. The "little executive" is discussed as someone who needs firm limits to allow this characteristic to become a positive drive instead of the driving force of an oppositional disorder. The parents are prepared for the third session, when the therapist explains that they need to pick their battles, but they need to win them.

The infant's sensitivity to external stimuli and his or her willfulness are the two main characteristics that need to be addressed in treatment. The parents may have some additional concerns about their infant. The therapist will deal with these concerns in the same fashion. A discussion of the infant's determination and willfulness introduces the next session, which will address the parents' concerns about how to deal with the infant's difficult behaviors.

Session 2. The overriding goal of this session is to build a strong therapeutic alliance with the parents, to help them understand their difficulties in dealing with their infant without feeling overwhelmed by guilt and shame, and to empower them to feel confident that they will work together to help their infant to learn internal regulation of eating.

Because many of the mothers in the previous study reported that they reexperienced with their infants feelings of ineffectiveness and helplessness that they themselves suffered during childhood with their own parents, this session focuses on both parents' upbringing and other significant experiences and the effect these experiences had on the parenting of their infant. After encouraging the parents to look at themselves as children of their own parents, the therapist gently introduces their role as parents. She might ask them whether certain aspects of parenthood have been particularly difficult for them. Many parents have difficulty balancing their desire to be always available and nurturing to their infant with the need to set limits to the infant's demanding behaviors. The therapist tries to help the parents link this conflict to their own parents' emotional unavailability or harsh discipline. Frequently, the parents want to be the parents they never had. This wish tends to push parents toward the other extreme of what they experienced with their own parents (e.g., if they perceive their own mother or father as intrusive or controlling, they tend to be permissive and indulgent; if their own parents were emotionally unavailable, they want to be there for their infant at all times).

For those parents who report secure relationships with their own parents, the therapist reinforces these positive experiences and further explores the reasons that parenting may be difficult. Other common factors that appear to burden these parents include the fear that the infant will starve to death (perhaps triggered by previous losses such as infertility problems, miscarriages, death of loved ones); conflicted and stressful relationships with the spouse, in-laws, or coworkers; and competing obligations to other children or professional associates. The therapist must be flexible and help the parents deal with whatever they perceive as their biggest problem, the reason that they are anxious and experiencing difficulty with the infant's food refusal.

Session 3. This session has three components: The therapist explains how infants learn internal versus external regulation of eating; the therapist explores the parents' own eating patterns and regulation of eating; and the therapist discusses specific feeding guidelines and limit-setting strategies with the parents.

First, the therapist explains that the transition to self-feeding is a critical time when infants can learn internal versus external regulation of eating. Infants who have an innate awareness of hunger and satiety send clear signals to their parents and are easy to feed. However, anorectic infants seem too distracted by their environment to notice when they are hungry. Consequently, these infants do not signal to their parents when they are hungry, and the parents begin to take over by trying to control externally how much these infants should eat. For these infants, however, interacting with their parents—who distract the infants just to slip some food in their mouths or run after them with food while the infants are at play—is more fun than eating. The parents become increasingly frustrated because eventually nothing seems to help. These intense interactions between the infant and his parents further interfere with the infant's awareness of hunger and lead to external regulation of the infant's eating, with the burden being on the parents whether the infant eats or does not eat.

Infants can become externally regulated in their eating through other ways, however. If the parents offer the infant the bottle or food whenever the infant is distressed, the infant will learn to associate feeding not only with the relief of feelings of hunger but also with emotional calming. Consequently, those children may want to drink from the bottle or eat when they are tense or distressed. When parents use food as a reward or as an expression of affection, children associate eating with feelings of parental love. Those children often confuse food with love. They may reject food when they are angry with the parent, or they may want to eat when they feel lonely or bored to regain feelings of affection through food.

Infants with anorexia seem particularly perceptive and readily make associations between their emotional experiences and eating. Consequently, the parents must exert a special effort to make the environment less stimulating during mealtime, to provide a neutral emotional experience during feeding, and to teach the infants self-calming techniques when they cannot get their way. This approach allows infants to pay more attention to their feeling of hunger.

After introducing the topic of eating regulation, the therapist explores the parents' own feeding histories and eating patterns. Frequently, one of the parents has experienced similar feeding problems as a child and still experiences emotional inhibition (e.g., not eating when upset, anxious, or angry; forgetting to eat when engaged with other things). The therapist helps the parents see the similarities in physiological reactivity between parent and child. The therapist then tells them that even individuals with high emotional and physiological reactivity can become more aware of their hunger feelings through a variety of techniques.

This is the opening to the feeding guidelines, which are concrete suggestions how to facilitate internal regulation of eating (Exhibit 13.1). The therapist should give the parents a copy of these guidelines and then discuss each guideline one by one. The parents may already be implementing some of the suggestions, or they may have difficulties with specific issues that should be discussed. The most important part of this session is to address the specific difficulties of the individual infant, to help the parents learn to use the "time-out" procedure to reinforce the rules, and to teach the infant self-calming when things do not go his or her way.

Session 4. This session takes place 1 week after the parents have been given the feeding guidelines. The goal of this session is to review feeding guidelines that the parents have been able to implement and areas in which they may still have difficulty. After identifying these areas, the therapist and the parents use problem-solving strategies to create a plan to deal with the infant's behavior. The parents may find it helpful to hear that in a previous study, only one quarter of the infants changed their eating pattern within days or weeks. The majority improved gradually over several months until they were able to clearly identify when they were hungry.

Session 5. This session takes place 4 weeks after the previous session. The goal of this session is to help the parents use problem-solving techniques and to identify any remaining difficulties the parents may have experienced since they implemented the feeding guidelines.

EXHIBIT 13.1
Feeding Guidelines for Teaching Your Child
How to Internally Regulate Eating

1. Schedule meals and snacks at regular times every day at 3- to 4-hour intervals to allow your child to get hungry.
2. Offer nothing between regular meals and snacks: no unplanned snacks, no bottles of milk or juice, no breastfeeding. If your child is thirsty, offer water.
3. If your child tends to fill up with milk or other liquids at meals, offer solids first and fluids last.
4. Encourage your child to feed him- or herself as much as possible (with fingers or spoon, etc.). Encourage him by commenting on self-feeding skills: "How good you are at getting the spoon in your mouth." and "Good job."
5. However, do not comment, positively or negatively, about the amount of food your child eats. He or she should learn to eat without approval or disapproval. His or her hunger should regulate his/her food intake.
6. Do not interfere with your child's process of learning new feeding skills by fussing over the mess. Use a sheet under the table to catch the mess. Wipe your child's mouth and clean up only after the meal is over.
7. Do not play games at mealtimes. Do not use toys to distract your child while he or she is eating. Do not watch television during mealtimes. Help your child refocus on eating when he or she gets distracted.
8. For older toddlers who want to get out of the highchair after a few minutes, make it a rule that he or she has to stay at the table in the chair until you are finished eating. For those toddlers who just want to play with the food without eating, limit meals to no more than 20 to 30 minutes.
9. Keep all the food that you want to offer for a particular meal on the table and serve small portions. Let your child ask for more to encourage him or her to listen to inner body signals instead of having to empty the plate.
10. Once you sit down, do not get up to get your child other food choices he or she may demand.
11. If your child engages in inappropriate behaviors that interfere with eating (e.g., throwing the food or feeding utensils, sliding down, standing in, or climbing out of the highchair), warn him or her once. The next time, give your child "time-out."
12. Do not use food as a present or reward, or for comfort.

Note. Parents control when, where, and what the child eats. The *child* controls how much is eaten. Try to relax; if you adopt a neutral attitude, your child will learn to eat when hungry.

Session 6. The last treatment session is scheduled 1 month after the previous session. The first goal is to explore any remaining difficulties in the infant's internal regulation of eating. The second goal is to prepare the parents to be able to deal with difficulties the infant might encounter in the future. By this time, the parents have worked with the infant on internal regulation for about 2 months, and they have a good sense of the infant's ability to perceive hunger and regulate his or her food intake internally. In many cases, the infant may have many good meals but continue to eat poorly at some meals. Most of these infants continue to be affected by changes in the time schedule and do best if meals are regular and set in routines. These infants continue to react to increased stimulation that is frequently part of everyday life (e.g., a relative is visiting, the family is going shopping, or the child is attending a birthday party). They tend to eat less under these circumstances. The parents are made aware of this vulnerability so that they will understand what is happening and not worry that, in spite of all their efforts, the infant has regressed.

Our pilot study (Chatoor et al., 1997) indicated that this vulnerability to increased social stimulation manifested by a lack of appetite continues to be a problem for many of these infants. Therefore, in this last session, the therapist discusses specific social triggers that the infants will encounter in the future. Transitions into playgroups or preschool are usually disruptive to their appetite. Frequently, these children tend to be so busy watching those around them that they forget to eat. Consequently, these transitions should be planned in stages to allow children to process the new information without losing their appetite.

At the end of this session, the parents should have gained enough insight to understand their infant's vulnerability. They are expected to have gained a sense of mastery when structuring the infant's environmental experiences to facilitate internal regulation of eating.

Treatment Measures

Assessment of Treatment Adherence and Treatment Competence. Improvements in outcome research can be attributed to the use of treatment manuals that specify the components of a given treatment and to the careful supervision and monitoring of therapists. Part of the monitoring of therapists involves ensuring that they continue to use the techniques that are appropriate to their treatment approach once they are trained in conducting the treatment according to manual specifications. The adherence measure developed for this study includes 30 items that describe the major components of the treatment modalities (control condition versus psychoeducational treatment). Videotapes of the second and sixth therapy sessions are used to assess whether the therapists follow the procedures outlined in the manuals. Two raters, trained to an interrater reliability of .70 on the measure, assess adherence of the therapists to the respective treatment modalities. Scores that are significantly higher for the modality in question than for the other modality indicate adherence.

Whereas adherence measures assess the degree to which the clinician practices the techniques as prescribed in the manual, competence measures assess how adequately the techniques are applied. Such measurement is vital because evidence suggests a significant relationship between measures of clinician performance and patient-rated change (O'Malley, Foley, & Rounsville, 1988). Again using the second and sixth hour from each intervention as was the case for the adherence ratings, two trained mental health professionals view the videotapes and score the sessions using a clinical observer's form for the competency measure. Competence and adherence ratings are regularly reviewed by the author. In the event that a clinician deviates from the treatment manual, retraining immediately takes place in a supervisory session.

Assessment of Treatment Process (Therapeutic Alliance). A long-standing debate in psychotherapy research focuses on the following question: What ingredients produce therapeutic success? On one side are those who propose that it is the specific technology associated with a particular approach that leads to positive change. On the other side are those who posit that nonspecific factors common to all treatments, such as the therapeutic relationship, produce therapeutic success. Krupnick and colleagues (1996) found not only that alliance was significantly related to outcome across all four treatments in the NIMH Collaborative Depression Study (interpersonal therapy, cognitive–behavioral therapy, pharmacotherapy, and pill-placebo plus clinical management) but also that alliance accounted for more of the variance in outcome than any specific treatment approach. To measure alliance, we use a modified form of the Vanderbilt Therapeutic Alliance Scale (Hartley & Strupp, 1983). Two raters independently view videotapes of the second and sixth sessions of treatment for each case in both interventions. The raters score mother–therapist and father–therapist alliance separately. The average of the two raters' scores is used to reflect the strength of the alliance for each case. In the analyses we will primarily focus on the mother–therapist alliance, but we plan to explore the effects of the father–therapist and the combined parental alliance as well.

Clinical Vignette

Anna was 26 months old when her pediatrician referred her to the Feeding Disorders Team for an evaluation. Her parents' main concerns were that she ate very little and had not been gaining weight appropriately. She never asked for food, usually took only a few bites, struggled to get them down, and ran around the room. Instead of eating her food, she often played and fed the dog with it. Anna's parents recalled that when she was about 9 months old and beginning to cruise around the house using the furniture, she became busy exploring and lost interest in feeding. However, the parents became truly concerned when Anna was 18 months old. The pediatrician noted that from 9 months to 18 months of age, she had fallen from the 50th percentile for weight to the 25th percentile. He suggested stopping her formula and bottles in order to encourage her to eat more solid food, but her intake of solid food did not improve, and her weight dropped further.

Family, Developmental, and Medical History

Anna is the second child of an upper-middle-class family. Both parents have postgraduate degrees. Despite her academic credentials, Anna's mother chose to stay at home and take care of her children. The older daughter, their biological child, was 8 years old. Anna, who was adopted shortly after birth, was born full-term, weighed 7 pounds and 6 ounces, and was delivered without complications. She ate well during the early months and developed appropriately for her age. She had some common childhood illnesses but was never hospitalized.

Assessments

Anna's physical examination was unremarkable, and all lab tests to screen for celiac disease and malabsorption were within normal limits.

Her nutritional evaluation revealed that her weight and height had dropped from the 50th percentile at 9 months, to the 25th at 18 months, to just under the 5th percentile at 26 months. However, her head circumference had remained at the 50th percentile. Her weight-to-height ratio was at 89% of the ideal, which placed her within the range of mild malnutrition. Anna's 3-day food record revealed that the variety of her diet appeared appropriate but the volume was too small.

The oral–motor assessment revealed that her oral patterns and movements were age-appropriate.

The observation of feeding revealed the same pattern described by the parents. Anna was distracted by the pictures on the wall and by the different chairs around the table. She ate a few bites, played with the food some more, and then slipped off the chair and ran around the room. The mother tried to encourage her to try some more food, but Anna was having too much fun looking in the mirror and behind the curtain and could not be persuaded to return to the table.

Treatment

The parents were eager to enroll Anna in the treatment study for infantile anorexia. They both came for the treatment sessions, forming a strong therapeutic alliance with the therapist. The therapist saw Anna as a sensitive, creative, but also very strong-willed child. The parents realized that because Anna was so precious to them and they had seen her as such a fragile baby, they had been ineffective in setting limits to her playful behavior that interfered with feeding. After discussion of the feeding guidelines, the parents changed the meal pattern for the whole family and instituted regular meal and snack times for everyone in the household. They also introduced the new time-out procedure for both children.

Follow-Up

At the first follow-up, a month after treatment was completed, the mother felt very encouraged by Anna's progress. She stated that Anna had stopped feeding the dog, that she stayed in the chair without protest until everyone was finished with the meal, and that she consumed at least one full meal a day. The mother was also pleased about the changes in her older daughter. Before treatment, the parents had tried to encourage Anna to eat more by making eating a competition between the children. The older daughter then started to eat more in order to please the parents, and she had gotten chubby. However, the new rules—no snacks between meals and no praise for eating—helped the older daughter to reduce her food intake.

At the last follow-up appointment, a year after treatment, the mother was delighted about the changes in Anna and in their family life. She announced, "Food is not an issue in our family anymore." She reported that in spite of all the girls' activities, she maintained a regular schedule for snacks and for family dinners. She also noted that the older daughter had slimmed down and that Anna was well-regulated in her eating and was gaining weight.

The observation of the meal revealed that Anna stayed seated and remained focused on her food while she was engaged in conversation with her mother. Mother and daughter looked relaxed and appeared to enjoy each other's company during feeding and during play. The nutritional assessment showed that Anna had returned to the 15th percentile for weight and height. Her 3-day food intake was adequate in nutritional variety and in calories.

Outcomes

At this point, the study is still ongoing, and only the results from the pilot study are available (Chatoor et al., 1997). During the interview at the time of follow-up 6 months to 2 years after treatment, 17 of the 20 mothers whose children had been treated for infantile anorexia reported that they had become more relaxed about their children's food intake. Three mothers confessed that they continued to worry about their children's poor eating patterns. Two of these mothers had put their children in day care, and every evening when they picked up their children, the daycare provider would inform each mother that her child had hardly eaten anything during the whole day. The third mother admitted that she was so overwhelmed by the care of three other young children that she was unable to implement the feeding guidelines.

When asked whether the intervention had increased their children's awareness of hunger, about two thirds of the mothers reported that their children seemed "often" or "always" aware of hunger, whereas one third noted "sometimes," and one mother "never." Three mothers considered their children to have become good eaters, and 11 mothers reported that their children were eating well generally but continued to have meals during which they ate poorly. Four children were having some good meals, and one child remained a poor eater.

When looking at more objective changes, we found that the 17 children whose mothers felt relaxed about their children's food intake showed no more dyadic conflict during feeding than a control group of healthy eaters. However, the three other children exhibited the same amount of conflict with their mothers as had been observed before treatment. In addition, the ideal body weight of the previously anorectic children increased significantly by an average of 7% ($p = .011$), whereas the controls maintained their previous growth pattern (Chatoor et al., 1997). When asked what aspect of treatment had been most helpful, the mothers clearly rated the validation and understanding of their children's special temperament as the most helpful. Also, the feeding guidelines were experienced by most mothers as somewhat-to-very helpful.

FUTURE CONSIDERATIONS

The pilot study and the preliminary results of individual cases of the ongoing study indicate that helping parents deal with the special temperament characteristics of children with infantile anorexia can facilitate the awareness of hunger and internal regulation of eating in these vulnerable infants. However, not all parents are able to follow through with the required regularity of meals and the consistency of limit-setting that these infants require. Although the treatment is short-term and easy to learn by practitioners, the challenge remains: how to help parents who are overwhelmed and unable to break the cycle of maladaptive interactions with their anorexic children.

REFERENCES

Abidin, R. R. (1983). Parenting Stress Index. In D. J. Keyser & R. C. Sweeland (Eds.), *Test critiques* (Vol. I, pp. 504–510). Kansas City, MO: Test Corporation of America.

American Psychiatric Association. (1994). *Diagnostic and statistical manual of mental disorders* (4th ed.). Washington, DC: Author.

Archer, L. A., & Szatmari, P. (1990). Assessment and treatment of food aversion in a four-year-old boy: A multidimensional approach. *Canadian Journal of Psychiatry, 35,* 501–505.

Bates, J. E., Freeland, C. A., Lounsbury, M. L. (1979). Measurement of infant difficultness. *Child Development, 50,* 794–803.

Beck, A. T., & Beamesderfer, A. (1974). Assessment of depression: The depression inventory. *Modern Problems in Pharmacopsychiatry, 7,* 151–169.

Beck, A. T., Steer, R. A., & Garbin, M. G. (1988). Psychometric properties of the Beck Depression Inventory: Twenty-five years later. *Clinical Psychology Review, 8,* 77–100.

Benoit, D. (1992). *Infant feeding behaviors questionnaires*. Unpublished scale.

Benoit, D. (1993). Phenomenology and treatment of failure to thrive. *Child and Adolescent Psychiatric Clinics of North America, 2*(1), 61–73.

Benoit, D. (August, 1996). *Diagnostic assessments of feeding disorders*. Paper presented at the Sixth World Congress, World Association for Infant Mental Health, New York, NY.

Bithoney, W. G., McJunkin, J., Michalek, J., Snyder, J., Egan, H., & Epstein, D. (1992). The effect of multidisciplinary team approach on weight gain in non-organic failure to thrive children. *Developmental and Behavioral Pediatrics, 12*, 254–258.

Burke, W. T. (1978). *The development of a technique for assessing the stresses experienced by parents of young children*. Unpublished doctoral dissertation, University of Virginia, Institute of Clinical Psychology.

Chatoor, I. (1989). Infantile anorexia nervosa: A developmental disorder of separation and individuation. *Journal of the American Academy of Psychoanalysis, 17*, 43–64.

Chatoor, I. (1991). Eating and nutritional disorders of infancy and early childhood. In J. Wiener (Ed.), *Textbook of child and adolescent psychiatry* (pp. 351–361). Washington, DC: American Psychiatry Press.

Chatoor, I. (2002). Feeding disorders in infants and toddlers: Diagnosis and treatment. *Child and Adolescent Psychiatric Clinics of North America, 11*, 163–183.

Chatoor, I., Dickson, L., Schaefer, S., & Egan, J. (1985). A developmental classification of feeding disorders associated with failure to thrive: Diagnosis and treatment. In D. Drotar (Ed.), *New directions in failure to thrive: Research and clinical practice* (pp. 235–238). New York: Plenum.

Chatoor, I., & Egan, J. (1983). Nonorganic failure to thrive and dwarfism due to food refusal: A separation disorder. *Journal of the American Academy of Child Psychiatry, 33*, 294–301.

Chatoor, I., Egan, J., Getson, P., Menvielle, E., & O'Donnell, R. (1988). Mother–infant interactions in infantile anorexia nervosa. *Journal of the American Academy of Child and Adolescent Psychiatry, 27*, 535–540.

Chatoor, I., Hamburger, E., Fullard, R., & Rivera, Y. (1994). A survey of picky eating and pica behaviors in toddlers. *Scientific proceedings of the annual meeting of the American Academy of Child and Adolescent Psychiatry, 10*, 50, New York.

Chatoor, I., Ganiban, J., Hirsch, R., Spurrell, E., & Reiss, D. (2000). Maternal characteristics and toddler temperament in infantile anorexia. *Journal of American Academy of Child and Adolescent Psychiatry, 39*, 743–751.

Chatoor, I., Getson, P., Menvielle, E., O'Donnell, R., Rivera, Y., Brasseaux, C., et al. (1997). A feeding scale for research and clinical practice to assess mother–infant interactions in the first three years of life. *Infant Mental Health Journal, 18*, 76–91.

Chatoor, I., Hirsch, R., Ganiban, J., Persinger, M., & Hamburger, E. (1998). Diagnosing infantile anorexia: The observation of mother–infant interactions.

Journal of the American Academy of Child and Adolescent Psychiatry, 37, 959–967.

Chatoor, I., Hirsch, R., & Persinger, M. (1997). Facilitating internal regulation of eating: A treatment model for infantile anorexia. *Infants and Young Children, 9,* 12–22.

Chatoor, I., Kerzner, B., Zorc, L., Persinger, M., Simenson, R., & Mrazek, D. (1992). Two-year-old twins refuse to eat: A multidisciplinary approach to diagnosis and treatment. *Infant Mental Health, 13,* 252–268.

Chatoor, I., McWade Paez, L., Simenson, R., & Ganiban, J. (1998). Semistructured interview. Unpublished interview, Children's National Medical Center, Washington, DC.

Culbert, T. P., Kajander, R. L., Kohen, D. P., & Reaney, J. B. (1996). Hypnobehavioral approaches for school-age children with dysphagia and food aversion: A case series. *Developmental Behavior Pediatrics, 17,* 335–341.

Emde, R., Bingham, R., & Harmon, R. (1993). Classification and the diagnostic process in infancy. In C. Zeanah (Ed.), *Handbook of infant mental health* (pp. 225–235). New York: Guilford Press.

Fosson, A., & Wilson, J. (1993). *Nutrition of normal infants.* St. Louis, MO: Mosby.

Frank, D., Silva, M., & Needlman, R. (1993). Failure to thrive: Mystery, myth, and method. *Contemporary Pediatrics, 10,* 114–133.

Galler, J. R., Ramsey, R. L., Solimano, G., Lowell, W. E., & Mason, E. (1988). The influence of early malnutrition on subsequent behavioral development: I. Degree of impairment in intellectual performance. *Journal of the American Academy of Child and Adolescent Psychiatry, 22,* 8–15.

Goldbloom, R. (1987). Growth in infancy. *Pediatrics Review, 9,* 151–166.

Hartley, D. E., & Strupp, H. H. (1983). The therapeutic alliance: Its relationship to outcome in brief psychotherapy. In J. Masling (Ed.), *Empirical studies of psychoanalytical theories* (Vol. I, pp. 1–37). Hillsdale, NJ: Erlbaum.

Homer, C., & Ludwig, S. (1981). Categorization of etiology of failure to thrive. *American Journal of Disabilities in Children, 135,* 848–851.

Jouriles, E. N., Murphy, C. M., Farris, A. M., Smith, D. A., Richters, J. E., & Waters, E. (1991). Marital adjustment, parent disagreements about child rearing, and behavior problems in boys: Increasing the specificity of the marital assessment. *Child Development, 62,* 1424–1433.

Kendall, P. C., Finch, A. J., Auerback, S. M., Hooker, J. F., & Mikula, P. J. (1976). The State Trait Inventory: A systematic evaluation. *Journal of Consulting and Clinical Psychology, 44,* 406–412.

Krupnick, J. L., Sotsky, S. M., Simmons, S., Meyer, J., Elkin, I., Watkins, J., et al. (1996). The role of therapeutic alliance in psychotherapy and pharmacotherapy outcome: Findings in the National Institute of Mental Health Treatment of Depression Collaborative Research Program. *Journal of Consulting and Clinical Psychology, 64,* 532–539.

Kuczmarski, R. J., Ogden, C. L., Grummer-Strawn, L. M., Fegal, K. M., Guo, S. S., Mei Z., et al. (2000). CDC growth charts: United States. *Advanced Data, 314*, 1–27.

Lindberg, L., Bohlin, G., & Hagekull, B. (1991). Early feeding problems in a normal population. *International Journal of Eating Disorders, 10*, 395–405.

Lindberg, L., Bohlin, G., Hagekull, B., & Palmerus, K. (1996). Interactions between mother and infants showing food refusal. *Infant Mental Health Journal, 17*, 334–347.

Loyd, B. (1983). Parenting Stress Index Statistical Characteristics. In R. R. Abidin (Ed.), *Parenting Stress Index—Clinical Manual Form #6* (pp. 8–25). Charlottesville, VA.

Marchi, M., & Cohen, P. (1990). Early childhood eating behaviors and adolescent eating disorders. *Journal of American Academy of Child and Adolescent Psychiatry, 29*, 112–117.

O'Malley, S. S., Foley, S. H., & Rounsville, B. J. (1988). Therapist competence and patient outcome in interpersonal psychotherapy of depression. *Journal of Consulting and Clinical Psychology, 56*, 496–501.

Patton, R. G., & Gardner, L. L. (1962). Influence of family environment on growth: The syndrome of "maternal deprivation." *Pediatrics, 12*, 957–962.

Patton, R. G., & Gardner, L. L. (1963). *Growth failure in maternal deprivation.* Springfield, IL: Charles C Thomas.

Pliner, P., & Lowen, E. R. (1997). Temperament and food neophobia in children and their mothers. *Appetite, 28*, 239–254.

Rydell, A. M., Dahl, M., & Sundelin, C. (1995). Characteristics of school children who are choosy eaters. *Journal of Genetic Psychology, 156*, 217–229.

Sanders, M. R., Patel, R. K., Le Grice, B., & Shepherd, R. W. (1993). Children with persistent feeding difficulties: An observational analysis of the feeding interactions of problem and non-problem eaters. *Health Psychology, 12*, 64–73.

Shore, B. A., Babbitt, R. L., Williams, K. E., Coe, D. A., & Snyder, A. (1998). Use of texture fading in the treatment of food selectivity. *Journal of Applied Behavioral Analysis, 31*, 621–633.

Siegel, L. J. (1988). Classical and operant procedures in the treatment of a case of food aversion in a young child. *Journal of Clinical Child Psychology, 27*, 105–110.

Singer, L., Ambuel, B., Wade, S., & Jaffe, A. (1992). Cognitive–behavioral treatment of health-impairing food phobias in children. *Journal of the American Academy of Child and Adolescent Psychiatry, 31*, 847–852.

Snyder, D. K. (1979). Multidimensional assessment of marital satisfaction. *Journal of Marriage and the Family, 41*, 813–823.

Snyder, D. K., Wills, R. M., & Keiser, T. W. (1981). Empirical validation of the Marital Satisfaction Inventory: An actuarial approach. *Journal of Consulting and Clinical Psychology, 49*, 262–268.

Spielberger, C. (1973). *Manual for the State-Trait Anxiety Inventory for Children.* Palo Alto, CA: Consulting Psychologists Press.

Timimi, S., Douglas, J., & Tsiftsopoulou, K. (1997). Selective eaters: A retrospective case note study. *Child: Care, Health and Development, 23,* 265–278.

Waterlow, J. C. (1972). Classification and definition of protein-calorie malnutrition. *British Medical Journal, 3,* 566–569.

Waterlow, J. C., Buzina, R., Keller, W., Lan, J. M., & Tanner, J. M. (1977). The presentation of height and weight data for comparing the nutritional status of groups of children under the age of 10 years. *Bulletin of the World Health Organization, 55,* 489–498.

IV

ATTENTION-DEFICIT/
HYPERACTIVITY DISORDER

INTRODUCTION:
ATTENTION-DEFICIT/
HYPERACTIVITY DISORDER

Attention-deficit/hyperactivity disorder (ADHD) may be the most commonly diagnosed of childhood Axis I mental disorders. ADHD is characterized by inappropriate levels of inattention, impulsivity, or hyperactivity and can have a detrimental impact on the child's psychosocial development. Prevalence estimates vary widely as a function of diagnostic criteria used, but reasonable estimates suggest that 3% to 5% of children nationwide are affected. Because ADHD accounts for a large proportion of all referrals for pediatric mental health services, at great economic and emotional expense, the development of effective treatments across the childhood and adolescent years is essential. In this section, four chapters present various treatment modalities for children with ADHD.

Arthur D. Anastopoulos and his colleagues describe two intervention projects dealing with kindergarten and preschool children who either have ADHD or are at risk for this condition. Next, they present the results of a treatment outcome study conducted with elementary school–age children who have either ADHD or ADHD and comorbid oppositional defiant disorder (ODD), followed by a description of a family-based treatment for adolescents with ADHD and ODD. For each study they discuss treatment benefits as well as limitations, emphasizing their findings suggesting that family-based psychosocial treatments produce clinically significant improvements.

Highlighting future directions, the authors call for multimodal treatment studies for preschool and adolescent ADHD populations.

Steven P. Hinshaw reviews the theoretical and clinical issues surrounding ADHD as a clinical disorder and describes his research program, which is based on the integration of behavioral therapy (BT) and cognitive–behavioral (CBT) interventions with pharmacological treatments for peer-related and interpersonal problems of children with ADHD. Hinshaw further describes the assessment measures, procedures, and intervention components in detail. In his research program, children receive positive reinforcement for self-monitoring, demonstrating appropriate responses during anger management exercises, and matching their own self-ratings with an objective adult observer's rating. He also describes the treatment's clinical implications as well as its limitations. In discussing future directions the author stresses the need for new types of psychosocial treatments based on different paradigms and the integration of diverse psychosocial treatments targeted at multiple domains over long periods of time, with these treatments coordinated with medication as needed. In addition, he draws attention to the need for group-based, rather than individual, treatments.

William E. Pelham and colleagues review the treatment for children with ADHD and describe their own intensive 8-week summer treatment program (STP), which is coupled with more traditional treatment programs that occur during the school year. The STP incorporates operant approaches, CBT, and pharmacological interventions. The STP emphasizes teaching and reinforcing self-efficacy and a range of social, academic, and recreational skills, all in the context of environments comparable to those children traditionally experience during the school year. The authors present in detail their assessment tools and treatment procedures, noting the impressive gains found at the end of the STP program. However, the authors caution that without continuing treatments during the school year, such gains may not be sustainable. In discussing future directions, the authors emphasize that STP is an evidence-based treatment and that such intensive and comprehensive treatments are needed to change the trajectory of most children with ADHD.

Lily Hechtman and her colleagues present their studies of medication and psychosocial interventions, in two different, controlled, randomized multimodal treatments (MMT) for children with ADHD. MMT entails the use of optimally titrated stimulant medication, academic study-skills training, remedial tutoring as needed, individual psychotherapy, social-skills training, parent management training, and strategies to provide home-based reinforcements for school behaviors and performance. In their research program, children receiving this impressive battery of treatments are compared with a conventional stimulant treatment group (CTG) and an attention control group (ACG). The authors also discuss and summarize the rationale and objectives of the MTA study, wherein many of the procedures developed in the MMT program were employed in a National Institute of Mental Health (NIMH)–supported six-site study of multimodal treatments. In anticipating future directions, the authors note the need for systematic studies of the timing of treatment components and their effects on outcomes, the need for multimodal designs to evaluate the efficacy of introducing psychosocial treatments before pharmacotherapy, the need for multimodal treatment regiments specifically tailored to the clinical needs of the children and their parents, and, lastly, for the need to evaluate treatments and treatment combinations for various types of patients.

As noted by each of the chapters' authors, abundant evidence suggests the short-term effects of various psychosocial treatments (especially BT and parent training [PT]) and medications. However, data concerning which of these treatments, alone or in combination, are effective for which children and in which functioning domains are insufficient. In addition, the authors note that the effects of longer-term treatments on the developmental outcomes of children with ADHD remain essentially unknown, and some experts have expressed the concern that short-term treatments may not, in fact, make much difference in the long run. To date, the few available long-term outcome studies have lacked adequate controls, failed to apply research-based state-of-the-art treatment, and failed to demonstrate long-term effects of treatment.

14

FAMILY-BASED PSYCHOSOCIAL TREATMENTS FOR CHILDREN AND ADOLESCENTS WITH ATTENTION-DEFICIT/ HYPERACTIVITY DISORDER

ARTHUR D. ANASTOPOULOS, TERRI L. SHELTON, AND RUSSELL A. BARKLEY

As recently as 10 years ago, it was not unusual to find people—lay people and health care professionals alike—who believed that attention-deficit/ hyperactivity disorder (ADHD; American Psychiatric Association, 1994) was a condition limited to school-age children. We now know that nothing could be further from the truth. Not only does ADHD occur during middle childhood; it can also be found among preschoolers, teenagers, and a significant number of adults. In light of these findings, most experts in the field today view ADHD to be a chronic and pervasive condition that persists across the life span (Barkley, 1998).

Whether young or old, individuals with ADHD are at increased risk for a multitude of psychosocial difficulties across the life span. The exact nature of these complications is determined in large part by a consideration of what is considered typical or normal at any given stage of development (Anastopoulos & Shelton, 2001). In addition to being affected by its primary symptoms, individuals with ADHD are at increased risk for having secondary or comorbid diagnoses (August, Realmuto, MacDonald, Nugent, & Crosby, 1996; Murphy & Barkley, 1996). In combination with ADHD, such comorbid conditions often increase the severity of an individual's overall psychosocial impairment, thereby making the prognosis for such individuals less favorable.

In light of such circumstances, understanding why singular treatment approaches generally do not meet all of the clinical management needs of individuals with ADHD is relatively easy. Consistent with the results of the recently completed multimodal treatment of ADHD (MTA) study, clinicians must use a combination of multiple treatment strategies, each of which addresses a different aspect of the individual's psychosocial difficulties. Which treatments should be used in combination? Therein lies the problem, because, apart from the MTA study, systematic investigation of multimodal treatments for school-age children with ADHD has been severely limited, with virtually no research of this kind having been conducted with preschoolers, adolescents, or adults with ADHD.

To begin investigating which combinations of treatments work best, clinicians must first identify which treatments show therapeutic promise and then determine the extent to which they produce therapeutic benefits when used alone (Pelham, Wheeler, & Chronis, 1998). It is in this spirit that we have conducted our own treatment outcome research. Recognizing that psychosocial treatments can play an important role in the overall clinical management of ADHD (especially when combined with pharmacotherapy), family-based psychosocial interventions have been the focus of our investigations. Most of this research was carried out in the ADHD Clinic in the Department of Psychiatry at the University of Massachusetts Medical Center. Some of it is also now under way through the first and second authors' affiliation with the Department of Psychology at the University of North Carolina at Greensboro.

In the previous edition of this text, we summarized the results of two completed psychosocial treatment outcome studies and described family-based treatment research that was ongoing at that time (Anastopoulos, Barkley, & Shelton, 1996). In this chapter, we will provide an update on the status of those projects.

INTERVENTIONS FOR YOUNG CHILDREN

Among many preschool children, the symptoms of ADHD are already disrupting the lives of their family. Although some behavioral problems in early childhood pass with time, many children do not outgrow these difficulties. The persistence of these problems from preschool until later years is quite common, and the problems tend to increase with age (e.g., Heller, Baker, Henker, & Hinshaw, 1996). In fact, an estimated 50% of preschoolers with significant disruptive or externalizing behaviors continue to have these difficulties when they are in elementary school and secondary school (Campbell, 1996). Several projects have been developed to address the difficulties that these young children, their families, and their teachers experience as a function of ADHD and other disruptive symptoms. The following sections describe two such projects involving kindergarten children and preschoolers in the Head Start program.

Rationale and Treatment Goals for the Kindergarten Project

The first project, funded by NIMH (Barkley et al., 2000), examined the effectiveness of multimethod psychoeducational interventions for kindergarten children at risk for ADHD and oppositional behavior. The main goals of the project were (a) to examine the degree to which a "total push" prevention–intervention program would reduce ADHD symptoms in kindergarten and (b) to determine the degree to which any benefits would reduce the need for supportive services later in elementary school.

Description of Study and Treatment Program

Participants

Parents of preschool children registering for kindergarten were asked to complete ratings of their children's disruptive behaviors. These annual screenings identified 158 children, ages 4.5 to 6 years, as having significantly high (i.e., greater than the 93rd percentile) levels of ADHD symptoms and oppositional behaviors. These children were randomly assigned to one of four treatment conditions imposed during kindergarten: no treatment, parent training only, full-day treatment classroom only, and a combination of parent training and classroom treatment.

Measures

Child outcomes were examined through a multimethod assessment including parent and teacher ratings of behavior and adaptive skills, evaluation of the child's cognitive and achievement levels, direct observation of child behavior in the classroom, lab measures of attention and activity, and direct observation of mother–child interaction in the lab. Information about parent outcomes included basic demographics, parenting stress, and parent psychological functioning.

Procedures

The kindergarten intervention program comprised several family and school-based treatment components, a summary of which appears in Table 14.1. The parent training component was based on the 10-week program developed by Barkley (1997). The individual sessions included the following: (a) overview of disruptive behavior disorders, including ADHD; (b) model of parent–child conflict and review of behavior management

TABLE 14.1
Treatment Components of NIMH Kindergarten Project

Parent training	• Overview of disruptive behavior disorders including ADHD • Model of parent–child conflict; review of behavior management principles • Using positive attending and ignoring skills during special play time • Using positive attending and ignoring skills to promote appropriate independent play and compliance with simple requests; discussion of how to give commands more effectively • Setting up a reward oriented home token/point system • Using response cost for minor noncompliance and rule violations • Using time-out for more serious rule violations • Handling problems in public • Handling future problems; working cooperatively with school and community agencies • Monthly follow-up session
Classroom management program	• Daily schedule for classroom events • Sign system: red (no talking), yellow (whispering), or green (inside voice) signs for activities to cue appropriate behavior) • Color chart: color coded, classroom-wide response cost system to provide frequent and immediate positive and negative feedback about child's following of classroom rules • Activity time/Friday reinforcement: range of daily and weekly activities whose access is dependent on progress on color chart • Individual and classroom visual prompts outlining critical steps of frequently occurring activities (e.g., lunch, recess, work, going home)
Social skills training	• Review 40 basic skills; develop common vocabulary • Practice through role play using concrete examples from classroom, bus, and recess • Integrate practice of skills into academic curriculum • Reinforce social skills in classroom through daily and weekly acknowledgment of progress • Communicate with family about target skills • Reward child for use of skills at home

principles; (c) use of positive attending and ignoring skills during special play time; (d) use of positive attending and ignoring skills to promote appropriate independent play and compliance with simple requests and discussion of ways to give commands more effectively; (e) establishment of a reward-oriented home token or point system; (f) use of response cost for minor noncompliance and rule violations; (g) use of time-out techniques for more serious rule violations; (h) use of appropriate strategies for problems in public; (i) ways of handling future problems and working cooperatively with school and community agencies; (j) monthly follow-up session.

The classroom component consisted of a comprehensive set of developmentally based, empirically supported behavior management techniques (e.g., token systems, response cost, use of natural consequences, and limited use of time out) adapting a previously successful classroom intervention program at the University of California—Irvine (Pfiffner & Barkley, 1998). The program also included a social skills intervention addressing 40 basic social skills. Using concrete examples from the classroom or recess and integrating them into the academic curriculum, the teacher taught social skills to increase the child's ability to generalize beyond the classroom. Children were rewarded for demonstrating social skills in the classroom, and the child's family received information about the skills so that they could reinforce them if the child used them at home.

Treatment Benefits and Limitations

At the end of the 1-year intervention, children who participated in the classroom component did experience significant improvement in their behavior in a number of areas (Barkley et al., 2000). Teacher ratings of ADHD symptoms as well as aggression and overall self-control significantly improved, as did the child's social skills. Direct observations of externalizing behavior in the classroom also reflected significant reductions in these disruptive behaviors. Children in the classroom treatment group were also rated by their parents as showing significant improvement in their adaptive skills. Children were not restricted from taking medication to control their symptoms; however, no children in the classroom intervention required any type of medication during kindergarten. Contrary to predictions, these improvements were not evident on laboratory measures of attention or impulse control or from mother–child interactions observed in the laboratory.

Despite the success of Barkley's parent training program in other projects, children who participated in the parent training component did not show any significant improvement at the end of the intervention (Barkley et al., 2000). Several reasons may explain this discrepancy. First, despite the fact that the parent training was free and transportation was provided, participation by parents was poor. Although all parents were required to give consent for their child's participation in the project, parents were not seeking mental health services at the time of their enrollment in the project. As a result, some of the parents may not have seen parent training as a priority. Other factors, such as scheduling and the need for child care, may have precluded participation even if families viewed the intervention as a priority.

To determine whether the results observed at the initial posttreatment assessment were maintained, children were followed for 3 years (Shelton et al., 2000; Barkley et al., 2002). Unfortunately, all the post-treatment gains at the end of the kindergarten year had faded by follow-up. Most children continued to have severe home and school behavioral difficulties as well as academic challenges, even though developmental maturation was noted, with some symptoms resolving in the intervention and control groups over time.

Discussion and Recommendations

Although the follow-up data are disappointing, these findings are consistent with our understanding of ADHD. Considerable evidence from this study and others suggests that psychosocial interventions can help minimize the impairment that ADHD symptoms cause, as well as limit the development of comorbid conditions. However, these interventions, including medication, cannot "cure" ADHD. Thus, expecting that a successful year-long intervention would be sufficient to eliminate future symptoms is unreasonable. These findings suggest that once successful interventions are identified, they must be monitored and adapted but not necessarily eliminated once the immediate difficulties are lessened.

Rationale and Treatment Goals for Project Mastery

Building on the successes of the kindergarten project and mindful of its limitations, we developed Project Mastery for the following reasons: (a) to evaluate whether the parent training interventions could be improved; (b) to assess whether the success of the kindergarten classroom interventions could be extended to preschool; and (c) to examine the effectiveness of delivering these interventions using a family-centered or system-of-care approach. The project was conducted in both Massachusetts and North Carolina Head Start programs, with the intervention phase ending in June 2001.

Participants

Over a 2-year period, parents in North Carolina were approached at centralized Head Start registration centers and asked to complete a behavioral screening similar to that used in the kindergarten project. Children whose parents rated them as having ADHD symptoms and aggression greater than the 93rd percentile were contacted about participation in the project. Close to 95% of the families contacted agreed to participate. Children attended the Head Start program associated with their geographical location, with some sites designated as intervention sites and some as control sites. Programs were matched for expertise of teaching and administrative staff and overall quality of the program as measured by the Early Childhood Environment Rating Scale—Revised. Fifty-nine children have participated in the comprehensive intervention, with another 45 serving as an assessment control group, receiving those interventions readily available in the community. Similar numbers have participated in the Massachusetts site. Of the North Carolina sample, 67% were males and 82% were African American. An additional 13% were Caucasian, with the remaining 5% other ethnicities (e.g., Hispanic, Asian). The families of all children met federal eligibility criteria for Head Start enrollment, based on family income and number in household.

Measures

Strengths and needs in multiple domains were measured to develop the child's individualized plan, as well as to evaluate the effectiveness of the intervention. Information on each child's behavioral, cognitive, and achievement status was obtained. Families provided information on parenting practices, parenting stress, family support, and psychiatric status. Teachers provided ratings on their knowledge of effective strategies and their attitudes toward using positive interventions and working collaboratively with families. Also assessed were the overall quality of the classroom and teacher–child interaction and the degree of interagency coordination.

Procedures

A summary of Project Mastery's major treatment components appears in Table 14.2. All components were based on knowledge of the developmental trajectories of young children with behavioral challenges, were developmentally supportive, used empirically supported strategies, and were delivered within a family-centered or system-of-care approach. The cornerstone of this approach is the development of an individualized service plan. Consistent with the basic tenets of a system-of-care approach (Stroul & Friedman, 1986), the plans were developed collaboratively with the family and the child's teacher; reflected the family's and teacher's priorities; were strength-based, using information gained from the baseline assessment, and were coordinated and community-based, integrating Project Mastery's interventions with any other interventions being provided to the child (e.g., speech and language therapy; community mental health services) and family (e.g., marital counseling).

TABLE 14.2
Treatment Components of Project Mastery

Parent training	• Discuss parent goals for child and develop service plan • Discuss success and limitations of current parenting strategies in meeting those goals • Review of triggers and payoffs of children's positive and negative behaviors • Introduce importance of play and how to help your child learn through play • Showing attention and appreciation • Giving praise and modeling self-praise • Giving commands effectively • Developing praise and reward programs • Setting limits effectively and ignoring inappropriate behavior • Using time out • Working collaboratively with your child's teacher
On-site classroom consultation	• Discuss teacher goals for child, review parent goals, finalize service plan • Using positive reinforcement of incompatible and alternative behaviors in the classroom • Using reminder strategies and positive reinforcement of successive approximations of target behaviors • Using natural consequences • Using time-out effectively • Developing individual or classroom based reward systems • Training on how to handle frequently occurring challenges in the classroom (e.g., biting, hitting) • Assisting teacher and modeling working collaboratively with families • Assisting teacher and modeling working collaboratively with other professionals serving the child and family
Social skills training	• Review basic skills; develop common vocabulary • Practice through role play using concrete examples from classroom and home • Reinforce social skills in classroom through daily and weekly acknowledgment of progress • Communicate with family about target skills • Reward child for use of skills at home
Community collaboration	• Integrating Project Mastery interventions with other family or child services • Facilitating cooperation with other agencies (e.g., special education, social service)

In contrast to the kindergarten project, wherein all children were in a special classroom, all classroom interventions were delivered on-site in the regular Head Start classrooms with regular Head Start staff. The interventions were based on the previous NIMH-funded kindergarten project (Shelton et al., 2000) and Webster-Stratton's Parents, Teachers and Children's

Videotape "Incredible Years" Series (1992). On-site consultation and teacher training focused on individual classroom-based practices that emphasized positive reinforcement of alternative behaviors, use of reminder strategies and positive reinforcement of successive approximations of target behaviors, use of natural consequences, and sparing use of time-out.

The parent training component was an extension and adaptation of Webster-Stratton's "Incredible Years" curriculum and mirrored the basic strength-based, collaborative approach of the classroom component. The 10 sessions reviewed the following: (a) parent goals and successes and limitations of current parenting strategies; (b) review of triggers and payoffs for children's positive and negative behaviors; (c) introduction to the importance of play and ways to help children learn through play; (d) ways of showing attention and appreciation; (e) ways to give praise and model self-praise; (f) review and development of praise and reward programs, identification of positive behavior, and use of reinforcements; (g) effective limit-setting and ignoring; (h) time out; (i) working with the child's teacher as a team. All parent training was provided on-site at the Head Start center in the evenings and on the day requested by most families. Dinner and child care were provided.

Social-skills groups were provided for the Project Mastery children concurrent with the parent training sessions. Targeted skills were chosen on the basis of the children's evaluation and parent and teacher priorities. The groups were conducted in the children's classrooms to promote generalization, and the content was a developmentally adapted version of the social-skills curriculum successfully used in the kindergarten project. Children received a small reward at the end of each session contingent on their behavior, and parents received verbal and written feedback about the content of the session and their child's progress to facilitate generalization of gains to the home.

Treatment Benefits and Limitations

With regard to child outcomes, goals on the service plan met or exceeded expectations for 85% of the children. In addition, children participating in the intervention classrooms demonstrated significant reductions in inattention, impulsivity, hyperactivity, and aggressive and oppositional behavior at home and at school (according to parent and teacher ratings on standardized behavior ratings scales) relative to those children in the assessment-only group. Some children experienced changes significant enough to no longer qualify them for ADHD and ODD diagnoses.

With regard to family outcomes, families participating in the intervention portion reported being extremely satisfied with the process by which the plan was developed, as well as the results. They reported significantly greater knowledge of effective and positive parenting strategies and increased confidence in their parenting abilities. More than half of the families participated in the parent training sessions—a rate that is considerably greater than other community-based parenting groups or the previous kindergarten project. Those that actually participated in the sessions showed a slightly greater reduction in parenting stress relative to the control group.

As for teacher outcomes, teachers receiving on-site training reported greater confidence in their ability to bring out the best in the child despite his or her challenging behaviors. They also reported increased knowledge and use of positive proactive interventions with the child and an increased likelihood of working collaboratively with the child's family.

With regard to system changes, the project has resulted in numerous increases in agency coordination not only for the children in the intervention group but for Head Start children in general. Referrals directly to Project Mastery from community agencies increased significantly from Year 1 to Year 2. With parental consent, information from the baseline assessments was used to facilitate the development of individualized educational plans and acquisition of developmental services for those children needing additional educational support. Efforts are under way to sustain the project now that the grant funding has ended. Parents who participated in the parent training have volunteered to serve as peer mentors and group facilitators for a parent training group to be run by Head Start staff. In addition, several agencies that provide mental health services to young children have contracted with Mastery staff to adopt the successful components.

Discussion and Recommendations

A key test is the degree to which the gains demonstrated during Head Start are maintained or at least minimize the need for supportive services in kindergarten and first grade. Follow-up data are currently being collected. It is likely, however, that the decrease in positive results observed over time in the NIMH kindergarten project will be observed in this intervention as well. If so, these findings, coupled with those from the kindergarten project, provide compelling evidence that services for children who display severe disruptive behaviors so early in life should have continued support that is adapted as their developmental needs change.

What is promising, however, is that positive outcomes could occur among children at high risk for difficulties because of the early and severe nature of their behavioral challenges as well as the economic stresses of their families. Families participating in Project Mastery demonstrated needs in multiple domains. Families experienced economic hardship, were generally headed by single parents, reported less social support and more stress related to parenting their children, and exhibited less knowledge of effective parenting skills. In addition, the children had lower-than-average cognitive abilities, academic achievement, and adaptive skills, as well as higher-than-average levels of externalizing behaviors. Given these multiple risk factors for child and family, another implication of the current findings is that a family-centered or system-of-care approach would seem to be an essential component of any intervention designed to effect changes in those children at highest risk for negative outcomes.

PARENT TRAINING FOR SCHOOL-AGE CHILDREN: THERAPEUTIC COMPONENT CONSIDERATIONS

Rationale and Treatment Goals

Although parent training (PT) is often used in the clinical management of ADHD, systematic investigation of its clinical efficacy has been limited. Surprisingly few studies have actually examined this form of treatment. Among those that have, cross-study comparisons have been complicated by numerous methodological variations, including differences in the type, format, and length of PT; the manner in which ADHD samples were defined; and the scope of the measures used to assess outcome.

In the absence of systematic investigation, many questions remain. Our understanding of how PT works is particularly limited. Most PT programs are multifaceted, typically including some combination of various contingency management techniques and counseling about ADHD. Which of these components is responsible for the observed therapeutic benefits of PT is not at all clear. Our knowledge of the scope of PT benefits is also limited. Although research has shown that PT brings about improvements in child behavior, parent–child relations, and parent functioning (Anastopoulos, Shelton, DuPaul, & Guevremont, 1993), little is known about its impact on a child's emotional functioning. Even less is known regarding the role of fathers.

The purpose of this study was to begin answering these questions. In particular, a therapeutic component analysis was conducted, comparing the effects of a complete PT program (i.e., contingency management plus ADHD counseling) versus ADHD counseling (AC) alone. We predicted that both forms of treatment would produce benefits, with the complete PT program clearly being the superior of the two. This study also included child emotional indices as outcome measures, based on the assumption that PT would improve this area of functioning as well. Input from fathers was obtained with the expectation that fathers' ratings would reflect relatively less change relative to mothers'.

Description of Study and Treatment Program

Participants

The sample for this study was drawn from a larger group of 138 clinic-referred children participating in an NIMH project examining comorbidity and ADHD parent training outcome. All carried a *Diagnostic and Statistical Manual of Mental Disorders, Third Edition, Revised (DSM–III–R)* diagnosis of ADHD as determined by the Diagnostic Interview Schedule for Children (DISC) and T-scores > 65 on the Attention Problems subscale of the Child Behavior Checklist (CBCL; Achenbach, 1991). Half also displayed ODD. Sample selection was further determined by parental psychopathology, with relatively equal numbers of mothers displaying either low or high levels on the Symptom Checklist 90–Revised (SCL-90-R; Derogatis, 1983). For the current project a subsample of 59 children (47 boys, 12 girls) and their parents served as participants. The children ranged in age from 6 to 11 years, with a mean of 106 months. All were of at least normal intelligence, and 49% received special education services. None was taking medication for behavior management purposes during the active portion of the study. Most (71%) were from two-parent, Caucasian, middle-class homes.

Measures

Parent-completed rating scales and coded observations of parent–child interactions were used to assess changes in parenting style. The Test of ADHD Knowledge (TOAK; Anastopoulos, 1992) and a modified version of the Knowledge of Behavioral Principles as Applied to Children (KBPAC) served as indices of changes in knowledge. Changes in child behavior were assessed by way of parent-completed rating scales and coded observations. Changes in child emotional functioning were determined by parent-completed rating scales, child self-report rating scales, and coded observations. Changes in parental and marital functioning were gauged primarily by parent self-report rating scales. Coded observations were used to address parent–child relations.

Procedure

Participants were randomly assigned either to a group receiving the complete PT program ($n = 35$) or to ADHD counseling ($n = 24$). A step-by-step summary of these treatment programs[1] appears in Table 14.3. The PT program followed the steps outlined in previous research (Anastopoulos et al., 1993). The therapeutic goal of the ADHD counseling program was threefold: to provide basic information about ADHD, to give parents an opportunity to describe how ADHD affected their child and family, and to

---

[1]Copies of the session-by-session outlines for these treatment programs may be obtained from the first author.

TABLE 14.3

Major Components of Parent Training and ADHD Counseling Programs

Parent training	Session	ADHD counseling
Program overview, overview of ADHD	1	Program overview, overview of ADHD
Four-factor model, behavior management principles	2	Four-factor model
Positive attending/ignoring, special time	3	Assessment and treatment issues
Extending positive attending, effective commands	4	School history and current school functioning
Home poker chip/point system	5	Impact of ADHD on child's home functioning
Response cost for minor problems	6	Impact of ADHD on child's social-emotional functioning
Time-out for serious misbehavior	7	Rights of children with ADHD in schools
Managing behavior in public	8	Overview of pharmacotherapy
School issues, handling future problems	9	Overview of social skills training
1-month booster session, termination and final disposition	10	1-month booster session, termination and final disposition

encourage parents to generate solutions to their child-management problems based on the knowledge they gained. No contingency management training was offered. Both groups received ten weekly 1-hour individually delivered treatment sessions over the course of 3 to 4 months. Experienced PhD-level psychologists delivered the treatments. Treatment integrity was addressed through the use of treatment manuals and expert review of audiotaped treatment sessions. Assessment data were gathered before treatment, immediately after treatment, and 6 months later.

Treatment Benefits and Limitations

Preliminary analyses indicated that the two groups were statistically equivalent at pretreatment with regard to all demographic dimensions and all but one outcome measure of interest (i.e., self-reported child depression).

To determine whether the experimental manipulation was effective, 2 (Group) × 3 (Time) repeated measures ANOVAs were performed on the TOAK, KBPAC, and parenting style measures (separately for mothers and fathers). As expected, knowledge of ADHD increased over time for mothers and fathers in both groups. Also in line with expectations, post-treatment knowledge of behavior management principles was greater for PT mothers ($p < .01$) and fathers ($p < .03$) than for parents receiving AC. PT mothers

($p < .001$) and fathers ($p < .10$) also reported using more effective parenting strategies at posttreatment, but these differences were not maintained at follow-up.

Contrary to expectations, repeated measures analyses of the various child, parent, and marital outcome data failed to produce any significant interactions. However, numerous trends ($p < .15$) did emerge, suggesting weak but consistent interactions favoring PT over AC. For example, PT mothers and fathers reported lower rates of ODD symptoms at posttreatment but not at follow-up. Coded observations of PT mothers interacting with their children revealed lower levels of child inattention and anger at posttreatment. PT fathers also reported lower rates of hyperactivity, impulsivity, and internalizing symptoms in their children, along with lower levels of parenting stress and greater parenting alliance. Of further interest is that children in PT reported greater improvement in their self-esteem.

Except for the parental depression and marital functioning measures, significant main effects across time were evident on all other parent self-report rating scale measures. The same was true for child self-esteem and for two of the coded behaviors from the mother–child observations (i.e., appropriate parenting, mutual enjoyment). Although the finding was not statistically significant, fewer PT parents (6%) dropped out of treatment relative to those receiving AC (17%).

Discussion and Recommendations

The obtained findings provided partial support for the study's hypotheses. As expected, PT and AC increased parental knowledge of ADHD. But PT was clearly superior to AC in increasing parental knowledge of behavior-management principles and improving parenting effectiveness. Although such changes indicated that the experimental manipulation was in fact successful, statistically significant group differences were not evident on any of the child, parent, or family functional outcome measures. Because both treatment groups produced a number of significant improvements over time, it would appear that giving parents knowledge of ADHD is far more therapeutically beneficial than previously thought. That said, it would be premature to conclude that ADHD counseling alone is sufficient. Numerous trends in the data pointed toward contingency management training as an important component of PT.

In addition to reducing children's behavior problems, PT produced anticipated changes in the child's emotional functioning. This result was evident by parent-reported reductions in internalizing symptoms and child-reported improvements in self-esteem. Although we can only speculate at this point, such changes may stem from increased parental use of positive attending and reinforcement strategies, which are emphasized throughout PT. Contrary to expectations, input from fathers revealed more treatment-related changes in home functioning than did similar input from mothers. The basis for this discrepancy is unclear. At the very least, this difference of parental opinion highlights the need for including fathers' input in outcome research.

TREATMENTS FOR REDUCING PARENT–ADOLESCENT CONFLICT: IS MORE BETTER?

Rationale and Treatment Goals

Little research exists on clinic-referred teens with ADHD. What does exist comes primarily from follow-up studies of hyperactive children into adolescence (e.g., Barkley, Fischer, Edelbrock, & Smallish, 1990). Such studies indicate that comorbid aggression, or ODD, is relatively common-place, occurring in 45% to 65% of cases diagnosed in childhood. This comorbidity has been found to bode poorly for these children's outcomes later as adolescents and young adults (Barkley, 1998). This comorbid condition is associated with greater family conflict and teen-management problems, rebelliousness, antisocial acts, and earlier substance experimentation and abuse than in normal adolescents or those having only ADHD (Barkley, Anastopoulos, Guevremont, & Fletcher, 1991). Research further suggests that the extent of such family conflict is a significant predictor of concurrent and later adolescent psychological well-being (Shek, 1998). Moreover, clinical evidence (Robin, 1999) also indicates that these parent–teen conflicts are a major reason that parents of teens with ADHD and ODD seek treatment.

Family therapy has consistently shown effectiveness in dealing with family conflicts, particularly among children and adolescents with ODD or conduct disorder (Dishion & Andrews, 1995). This fact, coupled with the previous findings concerning the high level of conflict and stress in families of teens with ADHD and ODD, served to encourage our earlier study of the efficacy of three different approaches to family therapy for these families (Barkley et al., 1992). One form of therapy was the Problem Solving Communication Training (PSCT) program developed by Robin and Foster (1989). This approach directly involves the adolescent as an active participant in treatment. PSCT includes instruction in family-based problem-solving, positive communication skills, and behavior-contracting procedures. The second therapy approach involved parent training in behavior management skills (BMT) using a modification of the program developed by Barkley (1997) with appropriate adjustments for adolescents. This program trains parents in positive reinforcement, token economies, response cost, grounding, and other traditional contingency management techniques. The third therapy was a more traditional approach—namely, Minuchin's Structural Family Therapy (SFT; Minuchin & Fishman, 1981).

The initial study of these three family-based treatment approaches for teens with ADHD showed that, at the group level of analysis, all treatment groups improved in association with treatment, with no differences in efficacy found among them. However, analyses of individual change (Jacobson & Truax, 1991) revealed that as many as 70% to 87% of the families did not change to any reliable degree as a function of these treatments. This indicated the need to investigate various means of improving the effectiveness of family-based treatment for parent–adolescent conflict in families of adolescents with ADHD. One way of doing so would be to increase the potency of these therapies by increasing the number of treatment sessions, providing treatment more intensively (more times per week), and examining combinations of these therapies.

The present NIMH-funded study sought to replicate and extend this earlier investigation by increasing the intensity of treatment in just these ways. Given that family conflicts are considerably greater in families of teens with ADHD and ODD than in families of teens with ADHD alone (Barkley et al., 1991), we focused on this ADHD group with comorbidity. These families have the greatest need for treatment and perhaps the best response to it as a result of their high initial levels of conflict. The prior study also found that the 8 to 10 weekly sessions of therapy were not sufficient to create a potent treatment for such long-standing family conflicts. Most families in that study did not demonstrate reliable change resulting from treatment with any form of therapy. This project therefore doubled the dosage of treatment to 18 sessions and increased its intensity through twice-weekly sessions.

To increase treatment potency still further, one treatment arm of this protocol involved a combination of PSCT with BMT whereas the other involved PSCT alone. The first nine sessions of treatment in one arm included only PSCT and in the other only BMT. By comparing these groups at the treatment midpoint, the present study provided a direct replication of the previous study. Thereafter, the PSCT-only group continued receiving that therapy for nine more sessions, and the BMT group went on to receive nine sessions of PSCT. By the end of treatment, the design compared PSCT alone with the combined BMT–PSCT treatment program.

Description of Study and Treatment Program

Participants

A total of 97 teens with ADHD between the ages of 12 and 18 years were recruited over a 3-year period. All met DSM–IV criteria for a dual diagnosis of ADHD, Combined Type, and ODD. In addition to these diagnostic requirements, participants (a) either could not be receiving psychoactive medication or, if receiving medication, be able to remain at a stable dose through the 18 sessions of therapy; (b) agreed not seek out any other form of mental health treatment during their participation in this project; (c) did not have any ongoing legal proceedings against them for criminal or status offenses by the local juvenile court authorities that would result in their removal from their family during the active treatment phase of the study.

Measures

Parents and teens completed various rating scales at the pre-treatment evaluation, at the midtreatment evaluation (after Session 9), after the final session of family therapy (Session 18), and 2 months after the termination of treatment. These rating scale measures included the Conflict Behavior Questionnaire (CBQ) and the Issues Checklist (IC; Robin & Foster, 1989). Also collected during these same assessment intervals were videotaped clinic-based observations of parents and teens engaging in neutral, conflictual, and positive discussions, which were then coded. Consumer satisfaction and treatment effectiveness ratings were collected as well but only at the end of treatment.

Procedure

Participants were assigned randomly to the two treatment groups, with a total of 58 families eventually assigned to PSCT and 39 to BMT–PSCT. A summary of these treatment programs (Barkley, Robin, & Edwards, 1999) appears in Table 14.4. Each treatment consisted of 18 60-minute sessions held approximately twice weekly. All families received a mid-treatment evaluation after the ninth session and then a posttreatment evaluation after the 18th and final session. The two groups then received a 2-month follow-up evaluation to examine the stability of treatment.

Doctoral-level clinical psychologists served as the therapists. Treatment integrity was addressed by way of pilot cases, use of session-by-session treatment manuals, and random reviews of treatment session audiotapes, which then served as a basis for providing therapists with ongoing feedback throughout the project.

Although both parents were strongly encouraged to attend therapy, one parent was required to attend these sessions consistently if it appeared that the second parent or partner would not be able to attend all of them. The adolescent was required to attend all PSCT sessions. In BMT–PSCT, teens did not attend the first nine BMT sessions but attended the remaining nine that focused on PSCT.

PSCT followed the outline by Robin and Foster (1989) and the manual developed in the earlier study (Barkley et al., 1992). This treatment program

TABLE 14.4
Major Components of Behavior Management Training
and Problem-Solving Communication Training

	Participants	Treatment goal/process	Techniques
Behavior management training	Parent(s)	• Positive parental attention to appropriate adolescent behavior • Home point system for reinforcing compliance with requests/rules • Grounding, loss of privileges for unacceptable behavior • Anticipating impending problems	Direct instruction, feedback, homework assignments
Problem-solving, communication training	Parent(s), teen	Problem-solving • Problem definition, generating solutions, negotiation, deciding on a solution, implementing the solution • Communication training • Using neutral voice tone, paraphrasing others' concerns, avoiding insults, put-downs, ultimatums Cognitive restructuring • Detecting/ restructuring irrational personal and family beliefs	Direct instruction, modeling, behavior rehearsal, role-playing, feedback, homework assignments

contained three major components for changing parent–adolescent conflict: (a) *problem-solving*, or training parents and teens in a 5-step problem-solving approach (i.e., problem definition, brainstorming of possible solutions, negotiation, decision-making about a solution, implementation of the solution); (b) *communication training*, or helping parents and teens to develop more effective communication skills while discussing family conflicts, such as speaking in an even tone of voice, paraphrasing others' concerns before speaking ones' own, providing approval to others for positive communication, and avoiding insults, put-downs, ultimatums, and other hallmarks of poor communication skills; (c) *cognitive restructuring*, or helping families detect, confront, and restructure irrational, extreme, or rigid belief systems held by parents or teens about their own or the other's conduct. The therapist supervised families practicing these skills during each session using direct instruction, modeling, behavior rehearsal, role-playing exercises, and feedback. The therapist also assigned between-session homework that involved the family's use of PSCT skills during a conflict discussion at home, which was audiotaped for later review by the therapist.

BMT followed the text by Barkley (1997) but was modified for teens as in the prior study (Barkley et al., 1992). In general, this approach taught parents to use contingency management methods for modifying inappropriate teen behavior or for increasing prosocial or acceptable behavior. Sessions dealt with the following areas: (a) use of positive parental attention to appropriate adolescent behavior; (b) development of a home point system for reinforcing the accomplishment of responsibilities (e.g., chores) and compliance with rules (e.g., curfew); (c) use of brief periods of grounding and loss of privileges for unacceptable behavior; (d) ways for parents to anticipate impending problem situations and establish plans to deal with them. Homework assignments were part of most sessions. This treatment always occurred for the first nine sessions and was then combined with PSCT for the second nine sessions.

Parents in both treatment conditions also received a 45-minute videotape on ADHD to review after the initial evaluation and discuss with the therapist during the first session of treatment. All teens were also encouraged to review this videotape at home.

Treatment Benefits and Limitations

Pretreatment Comparability. The family compositions were not found to differ between treatment groups. In terms of parental enrollment in treatment, the percentage of mothers participating in treatment was 97% for PSCT and 95% for BMT–PSCT. For fathers, this rate was 78% in PSCT and 87% in BMT–PSCT, an insignificant difference. Teens in the PSCT group were slightly but significantly older and thus were at a somewhat higher grade level in school than were the teens in the BMT–PSCT group. The PSCT teens were also slightly but significantly less intelligent than those assigned to BMT–PSCT. The medication status of the two groups was as follows: 62% of the PSCT group received some form of psychiatric medication at the beginning of treatment, whereas 49% of those in BMT–PSCT did so. This difference was not significant.

Treatment Outcome. By the midpoint, both treatments resulted in significant improvement at the group level of analysis according to participant ratings of various aspects of their behavior. Neither treatment was superior to the other in the degree of change that occurred. These improvements, however, could not be documented in the direct observations made of family conflict discussions. By the end of treatment, the same results were obtained after the number of treatment sessions were doubled and, in one treatment group, the two therapy approaches were combined. Both groups improved but did not differ from each other in degree of improvement. By this time, improvement was also documented through direct observation in the mothers' behavior, but not in the fathers' and teens' behaviors. Thus, the addition of BMT to PSCT did not appreciably increase the effectiveness of PSCT alone in these group level analyses. By the 2-month follow-up, continuing improvement was evident in both treatment groups according to both father and teen ratings but not to maternal ratings. In contrast, direct observations found that fathers in the BMT–PSCT group had worsened in their positive and negative behavior in the conflict discussion. At this level of analysis, both treatments appeared to be equally effective. Once treatment was withdrawn, however, fathers and teens in both groups rated themselves as improving further although direct observations documented a worsening of the fathers' interactive behavior in the combined therapy condition. No group differences were evident either with respect to how much participants liked the two treatments or with respect to their perceptions of treatment efficacy. Both groups reported relatively high levels of satisfaction.

Despite these relatively positive reports, such impressions of efficacy must be tempered by a consideration of the analyses that were done at the individual level. When the outcome data were examined using the Jacobson and Truax (1991) methodology, less than 25% of the participants in each therapy group demonstrated reliable change as a consequence of treatment. This finding is nearly identical to that found in our earlier research, signifying that only a small percentage of families actually benefited from either treatment. The significant improvements seen at the group level of analysis are therefore being driven by a small subset of families who were benefiting from treatment conflict. Individual analyses of the drop-out rates also revealed interesting findings. At the midpoint in treatment, significantly more families had dropped out of PSCT (15 families, or 26%) than BMT–PSCT (3 families, or 8%): $X^2 = 5.09$, $p = .024$. By the end of treatment, these numbers had risen to 22 (38%) in PSCT and just 7 (18%) in BMT–PSCT. This difference was again significant: $X^2 = 4.44$, $p = .035$. At the follow-up point, 25 families (46%) of those in PSCT alone did not attend this reevaluation whereas the figure was 10 families (23%) for BMT–PSCT.

Discussion and Recommendations

Our previous study (Barkley et al., 1992) compared these two forms of treatment given alone (PSCT versus BMT) for nine sessions and found them both equally effective. The midpoint of treatment in this study essentially served as a replication of that earlier project, revealing a very similar pattern of findings. Lengthening the treatment to 18 sessions did not produce the kinds of changes that had been anticipated. Likewise, the combination of PSCT and BMT was not superior to PSCT alone in terms of the improvements in family functioning that these two treatments generated. That said, it remains important to note that the drop-out rates for BMT–PSCT were significantly less than those observed in the PSCT condition alone. Thus, to ensure that higher percentages of families remain in treatment and experience the kinds of therapeutic changes that they desire, clinicians are advised to employ the combined BMT–PSCT approach.

What might account for this difference in drop-out rates? PSCT requires that the teen attend all sessions and immediately focuses on conflicts the parents and teens are having and ways to problem-solve them. In a sense, the family is immediately thrust into confrontations with each other at the initial stages of therapy so that they will know how to negotiate them more properly in the future. In contrast, BMT requires only the parents to attend the initial nine sessions of treatment and excludes the teen from these sessions. Moreover, it does not provoke parent–teen confrontations in the therapy sessions but instead focuses on conveying a set of skills to parents (largely contingency management). Although in the long run this treatment proved no more effective than PSCT among the families who stayed in treatment to the midpoint, far more families were willing to stay in treatment as a consequence of this means of introducing therapeutic management skills to them. This is a clinically important finding for therapists working with families of ADHD and ODD teens because it suggests an important issue in the staging of this combined therapeutic package. Such a finding supports the clinical admonition of the treatment developers of PSCT (Robin, 1999) that behavior-management training, involving only parents, may need to be initiated first before engaging in problem-solving training with both parents and teens. Robin (1999) has speculated that beginning with behavior-management training may be necessary because parents at this stage in treatment need some means of gaining control over the teens' disruptive, defiant, and otherwise hostile behavior, which is necessary before the parents can engage the teen in constructive attempts at discussing problems and resolving conflicts.

In sum, although some evidence of treatment efficacy is evident at both the group and individual levels of analysis, future research should focus on the development of alternative methods of service delivery to high-risk teens and their families.

SUMMARY

Taken together, our findings suggest that family-based psychosocial interventions do have some efficacy in the clinical management of children and adolescents with ADHD and its associated features. Although the magnitude of their therapeutic impact is much less than that resulting from stimulant medication and other forms of pharmacotherapy, our family-based treatments nonetheless produced clinically meaningful benefits for a small but significant percentage of the children and families who received them. The extent to which such benefits were realized seemed to vary as a function of age, with teens and their families displaying far fewer improvements after treatment than those observed among younger children. Such a developmental trend was not tested directly but can be inferred from the pattern of reported results. A more definitive statement about age-related psychosocial treatment effects must await the results of future research.

From the outset we emphasized that no treatment for ADHD should be used alone. Our findings lend further support to this contention. Whether the interventions that we tested would increase therapeutic benefits above and beyond that of other treatments (e.g., stimulant medication) remains to be seen. Such multimodal treatment research is especially needed among preschool and adolescent ADHD populations. Given the scope and magnitude of the therapeutic change that our psychosocial treatment programs can produce, they appear well suited for inclusion in future multimodal intervention studies, whether combined with pharmacotherapy or with other types of psychosocial interventions.

The verdict is still out on the role of family-based psychosocial interventions. Much more systematic research must be completed before any definitive conclusions may be drawn about the place of these interventions in the overall clinical management of children and adolescents with ADHD.

REFERENCES

Achenbach, T. M. (1991). *Manual for the Child Behavior Checklist/4-18 and 1991 profile*. Burlington: University of Vermont, Department of Psychiatry.

American Psychiatric Association. (1994). *Diagnostic and statistical manual of mental disorders* (4th ed.). Washington, DC: Author.

Anastopoulos, A. D. (1992). *Test of ADHD knowledge*. Unpublished manuscript, University of Massachusetts Medical Center.

Anastopoulos, A. D., Barkley, R. A., & Shelton, T. L. (1996). Family-based treatment: Psychosocial intervention for children and adolescents with attention deficit hyperactivity disorder. In E. D. Hibbs & P. S. Jensen (Eds.), *Psychosocial treatments for child and adolescent disorders: Empirically based approaches* (pp. 267–284). Washington, DC: American Psychological Association.

Anastopoulos, A. D., & Shelton, T. L. (2001). *Assessing attention-deficit/hyperactivity disorder*. New York: Kluwer Academic/Plenum Publishers.

Anastopoulos, A. D., Shelton, T. L., DuPaul, G. J., & Guevremont, D. C. (1993). Parent training for attention-deficit hyperactivity disorder: Its impact on parent functioning. *Journal of Abnormal Child Psychology, 21*, 581–596.

August, G. J., Realmuto, G. M., MacDonald, A. W., Nugent, S. M., & Crosby, R. (1996). Prevalence of ADHD and comorbid disorders among elementary school children screened for disruptive behavior. *Journal of Abnormal Child Psychology, 24*, 571–595.

Barkley, R. A. (1997). *Defiant children: A clinician's manual for parent training* (2nd ed.). New York: Guilford Press.

Barkley, R. A. (1998). *Attention-deficit hyperactivity disorder: A handbook for diagnosis and treatment* (2nd ed.). New York: Guilford Press.

Barkley, R. A., Anastopoulos, A. D., Guevremont, D. C., & Fletcher, K. E. (1991). Adolescents with attention deficit hyperactivity disorder: Patterns of behavioral adjustment, academic functioning, and treatment utilization. *Journal of the American Academy of Child and Adolescent Psychiatry, 30*, 752–761.

Barkley, R. A., Fischer, M., Edelbrock, C. S., & Smallish, L. (1990). The adolescent outcome of hyperactive children diagnosed by research criteria. I. An 8-year prospective follow-up study. *Journal of the American Academy of Child and Adolescent Psychiatry, 29*, 546–557.

Barkley, R. A., Guevremont, D. C., Anastopoulos, A. D., & Fletcher, K. F. (1992). A comparison of three family therapy programs for treating family conflicts in adolescents with attention deficit hyperactivity disorder. *Journal of Consulting and Clinical Psychology, 60*, 450–462.

Barkley, R. A., Robin, A. L., & Edwards, G. (1999). *Defiant teens.* New York: Guilford Press.

Barkley, R. A., Shelton, T. L., Crosswait, C. R., Moorehouse, M., Fletcher, K., Barrett, S., et al. (2000). Multi-method psycho-educational intervention for preschool children with disruptive behavior. *Journal of Child Psychology and Psychiatry and Allied Disciplines, 41*, 319–332.

Barkley, R. A., Shelton, T. L., Crosswait, C. R., Moorehouse, M., Fletcher, K., Barrett, S., et al. (2002). Preschool children with high levels of disruptive behavior: Three-year outcomes as a function of adaptive disability. *Development and Psychopathology, 14*, 45–67.

Campbell, S. B. (1996). Introduction to the special section young children at risk for psychopathology: Developmental and family perspectives. *Journal of Clinical Child Psychology, 25*, 372–375.

Derogatis, L. R. (1983). *Symptom checklist 90–revised manual.* Minnetonka: MN: NCS Assessments.

Dishion, T. J., & Andrews, D. W. (1995). Preventing escalation in problem behaviors with high-risk young adolescents: Immediate and 1-year outcomes. *Journal of Consulting and Clinical Psychology, 63*, 538–548.

Heller, T. L., Baker, B. L., Henker, B., & Hinshaw, S. P. (1996). Externalizing behavior and cognitive functioning from preschool to first grade: Stability and predictors. *Journal of Clinical Child Psychology, 25*, 376–387.

Jacobson, N. C., & Truax, P. (1991). Clinical significance: A statistical approach to defining meaningful change in psychotherapy research. *Journal of Consulting and Clinical Psychology, 59,* 12–19.

Minuchin, S., & Fishman, H. C. (1981). *Family therapy techniques.* Cambridge, MA: Harvard University Press.

Murphy, K., & Barkley, R. A. (1996). Attention deficit hyperactivity disorder in adults. *Comprehensive Psychiatry, 37,* 393–401.

Pelham, W. E., Wheeler, T., & Chronis, A. (1998). Empirically supported psychosocial treatments for attention deficit hyperactivity disorder. *Journal of Clinical Child Psychology, 27,* 190–205.

Pfiffner, L. J., & Barkley, R. A. (1998). Treatment of ADHD in school settings. In R. A. Barkley (Ed.), *Attention-deficit hyperactivity disorder: A handbook for diagnosis and treatment* (pp. 458–490). New York: Guilford Press.

Robin, A. L. (1999). *ADHD in adolescents: Diagnosis and treatment.* New York: Guilford Press.

Robin, A. L., & Foster, S. (1989). *Negotiating parent–adolescent conflict.* New York: Guilford Press.

Shek, D. T. L. (1998). A longitudinal study of the relations between parent–adolescent conflict and adolescent well-being. *The Journal of Genetic Psychology, 159,* 53–67.

Shelton, T. L., Barkley, R. A., Crosswait, C., Moorehouse, M., Fletcher, K., Barrett, S., et al. (2000). Multimethod psychoeducational intervention for preschool children with disruptive behavior: Two-year post-treatment follow-up. *Journal of Abnormal Child Psychology, 28,* 253–266.

Stroul, B. A., & Friedman, R. M. (1986). *A system of care for severely emotionally disturbed children and youth.* Washington, DC: Georgetown University Child Development Center CASSP Technical Assistance Center.

Webster-Stratton, C. (1992). *The parents, teachers and children's videotape Incredible Years series* [Videotape]. (Available from Seth Enterprises, 1411 8th Avenue West, Seattle, WA 98119)

15

ENHANCING SOCIAL COMPETENCE IN CHILDREN WITH ATTENTION-DEFICIT/HYPERACTIVITY DISORDER: CHALLENGES FOR THE NEW MILLENNIUM

STEPHEN P. HINSHAW

THE STATE OF THE ART REGARDING PSYCHOSOCIAL TREATMENTS FOR ATTENTION-DEFICIT/HYPERACTIVITY DISORDER

Since the appearance of the first edition of this volume, several large clinical trials appraising the efficacy and effectiveness of direct contingency management and clinical behavior therapy procedures for children with attention-deficit/hyperactivity disorder (ADHD) have appeared in the

Work on this chapter was supported, in part, by National Institute of Mental Health Grants MH45064 and MH50461. The author gratefully acknowledges the participation of the many children and families in the various summer research camp and treatment investigations described herein. Address correspondence to Stephen P. Hinshaw, Department of Psychology, Tolman Hall #1650, University of California, Berkeley, CA 94720-1650 (e-mail: hinshaw@socrates.berkeley.edu).

literature (Barkley et al., 2000; Klein & Abikoff, 1997; MTA Cooperative Group, 1999a, 1999b). In each case, the initial promise of these intensive psychosocial procedures was not borne out by the results of the trials. For example, both Klein and Abikoff (1997) and the MTA Cooperative Group (1999a) found that stimulant medication alone yielded significantly better outcomes (particularly related to core ADHD symptomatology) than did well-delivered behavioral procedures. In addition, Barkley et al. (2000) showed that whereas an intensive kindergarten classroom for preschoolers with externalizing (ADHD plus aggressive) behavior patterns provided some immediate benefits, these gains appeared to be short-lived. Furthermore, parent training alone was not a viable treatment for children in this age group. Overall, such results have prompted soul-searching on the part of advocates for behaviorally oriented treatments for ADHD (for a recent review, see Hinshaw, Klein, & Abikoff, 2002).

Yet a closer examination of such findings is essential to paint an accurate picture of the state of the art. First, the chief competitor to such behavioral treatments—namely, stimulant medications—shares a similar limitation with psychosocial strategies in that the benefits tend not to persist beyond the last dosage given (Hinshaw, 2000). Thus, there is a clear need to discover and implement strategies that can provide lasting gains. Second, the results of both the MTA Study (Conners et al., 2001; MTA Cooperative Group, 1999a, 1999b; Swanson et al., 2001) and the Klein and Abikoff (1997) trial are quite consistent with those from a host of other reports in the literature: All results indicate that combining behavioral treatments with stimulant medications provides an increment in outcome over either treatment alone, particularly regarding the potential for clinically significant gains. Specifically, whereas adding behavior therapy procedures to stimulant medications does not always produce a statistically significant boost in outcome, the incremental benefits are small in terms of effect size, yet real, and are especially likely to yield results closer to the normal range of functioning than those emanating from single-modality interventions. Thus, combination, or multimodal, treatments may become the field's standard. Third, with respect to important social outcomes (e.g., positive regard from peers, the attainment of social competence), reductions of problematic behavior yielded by pharmacological approaches are insufficient to teach and motivate the necessary prosocial skills and cooperative behaviors. Indeed, the controlled trial of Pfiffner and McBurnett (1997) has provided the initial empirical evidence regarding the effectiveness of social skills interventions for children with ADHD. Overall, although the need to develop new forms of alternative treatment strategies for children and adolescents with ADHD clearly exists, validated behavioral and social skills approaches clearly have a role in intervention, particularly regarding the promotion of social competence and positive family interactions (see Hinshaw et al., 2000; Wells et al., 2000).

This chapter begins by discussing the extreme levels of social difficulty faced by youths with ADHD and then describes a program of research, undertaken in the author's laboratory, on the types of intervention procedures that may enhance social competence in this population. Comparisons with medication-based interventions for ADHD are inevitable, given the prevalence and efficacy of such pharmacological treatments. Also, despite the promise of the interventions described herein, the clinical challenge of producing lasting benefits for youths with ADHD is daunting. Thus, the author's conclusions are only tentatively optimistic. Far more work is required to understand the core mechanisms of this disorder and to envision and configure the types of intervention and support needed for individuals with ADHD. In other words, self-management strategies for ADHD are emphasized, even when fully integrated with validated behavioral interventions, and are typically insufficient for the many facets of this complex disorder. To tackle the poor long-term course of ADHD, the field must (a) integrate diverse psychosocial treatments targeted at multiple domains and conducted over long time periods, (b) coordinate these treatments with medication in the majority of cases, and (c) probe for new paradigms of intervention.

ATTENTION-DEFICIT/HYPERACTIVITY DISORDER: A REAL (AND CONTROVERSIAL) DISORDER

One reason for the controversy surrounding the diagnosis of ADHD (see DeGrandpre & Hinshaw, 2000) is that the core symptoms of inattentiveness, impulsivity, and overactivity (American Psychiatric Association, 1994) are quite common in normal development, particularly in young children. Yet when youth display such behaviors (a) at extreme levels, (b) from an early age, and (c) in multiple settings, clear impairments in academic, behavioral, emotional, and interpersonal functioning typically result. Such youngsters are at risk for such diverse and troublesome problems as school failure, extreme peer rejection, and serious accidents related to impulsive behavior (see Hinshaw, 2002a). Furthermore, they are quite likely to persist with core symptoms and associated deficits throughout adolescence and even adulthood (Mannuzza & Klein, 1999). Thus, although ADHD has a long history, marked by shifting conceptualizations and changing terminology over the past century (Hinshaw, 1994; Schachar, 1986), when assessed carefully, it is a valid diagnosis, one that clearly requires systematic intervention.

Social Problems: Basis for Intervention

The interpersonal domain is particularly salient regarding ADHD (Whalen & Henker, 1985, 1992). In the first place, youngsters with this disorder are quite likely to be actively disliked by their peers, with such rejection occurring after extremely brief periods of exposure and highly prone to persist over time (Bickett & Milich, 1990; Erhardt & Hinshaw, 1994; Pelham & Bender, 1982). The reasons for such social rejection lie in the impulsive and socially aversive behavior patterns that children with ADHD often display, the frequent co-occurrence of aggression in children with the combined and hyperactive–impulsive types of this disorder, and the frequently displayed social isolation and social insensitivity of children with the inattentive type of ADHD (e.g., Hinshaw & Melnick, 1995). (It bears mention that children with the inattentive type of ADHD may be more likely to be socially neglected than socially rejected per se.) Crucially, disapproval by agemates during childhood has been strongly associated with risk for poor prognosis, including such maladaptive outcomes as school drop out, delinquency, and general risk for psychopathology (Parker & Asher, 1987). Although social disapprobation may be secondary to the underlying psychopathology of ADHD, peer rejection also appears to represent a causal factor for later maladjustment in its own right. Thus, intervention researchers have become increasingly concerned with the development of treatment strategies that directly target children's interpersonal problems (Asher & Coie, 1990).

For many years, the predominant modality for treating children's problems of attention regulation and hyperactivity—as well as nearly all other forms of child psychopathology—was individual, insight-oriented play therapy or verbal psychotherapy. Such expressive psychotherapies, however, produce few, if any, gains for either the core symptoms or the aggressive, school-related, or interpersonal features that typically accompany ADHD. By the 1960s, behavior therapists had begun systematic research on the application of operant and social learning principles to emotional and behavioral problems of children. In the 1970s, behavioral procedures for shaping more appropriate academic and social behaviors and for reducing defiant, aggressive behaviors were being evaluated for children with externalizing behavior problems.

Behavior-management programs for children with externalizing behavior problems fall into two major categories (Pelham & Hinshaw, 1992): (a) systematic programs of contingency management, in which reward-and-response cost procedures are implemented in classroom settings or special summer programs; and (b) clinical behavior therapy strategies, wherein the therapist teaches behavior-management procedures to parents and teachers, who implement targeted strategies in the child's natural environment. Despite the important gains yielded from both categories of behavioral programming, issues of generalization and maintenance of behavior change have continued to serve as key limitations (Pelham & Hinshaw, 1992). Partly in response to the challenge of providing lasting behavior change and partly related to the growing recognition of the importance of cognition in behavior change processes, a third class of behavioral intervention—cognitive–behavioral strategies—received wide attention in the 1970s and early 1980s.

The origins of cognitively oriented therapies are complex and variegated. Of particular note are the key influences of Ellis and Beck with respect to adult applications of directive cognitive therapies for problems of anxiety and mood and the influential writings of Bandura, Goldfried, Kanfer, and Meichenbaum regarding a cognitive reconceptualization of traditional operant behavioral strategies. With these procedures, the locus of interventions shifts from "programming" the environment to directing the client to solve problems via mediational techniques. Through use of such "portable coping strategies" (Meichenbaum, 1977), the hope is that gains will generalize and persist.

The developmental–linguistic theories of Luria and Vygotsky were quite influential in moving the field from a strict behavioral perspective to a model in which the child's alleged deficits in self-guiding, internalized speech are considered central. Self-instructional (SI) therapies soared in popularity in the 1970s and 1980s for children with hyperactivity or attention-deficit disorder (ADD; e.g., Douglas, Parry, Marton, & Garson, 1976). In the typical SI procedure, the therapist initially guides the child's actions with verbal commands and then fades such control (first to the child's overt speech, then to whispered speed, and finally to internalized verbalizations) as the child performs academic or social tasks. In the spirit of the times, and guided conceptually by the promise that cognitively based treatments could foster more lasting change than behavioral programs per se, I initiated my research program with cognitive–behavioral procedures as a key focus.

Because stimulant medication treatments are a mainstay in the field, I briefly highlight several key factors in their use and effectiveness. Used for child behavior disorders for over 60 years (Bradley, 1937), they have been subject to a large number of well-controlled investigations in recent decades, yielding impressive improvements in attention deployment, regulation of impulse, and control of extraneous motor movement (Greenhill & Osman, 2000). Importantly, such secondary features as aggression are reduced into normal ranges with pharmacological intervention (Hinshaw, 1991). Although the vast majority of diagnosed youngsters shows a favorable response to medication, pharmacological treatments are not without problems. First, evidence regarding improved school performance is decidedly mixed. Second, the time course of stimulant actions is quite short, and gains that are made while the medication is active tend not to persist once the medication has worn off (Hinshaw, 1994). Third, only in rare cases are the gains that accrue to stimulant treatment sufficient to yield full clinical improvement (Pelham & Hinshaw, 1992). Fourth, despite the short-term gains that typically accrue to medication treatments, no evidence exists supporting the long-term, carry-over benefits of pharmacological intervention in later life (e.g., Weiss & Hechtman, 1993). Thus, increasing focus has been placed on integrating pharmacological with psychosocial intervention strategies to extend the limited benefits of each single treatment modality.

Three major trends thus shaped the initiation of the current research program: (a) a reconceptualization of hyperactivity or ADHD as an attentional, self-regulatory disorder (e.g., Douglas, 1983); (b) increased focus on cognitive–behavioral therapies for self-management; and (c) heightened awareness of the problems as well as the promise of stimulant treatments. Yet I hasten to add several additional qualifications and findings. First, the enthusiastic push toward cognitive therapies for children with ADHD did *not* meet with continued support in the 1980s and 1990s. Indeed, despite the clear successes of cognitive and cognitive–behavioral therapies with adult disorders (e.g., depression, anxiety) and child disorders (e.g., aggression unaccompanied by ADHD), cognitive approaches for children— particularly those relying on SI procedures—have a rather dismal track record for children specifically diagnosed with attention deficits and hyperactivity (Abikoff, 1991; Hinshaw, 2000). In fact, despite some intriguing research underscoring the importance of delays of internalization of private speech in youngsters with ADHD (Berk & Potts, 1991), evidence in favor of the contention that SI procedures actually promote behavior change in this population is lacking. Such findings have prompted a renewed emphasis on blending validated mediational procedures with established behavioral strategies, as opposed to emphasizing weak SI methods.

Parallel to these findings has been another reconceptualization of the nature of ADHD. In recent research, deficits in sustained attention have been challenged as the underlying processes related to ADHD, with increased emphasis on impulse control, disinhibition, and associated "executive" deficits (e.g., Barkley, 1997). Such a concept renders questionable several of the premises of SI-based intervention (e.g., its use to extend attention span or simply to "slow" responses that are too fast) and places a premium on interventions that can foster controls on disinhibitory processes and behaviors. The full impact of such a reconceptualization on the development of innovative treatment strategies has not been felt.

A third line of research has amplified some of the limitations of medication treatments for the social difficulties of youngsters with ADHD. Specifically, even though stimulant treatments normalize such socially disruptive behavior patterns as physical and verbal aggression in classroom and playground settings (see Hinshaw, 1991), these pharmacological agents do not appear to produce comparably powerful effects on social reputations themselves (Hinshaw & McHale, 1991). Thus, although peer sociometric assessments show improvement when ADHD children receive stimulant medication as opposed to placebo, the gains fall short of clinical significance (e.g., Whalen et al., 1989). Peers may well be the "toughest audience" for detection of treatment-related gains. Interventions that serve chiefly to reduce problem behavior are not likely to be sufficient to promote full social competence; adjunctive psychosocial treatment strategies are necessary to produce clinically sufficient interventions for the crucial domain of interpersonal interactions (Hinshaw, 1992b).

Goals for Intervention Program

The goals and aims of the research program that I have pursued for two decades follow directly from the information presented above.

1. Because both traditional behavioral procedures and medication fail to provide lasting benefits for children with ADHD, the extension of behavioral treatments through mediational procedures designed to promote and extend the effects of contingency management strategies continues to be an important goal. Thus, an initial aim has been to understand whether specific mediational components (e.g., training in self-evaluation) can extend the benefits of operant behavioral procedures. Conversely, another aim has been to discover whether interventions that are behavioral in nature (e.g., graduated rehearsal of social skills) can enhance purely cognitive, mediational procedures for such important targets as anger control. The overriding objective is to develop integrated cognitive–behavioral treatments to self-management.

2. I have attempted to contrast the effectiveness of such cognitive–behavioral procedures with the gains in social relationships that accrue to medication interventions. Although investigations that compare psychosocial and pharmacological treatments are fraught with conceptual and methodological difficulties, the goal is an important one.

3. In keeping with the trend toward integration of medication treatment with psychosocial therapies, an additional goal has been to ascertain the combined efficacy of medication and self-management–based cognitive–behavioral intervention strategies. Indeed, given increasing evidence for the tenacity and persistence of ADHD-related symptomatology and accompanying impairment, and given the evidence for the clinical insufficiencies of either modality alone, attempts to integrate validated psychosocial procedures with pharmacological treatments are crucial endeavors.

As a graduate student, I was quite fortunate to have, as mentors for research and as guides for subsequent work, the influential research team headed by Barbara Henker of the University of California, Los Angeles, and Carol K. Whalen of the University of California, Irvine. Among many other contributions, their work has emphasized the social and ecological nature of the problems encountered by children with ADHD and the critical importance of understanding the interpersonal difficulties of hyperactive children (e.g., Whalen & Henker, 1992). Their influence also fostered an appreciation for the need to comprehend underlying mechanisms of psychopathology, work that I pursue actively (e.g., Hinshaw, 1987, 1992a). On the heels of a treatment study contrasting traditional behavioral interventions with cognitive–behavioral self-instructional treatments (Bugental, Whalen, & Henker, 1977), the team encouraged efforts to develop and implement self-management-oriented treatments for hyperactive youngsters.

The first investigations occurred during an after-school, clinic-based treatment program. Resulting from this work was a treatment manual (Hinshaw, Alkus, Whalen, & Henker, 1979) that incorporated elements of self-instructional training, problem-solving therapy, exercises to enhance self-evaluation abilities, and the explicit teaching of anger-management skills. From this early work came an appreciation of the critical need to perform self-management therapy in a group format; attempting to teach crucial self-management techniques to children individually does not allow either the appropriate level of affect or the opportunity for practice of social skills within the peer group (see Pfiffner & McBurnett, 1997). In addition, exposure to difficult group interactions fostered deeper interest in aggressive behavior and the clinically compelling processes involved in peer rejection.[1]

Because several components of this intervention showed particular promise, I then emphasized systematic evaluation of specific facets of training for self-evaluation and anger management. Work with the resulting manual (Hinshaw, Henker, & Whalen, 1981) yielded several empirical reports in which (a) the relative efficacy of behavioral versus cognitive components of self-management training were evaluated and (b) combinations of the psychosocial treatments with stimulant medication were performed.

At this point, self-evaluation and anger-management components were incorporated into the comprehensive curricula of (a) James Swanson at the day school program at the University of California, Irvine; (b) Russell Barkley for the comprehensive kindergarten curriculum in Massachusetts, discussed in Barkley et al. (2000), and (c) William Pelham in the Summer Treatment Program at the University of Pittsburgh (and now SUNY Buffalo; see Pelham & Hoza, 1996). In addition, I received funding from NIMH to examine the effects of medication with and without systematic clinic-based therapy (involving both parent management training plus child group treatment in self-management). Because, however, externalizing behavior patterns may be more akin to "chronic disease states" than to

---

[1]Pilot work in self-management training provided a sobering lesson in the importance of therapeutic work with children displaying impulse-control problems. In working with a cognitive–behavioral protocol as a first-year graduate student, I served as a therapist for a group of three boys from an elementary school, one of whom had been identified by school personnel as "impulsive." He was an 11-year-old boy with an IQ of approximately 130 but with serious parent- and teacher-reported impulse control problems. Some months later, following this brief intervention, I saw this youngster during a chance encounter in the community, with his hand severely bandaged. Despite warnings to the contrary, he had been playing with air compression pumps in the family garage and had literally blown off several fingers of one hand when the pump exploded. ADHD-related problems can therefore lead to extreme health consequences; self-regulation skills are clearly of major clinical importance.

358   STEPHEN P. HINSHAW

short-term infectious illnesses (see Kazdin, 1987), it is essential to evaluate intensive and long-term interventions that purport to effect socially competent functioning. Hence, the Multimodal Treatment Study of Children with ADHD (MTA Study; MTA Cooperative Group, 1999a) included the Summer Treatment Program model of Pelham and Hoza (1996), which, as just noted, incorporates the anger-management and self-evaluation components developed during earlier phases of my research.

Participants and Assessments

For all of the projects described herein, children were selected on the basis of stringent criteria for hyperactivity, ADD, or ADHD, depending on the year of the investigation. In other words, the samples comprised children of grade-school age (roughly 6 to 12 years of age), with intelligence in the normal range, who met inclusionary and exclusionary criteria for the disorder. Thus, youngsters with overt neurological handicaps, pervasive developmental disorders, psychosis, or severe emotional disturbance were excluded. To be included, a persistent pattern (extending for at least 6 months, with onset before 7 years of age) of inattention, impulsivity, and overactivity in home and school settings was required (American Psychiatric Association, 1994).

In addition, for most of the investigations discussed herein (with the exception of the MTA study), children were receiving stimulant medication in the community for at least 4 months before our work with them. Because of the previously medicated nature of the various samples, the children under investigation have been quite likely to respond positively to stimulant medication. Thus, any effects of psychosocial intervention, either alone or in combination with medication treatment, have been found in samples that are displaying a positive response to stimulants.

As is typical of clinical samples of children with ADHD, approximately half of the children met criteria for comorbid externalizing disorders such as oppositional defiant disorder (ODD) or, more rarely, conduct disorder (CD). Such comorbidity is quite important, given that many of the therapeutic interventions are targeted toward such interpersonal difficulties as anger control and overt aggression. The peer relations, family histories, and prognoses of children with overlapping ADHD and aggression are universally poor (Hinshaw, 1987); evaluating intervention strategies for this severely impaired subgroup is a major priority for the field (Hinshaw, 2000).

A limitation of the samples investigated is their largely or exclusively male composition (the MTA investigation does, however, include 20% girls). Certainly, males far outnumber females among clinical referrals for ADHD; it is quite difficult, for logistical and ethical reasons, to include a small number of girls in summer research programs or group-oriented treatment projects for youngsters with ADHD. Deliberate oversampling of girls would be a useful strategy in subsequent treatment programs (see Hinshaw, 2002b, for details of a large sample of preadolescent girls with ADHD under investigation by our laboratory).

Procedures

The types of self-management therapies under discussion have been performed in group therapy contexts. Small groups of 4 or 5 boys with ADHD meet, on a regular basis, with two leaders. The curricula have focused on a number of common goals, including the creation of a safe atmosphere for open disclosure and discussion of problems, the promotion of talk about the nature of ADHD and of medication treatments, and the regular rehearsal of cooperative social skills. The key components that have been put to empirical test—self-monitoring and self-evaluation skills, anger management exercises—are introduced only after a significant number of hours of initial trust building and relationship enhancement. Particularly with regard to the anger management assessments and training, in which children actively provoke and taunt one another with the end of fostering mutual self-control, group leaders must be sure that the exercises are performed after clear levels of trust and support have developed. On the other side of the coin, however, clinicians must remember that training will become a rather empty exercise (with no hope that the participants will eventually generalize their experiences) unless realistic levels of affect are produced. In other words, group leaders must maintain respect and safety while fostering realistic provocations from peers, a balance that is not always easy to maintain.

The training in self-management is fully integrated with established behavioral procedures. The participants receive regular systems of reinforcement during the therapy sessions, with contingencies in effect. Indeed, the work in self-evaluation explicitly integrates typical reinforcement programs with training in which the child learns to monitor his or her own behavior. Mediational procedures without the foundation of established behavioral procedures are simply not viable in samples composed of children with ADHD.

Many of the investigations described herein have occurred during summer research programs, settings in which relatively large numbers of boys with ADHD and comparison-group boys interact in class, playground, and small-group settings. A major advantage is that procedures learned during therapy groups can be evaluated through rigorous observational methodology in naturalistic settings that place a premium on social interchange. Indeed, given the short-term nature of most of the therapeutic interventions evaluated to date, perhaps the most important contributions from the overall research program relate to the various assessment measures that have been created to capture important peer interactions as well as the display of aggressive and antisocial behavior.

Intervention Components

Because of space limitations, the focus herein is on the two most validated components of the self-management protocols: (a) training in self-monitoring and self-evaluation and (b) anger management therapy.

Self-Evaluation Skills

Borrowing heavily from the careful work at Stony Brook of Drabman, Spitalnik, and O'Leary (1973) and Turkewitz, O'Leary, and Ironsmith (1975), I adapted exercises for the explicit teaching of self-monitoring and self-evaluation skills. Children with ADHD are notorious for the inaccuracy of self-reports of their own behavior: The intercorrelation between self-reported aggression and objectively observed aggression in the author's laboratory is $r = .44$ for boys in the control group and nearly zero for boys with ADHD. The hypothesis is that fostering accurate self-evaluation may help to promote more appropriate social behavior in class, play, and home settings.

The group begins by discussing a certain behavioral criterion (e.g., cooperation, paying attention) for the next period of activity. Specific examples, both positive and negative, are discussed and modeled; an operational definition of the criterion behavior is written out. As noted above, children receive reinforcement points at regular intervals for appropriate actions during the groups so that the newly defined behaviors can be specifically consequated. Next, self-monitoring and self-evaluation are taught using the "Match Game." Specifically, when it is time for the group leaders to give points at the end of a given interval, each child completes a self-evaluation form that lists the behavioral criterion of interest and a 5-point scale ranging from 1 (pretty bad) to 5 (great). As the adults privately complete their ratings of each child's performance in relation to the criterion, each child simultaneously rates himself or herself, attempting to appraise and match the adult rating. The essential part of the training occurs during the ensuing discussion: After each child reveals his or her reasons for the self-rating, the leaders present *their* rating and rationale. The objective here is to foster children's enhanced awareness of specific behaviors they have just performed.

To reinforce the accuracy of self-evaluation, extra points in the reinforcement system are given initially for the child's accurate matching, regardless of the value of the rating. Eventually, the extra reinforcement should require both a "match" *and* a rating above a certain, preannounced threshold. Without this added criterion, some children will learn to manipulate the system by intentionally misbehaving and earning full rewards by presenting a self-rating of "1." The Match Game can accompany nearly any academic, social, or solitary task of the child. It is intended to be repeated,

initially with high frequency and then faded to a less frequent schedule,throughout the group therapy. Eventually, parents and teachers can use
Match Game procedures to extend the benefits of reinforcement procedures
at home and school. For example, once a Daily Report Card system is
enacted in clinical behavior therapy, through which reinforcers at home are
earned for progress toward individualized behaviors at school, the child may
be able to self-evaluate with respect to the teacher's daily ratings.

Anger Management Training

Because of the severe peer-related difficulties encountered by most
youngsters with ADHD—particularly the repeated cycles of taunting from
peers and retaliatory aggression from the diagnosed child—I developed and
subsequently modified a curriculum to deal specifically with the enhancement
of anger control. The curriculum was strongly influenced by the theoretical
and empirical work of Novaco (1979) on anger management training for
adults; as such, it employs affective, cognitive, and behavioral components
designed to foster (a) recognition of internal and external cures signaling
incipient anger, (b) deployment of cognitive and behavioral strategies to
counteract the anger and ensuing aggressive responses, and (c) graduated
rehearsal of the chosen plans under increasingly realistic provocations from
peers (see Hinshaw et al., 1981).

The curriculum begins as each child reveals upsetting names and
phrases. Clearly, a safe atmosphere is necessary to foster meaningful disclosure along these lines. Group leaders must point out that, with the child's
permission, such phrases will later be used by the rest of the group to help
the child practice self-control (see the section on outcome measures later in
this chapter). Indeed, concepts of self-control are discussed by the group
before the specific training exercises.

In these specific strategies, the first skill taught is recognition of one's
own signs of impending anger. This exercise is particularly difficult for
younger children, but preadolescents can learn to recognize their own emotional, verbal, or behavioral cues. Next, each child selects, with guidance
from the leaders, a particular cognitive or behavioral strategy to employ
when provoked or teased. The goal here is not necessarily to prevent fighting back if retaliation is warranted. Rather, because of the impulsive tendencies of children with ADHD, the mediational strategies and alternative
responses are taught to foster the child's ability to choose a desired response,
in the hope of decreasing escalating cycles of impulsive fighting and resul-
tant peer rejection. Third, and critically, the chosen strategy is rehearsed
under increasingly realistic provocations from other members of the group.
It is important to note that reinforcement from the adult leaders—and self-
monitoring and self-evaluation of the child's new attempts at self-control—
are important therapeutic features of the curriculum.

Developmental issues are quite salient in anger-management training. Younger children are likely to select overt behavioral strategies to counteract provocation, whereas children approaching adolescence often prefer self-talk or other mediational approaches to aid with their self-control. Group leaders must be familiar with the types of strategies that children of differing ages are likely to select and implement.

Outcome Measures

Because the aims of the self-management therapies just described are to enhance social competence through reduction of negative and aggressive behaviors and the promotion of alternatives to retaliation, the use of outcome measures that directly tap both externalizing behaviors and more explicitly prosocial alternatives is critical. Thus, I have emphasized the development of observational methodologies that can tap specific behavioral responses. Although broader measures of social competence, including sociometric appraisals, are necessary for the evaluation of longer-term comprehensive therapy packages, the focus herein is on naturalistic, clinic-based, and laboratory-appropriate observational methodologies.

Live Observations of Social Behavior

A key goal for self-evaluation training is to promote improved social behavior with peers and adults beyond the therapy group—for instance, in classroom and playground situations. Yet appraising behavior change in relatively large social settings is fraught with difficulty, particularly because of the logistical problems inherent in making discrete, objective behavior counts across wide areas and in obtaining sufficient density of observations for each child in a setting as large as a classroom (with 20 or more classmates). Indeed, videotape coding is typically precluded when one is observing groups of this size.

Live observational procedures in this program of research began with the scan-sampled observation system of Hinshaw, Henker, and Whalen (1984a), in which teams of observers made extremely brief, sequential observations of children in repeated cycles throughout a class or play period. Because of the brief periods of observation—long enough for the observer to code a particular behavior before moving on to the next child—the number of categories was limited to broad classes of appropriate social behavior, negative social behavior, and nonsocial behavior. I subsequently modified this system to incorporate expansion of the number of codes, with negative social behavior subdivided into categories of physical and verbal aggression as well as noncompliance. These systems proved quite responsive to effects of both psychosocial and pharmacological interventions (Hinshaw, 1991; Hinshaw et al., 1984a). Yet the unpaced nature of the observations placed limits on code reliability.

I then reconfigured the system into a brief time-sampling procedure, in which observers (paced by headphones) have 3 or 4 seconds to find the child on their rosters, 3 seconds to observe, and 4 additional seconds to record the social behavior of interest (Hinshaw, 2002b). By this means, observers are yoked to the precise pacing schedule. Occurrence-only interobserver agreement figures are quite respectable with this system. Furthermore, the codes have served as important measures in nonintervention studies as well. For example, in Erhardt and Hinshaw (1994), aggression and prosocial behavior were important predictors of the initial peer status of children with ADHD. In Anderson, Hinshaw, and Simmel (1994), noncompliance was predicted by negative maternal behavior displayed during parent–child interactions, even with the child's level of negative and noncompliant behavior during the interaction statistically controlled. Finally, in Lee and Hinshaw (2004), noncompliance codes predicted the serenity of adolescent delinquency 5 to 7 years later in a longitudinal analysis.

Verbal Provocation Assessments of Anger Control

As a first-stage appraisal of the effects of the anger-management therapy procedures described earlier, I have devised verbal provocation assessments for the therapy groups in which training is performed. Specifically, using the upsetting names disclosed by each participant, the remainder of the group prepares to taunt the "target" child, who leaves the room during the group's preparations. When the target child returns, he or she sits in the middle of the group, attempting to withstand their taunts for a period of 1 or 2 minutes. Each successive session is videotaped, allowing subsequent coding of anger, aggressive retaliation, and the use of alternative coping strategies for self-control (see Hinshaw, Buhrmester, & Heller, 1989; Hinshaw, Henker, & Whalen, 1984b), plus more global codes of overall self-management.

In enforcing rules against touching and physical aggression, leaders must strike a balance between overexuberant provocation, on the one hand, and sterile, emotionless taunting on the other. Indeed, unless some real affect is generated in the assessments and in the rehearsal-based portions of the therapy, the procedures will have little likelihood of transcending mere cognitive exercises. A key goal for future research is to devise more naturalistic appraisals of response to provocation.

Laboratory Assessment of Covert Antisocial Behavior

Although it is not yet tied to outcomes of psychosocial therapy research, I devised an assessment procedure for appraising stealing, property destruction, and cheating in order to have a behaviorally specific referent for these acts of "covert," or clandestine, antisocial activity. Investigators in the field have long noted the distinction between overt (e.g., aggressive, defiant) and covert (e.g., stealing, firesetting, lying) manifestations (e.g., Loeber & Schmaling, 1985). In fact, covert antisocial behavior is a key predictor of later delin-quency. Yet such behavior occurs with a low base rate, and covert actions are, by their very nature, difficult to observe. Furthermore, global ratings of this domain are likely to be insensitive to longitudinal or therapeutic change and are quite likely to be conflated with overt aggression (Hinshaw, Simmel, & Heller, 1995). To redress the paucity of laboratory empirical data on covert behaviors, I devised an individual laboratory assessment in which children perform, in solitary fashion, worksheets geared to their developmental level.

In the room, small amounts of money and toys are left in view, and the experimenter leaves the answer key in the room (see Hinshaw, Heller, & McHale, 1992, for details). The amounts taken, the extent of property damage (e.g., destroyed classroom materials, graffiti), and evidence of cheat-ing can be coded from products left in the room (in early studies, surrepti-tious videotaping enhanced coding). Measures of stealing and property destruction show concurrent validity with parent and teacher ratings of covert or delinquent actions and with global staff appraisals; they form an empirical factor that is distinct from overt aggression and is far more likely to be shown by children with ADHD as opposed to nondiagnosed youths (Hinshaw et al., 1995). Furthermore, stealing and property destruction are dramatically reduced to normalized levels with stimulant medication (Hin-shaw, Heller, & McHale, 1992). Interestingly, however, cheating *increased* with medication treatment, possibly as a result of the participants' enhanced achievement motivation. Finally, the stealing variable was pre-dicted from maternal negativity during parent–child interactions that occurred before the summer program (Anderson et al., 1994); it also pre-dicts peer rejection (Hinshaw, Zupan, Simmel, Nigg, & Melnick, 1997) and severity of delinquency 5 to 7 years later (Lee & Hinshaw, 2004). In all, this brief laboratory assessment is a promising tool for needed multisource per-spectives on covert antisocial behaviors (Hinshaw et al., 1995).

Treatment Effectiveness

Self-Evaluation, Token Reinforcement, and Stimulant Medication

Hinshaw et al. (1984a) assessed the effects of adding the Match Game self-evaluation procedure to typical token reinforcement for boys with *Diag-nostic and Statistical Manual of Mental Disorders, Third Edition* (DSM–III) ADD with hyperactivity. Also, to ascertain the additive effects of medica-tion with the cognitive–behavioral self-evaluation procedure, children received either methylphenidate or a placebo. Results were assessed in the classroom and playground settings of a summer research program, with the scan-sampled observational system described previously.

After approximately 20 hours of group therapy, in which Match Game procedures had been taught and extensively practiced, boys with ADD were assigned to medication (low doses of methylphenidate) or placebo conditions for a 2-day evaluation period of naturalistic observations. Boys alternated between token reinforcement only and token reinforcement plus the addition of the Match Game; in both conditions, reinforcement was contingent on cooperative social behavior. In the Match Game condition, full reward value could be obtained only through accurate self-evaluation during each interval. No effects of the cognitive–behavioral procedure appeared in the classroom setting. On the playground, however, the following results were noted: (a) Medication was associated with fewer negative interactions than was placebo; (b) reinforced self-evaluation (Match Game plus points) yielded fewer negative interactions than did points alone; and (c) the combination of medication plus reinforced self-evaluation led to levels of social behavior that were identical to those of the boys in the comparison group. Thus, during the brief evaluation period, adding a cognitive mediational component enhanced social behavior relative to reinforcement alone, and at least in terms of rank ordering, the combination of pharmacological and cognitive–behavioral treatments produced the greatest benefit. Only this latter combination, in fact, brought levels of negative social behavior below those of the comparison boys. These results suggest strongly that the effects of behavioral reinforcement procedures can be extended through use of mediational strategies that aim to promote more active self-awareness. A valuable goal for subsequent research would be to ascertain the extent to which more extensive use of self-evaluation training—along with other cognitive–behavioral strategies—could extend the benefits of traditional reinforcement programs. In other words, the aim would not be to replace validated behavioral procedures with exclusively cognitive techniques but to integrate them with reinforcement, toward the goal of maintaining behavioral and interpersonal gains.

Anger Management Training

The initial test of the anger management curriculum took place in the afterschool treatment program described previously. In this uncontrolled evaluation, hyperactive youngsters displayed reductions in retaliation and increases in self-control following intervention (Hinshaw et al., 1984b). On the basis of these results, a controlled trial was next performed during a summer research program. Children with ADD were assigned randomly to receive (a) the cognitive–behavioral anger-management curriculum versus (b) a control condition comprising cognitive procedures (discussions of empathy and perspective-taking) but without active rehearsal of coping responses. Furthermore, this therapy manipulation was crossed with stimulant medication versus placebo status during both the treatment and evaluation procedures. Whereas low dosages of methylphenidate failed to produce any change in the posttreatment provocation assessments, the rehearsal-based cognitive–behavioral training proved superior to the cognitive-only intervention with respect to coping responses, reduction of retaliation, and global self-control (Hinshaw et al., 1984b). Within the limits of an immediate posttreatment assessment that took place in the same groups in which the training had occurred, integrated mediational–behavioral intervention procedures proved superior to methylphenidate regarding outcome domains linked to anger control.

In a partial replication, Hinshaw, Buhrmester, and Heller (1989) provided the cognitive–behavioral anger-management training to a new sample. In posttreatment verbal provocation assessments, the boys were assigned randomly to placebo versus moderate (0.6 mg/kg) dosages of methylphenidate. Here, medication facilitated the enhanced display of self-control and aggression reduction relative to placebo. Stimulant medication may therefore enable youngsters with ADHD to use previously learned cognitive–behavioral skills to display self-management; for the domain of anger control, moderate dosage levels of the pharmacological intervention may be necessary (see Hinshaw, 1991). The suggestion is that combinations of psychosocial and pharmacological treatments may yield optimal performance of critical social skills.

Strength of Effects

The within-subject nature of the comparisons between cognitive–behavioral and control conditions in the previously described research makes it difficult to use traditional measures of effect size to gauge the strength of benefits of these interventions. A more sensible and intuitive means of portraying the strength of effects for Hinshaw et al. (1984a) is to calculate the numbers of participants who showed improved levels of negative social behavior under the reinforced self-evaluation conditions versus the regular token-reinforcement conditions. Of the 21 boys with complete data, 14 showed optimal improvement with the self-evaluation procedures, 6 with the behavioral reinforcement alone, and 1 was equal in both conditions. As for enhancing appropriate social behavior, the respective numbers were 15 and 6. Thus, the self-evaluation condition led to 40% to 45% increments in success rate (see Hinshaw et al., 1984a, for details). On the other hand, in this same investigation, with respect to the absolute levels of negative social behavior displayed on the playground, the medication versus placebo change was from a mean of 10.40 instances to 5.68, an improvement of 45%; whereas the reinforced self-evaluation versus reinforcement only change was from a mean of 9.41 instances to 6.83, an improvement of 27%. Finally, and crucially, as noted above, the best indicator of overall improvement may lie in the domain of normative comparisons. Here, only the combination of medication plus reinforced self-evaluation led to rates of negative social behavior that were indistinguishable from those displayed by the boys in the comparison group.

In the study by Hinshaw et al. (1984b), one means of portraying the strength of the effect is to contrast the boys' overall scores on the global, 1-to-5–point "self-control" scale used by the raters (unaware of treatment condition) who coded videotaped responses to the provocations. For this scale, "1" signified aggressive, out-of-control reactions to the provocations, whereas "5" signaled optimal management of affect and the use of proactive strategies to combat the effects of the teasing. Here, the boys receiving the cognitive–behavioral anger-management training program improved from a mean score of 2.73 before intervention to 4.73 (nearly ideal self-control) after training, whereas the boys receiving the control intervention (that excluded active rehearsal in anger-management strategies) showed comparable mean ratings of 2.46 and 3.00. Thus, their improvement was minimal, with the mean level of "3" on the rating scale still indicating considerable problems in emotion regulation. In addition, the boys receiving the full intervention showed a rate of "purposeful alternate activities" in their posttreatment evaluations that was double that of the control participants. Thus, in this case, the active psychosocial intervention led to effects that were large and noticeable. Medication effects were nearly nonexistent in this paradigm; as indicated above, it may take larger dosage levels to achieve benefit for such social behaviors (Hinshaw et al., 1989). Yet in the absence of systematic probes for generalization and maintenance, the clinical significance of the anger management procedures cannot be proved.

Multimodal Treatments

Space does not permit a complete description of the efficacy and effectiveness of the multimodal treatment packages into which the previously described self-evaluation and anger-management procedures have been embedded. For relevant findings, see Barkley et al. (2000), MTA Cooperative Group (1999a, 1999b), and Pelham and Hoza (1996); for a current review, see Hinshaw et al. (2002). I point out, however, that the evaluation of multicomponent packages makes it difficult, if not impossible, to discern the benefits of specific treatment components unless dismantling studies are specifically undertaken. Also, as noted earlier, the effects of such multicomponent behavioral treatments are smaller than those from well-monitored pharmacological interventions, although a combination of these treatments and medication yields outcomes that approach clinical significance.

Therapist Measures

In the research discussed herein, group sessions are audiotaped or videotaped, affording careful appraisal of not only the group process but also the therapist's adherence to the protocol and competence in delivering the manualized interventions. I also point out that in the research described in

Hinshaw et al. (1984a, 1984b), the extensively trained and supervised graduate student therapists all participated in both the experimental and control treatments. Thus, it was the manualized treatment strategies per se and not the influence of particular therapist skills that yielded the positive outcomes that were found. In all, far more work is necessary to ensure that group therapists of cognitive–behavioral, self-management interventions for children with disruptive behavior disorders are adequately selected, trained, supervised, and monitored during the course of treatment.

Clinical Vignette

Travis [name changed] was 10.5 years old when he participated in one of the previously mentioned investigations of anger-management treatment. It is noteworthy that although he met full criteria for ADHD, he did not meet diagnostic criteria for ODD or CD. Indeed, program staff in general regarded Travis as a polite boy with excellent intentions but one whose inattention, disorganization, and impulsive style sometimes landed him in trouble.

One salient fact is that Travis had been adopted at an early age. Indeed, adoption is a frequent occurrence in the life histories of children with both ADHD and the other disruptive behavior disorders (Simmel, Brooks, Barth, & Hinshaw, 2001). Travis's adoptive parents were well educated and extremely earnest in their intentions to help their son and his difficulties with ADHD. During the early stages of self-control training, Travis appeared to relate well to his five compatriots in the group. At the time of the crucial session in which participants were asked to disclose those names that might upset them in the subsequent anger-control sessions, this boy eventually divulged that it sometimes made him angry when other kids teased him about being adopted. Again, this disclosure was made in the full knowledge that the words and names on the list would be used by the other children in the forthcoming group sessions, as a means of trying to provoke each child in turn and encourage him or her to use anger-management skills.

Over the next week of sessions (which were held daily in this program), Travis readily learned the "Match Game" in preparation for a separate evaluation of self-evaluation skills. His cooperation with the group was strong. Soon, it was time for the first "behavioral test"—the assessment trial held before the specific anger-management intervention began, in which the each child took turns spending 1.5 minutes in the "hot seat" at the center of the group, listening to group members' provocations derived from the names disclosed during the earlier session. Travis had been picked, by lot, to go third in this round-robin assessment session so that he was able to witness both a rather calm, self-controlled "model" and one whose levels of anger at the taunts was visibly higher. Just before it was Travis's turn to take the hot seat, he intimated to one of the group leaders that he was sure that the taunts and provocations would not be overly stressful because he knew that he was being videotaped and that the provocations were staged.

His prediction held true for the first 20 seconds or so of the assessment trial; he smiled placidly as the members of his peer group used names from his list in an attempt to upset him. He even weathered the term "adopted boy" with equanimity. Suddenly, however, one of the group members decided to "improvise" with his teasing, an inevitability in group sessions for children with ADHD, no matter how vigilantly group leaders monitor the process. This peer called out, in a loud voice that carried above those of the four other provocateurs, that the target boy's adoptive mother was a "b___ " (rhymes with "rich").

As the camera faithfully recorded, a brief pause ensued, during which time the group leaders registered this unexpected epithet and began to intervene by letting the provocateur know that he had stepped over the line. Within the next few seconds, however, an enraged Travis had leaped from his chair, grabbing the provocateur by the neck. The group leaders quickly separated the boys, reminded the group members that they could use only the words on the list for their teasing, and attempted to continue the assessment. But Travis was still furious and dumbfounded, hardly believing that his reaction had been so quick and violent.

In one sense, this unexpected turn of events was quite unfortunate, demonstrating that even the most carefully scripted assessments can quickly capsize in dealings with children referred for major problems with impulse control. At another level, however, it captured a clinical reality that is often not seen in the role-playing confines of group treatments for social skill or anger management. Although Travis was clearly miffed at this sudden turn of events, he became extremely motivated during subsequent training procedures in anger management to learn more about self-control. He seemed to realize that the safety and support of the videotaped and heavily supervised assessment session might not be duplicated in a comparable but unscripted session at school or in the neighborhood. The hope is that this vignette can impress upon readers the clinical gravity of the decision to undertake meaningful intervention for social competence among children with ADHD.

Limitations and Generalizability

As has been highlighted throughout this chapter, cognitive interventions for children with ADHD that are not explicitly linked to validated behavioral procedures are doomed to clinical failure. Self-instructional strategies should therefore *not* be used as primary treatment strategies for this population, and no one should expect that interventions based on social problem-solving or perspective-taking training alone will provide meaningful clinical benefit. Youngsters with ADHD—particularly those with co-occurring aggression—are particularly refractory to all but the most powerful treatment strategies (Hinshaw, 2000). Self-management treatments may be optimal for extending the benefits that can accrue to behavioral intervention.

In short, no clinically sufficient treatment strategies have yet been developed or validated for children with the difficult constellation of problems comprising ADHD. Thus, whereas self-management interventions share the same clinical limitations as other treatments, the hope is that they can be intentionally tied to reinforcement procedures and family treatments to enhance socially competent behavior.

Can therapists in clinical practice provide meaningful treatment for children with attention deficits and hyperactivity? The answer is a qualified "yes": As long as practitioners are willing to expand upon traditional notions of both assessment (i.e., by moving beyond the usual clinic-based evaluations) and intervention (i.e., by working to shape home and school environments and to actively promote self-management), academic and social competence can be forged. The typical forms of one-on-one therapy will require supplementation with group-based treatments, and the child will need to become actively involved in collaborative treatment efforts with parents and teachers. Self-management treatments can certainly be adopted by community practitioners, but their effective use by clinicians will require flexibility and a willingness to make active outreach into home, school, and peer settings.

Future Directions

As noted earlier, theories regarding the social difficulties of children with ADHD emphasize that such youngsters do not typically display deficits in knowledge of social situations or even in fundamental social skills (e.g., Barkley, 1998; Whalen & Henker, 1992). Rather, their chief difficulties appear to relate to social performance in natural interpersonal contexts (Hinshaw, 1992b). Furthermore, youngsters with ADHD—particularly those with aggression—appear to have social agendas and goals different from those of their peers (Melnick & Hinshaw, 1996). Also recall that recent conceptions of ADHD emphasize disinhibitory psychopathology and poor delay of gratification rather than attentional deficits per se (Barkley, 1997). The upshot is that treatments focusing simply on the teaching of "social skills" will, in all likelihood, fail to produce meaningful change for this population. Interventions must therefore facilitate (a) reductions of the externalizing behaviors that quickly shape negative reputations (Erhardt & Hinshaw, 1994); (b) contextualized performance of skilled interpersonal behavior (Pfiffner & McBurnett, 1997); (c) enhancement of inhibitory strategies (e.g., anger management); and (d) reformulation of the goals that ADHD children have for social interchange. In short, traditional notions of social skills intervention and SI treatments require substantial change if we are to alter the often dismal social prognoses of children with ADHD.

What can practitioners in the community learn from this research? One key implication is that much of the individual focus of therapy should shift to consideration of group-based treatments. Of course, without careful supervision, exposure of acting-out youths to others with similar tendencies may actually promote deviant behavior (Dishion, McCord, & Poulin, 1999). However, teaching important social skills to children individually is nearly impossible; only in the peer group can needed skills be meaningfully rehearsed. Also, the peer group can provide a safe sounding board for fears, anxieties, and goals. To be sure, performing therapy in groups requires explicit training for generalization and maintenance, as is the case for individual therapy. The persistent social difficulties of youngsters with ADHD mandate thorough, consistent programming involving the support and training of important people in the child's everyday environment. The personal and social devastation incurred by the deficits and excesses associated with ADHD demands nothing less.

REFERENCES

Abikoff, H. (1991). Cognitive training in ADHD children: Less to it than meets the eye. *Journal of Learning Disabilities, 24*, 205–209.

American Psychiatric Association. (1994). *Diagnostic and statistical manual of mental disorders* (4th ed.). Washington, DC: Author.

Anderson, C. A., Hinshaw, S. P., & Simmel, C. (1994). Mother–child interactions in ADHD and comparison boys: Relationships to overt and covert externalizing behavior. *Journal of Abnormal Child Psychology, 22*, 247–265.

Asher, S. R., & Coie, J. D. (1990). *Peer rejection in childhood*. New York: Cambridge University Press.

Barkley, R. A. (1997). *ADHD and the nature of self-control*. New York: Guilford Press.

Barkley, R. A. (1998). *Attention deficit hyperactivity disorder: A handbook for diagnosis and treatment* (2nd ed.). New York: Guilford Press.

Barkley, R. A., Shelton, T. L., Crosswait, C., Moorehouse, M., Fletcher, K., Barrett, S., et al. (2000). Multi-method psycho-educational intervention for preschool children with disruptive behavior: Preliminary results at post-treatment. *Journal of Child Psychology and Psychiatry, 41*, 319–332.

Berk, L. E., & Potts, M. (1991). Development and functional significance of private speech among attention-deficit hyperactivity disordered and normal boys. *Journal of Abnormal Child Psychology, 19*, 357–377.

Bickett, L., & Milich, R. (1990). First impressions formed of boys with attention deficit disorder. *Journal of Learning Disabilities, 23*, 253–259.

Bradley, C. (1937). The behavior of children receiving benzedrine. *American Journal of Psychiatry, 94*, 577–585.

Bugental, D. B., Whalen, C. K., & Henker, B. (1977). Causal attributions of hyperactive children and motivational assumptions of two behavior change approaches: Evidence for an interactionist position. *Child Development, 48,* 874–884.

Conners, C. K., Epstein, J. N., March, J. S., Angold, A., Wells, R. C., Klaric, J., et al. (2001). Multimodal treatment of ADHD in the MTA: An alternative outcome analysis. *Journal of the American Academy of Child and Adolescent Psychiatry, 40* 159–167.

DeGrandpre, R., & Hinshaw, S. P. (2000). Attention-deficit hyperactivity disorder: Psychiatric problem or American cop-out? *Cerebrum: The Dana Foundation Journal on Brain Sciences, 2,* 12–38.

Dishion, T., McCord, J., & Poulin, F. (1999). When interventions harm: Peer groups and problem behavior. *American Psychologist, 54,* 755–764.

Douglas, V. I. (1983). Attention and cognitive problems. In M. Rutter (Ed.), *Developmental neuropsychiatry* (pp. 280–329). New York: Guilford Press.

Douglas, V. I., Parry, P., Marton, P., & Garson, C. (1976). Assessment of a cognitive training program for hyperactive children. *Journal of Abnormal Child Psychology, 4,* 389–410.

Drabman, R., Spitalnik, R., & O'Leary, K. D. (1973). Teaching self-control to disruptive children. *Journal of Abnormal Psychology, 82,* 10–16.

Erhardt, D., & Hinshaw, S. P. (1994). Initial sociometric impressions of ADHD and comparison boys: Predictions from social behaviors and from nonbehavioral variables. *Journal of Consulting and Clinical Psychology, 62,* 833–842.

Greenhill, L. L., & Osman, B. (Eds.). (2000). *Ritalin: Theory and practice* (2nd ed.). Larchmont, NY: Mary Ann Liebert.

Hinshaw, S. P. (1987). On the distinction between attentional deficits/hyperactivity and conduct problems/aggression in child psychopathology. *Psychological Bulletin, 101,* 443–463.

Hinshaw, S. P. (1991). Stimulant medication and the treatment of aggression in children with attentional deficits. *Journal of Clinical Child Psychology, 20,* 301–312.

Hinshaw, S. P. (1992a). Externalizing behavior problems and academic underachievement in childhood and adolescence: Causal relationships and underlying mechanisms. *Psychological Bulletin, 111,* 127–155.

Hinshaw, S. P. (1992b). Intervention for social skill and social competence. *Child and Adolescent Psychiatric Clinics of North America, 1,* 539–552.

Hinshaw, S. P. (1994). *Attention deficits and hyperactivity in children.* Thousand Oaks, CA: Sage.

Hinshaw, S. P. (2000). Attention-deficit hyperactivity disorder: The search for viable treatments. In P. C. Kendall (Ed.), *Child and adolescent therapy: Cognitive–behavioral procedures* (2nd ed., pp. 88–128). New York: Guilford Press.

Hinshaw, S. P. (2002a). Is ADHD an impairing condition in childhood and adolescence? In P. S. Jensen & J. R. Cooper (Eds.), *Attention-deficit hyperactivity* disorder: State of the science, best practices (pp. 5-1–5-21). Kingston, NJ: Civic Research Institute.

Hinshaw, S. P. (2002b). Preadolescent girls with attention-deficit/hyperactivity disorder: I. Background characteristics, comorbidity, cognitive and social functioning, and parenting practices. *Journal of Consulting and Clinical Psychology, 70,* 1086–1098.

Hinshaw, S. P., Alkus, S. P., Whalen, C. K., & Henker, B. (1979). *STAR Program training manual.* Unpublished manuscript, University of California, Los Angeles.

Hinshaw, S. P., Buhrmester, D., & Heller, T. (1989). Anger control in response to verbal provocation: Effects of stimulant medication for boys with ADHD. *Journal of Abnormal Child Psychology, 17,* 393–407.

Hinshaw, S. P., Heller, T., & McHale, J. P. (1992). Covert antisocial behavior in boys with attention-deficit hyperactivity disorder: External validation and effects of methylphenidate. *Journal of Consulting and Clinical Psychology, 60,* 274–281.

Hinshaw, S. P., Henker, B., & Whalen, C. K. (1981). *A cognitive–behavioral curriculum for group training of hyperactive boys.* Unpublished manuscript, University of California, Los Angeles.

Hinshaw, S. P., Henker, B., & Whalen, C. K. (1984a). Cognitive–behavioral and pharmacologic interventions for hyperactive boys: Comparative and combined effects. *Journal of Consulting and Clinical Psychology, 52,* 739–749.

Hinshaw, S. P., Henker, B., & Whalen, C. K. (1984b). Self-control in hyperactive boys in anger-inducing situations: Effects of cognitive–behavioral training and of methylphenidate. *Journal of Abnormal Child Psychology, 12,* 55–77.

Hinshaw, S. P., Klein, R. G., & Abikoff, H. B. (2002). Nonpharmacologic treatments for ADHD and their combination with medication. In P. E. Nathan & J. Gorman (Eds.), *A guide to treatments that work* (2nd ed., pp. 3–23). New York: Oxford University Press.

Hinshaw, S. P., & McHale, J. P. (1991). Stimulant medication and the social interactions of hyperactive children: Effects and implications. In D. G. Gilbert & J. J. Connolly (Eds.), *Personality, social skills, and psychopathology: An individual differences approach* (pp. 229–253). New York: Plenum Press.

Hinshaw, S. P., & Melnick, S. (1995). Peer relationships in children with attention-deficit hyper-activity disorder with and without comorbid aggression. *Development and Psychopathology, 7,* 627–647.

Hinshaw, S. P., Owens, E. B., Wells, K. C., Kraemer, H. C., Abikoff, H. B., Arnold, L. E., et al. (2000). Family processes and treatment outcome in the MTA: Negative/ineffective parenting practices in relation to multimodal treatment. *Journal of Abnormal Child Psychology, 28,* 555–568.

Hinshaw, S. P., Simmel, C., & Heller, T. (1995). Multimethod assessment of covert antisocial behavior in children: Laboratory observations, adult ratings, and child self-report. *Psychological Assessment, 7,* 209–219.

Hinshaw, S. P., Zupan, B. A., Simmel, C., Nigg, J. T., & Melnick, S. M. (1997). Peer status in boys with and without attention-deficit hyperactivity disorder:

Predictions from overt and covert antisocial behavior, social isolation, and authoritative parenting beliefs. *Child Development, 64,* 880–896.

Kazdin, A. E. (1987). Treatment of antisocial behavior in children: Current status and future directions. *Psychological Bulletin, 102,* 187–203.

Klein, R. G., & Abikoff, H. (1997). Behavior therapy and methylphenidate in the treatment of children with ADHD. *Journal of Attention Disorders, 2,* 89–114.

Lee, S., & Hinshaw, S. P. (2004). Severity of adolescent delinquency among boys with and without attention-deficit hyperactivity disorder: Predictions from early antisocial behavior and peer status. *Journal of Clinical Child and Adolescent Psychology, 33,* 705–716.

Loeber, R., & Schmaling, K. B. (1985). Empirical evidence for overt and covert patterns of antisocial conduct problems: A meta-analysis. *Journal of Abnormal Child Psychology, 13,* 337–352.

Mannuzza, S., & Klein, R. G. (1999). Adolescent and adult outcomes in attention/deficit hyperactivity disorder. In H. C. Quay & A. E. Hogan (Eds.), *Handbook of disruptive behavior disorders* (pp. 279–294). New York: Kluwer Academic/Plenum.

Meichenbaum, D. H. (1977). *Cognitive–behavior modification: An integrative approach.* New York: Plenum Press.

Melnick, S., & Hinshaw, S. P. (1996). What they want and what they get: Social goals and peer acceptance in ADHD and comparison boys. *Journal of Abnormal Child Psychology, 24,* 69–185.

MTA Cooperative Group. (1999a). Fourteen-month randomized clinical trial of treatment strategies for attention–deficit hyperactivity disorder. *Archives of General Psychiatry, 56,* 1073–1086.

MTA Cooperative Group. (1999b). Moderators and mediators of treatment response for children with ADHD: The MTA Study. *Archives of General Psychiatry, 56,* 1088–1096.

Novaco, R. W. (1979). The cognitive regulation of anger and stress. In P. C. Kendall & S. D. Hollon (Eds.), *Cognitive–behavioral interventions: Theory, research, and procedures* (pp. 241–285). New York: Academic Press.

Parker, J. G., & Asher, S. R. (1987). Peer relations and later personal adjustment: Are low-accepted children at risk? *Psychological Bulletin, 102,* 357–389.

Pelham, W. E., & Bender, M. E. (1982). Peer relationships in hyperactive children: Description and treatment. In K. Gadow & I. Bialer (Eds.), *Advances in learning and behavioral disabilities* (Vol. 1, pp. 365–436). Greenwich, CT: JAI Press.

Pelham, W. E., & Hinshaw, S. P. (1992). Behavioral intervention for ADHD. In S. M. Turner, K. S. Calhoun, & H. E. Adams (Eds.), *Handbook of clinical behavior therapy* (2nd ed., pp. 259–283). New York: Wiley.

Pelham, W. E., & Hoza, B. (1996). Intensive treatment: A summer treatment program for children with ADHD. In E. D. Hibbs & P. S. Jensen (Eds.), *Psychosocial treatments for child and adolescent disorders: Empirically based strategies for clinical practice* (pp. 311–340). Washington, DC: American Psychological Association Press.

Pfiffner, L., & McBurnett, K. (1997). Social skills training with parent generalization: Treatment effects for children with attention deficit disorder. *Journal of Consulting and Clinical Psychology, 65*, 749–757.

Schachar, R. (1986). Hyperkinetic syndrome: Historical development of the concept. In E. A. Taylor (Ed.), *The overactive child* (pp. 19–40). London: MacKeith.

Simmel, C., Brooks, D., Barth, R. P., & Hinshaw, S. P. (2001). Prevalence of externalizing symptomatology in an adoptive sample: Pre-adoption risk factors and post-adoption functioning. *Journal of Abnormal Child Psychology, 29*, 101–116.

Swanson, J. M., Kraemer, H. C., Hinshaw, S. P., Arnold, L. E., Conners, C. K., Abikoff, H. B., et al. (2001). Clinical relevance of the primary findings of the MTA: Success rates based on severity of ADHD and ODD symptoms at the end of treatment. *Journal of the American Academy of Child and Adolescent Psychiatry, 40*, 168–179.

Turkewitz, H., O'Leary, K. D., & Ironsmith, M. (1975). Generalization and maintenance of appropriate behavior through self-control. *Journal of Consulting and Clinical Psychology, 43*, 577–583.

Weiss, G., & Hechtman, L. T. (1993). *Hyperactive children grown up* (2nd ed.). New York: Guilford Press.

Wells, K. C., Epstein, J. N., Hinshaw, S. P., Conners, C. K., Klaric, J., Abikoff, H. B., et al. (2000). Parenting and family stress treatment outcomes in attention-deficit hyperactivity disorder (ADHD): An empirical analysis in the MTA study. *Journal of Abnormal Child Psychology, 28*, 543–553.

Whalen, C. K., & Henker, B. (1985). The social worlds of hyperactive (ADHD) children. *Clinical Psychology Review, 5*, 447–478.

Whalen, C. K., & Henker, B. (1992). The social profile of attention-deficit hyperactivity disorder: Five fundamental facets. *Child and Adolescent Psychiatric Clinics of North America, 1*, 395–410.

Whalen, C. K., Henker, B., Buhrmester, D., Hinshaw, S. P., Huber, A., & Laski, K. (1989). Does stimulant medication improve the peer status of hyperactive children? *Journal of Consulting and Clinical Psychology, 57*, 545–549.

16

THE ROLE OF SUMMER TREATMENT PROGRAMS IN THE CONTEXT OF COMPREHENSIVE TREATMENT FOR ATTENTION-DEFICIT/ HYPERACTIVITY DISORDER

WILLIAM E. PELHAM JR., GREGORY A. FABIANO,
ELIZABETH M. GNAGY, ANDREW R. GREINER, AND BETSY HOZA

Children with attention-deficit/hyperactivity disorder (ADHD) have difficulties in attention, impulse control, and activity-level modulation that lead to serious impairment in daily life functioning, among classmates, peers, and family members. It has become increasingly evident that ADHD

We owe thanks to the hundreds of individuals who have contributed to the development of the summer treatment program and who have worked in it over the past 20 years and replicated it in other settings. We also thank the administrations of Florida State University (Psychology Department), the University of Pittsburgh (Department of Psychiatry), and the University at Buffalo (Department of Psychology) for their support. During the work described in this chapter and during the preparation of this manuscript, the authors were supported by grants from the National Institute on Drug Abuse (DA05605, DA12414); the National Institute on Alcohol Abuse and Alcoholism (AA06267, AA11873); the National Institute on Neurological Disorders and Stroke (NS39087); the National Institute of Mental Health (MH48157, MH47390, MH45576, MH50467, MH53554); and Shire Laboratories, Noven Pharmaceuticals, and ALZA Corporation.

377

should be viewed as a chronic disorder and that models of treatment should correspond to those appropriate for a chronic disease (American Academy of Pediatrics, 2001). Indeed, ADHD is more destructive, more costly for health plans and the educational system, and associated with considerably poorer long-term outcomes than are other chronic diseases, such as asthma (Kelleher, 1998; Weiss & Hechtman, 1993). Thus, interventions must be intensive, implemented across settings, and structured so that they can be conducted for years (Pelham & Fabiano, 2000).

The most common form of treatment for ADHD is medication with central nervous system (CNS) stimulants. Although they have a large evidence base and often result in short-term improvements, these medications have limitations (Swanson, McBurnett, Christian, & Wigal, 1995). Primary among these is that parents strongly prefer behavioral interventions to pharmacological ones (e.g., Pelham, Burrows-MacLean, Gnagy, Fabiano, et al., 2004) and are therefore more likely to continue them in the long run, which is necessary given the chronic nature of ADHD. Furthermore, medication alone does not result in improved adolescent and adult outcomes when used as the sole form of intervention (Weiss & Hechtman, 1993).

The second most common treatment for ADHD is behavior modification in the form of parent training and school interventions. Like medication, behavior modification has a large evidence base and extensively documented short-term efficacy (Pelham, Wheeler, & Chronis, 1998), but it also has limitations. It is expensive relative to medication and more difficult to implement and therefore continue over the long run (Pelham & Waschbusch, 1999). Unlike medication, however, behavioral interventions can teach skills that overcome some of the functional impairments associated with ADHD.

Research has suggested that *combining* medication and behavioral treatments offers significant incremental benefits beyond either treatment alone, and this is often the treatment of choice for ADHD (Pelham & Murphy, 1986; Pelham & Waschbusch, 1999). Combining treatment approaches offers the potential of more effective treatments at lower, and therefore less costly and safer, doses (both pharmacological and behavioral). In addition, multimodal treatments may yield better adherence over time, an obvious requirement for an effective chronic model of treatment.

According to another emerging belief, relatively more intensive psychosocial treatment programs are necessary to produce substantive behavioral changes (Hoza, Pelham, Sams, & Carlson, 1992; Pelham & Fabiano, 2000). Thus, the recent Multimodal Treatment Study for Children With ADHD (MTA) employed a psychosocial treatment package consisting of a summer treatment program, with a year-long behavioral school intervention and year-long parent training (Wells et al., 2000). A similar conclusion has been the consensus with regard to childhood conduct disorders (CD), which overlap with ADHD. Contemporary interventions for CD incorporate home, school, and peer environments and are implemented over years (e.g., Conduct Problems Prevention Group, 1999a, 1999b).

We have developed a comprehensive approach to the treatment of ADHD that is designed to overcome the limitations of existing interventions. We believe that an effective intervention for ADHD must focus on the child, the school, and the parents. Comprehensive treatments always include behavioral interventions and often include adjunctive pharmacological approaches, intensively implemented over long periods. Exhibit 16.1 lists key aspects of what we believe to be a comprehensive approach to intervention for ADHD.

As shown in Exhibit 16.1, our procedures for working with teachers and parents incorporate behavioral approaches that have been used for decades (e.g., O'Leary & O'Leary, 1977; Patterson, 1974), take a chronic approach to treatment, and focus on a broad view of the child's problems. In addition, our approach has three unique aspects. First, we believe that the role of medication, although important for many children, is most often that of an adjunctive, second-line treatment. Therefore, we begin intervention with a behavioral approach, adding medication when behavioral interventions are insufficient because of the severity of the problem, parent preferences, or resource limitations on the part of families or schools. Second, we focus our interventions on children's functional impairments rather than the *Diagnostic and Statistical Manual of Mental Disorders* (DSM) symptoms of the disorder. Finally, and most germane to this chapter, is our emphasis on intensive work with children with ADHD during the summers. Two issues are particularly relevant for this discussion: What should be the focus of treatment for ADHD, and why should summer programs be added to the treatment mix?

The first consideration in developing treatments for ADHD is selecting the targets of treatment. Many current researchers prefer to focus on reduction in DSM symptoms of the disorder (e.g., MTA Cooperative Group, 1999). However, we have argued that various domains of functional impairment are far more important to both short- and long-term functioning in ADHD than are symptoms and should be foremost among measures of treatment outcome (Pelham, 2001; Pelham & Fabiano, 2000, 2001). Parents seek out and obtain clinical services because of psychosocial impairment, regardless of diagnostic status (Angold, Costello, Farmer, Burns, & Erkanli, 1999). Further, impairment in peer relationships, parent–child interactions, and academic functioning predict a variety of negative long-term outcomes (Chamberlain & Patterson, 1995; Coie & Dodge, 1998; Lyon & Cutting, 1998). It is these areas of impairment rather than DSM symptoms that need to be explicitly targeted in treatment.

For example, difficulties in peer relations have long been among the most salient referring problems for children with ADHD (Pelham & Bender, 1982). Furthermore, problems in peer relations are among the problems for which standard ADHD treatments—such as traditional, office-

EXHIBIT 16.1
Comprehensive Treatment for
Attention-Deficit/Hyperactivity Disorder

Parent training

(a) Behavioral approach
(b) Focus on parenting skills, child behavior in the home and neighborhood, and family relationships (e.g., getting along with siblings, complying with parent requests)
(c) Skills taught to parents by therapists and implemented at home
(d) Typically group-based, weekly sessions with therapist initially (8–12 sessions); then faded to booster sessions (monthly, quarterly)
(e) Continual evaluation and modification of what is being done to identify what works best
(f) Plan for what will be done if parents or child backslides
(g) Contact reestablished with therapist for major developmental transitions (e.g., entry to middle school)

School Intervention

(a) Behavioral approach
(b) Focus on classroom behavior, academic performance, and peer relationships
(c) Teachers taught classroom management skills by a consultant (e.g., therapist, school psychologist or counselor); skills implemented with the child during school hours
(d) Two to 10 hours of training depending on the teacher's prior knowledge and skills, as well as the child's severity and responsiveness
(e) Continual evaluation and modification of what is being done to identify what works best
(f) Plan for backsliding and spread; all relevant school staff involved; integrated with parenting classes so parent learns to back up what the school is doing
(g) Integrate with school-wide plans and required, school-based programs (i.e., IEPs, 504 plans)
(h) Contact reestablished with consultant for major developmental transitions (e.g., entry to middle school)

Child intervention

(a) Behavioral and developmental approach
(b) Focus on teaching academic, recreational, and social–behavioral competencies, decreasing aggression, developing close friendships, and building self-efficacy
(c) Paraprofessional implemented, supervised by professionals
(d) Settings such as clinic-based weekly group sessions, after-school or Saturday sessions, and summer camps
(e) Typically *more* intensive rather than *less* intensive treatment necessary (e.g., weekly clinic social skills groups typically not effective)
(f) Monitoring and modification as needed based on what works best; treatment provided as long as necessary (e.g., multiple years or when deterioration occurs)
(g) Plan for what to do if backsliding occurs
(h) Integrate with school and parent treatments
(i) contact with consultant for major developmental transitions (e.g., middle school entry)

EXHIBIT 16.1 (Continued)
Comprehensive Treatment for
Attention-Deficit/Hyperactivity Disorder

Concurrent psychostimulant medication

(a) Only rarely used as first line treatment
(b) Need determined after initiation of behavioral treatments; timing of when to add medication dependent on child's severity and responsiveness to behavioral treatments
(c) Individualized, randomized, school-based medication trial conducted to determine need and minimal dose to complement the behavioral intervention
(d) Cycle through methylphenidate and amphetamine-based compounds, and then pemoline, before other drug classes
(e) Need for t.i.d. or long-acting medication also determined during initial assessment based on child's impairment across settings
(f) Repeated annual trials to adjust dosages and justify continued need; continued until no deterioration occurs when withdrawn

---

based approaches to therapy, including social skills training—have *not* proven efficacious (McFadyen-Ketchum & Dodge, 1998; Mrug, Hoza, & Gerdes, 2001). One reason for this failure is that it is difficult, if not impossible, to work on peer relationships in the office or in the classroom. However, peer relationships can be targeted in camp settings in which children learn not only appropriate behavior and social skills but also sports knowledge, sports skills, and appropriate sportsmanship. If children could learn these concepts and skills in office settings, soccer and little league practices would be held in coaches' offices rather than on the playing fields!

Regarding academic functioning, tutoring can be conducted during the school year. It has long been argued that all children, particularly children with learning problems, lose academic skills during summer vacations, and children clearly benefit from academic instruction during the summer months (Cooper, Charlton, Valentine, & Muhlenbruck, 2000). In the Multimodal Treatment Study of Children With ADHD (MTA), only children who attended a summer program with an academic component and also received stimulant medication made gains in standardized achievement scores (MTA Cooperative Group, 1999). However, attendance at *regular* summer school classes is modest at best, with daily absenteeism reaching rates as high as 40% (Goodnough, 2001). Arguably, if summer school were made more attractive by combining academic instruction with recreational activities focusing on peer relationships, children would be more motivated to attend and therefore derive greater academic benefit.

Third, deficits in parent–child relationships and parenting skills have long been known to predict dysfunctional outcomes for children with disruptive behavior disorders (Chamberlain & Patterson, 1995). Behavioral parent training is one of the most well-documented interventions for children with CD and ADHD (Brestan & Eyberg, 1998; Pelham et al., 1998), but it is infrequently provided in community mental health settings (Weisz & Weiss, 1993). The summer months afford an opportune time to interact and meet with parents because there is a dramatic reduction in school- and after-school-related activities.

In summary, summer time provides a unique opportunity to focus on the domains of impairment that are most critical to children with ADHD —peer relationships, parenting skills, and academic competencies. If treatment is interrupted during the summer, gains made during the school year may be lost as children and parents regress to old patterns of behavior. Children with ADHD are likely to experience failure in traditional summer camps, where they are often dismissed for their disruptive behavior or rejected by other children, and they will clearly have difficulties if they simply hang around the neighborhood. It is worth noting that *children spend as many hours interacting with peers, siblings, and parents during the summer as they spend in school during the entire rest of the year.* Thus, given a chronic care model, treatment in summer months is critical for children with ADHD.

Since 1980, we have included in our comprehensive treatment model for ADHD an intervention in a camplike setting in which children engage in a variety of activities with peers, along with academic instruction and parent training. Daily classroom periods enable both academic practice during the summer *and* assessment of the children's response to treatment in a classroom setting, enabling detailed treatment recommendations when the child returns to school. Parents are involved in the form of weekly evening training sessions, home backup for programs being implemented during the day, and daily contact with therapists. In addition, by conducting carefully controlled medication evaluations, we include the pharmacological approach that is necessary for some children with ADHD. In the fall following the summer program, parents can attend monthly booster parent training, and two consultations are held with the child's teacher to maximize generalization of treatment gains. This chapter describes the summer treatment program (STP) treatment components and presents information on the efficacy, social validity, and exportability of the STP.

SUMMER TREATMENT PROGRAM OVERVIEW

The STP is an 8-week program for children and adolescents between 5 and 15 years of age, who attend from 8:00 a.m. until 5:00 p.m. on weekdays. Children are placed in age-matched groups of approximately 12, and five student interns implement treatments for each group. Groups stay together throughout the summer so that children receive intensive experience in functioning as a group, making friends, and interacting appropriately with adults. Each group spends 3 hours daily in classroom sessions conducted by teachers and aides. The remainder of each day consists of recreationally based group activities.

Goals of Treatment

Our goals are to improve the children's peer relationships, interactions with adults, academic performance, and self-efficacy, while concurrently training their parents in behavior management. Using a social learning approach, we employ treatment components spanning the range from operant and cognitive–behavioral treatments to pharmacological interventions. We have modified the interventions so that they are age-appropriate and so that they can be tailored as necessary to the needs of each child. In addition, if the standard STP interventions do not produce the desired behavior change for a given child, staff members conduct a functional analysis and develop individualized programs. A treatment manual and multiple supporting documents describe the program in detail (see http://www.ctadd.org; Pelham, Greiner, & Gnagy, 1997a).

Point System

Using a systematic reward–response cost program, children continuously earn points for appropriate behavior and lose points for inappropriate behavior throughout the day (the youngest children earn and lose tokens). Such programs have an extensive history in behavior modification and have significant, acute effects on children's behavior (e.g., Kazdin, 2001; O'Leary, 1978). The behaviors included in the STP point system are those that are commonly targeted for development (e.g., following rules, paying attention) and elimination (e.g., teasing, noncompliance) in children with ADHD, oppositional defiant disorder (ODD), and CD. The points that children earn are exchanged for privileges (e.g., field trips), social honors, and home-based rewards.

Counselors record children's behavior throughout the day. Staff members receive intensive training to enable them to administer the point system reliably, thus eliminating the need for costly, independent observers to provide data for clinical research. Frequent checks are conducted to ensure that counselors' records are accurate reflections of the children's behavior and to ensure the clinical integrity of the program.

Positive Reinforcement and Appropriate Commands

Implicit in the implementation of all behavior management systems is the use of positive reinforcement to shape behavior (Martin & Pear, 2002; Kazdin, 2001). The forms of positive reinforcement employed in the STP include the point system, parental rewards, and social reinforcement. In particular, social reinforcement in the form of praise and public recognition (e.g., buttons, stickers, and posted charts) is used ubiquitously to provide a positive, supportive atmosphere. Each day begins with a warm greeting from the child's counselors. Even if the child has behaved poorly on the previous day, staff members start each day anew with a positive approach to the child. At the end of the day, each child's counselor meets briefly with the child and his or her parents to provide feedback about the day. Counselors systematically praise the children for appropriate behavior, modeling appropriate social reinforcement for the parents. If a child has misbehaved, counselors give feedback with a neutral, nonadmonishing tone. In addition to the liberal use of social reinforcement, staff members attempt to shape appropriate behavior by issuing commands with characteristics (e.g., brevity, specificity) that maximize compliance (see Figure 16.1; Forehand & Long, 1996; Walker & Walker, 1991).

Peer Interventions

Treatment also includes training in social skills that are thought to be necessary for effective peer-group functioning. Social-skills training is provided in brief (10 minute) daily group sessions. Sessions include instruction, modeling, role-playing, and practice in key social concepts (Oden & Asher, 1977), as well as more specific skills when necessary (Michelsen, Sugai, Wood, & Kazdin, 1983; Hinshaw, Henker, & Whalen, 1984). In addition to these sessions, children engage in cooperative group tasks (e.g., group art projects) that are designed to promote cooperation and contribute to cohesive peer relationships (Furman & Gavin, 1989). Children's implementation of the social-skills training programs is prompted and reinforced throughout the day using the point system, which targets numerous behaviors involving interactions with peers. The combination of a reward–cost program and social-skills training has been shown to be necessary to foster the development of social skills in children with externalizing disorders (e.g., Pelham & Bender, 1982). Blending these peer-focused components may be critical to enhancing change and generalization to the natural environment (McFayden-Ketchum & Dodge, 1998; Mrug et al., 2001; Walker, Hops, & Greenwood, 1986).

Children also learn group problem-solving skills using an approach developed by Spivak, Platt, and Shure (1976). This procedure has been applied in other camplike settings (Rickard & Dinoff, 1965) and is also the basis for individual social problem-solving skills that have been applied in work with aggressive boys (e.g., Conduct Problems Prevention Research Group, 1999b; Lochman & Curry, 1986).

Daily Report Cards

The delivery of daily report cards (DRCs) to parents is a common intervention for ADHD children (see Jacob & Pelham, 2000; Kelley, 1990), and numerous studies have documented their effectiveness (e.g., O'Leary, Pelham,

Counselor: _____

Counselor gave a command at an appropriate time.

If ___, place a checkmark beside the appropriate reason:

- Used a prompt in place of a command
- Gave a command instead of informing the child of a point loss or rule violation
- Ignored a behavior for which a command should have been given
- Gave a command rather than ignoring a mildly inappropriate behavior that was not attracting the attention of other group members
- Other: _____

Counselor obtained and maintained child's attention while giving the command.
- Command met criteria for an effective command
- Did not contain multiple behaviors
- Contained specific description of the desired behavior
- Used positive phrasing if possible
- Used clear wording and was not phrased in the form of a question
- Did not specify an extended time limit (except in the case of high-rate negative behavior)

Counselor followed the command sequence correctly (see diagram).
- Evaluated behavior
- Did not interrupt command sequence by issuing a prompt or repeated command without applying consequences
- Allowed sufficient time to elapse (10 seconds or time specified) before evaluating behavior
- Awarded points for compliance or deducted points for noncompliance
- Repeated command after noncompliance
- Assigned time out after repeated noncompliance

Score: ___ / ___ = ___

Figure 16.1. Sample treatment integrity and fidelity form. Supervisors complete these evaluation forms to measure adherence to treatment procedures and provide feedback, reinforcement, and correction to staff members.

Rosenbaum, & Price, 1976). In the STP, DRCs include individualized target behaviors across all settings. Target behaviors and criteria for meeting daily goals are set and revised regularly to ensure that they are at appropriate levels to challenge the child but still enable success most of the time if the child tries hard (Pelham et al., 1997a). Parents learn during training sessions to provide home-based rewards when their children reach DRC goals.

Sports Skills Training

Children receive intensive coaching and practice in sports skills. Children with ADHD typically do not follow the rules of games and have poor motor skills (Pelham et al., 1990), deficits that contribute to their social rejection and low self-esteem (Pelham & Bender, 1982). Involvement in sports is thought to enhance self-esteem and self-efficacy, which in turn are thought to play a role in behavior change (Smoll, Smith, Barnett, & Everett, 1993). For children with ADHD, who are at risk for low self-esteem, such skills training in a positive environment would appear to be particularly important. Indeed, sports competencies moderate peer status in children with ADHD (Chacko et al., 2000). Thus, 3 hours each day are devoted to small-group skills training and play in age-appropriate sports and games. Techniques that are designed to optimize skill training for young children are employed (e.g., Smoll & Smith, 1987). The intensive practice and time that are necessary to effect changes in sports skills highlight the value of the STP setting for this program component. In contrast, most children's sports involvement in North America consists of an hour or two of practice per week with an hour-long weekly game for a single sport "season"—typically 8 to 10 weeks.

Time-Out

Research by O'Leary and colleagues has shown that "prudent punishment" (e.g., appropriate verbal reprimands, privilege loss, time out) is necessary for effective intervention with children with ADHD (see Pfiffner & O'Leary, 1993, for a review). Thus, children are disciplined for certain prohibited behaviors (e.g., intentional aggression, intentional destruction of property, repeated noncompliance), with discipline taking the form of loss of privileges (e.g., loss of recess time) or time-out from positive reinforcement. Time-out is a technique that has been used for many years as an alternative to physical punishment (Kazdin, 2001; Martin & Pear, 2002; Ross, 1981). The time-out program used in the STP differs from others in current use in that the initial time assigned is relatively long (i.e., 10–30 minutes depending on the child's age), but a child may immediately earn a 50% reduction in time for "good behavior" (Pelham et al., 1997a). This puts the child in an earning situation even when he or she is being punished; that is, if the child controls his or her behavior, the punishment length is reduced (Fabiano et al., in press).

Classrooms

Children spend 2 hours daily in a classroom modeled after an academic special education classroom, and they spend a third hour in an art class. Behavior in the classrooms is managed using a relatively simple point system that includes both reward (earning points for work completion and accuracy) and response–cost (losing points for rule violations) components (Carlson, Pelham, Milich, & Dixon, 1992; Pelham et al., 1993). Public recognition and praise are given for assignment completion and accuracy, and the time-out system described previously is used. The behavior-management system in the classroom is designed to be implemented by a single teacher and a classroom aide and is therefore easily generalizable to regular school settings.

During the 2-hour classroom period, children engage in three structured academic activities. First, children complete a variety of seatwork assignments that are individualized according to each child's needs. Second, children are paired for a cooperative reading comprehension task, pairing a strong reader with a reader of lesser ability (Fuchs, Mathes, & Fuchs, 1993). This peer tutoring program has shown beneficial effects on reading ability and behavior in a regular classroom setting (Simmons, Fuchs, Fuchs, Mathes, & Hodge, 1995). Third, children work on individualized academic skills using computer-based instruction (Advanced Learning System, 1997). In the art class, children work on a variety of individual and group projects. Given that many children with ADHD have behavioral difficulties in special areas in school (e.g., art, music), this nonacademic class affords a unique opportunity to treat children's problems and build skills for transfer to these areas of the regular school setting.

Parent Involvement

Parents have almost daily contact with staff members and with each other when they pick up their children at the end of each day. To facilitate transfer of the gains children make in the STP to the home setting, their parents participate in weekly group training sessions that deal with implementation of behavior modification programs at home. The general procedures that parents learn in these sessions are the same as those employed in the STP, with modifications to make them practical for parents to implement. The parent training packages that we have employed have been validated as effective with children with externalizing disorders (e.g., Barkley, 1990; Cunningham, Bremner, & Secord-Gilbert, 1998; Forehand & Long, 1996; Forgatch & Patterson, 1989; Patterson & Forgatch, 1987). Since

1996, the parent training program that we have employed is a large-group problem-solving approach designed to improve maintenance of skills learned in parent training (Cunningham et al., 1998). At times, the children and their parents work jointly with the parent group leaders, using in vivo training situations. Parents may also participate in enhanced parent training classes aimed to prevent the occurrence of problems that interfere with the maintenance of treatment gains (e.g., mothers may participate in a course aimed to increase their skills for coping with stress or depression; Chronis, Gamble, Roberts, & Pelham, 2000).

Medication Assessment

The CNS stimulants frequently prescribed to children with ADHD tend to be inadequately assessed and monitored (Pelham, 1993). In the STP, children for whom it is appropriate undergo an extensive, placebo-controlled evaluation of the effects of stimulant medication—typically methylphenidate (see Pelham et al., 1997a; and Pelham & Smith, 2000, for a description of these procedures). Data gathered routinely in the STP (e.g., point system records) are evaluated, in addition to daily records of side effects, to determine whether medication was helpful, *beyond the effects of concurrent behavioral interventions*. If medication benefited the child in the areas of daily life functioning that are most important for him or her, without adverse effects, then medication may be recommended for follow-up as an adjunct to an ongoing behavioral intervention (see Pelham & Smith, 2000, for further discussion). Of 258 boys with ADHD who were treated in STPs from 1987 through 1992 (Pelham & Hoza, 1996), 88% participated in STP medication assessments. Continued treatment with psychostimulants was recommended for 68% of those children—a third of the children were thus thought to function adequately without medication. In cases in which higher doses of medication were compared with low doses, the low dose of medication (.3 mg/kg/dose or less, given twice daily), combined with behavior modification, was recommended 90% of the time (e.g., Carlson et al., 1992; Pelham et al., 1993).

Monitoring Treatment Response and Treatment Fidelity

Information is gathered daily from the point system; academic assignments; and counselor, teacher, and parent ratings and is entered daily into a customized database (Pelham, Gnagy, & Greiner, 1997a). The information is immediately available to staff members and supervisors to monitor children"s response to treatment and to make necessary modifications for individual children. In addition, counselors, teachers, and parents complete standardized measures of improvement at the end of the summer across a wide range of functional domains (e.g., compliance with adult directions, peer relations, sports skills, self-esteem, academic productivity). These ratings have been shown to be sensitive to treatment effects (Pelham et al., 2000).

An extensive set of documented procedures are implemented daily by staff members and supervisors to monitor and ensure treatment fidelity (Pelham, Greiner, & Gnagy, 1997b). A sample treatment integrity form, used to monitor whether staff members are following the manualized procedures for giving appropriate commands, is presented in Figure 16.1. Integrity materials include both lists of treatment procedures and ratings of the quality with which staff members are providing treatment, and 20 fidelity forms have been developed that cover every behavioral treatment component used in the STP. Staff members meet regularly to receive structured feedback from supervisors, who use the fidelity forms as guidelines for feedback.

RESEARCH-BASED CLINICAL TREATMENT: AN EVOLUTIONARY APPROACH

An additional strength of the STP is that its design facilitates clinical research. A limitation of some treatment outcome studies is that the measures collected (e.g., performance on a continuous performance task) or the interventions used (e.g., office-based social-skills training) do not reflect the everyday impairment experienced by a child with ADHD, or studies focus on symptom ratings as primary outcome measures. In contrast, the STP provides a wealth of information on the child's behavior in the very settings in which impairment is evident (e.g., in the classroom, playing baseball). Clinical records double as dependent measures in studies. Clinical observations generate research ideas, and results of empirical studies are used to modify subsequent treatment protocols. Through the summer of 2003, nearly 90 empirical studies have been conducted in the STP, many of them dissertations or grant-funded projects. Additionally, staff members from other STP sites have replicated some of our studies or initiated new programs of research. These studies have addressed a wide variety of questions regarding the nature and treatment of ADHD and have contributed a large information base to our knowledge of ADHD. As an illustration, some of the behavioral and combined treatment studies conducted within the context of the STP are briefly reviewed in subsequent sections. Although numerous studies on the pharmacological treatment of ADHD have also been conducted in the STP (e.g., Pelham et al., 1999), they are not reviewed here because of space limitations.

Studies of Behavioral Treatment for Attention-Deficit/ Hyperactivity Disorder

The intensive, comprehensive behavioral treatment components of the STP have been described in previous sections. A series of studies have demonstrated that these procedures produce significant, clinically meaning-ful changes in behavior. As reported in our previous version of this chapter (Pelham & Hoza, 1996), the STP typically results in significant improve-ments across multiple domains of functioning. Pelham & Hoza (1996) reported on 258 ADHD boys, ages 5 to 12, who participated in the STP. From pretreatment to posttreatment, significant improvements were found in parent ratings on a symptom-rating scale (Pelham, Gnagy, Greenslade, & Milich, 1992), an impairment rating scale (Fabiano et al., 1999), STP par-ent, teacher, and counselor improvement ratings in functional domains (Pelham et al., 2000), and self-perception (Harter, 1985). Results were con-sistent across a variety of demographic, diagnostic, and socioeconomic fac-tors (e.g., comorbid aggression, single- vs. two-parent households). Similar results were obtained across a variety of domains and measures in the STPs conducted as part of the MTA (MTA Cooperative Group, 1999; Wells et al., 2000). In that study (Pelham et al., 2000), the effects of the behavioral program alone were so great that minimal effects of medication were obtained in the STP setting despite substantial medication dosing (see also discussion in subsequent sections).

The effectiveness of the STP as a component of comprehensive behavioral treatment package has been evaluated in two large trials—one clinical trial (MTA Cooperative Group, 1999) and one prevention trial (August, Realmuto, Hektner, & Bloomquist, 2001). The STP was com-bined with behavioral parent training and a school-year behavioral inter-vention, and the behavioral treatment package produced beneficial effects in both studies. Although the role of the STP cannot be separated from the parent training and school intervention components in either study and should not be separated given the importance of a comprehensive, chronic-care model of treatment, some evidence suggests that the STP was one of the most potent components of the packages (Pelham et al., 2000) and pro-duced the highest degree of parent satisfaction (Pelham et al., under review; August et al., 2001).

A recent series of investigations are providing a wealth of evidence for the efficacy of the STP treatment package as a whole, compared with a no-treatment condition (Chronis et al., in press; Coles et al., under review; Fabiano et al., 2003; Pelham et al., 2002; Pelham et al., 2004). In a study of a 2-day withdrawal of the STP procedures (Chronis et al., under review), the withdrawal produced immediate and significant deterioration in behav-ior with very large effect sizes—regardless of whether the children were receiving a medication regimen. A subsequent investigation removed the behavioral treatment for 2 weeks in a BABAB design (Coles et al., under review; Pelham et al., 2002) and again showed significant effects of the STP treatment. These results have also been replicated in preliminary data from an ongoing investigation of single and combined treatment effects, in which the behavioral components were removed for a period of 3 consecutive weeks and a lower-intensity behavioral condition was added (see subsequent sections for a discussion of the combined treatment effects in these studies).

Given that the overall STP treatment package appears to produce behavioral changes with very large effect sizes, some studies have been conducted to determine the incremental contributions of individual treatment *components*. One such study investigated the incremental benefit of including time-out in the treatment package (Fabiano et al., in press), and the use of time-out in the STP resulted in a reduction of aggressive and noncompliant behavior. The classroom-based components of the STP were evaluated in two studies (Carlson et al., 1992; Pelham et al., 1993). In these studies, the classroom behavioral components resulted in clinically and statistically significant improvements across a variety of measures (e.g., disruptive behavior, teacher ratings, and classroom rule violations).

In the recreational setting, one explicit goal of the STP is to increase the children's knowledge of sports rules and improve sports skills, and children are encouraged to exhibit appropriate sportsmanship. The success of this approach was illustrated by improving sports skills, increasing attention to game situations, and decreasing unsportsmanlike behaviors in the context of the STP (e.g., Chronis et al., in press; Hupp & Reitman, 1999).

In all, the STP has provided a wealth of information on the effectiveness, utility, and influence of varying parameters of behavioral treatments for ADHD. Notably, the multiple settings and multiple measures available provide detailed information on improvement in behavior related to functional impairment (e.g., problems in peer relationships, compliance with adult commands, academic work completion)—the explicit target of treatment in behavior therapy (Pelham & Fabiano, 2000). Furthermore, two clinical trials have shown that a behavioral treatment package that includes the STP, parent training, and a school intervention produce substantial benefits that maintain over at least a 1-year period (August et al., 2001; MTA Cooperative Group, in press).

Studies of Combined Treatment for Attention-Deficit/ Hyperactivity Disorder

Researchers and clinicians have long understood that the single effects of behavior therapy or medication are often insufficient for normalizing behavior unless very intensive "doses" are employed (e.g., Klein & Abikoff, 1997; Pelham & Bender, 1982). For this reason, interest has turned to studying the effects of combining behavioral and stimulant treatments. There are reasons to believe that the combined treatment may result in incrementally greater improvement than use of either treatment alone (for discussion, see Pelham & Murphy, 1986; Pelham & Waschbusch, 1999). Notably, the vast majority of combined treatment studies of children with ADHD have occurred within or included the context of the STP. These studies include numerous case studies documenting the effects of combined treatment (Abramowitz, Eckstrand, O'Leary, & Dulcan, 1992; Chronis et al., 2001; Hoza et al., 1992; Reitman, Hupp, O'Callaghan, Gulley, & Northup, 2001); the MTA study (MTA Cooperative Group, 1999; Pelham et al., 2000); cross-over studies comparing the single and combined effects of behavior modification and stimulant medication in classroom settings (Carlson et al., 1992; Pelham et al., 1993; see also Northup et al., 1999, and Kolko, Bukstein, & Barron, 1999); and a new line of studies investigating the impact of treatment intensity on treatment response.

The case studies from the STP support the use of combined treatments for children with severe behavior problems, typically ADHD combined type and comorbid externalizing disorders. For example, Chronis et al. (2001) reported on the treatment of a child with ADHD over 3 years. Treatment included three summers of the STP, over 30 parent training classes, school interventions during the regular school year, and adjunctive psychological services for the child's mother. The child's behavior steadily improved over a period of 3 years. Similarly, Hoza et al. (1992) illustrated how a very non-compliant child required high-intensity behavior-modification procedures and substantial doses of medication to achieve meaningful behavior change.

The interactive effects of combined treatment intensity were clearly illustrated in the MTA study (MTA Cooperative Group, 1999; Pelham et al., 2000). Of 87 measures collected *during the STP*, the combined treatment group was only significantly different from the behavioral treatment group on *five* measures. The addition of medication did not increase the rates of normalization on most measures, which ranged from 25% (for positive peer relations) to 95% (for classwork productivity) with behavioral treatment alone. These results suggest that for parents who wish to avoid medication, implementing STP-like behavior-modification procedures is a viable alternative. The results contrast sharply with the endpoint analyses reported in the MTA study, at which point a nonintensive (at 14 months) behavioral intervention added relatively little incremental improvement on ADHD symptoms beyond that produced by an active, high dose of medication (MTA Cooperative Group, 1999).

In a more recent investigation (Pelham, Burrows-MacLean, Gnagy, Fabiano, et al., 2004), prior studies conducted in the STP classroom were extended to the entire STP and were crossed with 4 doses of medication (equivalent to 0, 5, 10, and 20 mg or oral immediate release MPH b.i.d.). Behavioral treatments were removed for alternating weeks for 4 weeks during the summer, and medication conditions varied across days for each child. Results showed significant effects of both medication and behavioral treatment across settings and also replicated the Carlson et al. (1992) findings regarding medication dose. Pelham et al. discovered that the lowest dose of medication combined with behavior modification produced effects similar to those associated with the highest dose of medication alone. Odds ratios were computed for combined treatments relative to unimodal treatments and showed that, for example, the addition of behavior modification to a low dose of medication improved the odds of obtaining a positive DRC by 10 times, whereas the addition of the low dose of medication to behavior modification improved DRC odds by 4 times. All odds ratios were significant, showing incremental benefit of the combined treatment. Notably, the dose at which performance was maximized in combined treatment was half that employed in Carlson et al. (1992) and one fourth that used in Klein and Abikoff (1997).

This study provides clear evidence that the behavioral treatments used in the STP have single effects that are as large or larger than those of medication and supports the hypothesis that dose, or intensity, of both medication and behavioral treatments need to be considered when evaluating studies of combined treatment. In an ongoing investigation, these results are being extended by including a lower-intensity version of the STP behavioral interventions (e.g., weekly home-based rewards, behavioral feedback without the point system) to more fully examine the relative efficacy of the more intensive STP components and individual differences in response to the STP treatment components and medication, alone and in various combinations. Preliminary data (Pelham et al., 2003) replicate the results of our previous study with relation to the high-intensity condition and provide evidence for the efficacy of these lower-intensity procedures in the STP context.

Clinical Research in the STP: The Interplay Between Research and Treatment

We view the STP as an excellent example of clinical research in which the ideas for studies grow out of a systematic approach to clinical work and the results of studies feed back into that clinical work. For example, we conducted a study of methylphenidate effects on the functioning of boys with ADHD during baseball games (Pelham et al., 1990). That study was prompted by parents' questions regarding whether they should medicate their children for Little League practice, as well as our observations of variability in children's baseball performance in the STP, which we suspected may have been a function of their medication status. To measure attention during baseball games, we developed two dependent measures: attention check questions about the game status and prompts to children to assume a "ready" position. In addition to being sensitive to MPH effects, these procedures improved attention independent of medication. Thus, we integrated these procedures into our standard STP procedures across a variety of settings and have shown that they improve attention in children with ADHD (Chronis et al., in press).

In the early 1990s, we responded to parents' requests by developing an STP for adolescents. The format and structure of the STP were adapted from pilot work with children in this age range (e.g., Evans & Pelham, 1991). One question that quickly emerged was whether we should be recommending medication for adolescents with ADHD, a point on which the literature was lacking. Thus, we conducted a study of stimulant effects on ADHD adolescents (Evans et al., 2001; Smith et al., 1998) that has also resulted in modifications to our adolescent STP and follow-up treatment regimens.

As another example, we became interested in friendship patterns in children with ADHD, specifically whether having a best friend might moderate difficulties in peer relationships as the child grows older (Mrug et al., 2001). We have subsequently evaluated aspects of our "buddy system" peer intervention and plan to incorporate it as a component of our peer interventions in future STPs (Hoza et al., 2003).

Follow-Up Treatment

Of course, not even intensive treatment such as the STP would be expected to have lasting effects without appropriate follow-up. Because ADHD is a chronic disorder, interventions must be continued in one form or another for very long time periods—perhaps indefinitely but modified as necessary across years. *We make it very clear to parents that without continued treatment, the gains their children make in the STP will be short-lived.* We have not systematically investigated the effects of follow-up treatment, but we have employed several different types. The follow-up treatment that we have offered has included a Saturday Treatment Program (SatTP) that employs the STP recreational procedures, school interventions in the classrooms to which children return after the STP, and booster parent training.

The SatTP is a biweekly program that runs from September through May. The format and goals are similar to those of the STP, with an emphasis on maintenance and generalization. Rather than the point system, counselors use behavioral feedback, time out, social reinforcement, natural consequences, and DRCs to modify behavior. Peer relationships and recreational and academic competencies continue to receive emphasis. Some sites have developed procedures for use in after-school programs as well. Booster parent training (Patterson, 1974) consists of sessions that continue working on the programs that parents have established during the STP and teaching the parents how to collaborate with school administrators and teachers.

Our follow-up school interventions are established by therapists working directly with teachers. Classroom management programs are developed that include changes in teacher attention, assignment structure, classroom structure, DRCs, and response cost–reward programs. Although these approaches typically involve 8 to 12 direct contacts and numerous telephone contacts (e.g., Wells et al., 2000), we have found that fewer contacts are needed when children have previously been in the STP.

When we have offered follow-up services on a fee-for-service basis, we have found that the amount of follow-up sessions in which families participate varies widely (see the discussion of barriers to treatment later in this chapter). Because active follow-up is so critical, we have structured our costs and payments for the STP to include (a) two parent group-booster training sessions that occur in the fall and (b) two school visits. This practice ensures that we have at least a minimal amount of continued contact with parents and that we are able to meet with the child's subsequent classroom teacher to facilitate maintenance of treatment gains in the child's regular classroom.

Rate of Treatment Completion and Consumer Satisfaction

Most outpatient treatment programs for children with disruptive behavior disorders have treatment completion rates *far* below this level, with dropout often approaching 50% (Miller & Prinz, 1990). A major difference between the STP and other treatment programs is that our dropout rate is *extremely low.* Of 1,204 ADHD children enrolled in an STP from 1987 through 2003, only 26 dropped out or were terminated early (a completion rate of 97.8%). Furthermore, children's attendance is routinely near 100%, as is parent training attendance. In our previous report in an earlier edition of this volume, we documented that the dropout rate in the STP is similarly low across socioeconomic status, race, and single-parent status, illustrating the utility of the STP across family characteristics that are reliably associated with poor adherence to treatment (Miller & Prinz, 1990). *A prerequisite to a successful long-term intervention is successful completion of the initial stage of treatment, and the STP virtually ensures that outcome.*

Perhaps contributing to the high rate of treatment completion, participants in the STP are overwhelmingly satisfied with the intervention. Converging evidence demonstrates the high rates of consumer satisfaction with the STP. We have already reported on the near-unanimous endorsement of the STP at our site (Pelham & Hoza, 1996). Table 16.1 illustrates that these results were replicated at five other STP sites across the United States. The high rate of consumer satisfaction has also been replicated in two large studies in which the STP has been used as a component of behavioral treatment—the MTA study and the Early Risers program (August et al., 2001; MTA Cooperative Group, 1999, Pelham et al., 2000).

Addressing Barriers to Treatment

To what might these high rates of treatment completion and near-unanimous parental endorsement of the STP be attributed? One explanation may be that the STP targets and removes barriers to treatment associated with ADHD (Pelham & Fabiano, 2000). This is a critical component of

TABLE 16.1
1998 End of Treatment Consumer Satisfaction Ratings for Five Summer Treatment Program Sites

	Cleveland Clinic Children's Hospital	Vanderbilt	Indiana University—PA	Butler, PA	Johnstown, PA
How much did your child benefit from participating in the STP?*	80	94	94	88	96
How much did you benefit from participating in the STP?*	93	95	75	88	100
How much did your child enjoy participating in the STP?*	80	89	94	99	97
Would you send your child to the STP again?†	90	95	100	99	100
Would you recommend the STP to other parents of a child with ADHD?†	97	100	94	100	96
How satisfied were you with STP treatment compared with other services you have received?‡	92	98	94	88	94
How effective was the STP treatment compared with other services you have received?‡	92	98	94	88	91

Note. STP = Summer treatment program; ADHD = Attention-deficit/hyperactivity disorder; PA = Pennsylvania. All values are percentages.
*Percent of parents responding "Much" or "Very much."
†Percent of parents responding "Probably" or "Definitely."
‡Percent of parents responding "Somewhat more" or "Much more."

effective treatments because research has shown that families are more likely to terminate treatment prematurely if barriers to treatment completion exist (e.g., the child does not like treatment; Kazdin, Holland, & Crowley, 1997). Furthermore, families who endorse barriers to treatment generally have poor treatment responses (Kazdin & Wassell, 1999).

The characteristics of a number of the families in the STP indicate that they may experience barriers to engaging in and completing treatment (e.g., single parenthood, high levels of life stress). However, as we discussed above, the impact of these barriers on treatment outcome is dramatically reduced or eliminated in the STP (Pelham & Hoza, 1996). For example, parent training sessions are conducted in the evenings, and STP staff provide structured child-care activities for the entire duration of the parent training class. The daily contact among counselors, parents, and children maximizes the therapeutic alliance that mental health professionals and parents must have for success in a long-term model of treatment. Another potential obstacle in treating children with externalizing disorders is that the children may refuse to attend or participate in treatment sessions (Kazdin et al., 1997). A treatment that includes engaging activities, interactions with peers, consistently responsive staff, and daily experiences of success results in children who *want* to come to the STP. Finally, the STP is conducted from 8:00 a.m. until 5:00 p.m. on weekdays for 8 weeks. Summer day camps are ubiquitous in every community in North America, providing summer activities for children in a manner that allows parents flexibility in their own activities and work schedules. By structuring the STP with the hours and length of a typical summer camp, we have adapted our mental health services for children with ADHD to match what is available for non-handicapped children. We believe that this approach removes a major barrier to treatment—making services fit with family schedules (Kazdin & Wassell 1999). In fact, if the STP were free, we would not be surprised if parents sent their children there every summer (see Table 16.1), a rate of engagement in and commitment to clinical services far surpassing any other clinical services we or others offer.

COSTS AND BENEFITS

We believe that these data go a long way toward suggesting that STPs are a useful component of a comprehensive approach to treating ADHD. However, among the primary considerations of the utility of such intensive treatment is whether it provides sufficient incremental effectiveness (beyond, for example, traditional outpatient treatment) to justify the cost of its use. Although we do not have data regarding this point, we are pursuing that question in our current research. We do, however, have considerable information about the cost of many STPs using our model. An 8-week STP in the United States can be provided for approximately $3,000 (in 2000 U.S. dollars) per child ($75.00 per day or $8.00 per hour). Innovative staffing arrangements (e.g., course credit rather than salary for some staff) and collaborative arrangements with local school districts (e.g., to loan space or computers) can often reduce this figure. Staffing arrangements depend heavily on college students working for credit and low salaries under the supervision of a small number of permanent staff members—a camp structure rather than a typical hospital or mental health structure. It should be noted that thousands of regular summer camps across the United States are staffed by high school and college students working under similar arrangements.

Comprehensive follow-up to an STP (as described in the previous sections) can be conducted for an additional $500 per year for parent–school interventions (e.g., six booster parent training group sessions, six teacher consultations) and an additional $500 for ten Saturday program booster sessions. The cost of follow-up treatment is relatively more expensive on a per-hour basis than the STP because treatment is shifted in part to individual, therapist-based treatment (e.g., school consultation). By employing large-group parent training formats (Cunningham et al., 1998), we have been able to reduce the cost of parent training to very low levels. We are currently working to develop procedures to reduce the follow-up costs—particularly with respect to teacher consultations. For example, BA-level clinicians with an educational background are as effective as clinicians with PhDs in working with teachers to implement classroom interventions for disruptive children (Kent & O'Leary, 1977), so we are attempting to lower our follow-up costs by hiring BA-level clinicians, who cost considerably less than clinicians with PhDs. We have developed stand-alone, downloadable programs that parents and teachers can use to develop school–home notes (http://wings.buffalo.edu/adhd). Our hope is to reduce or eliminate therapist visits to schools for many children with this approach. Thus, using the most cost-effective model, which costs $3,500 per child per year, we can provide an intensive and comprehensive treatment for ADHD that consists of an 8-week STP; a double-blind, placebo controlled medication assessment and recommendation; 18 sessions of parent training; 10 school-year Saturday sessions; and a year-long, consultant-assisted, teacher-implemented classroom intervention.

Although this might seem a large sum for a year of treatment, $3,500 ($67 per week) is considerably less than the cost of weekly sessions of individual or play therapy for one year—treatments that are commonly employed in community mental health settings but are not efficacious for ADHD (Weisz & Weiss, 1993). Bickman et al. (1995) reported annual costs for mental health services per child that ranged between $4,000 and $7,000 depending on year and site. Thus, our intervention package, which has demonstrated efficacy, is considerably more cost-effective than individual therapy, which costs much more and is not effective. Very few disorder-specific data exist regarding the costs of services for children with mental health problems. Kelleher (1998) has presented information from a Medicaid database showing that children with ADHD in western Pennsylvania were being treated at an average annual cost of $1,800 in 1994—slightly more than was spent on services for asthmatic children in the same database. Certainly, parents and physicians would not balk at spending $67 per week to treat a chronic disorder such as asthma, and we suggest treatment for ADHD is at least as important (Perrin, 2000). In school settings, Forness and Kavale (2003) estimate that it costs between $2,511 and $7,446 for a child with ADHD to receive special education services, depending on the child's placement (these costs are based on a 10-month school year and do not include the summer months). The lifetime cost to society for one juvenile offender who continues a criminal career into young adulthood is $2,000,000 in 1999 dollars (Office of Juvenile Justice and Delinquency Prevention, 1999).

We have outlined a comprehensive, intensive treatment that uses a chronic-care model and costs as much or less than less comprehensive and intensive treatments. The enormous cost of adjudicating and treating delinquency and associated problems (e.g., substance abuse, psychiatric hospitalization) and preventing recidivism in delinquent adolescents has spawned many intensive programs that are also costly (e.g., multisystemic therapy costing approximately $4,000 per adolescent in 1996 dollars; Henggeler, 1999). If participation in comprehensive treatment that includes an STP can be shown to decrease the probability that a child with ADHD will need special education services or have later contact with the juvenile justice system, both of which have enormous costs, then the utility and cost-effectiveness of comprehensive treatments that include an STP will be clear. For example, 570 children with ADD, ODD, and CD could be treated for 1 year with this intensive treatment for the same amount of money as the career cost of a single juvenile offender. If this intervention is effective in diverting one child out of the 570 from a negative trajectory, it would be cost-effective. By way of another example, 7 to 20 years of intensive treatment for one child could be provided for what 1 year of residential treatment for an adolescent typically costs—in the State of New York, which in 1999 was approximately $70,000 annually for noninstitutional, residential care. Surely, intensive programs such as the STP that start in childhood would be overwhelmingly justified if they reduced and eliminated later problems in adolescence and adulthood—returning enormous future cost savings and cost offsets and therefore being very cost-effective.

A final benefit of the STP is that it serves as a training site for students who are future professionals in mental health, health, and education. Through the summer of 2003, more than 1,100 students from more than 150 different colleges and universities have worked in the STP. Many of these students have gone on to graduate or medical school, faculty positions, and mental health or educational positions. All leave the STP trained in state-of-the-art behavior modification strategies for treating ADHD and other childhood problems.

REPLICABILITY

An important question regarding any intervention as comprehensive as the STP is whether it can be replicated. Internally, of course, we have replicated the STP more than 20 times with different staff members each time. In our previous version of this chapter, we reported on seven consecutive cohorts consisting of different children treated with common methods by seven different staff members (Pelham & Hoza, 1996). Since that report, we have conducted an additional nine replications, further documenting the internal validity of STP effects. The most basic requirement of programmatic replication is that the procedures be completely documented, and we have done that for the STP. The treatment procedures are detailed in a 400-page manual (Pelham et al., 1997a). The manual and all of the forms necessary to track a child's progress from intake through final report writing are developed.

In addition to our internal replications, the STP has been replicated in a number of academic and community settings, as well as across the seven different North American sites of the MTA Study—the University of California at Irvine and Berkeley, Duke University, Long Island Jewish Hospital, Montreal Children's Hospital, and Columbia University, in addition to our Pittsburgh site (Wells et al., 2000) and in the Early Risers Study at the University of Minnesota (August et al., 2001). Summer programs that utilize our model have also been conducted in settings ranging from university and medical center settings (Dalhousie University, Cleveland Clinic, New York University, Vanderbilt University) to community-based mental health agencies (including several in western Pennsylvania: Mercyhurst College, the Achievement Center in Erie, the Indiana County Guidance Center, and the Alternative Community Resource Program in Johnstown) and other agencies and private practices (in Denver, Colorado; Binghamton, New York; Ottawa, Canada; and Charleston, South Carolina).

We have typically provided consultation and training in the first year of operation for many of these STPs to supplement the program manual and materials; in subsequent years, other sites have taken over complete responsibility for the STP. A week-long, intensive centralized training session is provided annually for all interested sites by STP staff members with extensive experience each summer (see http://wings.buffalo.edu/adhd for information). The STP can be adapted to almost any setting where appropriate summer facilities (e.g., field space, pool, classrooms) and resources for follow-up are available, including mental health centers, school districts, group private practices, and hospitals. Perhaps reflecting our confidence in its efficacy and potential, in 1993 the STP was selected in a national competition as one of 20 Model Programs for Service Delivery for Child and Family Mental Health by the Section on Clinical Child Psychology (Section 1, Division 12) and Division of Child, Youth, and Family Services of the American Psychological Association. In 2003, the STP was named Innovative Program of the Year by Children and Adults With ADHD (CHADD), a national advocacy organization for people with ADHD.

The procedures and materials that have been developed for the STP can also be adapted for use in a variety of other treatment settings, and several STP sites have integrated STP components into many other services they routinely provide (Pelham, Manos, & Janakovic, 2000). For example, the Alternative Community Resource Center in Johnstown, Pennsylvania, routinely uses staff members trained in the STP and the procedures and treatment components across their entire range of services for a variety of populations.

SUMMARY

We have argued that effective treatment for ADHD should be comprehensive; be implemented across functional domains; be conducted long-term; focus on impairment rather than symptoms; be responsive to family needs; and be relatively more intensive than currently common interventions. As we have outlined above, summer treatment programs add to a comprehensive treatment model by offering the potential for unique combinations of treatment components that focus on self, peer, academic, and home domains and that make treatment especially palatable. Treatment that children and parents like is more likely to be continued for the time necessary in a chronic-care model than contemporary treatments for ADHD. Competencies such as sports skills that cannot be taught in traditional mental health settings can be regularly offered in STP contexts. Academic intervention can be given that yields the equivalent of 12-month schooling. Parent training can be combined with peer and academic interventions in a structure that minimizes barriers to treatment. The STP packs 360 hours of child treatment (equivalent, for example, to 7 years worth of weekly social skills training sessions, or as much training in sports skills as 3 years worth of regular children's soccer involvement) into an 8-week period, along with 18 hours of parent training, 80 hours of academic instruction, and a double-blind medication assessment. We believe that such comprehensive regimens are needed to change the long-term trajectory of most children with ADHD, and two clinical trials–prevention programs have provided support for this argument.

REFERENCES

Abramowitz, A. J., Eckstrand, D., O'Leary, S. G., & Dulcan, M. K. (1992). ADHD children's responses to stimulant medication and two intensities of a behavioral intervention. *Behavior Modification, 16,* 193–203.

Advanced Learning System [computer program]. (1997). Oklahoma City: The American Education Corporation.

American Academy of Pediatrics. (2001). Clinical practice guideline: Treatment of the school-aged child with attention-deficit/hyperactivity disorder. *Pediatrics, 108,* 1033–1044.

Angold, A., Costello, E. J., Farmer, E. M. Z., Burns, B. J., & Erkanli, A. (1999). Impaired but undiagnosed. *Journal of the American Academy of Child and Adolescent Psychiatry, 38,* 129–137.

August, G. J., Realmuto, G. M., Hektner, J. M., & Bloomquist, M. L. (2001). An integrated components preventive intervention for aggressive elementary school children: The Early Risers Program. *Journal of Consulting and Clinical Psychology, 69,* 614–626.

Barkley, R. A. (1990). *Attention deficit hyperactivity disorder: A handbook for diagnosis and treatment.* New York: Guilford Press.

Bickman, L., Guthrie, P. R., Foster, M. E., Lambert, E. W., Summerfelt, W. T., Breda, C. S., et al. (1995). *Evaluating managed mental health services: The Fort Bragg experiment.* New York: Plenum Press.

Brestan, E. V., & Eyberg, S. M. (1998). Effective psychosocial treatments of conduct-disordered children and adolescents: 29 years, 82 studies, and 5272 kids. *Journal of Clinical Child Psychology, 27,* 180–189.

Carlson, C. L., Pelham, W. E., Milich, R., & Dixon, M. J. (1992). Single and combined effects of methylphenidate and behavior therapy on the classroom behavior, academic performance and self-evaluations of children with attention deficit-hyperactivity disorder. *Journal of Abnormal Child Psychology, 20,* 213–232.

Chacko, A., Williams, A., Meichenbaum, D. L., Onyango, A. N., Fabiano, G. A., Coles, E. K., et al. (2000, November). *The moderating role of athleticism in children with ADHD.* Poster presented at the annual meeting of the Association for the Advancement of Behavior Therapy, New Orleans, LA.

Chamberlain, P., & Patterson, G. R. (1995). Discipline and child compliance in parenting. In M. Bornstein (Ed.), *Handbook of parenting: Applied and practical parenting.* (Vol. 4, pp. 205–225). Mahwah, NJ: Erlbaum.

Chronis, A. M., Fabiano, G. A., Gnagy, E. M., Onyango, A. N., Pelham, W. E., William, A., et al. (in press). An evaluation of the summer treatment program for children with attention-deficit/hyperactivity disorder using a treatment withdrawal design. *Behavior Therapy.*

Chronis, A. M., Fabiano, G. A., Gnagy, E. M., Wymbs, B. T., Burrows-MacLean, L., & Pelham, W. E. (2001). Comprehensive, sustained behavioral and pharmacological treatment for attention deficit hyperactivity disorder: A case study. *Cognitive and Behavioral Practice, 8,* 346–359.

Chronis, A. M., Gamble, S. A., Roberts, J. E., & Pelham, W. E. (2000, November). *Cognitive–behavioral therapy for mothers of children with ADHD: Changing distorted maternal cognitions about child behavior.* Paper presented at the annual meeting of the Association for the Advancement of Behavior Therapy, New Orleans, LA.

Coles, E. K., Pelham, W. E., Gnagy, E. M., Burrows-MacLean, L., Fabiano, G. A., Chacko, A., et al. (under review). *Treatment response to a comprehensive behavioral intervention.*

Coie, J. D., & Dodge, K. A. (1998). Aggression and antisocial behavior. In W. Damon (Series Ed.) & N. Eisenberg (Vol. Ed.), *Handbook of child psychology:*

Social, emotional, and personality development. (5th ed., Vol. 3, pp. 779–862). New York: Wiley.

Conduct Problems Prevention Research Group. (1999a). Initial impact of the fast track prevention trial for conduct problems: I. The high risk sample. *Journal of Consulting and Clinical Psychology, 67*, 631–647.

Conduct Problems Prevention Research Group. (1999b). Initial impact of the fast track prevention trial for conduct problems: II. Classroom effects. *Journal of Consulting and Clinical Psychology, 67*, 648–657.

Cooper, H., Charlton, K., Valentine, J. C., & Muhlenbruck, L. (2000). Making the most of summer school: A meta-analytic and narrative review. *Monographs of the Society for Research in Child Development, 65* (1, Serial No. 260).

Cunningham, C. E., Bremner, R., & Secord-Gilbert, M. (1998). *The community parent education (COPE) program: A school-based family systems oriented course for parents of children with disruptive behavior disorders.* Unpublished manual, McMaster University and Chedoke-McMaster Hospitals.

Evans, S. W., Pelham, W. E., Smith, B. H., Bukstein, O., Gnagy, E. M., Greiner, A. R., et al. (2001). Dose-response effects of methylphenidate on ecologically valid measures of academic performance and classroom behavior in adolescents with ADHD. *Experimental & Clinical Psychopharmacology, 9*, 163–175.

Evans, S. W., & Pelham, W. E. (1991). Psychostimulant effects on academic and behavioral measures for junior high school students in a lecture format classroom. *Journal of Abnormal Child Psychology, 19*, 537–552.

Fabiano, G. A., Pelham, W. E., Gnagy, E. M., Burrows-MacLean, L., Massetti, G. M., & Hoffman, M. T. (2003, November). *The single and combined effects of three intensities of behavior modification and four intensities of medication in a summer treatment program classroom.* Poster session presented at the 37th annual convention of the Association for the Advancement of Behavior Therapy, Boston.

Fabiano, G. A., Pelham, W. E., Gnagy, E. M., Kipp, H., Lahey, B. B., Burrows-MacLean, L., et al. (1999, November). *The reliability and validity of the children's impairment rating scale: A practical measure of impairment in children with ADHD.* Paper presented at the annual meeting of the Association for the Advancement of Behavior Therapy, Toronto, Ontario, Canada.

Fabiano, G. A., Pelham, W. E., Manos, M., Gnagy, E. M., Chronis, A. M., Onyango, A. N., et al. (in press). An evaluation of three time out procedures for children with attention-deficit/hyperactivity disorder. *Behavior Therapy.*

Forehand, R., & Long, N. (1996). *Parenting the strong-willed child: The clinically proven five-week program for parents of two- to six-year-olds.* Lincolnwood, IL: Contemporary Books.

Forgatch, M. S., & Patterson, G. R. (1989). *Parents and adolescents living together. Part 2: Family problem solving.* Eugene, OR: Castalia.

Forness, S. R., & Kavale, K. A. (2003). Impact of ADHD on school systems. In P. S. Jensen & J. R. Cooper (Eds.), *Attention-deficit/hyperactivity disorder: State of the science, best practices.* Kingston, NJ: Civic Research Institute.

Fuchs, D., Mathes, P. G., & Fuchs, L. S. (1993). *Peabody classwide peer tutoring reading methods*. Unpublished teacher's manual.

Furman, W., & Gavin, L. A. (1989). Peers' influence on adjustment and development: A view from the intervention literature. In T. J. Berndt & G. W. Ladd (Eds.), *Peer relationships in child development* (pp. 319–340). New York: Wiley.

Goodnough, A. (2001, July 14). Again, many empty seats in summer school classes. *The New York Times*.

Harter, S. (1985). *Self-perception profile for children*. Unpublished manuscript, University of Denver.

Henggeler, S. W. (1999). Multisystemic therapy: An overview of clinical procedures, outcomes, and policy implications. *Child Psychology and Psychiatry Review, 4*, 2–10.

Hinshaw, S. P., Henker, B., & Whalen, C. K. (1984). Self-control in hyperactive boys in anger inducing situations: Effects of cognitive–behavioral training and of methylphenidate. *Journal of Abnormal Child Psychology, 12*, 55–77.

Hoza, B., Mrug, S., Pelham, W. E., Greiner, A. R., & Gnagy, E. M. (2003). A friendship intervention for children with attention-deficit/hyperactivity disorder: Preliminary findings. *Journal of Attention Disorders, 6*, 87–98.

Hoza, B., Pelham, W. E., Sams, S. E., & Carlson, C. L. (1992). An examination of the "dosage" effects of both behavior therapy and methylphenidate on the classroom performance of two ADHD children. *Behavior Modification, 16*, 164–192.

Hupp, S. D. A., & Reitman, D. (1999). Improving sports skills and sportsmanship in children diagnosed with attention-deficit/hyperactivity disorder. *Child and Family Behavior Therapy, 21*, 35–51.

Jacob, R., & Pelham, W. E. (2000). Behavior therapy. In H. Kaplan & B. Sadock (Eds.), *Comprehensive textbook of psychiatry/VII* (7th ed., pp. 2080–2127). New York: Williams & Wilkins.

Kazdin, A. E. (2001). *Behavior modification in applied settings* (6th ed.). Belmont, CA: Wadsworth/Thomson Learning.

Kazdin, A. E., Holland, L., & Crowley, M. (1997). Family experience of barriers to treatment and premature termination from child therapy. *Journal of Clinical Child Psychology, 65*, 453–463.

Kazdin, A. E., & Wassell, G. (1999). Barriers to treatment participation and therapeutic change among children referred for conduct disorder. *Journal of Clinical Child Psychology, 28*, 160–172.

Kelleher, K. J. (1998). Use of services and costs for youth with attention deficit hyperactivity disorder and related conditions. *NIH Consensus Development Conference: Diagnosis and Treatment of Attention Deficit Disorder Programs and Abstracts*, 229–235.

Kelley, M. L. (1990). *School-home notes: Promoting children's classroom success*. New York: Guilford Press.

Kent, R. N., & O'Leary, D. (1977). Treatment of conduct problem children: B.A. and/or Ph.D. therapists. *Behavior Therapy, 8,* 653–658.

Klein R. G., & Abikoff, H. (1997). Behavior therapy and methylphenidate in the treatment of children with ADHD. *Journal of Attention Disorders, 2,* 89–114.

Kolko, D. J., Bukstein, O. G., & Barron, J. (1999). Methylphenidate and behavior modification in children with ADHD and comorbid ODD and CD: Main and incremental effects across settings. *Journal of the American Academy of Child and Adolescent Psychiatry, 38,* 578–586.

Lochman, J. E., & Curry, J. F. (1986). Effects of social problem-solving training and self-instruction training with aggressive boys. *Journal of Clinical Child Psychology, 15,* 159–164.

Lyon, G. R., & Cutting, L. E. (1998). Learning disabilities. In E. J. Mash & R. A. Barkley (Eds.), *Treatment of childhood disorders* (2nd ed., pp. 468–498). New York: Guilford Press.

Martin, G., & Pear, J. (2002). *Behavior modification: What it is and how to do it* (7th ed.). Upper Saddle River, NJ: Prentice Hall.

McFayden-Ketchum, S. A., & Dodge, K. A. (1998). Problems in social relationships. In E. J. Mash & R. A. Barkley (Eds.), *Treatment of childhood disorders.* (2nd ed., pp. 338–365). New York: Guilford Press.

Michelsen, L., Sugai, D., Wood, R., & Kazdin, A. E. (1983). *Social skills assessment and training with children and adolescents.* New York: Plenum Press.

Miller, G. E., & Prinz, R. J. (1990). Enhancement of social learning family interventions for childhood conduct disorder. *Psychological Bulletin, 108,* 291–307.

Mrug, S., Hoza, B., & Gerdes, A. C. (2001). Children with attention-deficit/hyperactivity disorder: Peer relationships and peer-oriented interventions. In D. W. Nangle & C. A. Erdley (Eds.), *The role of friendship in psychological adjustment: New directions for child and adolescent development* (pp. 51–77). San Francisco: Jossey-Bass.

MTA Cooperative Group. (1999). 14-month randomized clinical trial of treatment strategies for attention deficit hyperactivity disorder. *Archives of General Psychiatry, 56,* 1073–1086.

MTA Cooperative Group. (in press). The NIMH MTA follow-up: 24-month outcomes of treatment strategies for attention-deficit/hyperactivity disorder. *Pediatrics, 113,* 754–761.

Northup, J., Fusilier, I., Swanson, V., Huete, J., Bruce, T., Freeland, J., et al. (1999). Further analysis of the separate and interactive effects of methylphenidate and common classroom contingencies. *Journal of Applied Behavior Analysis, 32,* 35–50.

Oden, S., & Asher, S. R. (1977). Coaching children in social skills for friendship making. *Child Development, 48,* 495–506.

Office of Juvenile Justice and Delinquency Prevention. (1999). *OJJDP annual report.* Washington, DC: U.S. Department of Justice, Office of Justice Programs, Office of Juvenile Justice and Delinquency Prevention.

O'Leary, K. D. (1978). The operant and social psychology of token systems. In A. C. Catania & T. A. Brigham (Eds.), *Handbook of applied behavior analysis: Social and instructional processes* (pp. 179–207). New York: Irvington.

O'Leary, K. D., & O'Leary, S. G. (1977). *Classroom management: The successful use of behavior modification* (2nd ed.). New York: Pergamon Press.

O'Leary, K. D., Pelham, W. E., Rosenbaum, A., & Price, G. (1976). Behavioral treatment of hyperkinetic children: An experimental evaluation of its usefulness. *Clinical Pediatrics, 15,* 510–515.

Patterson, G. R. (1974). Interventions for boys with conduct problems: Multiple settings, treatments, and criteria. *Journal of Consulting and Clinical Psychology, 42,* 471–481.

Patterson, G. R., & Forgatch, M. S. (1987). *Parents and adolescents living together. Part 1: The basics.* Eugene, OR: Castalia.

Pelham, W. E. (1993). Pharmacotherapy for children with attention-deficit hyperactivity disorder. *School Psychology Review, 22,* 199–227.

Pelham, W. E. (2001). Are ADHD/I and ADHD/C the same or different? Does it matter? *Clinical Psychology: Science and Practice, 8,* 502–506.

Pelham, W. E. (2003). *A dose-ranging study of behavioral and pharmacological treatments for ADHD.* Poster session presented at the 2003 Association for the Advancement of Behavior Therapy Conference, Boston.

Pelham, W. E., & Bender, M. E. (1982). Peer relationships in hyperactive children: Description and treatment. In K. Gadow & I. Bialer (Eds.), *Advances in learning and behavioral disabilities* (Vol. 1, pp. 365–436). Greenwich, CT: JAI Press.

Pelham, W. E., Burrows-MacLean, L., Gnagy, E. M., Coles, E. K., Wymbs, B. T., Chacko, A., et al. (2003, November). *A dose-ranging study of behavioral and pharmacological treatment for children with ADHD.* Poster session presented at the 37th annual convention of the Association for Advancement of Behavior Therapy, Boston.

Pelham, W. E., Burrows-MacLean, L., Gnagy, E. M., Fabiano, G. A., Coles, E. K., Tresco, K. E., et al. (2004). *Transdermal methylphenidate, behavioral, and combined treatment for children with ADHD.* Manuscript submitted for publication.

Pelham, W. E., Carlson, C., Sams, S. E., Vallano, G., Dixon, M. J., & Hoza, B. (1993). Separate and combined effects of methylphenidate and behavior modification on the classroom behavior and academic performance of ADHD boys: Group effects and individual differences. *Journal of Consulting and Clinical Psychology, 61,* 506–515.

Pelham, W. E., & Fabiano, G. A. (2000). Behavior modification. *Psychiatric Clinics of North America, 9,* 671–688.

Pelham, W. E., & Fabiano, G. A. (2001). Treatment of attention-deficit hyperactivity disorder: The impact of comorbidity. *Journal of Clinical Psychology and Psychotherapy, 8,* 315–329.

Pelham, W. E., Gnagy, E. M., Chronis, A. M., Burrows-MacLean, L., Fabiano, G. A., Onyango, A. N., et al. (1999). A comparison of morning, midday, and late-afternoon methylphenidate with morning and late-afternoon Adderall in children with attention-deficit/hyperactivity disorder. *Pediatrics*, *104*, 1300–1311.

Pelham, W. E., Gnagy, E. M., Greenslade, K. E., & Milich, R. (1992). Teacher ratings of *DSM–III–R* symptoms for the disruptive behavior disorders. *Journal of the American Academy of Child and Adolescent Psychiatry*, *31*, 210–218.

Pelham, W. E., Gnagy, E. M., Greiner, A. R., Hoza, B., Hinshaw, S. P., Swanson, J. M., et al. (2000). Behavioral vs. behavioral and pharmacological treatment in ADHD children attending a summer treatment program. *Journal of Abnormal Child Psychology*, *28*, 507–526.

Pelham, W. E., Gnagy, E. M., Greiner, A. R., & the MTA Cooperative Group (under review). *Parent and teacher satisfaction with treatment and evaluation of effectiveness*.

Pelham, W. E., Greiner, A. R., & Gnagy, E. M. (1997a). *Summer treatment program manual*. Buffalo, NY: Comprehensive Treatment for Attention Deficit Disorders. Available at http://www.summertreatmentprogram.com

Pelham, W. E., Greiner, A. R., & Gnagy, E. M. (1997b). *Summer treatment program supervisor binder*. Buffalo, NY: Comprehensive Treatment for Attention Deficit Disorders, Inc. Available at http://www.summertreatmentprogram.com

Pelham, W. E., & Hoza, B. (1996). Intensive treatment: A summer treatment program for children with ADHD. In E. Hibbs & P. Jensen (Eds.), *Psychosocial treatments for child and adolescent disorders: Empirically based strategies for clinical practice* (pp. 311–340). Washington, DC: American Psychological Association.

Pelham, W. E., Hoza, B., Pillow, D. R., Gnagy, E. M., Kipp, H. L., Greiner, A. R., et al. (2002). Effects of methylphenidate and expectancy on children with ADHD: Behavior, academic performance, and attributions in a summer treatment program and regular classroom settings. *Journal of Consulting and Clinical Psychology*, *70*, 320–335.

Pelham, W. E., Manos, M., & Janakovic, F. (2000, August). Intensive behavioral treatment for children with ADHD. In J. R. Weisz (Chair) *Making evidence based treatments work in clinical practice*. Symposium conducted at the meeting of the American Psychological Association, Washington, DC.

Pelham, W. E., McBurnett, K., Harper, G., Milich, R., Clinton, J., Thiele, C., et al. (1990). Methylphenidate and baseball playing in ADD children: Who's on first? *Journal of Consulting and Clinical Psychology*, *58*, 130–133.

Pelham, W. E., & Murphy, H. A. (1986). Attention deficit and conduct disorders. In M. Hersen (Ed.), *Pharmacological and behavioral treatment: An integrative approach* (pp. 108–148). New York: Wiley.

Pelham, W. E., & Smith, B. H. (2000). Prediction and measurement of individual responses to Ritalin by children and adolescents with attention deficit hyperactivity disorder. In L. L. Greenhill & B. B. Osman (Eds.), *Ritalin: Theory and practice* (2nd ed., pp. 193–218). Larchmont, NY: Mary Ann Liebert.

Pelham, W. E., & Waschbusch, D. A. (1999). Behavioral intervention in attention-deficit/hyperactivity disorder. In H. C. Quay & A. E. Hogan (Eds.), *Handbook of disruptive behavior disorders* (pp. 255–278). New York: Kluwer Academic/Plenum Publishers.

Pelham, W. E., Wheeler, T., & Chronis, A. (1998). Empirically supported psychosocial treatments for attention deficit hyperactivity disorder. *Journal of Clinical Child Psychology, 27*, 190–205.

Perrin, J. M. (2000). Chronic illness in childhood. In R. E. Behrman, R. Kliegman, & H. B. Jenson (Eds.), *Textbook of pediatrics* (16th ed., pp. 120–123). Philadelphia: WB Saunders.

Pfiffner, L. J., & O'Leary, S. G. (1993). Psychological treatments: School-based. In J. L. Matson (Ed.), *Hyperactivity in children: A handbook*. London: Pergamon.

Reitman, D., Hupp, S. D. A., O'Callaghan, P., Gulley, V., & Northup, J. (2001). The influence of a token economy and methylphenidate on attention during sports with children diagnosed with ADHD. *Behavior Modification, 25*, 305–323.

Rickard, H. C., & Dinoff, M. (1965). Shaping adaptive behavior in a therapeutic summer camp. In L. P. Ullman & L. Krasner (Eds.), *Case studies in behavior modification* (pp. 325–328). New York: Holt, Rinehart, & Winston.

Ross, A. O. (1981). *Child behavior therapy: Principles, procedures, and empirical basis*. New York: Wiley.

Simmons, D. C., Fuchs, L. S., Fuchs, D., Mathes, P., & Hodge, J. P. (1995). Effects of explicit teaching and peer tutoring on the reading achievement of learning-disabled and low-performing students in regular classrooms. *The Elementary School Journal, 95*, 387–408.

Smith, B. H., Pelham, W. E., Evans, S., Gnagy, E. M., Molina, B., Bukstein, O., et al. (1998). Dosage effects of methylphenidate on the social behavior of adolescents diagnosed with attention deficit hyperactivity disorder. *Experimental and Clinical Psychopharmacology, 6*, 187–204.

Smoll, F. L., & Smith, R. E. (1987). *Sports psychology for youth coaches*. Washington, DC: National Federation for Catholic Ministry.

Smoll, F. L., Smith, R. E., Barnett, N. P., & Everett, J. J. (1993). Enhancement of children's self-esteem through social support training for youth sport coaches. *Journal of Applied Psychology, 78*, 602–610.

Spivak, G., Platt, J. J., & Shure, M. B. (1976). *The problem-solving approach to adjustment*. San Francisco: Jossey-Bass.

Swanson, J. M., McBurnett, K., Christian, D. L., & Wigal, T. (1995). Stimulant medication and treatment of children with ADHD. In T. H. Ollendick & R. J. Prinz (Eds.), *Advances in clinical child psychology* (Vol. 17, pp. 265–322). New York: Plenum Press.

Walker, H. M., Hops, H., & Greenwood, C. R. (1986). RECESS. In P. S. Strain, M. J. Guralnick, & H. M. Walker (Eds.), *Children's social behavior: Development, assessment, and modification*. New York: Academic Press.

Walker, H. M., & Walker, J. E. (1991). *Coping with noncompliance in the classroom: A positive approach for teachers*. Austin, TX: Pro-Ed.

Weiss, G., & Hechtman, L. (1993). *Hyperactive children grown up: ADHD in children, adolescents, and adults*. New York: Guilford Press.

Weisz, J. R., & Weiss, B. (1993). *Effects of psychotherapy with children and adolescents*. Newbury Park, CA: Sage.

Wells, K. C., Pelham, W. E., Kotkin, R. A., Hoza, B., Abikoff, H. B., Abramowitz, A., et al. (2000). Psychosocial treatment strategies in the MTA study: Rationale, methods, and critical issues in design and implementation. *Journal of Abnormal Child Psychology, 28,* 483–505.

17

MULTIMODAL THERAPY AND STIMULANTS IN THE TREATMENT OF CHILDREN WITH ATTENTION-DEFICIT/ HYPERACTIVITY DISORDER

LILY HECHTMAN, HOWARD B. ABIKOFF, AND PETER S. JENSEN

Most children with attention-deficit/hyperactivity disorder (ADHD) come to the attention of mental health professionals because of multiple difficulties in school and at home. For example, in spite of normal intelligence, youngsters with ADHD often perform poorly in school. This underachievement occurs because the primary symptoms of the disorder, excessive motor activity, poor sustained attention, and impulsivity, coupled with the children's distractibility, difficulty in following instructions, and disorganization, all contribute to academic difficulties. In addition, because children with ADHD frequently have poor social skills (Whalen & Henker, 1985), significant interpersonal problems with family, peers, and teachers are also common. Not surprisingly, these difficulties may give rise to poor self-esteem (Weiss, Hechtman, Perlman, Hopkins, & Wener, 1975). These problems are often compounded and amplified by significant comorbidity, such as oppositional defiant disorder; conduct disorder; and mood, anxiety, and learning disorders (Abikoff & Klein, 1992; August & Garfinkel, 1989; Biederman, Newcorn, & Sprich, 1991; Bird et al., 1988).

Thus, given the multiple difficulties that children with ADHD have, several different types of interventions may be required to address all these diverse problems.

MULTIMODAL THERAPY

Reports by James Satterfield and his colleagues support the usefulness and clinical efficacy of multimodal therapy in broad-based interventions with hyperactive children (Satterfield, Cantwell, & Satterfield, 1979; Satterfield, Satterfield, & Cantwell, 1980, 1981). These investigators, working with hyperactive children between ages 6 and 12 years, evaluated a treatment program consisting of methylphenidate, individual psychotherapy, group therapy, educational therapy, individual parent counseling, group counseling for parents, and family therapy. Children and their families received combinations of these treatments, depending on the needs and disabilities of the youths and their parents. In comparing these findings with other outcome studies, the investigators reported that the outcome of this comprehensively treated group was unusually good; the children showed improvement in home and school behavior and academic achievement and reduction in antisocial behavior as well. Moreover, improvements in the latter two areas were reportedly related to the length of treatment; children and family members who received 3 years of treatment showed better outcomes than those with less than 1 year of treatment.

The findings from the Satterfield et al. studies provided promising reports of a meaningful clinical intervention for youths with ADHD. However, the report of treatment efficacy needs to be tempered because the multimodal therapy received by these children was not provided within the context of a controlled, random assignment treatment study. However, such controlled, randomized, multimodal treatment studies were subsequently conducted by others, as described in the following sections.

Montreal–New York Study

The first study, supported by a grant from the National Institute of Mental Health, took place at two sites. The purpose of the study was to determine whether the provision of multimodal treatment (MMT) to children with ADHD who were also receiving methylphenidate resulted in better social, behavioral, emotional, and academic functioning than that associated with methylphenidate alone and whether exposure to MMT enables these children to continue to function adequately when medication is discontinued. Children participating in the study received their optimal dose of medication and were randomly assigned to either multimodal treatment (medication, academic study skills, tutoring, individualized remedial tutoring, individual psychotherapy, and parent training and counseling) or to one of two control groups: a conventional stimulant treatment group (CTG) or an attention control group (ACG) that controlled for time with and attention from professional staff received by the MMT group.

Method

Subjects and Selection: Inclusion Criteria. The study included boys and girls between the ages of 7 and 9 who met research diagnostic criteria for ADHD, including elevated scores on the Conners Teacher Rating Scale (CTRS; Goyette, Conners, & Ulrich, 1978) and the ascertainment of a diagnosis of ADHD according to the *Diagnostic and Statistical Manual of Mental Disorders, Third Edition, Revised* (DSM–III–R; American Psychiatric Association, 1987) and the parent version of the Diagnostic Interview Schedule for Children (DISC-P). Other inclusion criteria included an IQ of at least 85 on the Wechsler Intelligence Scale for Children—Revised (WISC–R), living at home with at least one parent, and the ability to travel to the clinic on a regular basis. In addition, to participate in the study, children had to be designated as stimulant responders.

Determination of Children's Response to Methylphenidate. Systematic procedures were used for establishing optimal clinical dosage and for determining responsivity to stimulants.

OPTIMAL DOSAGE. A specific titration (3 times per day) schedule was used. During titration, which on average requires 4 to 5 weeks, children were seen weekly at the clinic and dosage was increased gradually up to a maximum of 50 mg/day, on the basis of weekly assessments. Each week, the teachers completed the 10-item Abbreviated Conners Teacher Rating Scale (ACTRS) and a semistructured telephone interview to generate clinical information about aspects of the child's functioning and side effects on that dose. The teachers, parents, and psychiatrist also completed a weekly Global Improvement Scale (GIS).

The optimal dosage for each child was determined according to the following rules:

1. Dosage was increased (to a maximum of 50 mg/day) until there was no report of increased improvement with the higher dosage, at which point the child was returned to the previous dosage. Improvement was determined with a rating of "improved" by two of the three raters on the GIS, who compared the child's current functioning with his or her functioning during the pre-

vious week, and when the score on the ACTRS was within 1 standard deviation (SD) of the mean for the child's age.

2. If a child received a GIS rating of "completely well" by two raters and the ACTRS score was within 1 SD of the mean for age, then no further dosage increase occurred.
3. Teacher or parent reports of adverse side effects, determined from specific side effects questionnaire completed weekly, resulted in a return to a lower dosage.

METHYLPHENIDATE RESPONSIVITY. The determination of methylphenidate responsivity was based on two factors: positive clinical effects, confirmed by relapse on placebo, and the absence of negative cognitive effects.

Positive clinical response required that a child showed a reduction of at least 25% on the ACTRS score and be rated as improved by two of the three raters on the GIS.

Placebo confirmation of responsivity required that children who showed a positive clinical response also showed clinical deterioration during a placebo trial (blinded for child, parent, and teacher). In setting the criteria for relapse on placebo, we tried to select standards that were clinically meaningful and that provided objective criteria. These criteria were as follows:

1. Compared with functioning while on active medication, the child must receive a rating of at least "worse" by two of three raters (teacher, parent, or psychiatrist) on the GIS, which ranges from "completely well" to "very much worse."
2. The child must meet *DSM–III–R* criteria for ADHD, based on a *DSM–III–R* Symptom Checklist completed with the parent.
3. The child must receive a Hyperactivity factor score on the CTRS that is at least 25% higher than the score obtained on his or her optimal dosage.

Children who did not fulfill criteria for a positive clinical response and the criteria for placebo confirmation of responsivity did not participate in the study.

No consensus exists with regard to the standards for stimulant-induced cognitive impairment. To ascertain that cognitive functioning was not compromised at the child's optimal clinical dosage of methylphenidate, we initially administered an arithmetic test (an odd–even test developed by Schachar and Tannock to assess overfocusing dose–response effects of methylphenidate [R. Tannock, personal communication, July, 1989] at baseline and regularly during titration during the first 2 years of the study). Deleterious change in arithmetic performance was defined as a decrement of at least 20% in performance on two separate testings, relative to baseline. If such a change occurred, the most clinically effective dosage not associated with cognitive impairment was reinstituted. No such instances occurred. Children regularly showed higher accuracy with increasing dosage, confirming the findings regarding linear dose–response effects with methylphenidate (e.g., Douglas, Barr, O'Neill, & Britton, 1988; Pelham, 1986). Consequently, the study eliminated the formal cognitive-testing procedure during titration. Instead, during a telephone interview, teachers were asked each week about the child's academic and cognitive performance at given doses of medication to flag decrements.

EXCLUSION CRITERIA. The overall goal of the exclusionary criteria was to reduce diagnostic heterogeneity to permit clear generalizability of results. Children were excluded if they had (a) neurological disorders (e.g., cerebral palsy or seizures); (b) psychosis; (c) a current or recent history of physical abuse; (d) tic disorder or Tourette's syndrome; (e) a significant learning disability (defined as a standard score, in reading or mathematics on the Kaufmann Test of Educational Achievement [KTEA] of 85 or less [i.e., at least one SD below the population mean] and a KTEA score that was at least 15 points [1 SD] below their full scale IQ [Halperin, Gittelman, Klein, & Rudel, 1984]; these children were not included in the study because it is unreasonable, and possibly unethical, to withhold academic remediation for as much as 2 years from children assigned to the two control treatments); and (f) a DSM–III–R diagnosis of conduct disorder because these youths probably require targeting of different symptoms and different treatment strategies.

It is important to note that children with ADHD and additional conduct problems were not excluded. Children with comorbid oppositional defiant disorder (ODD), as well as youngsters with ADHD who would have met DSM–III criteria for conduct disorder (CD; one or two conduct problems rather than the more severe DSM–III–R criteria for CD [3 conduct problems]), entered the study. The inclusion of these children with conduct problems was intended not only to parallel the sample of hyperactive children who participated in Satterfield and colleagues' (1979) multimodal study but also to reflect the large percentage of school-aged children with ADHD who have comorbid disruptive behavior disorders (Hinshaw, 1987). In so doing, the results of this treatment study could be generalized to a childhood population that was representative of the ADHD spectrum.

TREATMENT ASSIGNMENT. Participants who met entry criteria were randomly assigned to one of the three treatment groups with group balancing for race, gender, IQ, and rate of oppositional disorders. Assignment was done in blocks of four children at a time to allow for those treatment components that require a group format.

Description of Study Treatments

Multimodal Interventions. The MMT interventions in the study were intended to address the major deficits associated with ADHD. Thus, the treatment program consisted of medication, academic study-skills training, individualized remedial tutoring, and individual psychotherapy. Social-skills training, parent management training and counseling, and a home-based reinforcement program for school behavior were also provided and integrated into a behavioral systems approach as part of the MMT regimen. These treatment components are described in the following sections.

STIMULANT TREATMENT. As noted previously, methylphenidate was adjusted to the most effective clinical dosage, to a maximum of 50 mg/day. Medication was prescribed 7 days per week, 3 times a day, with the smallest dosage (usually 5 or 10 mg) given at approximately 3:30 p.m. This regimen was designed to maximize attention and cooperation during the after-school treatment sessions. In general, this dosing procedure did not result in significant difficulties with sleep onset. The children were maintained on their clinically effective dosage throughout their participation in the study, although the development of side effects or drug tolerance resulted in dosage adjustments. To facilitate the appropriate management of each child's maintenance stimulant treatment, monthly feedback from parents, teachers, and the child (including behavioral ratings, descriptions of the child's functioning, and assessments of side effects) was obtained.

SOCIAL SKILLS TRAINING. Parents and teachers often complain that children with ADHD do not get along well with their peers. School observation indicates that children with ADHD are similar to other children with regard to the occurrence of neutral and positive peer interactions (Abikoff & Gittelman, 1982). What distinguishes students with ADHD from their peers is the higher frequency of negative social behaviors, such as bossiness, intrusiveness, and aggressiveness. Their awkward interpersonal exchanges with peers stem from a seeming lack of sensitivity to social cues, nuances, and demands; this behavior suggests the presence of social learning disability (Whalen & Henker, 1991).

The social-skills training focused on the development and enhancement of age-appropriate interpersonal skills. Embedded within the year-long training were components of two programs that have shown promise in improving children's social competency: Jackson, Jackson, and Monroe's (1983) *Getting Along With Others: Teaching Social Effectiveness to Children* program and the *Walker Social Skills Curriculum: The ACCEPTS Program* (Walker et al., 1983). These programs focus on social skills excesses and deficits and attempt to modify behavior using a variety of techniques, including direct instruction, modeling, behavioral rehearsal, feedback, reactions of others, and social reinforcement. We used elements of these established training programs, modified them when necessary to increase their relevance to children with ADHD, and added training features meant to enhance generalization.

The year-long curriculum addressed different social skills each week (e.g., joining a conversation, giving and receiving positive feedback, waiting for one's turn in games, cooperating in a group activity).

In-session training components included the use of modeling, role playing, and viewing previously videotaped training sessions. Homework assignments were given to increase skills mastery and to aid in generalization outside the treatment setting. Throughout the social-skills training, a behavior modification system was implemented that initially used concrete rewards to reinforce appropriate behavior in the session. Subsequently, the children self-evaluated their social behavior during the session (see Hinshaw, Henker & Whalen, 1984; Turkewitz, O'Leary, & Ironsmith, 1975), and the corresponding points earned or lost by the children were incorporated into the parent management program at home (described in more detail later in this chapter).

PARENT TRAINING AND FAMILY COUNSELING. Children with ADHD have problems adhering to adult rules and to the setting of limits. These difficulties are often characterized by noncompliant and oppositional behavior, frequently at levels severe enough to warrant a comorbid diagnosis of ODD. The resulting child management problems faced by parents (and teachers) are a common reason that these children are referred to mental health professionals. When noncompliance and defiance are among the child's symptoms, treatment directed at these behaviors seems indicated, especially because the presence of ODD in these children heightens their risk for the development of CD (Farrington, Loeber, & van Kammen, 1990). Accordingly, parent training, with an emphasis on behavior management strategies and a focus on dealing with the child's oppositional behavior (see Forehand & MacMahon, 1981), was included in the MMT program.

During the first year, the parents participated in a group format for the first 4 months and then in weekly individual sessions. The group sessions were based, in part, on Russell Barkley's (1987) behavior management training program for parents of defiant and hyperactive children. The parents learned how to use contingent praise, attention, time out, and response cost and how to set up and implement a token economy system at home. The latter consisted of a comprehensive point system, whereby daily privileges (e.g., TV, Nintendo games) and special activities and rewards were made contingent on points earned by the child in the social-skills sessions in the clinic, at school (based on the use of a daily report card format described later), and at home. Included in the behaviors targeted for increase at home were the completion of daily chores and compliance with parental requests. Children earned or lost points on the basis of whether they engaged in these positive behaviors. Similarly, negative behaviors, individualized for each child, were targeted for decrease (e.g., noncompliance, tantrums, fighting). A loss of points and, in some instances, time out resulted when these inappropriate behaviors occurred, whereas points were earned when the child did not display these negative behaviors at home.

After the group sessions, the parents participated individually for 8 months in once-weekly sessions, of which every fourth included the child with ADHD and the rest of the family. During the second year, treatment consisted of once-monthly sessions. The individual work with the parents served to reinforce, support, and clarify parental efforts to apply the behavior management techniques taught in the parent groups. The sessions also focused on any marital discord related to rearing and managing the child, and counseling for these conflicts was provided, if necessary. Although no studies have yet evaluated the effectiveness of such counseling in parents of children with ADHD, studies of parents of children with ODD and CD suggest that efforts to resolve marital conflict can produce positive behavioral changes in both the children and the parents (Dadds, Schwartz, & Sanders, 1987). During the family sessions, efforts are made to enhance communication among family members and to address such issues as parent–child alliances and scapegoating.

DAILY SCHOOL REPORT CARD. The report-card system is a cost-effective way to set goals and to monitor, reinforce, and modify the child's school behavior, without singling out or stigmatizing the child in the classroom or requiring excessive direct teacher and therapist involvement (see Atekeson & Forehand, 1979; Barkley, 1981; Lahey et al., 1977). Each child's report card contained a list of several behaviors that the teacher deemed important for that individual student (e.g., bringing completed homework to class, not interrupting). The teacher rated the child on each behavior and initialed the card. The children were required to bring the card home from school every day. The daily ratings were associated with a number of points earned or lost. The point totals were incorporated into the home-based reinforcement program managed by the parents and resulted in the gain or loss of privileges, activities, or other reinforcers at home. The target behaviors changed over time, reflecting changes in the child's comportment.

ACADEMIC SKILLS TRAINING AND REMEDIATION. The academic problems of children with ADHD are characterized typically by low or failing grades, repeating grades, lower-than-expected achievement test scores, and placement in resource rooms or special classes. These negative outcomes result from the interaction of several possible factors, including specific academic skills deficits, a concurrent learning disability, inattention during classroom lessons, and poor organizational and study skills.

The goal of the first 12 weeks of the academic treatment component was to improve organizational skills and strategies relevant to successful academic performance. To this end, the children were assigned to groups and exposed to a variety of tasks and activities, most of them academic in nature, that focus on following written and oral instructions, getting ready to work, organizing materials, efficient use of time, reviewing one's work, and so on.

During the subsequent 9 months, the participants received weekly remedial tutoring that targeted their specific skill deficits in reading, mathematics, and language. These prescriptive tutoring sessions, conducted by special education teachers, were individualized on the basis of diagnostic evaluations of each child.

Some children performed at grade level and did not require remediation. Training for these students focused on the mastery of academic skills and continued emphasis on the organizational and study skills described previously. The emphasis during these sessions was on the children's own schoolwork, although supplementary training materials and tasks for specific subskills were provided when needed.

PSYCHOTHERAPY. Unsurprisingly, given their multiple difficulties, children with ADHD often suffer from low self-esteem. The common experience of being shunned by other children, yelled at by parents and teachers, and chided for their poor scholastic performance and a lack of success in dealing with these problems on their own lead to feelings of demoralization, low self-worth, and a poor self-image. Often, these children also experience a great deal of underlying frustration, anger, and depression. To address these issues, the MMT program included an individual psychotherapy component that attempted to improve the child's self-esteem, promote a better understanding of the disorder, change the child's perception of the experienced rejection, and enhance self-effectiveness. A specific psychotherapy manual outlines interventions in these areas (Table 17.1).

Clinical Vignette

Robbie came to the clinic with a history of inattention in school, distractibility, and impulsivity. His self-esteem was generally poor; he lacked friends and showed a susceptibility to tears at the slightest provocation. For example, his mother complained that it took him hours to get anything done, such as getting dressed in the morning or doing homework, because he was not able to keep his mind on the task at hand. When chastised for this, Robbie would dissolve into tears and say that he never did anything right and that no one liked him. Robbie was put on stimulant medication, which significantly decreased his distractibility, impulsivity, and inattention, making it easier for him to complete tasks. In individual psychotherapy, his impulsive tendencies were the focus of cognitive–behavior therapy interventions, such as teaching him to tell himself to "hold his horses" and "give his brain time to think" before rushing to answer a question. Psycho-educational techniques were used to help him understand some of his difficulties and the benefits of medication. He also learned to identify and express his feelings adaptively, using supportive techniques, reflection, clarification, and interpretation. Gradually, as therapy progressed, Robbie developed a greater sense of competence and improved self-esteem. He began to make overtures to some classmates, and his crying episodes became less and less frequent. Throughout Robbie's individual psychotherapy, parent

TABLE 17.1
Montreal–New York Study
Components of Study Treatment Groups

Treatment group		
Multimodal	Attention control	Conventional stimulant
Medication • Methylphenidate • Individually titrated to optimal dose • 3 times per day • 7 days per week • Monthly medication monitoring visits	Medication • Methylphenidate • Individually titrated to optimal dose • 3 times per day • 7 days per week • Monthly medication monitoring visits	Medication • Methylphenidate • Individually titrated to optimal dose • 3 times per day • 7 days per week • Monthly medication visit, provided medication monitoring, and family support
Daily school report card Social skills training group* (weekly for 1 year)**	Peer activity group* (weekly for 1 year)**	
Academic organizational skills group* (weekly for 3 months)**	Working on projects (weekly for 3 months)**	
Academic remediation (dyads, weekly for remaining 8 months)**	Help with homework (dyads, weekly for remaining 8 months)**	
Parent training group* (weekly for 4 months)**	Parent support group* (weekly for 4 months)**	
Parent counseling (individual, weekly for remaining 8 months)**	Parental support (individual, weekly for remaining 8 months)**	
Individual psychotherapy of the child (weekly for 1 year)**	Individual supportive time with adult (weekly for 1 year)**	
Crisis intervention[†]	Crisis intervention[†]	Crisis intervention[†]

*Groups consisted of 4 to 5 children or families.
**All weekly interventions have monthly booster sessions in the second year.
[†]A total of eight crisis sessions were available, as needed (e.g., school consultation, intervention with parents or child).

counseling helped his parents to develop skills for managing his behavior more constructively and to support the progress that he was making in his individual therapy.

Procedures to Enhance Generalization

As noted earlier, treatment studies of children with ADHD indicate that clinical gains rarely transfer outside of the treatment setting. The achievement of treatment generalization is a daunting challenge, and no empirically established methods for achieving this goal exist yet. Nevertheless, the MMT program incorporated procedures that were intended to increase generalization.

For instance, the academic training sessions focused not only on materials and exercises deemed important by the clinical staff but also periodically included the student's actual classwork and homework assignments. In this manner, the child had the opportunity to practice organizational and academic skills on tasks that were directly linked to school demands.

As described previously, the children were given social-skills homework assignments between clinic sessions and were rewarded for following these assignments outside of the treatment setting. In addition, social-skills difficulties shown by a child in the clinic, if reported by the child's parents or teacher, were incorporated into the home and school-based programs. For example, if a child frequently interrupted others, the child would self-monitor and self-reinforce his or her behavior to refrain from interrupting when in the social-skills group. At home, the parent would monitor and reward the child's efforts to keep from interrupting, and progress toward this goal would also be included on the child's daily school report card. In this manner, the child was encouraged and rewarded for demonstrating specific social skills, not only in the clinic but at school and home as well.

Treatment Delivery

In the first year of treatment, the various MMT and ACG treatment sessions were conducted during two afternoons per week after school at the clinic; in the second year, each treatment component was provided once a month, in the form of booster sessions. The treatment arrangement was characteristic of treatment typically delivered within the context of a partial-day (after-school) treatment program, wherein professional staff members provided all the necessary interventions at one site and could readily share relevant treatment issues with one another.

CONTROL TREATMENTS

Attention Control

The attention-control interventions, while omitting the putative active treatment ingredients of the MMT interventions, were intended to control for the nonspecific treatment effects of the multimodal interventions that might be related to professional time and attention. The specific attention-control components are described briefly in the subsequent sections, and a comparison of the multimodal, attention-control, and conventional stimulant treatment group components may be found in Table 17.1.

1. *Projects.* The children concentrated on nonacademic projects (e.g., musical instruments, drawings of holiday plans), without formal instruction in organizational and study skills.

2. *Homework.* The children were provided with general assistance with homework assignments. No emphasis was placed on deficits in academic, organizational, or study skills, and remediation was not given.
3. *Peer activities.* The children were given opportunities to work together on tasks and activities and to play with appropriate structure and limit setting. No social-skills training was provided. The approach was similar to that of a community-based afterschool activity program.
4. *Parent psychoeducational and support group.* Parents were given psychoeducational information about ADHD (e.g., etiology, assessment, developmental issues). The parents also participated in a support group led by a therapist. Formal instruction in behavior management was not provided.
5. *Individual parent support.* A therapist helped to maintain a supportive, nondirective relationship with the parents and continued to serve as a resource for the provision of psychoeducational information and advice regarding ADHD. General parenting principles (e.g., need for consistency, structure, and clarity; avoidance of parental disagreements in front of child) were also dealt with, but specific behavioral management techniques were not taught.
6. *Individual child support.* Supportive, nondirective sessions focused on the child's unstructured discussion of life events and problems, providing an opportunity for the child to feel understood and accepted. Play and play-related activities were used to foster discussion. Play therapy or other psychotherapeutic interventions focusing on problems of ADHD symptomatology, social interactions, and self-esteem were not specifically used.

Conventional Stimulant Treatment Group

The children in the conventional stimulant control group received maintenance treatment with methylphenidate throughout their 2 years in the study. The individual monthly meetings lasted approximately 45 minutes and involved medication monitoring and nonspecific clinical management.

Crisis Intervention

Patients in all three groups had a bank of eight crisis intervention sessions that could be used during the 2 years to deal with whatever crises may arise.

MEDICATION WITHDRAWAL FEASIBILITY

As noted earlier, the positive effects of stimulant treatment are often not maintained when medication is discontinued, resulting in remedication for most children. Even when stimulants are combined with other interventions, such as cognitive training, more than 85% of children with ADHD resume medication within 1 month of cessation of stimulant treatment (Abikoff & Gittelman, 1985). One purpose of the current study was to determine whether exposure to long-term MMT enables youths with ADHD to be maintained off medication. To this end, blind placebo challenges were implemented after the first and second years of MMT. Children with ADHD in all three groups needed to restart medication within several days of medication withdrawal because of significant deterioration.

ASSESSMENT OF TREATMENT OUTCOME

Multimodal studies require multiple assessment procedures and measures to evaluate treatment efficacy. In this study, information regarding functioning in various domains was collected from parents, teachers, and children before the child's assignment to treatment, when the child was on and off medication, and subsequently at 6-month intervals.

The children's school behavior was evaluated using standardized teacher rating scales and observation procedures. At home, the children's behavior was assessed using parent rating scales. Changes in perceptions of parental self-efficacy, child management strategies, and knowledge of behavioral principles were assessed as well. The children also completed rating scales, which served as change measures of self-concept, social skills, and depression. Finally, testing procedures were used to assess changes in academic achievement and performance and in information processing skills. Table 17.2 lists the specific outcome measures used in the study.

The results have been published in Hechtmann et al. (2004a, 2004b) and Abikoff et al. (2004a, 2004b). Generally, findings suggest that all three groups improved significantly in most domains from baseline. The improvements were often seen after the titration of medication to optimal dose. The improvements were clearly seen at 6 months and were maintained without any deterioration at 12, 18, and 24 months. However, in general no significant difference was detected in the three groups.

In all clinical trials, inclusion and exclusion criteria delimit the scope of the study's generalizability. The current study is no exception. The results should be considered most relevant to children whose parents are willing to bring them to an after-school program two afternoons a week for a year. Findings are applicable to children of parents who agree to medication treatment (approximately 75% of referrals to the study) and to those who

TABLE 17.2
Montreal–New York Study
Domains Assessed and Study Outcome Measures

Domain	Instrument	What it measures	Type of measure	Informant
Child measures				
Social behavior	Social Skills Rating System (Gresham & Elliott, 1989)	Cooperation, assertion, responsibility, self-control, and total score	Rating scale, norms available	Parents
	Social Skills Rating System (Gresham & Elliott, 1989)	Cooperation, assertion, empathy, self-control, and total score	Self-rating scale, norm available	Child
	Taxonomy of Problem Situations (Dodge, McClaskey, & Feldman, 1985)	Six aspects of social competence in school, total score	Rating scale	Teacher
	Social Interaction Code (revised) (Abikoff, Martin, & Klein, 1989)	Child's social behavior toward peers and teacher and their response, peers' and teacher's social behavior toward child and child's response	Observation system	Observers (blinded)
ADHD behavior	Home Situations Questionnaire (Barkley, 1987)	Situations in which child shows problematic behaviors associated with ADHD	Rating scales, norms available	Parents
	Conners Parent Rating Scale–Revised (Goyette et al., 1978)	Impulsive-hyperactive factor, hyperkinesis index	Rating scales, norms available	Parents
	DSM–III–R Symptom Checklist	*DSM–III–R* ADHD symptoms	Interview questionnaire	Parents
	Conners Teacher Rating Scale (Goyette et al., 1978)	Hyperactivity factor, hyperkinesis index	Rating scales, norms available	Teacher

Domain	Instrument	What it measures	Type of measure	Informant
ADHD behavior (continued)	Conners Teacher Rating Scale (Goyette et al., 1978)	Hyperactivity factor, hyperkinesis index	Rating scales, norms available	Teacher
	School Situations Questionnaire (Barkley, 1987)	Situations in school in which child shows problematic behaviors associated with ADHD	Rating scales, norms available	Teacher
	Classroom Observation Code (Abikoff & Gittelman, 1985a)	12 classroom behaviors during structured work time	Observation system	Observers (blinded)
	Hillside Behavior Rating Scale	13 ADHD related behaviors	Rating scale	Observers (blinded)
	Conners Rating Scale	Hyperkinesis index, inattentive–overactive factors from IOWA Conners Rating Scale	Rating scale	Observers (blinded)
Academic performance	Homework Problem Checklist (Anesko & O'Leary, 1982)	26 homework related behaviors, total problem score	Rating scale	Parents
	Stanford Achievement Test (1989 edition)	Mathematics, reading, spelling, listening skills	Standardized achievement test	Child
	Arithmetic Test (Douglas et al., 1989)	Arithmetic productivity, accuracy, time spent, efficiency	Time performance test (alternate forms)	Child

continues

TABLE 17.2 (Continued)
Montreal–New York Study
Domains Assessed and Study Outcome Measures

Domain	Instrument	What it measures	Type of measure	Informant
Emotional indices	Piers-Harris Children's Self-Concept Scale (Piers, 1984)	Six aspects of self-concept and total score	Self-rating scale	Child
	Children's Depression Inventory (Kovacs & Beck, 1977)	Total score indicating level of self-reported depression	Self-rating scale	Child
Global indices	Global Improvement Scale	Global improvement in child functioning	8-point rating scale	Parents, teacher, physician
	Children's Global Assessment Scale (Shaffer et al., 1985)	Overall level of child's functioning	Rating scale	
Parent measures				
Emotional indices	Structured Clinical Interview for the *DSM–III–R* (Spitzer, Williams, Gibbon, & First, 1988)	Parental psychopathology	Clinical interview	Mother, father
Parenting indices	Being A Parent Scale (Johnston & Mash, 1989)	Parental satisfaction and efficacy	Rating scale	Parents
	Knowledge of Behavioral Principles (O'Dell, Tarler-Benlolol, & Flynn, 1979)	Parents' knowledge of behavioral principles as applied to children	Multiple choice test	Parents
	Parenting Practices Scale (Strayhorn & Weidman, 1988)	Parenting behaviors and parent-child interaction patterns	Self-rating scale	Parents
	Parenting Practices Scale (child report)	Child's report of mother's and father's parenting behaviors	Rating scale	Child

TABLE 17.2 (Continued)
Montreal–New York Study
Domains Assessed and Study Outcome Measures

Domain	Instrument	What it measures	Type of measure	Informant
Cognitive measures	Memory Scan Test (Swanson, Cantwell, Lerner, McBurnett, & Hanna, 1991)	Perceptual encoding and motor response times	Information-load processing task	Child
Other measures	Parent Satisfaction	Parental satisfaction with parenting groups	Rating scale	Parents
	Additional Therapeutic Contacts in Study	Number and type of crisis sessions provided by staff to child and parent	Log records	Staff

respond to methylphenidate (approximately 90% of the children considered for our study were found to respond to methylphenidate). Likewise, the study's findings may not be applicable to children with ADHD and severe learning disabilities or CD (diagnosed with *DSM–III–R* criteria) because these individuals were excluded from the trial. It is important to reiterate, however, that the study included children with ADHD who were comorbid for ODD, as well as those with less severe CDs and learning disabilities and those with anxiety and mood disorders. Given the overall representativeness of this sample, the study findings should be generalizable to a large segment of the elementary-school–aged population of children with ADHD.

The breadth of this multimodal clinical trial notwithstanding, a number of issues must be addressed in future studies. Treatment in the current study was provided within the context of an after-school program. Determining whether the delivery of treatment in nonclinical settings, especially schools, can maximize clinical efficacy is important. Another central question is whether intensive long-term psychosocial treatment alone can demonstrate clinical efficacy. Also pivotal are studies with sample sizes large enough to examine the interaction of treatment and patient characteristics. Studies of this kind are needed to generate essential information regarding which type of treatment is best for which type of patient. Especially pertinent are outcome data that address the implications of comorbidity for treatment planning in children with ADHD. Some of these and other important issues were addressed in the NIMH Collaborative Multisite Multimodal Treatment Study of Children With ADHD (the MTA Study; Richters et al., 1995; MTA Cooperative Group, 1999a, 199b).

RATIONALE AND OBJECTIVES OF THE MTA STUDY

The rationale of the MTA study has been described in detail by Richters et al. (1995). Basically, the MTA Cooperative Group posed three questions:

1. How do long-term medication and behavioral treatments compare with one another?
2. Are there additional benefits when they are used together?
3. What is the effectiveness of systematic, carefully delivered treatment versus routine community care?

Inclusion and Exclusion Criteria

For eligibility, children (of either sex) were between ages 7 and 9.9 years, in Grades 1 through 4, and in residence with the same primary caretaker or caretakers for the previous 6 months or longer. All met the *DSM–IV* criteria for ADHD Combined Type (the most common subtype in this age group), using the Diagnostic Interview Schedule for Children (DISC), parent report, version 3.0 (Shaffer et al., 1996) supplemented with up to two symptoms identified by children's teachers for cases falling just below the DISC diagnostic threshold. Exclusion criteria were limited to situations that would prevent families' full participation in assessments or treatment or that might require additional treatments incompatible with study treatments. The presence of comorbid conditions, such as ODD, CD, internalizing disorders, and specific learning disabilities, did not lead to exclusions per se; an important aim of the study was to examine their interactions with treatment outcomes.

Design

In a four-group parallel design, children were assigned randomly to medication management, behavioral treatment, combined treatment, or community care for 14 months. Rather than testing fixed single treatments, each MTA treatment arm was designed as a management strategy, such that each was sufficiently robust and flexible to stand on its own and to respond to individual patients' clinical needs throughout the study. For all three arms, subjects were eligible to receive up to eight additional sessions when needed to address clinical emergencies or instances of possible study attrition.

Behavioral Treatment

Behavioral treatment included parent training, child-focused treatment, and a school-based intervention organized and integrated with the school year. The parent training, based on work by Barkley (1987) and Forehand and MacMahon (1981), involved 27 group (six families per group) and eight individual sessions per family. It began weekly on randomization, concurrent with biweekly teacher consultation; both were tapered over time. The same therapist–consultant conducted parent training and teacher consultation, with each therapist–consultant having a caseload of 12 families.

The child-focused treatment was a summer treatment program (STP) developed by Pelham and described by Pelham and Hoza (1996) as a therapeutic summer camp. The 8-week, 5-days-per-week, 9-hours-per-day STP employed intensive behavioral interventions administered by counselors–aides, supervised by the same teacher–consultants who performed parent training and teacher consultation. Behavioral interventions were delivered in group-based recreational settings and included a point system tied to specific rewards, time out, social reinforcement, modeling, group problem-solving, sports skills, and social skills training. STP classrooms provided individualized practice of academic skills and reinforcement of appropriate classroom behavior.

The school-based treatment had two components: 10 to 16 sessions of biweekly teacher consultation focused on classroom behavior management strategies and 12 weeks (60 school days) of a part-time, behaviorally trained, paraprofessional aide working directly with the child (methods adapted from Swanson, 1992). The aides had been STP counselors, and the program continued in the fall classroom, which helped to generalize STP gains to classrooms. Throughout the school year, a daily report card linked home and school. The daily report card was a one-page teacher-completed checklist of the child's successes on specific preselected behaviors and was brought home daily by the child to be reinforced by the parents with home-based rewards (e.g., television time, snacks).

Consistent with the time-limited involvement of providers in clinical practice, the involvement of our personnel in the delivery of the behavioral treatments was gradually tapered, with the goal that parents would increasingly manage the child's behavioral treatment. In most cases, contact between therapists and parents had been reduced to once-monthly sessions or stopped altogether before end-point assessment.

Medication Management

Medication management has been described in detail by Greenhill et al. (1996). A brief summary follows.

Medication management started with a 28-day, double-blind, daily-switch titration of methylphenidate hydrochloride, using 5 randomly ordered repeats each of placebo, 5 mg, 10 mg, and 15 or 20 mg (higher doses for children >25 kg). Each of the doses listed was given at breakfast and lunch, with a half-dose (rounded to the nearest 5 mg) in the afternoon. Cross-site teams of experienced clinicians blindly reviewed graphs portraying parent and teacher ratings of responses to each of the 4 doses and by consensus selected each child's best dose. After agreement on best dose, the blind was broken, and the agreed-on dose (if not placebo) became the subject's initial maintenance dose. For subjects who did not respond adequately to methylphenidate during titration, alternate medications were titrated openly in the following order until a satisfactory one was found: dextroamphetamine, pemoline, imipramine, and, if necessary, others approved by a cross-site pharmacology panel.

During half-hour monthly medication maintenance visits, pharmacotherapists provided support, encouragement, and practical advice (but not behavioral treatment). When deemed necessary by the clinician or requested by the parent, readings from an approved list were supplied. After careful review of parent- and teacher-provided information, pharmacotherapists could make algorithm-guided dose adjustments of ±10 mg/d of methylphenidate (or an equipotent amount if the subject was taking another drug). Additional adjustments beyond ±10 mg/d could be authorized by a cross-site panel of experienced pharmacotherapists. In general, dose reductions were allowed only to address dose-related side effects.

Side effects were monitored monthly—not present, mild, moderate, or severe—using the parent-completed 13-item Pittsburgh Side Effects Rating Scale, reviewed by the pharmacotherapist.

Combined Treatment

Combined treatment provided all previously described treatments for medication management and behavioral treatment—namely, titration followed by monthly medication maintenance, parent group and individual sessions, teacher consultation, STP, and the classroom aide. However, to approximate clinical practice, we integrated the two treatment modalities; information was regularly shared between the teacher–consultant and pharmacotherapist and used to guide overall decisions. Manualized guidelines determined if and when an adjustment in one treatment should be made, as opposed to intervening first with the other. Consequently, the multimodal combination was not the simple addition of the two unimodal treatments.

Community Care

Community care participants received none of these treatments from study staff but were provided a report of their initial study assessments, along with a list of community mental health resources. They were subsequently reassessed in comparison with participants in our three treatment arms. At each assessment point, the types of treatments they obtained in the community were documented. Most community care subjects ($n = 97$ [67.4%]) received ADHD medications (principally one of the stimulants) from their own provider during the 14 months: methylphenidate ($n = 84$), pemoline ($n = 7$), amphetamine ($n = 6$), tricyclics ($n = 6$), clonidine/guanfacine ($n = 4$), and/or buproprion ($n = 1$). Ten subjects received more than 1 medication. In addition, 16 of these 97 children were treated by their physician with another antidepressant (not counting tricyclics or buproprion). For those treated with methylphenidate, the mean total daily dose at study completion was 22.6 mg, (versus 30.5 mg for MTA treated subjects), averaging 2.3 doses per day (vs 3.0 doses per day for MTA subjects).

Fidelity and Compliance

The MTA study achieved a high degree of adherence to protocol by cross-arm emphasis on subject rapport, manualization of all treatments, regular supervision of pharmacotherapists by skilled clinician investigators, cross-site weekly treatment panels, and audiotaping of all sessions. Good compliance (reflected by acceptance and attendance at treatment sessions) by patients with the protocol was facilitated by monthly pill counts, intermittent saliva measurements to monitor taking of methylphenidate, and encouragement of families to make up missed visits.

Results

All four groups showed sizable reductions in symptoms over time, with significant differences among them in degrees of change. For most ADHD symptoms, children in the combined treatment and medication management groups showed significantly greater improvement than those given intensive behavioral treatment and community care. Combined and medication management treatments did not differ significantly on any direct comparisons, but in several instances (oppositional–aggressive symptoms, internalizing symptoms, teacher-rated social skills, parent–child relations, and reading achievement) combined treatment proved superior to intensive behavioral treatment and community care or both, whereas medication management did not. The study's medication strategies were superior to community care treatments, despite the fact that two thirds of community-treated subjects received medication during the study period.

The study has also explored differential treatment effects on excellent responder status (Swanson et al., 2001) and a composite global outcome measure (Conners et al., 2001). In both instances, combined treatment was shown to be superior to the other treatment strategies, with modest incremental differences in effect sizes (.26 to .28) over medication management alone. The impact of various subject characteristics, such as comorbidity, ethnicity, and socioeconomic status, on differential treatment outcome has also been explored, with some evidence that children with ADHD and comorbid anxiety disorders or internalizing and externalizing disorders (e.g., anxiety disorder and OD or CD) responded best to combined treatment (MTA Cooperative Group, 1999b; Jensen et al., 2001). The sample is being systematically followed to explore questions such as maintenance of treatment effects over time; impact of treatments received on subsequent treatment choices; and outcome in adolescents, particularly with regard to substance use, antisocial behavior, and academic, social, and emotional functioning.

SUMMARY

This chapter reviews details of medication and psychosocial interventions in two different controlled, randomized MMT studies. Results from these studies have implications for the optimal treatment of children with ADHD. Stimulant medication is clearly effective, and with careful titration and monitoring, this efficacy does not attenuate. However, the MTA study findings indicated that medication treatment in the community is clearly less than optimal and needs to be improved. In fact, MTA analyses revealed that although 68% and 56% of MTA combined treatment and medication management subjects were "normalized," only 25% of community-treated subjects received similar benefit. Combined treatment was associated with lower dosages of medication and may be particularly useful in patients with comorbid anxiety, doubly comorbid conditions, single-parent families, lower SES, and, possibly, some ethnic minorities.

Systematic evaluations regarding the impact of the timing of treatment components on outcome are also needed. Children assigned to the combination of psychosocial and medication treatments in the Montreal–New York, and MTA multimodal studies begin the two treatments simultaneously in the latter and start with medication in the former. Multimodal designs that evaluate the efficacy of introducing psychosocial treatment before pharmacotherapy are warranted. Finally, these two studies use manualized, multipush treatment programs. Whether MMT regimens that are tailored specifically to the clinical needs of the children and their parents result in better outcomes than nontailored approaches remains unknown. Furthermore, studies that determine which treatments or combination of treatments are best for which type of patients are also needed.

REFERENCES

Abikoff, H., & Gittelman, R. (1982). *The social interactions of hyperactive and normal boys in unstructured school settings.* Unpublished manuscript.

Abikoff, H., & Gittelman, R. (1985). Classroom observation code: A modification of the Stony Brook code. *Psychopharmacology Bulletin, 21,* 901–909.

Abikoff, H., Hechtman, L., Klein, R. G., Gallagher, R., Fleiss, K., Etcovitch, L., et al. (2004a). Social functioning in children with ADHD treated with long-term methylphenidate and multimodal psychosocial treatment. *Journal of the American Academy of Child and Adolescent Psychiatry, 43,* 7, 820–829.

Abikoff, H., Hechtman, L., Klein, R. G., Weiss, K., Fleiss, J., Etcovitch, L., et al. (2004b). Symptomatic improvement in children with ADHD treated with long-term methylphenidate and multimodal psychosoial treatment. *Journal of the American Academy of Child and Adolescent Psychiatry, 43,* 7, 802–811.

Abikoff, H., & Klein, R. G. (1992). Attention deficit hyperactivity and conduct disorder. Comorbidity and implications for treatment. *Journal of Consulting and Clinical Psychology, 60,* 881–892.

Abikoff, H., Martin, D., & Klein, R. G. (1989). *Social interaction observation code* (Rev.). Unpublished manuscript.

American Psychiatric Association. (1987). *Diagnostic and statistical manual of mental disorders* (3rd ed., rev.). Washington, DC: Author.

Anesko, K. M., & O'Leary, S. G. (1982). The effectiveness of brief parent training for the management of children's homework problems. *Child and Family Behavior Therapy, 4,* 113–126.

Atekeson, B. M., & Forehand, R. (1979). Home-based reinforcement programs to modify classroom behavior: A review and methodological evaluation. *Psychological Bulletin, 86,* 1298–1308.

August, G., & Garfinkel, B. D. (1989). Behavioral and cognitive subtypes of ADHD. *Journal of the American Academy of Child and Adolescent Psychiatry, 28,* 739–748.

Barkley, R. A. (1981). *Hyperactive children: A handbook for diagnosis and treatment.* New York: Guilford Press.

Barkley, R. A. (1987). *Defiant children: A clinician's manual for parent training.* New York: Guilford Press.

Biederman, J., Newcorn, J., & Sprich, S. E. (1991). Comorbidity of attention-deficit/hyperactive disorder with conduct, depressive, anxiety, and other disorders. *American Journal of Psychiatry, 148,* 564–577.

Bird, H. R., Camino, G., Rubio-Stipic, M., Gould, M. S., Ribera, J., Sesman, M., et al. (1988). Estimates of the prevalence of childhood maladjustment in a community survey in Puerto Rico. *Archives of General Psychiatry, 45,* 1120–1126.

Conners, C. K., Epstein, J. N., March, J. S., Angold, A., Wells, K. C., Klaric, J., et al. (2001). Multimodal treatment of ADHD in the MTA: An alternative outcome analysis. *Journal of the American Academy of Child and Adolescent Psychiatry, 40,* 159–167.

Dadds, M. R., Schwartz, S., & Sanders, M. R. (1987). Marital discord and treatment outcome in behavioral treatment of child conduct disorders. *Journal of Consulting and Clinical Psychology, 55,* 396–403.

Dodge, K. A., McClaskey, C. L., & Feldman, E. (1985). A situational approach to the assessment of social competence in children. *Journal of Consulting and Clinical Psychology, 53,* 344–353.

Douglas, V. I., Barr, R. G., O'Neill, M. E., & Britton, B. G. (1988). Dosage effects and individual responsivity to methylphenidate in attention deficit disorder. *Journal of Child Psychology and Psychiatry, 29,* 453–475.

Farrington, D. P., Loeber, R., & van Kammen, W. B. (1990). Long-term criminal outcomes of hyperactivity-impulsivity-attention deficit and conduct problems in childhood. In L. N. Robins & M. Rutter (Eds.), *Straight and devious pathways to adulthood* (pp. 62–81). New York: Cambridge University Press.

Forehand, R. L., & McMahon, R. J. (1981). *Helping the non-compliant child: A clinician's guide to parent training.* New York: Guilford Press.

Goyette, C. H., Conners, C. K., & Ulrich, R. F. (1978). Normative data on revised Conners' Parent and Teacher Rating Scales. *Journal of Abnormal Child Psychology, 6,* 211–236.

Greenhill, L. L., Abikoff, H., Arnold, L. E., Cantwell, D. P., Conners, C. K., Elliott, G., et al. (1996). Medication treatment strategies in the MTA: Relevance to clinicians and researchers. *Journal of the American Academy of Child and Adolescent Psychiatry, 35,* 1304–1313.

Gresham, F. M., & Elliott, S. N. (1989). *Social skills rating system* (Parent and student forms). Circle Pines, MN: American Guidance Service.

Halperin, J. M., Gittelman, R., Klein, D. F., & Rudel, R. G. (1984). Reading-disabled hyperactive children: A distinct subgroup of attention deficit disorder with hyperactivity? *Journal of Abnormal Child Psychology, 12,* 1–14.

Hechtman, L., Abikoff, H., Klein, R. G., Greenfield, B., Etcovitch, J., Cousins, L., et al. (2004a). Children with ADHD treated with long-term methylphenidate and multimodal psychosocial treatment: Impact on parental practices. *Journal of the American Academy of Child and Adolescent Psychiatry, 43,* 830–838.

Hechtman, L., Abikoff, H., Klein, R. G., Weiss, G., Respitz, C., Kouri, J., et al. (2004b). Academic achievement and emotional status of children with ADHD treated with long-term methylphenidate and multimodal psychosocial treatment. *Journal of the American Academy of Child and Adolescent Psychiatry, 43,* 7, 812–819.

Hinshaw, S. P. (1987). On the distinction between attentional deficits/hyperactivity and conduct problems/aggression in child psychopathology. *Psychological Bulletin, 101,* 443–463.

Hinshaw, S. P., Henker, B., & Whalen, C. K. (1984). Cognitive–behavioral and pharmacologic interventions for hyperactive boys: Comparative and combined effects. *Journal of Consulting and Clinical Psychology, 52,* 739–749.

Jackson, N. F., Jackson, D. A., & Monroe, C. (1983). *Getting along with others: Teaching social effectiveness to children.* Champaign, IL: Research Press.

Jensen, P. S., Hinshaw, S. P., Kraemer, H. C., Lenora, N., Newcorn, J. H., Abikoff, H., et al. (2001). ADHD comorbidity findings from the MTA study: Comparing comorbid subgroups. *Journal of the American Academy of Child and Adolescent Psychiatry, 40,* 147–158.

Johnston, C., & Mash, E. J. (1989). A measure of parenting satisfaction and efficacy. *Journal of Clinical Child Psychology, 18,* 167–175.

Kovacs, M., & Beck, A. T. (1977). An empirical–clinical approach toward a definition of childhood depression. In J. G. Schulterbrandt & A. Raskin (Eds.), *Depression in childhood: Diagnosis, treatment, and conceptual models* (pp. 1–25). New York: Raven Press.

Lahey, B. B., Gendrich, J. G., Gendrich, S. I., Schnelle, J. F., Gant, D. S., & McNees, M. P. (1977). An evaluation of daily report cards with minimal teacher and parent contacts as an efficient method of classroom intervention. *Behavior Modification, 1,* 381–394.

MTA Cooperative Group. (1999a). A 14-month randomized clinical trial of treatment strategies for attention-deficit/hyperactivity disorder. *Archives of General Psychiatry, 56,* 1073–1086.

MTA Cooperative Group. (1999b). Moderator and mediator of treatment responses for children with ADHD: The MTA study. *Archives of General Psychiatry, 56,* 1088–1096.

MTA Cooperative Group. (2004). The NIMH MTA follow-up: 24-Month outcomes of treatment strategies for attention-deficit/hyperactivity disorder (ADHD). *Pediatrics, 113,* 754–761.

O'Dell, S. L., Tarler-Benlolol, L., & Flynn, J. M. (1979). An instrument to measure knowledge of behavioral principles as applied to children. *Journal of Behavioral Therapy and Experimental Psychiatry, 10,* 29–34.

Pelham, W. E. (1986). The effects of psychostimulant drugs on learning and academic achievement in children with attention deficit disorders and learning disabilities. In J. K. Torgensen & B. Y. L. Wong (Eds.), *Psychological and educational perspectives in learning disabilities* (pp. 259–295). New York: Academic Press.

Pelham, W. E., & Hoza, B. (1996). Comprehensive treatment for ADHD: A proposal for intensive summer treatment programs and outpatient follow-up. In E. Hibbs & P. Jensen (Eds.), *Psychosocial treatment research of child and adolescent disorders* (pp. 311–340). Washington, DC: American Psychiatric Press.

Piers, E. V. (1984). *Piers-Harris children's self-concept scale* (rev. manual). Los Angeles: Western Psychological Services.

Richters, J. E., Arnold, L. E., Jensen, P. S., Abikoff, H., Conners, C. K., Greenhill, L. L., et al. (1995). National Institute of Mental Health collaborative multisite, multimodal treatment study of children with attention deficit hyperactivity disorder (MTA): Part 1. Background and rationale. *Journal of the American Academy of Child and Adolescent Psychiatry, 34,* 987–1000.

Satterfield, J. H., Cantwell, D. P., & Satterfield, B. T. (1979). Multimodality treatment: A one-year follow-up of 84 hyperactive boys. *Archives of General Psychiatry, 36,* 965–974.

Satterfield, J. H., Satterfield, B. T., & Cantwell, D. P. (1980). Multimodality treatment: A two-year evaluation of 61 hyperactive boys. *Archives of General Psychiatry, 37,* 915–919.

Satterfield, J. H., Satterfield, B. T., & Cantwell, D. P. (1981). Three-year multimodality treatment study of 100 hyperactive boys. *Journal of Pediatrics, 98,* 650–655.

Shaffer, D., Fisher, P., Dulcan, M., Davies, M., Piacentini, J., Schwab-Stone, M., et al. (1996). The second version of the NIMH Diagnostic Interview Schedule for Children (DISC-2). *Journal of the American Academy of Child and Adolescent Psychiatry, 35,* 865–877.

Shaffer, D., Gould, M. S., Brasic, J., Ambrosini, P., Fisher, P., Bird, H., et al. (1985). CGAS (Children's Global Assessment Scale). *Psychopharmacology Bulletin, 21,* 747–748.

Spitzer, R. L., Williams, J. B. W., Gibbon, M., & First, M. B. (1988). *Instruction manual for the structured clinical interview for DSM–III–R (SCID).* New York: Biometrics Research.

Strayhorn, J. M., & Weidman, C. S. (1988). A parent practice scale and its relation to parent and child mental health. *Journal of the American Academy of Child and Adolescent Psychiatry, 27,* 613–618.

Swanson, J. M. (1992). *School-based assessments and interventions for ADD students.* Irvine, CA: KC Publications.

Swanson, J. M., Cantwell, D. P., Lerner, M., McBurnett, K., & Hanna, G. (1991). Effects of stimulant medication on learning in children with ADHD. *Journal of Learning Disablities, 24,* 219–230.

Swanson, J. M., Kraemer, H. C., Hinshaw, S. P., Arnold, L. E., Conners, C. K., Abikoff, H., et al. (2001). Clinical relevance of the primary findings of the MTA: Success rates based on severity of ADHD and ODD symptoms at the end of treatment. *Journal of the American Academy of Child and Adolescent Psychiatry, 40,* 168–179.

Turkewitz, H., O'Leary, K. D., & Ironsmith, M. (1975). Generalization and maintenance of appropriate behavior through self-control. *Journal of Consulting and Clinical Psychology, 43,* 577–583.

Walker, H. M., McConnell, S., Holmes, D., Todis, B., Walker, J. L., & Golden, N. (1983). *A curriculum for children's effective peer and teacher skills (ACCEPTS).* Austin, TX: Pro-Ed.

Weiss, G., Hechtman, L., Perlman, T., Hopkins, J., & Wener, A. (1975). Hyperactive children as young adults: A controlled prospective ten-year follow-up of 75 children. *Archives of General Psychiatry, 36,* 675–681.

Whalen, C. K., & Henker, B. (1985). The social worlds of hyperactive children. *Clinical Psychology Review, 5,* 1–32.

Whalen, C. K., & Henker, B. (1991). The social impact of stimulant treatment for hyperactive children. *Journal of Learning Disablities, 24,* 231–241.

V

SOCIALLY DISRUPTIVE BEHAVIORS AND CONDUCT DISORDERS

INTRODUCTION: SOCIALLY
DISRUPTIVE BEHAVIORS AND
CONDUCT DISORDERS

Disruptive behavior disorders (DBD) in childhood often progress to aggressive delinquent, criminal, and violent behaviors in adolescence and young adulthood. As a result, these conditions cause significant impairment in many areas, including academic, career, and social functioning in the individual's life. The prevalence-rate estimates for conduct disorder range widely, from 6% to 26% for boys younger than 18 years of age and from 2% to 9% for girls. Earlier onset appears to be associated with a worse prognosis, and conduct disorders seem to have both genetic and familial or environmental contributing factors. Therefore, intervening early in children's lives is likely to be the most parsimonious and cost-effective means to reverse this devastating developmental course. Although disruptive behavior disorders constitute a very important public health problem, little empirical research is available to guide health care providers as to which treatments are effective for which forms of DBD. In this section, five chapters propose various treatment strategies for the reduction of antisocial behaviors in children.

Alan E. Kazdin provides an overview of the treatment program and its key issues. His intervention is based on cognitive problem-solving skills training (PSST) and parent management training (PMT) for the treatment of aggressive and antisocial children. He describes the treatment implementation in detail. The goal of his research is to evaluate the treatment with clinically referred cases, to build an effective treatment package to address child and family dysfunction, to assess diverse domains of functioning in different contexts, to evaluate outcome in relation to nonreferred peers, and, finally, to evaluate follow-up functioning to at least 1 year posttreatment. The treatments are beneficial for the clinically referred patients and produce significant reduction in antisocial behaviors. Effects are maintained at least to 1-year follow-up assessment. In exploring future directions, he discusses the importance of understanding the mechanisms underlying treatment and child, parent, and family contextual factors that influence both the process and outcome of treatment.

David J. Kolko describes the application of several assessment and intervention findings obtained from his prior empirical studies of childhood firesetting. The components of his treatments consist of two skills-based interventions representing psychological (cognitive–behavioral therapy [CBT]) and fire service (Fire Safety Education), compared with a standard-practice condition (Home Visit for a Firefighter). The findings of these studies provide support for the feasibility and effectiveness of the interventions. Treatments were also found to be beneficial in that children showed reductions in their involvement in fire-related acts. The author suggests that future studies should examine carefully various clinical and methodological issues and implement novel interventions in order to enhance understanding in intervening with youth who exhibit this troublesome and potentially dangerous behavior.

Carolyn Webster-Stratton presents a series of studies designed to prevent and treat early onset oppositional and conduct disorders. This program is based on an interactive intervention program for families of young children. The treatment, which uses a videotape modeling method, consists of family training intervention, academic skills-training for parents, and training in problem solving and social skills for children. Webster-Stratton has followed children up to 3 years after treatment and is now assessing them at a 10- to 15-year follow-up. The posttreatment assessments indicate that this intervention is effective in significantly improving parental attitudes and parent–child interactions. Highlighting future directions, the author proposes that research should focus on the specific characteristics of the family and children using various combinations of treatment

Patricia Chamberlain and Dana K. Smith describe their project of Treatment Foster Care (TFC) for boys and girls with conduct disorders and delinquency referred by the Juvenile Justice. TFC is a community-based treatment model for out-of-home care constructed as an alternative to placement group care settings for youth. The components of the model include developing placement settings; preservice training and consultation for TFC parents; individual treatment for the youth; family therapy for both biological and foster parents; consultations with school, parole, and probation officers; and after-care services and support for all involved. TFC seems to be especially beneficial when all the components are implemented simultaneously. In outlining future directions, the authors propose to examine the applications and limitations of TFC with other populations.

Jane G. Querido and Sheila M. Eyberg present their treatment, parent–child interaction therapy (PCIT), for preschoolers with disruptive behavior disorders. The novelty of this study consists in parent–therapist contact and booster sessions as needed (maintenance treatment) after the completion of the standard treatment to maintain treatment gains following PCIT. The PCIT is a two-stage treatment model that includes child-directed interaction focused on strengthening the parent–child bond and parent-directed interaction that focuses on improving parents' expectations, ability to set limits, consistency, and fairness in discipline. The PCIT is an empirically supported treatment for the families of preschoolers with conduct problems. It has been replicated, and the results of all the studies indicate statistically and clinically significant outcomes of immediate treatment effects. The effects of maintenance treatment strategies remain unknown. This project is the first step in identifying strategies to improve long-term outcomes.

18

CHILD, PARENT, AND FAMILY-BASED TREATMENT OF AGGRESSIVE AND ANTISOCIAL CHILD BEHAVIOR

ALAN E. KAZDIN

For the past several years, our group has been treating aggressive and antisocial children and their families. The overall goal of our program is to identify and to develop effective interventions for youths referred for conduct disorder.[1] Completion of treatment outcome trials is a central part of

Research that forms the basis of this chapter was facilitated by generous research support of a Research Scientist Award (MH00353) and a MERIT Award (MH35408) from the National Institute of Mental Health (NIMH) and grants from NIMH (MH59029), the Leon Lowenstein Foundation, and the William T. Grant Foundation (98-1872-98). Several individuals have contributed greatly to the work, including past and current staff of Yale Child Conduct Clinic: Susan Breton, Elizabeth Brown, Susan Bullerdick, Justin Barsanti, Mary Cavaleri, Michael Crowley, Lisa Holland, Bernadette Lezca, Erin Levix, Paul Marciano, Molly McDonald, Jennifer Mazurick, Francheska Perepletchikova, Elif Tongul, Gloria Wassell, and Moira Whitley. The clinic has thrived through the support of others, especially the late Donald J. Cohen, MD, and Paula Armbruster, MSW, at the Yale Child Study Center. Both have greatly facilitated completion of the present work. Correspondence concerning this chapter should be directed to Alan E. Kazdin, Child Study Center, Yale University School of Medicine, 230 S. Frontage Road, New Haven, CT 06520-7900.

[1]In this chapter, conduct disorder refers generally to clinically severe antisocial behavior including aggression, lying, stealing, truancy, running away, and other behaviors. The term is used generically to refer to the constellation of symptoms rather than the diagnostic category specifically.

this work. At the same time, developing effective treatments requires a deeper understanding of the clinical dysfunction and the contexts in which it is embedded. Consequently, our program also examines diverse facets of children, parents, and families to acquire knowledge that can be integrated in the context of treatment trials. Also, developing effective treatments requires knowing a great deal about treatment and the ways in which change is produced, for whom, and under what conditions. This chapter provides an overview of our treatment research program, key issues, and current and future lines of research.[2]

TREATMENT OF CONDUCT DISORDER

Overview of the Problem

Conduct disorder (CD) refers to a broad pattern of functioning that includes diverse disruptive and rule-breaking behaviors. As a psychiatric disorder, CD requires the presence of at least three of 15 symptoms within the past 12 months (American Psychiatric Association, 1994). The symptoms include bullying others, initiating fights, using a weapon, being physically cruel to people or animals, stealing from others, forcing someone into sexual activity, fire setting, destroying property, lying, truancy, and running away. The behaviors come in various combinations and vary markedly in severity, chronicity, and frequency. The significance of the disorder stems from several critical features, including the following:

- a relatively high prevalence rate (conservatively between 2% and 6%, or approximately 1.4 to 4.2 million children in the United States);
- a high rate of clinical referrals (e.g., 33% to 50% of cases referred for outpatient treatment);
- untoward long-term outcomes of such children in adulthood (e.g., approximately 80% are likely to meet criteria for a psychiatric disorder in the future);
- untoward consequences for others, including siblings, peers, parents, and teachers, as well as strangers who are targets of antisocial and aggressive acts in childhood and in adulthood (e.g., engaging in crime, spouse and child abuse, and drunk driving at higher rates of such youths when they become adults); and

---

[2]Portions of this chapter have been adapted from Kazdin (2003a). From *Evidence-Based Psychotherapies for Children and Adolescents* (pp. 241–262), by A. E. Kazdin and J. R. Weisz, (Eds.), 2003, New York: Guilford Press. Copyright 2003 by Guilford Press. Adapted with permission.

- the monetary costs as youths traverse special education, mental health, juvenile justice, and social services over the course of their lives.

Each of these features could be elaborated to convey more persuasively the scope of the problem (Hill & Maughan, 2001; Kazdin, 1995b; Stoff, Breiling, & Maser, 1997). For example, the prevalence rates underestimate the extent of the problem. Research has demonstrated that youths who do not quite meet diagnostic criteria can show significant impairment and a poor long-term prognosis. Also, the central features of the disorder fail to convey the scope of the problems of children who come to treatment. Children who meet criteria for CD are likely to meet criteria for other disorders as well, especially oppositional defiant disorder and attention-deficit/hyperactivity disorder but also depression and anxiety disorders.

Several features associated with CD are relevant to treatment. For example, children with CD are also likely to

- show academic deficiencies, as reflected in achievement level, grades, being left behind in school, early termination from school, and deficiencies in specific skill areas, such as reading;
- have poor interpersonal relations, as reflected in diminished social skills in relation to peers and adults and higher levels of peer rejection;
- how deficits and distortions in cognitive processes related to interpersonal functioning; and
- live in families in which there is likely to be a history of criminal behavior and psychiatric dysfunction, child-rearing practices that contribute to the child's dysfunction (e.g., harsh punishment), unhappy marital relations, interpersonal conflict, aggression between the parents, poor family communication, and pervasive influences such as financial hardship (unemployment, significant debt, bankruptcy of the parent), untoward living conditions (dangerous neighborhood, small living quarters), transportation obstacles of the parent (no car or car in frequent repair, state-provided taxi service), high levels of parental stress (e.g., in relation to former spouses, living with relatives), and adversarial contact with outside agencies (e.g., schools, youth services, courts).

CD is conceived as a dysfunction of children and adolescents. The accumulated evidence regarding the symptom constellation, risk factors, and course over childhood, adolescence, and adulthood attests to the heuristic value of focusing on individual children. At the same time, there is a child-parent-family-context gestalt that includes multiple and reciprocal influences that affect each participant (i.e., child and parent) and the systems in which they operate (e.g., family, school).

Identifying and Developing Effective Treatments

Several advances have been made in developing effective treatments for CD. Treatments that have been identified and delineated as evidence based include parent management training, problem-solving skills training, and multisystemic therapy (Brestan & Eyberg, 1998; Kazdin, 2002). Our research group focuses on cognitive problem-solving skills training (PSST) and parent management training (PMT). Selection of these treatments is based on criteria we have adopted to sort through the myriad available options. These criteria include a conceptual model of the clinical dysfunction and its development, research that supports the model, and preliminary outcome research. PSST and PMT fare well on these criteria for treating CD. Several research programs have developed these treatments, as reviewed elsewhere (Kazdin & Weisz, 1998, 2003). This chapter focuses on our research program only. This focus is not intended to imply that our work is the only, the best, the first, or most interesting research in relation to these treatments.[3]

Problem-Solving Skills Training

Overview

The term *cognitive processes* refers to a broad class of constructs that pertain to the ways in which the individual perceives, codes, and experiences the world. Individuals who engage in conduct-disordered behaviors, particularly aggression, show distortions and deficiencies in various cognitive processes. These distortions and deficiencies are not merely reflections of intellectual functioning. Several cognitive processes have been studied. Examples include generating alternative solutions to interpersonal problems (e.g., different ways of handling social situations); identifying the means to achieve particular ends (e.g., making friends) or recognizing the consequences of one's actions (e.g., what could happen after a particular behavior); making attributions to others with regard to the motivation of their actions; perceiving how others feel; and developing expectations of the effects of one's own actions (Lochman, Whidby, & FitzGerald, 2000; Shirk, 1988; Shure, 1997, 1999; Spivack & Shure, 1982). Deficits and distortion among these processes relate to disruptive behavior, as reflected in

---

[3]Several investigators, some of whom have chapters in this book, have made enormous contributions to the treatment of CD and to the specific treatments discussed in this chapter (see Kazdin, 1997, in press; Kazdin & Weisz, 2003).

teacher ratings, peer evaluations, and direct assessment of overt actions (Lochman & Dodge, 1994; Rubin, Bream, & Rose-Krasnor, 1991).

An example of cognitive processes implicated in CD can be seen in the work on attributions and aggressive behavior. Aggression is not merely triggered by environmental events but rather through the way in which these events are perceived and processed. The processing refers to the child's appraisals of the situation, anticipated reactions of others, and self-statements in response to particular events. Attribution of intent to others represents a salient cognitive disposition critically important to understanding aggressive behavior. Aggressive children and adolescents tend to attribute hostile intent to others, especially in social situations wherein the cues of actual intent are ambiguous (Crick & Dodge, 1994). Understandably, when situations are initially perceived as hostile, children are more likely to react aggressively. Although many studies have shown that children with CD experience various cognitive distortions and deficiencies, the specific contribution of these processes to CD, as opposed to risk factors with which they may be associated (e.g., untoward living conditions, low IQ), has not been established. Nevertheless, research on cognitive processes among aggressive children has served as a heuristic base for conceptualizing treatment and for developing specific treatment strategies (Kendall, 2000).

Characteristics of Training

PSST consists of developing interpersonal cognitive problem-solving skills. Although many variations of PSST have been applied, several characteristics usually are shared. First, the emphasis is on the way children approach situations—that is, the thought processes in which the child engages to guide responses to interpersonal situations. The children are taught to engage in a step-by-step approach to solve interpersonal problems. They make statements to themselves that direct attention to certain aspects of the problem or tasks that lead to effective solutions. Second, the behaviors (solutions to the interpersonal problems) that are selected are important as well. Prosocial behaviors are fostered through modeling and direct reinforcement as part of the problem-solving process. Third, treatment uses structured tasks involving games, academic activities, and stories. Over the course of treatment, the cognitive problem-solving skills are increasingly applied to real-life situations. Fourth, therapists play an active role in treatment. They model the cognitive processes by making verbal self-statements, apply the sequence of statements to particular problems, provide cues to prompt use of the skills, and deliver feedback and praise to develop correct use of the skills. Finally, treatment combines several different procedures, including modeling and practice, role-playing, and reinforcement and mild punishment (loss of points or tokens), to develop increasingly complex response repertoires in the child.

In our program, PSST consists of weekly therapy sessions with the child, with each session usually lasting 30 to 50 minutes. The core treatment (12–20 sessions) may be supplemented with optional sessions, if the child requires additional assistance in grasping the problem-solving steps (early in treatment) or their application in everyday situations (later in treatment). (In separate projects, we have varied the duration of treatment.) Exhibit 18.1 presents the core treatment sessions and their foci. Central to treatment

EXHIBIT 18.1
Problem-Solving Skills Training: Overview of the Core Sessions

1. **Introduction and Learning the Steps.** The purpose of this initial session is to establish rapport with the child, to teach the problem-solving steps, and to explain the procedures of the cognitively based treatment program. The child is acquainted with the use of tokens (chips), reward menus for exchange of the chips, and response–cost contingencies. The child is trained to use the problem-solving steps as if they were a game; the therapist and child take turns learning the individual steps and placing them together in a sequence.

2. **and 3. Applying the Steps.** The second session reviews and continues to teach the steps, as needed. The child is taught to use the problem-solving steps to complete a relatively simple game. The child applies the steps to simple problems presented in a board-game fashion in which the therapist and child alternate turns. During the session, the therapist demonstrates how to use the problem-solving steps in decision making, how to provide self-reinforcement for successful performance, and how to cope with mistakes and failure. One of the goals of this session is to illustrate how the self-statements can be used to help the child stop and think rather than respond impulsively when confronted with a problem. The third session includes another game that leads to selection of hypothetical situations to which the child applies the steps. The therapist and child take turns, and further work is provided using prompts, modeling, shaping, and reinforcement to help the child be facile and fluid in applying the steps. The therapist fades prompts and assistance to shape proficient use and application of steps. A series of "supersolvers" (homework assignments) begins at this point; the child is asked to identify when the steps could be used, then to use the steps in increasingly more difficult and clinically relevant situations as treatment continues.

4. **Applying the Steps and Role Playing.** The child applies the steps to real-life situations. The steps are applied to the situation to identify solutions and consequences. Then the preferred solution, selected on the basis of likely consequences, is enacted through repeated role-playing exercises. Practice and role-playing exercises are continued to develop the child's application of the steps. Multiple situations are presented and practiced in this way.

5. **Parent–Child Contact.** The parent(s), therapist, and child are seen in the session. The child enacts the steps to solve problems. The parents learn more about the steps and various ways to provide attention and contingent praise for the child's use of the steps and selection and enactment of prosocial solutions. The primary goal is to develop the repertoire in the parent to encourage (prompt) use of the steps and to praise applications in a way that will influence the child's behavior (i.e., contingent, enthusiastic, continuous, verbal and nonverbal praise). Further contacts with the parents at the end of later sessions continue this aspect of treatment as needed.

6. to 11. Continued Applications to Real-Life Situations. In these sessions, the child uses the problem-solving steps to generate prosocial solutions to provocative interpersonal problems or situations. Each session concentrates on a different category of social interaction that the child might realistically encounter (e.g., peers, parents, siblings, teachers). Real-life situations generated by the child, parent, or others are enacted; hypothetical situations are also presented to elaborate themes and problem areas of the child (e.g., responding to provocation, fighting, being excluded socially, being encouraged by peers to engage in antisocial behavior). The child's supersolvers also become a more integral part of each session; they are re-enacted with the therapist at the beginning of each session in order to better evaluate how the child is transferring skills to his or her daily environment.

12. Wrap Up and Role Reversal. This wrap-up session is included for the following reasons: (1) to help the therapist generally assess what the child has learned in the session, (2) to clear up any remaining confusions the child may have concerning the use of the steps, and (3) to provide a final summary for the child of what has been covered in the meetings. The final session is based on a role reversal in which the child plays the role of the therapist and the therapist plays the role of a child learning and applying the steps. The purpose of this session is to have the child teach and benefit from the learning that teaching provides, to allow for any unfinished business of the treatment (spending remaining chips, completing final supersolvers), and to provide closure for the therapy.

Optional Sessions. During the course of therapy, additional sessions are provided to the child, as needed, if the child has special difficulty in grasping any features of the problem-solving steps or their application. For example, the child may have difficulty in applying the steps, learning to state them covertly, and so on. An additional session may be scheduled to repeat material of a previous session so that the child has a solid grasp of the approach. Optional sessions may be implemented at any point that the child's progress lags behind the level appropriate to the session that has been completed. For example, if a facet of treatment has not been learned (e.g., memorization of steps, fading of steps) associated with the particular session that has been completed, an optional session may be implemented. Also, if a problem or issue surfaces with regard to child or parent participation in supersolvers, a session will be scheduled with parent and child to shape the requisite behaviors in the session and to make assignments to ensure that this aspect of treatment is carried out.

Note. From *Evidence-Based Psychotherapies for Children and Adolescents* (pp. 245–246), by A. F. Kazdin and J. Weisz (Eds.), 2003, New York: Guilford Press. Copyright 2003 by Guilford Press. Reprinted with permission.

is developing the use of *problem-solving steps* (see Table 18.1) designed to break down interpersonal situations into units that permit identification and use of prosocial responses. The steps serve as verbal prompts the children deliver to themselves to engage in thoughts and actions that guide behavior. Each self-prompt or self-statement represents one step in solving a problem.

To assist the children in the acquisition and generalization of the problem-solving skills, several tasks are taught sequentially. The early sessions use simple tasks and games to teach the problem-solving steps, to help deter impulsive responding, and to introduce the reward system and

TABLE 18.1
The Problem-Solving Steps and Self-Statements

Self-statement steps to solve a problem	Purpose of the step
1. What am I supposed to do?	This step requires that the child identify and define the problem.
2. I have to look at all my possibilities.	This step asks the child to delineate or specify alternative solutions to the problem.
3. I'd better concentrate and focus in.	This step instructs the child to concentrate and evaluate the solutions (s)he has generated.
4. I need to make a choice.	During the fourth step (s)he chooses the answer which (s)he thinks is correct.
5. I did a good job (or) oh, I made a mistake.	This final step verifies whether the solution was the best among those available, whether the problem-solving process was correctly followed, or whether a mistake or less-than-desirable solution was selected, requiring that the process begin anew.

Note. The steps are taught through modeling; the therapist and child alternate turns in using and applying the steps, and each helps the other. Prompting, shaping, practicing, and effusively praising encourage the child's mastery of the steps, usually by the end of the first treatment session. As the child learns the steps, the therapist's modeling and prompting are faded and omitted or only used to help as needed. The steps evolve over the course of treatment in multiple ways. Among the most significant changes, they are abbreviated and combined. Also, the steps move from overt (made aloud) to covert (silent, internal) statements. By the end of treatment, use of the steps cannot be visibly seen; their overt features have completely disappeared by this time. From *Evidence-Based Psychotherapies for Children and Adolescents* (p. 246), by A. E. Kazdin and J. Weisz (Eds.), 2003, New York: Guilford Press. Copyright 2003 by Guilford Press. Reprinted with permission.

response cost contingencies (described in more detail later in the chapter). The greater part of treatment focuses on the child's use of the problem-solving steps to generate and to enact prosocial solutions to a range of interpersonal problems or situations. The interpersonal problems are presented in a variety of ways, using various approaches, materials, and tasks to encourage the child to think about multiple prosocial ways to handle problems with others. Role-playing is used extensively to give the child the opportunity to enact what he or she would do in a situation, thus making these interactions similar to real-life exchanges. Sessions concentrate on situations the child actually encounters (i.e., with peers, parents, siblings, teachers, and others) across multiple stimulus characteristics and conditions in an effort to promote generalization and maintenance (Kazdin, 2001b).

In a typical session, interpersonal problems (e.g., in relation to school) are addressed. The therapist models application of the steps to one situation, identifies alternative solutions, and selects one of them. The child and therapist enact that solution through a role-playing exercise. Throughout, the therapist prompts the child verbally and nonverbally to guide performance, provides a rich schedule of contingent social reinforcement, delivers concrete feedback for performance, and models improved ways of performing. Direct reinforcement of behavior is critical, and sessions draw heavily on the contingent and immediate delivery of social reinforcement (e.g., smiles, praise, "high five," applause).

Children begin each session with tokens (small plastic chips) that can be exchanged for small prizes at a "store" after each session. During the session, children can lose chips (response cost) for misusing or failing to use the steps. In fact, very few chips are provided or taken away in most of the sessions. Efforts to alter the child's behavior rely more on social reinforcement and extinction than token reinforcement. The chips present opportunities to address special issues or problems with the child, such as encouraging a particular type of prosocial solution that the child might find difficult.

Critical to treatment is the use of the problem-solving approach outside of treatment. In vivo practice, referred to as *supersolvers*, consists of systematically programmed assignments designed to extend the child's use and application of problem-solving skills to everyday situations. The parents are trained to help the child use the problem-solving steps. Parents are brought into sessions over the course of treatment to learn the problem-solving steps and to practice joint supersolver assignments with the child at home. Prompting, shaping, and praise are used by the therapist to develop the parent's behavior. Over time, the child and parent supersolvers increase in complexity and eventually relate to those problem domains that led to the child's referral to treatment.

Parent Management Training

Overview

In PMT, parents are trained to alter their child's behavior in the home (see Kazdin, in press). The parents meet with a therapist or trainer who teaches them to use specific procedures to alter interactions with their child, to promote prosocial behavior, and to decrease deviant behavior. Training reflects the general view that conduct problems are inadvertently developed and sustained in the home by maladaptive parent–child interactions and that altering these interactions can reduce these behaviors.

Multiple facets of parent–child interaction promote aggressive and antisocial behavior. These patterns include directly reinforcing deviant behavior, frequently and ineffectively using commands and harsh punishment, and failing to attend to appropriate behavior (Patterson, 1982; Patterson, Reid, & Dishion, 1992; Reid, Patterson, & Snyder, 2002). Among the many interaction patterns, those involving coercion have received the greatest attention. *Coercion* refers to deviant behavior on the part of one person (e.g., the child), which is rewarded by another person (e.g., the parent). Coercive interchanges between parent and child serve to reinforce aggressive behavior in the child, an aggressiveness that tends to increase over time. Also, parents tend to use punitive practices (e.g., corporal punishment) and many commands in ways that escalate problem behavior and tend to ignore prosocial behavior. Of course, this is not to say that all aggression and antisocial behavior are caused by mismanaged contingencies. Broader conceptual models have been suggested that integrate diverse facets related to parent and family functioning (e.g., parental stress, marital conflict) and their role in the unfolding of antisocial behavior (e.g., Dumas & Wahler, 1985; Patterson, 1988; Patterson et al., 1992; Reid et al., 2002). Parent–child interaction sequences remain pivotal in the models and have served as the basis for treatment of antisocial youth.

Characteristics of Training

Although many variations of PMT exist, they share several common characteristics. First, treatment is conducted primarily with the parent or parents, who directly implement several procedures at home. Usually, the therapist does not directly intervene with the child. Second, parents are trained to identify, define, and observe problem behaviors in new ways. Careful specification of the problem is essential for the delivery of reinforcing or punishing consequences and evaluation of progress. Third, the treatment sessions cover social learning principles, and the procedures that follow from them including positive reinforcement (e.g., the use of social praise and tokens or points for prosocial behavior), prompting and shaping, mild punishment (e.g., use of time-out from reinforcement, loss of privileges), negotiation, and contingency contracting. Fourth, the sessions provide opportunities for parents to see how the techniques are implemented, to practice using the techniques, and to review the behavior-change programs in the home.

In our program, the core treatment consists of 12 to 16 weekly sessions, with each session usually between 45 and 60 minutes (see Kazdin, in press, for the treatment manual). Exhibit 18.2 presents the core treatment sessions and their foci. As with the child, optional sessions are interspersed as needed to convey the approach, to develop or ensure the proper implementation of procedures at home and school, and to alter specific behavior-change programs. Meetings with the parent consist of developing behavior-change skills and programs that can be implemented at home and school. The program begins with relatively simple tasks for the parent. These build over the course of treatment to develop increasingly complex proficiencies in the parent's child-rearing repertoire and practices in everyday life.

A number of content and skill areas focus on treatment, as mentioned previously. The general format of the individual sessions is to convey content, to teach specific skills, and to develop use of the skill in the home in relation to child behavior. Thus, the session usually begins by discussing the general concept (e.g., positive reinforcement) and how it is to be implemented. Typically, a specific program is designed for implementation at home. Programs take into account special features of the family situation (others in the home,

1. **Introduction and Overview.** This session provides the parents with an overview of the program and outlines the demands placed upon them and the focus of the intervention.

2. **Defining and Observing.** This session trains parents to pinpoint, define, and observe behavior. The parents and trainer define specific problems that can be observed and develop a specific plan to begin observations.

3. **Positive Reinforcement (Point Chart and Praise).** This session focuses on learning the concept of positive reinforcement, examining factors that contribute to the effective application, and rehearsing applications in relation to the target child. Specific programs in which praise and points are to be provided for the behaviors observed during the week are outlined. An incentive (token or point) chart is devised, and the delivery of praise by the parent is developed through modeling, prompting, feedback, and praise by the therapist.

4. **Time-Out From Reinforcement.** Parents learn about time-out and the factors related to its effective application. Delivery of time-out is extensively role-played and practiced. The use of time-out is planned for the next week for specific behaviors.

5. **Attending and Ignoring.** In this session, parents learn about attending and ignoring and choose an undesirable behavior that they will ignore and a positive opposite behavior to which they will attend. These procedures are practiced within the session. Attention and praise for positive behavior are key components of this session.

6. **Shaping and School Intervention.** Parents are trained to develop behaviors by reinforcement of successive approximations and to use prompts and fading of prompts to develop terminal behaviors. Also in this session, plans are made to implement a home-based reinforcement program to develop school-related behaviors. These behaviors include individually targeted academic domains, classroom deportment, and other tasks (e.g., homework completion). Before the session, the therapist identifies domains of functioning, specific goals, and concrete opportunities to implement procedures at school. The specific behaviors are incorporated into the home-based reinforcement program. After this session, the school-based program continues to be developed and monitored over the course of treatment, with changes in foci as needed in discussion with the teachers and parents.

7. **Review of the Program.** Observations of the previous week and application of the reinforcement program are reviewed. Details about the administration of praise, points, and back-up reinforcers are discussed and enacted so the therapist can identify how to improve parent performance. Changes are made in the program as needed. The parent practices designing programs for a set of hypothetical problems. The purpose is to develop skills that extend beyond implementing programs devised with the therapist.

8. **Family Meeting.** At this meeting, the child and parents are brought into the session. The programs are discussed, including any problems. Revisions are made as needed to correct misunderstandings or to alter facets that may not be implemented in a way that is likely to be effective. The programs are practiced (through role-playing exercises) to see how they are implemented and to make refinements.

9 and 10. Negotiating, Contracting, and Compromising. The child and parent meet together to negotiate new behavioral programs and to place these in contractual form. In the first of these sessions, the therapist introduces the concepts of negotiating and contracting, and parent and child practice negotiation. In the second of these sessions, the child and parent practice with each other on a problem or issue in the home and develop a contract that will be used as part of the program. Over the course of the sessions, the therapist shapes negotiating skills in the parent and child, reinforces compromise, and provides increasingly less guidance (e.g., prompts) as more difficult situations are presented.

11. Reprimands and Consequences for Low-Rate Behaviors. Parents are trained in effective use of reprimands and how to deal with low-rate behaviors such as firesetting, stealing, and truancy. Specific punishment programs (usually chores) are planned and presented to the child as needed for low-rate behaviors.

12. and 13. Review, Problem Solving, and Practice. Material from other sessions is reviewed in theory and practice. Special emphasis is given to role-playing application of individual principles as they are enacted with the trainer. Parents practice designing new programs, revising ailing programs, and responding to a complex array of situations in which principles and practices discussed in previous sessions are reviewed.

Note. From *Evidence-Based Psychotherapies for Children and Adolescents* (pp. 250–251), by A. E. Kazdin and J. Weisz (Eds.), 2003, New York: Guilford Press. Copyright 2003 by Guilford Press. Reprinted with permission.

schedules), target behaviors of the child (e.g., noncompliance, fighting), available incentives, and parameters that are required for effective implementation (e.g., rich reinforcement schedule; shaping, immediacy, and contingency of consequences). The bulk of the treatment session is devoted to modeling by the therapist and role playing and rehearsal by the parent of such tasks as presenting the program to the child, providing prompts, and delivering consequences. As part of this rehearsal, therapist and parent may alternate roles of parent and child to develop the parent's proficiency. For example, delivery of reinforcement (e.g., praise) by the parent is likely to be infrequent, flat, delayed, and connected to parental nagging. Shaping begins with the initial parent repertoire and leads to more consistent, enthusiastic, and immediate praise; reduced nagging; clearer prompts; and so on.

In the home, the parent implements a token reinforcement system to provide a structured way of implementing the reinforcement contingencies. The tokens vary from stars, marks, points, coins, and other materials selected according to the age of the child, ease of delivery for the parent, and other practical issues. The tokens, paired with praise, are contingent on specific child behaviors. Among the many advantages of token reinforcement is the prompting function they serve for the parent to reinforce consistently. Also, tokens facilitate tracking of reinforcement exchanges between parent and child (earning and spending the tokens). The token reinforcement programs reflect an effort to shape both child (e.g., prosocial behaviors) and parent behavior (e.g., child-rearing practices). At the beginning of each treatment session, the therapist reviews precisely what occurred in the previous week or since the previous phone contact and in many cases re-enacts what the parent actually did in relation to the child.

PMT also focuses on child performance at school. Teachers are contacted to discuss individual problem areas, including deportment, grades, and homework completion. A home-based reinforcement system is devised in which the child's performance at school is monitored by the parents, who deliver consequences at home. The teachers may also implement programs in the classroom. The therapist monitors the school program through phone contact and discussions with the therapist in the treatment sessions.

Over the course of treatment, the child is brought into the PMT sessions to ensure that he or she understands the program and that the program is implemented as reported by the parent; the therapist also helps to negotiate behavioral contracts between parent and child. The review of the program focuses on concrete examples of what was done, by and to whom, and with what consequences. The therapist strives to identify ways in which parent and child behavior can be improved (shaping), practicing and providing feedback to the parent and refining or adapting programs as needed. Modeling, rehearsal, and role-playing exercises are used here as well.

Treatment Implementation

Common Treatment Characteristics

Both PSST and PMT emphasize changing the ways individuals perform (i.e., what they do in everyday life). In the case of PSST, treatment is directed specifically at changing the way the child responds in interpersonal situations at home, at school, and in the community and in interactions with teachers, parents, peers, siblings, and others. In the case of PMT, treatment focuses on altering a number of specific child–parent interaction practices by developing appropriate behavior and responding to inappropriate behavior. Both treatments emphasize the development of behavior and extension of behavior across diverse settings (e.g., home, school, and community). Much of the treatment is conducted in everyday life (i.e., outside of the treatment sessions). Tasks for the children (e.g., PSST) and behavior-change programs implemented by parents and teachers in everyday life are central. These are monitored carefully between sessions and regularly repaired or revised as needed to develop repertoires in the child and parents.

PSST and PMT draw heavily on learning theories and research findings. This emphasis has been useful because learning research provides vast and diverse literatures from which to draw, many of which focus specifically on how to develop, alter, and eliminate behavior and create the conditions necessary for change. In PSST and PMT, several procedures, drawn from basic as well as applied learning research, are used to develop behaviors of the child and parent. For example, each treatment session, whether for child or parent, includes extensive use of modeling, prompting and fading, shaping, positive reinforcement, practice and repeated rehearsal, extinction, and mild punishment (e.g., time-out from reinforcement, response cost). The demands for effective implementation of each of these are more complex than they appear. For example, delivering social reinforcement is not merely a matter of praising good behavior. The way praise is delivered along several dimensions dictates the effects (see Kazdin, 2001b).

Another feature of treatment pertains to monitoring of patient progress. As child and parent are trained, the therapist can readily assess how well they are doing in everyday life. During the sessions, the therapist monitors the child's and parent's efforts and use of the skills to see whether a program is being implemented, is having the desired effects, has obstacles, and so on. If little or no progress has occurred, the therapist can usually attend to obstacles immediately in the treatment sessions. The therapist revises programs, reduces or alters requirements on the parent or child, and makes the changes that are needed to improve implementation and to move toward the goals. The therapist obtains feedback from external sources (e.g., teachers, principles) during treatment. The therapist also monitors progress through telephone contact with children and parents during the week.

Finally, both PSST and PMT are manualized and individualized. A core set of themes and skill domains characterizes each treatment and treatment session. Within the core sessions, the therapist accommodates child, parent, and family circumstances, including problem areas, domains of dysfunction, and special conditions of the family (e.g., living conditions, job schedules, custody issues, presence of extended family members). The therapist achieves flexibility by providing optional sessions for the child or family to address specific problems or to work on a theme that was insufficiently conveyed in the core session. Thus, a session is not merely delivered; rather, the content and programs from that session are critically important to achieve change in the child and parent.

Underpinnings of Treatment

Several features underlying treatment delivery receive little attention in research reports and are often overlooked in efforts to extend treatment to clinical practice. To begin, therapist training is especially noteworthy. Full-time therapists (MA-level training in one of the mental health professions) provide treatment. They undergo an additional period of training of approximately 12 months. (We know that training can be readily achieved in this period but have not investigated, either systematically or unsystematically, whether this period can be greatly reduced with more concentrated attention.) The therapist engages in repeated practice, viewing of other therapists' sessions, and simulated treatment before assignment to a patient. Supervision of the initial treatment case consists of viewing live sessions (through video system) and discussing concretely all facets of the session. Modeling, role-playing exercises, practice, shaping, and reinforcement are used individually and in group format to train therapists.

Second, treatments are codified in manual form. The manuals provide the content and focus of individual sessions as well as the presentation, dialogue, and specific procedures to be used. Manuals facilitate therapist training. Also, the manuals are revised on the basis of research findings and the therapists' experience to better accomplish particular goals with children or parents.[4]

Third, therapist supervision, training, and feedback are ongoing. All sessions are videotaped, and routine as well as difficult sessions are reviewed. In addition, all treatment can be observed live from video monitor stations in the clinic. Review of tapes and live observation of sessions improve the quality of treatment because the entire treatment team can assist in deciding the focus of the next session and ways to improve on what has been accomplished.

Treatment Effectiveness: Clinical Trials and Tribulations

Our treatment outcome studies include several characteristics. First, we are interested in evaluating treatment with clinically referred cases. Our research is integrated in an outpatient clinical service. Second, we have adopted a constructive evaluation strategy (Kazdin, 2003b) to build an effective treatment package to address child and family dysfunction. Third, to evaluate treatment outcome, we assess diverse domains of functioning (e.g., antisocial behavior and delinquency, psychiatric symptoms, prosocial functioning) in different contexts (e.g., home, school, community) and with different informants (e.g., children, parents, teachers, therapists). Fourth, we evaluate outcome in relation to developmentally based normative functioning of nonreferred peers to examine the clinical significance of change and the outcome status of treated cases. Finally, we evaluate follow-up functioning up to at least 1 year after treatment is terminated. Although our focus is on developing an effective treatment package, the long-term objectives can be augmented by understanding children and families better

---

[4]Several manuals with variants of cognitive skills training (e.g., Feindler & Ecton, 1986; Finch, Nelson, & Ott, 1993; Santostefano, 1985; Shure, 1992) and parent management training (e.g., Cavell, 2000; Forehand & McMahon, 1981; Forgatch, 1994; Kazdin, in press; Sanders & Dadds, 1993) are available, only a small sample of which can be noted here. We have been hesitant to fix ours in a finalized version and instead use the results and accumulated experience to make regular revisions. A detailed description of our treatments is available.

and integrating this information into outcome research. Thus, we assess many child, parent, and family factors that we believe will significantly influence treatment outcome.

Setting and Participants

Children (≤13 years of age) referred for aggressive and antisocial behavior are seen at our clinic, the Yale Child Conduct Clinic. Children usually meet criteria for a primary diagnosis (using *Diagnostic and Statistical Manual of Mental Disorders* [DSM] criteria) of CD or ODD. Most youth fall within the normal range of intelligence, although a broad range is represented (e.g., full scale from about 60 to 135 on the Wechsler Intelligence Scale for Children—Revised). The families are European American, African American, or Hispanic American (approximately 60%, 30%, and 5%, respectively), with mixed races or Asian American forming the remainder. Approximately 60% of our cases come from two-parent families. Most cases are from lower and lower middle socioeconomic classes. Approximately 20% to 30% of these families receive social assistance.[5]

Assessment and Intervention

The goals of treatment are to reduce antisocial behavior; to improve the children's functioning at home, at school, and in the community; to reduce parental stress and dysfunction; and to improve family functioning. Several measures are administered immediately before and after treatment and at follow-up 1 year later. The primary measures related to our outcome studies are noted in Table 18.2.

TABLE 18.2
Primary Measures Related to Treatment Evaluation

Measures	Domains assessed
Intake measures	
General Information Sheet	Subject and demographic characteristics
Research Diagnostic Interview	Child diagnosis, number of conduct disorder symptoms, total number of symptoms
Risk Factor Interview	Child, parent, family, and contextual factors related to conduct disorder

---

[5]The Child Conduct Clinic and the research reported in this chapter initially began at the Western Psychiatric Institute and Clinic, University of Pittsburgh School of Medicine (1981–1989) and continued at Yale University (1989–present). Although screening criteria for the clinic have not changed appreciably over time, the demographic characteristics have changed to match the change in geographical locale. Consequently, the statistics describing the sample are approximate and are based on the overall characteristics of all cases. More precise descriptions of samples of individual studies can be obtained from the primary references themselves.

TABLE 18.2 (Continued)
Primary Measures Related to Treatment Evaluation

Measures	Domains assessed
Child functioning	
Wechsler Intelligence Scale for Children (Revised)	Verbal and performance scores, overall IQ
Wide Range Achievement Test	Reading ability
Interview for Antisocial Behavior	Child aggressive and antisocial behavior
Self-Report Delinquency Checklist	Child delinquent acts
Children's Action Tendency Scale	Child aggressiveness, assertiveness, submissiveness
Parent Daily Report	Parent evaluation of problems at home
Child Behavior Checklist (Parent)	Diverse behavior problems and social competence
Child Behavior Checklist—TRF (Teacher)	Diverse behavior problems and adaptive functioning
Peer Involvement Inventory	How well child gets along with peers in school
Parent and family functioning	
Dyadic Adjustment Scale	Perceived quality of marital relation
Family Environment Scale	Domains of family functioning
Parenting Stress Index	Perceived parental stress and life events
Beck Depression Inventory	Parent depression
Hopkins Symptom Checklist	Overall parent impairment
Quality of Life Inventory	Parent evaluation of quality of life
Treatment-related measures	
Parent Expectations for Child Therapy	Parents' expectations about treatment, their role, and child improvement
Barriers to Participation in Treatment	Barriers, obstacles, stressors that parents experience specifically in relation to treatment
Child, Parent, and Therapist Evaluation Inventories	Acceptability of and progress in treatment

Note. The assessment procedures and details of and references for individual measures are presented in Tables 18.3 and 18.4 later in this chapter. From *Evidence-Based Psychotherapies for Children and Adolescents* (p. 253), by A. E. Kazdin and J. Weisz (Eds.), 2003, New York: Guilford Press. Copyright 2003 by Guilford Press. Reprinted with permission.

Children who participate in our clinic are assigned randomly to alternative treatment conditions. Children up to age 6 receive PMT only; children 7 years and older receive PSST and PMT, alone or in combination. The different treatments are selected on the basis of the children's reading level, given the format of our PSST as well as suggestions from our work and the work of others that PSST may be more effective with older children (see Durlak, Fuhrman, & Lampman, 1991). When both PSST and PMT are provided to a family, two therapists are involved with each case. Child and parent are seen during the same visit.

Our early studies examined alternative treatment and control conditions and included both inpatient and outpatient cases. In our current work, each condition represents a viable, evidence-based treatment; also, we are only working with outpatients. The core treatment lasts from 4 to 8 months. The varied duration may depend on family progress, but more often, checkered family attendance slows the pace of treatment.

Treatment Effects

Several studies explore the effects of treatment and the factors that contribute to outcome. The studies and their foci are highlighted in Table 18.3. Overall, the main findings from our outcome studies indicate the following:

1. PSST alone and PSST in combination with PMT produce reliable and significant reductions in antisocial behavior and increases in prosocial behavior among children.
2. The combined treatment (PSST+PMT) tends to be more effective than either treatment alone.
3. Improvements are not plausibly explained by the passage of time, repeated contact with a therapist, or nonspecific (common) treatment factors associated with participation in treatment, given comparisons of treatment with other intervention and control conditions.
4. Youth referred for antisocial behavior who do not receive PSST or PMT or who receive relationship-based treatment usually do not change or deteriorate over time as a result of their conduct problem symptoms.
5. The effects of treatment are evident in performance at home, at school, and the community, both immediately after treatment and up to a 1-year follow-up assessment.
6. The effects of treatment have been obtained with both inpatient and outpatient cases.
7. Treatment outcome is influenced by multiple moderators; greater severity of child deviance, parent psychopathology and stress, and family dysfunction at pretreatment are associated with less therapeutic change.
8. Adding a treatment component to address parent sources of stress in everyday life improves treatment outcome of the child.

TABLE 18.3
Main Studies to Evaluate Treatment Outcome and Therapeutic Change

Investigation	Sample	Objective
Kazdin, Esveldt-Dawson, French, and Unis (1987a)	Inpatient children (ages 7–13, $n = 56$)	Evaluated PSST, relationship therapy, and treatment contact control
Kazdin et al. (1987b)	Inpatient cases (ages 7–12, $n = 40$)	Evaluated PSST and PMT combined and treatment contact control
Kazdin, Bass, Siegel, and Thomas (1989)	Inpatient and outpatient cases (ages 5–13, $n = 112$)	Compared PSST and PSST with in vivo practice and relationship therapy
Kazdin, Siegel, and Bass (1992)	Outpatient children (ages 7–13, $n = 97$)	Evaluated effects of PSST, PMT, and combination of both on child and parent functioning
Kazdin, Mazurick, and Siegel (1994)	Outpatient children (ages 4–13, $n = 75$)	Evaluated therapeutic change of completers and dropouts and factors that account for their different outcomes
Kazdin (1995a)	Outpatient children (ages 7–13, $n = 105$)	Replication of effects of combined treatment and child, parent, and family moderator of outcome
Kazdin and Crowley (1997)	Outpatient children (ages 7–13, $n = 120$)	Examined relation of intellectual functioning and severity of symptoms on responsiveness to treatment
Kazdin and Wassell (2000a)	Outpatient children (ages 2–14, $n = 169$)	Examined parent psychopathology and quality of life as moderators of therapeutic changes in children
Kazdin and Wassell (2000b)	Outpatient children (ages 2–14, $n = 250$)	Examined therapeutic changes in children, parents, and families and the predictors of these changes
Kazdin and Whitley (2003)	Outpatient children (ages 6–14, $n = 127$)	Examined the effects of addressing parental stress in treatment and the impact on perceived barriers to treatment and therapeutic changes

Note. From *Evidence-Based Psychotherapies for Children and Adolescents* (p. 254), by A. E. Kazdin and J. Weisz (Eds.), 2003, New York: Guilford Press. Copyright 2003 by Guilford Press. Reprinted with permission.

9. Treatment effects are evident not only in child behavior but also in reduced stress and maternal depression and improved family relations.

Unresolved Issues

Needless to say, many fundamental questions remain. Two questions that are especially salient concern whether the impact of treatment alters the lives of the children and families in palpable ways and whether these effects are long-term. Our studies have shown that children and families make statistically significant improvements with treatment and that the magnitude of these changes is rather large (e.g., mean effect size of change > 1.2; Kazdin & Wassell, 2000b). However, do the gains make a difference to the youth or to others in everyday life? *Clinical significance* refers to the practical value or importance of the effect of an intervention—that is, whether it makes any "real" difference to the clients or others—and can be measured in many ways. The myriad measures of clinical significance have become more sophisticated and even fancy (Kazdin, 2003b; Kendall, 1999). The most commonly used index of clinical significance in child therapy is whether treatment returns to normative levels of functioning relative to data from youths of the same age and sex who are functioning well in the community. Our treatment has demonstrated such changes.

A major obstacle that qualifies our enthusiasm about this finding stems from the fact that standard measures of clinical significance themselves have no clear meaning. For example, demonstrating that children return to normative levels of symptoms on a standardized measure (e.g., Child Behavior Checklist) does not necessarily mean that a genuine difference is evident in everyday life or that functioning is palpably improved. It might; however, little evidence supports the view that it does (Kazdin, 2001a). The entire matter of symptom change raises issues regarding the clinical significance of an outcome. It is easy to show that little, no, or a lot of change could mean clinically significant or no significant change depending on the clinical problem, goals of treatment, and contextual influences in the life of the client (Kazdin, 1999). Some researchers have evaluated among the outcomes arrest and reinstitutionalization and have shown treatment effects on such measures (e.g., Henggeler, Schoenwald, Borduin, Rowland, & Cunningham, 1998), and these efforts are laudable. In most outcome research with children, the impact on everyday functioning, whether on psychological measures (e.g., impairment) or direct measures of functioning in daily life, is not known.

No less significant is whether treatment effects are maintained. Obviously, follow-up assessment is critically important because developmental change is a strong competitor with treatment for many problems and because treatments that appear effective or more effective at one point in time (e.g., posttreatment assessment) may not be at another point in time (e.g., follow-up assessment; Kazdin, 2000c). Follow-up assessment in our program has focused primarily on evaluation of the child's functioning at home and at school for 1 year (and occasionally 2 years) after completion of the program. Therapeutic changes usually are maintained, as reflected in symptoms as well as prosocial functioning. Clearly, not knowing the long-term impact (e.g., 5 to 10 years after the intervention) and whether any outcome is due in whole or in part to the intervention is a limitation.

Related Lines of Research: Briefly Noted

As part of the task of developing and understanding treatment, we have had to take excursions along several fronts. Let me illustrate a few of these to convey the point and its relevance to our outcome research. First, we needed to measure for a number of constructs for which no standardized assessments exist. We have developed measures and attempted to provide sufficient validity information to address the question of initial interest. We have developed a few measures (Table 18.4) that have helped us identify potential moderators of treatment, subtype children or behavior, and understand key processes related to participation in treatment.

Second, a number of problems and issues emerge in the treatment of children with CD that are not easily neglected. For example, parental stress, harsh parenting practices and child abuse, domestic violence, and divorce

TABLE 18.4
Measures Developed or in Development to Assess Key Domains

Measure	Construct/domain	Key reference
Children's Hostility Inventory	Aggression (overt aggressive acts) and hostility (grudges or anger)	Kazdin, Rodgers, Colbus, and Siegel (1987)
Interview for Antisocial Behavior	Diverse symptoms of antisocial behavior; factors that include overt and covert aggression	Kazdin and Esveldt-Dawson (1986)
Risk Factor Interview	Family, parent, and child risk factors for poor long-term prognosis of the child	Kazdin, Mazurick, and Bass (1993)
Treatment Evaluation Inventories	Child, parent, and therapist versions of a scale to evaluate the extent to which the respondent (child, parent) finds treatment acceptable or the therapist (evaluates how acceptable that person found treatment)	Kazdin et al. (1987b)
Barriers to Participation in Treatment Scale	Perceived barriers and obstacles for participating in treatment	Kazdin, Holland, et al. (1997)
Parent Expectancies for Therapy Scale	Parents' initial expectations about treatment and participation in treatment	Nock and Kazdin (2001)
Management of Children's Behavior Scale	Parenting practices that contribute to or are associated with conduct problems in the home	Perepletchikova and Kazdin (in press)

Note. Measures referred to in citations before 2000 have been included in multiple studies; the references cited are those that describe the development of the measure.

are relatively common and play a role in administering treatment, leaving aside any role they may play in the maintenance and long-term course of CD. We have had to study a few of these. I say *had to*, because if one is interested in developing effective treatment in the context of clinical work, work on the treatment itself is, in my opinion, the easy part. The influences on treatment delivery are no less significant. For example, we have studied attrition from therapy (i.e., dropping out of treatment). In the United States, between 40% and 60% of children, adolescents, and adults who begin therapy drop out prematurely (Wierzbicki & Pekarik, 1993). Moreover, the rates tend to be higher as a function of clients' aggressiveness, which has been our clinical focus (Kazdin, 1996).

We completed a few studies to predict who drops out of treatment (Kazdin, 1990; Kazdin, Mazurick, & Bass, 1993), to examine the outcomes of families who drop out (Kazdin, Mazurick, & Siegel, 1994), to distinguish different types of families and circumstances among dropouts (Kazdin & Mazurick, 1994; Kazdin, Stolar, & Marciano, 1995), to develop a conceptual model about why families drop out (Kazdin, 1996), to develop measures of key constructs (Kazdin, Holland, Crowley, & Breton, 1997; Nock & Kazdin, 2001), to test the model (Kazdin, Holland, & Crowley, 1997; Kazdin & Wassell, 1999, 2000a), and to tinker with ancillary implications in relation to treatment acceptability (Kazdin, 2000b). We have learned a great deal, some of which is even interesting!

From clinical experience, we know that families sometimes leave treatment very early because the child is doing extremely well. Our research supports this finding when outcome is assessed among dropouts. For example, approximately 34% of dropouts have made important changes in their seemingly all-too-brief treatment period, as compared with 79% of those who complete treatment, according to data from parent evaluations (Kazdin & Wassell, 1998). Still, the percentage of dropouts who have made significant change is rather intriguing and has important conceptual and clinical implications on which I cannot elaborate here. In addition, our group has a better understanding or, equally and sometimes more comforting, the illusion of a better understanding of why people drop out. Families experience barriers to participation during their treatment, barriers that can affect their remaining in treatment, therapeutic change among those who do remain in treatment, and satisfaction with treatment. The next step is to test whether an intervention that addresses the putative bases for attrition can retain cases in treatment and influence outcome.

Third, a final illustration pertains to the evaluation of treatment outcome. Therapy outcome is complex for many reasons, often because multiple relevant domains of functioning (e.g., symptoms, impairment, prosocial behavior) are not all altered by treatment or change at the same rate. Another reason that outcome is complex is that changes evident on one informant's set of measures (e.g., parent, teacher, and child) may not be related to changes on another informant's set of the "same" measures. We have had to dip our toes into this puddle by looking at some of the complexities of therapeutic change. For example, we have looked at the relation of deviance and prosocial functioning and changes in each of these domains over time (Kazdin, 1993a) and the extent to which treatment of the child leads to changes in parent and family functioning (Kazdin, Siegel, & Bass, 1992; Kazdin & Wassell, 2000b). In addition, we have addressed methodological issues related to discrepancies among informants, including the contribution of method and construct variance in assessing child dysfunction and the implications for using different measures and perspectives in defining clinical dysfunction (Kazdin, 1989; Kazdin & Bass, 1988; Kazdin, Esveldt-Dawson, Unis, & Rancurello, 1983; Kazdin, French, Unis, & Esveldt-Dawson, 1983). The work has helped alert us to the scope of change and the interrelations among domains.

CURRENT DIRECTIONS AND RESEARCH PRIORITIES

Our Current Foci

Our work in progress focuses on a number of issues. Some of these are related to CD and its treatment; others are related to child therapy more generally. Three are especially high priorities. First, we are exploring *novel* models for delivering treatment. The current dominant model in therapeutic use consists of brief and time-limited treatment. Clinical dysfunction (e.g., CD, depression, ADHD) is likely to require more enduring interventions. We are currently exploring alternative models of treatment delivery that are designed to improve impact. Central to this work is evaluation of treatment of the usual duration, designed to address crises and to alter functioning at home, at school, and in the community. After initial treatment and demonstrated improvement in functioning in everyday life, treatment is suspended. At this point, the child's functioning begins to be monitored systematically and regularly (e.g., every month). Treatment is then provided *pro re nata* (PRN) based on the assessment data or emergent issues raised by the family, teachers, or others. The approach might be likened to the more familiar model of dental care in the United States in which regular checkups are recommended; an intervention is provided if and as needed on the basis of these periodic checks.

Second, we are trying to *understand treatment outcome* and the interrelations among domains in a more analytical way. We know now that treatment of the child has considerable impact on parent and family functioning, not in all domains we assess but in several of them (e.g., parent psychopathology, stress). Intricate relations are likely to exist among the domains at pretreatment (e.g., they moderate outcome), posttreatment (e.g., they are dependent variables), and, perhaps, follow-up (the new levels of the variables may moderate follow-up effects). There are likely to be relations that could inform treatment directly by identifying who is likely to respond to treatment and possible domains to target to improve responsiveness to treatments.

Third, we are *focusing in treatment more on parent sources of stress*. Parents and family sources of stress can play a role in child dysfunction as well as treatment. Specifically, socioeconomic disadvantage, marital conflict, parent psychopathology, stress, and social isolation are common characteristics among families of children with CD. Families who show adversity in one or more of these domains are more likely to drop out of treatment prematurely, to show fewer gains in treatment (among those who remain), and are less likely to maintain therapeutic gains (for a review, see Kazdin, 1995b). Also, stress can disrupt parents' discipline practices in ways that promote deviant child behavior (Dumas & Wahler, 1985; Patterson, 1988; Patterson et al., 1992). Our initial work suggests that explicit efforts to alleviate parental stress (e.g., by increasing the time parents have for themselves, for developing friendships, re-establishing a relationship that has gone awry, or pursuing something they consider as personally fulfilling) improves treatment outcome (Kazdin & Whitley, 2003). Improvements in the child and reductions in symptoms of psychopathology and stress in the parent are enhanced by this addition to treatment.

Fourth and most important, we are interested in *understanding the mechanisms of therapeutic change*. Perhaps the greatest weakness in psychotherapy literature is the paucity of research on reasons that treatment works. Current design and assessment practices in randomized controlled trials actually preclude drawing statements about the reasons that treatment works (Kazdin & Nock, 2003). Studying mechanisms of change is critically important to extend treatment to clinical settings and to optimize therapeutic change.

Other areas of research in our program include (a) the role of the therapeutic alliance in treatment and therapeutic change, (b) factors that influence patient adherence to treatment prescriptions, and (c) the impact of parents' expectations about the effects of treatment on their participation in treatment and therapeutic change. Each of these has emerged as a theme in the application of treatment with children and families or has been stimulated by specific findings in other work cited here. For example, we have reason to believe that a parent's perception of how demanding treatment influences therapeutic changes in the child (e.g., Kazdin & Wassell, 2000a). This connection contributes in part to our interest in the role parental expectations may play in diverse facets of treatment, including adherence to treatment prescriptions, therapeutic change, and satisfaction with treatment. The work may be pertinent to areas beyond the treatment of CD, but its relevance remains to be seen.

These remarks convey some of the concrete lines of work we are currently pursuing, stimulated largely by issues that emerge directly from treating children and families and from findings of research to date. More broadly, limited studies have helped provide a perspective and appreciation on the strengths and limitations of child psychotherapy beyond the confines of CD. Despite advances in child therapy (e.g., identifying evidence-based treatments), I have noted elsewhere that overall very little progress has been made in addressing key questions (e.g., Why does treatment work, for whom does treatment work and why?; see Kazdin, 2000a, 2000c). Progress in our own work and in child therapy more generally will require attention to a broader research agenda than is currently evident. Although that agenda cannot be considered here, it presents an important guide and context for directions we are pursuing.

EXTENDING TREATMENT TO CLINICAL PRACTICE

The implications of our research for clinical work can be discussed in different ways. The first and most obvious implication is that there are now evidence-based treatments for children referred for CD. In addition to the two techniques I have highlighted, other treatments are available as well (e.g., multisystemic therapy, functional family therapy; Brestan & Eyberg, 1998; Kazdin & Weisz, 2003; Sheldrick, Kendall, & Heimberg, 2001). One of these treatments ought to be the first line of attack in clinical work with children who have CD. In the case of PSST and PMT, many manuals are available to convey the procedures (see Kazdin, 1994, in press, 2000c). The paucity of training opportunities for mental health professionals to learn these techniques poses a difficulty. Furthermore, as I have noted, whether one is learning to fly a plane, play a musical instrument, or provide PMT or PSST, reading the manual is only a beginning.

Second, several procedures used routinely in research and considered to be unique to research may be equally critical for use in clinical practice. I have in mind some of the features of controlled clinical trials that are designed to augment treatment implementation and therapeutic effects. To begin, therapist training in the techniques is extensive. The delivery of treatment no doubt requires a great deal of skill and artistry. In our program, for example, we train therapists in the underlying principles of the treatments but much more extensively in the concrete procedures and programs that derive from these principles. We focus quite specifically on what the therapist says and does in each session, on contact with the child and family over the course of treatment, and on how to improvise the techniques as needed to address individual circumstances of the child and family (e.g., see Kazdin, in press). Therapists are trained to a level of mastery and supervised regularly to sustain and indeed even improve that level of mastery. Training therapists in this way, common among treatment research programs, departs greatly from the level of training and mastery of treatment in many clinical settings. The manner of training therapists, rehearsing treatment practices and skills, and providing ongoing feedback helps to ensure treatment integrity. In addition, treatment supervision also aids clinical care. In our own program and many other programs as well, all treatment is videotaped and can be viewed live to provide immediate feedback to a therapist and to problem solve. This kind of supervision not only maintains the integrity of treatment but also enhances quality of the treatment for the individual case.

The precise procedures we use to train and supervise therapists, to monitor treatment integrity, and to manage patient care may not be essential. However, some features to help establish and sustain the quality and integrity of treatment in clinical work are likely to have salutary effects in clinical practice. The results of treatments in research may rely on the quality of training, supervision, monitoring, and patient management that are often routine. Many of these practices could be implemented in clinical settings.

Some practices could improve both clinical research and practice. Systematic assessment of patient progress during treatment, rather than merely at the end of treatment, would be very helpful in establishing the effects of treatment in research and clinical work (Kazdin, 1993b). The absence of systematic evaluation in clinical practice is a great deficiency. Even if evidence-based treatments were used, the treatment is not likely to be effective or optimally effective for all cases. Some monitoring procedures are needed to provide an evaluation of progress during treatment and a basis for decisions about continuing, changing, augmenting, or ending treatment. A number of resources are available to suggest procedures that can be used in clinical work to evaluate progress in treatment (e.g., Clement, 1999; Cone, 2000; Kazdin, 1993b; Wiger, 1999). Ultimately, the quality of clinical work depends not only on using techniques supported by evidence but also on systematically examining their impact on individual patients.

Overall, discussions of improving patient care and disseminating the benefits of treatment research emphasize treatment techniques. Specifically, therapists look to research to evaluate techniques, with the idea that once they are identified, they can be disseminated to clinical practice. Perhaps this goal is attainable. However, from our experience (admittedly limited to only one program, primarily one disorder, and within a restricted age range), the effectiveness of treatment cannot be separated from the quality of therapist training, monitoring of treatment, and feedback to therapists. More broadly, a number of research practices can be adapted for clinical use to improve the quality of individual patient care. Also, extending treatment and ensuring its effectiveness greatly depends on understanding why and how treatments work. Dissemination without understanding is likely to produce quite checkered effects.

CLOSING COMMENTS

Our program is devoted to the treatment of children with CD and their families. We have focused on combined cognitive–behavioral procedures to focus on interpersonal cognitive processes of the child (PSST) and parent–child interactions (PMT). The treatments focus on facets within the individual (e.g., cognitive and behavioral repertoires, predisposition to respond to potentially problematic situations), as well as external and interactional events (e.g., antecedents and consequences from others), to promote prosocial behavior. With both of the treatments, altering performance outside of the treatment setting—specifically, at home, at school, and in the community—is emphasized. Although formal treatment sessions form the basis of the intervention, much of the treatment is conducted outside of the sessions. The child, parent, and teacher have separate but interrelated roles guided by the therapist. Treatment outcome studies—our own and those of others—have indicated that clinically referred patients improve with PSST and PMT and that effects are maintained at least to 1-year follow-up assessment.

CD represents a special challenge, given the multiple domains of functioning that are affected. Indeed, we consider CD a pervasive developmental disorder precisely because of the scope of dysfunction children exhibit. Even this characterization is inadequate in the context of clinical work because broader influences (parental, familial, and contextual) often must be considered in treatment. These influences have a demonstrated relevance to the child's antisocial behavior, participation and completion of treatment, and therapeutic change. In the process of developing treatment, we have been drawn into many other areas that are related to dysfunction and change. In this chapter, I have tried to highlight some of the work on treatment outcome, as well as some of the related areas that emerged as part of this work.

REFERENCES

American Psychiatric Association. (1994). *Diagnostic and statistical manual of mental disorders* (4th ed.). Washington, DC: Author.

Brestan, E. V., & Eyberg, S. M. (1998). Effective psychosocial treatments of conduct-disordered children and adolescents: 29 years, 82 studies, and 5,272 kids. *Journal of Clinical Child Psychology, 27,* 180–189.

Cavell, T. A. (2000). *Working with aggressive children: A practitioner's guide.* Washington, DC: American Psychological Association.

Clement, P. W. (1999). *Outcomes and incomes: How to evaluate, improve, and market your practice by measuring outcomes in psychotherapy.* New York: Guilford Press.

Cone, J. D. (2000). *Evaluating outcomes: Empirical tools for effective practice.* Washington, DC: American Psychological Association.

Crick, N. R., & Dodge, K. A. (1994). A review and reformulation of social information processing mechanisms in children's social adjustment. *Psychological Bulletin, 115,* 74–101.

Dumas, J. E., & Wahler, R. G. (1985). Indiscriminate mothering as a contextual factor in aggressive oppositional child behavior: "Damned if you do and damned if you don't." *Journal of Applied Behavior Analysis, 13,* 1–17.

Durlak, J. A., Fuhrman, T., & Lampman, C. (1991). Effectiveness of cognitive–behavioral therapy for maladapting children: A meta-analysis. *Psychological Bulletin, 110,* 204–214.

Feindler, E. L., & Ecton, R. B. (1986). *Adolescent anger control: Cognitive–behavioral techniques.* Elmsford, NY: Pergamon Press.

Finch, A. J., Jr., Nelson, W. M., & Ott, E. S. (1993). *Cognitive–behavioral procedures with children and adolescents: A practical guide.* Needham Heights, MA: Allyn & Bacon.

Forehand, R., & McMahon, R. J. (1981). *Helping the noncompliant child: A clinician's guide to parent training.* New York: Guilford Press.

Forgatch, M. S. (1994). *Parenting through change: A training manual.* Eugene, OR: Oregon Social Learning Center.

Henggeler, S. W., Schoenwald, S. K., Borduin, C. M., Rowland, M. D., & Cunningham, P. B. (1998). *Multisystemic treatment of antisocial behavior in children and adolescents.* New York: Guilford Press.

Hill, J., & Maughan, B. (Eds.). (2001). *Conduct disorders in childhood and adolescence.* Cambridge, England: Cambridge University Press.

Kazdin, A. E. (1989). Identifying depression in children: A comparison of alternative selection criteria. *Journal of Abnormal Child Psychology, 17,* 437–455.

Kazdin, A. E. (1990). Premature termination from treatment among children referred for antisocial behavior. *Journal of Child Psychology and Psychiatry, 3,* 415–425.

Kazdin, A. E. (1993a). Changes in behavioral problems and prosocial functioning in child treatment. *Journal of Child and Family Studies, 2,* 5–22.

Kazdin, A. E. (1993b). Evaluation in clinical practice: Clinically sensitive and systematic methods of treatment delivery. *Behavior Therapy, 24,* 11–45.

Kazdin, A. E. (1994). Psychotherapy for children and adolescents. In A. E. Bergin & S. L. Garfield (Eds.), *Handbook of psychotherapy and behavior change* (4th ed., pp. 543–594). New York: Wiley.

Kazdin, A. E. (1995a). Child, parent, and family dysfunction as predictors of outcome in cognitive–behavioral treatment of antisocial children. *Behaviour Research and Therapy, 33,* 271–281.

Kazdin, A. E. (1995b). *Conduct disorder in childhood and adolescence* (2nd ed.). Thousand Oaks, CA: Sage.

Kazdin, A. E. (1996). Dropping out of child psychotherapy: Issues for research and implications for practice. *Clinical Child Psychology and Psychiatry, 1,* 133–156.

Kazdin, A. E. (1997). Parent management training: Evidence, outcomes, and issues. *Journal of the American Academy of Child and Adolescent Psychiatry, 36,* 1349–1356.

Kazdin, A. E. (1999). The meanings and measurement of clinical significance. *Journal of Consulting and Clinical Psychology, 67,* 332–339.

Kazdin, A. E. (2000a). Developing a research agenda for child and adolescent psychotherapy research. *Archives of General Psychiatry, 57,* 829–835.

Kazdin, A. E. (2000b). Perceived barriers to treatment participation and treatment acceptability among antisocial children and their families. *Journal of Child and Family Studies, 9,* 157–174.

Kazdin, A. E. (2000c). *Psychotherapy for children and adolescents: Directions for research and practice.* New York: Oxford University Press.

Kazdin, A. E. (2001a). Almost clinically significant (p < .10): Current measures may only approach clinical significance. *Clinical Psychology: Science and Practice, 8,* 455–462.

Kazdin, A. E. (2001b). *Behavior modification in applied settings* (6th ed.). Pacific Grove, CA: Wadsworth.

Kazdin, A. E. (2002). Psychosocial treatments for conduct disorder in children and adolescents. In P. E. Nathan & J. M. Gorman (Eds.), *A guide to treatments that work* (2nd ed., pp. 57–85). New York: Oxford University Press.

Kazdin, A. E. (2003a). Problem-solving skills training and parent management training for conduct disorder. In A. E. Kazdin & J. R. Weisz (Eds.), *Evidence-based psychotherapies for children and adolescents* (pp. 241–262). New York: Guilford Press.

Kazdin, A. E. (2003b). *Research design in clinical psychology* (4th ed.). Needham Heights, MA: Allyn & Bacon.

Kazdin, A. E. (in press). *Parent management training: Treatment for oppositional, aggressive, and antisocial behavior in children and adolescents.* New York: Oxford University Press.

Kazdin, A. E., & Bass, D. (1988). Parent, teacher, and hospital staff evaluations of severely disturbed children. *American Journal of Orthopsychiatry, 58,* 512–523.

Kazdin, A. E., Bass, D., Siegel, T., & Thomas, C. (1989). Cognitive–behavioral treatment and relationship therapy in the treatment of children referred for antisocial behavior. *Journal of Consulting and Clinical Psychology, 57,* 522–535.

Kazdin, A. E., & Crowley, M. (1997). Moderators of treatment outcome in cognitively based treatment of antisocial behavior. *Cognitive Therapy and Research, 21,* 185–207.

Kazdin, A. E., & Esveldt-Dawson, K. (1986). The Interview for Antisocial Behavior: Psychometric characteristics and concurrent validity with child psychiatric inpatients. *Journal of Psychopathology and Behavioral Assessment, 8,* 289–303.

Kazdin, A. E., Esveldt-Dawson, K., French, N. H., & Unis, A. S. (1987a). The effects of parent management training and problem-solving skills training combined in the treatment of antisocial child behavior. *Journal of the American Academy of Child and Adolescent Psychiatry, 26*, 416–424.

Kazdin, A. E., Esveldt-Dawson, K., French, N. H., & Unis, A. S. (1987b). Problem-solving skills training and relationship therapy in the treatment of antisocial child behavior. *Journal of Consulting and Clinical Psychology, 55*, 76–85.

Kazdin, A. E., Esveldt-Dawson, K., Unis, A. S., & Rancurello, M. D. (1983). Child and parent evaluations of depression and aggression in psychiatric inpatient children. *Journal of Abnormal Child Psychology, 11*, 401–413.

Kazdin, A. E., French, N. H., Unis, A. S., & Esveldt-Dawson, K. (1983). Assessment of childhood depression: Correspondence of child and parent ratings. *Journal of the American Acdemy of Child Psychiatry, 22*, 157–164.

Kazdin, A. E., Holland, L., & Crowley, M. (1997). Family experience of barriers to treatment and premature termination from child therapy. *Journal of Consulting and Clinical Psychology, 65*, 453–463.

Kazdin, A. E., Holland, L., Crowley, M., & Breton, S. (1997). Barriers to Participation in Treatment Scale: Evaluation and validation in the context of child outpatient treatment. *Journal of Child Psychology and Psychiatry, 38*, 1051–1062.

Kazdin, A. E., & Mazurick, J. L. (1994). Dropping out of child psychotherapy: Distinguishing early and late dropouts over the course of treatment. *Journal of Consulting and Clinical Psychology, 62*, 1069–1074.

Kazdin, A. E., Mazurick, J. L., & Bass, D. (1993). Risk for attrition in treatment of antisocial children and families. *Journal of Clinical Child Psychology, 22*, 2–16.

Kazdin, A. E., Mazurick, J. L., & Siegel, T. C. (1994). Treatment outcome among children with externalizing disorder who terminate prematurely versus those who complete psychotherapy. *Journal of the American Academy of Child and Adolescent Psychiatry, 33*, 549–557.

Kazdin, A. E., & Nock, M. K. (2003). Delineating mechanisms of change in child and adolescent therapy: Methodological issues and research recommendations. *Journal of Child Psychology and Psychiatry, 44*, 1116–1129.

Kazdin, A. E., Rodgers, A., Colbus, D., & Siegel, T. (1987). Children's Hostility Inventory: Measurement of aggression and hostility in psychiatric inpatient children. *Journal of Clinical Child Psychology, 16*, 320–328.

Kazdin, A. E., Siegel, T., & Bass, D. (1992). Cognitive problem-solving skills training and parent management training in the treatment of antisocial behavior in children. *Journal of Consulting and Clinical Psychology, 60*, 733–747.

Kazdin, A. E., Stolar, M. J., & Marciano, P. L. (1995). Risk factors for dropping out of treatment among white and black families. *Journal of Family Psychology, 9*, 402–417.

Kazdin, A. E., & Wassell, G. (1998). Treatment completion and therapeutic change among children referred for outpatient therapy. *Professional Psychology: Research and Practice, 29*, 332–340.

Kazdin, A. E., & Wassell, G. (1999). Barriers to treatment participation and therapeutic change among children referred for conduct disorder. *Journal of Clinical Child Psychology, 28*, 160–172.

Kazdin, A. E., & Wassell, G. (2000a). Predictors of barriers to treatment and therapeutic change in outpatient therapy for antisocial children and their families. *Mental Health Services Research, 2*, 27–40.

Kazdin, A. E., & Wassell, G. (2000b). Therapeutic changes in children, parents, and families resulting from treatment of children with conduct problems. *Journal of the American Academy of Child and Adolescent Psychiatry, 39*, 414–420.

Kazdin, A. E., & Weisz, J. R. (1998). Identifying and developing empirically supported child and adolescent treatments. *Journal of Consulting and Clinical Psychology, 66*, 19–36.

Kazdin, A. E., & Weisz, J. R. (Eds.). (2003). *Evidence-based psychotherapies for children and adolescents*. New York: Guilford Press.

Kazdin, A. E., & Whitley, M. K. (2003). Treatment of parental stress to enhance therapeutic change among children referred for aggressive and antisocial behavior. *Journal of Consulting and Clinical Psychology, 71*, 504–515.

Kendall, P. C. (Ed.). (1999). Special section: Clinical significance. *Journal of Consulting and Clinical Psychology, 67*, 283–339.

Kendall, P. C. (Ed.). (2000). *Child and adolescent therapy: Cognitive–behavioral procedures* (2nd ed.). New York: Guilford Press.

Lochman, J. E., & Dodge, K. A. (1994). Social–cognitive processes of severely violent, moderately aggressive, and nonaggressive boys. *Journal of Consulting and Clinical Psychology, 62*, 366–374.

Lochman, J. E., Whidby, J. M., & FitzGerald, D. P. (2000). Cognitive–behavioral assessment and treatment with aggressive children. In P. C. Kendall (Ed.), *Child and adolescent therapy: Cognitive–behavioral procedures* (2nd ed., pp. 31–87). New York: Guilford Press.

Nock, M. K., & Kazdin, A. E. (2001). Parent expectancies for child therapy: Assessment and relation to participation in treatment. *Journal of Child and Family Studies, 10*, 155–180.

Patterson, G. R. (1982). *Coercive family process*. Eugene, OR: Castalia.

Patterson, G. R. (1988). Stress: A change agent for family process. In N. Garmezy & M. Rutter (Eds.), *Stress, coping, and development in children* (pp. 235–264). Baltimore: The Johns Hopkins University Press.

Patterson, G. R., Reid, J. B., & Dishion, T. J. (1992). *Antisocial boys*. Eugene, OR: Castalia.

Perepletchikova, F., & Kazdin, A. E. (in press). Assessment of parenting practices related to conduct problems: Development and validation of the Management of Children's Behavior Scale. *Journal of Child and Family Studies*.

Reid, J. B., Patterson, G. R., & Snyder, J. (Eds.). (2002). *Antisocial behavior in children and adolescents: A developmental analysis and model for intervention*. Washington, DC: American Psychological Association.

Rubin, K. H., Bream, L. A., & Rose-Krasnor, L. (1991). Social problem solving and aggression in childhood. In D. J. Pepler & K. H. Rubin (Eds.), *The development and treatment of childhood aggression* (pp. 219–248). Hillsdale, NJ: Erlbaum.

Sanders, M. R., & Dadds, M. R. (1993). *Behavioral family intervention*. Needham Heights, MA: Allyn & Bacon.

Santostefano, S. (1985). *Cognitive control therapy with children and adolescents*. Elmsford, NY: Pergamon Press.

Sheldrick, R. C., Kendall, P. C., & Heimberg, R. G. (2001). Assessing clinical significance: A comparison of three treatments for conduct disordered children. *Clinical Psychology: Science and Practice, 8,* 418–430.

Shirk, S. R. (Ed.). (1988). *Cognitive development and child psychotherapy*. New York: Plenum.

Shure, M. B. (1992). *I can problem solve (ICPS): An interpersonal cognitive problem solving program*. Champaign, IL: Research Press.

Shure, M. B. (1997). Interpersonal cognitive problem solving: Primary prevention of early high-risk behaviors in the preschool and primary years. In G. W. Albee & T. P. Gulotta (Eds.), *Primary prevention works* (pp. 167–188). Thousand Oaks, CA: Sage.

Shure, M. B. (1999). Preventing violence the problem-solving way. *Juvenile Justice Bulletin, April, 1-11*. Publication of the U.S. Department of Justice, Office of Juvenile Justice and Delinquency Prevention, Washington, DC.

Spivack, G., & Shure, M. B. (1982). The cognition of social adjustment: Interpersonal cognitive problem solving thinking. In B. B. Lahey & A. E. Kazdin (Eds.), *Advances in clinical child psychology* (Vol. 5, pp. 323–372). New York: Plenum.

Stoff, D. M., Breiling, J., & Maser, J. D. (Eds.). (1997). *Handbook of antisocial behavior*. New York: Wiley.

Wierzbicki, M., & Pekarik, G. (1993). A meta-analysis of psychotherapy dropout. *Professional Psychology: Research and Practice, 24,* 190–195.

Wiger, D. E. (1999). *The psychotherapy documentation primer*. New York: Wiley.

19

TREATMENT AND EDUCATION FOR CHILDHOOD FIRESETTING: DESCRIPTION, OUTCOMES, AND IMPLICATIONS

DAVID J. KOLKO

THE PROBLEM OF FIRESETTING IN CHILDREN AND YOUTH

Scope and Impact

Firesetting by children or youths is a common and costly problem that causes significant individual and societal consequences. Data collected by the National Fire Incident Reporting System (NFIRS) for 1997 found that

Preparation of this chapter was supported, in part, by a renewal of grant MH-39976 from the National Institute of Mental Health. The author acknowledges the collaboration of the Pittsburgh Bureau of Fire, especially Lt. Varnell Lewis, and the contribution of the staff of Project SAFETY (Services Aimed at Fire Education and Training for Youth). Many of the background studies reviewed herein were conducted in collaboration with Alan E. Kazdin, PhD. Much of the evidence presented in the section on background research in firesetting was based on a grant awarded to David J. Kolko and Alan E. Kazdin that compared and followed firesetting children and their nonfiresetting peers (NIMH #39976; 1985-1990).

children playing with fire accounted for 65,000 fires that resulted in 2,158 civilian injuries and 284 civilian deaths (Hall, 2000a). Such figures are likely to be underestimated given the large number of fires that never come to the attention of the fire service; estimates suggest that the ratio of reported fires to unreported fires is about three to one. During a 12-month period (September 1999 to September 2000), 1,283 children and adolescents were referred for firesetting behavior to a state-wide intervention program in Massachusetts (Massachusetts Coalition for Juvenile Firesetter Programs, 2000).

Children's fireplay is responsible for many fire injuries and deaths in both children and adolescents. As reported by NFIRS (Hall, 2000a), the majority of all injuries and deaths in children are related to playing with fire. Nearly two fifths of all preschool deaths are due to fireplay, a level of risk that exceeds twice that for all other age groups combined. Among fatal victims of home fires between 1993 and 1997, 86.3% involved a child or adolescent. Young children (ages 1–4 years) accounted for 60% of all reported fire-related deaths for children in 1994.

An estimated 9,200 juveniles were arrested for arson in 1999, 89% of whom were males and 67% of whom were under the age of 15 (*Crime in the United States 1999*, 2000). Juveniles accounted for 54% of all arrests for arson that year, making arson the only crime for which juveniles make up a majority of all arrests. The number of arrests increased by 9% from 1990 to 1999 but decreased by 19% from 1995 to 1999. Other evidence suggests that the incidence of juvenile firesetting has shown a general decline in past decades, with reports of the number of civilian deaths and civilian injuries attributed to children's fireplay showing a more variable pattern; this reduction was found between 1994 and 1997 (Hall, 2000b). Despite these somewhat optimistic trends, however, firesetting and arson among youths are still serious health and social problems.

The overall magnitude of the impact of firesetting and arson attributable to youths in this country is difficult to ascertain, but some reports provide an understanding of the general impact of firesetting in this age group. Reports of property damage resulting from incendiary and suspicious fires in 1998 were estimated at $1.249 billion dollars, with a loss of 470 civilian lives (Hall, 2000b). Direct property damage caused by juvenile firesetting was estimated at $283.3 million (Hall, 2000a).

Scientific and Practice Perspectives

The problem of childhood firesetting in various communities across the country has received greater attention in recent years. However, the volume of programmatic efforts reported far exceeds the availability of new scientific studies and clinical reports in this area. A scientific impediment to studying and treating the problem is the variability that exists in the description and definition of childhood firesetting, or firestarting (Kolko, 2002a). Although a standard definition does not exist, the need to explicate any criteria used (e.g., nature and severity of a child's involvement with fire) in the selection of cases for study or service remains. In our research, children who acknowledge, or those whose parents acknowledge, any unsanctioned use of fire that produces at least some damage to property have been classified as firesetters. Accordingly, we classified matchplayers who caused no property damages as nonfiresetters. Of course, subsequent evidence from our work has shown that the matchplayers share certain characteristics with both nonfiresetters and firesetters. Clearly, the way we classify cases varying in level of fire involvement may affect a study's outcomes. The variability that exists in subject samples on this one parameter alone suggests that caution be exercised in evaluating research evidence in the area.

A second consideration in examining this literature reflects the fact that the cases described in the literature and news media are quite diverse. Because no single profile of the firesetter or arsonist has been identified, the fact that cases vary according to age, history, frequency, and severity of firesetting, firesetting motives and precipitants, and level of child, parent, and family dysfunction, among other characteristics, is unsurprising. The extent to which these characteristics influence the severity of the child's firesetting history or other clinical problems is still virtually unknown.

One topic likely to be advanced by an understanding of the interplay among these fire-related and clinical characteristics involves the identification of subtypes of firesetters. Clinical reports and experience continue to emphasize the presence of certain subgroups, such as the curious, cry-for-help, pathological, or delinquent firesetter, despite the absence of any clear scientific evaluations of these subgroups. Some children have exhibited serious firesetting characterized by frequent, intentional, concealed, and destructive incidents (Bumpass, Fagelman, & Brix, 1983; Jacobson, 1985; Kuhnley, Hendren, & Quinlen, 1982; Lewis & Yarnell, 1951; Stewart & Culver, 1982), whereas others have set a single fire at home that appeared to be accidental or due to curiosity or experimentation, which may be among the most common motives for children (Lewis & Yarnell, 1951). If such subgroups exist, personal motives, related antecedents, and key consequences are likely to influence the likelihood of recidivism. Unfortunately, few empirical studies have examined this topic (Kolko, 2002a). The relative absence of prospective studies has limited our understanding of those children who set additional fires and the interventions they should receive.

This chapter describes the application of several assessment and intervention findings obtained from prior empirical studies of childhood firesetters to the development and evaluation of an intervention outcome study. In this clinical trial, firesetters (ages 5–13 years) were assigned randomly to intervention conditions that reflect contemporary methods used by both fire service officials (community: fire safety education) and mental health practitioners (clinic: psychological counseling). Some children were assigned to a standard practice condition. Both short-term and long-term comparisons have been reported. By way of introduction, evidence to suggest the need for such a study is reviewed.

BACKGROUND RESEARCH ON FIRESETTING

Descriptive and Follow-Up Studies

The scientific goals of that application were to (a) describe empirically the clinical characteristics of firesetting children; (b) examine the antecedents, characteristics, and consequences of firesetting incidents; and (c) develop predictors of the continuation and cessation of firesetting. As an overview to the present treatment study, the results of related studies are briefly reported in this section. A more complete description of this work is found in the original version of this chapter (Kolko, 1996).

Prevalence and Recurrence

In terms of clinically referred children, prevalence rates based on structured assessment interviews have been reported for firesetting (an incident of burning with property damages) and matchplay (play with matches or lighters with no damages) in a sample of 164 outpatients (19.4%, 24.4%) and 136 inpatients (34.6%, 52.0%), respectively, in Pittsburgh, Pennsylvania (Kolko & Kazdin, 1988b). High rates of recurrent firesetting also were reported for these two respective samples (52%, 72%). A related study found moderate-to-high parent–child agreement (kappas, .58 to .86) in rating these behaviors and other firesetting characteristics from a firesetting history interview that serves as the basis for classification of many of the samples to be reported in subsequent studies (Kolko & Kazdin, 1988a).

Characteristics of Children's Firesetting Incidents

Details of children's firesetting incidents were reported in two studies. In one study, parents completed the Fire Incident Analysis (FIA) to document parameters of their children's most serious incidents (Kolko & Kazdin, 1991c). Firesetters were classified as "high" and "low" on each of two primary motives (curiosity, anger). Heightened curiosity was associated with greater psychopathology, firesetting risk, and fire involvement, whereas heightened anger was associated with firesetting risk measures and behavioral problems. A parallel study of 95 firesetters is described in the Fire Incident Analysis for Children (FIA-C; Kolko & Kazdin, 1994). Access to incendiaries, lack of child remorse and parental consequences, and motives of curiosity and fun were commonly reported characteristics. Four fire characteristics predicted their overall severity of involvement in fire at follow-up: fires set away from the home, acknowledgment of being likely to set another fire, a neutral or positive reaction to the fire, no parental response to the fire.

Fire-Specific and Clinical Correlates

Initial efforts were directed toward operationalizing several potential fire-specific risk factors for parents (the Firesetting Risk Inventory, or FRI; Kolko & Kazdin, 1989a) and children (Children's Firesetting Inventory, or CFI; Kolko & Kazdin, 1989b). Parents of firesetters acknowledged significantly higher scores on measures of firesetting contact (e.g., curiosity about fire, involvement in fire-related acts, exposure to firesetting models among peers or family members) and general child–parent behavior (e.g., negative behavior) or family environment (e.g., use of harsh punishment, less effective mild punishment). On the CFI, firesetters acknowledged more attraction to fire, past fireplay, family interest in fire, exposure to friends or family who smoke, and, somewhat surprisingly, knowledge of things that burn; however, they tended to show less fire competence (skill) in role-playing exercises than nonfiresetters.

Other clinical studies have documented a relationship between childhood firesetting and child dysfunction, such as heightened aggression, psychopathology, and social-skills deficits (Kolko, Kazdin, & Meyer, 1985). In an extension of this study (Kolko & Kazdin, 1991b), firesetters were reported to exhibit more covert behavior than both matchplayers and nonfiresetters, and firesetters and matchplayers received more extreme scores than nonfiresetters on measures of aggression, externalizing behaviors, impulsivity, emotionality, and hostility, although they did not differ from one another otherwise. In contrast, child report measures revealed only a few differences associated with firesetting (e.g., aggression, unassertiveness, low self-esteem) relative to nonfiresetters. Although firesetting has been associated with Conduct Disorder in some studies (American Psychiatric Association, 1987; Heath, Hardesty, Goldfine, & Walker, 1985; Kelso & Stewart, 1986), other studies have not supported this association (Kolko et al., 1985; Kolko & Kazdin, 1989a, 1989b).

Parental correlates of firesetting have included heightened personal psychiatric distress; marital disagreement; exposure to stressful life events; and less child acceptance, monitoring, discipline, and involvement in activities that enhance the child's personal development and family relationships (Kazdin & Kolko, 1986; Kolko & Kazdin, 1991a). Firesetters have characterized their parents' child-rearing practices as involving laxness in discipline, nonenforcement of rules, and induction of anxiety, with scores for matchplayers generally falling between those of firesetters and nonfiresetters.

Recidivism and Follow-Up

A prospective study that followed a sample of 138 children for 1 year showed that 14 of 78 nonfiresetters (18%) had set a fire later and that 21 of 60 firesetters (35%) had set an additional fire by follow-up (Kolko & Kazdin, 1992). Late starting was associated only with limited family sociability, whereas recidivism was associated with the child's knowledge of combustibles and involvement in fire-related activities, community complaints about fire contact, child hostility, lax discipline, family conflict, and limited parental acceptance, family affiliation, and organization. Some of these variables are parallel to those that have been associated with adult arson (Rice & Harris, 1991).

A 2-year follow-up study of 268 pediatric patients and nonpatients (ages 6–13) that included some of the sample reported above used fire history reports to classify cases into one of three mutually exclusive categories and thereby determine the number of children who engaged in firesetting or matchplay only (Kolko, Day, Bridge, & Kazdin, 2001). According to the aggregated reports of children and their parents, both patients and nonpatients reported high levels of follow-up firesetting (49%, 64%) and matchplay (57%, 76%), although the frequency of each behavior was generally higher for patients than nonpatients for both firesetting (M's = 4.2 vs. 1.0) and matchplay (M's = 3.1 vs. 0.9), respectively. In these samples, 25 of 50 nonpatients (50%) and 26 of 44 patients (59%) were recidivists, whereas 14 of 110 nonpatients (13%) and 11 of 42 patients (26%) became late starters. Such findings highlight the prevalence of firesetting in clinic and nonclinic samples and the continuity of firesetting over time.

This study also examined fire-specific and general psychosocial measures as predictors of follow-up firesetting and matchplay separately for patients and nonpatients (Kolko et al., 2001). Early firesetting and matchplay were significant predictors of follow-up fire involvement in both samples. The psychosocial predictors of firesetting that added incremental variance beyond this fire history varied by sample. In the nonpatients, two other predictors were found (i.e., exposure to fire models, parental psychological control). In the patients, several variables served as predictors (e.g., fire competence, complaints about the child, parental distress, harsh punishment, social service contact). These findings highlight some of the potential risk factors for later involvement with fire that included, not surprisingly, prior firesetting and matchplay. Other studies have examined recidivism rates in forensic samples that include adolescent and young adult arsonists (Repo & Virkkunen, 1997).

Research Summary

The aforementioned research suggests that factors associated with the onset and continuation of firesetting generally fall into two domains

(Kolko, 1996). The first, *involvement with, interest in, or awareness of fire*, includes matchplay and firesetting and circumstances that support fireplay, such as curiosity about or attraction to fire and limited fire competence (Grolnick, Cole, Laurenitis, & Schwartzman, 1990). The second domain, *general behavioral and environmental dysfunction or conditions*, reflects factors that may increase children's involvement in deviant behavior. Such characteristics reflect various forms of child (e.g., aggression), parent (e.g., poor monitoring), and family dysfunction (e.g., conflicts) likely to increase interpersonal problems and limit positive family interactions (Kolko, 1999). Similar characteristics have been found in adult arsonists (Kolko, 2001b).

Intervention and Treatment Studies

Description of Intervention Services

Background information used to support various aspects of the intervention studies reported herein derive from the results of an original national survey of 16 programs sponsored by FEMA and 13 affiliates of the FireHawks program that were surveyed in 1984 (Kolko, 1988). The report describes the characteristics, functions, and service-delivery issues associated with community treatment. The findings suggested the importance of teaching fire safety skills and making psychosocial intervention available, assessing child and family variables associated with firesetting, basing interventions on conceptual models and empirically supported procedures, and conducting a formal follow-up to assess outcome and evaluate its predictors.

Fire Service and Educational Approaches

Contemporary approaches to intervention and treatment for children who set fires and their families vary in the degree to which they target the two primary domains. Although the fire service has offered other services in recent years, fire service personnel generally rely on a few types of services. Some programs offer a firehouse orientation and tour for the typical young and curious firesetter (Gaynor, McLaughlin, & Hatcher, 1984), or the firefighter may visit or call the home to provide a brief educational session. Because such brief and informal contact with a firefighter may be insufficient, training in fire safety skills or treatment designed to alter the child's cognitive–behavioral repertoire may be a more effective intervention.

With its more extensive focus on the child's experience with, exposure to, and interest in fire, fire safety education (FSE) generally consists of instruction in safety skills and practices (Federal Emergency Management Agency [FEMA], 1983; see Pinnsoneault, 2002). The materials include risk interviews and technical materials for intervention (Interviewing and Counseling Juvenile Firesetter Program [ICJF]; Federal Emergency Management, 1979, 1983). The Learn Not To Burn [LNTB] program (National Fire Protection Association, 1979), which emphasizes various protection (e.g., fire drills), prevention (e.g., safe use of matches), and persuasion (e.g., safe smoking practices), may be the only program that has demonstrated its impact on fire safety knowledge relative to controls (National Fire Protection Association, 1978). Other approaches provide training in fire evacuation and assistance skills (Jones, Kazdin, & Haney, 1981; Jones, Ollendick, & Shinske, 1989). Pinsonneault (2002) provides one of the more comprehensive descriptions of fire safety principles and materials for general application.

One study with young hospitalized firesetters found that training in group fire safety and prevention skills (FSST) was more effective than individual fire awareness and discussion (FAD) in reducing contact with fire-related materials, increasing fire safety knowledge, and reducing any follow-up fireplay (Kolko, Watson, & Faust, 1991). Parent-report measures at 6-month follow-up showed that children who received FSST were less frequently engaged in all four forms of involvement with fire than children who received FAD (16.7% vs. 58.3%). Despite these preliminary findings, the study was quasiexperimental in design and used a limited four-session manual. Another fire safety education program administered during residential treatment found that only one of 35 children had set another fire by 1-year follow-up (DeSalvatore & Hornstein, 1991).

Psychological Services and Treatment Approaches

Treatment applications designed to alter behavioral dysfunction and environmental conditions have incorporated several cognitive–behavioral treatment (CBT) procedures, at times in conjunction with fire safety training (see Kolko, 2002b). These methods include graphs that depict the personal context of a fire (Bumpass, Brix, & Preston, 1985), prosocial and assertive skills training (Kolko & Ammerman, 1988; DeSalvatore & Hornstein, 1991; McGrath, Marshall, & Prior, 1979), contingency management (Adler, Nunn, Northam, Lebnan, & Ross, 1994; Kolko, 1983), and both parental and medication treatment (Cox-Jones, Lubetsky, Fultz, & Kolko, 1990). In general, treatment has emphasized child self-control, parent management skills, and positive family interactions, with some interventions incorporating several procedures (e.g., contingencies and behavioral training skills). Reduced firesetting has been found in these applications, but they reflect single-case, anecdotal reports and include no controlled designs or follow-up data. These reports highlight the need to consider the behavioral and functional context of firesetting, its relationship to the child's interpersonal repertoire, and the use of punishment and reinforcement procedures.

An Australian study provides the only known controlled evaluation of similar approaches to working with firesetters (ages 5–16) classified as either curiosity-driven or pathological (Adler et al., 1994). Although the number of fires reported after intervention was reduced, no significant effects for the combined experimental interventions that were used with either firesetter group could be demonstrated. Curious (as opposed to pathological) cases tended to show greater improvement (73% vs. 52%) and a lower dropout percentage (20% vs. 35%). The overall dropout rate of 28% and the absence of data on treatment integrity and child behavior notwithstanding, this initial outcome study shows that even minimal intervention may be effective in reducing firesetting behavior.

Summary of Intervention and Treatment Procedures

The aforementioned anecdotal, clinical, and limited empirical evidence highlights the role of two primary domains associated with firesetting: (a) experience with, exposure to, and interest in fire (fire-specific involvement); and (b) individual or family conditions that influence child behavior (behavioral–environmental control). Accordingly, fire safety education targets the former and psychosocial intervention targets the latter; each approach addresses specific characteristics associated with increased firesetting risk (Kolko, 2002b). Only anecdotal or limited empirical support for the utility of these approaches exists. A comparative evaluation of both interventions would advance the treatment of childhood firesetters. This population is suitable for the proposed treatments because children who set multiple fires are prevalent, firesetters are referred to fire service and mental health systems for intervention, and factors in the two risk factor domains can be effectively translated into procedures applied to reduce firesetting behavior.

TREATMENT OUTCOME STUDY: DESIGN AND METHODS

Study Rationale and Design

The search for effective interventions for child firesetters is important given the seriousness of this behavior; the frequent referral of children for fire service and mental health intervention; and the uncertainties about who is likely to set another fire, what factors should be targeted during intervention, and how children vary in clinical response. Still, no efficacy studies comparing fire safety education and psychological treatment for a representative sample of referred cases existed at the time this study was conducted (see Cole, Grolnick, & Schwartzman, 1993; Kolko, 1999). Further, the precise way that these alternative interventions affect key correlates and risks for firesetting (e.g., matchplay, attraction to fire) or other fire-related activities is virtually unknown.

In this three-arm, parallel groups design study, firesetting boys and their parents were randomly assigned to one of the two previously mentioned conditions that reflect contemporary methods used by community-based fire service programs (i.e., Fire Safety Education, or FSE) or mental health clinics (CBT). Each of these skills-based interventions was compared with a third condition that was selected to reflect the most common fire service intervention for this population (Kolko, 1988)—namely, a home visit from a firefighter (HVF). Administered across the same overall time interval as these other two conditions, HVF reflected the primary content of these educational practices by providing information to heighten the child's awareness of the dangers of fire and a follow-up visit, but the treatment was intended to be brief (two contacts). This condition was considered the only ethical and feasible minimal intervention to which families already scheduled to receive fire department services upon study referral could be assigned; pilot testing confirmed that some parents were not willing to be randomized to HVF when these alternative interventions were also available. The latter cases could not be randomized because of either logistic considerations or referral patterns. Thus, two intensive programs parallel to the methods used by fire service and mental health programs in the community (FSE and CBT, respectively) were compared with each other and then with a third, minimal-contact condition (HVF) without the use of a no-treatment or wait-list control group.

Study Objectives

The primary aim of the study is to compare two intensive skills training procedures derived from firesetting research findings that reflected contrasting conceptual models and to determine whether they were more efficacious than a routine practice condition that provided brief exposure to a firefighter. Each intervention was designed to be short-term, executed by trained specialists using program manuals, monitored to ensure therapeutic integrity, and evaluated on multiple measures. Given the importance of assessing several activities related to a child's involvement with fire (see Cole et al., 1993; Kolko, 1999), measures were evaluated in domains related to the frequency of firesetting and matchplay, other fire-related activities, and the children's interest in or attraction to fire. Both the short- and long-term effects of treatment are evaluated. It was hypothesized that CBT and FSE would result in a significant reduction in child involvement with fire and the severity of firesetting, relative to HVF, for comparisons at both post-treatment and follow-up. The full results of these primary analyses were reported in Kolko (2001a).

Secondary hypotheses to be evaluated in this chapter were directed toward understanding the specificity of the two intensive interventions. Specifically, FSE was expected to be superior to CBT or HVF in improving fire safety knowledge and skill, whereas CBT was expected to be superior to FSE or HVF in reducing the psychosocial or clinical correlates of firesetting.

Participants

Seventy boys were referred for services by the City of Pittsburgh Bureau of Fire (e.g., arson investigators), parental solicitation, or a mental health practitioner. Of this group of boys 54 met study inclusion criteria, completed the preassessment, and were assigned to an intervention condition. The boys met the following criteria: (a) 5 to 13 years of age, (b) current residence with at least one parent or legal guardian, (c) documented firesetting within the past 2 months in which property was burned or otherwise damaged, (d) normal intelligence level (>70 on two WISC–R subtests), and (e) parent consent and child assent for participation. Cases were excluded for the following reasons: (a) a medical condition that would complicate participation; (b) participation in a related treatment program; (c) identification of a major stressor or crisis that could precipitate family instability (disruption), complicate involvement in treatment, or entail highly burdensome case management requirements (e.g., recent physical or sexual abuse, residence in a shelter); and (d) current psychosis, suicidality, or a diagnosis of an affective disorder (e.g., major depression) based on a semistructured clinical interview.

A total of 46 of the 54 cases (85%) completed treatment. The average age of these 46 children was 9.6 years (SD = 2.1), with a mean WISC–R full-scale IQ composite of 89.6 (SD: 19.7; range: 76–128). Twenty-seven (59%) were African American, 15 (32%) were Caucasian, and four were biracial (9%). Twelve children (43%) were in special classes. Thirty-eight (83%) of the children received a *Diagnostic and Statistical Manual of Mental Disorders, Third Edition, Revised (DSM–III–R)* Axis I diagnosis, the most common of which were attention deficit hyperactivity disorder (ADHD; 25, or 54%) and conduct disorder (CD; 13, or 28%). Twenty-two children (48%) lived with their biological mothers, 13 (28%) with biological parents, five (11%) with adoptive parents, and 6 (13%) in other arrangements. Incomes for 25 families (54%) were below $1,000 per week. Twenty-six families (57%) received public assistance.

Cases were accepted if there was documentation of the child's involvement in a fire that resulted in property damages after a formal investigation (Cause and Origin Report) by a city arson investigator or confirmation of an incident by the child or parent. According to parent reports at intake, 10 (22%) of the children set fires in community buildings, 28 (61%) in residential buildings, and eight (17%) in yards or parks. Almost half of the fires involved household property or structures. The children reported motives such as curiosity, attraction, or boredom (58%) or some form of manipulation, control, or revenge (42%). About one third (37%) of the children said the fires were accidental.

Parents whose children met preliminary background inclusion criteria were informed of the purpose, procedures, and benefits of the project. Further details of the fire (e.g., characteristics, consequences) and information about family structure or status were obtained through phone screens to select appropriate candidates. A clinical interview later evaluated intelligence (WISC–R subtests) and the presence of a psychiatric disorder. Upon determining eligibility and documenting motivation, clinicians taught children and parents about all study procedures and asked them to provide written assents and consents for participation. When appropriate, the clinicians also discussed referral for treatment of child or parent dysfunction.

Intake or screening and all subsequent assessments were conducted at Western Psychiatric Institute and Clinic (WPIC). Program interventions were conducted in the outpatient clinic at WPIC (FSE and CBT) or the child's home (HVF). The firefighter–educators and therapists were responsible for implementation of the intervention conditions. Firefighters were selected on the basis of several criteria (e.g., college equivalent to 4-year baccalaureate degree, at least 2 years of experience as firefighter, potential to serve as an effective educator). The mental health therapists had BA, MA, and MSW degrees; clinical experience with children with behavior problems; and prior training in cognitive–behavioral procedures. Staff gender and ethnicity were balanced across intervention conditions. Because of time constraints and the selection of staff with specialized expertise, staff members were assigned to one condition only (i.e., nested), which eliminated the potential confounding of intervention conditions and capitalized on their respective expertise. Accordingly, each fire service condition (FSE, HVF) was staffed by a separate group of three firefighters each, whereas three therapists were assigned to the CBT condition.

Assessment Procedures

Research associates administered self-report instruments and interviews to children and their caretakers in a separate designated assessment area. Measures also were obtained from juvenile court and social service records. The measures were administered at (a) pretreatment (intake), (b) posttreatment (on average approximately 13 weeks later), and (c) one-year follow-up. Details of firesetting incidents were obtained at initial assessment and, for subsequent incidents, from either informant using the Fire Incident Analysis (Kolko & Kazdin, 1991c, 1994). Exhibit 19.1 lists representative measures in each domain and their schedule of administration. Selected measures in each domain are briefly described in subsequent sections.

Primary (Fire-Specific) Outcome Measures

Firesetting and Matchplay Behavior. Questions from the Fire History Screen (FHS; Kolko & Kazdin, 1988a, 1988b) were administered to both informants to document the child's involvement in matchplay and firesetting in the past 6 months. The frequencies of each behavior were recorded within

EXHIBIT 19.1
Primary Outcome and Treatment Specificity Measures (by Topic and Source)

Fire involvement/interest/risk

Child: Fire history screen, fire incident analysis, children's firesetting interview, Firesetting Attraction and Interest Scale

Parent: Fire history screen, fire incident analysis, firesetting risk interview, Firesetting Attraction and Interest Scale

Fire competency/skill

Child: Fire knowledge test, CFI fire competency/skill factor

Parent: Parent questionnaire, FRI fire knowledge factor

Psychosocial or clinical functioning

Child: Social problem-solving interview, children's hostility interview, parent perception inventory

Parent: Child behavior checklist, child rearing interview, conflict behavior questionnaire, family assessment device

Status based on official records

Children/youth service records, juvenile court records

Note. From "Efficacy of Cognitive Behavioral Treatment and Fire Safety Education for Children Who Set Fires: Initial and Follow-Up Outcomes," by D. Kolko, 2001, *Journal of Child Psychology and Psychiatry and Allied Disciplines, 42,* p. 365. Copyright 2001 by Blackwell. Reprinted with permission.

each time period. From this information, a dichotomous variable was created to reflect the presence or absence of each behavior. Given the importance of these two variables, both separate and aggregate self-report variables were examined. In addition, an aggregate of the two informant's reports was developed indicating whether the child had been seen with any matches or lighters.

Individualized Child Problems With Fire. To foster the effort and motivation required for improvement, the children were asked to estimate how difficult it would be to stop their fireplay using a 3-point scale (1 = not at all; 3 = very much). Correspondingly, parents were asked to evaluate the severity of their children's individualized problems with fire on a 10-point scale (1 = no problem at all; 10 = very serious problem). Most parents reported one problem reflecting the child's use of or interest in firesetting. Similar measures have been used to evaluate treatment for physical abuse of children (Kolko, 1996). Because this measure was introduced later in the study, only a subset of data is available.

Fire-Related Activities. Factors from the child-reported Child Firesetting Interview (CFI; Kolko & Kazdin, 1989a) and parent-reported Firesetting Risk Interview (FRI; Kolko & Kazdin, 1989b) were completed, only some of which are reported herein. Specifically, the two informants rated the child's level of involvement in fire-related acts, and the higher of the two ratings was selected for analysis. This scale includes four items, each rated on a 1-to-five–point scale (e.g., hide matches).

The Safe and Unsafe Fire Activities (SUFA) measure was developed for this study to complement the CFI and FRI by evaluating the occurrence (presence or absence) of specific high-risk fire-related behaviors in four domains within the past 2 weeks (see Kolko, 2001a). Deviant fire behaviors were evaluated in three domains (i.e., inappropriate interest in fire, deviant fire activities, and negative peer influences). Because few items per domain were endorsed, an alternative scoring procedure was used whereby a report by either informant of any behavior in that domain yielded a domain score of 1. Scores were then aggregated to form an overall deviant fire activity score ($M = 1.07$; $SD = .84$; range: 0.00–3.00).

An exploratory analogue task was designed to determine in what ways a subset of children ($n = 25$) would respond to a hidden pack of matches situated in one of the assessment rooms. The child was led to a room with a one-way mirror and asked to sit down before the assessment interview while the staff member left for about 2 minutes. A simulated pack of matches was situated near the back corner of a small figurine and was visible from the chair. Observations were made for the following behaviors during this time period: (a) child noticing pack; (b) child touching pack; (c) child picking up the pack; (d) child attempting to strike a match; and (e) child attempting to keep the pack. A final rating determined whether the child seemed to be aware of the purpose of the task and of the possibility of being monitored (task reactivity).

Fire Interest and Attraction. Child and parent reports were aggregated for all three measures in this section. The first measure asked whether the child was interested in fire (FHS; Kolko & Kazdin, 1989b). The two informants also rated seven identical items on the scale measuring the child's curiosity about fire on the CFI and FRI (e.g., likes to talk about fire), and the higher score was selected for analysis. Heightened curiosity is associated with increased risk for later fire involvement (Kolko & Kazdin, 1991c) but has rarely been examined as an outcome variable (Kolko, 1996). Finally, the 23-item Fire Attraction and Interest Scale (FAIS; Kolko & Kazdin, 1992) was administered to both children (alpha = .83) and parents (alpha = .91), and the higher score was selected for analysis. The measure evaluates various aspects of fire that children may like or exhibit (e.g., watching fire). The FAIS differentiates children with firesetting recidivism from children without.

A second measure piloted for this study, the Fire Video Analogue Task, involved showing the children four 5-minute video segments depicting different types of stimuli (e.g., boxing match between two professional fighters, kids playing with fire). The segments were counterbalanced across children. Each scene was rated on three 5-point scales (1 = not at all; 5 = very much): (1) how much the child liked the scene; (2) how great the child's excitement; (3) how much the child wanted to see the scene again. Exploratory analyses examined ratings for the fire scene only.

Official Juvenile Court Records

A separate outcome related to the children's referral for firesetting is whether they had any juvenile court involvement for arson or a related crime at any point during their involvement in the study. Official records from the juvenile court were reviewed for any charges or convictions resulting from arson.

Other Measures

A recent study has also examined the specificity of each primary intervention (Kolko, 2003). FSE was hypothesized to result in the greatest improvement in measures of fire education and competence in the children and, secondarily, their parents relative to CBT or HVF. Related measures included the 25-item Fire Knowledge Test (FKT; National Fire Protection Association, 1979); the parallel Parent Questionnaire (PQ; National Fire Protection Association, 1978), which measures child involvement in various fire safety and prevention activities; the child's level of fire competency and skill on the CFI (Kolko & Kazdin, 1989a); and the fire knowledge scale on the parallel FRI (Kolko & Kazdin, 1989b).

CBT was hypothesized to result in the greatest improvement on measures of clinical functioning relative to FSE and HVF. The child-directed measures included the number of aggressive solutions proposed in response to several hypothetical problem-solving situations (Dodge & Coie, 1987), the 38-item Children's Hostility Inventory (CHI; Kazdin, Rodgers, Colbus, & Siegel, 1987), and the Child Behavior Checklist aggression and delinquency subscales (CBCL; Achenbach & Edelbrock, 1983; Kolko et al., 1985). Parental measures reflected child-rearing practices (monitoring and discipline) on the Child Rearing Inventory (Loeber & Dishion, 1984; Stouthamer-Loeber & Loeber, 1985) and the Parent Perception Inventory (PPI) to evaluate positive management and interactional behavior (Hazzard, Christensen, & Margolin, 1983). For family measures, the parent completed the Conflict Behavior Questionnaire (CBQ) to capture parent–child conflict (Robin & Foster, 1989) and the general functioning subscale from the Family Assessment Device (FAD; Epstein, Baldwin, & Bishop, 1983; Miller, Epstein, Bishop, & Keitner, 1985).

Characteristics and Administration of Intervention

Overview

Children were randomly assigned to FSE or CBT in an effort to compose groups comparable in developmental or family background status. Children in the HVF group were not randomized because many of them were already assigned to receive services in the fire department upon study referral. To ensure comparability on certain key variables that relate to fire-setting behavior, risk for recidivism, or response to treatment (Cole, Grolnick, McAndrews, Matkoski, & Schwartzman, 1986; Kolko, 1989; Kolko & Kazdin, 1989a; Wooden & Berkey, 1984), Efron's biased coin toss (Efron, 1980) was used to balance the groups on age (7–9 vs. 10–12), low socioeconomic status (<II; based on Hollingshead & Redlich, 1958), and number of parents in household (one vs. two).

Treatment commenced approximately 1 week subsequent to completion of the pretreatment assessment interview. Participants met individually with a trained staff member in semistructured sessions using material in manual form. Staff members in the FSE and CBT conditions employed instructions, modeling, role-playing exercises or behavioral rehearsal, feedback, and social reinforcement, which were supplemented with supervision sessions for discussion of case issues. All conditions required parent and child involvement. FSE and CBT were designed to be comparable in session length (1-hour sessions) and treatment duration (8 weekly sessions). HVF consisted of an initial 1-hour session and follow-up visit (or call) that were also spaced about 8 weeks apart. An average of 7.4 (SD = 2.9) and 5.5 (SD = 2.1) sessions were conducted in CBT and FSE, respectively. Children in these two conditions participated for 7.3 (SD = 3.6) and 7.5 (1.8) hours, respectively, and parents for 4.5 (2.0) and 5.7 (1.9) hours, respectively. The number of weeks in treatment was 8.7 (SD = 3.5) and 8.7 (5.8) for the CBT and FSE conditions, respectively.

Intervention Conditions

Cognitive–Behavioral Treatment. CBT involves the application of cognitive–behavioral procedures designed to modify the characteristics and correlates of firesetting noted in the clinical literature (see Adler et al., 1994; Federal Emergency Management Agency, 1979, 1983; Gaynor & Hatcher, 1987; Kolko, 1983, 2001b; Kolko & Ammerman, 1988; Wooden & Berkey, 1984). By teaching aspects of generalized self-control and establishing environmental conditions that encourage behaviors other than firesetting, these procedures seek to alter the psychological significance of firesetting, the child's social–cognitive repertoire, and the functional context in which it occurs. Children and parents participated both separately and together in different sessions with a mental health therapist (see Exhibit 19.2 for outline of content).

Children were helped to create a graph showing their recent fires (see Bumpass et al., 1983, 1985; Kolko & Ammerman, 1988) so that they might understand how their motives for the fire were related to specific events or affective states. Children received three training sessions in general problem-solving skills in different steps (e.g., problem identification, generation of alternative solutions) and self-instructions (see Weissberg, Gesten,

EXHIBIT 19.2
Outlines of Content for Each Primary Intervention Condition

Cognitive–behavioral treatment condition (CBT)

SESSION 1

Child: Interests/problems and review of fire incident

Parent: Family characteristics and stress management

SESSION 2

Parent: Monitoring, attending/ignoring/positive reinforcement

SESSION 3

Child: Feelings, automatic/balanced thoughts/introduction to problem-solving (define, goal, think)

SESSION 4

Child: Generating alternatives, considering consequences, and choosing the best solution

SESSION 5

Parent: Logical consequences, removing privileges/fines/home contingencies/ allowances/point systems

SESSION 6

Child: Applications to problems, leisure activities and fire activities

SESSION 7

Child and Parent: Home contingency program/family contract

SESSION 8

Child: Assertion/complaints/requests and review of home program

Fire safety/education (FSE)

SESSION 1

Child and Parent: Fire facts/causes of fires/review details of fire; overview of session and intervention

SESSION 2

Child or Parent: How fires start/impact of fire/children's motives/film/worksheet

SESSION 3

Child: Matches are tools/helpers and hazards/firefighters and equipment

SESSION 4

Child: Fire evacuation and reporting

SESSION 5

Child: Home fire escape plan/injury prevention/first aid

SESSION 6

Parent: Home fire safety and match safety/smoke detectors/fire extinguishers/other fire risks

SESSION 7

Child: Fire safety concepts

Child and Parent: Fire safety project

SESSION 8

Child and Parent: Discussion of fire safety project/fire safety achievement certificate

---

Note. From *Handbook on Firesetting in Children and Youth,* by D. J. Kolko (Ed.), 2002, New York: Kluwer. Copyright 2002 by Kluwer. Reprinted with permission.

Liebenstein, Doherty-Schmid, & Hutton, 1980; Weissberg, Gesten, Rapkin, Cowen, Davidson, Flores de Apodaca, & McKim, 1981) before being taught how to apply the skills to personally challenging situations. Children also received training in assertion skills and were encouraged to use specific prosocial responses to interpersonal conflicts.

Parents were taught about the environmental context of firesetting (e.g., motives) and the need to monitor their children's behavior and promote their children's involvement in prosocial activities. They learned basic child management principles (e.g., attending, ignoring, praise) and ways to apply them in response to specific behaviors. Parents reviewed methods to establish contingencies to address both positive (e.g., reinforcement; Adler et al., 1994; Holland, 1969; Kolko, 1983) and fire-related behaviors (response cost or forfeiture of privileges; Holland, 1969; Kolko, 1983). A home-based contingency is jointly developed (e.g., duration criterion, types of reinforcers, types of alternative activities such as athletics and recreation), along with the criteria to be used to gradually withdraw the contingency.

Fire Safety Education. FSE incorporates procedures based on the descriptive differences between firesetters and nonfiresetters identified earlier (e.g., knowledge of combustibles, role-playing exercises related to emergency responses), the content of the initial FSST intervention, and other procedures to promote fire safety prevention and evacuation (e.g., Cole et al., 1986; Federal Emergency Management Agency, 1979; Jones & Haney, 1985; National Fire Protection Association, 1979, 1982). In general, FSE provides instruction in fire safety skills designed to inhibit the child's continued involvement in firesetting or fireplay activities. The children and parents meet together or, at other times, separately with a firefighter–educator. Session content is outlined in Exhibit 19.2.

Briefly, early sessions involved a review with the child of selected details of the fire (e.g., motive, format, role of peers) and a discussion with parents of the causes of firesetting. Sessions were devoted to child training in fire safety education principles and exercises (Adler et al., 1994; Gaynor et al., 1984), fire protection and evacuation strategies (e.g., stop–drop–roll, emergency phone calls, exiting a burning house to contact a neighbor; Federal Emergency Management Agency, 1979; Gaynor et al., 1984; Jones & Haney, 1985), and methods to identify, report, and control a fire (National Fire Protection Association, 1979). The program emphasized an array of preventive information and strategies (e.g., uses and abuses of fire, giving matches to an adult), including participation in a concluding fire safety project. Parents received a similar overview of fire prevention and additional materials (e.g., home fire safety guidelines) and participated in the child's fire safety project (Federal Emergency Management Agency, 1979). Role-playing exercises were used to enhance retention of all material (Jones et al., 1989). Children then received a certificate of achievement.

Home Visit From a Firefighter. This brief two-contact condition was designed to reflect an enhanced version of some of the routine practices found in most fire departments. Based on field surveys of existing programs and local firefighters and the author's national survey, the content included the danger of fires (e.g., to firesetters themselves, their families, and their pets), functions of firefighters, a "no-fire contract," and safety materials (e.g., coloring book on fire safety, plastic fire helmet). The child's parent also was encouraged to participate in the session and received a home fire safety handout. In the second contact, the firefighter contacted the child and parent to review and then elaborate on these concepts, as necessary (e.g., play with matches or lighters begins as a simple activity).

Intervention Measures: Credibility, Adherence, and Integrity

Information regarding both participants' expectations of the credibility and utility of each treatment condition were solicited before their randomization to treatment (Kolko, 2001a). At pretreatment, children and parents in each condition were found to perceive all three conditions as generally credible and of potential benefit in reducing involvement in firesetting.

Several procedures were designed to uphold the integrity of each distinct intervention, including extensive training, pilot cases, and videotape reviews (Kolko, 2001a). Weekly treatment team reviews were conducted throughout intervention. To evaluate treatment integrity, the session material was written into individual objectives and tasks. A trained independent observer viewed randomly selected session tapes per condition and rated each session item on a 3-point scale of correctness and completeness (1 = content not covered during the session; 2 = content was covered only minimally or partially or was somewhat unclear, confusing, or disorganized; 3 = most or all of the content was covered as stated and in a clear way), and ratings were used to compute the percentage of correctly administered items per session. The overall means (and ranges) for these correctness ratings were generally high for CBT ($M = .92$; $SD = .07$; range: .85–.99) and FSE ($M = .86$; $SD = .10$; range: .81–.98).

Treatment adherence (process) was monitored by therapists or firefighter educators who completed individual session summary ratings (1 = not at all; 5 = very much) to document important aspects of the administration of intervention. The mean ratings for patients in the CBT and FSE conditions, respectively, did not differ significantly for any of the individual items, such as on task or attentiveness (4.2, 4.0); level of participation or involvement (4.3, 4.2); level of compliance (4.6, 4.3); and level of understanding of material (4.2, 4.4). In general, participants were engaged in and responsive to their respective interventions.

Clinical Vignette

Robert was a 12-year-old biracial male who was referred with his second foster mother after he lit a quilt with a match and set his bed on fire. His current firesetting history included burning holes in his bedspread, burning newspapers and books, burning paper towels using the stove, and burning paper towels in a waste can. His current foster mother reported that Robert had set fire in the past to three different houses, which precipitated his removal from his biological mother's home. He also set a fire in the home of his first foster mother, which led to his removal from her home. He was placed temporarily in a residential setting operated by the foster care program, where a camera in his room monitored his activities.

Robert had a history of antisocial behavior (theft, lying, vandalism, fighting with adults, use of weapons, cruelty) and oppositional symptoms (losing his temper, arguing with adults, defying requests, annoying others on purpose, swearing, being resentful). His foster mother reported that he was sexually abused by his biological mother's paramour but provided no further details of the abuse. Limited developmental information indicated that he had experienced no major illnesses, hospitalizations, or surgeries and only one broken leg after a car accident. He completed the sixth grade upon referral and was in special education classes. He was described as having good peer, but poor teacher, relationships.

No evidence suggested substance abuse or suicidal or homicidal ideation or behavior. He was well groomed and showed no signs of agitation or psychomotor retardation. His mood was flat but appropriate. His content and perception were appropriate, and he was well oriented. His general level of functioning was limited. He had a 1-year history of being treated with Ritalin (5 mg tid) for ADHD and a sporadic 6-year history of occasional participation in outpatient services. He was reported to have been doing well in treatment at the time of referral.

Robert was assigned randomly to the CBT condition. He and his second foster mother received 7.6 hours of treatment across 9 weeks, with four no-show appointments. His treatment emphasized training in self-control and anger-control skills, and her treatment emphasized the use of effective contingencies and monitoring strategies. Both participants learned these skills easily, but Robert found it difficult to apply them with friends, and his foster mother found it challenging to be consistent at home. A home program was established that included targets and opportunities related to peer activities. Robert and his foster mother also had difficulty attending appointments because of conflicting appointments and schedule demands, which required considerable flexibility on the part of their clinician.

The outcome assessment revealed that Robert had been exposed to peers who were playing with fireworks over the July 4th holiday, but he had not lit them himself. He and his foster mother reported no other involvement with fire at posttreatment or follow-up. Other data showed that he was responding well to the home program, although he did continue to exhibit a modest level of behavior problems.

TREATMENT OUTCOME

Data Reduction and Analysis

Given the minimal overlap among measures, intervention outcomes were examined using group (HVF, CBT, FSE) by time (pretreatment versus posttreatment) repeated measures analyses of variance (ANOVAs) and follow-up multiple comparisons ($p < .05$) for individual continuous measures. Dichotomous data were examined using chi-square or McNemar tests. Separate analyses evaluated 1-year follow-up effects (pretreatment versus follow-up). Because this section only summarizes these outcomes, the reader is referred to the original outcome study on which these findings are based (Kolko, 2001a).

Primary Outcomes: Immediate and Follow-Up Effects

Firesetting and Matchplay Behavior

In terms of the number of firesetting and matchplay incidents reported on the FHS, there was a significant reduction in firesetting over time and a near-significant interaction that reflected greatest improvement for CBT. There was also a significant reduction over time in the frequency of matchplay incidents. Parent reports revealed a significant reduction over time in the frequency of firesetting and matchplay.

Reports from the two informants were aggregated and then dichotomized to examine changes over time in the proportion of children in each condition exhibiting each behavior. Fewer children in each condition had reports of any firesetting by posttreatment, but only CBT was associated with fewer matchplay incidents. For FSE, the reduction in number of children who played with matches or had been seen with matches or lighters only approached significance. Analyses of the proportion of cases who exhibited *either* behavior also revealed no significant between-group differences at either time period for child reports and for parent reports.

Separate analyses examined pretreatment follow-up outcomes. For child reports on the FHS, fewer fires were reported by follow-up and the reduction tended to be greater for CBT and FSE. Similarly, fewer incidents of matchplay were reported over time. Parent reports confirmed the reduction in firesetting and matchplay incidents. Fewer children in each condition had set a fire at follow-up, but only CBT and FSE were associated with a reduction in the number of children who played with matches. Fewer children in the CBT and FSE groups were seen with matches or lighters by follow-up. Significantly fewer children in the CBT and FSE groups reported either behavior at follow-up relative to the children in the HVF group; parent reports showing this improvement only approached significance.

Individualized Problems With Fire

The children reported that it would be easier to stop their fireplay by posttreatment. Parents reported a significant reduction over time in the severity ratings of the child's primary problem with fire, and this reduction was significantly greater in the CBT and FSE groups than in the HVF group. At 1-year follow-up, a significant reduction occurred over time in the children's ratings of the difficulty in stopping inappropriate fire use. Likewise, parents reported a significant reduction over time in the severity ratings of the child's primary (individualized) problem with fire.

Fire-Related Activities

Aggregate CFI and FRI reports showed a significant reduction over time in the child's involvement in fire-related acts. On the SUSA, CBT cases showed a decrease and HVF cases an increase on the aggregated deviant fire behavior subscale by posttreatment. On the exploratory analogue hidden-matches task, at pretreatment nine children noticed and touched the matches, five children picked up the pack, and none attempted to strike or take the matchpack. Five children each were rated as interested in the pack and were reactive to the task. At posttreatment, nine children each noticed and picked up the matches pack, and five picked it up. No significant reductions in any of these behaviors were found, owing primarily to the low number of reported incidents for each item.

For the pretreatment follow-up comparisons, scores on the CFI–FRI aggregate involvement in fire-related acts factor showed a significant reduction by follow-up, and the interaction was greatest for CBT cases. On the aggregate SUFA deviant fire behavior variable, CBT cases showed a significant reduction, whereas HVF cases showed an increase, by follow-up. The hidden-matches task was not repeated at follow-up because of questions about its utility and the potential for heightened reactivity upon repetition.

Fire Interest or Attraction

The three conditions showed comparable levels on the aggregate FHS interest-in-fire item at pretreatment and posttreatment. By posttreatment, there was a significant reduction in the proportion of endorsements of interest in fire for the FSE group and a trend for the CBT group. Scores on the aggregate curiosity-about-fire factor and the FAIS also decreased by posttreatment. On the exploratory Fire Video Analogue Task, posttreatment analyses revealed no significant main effects of condition or time ($p < .26 -$ .89) and no significant interactions ($p < .50 - .52$), on the ratings of interest, excitement, and repetition in response to the fire scene. If anything, the ratings were somewhat higher at posttreatment. Most of the ratings were similar (modest) for all conditions at both times.

In terms of the 1-year analyses, fewer children in the CBT and FSE groups reported an interest in fire at follow-up, with significantly fewer children in the CBT and FSE groups showing such an interest by follow-up. By follow-up, lower scores over time were found on the combined CFI–FRI curiosity-about-fire factor and the combined FAIS, but the reduction in FAIS scores was greatest for the CBT group, followed next by the FSE group. Although fewer children were willing to participate in the Fire Video Analogue Task at follow-up, prefollow-up comparisons revealed that the ratings decreased for all three scales, F's (1, 16) = 3.69 – 5.70, $p < .076 - .03$, with the CBT and FSE groups tending to show more of a reduction over time.

Court and Social Service Records

In terms of official juvenile court records, only two children each were adjudicated of a delinquent offense in HVF (arson, theft) and FSE (arson, indecent sexual assault) before the study. By posttreatment, delinquent offenses (stealing and breaking and entering) were documented for two children in the FSE group. By follow-up, no child had been adjudicated of any delinquent act, and no reports of any charges for a delinquent behavior existed.

Other Analyses

Briefly, recent analyses were conducted to evaluate treatment specificity based on pretreatment and posttreatment group comparisons using repeated measures ANOVAs examining time effects and condition multiplied by time interactions (see Kolko, 2003). These findings indicated that FSE was associated with higher scores than CBT or HVF on three of the four fire competence–skill measures (PQ, CFI fire competence–skill factor, FRI fire knowledge factor). In terms of the psychosocial or clinical functioning measures, the analyses revealed several reductions over time but only one significant interaction. Specifically, children in the CBT group showed a greater increase than children in the FSE and HVF groups in the number of assertive solutions given to problem situations.

SUMMARY AND FUTURE DIRECTIONS

This chapter examined the outcomes associated with intervention conditions based on the findings of prior empirical assessment and follow-up studies and existing fire safety programs. Specifically, two skills-based interventions representing psychological (CBT) and fire service (FSE) approaches were compared with a third, standard-practice condition (HVF). In general, several improvements were noted over time on measures of fire involvement, interest, and risk for all three conditions. For example, children in the three conditions reported less difficulty in stopping their inappropriate use of fire and showed reductions in their involvement in fire-related acts, curiosity about fire, and attraction to fire at posttreatment.

However, some key group differences and near-significant trends on measures of fire involvement and interest favoring CBT or FSE were evident. For example, CBT and FSE were more efficacious than HVF on certain measures, including the proportion of children exhibiting any firesetting or matchplay, the severity of their individual problems with fire, their involvement in fire-related acts and other deviant fire activities, and their attraction to or interest in fire. These and other group differences were evident at follow-up, suggesting that the effect of HVF was not as fully maintained as the effects for the other interventions. Such improvements were demonstrated after exposure to two brief but very different interventions, one drawing upon instruction in cognitive–behavioral techniques emphasizing self-management and interpersonal behavior and the other on training in fire safety and prevention.

Evidence was found for the specific effects of FSE, but there was limited evidence for CBT. FSE was more successful in increasing children's involvement in various fire safety and preventive behaviors. The incorporation in FSE of many of the concepts evaluated by the specificity measures may have promoted this outcome. CBT was associated with greater improvement in prosocial problem-solving skills but not in other child behaviors or parental practices targeted by this intervention. The brevity of CBT may have restricted the gains made on these specific outcomes, especially because several complicated skills were targeted. Further, specificity was demonstrated for FSE, which was based on several measures of new skills to be taught during intervention, whereas specificity measures for CBT primarily examined deviant behaviors designed to be reduced. All told, specificity has been difficult to document even when studies include larger samples, longer treatment durations, and more conceptually specific intervention content (Kolko, Brent, Baugher, Bridge, & Birmaher, 2000).

From a practitioner's perspective, this work may be beneficial in a few ways. First, various methods are described that can evaluate a child's firesetting history and other important psychosocial characteristics (see Wilcox & Kolko, 2002). For example, the findings reported by Kolko et al. (2001) suggest that a few fire history and background characteristics associated with recidivism may facilitate risk assessment. Additionally, the present study highlights key outcome and treatment process measures, such as the children's contact with and use of fire, as well as their behavioral competencies and dysfunction. Other measures of firesetting involvement, interest, or exposure are needed for use in large-scale descriptive and predictive studies that evaluate the reliability, factor structure, and validity of these instruments and their relationship to firesetting behavior (see Kolko, Wilcox, Nishi-Strattner, & Kopet, 2002). The fact that firesetting is a covert and low-frequency behavior often requires the use of multiple measures and informants. In this outcome study, self-reports from children and parents were supplemented with analogue tasks as have been used elsewhere to evaluate clinical outcome (see Kolko et al., 1991).

The findings also bear implications for the implementation of effective interventions. Given that CBT and FSE had certain common and separate effects beyond HVF, it seems logical to consider their integration when appropriate, especially with heterogeneous and complicated cases. Indeed, many cases referred for services since this study was completed have received a combination of both of these interventions, and their integration may be evident in some community programs (Kolko, 1999). Research is still needed to determine whether the combination of both interventions is more efficacious than either one alone or whether training in FSE is more effective for curious children, whereas CBT or its derivatives are more useful with behaviorally dysfunctional children. Such findings would offer clear directions for matching cases to appropriate interventions. At the same time, the presence of several time effects suggests that HVF still offers some advantages because it was less intensive and was conducted by a firefighter in the home where family access may be maximized (Adler et al., 1994). Thus, HVF may serve as an alternative when intensive interventions are not available or feasible.

Future studies must address the key limitations of the outcome study, such as the fact that children were not randomized to all conditions, the length of intervention was fairly brief, and the small sample size may have limited power to demonstrate significant group differences. Additional studies are also needed to evaluate other features of these treatments and their therapeutic effectiveness. Certainly, studies are needed to evaluate the specific and nonspecific effects of intervention for this particular behavior problem. These studies should include investigations of the benefit of multimodal interventions that combine various approaches or that are more intensive, the use of paraprofessionals to apply treatment, and the use of specialized audiovisual curricula. Identification of effective methods to reduce a child's attraction to fire also await further experimentation. Finally, future studies should determine whether intervention is more effective when it targets the child's firesetting behavior or its presumed correlates.

In summary, the findings of this study provide initial support for the feasibility and effectiveness of two alternative interventions with children who have set a recent fire. Further information of this nature is needed to help practitioners apply efficacious interventions and, ultimately, to efficiently modify the most critical intervention targets (see Kolko, Pinsonneault, & Okulitch, 2002). Studies that carefully examine various clinical and methodological issues may enhance our understanding and the implementation of novel interventions with children and youth who exhibit with this troublesome and potentially dangerous behavior.

REFERENCES

Achenbach, T. M., & Edelbrock, C. (1983). *Manual for the Child Behavior Checklist and revised child behavior profile*. Burlington: University of Vermont Department of Psychiatry.

Adler, R. G., Nunn, R. J., Northam, E., Lebnan, V., & Ross, R. (1994). Secondary prevention of childhood firesetting. *Journal of the American Academy of Child and Adolescent Psychiatry, 33*, 1194–1202.

American Psychiatric Association. (1987). *Diagnostic and statistical manual of mental disorders—revised* (3rd ed., rev.). Washington, DC: Author.

Bumpass, E. R., Brix, R. J., & Preston, D. (1985). A community-based program for juvenile firesetters. *Hospital and Community Psychiatry, 36*, 529–533.

Bumpass, E. R., Fagelman, F. D., & Brix, R. J. (1983). Intervention with children who set fires. *American Journal of Psychotherapy, 37*, 328–345.

Cole, R. E., Grolnick, W., McAndrews, M. M., Matkoski, K. M., & Schwartzman, P. (1986). *Rochester Fire Related Youth Project: Progress report* (Vol. 2). Rochester: Office of Fire Prevention and Control, New York Department of State.

Cole, R., Grolnick, W., & Schwartzman, P. (1993). Fire setting. In R. T. Ammerman & C. G. Last (Eds.), *Handbook of perspective treatments for children and adolescents* (pp. 332–346). Needham Heights, MA: Allyn & Bacon.

Cox-Jones, C., Lubetsky, M., Fultz, S. A., & Kolko, D. J. (1990). Inpatient treatment of a young recidivist firesetter. *Journal of the American Academy of Child Psychiatry, 29*, 936–941.

Crime in the United States 1999. (2000). Washington, DC: U.S. Government Printing Office.

DeSalvatore, G., & Hornstein, R. (1991). Juvenile firesetting: Assessment and treatment in psychiatric hospitalization and residential placement. *Child and Youth Care Forum, 20*, 103–114.

Dodge, K. A., & Coie, J. D. (1987). Social-information-processing factors in reactive and proactive aggression in children's peer groups. *Journal of Personality and Social Psychology, 53*, 1146–1158.

Efron, B. (1980). *Biostatistics casebook*. Palo Alto, CA: Stanford University Press.

Epstein, N. B., Baldwin, L. M., & Bishop, D. S. (1983). The McMaster Family Assessment Device. *Journal of Marital and Family Therapy, 9*, 171–180.

Federal Emergency Management Agency. (1979). *Interviewing and counseling juvenile firesetters*. Washington, DC: U.S. Government Printing Office.

Federal Emergency Management Agency. (1983). *Juvenile firesetter handbook: Dealing with children ages 7–13*. Washington, DC: U.S. Government Printing Office.

Gaynor, J., & Hatcher, C. (1987). *The psychology of child firesetting: Detection and intervention*. New York: Brunner/Mazel.

Gaynor, J., McLaughlin, P. M., & Hatcher, C. (1984). *The Firehawk Children's Program: A working manual*. San Francisco: National Firehawk Foundation.

Grolnick, W., Cole, R. E., Laurenitis, L. R., & Schwartzman, P. (1990). Playing with fire: A developmental assessment of children's fire understanding and experience. *Journal of Clinical Child Psychology, 19*, 128–135.

Hall, J. R. (2000a). *Children playing with fire*. Quincy, MA: National Fire Protection Association.

Hall, J. R. (2000b). *U.S. arson trends and patterns*. Quincy, MA: National Fire Protection Association.

Hazzard, A., Christensen, A., & Margolin, G. (1983). Children's perceptions of parental behaviors. *Journal of Abnormal Child Psychology, 11*, 49–59.

Heath, G. A., Hardesty, V. A., Goldfine, P. E., & Walker, A. M. (1985). Diagnosis and childhood firesetting. *Journal of Clinical Psychology, 41*, 571–575.

Holland, C. J. (1969). Elimination by the parents of firesetting behaviour in a 7-year-old boy. *Behaviour Research and Therapy, 7*, 135–137.

Hollingshead, A., & Redlich, F. (1958). *Social class and mental illness: A community study*. New York: Wiley.

Jacobson, R. R. (1985). Child firesetters: A clinical investigation. *Journal of Child Psychology and Psychiatry, 26*, 759–768.

Jones, R. T., & Haney, J. I. (1985). Behavior therapy and fire emergencies: Conceptualization, assessment, and intervention. In M. Hersen, R. Eisler, & P. Miller (Eds.), *Progress in behavior modification* (Vol. 19, pp. 177–216). New York: Academic Press.

Jones, R. T., Kazdin, A. E., & Haney, J. I. (1981). Social validation and training of emergency fire safety skills for potential injury prevention and life saving. *Journal of Applied Behavior Analysis, 14*, 249–260.

Jones, R. T., Ollendick, T. H., & Shinske, F. K. (1989). The role of behavioral versus cognitive variables in skill acquisition. *Behavior Therapy, 20*, 293–302.

Kazdin, A. E., & Kolko, D. J. (1986). Parent psychopathology and family functioning among childhood firesetters. *Journal of Abnormal Child Psychology, 14*, 315–329.

Kazdin, A. E., Rodgers, A., Colbus, D., & Siegel, T. (1987). Children's Hostility Inventory: Measurement of aggression and hostility in psychiatric inpatient children. *Journal of Clinical Child Psychology, 16*, 320–328.

Kelso, J., & Stewart, M. A. (1986). Factors which predict the persistence of aggressive conduct disorder. *Journal of Child Psychology and Psychiatry, 27*, 77–86.

Kolko, D. J. (1983). Multicomponent parental treatment of firesetting in a developmentally-disabled boy. *Journal of Behavior Therapy and Experimental Psychiatry, 14*, 349–353.

Kolko, D. J. (1988). Community interventions for childhood firesetters: A comparison of two national programs. *Hospital and Community Psychiatry, 39*, 973–979.

Kolko, D. J. (1989). Fire setting and pyromania. In C. Last & M. Hersen (Eds.), *Handbook of child psychiatric diagnosis* (pp. 443–459). New York: Wiley.

Kolko, D. J. (1996). Education and counseling for child firesetters: A comparison of skills training programs with standard practice. In E. D. Hibbs & P. S. Jensen (Eds.), *Psychosocial treatments for child and adolescent disorders: Empirically based strategies for clinical practice* (pp. 409–433). Washington, DC: American Psychological Association.

Kolko, D. J. (1999). Firesetting in children and youth. In M. Hersen & V. V. Hasselt (Eds.), *Handbook of psychological approaches with violent offenders: Contemporary strategies and issues* (pp. 95–115). New York: Plenum Press.

Kolko, D. J. (2001a). Efficacy of cognitive–behavioral treatment and fire safety education for firesetting children: Initial and follow-up outcomes. *Journal of Child Psychology and Psychiatry and Allied Disciplines, 42*, 359–369.

Kolko, D. J. (2001b). Firesetters. In C. R. Hollin (Ed.), *Handbook of offender assessment and treatment* (pp. 391–413). New York: Wiley.

Kolko, D. J. (2002a). Research studies on the problem. In D. J. Kolko (Ed.), *Handbook on firesetting in children and youth* (pp. 33–56). New York: Kluwer/Academic Press.

Kolko, D. J. (2002b). Child, parent, and family treatment: Cognitive–behavioral interventions. In D. J. Kolko (Ed.), *Handbook on firesetting in children and youth* (pp. 305–336). New York: Kluwer/Academic Press.

Kolko, D. J. (2003). *Interventions for children who set fires: Treatment specificity, moderation, and mediation.* Manuscript submitted for publication.

Kolko, D. J., & Ammerman, R. T. (1988). Firesetting. In M. Hersen & C. Last (Eds.), *Child behavior therapy casebook* (pp. 243–262). New York: Plenum.

Kolko, D. J., Brent, D. A., Baugher, M., Bridge, J., & Birmaher, B. (2000). Cognitive and family therapies for adolescent depression: Treatment specificity, mediation, and moderation. *Journal of Consulting and Clinical Psychology, 68*, 603–614.

Kolko, D. J., Day, B. T., Bridge, J., & Kazdin, A. E. (2001). Two-year prediction of children's firesetting in clinically-referred and non-referred samples. *Journal of Child Psychology and Psychiatry and Allied Disciplines, 42*, 371–380.

Kolko, D. J., & Kazdin, A. E. (1988a). Parent–child correspondence in identification of firesetting among child psychiatric patients. *Journal of Child Psychology and Psychiatry, 29*, 175–184.

Kolko, D. J., & Kazdin, A. E. (1988b). Prevalence of firesetting and related behaviors in child psychiatric inpatients. *Journal of Consulting and Clinical Psychology, 56*, 628–630.

Kolko, D. J., & Kazdin, A. E. (1989a). Assessment of dimensions of childhood firesetting among child psychiatric patients and nonpatients. *Journal of Abnormal Child Psychology, 17*, 609–624.

Kolko, D. J., & Kazdin, A. E. (1989b). The Children's Firesetting Interview with psychiatrically referred and nonreferred children. *Journal of Abnormal Child Psychology, 17,* 609–624.

Kolko, D. J., & Kazdin, A. E. (1991a). Matchplaying and firesetting in children: Relationship to parent, marital, and family dysfunction. *Journal of Clinical Child Psychology, 19,* 229–238.

Kolko, D. J., & Kazdin, A. E. (1991b). Aggression and psychopathology in match-playing and firesetting children: A replication and extension. *Journal of Clinical Child Psychology, 20,* 191–201.

Kolko, D. J., & Kazdin, A. E. (1991c). Motives of childhood firesetters: Firesetting characteristics and psychological correlates. *Journal of Child Psychology and Psychiatry, 32,* 535–550.

Kolko, D. J., & Kazdin, A. E. (1992). The emergence and recurrence of child fire-setting: A one-year prospective study. *Journal of Abnormal Child Psychology, 20,* 17–37.

Kolko, D. J., & Kazdin, A. E. (1994). Children's descriptions of their firesetting incidents: Characteristics and relationship to recidivism. *Journal of the American Academy of Child Psychiatry, 33,* 114–122.

Kolko, D. J., Kazdin, A. E., & Meyer, E. C. (1985). Aggression and psychopathology in childhood firesetters: Parent and child reports. *Journal of Consulting and Clinical Psychology, 53,* 377–385.

Kolko, D. J., Pinsonneault, I., & Okulitch, J. S. (2002). Further considerations and future directions. In D. J. Kolko (Ed.), *Handbook on firesetting in children and youth* (pp. 395–406). New York: Kluwer/Academic Press.

Kolko, D. J., Watson, S., & Faust, J. (1991). Fire safety/prevention skills training to reduce involvement with fire in young psychiatric inpatients: Preliminary findings. *Behavior Therapy, 22,* 269–284.

Kolko, D. J., Wilcox, D. K., Nishi-Strattner, L., & Kopet, T. (2002). Clinical assessment of juvenile firesetters and their families: Tools and tips. In D. J. Kolko (Ed.), *Handbook on firesetting in children and youth* (pp. 177–212). New York: Kluwer/Academic Press.

Kuhnley, E. J., Hendren, R. L., & Quinlan, D. M. (1982). Firesetting by children. *Journal of American Academy of Child Psychiatry, 2,* 560–563.

Lewis, N. O. C., & Yarnell, H. (1951). Pathological firesetting (pyromania). *Nervous and Mental Disease Monograph* (Vol. No. 82). Nicolasville, KY: Coolidge Foundation.

Loeber, R., & Dishion, T. (1984). Boys who fight at home and school: Family conditions influencing cross-setting consistency. *Journal of Consulting and Clinical Psychology, 52,* 759–768.

Massachusetts Coalition for Juvenile Firesetter Programs. (2000). *Children and fire.* Fall River: Massachusetts Coalition for Juvenile Firesetter Programs.

McGrath, P., Marshall, P. T., & Prior, K. (1979). A comprehensive treatment program for a firesetting child. *Journal of Behavior Therapy and Experimental Psychiatry, 10,* 69–72.

Miller, I. W., Epstein, N. B., Bishop, D. S., & Keitner, G. I. (1985). The McMaster Family Assessment Device: Reliability and validity. *Journal of Marital and Family Therapy, 11*, 345–356.

National Fire Protection Association. (1978). *Executive summary report of the Learn Not to Burn Curriculum.* Quincy, MA: Author.

National Fire Protection Association. (1979). *Learn Not to Burn Curriculum.* Quincy, MA: Author.

National Fire Protection Association. (1982). *Sparky's coloring book.* Quincy, MA: Author.

Pinsonneault, I. (2002). Developmental perspectives on children and fire. In D. J. Kolko (Ed.), *Handbook on firesetting in children and youth* (pp. 15–31). New York: Kluwer/Academic Press.

Repo, E., & Virkkunen, M. (1997). Young arsonists: History of conduct disorder, psychiatric diagnoses and criminal recidivism. *The Journal of Forensic Psychiatry, 8*, 311–320.

Rice, M. E., & Harris, G. T. (1991). Firesetters admitted to a maximum security psychiatric institution: Offenders and offenses. *Journal of Interpersonal Violence, 6*, 461–475.

Robin, A. L., & Foster, S. L. (1989). *Negotiating parent/adolescent conflict: A behavioral–family systems approach.* New York: Guilford Press.

Stewart, M. A., & Culver, K. W. (1982). Children who set fires: The clinical picture and a follow-up. *British Journal of Psychiatry, 140*, 357–363.

Stouthamer-Loeber, M., & Loeber, R. (1985). *Child-rearing practices—Pilot version.* Unpublished instrument, Pittsburgh Youth Study, University of Pittsburgh, Western Psychiatric Institute and Clinic, Pittsburgh, PA.

Weissberg, R. P., Gesten, E. L., Liebenstein, N. L., Doherty-Schmid, K., & Hutton, H. (1980). *The Rochester Social Problem-Solving (SPS) Program: A training manual for teachers of 2nd–4th grade children.* Rochester, NY: University of Rochester.

Weissberg, R. P., Gesten, E. L., Rapkin, B. D., Cowen, E. L., Davidson, E., Flores de Apodaca, R., et al. (1981). Evaluation of a social-problem-solving training program for suburban and inner-city third-grade children. *Journal of Consulting and Clinical Psychology, 49*, 251–261.

Wilcox, D. K., & Kolko, D. J. (2002). Assessing recent firesetting behavior and taking a firesetting history. In D. J. Kolko, (Ed.), *Handbook on firesetting in children and youth* (pp. 161–176). New York: Kluwer/Academic Press.

Wooden, W., & Berkey, M. L. (1984). *Children and arson: America's middle-class nightmare.* New York: Plenum.

20

THE INCREDIBLE YEARS: A TRAINING SERIES FOR THE PREVENTION AND TREATMENT OF CONDUCT PROBLEMS IN YOUNG CHILDREN

CAROLYN WEBSTER-STRATTON

OVERALL GOALS

The ultimate purpose of the University of Washington Parenting Clinic's program of research is to develop, evaluate, and improve cost-effective, widely applicable, and theory-based early intervention programs that are designed to prevent and treat early onset oppositional defiant disorder (ODD) and conduct disorder (CD) in children. Children with these disorders typically exhibit a broad range of antisocial behaviors (e.g., lying, cheating, stealing, fighting, oppositional behaviors, and noncompliance to parental requests) at higher-than-normal rates. Our interest in such children was stimulated by

This research was supported by the National Institute of Mental Health (NIMH) National Center for Nursing Research Grant #5 R01 NR01075 and Research Scientist Development Award MH00988 from NIMH. Correspondence concerning this chapter should be addressed to Carolyn Webster-Stratton, University of Washington, School of Nursing, Parenting Clinic, Box 354801, Seattle, WA 98195.

research showing the high prevalence rates for conduct problems—rates that are increasing at younger ages. Between 1988 and 1997, arrests of young offenders (between 7 and 12 years of age) for violent crimes increased by 45% and for drug violation by 156% (Snyder, 2001). Research indicates that aggressive children are at increased risk for being abused by their parents, as well as for school dropout, depression, drug abuse, juvenile delinquency, violence, adult crime, antisocial personality, marital disruption, and other diagnosable psychiatric disorders (Dishion, French, & Patterson, 1995; Loeber et al., 1993; Patterson, Capaldi, & Bank, 1991). Conduct problems (hereafter this term will be used to refer to young children with ODD and CD or both) are one of the most costly of mental disorders to society because such a large proportion of antisocial children remain involved with mental health agencies or criminal justice systems throughout the course of their lives.

Developmental theorists have suggested that there may be two developmental pathways related to conduct disorder: the "early-starter" versus "late-starter" models (Loeber et al., 1993; Patterson et al., 1991). The hypothesized "early-onset" pathway begins formally with the emergence of ODD in early preschool years, progresses to aggressive and nonaggressive (e.g., lying, stealing) symptoms in middle childhood, and then develops into the most serious symptoms by adolescence, including interpersonal violence, substance abuse, and property crimes (Lahey, Loeber, Quay, Frick, & Grimm, 1992). In contrast, the late-starter pathway first begins with a history of normal social and behavioral development during the preschool and early school years and progresses to symptoms of CD during adolescence. The prognosis for late-starter adolescents appears to be more favorable than for adolescents who have a history of CD beginning in their preschool years. For example, Snyder (2001) has shown that if the child was age 15 when first referred for problems, he or she has a 13% chance of becoming a chronic offender. If, on the other hand, the child was age 9 when first referred, he or she had a 36% chance of continuing as a chronic offender. Adolescents who first exhibited ODD symptoms in the preschool years followed by an early onset of CD have a two- to three-fold risk of becoming tomorrow's serious violent and chronic juvenile offenders. These children with early-onset CD also account for a disproportionate share of delinquent acts in adolescence. Thus, ODD is a sensitive predictor of CD. Indeed, the primary developmental pathway for serious conduct disorders in adolescence and adulthood appears to be established during the preschool period (Campbell, 1995; Loeber, 1991).

Theories regarding the causes of child conduct problems include ineffective parenting (e.g., harsh discipline, low parent involvement in school activities); family factors (e.g., marital conflict, depression, drug abuse, criminal behavior in parents); child biological and developmental risk factors (e.g., attention deficit disorders, learning disabilities, and language delays); school risk factors (e.g., teachers' use of poor classroom management strategies, classroom level of aggression, large class sizes, low teacher involvement with parents); and peer and community risk factors (e.g., poverty and gangs). For reviews of risk factors, see Coie et al. (1993) and Loeber and Farrington (2000).

Because CD becomes increasingly resistant to change over time, intervention that begins in the early school years is clearly a strategic way to prevent or reduce aggressive behavior problems. Our decision to focus our interventions on the period consisting of preschool and early school years was based on several considerations. First, evidence suggests that children with ODD and CD are clearly identifiable at this age. *Our prior studies have revealed that children as young as age 4 have already been expelled from two or more preschools and have experienced considerable peer and teacher rejection.* Second, evidence suggests that the younger the child at the time of intervention, the more positive the child's behavioral adjustment at home and at school (Strain, Steele, Ellis, & Timm, 1982). Third, the move to school—from preschool through the first years of elementary school—is a major transition and a period of great stress for many children and their parents. The child's early success or failure in adapting to school sets the stage not only for the child's future behavior at school and his or her relationships with teachers and peers but also for parents' future attitudes toward their child's schools and their own relationships with teachers and administrators. Fourth, recent projections suggest that approximately 70% of the children who need services for conduct problems—in particular, young children—do not receive them. And very few of those who do receive intervention ever receive an intervention that has been empirically validated (Brestan & Eyberg, 1998). We believe that early intervention, if placed strategically during the high-risk child's first major transition point, can counteract risk factors and reinforce protective factors, thereby helping to prevent a developmental trajectory from conduct problems to increasingly aggressive and violent behaviors, negative reputations, and spiraling academic failure.

In order to address the parenting, family, child, and school risk factors, we have developed three types of interlocking training curriculums, known as the Incredible Years Training Series, each of which is targeted at either parents or teachers or children (ages 2–8 years). This chapter reviews these training programs and their associated research (Table 20.1).

INCREDIBLE YEARS PARENT INTERVENTIONS

Parent Training Intervention

Rationale for Parent Training

One of the major intervention strategies shown to be successful for reducing ODD and CD symptoms in children involves parent training. This

TABLE 20.1
Overview of the Incredible Years Parent, Teacher, and Child Training Programs

Interventions	Skills targeted	Person trained	Settings targeted
Incredible Years BASIC Parent Training Programs	Parenting skills • Play/involvement • Praise/rewards • Limit setting • Discipline	Parent	Home
Incredible Years ADVANCE Parent Training Programs	Interpersonal skills • Problem solving • Anger management • Communication • Depression control • Giving and getting support	Parent	Home, work, and community
Incredible Years EDUCATION Parent Training Programs (a.k.a. Supporting Your Child's Education)	Academic skills • Academic stimulation • Learning routine after school • Homework support • Reading • Limit setting • Involvement at school • Teacher conferences	Parent	Home–school connection
Incredible Years Teacher Training Programs	Classroom management skills; promoting parent involvement	Teacher	School
Incredible Years Child Training Programs (Dina Dinosaur Social Skills and Problem-Solving Curriculum)	Social skills • Friendship • Teamwork • Cooperation/helping • Communication Problem solving • Anger management • Steps of problem solving Classroom behavior • Quiet hand up • Compliance • Listening • Stop-look-think-check • Concentrating	Child	Home and school

approach assumes a model in which ineffective parenting skills are the most important risk factor and intervening variable in the development and maintenance of conduct problems. We have been strongly influenced by Patterson's (1982, 1986) seminal work and theoretical formulations concerning the development of conduct disorder and problem behaviors. His social learning, interactional-based model emphasizes the importance of the family socialization processes. Patterson developed the coercion hypothesis, which postulates that children learn to get their own way and escape (or avoid) parental criticism by escalating their negative behaviors; this, in turn, leads to increasingly aversive parent interactions. As this coercive training in a family continues over time, the rate and intensity of aggressive behaviors—on the part of parents and children—increase. Moreover, as the child observes increasingly frequent parental anger and negative discipline, the child is provided with further modeling (observational learning) of aggression (Patterson, 1982). The pioneering research of Patterson and others has found that parents of children with conduct problems exhibit fewer positive behaviors; use more violent disciplinary techniques; are more critical, more permissive, and less likely to monitor their children's behaviors; and are more likely to reinforce inappropriate behaviors while ignoring or even punishing prosocial behaviors.

In addition to social learning theory, attachment theory (Bowlby, 1980) has elucidated the importance of the affective nature of the parent–child relationship. Considerable evidence indicates that a warm, positive bond between parent and child leads to a more socially competent child, whereas high levels of negative affect and hostility on the part of parents is disruptive to children's ability to regulate their emotional responses and manage conflict appropriately. For example, research has shown that the relationship between harsh discipline and externalizing problems occurred only among children in homes in which a warm child–parent relationship was lacking (Deater-Deckard, Dodge, Bates, & Pettit, 1996). Likewise, in a recent review of research on risk and resilience, Doll and Lyon (1998) concluded that a warm relationship with at least one caregiver was a strong protective factor against the negative influences of family dysfunction. This finding was supported by results of a large national study of adolescent development that showed that youth who report positive relationships and bonding with their families and schools engage in less risky and few antisocial behaviors (Resnick et al., 1997). Accordingly, we hypothesized that if we could intervene with parents to enhance their relationships while children were still very young and their families' negative styles of interaction were still malleable, we could improve the poor long-term prognoses for these children.

Videotape Modeling Methods

We were particularly interested in determining which *methods* of training parents were most effective—that is, cost-effective, widely applicable, and sustaining. Cost-effectiveness is vital because conduct problems are increasingly widespread, creating a need for service that far exceeds available personnel and resources. Most of the early parent training programs largely relied on verbal methods such as didactic lectures, brochures, and group discussions. Although these methods are cost-effective, they have been shown to be ineffective for inducing behavioral changes in parents, particularly in parents whose educational level or general intellectual level is deficient. On the other hand, performance training methods such as live modeling, role rehearsal, and individual video feedback had proven effective in producing behavioral changes in parents and children (O'Dell, 1985); however, implementation was time-consuming and costly, making them impractical in the face of increasing demand. Videotape modeling, on the other hand, was one method that promised to be practical and cost-effective.

In accordance with Bandura's (1989) modeling and self-efficacy theories of learning, we hypothesized that parents could develop their parenting skills by watching (and modeling) videotape examples of parents interacting with their children in ways that promoted prosocial behaviors and decreased inappropriate behaviors. We theorized that videotape would provide a more flexible method of training than didactic instruction or role-playing exercises because of its ability to portray a wide variety of models and situations. We hypothesized that this flexible modeling approach would result in better generalization of the training content and therefore better long-term maintenance. Further, it would be a better method of learning for less verbally sophisticated parents. Finally, such a method, if proven effective, would have the advantage not only of low individual training cost when used in groups but also of possible mass dissemination. Thus, in 1979 we initiated our program of research to develop and evaluate videotape modeling parent intervention programs for families of young children with ODD and CD. We were interested both in evaluating the parent program's efficacy and in testing a theory of behavior change processes.

Content and Process of the Incredible Years Parent
Training Programs

First, we developed an interactive, videotape-based parent intervention program (BASIC) for parents of children from between the ages of 2 and 6 years. Subsequently, we added a school-age version of the BASIC parent training series (developed with a more culturally diverse population) for use with parents of children from between the ages of 6 and 10 years. Heavily guided by the modeling literature, the BASIC program aims to promote modeling effects for parents by creating positive feelings about the videotape models. For example, the videotapes show parents and children of differing ages, cultures, socioeconomic backgrounds, and temperaments so that parents will perceive at least some of the models as similar to themselves and their children and will therefore accept the tapes as relevant. Videotapes show parent models (unrehearsed) in natural situations with their children, such as eating meals, going to bed, or being potty trained and are used to stimulate group discussion, problem solving and interactive learning. This approach emphasizes our belief in a coping and interactive model of learning (Webster-Stratton & Herbert, 1994); that is, parents view a videotape vignette and then discuss what they liked about the parents' approach or role-playing exercise and how they might have handled the interaction more effectively. This approach serves not only to enhance parents' confidence in their own ideas but also to develop their ability to analyze different situations with their children and select an appropriate parenting strategy.

The BASIC parent training program takes 26 hours, or 13 to 14 weekly 2-hour sessions. It encompasses videotape programs of modeled parenting skills (250 vignettes, each of which lasts approximately 1 to 2 minutes) shown by a therapist to groups of parents (10–14 parents per group). The program is also designed to help parents understand normal variations in children's development, emotional reactions, and temperaments. We see the therapist's role as one of supporting and empowering parents by teaching, leading, reframing, predicting, and role playing, always within a collaborative context (Webster-Stratton & Hancock, 1998; Webster-Stratton & Herbert, 1994). The collaborative context is designed to ensure that the intervention is sensitive to individual cultural differences and tailored to each family's individual needs and goals (identified in the first session) as well as to each child's personality and behavior problems.

The program encourages a commitment to parental self-management. We believe that this approach empowers parents in that it gives back dignity, respect, and self-control to parents who are often seeking help for their children's problems at a vulnerable time of low self-confidence and intense feelings of guilt and self-blame (Webster-Stratton & Spitzer, 1996). By using a group process, the program not only is more cost-effective but also addresses an important risk factor for children with conduct problems— namely, the family's isolation and stigmatization. The parent groups provide support and become a model for parent support networks. (For details of therapeutic processes, please see Webster-Stratton & Herbert [1994].)

The first two segments of the BASIC program focus on teaching parents to play with their children, fostering interactive and reinforcement skills. This material is derived from the early research of Hanf and Kling (1973) and Eyberg, Boggs, and Algina (1995). The third and fourth segments teach parents a specific set of nonviolent discipline techniques including commands, time-out, and ignoring, as described by Patterson (1976) and Forehand and McMahon (1981), as well as logical and natural consequences and monitoring. The fourth segment also shows parents ways to teach their children problem-solving skills (Shure, 1994). Tables 20.2 and 20.3 provide a brief description of the content of each of the parenting programs.

TABLE 20.2
Content and Objectives of the Incredible Years
BASIC Parent Training Programs (Ages 2–7 Years)

Content	Objectives	Content	Objectives
Program One: Play			
Part 1: How to Play With a Child	• Recognizing children's capabilities and needs • Providing positive support for children's play • Helping children develop imaginative and creative play • Building children's self-esteem and self-concept • Handling children's boredom • Avoiding power struggles with children • Understanding the importance of adult attention	Part 2: Helping Children Learn	• Talking with children • Understanding ways to create faster language development • Building children's confidence in learning ability • Helping children learn to problem solve • Helping children deal with frustration • Avoiding the criticism trap • Making learning enjoyable through play
Program Two: Praise and Rewards			
Part 1: The Art of Effective Praising	• Understanding ways to praise more effectively • Avoiding praise of perfection only • Recognizing common traps • Handling children who reject praise • Providing physical warmth • Recognizing child behaviors that need praise • Understanding the effects of social rewards on children • Doubling the impact of praise • Building children's self-esteem	Part 2: Tangible Rewards	• Providing unexpected rewards • Understanding the difference between rewards and bribes • Recognizing when to use the "first-then" rule • Providing ways to set up star and chart systems with children • Recognizing ways to carry out point programs • Understanding how to develop programs that are age appropriate • Understanding ways to use tangible rewards for reducing or eliminating problems such as dawdling, not dressing, noncompliance, not sharing, fighting with siblings, picky eating, messy rooms, not going to bed, and messy diapers

Content	Objectives	Content	Objectives
Program Three: Effective Limit Setting			
Part 1: How to Set Limits	• Identifying important household rules • Understanding ways to give more effective commands • Avoiding unnecessary commands • Avoiding unclear, vague, and negative commands • Providing children with positive alternatives • Understanding when to use the "when-then" command • Recognizing the importance of warnings and helpful reminders • Understanding ways to use problem-solving approaches	Part 2: Helping Children Learn to Accept Limits	• Dealing with children who test the limits • Understanding when to divert and distract children • Avoiding arguments and "why games" • Recognizing traps children set for parents • Ignoring inappropriate responses • Following through with commands effectively • Helping children to be more compliant
Part 3: Dealing With Non-compliance	• Understanding how to implement time-out for noncompliance • Understanding ways to explain time-out to children • Avoiding power struggles • Dealing with children who refuse to go to time-out or refuse to stay in time-out • Ignoring children's inappropriate responses • Following through effectively and consistently • Avoiding common mistakes concerning time-out		

continues

TABLE 20.2 (Continued)
Content and Objectives of the Incredible Years
BASIC Parent Training Programs (Ages 2–7 Years)

Content	Objectives	Content	Objectives
Program Four: Handling Misbehavior			
Part 1: Avoiding and Ignoring Misbehavior	• Anticipating and avoiding frustration • Showing disapproval • Ignoring and distracting • Handling noncompliance, screaming, arguing, pleading, and tantrums • Handling crying, grabbing, not eating, and refusing to go to bed	Part 2: Time-Out and Other Penalties	• Explaining time-out to a school-age child. • Using time-out for hitting behaviors • Using the time-out chair with a toddler • Explaining time-out to a toddler • Using a time-out room with a toddler • Using time-out to help stop sibling fights • Following through when a child refuses to go to time-out • Dealing with spitting • Dealing with threats • Understanding and establishing logical consequences • Coping when discipline doesn't work • Dealing with the telephone syndrome • Dealing with the TV syndrome
Part 3: Preventive Strategies	• Encouraging sharing and cooperation among children • Using puppets and story books to teach children social skills • Talking and listening effectively • Problem solving with children • Reviewing points to remember when using time-out		

TABLE 20.3
Content and Objectives of the Incredible Years
BASIC Parent Training Programs (Ages 5–12 Years)

Content	Objectives	Content	Objectives
Program Nine: Promoting Positive Behaviors in School-Age Children			
Part 1: The Importance of Parental Attention	• Providing positive support for children's play • Helping children develop imaginative and creative play • Building children's self-esteem and self-confidence through supportive parental attention • Understanding the importance of adult attention for promoting positive child behaviors • Understanding how lack of attention and interest can lead to child misbehaviors	Part 2: Effective Praise	• Knowing how to use praise more effectively • Avoiding praising only perfection • Recognizing common traps • Knowing how to deal with children who reject praise • Providing physical warmth • Recognizing child behaviors that need praise • Understanding the effects of social rewards on children • Doubling the impact of praise • Building children's self-esteem and self-concept
Part 3: Tangible Rewards	• Understanding the difference between rewards and bribes • Recognizing when to use the "first-then" rule • Understanding how to set up star and point systems with children • Understanding how to design programs that are age-appropriate • Understanding ways to use tangible rewards for problems such as dawdling, not dressing, noncompliance, not sharing, sibling fighting, picky eating, messy room, not going to bed, and toilet training		

continues

Content	Objectives	Content	Objectives
Program Ten: Reducing Inappropriate Behaviors in School-Age Children			
Part 1: Clear Limit Setting	• The importance of household rules • Guidelines for giving effective commands • How to avoid using unnecessary commands • Identifying unclear, vague, and negative commands • Providing children with positive alternatives • Using "when/then" commands effectively • The importance of warnings and helpful reminders	Part 2: Ignoring Misbehavior	• Dealing effectively with children who test the limits • Knowing when to divert and distract children • Avoiding arguments and "why games" • Understanding why it is important to ignore children's inappropriate responses • Following through with commands effectively • Recognizing how to help children be more compliant
Part 3: Time-Out Con-sequences	• Guidelines for implementing time-out for noncompliance, hitting, and destructive behaviors • How to explain time-out to children • Avoiding power struggles • Techniques for dealing with children who refuse to go to time-out or won't stay in time-out • Recognizing common mistakes using time-out • Understanding the importance of strengthening positive behaviors	Part 4: Con-sequences, Extra Chores, and Start-Up Commands	• Guidelines for avoiding power struggles • Recognizing when to use logical consequences, privilege removal, or start up commands • Understanding what to do when discipline doesn't seem to work • Recognizing when to ignore children's inappropriate responses and how to avoid power struggles • Understanding how natural and logical consequences increase children's sense of responsibility • Understanding when to use work chores with children • Understanding the importance of parental monitoring at all ages

Content	Objectives	Content	Objectives
Part 5: Problem Solving With Children	• Understanding the importance of adults not imposing solutions on children but rather fostering a "thinking process" about conflict • Recognizing how and when to use "guided solutions" for young children • Recognizing how to foster children's empathy skills • Understanding ways to encourage children's generation of solutions to problems • Learning how to help children think about and evaluate consequences to proposed solutions • Recognizing when children may be ready to problem solve on their own • Understanding how to use the problem-solving strategies in a family meeting	Part 6: Special Problems: Lying, Stealing, and Hitting	• Promoting open communication between adults and children • Understanding the problem steps: (1) problem definition, (2) brainstorming, (3) evaluating, (4) planning and follow up • Avoiding "blocks" to effective problem solving with children such as lectures, negative or quick judgments about solutions, excessive focus on the "right" answer, and the failure to validate a child's feelings • Exploring the advantages and disadvantages of spanking versus grounding, versus time-out versus loss of privileges

Family Training Interventions

Rationale for Broader-Based Training

Besides parenting behavior per se, other aspects of parents' behavior and personal lives constitute risk factors for child conduct problems. Researchers have demonstrated that factors such as parental depression, marital discord, lack of social support, and environmental stressors disrupt parenting behavior and contribute to relapses subsequent to parent training (for review see Webster-Stratton, 1990c). In our own analysis of the marital status of 218 parents of children with ODD and CD, we found that 75% of the sample had been divorced at least once or were currently in stressful marriages. Half of the married couples reported current experiences with spouse abuse. Further analyses revealed a direct link between negative marital conflict management style and children's patterns of social interactions and conflict management with peers (Webster-Stratton & Hammond, 1999), in addition to an indirect path through the parenting style. Other studies also suggested that factors such as children's exposure to marital conflict (Grych & Finchman, 1992), physical aggression between spouses, and disagreements over child rearing (Jouriles, Norwood, McDonald, Vincent, & Mahoney, 1996) were key factors influencing the development of conduct disorders.

This evidence linking family risk factors other than parenting behavior—such as marital distress and poor communication and problem-solving ability—to child conduct problems and treatment relapses led us to expand our theoretical and causal model concerning conduct problems. For example, rather than the child's conduct problems being the result of parenting deficits per se, we hypothesized that the child's conduct in general and poor peer interactions in particular are modeled from the marital interactions and parents' interpersonal skills with other adults. The child learns communication and problem-solving styles directly from observing his or her parents' interactions. In our revised model—a conflict-resolution–deficit model—we hypothesized that parents with children with ODD and CD have more general relational deficits in communication, conflict resolution, and affect regulation. We believe that these deficits are manifested in marital and interpersonal difficulties, inability to get support or cope with life stressors, problematic parenting, and difficulty in coping with child misbehaviors. These in turn exacerbate ineffectual parenting and thereby contribute to the coercive process leading to the development of child conduct problems (Dadds & Powell, 1991; Griest et al., 1982).

Content of ADVANCE Training Program

In light of this research, plus the results of our long-term follow-ups indicating the potency of marital distress and divorce as predictors of treatment relapse, we developed the ADVANCE treatment program. We theorized that a broader-based training model (i.e., one involving more than parenting training) would help mediate the negative influences of these interpersonal factors on parenting skills and promote increased maintenance and generalizability of treatment effects. This program has the same theoretical basis as the BASIC parent skills training program—namely, cognitive social learning theory and a strong relationship focus. The therapeutic process and methods are also the same as for the BASIC program because our prior research had indicated that therapist-led parent group discussions and interactive videotape modeling techniques were highly effective methods of producing behavioral change and promoting interpersonal support. Moreover, we theorized that it would be a cost-effective alternative to the conventional format of individual marital or interpersonal therapy.

The content of this 14-session videotape program (60 vignettes), which is offered after the completion of the BASIC training program, involves four components:

1. *Personal self-control:* Parents are taught to substitute coping and positive self-talk for their depressive, angry, and blaming self-talk. This therapy component builds on well-established research and clinical writings (Beck, 1979; Lewinsohn, Antonuccio, & Teni, 1984; Meichenbaum, 1993). In addition, parents are taught specific anger management techniques.

2. *Communication skills:* Parents are taught to identify blocks to communication and to learn the most effective communication skills for dealing with conflict. This component builds on the communication work of Gottman, Notarius, Gonso, and Markman (1976) and the social learning–based marital treatment developed by Jacobson and Margolin (1979).

3. *Problem-solving skills:* In this component, parents are taught effective strategies for coping with conflict—whether with spouses, employers, extended family members, or children. These components build on the research by D'Zurilla and Nezu (1982) but are also influenced by the marital programs of Jacobson and Margolin (1979).

4. *Strengthening social support and self-care:* This concept is woven throughout all of the group sessions and components by encouraging the group members to ask for support when necessary and to give support to others. The content of both the BASIC and ADVANCE programs is also provided in the text that the parents use for the program entitled *The Incredible Years: A Troubleshooting Guide for Parents* (Webster-Stratton, 1992a; see Table 20.4).

Academic Skills Training Intervention for Parents (SCHOOL)

Rationale for Academic Skills Training

In follow-up interviews with parents who had completed our parent training programs, 58% requested guidance on how to encourage their children to do their homework; how to communicate with teachers concerning their children's behavior problems at school; and how to promote their children's reading, academic, and social skills. These data suggested a need for teaching parents how to access schools, collaborate with teachers, and supervise children's peer relationships. Clearly, integrating interventions across settings (home and school) and agents (teachers and parents) to target school and family risk factors fosters greater between-environment consistency and offers the best chance for long-term reduction of antisocial behavior.

TABLE 20.4
Content and Objectives of the Incredible Years
ADVANCE Parent Training Programs (Ages 4–10 Years)

Content	Objectives	Content	Objectives
Program Five: How to Communicate Effectively With Adults and Children			
Part 1: Active Listening and Speaking Up	• Understanding the importance of active listening skills • Learning how to speak up effectively about problems • Recognizing how to validate another's feelings • Knowing how and when to express one's own feelings • Avoiding communication blocks such as not listening, storing up grievances, and angry explosions	Part 2: Communicating More Positively to Oneself and to Others	• Understanding the importance of recognizing self-talk • Understanding how angry and depressive emotions and thoughts can affect behaviors with others • Learning coping strategies to stop negative self-talk • Learning coping strategies to increase positive self-talk • Increasing positive and polite communication with others • Avoiding communication blocks such as put-downs, blaming, and denials • Understanding the importance of seeing a problem from the other person's point of view
Part 3: Giving and Getting Support	• Understanding the importance of support for a family or an individual • Recognizing communication styles or beliefs that block support • Fostering self-care and positive self-reinforcement strategies in adults and children • Avoiding communication blocks such as defensiveness, denials, cross complaints, and inconsistent or mixed messages • Knowing how to get feedback from others		

Content	Objectives	Content	Objectives
Part 3: Giving and Getting Support (continued)	• Understanding how to turn a complaint into a positive recommendation • Promoting consistent verbal and nonverbal messages • Knowing how to make positive requests of adults and children • Understanding why compliance to another's requests is essential in any relationship • Learning how to be more supportive to others		

Program Six: Problem Solving for Parents

Content	Objectives	Content	Objectives
Part 1: Adult Problem Solving	• Recognizing when to use spontaneous problem-solving skills • Understanding the important steps to problem solving • Learning how and when to collaborate effectively • Avoiding blocks to effective problem solving such as blaming, attacks, anger, side-tracking, lengthy problem definition, missed steps, and criticizing solutions • Recognizing how to use problem-solving strategies to get more support • Learning how to express feelings about a problem without blaming.	Part 2: Family Problem- Solving Meetings	• Understanding how to use the problem-solving steps with school-age children • Recognizing the importance of evaluating plans during each problem-solving session • Understanding the importance of rotating the leader for each family meeting • Learning how to help children express their feelings about an issue • Reinforcing the problem-solving process

continues

Content	Objectives	Content	Objectives
Program Seven: Problem Solving With Young Children			
Part 1: Teaching Children to Problem Solve Through Stories and Games	• Understanding that games and stories can be used to help children begin to learn problem-solving skills • Appreciating the developmental nature and process of problem solving and learning how to enhance these skills in children • Strengthening a child's beginning empathy skills or ability to understand a problem from another person's viewpoint • Recognizing why aggressive and shy children need to learn these skills • Learning how to help children think about the emotional and behavioral consequences to proposed solutions • Knowing how to help older children evaluate their proposed solutions • Understanding the importance of validating children's feelings • Learning how to help children make more positive attributions about another person's intentions • Recognizing the value of adults modeling their ability to problem solve for children to observe	Part 2: Teaching Children to Problem Solve in the Midst of Conflict	• Understanding the importance of not imposing solutions upon children but of fostering a thinking process about conflict • Recognizing how and when to use guided solutions for very young children or for children who have no positive solutions in their repertoire • Discovering the value of obtaining the child's feelings and view of the problem before attempting to problem solve • Learning how to foster children's skills to empathize and perceive another's point of view • Recognizing when children may be ready to problem solve on their own • Avoiding blocks to effective problem solving with children, such as lectures, quick judgments, exclusive focus on the right answer, and failure to validate a child's feelings

Content of Academic Skills Training

In 1990 we developed an intervention using interactive videotape modeling skills training (SCHOOL) as an adjunct to our BASIC and ADVANCE interventions. This intervention consists of four to six additional sessions that are usually offered after the BASIC program. It focuses on parents' collaboration with teachers and their ability to foster their children's academic readiness and school success through involvement in school activities, homework, and peer monitoring. This program's methods are consistent with the BASIC and ADVANCE interventions (see Table 20.5).

This 6-session program involves six components:

1. *Promoting children's self-confidence:* Parents are taught to lay the foundation for their children's success at school by helping their children feel confident in their own ideas and in their ability to learn. Specifically, in this program we teach parents how to prepare their children for reading by teaching them the dialogic-reading approach (Whitehurst et al., 1988), ways to foster language development and problem solving, and ways to promote children's reading, writing, and story-telling skills.

2. *Fostering good learning habits:* Parents are taught to establish a predictable homework routine, set limits on time spent on television and computer games, and follow through with consequences for children who test these limits.

3. *Dealing with children's discouragement:* Parents are taught how to set realistic goals for their child and how to gradually increase the difficulty of the learning task as the child acquires mastery, using praise, tangible rewards, and attention to motivate and reinforce progress.

4. *Participating in homework:* Parents are taught ways to play a positive and supportive role in their children's homework.

5. *Using teacher–parent conferences to advocate for the child:* This segment shows parents how to collaborate with their children's teachers to jointly develop plans to address their children's difficulties, such as inattentiveness, tardiness, and aggression in school.

6. *Discussing a school problem with the child:* Parents discuss how to talk with their children about academic problems and how to set up a plan with them to maximize their success at school.

TABLE 20.5
Content and Objectives of the Incredible Years
Supporting Your Child's Education Parent Training Program

Content	Objectives	Content	Objectives
Program Eight: How to Support Your Child's Education			
Part 1: Promoting Your Child's Self-Confidence	• Recognizing the capabilities of young children • Providing positive support for children's play • Helping children develop imaginative and creative play • Building children's self-esteem and self-confidence in their learning ability • Making learning enjoyable through play • Teaching children to problem solve • Understanding the importance of adult attention and listening skills for children • Fostering children's reading skills and story telling through interactive dialogue, praise, and open-ended questions	Part 2: Fostering Good Learning Habits	• Setting up a predictable routine • Understanding how television interferes with learning • Incorporating effective limit-setting regarding homework • Understanding how to follow through with limits • Understanding the importance of parental monitoring • Avoiding the criticism trap
Part 3: Dealing With Children's Discouragement	• Helping children avoid a sense of failure when they can't do something • Recognizing the importance of children learning according to their developmental ability and learning style • Understanding how to build on children's strengths • Knowing how to set up tangible reward programs to help motivate children in difficult areas • Understanding how to motivate children through praise and encouragement	Part 4: Participating in Children's Homework	• Understanding the importance of parental attention, praise, and encouragement for children's homework activities • Recognizing that every child learns different skills at different rates according to their developmental ability • Understanding how to build on children's strengths • Understanding how to show active interest in children's learning at home and at school

TABLE 20.5 (Continued)
Content and Objectives of the Incredible Years
Supporting Your Child's Education Parent Training Program

Content	Objectives	Content	Objectives
Part 5: Using Parent–Teacher Conferences to Advocate for Your Child	• Understanding the importance of parental advocacy for their children in school • Understanding how to focus on finding solutions to children's school difficulties (rather than blame) • Recognizing effective communication and problem-solving strategies in talking with teachers • Knowing ways to support teachers in their teaching efforts • Recognizing strategies to motivate children at school • Understanding the importance of continuity from home to school		

Effectiveness of Parent and Family Interventions for Children With Oppositional Defiant Disorder or Conduct Disorder

Short- and Long-Term Outcomes

The efficacy of the Incredible Years BASIC parent program as an indicated intervention or treatment program for children (ages 3–8 years) diagnosed with ODD and CD has been demonstrated in six published randomized control-group trials (Webster-Stratton, 1981, 1982, 1984, 1990a, 1994, 1998; Webster-Stratton & Hammond, 1997; Webster-Stratton, Hollinsworth, & Kolpacoff, 1989; Webster-Stratton, Kolpacoff, & Hollinsworth, 1988). The program has been shown to be effective in significantly improving parental attitudes and parent–child interactions, along with significantly reducing parents' reliance on violent and critical disciplinary approaches and reducing child conduct problems, when compared with control groups and other treatment approaches. In addition, the program has been replicated by independent investigators in mental health clinics treating families of children with conduct problems (Scott, 1999; Spaccarelli, Cotler, & Penman, 1992; Taylor, Schmidt, Pepler, & Hodgins,

1998). Further, two of these replications were effectiveness trials—that is, they were conducted in applied settings, not a university research clinic, and the therapists were typical therapists at the center.

Several of the early studies used component analyses in an effort to discern the most effective ingredient of the treatment program. In the second randomized study with low-income single mothers of children with conduct problems, the therapist-led, group-discussion BASIC program was compared with the individualized one-to-one parent training approach with a therapist using "bug-in-the-ear" (i.e., small microphone worn in parent's ear so that therapist can coach parent while interacting with his or her child) feedback and individual coaching (Webster-Stratton, 1984). Results indicated that the BASIC program was more effective than the one-to-one program and was found to be five times more cost-effective, using 48 hours of therapist time versus 251 hours in the one-to-one program. A third study was conducted to ascertain which element of the overall BASIC program (i.e., group support and discussion, therapist leadership, or videotape modeling) contributed most to its effectiveness. Results indicated that the combined treatment condition that included videotape modeling plus therapist-led group discussion was consistently favored over the other approaches, which used group discussion only or individualized self-administered video modeling (IVM; Webster-Stratton et al., 1988; Webster-Stratton et al., 1989). One year later, results from 93% of the original sample indicated that all the significant improvements reported immediately after treatment were maintained. Moreover, two thirds of the sample showed clinically significant improvements. Of particular interest was the finding that the IVM—that is, the intervention without therapist feedback or group support—was also shown to be modestly effective (Webster-Stratton, 1990a, 1992b).

Three years after treatment, by which time all the children were enrolled in school, we assessed 82.1% of the families again to determine any long-term differences between treatment groups in terms of numbers of relapses and children's functioning at school and home. Follow-up reports from parents and teachers indicated that only the combined videotape modeling group discussion treatment achieved stable improvements; the other two treatment groups showed significant relapses. These data suggested the importance of therapist leadership and parent group support in conjunction with videotape modeling in producing the most effective results in terms of producing significant behavior change that not only generalizes across settings and over time but is also highly cost-effective, with good consumer satisfaction.

Nonetheless, evaluation of the clinical significance of the treatment programs indicated that, after 3 years, 25% to 46% of parents were concerned about school-related problems, such as peer relationships, aggression, noncompliance, and academic underachievement. Data from parents pointed to a need to help parents become more effective in supporting their child's education and in collaborating with their child's teacher in addressing their child's social and academic problems. Data from teachers revealed a need to expand the intervention to include training for teachers in ways to manage classroom behavior problems and in ways to collaborate with parents (Webster-Stratton, 1990b). These data led us to develop the parent academic skills training intervention (SCHOOL) described earlier, as well as the teacher training intervention, which will be described shortly.

Of particular interest were the findings in the third study regarding the IVM. In contrast to the control families, the IVM treatment resulted in significant improvements in child conduct problems (as reported by parents) and in parent–child interactions (according to independent observers). These findings are rather remarkable in light of the fact that these multiproblem families had no direct therapist contact or group support throughout the entire training series, and they suggest that parents who are motivated can learn to change their own and their children's behaviors by means of a self-administered program. Clearly, this is the most cost-effective alternative and has major implications for treatment and prevention. In a fourth randomized study, we evaluated the added effects of combining brief therapist consultation to IVM treatment in an attempt to enhance its effectiveness while maintaining its cost-effectiveness. Comparing IVM, IVM plus therapist consultation (IVMC), and a wait-list control group at pretreatment, posttreatment, and 1 year later, our fourth study found that both treatment groups of mothers reported significantly fewer child behavior problems, reduced stress levels, and less use of spanking than the control group. Home visit data indicated that both treatment groups exhibited significant behavioral changes that were maintained 1 year later. There were relatively few differences between the two treatment conditions on the outcome measures. However, the children in the IVMC group were significantly less deviant than the children in the IVM group, suggesting that therapist consultation improves this treatment approach (Webster-Stratton, 1990a, 1992b). These findings have implications for reaching many more families in cost-effective treatment or prevention programs to help prevent behavior problems from escalating in the first place.

In a fifth study, we examined the effects of adding the ADVANCE intervention component to the BASIC intervention (Webster-Stratton, 1994). Parents of 78 families with children with ODD and CD received the initial BASIC parent training and then were randomly assigned to either ADVANCE training or no further contact. In both treatment groups, significant improvements were noted in child adjustment and parent–child interactions, as well as a decrease in parental distress and child behavior problems. These changes were maintained at follow-up. Children in the ADVANCE group showed significant increases in the total number of solutions generated during problem solving, most notably in prosocial solutions (as compared to aggressive solutions), compared with their counterparts.

Observations of parents' marital interactions indicated significant improvements in ADVANCE parents' communication, problem solving, and collaboration skills when compared with parents who did not receive ADVANCE. Only one family dropped out of the ADVANCE program, which attests to its perceived usefulness by families. All the families attended more than two thirds of the sessions, with the majority attending over 90% of sessions. Parents in the ADVANCE group reported significantly greater consumer satisfaction than did parents who did not receive ADVANCE, with parents reporting the problem-solving skills to be the most useful and anger management the most difficult.

Next we looked at the ways in which clinically significant improvements (30%) in parents' communication and problem-solving skills were related to improvements in their parenting skills. We found that, in the case of fathers, improvement in marital communication skills was associated with a significant reduction in the number of criticisms in their interactions with their children; fathers' improved marital communication was also related to improvements in the child's prosocial skills. These results indicate the importance of fathers' marital satisfaction as a determining factor in their parenting skills.

Overall, these results suggest that focusing on helping families to manage personal distress and interpersonal issues through a videotape modeling group discussion treatment (ADVANCE) is highly promising in terms of (a) improvements in marital communication, problem solving, and coping skills; (b) improvements in parenting skills; (c) improvements in children's prosocial skills; and (d) consumer satisfaction—that is, being highly acceptable and perceived as useful by families (Webster-Stratton, 1994). As a result of these findings. we combined BASIC plus ADVANCE plus SCHOOL into an integrated 22- to 24-week program for parents, which has become our core treatment protocol for parents of children with conduct problems.

In a sixth study, we compared the effects of combining a child training intervention using the broader parent training program (BASIC + ADVANCE) with the broader parent training program without child training. With the broader parent training focus, we replicated our results from the prior ADVANCE study and were able to determine the added advantages of training children as well as parents. (See description of these study results later in this chapter, in the section on child training results.)

Parent Training Treatment—Who Benefits and Who Doesn't?

As reported in the previous sections, we have followed families longitudinally (1, 2, and 3 years posttreatment) and are currently engaged in a 10- to 15-year follow-up. We have assessed not only the statistical significance of treatment effects but also the clinical significance of treatment effects. In our 3-year follow-up of 83 families treated with the BASIC program, we found that 25% to 46% of parents and 26% of teachers still reported clinically significant child behavior problems (Webster-Stratton, 1990b). These findings are similar to other long-term treatment outcome studies that suggest that 30% to 50% of families relapse or fail to show continuous long-term benefits from treatment (e.g., Jacobson, Schmaling, & Holtzworth-Monroe, 1987; McMahon & Forehand, 1984; Wahler & Dumas, 1984). We also found that the families of children who had continuing externalizing problems (according to teacher and parent reports) at our 3-year follow-up assessments were characterized by maritally distressed or single-parent status; increased maternal depression; lower social class; high levels of negative life stressors; and family histories of alcoholism, drug abuse, and spouse abuse (Webster-Stratton, 1990b; Webster-Stratton & Hammond, 1990). We found that the best predictor of the amount of child deviance at home was single-parent status or marital adjustment. For families in which a father was present, the degree of negative life stress experienced by the father in the year after treatment was the best predictor of child deviance. Marital status was the best predictor of teacher reports of child adjustment. Thus, divorce, marital distress, and negative life stress were key predictors in determining the child's long-term treatment outcome (Webster-Stratton, 1990b; Webster-Stratton & Hammond, 1990).

Recently Hartman, Stage, and Webster-Stratton (2003) examined whether child risk factors (i.e., inattention, hyperactivity, and impulsivity problems) predicted less effective results from the parent training intervention (BASIC). Contrary to the researchers' hypothesis, the child factors made a significant contribution to decreasing conduct problems over time, suggesting that the children with ODD and CD who were comorbid for problems such as inattention, impulsivity, and hyperactivity made even greater gains in reducing conduct problems than children without these risk factors.

Parent Training Prevention Studies

Effectiveness of Parent Training Prevention Programs

In the past decade, we have evaluated the BASIC parent program as a selective prevention program in two randomized studies with Head Start families. In the first study, seven Head Start centers were randomly assigned to two conditions: (a) an experimental condition in which all parents were invited to participate in the parent intervention (BASIC), in addition to receiving the regular center-based Head Start program ($n = 296$); and (b) a control condition in which parents participated in the regular center-based Head Start program offerings ($n = 130$). Parent groups were led by trained facilitators who were family service workers employed by Head Start. At postassessment, blinded observer reports indicated that mothers participating in the intervention improved in all four parent behaviors during interactions with their children; mothers made significantly fewer critical remarks and commands, used less harsh discipline, and were more nurturing, reinforcing, and competent compared with mothers in the control group (who remained stable). Mothers participating in the intervention reported that their discipline strategies also improved; mothers were more consistent, used fewer physical and verbally negative discipline techniques, and were more appropriate in their limit-setting techniques. In turn, the children of mothers in the intervention group exhibited significantly less misbehavior, noncompliance, deviance, and negative affect and more positive affect, whereas the control children's behavior remained unchanged. Similarly, teachers reported that the children participating in the intervention showed increased social competence, whereas the children in the control group remained stable. Teachers reported significant increases in parents' involvement and contact with school, whereas reports by teachers or parent involvement in the control group remained stable. One year later, when children were in kindergarten, improvements in the mothers' parenting skills and in their children's affect and behavior were maintained and continued to be significantly improved compared with families (Webster-Stratton, 1998). Furthermore, in a subsequent study we replicated these results with 272 Head Start mothers (Webster-Stratton, Reid, & Hammond, 2001a), as have two other independent investigators using the program as a prevention programs with Hispanic families in New York (Miller & Rojas-Flores, 1999; Brotman et al., 2003) and with day care providers and low-income African American mothers who had enrolled their toddlers in day care centers in Chicago (Gross, Fogg, Webster-Stratton, Gavey, & Grady, 2003).

Recently, we completed analyses of the combined data from both previously described Head Start studies in order to evaluate the effectiveness of the Incredible Years parenting program with four cultural groups. The sample included 634 families (370 Caucasian, 120 African American, 73 Asian, and 71 Hispanic) enrolled in 23 Head Start centers. Results indicated that, although there were some baseline differences in risk factors and parenting and child behaviors, there were few differential treatment responses according to ethnicity. All groups showed positive improvements that were sustained 1 year later relative to controls. There was also evidence that the effects of intervention on teachers' bonding with parents was more pronounced for minority mothers than for Caucasian mothers. Parents from all ethnic groups reported high satisfaction levels after the parenting program. Minority parents had even higher attendance rates at parenting groups than Caucasian parents. Results indicated that this program is acceptable and effective for use with diverse populations (Reid & Webster-Stratton, 2001).

In another study using the same combined Head Start population, we analyzed the effect of mothers' mental health risk factors on their engagement in the program and their ability to make positive changes in their parenting skills and children's behaviors. Although mothers with mental health risk factors (i.e., depression, high levels of anger, history of abuse or harsh parenting as a child, and history of substance abuse) exhibited poorer parenting skills than mothers without these risk factors, these risk factors did not prevent the mothers from becoming engaged in the parenting training program. Furthermore, the mothers who had mental health risk factors benefited from the parenting training program at levels that were comparable to the mothers who did not have mental health risk factors, as did their children (Baydar, Reid, & Webster-Stratton, 2003).

Summary and Significance of Parent Training

We hypothesized that because parents are the most powerful—and potentially malleable—influence on young children's social development, intervening with parents would be the most strategic first step. Indeed, our studies have shown that parent training is highly promising as an effective therapeutic method for producing significant behavior change in children with high-risk behaviors (i.e., conduct problems) and with high-risk populations (e.g., socioeconomically disadvantaged children). These findings (Reid, Webster-Stratton, & Baydar, 2004) provide support for the theory that parenting practices play a key role in children's social and emotional development. The parent intervention approach is also inexpensive, with good consumer satisfaction, regardless of parents' educational or socioeconomic background. Approximately 65% of families treated in the clinic achieved sustained improvements in their children's conduct problems. Moreover, our effects were further enhanced when we targeted other parental risk factors, such as marital distress, anger management, and maternal depression, in our ADVANCE intervention. These interventions strengthened parental coping skills and helped buffer the disruptive effects of these personal and interpersonal stressors on parenting and on children's social development. Nonetheless, when we looked at predictors of relapse and the failure of improvements in child behaviors to generalize beyond home to school and peer relationships, our long-term data suggested that our model concerning the development of conduct problems was incomplete. Collaboration with teachers to promote more sustained effects across the home and school settings seemed to be imperative.

Incredible Years Teacher Training Intervention

Rationale for Teacher Training

Once children with behavior problems enter school, negative academic and social experiences make key contributions to the further development of conduct problems. Aggressive, disruptive children quickly become socially excluded. This isolation leads to fewer opportunities to interact socially and to learn appropriate friendship skills. Over time, peers become mistrustful and respond to aggressive children in ways that increase the likelihood of reactive aggression. Evidence suggests that peer rejection eventually leads to these children's association with deviant peers. Once children have formed deviant peer groups, the risk for drug abuse and antisocial behavior is even higher (for a review of this research see Coie, 1990).

Furthermore, researchers (e.g., Brophy, 1996) have found that teacher behaviors and school characteristics (e.g., low emphasis of teachers on social and emotional competence, infrequent praise, little attention to individualizing goals regarding specific social and academic needs for particular children, and high student–teacher ratio) were related to classroom aggressive behaviors, delinquency, and poor academic performance. High-risk children are often clustered in classrooms with a high density of other high-risk students, thus presenting the teacher with additional management challenges. Rejecting and nonsupportive responses from teachers further exacerbate the problems of aggressive children. Such children often develop poor relationships with teachers and receive less support, nurturing, and teaching and more criticism in the classroom. Some evidence suggests that teachers retaliate in a manner similar to parents and peers. Walker, Colvin, and Ramsey (1995) reported that antisocial children were less likely to receive encouragement from teachers for appropriate behavior and more likely to be punished for negative behavior than well-behaved children. Aggressive children are also frequently expelled from classrooms. The lack of teacher support and exclusion from the classroom exacerbate not only these children's social problems but also their academic difficulties; they also contribute to the likelihood of school dropout. Finally, recent research has shown that poorly managed classrooms have higher levels of classroom aggression and rejection that, in turn, influence the continuing escalation of individual child behavior problems (Kellam, Ling, Merisca, Brown, & Ialongo, 1998). A spiraling pattern of negative behavior in the child and reactivity in the teacher can ultimately lead to parent demoralization, withdrawal, and a lack of connection and consistency between the socialization activities of school and home. Although most teachers want to be active partners in facilitating the bonding process with parents, many lack the confidence, skills, or training to work collaboratively with families. Teacher education programs also devote scant attention to ways to build relationships and partnerships with parents and ways to successfully integrate social and emotional literacy curriculum in the academic curriculum.

This literature suggests that for high-risk children to benefit, intervention programs must promote healthy bonds or supportive networks between teachers and parents and between children and teachers. Strong family–school networks benefit children as a result of parents' increased expectations, interest in, and support for their child's social and academic performance and create a consistent socialization process across home and school settings. The negative cycle described previously can be prevented when teachers develop nurturing relationships with students, establish clear classroom rules about bullying, prevent social isolation by peers, and offer a curriculum that includes training students in emotional literacy, social skills, and conflict management. Considerable research has demonstrated that effective classroom management can reduce disruptive behavior and enhance social and academic achievement (Brophy, 1996; Walker, Colvin, & Ramsey, 1995). Well-trained teachers can help aggressive, disruptive, and uncooperative children to develop the appropriate social behavior that is a prerequisite for their success in school.

Content of the Incredible Years Teacher Training Program

The teacher training program is a 4- to 6-day (or 42-hour) program for teachers, school counselors, and psychologists that involves group-based training. Group-based training targets teachers' use of effective classroom management strategies for dealing with misbehavior; promoting positive relationships with difficult students; strengthening social skills in the class-room, as well as the playground, bus, and lunchroom; and strengthening teachers' collaborative process and positive communication with parents (e.g., the importance of positive home phone calls, regular meetings with parents, home visits, and successful parent conferences). For indicated children (i.e., children with conduct disorder), teachers, parents, and group facilitators will jointly develop transition plans detailing classroom strategies that are successful with that individual child; goals achieved and goals still to be worked on; characteristics, interests, and motivators for the child; and ways parents would like to be contacted by teachers. This information is passed on to the following year's teachers. Additionally, teachers learn how to prevent peer rejection by helping the aggressive child learn appropriate problem-solving strategies and helping his or her peers to respond appropriately to aggression. Teachers are encouraged to be sensitive to individual developmental differences (e.g., variation in attention span and activity level) and biological deficits in children (e.g., unresponsiveness to aversive stimuli, heightened interest in novelty) and the relevance of these differences for enhanced teaching efforts that are positive, accepting, and consistent. Physical aggression in unstructured settings (e.g., playground) is targeted for close monitoring, teaching, and incentive programs. A complete description of the content included in this curriculum is described in the book that teachers use for the course, *How to Promote Social and Emotional Competence in Young Children* (Webster-Stratton, 2000; see Table 20.6).

TABLE 20.6
Content and Objectives of the Incredible Years
Teacher Training Program (Ages 4–10 years)

Content	Objectives	Content	Objectives
Program One: The Importance of Teacher Attention, Encouragement, and Praise		**Program Two: Motivating Children Through Incentives**	
	• Using praise and encouragement more effectively • Building children's self-esteem and self-confidence by teaching children how to praise themselves • Understanding the importance of general praise to the whole group as well as individual praise • Knowing the importance of praising social and academic behaviors • Recognizing common traps • Using physical warmth as a reinforcer • Providing nonverbal cues of appreciation • Doubling the impact of praise by involving other school personnel and parents • Helping children learn how to praise others and enjoy others' achievements		• Understanding why incentives are valuable teaching strategies for children with behavior problems • Understanding ways to use an incentive program for social problems such as noncompliance, inattentiveness, lack of cooperation, and hyperactivity as well as for academic problems • Setting up individual incentive programs for particular children • Using group or classroom incentives • Designing programs that have variety and build on the positive relationship between the teacher, child, and parent • Using incentives in a way that fosters the child's internal motivation and focuses on the process of learning rather than the end product • Providing unexpected rewards • Appreciating the importance of involving parents in incentive programs

Content	Objectives	Content	Objectives

Program Three: Preventing Behavior Problems—The Proactive Teacher

- Preparing children for transitions
- Establishing clear, predictable classroom rules
- Using guidelines for giving effective commands or instructions
- Identifying unclear, vague, and negative commands
- Understanding the value of warnings and helpful reminders, especially for distractible and impulsive children
- Engaging children's attention
- Using nonverbal signals and cues for communication
- Recognizing the need for ongoing monitoring and positive attention

Program Four: Decreasing Students' Inappropriate Behavior

- Knowing how to redirect and engage children
- Knowing how and when to ignore inappropriate responses from children
- Using verbal and non-verbal cues to reengage off-task children
- Understanding the importance of reminders and warnings
- Using guidelines for setting up time-out in the classroom
- Avoiding common mistakes in using time-out
- Handling common misbehaviors such as impulsivity, disengagement, noncompliance, tantrums, and disruptive behaviors
- Using the color cards system
- Recognizing when to use logical consequences or removal of privileges as discipline

continues

Content	Objectives	Content	Objectives
Program Five: Building Positive Relationships With Students		**Program Six: How to Teach Social Skills, Problem Solving, and Anger Management in the Classroom**	

Program Five: Building Positive Relationships With Students

- Building positive relationships with difficult students
- Showing students you trust and believe in them
- Fostering students' sense of responsibility for the classroom and their involvement in other students' learning as well as their own
- Giving students choices when possible
- Teaching students how to ask for what they want in appropriate ways
- Fostering listening and speaking skills between students
- Teaching students how to problem solve through role-plays and examples
- Promoting positive self-talk
- Implementing strategies to counter students' negative attributions
- Promoting positive relationships with students' parents

Program Six: How to Teach Social Skills, Problem Solving, and Anger Management in the Classroom

- Helping increase children's awareness of different feelings and perspectives in social situations
- Building children's emotional vocabulary
- Understanding how to help children identify a problem and to generate possible solutions
- Helping children learn to think ahead to different consequences and to different solutions and how to evaluate the most effective solutions
- Helping children recognize their anger and learn ways to manage it successfully
- Using puppets to present hypothetical problem situations such as being teased, bullied, or isolated by other children
- Providing small-group activities to practice friendship, group entry, play, and problem-solving skills
- Helping children learn how to use friendly talk such as giving compliments, providing suggestions, offering apologies, asking for help, and sharing ideas and feelings
- Helping children learn classroom behavior such as listening, quiet hand up, cooperating, and following teacher's directions

Effectiveness of Teacher Training Program With Selective
and Indicated Populations

Our first evaluation of the teacher training curriculum was conducted with teachers of children who had been diagnosed with ODD and CD. The randomized trial included 133 clinic-referred families, the majority (85%) of whom were Caucasian. Families were admitted to the study if their children (ages 4–8) met the *Diagnostic and Statistical Manual of Mental Disorders, Fourth Edition (DSM–IV)* criteria for early onset ODD or CD. Families were randomly assigned to one of six groups: (a) Parent training only (BASIC + ADVANCE) (n = 23); (b) Child training only (Dina Dinosaur Curriculum); (c) Parent training, academic skills training, and teacher training (BASIC + ADVANCE + SCHOOL + TEACHER); (d) Parent training, academic skills training, teacher training, and child training (BASIC + ADVANCE + SCHOOL + TEACHER + CHILD) (n = 22); (e) Child training and teacher training (CHILD + TEACHER) (n = 40); and (f) wait-list control group.

The parent training–only group received 22 two-hour weekly sessions covering the BASIC and ADVANCE components described previously. Those assigned to the child training–only group received 18 to 22 weeks of the Dina Dinosaur curriculum described in the next section. The third condition included the BASIC and ADVANCE program, as well as the academic skills (SCHOOL) and teacher training (TEACHER) programs. In this evaluation, the teacher program consisted of four full-day workshops offered monthly and a minimum of two school consultations, in which the parent and group facilitator met with the teacher to create an individual behavior plan for the targeted child. Clinic therapists made periodic phone calls to teachers to support their efforts and keep them apprised of the progress of the child at home. Families in the wait-list control condition were randomly assigned to the parent training condition after 8 or 9 months.

Immediately after testing, results indicated that combining parent academic-skills training with training for teachers improves children's outcomes by strengthening academic and social skills in the classroom, promoting more positive peer relationships, and reducing behavior problems at school and home. Classroom observations of teacher behavior showed that trained teachers were rated as less critical, harsh, and inconsistent and more nurturing than control teachers. Classroom atmosphere was also consistently better for those receiving teacher training. In addition, children in the teacher-training conditions showed significant increases in prosocial behaviors and academic competence and decreases in aggressive and antisocial behaviors, according to teacher report. Children whose teachers received the training were also observed by independent raters to improve in measures of peer aggression during structured and unstructured situations compared with children in the control group. In summary, short-term results indicated that when teacher training was added to either parent training or child training, the effects on children's behaviors were enhanced at school over and above what would have been achieved by either intervention alone. Not only was aggressive behavior apparently reduced, social and academic behaviors were strengthened in the intervention conditions that added teacher training (Webster-Stratton, Reid, & Hammond, 2004).

Our second study evaluating the teacher training curriculum was conducted with 61 Head Start teachers and 272 mothers. Fourteen Head Start centers (34 classrooms) were randomly assigned to (a) an experimental condition in which parents, teachers, and family service workers participated in the prevention program (Incredible Years parent and teacher programs) or (b) a control condition consisting of the regular Head Start program (control). Results indicated that parent–teacher bonding was significantly higher for mothers in the experimental group than for mothers in the control group. Children in the experimental group showed significantly fewer conduct problems at school than children in the control group. After training, teachers in the experimental group showed significantly better classroom management skills than teachers in the control group (Webster-Stratton & Hammond, 1997). The teacher training curriculum has also been evaluated by an independent investigator studying its use among day care providers in Massachusetts, with significant results according to teacher reports (Arnold, Griffith, Ortiz, & Stowe, 1998).

Incredible Years Child Training Intervention

Rationale for Child Training

Moffit and Lynam (1994) have argued that some abnormal aspect of the child's internal organization at the physiological, neurological, and neuropsychological levels (which may be genetically transmitted) is linked to the development of CD, particularly for those whose conduct problems begin early in life. Children with conduct problems have been reported to be more likely to have certain temperamental characteristics, such as inattentiveness, impulsivity, and attention-deficit/hyperactivity disorder (ADHD; Lillenfield & Waldman, 1990). Researchers interested in the biological aspects of the development of conduct problems have investigated variables such as neurotransmitters, autonomic arousal system, skin conductance, and hormonal influences, and some findings suggest that such children may have low autonomic reactivity (i.e., low physiological response to stimuli). Other factors have also been implicated in child conduct disorder. For example, deficits in social–cognitive skills have been shown to contribute to poor emotional regulation and aggressive peer interactions (Dodge & Price, 1994). Additionally, studies indicate that children with conduct problems have significant delays in their peer play skills—in particular, difficulty with reciprocal play, cooperative skills, turn taking, waiting, and giving suggestions (Webster-Stratton & Lindsay, 1999).

Finally, reading, learning, and language delays are also implicated in children with conduct problems, particularly for early life course persisters (Moffitt & Lynam, 1994). Low academic achievement often manifests itself in these children during the elementary grades and continues through high school. The relationship between academic performance and ODD or CD is bidirectional. Academic difficulties may cause disengagement, increased frustration, and lower self-esteem, which contribute to the child's behavior problems. At the same time, noncompliance, aggression, elevated activity levels, and poor attention limit a child's ability to be engaged in learning and achieve academically. Thus, a cycle is created in which one problem exacerbates the other. This combination of academic delays and conduct problems appears to contribute to the development of more severe CD and school failure.

The current research concerning the possible biological, sociocognitive, and academic or developmental deficits in children with conduct problems suggests the need for training programs that help parents and teachers understand children's biological deficits (their unresponsiveness to aversive stimuli and heightened interest in novelty) and support their use of effective parenting and teaching approaches so that they can continue to provide positive, consistent responses. The data regarding autonomic underarousal theory suggest that these children may require overteaching (i.e., repeated learning trials) to learn to inhibit undesirable behaviors and manage emotion. Parents and teachers must use consistent, clear, specific limit setting that uses simple language and concrete cues and reminders. Additionally, this information suggests the need to directly intervene with children, focusing on their particular social learning needs, such as problem solving, perspective taking, and play skills, as well as literacy and special academic needs.

One reason that the improvements in child behavior resulting from parenting training does not reliably generalize from home to schools might be the exclusive focus on parent skills as the locus of change—that is, the lack of attention in intervention programs to the role that child factors play in the development of conduct problems.

Content and Process of the Child Social Skills and Problem-Solving Training Intervention (Dinosaur Curriculum)

Our efforts to create a developmentally appropriate, theory-based intervention for aggressive preschool and early school-aged children were guided both by the available literature and by our own observations comparing children with OD and CD with behaviorally normal children (Webster-Stratton & Lindsay, 1999). Traditional social skills training programs typically did not have content directly relevant to CD and aggression. Our program targets selected child risk factors (problem-solving and social skills deficits, peer rejection, loneliness, and negative attributions) and directly uses the child as an agent of change. The intervention is designed to enhance children's school behaviors and promote social competence and positive peer interactions, as well as nonaggressive conflict management strategies. In addition, the program teaches children how to successfully integrate themselves into the classroom, how to develop friendships, and how to play successfully with peers.

This 22-week program consists of a series of nine videotape programs (over 100 vignettes) that teach children problem-solving and social skills. Organized to dovetail with the content of the parent training program, the program consists of seven main components: (a) introduction and rules (1–2 sessions); (b) empathy training (2–3 sessions); (c) problem-solving training (3–4 sessions); (d) anger control (2–3 sessions); (e) friendship skills (3–4 sessions); (f) communication skills (2–3 sessions); and (g) school training. The children come to our clinic once a week to meet in small groups of six children for 2 hours. In this curriculum, we use videotape modeling examples in every session to foster discussion, problem solving, and modeling of prosocial behaviors. To enhance generalization, the scenes selected for each of the units involve real-life conflict situations at home and at school (playground and classroom). The tapes are paused so that the children can discuss feelings, generate ideas for more effective responses, and create alternative scenarios through role-playing exercises. In addition to interactive videotape modeling teaching, the therapists use life-size puppets to model appropriate behavior and thinking processes for the children. The use of puppets appeals to children on the fantasy level, which is very important for children in this preoperational age group. Because young children are more vulnerable to distraction, are less able to organize their thoughts, and have poorer memories, we use a number of strategies for reviewing and organizing the material to be remembered: (a) playing "copy cat" to review skills learned; (b) using many videotape examples of the same concept in different situations and settings; (c) using cartoon pictures and specially designed stickers as cues to remind children of key concepts; (d) engaging in role-playing exercises with puppets and other children to provide not only practice opportunities but also experience with different perspectives; (e) re-enacting videotape scenes; (f) acting out visual story examples of key ideas; (g) rehearsing skills with play, art, and game activities; (h) sending homework so children can practice key skills with parents; and (i) sending letters to parents and teachers that explain the key concepts children are learning and asking them to reinforce these behaviors whenever they see them occurring throughout the week. For example, if the concept being taught is teamwork, teachers and parents will be asked to reinforce any examples they see of children sharing, helping, and cooperating during the week and to give the child a note about these behaviors, which is to be brought to the next session. (Teachers and parents receive special Dinosaur notes that they may use with the children.) More details about this intervention can be found in Webster-Stratton and Reid (2003); see also Table 20.7.

Child Dinosaur School Effectiveness With Indicated Populations (Children With ODD and CD)

To date, two randomized studies have evaluated the effectiveness of the child training program for reducing conduct problems and promoting social competence in children diagnosed with ODD and CD. In the first study, 97 clinic-referred children (72 boys and 25 girls), ages 4 to 7, and their parents (95 mothers and 71 fathers) were randomly assigned to one of four groups: a parent training treatment group (PT: BASIC + ADVANCE), a child training group (CT), a child and parent training group (CT + PT), or a wait-list control group (CON). Posttreatment assessments indicated that all three treatment conditions had resulted in significant improvements in comparison with controls. Comparisons of the three treatment conditions indicated that children in the CT and CT + PT groups showed significant improvements in problem solving as well as conflict management skills, as measured

TABLE 20.7
Content and Objectives of the Incredible Years
Child Training Programs (a.k.a. Dina Dinosaur Social Skills
and Problem-Solving Curriculum) (Ages 4–8 Years)

Content	Objectives	Content	Objectives
Program One: Making Friends and Learning School Rules		**Program Two: Understanding and Detecting Feelings**	
Introduction to Dinosaur School	• Understanding the importance of rules • Participating in the process of rule making • Understanding what will happen if rules are broken • Learning how to earn rewards for good behaviors • Learning to build friendships	Part 1: Wally Teaches Clues to Detecting Feelings Part 2: Wally Teaches Clues to Understanding Feelings	• Learning words for different feelings • Learning how to tell how someone is feeling from verbal and nonverbal expressions • Increasing awareness of nonverbal facial communication used to portray feelings • Learning different ways to relax • Understanding why different feelings occur • Understanding feelings from different perspectives • Practicing talking about feelings

continues

TABLE 20.7 (Continued)
Content and Objectives of the Incredible Years
Child Training Programs (a.k.a. Dina Dinosaur Social Skills
and Problem-Solving Curriculum) (Ages 4–8 Years)

Content	Objectives	Content	Objectives
Program Three: Detective Wally Teaches Problem-Solving Steps			
Part 1: Identifying Problems and Solutions Part 2: Finding More Solutions Part 3: Thinking of Consequences	• Learning how to identify a problem • Thinking of solutions to hypothetical problems • Learning verbal assertive skills • Learning how to inhibit impulsive reactions • Understanding what apology means • Thinking of alternative solutions to problem situations such as being teased and hit • Learning to understand that solutions have different consequences • Learning how to critically evaluate solutions—one's own and others	Part 4: Detective Wally Teaches How to Control Anger Part 5: Problem Solving	• Recognizing that anger can interfere with good problem solving • Understanding Tiny Turtle's story about managing anger and getting help • Understanding when apologies are helpful • Recognizing anger in themselves and others • Understanding anger is okay to feel "inside" but not to act out by hitting or hurting someone else • Learning how to control anger reactions • Understanding that things that happen to them are not necessarily hostile or deliberate attempts to hurt them • Practicing alternative responses to being teased, bullied, or yelled at by an angry adult • Learning skills to cope with another person's anger

TABLE 20.7 (Continued)
Content and Objectives of the Incredible Years
Child Training Programs (a.k.a. Dina Dinosaur Social Skills
and Problem-Solving Curriculum) (Ages 4–8 Years)

Content	Objectives	Content	Objectives
Program Four: Molly Manners Teaches How to Be Friendly		**Program Five: Molly Manners Explains How to Talk With Friends**	
Part 1: Helping Part 2: Sharing Part 3: Teamwork at School Part 4: Teamwork at Home	• Learning what friendship means and how to be friendly • Understanding ways to help others • Learning the concept of sharing and the relationship between sharing and helping • Learning what teamwork means • Understanding the benefits of sharing, helping and teamwork • Practicing friendship skills		• Learning how to ask questions and tell something to a friend • Learning how to listen carefully to what a friend is saying • Understanding why it is important to speak up about something that is bothering you • Understanding how and when to give an apology or compliment • Learning how to enter into a group of children who are already playing • Learning how to make a suggestion rather than give commands • Practicing friendship skills

Program Six: Dina Dinosaur Teaches You How to Do Your Best in School

Content	Objectives
Part 1: Listening, Waiting, Quiet Hands Up Part 2: Concentrating, Checking, and Co-operating	• Learning how to listen, wait, avoid interruptions, and put up a quiet hand to ask questions in class • Learning how to handle other children who poke fun and interfere with the child's ability to work at school • Learning how to stop, think, and check work first • Learning the importance of cooperation with the teacher and other children • Practicing concentrating and good classroom skills

by observations of their interactions with a best friend; differences among treatment conditions on these measures consistently favored the CT condition over the PT condition. As for parent and child behavior at home, parents and children in the PT and CT + PT groups had significantly more positive interactions in comparison with parents and children in the CT group.

One-year follow-up assessments indicated that all the significant changes noted immediately after treatment had been maintained over time. Moreover, child conduct problems at home had significantly lessened over time. Analyses of the clinical significance of the results suggested that the combined CT + PT condition produced the most significant improvements in child behavior at 1 year follow-up (Webster-Stratton & Hammond, 1997).

Who Benefits From Dinosaur Child Training?

Families of 99 children (ages 4–8 years) with ODD and CD, who were randomly assigned to either the child training treatment group or the control group, were examined in terms of the impact of three categories of risk factors (child hyperactivity, parenting style, and family stress) on treatment outcome. The hyperactivity and family stress risk factors did not seem to affect the children's ability to benefit from the child treatment program. By far the most important risk factor was negative parenting. Fewer children who had parents with one of the negative parenting risk factors (high criticisms or physical spanking) showed clinically significant improvements compared with children who did not have a negative parenting risk factor. This finding suggests that for children whose parents exhibit harsh and coercive parenting styles, a parenting intervention in addition to a child intervention is necessary (Webster-Stratton, Reid, & Hammond, 2001b).

RECOMMENDATIONS AND FUTURE DIRECTIONS

In light of the research on risk factors over the past decade, which indicate the relationships between child and school risk factors and child conduct problems, treatment programs for children's conduct problems must address these risk factors as well as family and parent factors. Our latest studies with clinic populations suggest that adding teacher and child training components significantly enhances the effectiveness of treatment for such children.

We hypothesize that the more proactive and powerful approach to the problem of escalating aggression in young children would be to offer parent, teacher, and child training curriculum in strengthening social and emotional competence in schools as a school-based prevention intervention model for all children. Our reasons for this are threefold: First, offering interventions in schools makes programs more accessible to families and eliminates some of the stigma associated with services offered in traditional mental health settings, as well as some practical and social barriers (e.g., lack of transportation). Second, offering interventions in schools allows such programs to be available before children's common behavior problems have escalated to the point that they require extensive clinical treatment. Moreover, when intervention is offered in natural communities, these communities become strengthened as a source of support for teachers and parents. A third advantage of interventions delivered by on-site school staff is the sheer number of high-risk families and children who can be reached at comparatively low cost. Finally, offering a social and emotional curriculum such as the Dinosaur School program to the entire class is less stigmatizing than creating a separate group and more likely to result in sustained effects across settings and time. Although we have shown that a child can learn new skills in separate sessions, the skills do not necessarily generalize back to the classroom. Because the peers have not been part of the intervention, peers will still react to the target child in negative ways because of his or her negative reputation. Including all the children in the intervention provides more opportunity for more prosocial children to model appropriate social and conflict management skills and provides the entire classroom with a common vocabulary and problem-solving steps to use in resolving everyday conflicts. Thus, social competence is strengthened for the lower-risk children, those with internalizing problems (e.g., social withdrawal and anxiety), as well as for the aggressive children, and the classroom environment generally fosters appropriate social skills on an ongoing basis. Additionally, with a classroom-based model, the dosage of intervention is magnified as teachers provide reinforcement of the key concepts throughout the day and week.

We are currently engaged in a randomized study evaluating the effects of a school-based intervention with two levels of intervention: (a) a universal intervention that includes teacher training and the Dinosaur School for all children in the classroom via a curriculum spanning preschool through second grade and (b) an indicated intervention that includes parent training (BASIC + SCHOOL + ADVANCE) offered over two grade levels for parents of the children who are exhibiting high-risk behaviors. Preliminary results are very promising. More information about the classroom-based version of Dinosaur School can be found elsewhere (Webster-Stratton & Reid, 2004).

Future research on children with ODD and CD should focus on the specific characteristics of families and children and how they relate to treatment outcome using various combinations of treatments. For example, because approximately 40% to 50% of young children with ODD and CD are also co-morbid for attention deficit disorder, learning delays, and internalizing problems, knowing how these children respond to treatment and whether these are the children that would benefit from the multifaceted interventions would seem particularly important. Long-term follow-ups of these interventions are also needed to assess their ultimate impact on later development of delinquency, substance abuse, and antisocial behavior.

SUMMARY

In summary, a review of our own research suggests that comprehensive interactive videotape training methods are highly promising, especially for training those who work with young children with conduct problems and for high-risk populations such as Head Start. Our most effective parent intervention involved videotape training not only in parenting skills but also in marital communication, problem solving and conflict resolution, and ways to foster children's academic competence, as well as their social and emotional competence. These findings have pointed to the need for interventions that help strengthen families' protective factors—specifically, parents' interpersonal skills and coping skills—so that they can cope more effectively with their added stresses. Our research has also suggested that child and teacher training is a highly effective strategy for building social skills, problem-solving strategies, and peer relationships in young children with conduct problems. The child training program seems to be particularly helpful for children with conduct problems who are comorbid for ADHD and for children with peer relationship difficulties.

Our intervention studies, which target different combinations of risk factors, can be seen as an indirect test of the different theoretical models regarding the development of conduct disorders. We started with a simple parenting skills deficit model and have evolved to a more complex interactional model. In our current model, we hypothesize that the child's eventual outcome will depend on the interrelationship between child, parent (or parents), teacher (or teachers), and peer risk factors. Therefore, the most effective interventions should be those that involve schools, teachers, and the child's peer group. Optimally, one would assess these risk factors and determine the right match of program to the particular needs or risk factors of the family, child and school. Table 20.8 demonstrates the way treatment components may be combined depending on the risk status of the population and the pervasiveness of the child's problems.

Ideally a continuum of services should be provided to young children that assist children and families before diagnosed problems emerge; these services should also prevent those children who do have conduct problems from continuing on that trajectory. Given the increasing rates of aggression in younger children and the continuity of the problem from early childhood through adolescence and often into adulthood—with its implication for the intergenerational transmission of violence—the chance of breaking the link in the cycle of disadvantage is a public health matter of the utmost importance.

TABLE 20.8
Selecting Program Components According to Risk Status of Population,
Age, and Pervasiveness of Child's Problems

Settings	Minimum core program	Recommended supplemental programs for special populations
Prevention Programs for Selected Populations*		
Preschool, day care, Head Start, schools— grades K–3, public health centers	BASIC (12 to 14, 2-hour weekly sessions)	ADVANCE Parent Program for highly stressed families
		SCHOOL Parent Program for children, kindergarten to Grade 3
		Child Dinosaur Program if child's problems are pervasive at home and school
		TEACHER Classroom Management Program if teachers have high numbers of students with behavior problems or if teachers have not received this training previously
Treatment Programs for Indicated Populations**		
Mental health centers, pediatric clinics, HMOs	BASIC and ADVANCE (22 to 24, 2-hour weekly sessions)	Child Dinosaur Program if child's problems are pervasive at home and at school
		TEACHER Program if child's problems are pervasive at home and at school
		SCHOOL Program for parents if child has academic problems.

*"High-risk" populations without overt behavior or conduct problems.
**Children exhibiting behavior problems or diagnosed conduct disorders.

REFERENCES

Arnold, D. H., Griffith, J. R., Ortiz, C., & Stowe, R. M. (1998). Day care interactions and teacher perceptions as a function of teacher and child ethnic group. *Journal of Research in Childhood Education, 12,* 143–154.

Bandura, A. (1989). Regulation of cognitive processes through perceived self-efficacy. *Developmental Psychology, 25,* 729–735.

Baydar, N., Reid, J. B., & Webster-Stratton, C. (2003). Who benefits from school-based preventive parent training programs? The role of mother mental health factors and program engagement. *Child Development, 74,* 279–291.

Beauchaine, T. P., Webster-Stratton, C., & Reid, M. J. (in press). Mediators, moderators, and predictors of one-year outcomes among children treated for early-onset conduct problems: A latent growth curve analysis. *Journal of Consulting and Clinical Psychology.*

Beck, A. T. (1979). *Cognitive therapy and emotional disorders*. New York: New American Library.

Bowlby, J. (1980). *Attachment and loss: Loss, sadness, and depression*. New York: Basic Books.

Brestan, E. V., & Eyberg, S. M. (1998). Effective psychosocial treatments of conduct-disordered children and adolescents: 29 years, 82 studies, and 5,272 kids. *Journal of Clinical Child Psychology, 27*, 180–189.

Brophy, J. E. (1996). *Teaching problem students*. New York: Guilford Press.

Brotman, L. M., Klein, R. G., Kamboukos, D., Brown, E. J., Coard, S. I., & Sosinsky, L. S. (2003). Preventive intervention for urban, low-income preschoolers at familial risk for conduct problems: A randomized pilot study. *Journal of Clinical Child and Adolescent Psychology, 32*, 246–257.

Campbell, S. (1995). Behavior problems in preschool children: A review of recent research. *Journal of Child Psychology and Psychiatry and Allied Disciplines, 36*, 113–149.

Coie, J. D. (1990). Toward a theory of peer rejection. In S. R. Asher & J. D. Coie (Eds.), *Peer rejection in childhood* (pp. 365–398). Cambridge, England: Cambridge University Press.

Coie, J. D., Watt, N. F., West, S. G., Hawkins, D., Asarnow, J. R., Markman, H. J., et al. (1993). The science of prevention: A conceptual framework and some directions for a national research program. *American Psychologist, 48*, 1013–1022.

D'Zurilla, T. J., & Nezu, A. (1982). Social problem-solving in adults. In P. C. Kendall (Ed.), *Advances in cognitive behavioral research and therapy* (Vol. 1). New York: Academic Press.

Dadds, M. R., & Powell, M. B. (1991). The relationship of interpersonal conflict and marital adjustment to aggression, anxiety and immaturity in aggressive and nonclinic children. *Journal of Abnormal Child Psychology, 19*, 553–567.

Deater-Deckard, K., Dodge, K. A., Bates, J. E., & Pettit, G. S. (1996). Physical discipline among African-American and European-American mothers: Links to children's externalizing behaviors. *Developmental Psychology, 32*, 1065–1072.

Dishion, T. J., French, D. C., & Patterson, G. R. (1995). The development and ecology of antisocial behavior. In D. Cicchetti & D. J. Cohen (Eds.), *Developmental psychopathology, Vol. 2: Risk disorder and adaptation* (pp. 421–471). New York: Wiley.

Dodge, K. A., & Price, J. M. (1994). On the relation between social information processing and socially competent behavior in early school-aged children. *Child Development, 65*, 1385–1397.

Doll, B., & Lyon, M. A. (1998). Risk and resilience: Implications for the delivery of educational and mental health services in schools. *School Psychology Review, 27*, 348–363.

Eyberg, S. M., Boggs, S., & Algina, J. (1995). Parent–child interaction therapy: A psychosocial model for the treatment of young children with conduct problem behavior and their families. *Psychopharmacology Bulletin, 31*, 83–91.

Forehand, R. L., & McMahon, R. J. (1981). *Helping the noncompliant child: A clinician's guide to parent training*. New York: Guilford Press.

Gottman, J., Notarius, C., Gonso, J., & Markman, A. (1976). *A couple's guide to communication*. Champaign, IL: Research Press.

Griest, D. L., Forehand, R., Rogers, T., Breiner, J., Furey, W., & Williams, C. A. (1982). Effects of parent enhancement therapy on the treatment of outcome and generalization of a parent training program. *Behaviour Research and Therapy, 20*, 429–436.

Gross, D., Fogg, L., Webster-Stratton, C., Garvey, C. W. J., & Grady, J. (2003). Parent training with families of toddlers in day care in low-income urban communities. *Journal of Consulting and Clinical Psychology, 71*, 261–278.

Grych, J. H., & Finchman, F. D. (1992). Interventions for children of divorce: Toward greater integration of research and action. *Psychological Bulletin, 111*, 434–454.

Hanf, E., & Kling, J. (1973). *Facilitating parent–child interactions: A two-stage training model*. Portland: University of Oregon Medical School.

Hartman, R. R., Stage, S., & Webster-Stratton, C. (2003). A growth curve analysis of parent training outcomes: Examining the influence of child factors (inattention, impulsivity, and hyperactivity problems), parental and family risk factors. *The Child Psychology and Psychiatry Journal, 44*, 388–398.

Jacobson, N., Schmaling, K. B., & Holtzworth-Monroe, A. (1987). Component analyses of behavioral marital therapy: Two-year follow-up and prediction of relapse. *Journal of Consulting and Clinical Psychology, 13*, 187–195.

Jacobson, N. S., & Margolin, G. (1979). *Marital therapy: Strategies based on social learning and behavior as exchange principles*. New York: Brunner/Mazel.

Jouriles, E. N., Norwood, W. D., McDonald, R., Vincent, J. P., & Mahoney, A. (1996). Physical violence and other forms of marital aggression: Links with children's behavior problems. *Journal of Family Psychology, 10*, 223–234.

Kellam, S. G., Ling, X., Merisca, R., Brown, C. H., & Ialongo, N. (1998). The effect of the level of aggression in the first grade classroom on the course and malleability of aggressive behavior into middle school. *Development and Psychopathology, 10*, 165–185.

Lahey, B. B., Loeber, R. L., Quay, H. C., Frick, P. J., & Grimm, J. (1992). Oppositional defiant and conduct disorders: Issue to be resolved for DSM–IV. *Journal of the American Academy of Child and Adolescent Psychiatry, 31*, 539–546.

Lewinsohn, P. M., Antonuccio, D. O., Steinmetz, S. L., & Teni, L. (1984). *The coping with depression course*. Eugene, OR: Castalia.

Lillenfield, S. O., & Waldman, I. D. (1990). The relation between childhood attention-deficit hyperactivity disorders and adult antisocial behavior reexamined: The problem of heterogeneity. *Clinical Psychology Review, 10*, 669–725.

Loeber, R. (1991). Antisocial behavior: More enduring than changeable? *Journal of the American Academy of Child and Adolescent Psychiatry, 30*, 393–397.

Loeber, R., & Farrington, D. P. (2000). Young children who commit crime: Epidemiology, developmental origins, risk factors, early interventions, and policy implications. *Developmental Psychopathology, 12*, 737–762.

Loeber, R., Wung, P., Keenan, K., Giroux, B., Stouthamer-Loeber, M., Van Kammen, W. B., et al. (1993). Developmental pathways in disruptive child behavior. *Development Psychopathology, 5*, 103–133.

McMahon, R. J., & Forehand, R. (1984). Parent training for the noncompliant child: Treatment outcome, generalization, and adjunctive therapy procedures. In R. F. Dangel & R. A. Polster (Eds.), *Parent training: Foundations of research and practice* (pp. 298–328). New York: Guilford Press.

Meichenbaum, D. (1993). Changing conceptions of cognitive behavior modification: Retrospect and prospect. *Journal of Consulting and Clinical Psychology, 61*, 202–204.

Miller, L. S., & Rojas-Flores, L. (1999). *Preventing conduct problems in urban, Latino preschoolers through parent training: A pilot study.* New York: New York University Child Study Center.

Moffitt, T. E., & Lynam, D. (1994). The neuropsychology of conduct disorder and delinquency: Implications for understanding antisocial behavior. In D. C. Fowles, P. Sutker, & S. H. Goodman (Eds.), *Progress in experimental personality and psychopathology research* (pp. 233–262). New York: Springer.

O'Dell, S. L. (1985). Progress in parent training. *Progress in Behavior Modification, 19*, 57–108.

Patterson, G. R. (1976). *Living with children: New methods for parents and teachers.* Champaign, IL: Research Press.

Patterson, G. R. (1982). *Coercive family process.* Eugene, OR: Castalia.

Patterson, G. R. (1986). Performance models for antisocial boys. *American Psychologist, 41*, 432–444.

Patterson, G. R., Capaldi, D., & Bank, L. (1991). An early starter model for predicting delinquency. In D. J. Pepler & K. H. Rubin (Eds.), *The development and treatment of childhood aggression* (pp. 139–168). Hillsdale, NJ: Erlbaum.

Reid, M. J., & Webster-Stratton, C. (2001). Parent training with low-income, minority parents: A comparison of treatment response in African American, Asian American, Caucasian and Hispanic mothers. *Prevention Science, 2*, 209–227.

Reid, M. J., Webster-Stratton, C., & Baydar, N. (2004). Halting the development of externalizing behaviors in Head Start children: The effects of parenting training. *Journal of Clinical Child and Adolescent Psychology, 33*, 279–291.

Reid, M. J., Webster-Stratton, C., & Hammond, M. (in press). Follow-up of children who received the Incredible Years Intervention for Oppositional Defiant Disorder: Maintenance and prediction of 2-year outcome. *Journal of Abnormal Child Psychology.*

Resnick, M. D., Bearman, P. S., Blum, R. W., Bauman, K. E., Harris, K. M., & Jones, R. (1997). Protecting adolescents from harm: Findings from the National Longitudinal Study on Adolescent Health. *Journal of the American Medical Association, 278*, 823–832.

Scott, S., Spender, Q., Doolan, M., Jacobs, B., & Aspland, H. (2001). Multicentre controlled trial of parenting groups for child antisocial behaviour in clinical practice. *British Medical Journal, 323,* 1–5.

Shure, M. (1994). *I can problem solve (ICPS): An interpersonal cognitive problem-solving program for children.* Champaign, IL: Research Press.

Snyder, H. (2001). Epidemiology of official offending. In R. Loeber & D. Farrington (Eds.), *Child delinquents: development, intervention and service needs* (pp. 25–46). Thousand Oaks, CA: Sage.

Spaccarelli, S., Cotler, S., & Penman, D. (1992). Problem-solving skills training as a supplement to behavioral parent training. *Cognitive Therapy and Research, 16,* 1–18.

Strain, P. S., Steele, P., Ellis, T., & Timm, M. A. (1982). Long-term effects of oppositional child treatment with mothers as therapists and therapist trainers. *Journal of Applied Behavior Analysis, 15,* 1163–1169.

Taylor, T. K., Schmidt, F., Pepler, D., & Hodgins, H. (1998). A comparison of eclectic treatment with Webster-Stratton's parents and children series in a children's mental health center: A randomized controlled trial. *Behavior Therapy, 29,* 221–240.

Wahler, R. G., & Dumas, J. E. (1984). Changing the observational coding styles of insular and noninsular mothers: A step toward maintenance of parent training effects. In R. F. Dangel & R. A. Polster (Eds.), *Parent training: Foundations of research and practice* (pp. 379–416). New York: Guilford Press.

Walker, H. M., Colvin, G., & Ramsey, E. (1995). *Antisocial behavior in school: Strategies and best practices.* Pacific Grove, CA: Brooks/Cole.

Webster-Stratton, C. (1981). Modification of mothers' behaviors and attitudes through a videotape modeling group discussion program. *Behavior Therapy, 12,* 634–642.

Webster-Stratton, C. (1982). Teaching mothers through videotape modeling to change their children's behaviors. *Journal of Pediatric Psychology, 7,* 279–294.

Webster-Stratton, C. (1984). Randomized trial of two parent-training programs for families with conduct-disordered children. *Journal of Consulting and Clinical Psychology, 52,* 666–678.

Webster-Stratton, C. (1990a). Enhancing the effectiveness of self-administered videotape parent training for families with conduct-problem children. *Journal of Abnormal Child Psychology, 18,* 479–492.

Webster-Stratton, C. (1990b). Long-term follow-up of families with young conduct problem children: From preschool to grade school. *Journal of Clinical Child Psychology, 19,* 144–149.

Webster-Stratton, C. (1990c). Stress: A potential disruptor of parent perceptions and family interactions. *Journal of Clinical Child Psychology, 19,* 302–312.

Webster-Stratton, C. (1992a). *The incredible years: A trouble-shooting guide for parents of children ages 3–8 years.* Toronto, Canada: Umbrella Press.

Webster-Stratton, C. (1992b). Individually administered videotape parent training: Who benefits? *Cognitive Therapy and Research, 16,* 31–35.

Webster-Stratton, C. (1994). Advancing videotape parent training: A comparison study. *Journal of Consulting and Clinical Psychology, 62*, 583–593.

Webster-Stratton, C. (1998). Preventing conduct problems in Head Start children: Strengthening parent competencies. *Journal of Consulting and Clinical Psychology, 66*, 715–730.

Webster-Stratton, C. (2000). *How to promote social and academic competence in young children.* London: Sage.

Webster-Stratton, C., & Hammond, M. (1990). Predictors of treatment outcome in parent training for families with conduct problem children. *Behavior Therapy, 21*, 319–337.

Webster-Stratton, C., & Hammond, M. (1997). Treating children with early-onset conduct problems: A comparison of child and parent training interventions. *Journal of Consulting and Clinical Psychology, 65*, 93–109.

Webster-Stratton, C., & Hammond, M. (1999). Marital conflict management skills, parenting style, and early-onset conduct problems: Processes and pathways. *Journal of Child Psychology and Psychiatry, 40*, 917–927.

Webster-Stratton, C., & Hancock, L. (1998). Parent training: Content, methods and processes. In E. Schaefer (Ed.), *Handbook of parent training, second edition* (pp. 98–152). New York: Wiley.

Webster-Stratton, C., & Herbert, M. (1994). *Troubled families—problem children: Working with parents: A collaborative process.* New York: Wiley.

Webster-Stratton, C., Hollinsworth, T., & Kolpacoff, M. (1989). The long-term effectiveness and clinical significance of three cost-effective training programs for families with conduct-problem children. *Journal of Consulting and Clinical Psychology, 57*, 550–553.

Webster-Stratton, C., Kolpacoff, M., & Hollinsworth, T. (1988). Self-administered videotape therapy for families with conduct-problem children: Comparison with two cost-effective treatments and a control group. *Journal of Consulting and Clinical Psychology, 56*, 558–566.

Webster-Stratton, C., & Lindsay, D. W. (1999). Social competence and early-onset conduct problems: Issues in assessment. *Journal of Child Clinical Psychology, 28*, 25–93.

Webster-Stratton, C., & Reid, M. J. (2003). Treating conduct problems and strengthening social emotional competence in young children (ages 4–8 years): The Dina Dinosaur treatment program. *Journal of Emotional and Behavioral Disorders, 11*, 130–143.

Webster-Stratton, C., & Reid, M. J. (2004). Strengthening social and emotional competence in young children—The foundation for early school readiness and success: Incredible Years classroom social skills and problem-solving curriculum. *Journal of Infants and Young Children, 17*, 96–113.

Webster-Stratton, C., Reid, M. J., & Hammond, M. (2001a). Preventing conduct problems, promoting social competence: A parent and teacher training partnership in Head Start. *Journal of Clinical Child Psychology, 30*, 283–302.

Webster-Stratton, C., Reid, M. J., & Hammond, M. (2001b). Social skills and problem solving training for children with early-onset conduct problems: Who benefits? *Journal of Child Psychology and Psychiatry, 42,* 943–952.

Webster-Stratton, C., Reid, M. J., & Hammond, M. (2004). Treating children with early-onset conduct problems: Intervention outcomes for parent, child, and teacher training. *Journal of Clinical Child and Adolescent Psychology, 33,* 105–124.

Webster-Stratton, C., & Spitzer, A. (1996). Parenting a young child with conduct problems: New insights using grounded theory methods. In T. H. Ollendick & R. S. Prinz (Eds.), *Advances in clinical child psychology* (pp. 333–355). Hillsdale, NJ: Erlbaum.

Whitehurst, G. J., Falco, F., Lonigan, C. J., Fischel, J. E., Valdez-Menchaca, M. C., & Caulfield, M. (1988). Accelerating language development through picture book reading. *Developmental Psychology, 24,* 552–558.

21

MULTIDIMENSIONAL TREATMENT FOSTER CARE: A COMMUNITY SOLUTION FOR BOYS AND GIRLS REFERRED FROM JUVENILE JUSTICE

PATRICIA CHAMBERLAIN AND DANA K. SMITH

INTRODUCTION

In most communities, the options for treating children and adolescents with severe conduct problems are limited and costly, and their effectiveness is untested. In severe cases, in which family members are unable to prevent their youngsters from committing illegal and sometimes violent acts in the community, the need for effective models of out-of-home care is evident. Although numerous and diverse types of treatment models are cur-

This chapter was written with support provided by the National Institute of Mental Health (NIMH) Grants No. R01 MH 54257, Center for Studies of Violent Behavior and Traumatic Stress, NIMH, U.S. PHS; R01 MH60195, Child and Adolescent Treatment and Preventive Intervention Research Branch, DSIR, NIMH, U.S. PHS; P30 MH 46690, Prevention and Behavioral Medicine Research Branch, Division of Epidemiology and Services Research, NIMH, U.S. PHS and the Office of Research on Minority Health. Correspondence concerning this chapter should be addressed to Patricia Chamberlain, Oregon Social Learning Center, 160 East 4th Avenue, Eugene, OR 97401. Electronic mail may be sent to pattic@oslc.org.

rently used to provide a wide array of services in a variety of placement settings (e.g., hospital inpatient units, residential care centers, state training schools), few controlled studies have evaluated the effectiveness and limitations of these settings or models of care. In fact, relative to the large and escalating numbers of children and adolescents living in out-of-home care, the lack in amount and quality of empirical work that has occurred in this area is somewhat startling (see review by Curry, 1991). With a few isolated exceptions, studies assessing the effectiveness of residential treatment models use no comparison or control groups and rely only on examining participants' changes before and after treatment.

In this chapter, we describe a community-based treatment model for out-of-home care that is an alternative to placement in group care settings. The Multidimensional Treatment Foster Care (MTFC) model described here uses a series of multicomponent, multilevel interventions that occur in family, school, and community settings. Like other treatment models developed in the 1980s for treating adolescents with severe and chronic problems (e.g., Henggeler et al., 1986), the MTFC model recognizes that conduct problems are determined by multiple causes and factors (Reid & Eddy, 1997). Therefore, the intervention focuses on the most relevant factors for each youth and family member and occurs in all of the key settings in which the adolescent interacts. Typically, these include the teenager's daily interchanges with parents, peers, and teachers, with the recognition that these key relationships are embedded and influenced by broad social contexts such as neighborhoods and schools.

In addition to the standard normative social contexts that adolescents experience, those in out-of-home care are influenced by the ecology of their placement setting. Several reviews (e.g., Pfeiffer & Strzelecki, 1990; Small, Kennedy, & Bender, 1991; Wells, 1991) of residential care describe varying characteristics of placement living settings on key dimensions such as level of restrictiveness, amount and type of supervision and discipline, importance of peer relations, and types and amounts of transactions with adults. Although the residential care literature contains several excellent descriptions of the therapeutic milieus (e.g., Redl & Wineman, 1957), along with theoretically grounded hypotheses about what the salient change mechanisms are, no data exist that directly connect the way these factors influence adolescents' adjustment and progress in care, let alone their postplacement outcomes. Later in this chapter, we present a model that connects key aspects of the placement settings to adolescent outcomes.

OVERVIEW OF THE MTFC MODEL

Since the early 1980s, the Oregon Social Learning Center (OSLC) has conducted the MTFC program, which serves youths who have problems with chronic antisocial behavior and delinquency and who were referred from local juvenile justice departments. Adolescents (12–18 years) who are in need of out-of-home placement are referred to MTFC as an alternative to placement in group care or the state training schools. Other populations of youngsters served by the OSLC MTFC model have included children and adolescents leaving the state mental hospital (Chamberlain & Reid, 1991), youths with low cognitive functioning and inappropriate sexual behavior (Chamberlain, 2003), children in conventional state-supported foster care who have behavioral and emotional problems (Smith, Stormshak, Chamberlain, & Bridges Whaley, 2001), and children in an early intervention program for preschoolers in foster care (Fisher, Gunnar, Chamberlain, & Reid, 2000). The MTFC program for youths referred from juvenile justice is the focus of this chapter.

In the Oregon MTFC model, foster families are recruited, trained, and supervised to provide daily treatment to the adolescents placed with them. Daily treatment in the foster home is augmented by six other service elements:

1. individual therapy and skill training;
2. family therapy for the adolescent's biological (or adoptive) relatives;
3. regular school consultations, including on-site observations and school-based interventions, as needed;
4. consultation with parole and probation officers;
5. psychiatric consultation, as needed; and
6. case management services to coordinate all aspects of the program and to provide daily contact, supervision, and consultation to the treatment foster parents.

Regular home visits are scheduled throughout the youth's placement in most instances (i.e., 85%) in which the goal is to return the adolescent to his or her family of origin following placement in MTFC. Those families and teenagers also participate in a 12-month aftercare program.

The average placement period is from 6 to 9 months. Typically, only one adolescent is placed in each MTFC home. MTFC parents are paid $1,200 per month, which is approximately twice the rate for regular foster care paid by the State of Oregon. The program is funded through a state contract that pays $130 per day per child. Aftercare and school-based services, as well as research on those components, have been funded separately through federal grants (i.e., Chamberlain, 1990, 1992).

Since the early 1980s, widespread implementation of various versions of the MTFC model has occurred in the United States. MTFC was included in the National Institute of Mental Health (NIMH)–sponsored Child and Adolescent Services System for severely emotionally disturbed youngsters (Stroul & Friedman, 1986). The OSLC MTFC program has been featured in two recent Surgeon's General reports: one on Mental Health Services for

Children and Adolescents (U.S. Department of Health and Human Services, 2000a) and another on the Prevention of Violence (U.S. Department of Health and Human Services, 2000b). Because of the accumulating body of evidence on the relative effectiveness of MTFC, the flexibility of the MTFC model to address individual and family circumstances and needs, the relative low cost (compared with inpatient or residential care), and cost-benefit (Aos, Phipps, Barnoski, & Lieb, 2002), policy makers have become increasingly interested in implementing MTFC in their local communities.

COMPONENTS OF MTFC

More complete descriptions of the MTFC model are provided in Chamberlain (1994) and Chamberlain (2003). An overview is provided here.

Developing the Placement Setting: Recruiting, Screening, and Hiring Treatment Foster Parents

One- and two-parent families from diverse social, ethnic, cultural, and economic backgrounds have served as successful MTFC parents. We attempt to select families that are strong both in terms of stability and parenting skills. The four-stage selection and hiring process consists of an initial telephone interview, followed by a written application, a home visit, and preservice training. Because of the magnitude of the problems presented by adolescents who are served, MTFC parents must be well trained, closely supervised, and willing to work actively as part of a treatment team. This aspect of the program appeals to many experienced foster parents, whereas others, who prefer their own ways of conducting foster care, are not interested. Foster parents are recruited through word-of-mouth referrals and newspaper advertising. Current MTFC parents are paid a $100 finder's fee for referring families that we eventually train.

Preservice training for treatment foster parents is adapted from the social learning parent training model developed at our center and elsewhere (Miller & Prinz, 1990; Wahler & Sansbury, 1990; Webster-Stratton & Hammond, 1990). The treatment model requires that MTFC parents engage in specific activities that are centered on providing the adolescent with frequent reinforcement and clear and consistent consequences and limits. The training focuses on examples of how these processes can be tailored to fit the adolescent's individual needs, as well as the foster family's daily living schedule and priorities. All MTFC parents complete 20 hours of training before a youngster is placed with them. Ongoing consultation with MTFC parents is the treatment model's cornerstone. Without ongoing consultation, adolescents tend to manipulate the MTFC parents into responding in negative ways, often relying on punitive or anger-based methods of control. For example, in the face of adolescent rule violations or other misbehaviors, the most common adult reaction is anger and irritability. In such situations, these types of reactions have been shown to function in a way that actually increases the probability that the youngster's problem behavior will continue and escalate (Patterson, 1982). The adult then avoids teaching or relating positively to the teenager. Eventually, problem behaviors escalate until, finally, the adolescent is rejected from the home. Preservice training alone is not sufficient to maintain foster parent motivation or performance.

Program supervisors, who are trained in both the social learning treatment model and developmental psychopathology and who are experienced with adolescents, act as consultants to the MTFC parents. They provide support and supervision in a formal, weekly meeting attended by six to eight sets of MTFC parents. They also have daily telephone contact with MTFC parents to collect data on the youths' problems and progress during the past 24 hours using the Parent Daily Report (PDR) Checklist (Chamberlain & Reid, 1987). PDR data are also used in weekly supervision meetings with MTFC parents to review cases and make adjustments in the teenagers' daily treatment plans. During frequent telephone contacts, program supervisors provide support and supervision as needed and help MTFC parents troubleshoot anticipated problems.

Program supervisors consult with MTFC parents to develop an individualized Daily Treatment Plan (DTP) for each youth in the program. The DTP is based on a point-and-level system that MTFC parents use to provide youths with frequent reinforcement for accomplishing normative daily tasks, such as self-care, homework completion, and punctuality, and for specifically targeted behaviors indicated in their treatment plans. Points are exchanged for privileges that expand increasingly as the adolescent progresses through the program. Points are lost for minor rule breaking and problem behaviors.

Individual treatment and skill training sessions are provided to youths at least weekly. The aim is to help them cope with the stress and anxiety associated with being in out-of-home care, to teach them skills for dealing with social problems with peers and adults, to provide support and advocacy within the program, and to provide treatment around case-specific issues. Issues such as coping with rejection, past abuse, and parental abandonment and problems with making friends and dealing with authority are typically addressed. The individual therapist is available to each youth by telephone at all times and, in coordination with the program supervisor, conducts crisis intervention, as needed. Youths are encouraged to bring up any difficulties that they are experiencing in the program, including problems in the foster home, in school, or with the daily program.

Individual therapists help the adolescents negotiate changes in their programs and, in the process of this work, focus on teaching and modeling good problem-solving skills. Other interventions in individual treatment are coordinated with the treatment occurring in the MTFC home and at school. For example, if developing alternatives to swearing is a target behavior in the MTFC home, the therapist would discuss and enact through role-playing exercises various options with the teenager and support the practice of these approaches between individual sessions.

Family therapy with the youth's biological, adoptive, or other after-program living resource takes place weekly. Treatment content and methods are based on the social learning family treatment model developed by Patterson (1985). Parents are taught to implement the same daily program (i.e., the DTP) that their child is experiencing in the MTFC home. During regularly scheduled home visits, parents practice using this system; ideally, they will have become well versed in its use by the time the child returns home after completing the program.

Families are often difficult to engage in treatment. They have often had negative contacts with social service agencies and tend to be suspicious of organized efforts to address their child's problems, which makes them hesitant to participate. We see it as part of our mandate to find a way to productively engage families and have developed several strategies to do so. Family therapists are all experienced clinicians who have been trained and supervised in the social learning treatment approach. Treatment usually consists of a balance between helping parents to implement effective encouragement, supervision, and discipline practices and to deal with the personal and family system barriers they face. The family therapist usually conducts a series of initial sessions with the parent (or parents) alone and then brings in other family members (e.g., siblings, program youth) after they have established a collaborative relationship.

Consultation with schools and parole or probation officers is conducted regularly by the program supervisor. The youth carries a daily school card that is filled out by each teacher. Attendance, behavior in class, and assignments are tracked on the card, which is returned to the MTFC parents each day. The youth receives points for carrying the card and for appropriate in-school behavior. When this monitoring system is not enough to meet the adolescent's behavioral or academic needs (or both), in-school consultation is conducted. Intensive involvement by MTFC program staff allows the majority of the program youths to attend public schools, often in special educational settings. Program supervisors have regular telephone contact with the parole and probation officers assigned to the cases and send them copies of youths' weekly PDR Checklist data. When serious rule infractions or law violations occur, parole and probation officers are consulted for input regarding the adolescents' consequences. In these instances, point loss, work chores, and sometimes short-term stays in juvenile detention may be used as consequences.

The program supervisor is the key staff person who coordinates the program components. Program supervisors handle a maximum caseload of 10 to 12 youths. In addition to having the necessary training and experience, they must be able to interact effectively with, and keep in perspective, the viewpoints of a diverse group of individuals, including the youth, his or her parents, the MTFC parents, school personnel, individual and family therapists, juvenile judges, consulting psychiatrists, and parole or probation officers. Program supervisors are responsible for the development and implementation of the overall treatment plan. They make all decisions on modifications and revisions to the plan and act as advocate and supervisor for the MTFC parents. They also supervise the individual and family therapists. Program supervisors conduct two management meetings per week, one with the MTFC parents and one with the program director and the individual and family therapists.

Aftercare services and support are provided to the youth's parents or other adults in his or her postprogram living setting for the year after treatment. These services include weekly parent group meetings, family therapy sessions (as needed), and ongoing school consultation

OUTCOMES AND RESEARCH EVIDENCE

Three studies on the effectiveness of MTFC using comparison or control groups have been conducted at OSLC (Chamberlain, 1990; Chamberlain & Reid, 1991, 1998). The third study that compared the effectiveness of MTFC to group care for chronic male juvenile offenders and a fourth parallel study currently under way with female adolescent offenders will be briefly described here.

MTFC for Adolescent Boys

In 1990, 79 boys were referred to our study by the juvenile justice system because of chronic and serious delinquency. After obtaining appropriate consents to participate, we randomly assigned boys to placement in MTFC or to one of eleven group care programs (GC) located throughout Oregon. The primary outcomes that were examined in this study were police reports of offenses and self-reported delinquency rates. In addition to examining outcomes, we measured four variables that were hypothesized to mediate the effectiveness of treatment regardless of whether boys were placed in MTFC or GC. We completed this measure when boys were in their MTFC or GC placements for 3 months (i.e., halfway through the placement period). We hypothesized that to the extent that these mediating variables were in place, boys' outcomes on antisocial and criminal behaviors would be more positive. The four mediators were adult supervision; the use of fair and consistent discipline; the presence of a positive relationship with a mentoring adult; and lower levels of association with delinquent peers, especially when unsupervised (for a full description, see Chamberlain, Ray, & Moore, 1996).

Participating boys were on average 14 years old and had been arrested more than 14 times before entering the study. They averaged 1.3 previous out-of-home placements, excluding detention stays, and had spent an average of 73 days in detention during the previous year. Fifteen percent had been charged with a sex offense, and 18% had been arrested for fire setting.

The MTFC program consisted of placing boys (usually one per home) in a trained and supported community family where they underwent a structured daily program using the point-and-level system. Boys also participated in weekly individual therapy that was skill focused, and their parents (or other aftercare resource) participated in family treatment. Frequent contact between boys and parents or relatives was promoted, as were weekly home visits, in which parents were taught to use a management system parallel to the one used in the MTFC home. Psychiatric consultation and medication management were provided as needed. The MTFC placements lasted an average of 6.8 months. Detailed descriptions of the program model are given in Chamberlain (1994) and Chamberlain (2003).

In GC programs, boys lived with 6 to 15 other boys in family-style group homes, in stand-alone group homes, or in cottages on the grounds of larger institutions. In GC, most boys participated in daily group therapy. Most programs used variations of the Positive Peer Culture model (Vorrath & Brendtro, 1985), wherein peers were expected to participate in daily governance and decision making. Boys' families participated in family therapy in 40% of the cases, and boys participated in individual therapy in 53% of the cases. Eleven group homes located throughout the state participated in the study.

Data on official arrest rates 1 year after discharge showed that boys in MTFC had significantly fewer arrests (MTFC mean = 2.6 arrests; GC mean = 5.4 arrests). Postdischarge self-reports of delinquent activities also showed that MTFC boys reported engaging in significantly fewer delinquent activities, including serious and person crimes (MTFC mean = 12.8 self-reported criminal activities; GC mean = 28.9 self-reported criminal activities). MTFC boys also spent fewer days incarcerated than did boys in the GC group (means = 53 versus 129 days, respectively), ran away from their placements less often (means = 18 days versus 36 days, respectively), and completed their programs more often. In addition, MTFC boys reported using hard drugs less frequently at follow-up. Additional follow-up analyses on arrest rates have been completed for 3 years after discharge. Table 21.1 shows the cumulative number of arrests for boys in both groups through Year 3 postdischarge. As can be seen there, boys in MTFC continued to be arrested significantly fewer times each year through Year 3 of follow-up.

The four treatment factors (i.e., supervision, discipline, positive relationship with a mentoring adult, decreased association with delinquent peers) hypothesized to mediate treatment effectiveness were also examined. As hypothesized, these four treatment factors were shown to play a mediational

TABLE 21.1
Cumulative Number of Arrests Postdischarge

Follow-up year	GC	MTFC	Significance level
1	5.4 (4.2)	2.6 (3.1)	$p < .01$
2	8.4 (6.4)	4.5 (5.0)	$p < .01$
3	10.1 (6.7)	6.8 (6.1)	$p < .05$

role in explaining offense outcomes and self-reports of criminal behavior for chronically delinquent boys (Eddy & Chamberlain, 2000). Not only was MTFC more effective than GC; a significant part of the treatment effect relied on the presence of these four factors. These findings highlight the important role that family management skills can play in changing the negative trajectory of antisocial behavior and preventing further offending—even for serious offending behavior that has extended into the adolescent years.

Multidimensional Treatment Foster Care for Adolescent Girls

In the early 1980s, we began accepting referrals from the juvenile justice system for girls. From the outset, their treatment needs differed in obvious ways from those of boys. In 1994, we looked systematically at the differences in risk factors and adjustment for female and male delinquents referred to our MTFC program (Chamberlain & Reid, 1994) and discovered some interesting patterns that have helped to guide our current work.

A review of the literature on female delinquency led to the realization that nearly all of the previous work on understanding the development and escalation of serious forms of antisocial behavior has been conducted on male samples. Little is known about the antecedents of serious antisocial behavior for females and even less about effective methods of intervention. Our review of 88 consecutive referrals of girls and boys to MTFC showed that girls did as well as boys on arrest outcomes but experienced a different pattern of adjustment to the program. Whereas boys gradually improved over time in terms of daily problem behaviors in the MTFC homes, girls started out with a relatively low rate of daily problems and became more difficult over time. These data, in concert with discussions with MTFC parents, helped us to understand that there were specific dynamics occurring with girls that we needed to attend to differently than we had for boys.

In 1998 we began conducting a randomized study with girls parallel to the previously discussed one for boys. That study is currently under way. With half of the final sample in, the girls participating in the study are on average 14.8 years old and have been arrested an average of 11 times on referral. Compared with boys (who were also referred from the juvenile justice system), girls are slightly older at age of referral and have fewer previous arrests. A comparison of some of the characteristics of boys and girls are shown in Table 21.2. Girls tended to have more chaotic family backgrounds, as revealed by higher rates of parental criminality, and more frequent placements out of their family homes. We have interviewed girls to obtain a history of their living situations throughout their lives. Each time a parent figure went in or out of their lives, we counted a parental transition (e.g., "my mom went to prison, so I was put in foster care"). So far, girls in the study have had an average of 16 such parental transitions—more than one per year. Unfortunately, we did not collect similar data from the boys, so no cross-gender comparisons can be made.

Girls also appear to have higher rates of mental health symptoms than boys. For example, looking at the percentage of youths in the study who met the clinical cut-off level on the Brief Symptom Inventory (Derogatis & Spencer, 1982), more girls scored in the clinical range for depression (19% vs. 8% for the boys), anxiety (26% vs. 11%), somatic problems (20% vs. 5%), and paranoid ideation (20% vs. 10%). Three quarters of the girls that we have interviewed so far have met criteria for three or more *Diagnostic and Statistical Manual of Mental Disorders, Fourth Edition* (DSM–IV) Axis I diagnoses.

In many ways, the focus of the intervention for girls parallels key components used with boys. The same four variables that mediated treatment effects for boys appear to be just as relevant for girls. These are adult supervision; clear and effective limits and discipline; relationship with an adult

TABLE 21.2
Gender and Risk: Preliminary Findings
From Two NIMH Studies of Youth From Juvenile Justice

Characteristics	Boys ($n = 79$)	Girls ($n = 61$)
Average age at referral	14.4	14.8*
Number of previous placements	1.3	3.0*
Number of crimes committed (by self)	13.5	13.1
Number of days in previous year spent in detention	73.0	72.0
Percentage who have run away once or more	73.7	91.7*
Percentage with mother convicted of a crime	21.6	46.7*
Percentage with father convicted of a crime	31.3	63.2*
Percentage with at least one parent convicted	41.1	70.0*
Documented suicide attempt	2.6	58.3*

*$p < .01$.

mentor; and not associating with delinquent peers, especially older male delinquent peers. We have augmented this basic model for girls to add work on methods for helping girls stabilize their relationships with adult caretakers and friends, for preparing for their futures through planning and goal setting, and for understanding past trauma and abuse experiences to assist them in overcoming challenges to daily living.

Preliminary outcomes for girls randomly assigned to MTFC or GC show that girls in the MTFC condition spent more days in treatment and fewer days in detention than girls in GC at both 6 months and 12 months after referral. Girls in MTFC also have spent fewer days in locked (detention and state training school) settings than girls in GC (see Figure 21.1 and Figure 21.2).

Cost-Effectiveness of the Multidimensional Treatment Foster Care Approach

In an independent evaluation of the cost-effectiveness of 31 violence prevention programs and other approaches to reducing criminal and at-risk behavior in youths and adults, the Washington State Institute for Public Policy (Aos et al., 2002) found that the OSLC MTFC program was among the approaches that resulted in the greatest savings to taxpayers (an average of over $27,000 per youth in saved criminal justice and victim costs). This

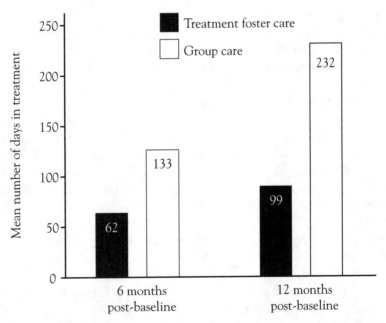

Figure 21.1. Mean number of days spent in treatment at 6 and 12 months post-baseline.

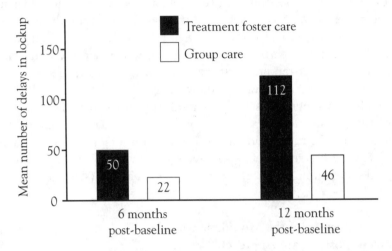

Figure 21.2. Mean number of days spent in lockup at 6 and 12 months post-baseline.

savings was the result of a decrease in the arrest and incarceration rates for the high-risk youths in the program. The benefit per dollar of cost for MTFC was calculated at $22.58. This compared to negative benefits per dollar costs of more widely used program models such as boot camps or juvenile intensive supervision (parole). The relative effectiveness and cost-effectiveness of MTFC caused it to be chosen as one of 10 Blueprint for Violence Prevention programs by the Center for the Study and Prevention of Violence at the University of Colorado (Elliott, 1997) and as one of nine national Exemplary Safe and Drug-Free Schools Programs by the U.S. Department of Education in 2001. Implementations of the Oregon MTFC model are now being conducted in several sites in the United States and in Sweden.

Clinical Vignette

Like many youths in the MTFC program, Kelly had a long history of instability and family chaos. By the time she entered the program at age 16, she had moved so many times that she had lost count. Kelly was shuttled back and forth between family members as her mother struggled to manage clinical depression and drug abuse. Between moves, Kelly was often left to care for her younger siblings for days at a time. Even when her mother was physically present, her struggles to manage her own mental health problems and substance use were so difficult that the needs of Kelly and her siblings were routinely neglected. The combination of inconsistent care, a chronically unstable living situation, and harsh physical discipline appeared to have shaped Kelly into a negative, pessimistic, self-critical teenager with no hope for her future.

Kelly was referred to MTFC following a lengthy referral history for law violations and unsuccessful placements in treatment programs. Before her placement in MTFC, she had received charges of Burglary II, Theft II, Assault IV, Harassment, and three charges of Menacing. Although she was very bright (IQ in the above-average-to-superior range), Kelly had not attended school in the year before placement because she had been expelled for threatening a student with a weapon. And Kelly wasn't all talk. During at least one incident, she actually followed through with a threat, stabbing a peer and receiving an assault charge.

Despite having experienced a very traumatic, chaotic, and violent history, Kelly made tremendous gains during her stay in MTFC. Initially appearing depressed, irritable, intimidating, and extremely defiant, Kelly slowly blossomed into a bright, articulate young lady with prosocial goals and aspirations for her future. One of the most difficult behaviors for Kelly to change was her verbal response to frustration or disagreement. Kelly apparently had become so accustomed to using vulgar, threatening language when upset that she was not even aware of this behavior or its effect on others. To this end, the point system was a particularly valuable tool with Kelly. The point system provided Kelly the opportunity to receive feedback in a nonreactive, unemotional manner. Through the loss of points for small verbal infractions (e.g., swearing, rude comments) made at school, in the community, or in the foster home, Kelly slowly began to make the connection that her behaviors were related to consequences. As Kelly progressed in the program and demonstrated better problem-solving skills, this behavior was shaped to encourage more appropriate expression of emotions. For instance, as Kelly's use of inappropriate or threatening verbal responses to others decreased, her lack of skill in appropriately discussing her negative feelings became apparent. As a way to encourage and practice age-appropriate discussions of feelings, a system was set up whereby Kelly received a daily phone call from her skills trainer to discuss her day. Clear limits were set by the program supervisor regarding behavioral expectations for these phone calls, and Kelly was informed that her skills trainer was instructed to terminate the phone call if Kelly was rude, overly negative, or aggressive in her talk. Kelly earned $1 per phone call and was not paid for calls that were terminated for inappropriate talk.

This intervention was powerful in that it reinforced Kelly for age-appropriate, desired behavior in an overall context that was reinforcing (i.e., she enjoyed contact with her skills trainer). Because calls took place in the foster home and during home visits, the intervention also allowed for the practice and reinforcement of adaptive behaviors across multiple settings. In addition, because Kelly had little practice in relating to prosocial peers, this intervention allowed for the practice of appropriate, prosocial conversation that could be easily generalized to phone calls and supportive discussions with peers.

Because of Kelly's complex family dynamics (e.g., mother's mental illness, mother's and father's substance use) and her tumultuous relationship with her mother, the courts identified Kelly's maternal grandmother as her long-term placement resource. Although Kelly's grandmother lived 90 minutes away, she attended weekly family therapy sessions and participated actively in learning and practicing use of the point-and-level system, methods of reinforcement and limit-setting, and use of consequences for negative behaviors. Kelly's grandmother had difficulty reading and writing, so parenting techniques were demonstrated using video clips of family interactions and were practiced using role playing exercises during family sessions. Despite her relatively rough exterior, Kelly's grandmother was extremely caring, kind, and loving toward Kelly. She slowly learned to use methods of reinforcement and limit-setting that were found to be successful with Kelly in the foster home and ultimately became proficient in the use of the point system as a basic tool to provide feedback on Kelly's daily behavior.

By the time Kelly successfully completed MTFC, she had become involved in several prosocial activities (i.e., weekly horseback riding lessons, volunteering at the local Humane Society), had developed a positive relationship with her foster family, had completed her GED at the local community college, and had identified a career path in the animal care industry (i.e., veterinarian assistant). Although Kelly's family continues to struggle to reinforce positive behavior and set appropriate limits with Kelly and her siblings, her grandmother continues to participate in aftercare and actively involves the family therapist in discussions regarding use of the point system and the appropriate application of consequences for undesirable behaviors.

SUMMARY AND LIMITATIONS

MTFC is a multifaceted model and therefore is complicated to implement and supervise. However, research to date suggests that MTFC has the potential to be an effective treatment approach for a variety of difficult-to-treat youth populations (Chamberlain, 1990; Chamberlain & Reid, 1991, 1998; Moore, 2000; Smith et al., 2001). In addition, recent research on the Oregon Model of MTFC has identified specific components of MTFC (i.e., supervision, discipline, positive relationship with mentoring adult, limited associations with delinquent peers) that make it work as it was intended (i.e., Eddy & Chamberlain, 2000). These research findings are important not only in demonstrating the effectiveness of MTFC with specific populations but also in providing preliminary evidence suggesting that the MTFC model functions optimally when all components are implemented simultaneously. Although MTFC programs throughout the United States are extremely variable in the ways they implement key aspects of MTFC and many program directors are tempted to select one element of the model to the exclusion of other key services, preliminary research and clinical examinations of the model suggest that such an approach is unwise. In fact, the power of MTFC is believed to come from the multidimensional format that relies on well-coordinated interventions across multiple settings. Requesting that the various treatment agents network is not enough. Cases involving complex clinical issues require decisions that consider the system as a whole rather than one aspect (e.g., overall treatment goals and the coordination of treatment across settings need to be kept in mind when decisions regarding the goals of family therapy are established or refined).

MTFC has the potential to be widely generalizable not only because it is cost-effective and appears to be associated with positive outcomes but also because it has the flexibility to be adapted to fit the needs of individual youths, families, and communities. At this point, however, little is known about how best to replicate or disseminate effective MTFC programs to other populations and areas. Questions remain regarding the degree to which individual programs may diverge from the strict parameters of MTFC models already shown to be effective and the best ways to train and supervise new MTFC programs to maintain treatment fidelity. In an effort to examine specifics of the dissemination process, a current study is under way in San Diego County (Chamberlain, 2000) wherein aspects of the MTFC model are being applied and tested in the context of conventional state-supported foster care. In particular, researchers are examining factors that facilitate or impair dissemination of intervention models developed under well-controlled research conditions into community settings.

The MTFC approach appears to be a promising method for providing services, placement, and care to severely troubled youths and families. Although much work remains in examining the applications and limitations of MTFC, we hope that continued research on implementation and dissemination practices will broaden our understanding of this treatment approach and inform further theory-based replications and adaptations of the MTFC model.

REFERENCES

Aos, S., Phipps, P., Barnoski, R., & Leib, R. (2002). *The comparative costs and benefits of programs to reduce crime: A review of national research findings with implications for Washington state*. Olympia: Washington State Institute for Public Policy.

Chamberlain, P. (1990). *Teaching and supporting families: A model for reunification of children with their families*. Grant No. 90CW0994, Administration for Children, Youth, and Families, Child Welfare Services, HDS, DHHS.

Chamberlain, P. (1992). *Family alliances change teens (FACT): A research study.* Grant No. H237E22018, Office of Special Education Programs, U.S. Department of Education.

Chamberlain, P. (1994). *Family connections.* Eugene, OR: NW Media.

Chamberlain, P. (2000). *Cascading dissemination of a foster parent intervention.* Grant No. R01 MH 60195, Services Research and Clinical Epidemiology Branch, NIMH, U.S. PHS.

Chamberlain, P. (2003). *Treating chronic juvenile offenders.* Washington, DC: American Psychological Association.

Chamberlain, P., Ray, J., & Moore, K. J. (1996). Characteristics of residential care for adolescent offenders: A comparison of assumptions and practices in two models. *Journal of Child and Family Studies, 5,* 259–271.

Chamberlain, P., & Reid, J. B. (1987). Parent observation and report of child symptoms. *Behavioral Assessment, 9,* 97–109.

Chamberlain, P., & Reid, J. B. (1991). Using a specialized foster care treatment model for children and adolescents leaving the state mental hospital. *Journal of Community Psychology, 19,* 266–276.

Chamberlain, P., & Reid, J. B. (1994). Differences in risk factors and adjustment for male and female delinquents in Treatment Foster Care. *Journal of Child and Family Studies, 3,* 23–39.

Chamberlain, P., & Reid, J. B. (1998). Comparison of two community alternative to incarceration for chronic juvenile offenders. *Journal of Consulting and Clinical Psychology, 6,* 624–633.

Curry, J. (1991). Outcome research on residential care treatment: Implications and suggested directions. *American Journal of Orthopsychiatry, 61,* 348–358.

Derogatis, L. R., & Spencer, P. M. (1982). *The brief symptom inventory (BSI) administration, scoring, and procedures manual—I.* Baltimore: Clinical Psychometric Research.

Eddy, J. M., & Chamberlain, P. (2000). Family management and deviant peer association as mediators of the impact of treatment condition on youth antisocial behavior. *Journal of Consulting and Clinical Psychology, 5,* 857–863.

Elliott, D. S. (Series Ed.). (1997). *Blueprints for violence prevention.* Boulder: Institute of Behavioral Science, University of Colorado at Boulder.

Fisher, P. A., Gunnar, M. R., Chamberlain, P., & Reid, J. B. (2000). Preventive intervention for maltreated preschool children: Impact on children's behavior, neuroendocrine activity, and foster parent functioning. *Journal of the American Academy of Child and Adolescent Psychiatry, 39,* 1356–1364.

Henggeler, S. W., Rodick, J. D., Borduin, C. M., Hanson, C. L., Watson, S. M., & Urey, J. R. (1986). Multisystemic treatment of juvenile offenders: Effects on adolescent behavior and family interactions. *Developmental Psychology, 22,* 123–141.

Miller, G. E., & Prinz, R. J. (1990). Enhancement of social learning family interventions for childhood conduct disorder. *Psychological Bulletin, 108,* 291–307.

Moore, K. J. (2000, March). Multidimensional Treatment Foster Care with children and youth who have borderline cognitive functioning. In P. Chamberlain (Chair), *The Oregon Multidimensional Treatment Foster Care Model: Applications and outcomes*. Symposium conducted at the Research and Training Center for Children's Mental Health's 13th Annual Research Conference, Clearwater Beach, FL.

Patterson, G. R. (1982). *Coercive family process*. Eugene, OR: Castalia.

Patterson, G. R. (1985). Beyond technology: The next stage in the development of a parent training technology. In L. L'Abate (Ed.), *Handbook of family psychology and therapy* (Vol. 2, pp. 1344–1379). Homewood, IL: Dorsey Press.

Pfeiffer, S. I., & Strzelecki, S. C. (1990). Inpatient psychiatric treatment of children and adolescents: A review of outcome studies. *Journal of the American Academy of Child and Adolescent Psychiatry, 29*, 847–853.

Redl, F., & Wineman, D. (1957). *The aggressive child*. New York: Free Press.

Reid, J. B., & Eddy, J. M. (1997). The prevention of antisocial behavior: Some considerations in the search for effective interventions. In D. M. Stoff, J. Breiling, & J. D. Maser (Eds.), *Handbook of antisocial behavior* (pp. 343–356). New York: Wiley.

Small, R., Kennedy, K., & Bender, B. (1991). Critical issues for practice in residential treatment: The view from within. *American Journal of Orthopsychiatry, 61*, 327–338.

Smith, D. K., Stormshak, E., Chamberlain, P., & Bridges Whaley, R. (2001). Placement disruptions in treatment foster care. *Journal of Emotional and Behavioral Disorders, 9*, 200–205.

Stroul, B. A., & Friedman, R. M. (1986). *A system of care for severely emotionally disturbed children and youth*. Washington, DC: Georgetown.

U.S. Department of Health and Human Services. (2000a). Children and mental health. In *Mental health: A report of the Surgeon General* (DHHS publication No. DSL 2000-0134-P, pp. 123–220).Washington, DC: U.S. Government Printing Office.

U.S. Department of Health and Human Services. (2000b). Prevention of violence. In *Mental health: A report of the Surgeon General* (DHHS publication No. DSL 2000-0134-P). Washington, DC: U.S. Government Printing Office.

Vorrath, H., & Brendtro, L. K. (1985). *Positive peer culture*. Chicago: Aldene.

Wahler, R. G., & Sansbury, L. E. (1990). The monitoring skills of troubled mothers: Their problems in defining child deviance. *Journal of Abnormal Child Psychology, 18*, 577–589.

Webster-Stratton, C., & Hammond, M. (1990). Predictors of treatment outcome in parent training for families with conduct problem children. *Behavior Therapy, 21*, 319–337.

Wells, K. (1991). Placement of emotionally disturbed children in residential treatment: A review of placement criteria. *American Journal of Orthopsychiatry, 61*, 339–347.

22

PARENT–CHILD INTERACTION THERAPY: MAINTAINING TREATMENT GAINS OF PRESCHOOLERS WITH DISRUPTIVE BEHAVIOR DISORDERS

JANE G. QUERIDO AND SHEILA M. EYBERG

DISRUPTIVE BEHAVIORS IN YOUNG CHILDREN

Disruptive behavior refers to a cluster of externalizing behaviors that includes noncompliant, aggressive, and destructive behaviors. It is the most common reason for referral of young children to mental health services (Chamberlain & Smith, 2003). Without treatment, disruptive behavior persists from an early age to adulthood and tends to worsen with time (Cicchetti & Richters, 1993; Lahey et al., 1995). Risk factors found to influence the development and maintenance of disruptive behavior include personality or biological characteristics of the child, such as difficult temperament (Bates, Bayles, Bennett, Ridge, & Brown, 1991) and neuropsychological abnormalities affecting social information processing (Crick & Dodge, 1994), as well as parental and familial characteristics such as maternal depression (Webster-Stratton & Hammond, 1997), social isolation (Dumas & Wahler, 1983), anger (Wolfe, 1987), single-parent status, and poverty (Forehand, Furey, & McMahon, 1984). Parent and family factors influence child behavior through their effect on parenting behaviors, which have been found to play a critical role in the maintenance of disruptive behavior throughout a child's development (McMahon & Estes, 1997).

Early intervention programs for families of children with disruptive behavior have resulted in statistically significant improvements in children's behavior and in family functioning after treatment completion (Brinkmeyer & Eyberg, 2003; Webster-Stratton & Reid, 2003). Research suggests, however, that families characterized by multiple risk factors may be less likely to maintain short-term treatment gains (Kazdin, Mazurick, & Bass, 1993). Although studies have examined long-term outcomes associated with treatments for disruptive behavior, reviews of the long-term follow-up results have suggested that positive outcomes may be maintained for only half of the families who complete treatment (Eyberg, Edwards, Boggs, & Foote, 1998; Webster-Stratton, 1990). Treatment gains that fail to endure during follow-up may indicate the need for additional administrations of the treatment to consolidate gains. Booster sessions have been advocated as practical and cost-effective in regaining treatment effects, although empirical data on the effect of booster sessions on parent training outcomes are lacking. Clearly, a model of maintenance treatment for young children with disruptive behavior needs to be developed and tested empirically.

PARENT–CHILD INTERACTION THERAPY

Parent–child interaction therapy (PCIT) is a treatment for disruptive behavior in young children that is based on the two-stage treatment model developed by Hanf (1969). In PCIT, parents are taught skills to establish a nurturing and secure relationship with their child while increasing the child's prosocial behavior and decreasing his or her negative behavior. Treatment progresses through two distinct phases. The first, the child-directed interaction (CDI) phase, resembles traditional play therapy and focuses on strengthening the parent–child bond, increasing positive parenting, and improving child social skills, whereas the second phase, parent-directed interaction (PDI), resembles cognitive–behavioral therapy and focuses on improving parents' expectations, ability to set limits, and consistency and fairness in discipline and reducing child noncompliance and other negative behavior.

PCIT was influenced by Baumrind's (1967) developmental research associating parenting styles with child outcomes. Baumrind formulated the authoritative–authoritarian–permissive parenting theory and later transformed this typology of parenting styles into one based on two orthogonal constructs, parent responsiveness and parent demandingness (Baumrind, 1991). She demonstrated that parents who do not adequately meet young children's needs for nurturance and limits are less likely to have successful and healthy adolescents. The strong and consistent relationship between certain parenting styles and problematic child outcomes has been shown in many studies (e.g., Azar & Wolfe, 1989; Calzada & Eyberg, 2003; Querido, Bearss, & Eyberg, 2002). Consistent with this literature, PCIT assumes that treatment must focus on promoting optimal parenting styles and parent–child interactions to achieve optimal child outcomes. To define this focus, PCIT draws on both attachment and social learning theories (Foote, Eyberg, & Schuhmann, 1998).

A secure, stable attachment relationship and healthy parent–child interactions play key roles in promoting optimal social, emotional, and behavioral development in children. Attachment theory asserts that sensitive and warm parenting leads to the development of a secure attachment. Children who develop a maladaptive attachment with their caregiver show more severe levels of aggressive behavior, low social competence, poor coping skills, low self-esteem, and poor peer relationships (Coie, Watt, West, & Hawkins, 1993; Richman, Stevenson, & Graham, 1982). The combination of maladaptive parent–child attachment and poor child management skills has been consistently linked to the severity of disruptive behavior (Loeber & Schmaling, 1985; Patterson, 1982). On the basis of such findings, CDI aims to develop a secure parent–child relationship and stable attachment.

Patterson's (1982) coercion theory provides a transactional account of early conduct problems (Eyberg, Schuhmann, & Rey, 1998) in which children's behavior problems are inadvertently established or maintained by parent–child interactions. Social learning theorists emphasize the contingencies that shape dysfunctional interactions between children and their parents. Aversive interactions must be interrupted by a change in parent behavior that involves clear limit-setting that is firmly and consistently established early in the child's life (Baumrind, 1996; Patterson, 1982). PDI addresses these processes by establishing consistent contingencies for child behaviors that are implemented within the context of the positive parent–child relationship established through CDI interactions.

Methods

Screening

PCIT is suitable for families of children between the ages of 2 and 7 who are showing disruptive behavior. An initial screening is conducted to ensure that the treatment matches the needs of the family. In our outcome studies, we require children to meet diagnostic criteria for oppositional defiant disorder (ODD) and to score in the clinical range on a parent rating scale of child disruptive behavior. We also require parents to score within normal limits (standard score >75) on a cognitive screening measure.

Assessment

The goal of the intake assessment for PCIT is to obtain an accurate representation of the child's behavior using multiple informants and methods, including interviews with parents and teachers, behavior rating scales, and behavioral observation in the clinic and school setting. The assessment information is integrated in PCIT to delineate the treatment needs, guide the course of treatment, and evaluate treatment outcome.

The PCIT intake assessment begins with a semistructured clinical interview with the parent (or parents) that is designed to obtain information about the child's behavior problems and the contexts in which they occur, to identify child and family factors that will affect treatment, to understand the family's goals and expectations for treatment, and to describe for the parent the the structure of PCIT. The interview is also used as a time to establish an alliance with the parents. It enables them to ask questions and helps them decide whether they are ready to commit to the demands of treatment.

After the clinical interview, the therapist administers a structured diagnostic interview, such as the Diagnostic Interview Schedule for Children—IV (DISC–IV–P; Shaffer, Fisher, Lucas, Dulcan, & Schwab-Stone, 2000), to determine whether the child meets diagnostic criteria for ODD and to identify comorbid disorders for consideration in treatment planning. Children with subclinical expressions of disruptive behavior disorders can be treated effectively with PCIT, but these children and their families may also do well in less intensive treatments. Consequently, the therapist may suggest alternative treatment options to the parents, particularly if the child is age 4 or younger and can return to PCIT at a later time if the problems persist.

Parents are asked to complete several parent rating scales to assess a broad range of child behavior. One behavior rating scale used during the assessment is the Eyberg Child Behavior Inventory (ECBI; Eyberg & Pincus, 1999). This 36-item instrument permits a fine-grained analysis of the child's disruptive behavior and contains two scales. The intensity scale measures the frequency of current behavior problems similar to most behavior rating scales, and the problem scale measures the extent to which the child's behavior is problematic for the parent, which is related to parent tolerance (Brestan, Eyberg, Algina, Johnson, & Boggs, 2003). The intensity and problem scales of the ECBI are highly reliable, and studies have supported their construct and discriminative validity, as well as sensitivity to treatment change in clinic-referred children (Rich & Eyberg, 2001; Taylor, Schmidt, Pepler, & Hodgins, 1998; Webster-Stratton & Hammond, 1997). The intensity scale cutoff score of 132 is used as one index in determining whether the child's behavior problems are severe enough to warrant PCIT.

PCIT takes into account the transactional nature of psychological functioning in the parent–child relationship and other family relationships. For this reason, parents are asked to complete self-report scales of individual, parent, and family functioning, such as the Parenting Stress Index—Short Form (PSI–SF; Abidin, 1997), Parenting Alliance Measure (PAM; Abidin & Konold; 1999), Parenting Locus of Control—Short Form (PLOC–SF; Rayfield, Eyberg, Boggs, & Roberts, 1995), Child Rearing Inventory (CRI; Brestan et al., 2003), and Beck Depression Inventory—II (BDI–II; Beck, Steer, & Brown, 1996). These scales extend and quantify information from the interview and enable the therapist to anticipate ways in which treatment may need to be tailored to meet the needs of the family.

Finally, to determine whether the child's problems are consistent across informants and situations, data are collected from the child's teacher or daycare provider. The teacher–provider is asked to complete the Sutter-Eyberg Student Behavior Inventory—Revised (SESBI–R; Eyberg & Pincus, 1999), which is a 38-item teacher rating scale of disruptive classroom behaviors. Like the ECBI, it contains an intensity scale and a problem scale that yield similar information from the school setting. Studies have shown high reliability and predictive validity with school conduct referrals and suspensions across 2 subsequent years (Lea, Storch, & Eyberg, 2003).

The final component of the PCIT intake assessment involves behavioral observations of parent–child interactions conducted in the clinic playroom and child classroom behaviors conducted at the child's school. These observations provide information about the severity and extent of the child's behavior problems, provide the therapist with a clearer understanding of the parent and teacher reports, and clarify ways in which the child's interactions with important adults may need to be modified.

The Dyadic Parent–Child Interaction Coding System—II (DPICS–II; Eyberg, Bessmer, Newcomb, Edwards, & Robinson, 1994) is a behavioral coding system used in the clinic that measures the quality of parent–child social interactions. The parent–child interactions are coded twice, on separate days, during three 5-minute standard situations (child-directed interaction, parent-directed interaction, clean-up) that vary in the degree of parental control required. The behaviors that are coded include child and parent verbalizations as well as selected vocalizations (e.g., whine, yell) and physical behaviors (e.g., positive and negative touch). Several sequences of behavior are also coded, which emphasize parental antecedents (e.g., commands) and consequences (e.g., praise) for important child behaviors.

The Revised Edition of the School Observation Coding System (REDSOCS; Jacobs et al., 2000) is used to assess the child's disruptive behavior in the classroom. REDSOCS is an interval coding system that measures inappropriate, noncompliant, and off-task behaviors. The system allows for a variable number of children to be coded alternately during an observation session and results in 10 minutes of observed behavior per child during each session. A child is observed on three different school days, yielding 30 minutes of observation time in total.

After the interview, parent and teacher report measures and behavioral observations are completed, and the PCIT therapist integrates the information for initial treatment planning. The data also serve as a baseline against which treatment progress can be monitored. Progress in PCIT is assessed weekly using the DPICS to determine the parents' skill acquisition, set the session goals, and guide the course of treatment. Parents also complete the ECBI Intensity Scale each week before treatment sessions to track changes in the child's behavior at home. When these measures show that the parents have mastered the interaction skills and the child's behavior problems are within the normal range, the standard treatment is successfully completed. Many of the measures administered at treatment intake are then repeated to assess the generalized effects of treatment and to plan for follow-up.

Treatment Procedure

PCIT sessions are conducted once a week and are 1 hour in length. The principles and skills of each phase of treatment are first presented to the parents alone in a didactic session that involves modeling the skills and engaging in role-playing exercises. At the end of each *didactic session*, handouts summarizing the basic CDI or PDI techniques are given to parents for their review. In subsequent *coaching sessions*, parents take turns being coached in the skills with their child and observing their spouse being coached with the child. The average length of PCIT treatment is 13 sessions (Werba, Eyberg, Boggs, & Algina, 2003).

CDI emphasizes changing the quality of the parent–child interaction by creating or strengthening a positive parent–child relationship. CDI incorporates the techniques of differential social attention and nondirective play therapy with the parent in the role of the therapist. During CDI, the parents learn to follow the child's lead in play by using the nondirective PRIDE skills: Praising the child, Reflecting the child's statements, Imitating the child's play, Describing the child's behavior, and using Enthusiasm in the play. Differential reinforcement of child behavior, by directing the PRIDE skills to the child's appropriate play and actively ignoring undesirable behavior, provides a positive form of behavior management throughout this phase. Table 22.1 shows a selection from the CDI handout, which describes the CDI rules, their rationale, and examples of each rule. Parents are asked to practice CDI skills at home during daily 5-minute play sessions with their child. Additional handouts addressing general behavioral management skills, social support, and modeling of appropriate behavior are provided to parents during the course of CDI if discussion indicates that these would be applicable to the family's areas of concern.

During CDI coaching sessions, therapists coach parents in their use of the PRIDE skills until parents meet criteria for skill mastery, as assessed

TABLE 22.1
Selections From the Child-Directed Interaction Handout (PRIDE)

Rules	Reason	Examples
PRAISE appropriate behavior.	Causes your child's good behavior to increase.	Good job of putting the toys away!
REFLECT appropriate talk.	Shows your child that you are listening.	Child: I drew a tree. Parent: Yes, you made a tree.
IMITATE appropriate play.	Lets your child lead. Shows your child that you approve of her game.	Child: I put a nose on the potato head. Parent: I'm putting a nose on Mr. Potato Head too.
DESCRIBE appropriate behavior.	Shows your child that you are interested in what he does.	You're making a tower. You drew a square.
Be ENTHUSIASTIC.	Lets your child know that you are enjoying the time you are spending together.	Parent: You are REALLY being gentle with the toys.

Note. From *Comprehensive Handbook of Psychotherapy, Vol. 2: Cognitive/Behavioral/Functional Approaches* (pp. 97–100), by T. Patterson and F. Kaslow (Eds.), 2002, New York: Wiley. Copyright 2002 by Wiley. Adapted with permission.

during a 5-minute coding interval at the start of each session. Criteria consist of 10 behavioral descriptions, 10 reflective statements, 10 labeled praises, and no more than three questions, commands, or criticisms during the interval. Parents must also ignore nonharmful inappropriate behavior. It is through the CDI coaching that therapists reinforce parent skill acquisition and understanding of the principles ("Another great praise for quiet play! Notice how much quieter his play is since you started praising that."). Therapists also use reframing to change negative attributions of child behavior and may include in vivo stress- or anger-management skills coaching if needed.

PDI emphasizes decreasing inappropriate child behaviors that are too harmful to be ignored, are controlled by reinforcers other than parental attention, or do not extinguish easily. During PDI, parents continue to give positive attention to appropriate behavior and to ignore inappropriate behavior. However, they learn to direct the child's behavior when necessary with effective commands and specific consequences for compliance and noncompliance.

In PDI, parents first learn to use *running commands*—commands for behaviors that come to mind "on the run." Parents first practice simple running commands ("Put the green block on that side") and then learn to focus on "positive opposites," such as telling a child who starts climbing on the table to "please come sit here by me." Parents are taught the "Eight Rules of Effective Commands" (Table 22.2) and a simple algorithm of precise steps to follow after a command is given (Figure 22.1). Specifically, they are taught to pay attention only to whether the child obeys or disobeys and to

Example: "Please put the block in the box."

"If you don't _____ you will have to sit on the chair."

Stay Calm. Take the child immediately to the chair. "You didn't do what I told you to do, so you have to sit on the chair. Stay on the chair until I tell you that you can get off." (3 min + 5 sec. quiet)

Take child to the chair. "You got off the chair again before I told you you could. If you get off the chair again before I tell you to, I will have to put you in the time-out room. Stay on the chair until I tell you you can get off." (This time-out warning occurs only once.)

Take the child to time-out room. "You got off the chair before I told you you could, so you're going to the time-out room." (1 minute + 5 seconds of quiet.) "Stay on the chair until I tell you that you can get off."

Take child to chair. "You got off the chair before I told you you could, so you're going to the time-out room." (1 minute + 5 seconds of quiet.) "Stay on the chair until I tell you that you can get off."

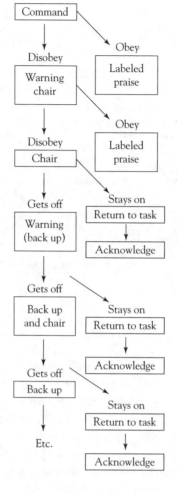

Example: Good minding.

Example: "I like it when you do what I tell you to."

Go to chair and say: "Are you ready to come back and put the block in the box?"
    If no, "All right. Then stay on the chair until I tell you you can get off."
If yes, "All right." (Back to table; repeat command if necessary.)
Example: "Thank you."

Go to chair and say: "Are you ready to come back and put the block in the box?"
If no, "All right. Then stay on the chair until I tell you that you can get off."
If yes, "All right." (Back to table; repeat command if necessary.)
Example: "Thank you."

Go to chair and say: "Are you ready to come back and put the block in the box?"
If no, "All right. Then stay on the chair until I tell you that you can get off."
If yes, "All right." (Back to table; repeat command if necessary.)
Example: "That's it."

Figure 22.1. Time-out diagram.

give a labeled praise if the child obeys or initiate the time-out procedure if the child disobeys.

The time-out procedure begins with a warning and may proceed to a time-out chair and then to a time-out room. The time-out room is used only when the child gets off the time-out chair without permission, and its use

582   QUERIDO AND EYBERG

TABLE 22.2
The Eight Rules for Effective Commands in Parent-Directed Interaction

Rule	Reason	Examples
1. Commands should be direct.	Leaves no question that the child is being told to do something.	Please hand me the block. *Instead of* Will you hand me the block?
2. Commands should be *positively stated.*	Tells child what to do rather than what not to do.	Come sit beside me. *Instead of* Don't run around the room!
3. Commands should be given *one at a time.*	Helps child to remember the whole command.	Put your shirt in the hamper. *Instead of* Clean your room.
4. Commands should be *specific.*	Permits children to know exactly what they're supposed to do.	Get down off the chair. *Instead of* Be careful.
5. Commands should be *age-appropriate.*	Makes it possible for children to understand the command.	Draw a square. *Instead of* Draw a hexagon.
6. Commands should be given *politely.*	Teaches children to obey polite and respectful commands.	Parent: Please hand me the block. *Instead of* Parent: (loudly) Hand me that block this instant!
7. Commands should be explained *after* they are obeyed.	Avoids encouraging child to ask "why" after a command as a delay tactic.	Parent: Go wash your hands. Child: (obeys) Parent: You did a nice job of getting all the mud off. Now you won't get your new shirt dirty.
8. Commands should be used *only* when *necessary.*	Decreases the child's frustration.	[Child is running in the house.] Please sit in this chair. (Good time for this command)

Note. From *Comprehensive Handbook of Psychotherapy, Vol. 2: Cognitive/Behavioral/Functional Approaches* (pp. 97–100), by T. Patterson and F. Kaslow (Eds.), 2002, New York: Wiley. Copyright 2002 by Wiley. Adapted with permission.

decreases rapidly. At specific points in the time-out procedure, the child is given the opportunity to end time-out, which continues until the child obeys the original command.

During the PDI didactic session, the time-out procedure is modeled through role-playing exercises with the parents, and the parents are given handouts illustrating the procedures to review during the week. They are instructed not to practice the PDI with their child until the next therapy session, however, so that they can be coached during their first PDI with the child and will have the emotional support of the therapist if they find the procedure difficult.

Subsequent PDI sessions are tailored to the child's unique problems as described by the parents. If a treatment goal includes increasing certain behaviors, the therapist coaches the parents to give commands for those target behaviors. For example, to increase a child's use of an inside voice, the parent might give a command directing the child to repeat a statement using an inside voice and then follow with enthusiastic labeled praise that explains the reason the behavior is important, such as "Thanks for using your inside voice. When you use your inside voice, it's easier for me to understand what you're saying." In PDI coaching sessions, parents work toward meeting the mastery criteria of PDI skills that serve as an indicator of their consistency. During the 5-minute coded observation at the beginning of the session, at least 75% of parent commands must be effective, and parents must show 75% correct follow-through after commands (labeled praise after the child obeys and warning after the child disobeys). Parents must also rate their child within one-half standard deviation of the normative mean (114) on the ECBI intensity scale and must indicate that they feel confident in their ability to manage their child's behavior on their own.

Throughout the PDI phase of treatment, the therapist guides the parents in applying the principles and procedures of CDI and PDI to the child's behavior at home and in other settings. Initially, parents are instructed to practice the PDI skills in brief 5- to 10-minute daily practice sessions after the daily CDI play session. Homework assignments proceed gradually to use of the PDI procedure only at times when it is important that the child obey a specific command. Parents are then often taught "house rules"—a *standing command* variation of the PDI algorithm that is used primarily to deal with aggressive child behavior (Exhibit 22.1). Other variations of the basic PCIT procedures for problems encountered in public situations are reviewed with parents in the last few sessions of treatment as parents assume increasing responsibility for applying the principles creatively to new situations and practice problem solving future situations that may occur as their children become older.

Two primary methods are used to maintain treatment gains after PCIT. The first, which is always included in PCIT, is to teach and use a problem-solving approach to the family's unique problems that arise during treatment. Family members are then able to use the problem-solving method on their own to maintain treatment gains after treatment has ended. The second method, which we are currently studying empirically, is to continue therapist–parent contact after completion of the standard treatment program, with brief, monthly telephone check-up calls and booster sessions as needed. Specifically, following successful completion of PCIT and remission of disruptive behavior disorders, the families in our study are randomly

EXHIBIT 22.1
House Rules Handout

Types of behaviors that house rules address

Behaviors that persist despite praising incompatible (opposite) behaviors.
Behaviors that occur unpredictably and before a command can be given.
Behaviors that cannot be ignored because of potential harm.

Steps to developing a house rule

1. Select the misbehavior to be stopped.
2. If possible, choose a word for the misbehavior that your child understands.
3. If not possible, teach your child a word for it before proceeding.
4. Explain the new house rule to the child at a neutral time.

House rule cautionary reminders

Do not use a warning if the child breaks a house rule. When the misbehavior occurs, take your child immediately to the chair for 3 minutes plus 5 seconds of quiet.
Take your child to the chair every time the misbehavior occurs.

Beginning another house rule

A new house rule may be implemented after your child has learned to obey the previous one.

Your child should have no more than two "active" house rules at a time. (Once your child has learned to obey a house rule, it is no longer "active" but it is still a house rule.)

assigned to assessment-only or to a 2-year maintenance phase of treatment. During PCIT maintenance treatment, a family's therapist calls the family each month to provide support and encouragement for the parents' continued use of the PCIT skills and to monitor their general functioning, their follow-through with techniques learned in treatment, and their child's behavior. Using a semistructured interview to gather and quantify information from the family, the therapist determines which level of intervention fits the family's current needs. A Level 1 intervention is a brief, 15- to 20-minute telephone call that involves reinforcing the parents' consistency and maintenance of treatment gains, support or problem solving if needed, and encouragement to continue participation in the maintenance treatment. A Level 2 intervention is indicated if a decline in child or family functioning is identified. Level 2 involves a longer, 25- to 60-minute discussion that involves empathic listening, problem solving, and implementing a plan or solution. The therapist then contacts the family a week later to assess the intervention effect. If the situation has not improved, a Level 3 intervention is indicated. Level 3 is a clinic session that includes observation of parent–child interactions followed by coaching, if necessary, and development of a plan for problem resolution. This continuing care model of maintenance treatment is based on the conceptualization of disruptive behavior as a chronic, recurrent condition requiring periodic monitoring and treatment as needed. For further understanding and improvement of the durability of treatment change, maintenance treatment models must be developed and tested for long-term effects.

Posttreatment Measures

After completion of treatment, parents are asked to complete several measures in addition to those that were part of the intake assessment. The Barriers to Treatment Participation Scale (Kazdin, Holland, Crowley, & Breton, 1997) assesses barriers experienced by the family throughout treatment, including treatment demands, perceived relevance of treatment, and the family's relationship with the therapist. Parents are also asked to complete a measure of consumer satisfaction, the Therapy Attitude Inventory (Brestan, Jacobs, Rayfield, & Eyberg, 1999), which assesses parents' satisfaction with the process and outcome of PCIT. These measures are used to guide the development of PCIT toward preventing barriers to treatment and improving the satisfaction of families who participate in this treatment.

Clinical Vignette

Background Information

Brandon is a 4-year-old boy who was referred by his pediatrician for treatment of oppositional behavior at home and in public. Brandon lives with his biological mother, Ms. C, who attends the local community college on a half-time basis, and his 2-year-old sister, Kristy. Brandon's father left the family just before Kristy was born, moved back to his country of origin, and has not had contact with the family since that time.

During the initial evaluation, Ms. C said that she was primarily concerned about Brandon's anger. She described Brandon as overly sensitive to perceived slights and reacting to many seemingly neutral events with angry outbursts that included hitting, pinching, and biting others. She reported that Brandon required constant supervision, especially in public areas, because he might bite or hit strangers. She described her primary method of discipline as time-out, although she reported occasional use of spanking for Brandon's aggressive behaviors, noting that neither disciplinary method had been effective in achieving positive changes in his behavior.

Ms. C described Brandon's development as slightly delayed. He walked alone at 15 months and began using two-word sentences at about 30 months. During the intake evaluation, Brandon was active and had difficulty staying focused on the task at hand. Several times during the assessment, he threw the toys around the room, hitting the walls, his mother, and the therapists. Results of the DISC–IV–P indicated that Brandon met criteria for ODD at the time of the evaluation. On the ECBI, Ms. C had an intensity scale score of 163 and a problem scale score of 19, indicating significant disruptive behavior, almost two standard deviations above the mean. Ms. C identified several behavior problems on the ECBI, including whining, sassing, getting angry when he doesn't get his way, arguing, throwing temper tantrums, and hitting. Brandon was observed in his classroom for 10 minutes on three separate days during circle time, using REDSOCS. Brandon showed inappropriate and off-task behavior most of the time he was observed and did not obey any of his teacher's commands. Ms. R, Brandon's teacher, also completed the SESBI–R, and her scores were consistent in showing significant disruptive behavior at school. She endorsed many behaviors similar to those endorsed by Ms. C on the ECBI, and she noted on the form her concern that Brandon would be asked to leave the preschool if his biting continued.

During the clinic evaluation, Ms. C was observed with Brandon in three play situations. When Ms. C was asked to follow Brandon's lead and play along with his game, they both seemed to enjoy the play, and Ms. C was warm and affectionate with Brandon. When Ms. C was asked to lead the play and get Brandon to play along with her game, Brandon whined that the first game was more fun and that he didn't want to play the new game. Ms. C then told Brandon that he had a good point, and she suggested that they return to the first game, after which Brandon's behavior was again positive. During the third situation, Ms. C was asked to tell Brandon to clean up the toys by himself. Brandon ignored his mother's requests throughout the 5-minute interaction. Ms. C tried to entice Brandon with promises of ice cream and other treats on the way home, but he moved the toys to the other side of the playroom and continued playing until the end of the observation. Ms. C reported that Brandon's behavior during these structured interactions had been somewhat better than his usual behavior at home, in that he usually became more argumentative and angry when asked to put away his toys.

Summary of Therapy

Ms. C was motivated to begin PCIT, and the first session was scheduled the following week. Ms. C arrived promptly for the CDI didactic session and paid close attention as the therapists demonstrated the PRIDE skills and described the reasons for using each of them. Ms. C showed good understanding of CDI when asked to recall the skills but seemed hesitant and shy during role-playing exercises with the therapists. The therapists gave Ms. C a handout summarizing the CDI skills (see Table 22.1) and joked with her about the likelihood that she would feel much more comfortable playing blocks with Brandon. She was able to identify a place and time for the home practice sessions, and the therapists gave her a homework sheet to record the sessions and any problems or questions that came up during the practice.

Over the next 3 weeks, Ms. C acquired the CDI skills and became effective at ignoring and decreasing Brandon's attention-seeking behaviors that had initially escalated, including whining and resisting (by pushing his mother's hand away) his mother's attempts to enter his game too actively. At the fourth CDI session, Ms. C reported that her PRIDE skills had begun to feel very natural and that she often noticed herself praising, reflecting, and describing Brandon's behavior during the day. She also reported that Brandon had started talking more, which was helping his speech development. Upon meeting the CDI mastery criteria, Ms. C was congratulated and informed that the next session would focus on a new set of skills, although continuing her daily CDI sessions with Brandon would be essential.

Ms. C's score on the ECBI Intensity Scale had decreased gradually during CDI and was 147 just before the PDI didactic session. She commented on the number of behavior ratings that had shifted to the less-frequent side of the scale since treatment started and described Brandon as seeming less angry than he had been initially, although she expressed concern about his continued aggressive behavior with peers. The therapists then suggested that they begin reviewing the PDI skills. Ms. C engaged actively in discussion of the "Eight Rules for Effective Commands" and the steps of the PDI procedure. The therapists first modeled the PDI scenarios and then asked Ms. C to engage in role-playing scenarios with them. Unlike the earlier role-playing exercises with the therapists, Ms. C appeared comfortable adopting her role and laughed with the therapists when they exaggerated some of the child behaviors that could occur. Ms. C picked up the skills quickly during the role-playing scenarios and said she was eager to begin using the skills with Brandon. The therapists clarified that the first PDI practice session with Brandon would not actually take place until the following week in the therapy session. They explained that this would give them all the opportunity to describe the procedure to Brandon together before they started and that the therapists would be able to coach Ms. C to ensure that their first experience with the new procedure would go well. At the end of the session, Ms. C was given the PDI summary handouts to review before the next session. The therapists explained that this next week would be the most important week to have CDI sessions faithfully every day so that Brandon's first experience with the time-out procedure would be a true time-out from positive reinforcement (CDI).

During the next 4 weeks of PDI, Ms. C reported feeling increasingly confident in her ability to manage Brandon's behavior at home. Although the first PDI coaching session was lengthy because of Brandon's defiant behavior, he did not go to the time-out room after the second week of PDI, and during the next 3 weeks he required increasingly fewer warnings. Ms. C was pleased with their progress and each week reported new changes that she had not anticipated. For example, she noticed that Brandon had become more polite, often saying "please" when asking her permission to do something. Ms. C also reported that Brandon had stopped attempting to bite her and was less aggressive with peers at school; he seemed to have stopped biting other children as well. As Ms. C became confident in her parenting, she was encouraged to begin using her PDI skills for four or five selected commands throughout the day and to follow through consistently with labeled praise every time that Brandon complied and with the time-out procedure every time he did not comply.

In subsequent PDI coaching sessions, the house-rules procedure was introduced for Brandon's remaining aggressive behaviors. At the ninth session, Ms. C reported that although he was hitting much less often since the beginning of treatment, Brandon still hit his sister two or three times a week. The therapists described the usual procedure of labeling a behavior for 2 or 3 days before targeting it as a house rule so that Brandon would know clearly what behavior would result in automatic time-out. However, Ms. C was certain that Brandon understood precisely what "hit your sister" meant, and the therapists agreed that the labeling procedure would not be necessary for this house rule with Brandon. Brandon had behaved well during coaching, and Ms. C decided to describe the new rule to Brandon before they left the session. She did a nice job of getting his attention and describing the house rule to him at a level he could understand. As she explained the rule, Brandon listened with wide eyes, and then told her that he wasn't going to hit Kristy anymore. At the next session, Brandon told the therapists in the waiting room that he had not hit Kristy and that his mother took him to see Santa Claus so he could tell him, too.

At the 11th session, the major presenting problems seemed to be close to resolution. In addition, Brandon's ECBI Intensity score was down to 99, well below the criterion for termination, and Ms. C's CDI and PDI skills had been at criterion levels for several weeks. Ms. C's homework sheets further indicated that Brandon was requiring warnings for fewer than 10% of her commands and had not gone to the time-out room since the second week after starting PDI. Ms. C reported that Brandon was no longer engaging in any aggressive behaviors at school or in other situations. The only concern Ms. C noted with public behavior was that Brandon sometimes ran away from her in the grocery store. The therapists asked Ms. C to think of all the strategies she had learned in CDI and PDI and how they might be applied to this problem. The therapists jotted down the ideas she mentioned and then encouraged her to think through what might happen as a result of each idea. One solution Ms. C thought of was to use a command for an incompatible ("positive opposite") behavior—specifically, "Please hold my hand in the store." When she described the way that she anticipated this would work, she seemed optimistic about her solution, as did the therapists. The therapists suggested to Ms. C that it seemed as if she and Brandon were close to treatment graduation, and Ms. C seemed pleased. They decided together to discuss at the next session whether it might be the last.

At that next session, which was the fifth PDI coaching session, Ms. C reported that her solution for the grocery store had worked well and that she actually found the shopping trip with Brandon fun. During the session, Ms. C continued to show mastery of the CDI and PDI skills and reported being very confident in her ability to manage Brandon's behavior. Therefore, Ms. C and the therapists mutually agreed to end regular treatment. The therapists reviewed the study's randomization procedures, assuring Ms. C that even if she fell into the assessment-only group, she could still call her therapists any time she had questions or concerns. The therapists gave Ms. C a handout describing several alternative discipline procedures that could be used for minor misbehaviors as Brandon got older (e.g., token chart). They also gave Ms. C (and Brandon) a certificate for successful completion of PCIT and gave Brandon a big blue ribbon for good behavior ("for being so good at school, being so polite, and for not hitting your sister anymore"). Ms. C said she hoped to be in the maintenance treatment group but didn't really expect to have any problems she couldn't handle.

Randomization resulted in assignment to the maintenance treatment group, and therefore the primary therapist called Ms. C monthly for the next 2 years to monitor Brandon's behavior and family stressors that might affect the family's ability to maintain treatment gains. Only Level 1 interventions were indicated for all monthly calls during the first year. During a call in the second follow-up year, however, Ms. C reported that Brandon had started to hit other children at school after an incident in which he was hit by a classmate on the playground. At that time, a Level 2 intervention was indicated, and the therapist engaged Ms. C in a discussion of possible solutions that were consistent with the skills she learned during the treatment program. The plan that was developed involved Ms. C calling Brandon's teacher for a daily update on his behavior. Ms. C decided to take Brandon to the children's library on the way home from school and select a story book she would read to him before bed each day he kept his hands to himself at school. She also decided that he would not be allowed to watch a favorite cartoon show on television after school on any day that he hit a classmate at school. When the therapist called Ms. C the following week to assess the effectiveness of the plan, Ms. C reported that Brandon had hit a classmate the first day that the school plan had gone into effect but that he had not hit a classmate in the past 6 days. Ms. C was pleased with how rapidly she had brought the problem under control, and during the next monthly call, she reported no further occurrences of hitting at school. Ms. C reported no other problems during the remaining monthly calls.

Treatment Outcomes

Several studies have demonstrated positive outcomes following PCIT for families of preschoolers with disruptive behavior, including statistically and clinically significant improvements in children's behavior on parent and teacher rating scales and direct observations in the clinic and at school. Specifically, these studies have documented the superiority of PCIT to wait-list controls (Nixon, Sweeney, Erickson, & Touyz, 2003; Schuhmann, Foote, Eyberg, Boggs, & Algina, 1998), to classroom controls (McNeil, Eyberg, Eisenstadt, Newcomb, & Funderburk, 1991), and to group parent training (Eyberg & Matarazzo, 1980). PCIT outcome studies have demonstrated important changes in parents' interactions with their children, including increased reflective listening, physical proximity, and prosocial verbalization and decreased criticism and sarcasm at treatment completion (Eisenstadt, Eyberg, McNeil, Newcomb, & Funderburk, 1993). Maternal Q-set scores on attachment security and attachment dependency have shown significant changes during both CDI and PDI (Floyd & Eyberg, 2003). Table 22.3 provides effect sizes from a recent study (Schuhmann et al., 1998) to illustrate the magnitude of change in parents' reports of personal distress, parenting locus of control, and child behavior problems, as well as observations of parenting behavior.

The effects of PCIT have been found to generalize to other family members and other settings. For example, the behavior of untreated siblings has improved relative to siblings of wait-list families, suggesting generalization of treatment effects on parent behavior to other interactions within the family (Brestan, Eyberg, Boggs, & Algina, 1997). The behaviors of the referred children have also been shown to generalize to the school setting, with referred children showing significantly greater improvements than two control groups on teacher rating scales and observational measures of classroom behavior (McNeil et al., 1991).

A few studies have addressed the issue of maintenance, without further treatment, following completion of PCIT (Boggs et al., 2003; Eisenstadt et al., 1993; Eyberg et al., 2001; Funderburk et al., 1998; Hood & Eyberg, 2003). In a short-term follow-up study of 14 families, all families maintained treatment gains on observational measures of child compliance, parent-rating scale measures of conduct problems, internalizing problems, activity level, maternal stress, and child self-report of self-esteem at 6-week follow-up (Eisenstadt et al., 1993). Treatment gains were maintained at 1-year follow-up, but at 2-year follow-up, although measures of child behavior problems and parenting stress remained significantly below pretreatment levels, they showed worsening during the second follow-up year (Eyberg et al., 2001).

Evidence of long-term maintenance of treatment effects at school has also been provided. Funderburk et al. (1998) conducted 12- and 18-month follow-up school assessments with 12 boys referred to PCIT for behavior problems both at home and at school. At the 12-month follow up, 11 of the 12 boys maintained all posttreatment improvements on observational and teacher rating scale measures of classroom behavior problems. At the 18-month follow

TABLE 22.3
Effect Sizes of Changes From Pre- to Posttreatment for Families Completing Parent–Child Interaction Therapy (Schuhmann et al., 1998)

| | Mothers | | | | | |
| | Pretreatment | | | Posttreatment* | | |
Assessment Measure	n	M	SD	M	SD	d
Beck Depression Inventory	22	8.2	7.2	6.7	7.5	0.2
Parenting Stress Inventory						
Total score	22	282.7	31.3	239.9**	29.3	1.4
Child domain	22	142.5	15.0	113.5**	18.4	1.7
Parent domain	22	140.2	21.9	126.4†	17.9	0.7
Parental Locus of Control	22	69.9	8.2	60.2**	8.9	1.1
Eyberg Child Behavior Inventory						
Intensity Scale	22	170.3	26.4	117.6**	40.4	1.5
Problem Scale	22	21.9	6.5	10.9**	9.6	1.3
DPICS–II (%)						
Praise	23	3.0	2.0	17.0†	9.0	2.2
Criticisms	23	6.0	4.0	2.0†	3.0	1.1
Behavioral Descriptions	23	1.0	1.0	8.0†	1.0	7.0

| | Fathers | | | | | |
| | Pretreatment | | | Posttreatment | | |
Assessment Measure	n	M	SD	M	SD	d
Beck Depression Inventory	12	8.0	4.7	3.4	2.6	1.2
Parenting Stress Inventory						
Total Score	12	270.4	27.6	239.4	26.5	1.1
Child Domain	12	136.3	15.3	114.3†	18.6	1.3
Parent Domain	12	134.8	18.9	125.1	11.6	0.6
Parental Locus of Control	12	66.1	7.1	56.9**	9.1	1.6
Eyberg Child Behavior Inventory						
Intensity Scale	12	159.6	25.2	126.8†	30.2	1.2
Problem Scale	12	20.5	5.0	10.2	8.9	1.4
DPICS–II (%)						
Praise	12	4.0	3.0	20.0†	10.0	2.2
Criticisms	12	6.0	4.0	2.0†	2.0	1.3
Behavioral Descriptions	12	2.0	2.0	14.0†	10.0	1.7

Note. DPICS–II: Dyadic Parent–Child Interaction Coding System–II. Unadjusted DPICS–II posttreatment means are reported for interpretive clarity.
*Asterisks in this column indicate the statistical significance level of differences between the pretreatment and posttreatment scores for parents in the treatment group, based on t tests.
**$p < .01$.
†$p < .05$.

up, the children maintained their improvements in compliance, but other measures of school behavior showed declines back into the pretreatment range.

Differences in long-term outcomes associated with either completing or dropping out of PCIT have also been examined. Boggs et al. (2003) conducted telephone follow-up assessments of 23 children from the Eyberg, Boggs, and Algina (1995) study who had completed treatment and 23 children who had dropped out 10 to 30 months earlier. At the follow-up, families who completed treatment had significantly fewer symptoms of the disruptive behavior disorders and significantly less parenting stress. The children who completed treatment were also assessed 4 to 6 years after treatment, and as a group, these children remained within the normal range of disruptive behavior (Hood & Eyberg, 2003). However, one notable finding showed that scores for one quarter of these children were above normal limits at this follow-up.

FUTURE CONSIDERATIONS

PCIT is an empirically supported intervention for young children with disruptive behavior that has abundant evidence of immediate treatment effects and promising evidence of long-term effectiveness for most children. Research on long-term follow-up of child treatments generally is still in the early stages, and recent increases in violent crime by children make the study of treatment maintenance for children with disruptive behavior a research priority. The few long-term follow-up studies of PCIT to date suggest that most families who complete treatment maintain their gains, but little is known about the 25% of families who complete treatment successfully and then relapse in the second follow-up year—or how to reduce this percentage further. By monitoring families during the initial 2-year period after treatment and identifying the earliest signs of relapse, we hope to engage these parents in effective problem-solving before the negative parent–child interactions escalate out of control. Once parents learn that they are able to reestablish authoritative parenting patterns and reverse early setbacks, future escalations may be less threatening to long-term maintenance of treatment gains.

REFERENCES

Abidin, R. R. (1997). Parenting Stress Index: A measure of the parent–child system. In C. P. Zalaquett & R. J. Wood (Eds.), *Evaluating stress: A book of resources* (pp. 277–291). Lanham, MD: Scarecrow Press.

Abidin, R. R., & Konold, T. R. (1999). *Parenting Alliance Measure: Professional manual*. Odessa, FL: Psychological Assessment Resources.

Azar, S. T., & Wolfe, D. A. (1989). Child abuse and neglect. In E. J. Mash, R. A. Barkley, et al. (Eds.), *Treatment of childhood disorders* (pp. 451–489). New York: Guilford Press.

Bates, J. E., Bayles, D., Bennett, D. S., Ridge, B., & Brown, M. (1991). Origins of externalizing behavioral problems at eight years of age. In D. J. Pepler & K. H. Rubin (Eds.), *The development and treatment of childhood aggression* (pp. 93–119). Hillsdale, NJ: Erlbaum.

Baumrind, D. (1967). Child care practices anteceding three patterns of preschool behavior. *Genetic Psychology Monographs, 75,* 43–88.

Baumrind, D. (1991). The influence of parenting style on adolescent competence and substance use. *Journal of Early Adolescence, 11,* 56–95.

Baumrind, D. (1996). The discipline controversy revisited. *Family Relations: Journal of Applied Family and Child Studies, 45,* 405–414.

Beck, A. T., Steer, R. A., & Brown, G. K. (1996). *Manual for the Beck Depression Inventory–II.* San Antonio, TX: Psychological Corporation.

Boggs, S. R., Eyberg, S. M., Edwards, D. L., Rayfield, A., Jacobs, J., Bagner, D., et al. (2003). *Long-term treatment outcome: A comparison of treatment completers and treatment dropouts from parent-child interaction therapy.* Manuscript submitted for publication.

Brestan, E. V., Eyberg, S. M., Algina, J., Johnson, S. B., & Boggs, S. R. (2003). How annoying is it? Defining parental tolerance for child misbehavior. *Child and Family Behavior Therapy, 25,* 1–15.

Brestan, E. V., Eyberg, S. M., Boggs, S. R., & Algina, J. (1997). Parent–child interaction therapy: Parents' perceptions of untreated siblings. *Child and Family Behavior Therapy, 19,* 13–28.

Brestan, E. V., Jacobs, J., Rayfield, A., & Eyberg, S. M. (1999). A consumer satisfaction measure for parent–child treatments and its relationship to measures of child behavior change. *Behavior Therapy, 30,* 17–30.

Brinkmeyer, M., & Eyberg, S. M. (2003). Parent–child interaction therapy for oppositional children. In A. E. Kazdin & J. R. Weisz (Eds.), *Evidence-based psychotherapies for children and adolescents* (pp. 204–223). New York: Guilford Press.

Calzada, E. J., & Eyberg, S. M. (2003). *Parenting practices and child conduct problems in preschool-age Latino children.* Manuscript submitted for publication.

Chamberlain, P., & Smith, D. K. (2003). Antisocial behavior in children and adolescents: The Oregon multidimensional treatment foster care model. In A. E. Kazdin & J. R. Weisz (Eds.), *Evidence-based psychotherapies for children and adolescents* (pp. 282–300). New York: Guilford.

Cicchetti, D., & Richters, J. E. (1993). Developmental considerations in the investigation of conduct disorder. *Development and Psychopathology, 5,* 331–344.

Coie, J. D., Watt, N. F., West, S. G., & Hawkins, J. D. (1993). The science of prevention: A conceptual framework and some directions for a national research program. *American Psychologist, 48,* 1013–1022.

Crick, N. R., & Dodge, K. A. (1994). A review and reformulation of social information-processing mechanisms in children's social adjustment. *Psychological Bulletin, 115,* 74–101.

Dumas, J. E., & Wahler, R. G. (1983). Predictors of treatment outcome in parent training: Mother insularity and socioeconomic disadvantage. *Behavioral Assessment, 5,* 301–313.

Eisenstadt, T. H., Eyberg, S. M., McNeil, C. B., Newcomb, K., & Funderburk, B. W. (1993). Parent–child interaction therapy with behavior problem children: Relative effectiveness of two stages and overall treatment outcome. *Journal of Clinical Child Psychology, 22,* 42–51.

Eyberg, S. M., Bessmer, J., Newcomb, K., Edwards, D., & Robinson, E. A. (1994). *Dyadic Parent-Child Interaction Coding System II: A manual.* Social and Behavioral Sciences Documents (Ms. No. 2897). Retrieved September 27, 2004, from http://www.pcit.org

Eyberg, S. M., Boggs, S. R., & Algina, J. (1995). Parent–child interaction therapy: A psychosocial model for the treatment of young children with conduct problem behavior and their families. *Psychopharmacology Bulletin, 31,* 83–91.

Eyberg, S. M., Edwards, D., Boggs, S., & Foote, R. (1998). Maintaining the treatment effects of parent training: The role of booster sessions and other maintenance strategies. *Clinical Psychology: Science and Practice, 5,* 544–554.

Eyberg, S. M., Funderburk, B. W., Hembree-Kigin, T. L., McNeil, C. B., Querido, J. G., & Hood, K. (2001). Parent–child interaction therapy with behavior problem children: One- and two-year maintenance of treatment effects in the family. *Child and Family Behavior Therapy, 23,* 1–20.

Eyberg, S. M., & Matarazzo, R. G. (1980). Training parents as therapists: A comparison between individual parent–child interaction training and parent group didactic training. *Journal of Clinical Psychology, 36,* 492–499.

Eyberg, S. M., & Pincus, D. (1999). *Eyberg Child Behavior Inventory and Sutter-Eyberg Student Behavior Inventory: Professional manual.* Odessa, FL: Psychological Assessment Resources.

Eyberg, S. M., Schuhmann, E. M., & Rey, J. (1998). Child and adolescent psychotherapy research: Developmental issues. *Journal of Abnormal Child Psychology, 26,* 71–82.

Floyd, E. N., & Eyberg, S. M. (2003, August). *Testing the attachment theory of parent-child interaction therapy.* Poster presented at the annual meeting of the American Psychological Association, Toronto, Canada.

Foote, R., Eyberg, S., & Schuhmann, E. (1998). Parent–child interaction approaches to the treatment of child behavior problems. *Advances in Clinical Child Psychology, 20,* 125–151.

Forehand, R., Furey, W. M., & McMahon, R. J. (1984). The role of maternal distress in a parent training program to modify child non-compliance. *Behavioral Psychotherapy, 12,* 93–108.

Funderburk, B. W., Eyberg, S. M., Newcomb, K., McNeil, C. B., Hembree-Kigin, T. L., & Capage, L. (1998). Parent–child interaction therapy with behavior problem children: Maintenance of treatment effects in the school setting. *Child and Family Behavior Therapy, 20,* 17–38.

Hanf, C. (1969, June). *A two-stage program for modifying maternal controlling during mother-child (M-C) interaction.* Paper presented at the meeting of the Western Psychological Association, Vancouver, BC.

Hood, K. K., & Eyberg, S. M. (2003). Outcomes of parent–child interaction therapy: Mothers' reports on maintenance three to six years later. *Journal of Clinical Child and Adolescent Psychology, 32,* 419–429.

Jacobs, J. R., Boggs, S. R., Eyberg, S. M., Edwards, D. L., Durning, P., Querido, J. G., et al. (2000). Psychometric properties and reference point data for the Revised Edition of the School Observation Coding System. *Behavior Therapy, 31,* 695–712.

Kazdin, A. E., Holland, L., Crowley, M., & Breton, S. (1997). Barriers to Participation in Treatment Scale: Evaluation and validation in the context of child outpatient treatment. *Journal of Child Psychology and Psychiatry and Allied Disciplines, 38,* 1051–1062.

Kazdin, A. E., Mazurick, J. L., & Bass, D. (1993). Risk for attrition in treatment of antisocial children and families. *Journal of Clinical Child Psychology, 22,* 2–16.

Lahey, B., Loeber, R., Hart, E. L., Frick, P., Applegate, B., Zhang, Q., et al. (1995). Four-year longitudinal study of conduct disorder in boys: Patterns and predictors of persistence. *Journal of Abnormal Psychology, 104,* 83–93.

Lea, E. S., Storch, E. A., & Eyberg, S. M. (2003). *Prediction of school behavior and learning problems from the Sutter-Eyberg Student Behavior Inventory–Revised.* Manuscript submitted for publication.

Loeber, R., & Schmaling, K. B. (1985). The utility of differentiating between mixed and pure forms of antisocial child behavior. *Journal of Abnormal Child Psychology, 13,* 315–335.

McMahon, R. J., & Estes, A. M. (1997). Conduct problems. In E. J. Mash & L. G. Terdal (Eds.), *Assessment of childhood disorders* (3rd ed., pp. 130–193). New York: Guilford Press.

McNeil, C. B., Eyberg, S., Eisenstadt, T. H., Newcomb, K., & Funderburk, B. (1991). Parent–child interaction therapy with behavior problem children: Generalization of treatment effects to the school setting. *Journal of Clinical Child Psychology, 20,* 140–151.

Nixon, R. D. V., Sweeney, L., Erickson, D. B., & Touyz, S. W. (2003). Parent–child interaction therapy: A comparison of standard and abbreviated treatments for oppositional defiant preschoolers. *Journal of Consulting and Clinical Psychology, 71,* 251–260.

Patterson, G. R. (1982). *A social learning approach to family intervention. III. Coercive family process.* Eugene, OR: Castalia.

Querido, J. G., Bearss, K., & Eyberg, S. M. (2002). Theory, research, and practice of parent–child interaction therapy. In F. W. Kaslow & T. Patterson (Eds.), *Comprehensive handbook of psychotherapy, Vol. 2: Cognitive/behavioral/functional approaches* (pp. 91–113). New York: Wiley.

Rayfield, A., Eyberg, S. M., Boggs, S., & Roberts, M. (1995, November). *Development and validation of the Parenting Locus of Control–Short Form*. Paper presented at the annual meeting of the Association for the Advancement of Behavior Therapy Preconference on Social Learning and the Family, Washington, DC.

Rich, B. A., & Eyberg, S. M. (2001). Accuracy of assessment: The discriminative and predictive power of the Eyberg Child Behavior Inventory. *Ambulatory Child Health, 7*, 249–257.

Richman, N., Stevenson, J., & Graham, P. J. (1982). *Pre-school to school: A behavioural study*. London: Academic Press.

Schuhmann, E. M., Foote, R. C., Eyberg, S. M., Boggs, S. R., & Algina, J. (1998). Efficacy of parent–child interaction therapy: Interim report of a randomized trial with short-term maintenance. *Journal of Clinical Child Psychology, 27*, 34–45.

Shaffer, D., Fisher, P., Lucas, C. P., Dulcan, M. K., & Schwab-Stone, M. E. (2000). NIMH Diagnostic Interview Schedule for Children Version IV (NIMH DISC–IV): Description, differences from previous versions, and reliability of some common diagnoses. *Journal of the American Academy of Child and Adolescent Psychiatry, 39*, 28–38.

Taylor, T. K., Schmidt, F., Pepler, D., & Hodgins, C. (1998). A comparison of eclectic treatment with Webster-Stratton's parents and children series in a children's mental health center: A controlled trial. *Behavior Therapy, 29*, 229–240.

Webster-Stratton, C. (1990). Long-term follow-up of families with young conduct problem children: From preschool to grade school. *Journal of Clinical Child Psychology, 19*, 144–149.

Webster-Stratton, C., & Hammond, M. (1997). Treating children with early-onset conduct problems: A comparison of child and parent training interventions. *Journal of Consulting and Clinical Psychology, 65*, 93–109.

Webster-Stratton, C., & Reid, M. J. (2003). The incredible years parents, teachers, and children training series: A multifaceted treatment approach for young children with conduct problems. In A. E. Kazdin & J. R. Weisz (Eds.), *Evidence-based psychotherapies for children and adolescents*. New York: Guilford Press.

Werba, B., Eyberg, S. M., Boggs, S. R., & Algina, J. (2003). *Predicting outcome in parent–child interaction therapy: Responsiveness and attrition*. Manuscript submitted for publication.

Wolfe, D. A. (1987). *Child abuse: Implications for child development and psychopathology*. Newbury Park, CA: Sage.

VI

AUTISTIC DISORDERS

INTRODUCTION:
AUTISTIC DISORDERS

Autistic disorder is characterized by impairments in communication and social skills and a marked absence of interest in participating in age-appropriate social activities. In addition, cognitive skills are usually impaired, and comorbid conditions such as aggressiveness, self-injurious behaviors, hyperactivity, and affective variability, as well as stereotypical rocking, compulsive ritualistic behavior, and mental retardation may be present. The autistic symptoms may be expressed in different forms depending on the age and developmental level of the child. The incidence of autism is 6.6 to 13.6 per 10,000 individuals, and the rates for males are 4 to 5 times more than those for females. One aim of psychosocial interventions is to reverse these dysfunctional aspects by intervening as early as possible in the course of the child's development, often by building therapeutic strategies into the approaches used by primary caregivers and other individuals in the child's milieu. In this section, three chapters present various intervention strategies.

Laura Schreibman and Robert L. Koegel are investigating the effectiveness of an individualized intervention addressing specific child and family characteristics in order to maximize the effectiveness of the treatment. They use parent training as an avenue for the treatment of children with autism. In their chapter they describe how parents are trained to identify and target a few pivotal behaviors of self-management for the intervention with the goal of encouraging children's increased independence. The authors present in detail the treatment components and the delivery of intervention. Analyses indicate that the experimental group is superior to control condition. The authors recommend further refinement of the intervention to effect generalizability and wider replicability across children, and they call for additional studies to identify the various parent and child characteristics that affect treatment outcomes.

Lynn Kern Koegel, Robert L. Koegel, and Lauren I. Brookman review empirically supported interventions for children with communication difficulties and present their work, which focuses on a reciprocal parent–child dyad communication approach. They present in detail their model of interactive communication accentuating the child's role as an active communicative partner to enhance language procedures. They also outline the techniques used for teaching children to be active communicators. Preliminary results indicate the promising nature of this procedure, with some evidence of generalization to home settings. The treatment was successful in improving communication with widespread concomitant decreases in disruptive and inappropriate behaviors. The authors recommend that future techniques be designed to promote self-learning and independence to develop more efficient treatments for children with autism, more significant generalization and maintenance treatment gains, and greater reduction of parental stress.

Frank W. Kohler and his collaborators review empirically supported interventions for children with autism and discuss their therapeutic strategy, Learning Experience . . . an Alternative Program (LEAP), for preschoolers with autism. Parents of children participate in a parent program designed to teach more effective ways of interacting with their preschoolers in school, at home, and community environments, in addition to classroom-based interventions. The LEAP intervention also involves cooperation with peers in playing, hanging out together, and sharing toys. The authors discuss in detail their treatment procedure. The outcomes are quite encouraging, and the peer-mediated intervention technique appears to be beneficial for children with autism. In highlighting future directions, the authors recommend that future studies should design, implement and evaluate longitudinal community-based interventions to achieve the magnitude, breadth, and longevity of behavior change that children need to function in a complex social structure.

All the therapeutic modalities included in this section involve the training of parents to actively participate in the treatment of their children. Although treatment effects appear beneficial, many unanswered questions remain. Could these interventions be used with other more at-risk populations (i.e., children of lower socioeconomic levels, various ethnic groups, various levels of impairment, or various ages and levels of functioning)? Could these interventions be beneficial when performed outside of laboratory settings? Because children with developmental disorders can precipitate stress and discord in their families, should parent and family treatment be an integral part of the children's interventions? These studies provide just an introduction to the larger amount of work that is continuing in this area. Future studies must not only address the previously mentioned issues but must also embrace more comprehensive approaches to the treatment of autism, such as the use of combinations of therapeutic interventions across modalities and settings.

23

TRAINING FOR PARENTS OF CHILDREN WITH AUTISM: PIVOTAL RESPONSES, GENERALIZATION, AND INDIVIDUALIZATION OF INTERVENTIONS

LAURA SCHREIBMAN AND ROBERT L. KOEGEL

INTRODUCTION

This chapter describes a systematic line of clinical research focusing on the involvement of parents as intervention providers for their children with autism. We begin with a brief description of autism and the impact of such children on their parents. The next section of the chapter describes

Preparation of this chapter and the research reported herein were supported by USPHS Research Grants MH 39434 and MH 28210 from the National Institute of Mental Health.

the advantage of parent training over a program in which the child is treated exclusively by clinicians in a clinic setting. Next, we discuss the evolution of an optimal form of parent training. The core of this research begins with a comparison of a parent training program that treats only individual target behaviors with a parent training program that focuses on pivotal behaviors in autism (i.e., motivation and responsivity to multiple cues). Because of limitations in the generalization of this approach and continued reported high stress in parents, a third pivotal behavior, self-management, was added. Although it improved overall general intervention success, remaining heterogeneity in intervention outcome suggests the need to develop individualized intervention protocols tailored to individual children and families.

AUTISM

Autistic disorder (*Diagnostic and Statistical Manual of Mental Disorders, Fourth Edition* [DSM–IV], American Psychiatric Association, 2000) is a severe form of psychopathology often apparent from the beginning of life and diagnosable by the age of 3 years. It is characterized primarily by severe and pervasive deficits in social attachment, social behaviors, and communication. It is also characterized by restricted patterns of behavior (e.g., stereotypical rocking, flapping) and restricted interests (e.g., compulsive and ritualistic behaviors), attentional deficits, disturbances of affect, and, in approximately 75% of cases, mental retardation. The incidence of strictly defined autistic disorder was typically reported to be approximately 4 per 10,000 children (with autistic-like symptoms occurring in many more children), and it is found in males versus females at the ratio of 4 or 5:1. For as yet unknown reasons, some estimates suggest that the current incidence of autism in the general population has increased to as many as 1 per 200 children (Wing & Potter, 2002) and may be rising.

Understandably, raising a child with such a severe developmental disorder places an extreme burden on parents. Added to this difficulty is the historical fact that for many years parents were implicated in the etiology of the disorder (e.g., Bettelheim, 1967). The severity of the disorder and the erroneous conception of autism as a psychogenically based disorder essentially prevented parents from being considered as intervention agents for their children with autism. However, recent research indicating that autism is a neurodevelopmental disorder (e.g., Akshoomoff, Pierce, & Courchesne, 2002; Denckla & James, 1991; Lamb, Moore, Bailey, & Monaco, 2000; Minshew, Sweeney, & Bauman, 1997) and the development of behavioral parent training programs has allowed for the successful use of parents as an important clinical resource.

DESCRIPTION OF PROGRAM

The focus of this chapter is on research exploring the effectiveness of parent training as an avenue for the delivery of treatment for autism. In early studies (Koegel, Schreibman, Britten, Burke, & O'Neill, 1982; Lovaas, Koegel, Simmons, & Long, 1973) researchers systematically compared behavioral interventions delivered by a trained clinician with the same interventions delivered by a parent trained in the implementation of the treatment. Results consistently showed that parents typically produced as much or greater initial behavioral gains in their children and far greater generalization and maintenance of treatment gains. Further, this avenue of intervention delivery improved the overall pattern of family interactions, permitting far greater freedom and pursuit of leisure-time family activities than when an equivalent intervention was provided by a clinician instead of the parent. Because this approach appears to be more effective for the child and more economical and satisfying for the family, and because it provides for the feasibility of intervention delivery to children living in areas remote from clinical centers, we have embarked on a large scale research program to identify the most effective forms and content of parent training in order to have a maximum impact on autism per se, as well as on overall family functioning.

In spite of the very positive results, one rather serious limitation to date has been that the children can become extremely dependent upon their treatment provider (in this case, their parents) and may continue to exhibit relatively limited autonomous responding even after extensive intervention. On the basis of the literature and our pilot data, we hypothesized that the most productive parent training avenue is one that involves the child as a major contributor to his or her own intervention. Specifically, we feel that parent training programs involving content focused on intervention that *motivates* the children to initiate and maintain social interactions and to *self-manage* their own behaviors are critical to the children's long-term development. The types of changes that are required of the children over the years are those that need to be manifested in an infinite number of environments, including many where their parents are not present. Further, as the children mature, their need for independent functioning becomes greater.

GOALS AND ISSUES

The literature (e.g., Freeman & Ritvo, 1976; Koegel, Glahn, & Nieminen, 1978; Wing, 1972) and results of our previous research (Koegel et al., 1982; Koegel, Schreibman, Johnson, O'Neill, & Dunlap, 1984; Koegel,

Schreibman, O'Neill, & Burke, 1983; Runco & Schreibman, 1983; Runco & Schreibman, 1988; Schreibman, Koegel, Mills, & Burke, 1981; Schreibman, Runco, Mills, & Koegel, 1982) suggest that although parent training proved to be superior to clinic intervention on a variety of dependent measures, there remained limitations to the effectiveness of parent training. These limitations related strongly to problems in generalization, with intervention gains evident in the presence of the parents but often not evident in the parents' absence. Also, intervention gains were very specific, showing little or no generalization to nontreated behaviors. Our research into these impediments to generalization implicated deficits in motivation and responsivity as important variables. Deficits in motivation were noted when the child would learn a behavior but not perform the behavior spontaneously. Deficits in responsivity were noted when the child's breadth of attention was too narrow to allow observational learning in the home environment. The child usually learned only when the parents directly taught the behavior.

Subsequent advances have shown that intervention delivered in naturalistic conditions that focused on improving motivation had a major impact on improving the breadth of treatment gains. Rather than improving only single behaviors at a time, such interventions appeared to influence widespread areas of the children's functioning. Because so many untreated behaviors also were affected, we called this type of intervention pivotal response training. This new pivotal parent training program involved teaching the parents specific procedures that have been reported in the research literature to enhance motivation and to increase the children's responsivity to cues in the environment (Dunlap, 1984; Koegel, Camarata, & Koegel, 1994; Koegel, Camarata, Koegel, Ben-Tall, & Smith, 1998; Koegel, Dyer, & Bell, 1987; Koegel, Koegel, Harrower, & Carter, 1999; Koegel, Koegel, Shoshan, & McNerney, 1999; Koegel, O'Dell, & Dunlap, 1988; Koegel, O'Dell, & Koegel, 1987; Koegel & Schreibman, 1977; Koegel & Williams, 1980; Laski, Charlop, & Schreibman, 1988; Pierce & Schreibman, 1995; Schreibman, Charlop, & Koegel, 1982; Stahmer, 1999). These interventions provided not only widespread response generalization in that many behaviors improved, but the speed of teaching parents was faster, the rate of acquisition of new behaviors on the part of the children was faster, disruptive behaviors decreased to almost zero without the need for separate intervention, and the affect of the children and their parents was considerably more positive during both intervention and nonintervention interactions (Koegel, Bimbela, & Schreibman, 1996; Schreibman, Kaneko, & Koegel, 1991). However, in spite of the considerable optimism over these achievements, the significant problem of the children's apparent dependence on cues from adults, and on continued intervention from adults, remained. The children failed to exhibit the autonomy required to function normally in most social contexts.

Accordingly, we and others have extended this line of pivotal response training to include the pivotal behavior of *self-management* as a major intervention target (Koegel & Koegel, 1988). This type of teaching is a direct and logical outgrowth of the previous pivotal response training, which is based heavily on naturalistic intervention procedures. Self-management continues to extend this research in several ways. For example, the use of natural reinforcers intrinsic to the child-selected activities provides the opportunity for the child to naturally provide self-reinforcement.

Self-management has several advantages as a means of facilitating generalized and independent responding for children with autism. First, the procedures allow the child to take an active role in his or her therapy, reducing the need for constant clinician vigilance (Fowler, 1984). Second, by teaching the child the skill of self-management as a pivotal behavior, an indefinite number of behaviors can be targeted in virtually any environment the child enters. Third, many factors that are included in self-management programs have previously been shown to be successful in promoting generalization. These include the administration of delayed rewards (e.g., Dunlap, Koegel, Johnson, & O'Neill, 1987) and of unpredictable rewards (Koegel & Rincover, 1977). Fourth, the use of the self-management techniques or the occurrence or improvement of the target behavior (or both) may encourage other individuals in the natural environment to provide reinforcers (Baer, Fowler, & Carden-Smith, 1984), initiating a favorable cycle of steadily improving environmental interactions. Fifth, the child's use of a recording device (to monitor his or her behavior) may lead to the device acquiring discriminative stimulus properties such that it acquires stimulus control for the occurrence or improvement of the desired target behaviors (Nelson & Hayes, 1981). Other factors discussed by Stokes and Baer (1977) that may contribute to generalization and that are also included in many self-management programs are loose teaching, including multiple exemplars, and teaching in multiple environments. As mentioned, self-management is a widely researched intervention technique that uses the client as an active participant in the intervention process. These procedures have not only been shown to be effective with populations of typical individuals (e.g., Drabman, Spitalnik, & O'Leary, 1973; O'Brien, Riner, & Budd, 1983; Sagotsky, Patterson, & Lepper, 1978) but have also been used successfully with persons exhibiting symptoms of mild to moderate mental retardation (Gardner, Cole, Berry, & Nowinski, 1983; Horner & Brigham, 1979; Shapiro & Klein, 1980; Shapiro, McGonigle, & Ollendick, 1980; Sugai & Rowe, 1984).

Working with children with autism, Koegel and Koegel (1990) demonstrated that severely handicapped autistic children could successfully reduce a difficult behavior (self-stimulation) using self-management procedures. Stahmer and Schreibman (1992) used self-management to increase appropriate play in unsupervised environments. For lower-functioning children with autism for whom language-based self-management was typically unsuccessful, Pierce and Schreibman (1994) demonstrated the effectiveness of pictorial self-management. Koegel, Harrower, and Koegel (1999) used self-management to facilitate participation in full-inclusion classrooms by children with disabilities.

Thus, to address the remaining generalization problems still evident in parent training, we directed our research toward the comparison of two parent training programs. One consists of a typical parent training approach where the parents are taught to manage their children's behavior. The other is an approach wherein the parents are taught to include their child as a central part of the intervention delivery through self-management techniques. We hypothesized that the new parent training approach would remediate the limitations and allow the achievement of generalized gains in the children's behavior and allow them to function more independently in their social environments.

METHOD

As discussed above, a main issue in the treatment of children with autism is the generalization of intervention effectiveness. Thus, we seek to develop interventions that will be expressed (a) in a wide variety of stimulus situations, (b) across a range of individual behaviors, and (c) over extended periods of time. Focusing on pivotal behaviors means a greater economy and efficiency in our efforts because we assume a greater overall impact as a function of targeting a few (pivotal) behaviors.

Assessments

As with the development of any effective behavioral intervention plan, accurate, comprehensive, and appropriate assessment is an integral part of the process. We divide our assessments along two lines of dependent measures: assessments designed to directly evaluate the effects of the training on a wide range of relevant *child* variables and assessments designed to evaluate the impact of the training on the *parents and the family*. We consider this second group of assessments particularly important because ours is a parent training program, and no matter how effective with the children, the parents will be disinclined to use the intervention if they find it too difficult, too disruptive to family life, or ineffective. Assessments are conducted before and after the intervention and at follow-up intervals.

Child Measures

The measures of the child's behavior are divided into two subareas reflecting stimulus and response generalization: (a) social adaptation, an index of the child's level of functioning relative to his or her social environment, along nonverbal dimensions; and (b) language development, which deals with both receptive and expressive dimensions. These subareas were chosen because impairments in the social and language areas encompass the majority of the major symptoms of autism (Kanner, 1943; Rimland, 1964; Rutter, 1971; Schreibman, 1988).

Social Adaptation. We use both a behavioral measure and a standardized questionnaire. The behavioral measure consists of a structured observation wherein the child is observed in a large living room–type environment equipped with several toys, couch, table, and so forth. The child is observed with a therapist and with an unfamiliar adult to assess the child's behavior independent of the parent. These sessions are videotaped, and later analysis and scoring of multiple responses provides for a quantitative description of the degree to which specified behaviors are present or absent in a free-play setting (e.g., Lovaas, et al., 1973). Four behaviors characteristic of autism are scored. These include (a) self-stimulation, (b) appropriate play, (c) social nonverbal behavior (e.g., responding to request, imitating), and (d) tantrum or crying.

The standardized measure of social adaptation is the Vineland Adaptive Behavior Scales (Sparrow, Balla, & Cicchetti, 1984), which yields scores relating to socialization, communication, daily living skills, an adaptive behavior composite, and level of maladaptive behavior. This generalization measure reflects the child's competence and independence in his or her social environment.

Language Development. We obtain both behavioral measures and standardized test measures in the area of language development. For the behavioral measure, we use the structured playroom setting procedure (described in the previous section), scoring several categories of verbal behavior. These include appropriate imitation of others' speech, ability to answer questions posed by others, spontaneous speech, and other appropriate speech. We also score inappropriate speech (e.g., echolalia, neologisms, and, idiosyncratic language).

For our standardized measures of language development, we use the Assessment of Children's Language Comprehension (Foster, Giddan, & Stark, 1973), which provides a detailed, in-depth analysis of the child's level of generalized language development with respect to population norms with information regarding the amount of simultaneous language components a child is able to use (this method also provides a generalization assessment regarding our responsivity to multiple cues pivotal behavior). We also administer the Peabody Picture Vocabulary Test (Dunn & Dunn, 1981) to assess the child's receptive language level and the Expressive One-Word Picture Vocabulary Test—Revised (EOWPVT; Gardner, 1990), which provides a measure of the child's expressive vocabulary with respect to population norms.

Parent and Family Measures

Because we are interested in the impact of our treatment conditions on the family system, we obtain data on dependent measures designed to provide information on important family variables. The specific measures we use are those that have been shown to be sensitive to important clinical aspects of the family (e.g., Koegel et al., 1982; Schreibman & Koegel, 1989) and that are likely to show changes as the child shows increasing amounts of independent behavior.

Family Environment and Interaction. We use several indices of the atmosphere of the whole family system and the specific nature of parent–child interactions. To obtain information about how the families budget their time over a day, parents are asked to keep a 24-hour Time Activity diary (e.g., Berk & Berk, 1979) for one weekday and for one weekend day. The diary asks the parents to indicate how much time they spent in various activities (e.g., teaching their child, leisure activity, custodial care of child) and who was with them during the activity. It also asks for their perception of the valence of each activity (e.g., "pleasant," "work"). We then systematically review the forms and tabulate the amount of time the parents are involved in various types of activities, the ratings to which the parents assign the particular activity, and other important information. This information gives us a clearer picture of the influence of our program on family interactions and structure. We consider the inclusion of this measure very important because it has provided extremely interesting results during our research (Koegel et al., 1982), indicating its sensitivity to changes in the ways that parents change the structure of their time as a function of the parent training.

A video assessment is conducted during the dinner hour. This unstructured home observation allows us to gather information on changes in both the child's and the parents' behavior as a function of the teaching of our different treatment packages (e.g., motivation, responsivity to multiple cues, self-management). We score these videotapes for style of family interactions. Specifically, we assess (a) level of happiness of the interaction, (b) level of parental interest in the interaction, (c) level of stress in the interaction, and (d) level of sternness or pleasantness of the interaction.

To obtain generalized effects of the parent training in a more structured setting, we use the previously described structured laboratory observations in the context of the child measures. During the assessments relating to the parent, the parent is the adult present with the child in the room. The parent is instructed to engage in specific interactions that enable us to determine the extent to which the child exhibits appropriate and psychopathological spontaneous independent behavior in a free-play setting with the parent. We also can determine the extent to which the child engages in social interactions with the parent and the nature of these interactions.

Parenting a child with autism is a challenging task, and we wish to acquire information relating to the perceived stress of these parents as a function of teaching. We have chosen an assessment that allows us to easily compare our results with those of other researchers. The *Questionnaire* on Resources and Stress (QRS; Holroyd, 1974; Holroyd, Brown, Wikler, & Simmons, 1975) is a paper-and-pencil, true–false item questionnaire designed to measure variables pertinent to families with handicapped family members (Holroyd, 1982). The short form of the questionnaire has a total of 66 questions measuring parent stress along 11 subscales, including (1) dependency and management, (2) cognitive impairment, (3) limits on family opportunity, (4) life-span care, (5) family disharmony, (6) lack of personal reward, (7) terminal illness stress, (8) physical limitations, (9) financial stress, (10) preference for institutionalization, and (11) personal burden. The QRS is a multidimensional, quantifiable, and simple-to-administer assessment that has been validated against several clinical populations, including children with autism (Holroyd et al., 1975; Holroyd & McArthur, 1976; Koegel et al., 1992).

We also administer the Parenting Stress Index (PSI; Loyd & Abidin, 1985), which is a self-report measure designed to yield a measure of the relative magnitude of stress in the parent–child system. The PSI is divided into a Child Characteristics Domain and a Parent Characteristics Domain. The six subscales composing the Child Domain (adaptability, acceptability, demandingness, mood, distractibility, hyperactivity, and reinforces parent) assess the presence of child behaviors and characteristics that are presumed to be stressful for parents. A separate Parent Domain score is derived from seven subscales (depression, attachment, restriction of role, sense of competence, social isolation, relationship with spouse, and parent health) that assess dimensions of parenting stress pertinent to personal adjustment and family functioning. Scores below the 15th percentile and above the 75th percentile are judged to be clinically elevated and may warrant referral for relevant services.

To assess whether and how parental depression levels affect participation in the intervention, we have chosen a widely used measure of depression, the Beck Depression Inventory (BDI; Beck, 1978). The BDI is a paper-and-pencil questionnaire used with many different adult populations. The BDI contains groups of statements. Each group of statements includes answers that range from nondepressed to severely depressed. The individual must choose the statement from each group that best describes the way he or she has been feeling in the past week. The BDI is quantifiable and very easy to administer and has been used and validated with many different populations.

Intervention Procedures

Because *motivation, responsivity to multiple cues, and self-management* have each been shown to affect generalized intervention gains in these children, these are the specific targets of teaching for the parents who participate in our program.

Motivation

The parents are taught to increase their child's motivation by using several individual strategies that have each been demonstrated to increase motivation and enhance learning (Koegel & Egel, 1979; Koegel et al., 1987; Koegel & Williams, 1980; Koegel, Carter, & Koegel, 2003; Koegel, Koegel, Frea, & Green-Hopkins, 2003; O'Dell, Dunlap, & Koegel, 1983; O'Dell & Koegel, 1981; Turner, 1978). The strategies include the following:

1. *Clear instructions and questions.* Here the parent is taught to present instructions only when the child is attending; to present the instructions in a clear, unambiguous manner; and to present instructions that are relevant and appropriate to the task.
2. *Intersperse maintenance tasks.* To enhance motivation by keeping the overall success and reinforcement levels high, previously mastered tasks are interspersed frequently among more difficult tasks.
3. *Child choice.* To maximize the child's interest in the learning situation, he or she is given a great deal of input in determining the specific stimuli and the nature of the learning interaction. A variety of materials (e.g., toys, games, snacks) are presented, and the child is allowed to select an activity or object about which the learning interaction will take place. The parent is encouraged to be alert to the child's changing interests and allow the child to change to another preferred activity.
4. *Direct and natural reinforcers.* Direct, rather than indirect, reinforcers are used. Direct reinforcers are consequences that are directly related to the response they follow. A direct reinforcer for the verbal response "car" might be access to a toy car as opposed to a food or token reinforcer. Access to a toy car is a direct and natural consequence of saying "car," whereas food is not.
5. *Reinforcement of attempts.* To maximize reinforcement and therefore enhance the child's motivation to respond, we train the parents to reinforce all reasonable attempts made by the child to respond. Thus, reinforcers are contingent upon attempts that may not be completely correct and may not be

quite as good as previous attempts, but are within a broader range of correct responses.

Responsivity to Multiple Cues

Prior research has identified an attentional deficit, *stimulus overselectivity*, characterizing many children with autism. This pattern of attention is characterized by a failure to respond to simultaneous multiple cues that typically occur in a learning situation (see Schreibman, 1988, and Rosenblatt, Bloom, & Koegel, 1995, for reviews of this literature). This deficit has been implicated in a wide range of behavioral deficits including failure to generalize (e.g., Lovaas, Koegel, & Schreibman, 1979; Schreibman, 1988). We also know that for many of these children overselectivity may be remediated by teaching the children a series of successive *conditional discriminations* (Koegel & Schreibman, 1977; Schreibman et al., 1982). A conditional discrimination is one that *requires* response to multiple cues. For example, asking a child to go get her red sweater is a conditional discrimination task because the child undoubtedly has more than one red item of clothing and more than one sweater. Correct responding depends on attention to *both* color and object. In our training, parents learn to present their children with tasks involving conditional discriminations. We reason that as the children learn to respond on the basis of multiple cues, their attention is more normalized, allowing for more environmental cues to become functional. Because stimulus control of behavior is no longer as restricted, enhanced generalization should result.

Self-Management

The third pivotal behavior that contributes to generalization of intervention effects is self-management. Once children have learned to use self-management to control their own behavior, they can take this skill into any setting and apply it to any behavior. In other words, generalization is systematically programmed. To accomplish this, we teach the parents a series of steps to train their child to use self-management.

1. *Identification of target behavior and reinforcer.* To begin, parents choose and define a target behavior to be self-managed. Ideally the child would choose the target behavior, but this is often not possible, especially during the initial self-management programs. The parent is encouraged to allow the child to participate as much as possible in choosing behaviors to maximize their quality of life (Turnbull, Bateman, & Turnbull, 1993). Also, the parent allows the child to choose the reinforcer (again maximizing motivation) for appropriate self-management.

2. *Identification of target behavior by the child.* Here the parents teach their child to identify the target behavior. They present to the child appropriate and inappropriate examples of the behavior and reinforce the child for correct identifications of the behavior. This process continues until the child can correctly discriminate the behavior on a minimum of 80% of random presentations. Next, the child is asked to provide examples of appropriate and inappropriate behavior (to ensure that the child knows it is his or her own behavior that is to be monitored). The parents are taught to reinforce the child's correct responses on a continuous reinforcement schedule.

3. *Teaching self-monitoring of the target behavior.* Once the child can correctly identify the target behavior, the parent begins implementation of self-management proper. Depending on the target behavior, the child is taught to record instances of the behavior (e.g., responses to social initiations) or the occurrence of the behavior within an interval (e.g., an interval of appropriate play). Specifically, the parents learn to teach their child to record (on a wrist counter or a checksheet) by pushing a button, making a checkmark, or affixing a sticker (depending on the child's level of ability and coordination) occurrences of the appropriate behavior. Initially, each time the child engages in the behavior, the parent is taught to prompt the child to conduct the relevant self-management activity. For example, the parent might say at the end of a previously established interval, "It's time! Did you do behavior X?" The child is then verbally or physically prompted to record the behavior. Accurate recording of the behavior is reinforced. Similarly, accurate recording (or withholding of recording) of inappropriate behavior also is reinforced. The previously selected reinforcer is available to the child after a predetermined interval or number of correct responses. Initially the intervals or required number of responses is set at a very low level to ensure the child's success.

4. *Increasing self-management independence.* After successful implementation of these procedures, the parents learn to increase self-management independence. Thus, parental prompts to self-record are gradually faded. Prompts for the child to exchange recorded points for reinforcers are also faded. Moreover, the schedule of reinforcement is gradually thinned by increasing the number of recorded points required for a reinforcer or by increasing the time interval required for self-managing until the child is able to self-manage his or her behavior for periods of up to several hours. Next, parents learn to fade their supervision of the child by fading their presence and, if possible, the

presence of the self-management materials (e.g., recording devices). Finally, parents learn to validate their child's appropriate use of self-management in the parent's absence by communicating with significant others in the child's environment. Specifics of each of these steps is provided in a self-management training manual (Koegel, Koegel, & Parks, 1990).

Intervention Delivery

Our research suggests that 25 hours of training is typically adequate for teaching the three pivotal behaviors, although some parents acquire the skills more quickly, and some take much longer. The initial teaching session is devoted to assessments (see subsequent sections) of both the child's level of naturalistic language use and social interaction and level of appropriate responding in a more structured situation. The first session usually entails a 15-minute unstructured interview with the child's parents to determine the conditions under which the child typically exhibits appropriate spontaneous behavior and at what level of sophistication and success. The child is typically present and given access to a wide variety of age-appropriate activities; he or she may be provided various opportunities for language and social interaction in unstructured situations with unfamiliar persons.

At the end of the first session, the parent is given the *Pivotal Response Training Manual* (Koegel et al., 1989), which covers the motivation and responsivity pivotal behaviors, and a homework reading assignment to be completed by the next training session. The next sessions are designed to ensure that parents understand the general principles and can apply them in the home. During each session, the trainer reviews the exercises in the manual with the parent and answers questions.

When the parents have completed the *Pivotal Response Training Manual*, they are brought into the training situation with their child. Here they first observe a trained therapist using the pivotal response training components, and then they are gradually introduced into the teaching sessions, with responsibility for implementing the training gradually transferred to the parent. This transition rate depends on the parent's rate of mastery of the procedures and usually requires several sessions. Parents are given immediate feedback about their use of the training procedures. The training continues until the parent demonstrates a minimum of 80% correct usage of each of the procedures (e.g., child choice, direct reinforcers) during a 10-minute fidelity of implementation assessment. When parents have completed this training, they begin training in self-management.

Training in self-management parallels the training of the other two pivotal behaviors. The parents read the self-management manual (Koegel et al., 1990), which covers in detail the specific procedures outlined above (e.g., training in identification of target behavior). As with training on the other pivotal behaviors, the parents read sections of the manual focusing on each procedure and then discuss the procedures during the following training sessions. Once the manual is completed, the parents begin teaching their child in self-management. The parent trainer models implementation of the specific procedures, and the parents begin implementation, with appropriate feedback from the trainer. Training is considered complete when the parent has independently trained two target behaviors via self-management. To ensure that self-management procedures are actually being implemented in the home setting, we conduct three 2-hour home probes 2 weeks, 6 months, and 12 months after training. Again, the criterion is a minimum of 80% correct use of self-management procedures for clinic and in-home fidelity of implementation assessments.

Clinical Vignette

An example of the way an intervention may be provided is described in the following vignette. Jenny, age 8, is referred to our intervention program by the local developmental disabilities center. She received an autism diagnosis from a child psychologist with expertise in autism. She is a beautiful little girl with brown hair and large blue eyes. Her language consists primarily of echolalia and some functional phrases averaging about four words in length. She occasionally exhibits stereotypical repetitions of sound combinations and body rocking. She is socially avoidant of others, particularly peers. She engages in some functional toy play but very little symbolic or imaginative play. She tends to become stereotyped and ritualistic in her play, for example, lining up pictures of characters from her favorite movies. Upon referral, the parents' main concerns centered on Jenny's rudimentary and stigmatizing language behavior, her social avoidance, her frequent and intense temper tantrums, and her stereotyped engagement with toys.

Jenny's father manages a local fast-food restaurant and is away from home a good deal of the day. He is exhausted when he comes home. Although he is quite concerned about his daughter, it is difficult for him to find the time to spend time with her, and he expresses frustration that he "doesn't know what to do with her anyway." Jenny's mother, a homemaker, has two younger children at home but is deeply committed to Jenny's treatment and always finds the time to take her to her various appointments.

Upon acceptance into our program, Jenny is given our child assessment battery, and her parents are given the parent assessment battery. Jenny scores a 60 on the Stanford-Binet and a 75 on the Leiter International Performance Scales. She receives a standard score of 45 on the PPVT, and her standard score on the Vineland Adaptive Behavior Scales is 55. Scores on these standardized assessments indicate that Jenny is functioning in the mildly mentally retarded range overall, with strengths in the area of nonverbal functioning and particular difficulty with language and communication. Additionally, her adaptive functioning is moderately delayed.

Both parents score in the 2.5 to 3.5 range on the first four subscales of the QRS and 121 on the PSI. This indicates a moderate-to-high level of stress. The score is consistent with the Time Activity Diaries, which indicate that the mother spends a good deal of every day attending to Jenny's needs while the father spends relatively little time with her (as was apparent by his complaint that he did not know what to do with her). Parent measures indicate that the home environment is not severely disrupted but that both parents are experiencing moderate stress. The mother also is moderately depressed, as evident by her score of 40 on the BDI.

We begin intervention with PRT to increase Jenny's language and play skills. Because she is motivated to interact with a variety of play materials, access to these materials provides an excellent reinforcer (i.e., direct reinforcement). Access to play activities is contingent on increasingly advanced language and social behaviors, such as eye contact with the therapist and sharing. Because the father is typically unavailable to come to the clinic for training sessions, the mother is trained. According to the intervention plan, she reads the PRT training manual and discusses the various points in the manual with her parent trainer. She observes a trained therapist working with Jenny and then gradually takes on more and more responsibility for working directly with Jenny. Both mother and child respond well to the intervention, and within the first two months, the PRT sessions are proving enjoyable for both. We also note a consistent increase in Jenny's language skills, and both parents feel more optimistic about her potential. After these 2 months, the father asks to be trained in PRT. He arranges to come into the clinic for training, and the mother gives him additional feedback when he works with Jenny at home. He is delighted that he now knows "what to do with her" and feels more confident that his time with her is more fruitful. Both parents note a significant reduction in Jenny's tantrum behavior because she is more able to use her language functionally.

Because this child is a good candidate for self-management training, we discuss a potential target behavior with the parents. They both indicate that it would be helpful if Jenny could occupy herself in an appropriate manner without constant adult supervision. They decide to target appropriate toy play as the self-management behavior. The mother is given the self-management training manual, and the parent trainer discusses each of the self-management steps. The mother begins by modeling appropriate and inappropriate play behaviors and teaches Jenny to correctly identify them. Jenny is then prompted to engage in appropriate and inappropriate play behaviors and to identify them. She is subsequently taught how to self-monitor and record her own behavior during intervals of increasing length. According to the self-management plan, increasing intervals of appropriate toy play are required and adult supervision is faded. Finally the self-management materials are faded, and Jenny is able to play appropriately, unsupervised, for periods of approximately 90 minutes.

Posttreatment assessments mirror the parents' positive impressions of the intervention. Jenny now scores a 75 on the Stanford-Binet and an 87 on the Leiter International Performance Scales. She is now functioning in the borderline range of intelligence on scales that require language and in the low–average range on the nonverbal assessment. After intervention, she receives a standard score of 65 on the PPVT, and her standard score on the Vineland Adaptive Behavior Scales is 75. Jenny is now using language more appropriately in her environment and has increased her vocabulary skills. Additionally, she is now engaging in more appropriate communication and social skills in the home, as shown by her increased scores on the Vineland Scale.

At posttreatment, parent measures indicate a reduction in stress levels on the QRS (1.5–2.1 range) and the PSI measures (107). Both parents now report (on the Time Activity Diary) spending more time with Jenny, but the nature of the time has changed from being almost exclusively custodial-type activities to more teaching and recreational activities. Both mother and father express satisfaction with their training in that they now feel more able to help their daughter. Consistent with this attitude is a reduction of the mother's stress level as recorded on the BDI (a score of 29).

OUTCOMES

Throughout these stages of our research, we have been able to make substantial and empirically measurable improvements in intervention delivery. However, with every individual intervention technique we have always been able to describe a subgroup of children who have not responded favorably to the treatment. We believe that this difficulty does not relate to the effectiveness of a particular intervention but to a complex set of issues involving child characteristics, family variables, and the specific targeted behavior. Thus, we have begun a line of research that addresses the NIH priority of individualizing the intervention of autism (Bristol et al., 1996).

In relation to child characteristics, recent interest in the heterogeneity of autism has supported our substantial database that indicates that considerable variability exists within the diagnosis of autism. Researchers in the content areas of both behavioral and neurological characteristics of autism have suggested the importance of identifying individualized interventions (Asarnow & Koegel, 1994; Bristol et al., 1996; Courchesne et al., 1994; Damasio & Maurer, 1978; Gillberg & Gillberg, 1983; Mrazek & Haggerty, 1994; Ritvo, Ritvo, & Brothers, 1982; Rosenberger-Debiesse & Coleman, 1986; Schreibman, 1997; Schreibman, 2000). Related specific characteristics such as cognitive ability (Fein, Waterhouse, Lucci, & Snider, 1985), communication and social skills, and behavior such as activity level and aggression (Eaves, Eaves, & Ho, 1994) vary greatly across children. Further, the clinical picture within the children themselves changes throughout development (Waterhouse, Fein, Nath, & Snyder, 1987). Such heterogeneity of behavioral characteristics and variability in the course of the disability makes comparison of specific interventions difficult. Individualization of intervention can therefore be approached from the neurological arena or the behavioral arena. At this time, our knowledge of important variables relating to prognosis and treatment are behavioral, and it is to this approach that our research has been directed. This behavioral focus suggests the importance of shifting attention to the *individualization* of intervention techniques to correspond with specific child and family characteristics to maximize the effectiveness of the necessary comprehensive intervention programs.

A strong basis for the argument for individualization of treatment relates to data collected on self-management during our previous funding period. These data suggest that specific quantifiable variables (e.g., IQ over 50) influence the effectiveness of the specific treatment. In other words, children with higher cognitive abilities seem to make more significant gains when self-management is used. In contrast, children with lower cognitive skills seem to demonstrate greater gains when the skills are taught in the context of a parent-management program.

Further, a potentially important first step is provided by recently completed studies in our laboratory. Sherer and Schreibman (in press) identified a specific profile of child behaviors that seems to predict successful treatment outcome with PRT. The fact that this profile's predictive ability is specific to PRT is suggested by the fact that the profile does not predict child response to another behavioral intervention, Discrete Trial Training (Schreibman, Stahmer, & Cestone 2002). This work gives us hope that with continued research we will be able to refine our ability to develop specific intervention protocols for children on the basis of their individual behavioral characteristics. In a second study (Ingersoll, Stahmer, & Schreibman, 2001), a child characteristic of peer social avoidance was found to predict child outcome in an integrated preschool environment.

A second area of importance relates to family characteristics. Several variables have been studied in relation to family characteristics. Data collected in our clinics and others (Robbins, Dunlap, & Pleinis, 1991; Moes, Koegel, Schreibman, & Loos, 1992) show that parents of children with autism, particularly mothers, experience significant stress for themselves, family members, and the family as a whole in areas related to caring for the child with autism. In relation to treatment, the mothers feel that increased family support and cooperation would be likely to reduce their stress. Literature in the area of parent training suggests that some types of parent training may actually increase the stress parents experience (Benson & Turnbull, 1986; Gallagher, Beckman, & Cross, 1983). This finding is supported by data from our clinics suggesting that providing *certain* types of parent training, such as teaching procedures that are efficient, easy to implement, and easily fit into daily routines (e.g., PRT), actually *reduce* parental stress (Moes, Koegel, & Schreibman, 1993). These methods of training are in contrast to methods that require special times set aside to work one-on-one with a particular family member with autism, which do not reduce parental stress.

In the area of autism, parental stress highly correlates with the amount of progress demonstrated by the child in family-oriented training programs. Specifically, the relative magnitude of stress in the parent–child system, relating to child behaviors and characteristics that are presumed to be stressful for parents, and dimensions of parenting stress pertinent to personal adjustment and family functioning are highly correlated with child improvement in a parent intervention program. Such variables relate specifically to intervention effectiveness and should be considered in relation to treatment type (Robbins et al., 1991). Other variables that may relate to the effectiveness of parent training programs of parents of disabled children may be educational level, socioeconomic status, and marital status (Clark & Baker, 1983).

Directly related to the extreme variability in child and family characteristics is the implicit necessity of individualizing the intervention according to the particular goals addressed. This individualization is necessary because the specific target behaviors also seem to have an interactive effect with intervention type. For example, as previously discussed, our data suggest that interventions focusing on behavior management (e.g., dressing, self-stimulation) may respond better with self-management if the child has higher cognitive functioning. However, another phenomenon may occur with language structures—that is, a first lexicon responds significantly better when variables of natural language paradigms are incorporated (Koegel, O'Dell, & Koegel, 1987; Laski et al., 1988). In contrast, some structures such as question-asking (Koegel, 1995) and grammatical features that occur infrequently (Camarata & Nelson, 1992) appear to be enhanced with at least some components of an individualized target-behaviors model. Such individualization, depending on child characteristics (Yoder, Kaiser, & Alpert, 1991), family variables, and target behaviors are likely to result in an individualized prescriptive treatment, enhancing outcomes for all children with autism.

One important reason that we are optimistic about the generalizability of our intervention program is that it is implemented by parents. As has already been well documented in the behavioral literature, parent training is an important means of achieving generalization because the parents are in many of the children's environments, and thus intervention is provided in a variety of settings, across a variety of behaviors, and across times of the day. However, it must be acknowledged that our research, as well as that of most other researchers, involves programs wherein parents voluntarily commit to participation in a research program, often in a university setting. These parents are thus motivated to enter the parent training program. In addition, most of these parents are literate and can benefit from our written manuals. However, what we do not yet know is how our intervention may be differentially effective with parents who do not come to us but instead are randomly picked from schools, for example. We also do not know how effective our program would be if parents were illiterate and were provided the training via vocal instructions or other means. Again, these points speak to the issue of generalizability of our training program.

Another issue, and one that is underrepresented in the parent training literature, is the issue of different ethnicities and cultures. That cultural differences might affect the ways in which parents perceive, use, and evaluate our training programs is certainly not surprising. For instance, specific cultures differentially value target behaviors. Thus, a child's independence may be considered a very important intervention goal by one culture, whereas another culture may find it of less significance. Parents of different cultures may find certain specific aspects of intervention more or less acceptable or easy to implement. The possibilities for variability here are almost endless, and we must address these issues if we are to maximize the generalization of our intervention applicability.

FUTURE CONSIDERATIONS

Given the issues under discussion, our next research emphases are obvious. The issues of refining intervention procedures to affect wider availability and applicability across children is crucial (e.g., Koegel, Symon, & Koegel, 2002). Further, a more detailed understanding of child and parent variables is essential (e.g., Santarelli, Koegel, Casas, & Koegel, 2001). All of these issues relate to improved generalization of treatment applicability and intervention effects.

Judging from our research to date, and that of other researchers, we feel our future direction is clear. To provide the most effective and generalized intervention, we will need to identify the interaction of child, treatment, and parent or family variables so that ultimately we may be able to individually prescribe specific interventions for specific cases. Thus, child characteristics such as cognitive and verbal abilities may affect intervention presentation and success. Similarly, parent and family characteristics, such as motivation, education level, stress, number of children, culture, and social and financial resources, may be expected to affect the ways in which parents learn and implement treatment. We already know that different intervention procedures may have differential success with various child characteristics and parent or family variables. Therefore, what should be available in the future is a means for assessing these variables and the way they interact so as to allow us to design and implement an intervention program that is maximally beneficial to the child and to the entire family. Fortunately, the behavioral approach to intervention, by definition, is designed to continually assess and refine procedures. We anticipate that further research along the lines dictated by current efforts will make even greater advances toward improving the lives of these families.

In summary, our ongoing research has led us to delineate specific gaps that exist in the intervention for children with autism—that is, research suggests that specific variables associated with outcomes relate to the complex interactions of child characteristics, family variables, and target behaviors. Specifically, an individualized intervention that addresses these variables appears to have the potential to result in a prescriptive approach for individual children, so that implementation of treatment should show significant improvements for almost all individual children and their families. Thus, we expect an individualized intervention package to produce a major advance in the treatment of autism.

REFERENCES

Akshoomoff, N., Pierce, K., & Courchesne, E. (2002). The neurobiological basis of autism from a developmental perspective. *Developmental Psychopathology, 14,* 613–634.

American Psychiatric Association. (2000). *Diagnostic and statistical manual of mental disorders* (4th ed.). Washington, DC: Author.

Asarnow, J., & Koegel, R. L. (1994). Prevention of mental health disorders in children. In P. J. Mrazek & R. J. Haggerty (Eds.), *Background materials for reducing risks for mental disorders.* Washington, DC: National Academy Press.

Baer, M., Fowler, S. A., & Carden-Smith, L. (1984). Using reinforcement and independent-grading to promote and maintain task accuracy in a mainstreamed class. *Analysis and Intervention in Developmental Disabilities, 4,* 157–170.

Beck, A. T. (1978). *Beck Depression Inventory.* Philadelphia: Center for Cognitive Therapy.

Benson, H. A., & Turnbull, A. P. (1986). Approaching families from an individualized perspective. In R. H. Horner, L. H. Meyer, & H. D. B. Fredericks (Eds.), *Education of learners with severe handicaps: Exemplary service strategies.* Baltimore: Brookes.

Berk, R. A., & Berk, S. F. (1979). *Labor and leisure at home: Content and organization of the household day.* Beverly Hills, CA: Sage.

Bettelheim, B. (1967). *The empty fortress.* New York: Free Press.

Bristol, M. M., Cohen, D. J., Costello, E. J., Denckla, M., Eckberg, T. J., Kalleln, R., et al. (1996). State-of-the-science in autism: A report to the National Institutes of Health. *Journal of Autism and Developmental Disorders, 26,* 121–154.

Camarata, S. M., & Nelson, K. E. (1992). Treatment efficiency as a function of target selection in the remediation of child language disorders. *Clinical Linguistics and Phonetics, 6,* 167–178.

Clark, D. B., & Baker, B. L. (1983). Predicting outcome in parent training. *Journal of Consulting and Clinical Psychology, 51*, 309–311.

Courchesne, E., Townsend, J. P., Akshoomoff, N. A., Yeung-Courchesne, R., Press, G. A., Murakami, J. W., et al. (1994). Impairment in shifting attention in autistic and cerebellar patients. In S. H. Broman & J. Grafman (Eds.), *Atypical cognitive deficits in developmental disorders: Implications for brain function* (pp. 107–137). Hillsdale, NJ: Erlbaum.

Damasio, A. R., & Maurer, R. G. (1978). A neurological model for childhood autism. *Archives of Neurology, 35*, 777–786.

Denckla, M. B., & James, L. S. (1991, May). An update on autism: A developmental disorder. *Pediatrics, 87*, 751–796.

Drabman, R. S., Spitalnik, R., & O'Leary, K. D. (1973). Teaching self-control to disruptive children. *Journal of Abnormal Psychology, 82*, 10–16.

Dunlap, G. (1984). The influence of task variation and maintenance tasks on the learning and affect of autistic children. *Journal of Experimental Child Psychology, 37*, 41–64.

Dunlap, G., Koegel, R. L., Johnson, J., & O'Neill, R. E. (1987). Maintaining performance of autistic clients in community settings with delayed contingencies. *Journal of Applied Behavior Analysis, 20*, 185–191.

Dunn, L. M., & Dunn, L. M. (1981). *Peabody Picture Vocabulary Test–revised.* Circle Pines, MN: American Guidance Service.

Eaves, L. C., Eaves, D. M., & Ho, H. H. (1994). Subtypes of autism by cluster analysis. *Journal of Autism and Developmental Disorders, 24*, 3–22.

Fein, D., Waterhouse, L., Lucci, D., & Snyder, D. (1985). Cognitive subtypes in developmentally disabled children: A pilot study. *Journal of Autism and Developmental Disorders, 15*, 77–95.

Foster, R., Giddan, J. J., & Stark, J. (1973). *Assessment of Children's Language Comprehension.* Palo Alto, CA: Consulting Psychologists Press.

Fowler, S. (1984). Introductory comments: The pragmatics of self-management for the developmentally disabled. *Analysis and Intervention in Developmental Disabilities, 4*, 85–89.

Freeman, B. J., & Ritvo, E. R. (1976). Parents as paraprofessionals. In E. R. Ritvo (Ed.), *Autism: Diagnosis, current research, and management* (pp. 277–285). New York: Spectrum Publications.

Gallagher, J. J., Beckman, P. J., & Cross, A. H. (1983). Families of handicapped children: Sources of stress and its amelioration. *Exceptional Children, 50*, 10–19.

Gardner, M. (1990). *The expressive one word picture vocabulary test* (rev. ed.). Novato, CA: Academic Therapy Publications.

Gardner, W. I., Cole, C. L., Berry, K. L., & Nowinski, J. M. (1983). Reduction of disruptive behaviors in mentally retarded adults. *Behavior Modification, 7*, 76–96.

Gillberg, C., & Gillberg, I. C. (1983). Infantile autism: A total population study of reduced optimality on the pre-, peri-, and neonatal period. *Journal of Autism and Developmental Disorders, 13*, 153–166.

Holroyd, J. (1974). Questionnaire on Resources and Stress: An instrument to measure family response to a handicapped family member. *Journal of Community Psychology, 2,* 92–94.

Holroyd, J. (1982). *Questionnaire on Resources and Stress.* Draft manual.

Holroyd, J., Brown, N., Wikler, L., & Simmons, J. Q. (1975). Stress in families of institionalized and noninstitutionalized autistic children. *Journal of Community Psychology, 3,* 26–31.

Holroyd, J., & McArthur, D. (1976). Mental retardation and stress on the parents: A contrast between Down's syndrome and childhood autism. *American Journal of Mental Deficiency, 80,* 431–436.

Horner, R. H., & Brigham, T. A. (1979, February). The effects of self-management procedures on the study behavior of two retarded children. *Education and Training of the Mentally Retarded,* 18–24.

Ingersoll, B., Stahmer, A., & Schreibman, L. (2001). Differential treatment outcomes for children with autistic spectrum disorder based on level of peer social avoidance. *Journal of Autism and Developmental Disorders, 31,* 343–349.

Kanner, L. (1943). Autistic disturbances of affective contact. *The Nervous Child, 3,* 217–250.

Koegel, L. K. (1995). Communication and language intervention. In R. L. Koegel & L. K. Koegel (Eds.), *Teaching children with autism: Strategies for initiating positive interactions and improving learning opportunities* (pp. 17–32). Baltimore: Brookes.

Koegel, R. L., Bimbela, A., & Schreibman, L. (1996). Collateral effects of parent training on family interactions. *Journal of Autism and Developmental Disorders, 26,* 347–359.

Koegel, R. L., Camarata, S. M., & Koegel, L. K. (1994). Aggression and noncompliance: Behavior modification through naturalistic language remediation. In J. L. Matson (Ed.), *Autism in children and adults: Etiology, assessment, and intervention* (pp. 165–180). Sycamore, IL: Sycamore Press.

Koegel, R. L., Camarata, S., Koegel, L. K., Ben-Tall, A., & Smith, A. (1998). Increasing speech intelligibility in children with autism. *Journal of Autism and Developmental Disorders, 28,* 241–251.

Koegel, L. K., Carter, C. M., & Koegel, R. L. (2003). Teaching children with autism self-initiations as a pivotal response. *Topics in Language Disorders, 23,* 134–145.

Koegel, R. L., Dyer, K., & Bell, L. K. (1987). The influence of child preferred activities on autistic children's social behavior. *Journal of Applied Behavior Analysis, 20,* 243–252.

Koegel, R. L., & Egel, A. (1979). Motivating autistic children. *Journal of Abnormal Psychology, 88,* 418–426.

Koegel, R. L., Glahn, T. J., & Nieminen, G. S. (1978). Generalization of parent training results. *Journal of Applied Behavior Analysis, 11,* 95–109.

Koegel, L. K., Harrower, J., & Koegel, R. L. (1999). Support for children with disabilities in full-inclusion classrooms through self-management. *Journal of Positive Behavior Interventions, 1,* 26–34.

Koegel, R. L., & Koegel, L. K. (1988). Generalized responsivity and pivotal behaviors. In R. H. Horner, G. Dunlap, & R. L. Koegel (Eds.), *Generalization and maintenance: Life-style changes in applied settings* (pp. 41–66). Baltimore: Brookes.

Koegel, R. L., & Koegel, L. K. (1990). Extended reductions in stereotypic behavior through self-management in multiple community settings. *Journal of Applied Behavior Analysis, 23,* 119–127.

Koegel, L. K., Koegel, R. L., Frea, W., & Green-Hopkins, I. (2003). Priming as a method of coordinating educational services for students with autism. *Language, Speech, and Hearing Services in Schools, 34,* 228–235.

Koegel, L. K., Koegel, R. L., Harrower, J. K., & Carter, C. M. (1999). Pivotal response intervention. I: Overview of approach. *Journal of the Association for Persons with Severe Handicaps, 24,* 174–186.

Koegel, R. L., Koegel, L. K., & Parks, D. R. (1990). *How to teach self-management skills to individuals with severe handicaps: A training manual.* Santa Barbara: University of California.

Koegel, L. K., Koegel, R. L., Shoshan, Y., & McNerney, E. (1999). Pivotal response intervention. II: Preliminary long-term outcome data. *Journal of the Association for Persons with Severe Handicaps, 24,* 186–198.

Koegel, R. L., O'Dell, M. C., & Dunlap, G. (1988). Producing speech use in nonverbal autistic children by reinforcing attempts. *Journal of Autism and Developmental Disorders, 18,* 525–538.

Koegel, R. L., O'Dell, M. C., & Koegel, L. K. (1987). A natural language teaching paradigm for nonverbal autistic children. *Journal of Autism and Developmental Disorders, 17,* 187–200.

Koegel, R. L., & Rincover, A. (1977). Some research on the difference between generalization and maintenance in extra-therapy settings. *Journal of Applied Behavior Analysis, 10,* 1–16.

Koegel, R. L., & Schreibman, L. (1977). Teaching autistic children to respond to simultaneous multiple cues. *Journal of Experimental Child Psychology, 24,* 299–311.

Koegel, R. L., Schreibman, L., Britten, K. R., Burke, J. C., & O'Neill, R. E. (1982). A comparison of parent training to direct clinic treatment. In R. L. Koegel, A. Rincover, & A. L. Egel (Eds.), *Educating and understanding autistic children* (pp. 260–279). San Diego, CA: College Hill Press.

Koegel, R. L., Schreibman, L., Good, A., Cerniglia, L., Murphy, C., & Koegel, L. L. (1989). *How to teach pivotal behaviors to children with autism: A training manual.* Santa Barbara: University of California.

Koegel, R. L., Schreibman, L., Johnson, J., O'Neill, R. E., & Dunlap, G. (1984). Collateral effects of parent training on families with autistic children. In R. G. Dangel & R. A. Polster (Eds.), *Parent training: Foundations of research and practice* (pp. 358–378). New York: Guilford Press.

Koegel, R. L., Schreibman, L., Loos, L. M., Dirlich-Wilhelm, H., Dunlap, G., Robbins, F. R., et al. (1992). Consistent stress profiles in mothers of children with autism. *Journal of Autism and Developmental Disorders, 22,* 205–216.

Koegel, R. L., Schreibman, L., O'Neill, R. E., & Burke, J. C. (1983). The personality and family-interaction characteristics of parents of autistic children. *Journal of Consulting and Clinical Psychology, 51*, 683–692.

Koegel, R. L., Symon, J. B., & Koegel, L. K. (2002). Parent education for families of children with autism living in geographically distant areas. *Journal of Positive Behavioral Interventions, 4*, 88–103.

Koegel, R. L., & Williams, J. (1980). Direct vs. indirect response–reinforcer relationships in teaching autistic children. *Journal of Abnormal Child Psychology, 4*, 536–547.

Lamb, J., Moore, J., Bailey, A., & Monaco, A. (2000). Autism: Recent molecular genetic advances. *Human Molecular Genetics, 9*, 861–868.

Laski, K. E., Charlop, M. H., & Schreibman, L. (1988). Training parents to use the natural language paradigm to increase their autistic children's speech. *Journal of Applied Behavior Analysis, 21*, 391–400.

Lovaas, O. I., Koegel, R. L., & Schreibman, L. (1979). Stimulus overselectivity in autism: A review of research. *Psychological Bulletin, 86*, 1236–1254.

Lovaas, O. I., Koegel, R. L., Simmons, J. Q., & Long, J. S. (1973). Some generalization and follow-up measures on autistic children in behavior therapy. *Journal of Applied Behavior Analysis, 6*, 131–166.

Loyd, B. H., & Abidin, R. R. (1985). Revision of the Parenting Stress Index. *Journal of Pediatric Psychology, 10*, 169–177.

Minshew, N. J., Sweeney, J. A., & Bauman, L. L. (1997). Neurological aspects of autism. In D. J. Cohen & F. R. Volkmar (Eds.), *Handbook of autism and pervasive developmental disorders* (2nd ed., pp. 344–369). New York: Wiley.

Moes, D., Koegel, R. L., & Schreibman, L. (1993). *Behavior therapy paradigms and parenting stress.* Paper presented at the 1993 Annual Convention of the Association for the Advancement of Behavior Therapy, Atlanta, GA.

Moes, D., Koegel, R. L., Schreibman, L., & Loos, L. M. (1992). Stress profiles for mothers and fathers of children with autism. *Psychological Reports, 3*, 1272–1274.

Mrazek, P. J., & Haggerty, R. J. (1994). *Reducing risks for mental disorders.* Washington, DC: Institute of Medicine, National Academy Press.

Nelson, R. O., & Hayes, S. C. (1981). Theoretical explanations for reactivity in self-monitoring. *Behavior Modification, 5*, 3–14.

O'Brien, T. P., Riner, L. S., & Budd, K. (1983). The effects of a child's self-evaluation program on compliance with parental instructions in the home. *Journal of Applied Behavior Analysis, 16*, 69–79.

O'Dell, M. C., Dunlap, G., & Koegel, R. L. (1983, August). *The importance of reinforcing verbal attempts during speech training with nonverbal children.* Paper presented at the Annual Convention of the American Psychological Association, Los Angeles.

O'Dell, M. C., & Koegel, R. L. (1981, November). *The differential effects of two methods of promoting speech in nonverbal autistic children.* Paper presented at the American Speech-Language-Hearing Association, Los Angeles.

O'Neill, R. E. (1987). *Environmental interactions of normal children and children with autism*. Unpublished doctoral dissertation, University of California, Santa Barbara.

Pierce, K., & Schreibman, L. (1994). Teaching children with autism daily living skills in unsupervised settings through pictorial self-management. *Journal of Applied Behavior Analysis, 27,* 471–481

Pierce, K., & Schreibman, L. (1995). Increasing complex social behaviors in children with autism: Effects of peer-implemented Pivotal Response Training. *Journal of Applied Behavior Analysis, 28,* 285–295.

Rimland, B. (1964). *Infantile autism*. New York: Appleton-Century-Crofts.

Ritvo, E. R., Ritvo, E. C., & Brothers, A. M. (1982). Genetic and immunohematologic factors in autism. *Journal of Autism and Developmental Disorders, 12,* 109–114.

Robbins, F. R., Dunlap, G., & Plienis, A. J. (1991). Family characteristics, family training, and the progress of young children with autism. *Journal of Early Intervention, 15,* 173–184.

Rosenberger-Debiesse, J., & Coleman, M. (1986). Brief report: Preliminary evidence for multiple etiologies in autism. *Journal of Autism and Developmental Disorders, 16,* 385–392.

Rosenblatt, J., Bloom, P., & Koegel, R. L. (1995). Overselective responding: Description, implications and intervention. In R. L. Koegel & L. K. Koegel (Eds.), *Teaching children with autism* (pp. 33–42). Baltimore: Brookes.

Runco, M. A., & Schreibman, L. (1983). Parental judgments of behavior therapy efficacy with autistic children: A social validation. *Journal of Autism and Developmental Disorders, 13,* 237–248.

Runco, M. A., & Schreibman, L. (1988). Children's judgments of autism and social validation of behavior therapy efficacy. *Behavior Therapy, 19,* 565–576.

Rutter, M. (1971). The description and classification of infantile autism. In D. W. Churchill, G. D. Alpern, & M. K. DeMyer (Eds.), *Infantile autism* (pp. 8–28). Springfield, IL: Charles C Thomas.

Sagotsky, G., Patterson, C. J., & Lepper, M. R. (1978). Training children's self-control: A field experiment in self-monitoring and goal setting in the classroom. *Journal of Experimental Child Psychology, 25,* 242–253.

Santarelli, G., Koegel, R. L., Casas, J. M., & Koegel, L. K. (2001). Culturally diverse families participating in behavior therapy parent education programs for children with developmental disabilities. *Journal of Positive Behavior Interventions, 3,* 120–123.

Schreibman, L. (1988). *Autism*. Newbury Park, CA: Sage.

Schreibman, L. (1997). Theoretical perspectives on behavioral intervention for individuals with autism. In D. J. Cohen & F. R. Volkmar (Eds.), *Handbook of autism and pervasive developmental disorders* (2nd ed., pp. 920–933). New York: Wiley.

Schreibman, L. (2000). Intensive behavioral/psychoeducational treatments for autism: Research needs and future directions. *Journal of Autism and Developmental Disorders, 30,* 373–378.

Schreibman, L., Charlop, M. H., & Koegel, R. L. (1982). Teaching autistic children to use extra-stimulus prompts. *Journal of Experimental Child Psychology, 33*, 475–491.

Schreibman, L., Kaneko, W. M., & Koegel, R. L. (1991). Positive affect of parents of autistic children: A comparison across two teaching techniques. *Behavior Therapy, 22*, 479–490.

Schreibman, L., & Koegel, R. L. (1989, May). *Assessment of subareas of high stress in mothers of autistic children: A comparison across three populations.* Paper presented at the 15th Annual Convention of the Association for Behavior Analysis, Milwaukee, WI.

Schreibman, L., Koegel, R. L., Mills, J. I., & Burke, J. C. (1981). The social validation of behavior therapy with autistic children. *Behavior Therapy, 12*, 610–624.

Schreibman, L., Runco, M. A., Mills, J. I., & Koegel, R. L. (1982). Teachers' judgments of improvements in autistic children in behavior therapy: A social validation. In R. L. Koegel, A. Rincover, & A. L. Egel (Eds.), *Educating and understanding autistic children* (pp. 78–87). San Diego, CA: College Hill Press.

Schreibman, L., Stahmer, A., & Cestone, V. (2002, May). *Pretreatment behavioral profiles as predictors of treatment outcome in children with autism.* Paper presented at the annual meeting of the Association for Behavior Analysis, Toronto, Canada.

Shapiro, E. S., & Klein, R. D. (1980). Self-management of classroom behavior with retarded/disturbed children. *Behavior Modification, 4*, 83–97.

Shapiro, E. S., McGonigle, J. J., & Ollendick, T. H. (1980). An analysis of self-assessment and self-reinforcement in a self-managed token economy with mentally retarded children. *Applied Research in Mental Retardation, 1*, 227–240.

Sherer, M., & Schreibman, L. (in press). Individual behavior profiles and predictions of treatement effectiveness for children with autism. *Journal of Consulting and Clinical Psychology.*

Sparrow, S. S., Balla, D. A., & Cicchetti, D. V. (1984). *Vineland Adaptive Behavior Scales.* Circle Pines, NM: American Guidance Service.

Stahmer, A. C. (1999). Using pivotal response training to facilitate appropriate play in children with autistic spectrum disorders. *Child Language Teaching and Therapy, 15*, 29–40.

Stahmer, A. C., & Schreibman, L. (1992). Teaching children with autism appropriate play in unsupervised environments using a self-management treatment package. *Journal of Applied Behavior Analysis, 25*, 447–459.

Stokes, T. F., & Baer, D. M. (1977). An implicit technology of generalization. *Journal of Applied Behavior Analysis, 10*, 347–367.

Sugai, G., & Rowe, D. (1984). The effect of self-recording on out-of-seat behavior of an EMR student. *Education and Training of the Mentally Retarded, 19*, 23–28.

Turnbull, H. R. III, Bateman, D. F., & Turnbull, A. P. (1993). Family empowerment. In P. Wehman (Ed.), *The ADA mandate for social change* (pp. 157–173). Baltimore: Brookes.

Turner, B. L. (1978). *The effects of choice of stimulus materials on interest in the remediation process and the generalized use of language training.* Unpublished master's thesis, University of California, Santa Barbara.

Waterhouse, L., Fein, D., Nath, J., & Snyder, D. (1987). Pervasive developmental disorders and schizophrenia occurring in childhood: A review of critical commentary. In G. L. Tischler (Ed.), *Diagnosis and classification in psychiatry: A critical appraisal of DSM–III* (pp. 335–368). New York: Cambridge University Press.

Wing, L. (1985). *Autistic children: A guide for parents and professionals.* Levittown, PA: Brunner/Mazel.

Wing, L., & Potter, D. (2002). The epidemiology of autistic spectrum disorders: Is prevalence rising? *Mental Retardation and Developmental Disabilities Research Reviews. Special Issue: The Epidemiology of Neurodevelopmental Disorders, 8,* 151–161.

Yoder, P. J., Kaiser, A. P., & Alpert, C. L. (1991). An exploratory study of the interaction between language teaching methods and child characteristics. *Journal of Speech and Hearing Research, 34,* 155–167.

24

CHILD-INITIATED INTERACTIONS THAT ARE PIVOTAL IN INTERVENTION FOR CHILDREN WITH AUTISM

LYNN KERN KOEGEL, ROBERT L. KOEGEL, AND LAUREN I. BROOKMAN

Increasingly effective interventions are now used for children diagnosed with autism, and recent clinical reports suggest that at least some children may make very large gains. However, considerable ambiguity remains with respect to defining the nature of the gains and specific intervention variables that produce the most clinically significant gains.

The literature suggests that several important areas relating to intervention require further research. These areas include (a) the need to obtain

Preparation of this manuscript was supported in part by U.S. Public Health Service Research Grant MH28210 from the National Institute of Mental Health; U.S. Department of Education, National Institute on Disability and Rehabilitation Research Cooperative Agreement No. G0087C0234; and U.S. Department of Education Research Grant No. H023C30070. In addition, proceeds from the book *Same As It Never Was*, by Claire Scovell LaZebnik, were also used to fund the preparation of this manuscript.

The treatment manuals used in the studies mentioned in this chapter can be obtained by sending requests to the first author: Lynn Kern Koegel, Clinical Director, Autism Research and Training Center, Graduate School of Education, University of California, Santa Barbara, CA 93106.

socially significant measurements regarding the types of gains the children make during intervention; and (b) the need to define and control individual components of the intervention that the literature suggests are likely to be associated with the best outcomes. In other words, the literature currently lacks systematic controlled experimental studies examining specific modifiable characteristics of the children's behavior during intervention that reliably produce highly positive postintervention outcomes. The literature and our pilot data suggest that targeting child-initiated interactions during intervention may be particularly important. Thus, this chapter will discuss the use of specific child initiations as the focus of intervention.

This intervention extends presently available language intervention procedures for children with autism, which emphasize the adult as the initiator of language, to focus instead on interventions that teach the child to be an active communicative partner in the dyad. Preliminary data are presented on important linguistic structures that show improvement as a result of such language intervention, in addition to concomitant improvements in a number of other disruptive and interfering behaviors. These data suggest that for children with autism, treatment is vastly enhanced if the children are recruited as active participants in the habilitation process. By providing them with self-initiated procedures to obtain language learning, the need for extensive adult initiations is greatly reduced, with widespread language improvements and increases in independence and autonomy for the child.

LITERATURE REVIEW

Communication difficulties are pathognomonic to children with autism and have been reported to precipitate many severe behavior problems. Amelioration of communication problems in young children with autism is particularly important because the literature has clearly demonstrated that children who fail to meet developmental milestones in the area of expressive language skills by the age of 2 are very likely to exhibit a variety of related disabilities, including delayed phonological development (Paul & Jennings, 1992), delayed receptive language skills, and deficits in socialization (Paul, 1991). Perhaps more alarming is the fact that longitudinal studies suggest that many preschoolers with language disabilities continue to present speech and language delays over extended periods of time (Aram & Nation, 1980) and are at risk for a variety of social and academic difficulties. One follow-up study that assessed children diagnosed as having language impairments (without hearing impairment or neurological or craniofacial abnormalities) during the preschool years found significant academic, social, and behavior problems 10 years later. In fact, 89% of the children received some type of specialized services, such as tutoring and special class placement, or were required to repeat a grade. Further, the majority of these children were rated as being less socially competent and having more behavioral problems than their peers (Aram, Ekelman, & Nation, 1984).

In short, early communication problems often antedate serious psychosocial problems and therefore can be a major health problem for young children. In fact, recent epidemiological studies suggest that as many as 75% to 80% of problem behaviors have a communicative function (Derby et al., 1992; Iwata et al., 1994). A growing body of scientific research demonstrates that teaching functionally equivalent communicative behaviors can result in dramatic improvements in behavior (Wacker, Berg, Asmus, Harding, & Cooper, 1998). In addition to preventing a wide variety of problems that may directly or indirectly correlate with difficulties in communication (Koegel, 2000), such interventions can also simultaneously improve general family harmony and affect (Koegel, Steibel, & Koegel, 1998). Thus, accumulating research indicates a clear and important need for psychosocial studies assessing linguistic areas that, when treated, may result in the greatest and most widespread effects.

The importance of language acquisition and its fluent use has led a number of researchers to assess variables relating to how children learn language. Logically, a focus has been mother–child interactions and maternal input to toddlers. Initially, authors suggested that expressive language difficulties may result from language-impoverished environments. Although this certainly may be the case for children who suffer from neglect, accumulating data suggest that children demonstrating language delays may be providing their mothers with a different set of stimuli to which to respond, which in turn affects the mother's input to the child. One study of play behavior in children with autism showed that mothers and fathers exhibited more play behaviors towards their children with autism than toward their nondisabled children. This level of adult-initiated interactions was negatively correlated with the child's level of functioning—that is, children whose scores were higher on the Vineland Adaptive Behavior Scales demonstrated greater numbers of child-initiated interactions with their parents, thereby reducing the need for the parents to initiate an interaction. The findings of this study suggested that parents may attempt to compensate for the child's disability level by providing more adult-initiated play interactions (El-Ghoroury & Romanczyk, 1999). In assessing the quality of interactions, Whitehurst et al. (1988) found that even though mothers' linguistic input to their children with language delays was different from that afforded to age-matched peers, it was similar to that of mothers' of children who had the same expressive language age. One specific difference is the number of expansions and extensions that adults provide to their children. Mothers of children with language delays do not provide expansions and extensions as often as mothers of typical language developers. However, if one assesses the proportion of expansions and extensions to child utterances (as opposed to the proportion of maternal utterances containing expansions and extensions), the difference disappears (Paul & Elwood, 1991). In other words, when children with language delays give their mothers something to expand, the mothers do so, but this cycle occurs much less frequently than with typical language developers. Therefore, it is becoming increasingly evident that children with language disabilities converse less frequently and provide adults with fewer sophisticated structures to which to respond, thereby limiting their ability to obtain environmental learning. This reduced conversational interaction and sophistication in the very early years can cause problems for future language and discourse development (Yoder, Davies, Bishop, & Munson, 1994).

As a result of this apparent lack of motivation to communicate, which appears to be either caused or affected by functioning level, a major change has arisen in approaching language intervention, one that differs in emphasis from the more traditional, highly imitative, and adult-controlled procedures. This change emphasizes the reciprocal interactive nature of communication and therefore accentuated the child's role as an active communicative partner in the dyad (Camarata & Nelson, 1992; Hart & Risley, 1968; Kaiser, Yoder, & Keetz, 1992; Koegel, O'Dell, & Koegel, 1987; Yoder, Kaiser, Alpert, & Fischer, 1993). This represents a shift from the previous techniques that failed to consider the reciprocal nature of interactions; the child's role in developing goals, selecting stimulus items, and so forth; the social environment; and the interaction between the child and his or her environment over time (Prizant, Wetherby, & Rydell, 2000).

Motivational Techniques

One successful approach incorporating these techniques has been an emphasis on improving the child's motivation to communicate. This improved motivation is frequently accomplished by arranging the child's environment to increase the number of opportunities to use language during natural ongoing activities. Table 24.1 summarizes the major variables in this approach to treatment (Koegel et al., 1987). The procedures appear to be especially suited to providing treatment for children in the early stages of language learning, particularly children who do not verbalize frequently and who are developing an initial lexicon. For example, Yoder et. al. (1993) showed that following the child's lead, whereby teaching episodes occurred only when the child had sustained attention to a target object or intentionally communicated something about the target object, resulted in considerably greater noun acquisition than when the treatment provider intrusively recruited the child's attention before attempting to teach. This type of teaching provides the child with natural intrinsic reinforcers, and because the teaching is embedded in naturally occurring activities throughout the day, it incorporates task variation (rather than drill sequences), which leads to more rapid acquisition.

TABLE 24.1
Differences Between the Analogue and the Natural Language Paradigm

	Analogue condition	Motivational condition
Stimulus items	Chosen by clinician	Chosen by child
	Repeated until criterion is met	Varied every few trials
	Phonologically easy to produce, irrespective of whether they were functional in the natural environment	Age-appropriate items that can be found in child's natural environment
Prompts	Manual (e.g., touch tip of tongue, hold lips together)	Clinician repeats item
Interaction	Clinician holds up stimulus item; stimulus item not functional within interaction	Clinician and child play with stimulus item (i.e., stimulus item is functional within interaction)
Response	Correct responses or successive approximations reinforced	Looser shaping contingency so that attempts to respond verbally (except self-stimulation) are also reinforced
Consequences	Edible reinforcers paired with social reinforcers	Natural reinforcer (e.g., opportunity to play with the item) paired with social reinforcers

Teaching approaches that specifically incorporate motivational techniques have demonstrated that 85% to 90% of children diagnosed with autism who begin intervention before the age of 5 can learn to use verbal communication as their primary mode of communication (Koegel, 1995; Koegel, 2000; McGee, Daly, & Jacobs, 1994). These statistics are impressively higher than they were 2 decades ago, when intervention programs reported that approximately 50% of the children remained nonverbal (Prizant, 1983).

However, several linguistic areas must be emphasized if children with autism are to achieve communicative competence. First, a high degree of clinician control, which often involves withholding a desired item until the child requests it, can result in excessive and restrictive control of the interaction. This restrictiveness can present several problems. For example, the child may become excessively dependent on the clinician prompt (e.g., withholding the item or asking the child "What's this?" or "What do you want?") to evoke expressive words or language. Further, researchers have shown that for children with language disabilities, many opportunities for language use do not occur or occur only infrequently. These opportunities can be increased by teaching treatment providers and other significant individuals in the children's natural environment to provide or increase opportunities for such language interactions (Peck, 1985; Sigafoos, Roberts, Kerr, Couzens, & Baglioni, 1994).

Self-Initiations

Although some significant increases in language and vocabulary acquisition may be demonstrated with adult-driven approaches, the result is that the child still has language limitations in that the vocabulary growth under such procedures typically encompasses only highly desired items rather than a wide variety of linguistic forms. This finding is important when one considers that the utterances of children with autism and other language delays lack both adequate quantitative and qualitative aspects compared with the language of typical children (Wetherby & Prutting, 1984; Paul & Shiffer, 1991; Yoder et al., 1994). For example, initiations to peers may be a useful index of social development in children with autism (Hauck, Fein, Waterhouse, & Feinstein, 1995). However, very few studies in the area of autism have focused on the qualitative aspects of language, such as the types of communicative intentions a child uses with various communicative partners. The use of child initiations—which further linguistic competence, increase spontaneous language use, and promote topic continuity that results in sustained engagement in social interactions—are areas where deficits seem to persist for children with autism. This topic warrants further research.

Preliminary work (Koegel, Koegel, Shoshan, & McNerney, 1999; Koegel, Carter, & Koegel, 2003) suggests that teaching young children with autism to evoke language learning from their environments may be especially likely to result in rapid language growth. This line of research also suggests that when such efforts are made to improve self-initiated communicative strategies, desirable concomitant changes are likely to occur, including reductions in aggression, self-stimulation, self-injury, and tantrums. Thus, self-initiations have been referred to as *pivotal*.

Given the likely importance of social initiations as prognostic indicators, more specific information on the types and amounts of these initiations that lead to positive outcomes for children with autism might greatly enhance our research base—that is, unlike typically developing children, verbal and preverbal children with autism exhibit a pervasive lack of social initiations (Bates, Thal, & Marchman, 1991; Stone, Ousley, Yoder, Hogan, & Hepburn, 1997). For example, a common child-initiated social verbalization that occurs early in typical child development is "that?" (/daet/), which is often used in conjunction with pointing to items. With nonverbal cues, such as pointing, this interrogative verbalization can be a specific prompt for a parent to label the item for the child (Halliday, 1975). Over time, this type of utterance becomes increasingly more sophisticated and varied, resulting in steadily more sophisticated social queries (who, where, when, why, etc.). Instead of exhibiting these typical developmental milestones, children with autism emit fewer utterances and typically do not engage in meaningful social initiation (Calloway, Myles, & Earles, 1999).

Such assessment data have led researchers to begin to develop intervention procedures to teach these child-initiated utterances. For example, Yoder and Warren (1999) have begun to develop interventions to increase the generalized use of self-initiated protodeclaratives and protoimperatives in preschool children with autism. Also, a number of researchers have designed intervention procedures to improve the use of self-initiated questions and other spontaneous initiations (Hung, 1977; Koegel, Camarata, Valdez-Menchaca, & Koegel, 1998; Taylor & Harris, 1995; Warren, Baxter, Anderson, Marshall, & Baer, 1981). Preliminary research suggests that teaching these skills may result in more widespread clinical gains and more favorable long-term outcomes (Koegel, Koegel, Shoshan, & McNerney, 1999).

With steadily increasing numbers of children being diagnosed with autism, the need to develop more efficient intervention programs that are accessible to more children is critical. Addressing this need is likely to necessitate identification of specific intervention variables that are associated with the most successful outcomes. Researchers have suggested that intervention programs would be enhanced if pivotal behaviors, or interventions in specific areas that lead to collateral changes in a broader range of behaviors, were identified. Most researchers and practitioners identify some type of social–communicative function as problematic across subgroups in the spectrum of autism (Koegel & Koegel, 1995; Volkmar, Carter, Sparrow, & Cicchetti, 1993). Therefore, researchers have discussed the need for intervetion in areas such as social communication as a priority in intervention research (Mundy & Crowson, 1997). Competence in these areas requires reciprocal interactions with active initiations on the part of both partners in a communicative dyad. However, many previous intervention programs for children with autism have relied almost exclusively on an adult-initiated model, with the child primarily responding to questions or commands from the adult rather than taking an active role in initiating learning interactions. Current research strongly suggests that intervention for child initiations is a pivotal behavior to achieve broad socially significant improvement in the condition of autism.

PROCEDURES

Teaching Self-Initiated Queries

One area of research relates to instating or increasing linguistic structures, such as queries, that will result in access to *further* learning. Therefore, researchers have begun assessing the effects of teaching a variety of queries such as, "What's that?", "Where is it?", and "Whose is it?", that are targeted for child initiations. "What" and "Where" questions emerge within the second year of life, and "Whose" questions appear by age 3 in most typical language developers. These structures, often used for both social purposes and as a means of accruing additional linguistic information, appear to be important for widespread communication development. A number of studies demonstrate procedures for teaching question asking (Hung, 1977; Koegel et al., 1998; Taylor & Harris, 1995; Warren et al., 1981) and other verbal initiations (Koegel, Koegel, Shoshan, & McNerney, 1999). The following strategies incorporate motivational components into the teaching of child-initiated information-seeking interrogatives:

1. *Teaching vocabulary through the child-initiated interrogative "What's that?"* One component of teaching the child to initiate learning interactions focuses on teaching the interrogative "What's that?" to increase expressive vocabularies (noun labels). The initial treatment step focuses on improving the children's motivation to engage in self-initiated queries by incorporating motivational components (see Table 24.1) proven to be effective in improving responsivity. The goal of this procedure is to teach the child the pragmatic intent of information seeking in order to evoke linguistic information from the communicative partner. To do this, the children's pretreatment videotapes are analyzed for items that are likely to be highly desired, such as pieces to favorite puzzles, food treats, and so on. To encourage the children to use the queries, the items are hidden in a brown or opaque bag, and the children are prompted to ask, "What's that?" and then are shown or given the desired item. Gradually, the prompt is faded until the children are frequently asking the question during the session.

   Once the children are asking the question and repeating the noun at a high rate, new (neutral) items, with unknown labels, are gradually incorporated into the sessions. These items, which appear to have no special appeal to the child according to pretreatment analysis and testing, are gradually added until almost all neutral items, which the child is unable to label according to the same pretests, are presented. In addition, the opaque bag is gradually faded so that unknown items are merely sitting around the room. This is an important step because it represents the transition from the use of only highly desired items to the use of a larger variety of items and promotes the child's general curiosity about the environment.

2. *Teaching prepositions through the child-initiated interrogative "Where is it?"* To expand the children's self-initiated questions to later emerging forms, a second procedure focuses on teaching the children to ask "where" questions to understand the use of prepositions. The child's favorite items are selected and hidden in *specific* locations; the child is prompted to ask "Where is it?", and the adult tells the child the location of the item and allows the child to take it from that location.

3. *Teaching pronouns and possessives through the child-initiated interrogative "Whose is it?"* To teach pronouns and possessives, parents bring in a variety of items that their children clearly associate with a particular member of the family. The children are prompted to ask "Whose is it?"; the clinician responds and gives the child the item. Eventually, the child is prompted to repeat the possessive form.

   Teaching "yours" and "mine" is accomplished by similar means. Highly desired objects are used (e.g., candies, favorite toys); however, when the clinician says, "It's yours," the child is prompted to say "mine" and is then presented with the item. This reversal is notably difficult for children with autism to acquire, but using highly desired objects greatly facilitates acquisition. Again, the procedure involves teaching the child to obtain the linguistic skill through a child-initiated strategy rather than an adult-initiated strategy.

Clinical Vignette

After the previously discussed steps have been completed and all prompts have been removed, the procedures occur as follows. The following excerpts are from intervention programs that focus on teaching information-seeking child initiations. On the basis of the previously described treatment procedures, which systematically move the children through a series of queries in developmental order, the session may resemble the following:

> *Child:* "What dat?" (The treatment provider has, through a systematic prompting and fading process, taught the child to spontaneously self-initiate the interrogative without an adult initiation.)

> *Treatment provider:* "It's an A." (This is said while removing a puzzle piece from the bag. The treatment labels the item. To provide predictability without further verbal demands that may

> lead to avoidance and disruptive behavior, the treatment provider does not respond with another instruction.)

> *Child:* "A."

The treatment provider shows the child the puzzle piece, which the child may take if desired. (This sequence provides the child with a naturally and inherently reinforcing stimulus contingent on an initial child initiation and the reciprocal social–verbal interaction that followed.)

Once the child has learned to ask "What's that?" the treatment sessions focus on teaching "Where" questions. A typical session may resemble the following:

> *Child:* "Where cracker?" (unprompted spontaneous interrogative)

> *Clinician:* "Under the napkin." (includes target preposition)

The child looks under the napkin and takes the cracker. (Natural consequence is provided contingent on query that will result in acquisition of linguistic target during the social–communicative interchange.)

As with the first question type, all of the children are taught to use "Where" questions under a variety of conditions to elicit learning of a variety of prepositions (e.g., in, on, under, behind, in front).

The next query, "Whose," is targeted to teach a child-initiated strategy for learning "yours" and "mine" and the possessive. A sample dialogue resembles the following:

> *Child:* "Whose is it?" (Child initiates interrogative.)

> *Clinician:* "It's Mommy's." (Mother holds up her purse. The adult response provides targeted linguistic structure during the social–verbal interchange.)

> *Child:* "Mommy's purse."

> *Clinician:* "Right, it's Mommy's." (The clinician gives child the purse, providing natural reinforcer.)

Functional Analysis and Teaching Functionally Equivalent Behaviors

Preliminary research suggests that self-initiated queries such as those described in the preceding vignette excerpts can result in furthering linguistic and social learning and decreasing problem behaviors. However, children with autism seem to need additional child-initiated skills to deal with existing crisis situations that have developed and been maintained as a result of their failure to use appropriate communication. Child-initiated verbalizations that occur frequently in typically developing children—such as strategies to seek attention (e.g., "Look, Mommy!" and "Mommy!"), request actions (e.g., "Help!"), and request clarification (e.g., "What?" and "Huh?")—occur at a much lower frequency in children with language disabilities (Paul & Shiffer, 1991). Similar functions of communication can be seen in children with disabilities in the form of inappropriate behavior (Carr & Durand, 1985; Horner & Budd, 1985; Kern, & Vorndran, 2000). Epidemiological studies suggest that the communicative function can be determined for approximately 75% to 80% of disruptive behaviors (Derby et al., 1992; Iwata et al., 1994). Although a number of assessment procedures are currently available (O'Neill & Johnson, 2000), many agencies do not routinely conduct functional assessment as a component of a behavior support plan (Reid, 2000).

The purpose of a functional analysis is to attempt to determine why a disruptive or inappropriate behavior occurs and to *replace* the undesired behavior with an equivalent appropriate communicative behavior. To functionally analyze a behavior, the clinician must operationally describe the undesirable behavior or behaviors, predict the times and situations when this behavior or behaviors will and will not be performed across the range of typical daily routines, and define the function or functions or maintaining variables that the undesirable behavior or behaviors produce for the individual (Frea & Hughes, 1997; Frea, Koegel, & Koegel, 1994; Koegel, Koegel, & Carter, 1999; O'Neill, Horner, Albin, Storey, & Sprague, 1989). Researchers have raised concerns that problems may occur if assessments are implemented by individuals who are unfamiliar with the settings and routines of the individual with challenging behavior. Therefore, it is important for the intervention plan to lead to changes in environmental conditions and programmatic supports so that significant reductions in challenging behavior occur with concomitant improvements in life quality for the individual with disabilities (Reid, 2000). In addition, individuals with disabilities are assumed to acquire functionally equivalent self-initiated responses in their progress toward independence. This acquisition necessitates performing functional assessments in typical settings on a routine basis and teaching the individual with disabilities to initiate these responses in everyday settings.

In addressing this issue, our preliminary work suggests that parents, who are familiar with the child's settings and routines and replacement behaviors that are likely to result in lifestyle changes, can be extremely useful as adjuncts in the functional analysis process. In a preliminary study, parents collected data relating to four areas. First, they describe the disruptive behavior (e.g., hit, turned off light, threw toy) and note the time and the place that the particular behavior or behaviors occurred. Second, parents note what happens immediately before the occurrence of the disruptive act (a checklist is provided so that the parents can check a box that contains likely setting events, such as the child's being alone or ignored). Third, parents record what occurs after the disruptive behavior (a checklist is provided that contains likely consequences of the child's behavior, such as engaging in actions that provide the child with attention). The final section of the recording sheet contains a checklist with items that attempt to evaluate and explain why the disruptive behavior occurred. This checklist provides common reasons for disruptive behavior, including (a) to get out of something, (b) a create a transition, (c) to obtain something, (d) to gain attention, and (e) to avoid a person or a place.

Then, a functionally equivalent replacement behavior is taught based on the function of the behavior. For example, in the case of a child engaging in inappropriate behaviors to gain attention, the child might be taught appropriate self-initiated replacement communicative behaviors, such as saying, "Look!" or "Let's play!" This technique provides the child with an efficient form of appropriate verbal communication that is likely to be effective in obtaining attention. The goal is to reach the point at which the child will self-initiate the appropriate verbal behavior when the need for that particular function (to obtain attention) arises under natural conditions. Parents work to teach the replacement behavior daily (repeatedly throughout the day) when a disruptive behavior is not occurring. The child is also prompted to engage in the appropriate replacement behavior when disruptive behavior is likely to occur.

OUTCOMES

Communication treatment for individuals with autism must be comprehensive, coordinated, and multifaceted. Several components are pivotal if communicative competence is to be achieved. First, motivating the child to solicit language-teaching interactions from the natural environment both accelerates language development and reduces the need for adult-driven treatments. For example, spontaneous information-seeking strategies seem to be necessary for language development and provide reciprocal interactions that enhance social skills. Second, providing the child with self-initiated communicative skills to replace disruptive behaviors needs to be an ongoing process; determining the communicative function of disruptive behaviors and replacing these problem behaviors with communicatively equivalent appropriate behaviors can result in durable decreases in problem behaviors and reduces the need for punitive measures. Furthermore, self-initiations can be considered pivotal because they have the potential to provide widespread spontaneous learning opportunities in natural environments throughout the child's day, without the need for adult-initiated interventions (Koegel, 2000; Koegel, Koegel, Harrower, & Carter, 1999; Yoder & Warren, 1999). Third, research suggests that unbiased observers do not judge children as being pragmatically appropriate if they do not show initiations during unstructured interactions (Koegel, Koegel, Shoshan, & McNerney, 1999).

In a preliminary study (Koegel, 1993), we taught three children with autism, significant language delays, and associated severe behavior problems (e.g., self-injury, aggression) to ask, "What's that?" in response to unfamiliar items with unknown labels. Before starting treatment, the children typically used no queries at all, and all had extremely limited expressive vocabularies. The purpose of this study was not only to teach the children to use queries but also to assess the effect of this information-seeking strategy on subsequent language skills (in this study, expressive vocabulary development). Results demonstrated that the children learned to use the query "What's that?" and all demonstrated significant increases in expressive vocabulary as a result of this self-initiated strategy. The children who participated in this research were able to learn the query in one or two sessions, and completion of the treatment was typically accomplished after 8 to 15 sessions. Vocabulary assessments showed that the children were learning an average of six words per every hour of treatment. Although other studies have taught question asking, generalization of the questions has been limited or nonexistent. Generalization data collected in this study demonstrated that incorporating motivational procedures resulted in the children's continued and appropriate use of the query with their mothers at home, and the resulting maternal response (labeling) also resulted in new vocabulary acquisition for the children. This outcome was especially important because baseline assessments obtained before treatment indicated that the children *never* used these queries with their mothers and demonstrated no new vocabulary acquisition at all.

A second study attempted to teach the children to ask, "Where is it?" to elicit prepositions. The children all acquired the query during the first session and showed generalized use of the query to acquire two to four prepositions after four half-hour sessions. Further, cumulative acquisition of other prepositions continued after subsequent sessions. Similarly, the children who participated in a preliminary study learned to ask, "Whose is it?" in one or two sessions, and probes after every four sessions (2 hours of treatment) indicated that the children learned the query to acquire possessives in an average of 10 half-hour sessions.

Interestingly, before the implementation of treatment, the children demonstrated high levels of disruptive behavior, such as self-injury, aggression, and self-stimulation. In contrast, after the implementation of treatment, all children demonstrated decreased levels of these behavior problems, suggesting that their ability to take control over learning may have reduced the frustration associated with such interactions.

Another study (Koegel, Carter, & Koegel, 2003) demonstrated the utility of using self-initiated queries to facilitate the acquisition and generalization of grammatical morphemes in children with autism. In this study, children were taught to ask questions such as "What happened?" and "What's happening?" while reading pop-up books with an adult. The adult responded to the child's query using the appropriate verb stem and targeted verb ending (e.g., -ing or the past tense) and prompted the child to repeat the verb. The children were able to learn the self-initiated strategy and acquired the targeted morpheme. Moreover, the children's language samples demonstrated that they generalized the target morpheme to novel verbs.

PILOT STUDY

The aforementioned studies led us to assess whether a series of initiations could be taught to children diagnosed with autism who were verbal but who had significant language delays and demonstrated few or no spontaneous initiations of any type (verbal or nonverbal) before intervention (Koeegel, Koegel, Shoshan, & McNerney, 1999). In the first phase of this study, analysis of archival data showed that children with few or no initiations had less favorable outcomes than those who did initiate. Therefore, in Phase 2 of the study, we assessed whether the children would have highly favorable outcomes once they were taught to initiate using a programmatic intervention plan. Results showed increases in pragmatic ratings, adaptive behavior, and social and community functioning when child initiations occurred. Additionally, the postmeasures suggested considerable improvements in the condition of autism (some had been removed from state agency lists of children with developmental disabilities).

Logically, long-term outcomes of general functioning in a variety of areas, including communication, daily living areas, maladaptive behavior, and social areas, are of critical importance in our research. To provide a more comprehensive outcome evaluation on the effects of teaching a variety of self-initiations, we assessed a number of areas in our dependent measures, analyzing both direct effects of the interventions and collateral changes in the children's symptoms and overall condition. The dependent measures included (a) direct changes in the targeted behavior of child initiations, (b) collateral changes in the three primary deficit areas in autism (i.e., impaired communication, impaired social interaction, and restricted stereotyped patterns of behavior), and (c) global measures of changes in the children's condition in each group as compared with those of typically developing children. Specific data for this preliminary study are presented in the next section. We are extremely optimistic about the long-term positive outcomes of this pilot study.

Postintervention Judgments of Pragmatics by Naïve Observers[1]

The first panel of Figure 24.1 presents the outcome data with respect to naïve ratings of pragmatics for the six children selected for Phase 1 of the study. The data in this first panel illustrate that three of the children were

---

[1]Observers who were naïve to the experimental hypothesis.

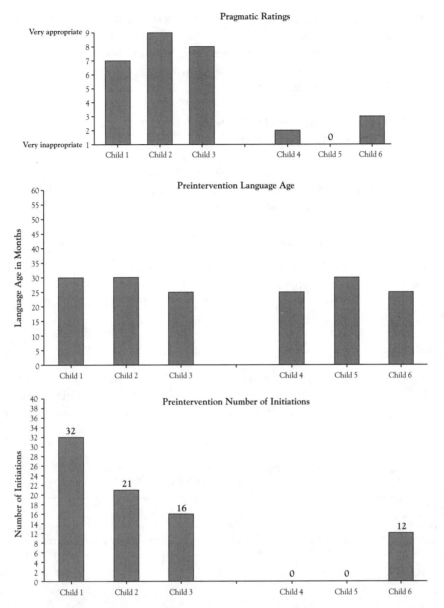

Figure 24.1. The children's postintervention outcome ratings on the pragmatics scale, preintervention language ages, and preintervention number of spontaneous initiations for Children 1 through 6. From "Pivotal Response Intervention I: Overview of Approach," by L. K. Koegel, R. L. Koegel, Y. Shoshan, and E. McNerney, 1999, *Journal of the Association for Persons With Severe Handicaps, 24,* p. 190. Copyright 1999 by Research and Practice for Persons With Severe Disabilities. Reprinted with permission.

scored as having very high ratings of pragmatics, and three of the children were judged to have very low ratings. Specifically, Children 1, 2, and 3, who exhibited higher numbers of child initiations, received ratings of 7, 9, and 8 respectively, indicating that they were judged by naïve raters as appearing very appropriate on the pragmatics scale during unstructured social interactions. In contrast, Children 4, 5, and 6 received ratings of only 2, 1, and 3, respectively, indicating that in addition to exhibiting low or no initiations, they were judged by naïve raters as appearing very inappropriate on the pragmatics scale during unstructured social interactions.

Preintervention Similarities Between the Children With Positive and Poor Outcomes

Although the children with positive and poor outcomes showed large postintervention differences, at preintervention they had similar language ages and scored at comparable levels on adaptive behavior scales.

Preintervention Language Ages

The second panel of Figure 24.1 shows preintervention language ages for the children with positive and poor outcomes. Language ages for the six children were about the same before intervention, ranging from 2 years to 2 years and 6 months.

Preintervention Adaptive Behavior Scales Scores

Adaptive behavior scales scores for the children are shown in Tables 24.2 and 24.3. These data suggest that although all of the children scored at a similar level relatively early on (averaging 12 to 14 months below their

TABLE 24.2

Chronological Ages and Adaptive Behavior Scale Scores at Preintervention and Postintervention for the Children in Preliminary Initiations Study Phase 1

Child	Pre-		Post-	
Positive outcome (Study 1)	Chronological age	Adaptive behavior composite	Chronological age	Adaptive behavior composite
Child #1	3;9	2;11	12;5	11;4
Child #2	3;5	2;4	13;1	13;4
Child #3	3;1	1;7	12;2	13;0
Poor Outcome (Study 1)				
Child #4	3;6	2;6	15;4	3;11
Child #5	3;4	3;0	12;10	2;3
Child #6	3;10	2;1	10;9	6;1

Note. From "Pivotal Response Intervention I: Overview of Approach," by L. K. Koegel, R. L. Koegel, Y. Shoshan, and E. McNerney, 1999, *Journal of the Association for Persons With Severe Handicaps, 24,* p. 192. Copyright 1999 by Research and Practice for Persons With Severe Disabilities. Reprinted with permission.

TABLE 24.3
Social and Community Functioning: Outcome Data
from the Children in Phase 1

Children	School or postschool placement	Academic achievement	Social circles	Extracurricular activities
(Study 1) Positive Outcome Children 1, 2, 3	Regular education	Grades above average. Mostly As and Bs.	Have typically developing friends, sleep-overs, and birthday parties; use the tele-phone socially; Child 2 spoke at 6th grade graduation.	Child 1 com-petes in races; participates in rock climbing; and summer camps; plays adult level violin. Child 2 plays the cello; writes and illustrates; baby-sits; posts reviews on Internet. Child 3 plays team soccer; competes in state tennis competitions.
(Study 1) Poor Outcome Children 4, 5, 6	Children 4 and 5 Special Edu-cation; Child 6 removed from public school as a result of parent dissatis-faction; takes part in home schooling.	Children 4 and 5 institutionalized in residential facility, level IV; Child 6 academics at a 2nd grade level (is currently in 5th grade).	All three children demonstrate aggression, self-injury, tantrums, and other inap-propriate behaviors; none interacts socially with peers; all three require high levels of adult super-vision.	No extra-curricular activities.

chronological age), significant differences between the children with positive and poor outcomes occurred over time.

Preintervention Differences in Spontaneous Initiations Between Children With Positive and Poor Outcomes

The third panel of Figure 24.1 shows the preintervention number of spontaneous initiations for each child during the 15-minute videotape samples of social play interactions. As can be seen, the six children differed in terms of the number of spontaneous initiations they exhibited during the

videotaped social play interactions. Specifically, the preintervention number of spontaneous initiations exhibited during the unstructured language
interactions averaged 23 (32, 21, and 16, respectively) for Children 1, 2,
and 3, who had favorable outcomes. In contrast, Children 4, 5, and 6, who
had poor intervention outcomes, showed fewer spontaneous child initiations during the videotaped social play interactions, with Children 4 and 5
demonstrating no spontaneous initiations at all.

On the basis of the post hoc results of Study 1 and the results of
preliminary studies showing the feasibility of teaching a generalized
child-initiated response, Phase 2 assessed whether a series of initiations
could be taught to children with autism who demonstrated few or no spontaneous initiations before intervention and whether these children who
received intervention for initiations would have highly favorable postintervention outcomes. Subjects in this phase were selected because they had
preintervention characteristics similar to those of the poor outcome children in Phase 1. All children attended regular education preschools with
special education assistants in their classrooms but had been recommended
for Special Day Class placement because of their poor social, academic, and
communicative behaviors. The children did not participate in extracurricular activities, were rarely taken outside of their homes, and had no sustained
peer relationships. The children in this study also demonstrated disruptive
behaviors and aggressive behavior toward adults and peers.

Intervention for this group was similar to the intervention in Phase 1,
except that it focused on teaching a series of child initiations rather than
targeting the same structures through an adult-driven approach. These initiations were designed to be strategies (such as question asking, described
above) that would be likely to evoke an adult response resulting in
social–communicative development. A variety of initiations were taught in
a general developmental sequence, as they are acquired by typically developing children. As can be seen in Figure 24.2, the results suggest that before
intervention the children had similar characteristics in terms of language
ages and number of initiations as had the children with poor outcomes in
Phase 1. In addition, adaptive behavior scale scores showed similar developmental delays. The light-colored bars (preintervention ratings of pragmatics) in the third panel of this figure show that before intervention the
children were judged to be in the "very inappropriate" range, appearing very
abnormal (with scores between 1 and 2 on the 9-point Likert scale).

In contrast, the dark-colored bars in this figure show the postintervention data for spontaneous child initiations and for ratings of pragmatics. Specifically, the second panel of Figure 24.2 shows that after the
child-initiation intervention the number of spontaneous initiations
increased considerably. Further, postintervention ratings of pragmatics
(dark bars in the third panel), rated by individuals who were blinded to the
experimental hypotheses and who did not have experience working with

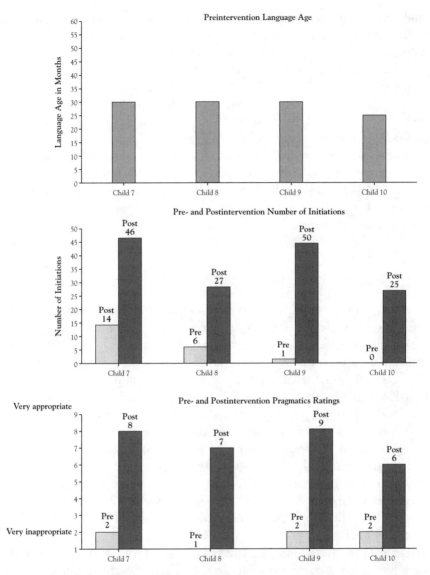

Figure 24.2. The preintervention language ages, the preintervention and postinter-vention number of initiations, and the preintervention and postintervention pragmatic ratings for Children 7 through 10. From "Pivotal Response Intervention I: Overview of Approach," by L. K. Koegel, R. L. Koegel, Y. Shoshan, and E. McNerney, 1999, *Journal of the Association for Persons With Severe Handicaps, 24,* p. 194. Copyright 1999 by Research and Practice for Persons With Severe Disabilities. Reprinted with permission.

people with disabilities, suggest that the children were rated as exhibiting "very normal, appropriate" pragmatic behavior. These scores are similar to those of the children with very favorable outcomes in Phase 1.

In addition, after intervention the children were all participating in regular education classes, did not qualify for special education classes, had grades at or above average (in their regular education classes), had social circles with typically developing peers outside of school hours, and participated in a variety of extracurricular activities without support. These results are consistent with the gains reported for the children with positive outcomes in Phase 1.

With respect to diagnoses from outside agencies, at the time of the postmeasures none of the children had diagnoses of autism, and all had been removed from state agency lists of children with developmental disabilities. Half of these children did not qualify for any type of special education services whatsoever, and one child received speech services only. Again, the results of this pilot research support the notion of self-initiations as another pivotal behavior because teaching the initiations appears to result in widespread gains in other areas.

FUTURE CONSIDERATIONS

The aforementioned results draw attention to an important question regarding the early acquisition of language: "Does an understanding of how typical language-developers learn language help in devising communication interventions for individuals with autism?" Of importance here is the fact that research shows that typically developing children gain considerable social and communicative competence through child initiations and reciprocal participation in communicative interactions. Strategies such as question asking that enhance linguistic competence are some of the earliest emerging forms of speech emitted by typically developing children. Even later in the preschool years, when most children have learned to use complex grammatical structures, children continue to use a large number of questions with both adults and peers (Hart & Risley, 1968). In contrast, the extremely restricted style of interacting that children with autism exhibit severely limits the types of interactions to which they are exposed. Because utterances are emitted infrequently, the children are likely to be involved in very few communicative interactions. Further, the communicative functions most frequently used by children with autism (requesting and protesting) are likely to result only in getting their needs met, rather than evoking the social use of language. In contrast, the aforementioned preliminary research suggests that interventions emphasizing self-initiations result in quantitative and qualitative improvements in communication, with widespread concomitant decreases in disruptive and inappropriate behavior.

In summary, a number of highly specialized intervention strategies have evolved to improve the communication of children with autism (Wetherby & Prizant, 2000). Early approaches were highly analogue in nature and imitation based. They typically involved decreasing inappropriate behaviors through punishment, then attempting to teach appropriate behaviors, beginning with nonverbal imitation and gradually focusing on verbal imitation. Whereas many general skills improved under such conditions, the children often failed to show generalized use of newly learned language and spontaneous use of language with the highly structured aspects of this treatment (Lovaas, 1977; Schreibman, 1988). As a result, a major change arose in approaching language intervention that built on, but differed in emphasis from, the more traditional, highly imitative, and adult-driven techniques. This change emphasized the reciprocal, interactive nature of the communicative interaction and therefore accentuated the child's role as an active communicative partner in the dyad (Camarata & Nelson, 1992; Hart & Risley, 1968; Kaiser et al., 1992; Koegel et al., 1987; Wetherby & Prizant, 2000; Yoder et al., 1993).

These naturalistic and child-initiated procedures have the simultaneous benefit of not only improving communication and decreasing disruptive behaviors but also reducing the inordinate number of hours of adult-driven treatment in a formal clinical session. This may alleviate the great financial burden for families and other agencies in providing costly long-term services, which may be completely inaccessible for families who do not receive specialized services. In contrast, teaching self-initiated learning techniques are both cost- and time-efficient because the child continues to exhibit therapeutic interactions with the environment both within and outside of the formal therapy sessions. Procedures such as teaching question asking and procedures in which the children take an active role in their own treatment not only create independence on the part of the child but also parallel procedures that typically developing children use regularly and continuously throughout the day and throughout their development. The results of ongoing research suggest that future development of techniques designed to promote self-learning and independence will likely result in more efficient treatments for children with autism, more significant generalization and maintenance of treatment gains, greater reductions in parental stress, and more favorable long-term outcomes.

REFERENCES

Aram, D., Ekelman, B., & Nation, J. (1984). Preschoolers with language disorders: 10 years later. *Journal of Speech and Hearing Research, 27*, 232–244.

Aram, D., & Nation, J. (1980). Preschool language disorders and subsequent language and academic difficulties. *Journal of Communication Disorders, 13*, 159–170.

Bates, E., Thal, D., & Marchman, V. (1991). Symbols and syntax: A Darwinian approach to language development. In N. A. Krasnegor & D. M. Rumbaugh (Eds.), *Biological and behavioral determinants of language development* (pp. 29–65). Hillsdale, NJ: Erlbaum.

Calloway, C. J., Myles, B. S., & Earles, T. L. (1999). The development of communicative functions and means in students with autism. *Focus on Autism and Other Developmental Disabilities, 14*, 140–149.

Camarata, S. M., & Nelson, K. E. (1992). Treatment efficiency as a function of target selection in the remediation of child language disorders. *Clinical Linguistics and Phonetics, 6*, 167–178.

Carr, E. G., & Durand, V. M. (1985). Reducing behavior problems through functional communication training. *Journal of Applied Behavior Analysis, 18*, 111–126.

Derby, K. M., Wacker, D. P., Sasso, G., Steege, M., Northup, J., Cigrand, K., et al. (1992). Brief functional assessment techniques to evaluate aberrant behavior in an outpatient setting: A summary of 79 cases. *Journal of Applied Behavior Analysis, 25*, 713–721.

El-Ghoroury, N. H., & Romanczyk, R. G. (1999). Play interactions of family members towards children with autism. *Journal of Autism and Developmental Disorders, 29*, 249–258.

Frea, W. B., & Hughes, C. (1997). Functional analysis and treatment of social–communicative behavior of adolescents with developmental disabilities. *Journal of Applied Behavior Analysis, 30*, 701–704.

Frea, W. D., Koegel, L. K., & Koegel, R. L. (1994). *Understanding why problem behaviors occur: A guide for assisting parents in assessing causes of behavior and designing treatment plans.* Santa Barbara: University of California.

Halliday, M. A. K. (1975). *Learning how to mean: Explorations in the development of language.* New York: Elsevier–North Holland.

Hart, B. M., & Risley, T. R. (1968). Establishing the use of descriptive adjectives in the spontaneous speech of disadvantaged preschool children. *Journal of Applied Behavior Analysis, 1*, 109–120.

Hauck, M., Fein, D., Waterhouse, L., & Feinstein, C. (1995). Social initiations by autistic children to adults and other children. *Journal of Autism and Developmental Disorders, 25*, 579–595.

Horner, R. H., & Budd, C. M. (1985). Acquisition of manual sign use: Collateral reduction of maladaptive behavior, and factors limiting generalization. *Education and Training of the Mentally Retarded, 20*, 39–47.

Hung, D. W. (1977). Generalization of "curiosity" questioning behavior in autistic children. *Journal of Behavior Therapy and Experimental Psychiatry, 8*, 237–245.

Iwata, B. A., Pace, G. M., Dorsey, M. F., Zarcone, J. R., Vollmer, T. R., Smith, R. G., et al. (1994). The functions of self-injurious behavior: An experimental–epidemiological analysis. *Journal of Applied Behavior Analysis, 27*, 215–240.

Kaiser, A. P., Yoder, P. J., & Keetz, A. (1992). Evaluating milieu teaching. In S. F. Warren & J. Reichle (Eds.), *Causes and effects in communication and language intervention.* Baltimore: Brookes.

Kern, L., & Vorndran, C. M. (2000). Functional assessment and intervention for transition difficulties. *Journal of the Association for Persons with Severe Handicaps, 25*, 212–216.

Koegel, L. K. (1993). *Teaching children with autism to use a self-initiated strategy to learn expressive vocabulary*. Unpublished dissertation, University of California, Santa Barbara.

Koegel, L. K. (1995). Communication and language intervention. In R. L. Koegel & L. K. Koegel (Eds.), *Teaching children with autism: Strategies for initiating positive interaction and improving learning opportunities* (pp. 17–32). Baltimore: Brookes.

Koegel, L. K. (2000). Interventions to facilitate communication in autism. *Journal of Autism and Developmental Disorders, 30,* 383–391.

Koegel, L. K., Camarata, S. M., Valdez-Menchaca, M. C., & Koegel, R. L. (1998). Teaching children with autism to use self-initiated strategy to learn expressive vocabulary. *American Journal of Mental Retardation, 102,* 346–357.

Koegel, L. K., Carter, C. M., & Koegel, R. L. (2003) Teaching children with autism self-initiations as a pivotal response. *Topics in Language Disorders, 23,* 134–145.

Koegel, R. L., & Koegel, L. K. (Eds.). (1995). *Autism: Assessment, support, and trends.* Baltimore: Brookes.

Koegel, L. K., Koegel, R. L., Harrower, J. K., & Carter, C. M. (1999). Pivotal response intervention. I: Overview of approach. *Journal of the Association for Persons with Severe Handicaps, 24,* 174–185.

Koegel, R. L., Koegel, L. K., & Carter, C. M. (1999). Pivotal teaching interactions for children with autism. *School Psychology Review, 28,* 576–594.

Koegel, L. K., Koegel, R. L., Shoshan, Y., & McNerney, E. (1999). Pivotal response training. II: Preliminary long-term outcome data. *Journal of the Association for Persons with Severe Handicaps, 24,* 186–198.

Koegel, R. L., O'Dell, M. C., & Koegel, L. K. (1987). A natural language paradigm for teaching non-verbal autistic children. *Journal of Autism and Developmental Disorders, 17,* 187–199.

Koegel, R. L., Schreibman, L., Loos, L. M., Dirlich-Wilhelm, H., Dunlap, G., Robbins, F. R., et al. (1992). Consistent stress profiles in mothers of children with autism. *Journal of Autism and Developmental Disorders, 22,* 205–216.

Koegel, L. K., Steibel, D., & Koegel, R. L. (1998). Reducing aggression in children with autism toward infant or toddler siblings. *Journal of the Association for Persons with Severe Handicaps, 23,* 111–118.

Lovaas, O. I. (1977). *The autistic child: language development through behavior modification.* New York: Irvington.

McGee, G. G., Daly, T., & Jacobs, H. A. (1994). The Walden Preschool. In S. L. Harris & J. S. Handleman (Eds.), *Preschool education programs for children with autism* (pp. 127–162). Austin, TX: Pro-Ed.

Mundy, P., & Crowson, M. (1997). Joint attention and early social communication: Implications for research on intervention with autism. *Journal of Autism and Developmental Disorders, 27,* 653–676.

O'Neill, R. E., & Johnson, J. W. (2000). Brief description of functional assessment procedures reported in JASH (1983–1999). *Journal of the Association for Persons with Severe Handicaps, 25,* 197–200.

Paul, R. (1991). Profiles of toddlers with slow expressive language development. *Topics in Language Disorders, 11*, 1–13.

Paul, R., & Elwood, T. (1991). Maternal linguistic input to toddlers with slow expressive language development. *Journal of Speech and Hearing Research, 34*, 982–988.

Paul, R., & Jennings, P. (1992). Phonological behavior in toddlers with slow expressive language development. *Journal of Speech and Hearing Research, 35*, 99–107.

Paul, R., & Shiffer, M. E. (1991). Communicative initiations in normal and late-talking toddlers. *Applied Psycholinguistics, 12*, 419–431.

Peck, C. A. (1985). Increasing opportunities for social control by children with autism and severe handicaps: Effects on student behavior and perceived classroom climate. *Journal of the Association for Persons with Severe Handicaps, 10*, 183–193.

Prizant, B. M. (1983). Language acquisition and communicative behavior in autism: Toward an understanding of the "whole" of it. *Journal of Speech and Hearing Disorders, 48*, 296–307.

Prizant, B., Wetherby, A., & Rydell, P. (2000). Communication intervention issues for children with autism spectrum disorders. In A. Wetherby & B. Prizant (Eds.), *Autism spectrum disorders: A transactional developmental perspective* (pp. 193–224). Baltimore: Brookes.

Reid, D. H. (2000). Enhancing the applied utility of functional assessment. *Journal of the Association for Persons with Severe Handicaps, 25*, 241–244.

Schreibman, L. (1988). *Autism. Vol. 15: Developmental clinical psychology and psychiatry.* Newbury Park, CA: Sage.

Sigafoos, J., Roberts, D., Kerr, M., Couzens, D., & Baglioni, A. J. (1994). Opportunities for communication in classrooms serving children with developmental disabilities. *Journal of Autism and Developmental Disorders, 24*, 259–279.

Stone, W. L., Ousley, O. Y., Yoder, P. J., Hogan, K. L., & Hepburn, S. L. (1997). Non-verbal communication in two- and three-year-old children with autism. *Journal of Autism and Developmental Disorders, 27*, 677–696.

Taylor, B. A., & Harris, S. L. (1995). Teaching children with autism to seek information: Acquisition of novel information and generalization of responding. *Journal of Applied Behavior Analysis, 28*, 3–14.

Volkmar, F., Carter, A., Sparrow, S., & Cicchetti, D. (1993). Quantifying social development in autism. *Journal of the American Academy of Child and Adolescent Psychiatry, 32*, 627–632.

Wacker, D. B., Berg, W. K., Asmus, J. M., Harding, J. W., & Cooper, L. J. (1998). Experimental analysis of antecedent influences on challenging behaviors. In J. K. Luiselli & M. J. Cameron (Eds.), *Antecedent control: Innovative approaches to behavioral support* (pp. 67–86). Baltimore: Brookes.

Warren, S. F., Baxter, D. K., Anderson, S. R., Marshall, A., & Baer, D. M. (1981). Generalization of question-asking by severely retarded individuals. *Journal of the Association for Persons With Severe Handicaps, 6*, 15–22.

Wetherby, A. M., & Prizant, B. M. (2000). *Autism spectrum disorders: A transactional developmental perspective*. Baltimore: Brookes.

Wetherby, A. M., & Prutting, C. A. (1984). Profiles of communicative and cognitive–social abilities in autistic children. *American Speech-Language-Hearing Association, 27*, 364–377.

Whitehurst, G., Fischel, J., Lonigan, C., Valdez-Menchaca, M. C., DeBaryshe, B., & Caulfield, M. (1988). Verbal interaction in families of normal and expressive-language-delayed children. *Developmental Psychology, 24*, 690–699.

Yoder, P. J., Davies, B., Bishop, K., & Munson, L. (1994). Effect of adult continuing questions on conversational participation in children with developmental disabilities. *Journal of Speech and Hearing Research, 37*, 193–204.

Yoder, P. J., Kaiser, A. P., Alpert, C. L., & Fischer, R. (1993). Following the child's lead when teaching nouns to preschoolers with mental retardation. Journal of *Speech and Hearing Research, 36*, 158–167.

Yoder, P. J., & Warren, S. F. (1999). Facilitating self-initiated proto-declaratives and proto-imperatives in prelinguistic children with developmental disabilities. *Journal of Early Intervention, 22*, 79–96.

25

LEARNING EXPERIENCES . . . AN ALTERNATIVE PROGRAM FOR PRESCHOOLERS AND PARENTS: PEER-MEDIATED INTERVENTIONS FOR YOUNG CHILDREN WITH AUTISM

FRANK W. KOHLER, PHILLIP S. STRAIN, AND HOWARD GOLDSTEIN

Peer-mediated interventions for young children with autism have as their theoretical foundation the following notions: (a) Peers can be as effective as, or perhaps more effective than, direct adult intervention agents; (b) for many skill domains, the contexts created by peer-mediated interventions are closer to the everyday, clinically relevant environments where clients must ultimately be able to function; (c) the abundance of peers in most settings creates natural opportunities for clients to learn from multiple examples (a technique generally recognized to improve generalizations of intervention gains); and (d) the natural variability of peers' adherence to intervention agent roles creates many opportunities for clients to learn under flexible training conditions (another feature of instruction widely held to facilitate generalized outcomes).

In application, the peer-mediated interventions detailed in this chapter can be traced historically to Harlow's pioneering work with primates reared in isolation. A series of landmark studies (e.g., Novak & Harlow, 1975; Suomi & Harlow, 1972) showed that pairing isolate monkeys with slightly younger but socially normal monkeys largely remediated the profound social deficits displayed by the isolate-reared primates. Significantly, pairing them with same-age and adult monkeys had no therapeutic effect. Later, Furman, Rahe, and Hartup (1979) showed similar effects by pairing withdrawn preschoolers with socially competent peers.

Another line of clinical research relevant to the current use of peer-mediated interventions began with Wahler's (1967) early study of peers as social-reinforcement agents. From Wahler's initial study, a large body of research has emerged on the power of peer reinforcement, either mediated by individuals or by groups (Furman et al., 1979; Greenwood, Todd, Hops, & Walker, 1982; Odom, Hoyson, Jamieson, & Strain, 1985). Although the data are somewhat mixed, one significant finding is that when a direct comparison is made, peer-based group contingencies yield better outcomes than do adult-mediated approaches (Sancilio, 1987).

The programmatic research on peer-mediated interventions described in this chapter was conducted within the context of a comprehensive early intervention program for preschoolers and parents known as Learning Experiences . . . An Alternative Program (LEAP). In effect, LEAP represents an attempt to test the limits of peer-mediated interventions by applying these tactics for extended periods of time to a wide variety of behavior goals. When LEAP began in 1980, the inclusion of young children with autism with typical peers was a very controversial practice. To some extent, the controversy still exists today. Before providing an overview of the LEAP model and specific intervention studies, a brief discussion of the inclusion debate is offered.

DEBATE OVER INCLUSION

Although almost all those involved in early intervention claim some allegiance to inclusion (e.g., Harris & Handleman, 1993), fundamental philosophical and clinical differences are obvious. In the LEAP model, children do not earn access to typical peers when they are behaviorally ready. Conversely, children have immediate and daily access to this powerful source for behavioral change. One important reason for having high-quality inclusionary options for children with autism is the free appropriate public education (FAPE) right as written in the federal law controlling special education and related services, Individuals With Disabilities Education Act Amendments of 1997. Specifically, the FAPE requirement may be difficult to achieve if children with significant social deficits are denied regular and plentiful access to socially competent peers.

Regrettably, the inclusion issue is characterized more by myths than by sound logic and empirical evidence. The following myths are typical: (a) Children with autism require a certain level of readiness before receiving functional instruction; (b) one-to-one instruction is necessary to ensure that children achieve developmental gains; (c) children with autism are overstimulated in typical settings; and (d) in typical settings, educators cannot perform the necessary behavioral-control procedures directed toward reducing challenging behaviors.

The Readiness Myth

The readiness notion has many manifestations, including (a) an initial curriculum that focus almost entirely on child compliance during simple motor-imitation tasks; (b) systematic movement of children from developmentally segregated settings to inclusionary settings once certain skills are achieved; and (c) beginning of intervention with the most directive, adult-driven teaching methods, followed by more child-initiated tactics. Because children with autism do demonstrate developmental growth in readiness models, it does not follow that this approach is mandatory or superior to others.

As described by Strain, McGee, and Kohler (2001), the most relevant data that refute the readiness notion are as follows:

1. peer-mediated intervention studies in which some 80 young children with autism have acquired important social skills without any readiness training in the forms of curricular or teaching tactics (see review by Strain & Kohler, 1998);
2. self-control interventions conducted by Koegel, Koegel, and Carter (1998) in which some 500 behaviors have been brought under the influence of tactics that are independent of readiness training;
3. many language studies (e.g., Kaiser & Hester, 1994; Koegel et al., 1998; McGee, Krantz, & McClannahan, 1985; Yoder et al., 1995) in which child-initiated tactics have been effective;
4. behavior–analytical comparison studies in which more incidental, learner-initiated tactics *are equal or superior to* more adult-directed tactics in producing generalized responding and positive affect among teachers and learners (Elliott, Hall, & Sopher, 1991; Koegel, O'Dell, & Dunlap, 1988; Schreibman, Kaneko, & Koegel, 1991).

At this point, the question is not what data support the readiness notion but how many cases of invalidity are enough to dispel the notion?

The Tutorial-Like Instruction Myth

Closely tied to the readiness myth is the notion that children with autism require tutorial-based one-on-one instruction to learn new skills. One-on-one instruction is often considered the primary tactic to achieve a high level of intervention intensity. The efficacy of tutorial instruction cannot be disputed. However, the fact that children learn under this approach does not mean that it is mandatory *or* superior. Moreover, numerous cases of invalidity should cause educators to question the soundness of the one-to-one myth. As Strain et al. (2001) point out, data that contradict the tutorial instruction myth are as follows:

1. studies in which self-management techniques have been applied successfully in the context of ongoing routines in full inclusion settings to improve task engagement, appropriate behavior, and academic responses (e.g., Callahan & Rademacher, 1998; Koegel, Harrower, & Koegel, 1998; Sainato, Strain, Lefebvre, & Rapp, 1990);

2. studies in which adult-mediated behavioral teaching strategies are embedded in ongoing, group-based class routines to improve cognitive skills, early reading skills, imitation, and a variety of specific Individual Education Plan (IEP) objectives (e.g., Hoyson, Jamieson, & Strain, 1984; Kamps, Barbetta, Leonard, & Delquadri, 1994; Kohler, Strain, Hoyson, & Jamieson, 1997; Venn, Wolery, Werts, et al., 1993);

3. studies in which typical peers have learned to engage peers with autism in social and instruction exchanges during routine activities to enhance communicative skills, object use, and toy play skills (e.g., Goldstein, Kaczmarek, Pennington, & Shafer, 1992; McGee, Paradis, & Feldman, 1993; Pierce & Schreibman, 1997);

4. studies in which high levels of child engagement and many instructional opportunities have been achieved within the context of routine preschool activities involving large numbers of children (e.g., Kohler et al., 1997; Strain, Danko, & Kohler, 1994; Venn, Wolery, Fleming, et al., 1993).

The Overstimulation Myth

Although the overstimulation myth has seldom found its way into the literature, it is often used to deny children access to typical settings. The overstimulation myth has multiple origins. For example, the difficulty that some children with autism have with changing activities, the fact that some children are easily distracted from performing requested tasks, the tendency of children with autism to ignore important environmental cues, and the paucity of challenging behaviors that some children exhibit when taught in isolated settings all may lead to an overstimulation hypothesis. Although many children with autism do display limited attention to important cues, no evidence suggests that these challenges have a neurobehavioral basis akin to overstimulation. Furthermore, although many children with autism have unusual sensory preferences and dislikes, no data support an overstimulation origin to these behavioral patterns either.

Despite the absence of data suggesting that children with autism are understimulated in a neurobehavioral sense, several data sources may undercut the overstimulation hypothesis:

1. studies in which programmed variations in instructional stimuli, choice making, and reinforcers lead to higher levels of engagement, appropriate behavior, and developmental outcomes (e.g., Dunlap, 1984; Dunlap et al., 1994; Koegel, Dyer, & Bell, 1987);

2. studies in which chronic, high-amplitude challenging behaviors have been reduced successfully in typical (presumably highly stimulating) settings (Carr et al., 1999; Dunlap & Fox, 1999; Fox, Dunlap, & Philbrick, 1997; Vaughn, Clarke, & Dunlap, 1997);

3. studies of children's social skill acquisition in which day-one intervention effects co-occur with the onset of increased social stimuli (e.g., Odom, Strain, Karger, & Smith, 1986; Strain, 1977; Strain, Kohler, Storey, & Danko, 1994);

4. studies wherein older children and adults with autism experience significant reductions in challenging behavior as a result of receiving nonaversive behavioral intervention and a more varied, stimulating, and independent lifestyle (e.g., Bellamy, Newton, LeBaron, & Horner, 1990; Carr et al., 1999; Lucyshyn, Olson, & Horner, 1995).

Taken together, the results of research pointing to invalidity suggest the presence of redundant, inappropriate, and uninteresting stimuli in the lives of many young children with autism.

The Behavioral-Control Limitation Myth

This myth asserts that inclusionary settings do not allow for the types and intensity of interventions needed to control the challenging behaviors of children with autism. To a certain extent, this view is valid. In fact, many inclusionary programs promote the use of normalized interventions, prohibit the use of tactics considered disrespectful of children, and focus on skill building rather than behavioral reduction. It is true that placement in an inclusionary setting may be incompatible, in a sociopolitical fashion, with the use of behavior-control tactics that would not be readily used for typical preschool children. However, the question of fundamental importance is whether, for example, a prohibition on exclusionary time out, physical aversives, overcorrection, and the like deprives children with autism of a necessary and appropriate educational program. Judging by the extensive and successful use of more normalized, positive strategies, we would submit that the answer to this question is no. As Strain et al. (2001) suggest, the following data sources support the use of more normalized strategies to reduce challenging behaviors:

1. studies in which a response substitution strategy has been used successfully to reduce challenging behaviors (Carr & Carlson, 1993; Dunlap & Fox, 1999);
2. studies in which a variety of curricular modifications have been used successfully to prevent or reduce challenging behaviors (Dyer, 1987; Mason, McGee, Farmer-Dougan, & Risley, 1989; Strain & Sainato, 1987);
3. studies in which children with autism have self-managed their behavior (Dunlap, Dunlap, Koegel, & Koegel, 1991; Koegel, Koegel, Hurley, & Frea, 1992);
4. studies in which various strategies have emerged from ongoing functional analysis and then successfully applied to reduce challenging behaviors (Durand & Crimmins, 1988; Storey, Lawry, Danko, & Strain, 1994).

OVERVIEW OF THE LEAP PROGRAM

The LEAP research and demonstration program is designed to meet the needs of both typical preschoolers and those with autism in an integrated setting. LEAP offers parents a free program that operates five days per week in a local community center. A master's-level teacher and an assistant provide individualized educational programming to 10 normally developing children and three to four children with autism. Six classrooms of this composition are in operation. In addition, a full-time speech and language pathologist, supervisory staff, and contracted occupational and physical therapists work directly with the children in their classrooms. Parents of children with autism participate in a program designed to teach more effective skills for interacting with their preschoolers in the school, home, and community. LEAP also arranges consultation services to parents from physicians, child development specialists, and mental health providers. Moreover, parents of all children in the LEAP program operate their own education and support group.

LEAP comprises four program components: (a) referral process, (b) classroom instruction, (c) parent involvement and education, and (d) future educational placement. These components are briefly described here, followed by a synopsis of overall program outcomes.

Referral Process

Referrals for typical preschoolers originate from families whose children have attended the program. Referrals for children with autism originate from (a) preschools serving children with disabilities, (b) residential treatment programs, (c) local medical and mental health specialists, (d) local educational agencies, and (e) parental contact.

During the initial contact with a family, information regarding the child's existing medical condition, any general parental concerns, provisions for transportation, and parental availability and interest in involvement is obtained. An initial visit is then scheduled for interested parents. During the visit, prospective parents are provided with a detailed description of the program. Specific information relating to the child's current level of functioning and parental concerns are reviewed and discussed.

For families of children with autism, the local education agency and LEAP staff conduct an IEP meeting to determine placement. Children who are considered candidates for LEAP typically display at least three of the following criteria: (a) significantly delayed social skills, (b) significantly delayed language, (c) excessive levels of disruptive or stereotypical behaviors, and (d) minimal level of preacademic competencies. In addition to these behavioral criteria, children in the research protocol meet *Diagnostic and Statistical Manual of Mental Disorders, Fourth Edition* (DSM–IV) criteria (American Psychiatric Association, 1994) for autism on the basis of independent evaluations. In effect, then, these criteria serve as our operational definition of autism. Assistance is provided in the alternative placement of families for whom the LEAP preschool program is not deemed appropriate.

Classroom Instruction

The first 4 weeks of each child's placement within the LEAP classroom is devoted, in part, to assessing the child's current level of functioning. Standardized instruments used include the Battelle Developmental Inventory (Newborg, Stoek, & Wenck, 1984) and the McCarthy Scales of Children's Abilities (McCarthy, 1972). In addition, observations are conducted on prerequisite learning, independent functioning, and social interaction skills. A speech and language consultant also evaluates each child who demonstrates delays in language development. At the end of this assessment period, an IEP meeting is scheduled. Short-term objectives for each child are developed from checklists completed by the parents. Individualized plans are then developed for each child and reviewed weekly by the staff. A formal IEP update occurs every 3 to 4 months.

The Creative Curriculum for Early Childhood (Dodge & Colker, 1988) is used as a guide for instructional planning. The physical environment of each classroom is arranged so that there are clearly defined interest areas to support child-directed play. Themes such as dinosaurs, transportation, and families are used to help children learn about the world around them and acquire valuable information and concepts. The classroom schedule provides a balance of quiet and active approaches; individual, small, and large groups; child- and teacher-directed tasks; large- and small-muscle exercises; and indoor and outdoor activities.

To meet the needs of children with autism, the early childhood curriculum is supplemented to facilitate the development of functional skills. Instruction focuses on skills such as selecting and transitioning to new activities, following classroom routines, and participating in group activities. The early childhood curriculum also is adapted to prevent and address challenging behaviors (e.g., effective use of rules, environmental arrangements, scheduling, activities, and materials) as well as the use of positive procedures for conducting functional analyses of behaviors.

Instructional strategies used by teachers reflect both a developmentally appropriate practice approach to early childhood education as well as a best-practices approach to early intervention. Teachers facilitate all children's learning by (a) providing opportunities for the children to choose from a variety of activities, materials, and equipment; (b) facilitating their engagement with materials by assisting and guiding children; and (c) extending their learning by asking questions or making suggestions that stimulate their learning.

The following guidelines are used by classroom teachers when making decisions about instructional strategies for young children with autism:

1. Instructional strategies for children with disabilities should be as normal as possible (i.e., approximating the strategies used with same-age typical peers).
2. Instructional strategies should focus on teaching functional skills during naturally occurring routines and events in the classroom.
3. Instructional strategies should incorporate learning objectives into child-selected activities and teach necessary skills (e.g., choice making, independent work and play skills) because children with disabilities need to participate in activities.
4. Instructional strategies should be individually determined for the child, for the task, and for the child's level in the learning process.
5. Instructional strategies should include multiple methods for enhancing the probability of skill generalization.

6. Instructional strategies should be effective (i.e., they should result in children successfully learning desired skills).

Each child's progress toward identified objectives is monitored on an ongoing basis. Skill acquisition is evaluated frequently, focusing on the amount of time, the way, the level of assistance needed (e.g., level of prompts), and the conditions (e.g., materials, adults, activities, settings, etc.) under which the child performs desired skills. Progress is monitored via direct observation. For preschoolers with autism, performance in the classroom is compared with similar competencies demonstrated in the home and community. Multiple baseline designs are used to evaluate long-term maintenance and generalization of intervention gains.

Family Involvement

Family involvement is essential to the success of the LEAP program. All families participate in the program in some capacity. In the classroom, parents may choose to participate in a variety of activities that include (a) construction of instructional materials, (b) preparation of activity centers, and (c) provision of direct intervention. Parents of children with autism may choose to participate in a parent education program up to 3 times per week in home and community environments. Parents of children who are LEAP graduates may provide support and information to new parents.

We begin with an assessment of parent and child entry-level skills. Specific parent and child target behaviors are assessed through several initial play-observation sessions. Child target behaviors are also determined by having parents select specific behaviors that they would like to see either increased or decreased in their children. Although parents may acquire a range of different skills, all parents receive a curriculum to address core skills such as giving clear directions, prompting and shaping successive approximations, and providing consistent consequences. Parents also learn procedures that teachers have found effective. Along with individualized work with families in the home, school, and community, parents may elect to apply their new skills in the classroom setting.

Evaluation of project participation is conducted by assessing a range of parent and child outcomes. Changes in social functioning are assessed through preintervention and follow-up assessment of stress variables within the family and extrafamilial social contacts. These areas of family functioning were selected because of the high incidence of reported stress and insularity among parents of children with autism. Staff also assess the generalization and maintenance of parents' newly learned skills (Schreibman, 1988).

Future Education Placement Planning

Staff and parents collaborate to consider the future placement of LEAP graduates. Various options are considered by a staff–parent team. Leap staff work cooperatively with professionals who will serve the child in follow-up settings. Future teachers are invited to observe the child at LEAP and become familiar with intervention strategies that LEAP staff have found effective. Follow-up visits are scheduled with future teachers to monitor maintenance and generalization of child intervention gains.

Overall Program Outcomes

The data summarized below represent a completed analysis on 22 initial clients who have completed the experimental protocol. For this group we have shown the following:

1. Using the Childhood Autism Rating Scale (Schopler, Reichler, & Renner, 1988), many children receive a moderate-to-severe autism-level rating at program entry and then move to a non-autistic rating after 2 years of intervention. These results have been shown to persist up to age 10 (Strain & Kohler, 1998).
2. Children's overall cognitive growth improves, on average, from a delay of 12 to 18 months on entry to the normal range after 2 years of intervention. Stanford-Binet scores for this group range from 68 to 122 at age 10, with a mean of 98 (Kohler et al., 1997; Strain & Cordisco, 1993).
3. On the basis of direct observation of mother–child intervention, children's appropriate behavior improves, on average, from an entry level of 47% to 96% at program exit. At age 10, the level remains at 96% (Cordisco & Strain, 1986; Strain & Danko, 1995).
4. On the basis of observed child interactions, positive peer behaviors increase, on average, from an entry level of 2% to 26% at exit and 27% at age 10. At exit and age 10, positive social interaction levels were found to be similar to interaction patterns involving typical peers only. Twelve of the 22 children completed their public education in typical settings, graduating on time with their cohorts.

PEER-MEDIATED INTERVENTIONS: OPTIONS AND OUTCOMES

Peer interaction is an important part of preschool life. Children are expected to socialize and communicate with one another, play together, share toys and materials, and enjoy one another's company. The behavioral demands involved in these activities should not be underestimated. Playing together often requires making a graceful entry into an ongoing activity. It may involve identifying possible roles to play within an activity. Sharing toys often entails keeping one's immediate desires in check, negotiating for time with a desired toy, taking turns, and tracking how long one is entitled to play with a toy before offering it to a peer. Children with autism tend to have behavioral deficiencies that lead them to be socially withdrawn, to incite conflict or display aggression, or to be ostracized by their classmates (Kohler & Strain, 1993; Kohler, Strain, & Shearer, 1992).

When children with autism participate in routine preschool settings, more of their peers are present than adults. Thus, peers are more readily available to children as a source of stimulation, purveyors of reinforcement, and presenters of behavior to which children with special needs can react. Peers naturally serve as models and thus have a robust influence on the observational learning of social and communication skills. The pervasiveness of peers also means that their reactions to the behavior of children with special needs are likely to serve as immediate and natural consequences.

Another advantage of involving typical peers is that they can learn to be mediators of intervention with relative ease. In fact, one can argue that we researchers have progressed further in identifying profitable behaviors to teach peers that in turn promote changes in social interaction than we have in identifying target behaviors to teach to children with special needs. Because social interaction involves a large, complex, conditional behavioral repertoire, discerning the skills that should be taught to children with special needs for positive social interactions and successful relationships with peers is difficult. Teaching pivotal social skills alone may not be effective unless children have a receptive, reinforcing environment within which to practice those new skills.

We have developed five types of peer-mediated interventions at LEAP Preschool: (a) peers as models for observational learning; (b) social skills training for children with autism and their peers; (c) peers as facilitators of sociodramatic play; (d) peers as facilitators of social and communication skills; and (e) use of naturalistic teaching tactics to facilitate children's social interaction with peers.

Peer as Models for Observational Learning

Observational learning has long been recognized as a basic process for acquiring a host of language and social interaction skills (Bandura, 1977; Bijou, 1993; Browder, Schoen, & Lentz, 1986–87; Flavell, 1977; Glidden & Warner, 1982; Piaget, 1952). Inclusive preschool settings provide opportunities for children with autism to imitate typical peers. However, it is not a given that observational learning will occur when children with disabilities simply are presented the opportunity (Peck & Cooke, 1983). Investigations of observational learning resulting from group instruction have produced mixed results (Biberdorf & Pear, 1977; Hanley-Maxwell, Wilcox, & Heal, 1982; LeBlanc, Etzel, & Domash, 1978). A number of strategies can maximize the chances that observational learning will occur:

1. Focus on functional skills that produce salient consequences. The more obvious it is that demonstration of skills produces desirable consequences to both the peer model and the child with disabilities who observes the episodes, the more likely it is that observational learning will take place.

2. Have peers model communication behaviors that are developmentally appropriate. Goldstein and Brown (1989) suggest that the greater the mismatch between the child's response and the behavior being modeled, the less the chance that observational learning will be demonstrated. This principle also could be derived from Vygotsky's (1978) concept of the zone of proximal development.

3. Use models who are perceived as similar to target children and who enjoy high social status in their group. Children are more likely to imitate peers than adults and same- rather than opposite-gender models. The more similar the peer, the greater the likelihood of imitation (Hosford, 1980; Rosekrans, 1967). High-status peers tend to be imitated more often than low-status peers.

4. Incorporate modeling and assessment of observational learning into structured learning activities. Common preschool activities such as circle time, story reading, and lesson time all are conducive to observational learning. The teacher needs to monitor the effects by asking the child with disabilities to provide an observed response later in the activity, later in the day, or the next day.

5. Provide ample opportunities for modeling. The likelihood of observational learning is increased when more opportunities are presented. Of course, these opportunities benefit children only if they are attending (Strain, McGee, & Kohler, 2001).

6. Progress from immediate to increasingly delayed imitation. Goldstein and Brown (1989) used adjacent trial observational training to teach syntactic responses to children with disabilities. Adjacent trial observational training occurred when the peer model performed the desired receptive (e.g., "put the shoe under the bed") or expressive language response just

before asking the child with a disability to perform the same response. This procedure differs from the standard paradigm in which children are asked to perform long after they have observed the desired behavior. Adjacent trials resulted in immediate imitation and learning. Children subsequently demonstrated observational learning of other responses modeled in nonadjacent trials. Thus, immediate imitation can serve as a springboard for delayed imitation and eventually for conventional forms of observational learning.

7. Reinforce peers for modeling appropriate behavior. Praising the model for showing classmates how to respond can make the episode more salient.

8. Reinforce children for imitating peers incidentally. Target children can be reinforced for attending to the peer models as well as for imitating peers. Teachers do not want to miss an opportunity for reinforcing children with disabilities when spontaneous, delayed imitation occurs incidentally during the day.

9. Frequently assess behaviors targeted for observation. Maintaining high expectations and providing opportunities for children with disabilities to attempt newly learned social and communication skills is key to success.

Social Skills Training for Children With Autism and Their Peers

Teachers use a formal program to teach children to engage in positive interaction (Kohler, Shearer, & Strain, 1990). All preschoolers in the classroom, including children with autism and typical peers, participate in training, which occurs within a range of structured play activities on a daily basis (Kohler & Strain, 1993). Five skills are learned and practiced in these sessions: (a) playing organizer suggestions, (b) sharing of offers and requests, (c) assistance with offers and requests, (d) compliments, and (e) affection. These skills are learned in this sequence through three different strategies. First, each skill is used to *initiate and extend or continue* play interactions with another child. For example, children might offer to share something with a youngster who is playing alone. Second, children learn to *respond positively* by accepting or agreeing with their playmate's overture. Finally, children learn *to be persistent* in their use of initiations and responses. Overtures that are ignored or refused are followed by different or more elaborate offers or requests.

Social-skills training occurs throughout the year and entails three stages. Teachers introduce and model individual skills during Stage 1, which lasts 1 or 2 sessions. During Stage 2 (1 or 2 days), children rehearse that skill with the teacher, who provides ongoing instructions, models, and feedback (correction and praise) to individual children. Children practice the skill with one another independent of close teacher directions during Stage 3. Two criteria are set for terminating the final stage of training for each skill: (a) Children with autism and their peers can produce at least four exchanges using the newly taught skill during a 6-minute period; and (b) typical children exhibit at least 50% of their skills independently of adult prompts. After these two criteria are met, the teacher begins Stage 1 with a new social skill (e.g., training for sharing begins after children have completed all three stage of training for play organizers).

The protocol is designed to accommodate a variety of activities that are rotated daily. For example, play organizer, sharing, and assistance overtures are suited to dramatic, manipulative, and gross motor activities. The sequence and scope of training are also tailored to meet children's individual needs. For example, children with spontaneous language practice directing play organizer suggestions and assistance offers or requests to peers. Conversely, youngsters lacking language skills might learn to exhibit nonverbal share requests or offers and to respond positively to other children's overtures.

During and after training, children participate in daily play activities to exchange and further refine their newly taught overtures. The teacher begins each session by reviewing the various play materials and roles with a group of 3 or 4 youngsters, including one child with autism and 2 or 3 typical peers. Children rehearse a range of designated skills or strategies with the teacher, who provides instructions and models. After this introduction, the children begin their play session while the teacher monitors and facilitates children's interactions with prompts, visual cues, and reinforcement (Strain, 1977).

Peers as Facilitators of Sociodramatic Play

Many preschool settings provide opportunities for children to engage in sociodramatic play. They provide areas equipped with materials and props that relate to familiar activities (e.g., cooking, going to the grocery store) and sometimes less familiar activities (e.g., going camping or to a magic show). For a group of children to engage in this sophisticated form of play, they must identify the various characters or roles present in those real-life settings, figure out what those characters do, and enact the activities that typically compose the particular sociodramatic play theme.

Many young children have limited awareness of some of the themes and roles that might be appropriate for a particular play activity. Therefore, teachers introduce these themes and use stories to discuss various roles and scenarios that could be enacted. Goldstein and Cisar (1992) set up such situations in which two typical peers were grouped with a child with autism. The teacher began by assigning children roles, giving them materials, and providing an overview of expectations for children's actions. The teachers did not provide any further directions about what each child should say or do, however. Although the typical peers nearly doubled their interaction in this situation, they (as did their peers with disabilities) engaged in social behavior that was mainly unrelated to the theme. To improve the quality and quantity of social interaction, Goldstein and Cisar (1992) provided more specific training developed from loosely conceived scripts. Rather than lines of a play, however, these scripts outlined a set of acts for children to say or do. The scripts balanced the number of acts for each role in hopes of avoiding the passive role often delegated to the child with disabilities if children are left on their own (i.e., the patient when playing doctor or the passenger on a bus trip). After a rather minimal amount of training on these scripts (about 1 or 2 hours total), unrelated social behavior was virtually nonexistent and all children exhibited impressive rates of targeted and theme-related social behavior. Recommendations for facilitating social interaction follow:

1. Introduce sociodramatic routines through a variety of strategies.
2. Build shared expectations among children by explaining the roles in a given theme, reading and discussing stories related to themes, and describing various actions that children can perform in that activity.
3. When describing the actions associated with given roles, try to balance the number of possible actions for each role. Minimize the problem of the child with disabilities being relegated to the most passive role by requiring the children to take turns playing each of the roles.
4. Provide examples of different levels of actions (e.g., nonverbal, minimal verbal, elaborated verbal) so the children learn to tailor the interaction to different developmental levels. In this way, the script could easily be individualized for children with varying abilities so as to ensure that more elaborate responses are modeled by peers for the children with disabilities.
5. Teach peers to prompt and reinforce one another's efforts to facilitate social interactions and provide ongoing support to maintain their efforts. Having them identify reinforcers that the entire group will enjoy if a classmate with disabilities engages in a predetermined level of social interaction can enhance collaborative support among peers.

Peers as Facilitators of Social and Communication Skills

An extensive literature has developed since Strain and Shores (1977) first argued for using social reciprocity to develop procedures that increase interaction among peers. Early research demonstrated that social reinforcement on the part of both typically developing children and children with disabilities had positive reciprocal effects on rates of social interaction (e.g., Charlesworth & Hartup, 1967; Hartup, Glazer, & Charlesworth, 1967; Strain, Shores, & Kerr, 1976; Strain & Timm, 1974; Wahler, 1967). Because adults' praise for interacting can have the immediate effect of interrupting peer interaction (Shores, Hester, & Strain, 1976), an emphasis on natural reinforcement is preferred. Potential natural peer reinforcement can take several forms (e.g., smiles, eye contact, gestural expressions, verbal compliments, verbal responses, sharing toys, physical contact). Nonetheless, educators need to monitor the effects of putative reinforcers to determine whether they are effective with individual children with disabilities.

The literature has focused on the other directive forwarded by Strain and Shores (1977), which was to develop interventions that rely on social initiations to facilitate the social interactions of children with significant social impairments. Strain, Shores, and Timm (1977) instructed a peer to try his best to engage a fellow preschooler who was socially withdrawn in social play. This study showed the powerful effect that peers' social initiations can have on teaching children with disabilities to play and interact socially. Subsequent studies showed that peers' use of social initiation strategies almost invariably had positive effects on the social interaction of children who were socially withdrawn as well as those who exhibited autism (e.g., Day, Powell, & Dy-Lin, 1982; Hendrickson, Strain, Tremblay, & Shores, 1982; Ragland, Kerr, & Strain, 1978).

Researchers have identified a range of strategies that peers can use to facilitate the social interaction of children with mild to severe social impairments. Some of these strategies are predominantly motor or gestural overtures (e.g., sharing toys, providing assistance, displaying affection); others are verbal behaviors (e.g., play organizers, compliments, offering assistance). General comments and statements are often used to promote social interactions. Peers can describe their own play (e.g., "I'm baking a cake"), that of the focal child (e.g., "You're cooking pasta"), or that of another child (e.g., "Max is going up the slide"). Although such comments do not obligate a response, children with autism often do respond (Goldstein & Kaczmarek, 1992). Peers also can question and make requests of children with disabilities. Such requests might focus on acquiring a child's attention (e.g., "Hey, Joe, look at this"), an object (e.g., "Please hand me the scarf"), or information (e.g., "What toy did you give Jack?"). Finally, peers can request clarification if a child says something that they do not understand (e.g., "Tell me again").

Many of the behaviors described above are considered initiations. As such, they are excellent ways of getting an interaction started when no interaction has occurred for some time. However, peers also should be encouraged to respond to children with disabilities. Responsive behaviors include accepting or exchanging toys; complying with requests for assistance, attention, information, or objects; returning affectionate behaviors; and taking another turn in a conversation or social exchange to keep the interaction going.

Perhaps the most important consideration is to select strategies for which peer implementation can be sustained. Goldstein and his colleagues have sought to package facilitative strategies in hopes of simplifying peer training, implementation, and retention of strategies (English, Goldstein, Shafer, & Kaczmarek, 1997; Goldstein, English, Shafer, & Kaczmarek, 1997; Goldstein, Kaczmarek, Pennington, & Shafer, 1992). Their notion of "stay–play–talk" comprises a number of the strategies discussed above. "STAY" implies establishing close proximity and following the target child's lead. "PLAY" encompasses establishing mutual attention or getting the child's attention, joint play suggestions or play organizers, and talking about the ongoing play activity. "TALK" includes being responsive to what the target child says or does and keeping the play activity going (redirecting the child or re-using the previous behaviors).

We generally encourage teachers to involve all typically developing children in daily intervention. In fact, typically developing children with less sophisticated social skills may derive the most direct benefit of learning an array of social strategies. Goldstein and Ferrell (1987) attempted to balance play triads by selecting pairs of typical peers who progressed most and least quickly through training. They determined that peers' rates of strategy use was unrelated to their success in daily intervention sessions. Although some initial benefits may accrue in selecting peers who have the richest repertoires of social skills for their age, small amounts of training appear to cancel out those initial differences.

Another factor has to do with the willingness and availability of peers. Although not compared directly, English et al. (1997) surmised that consistent pairing of a peer buddy with a child with a disability was likely to have more positive effects on relationship development than systematically varied pairings. Selecting peers who have a good attendance, as well as similar interests to the child with a disability, appears to be the best method. Peers are also more willing to engage in an intervention if they have shared positive experiences with the child with a disability. Finding out what activities the child with a disability prefers and matching those with the preferences demonstrated by a peer is an important consideration.

English et al. (1997) provide a protocol for supporting peers' use of "buddy skills" during routine preschool activities. This protocol includes 11 steps, beginning with performing an initial assessment and followed by teaching children their roles and strategies, implementing daily sessions, and conducting evaluations. General guidelines for implementing the steps of this protocol follow:

1. Select facilitative strategies to teach peers, such as the "stay–play–talk" strategies, which can be taught successively in a cumulative fashion.

2. Teach facilitative strategies to peers in small group sessions, eventually requiring peers to demonstrate the strategies as the teacher or an assistant performs a role-playing exercise with the child with a disability (see the description of social-skills training provided earlier).
3. Assign peers to be buddies with children with autism, and provide opportunities for them to use the strategies in play settings and other activities throughout the day.
4. Remind peers to use the facilitative strategies before activities suitable for strategy use, and encourage peers to generate examples or goals for using the strategies.
5. Prompt peers, as necessary (but not too often or intrusively) in selected activities to display the facilitative strategies, and then fade prompts over time.
6. Reinforce peers for strategy use and children with disabilities for appropriate social interactions after play and other activities. Encourage peers to provide supportive remarks to one another to prompt and reward strategy use.

Naturalistic Teaching Tactics

LEAP teachers also use naturalistic teaching tactics to facilitate children's interaction with peers. Table 25.1 lists the strategies that teachers use throughout the day. These tactics rely on the provision of antecedent variables to accomplish two objectives: (a) stimulate children's interest, enjoyment, and play in an activity, and (b) facilitate communication and interaction with others. Many tactics in Table 25.1 accomplish both of these functions. For example, the use of novel materials may enhance a child's interest in an activity, as well as generate overtures to both the teacher and peers. In contrast to practices that place children in the passive role of responding to adult directions, the tactics in Table 25.1 attempt to follow or respond to a child's lead within an activity (Bricker & Woods-Cripe, 1992; Kaiser, Hendrickson, & Alpert, 1991; Kohler, Anthony, Steighner, & Hoyson, 2001).

Typically developing peers assume a variety of roles in the naturalistic teaching process. First, teachers use these tactics during activities that include all children in the class. Second, many tactics are designed to facilitate interaction with peers rather than the teacher. For example, the teacher might use comments and questions to facilitate children's interest and attention to peers (e.g., "Katie is taking her baby for a walk"). Finally, the last tactic in Table 25.1 refers to the process of prompting peers to direct explicit overtures to a child with autism.

A critical step in using this approach is learning how to stimulate children's natural interest and motivation. This requires teachers to make a host

TABLE 25.1
Description of Naturalistic Teaching Strategies

Tactic strategy	Description
Use novel materials	Incorporate materials that are novel or unique into the activity. These may be items in which the child has shown a previous interest, such as Winnie the Pooh characters, balloons, and bubbles.
Join the activity	The teacher joins the activity and engages in play-related actions and themes with the children.
Invite child to make choices	The teacher invites the child to make choices about desired actions or materials. This can be done through questions or nonverbal overtures (e.g., holding out a container of markers so the child can select one).
Use incidental strategies	Place items out of reach, block the child's access to desired items, sabotage materials, and act in ways that violate the child's expectations (i.e., respond to child' overtures in the wrong way).
Use comments and questions	Use comments and questions to facilitate the child's interest and play-related talk (e.g., "I think that I'll put my baby right next to yours" or "Why are you coloring your turtle purple?").
Require expansion of talk	Respond to the child's talk in a manner that generates elaboration. If the child requests a ball, the teacher might ask "What are you going to do with it?" before giving the child the ball.
Invite interaction with peers	The teacher encourages interaction with other children by drawing the child's attention to peers or prompting peers to direct overtures to the focal child (e.g., "Maybe you could ask Sam to play with you").

of spontaneous judgments, such as (a) what action, theme, or material is the child interested in?; (b) if the child is not displaying interest, how might I occasion this?; (c) if the child is showing some form of interest and engagement, then what methods can I use to facilitate high-quality play with others? Teachers address Question 2 by searching for novel materials that capture children's interest. Once stimulating materials are identified, teachers use the other tactics in Table 25.1 to facilitate children's interaction. For example, a teacher might carry Pooh Bear characters in her pocket in hopes of eliciting interest and some form of request from a child. The teacher might respond to the request by asking the child which animal he wants first, having the child describe how he is going to use the animal, and other such gambits.

Teachers' initial efforts to use the tactics in Table 25.1 are often met with child indifference and opposition. Subsequently, teachers often receive support or guidance from another individual who provides on-the-spot coaching. In addition, teachers also examine videotapes of their sessions to evaluate their progress and make decisions about necessary modifications. Our experience is that most teachers require 6 to 12 sessions before they become comfortable and successful following a child's lead within an activity.

EXPERIMENTAL RESULTS FOR THE PEER-MEDIATED INTERVENTIONS

Approximately three dozen studies have been conducted to examine the peer-mediated interventions developed at LEAP Preschool. The following findings have been obtained:

1. Typically developing peers as young as 36 months can be readily taught to engage in persistent social approaches toward their socially withdrawn peers (Strain, 1977; Strain, Shores, & Timm, 1977).
2. Peer-mediated interventions often yield Day 1 effects, suggesting that the poor social abilities characteristic of young children with autism may be attributable, in part, to the socially unresponsive contexts in which they are often educated (Strain, 1977; Strain & Odom, 1986).
3. For many target children, the level of positive peer behavior falls within normative limits for age and social context (Strain, 1987).
4. Teachers' use of naturalistic tactics have produced increases in children's social interaction and play across the full spectrum of preschool activities (Kohler et al., 2001; Kohler et al., 1997). These tactics can also be combined with the formal strategies of peer modeling and facilitation of sociodramatic and communication skills.
5. Cross-setting behavior change is achievable with relatively minor alterations in the social responsiveness of generalized settings (Strain, 1985).
6. Typical peers have experienced no negative outcomes from participation as intervention agents. To the contrary, their social relations with other typical children and their general class deportment may improve (Strain, 1987).

Ensuring that peers interact with and facilitate the development of children with autism is a significant challenge in all preschool programs that serve children with varying needs and abilities. Our knowledge of peer-mediated interventions has grown considerably since the first version of this chapter (Strain, Kohler, & Goldstein, 1996). Before the mid 1990s, the peer interventions at LEAP focused exclusively on the social and communication skills of children with autism. Furthermore, these interventions required high levels of adult involvement and were limited to only 1 or 2 periods of the day. Since that time, we have focused on expanding interventions into the full spectrum of LEAP activities to address a wide range of skills.

DISCUSSION AND FUTURE DIRECTIONS

The field of peer-mediated intervention for preschool-age children with autism is at a crossroads—a crossroads marked on one side by our meager short-term successes and on the other by our lack of success when it comes to reliably and consistently producing truly powerful and long-term effects. What are the hallmarks of our success or lack thereof, and which path might we choose for the future?

If the universe of social contexts, demands, and challenges is defined by our prevailing, single-case experimental paradigm, we do pretty well as intervention agents for children's social and communication skills—that is, we almost always improve skills to above the pretraining level of performance (e.g., Strain et al., 1977). We almost always find that individuals do more than they are directly taught to do; when this happens we do not see the phenomenon as a problem of experimental control, incidentally (Goldstein, Wickstrom, Hoyson, Jamieson, & Odom, 1988). Of course, when individuals perform poorly and not as they are taught, we resort to experimental control issues (e.g., lack of fidelity of treatment, specific intervention agent effects) as our explanatory mechanism of choice. More rarely, we show that individuals continue, to some extent, to behave more socially when there are no obvious incentives offered by the experimenters to do so (e.g., Day et al., 1982). Not surprisingly, we do not tend to interpret this event as an issue of poor experimental control either.

So what are the limitations or problems with these kinds of effects? The problems are not so much a lack of behavioral effect as such; rather, they extend to the context and time frame within which our interventions most often occur. Stated simply, many social interventions with preschoolers are analogous to the use of a bandage to close a wound from a grenade. Our interventions are often too infrequent and too trivial. Presuming for the moment, however, that our intervention methods and foci for change are correct, let us explore the more simple problem of intensity.

Consider the answers to the following questions:

1. Where do clients need good communicative and social relations? All settings.
2. With whom must clients engage communicatively and socially? Everyone.
3. During what times do clients need to engage communicatively and socially? Most of the time.

If, in fact, social and communicative skillfulness have a certain universality; if, in fact, these skills, to some extent, are needed by everyone, at most times, and in all contexts, then how do our standard interventions meet this challenge? Most experimental demonstrations offer, within school-only contexts, perhaps 20 minutes of intervention per day, at most in two settings, with the involvement of a couple of intervention agents. Moreover, given that most experiments last 3 to 5 months, they provide about 24 hours of cumulative intervention time toward altering the way a young child will interact with others.

The preceding commentary in no way dismisses the value of the work done to date. Much has been discovered about functional social skills (Strain, 1984, 1985), about motivational mechanisms to enhance skill display (McConnell, Sisson, Cort, & Strain, 1991), about the influence of socially responsive environments (Fox et al., 1984), and about the myriad ways to assess social relationships (Greenwood, Todd, Hops, & Walker, 1982). The argument here simply is this: The easy experimental demonstrations of effect are now behind us, and we should proceed with designing, implementing, and evaluating the longitudinal, community-wide interventions that are necessary to achieve the magnitude, breadth, and longevity of behavior change that our clients need and the contextually complex social world demands.

REFERENCES

American Psychiatric Association. (1994). *Diagnostic and statistical manual of mental disorders* (4th ed.). Washington, DC: Author.

Bandura, A. (1977). *Social learning theory*. Englewood Cliffs, NJ: Prentice-Hall.

Bellamy, G. T., Newton, J. S., LeBaron, N., & Horner, R. H. (1990). Quality of life and lifestyle outcomes: A challenge for residential programs. In R. Schalock (Ed.), *Quality of life: Perspectives and issues* (pp. 127–137). Washington, DC: American Association on Mental Retardation.

Biberdorf, J. R., & Pear, J. J. (1977). Two-to-one versus one-to-one student–teacher ratios in the operant verbal training of retarded children. *Journal of Applied Behavior Analysis, 10*, 506.

Bijou, S. W. (1993). *Behavior analysis of child development* (2nd ed.). Reno, NV: Context Press.

Bricker, D., & Woods-Cripe, J. J. (1992). *An activity-based approach to early intervention*. Baltimore: Brookes.

Browder, D., Schoen, S., & Lentz, F. (1986–87). Learning to learn through observation. *Journal of Special Education, 20*, 447–461.

Callahan, K., & Rademacher, J. A. (1998). Using self-management strategies to increase the on-task behavior of a student with autism. *Journal of Positive Behavioral Interventions, 1*, 117–122.

Carr, E. G., & Carlson, J. I. (1993). Reduction of severe behavior problems in the community using a multicomponent treatment approach. *Journal of Applied Behavior Analysis, 26*, 157–172.

Carr, E. G., Levin, L., McConnachie, G., Carlson, J. I., Kemp, D. C., Smith, et al. (1999). Comprehensive multinstructional intervention for problem behavior in the community: Long-term maintenance and social validation. *Journal of Positive Behavioral Interventions, 1*, 5–25.

Charlesworth, R., & Hartup, W. W. (1967). Positive social reinforcement in the nursery school peer group. *Child Development, 38*, 993–1002.

Cordisco, L. K., & Strain, P. S. (1986). Assessment and generalization and maintenance of a multicomponent parent training program. *Journal of the Division of Early Childhood, 10*, 10–24.

Day, R., Powell, T., Dy-Lin, E., & Stowitschek, J. (1982). An evaluation of the effects of a social interaction training package on mentally handicapped preschool children. *Education and Training of the Mentally Retarded, 17*, 125–130.

Dodge, D. T., & Colker, L. J. (1988). *The creative curriculum* (3rd ed.). Washington, DC: Teaching Strategies.

Dunlap, G. (1984). The influence of task variation and maintenance tasks on the learning and affect of autistic children. *Journal of Experimental Child Psychology, 37*, 41–64.

Dunlap, G., dePerczel, M., Clarke, S., Wilson, D., Wright, S., White, R., et al. (1994). Choice making to promote adaptive behavior for students with emotional and behavioral challenges. *Journal of Applied Behavior Analysis, 24*, 505–518.

Dunlap, L. K., Dunlap, G., Koegel, L. K., & Koegel, R. L. (1991). Using self monitoring to increase students' success and independence. *Teaching Exceptional Children, 23*, 17–22.

Dunlap, G., & Fox, L. (1999). A demonstration of behavioral support for young children with autism. *Journal of Applied Behavior Analysis, 1*, 77–87.

Durand, V. M., & Crimmins, D. B. (1988). Identifying the variables maintaining self-injurious behavior. *Journal of Autism and Developmental Disorders, 18*, 99–117.

Dyer, K. (1987). The competition of autistic stereotyped behavior with usual and specially assessed reinforcers. *Research in Developmental Disabilities, 8*, 607–626.

Elliott, R., Hall, K., & Sopher, H. (1991). Analog language teaching vs. natural language teaching: Generalization and retention of language learning for adults with autism and mental retardation. *Journal of Autism and Developmental Disorders, 21*, 433–447.

English, K., Goldstein, H., Shafer, K., & Kaczmarek, L. (1997). Promoting interactions among preschoolers with and without disabilities: Effects of a buddy system skills-training program. *Exceptional Children, 63*, 229–243.

Flavell, J. H. (1977). *Cognitive development*. Englewood Cliffs, NJ: Prentice-Hall.

Fox, L., Dunlap, G., & Philbrick, L. A. (1997). Providing individualized supports to young children with autism and their families. *Journal of Early Intervention, 21*, 1–14.

Fox, J. J., Gunter, P., Brady, M. P., Bambara, L., Spiegel-McGill, P., & Shores, R. E. (1984). Using multiple peer exemplars to develop generalized social responding of an autistic girl. In R. Rutherford & C. M. Nelson (Eds.), *Monograph on Severe Behavioral Disorders of Children and Youth, 7,* 17–26.

Furman, W., Rahe, D. F., & Hartup, W. W. (1979). Rehabilitation of socially withdrawn preschool children through mixed-age and same-age socialization. *Child Development, 50,* 915–922.

Glidden, L. M., & Warner, D. A. (1982). Research on imitation in mentally retarded persons: Theory-bound or ecological validity run amuck? *Applied Research in Mental Retardation, 3,* 383–395.

Goldstein, H., & Brown, W. H. (1989). Observational learning of receptive and expressive language by handicapped preschool children. *Education and Treatment of Children, 12,* 5–37.

Goldstein, H., & Cisar, C. L. (1992). Promoting interaction during sociodramatic play: Teaching scripts to typical preschoolers and classmates with disabilities. *Journal of Applied Behavior Analysis, 25,* 265–280.

Goldstein, H., English, K., Shafer, K., & Kaczmarek, L. (1997). Interaction among preschoolers with and without disabilities: Effects of across-the-day peer intervention. *Journal of Speech, Language, and Hearing Research, 40,* 33–48.

Goldstein, H., & Ferrell, D. (1987). Augmenting communicative interaction between handicapped and nonhandicapped preschool children. *Journal of Speech and Hearing Disorders, 52,* 200–211.

Goldstein, H., & Kaczmarek, L. (1992). Promoting communicative interaction among children in integrated intervention settings. In S. F. Warren & J. Reichle (Eds.), *Communication and language intervention series: Vol. 1. Causes and effects in communication and language intervention* (pp. 81–112). Baltimore: Brookes.

Goldstein, H., Kaczmarek, L., Pennington, R., & Shafer, K. (1992). Peer-mediated intervention: Attending to, commenting on, and acknowledging the behavior of preschoolers with autism. *Journal of Applied Behavior Analysis, 25,* 289–305.

Goldstein, H., Wickstrom, S., Hoyson, M., Jamieson, B., & Odom, S. (1988). Effects of sociodramatic play training on social and communicative interaction. *Education and Treatment of Children, 11,* 97–117.

Greenwood, C. R., Todd, N. M., Hops, H., & Walker, H. M. (1982). Behavior change targets in the assessment and treatment of socially withdrawn preschool children. *Behavioral Assessment, 4,* 273–297.

Hanley-Maxwell, C., Wilcox, B. L., & Heal, L. W. (1982). A comparison of vocabulary learning by moderately retarded students under direct instruction and incidental presentation. *Education and Training of the Mentally Retarded, 17,* 214–221.

Harris, S. L., & Handleman, J. S. (Eds.). (1993.) *Preschool education programs for children with autism.* Austin, TX: Pro-Ed.

Hartup, W. W., Glazer, J., & Charlesworth, R. (1967). Peer reinforcement and sociometric status. *Child Development, 38,* 1017–1024.

Hendrickson, J. M., Strain, P. S., Tremblay, A., & Shores, R. E. (1982). Functional effects of peer social initiations on the interactions of behaviorally handicapped children. *Behavior Modification, 6,* 323–353.

Hosford, R. E. (1980). Self-as-model: A cognitive social learning technique. *The Counseling Psychologist, 9,* 45–62.

Hoyson, M., Jamieson, B., & Strain, P. S. (1984). Individualized group instructions of normally developing and autistic-like children: The LEAP curriculum model. *Journal of the Division for Early Childhood, 8,* 157–172.

Kaiser, A., Hendrickson, J., & Alpert, K. (1991). Milieu language teaching: A second look. In R. Gable (Ed.), *Advances in mental retardation and developmental disabilities* (Vol. 4, pp. 63–92). London: Jessica Kingsley.

Kaiser, A., & Hester, P. (1994). Generalized effects of enhanced milieu teaching. *Journal of Speech and Hearing Research, 37,* 63–92.

Kamps, D. M., Barbetta, P. M., Leonard, B. R., & Delquadri, J. (1994). Classwide peer tutoring: An integration strategy to improve reading skills and promote peer interactions among students with autism and general education peers. *Journal of Applied Behavior Analysis, 25,* 49–61.

Koegel, L. K., Harrower, J. K., & Koegel, R. L. (1998). Support for children with developmental disabilities in full inclusion classrooms through self-management. *Journal of Positive Behavior Interventions, 1,* 26–33.

Koegel, L. K., Koegel, R. L., & Carter, C. M. (1998). Pivotal responses and the natural language teaching paradigm. *Seminars in Speech and Language, 19,* 355–372.

Koegel, L. K., Koegel, R. L., Hurley, C., & Frea, W. D. (1992). Improving social skills and disruptive behavior in children with autism through self-management. *Journal of Applied Behavior Analysis, 25,* 341–353.

Koegel, R. L., Dyer, K., & Bell, L. (1987). The influence of child-preferred activities on autistic children's social behavior. *Journal of Applied Behavior Analysis, 20,* 243–252.

Koegel, R. L., O'Dell, N., & Dunlap, G. (1988). Producing speech use in nonverbal autistic children by reinforcing attempts. *Journal of Autism and Development Disorders, 18,* 525–538.

Kohler, F. W., Anthony, L. J., Steighner, S. A., & Hoyson, M. (2001). Teaching social interaction skills in the integrated preschool: An examination of naturalistic tactics. *Topics in Early Childhood Special Education, 21,* 93–103.

Kohler, F. W., Shearer, D., & Strain, P. S. (1990). *Peer mediated intervention manual.* Pittsburgh, PA: University of Pittsburgh.

Kohler, F. W., & Strain, P. S. (1993). Teaching preschool children to make friends. *Teaching Exceptional Children, 25,* 41–43.

Kohler, F. W., Strain, P. S., Hoyson, M., & Jamieson, B. (1997). Merging naturalistic and peer-based strategies to address the IEP objectives of preschoolers with autism: An examination of structural and child behavior outcomes. *Focus on Autism and Other Developmental Disabilities, 12,* 196–206.

Kohler, F. W., Strain, P. S., & Shearer, D. D. (1992). The overtures of preschool social skill intervention agents: Differential rates, forms, and topographies. *Behavior Modification, 16*, 525–542.

LeBlanc, J., Etzel, B., & Domash, M. (1978). A functional curriculum for early intervention. In K. E. Allen, V. A. Holm, & R. L. Schiefelbusch (Eds.), *Early intervention—A team approach* (pp. 331–381). Baltimore: University Park Press.

Lucyshyn, J. M., Olson, D., & Horner, R. H. (1995). Building an ecology of support: A case study of one woman with severe problem behaviors living in the community. *Journal of the Association for Persons With Severe Handicaps, 20*, 16–30.

Mason, S. A., McGee, G. G., Farmer-Dougan, V., & Risley, T. R. (1989). A practical strategy for reinforcer assessment. *Journal of Applied Behavior Analysis, 22*, 171–179.

McCarthy, D. A. (1972). *Manual for the McCarthy Scales of Children's Abilities*. San Antonio, TX: The Psychological Corporation.

McConnell, S. R., Sisson, L. A., Cort, C. A., & Strain, P. S. (1991). Effects of social skills training and contingency management on reciprocal interaction of behaviorally handicapped preschool children. *Journal of Special Education, 24*, 473–495.

McGee, G. G., Krantz, P. J., & McClannahan, L. E. (1985). The facilitative effects of incidental teaching on preposition use by autistic children. *Journal of Applied Behavior Analysis, 18*, 17–31.

McGee, G. G., Paradis, T., & Feldman, R. S. (1993). Free effects of integration on levels of autistic behavior. *Topics in Early Childhood Special Education, 13*, 57–67.

Newborg, J., Stock, J. R., & Wenck, L. (1984). *Battelle Developmental Inventory*. Allen, TX: DLM Teaching Resources.

Novak, M. A., & Harlow, H. F. (1975). Social recovery of monkeys isolated for the first year of life. I: Rehabilitation and therapy. *Developmental Psychology, 11*, 453–465.

Odom, S. L., Hoyson, M., Jamieson, B., & Strain, P. S. (1985). Increasing handicapped preschoolers' peer social interactions: Cross-setting and component analysis. *Journal of Applied Behavior Analysis, 18*, 3–16.

Odom, S. L., Strain, P. S., Karger, M. A., & Smith, J. D. (1986). Using single and multiple peers to promote social interactions of preschool children with severe handicaps. *Journal of the Division for Early Childhood, 10*, 53–64.

Peck, C. A., & Cooke, T. P. (1983). Benefits of mainstreaming at the early childhood level: How much can we expect? *Analysis and Intervention in Developmental Disabilities, 3*, 1–22.

Piaget, J. (1952). *The origins of intelligence in children*. New York: International Universities Press.

Pierce, K., & Schreibman, L. (1997). Multiple peer use of PRT to increase social behavior of classmates with autism: Results from trained and untrained peers. *Journal of Applied Behavior Analysis, 28*, 157–160.

Ragland, E. U., Kerr, M. M., & Strain, P. S. (1978). Effects of social initiations on the behavior of withdrawn autistic children. *Behavior Modification, 2,* 565–578.

Rosekrans, M. A. (1967). Imitation in children as a function of perceived similarity to a social model and vicarious reinforcement. *Journal of Personality and Social Psychology, 7,* 307–314.

Sainato, D. M., Strain, P. S., Lefebvre, D., & Rapp, N. (1990). Effects of self-evaluation on the independent work skills of preschool children with disabilities. *Exceptional Children, 56,* 540–551.

Sancilio, M. F. M. (1987). Peer intervention as a method of therapeutic intervention with children. *Clinical Psychology Review, 7,* 475–500.

Schopler, E., Reichler, R. J., & Renner, B. R. (1988). *Childhood Autism Rating Scale.* Circle Pines, MN: AGH Publishing.

Schreibman, L. (1988). *Autism.* Thousand Oaks, CA: Sage.

Schreibman, L., Kaneko, W., & Koegel, R. (1991). Positive affect of parents of autistic children: A comparison across two teaching techniques. *Behavior Therapy, 22,* 479–490.

Shores, R. E., Hester, P., & Strain, P. S. (1976). The effects of amount and type of teacher–child interaction on child–child interaction during free-play. *Psychology in the Schools, 13,* 171–175.

Storey, K., Lawry, J., Danko, C., & Strain, P. S. (1994). Functional analysis and intervention for disruptive behaviors of a kindergarten student. *Journal of Education Research, 30,* 8–19.

Strain, P. S. (1977). Training and generalization effects of peer social initiations on withdrawn preschool children. *Journal of Abnormal Child Psychology, 5,* 445–455.

Strain, P. S. (1984). Social behavior patterns of nonhandicapped and nonhandicapped developmentally disabled friend pairs in mainstreaming preschools. *Analysis and Intervention in Developmental Disabilities, 4,* 15–28.

Strain, P. S. (1985). Social and non-social determinants of acceptability in handicapped preschool children. *Topics in Early Childhood Special Education, 4,* 47–58.

Strain, P. S. (1987). Comprehensive evaluation of young autistic children. *Topics in Early Childhood Special Education, 7,* 97–110.

Strain, P. S., & Cordisco, L. (1993). LEAP Preschool. In S. L. Harris & J. S. Handleman (Eds.), *Preschool education programs for children with autism* (pp. 127–162). Austin, TX: Pro-Ed.

Strain, P. S., & Danko, C. D. (1995). Caregivers' encouragement of positive interaction between preschoolers with autism and their siblings. *Journal of Emotional and Behavioral Disorders, 3,* 2–12.

Strain, P. S., Danko, C., & Kohler, F. W. (1994). Activity engagement and social interaction development in young children with autism: An examination of "free" intervention effects. *Journal of Emotional and Behavioral Disorders, 2,* 15–29.

Strain, P. S., & Kohler, F. W. (1998). Peer-mediated social intervention for young children with autism. *Seminars in Speech and Language, 19*, 391–405.

Strain, P. S., Kohler, F. W., & Goldstein, H. (1996). Learning experiences . . . an alternative program: Peer-mediated interventions for young children with autism. In E. Hibbs & P. Jensen (Eds.), *Psychosocial treatments for child and adolescent disorders: Empirically based strategies for clinical practice* (pp. 573–587). Washington, DC: American Psychological Association.

Strain, P. S., Kohler, F. W., Storey, K., & Danko, C. (1994). Teaching preschoolers with autism to self-monitor their social interaction. *Journal of Emotional and Behavioral Disorders, 2*, 78–88.

Strain, P. S., McGee, G., & Kohler, F. W. (2001). Inclusion of children with autism in early intervention: An examination of rationale, myths, and procedures. In M. J. Guralnick (Ed.), *Early childhood inclusion: Focus on change* (pp. 337–363). Baltimore: Brookes.

Strain, P. S., & Odom, S. L. (1986). Peer social initiations: An effective intervention for social skills deficits of exceptional children. *Exceptional Children, 52*, 543–551.

Strain, P. S., & Sainato, D. M. (1987). Preventative discipline in the preschool class. *Teaching Exceptional Children, 19*, 26–30.

Strain, P. S., & Shores, R. E. (1977). Social reciprocity: Review of research and educational implications. *Exceptional Children, 43*, 526–531.

Strain, P. S., Shores, R. E., & Kerr, M. M. (1976). An experimental analysis of "spillover" effects on the social interaction of behaviorally handicapped preschool children. *Journal of Applied Behavior Analysis, 9*, 31–40.

Strain, P. S., Shores, R. E., & Timm, M. A. (1977). Effects of peer initiations on the social behavior of withdrawn preschoolers. *Journal of Applied Behavior Analysis, 10*, 289–298.

Strain, P. S., & Timm, M. A. (1974). An experimental analysis of social interaction between a behaviorally disordered preschool child and her classroom peers. *Journal of Applied Behavior Analysis, 7*, 583–590.

Suomi, S. J., & Harlow, H. F. (1972). Social rehabilitation of isolate-reared monkeys. *Developmental Psychology, 6*, 487–496.

Vaughn, B. J., Clarke, S., & Dunlap, G. (1997). Assessment-based intervention for severe behavior problems in a natural family context. *Journal of Applied Behavior Analysis, 30*, 713–716.

Venn, M. L., Wolery, M., Fleming, L. A., DeCesare, L. D., Morris, A., Sigesmund, M. H. (1993). Effects of teaching preschool peers to use the hand-model procedure during snack activities. *American Journal of Speech-Language Pathology, 2*, 38–46.

Venn, M. L., Wolery, M., Morris, A., DeCesare, L. D., & Cuffs, M. S. (in press). Use of progressive time delay to teach in-class transitions to preschoolers with autism. *Journal of Autism and Developmental Disorders.*

Venn, M. L., Wolery, M., Werts, M. G., Morris, A., DeCesare, L. D., & Cuffs, M. S. (1993). Embedding instruction in art activities to teach preschoolers with disabilities to imitate their peers. *Early Childhood Research Quarterly, 8*, 277–294.

Vygotsky, L. S. (1978). *Mind and society: The development of higher psychological processes*. Cambridge, MA: Harvard University Press.

Wahler, R. G. (1967). Child–child interactions in free-field settings: Some experimental analyses. *Journal of Experimental Child Psychology, 5*, 278–293.

Yoder, P. J., Kaiser, A. P., Goldstein, H., Alpert, C. Mousetic, L., Kaczmarek, L., et al. (1995). An exploratory comparison of milieu teaching and responsive interaction in classroom applications. *Journal of Early Intervention, 19*, 218–242.

VII

TREATMENTS NOT SPECIFIC TO A PARTICULAR DISORDER

INTRODUCTION:
TREATMENTS NOT SPECIFIC
TO A PARTICULAR DISORDER

Sometimes people seek treatment not because they meet *Diagnostic and Statistical Manual of Mental Disorders* (DSM) diagnostic criteria for major psychiatric disorders but because of life's stresses, external events that affect their well-being, difficulty in adjusting to a new cultural milieu, low self-esteem not related to depression, or personality traits that prevent self-actualization. This section consists of three chapters, each presenting innovative approaches to the treatment of various types of psychological problems that afflict children and adolescents. These treatments employ theoretically based techniques, blending multiple approaches when required. The development of comprehensive combined techniques has become a "must" for this area of treatment research and offers the promise of greater applicability of findings to the needs of clinicians.

Frederick D. Frankel presents a review of existing literature on social-skills training programs for children who are rejected or neglected by their peers and discusses the UCLA Friendship Study. The aim of the intervention is to improve the social skills of rejected children and help them achieve good sportsmanship, self-confidence, group cooperation, and good host behavior. Several techniques are used for this purpose, such as didactic presentation and behavioral rehearsals, coached play (through providing structured activities such as group sports), and the involvement of parents as partners in social-skills training. Children with attention-deficit/hyperactivity disorder (ADHD) and oppositional defiant disorder (ODD) were assigned to three groups:

medication (prescribed by physicians in the community), other medications, and no medication. Although the study results are promising for rejected children, an important aim of this study is to develop measures that can be readily applied to community settings and to examine the interactions of social-skills training and stimulant medication. In anticipating future directions, the author notes the need for studies with larger numbers of children to analyze individual medication responses and the differential impact of various diagnoses, such as anxiety and mood disorders.

Giuseppe Costantino and his colleagues discuss the use of a culturally sensitive Cuento (folktale) and hero–heroine modeling therapy for the treatment of Hispanic children and adolescents with conduct disorders, anxiety, and phobias. The folktales and biographies, which convey a message or moral to be emulated, are techniques based on the principles of social learning theory. The study lends support to the effectiveness of using culturally sensitive modalities to treating Hispanic youngsters with anxious and fearful symptoms and conduct problems at school. Treatment outcomes were demonstrated across genders and several Hispanic nationalities. Story telling of cultural material, using folktales with very young children and heroic biographies with adolescents, appears to be an effective modality. However, no significant treatment effects were found for depression outcomes. In highlighting limitations and future directions, the authors indicate that the cultural uniqueness of such interventions needs to be established empirically. They also note that multiple control groups, as well as stronger tests of the efficacy of culturally sensitive interventions, are needed.

Judith A. Cohen and her colleagues discuss their projects of trauma-focused cognitive–behavioral therapy (CBT) for sexually abused children. Many abused children develop behavioral or emotional symptoms, including posttraumatic stress disorder (PTSD). The authors summarize the methods from four research projects and present in detail their assessment measures and the treatment procedures. Children experienced significant improvement on both the frequency and the number of PTSD symptoms, as well as in internalizing and externalizing behavior problems. Children also experienced significant improvements in their ability to trust others. Trauma-focused CBT appears to be clinically effective with sexually abused children. In highlighting future directions, the authors suggest that greater attention should be given to the impact of culture, ethnicity, gender, and developmental factors on treatment response, as well as to the acceptability of different types of treatments. Research should also expand to include children from typical clinical settings. The authors note the need for dismantling studies to examine whether gradual exposure and cognitive processing are necessary for trauma-focused CBT to be effective and, if so, for which child capacities. Finally, the authors noted that studies should examine the length of treatment and varying degrees or dosage of the CBT, as well long-term follow-up outcome studies.

26

PARENT-ASSISTED CHILDREN'S FRIENDSHIP TRAINING

FREDERICK D. FRANKEL

INTRODUCTION

The goals of this chapter are to describe the evolution of an evidence-based intervention for children's friendships by briefly reviewing the following: (a) the importance of friendships and their role in the overall adjustment of children, (b) the types of interventions developed to remediate problems in peer relationships, and (c) the structure and development of an evidence-based intervention that fully integrates parents into treatment. Treatment development has involved the interplay between the manualized delivery of treatment (to maintain consistency) and subsequent analysis of potential moderating factors. Initial analysis revealed diminished responsiveness of children with oppositional defiant disorder (ODD). Subsequent analyses showed that this diminished responsiveness was overcome by further developing parent modules, but significant effects of concurrent medications upon treatment outcome were also revealed.

Many mental health practitioners are not adequately prepared to consider or detect peer problems in clinical practice. Consequently, diagnostic schemas have only peripherally included peer problems. Children in therapy are twice as likely to have peer problems than children not in therapy (Malik & Furman, 1993; Rutter & Garmezy, 1983). Often, when the presenting psychopathology has been treated, peer problems remain but are not usually addressed by further treatment.

An estimated 10% of children without any known risk factors have problems making and keeping friendships (Asher, 1990). In their 12-year follow-up study into young adulthood, Bagwell, Newcomb, and Bukowski (1998) found that peer rejection and lack of at least one best friend both contributed equally to psychopathology of young adults. According to Malik & Furman (1993), ". . . peers are not only playmates but also confidants, allies and sources of support in times of stress." (p. 1303). To form high-quality friendships, children must suspend egoism, treat the friend as an equal, and deal effectively with conflict (Hartup, 1996). Friendships are the context for learning social skills and learning about and feeling good about oneself, and they also provide resources for support (Hartup, 1993). In a 1-year follow-up study of 10-year-olds, Bukowski, Hoza, and Newcomb (1991; cited in Hartup, 1996) demonstrated that having friends has positive effects on self-esteem. Children's group problem-solving skills are generally better when done with friends rather than nonfriends (Azmitia & Montgomery, 1993). Friends share a climate of agreement much greater than that among nonfriends (Gottman, 1983). This foundation of accord is probably why friends resolve disagreements more easily than nonfriends (Hartup & Laursen, 1993). Friendships may also moderate the negative impact of divorce (Wasserstein & La Greca, 1996). These important benefits are among the reasons professionals should consider children's friendships.

REVIEW OF TREATMENT TO ENHANCE FRIENDSHIPS

Social-skills training programs are designed to improve the skills of children who are rejected or neglected by their peers. The most common intervention setting has been the child's school. Bierman (1989) has concluded that school-based interventions may demonstrate immediate changes in children's social behavior within the treatment situation but not durable changes that generalize to the child's social environments. In a recent meta-analysis of social skills programs, Quinn, Kavale, Mathur, Rutherford, and Forness (1999) found that the mean effect size (effect size, ES = [Treatment group mean – Control group mean]/Control group SD) for all group studies was .199. This finding indicated that the average treated subject was better off than 58% of subjects receiving no training (i.e., an 8% improvement over no training).

Most social-skills intervention studies have been done in research settings with volunteer subjects. In contrast, the few studies of social-skills training in outpatient clinic settings have failed to demonstrate convincing evidence of improvement (Kolko, Loar, & Sturnick, 1990; Michelson et al., 1983; Yu, Harris, Solovitz, & Franklin, 1986). Two studies exemplify the problems: Yu et al. (1986) failed to replicate effects across two experimental groups of outpatient boys, each having small *ns*. Michelson et al. (1983) demonstrated significant effects but used measures with unknown discriminative or predictive validity with regard to peer adjustment.

One problem may be in the content of the interventions. Few intervention components used in social-skills training studies have been assessed for social validity (Budd, 1985) or for effectiveness in enhancing peer acceptance. An intervention is said to have social validity when it targets behaviors that discriminate children having peer difficulties from children who do not. Evidence suggests that focus on socially valid target behaviors enhances the likelihood that children will be better accepted by peers after training. For instance, cooperation with peers and peer support skills (e.g., active listening skills) have been shown to differentiate accepted children from rejected ones. Studies that provided training in these skills have demonstrated improved peer sociometric ratings (Bierman & Furman, 1984; Gresham & Nagle, 1980; Hepler & Rose, 1988; Oden & Asher, 1977; Tiffen & Spence, 1986). Oden and Asher (1977) focused on coaching children to have fun and make sure the game partner had fun as well. The children chosen were initially the least popular within their class, as derived from peer sociometric ratings. At 1-year follow-up, these authors found lasting improvement in peer acceptance.

Training in a select set of socially valid behaviors may help generalization in three ways. First, children may be better able to focus on key behaviors to observe in their social milieu. Second, they are more likely to observe better-accepted children perform these behaviors with desirable social outcomes. Third, they are more likely to have successful outcomes when they perform these behaviors.

Perhaps as a result of the lack of clear findings for comprehensive social-skills intervention programs, clinicians have considered alternative approaches. They have attempted individual treatment for friendship problems, employed strategies to pair the friendless child with a socially competent peer, and recommended that the friendless child be enrolled in more structured play activities. Each of these approaches is briefly reviewed.

Individual Treatment to Enhance Friendships

Arguments in favor of conducting therapy sessions in which one child meets with one adult have been weak. Bierman and Furman (1984) found that small group training of conversational skills was more effective in changing peer sociometrics than individual coaching. Malik and Furman (1993) in commenting on group versus individual approaches to social skills enhancement concluded, "Although inclusion of peers makes this approach much less practical for individual practitioners, we have found little evidence that training sessions with adults will generalize to interactions with peers" (p. 1316).

One interesting variant of individual treatment for social skills problems was a study by Kehle, Clark, Jenson, and Wampold (1986). They videotaped four male subjects with behavior and hyperactivity disorders who were between the ages of 10 and 23. The subjects were shown an 11-minute videotape in which their disruptive behaviors had been edited out. Three subjects decreased disruption through 6 weeks of follow-up, whereas one subject who viewed the unedited tape of his behavior increased disruption. Although promising, this technique has obtained limited replication in one other small sample of subjects (Possell, Kehle, Mcloughlin, & Bray, 1999). No evidence suggested that these individuals were better accepted by their peers.

Peer Pairing

Peer pairing is another approach used to improve the social status of disliked children. The motivation seems to be twofold: (a) to have more socially competent peers help to improve the behaviors of disliked children, and (b) to promote friendships between the popular peer mentors and the unpopular children, thus elevating them in social status.

When used as a vehicle for specific skill instruction, this method has shown some success in improving the behaviors of disliked children. In support of this assertion, simply pairing unpopular children with more popular peers was less effective than peer pairing and concomitant social-skills training (Bierman, 1986; Oden & Asher, 1977). Prinz, Blechman, and Dumas (1994) paired four aggressive children with four socially competent children during a median of twenty-two 50-minute sessions (each with one adult supervising). Each session employed role-playing exercises in which the competent child first demonstrated the correct example. Although aggressive behavior decreased in comparison with an attention control group, changes in sociometric rankings failed to materialize.

The other rationale for the pairing of competent peers with aggressive children—the hope that the competent peers would become friends with the aggressive children—was not observed by Prinz et al. No support has been found in any studies of this method in promoting the friendships between children involved as mentors and their protégés. For example, developmentally disabled children were paired with more popular nonretarded children (Chennault, 1967; Lilly, 1971; Rucker & Vincenzo, 1970). Once the pairing stopped, social relationships were not maintained.

Structured Activities and Friendships

Structured activities such as organized team sports and scouting typically play a large part in the social lives of elementary school children and their parents. Ladd and Price (1987) found that 83% of parents of kindergartners involve their children in adult-structured activities. Parke and Bhavnagri (1989) report that 78% of mothers report volunteering to help out at least occasionally in one such activity. They report increased participation in these activities as the child ages, with participation peaking during preadolescence. Many practitioners recommend the involvement of withdrawn and rejected children in these activities.

Research (Bryant, 1985; Ladd & Price, 1987) has failed to show that involvement in structured activities is significantly related to social adjustment. However, some evidence suggests that these activities may produce indirect benefits. Dishion, Andrews, and Crosby (1995) found that 73% of best friends in their study originally met in school or some other structured activity (71% lived within three blocks of their best friends). They found that best friends who met through school and organized activities were at less risk for problematic behavior than were those who met through unsupervised settings. However, no evidence exists that introducing the rejected child to these activities will improve peer relationships. To the contrary, rejected children quickly reestablish their social status with a new peer group (Coie & Kupersmidt, 1983). Therefore, the most important contributions to a child's social adjustment seem to occur immediately before and after these activities (arranging play dates and meeting new acquaintances; Frankel, 1996).

Sports participation is heterogeneous with respect to fostering social skills. According to Smoll and Smith (1987), coaches approach teaching sports to children in one of two ways: (a) values oriented, in which good sportsmanship, self-confidence, group cooperation, and leadership skills are emphasized or (b) professional, in which winning is paramount. In contrast to the professional approach to coaching, the authors showed that child's positive evaluation of a sports experience did not correlate with win–loss records. This finding contrasts sharply with incidents that have been in the news: Both teams of 7-year-old Tee-ball players watch helplessly as their parents brawl with one another; family members of a high school football player assaulted the coach for not putting a particular boy in a game. Children in our groups describe coaches who promote the views that "winning is everything" and "the end justifies the means." They encourage their team to taunt their opponents before the game. In cases like these, the adults' behavior seems more problematic than the children's, which lends additional support to the involvement of parents in social-skills interventions.

THE PARENT'S ROLE IN CHILDREN'S FRIENDSHIPS

According to Ladd, LeSieur, and Profilet (1993), parents may directly influence children's peer relations in four ways: First, they integrate their child into social environments outside the home; second, they help their child select playmates and arrange play dates; third, they supervise interactions with peers; and fourth, they help their child solve interpersonal problems. Parents must not only maintain community networks but must also ensure that their children use these networks as a springboard to more intimate friendships (Parke & Bhavnagri, 1989).

In addition to the positive influence that parents have upon peer acceptance of their child, they may inadvertently promote peer rejection. Mothers of rejected children were less likely to appropriately monitor play experiences than were mothers of accepted children (Ladd, Profilet, & Hart, 1992; Pettit, Bates, Dodge, & Meece, 1999) and were themselves less socially competent (Prinstein & LaGreca, 1999). Dodge, Schlundt, Schocken, and Delugach (1983) found that mothers of rejected children were more likely to dominate a group of children at play than were parents of popular children. Mothers of rejected children may fail to teach their child conflict management skills and rules of behavior (Kennedy, 1992), unwittingly train their child to ignore peer etiquette for entry into play group situations (Russell & Finnie, 1990), or allow coercive control of play (Ladd, 1992).

Despite the major influence of parents on their children's friendships, parents have been notably absent from social-skills training programs (La Greca, 1993; Sheridan, Dee, Morgan, McCormick, & Walker, 1996). The expectation that parent involvement in social-skills training enhances treatment generalization is reasonable (Frankel & Myatt, 2002; Ladd et al., 1992). Such inclusion might also address the social errors of parents that adversely affect their children's social acceptance. However, researchers have been slow to realize the full potential of parents as partners in social skills training.

Early Approaches to Integrating Parents Into Social-Skills Treatment

Two early studies incorporated parents in helping children solve problems and decreasing aggressive behavior. Shure and Spivak (1978) found that popular kindergartners generated higher-quality solutions to verbal vignettes of the Preschool Interpersonal Problem Solving (PIPS) measure than rejected children. Shure and Spivak (1978) trained parents to be surrogate teachers of a prepackaged social problem-solving program. The program focused on decreasing aggression in children rather than increasing peer acceptance and friendships. This was a very ambitious program that intensively trained parents. It demonstrated that parents could be counted on to institute detailed programs. Results clearly indicated improved problem solving in the children.

Middleton and Cartledge (1995) selected four male first- and second-graders who had low prosocial skills and high rates of aggression and classroom disruption. Project staff instructed each target child together with two or three socially competent peers. The program focused on reduction of aggression rather than improvements in the number and quality of friendships. Parents received a single 1 1/2 hour training session and continued involvement with a note home (outlining home practice of the social skill being taught). Project staff followed up with daily phone calls. The parent of one boy did not cooperate. His behavior deteriorated to the point that he had to be placed in a special education classroom. Parents of three boys complied an average of 77% of the time with this program. Results for these boys were encouraging; all showed substantial decreases in aggressive behaviors. However, peer acceptance was not measured.

Teaching Parents to Better Manage Their Child's Friendships

Perhaps the view that parents of less socially competent children may themselves lack social skills has inhibited development of interlocking programs for parents and children (Budd, 1985; Cousins & Weiss, 1993). But this view has not deterred some investigators. For instance, Cousins and Weiss (1993) spent 45 sessions training children in social skills while simultaneously training parents in management skills relevant to peer relationships. According to the authors, "In these groups, the children are taught about relationships with adults and peers, social skills for relating to their parents, skills necessary for solving problems with parents and teachers, and point systems used by parents and teachers." (p. 450). The authors advocated teaching parents to organize their child's social agenda and debrief their child after social contacts. Pfiffner and McBurnett (1997) also demonstrated that social-skills training benefits were readily transferred to the home when parents were trained to promote this generalization.

Sheridan et al. (1996) combined stimulant medication and social-skills training for five boys with ADHD between the ages of 8 and 10 years. The boys participated in 10 weekly sessions focusing on social entry, maintaining interactions, and solving problems. Parents were trained in using supportive listening skills, helping their children solve social problems, setting social goals, and helping their children transfer skills to home environment. Parent and teacher reports suggested general improvement for most boys.

Researchers have long known the importance of parents in the development of their child's friendships. Clinicians can take advantage of this knowledge in fully integrating parents into programs aimed at improving children's friendships. We have found that most parents possess adequate skills in most areas of functioning, with the exception of a few localized blind spots. In a group and with a little information from us, parents can help each other improve the way they manage their children's peer relations.

DESCRIPTION OF THE UCLA CHILDREN'S FRIENDSHIP PROGRAM

Over the past 14 years we have seen over 1,000 children in our outpatient program. The details of the program, including session outlines and vignettes (exemplifying typical and problematic patient responses), have been presented elsewhere (Frankel & Myatt, 2002). Therefore only a brief description follows.

We have adopted a process-oriented perspective of social competence (Taylor & Asher, 1984) in which we select important social-interaction processes and address the specific components that contribute to successful social transactions. Our goal is to teach children the skills to have mutually satisfying social interactions that lead to higher regard within the peer group and the development of satisfying dyadic friendships. Parents are taught to monitor these skills during weekly homework assignments. Our program addresses the rejected and neglected child's interactions with peers in five crucial areas: (a) abating the effects of the child's reputation within his current peer group (Bierman, 1989) by reducing intrusive and inappropriate behaviors; (b) diminishing the importance of the rejecting peer group by giving the child and parents skills to work together to expand the child's associates; (c) instructing parents and children in ways to work together to promote more successful play dates and continue acquisition of social skills, such as through best friends (Hartup, 1983); (d) having the parents support the child's efforts to keep a low profile in the peer group in which the child has a bad reputation (Nangle, Erdley, & Gold, 1996); (e) preventing continuing provocation from peers by improving the child's competence in nonaggressive responses to teasing and conflicts with adults.

Method

Procedures

Although we have reported the results of our intervention for children with ADHD, ODD, and those who do not fit criteria for any diagnosis, our clinical intervention is open to all children who fit our entry requirements. Entry requirements are (a) the ability to share a common conversational focus, (b) rudimentary sports and play skills (e.g., bouncing a ball, shooting baskets, and knowledge of how to play several common board games), (c) no more than 2 years below age level in cognitive skills and social maturity, and

(d) ability to sit for 20 minutes of instruction in a classroom situation. We assess this by asking about educational placement (regular or special class) and other behavioral problems and interviewing the child for a standard 20-minute mental status exam.

Assessments

Our approach is to put available adult informants to best use. Parents are given a standardized assessment inquiring about social behaviors they observe in the home. Teachers are given an assessment of behaviors they might observe in the classroom and play yard.

Social Skills Rating System—Parent. The Social Skills Rating System–Parent (SSRS; Gresham & Elliott, 1990) is a questionnaire consisting of 55 items for which mothers assigned ratings such as "never," "sometimes," and "very often." Among the seven subscales that compose this instrument, only assertion and self-control subscales measure friendship skills. The assertion subscale measures making friends and playing well with them. The self-control subscale measures appropriate response to provocation by others.

Pupil Evaluation Inventory—Teacher. The Pupil Evaluation Inventory (PEI; Pekarik, Prinz, Liebert, Weintraub, & Neil, 1976) consists of 35 items, each rated as "describes child" or "does not describe child." We employed the 42-item teacher-rated PEI revised by Pope, Bierman, and Mumma (1991), which contains the following scales: withdrawal (9 items) assesses shyness and sadness; likability (5 items) assesses highly prosocial behavior; aggression (10 items) assesses teasing and physical aggression; hyperactivity (15 items) assesses impulsive and disruptive behavior; inattention (6 items) assesses immaturity. Teacher responses are collected by telephone interview. Teachers are not informed of the treatment status of the child on whom they are asked to report.

Correlations between peer and teacher PEI ratings have exceeded .54 (Ledingham, Younger, Schwartzman, & Bergeron, 1982). Teacher and peer PEI assessments in first grade have been shown to be equally good predictors of antisocial behavior 7 years later (Tremblay, LeBlanc, & Schwartzman, 1988). Frankel and Myatt (1994) have demonstrated that the withdrawal and likability scales tap a dimension of social competence, whereas the aggression scale taps a dimension of externalizing behavior.

Child Sessions

Session Structure. Each child session (except for the first and last) is broken down into four segments. During the first segment, children report on the results of the socialization homework assignment given in the previous session. The second segment consists of a didactic presentation, related behavioral rehearsal, and coaching. The third segment consists of coached play. In the fourth segment, children and parents are reunited. The group leaders help parent and child to formalize the child's socialization homework assignment.

Didactic Presentation and Behavioral Rehearsal. In Session 1, children are introduced to the rules of the sessions (e.g., raise hand before talking, be serious when first meeting someone) and then taught communication techniques, such as voice volume, smiling, and physical closeness (Bierman & Furman, 1984). Session 2 introduces good times and places (e.g., playgrounds) and bad times and places (e.g., in the class, while teacher is talking) to make friends. These rules are enforced throughout the sessions (i.e., no talking during the didactic part of the sessions, but talking is encouraged during the coaching activities). Session 2 also introduces information-exchange techniques under the rubric of trading information (Gottman, 1983; Gottman, Gonso, & Rasmussen, 1975). Each child is taught to exchange information with another child regarding their play interests. Techniques for group entry (e.g., Garvey, 1984; Putallaz, 1983; Putallaz & Gottman, 1981) and "slipping in" (acting in concert with other children playing) are introduced in Sessions 3 and 4, respectively. Reasons for being turned down from group entry (Corsaro, 1981) and ways to address the problem are added in Session 4. Praising other children (e.g., "good shot;" Gottman et al., 1975), techniques of persuasion (Dodge, Coie, Pettit, & Price, 1990), and negotiation to allow children to change activities that no longer interest them (Gottman & Parkhurst, 1980) are added in Sessions 5 and 6. Session 7 is devoted to skills needed during the play date (the rules of a good host). In Session 8, children learn to react neutrally or humorously to teasing. Several responses to teasing, which are intended to tease the perpetrator about their inability to tease well, are modeled (e.g., "When I first heard that, I fell off my dinosaur;" "Tell me when you get to the funny part;" Perry, Williard, & Perry, 1990). Session 9 deals with respectful responses to adults during confrontations (e.g., don't argue or roll your eyes, remain quiet and attentive). Session 10 deals with being a good winner (e.g., praise teammates, pretend winning was not important) and organizing competitive games with children of equal abilities on both sides. Session 11 deals with avoiding physical fights: Group pressure is used to label physical fighting as undesirable. Techniques to avoid bullies are also presented (e.g., stay out of their reach, stay with other children, don't tease or antagonize them). Session 12 consists of a graduation ceremony, party for the children, and post-treatment evaluation.

Coached Play. Coached play begins during Session 2. In addition to the more obvious goal of teaching and rewarding good sportsmanship, this session segment also provides an opportunity to assess and improve the child's collection of toys, knowledge of how and when to use them, and willingness to play with them. Coaches are prohibited from taking a direct part in the children's play, but they watch, dispense token and verbal reinforcement, and provide consequences for misbehavior (Ladd & Golter, 1988). The coach identifies and praises appropriate behavior (Bernhardt & Forehand, 1975). Beginning with Session 2, children bring toys suitable for outside play from home. Parents sometimes need to purchase toys (e.g, balls, jump ropes) if children do not have them at home or do not seem inclined to play with the ones they have. During Sessions 3 and 4, children practice entering the group and making relevant comments in the following manner: Children play together as a group, with the coach structuring the game. One or two children are pulled out as onlookers. Children take turns being the outsider and are coached to watch until they understand the game structure. Then they are coached to join the game in progress by making relevant comments, praising other children (Black & Hazen, 1990), asking to join the side that needs the most help, and acting in concert with them. Sessions 5 and 6 focus on praising others and negotiating switches in games when the participants seem bored.

The focus is turned to play dates in Sessions 7, 8, and 9. Children bring indoor interactive games and take turns being the host and the guest. Highly competitive outdoor games are avoided until their introduction in Session 10 (Tryon & Keane, 1991) and continued until Session 11. Pseudoconfrontations with adults during deck play to practice instructed techniques (e.g., a coach wrongly accusing them of cheating) after they are warned during the didactic portion of the session that coaches will do this.

Child Socialization Homework. Homework assignments always follow at least one session of discussion and behavioral rehearsal. Socialization homework assignments have three major components.

The first component involves a telephone call to practice conversational skills. After Session 2 and all subsequent sessions, children are to use the call to practice trading information. At first, they call only group members. Beginning with Session 4, they include a child not in the group.

The second component involves bringing a toy to session to help children and parents cultivate a selection of toys that will help with socialization. When children have no such toys, the parent group leader makes suggestions to these parents about appropriate purchases. Toys with violent or provocative themes, such as toy guns and water pistols, are prohibited, as are solitary toys such as books and electronic toys. Occasionally, children will bring a toy with which they seem too interested, which leads to solitary play that does not encourage the participation of other children. In these cases, the children are prompted to join the group. Parents and children are instructed to avoid this toy for subsequent interaction with peers. Toy assignments given in Sessions 1 through 5 concentrate on playing with outdoor toys and augmenting the child's associates. Toy assignments given in Sessions 6 through 8 are devoted to enhancing play dates and augmenting best friendships. Toy assignments given in Sessions 9 through 11 focus on toys to be used in competitive (team) games.

The third component involves socialization with neighborhood peers. Homework assignments given in Sessions 5 and 6 put into practice the instruction on group entry. Each parent and child agrees on a place and time that the child will attempt to join an ongoing play group of children who are not currently their associates. Parents of younger children (ages 7 to 9) are to observe from afar (e.g., pretending to read a newspaper on a bench a short distance away). Parents of older children set the date when the homework is to be attempted (usually at school) and remind their child that day to do the assignment. After Sessions 7 through 11, children are to pick someone they had met during the group entry homework assignment and trade information with him or her to establish activities of mutual interest for a play date. They are then asked to invite the other child to their house or a similar place where they can be alone to play with each other. If the invitation for the play date is accepted, the parent is to arrange the date and time. Immediately before the time of the play date, the parents' tasks are to remind the child of the rules of a good host, to exclude noninteractive activities (e.g., watching television, playing electronic games, and playing with toys that cannot be shared). At the time of the play date, parents are to monitor the play date from afar (Ladd & Golter, 1988) and to enforce rules. Play dates continue throughout the remainder of the program.

After Sessions 8, 9, and 10, children are asked to practice responses to being teased with a selected child who had teased them or to participate in a role-playing exercise with their parents (e.g., a mother might pretend to be a peer and say "Your mother's ugly,"). After Sessions 9 and 10, children are to practice respectful ways to handle confrontations with adults.

Parent Sessions

Session Structure. Each parent session (except for Sessions 1 and 12) is broken down into four segments. In the first segment, parents report their own and their child's performances on the homework assignment. Obstacles to compliance are addressed. In the second segment, an informational handout is presented. In the third segment, the content of the concurrent child session is briefly reviewed, and the homework assignment for the following week is presented. Potential obstacles to homework compliance are discussed. In the fourth segment, the parent and child are reunited, and agreements for specific homework assignments are negotiated between them. Phone calls between group members (to practice conversational skills taught in sessions) are facilitated by having parents arrange the date and time for the call before they leave the session.

No play dates or other social contacts are allowed among group members for the following reasons:

1. Children with ADHD or Asperger's syndrome should not be friends with one another because they typically behave more poorly on play dates together than on play dates with typically developing peers.

2. Asking for play dates with other group members may involve an element of coercion. One of the children may not actually want to play with the other. One or both sets of parents may rightfully feel the children should not be friends with each other. Allowing such play dates may make it difficult for the parties to say no because they might face hurt feelings for the rest of the sessions.

3. After-session social contacts introduce competition (e.g., "They're getting together and we're not") and bad feelings among some group members (e.g., "She's having a play date without me").

4. Prohibiting after-session contacts allows parents and children to speak their minds without worrying about alienating a potential friend and to maintain credibility in their efforts to help one another solve social problems.

Didactic Presentation and Handouts. The goals of these presentations are to (a) inform parents of their roles in peer acceptance of their children, (b) ensure that parents take their assigned roles in the child socialization homework, (c) ensure that parents provide supportive feedback for the principles the children are being taught, and (d) allow discussion of potential obstacles to homework completion. Over the years, we have learned much from parents during this period, both in terms of possible obstacles as well as suggestions for solutions.

Nine sessions include instructional handouts. Session 1 delineates the goals of treatment, the methods to be used, and the parent requirements. Session 2 focuses on the parents' encouragement of their children and their children's friendships and ways to trade information. Session 3 reviews the parents' sources for potential playmates for their child and physical resources for play dates. Deficiencies in these areas are discussed and advice offered to facilitate implementation. Session 4 informs the parents about the group entry skills their children have learned. Session 5 focuses on the way to accomplish the group entry assignment. Session 7 presents the structure of, and parent responsibilities for, the play date. Session 8 informs parents of the "making fun of the tease" technique for resisting teasing. Session 9 reviews parents' options for defusing repeated confrontations between their child and another adult. Session 11 reviews ways parents should support their children, avoidance of physical fights, and guidelines for providing decelerative consequences for fighting. Session 12 is a review of the major points of the intervention and ways to maintain treatment gains.

Generalization

Homework assignments are the key to generalization. Five features of the intervention facilitate the performance of the homework: (a) The date and time and other party to the assignment are pre-arranged between parent and child before they leave the session; (b) the parent's role is clearly delineated; (c) children and parents are accountable for their parts of the homework assignments—they report the results of the assignment at the beginning of the next session; (d) the assignments are easy at first and gradually become more difficult; (e) high compliance for the easier assignments, together with pressure from the group, sets an expectation for homework compliance.

In addition to the social validity of session content previously discussed, three other features of the intervention may enhance generalization. The intervention is presented to the children as a class intended to teach them how to make and keep friends. It was hypothesized that the classroom situation (6 to 10 children with didactic and homework components) would facilitate the acquisition of knowledge and help generalize certain programmatic features to the school situation (e.g., don't try to make friends while the teacher is talking). The coached play segment is held in a large outside area with a basketball court and swings, similar to a playground. This resemblance may facilitate generalization to recess at school and playgrounds. Children are required to bring in their own toys, which they would be able to use when the group was not in session.

OUTCOME OF PREVIOUS STUDIES

The original 12-session treatment program (Frankel, Myatt, & Cantwell, 1995) consisted of child didactic lessons, socialization homework, and free play coaching modules, but only the beginning steps of parent involvement. Informational presentations were made to parents during the first two sessions. Parents were encouraged to wait in a meeting room and socialize with one another until the last 15 minutes of Sessions 3 through 11. During these last 15 minutes, a brief review was made of the contents of the child session, and parents were given a handout covering guidelines for the child's socialization homework assignment. Potential problems with compliance were briefly discussed. Our results suggested generalization had occurred outside the treatment situation. We compared 36 boys receiving treatment with 17 boys on the waiting list over the same period of time. Significantly greater mean improvement for the SSRS (social scale) was obtained for boys receiving treatment. Child diagnosis of ADHD did not affect any outcome measures. This finding was a surprise because we thought that boys diagnosed with ADHD might have more difficulty in following the rules and therefore would not show improvement at home. Changes in school were also noted. Mean improvement on the teacher-reported PEI withdrawal and aggression scales was statistically significant for boys without ODD ($n = 18$ in the treatment group). Again, we were surprised that the presence of ADHD ($n = 40$) did not have a significant impact on outcome.

We were able to develop models for predicting teacher-reported outcome on the withdrawal, likability, and aggression scales of the PEI (Frankel, Myatt, Cantwell, & Fineberg, 1997a). Fifty-two subjects were divided into treatment responders and nonresponders using a double median split procedure (eliminating subjects improving at the median of each outcome measure). Completed Achenbach Child Behavior Checklists (CBCL; Achenbach, 1991) were assessed before treatment and used as a potential moderator variable. CBCL ratings and *Diagnostic and Statistical Manual of Mental Disorders, Third Edition, Revised (DSM–III–R)* diagnosis for boys completing our original intervention were submitted to multiple logistic regression analysis (Afifi & Clark, 1984; Frankel & Simmons, 1992). We confirmed that the *DSM–III–R* diagnosis of ODD predicted poorer response to treatment on the teacher-rated withdrawal measure (69.94% accuracy). No significant effects on outcome were noted for any demographic variable. Scores on the CBCL thought problems factor were significantly related to whether a subject was a treatment responder in PEI aggression, whereas the absence of the *DSM–III–R* diagnosis of ODD predicted that the subject would be a treatment responder in PEI withdrawal. A majority of nonresponding subjects who were predicted to be responders for either aggression or withdrawal came from only two of the 12 treatment groups (randomization tests, $p < .05$). Parents in these treatment groups chose not to stay and socialize during the unstructured time but did attend the last segment of each session as required.

The preceding results prompted enhancement of the structure of the parent component. Parent attendance was now required for the entire session. We developed seven additional parent modules and accompanying handouts, which gave the parents the script that the children received for key social situations and enabled parents to remind children of this script before execution of homework assignments. Parents reviewed their attempts to have their child complete socialization homework during the first portion of each session. Our hypothesis was that this step would help parents deal with compliance issues surrounding socialization homework.

Four treatment groups, totaling 16 boys and 5 girls, completed this enhanced program (Frankel, Cantwell, & Myatt, 1996). These results were compared with the outcome obtained on the original program with 26 additional treated subjects (total $n = 50$ boys and 12 girls, original program). A reliability of change (RC) score (RC = [pretreatment – posttreatment]/SE$_{ds}$, where SE$_{ds}$ was the standard error of the difference scores for each measure) was calculated for each subject in the pathological range on each measure at baseline. An RC greater than 2 was designated as indicating reliable change. Results revealed that significantly more teachers reported reliable change in PEI aggression and likability after the enhanced versus original program. A nonsignificant trend was also apparent for the proportion of parents reporting reliable change on the SSRS after the enhanced program: RCs after the enhanced program were substantially above wait-list control levels (22 boys and 4 girls), except for PEI withdrawal.

A third study (Frankel, Myatt, Cantwell, & Feinberg, 1997b) used the enhanced parent modules to effect social skills training. This study compared 35 children with ADHD, who began stimulant medication before the start of the study, and 14 children without ADHD, who received social-skills treatment with respective wait-list groups (12 children in each group). Subjects in both diagnostic groups showed comparable benefits over their peers in the wait-list control group on both parent and teacher ratings. Children with ODD were not different from those without ODD on most outcome measures. Effect sizes ranged from 0.93 to 1.34.

SYNERGISTIC EFFECTS BETWEEN STIMULANT MEDICATION AND TREATMENT

Children who enter our program are prescribed medication by physicians in the community. To assess possible synergistic effects between existing prescriptions for medication and treatment response to our program, consecutive admissions to our program for the past 5 years were selected who met the following criteria: (a) diagnosis of ADHD with or without ODD using the SNAP–IV (Swanson, 1992); (b) failure to meet any other diagnosis using the Diagnostic Interview for Children and Adolescents (DICA–IV; Welner, Reich, Herjanic, & Jung, 1987), (c) failure to meet screening criteria for autism spectrum disorder either by history or use of the Autism Spectrum Screening Questionnaire (Ehlers, Gillberg, & Wing, 1999). The mean age was 8.5 years. Seventeen children satisfied criteria for ADHD alone, and 31 children met criteria for ADHD and ODD. Eight were girls, and 40 were boys. Medication status was broken into three groups: no medication ($n = 11$); stimulants only ($n = 27$); and other medication ($n = 21$). Ritalin was the most commonly prescribed stimulant ($n = 19$); Dexedrine was next ($n = 7$); Adderall was next ($n = 2$); and Cylert was the least ($n = 1$). The most commonly prescribed other medications were Zoloft ($n = 8$), Depakote ($n = 5$), Prozac ($n = 5$), and Clonidine ($n = 3$), either alone ($n = 10$) or in combination with one or two other medications ($n = 18$).

The results of the teacher PEI were emphasized because teachers were blind to the treatment status of children. Baseline scores of the withdrawal and likability scales were submitted to a 2 × 3 (Diagnosis × Medication) fixed effects ANOVA. No main effects or interactions were significant. Difference scores (DSs) were constructed as pretreatment minus posttreatment scores for each teacher measure (subjects with zero baseline scores were not included in the analysis). Positive DSs indicated improvement. The DSs were submitted to a 2 × 3 (Diagnosis × Medication) fixed effects ANOVA. Results revealed that subjects who were prescribed stimulants only (mean DS = +.16) demonstrated marginally greater improvement on their aggression scores than subjects prescribed no medication (mean DS = .02) or other medications (mean DS = −.03; $F[2, 49] = 2.86$, $p = .06$]. When the analysis was conducted with only the two medicated groups, the results reached statistical significance ($F[1, 35] = 5.43$, $p < .05$). No other main effects or interactions were significant. Examination of individual DSs revealed that 74% of subjects in the stimulant group (17/24) displayed improvement versus 37.5% (6/16) of unmedicated children and 25% (5/20) of children prescribed other medications. Of the five children who improved and were prescribed other medications, four were prescribed stimulants in combination with other medications.

These results suggest that there may be a synergistic effect between stimulant medication and the present program for children with ADHD. Because the children were not randomly assigned to medication condition, confounding variables are possible. For instance, children who receive more severe ratings on some behavioral dimension relevant to friendships may be more likely to be prescribed multiple medications or medication other than stimulants. However, baseline scores were not significantly different. Regardless of the reasons for group differences, it is clear that children entering our program who were prescribed only stimulants had the best chance of responding to our treatment. This finding suggests the need for a controlled study.

SUMMARY

Our analysis of treatment outcome has resulted in enhancement of the intervention. As moderating variables are identified, strategies have been developed to change the effectiveness for the patients not realizing maximal benefits, as with children with ODD. The synergistic effects of stimulant medication suggest that if the pretreatment diagnostic workup yields a diagnosis of ADHD, parents should be counseled on this synergy and treatment delayed until after a stimulant trial.

The implications for children with ADHD on medications other than stimulants are not as clear. First, the *ns* for nonstimulant medications are small. We plan to continue to collect data with the goals of aggregating sufficient *ns* so that we may make recommendations to parents before they begin our treatment.

REFERENCES

Achenbach, T. M. (1991). *Integrative guide for the 1991 CBCL/4-18, YSR, and TRF profiles*. Burlington: University of Vermont Department of Psychiatry.

Afifi, A., & Clark, V. (1984). *Computer-aided multivariate analysis*. Toronto, Canada: Lifetime Learning.

Asher, S. R. (1990). Recent advances in the study of peer rejection. In S. R. Asher & J. D. Coie (Eds.), *Peer rejection in childhood* (pp. 3–14). Cambridge, England: Cambridge University Press.

Azmitia, M., & Montgomery, R. (1993). Friendship, transactive dialogues, and the development of scientific reasoning. *Social Development, 2,* 202–221.

Bagwell, C. L., Newcomb, A. F., & Bukowski, W. M. (1998). Preadolescent friendship and peer rejection as predictors of adult adjustment. *Child Development, 69,* 140–153.

Bernhardt, A. J., & Forehand, R. (1975). The effects of labeled and unlabeled praise upon lower and middle class children. *Journal of Experimental Child Psychology, 19,* 536–543.

Bierman, K. L. (1986). Process of change during social skills training with preadolescents and its relation to treatment outcome. *Child Development, 57,* 230–240.

Bierman, K. L. (1989). Improving the peer relationships of rejected children. In B. B. Lahey & A. E. Kazdin (Eds.), *Advances in clinical child psychology* (Vol. 12, pp. 53–85). New York: Plenum Press.

Bierman, K. L., & Furman, W. (1984). The effects of social skills training and peer involvement in the social adjustment of preadolescents. *Child Development, 55,* 151–162.

Black, B., & Hazen, N. L. (1990). Social status and patterns of communication in acquainted and unacquainted preschool children. *Developmental Psychology, 26,* 379–387.

Bryant, B. K. (1985). The neighborhood walk: Sources of support in middle childhood. *Monographs of the Society for Research in Child Development, 50*(3, Serial No. 210).

Budd, K. S. (1985). Parents as mediators in the social skills training of children. In L. L'Abate & M. A. Milan (Eds.), *Handbook of social skills training and research* (pp. 245–262). New York: Wiley.

Chennault, M. (1967). Improving the social acceptance of unpopular educable mentally retarded pupils in special classes. *American Journal of Mental Deficiency, 72,* 455–458.

Coie, J. D., & Kupersmidt, J. B. (1983). A behavioral analysis of emerging social status. *Child Development, 54,* 1400–1416.

Corsaro, W. A. (1981). Friendship in the nursery school: Social organization in a peer environment. In S. R. Asher & J. M. Gottman (Eds.), *The development of children's friendships* (pp. 207–241). New York: Cambridge University Press.

Cousins, L. S., & Weiss, G. (1993). Parent training and social skills training for children with attention-deficit hyperactivity disorder: How can they be combined for greater effectiveness? *Canadian Journal of Psychiatry, 38,* 449–457.

Dishion, T. J., Andrews, D. W., & Crosby, L. (1995). Anti-social boys and their friends in early adolescents: Relationship characteristics, quality, and interactional process. *Child Development, 66,* 139–151.

Dodge, K. A., Coie, J. D., Pettit, G. S., & Price, J. M. (1990). Peer status and aggression in boys' groups: Developmental and contextual analysis. *Child Development, 61,* 1289–1309.

Dodge, K. A., Schlundt, D. C., Schocken, I., & Delugach, J. D. (1983). Social competence and children's sociometric status: The role of peer group entry strategies. *Merrill-Palmer Quarterly, 29,* 309–336.

Ehlers, S., Gillberg, C., & Wing, L. (1999). A screening questionnaire for Asperger syndrome and other high-functioning autism spectrum disorders in school-age children. *Journal of Autism and Developmental Disorders, 29,* 129–141.

Frankel, F. (1996). *Good friends are hard to find: Help your child find, make, and keep friends.* Los Angeles: Perspective Publishing.

Frankel, F., Cantwell, D. P., & Myatt, R. (1996). Helping ostracized children: Social skills training and parent support for socially rejected children. In E. D. Hibbs & P. S. Jensen (Eds.), *Psychosocial treatments for child and adolescent disorders: Empirically based strategies for clinical practice* (pp. 591–617). Washington, DC: American Psychological Association.

Frankel, F., & Myatt, R. (1994). A dimensional approach to the assessment of social competence in boys. *Psychological Assessment, 6,* 249–254.

Frankel, F., & Myatt, R. (2002). *Children's friendship training.* New York: Brunner-Routledge.

Frankel, F., Myatt, R., & Cantwell, D. P. (1995). Training outpatient boys to conform with the social ecology of popular peers: Effects on parent and teacher ratings. *Journal of Clinical Child Psychology, 24,* 300–310.

Frankel, F., Myatt, R., Cantwell, D. P., & Feinberg, D. T. (1997a). Use of child behavior checklist and *DSM–III–R* diagnosis in predicting outcome of children's social skills training. *Journal of Behavior Therapy and Experimental Psychiatry, 28,* 149–161.

Frankel, F., Myatt, R., Cantwell, D. P., & Feinberg D. T. (1997b). Parent-assisted children's social skills training: Effects on children with and without attention-deficit hyperactivity disorder. *Journal of the Academy of Child and Adolescent Psychiatry, 36,* 1056–1064.

Frankel, F., & Simmons, J. Q. (1992). Parent behavioral training: Why and when some parents drop out. *Journal of Clinical Child Psychology, 21,* 322–330.

Garvey, C. (1984). *Children's talk*. Cambridge, MA: Harvard University Press.

Gottman, J. M. (1983). How children become friends. *Monographs of the Society for Research in Child Development, 48*(Serial No. 201).

Gottman, J. M., Gonso, J., & Rasmussen, B. (1975). Social interaction, social competence and friendship in children. *Child Development, 46*, 709–718.

Gottman, J. M., & Parkhurst, J. T. (1980). A developmental theory of friendship and acquaintanceship processes. In W. A. Collins (Ed.), *Development of cognition, affect and social relationships: Minnesota Symposium on Child Psychology* (Vol. 13, pp. 197–253). Hillsdale, NJ: Earlbaum.

Gresham, F. M., & Elliott, S. N. (1990). *Social skills rating system: Manual*. Circle Pines, MN: American Guidance Service.

Gresham, F. M., & Nagle, R. J. (1980). Social skills training with children: Responsiveness to modeling and coaching as a function of peer orientation. *Journal of Consulting and Clinical Psychology, 48*, 718–729.

Hartup, W. W. (1983). Peer relations. In E. M. Hetherington (Ed.) & P. H. Mussen (Series Ed.), *Handbook of child psychology*. Vol 4. *Socialization, personality and social development* (pp. 103–196). New York: Wiley.

Hartup, W. W. (1993). Adolescents and their friends. In B. Laursen (Ed.), *Close friendship in adolescence: New directions for child development* (pp. 3–22). San Francisco: Jossey-Bass.

Hartup, W. W. (1996). The company they keep: Friendships and their developmental significance. *Child Development, 67*, 1–13.

Hartup, W. W., & Laursen, B. (1993). Conflict and context in peer relations. In C. H. Hart (Ed.), *Children on playgrounds* (pp. 44–84). Albany: State University of New York Press.

Hepler, J. B., & Rose, S. F. (1988). Evaluation of a multi-component group approach for improving social skills of elementary school children. *Journal of Social Service Research, 11*, 1–18.

Kehle, T. J., Clark, E., Jenson, W. R., & Wampold, B. E. (1986). Effectiveness of self-observation with behavior disordered elementary school children. *School Psychology Review, 15*, 289–295.

Kennedy, J. (1992). Relationship of maternal beliefs and childrearing strategies to social competence in preschool children. *Child Study Journal, 22*, 39–55.

Kolko, D. J., Loar, L. L., & Sturnick, D. (1990). Inpatient social–cognitive skills training with conduct disordered and attention deficit disordered children. *Journal of Child Psychology and Psychiatry, 31*, 737–748.

Ladd, G. W. (1992). Themes and theories: Perspectives on processes in family–peer relationships. In R. D. Parke & G. W. Ladd (Eds.), *Family-peer relationships: Modes of linkages* (pp. 3–34). Hillsdale, NJ: Erlbaum.

Ladd, G. W., & Golter, B. S. (1988). Parents' management of preschoolers peer relations: Is it related to children's social competence? *Developmental Psychology, 24*, 109–117.

Ladd, G. W., LeSieur, K., & Profilet, S. (1993). Direct parental influences on young children's peer relations. In S. W. Duck (Ed.), *Understanding relationship processes 2: Learning about relationships*. London: Sage.

Ladd, G. W., & Price, J. M. (1987). Predicting children's social and school adjustment following the transition from preschool to kindergarten. *Child Development, 58*, 1168–1189.

Ladd, G. W., Profilet, S. M., & Hart, C. H. (1992). Parents' management of children's peer relations: Facilitating and supervising children's activities in the peer culture. In R. D. Parke & G. W. Ladd (Eds.), *Family-peer relationships: Modes of linkages* (pp. 215–253). Hillsdale, NJ: Erlbaum.

La Greca, A. M. (1993). Social skills training with children: Where do we go from here? *Journal of Clinical Child Psychology, 22*, 288–298.

Ledingham, J. E., Younger, A., Schwartzman, A., & Bergeron, G. (1982). Agreement among teacher, peer and self-ratings of children's aggression, withdrawal and likability. *Journal of Abnormal Child Psychology, 10*, 363–372.

Lilly, M. S. (1971). Improving social acceptance of low sociometric status, low-achieving students. *Exceptional Children, 37*, 341–347.

Malik, N. M., & Furman, W. (1993). Practitioner review: Problems in children's peer relations: What can the clinician do? *Journal of Child Psychology and Psychiatry, 34*, 1303–1326.

Michelson, L., Mannarino, A. P., Marchione, K. E., Stern, M., Figeroa, J., & Beck, S. (1983). A comparative outcome study of behavioral social-skills training, interpersonal-problem-solving, and non-directive control treatments with child psychiatric outpatients. *Behaviour Research and Therapy, 21*, 545–556.

Middleton, M. B., & Cartledge, G. (1995). The effects of social skills instruction and parental involvement on the aggressive behaviors of African American males. *Behavior Modification, 19*, 192–210.

Nangle, D. W., Erdley, C. A., & Gold, J. A. (1996). A reflection of the popularity construct: The importance of who likes or dislikes a child. *Behavior Therapy, 27*, 337–352.

Oden, S., & Asher, S. R. (1977). Coaching children in social skills for friendship making. *Child Development, 48*, 495–506.

Parke, R. D., & Bhavnagri, N. P. (1989). Parents as managers of children's peer friendships. In D. Belle (Ed.), *Children's social networks and social supports* (pp. 241–259). New York: Wiley.

Pekarik, E., Prinz, R., Liebert, D., Weintraub, S., & Neil, J. (1976). The pupil evaluation inventory: A sociometric technique for assessing children's social behavior. *Journal of Abnormal Child Psychology, 4*, 83–97.

Perry, D. G., Williard, J. C., & Perry, L. C. (1990). Peer perceptions of the consequences that victimized children provide aggressors. *Child Development, 61*, 1310–1325.

Pettit, G. S., Bates, J. E., Dodge, K. A., & Meece, D. W. (1999). The impact of after-school peer contact on early adolescent externalizing problems is moderated by parental monitoring, perceived neighborhood safety, and prior adjustment. *Child Development, 70,* 768–778.

Pfiffner, L. J., & McBurnett, K. (1997). Social skills training with parent generalization: Treatment effects for children with attention deficit disorder. *Journal of Consulting and Clinical Psychology, 65,* 749–757.

Pope, A. W., Bierman, K. L., & Mumma, G. H. (1991), Aggression, hyperactivity, and inattention-immaturity: Behavior dimensions associated with peer rejection in elementary school boys. *Developmental Psychology, 27,* 663–671.

Possell, L. E., Kehle, T. J., Mcloughlin, C. S., & Bray, M. A. (1999). Self-modeling as an intervention to reduce disruptive classroom behavior. *Cognitive and Behavioral Practice, 6,* 99–105.

Prinstein, M. J., & La Greca, A. M. (1999). Links between mothers' and children's social competence and associations with maternal adjustment. *Journal of Clinical Child Psychology, 28,* 197–210.

Prinz, R. J., Blechman, E., & Dumas, J. E. (1994). An evaluation of peer coping-skills training for childhood aggression. *Journal of Clinical Child Psychology, 23,* 193–203.

Putallaz, M. (1983). Predicting children's sociometric status from their behavior. *Child Development, 54,* 1417–1426.

Putallaz, M., & Gottman, J. M. (1981). An interactional model of children's entry into peer groups. *Child Development, 52,* 986–994.

Quinn, M. M., Kavale, K. A., Mathur, S. R., Rutherford, R. B., & Forness, S. R. (1999). Meta-analysis of social skills interventions for students with emotional and behavior disorders. *Journal of Emotional and Behavior Disorders, 7,* 54–64.

Rucker, C. N., & Vincenzo, F. M. (1970). Maintaining social acceptance gains made by mentally retarded children. *Exceptional Children, 36,* 679–680.

Russell, A., & Finnie, V. (1990). Preschool children's social status and maternal instructions to assist group entry. *Developmental Psychology, 26,* 603–611.

Rutter, M., & Garmezy, N. (1983). Developmental psychopathology. In E. M. Hetherington (Ed.) & P. H. Mussen (Series Ed.), *Handbook of child psychology: Socialization, personality and social development* (Vol. 4, pp. 775–911). New York: Wiley.

Sheridan, S. M., Dee, C. C., Morgan, J. C., McCormick, M. E., & Walker, D. (1996). A multimethod intervention for social skills deficits in children with ADHD and their parents. *School Psychology Review, 25,* 57–76.

Shure, M. B., & Spivak, G. (1978). *Problem-solving techniques in childrearing.* San Francisco: Jossey-Bass.

Smoll, F. L., & Smith, R. E. (1987). *Sports psychology for youth coaches.* Washington, DC: National Federation for Catholic Ministry.

Swanson, J. M. (1992). *School-based assessments and interventions for ADD students.* Irvine, CA: KC Publishing.

Taylor, A. R., & Asher, S. R. (1984). Children's goals and social competence: Individual differences in a game-playing context. In T. Field, J. L. Roopnarine, &

M. Segal (Eds.), *Friendships in normal and handicapped children* (pp. 53–78). Norwood, NJ: Ablex.

Tiffen, K., & Spence, S. H. (1986). Responsiveness of isolated versus rejected children to social skills training. *Journal of Child Psychology and Psychiatry, 27,* 343–355.

Tremblay, R. E., LeBlanc, M., & Schwartzman, A. E. (1988). The predictive power of first-grade peer and teacher ratings of behavior: Sex differences in antisocial behavior and personality at adolescence. *Journal of Abnormal Child Psychology, 16,* 571–583.

Tryon, A. S., & Keane, S. P. (1991). Popular and aggressive boys' initial social interaction patterns in cooperative and competitive settings. *Journal of Abnormal Child Psychology, 19,* 395–406.

Wasserstein, S. B., & La Greca, A. M. (1996). Can peer support buffer against behavioral consequences of parental discord? *Journal of Clinical Child Psychology, 25,* 177–182.

Welner, Z., Reich, W., Herjanic, B., & Jung, K. G. (1987). Reliability, validity, and parent-child agreement studies of the Diagnostic Interview for Children and Adolescents (DICA). *Journal of the American Academy of Child and Adolescent Psychiatry, 26,* 649–653.

Yu, P., Harris, G. E., Solovitz, B. L., & Franklin, J. L. (1986). A social problem-solving intervention for children at high risk for later psychopathology. *Journal of Clinical Child Psychology, 15,* 30–40.

27

TEMAS NARRATIVE TREATMENT: AN EVIDENCE-BASED CULTURALLY COMPETENT THERAPY MODALITY

GIUSEPPE COSTANTINO, ROBERT G. MALGADY, AND ELSA CARDALDA

PSYCHIATRIC EPIDEMIOLOGY OF HISPANIC YOUTH

According to the United States Census, there were nearly 35.3 million Hispanics living in this country in 2000, which represents a growth rate of over 60% compared with the 1990 census ("New Census," March 8, 2001; U.S. Bureau of the Census, 2000). This growth rate is more than eight times that of any other ethnic population in the United States, which has been attributed to high birth rates, youthful age distribution, and high

Parts of this chapter were published in "Storytelling Through Pictures: Culturally Sensitive Psychotherapy for Hispanic Children and Adolescents," by G. Costantino, R. Malgady, and L. Rogler, 1994, *Journal of Clinical Child Psychology, 23*, pp. 13–20. Copyright 1994 by Lawrence Erlbaum Associates. Reprinted with permission. The authors would like to thank Dr. William Bracero; Dr. Maria Sesin; Tania Hernandez, CSW; and Drs. Pilar Hernandez, Maria Ranson, Frances Leon, Carolyn Alto, and Yvette Montalvo Roca, who conducted the early clinical research on the utility of the TEMAS narrative therapy. Additionally, the authors would like to thank Professors Daniel G. Dupertuis and Maria de los Angeles of Buenos Aires University, Buenos Aires, Argentina. Drs. Jacqueline Guajardo, Melanie Perez, Gloria Montes de Oca, MA, Carolina Meucci, MA, Luiggi Caprino, MA, Marie Borges, MPH, who conducted the most recent therapy research.

levels of immigration ("New Census," March 8, 2001). The census estimate of the Hispanic population may be conservative because it does not take into account members of undocumented Hispanics. Nevertheless, these figures indicate that Hispanics have surpassed African Americans—who increased only by 16%, to 34.7 million, from the 30 million counted in the 1990 census—as the largest minority population.

Epidemiological studies of psychiatric prevalence rates and symptomatology have, for the most part, neglected the rapidly growing population of Hispanic children and adolescents. In New York City, for example, the Hispanic population is a youthful one, with 32% of Puerto Ricans and Dominicans under the age of 18 compared with 16% of non-Hispanic Whites ("New Census," March 8, 2001). Some early studies found lower self-esteem among Hispanic children compared with African American or non-Hispanic Caucasian children (Anderson & Johnson, 1971; Fisher, 1974), whereas others reported more behavioral problems among Hispanic children and adolescents compared with their Caucasian counterparts (Langer, Gersfen, & Eisenberg, 1974). Later, Canino, Gould, Prupis, and Schafer (1986) found that Hispanic children and adolescents reported more depression and anxiety symptoms than did their African American peers. However, the literature on depression is inconsistent with some studies, which report more severe depressive symptoms among Hispanic youth relative to other ethnic groups (Emslie, Weinberg, Rush, Adams, & Reintelmann, 1990), and other studies that do not report (Garrison, Jackson, Marsteller, McKeon, & Addy, 1990). Roberts (1992) reported that Hispanic adolescents express somatic complaints more frequently than their Caucasian and African American counterparts. In a nationwide epidemiological study, Kessler, McGonagle, Zhao, and Nelson (1994) reported that Hispanics have the highest rates of depression and other affective disorders (and the highest rates of comorbidity) among all ethnic groups.

According to some estimates (Aspira, 1993; New York City Department of City Planning, 1994), Hispanic youngsters exhibit the highest high-school dropout rate of all ethnic groups and alarming rates of referral to mental health clinics for problems such as social and emotional disorientation, conduct and anxiety disorders, adjustment reactions with anxiety features, and low self-esteem. Estimates of Puerto Rican dropout rates have ranged as high as 60%, and comparative data indicate that New York City rates are as bad as or worse than the national average (National Puerto Rican Forum, 1990; New York City Board of Education, 1990; New York State Office of Mental Health, 1994). A recent survey confirms that nationwide the Hispanic drop-out rate is three times that of Caucasians and twice that of African Americans ("Dropout Rates," 2003, June 13). Studying prevalence and risk factors among a multinational group of Hispanic early adolescents, Vega, Zimmerman, Warheit, Apospori, and Gil (1993) found a high prevalence of drug use. One study with therapeutic implications indicated that adherence to more traditional Hispanic cultural values were associated with a lower risk of drug use among Hispanic youth (Pumariega, Swanson, Holzer, Linskey, & Quintero-Salinas, 1992). Related to school dropout rate and substance abuse, Hispanic youths were the most rapidly increasing incarcerated population in the U.S., according to an earlier study (Martinez, 1987). Delinquency and mental illness have been shown to have a high rate of co-occurrence in the general adolescent population (Stoep, Evens, & Taub, 1997). A study of incarcerated minority youth showed that 72% of these offenders had emotional disorders (Pumariega et al., 1995). With respect to the severity of disorders among the juvenile offenders, Hispanic female adolescents exhibited higher rates of generalized anxiety than did their African American and Caucasian counterparts, and they also showed higher rates of all disruptive disorders and alcohol and substance use disorders than did their African American peers (Teplin, Abram, McClelland, Dulcan, & Mericle, 2002). According to the New York State Office of Mental Health (1994), among the primary *Diagnostic and Statistical Manual of Mental Disorders* (*DSM–III–R*; American Psychiatric Association, 1987) diagnoses of nearly 8,000 children and adolescents enrolled in community-based services, the rate of disruptive behavior disorders (46.9%) eclipses all others for the Hispanic youth. Furthermore, these disorders are nearly equally distributed between conduct and oppositional disorders. Environmental, social, and health disparities experienced by minority urban youths put them at high risk for mental illness; compared with Caucasians, a disproportionately higher number of Hispanic and African American youth exhibit behavior and psychiatric disorders from age 5 to 16 (Saravanabhavan & Walker, 1999). The dramatic increase in the Hispanic population during the last decade is likely to continue, making the need for evidence-based, culturally competent mental health assessment and treatment more urgent (Padilla, Ruiz, & Alvarez, 1975). This chapter reports the development of TEMAS narrative, an evidence-based, culturally competent modality designed for use with Hispanic youth (Costantino & Malgady, 1994; Malgady & Costantino, 2003).

CULTURALLY SENSITIVE *CUENTO* AND HERO–HEROINE MODELING THERAPY MODALITIES PROGRAM

The need for culturally competent mental health services addressing the special problems of Hispanic adults and youngsters is a widely acknowledged issue in the mental health literature on the treatment of minorities (Dana, 2003; Kazdin & Weisz, 1998, 2003; Malgady & Costantino, 1999; Malgady, Rogler, & Costantino, 1987; Rogler et al., 1983). At the root of this issue, the cultural distance experienced by Hispanic clients when seeking mainstream mental health services has prompted efforts to increase the sensitivity and competence of services to Hispanic culture. Indeed, mental health services have become more culturally sensitive and culturally competent in several ways: by matching clients with Spanish-speaking Hispanic therapists, by matching the theoretical orientation of therapy to clients' cultural values, and by introducing culture directly into the therapeutic process (Costantino & Malgady, 1996; Rogler, Malgady, Costantino, & Blumenthal, 1987). Yet limited empirical evidence suggests that such efforts, which have largely been directed toward adults, result in reduced treatment dropout rates, increased retention, and more effective outcomes (Sue, Fujino, Hu, & Zane, 1991; Kazdin & Weisz, 2003). Researchers at the Hispanic Research Center (at Fordham University in collaboration with the Sunset Park Mental Health Center of Lutheran Medical Center, New York) have developed a program of culturally competent treatment research in which they have evaluated experimental mental health interventions for Hispanic children and adolescents over the course of the past 2 decades. These studies were preventive interventions developed on the basis of narrative therapy, using cultural–cognitive behavioral role modeling in conjunction with behavioral reinforcement strategies to influence high-risk indicators such as anxiety, acting-out behavior, and poor ethnic identity and self-concept (Costantino & Malgady, 1996; Costantino, Malgady, & Rogler, 1986, 1988; Malgady & Costantino, 2003; Malgady, Rogler, & Costantino, 1990a, 1990b). This research is one of only two such programmatic efforts identified in a recent search of the literature over the past 20 years (American Psychological Association, 2003; Bernal & Scharron-Del-Rio, 2001; Coatsworth, Szapocznik, Kurtines, & Santisteban, 1997).

Culturally Competent Adaptation of Narrative Therapy

Our program of culturally competent treatment of Hispanic children and adolescents has paved the path for the Guidelines on Multicultural Education, Training, Research, Practice, and Organizational Change for Psychologists (American Psychological Association, 2003). Consequently, our *cuento* and Tell-Me-A-Story (TEMAS) narrative therapies have been recognized as culturally competent evidence-based treatments for Hispanic youth (American Psychological Association, 2003; Bernal & Scharrón-Del-Rio, 2001; Dana, 2003; Kazdin & Weisz, 2003; U.S. Department of Health and Human Services, 2001). Our culturally competent adaptation of narrative treatment research was conceptualized in the cognitive–behavioral theory process and rooted in social learning theory principles (e.g., social modeling). Narrative psychotherapy is rapidly gaining acceptance as a culturally sensitive treatment modality (Bracero, in press; Howard, 1991). Cognitive psychologists such as Bruner (1986) and Mair (1989) have affirmed that identity development occurs as a result of life-story construction. Howard

(1991) conceptualizes psychopathology as an incoherent story with an incorrect ending; consequently, the goal of psychotherapy is to reconstruct a coherent story with a correct ending. Further, he describes storytelling as the most adept process in understanding culturally diverse individuals and in conducting cross-cultural psychotherapy. Furthermore, Bracero (in press) indicates that narrative therapy is a valid modality for Hispanic clients. Evidence for this validity can be seen in the work of Inclan and Hernandez (1992) on culture–migration dialogue technique as a narrative therapy for Hispanic families; in Costantino's work on the use of Puerto Rican folktales in *cuento* therapy treatment of multiple family groups; in TEMAS storytelling techniques in the group therapy of Latino children; and in our own clinical research using both TEMAS pictures and selected artwork of Frida Kahlo in the treatment of depressed Hispanic female clients (Bracero, in press) Our early and later development of narrative treatment coincides with the rise of narrative therapy, which was formally introduced by White and Epston (1999), who hypothesized that patients' problem-saturated life stories of failure and emotional distress can be transformed into hopeful and solution-focused life stories.

In our initial study of bicultural intervention with young children, Costantino, Malgady, and Rogler (1986) developed a storytelling modality using Puerto Rican *cuentos*, or folktales, as a cognitive–behavioral modeling intervention. In this approach, the characters in the folktales were posed as therapeutic peer models conveying the theme and moral of the stories. The content of such stories motivated children's attention to the models, which is critical in the first stage of the modeling process. Second, the stories were rewritten to present settings, attitudes, values, and behaviors that reflect adaptive responses to the designated targets of therapeutic intervention, such as acting out, anxiety symptoms, and negative self-concept. The original folktales were adapted to bridge both Puerto Rican and European American cultural values and settings. Reinforcement of children's imitation of the models through active therapeutic role-playing exercises facilitated social learning of adaptive responses, which were targeted in the stories' themes. In this manner, the modality was rooted in the children's own cultural heritage, presented in a format with which they could readily identify, and therapeutically aimed to improve adjustment to mainstream cultural demands. The intervention was conducted with the children in a dyadic format, with their mothers in small group sessions led by bilingual Hispanic therapists. This intervention was designed to be preventive because the children were presenting significant emotional and behavior problems in school and at home, but they did not reach the threshold of diagnostic criteria for *DSM–III–R* (American Psychiatric Association, 1987) disorders. In addition, their uniformly low socioeconomic status and the high rate of single-parent household composition also characterized these children as a high-risk group.

The effectiveness of the bicultural folktale modality was determined by comparing the treatment outcomes of a second folktale condition, in which the same stories were true to their original themes and not adapted to bridge cultural conflict, with those of a mainstream play therapy. The evaluation of treatment outcomes indicated that the bicultural folktale intervention led to the greatest improvement in social judgment and greatest reduction in anxiety symptoms, improvements that persisted at 1-year follow-up.

A related cognitive–behavioral modeling intervention appropriate for adolescents was based on heroic adult role models (Costantino & Malgady, 1996; Malgady, Rogler, & Costantino, 1990a, 1990b). A major consideration in developing this modality was that Puerto Rican adolescents often live in single-parent households; hence, they lack appropriate adult male role models with whom they can identify and adaptive values and behaviors that they can imitate during adolescence, when critical psychosocial development occurs. National figures indicate that 41% of Hispanic households are headed by females (U.S. Bureau of the Census, 1991); estimates specific to Puerto Ricans in New York City are somewhat higher (44%, according to Mann & Salvo, 1985). Our own samples drawn from New York City public schools in Hispanic communities showed rates of female-headed households exceeding 60% (Costantino & Malgady, 1996). Consequently, Puerto Rican adolescents appeared to be suitable candidates for a modeling therapy that fulfills their need for adaptive role models in a culturally sensitive and competent manner.

We developed and evaluated a *cuento*, or narrative, therapy using biographical stories of heroic Puerto Ricans in an effort to bridge the bicultural, intergenerational, and identity conflicts faced by Puerto Rican adolescents. This modality sought to enhance the relevance of therapy for adolescents by exposing them to successful male and female adult models in their own culture, fostering ethnic pride and identity and modeling achievement-oriented behavior and adaptive coping with skills appropriate to life in the urban Hispanic community. The content of the biographies embodied themes of cultural conflict and adaptive coping with stress. This intervention was also considered preventive because, although the adolescents were screened for behavior problems in school, they did not meet *DSM–III–R* diagnostic criteria. Treatment outcomes were assessed relative to an attention control group participating in a school-based dropout prevention program. Evaluation of treatment effectiveness revealed that the culturally sensitive modeling intervention generally decreased anxiety symptoms and increased ethnic identity. However, treatment interacted with household composition and participants' gender. Consistent with the intention of the intervention, the role models promoted greater cultural identity in the absence of a male adult in the adolescents' households—but only among male adolescents. Female adolescents had stronger Puerto Rican identities than males regardless of treatment, possibly because of stable maternal identification. Similarly, the role models promoted greater self-esteem among male and female adolescents from female-headed households; however, although females from intact families felt "more Puerto Rican," their self-image diminished in the process. One explanation of this unexpected finding is that they may have perceived the role models presented in treatment in an idealized manner, which generated emotional conflict concerning their real parents, so that parental identification led to lower self-esteem. This process may have occurred only among females because the female role models often demonstrated untraditional female sex roles.

The interactions influencing treatment outcomes point to the importance of adolescents' social context in considering the therapeutic value of culturally sensitive behavioral interventions. This finding suggests the need to investigate both the integrity and quality of intrafamilial relations as potential mediators or moderators of treatment outcomes. The introduction of cultural sensitivity in the treatment process is a promising approach to addressing the special mental health needs of Hispanic adolescents; however, a need remains for further research investigating the ways in which culturally sensitive services can be implemented more effectively, given that dynamic processes may intervene to enhance or diminish their effectiveness. One objective of this research program will be to investigate the dynamic interplay between a culturally sensitive narrative intervention and the familial context of male and female Hispanic adolescents, resulting in gender- and family-specific refinements in treatment protocols.

The present study pursued several new directions in this program of culturally sensitive treatment outcome research. First, whereas in previous studies inclusion criteria were based on teacher ratings of school behavior, research participants in the present study were screened for symptoms using the third and revised edition of the *DSM–III–R* (American Psychiatric Association, 1987) using a standardized structured clinical interview. Second, the present study included older children and young adolescents from 9 to 13 years old, an age range not addressed in previous studies that presented written and verbal modeling stimuli. This study presented pictures, which were thought to be more effective in communicating with a more psychologically disturbed and educationally disadvantaged group. Fourth, this study included diverse Hispanic groups, whereas previous studies focused exclusively on Puerto Ricans.

The rationale for changing therapy format from verbally presented stimuli (*cuentos*) to visual stimuli in TEMAS (an acronym for "Tell me a story") was dictated by the fact that the second modality is readily adaptable to culturally diverse groups, thus affording the clinician a culturally sensitive, culturally competent modality that can be administered to multicultural youths.

Participants and Setting

The participants in the study were recruited from a public school in Brooklyn, New York. The school is located in a community of 102,000 residents, mostly Hispanics (over 60%) and mostly Hispanics of Puerto Rican descent and of low socioeconomic status. In recent years, however, the diversity of the Hispanic population has increased rapidly as a result of immigration from the Dominican Republic and Central and South America. The school had a population of approximately 1,400 students, 95% of whom were Hispanic.

Over 500 students in Grades 4 through 6 whose self-reported ethnicity was Hispanic were contacted for participation. Student and parental consent was obtained from 363 respondents, who were subsequently screened for *DSM–III–R* symptomatology using a structured clinical interview, the Child Assessment Schedule (CAS; Hodges, 1986). Interviewers were two doctorate-level psychology students who were trained to administer the CAS. None of the students satisfied the diagnostic criteria of the selected *DSM–III–R* disorders assessed by the CAS. However, the students satisfied clinically derived *DSM–III–R* diagnostic criteria. The three most prevalent categories of symptomatology, however, were associated with anxiety, conduct, and phobic disorders. Forty-nine students presenting symptoms that were primarily in categories other than these were excluded. The three categories of symptoms were highly comorbid; most (n = 276) students presented at least three symptoms in at least two of the three categories. Among the screened students, the 30 most symptomatic males and females in each of the three primary diagnostic categories (n = 90) were randomly selected for the study. The number of the symptoms presented per diagnostic category ranged from five to 11 on any one of these three disorders and at least three on a second disorder. The most prevalent subdiagnostic symptoms were in the conduct disorder category, followed by anxiety and then phobic disorder symptoms. The most common pattern of comorbidity was conduct–phobic symptomatology, followed by conduct–anxiety and phobic–anxiety symptomatologies. About 60% of the participants were of Puerto Rican descent (n = 55); 25% were Dominican (n = 22); and 15% were Colombian, San Salvadorian, Nicaraguan, or Peruvian. All students were bilingual, according to self-reports and teacher reports.

Procedures

Participants were stratified by sex and grade level and then randomly assigned to either the experimental intervention or an attention control group (n = 45 per treatment group). The experimental group underwent TEMAS narrative treatment, whereas the attention control group received psychoeducational treatment (e.g., watching videos such as *The Adventures of Tom Sawyer*). The experimental and attention control groups were randomly subdivided into six subgroups of seven to eight participants each. Members of each group participated in eight 90-minute sessions, which took place weekly. Sessions were videotaped to monitor the fidelity of treatments and provide immediate feedback to therapists. These videotapes were also discussed among group therapy members. Sessions were conducted by six Hispanic graduate psychology trainees (PhD and PsyD students) in a private classroom in the participating school after school hours. All therapists had completed at least 3 years of graduate study and were trained with videotape feedback by the first author. Three therapists conducted experimental sessions, and three conducted the control sessions, each therapist administering two subgroups. Both groups were pretested before the first session and posttested after the eighth session with a battery of outcome measures. To promote attendance, participants in both groups were given token rewards, such as T-shirts and school supplies, each time they attended two consecutive sessions.

Treatment Outcome Measures

Measures of treatment outcome included the anxiety and phobia symptom scales of the Symptom Check List (SCL–90; Derogatis, 1983), the National Institute of Mental Health Center for Epidemiological Studies—Depression Scale (CES–D; Radloff, 1977), and the Conners Teacher Behavior Rating Scale (BRS; Conners, 1989). The SCL–90 and CES–D instruments are self-report measures that were developed for use with adult populations. They also have been used, however, with teenagers and young adolescents. Participants were instructed to ask for clarification if they did not understand the meaning of any of the items. The BRS was completed by participants' teachers, who were blinded to the students' intervention group membership. Use of the BRS also provided continuity with our previous research on Hispanic eighth and ninth graders. Alpha reliability of the teachers' BRS ratings was .92 in the present study.

Because epidemiological research on adult Hispanic populations has frequently used the CES–D to assess depression, and because comparable data on Hispanic children are lacking, we selected this scale for consistency with adult research. The CES–D was pilot tested for readability and understanding with a small group of students who were screened for this study but who chose not to participate. Only minor changes in wording were required on four of the 20 items (Items 3, 4, 9, and 20). Alpha reliability computed for the 20-item CES–D was moderate for the total sample ($n = .81$), nearly equal within each treatment group (.78 and .82), and decreased slightly by grade level (.84 at Grade 6; .79 at Grade 5; and .69 at Grade 4).

The SCL–90 has been used reliably in our earlier study with eighth and ninth graders and in pilot studies, which we conducted with sixth and seventh graders. To ensure the consistency of data, the SCL–90 was also administered in the present study. In addition, our previous studies used the Trait Scale of the State–Trait Anxiety Inventory for Children (STAI-C; Spielberger, Edwards, Lushene, Montuori, & Platzek, 1973), which is somewhat redundant in content with the CES–D items and highly correlated (over $r =$ .70) with the total CES–D score. The SCL–90 anxiety scale and the CES–D ($r = .35$) showed far less overlap. No vocabulary problems with the brief symptom descriptions were evident in a pilot study conducted with the present population. However, a panel of parents who reviewed the study instruments, including the entire SCL–90, required the deletion of three items that they found objectionable for their children (e.g., a reference to "tingling" sensations in parts of the body). Alpha reliability for the total SCL–90 score exceeded .90 for the total sample within treatment groups and within grade levels. The subscale scores used in the data analysis (anxiety and phobia) showed similar patterns of internal consistency reliability, much like the CES–D: total (as = .74–.76), treatments (as = .71–.78), and grade levels (as = .77–.79, Grade 6; .74–.77, Grade 5; .64–.67, Grade 4).

Scores on the CES–D, SCL–90 and BRS were transformed into standardized T-Scores (M = 50, SD = 10) for ease of interpretation and for comparability across the measures. The nature of the standard score transformation was linear, preserving slight skewness. All measures were scaled such that increasing scores reflect increasing severity of psychopathology. Participants were given the choice of completing the instruments in English or Spanish; only 12 participants born in the Dominican Republic, El Salvador, Nicaragua, and Peru chose to complete the Spanish versions (i.e., other participants who were born in the United States chose to take the English version, whereas these 12 participants, all of whom were born in the preceding countries, chose to take the Spanish versions). The Spanish versions of the instruments were back-translations prepared at the Hispanic Research Center of Fordham University.

Interventions: Narrative Therapy Sessions

The theory behind and description of cultural sensitive competent therapy are described in more detail elsewhere (Costantino & Malgady, 1996: Malgady, Rogler, & Costantino, 1990a, 1990b); presented here is a brief overview of the process applied to narrative therapy. The fundamental idea behind this therapy is that the observer must pay attention to a model if he or she is to imitate the targeted symbolic behavior. Hence, the cultural familiarity of the models is expected to increase attention to the model's target behaviors and, consequently, the probability of imitation. Second, elements of narrative therapy are fundamental to the behavior change. Target adaptive behavior that is imitated from the role model presented is repeatedly followed by positive reinforcement. Thus, the acquired behaviors become cognitively and behaviorally instantiated. In the absence of the model, verbal labeling of imitative behavior followed by reinforcement facilitates acquisition and learning. In addition to verbal reinforcement by the therapist, according to the cognitive–behavioral component of the protocol, merit reinforcers, such as a score of "very good" on special report cards, are given to reward adaptive target behavior. Moreover, spontaneous verbal peer reinforcement occurs as group members form bonds, which is common. Within this theoretical framework, the symbolic models of adaptive emotional and behavioral functioning are presented within the various Hispanic cultures in which the adolescents live. The stories motivate attention processes by presenting culturally familiar characters of the same ethnicity as the adolescents by changing cognition, modeling beliefs, values, and behaviors with which the adolescents can identify, and by modeling functional relationship with peers and authority figures. This modality seems to be particularly appropriate for adolescents with symptoms bordering on conduct disorders.

The experimental intervention consisted of a storytelling modality based on pictorial stimuli depicting Hispanic cultural elements (e.g., traditional foods, games, sex roles) and Hispanic families and neighborhoods (e.g., stores, or *bodegas*) in urban settings. These stimuli were eight pictures from the TEMAS Thematic Apperception Test (Costantino, 1987) portraying multiracial Hispanic characters interacting in a variety of urban, familial, and school settings. The TEMAS pictures were developed by a professional artist who attempted to capture elements of Latino culture as described by a panel of cultural experts (Costantino, Malgady, & Rogler, 1988). Research on TEMAS also indicates that Hispanic children and adolescents readily identify the characters and families in the pictures as Hispanic and the settings as similar to their own neighborhoods and that children and adolescents tell substantially longer stories about TEMAS pictures than about stimuli with less of a cultural emphasis, such as the Thematic Apperception Test (TAT) cards (Costantino & Malgady, 1983; Costantino, Malgady, & Vazquez, 1981).

The TEMAS pictures have been empirically shown to evoke stories based on designated themes among Hispanic children and adolescents (Costantino, Malgady, & Rogler, 1988). The pictures chosen were particularly likely to evoke storytelling related to anxious, depressed, and fearful feelings and disruptive–cooperative, aggressive–nonaggressive, and achieving–failing behaviors. Some TEMAS pictures are designated for both sexes, whereas others are pairs of parallel sex-specific pictures. In the therapy sessions, either a single picture portraying a boy and girl or a pair of pictures (one boy, one girl) was presented. A series of multicultural and cross-cultural studies have documented the multicultural and cross-cultural validity of the TEMAS test, in both minority and nonminority versions, as shown by the research of Bernal (1991); Cardalda, Sayers, and Machado (2001); Cardalda, Santiago-Negron, Costantino, and Malgady (1999b); Cardalda et al. (2000); Cardalda, Quintero, Costantino, and Malgady (1999a); Costantino and Malgady (2001); Costantino and Malgady (1983); Costantino, Malgady, Casullo, and Castillo (1991); Dana (1996); Gomez-Dupertuis and Ropaldo (2001); Sardi

(2000); Sardi and Summo (2001); and Walton, Nuttall, and Vazquez-Nuttall (1997, 1998).

Therapy sessions were conducted in three phases. The goal of the first phase, which averaged about 30 minutes, was for the group members to develop a composite story in response to the preselected TEMAS picture. The participants told stories about the pictures, either spontaneously or, when necessary, with prompting, identifying the picture's characters, setting, plot, and resolution. After the third session, as therapeutic alliance rapport were established, little prompting by the therapist was required. The therapist attempted to capture those thematic elements in the individual narratives that provided the most adaptive solution to synthesize the most therapeutic composite story.

In the second phase of the sessions, which averaged about 40 minutes, group members were motivated to share their personal experiences as related to the composite story. The therapist emphasized that the members should share their true experiences and be respectful of the self-disclosures of others. With the building of rapport, personal experiences, feelings, and significant life events were readily projected onto the participants' storytelling, requiring very little prompting on the part of the therapist. The therapist then compared the behaviors, attitudes and feelings expressed in the personal disclosures with the corresponding elements of the composite story constructed in the first phase. The therapist verbally reinforced themes in the participants' personal narratives that were adaptive or consistent with the composite story. The therapist referred maladaptive themes to the group for discussion of alternative, more adaptive resolutions of personal conflict and problem solving. In this process, participants were encouraged to express their own value judgments about their peers' experiences. The most common reactions expressed were judgments of good or bad behavior, verbal reinforcement, disapproval, socially supportive encouragement, and empathy. Thus, this phase engaged the participants in verbalizing personal conflicts in their lives and ways that they coped with them, thereby seeking to reinforce and symbolically internalize adaptive resolutions of stressful situations.

In the third phase, which averaged about 20 minutes, the participants dramatized the composite story by performing the roles of the characters in the original picture and of the characters that had been constructed in the group interaction. The therapist and peers provided verbally supportive reinforcement of imitative target behaviors (e.g., confronting one's fears, proper behavior, adaptive coping with stress) during the dramatization. The psychodrama was videotaped and played back to the group for critical review and reinforcement of the desired behaviors. Thus, the goal of this phase was to provide reinforcement through personal dramatization of adaptive symbolic narrative models.

The attention control group engaged in discussion sessions with an emphasis on psychoeducational content. Four different children's videos were shown in alternate weeks: *The Adventures of Tom Sawyer, Pinocchio, The Black Stallion,* and *Star Wars.* A video was shown during the first session, and participants were told to pay close attention because the following week they would be discussing and drawing pictures about what they saw. Both a schoolteacher and a teaching assistant, whose main task was to promote participants' attention to the video while managing their behavior and minimizing disruptions, conducted the video sessions.

A different schoolteacher and a therapist conducted the sessions following the video presentation. The schoolteachers and therapists conducting these sessions were not involved in conducting the TEMAS narrative therapy sessions. The participants were first asked to recall the content of the movie. Much like the discussion of TEMAS pictures, the participants recounted the characters, setting, events, and story ending. As in the therapy condition, the teacher and therapist facilitated the recollection of the movie content, when necessary, by prompting. The participants were then asked to share with the group the themes and characters in the video that they liked the best, and then they were asked to draw them. Last, the participants dramatized the theme or the actions of their favorite characters in the movie. Consistent with the procedures in the experimental group, the skits were videotaped and played back to the participants. In the attention control group, symbolic models, such as Pinocchio or Tom Sawyer, were presented, thus fostering cognitive functioning without direct therapeutic impact. Drawing and dramatization were activities resembling play therapy. Otherwise, the TEMAS therapy and the attention control sessions were structured to be as similar as possible.

Format of TEMAS Narrative Sessions

A step-by-step format and time frame for development of a composite TEMAS group narrative session is outlined below:

1. Create a composite TEMAS Group Narrative Session (15–20 minutes).
    1.1. Group members take turns creating a story about the picture presented.
    1.2. Therapist uses structured questioning to hold attention and promote identification (e.g., What was the main character's motivation to act? What were his or her feelings? What were his or her conflicts and problems? What did he or she do to resolve them?).
    1.3. Therapist highlights important issues.
    1.4. Therapist uses structured inquiries to hold attention and promote identification with the main character (e.g., What conflicts and problems did the main character confront? What was the

main character feeling? What obstacles did he or she encounter and overcome? What did the main character do to master them?

Therapist administers behavioral reinforcers (e.g., "excellent insight," "very good interpretation," "it appears that you fully understand") throughout 1.1 through 1.4.

2. Elicit similar personal experiences (20–30 minutes).
    2.1. Introductory question: Did any of you have (or know a person with) a similar experience? Discuss responses.
    2.2. Identify participants who were emotionally supportive during this experience.
    2.3. Compare personal stories with the narrative (e.g., the main character faced obstacles and conflicts; what are you doing about this problem?).
    2.4. Create a composite–adaptive story made up of all positive segments of personal stories given. Identify positive ideas, behaviors, and consequences.

Therapist administers behavior reinforcers (e.g., "excellent understanding . . . very good identification with the main character . . .") throughout steps 2.1 through 2.4.

3. Role playing (15–20 minutes).
    3.1. Present semistructured scenario, characters, and dilemma, and select volunteers for roles.
    3.2. Enact story spontaneously with regard to the given narrative, achieving a solution of the problems and conflicts presented.
    3.3. Participants are administered appropriate verbal reinforcements and given excellent grades.
    3.4. Review and discuss videotape (reinforcement).
    3.5. Provide summary evaluation of session.

Results

Because multiple outcome measures were present, the data were analyzed first by a multivariate analysis of covariance to maintain a .05 family-wise significance level. The design underlying the analysis was Treatment × Sex × Grade Level (2 × 2 × 3 factorial) controlling the pretest scores as covariates. Multivariate main and interaction effects involving the treatment factor were significant at the .05 and .01 levels. Therefore, univariate analyses of covariance were pursued separately for each outcome measure.

The results of univariate analysis revealed that no significant differences existed among treatment groups or grade or sex interactions involving treatments, with respect to depression as measured by the CES–D. The results did, however, reveal varying patterns of univariate treatment effects on teacher ratings of school conduct and participant self-reported SCL–90 measures of anxiety and phobic symptoms.

With regard to conduct disorders measured by the BRS, there was significant Treatment Group × Grade Level interaction effect ($p < .01$) explaining 11% of the variance independent of pretest scores. On the basis of Scheffé tests (Scheffé, 1959), the nature of the interaction was such that no significant treatment group differences were noted at Grades 4 or 5 ($p > .05$), but a significant difference was observed among sixth graders ($p < .05$) in favor of the experimental storytelling intervention. The two treatment groups' mean posttest T-scores, adjusted for pretest differences, are shown in Figure 27.1 as a function of grade level. Figure 27.1 shows that the storytelling treatment improved sixth graders' conduct, according to teachers' ratings of severity (adjusted posttest M = 55.2), about half a standard deviation more than the attention control treatment (adjusted posttest M = 60.3). A similar pattern of findings was evident on two of the four BRS subscales: conduct problem and hyperactivity. No significant differences between treatments were noted at any grade level, however, with respect to the inattentive–passive and tension–anxiety subscales.

There was a significant main effect of treatment group on the self-reported SCL–90 Anxiety subscale ($p < .05$) explaining a modest 4% of the residual posttest variance. There were no significant interaction effects on anxiety (adjusted posttest M = 55.5) in the treatment group compared with those of the attention control group (adjusted posttest = 60.8), but the differences corresponded to about half a standard deviation in magnitude.

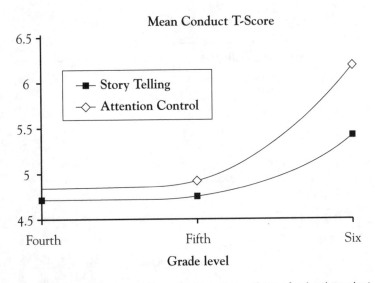

Figure 27.1. Mean posttreatment T-score of teacher ratings of school conduct, adjusted by pretest covariate, for treatment groups as a function of grade level.

Effects on phobic symptomatology were more complex. The three-way Treatment × Sex × Grade Level interaction was significant ($p < .01$), explaining 9% of the variance. The adjusted posttest means of the two treatment groups as a function of grade level are shown for males in Figure 27.2 and for females in Figure 27.3. Scheffé tests revealed that for males, the storytelling treatment significantly reduced phobic symptoms (adjusted posttest M = 55.4) relative to the attention control treatment (adjusted posttest M =

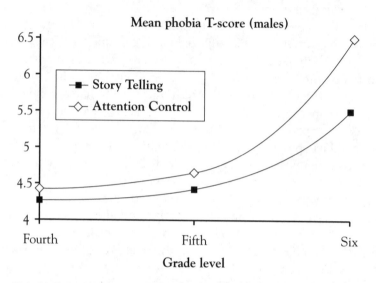

Figure 27.2. Males' mean posttreatment T-score of self-reported SCL–90 Phobic symptoms, adjusted by pretest covariate, for treatment groups as a function.

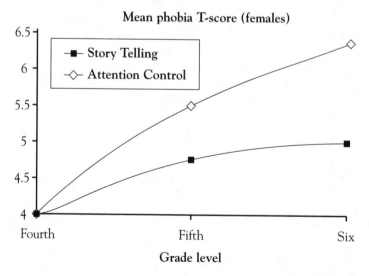

Figure 27.3. Females' mean posttreatment T-score of self-reported SCL–90 Phobic symptoms, adjusted by pretest covariate, for treatment groups as a function.

62.5) only at the sixth grade level ($p < .05$). On the other hand, for females, the storytelling treatment was more effective than the attention control treatment ($p < .05$) at both the fifth grade (adjusted posttest M = 50.6 versus 55.4) and the sixth grade (adjusted posttest M = 54.8 versus 63.3) levels. These standardized differences correspond to effect sizes ranging from about one half to three quarters of a standard deviation.

To check for differential therapist effects, a one-way analysis of covariance between the three therapists conducting each intervention was computed for each treatment outcome measure, with the pretest as a covariate. No significant differences among participants treated by the three experimental group therapists were observed. Similarly, we detected no significant adjusted mean posttest differences among participants treated by the three control group therapist–teacher pairs.

DISCUSSION

Research on risk factors associated with mental health problems indicates a pressing need to develop and evaluate preventive and therapeutic interventions for Hispanic children and adolescents. The present study, which forms part of a program of research toward this goal (Malgady, Rogler, & Costantino, 1990b), lends support to the effectiveness of using culturally competent modalities to treat Hispanic youngsters' conduct problems in school and their anxious and fearful symptoms. Treatment outcomes were demonstrated across several Hispanic nationalities, across genders, and for three patterns of symptomatology at the threshold of DSM–III–R disorders. However, no significant treatment effect on depression was observed.

The lack of a significant depression outcome is probably due to the fact that participants had very low CES–D scores on the pretest and fewer CAS depression symptoms relative to the other three symptom categories. When the CES–D is scored for DSM–III–R disorders, a score of 16 or higher (maximum = 60) is considered the diagnostic threshold (Moscicki, Rae, Reiger, & Locke, 1987). In the present study, the mean pretest CES–D raw score was only 6.70 (SD = .89), which is significantly lower than the mean levels reported for both adult Hispanic males and females (Moscicki et al., 1987).

The ultimate therapeutic value of culturally competent modalities, such as the present one, has not been formally evaluated. However, the TEMAS narrative study presents sufficient culturally competent validity to be deemed an evidence-based treatment (American Psychological Association, 2003; Bernal & Scharrón-Del-Rio, 2001; Kazdin & Weisz, 1998; U.S. Department of Health and Human Services, 2001). A more formidable test of the preventive mental health merits of culturally sensitive modalities would be to follow culturally treated groups of high-risk children and adolescents, compared with cohorts who are untreated and treated by standard modalities, to assess whether the amelioration of symptoms is related to reducing child rates of *DSM–III–R* disorders.

Other rigorous testing of the effectiveness of culturally sensitive interventions should involve two additional considerations. The first is that the cultural uniqueness of such interventions needs to be established empirically. The cultural sensitivity of the present intervention has at its premise the fact that the TEMAS pictures portray Hispanic culture, as depicted in the family scenes, neighborhoods, and multiracial characters. However, the stimuli also portray impoverished, inner-city settings, which are not uniquely Hispanic. Moreover, the expression of feelings, personal involvement in storytelling, or general therapy variables may have accounted for the treatment change. Thus, further experimental control is needed to isolate the primary sources of therapeutic change.

The second limitation of this and other culturally sensitive treatment research is that multiple control groups are required. In the present study, for example, the control group received attention equivalent to the TEMAS intervention group. The activities conducted in the two groups were also similar, but they were not therapeutically directed in the control group. Thus, this design controlled for structural similarity between the two intervention groups. However, stronger tests of the efficacy of culturally sensitive interventions are needed to demonstrate empirically incremental treatment outcomes relative to standard modalities, such as cognitive–behavioral therapy or play therapy.

Consistent with previous studies, age-dependent outcomes emerged in the present study. After studying diverse age bands in several studies, we can conclude that storytelling of cultural material is an effective modality using folktales with very young children (Costantino et al., 1986); using heroic biographies with older adolescents (Malgady et al., 1990a); and, as shown in the present study, composing stories about familial and ethnic pictures with older children and early adolescents. The specificity of these treatment outcomes invites further inquiry to explain what developmental experiences affect responsiveness to therapeutic intervention.

The pattern of age-related findings also showed substantial main effects (see Figures 27.1 through 27.3). Indeed, the analyses of conduct, anxiety, and phobia scores revealed significant main effects of age. This effect across treatments suggests that the sixth graders were more responsive to treatment in general than were the younger participants. One possible reason for this finding may be the lower reliability of the CES–D and SCL–90 with the fourth graders (9- and 10-year-olds). The internal consistency estimates for these measures were marginal (in the high .60s). Thus, although some attenuation of treatment effects may have occurred among the fourth graders, a sufficient potential for explanation of treatment variance existed, even within the ceiling imposed by the modest reliabilities. Underlying these findings runs a common thread: the abiding interest of youngsters to participate actively in symbolic modeling activities that enmesh culture. One intriguing question that warrants furthur inquiry is whether cultural sensitivity operates like a catalyst, enabling the effectiveness of a standard therapeutic technique such as modeling therapy in the present case, or whether cultural sensitivity itself is therapeutic, fostering anticipatory socialization skills in youngsters that confront otherwise confusing demands. This is an intriguing question warranting further inquiry.

Notwithstanding the limitations of this study, a program of clinical research, which is being conducted at the Sunset Park Mental Health Center of Lutheran Medical Center (Bracero, in press; Bracero, Sesin, Hernandez, Costantino, & Malgady, 1998, 1999; Bracero, Sesin, Hernandez, Ranson, & Hernandez, 2000) has shown the clinical utility of this TEMAS narrative therapy in the treatment of Hispanic women. Results of these studies indicate a significant reduction in depression among the TEMAS narrative therapy group compared with two other groups receiving traditional group therapy. The authors emphasized the need to develop brief, solution-focused treatment intervention that is both culturally competent and facilitates a sense of empowerment in Hispanic women. The women in the TEMAS groups were able to construct realistic solutions to personal and cross-cultural life conflicts while maintaining their diverse cultural heritage. The TEMAS narrative therapy is presently undergoing further validation as a cultutally competent, evidence-based treatment with youths affected by traumatic stress (Costantino, 2002; Costantino, Guajardo, Hernandez, Borges, Perez, Meucci, et al., 2004; Costantino, Malgady, Stiles, Borges, Costantino, Hernandez, et al., 2003). The Sunset Park Mental Health Center with Dr. Giuseppe Costantino as the Principal Investigator is participating in a multisite study with other organizations in New York City such as New York University, Columbia University, and Mount Sinai Medical Center in treating school-age children affected by the 9/11 events. The Sunset Park study site assesses the validity of the TEMAS Narrative Therapy, an evidence-based, culturally sensitive treatment (Costantino, Malgady, & Cardalda, in press; Malgady & Costantino, 2003) vs. traditional cognitive–behavioral therapy (CBT) for traumatized schoolchildren. Thirty percent of the 600 children tested (180) have screened positive for trauma symptomatology, whereas 50 percent of the positive screens (90) tested positive for posttraumatic stress disorders. These children have been assigned to TEMAS narrative and cognitive behavior therapies and are undergoing 20 therapy sessions. Analyses will focus on the main effects of gender and their potential intercation effects involving treatment, CBT, and TEMAS narrative as indicators of treatment processes and outcomes. This recent development of TEMAS narrative therapy as evidence-based treatment has revealed that the technique appears to be a valid treatment for culturally diverse adults and young adults. In addition to showing direct clinical utility in an in vivo clinical setting, these studies indicate that the format of the TEMAS narrative therapy session can be streamlined by deleting the videotaping of of the original session format and replacing it by a session in which the participants compare their own emotional distress, feelings, and attitudes as revealed in their own personal narratives with the adaptive behaviors, feelings, attitudes, and solutions of conflicts exhibited by the characters in the composite story. The TEMAS narrative technique has the advantages of being less cumbersome, less technical (thus not requiring a technical assistant), and less intrusive than traditional therapy modality; it can be easily replicated as a culturally sensitive and culturally competent group therapy modality. In addition, this modality can be readily duplicated with and applied to culturally diverse youths.

In the tradition of psychologists who have proposed a narrative conceptualization of human thinking, Howard (1991, pp. 187, 196) suggested that storytelling is fundamental to the development of identity, which he calls "life-story construction." Psychopathology occurs when life stories go awry. Thus, the effectiveness of culturally sensitive storytelling techniques may correspond to Howard's view of psychotherapy as an "exercise in story repair." This may help to explain the age-specific effects of the diverse modalities. Perhaps storytelling is connected to the self-identity that is appropriate for a given age. As children mature, the complexity of their stories progress from, for example, folktales about fictional characters to biographies of historical characters, and from a preferred visual–pictorial modality to a verbal–written one. Cultural sensitivity and cultural competence in psychotherapy, then, might be viewed as the composition and narration of an age-appropriate story fitting the functional demands imposed on culturally and linguistically diverse youngsters to "repair" their own dysfunctional stories, and by analogy to "repair" their dysfunctional lives.

REFERENCES

American Psychiatric Association. (1987). *Diagnostic and statistical manual of mental disorders* (3rd ed., rev.). Washington, DC: Author.

American Psychological Association. (2003). Guidelines on multicultural education, training, research, practice, and organizational change for psychologists. *American Psychologist, 58,* 377–402.

Aspira Inc. of New York. (1983). *Racial and ethnic high school dropout rate in New York City.* New York: Author.

Anderson, J. F., & Johnson, W. H. (1971). Stability and change among three generations of Mexican-Americans: Factors affecting achievement. *American Educational Journal, 8,* 285–307.

Bernal, I. (1991). *The relationship between level of acculturation, the Robert's Apperception Test for Children, and the TEMAS (Tell-Me-A-Story test).* Unpublished dissertation, California School of Professional Psychology, Los Angeles.

Bernal, G., Scharrón-Del-Rio, M. (2001). Are empirically supported treatments valid for ethnic minorities? Toward an alternative approach for treatment research. *Cultural Diversity and Ethnic Minority Psychology, 7,* 328–342.

Bracero, W. (in press). *Between the two worlds: The assessment and treatment of the culturally diverse.* Northvale, NJ: Jason Aronson.

Bracero, W., Sesin, M., Hernandez, T., Costantino, G., & Malgady, R., (1998, August). *TEMAS narrative therapy with Latino depressed women.* Poster presented at the 106th Convention of the American Psychological Association, San Francisco.

Bracero, W., Sesin, M., Hernandez, T., Costantino, G., & Malgady, R. (1999, August). *TEMAS narrative therapy with Hispanic women with at-risk children.* Poster presented at the 107th Convention of the American Psychological Association, Boston.

Bracero, W., Sesin, M., Hernandez, P., Ranson, M., & Hernandez, T. (2000, August). *TEMAS therapy: TEMAS narratives as cultural discourse and therapeutic metaphors.* Symposium presented at the 108th Convention of the American Psychological Association, Washington, DC.

Bruner, J. (1986). *Actual minds, possible worlds.* Cambridge, MA: Harvard University Press.

Canino, I. A., Gould, M. S., Prupis, M. A., & Shafer, D. (1986). A comparison of symptoms and diagnoses in Hispanic and Black children in an outpatient mental health clinic. *Journal of American Academy of Child Psychiatry, 25,* 254–259.

Cardalda, E., Orobitig, D., Gonzalez, M., Fields, C., Costantino, G., & Malgady, R. G. (2000, August). *Racial description in TEMAS narratives by Puerto Rican children.* Poster presented at the 108th Convention of the American Psychological Association, Washington, DC.

Cardalda, E., Quintero, J., Costantino, G., & Malgady, R. (1999a, August). *The development of achievement motivation among Hispanic students.* Poster presented at the 107th Convention of the American Psychological Association, Boston.

Cardalda, E., Santiago-Negron, S., Costantino, G., & Malgady, R. (1999b, July). *Cross-cultural standardization of TEMAS with Puerto Rican children.* Paper presented as part of symposium: Psychological tests in cross-cultural perspective, S. L. Nielsen, (Chair), XXVII International Congress of Psychology, Stockholm, Sweden.

Cardalda, E., Sayers, S., & Machado, W. (2001, August). *Clinical utility of TEMAS with sexually abused children in Puerto Rico.* Paper presented as part of the poster session: Cross-cultural validation of TEMAS: A multicultural projective–narrative test at the 109th Convention of the American Psychological Association, San Francisco.

Coatsworth, J. D., Szapocznik, J., Kurtines, W., & Santisteban, D. A. (1997). Culturally competent psychosocial intervention with antisocial problem behavior in Hispanic youths. In D. M. Stoff, J. Breiling, & J. Maser (Eds.), *Handbook of antisocial behavior* (pp. 395–404). New York: Wiley.

Conners, C. K. (1989). *Manual for Conners Rating Scales.* North Tonawanda, NY: Multi-Health Systems.

Costantino, G. (1987). *TEMAS (Tell-Me-a-Story) test: Stimulus cards*. Los Angeles: Western Psychological Services.

Costantino, G. (2002) *Evidence-based mental health treatment and services for youths affected by September 11 terrorist attacks*. Brooklyn, NY: Lutheran Medical Center, Sunset Park Mental Health Center.

Costantino, G., Guajardo, J., Hernandez, T., Borges, M., Perez, M., Meucci, C., et al. (2004, June). *TEMAS narrative therapy v. Cognitive/behavior therapy for children affected by September 11 terrorist attacks*. Paper presented at the 2nd annual Mental Health Conference on Latino Health Disparities, Carlos Albizu University, San Juan, Puerto Rico.

Costantino, G., & Malgady, R. (1983). Verbal fluency of Hispanic, black and white children on TAT and TEMAS, a new thematic apperception test. *Hispanic Journal of Behavioral Sciences, 5*, 199–206.

Costantino, G., & Malgady, R. (1994). Storytelling-through-pictures: Culturally sensitive psychotherapy for Hispanic children and adolescents. *Journal of Clinical Child Psychology, 23*, 13–20.

Costantino, G., & Malgady, R. (1996). Culturally sensitive treatment: Cuento and hero/heroine modeling therapies for Hispanic children and adolescents. In P. Jensen & E. Hibbs (Eds.), *Psychosocial treatments for child and adolescent disorders: Empirically based strategies for clinical practice* (pp. 639–697). Washington, DC: American Psychological Association.

Costantino, G., & Malgady, R. (2001, July). *Multicultural and cross-cultural validation of TEMAS, a multicultural projective–narrative test*. Presentation as part of the symposium Multicultural and Cross-cultural Validation of TEMAS, (R. Dana, Chair), VIIth European Congress of Psychology, London.

Costantino, G., Malgady, R., Casullo, M. M., & Castillo, A. (1991). Cross-cultural standardization of TEMAS in three Hispanic subcultures. *Hispanic Journal of Behavioral Sciences, 13*, 48–62.

Costantino, G., Malgady, R. G., & Rogler, L. H. (1986). Cuento therapy: A culturally sensitive modality for Puerto Rican children. *Journal of Consulting and Clinical Psychology, 54*, 739–746.

Costantino, G., Malgady, R. G., & Rogler, L. H. (1988). *Technical manual: The TEMAS test*. Los Angeles: Western Psychological Services.

Costantino, G., Malgady, R. G., Stiles, J., Borges, M., Costantino, E., Hernandez, A., et al. (2003, August). *TEMAS narrative for Latino children affected by WTC disaster*. Poster session presented at the 111th Convention of the American Psychological Association, Toronto, Canada.

Costantino, G., Malgady, R., & Vazquez, C. (1981). A comparison of the Murray TAT and a new thematic apperception test for urban Hispanic children. *Hispanic Journal of Behavioral Sciences, 3*, 291–300.

Dana, R. (1996). Culturally competent assessment practice in the United States. *Journal of Personality Assessment, 66*, 472–487.

Dana, R. (2003, August). *Bridging the gap between standard and multicultural assessment practice: An agenda for research and training*. Address presented at the

111th Convention of the American Psychological Association, Toronto, Canada.

Derogatis, L. R. (1977). *SCL–90-R, administration, scoring, and procedures manual-I for the (revised) version*. Johns Hopkins University School of Medicine

Derogatis, L. R. (1983). Misuse of the Symptom Checklist 90. *Archives of General Psychiatry, 40,* 1152–1160.

Dropout rates higher for Hispanic students than other groups, study says. (2003, June 13). *Knight Ridder Tribune News,* pp. 1–3.

Emslie, G. J., Weinberg, W. A., Rush, A. J., Adams, R. M., & Rentelmann, J. W. (1990). Depressive symptoms by self-report in adolescence: Phase 1 of the development of a questionnaire for depression by self-report. *Journal of Child Neurology, 5,* 114–121.

Fisher, R. I. (1974). A study of non-intellectual attributes of children in a first grade bilingual–bicultural program. *Journal of Educational Research, 67,* 323–328.

Garrison, C., Jackson, K., Marsteller, F., McKeon, R., & Addy, C. (1990). A longitudinal study of depressive symptomatology in young adolescents. *Journal of the American Academy of Child Adolescent Psychiatry, 29,* 581–585.

Gomez-Dupertuis, G., & Ropaldo, M. A. (2001, August). *Differences and similarities between Argentine and American children on the TEMAS.* Presentation as part of the symposium Multicultural and Cross-cultural Validation of TEMAS (R. Dana, Chair), VIIth European Congress of Psychology, London.

Hodges, K. (1986). *Child assessment schedule (CAS) Modified for DSM–III–R.* Ypsilanti: Eastern Michigan University, Department of Psychology.

Howard, G. S. (1991). Culture tales: A narrative approach to thinking, cross-cultural psychology, and psychotherapy. *American Psychologist, 46,* 187–197.

Inclan, V., & Hernandez, M. (1992). Cross cultural perspectives and codependence: The case of poor Hispanics. *American Journal of Orthopsychiatry, 62,* 245–254.

Kazdin, A. E., & Weisz, J. R. (1998). Identifying and developing empirically supported child and adolescent treatment. *Journal of Consulting and Clinical Psychology, 66,* 19–36.

Kazdin, A. E., & Weisz, J. R. (2003). *Evidence-based psychotherapies for children and adolescents.* New York: Guilford Press.

Kessler, R. C., McGonagle, K. A., Zhao, S., & Nelson, C. B., (1994). Lifetime and 12-month prevalence of *DSM–III–R* psychiatric disorders in the United States: Results from the National Comorbity Study. *Archives of General Psychiatry, 51,* 8–19.

Langer, T., Gersfen, J., & Eisenberg, J. (1974). Approaches to measurement and definition in the epidemiology of behavior disorders: Ethnic background and child behavior. *Journal of Health Services, 4,* 483–501.

Mair, M. (1989). *Between psychology and psychotherapy.* London: Routledge.

Malgady, R. G., Rogler, L. H., & Costantino, G. (1987). Ethnocultural and linguistic bias in mental health evaluations of Hispanics. *American Psychologist, 42,* 228–234.

Malgady, R. G., Rogler, L. H., & Costantino, G. (1990a). Hero/heroine modeling for Puerto Rican adolescents: A preventive mental health intervention. *Journal of Consulting and Clinical Psychology, 58*, 469–474.

Malgady, R. G., Rogler, L. H., & Costantino, G. (1990b). Culturally sensitive psychotherapy for Puerto Rican children and adolescents: A program of treatment outcome research. *Journal of Consulting and Clinical Psychology, 58*, 704–712.

Malgady, R. G., & Costantino, G. (1999). Ethnicity and culture: Hispanic youth. In W. K. Silverman & T. H. Ollendik (Eds.), *Development issues in the clinical treatment of children* (pp. 231–250). Boston: Allyn and Bacon.

Malgady, R. G., & Costantino, G. (2003). Narrative therapy for Hispanic children and adolescents. In A. E. Kazdin & J. R. Weisz (Eds.), *Evidence-based psychotherapies for children and adolescents* (pp. 425–435). New York: Guilford Press.

Mann, E. S., & Salvo, J. J. (1985). *Characteristics of new Hispanic immigrants to New York City: A comparison of Puerto Rican and non-Puerto Rican Hispanics* (Research bulletin). New York: Hispanic Research Center, Fordham University.

Martinez, O. (1987). Minority youth and crime. *Crime and Delinquency, 33*, 325–328.

Moscicki, E. K., Rae, D. S., Reiger, D. A., & Locke, B. Z. (1987). The Hispanic health and nutrition examination survey: Depression among Mexican Americans, Cuban Americans, and Puerto Ricans. In M. Gaviria & J. D. Arana (Eds.), *Health and behavior: Research agenda for Hispanics* (pp. 145–159). Chicago: University of Illinois.

National Puerto Rican Forum. (1990). *The next step toward equality*. New York: Author.

New census shows Hispanics are even with blacks in U.S. (2001, March 8). *The New York Times*, pp. 1, A21.

New York City Board of Education, Office of Resources, Education, and Assessment. (1990). *The cohort report: Four-year results for class of 1990. The 1989–90 annual dropout rate*. New York: Author.

New York City Department of City Planning. (1994). *City planning report*. New York: Author.

New York State Office of Mental Health. (1994). *Primary diagnoses of children in CDF database*. Albany, NY: Author.

Padilla, A. M., Ruiz, R. A., & Alvarez, R. (1975). Community mental health services for the Spanish-speaking surnamed population. *American Psychologist, 30*, 892–905.

Pumariega, A., Atkins, L., Montgomery, L., Kowalski, T., & Culley, D. (1995). *Psychopathology and symptomatology in incarcerated versus hospitalized youth. A system of care for children's mental health: Expanding the research base*. Proceedings of the 8th Annual Mental Health Conference at the Florida Mental Health Institute, Tampa, FL.

Pumariega, A. J., Swanson, J. W., Holzer, C. E., Linskey, A. O., & Quintero-Salinas, R. (1992). Cultural context and substance abuse in Hispanic adolescents. *Journal of Child and Family Studies, 1*, 75–92.

Radloff, L. S. (1977). The CES–D scale: A self-report depression scale for research in the general population. *Applied Psychological Measurement, 1*, 385–401.

Roberts, R. E. (1992). Manifestation of depressive symptoms among adolescents. *The Journal of Nervous and Mental Diseases, 180*, 627–633.

Rogler, L. H., Cooney, R., Costantino, G., Early, B., Grossman, B., Gurak, D., et al. (1983). *A conceptual framework for mental health research on Hispanic populations* (Monograph No. 10). New York: Hispanic Research Center, Fordham University.

Rogler H. R., Malgady, R. G., Costantino, G., & Blumenthal, R. (1987). What does culturally sensitive mental health services mean? The case of Hispanics. *American Psychologist, 42*, 565–570.

Saravanabhavan, R. C., & Walter, S. (1999). Prevalence of disabling conditions among African-American children and youth. *Journal of National Medical Association, 91*, 265–272.

Sardi, G. M. (2000). *Aggressivita e funzioni cognitive nella risoluzione dei conflitti nei bambini fra i 7 e gli 8 anni* [Aggression and cognitive functions in the resolution of conflict in children aged 7 to 8]. Unpublished dissertation, Universita degli Studi di Roma, "La Sapienza," Rome, Italy.

Sardi, G. M., & Summo, B. (2001, August). *Relationship between aggression, cognition and moral judgment in problem solving among Italian 7- and 8-year-old children.* Paper presented as part of the Poster session: Cross-cultural validation of TEMAS: A multicultural Projective–Narrative test, at the 109th Convention of the American Psychological Association, San Francisco.

Scheffé, H. (1959). *The analysis of variance.* New York: Wiley.

Spielberger, C. D., Edwards, C. D., Lushene, R. E., Montuori, J., & Platzek, D. (1973). *Preliminary test manual for State-Trait Anxiety Inventory for Children (STAIC).* Palo Alto, CA: Consulting Psychologist Press.

Stoep, A., Evens, C., & Taub, J. (1997). Risk juvenile justice system referral minority children among in a public mental health system. *The Journal of Behavioral Health Services and Research, 24*, 428–440.

Sue, D. W. (1981). *Counseling the culturally different: Theory and practice.* New York: Wiley.

Sue, S. (1988). Psychotherapeutic services for ethnic minorities. *American Psychologist, 43*, 301–308.

Sue, S., Fujino, D. C., Hu, L. T., & Zane, N. W. S. (1991). Community mental health services for ethnic minority groups: A test of the cultural responsiveness hypothesis. *Journal of Consulting and Clinical Psychology, 59*, 533–540.

Teplin, L., Abram, K., McClelland, G., Dulcan, M., & Mericle, A. (2002). Psychiatric disorders in youth in juvenile detention. *Archives of General Psychiatry, 59*, 1133–1144.

U.S. Bureau of the Census. (1991). *1990 Census of Population and Housing* (Summary Type File 1A, Data User Services Division), Washington, DC: Author.

U.S. Bureau of the Census. (2000). *Current population reports, population characteristics.* Washington, DC: Author.

U.S. Department of Health and Human Services. (2001). *Culture, race and ethnicity. A supplement to mental health: A report of the Surgeon General.* Washington, DC: Author.

Vega, W. A., Zimmerman, R. S., Warheit, G. J., Apospori, E., & Gil, A. G. (1993). Risk factors for early adolescent drug use in four ethnic and racial groups. *American Journal of Public Health, 83,* 185–189.

Walton, J. R., Nuttall, R. L., & Vazquez-Nuttall, E. (1997). The impact of war on the mental health of children: A Salvadorian study. *Child Abuse and Neglect, 21,* 737–749.

Walton, J. R., Nuttall, R. L., & Vazquez-Nuttall, E. (1998, August). Effects of war on children's motivation reflected in TEMAS stories. In G. Costantino (Chair), *Multicultural/cross-cultural motivation as assessed by TAT & TEMAS.* Symposium presented at the 106th Convention of the American Psychological Association, San Francisco.

White, M., & Epston, D. (1999). *Narrative means to therapeutic ends.* New York: Norton.

28

TRAUMA-FOCUSED COGNITIVE–BEHAVIORAL THERAPY FOR SEXUALLY ABUSED CHILDREN

JUDITH A. COHEN, ESTHER DEBLINGER,
AND ANTHONY P. MANNARINO

BACKGROUND

Sexual abuse is a common experience for children and adolescents (Sedlak & Broadhurst, 1996). Studies have indicated that up to 25% of girls and 15% of boys in the United States experience some form of sexual abuse before age 18 (Finkelhor, 1998). Sexual abuse occurs across educational, socioeconomic, racial, and ethnic groups (Alter-Reid, Gibbs, Lachenmeyer, Sigal, & Massoth, 1986; Wyatt & Peters, 1986). Many children who have experienced such abuse develop behavioral or emotional symptoms, including posttraumatic stress disorder (PTSD; Deblinger, McLeer, Atkins, Ralph, & Foa, 1989; McLeer, Deblinger, Henry, & Orvashel, 1992); other anxiety symptoms (Mannarino, Cohen, & Gregor, 1989); depressive symptoms (Wozencroft, Wagner, & Pelligrin, 1991); and various behavioral problems, including sexually inappropriate behaviors (Einbender & Friedrich, 1989; Friedrich et al., 1992).

PTSD was first included in the official psychiatric nomenclature in the third edition of the *Diagnostic and Statistical Manual of Mental Disorders* (*DSM–III*; American Psychiatric Association, 1980). The diagnosis of this disorder requires exposure to a serious stressor and a specified number of symptoms in each of three clusters: reexperiencing, avoidance and numbing, and hyperarousal (American Psychiatric Association, 2000). Because the diagnosis of PTSD in childhood is particularly complex (American Academy of Child and Adolescent Psychiatry, 1998), and possibly because children are reticent to disclose or discuss sexual abuse, this disorder may be underdiagnosed in abused children and may only be identified when the child has developed significant comorbid symptoms, such as substance abuse, suicidality, or violence toward others (Steiner, Garcia, & Matthews, 1997). PTSD in children is frequently accompanied by comorbid psychiatric conditions such as depression (American Academy of Child and Adolescent Psychiatry, 1998), and recent research suggests that once PTSD symptoms are present in children or adolescents, they may be long-standing, chronic, and resistant to change (Rothbaum & Foa, 1993; Kilpatrick, Saunders, & Veronen, 1987; American Academy of Child and Adolescent Psychiatry, 1998). Several studies that have examined the incidence of PTSD among children who have experienced sexual abuse have found that although many do not meet full *DSM–IV* diagnostic criteria for this disorder, the majority have some PTSD symptoms that deleteriously affect daily functioning (McLeer, Callaghan, Henry, & Wallen, 1994). Recent practice guidelines for childhood PTSD have suggested that such children should be offered trauma-focused treatment, even in the absence of full-blown PTSD symptomatology (American Academy of Child and Adolescent Psychiatry, 1998; Cohen, Berliner, & March, 2000). As previously noted, many sexually abused children may not have significant PTSD but may exhibit significant depressive, anxiety-related, or behavioral symptoms. Treatment approaches for symptomatic sexually abused children must therefore address a wide range of potential psychiatric symptoms rather than targeting a single psychiatric disorder.

Cognitive–behavioral treatment approaches (CBT) have been used for several years to treat sexually abused adults with PTSD. For example, Foa, Rothbaum, Riggs, and Murdock (1991); Frank, Anderson, Stuart, Dancu, Hughes, and Wert (1988); and Resick and Schnicke (1992) all successfully used techniques such as exposure and cognitive restructuring in treating adult rape victims. Some of the early descriptive treatments for sexually abused children included cognitive and behavioral components, although these interventions were not identified as CBT (e.g., Sgroi, 1982; MacFarland, Waterman, Conerly, Damon, Durfee, & Long, 1986). In the early 1990s, researchers began to empirically evaluate outcomes in the treatment of children exposed to sexual abuse. Most of these studies examined the efficacy of trauma-focused CBT (TF-CBT), and thus a number of treatment manuals for this form of CBT were developed and published (e.g., Cohen & Mannarino, 1993; Deblinger & Heflin, 1996; Cohen, Mannarino, & Deblinger, 2002). These interventions have been increasingly used and empirically evaluated since the mid-1990s.

DESCRIPTION OF PROGRAMS

The Center for Traumatic Stress in Children and Adolescents (CTSCA) at Allegheny General Hospital was established in February 1994 as a clinical research specialty program to address the needs of children and youths experiencing traumatic life events. Its founders had previously directed a specialty program for sexually abused children at the University of Pittsburgh Medical Center, Western Psychiatric Institute and Clinic and were given the opportunity to significantly expand the scope of the program through this relocation. Currently CTSCA is codirected by a clinical child psychologist and a child and adolescent psychiatrist and is staffed by PhD-level psychologists, MSW-level clinical social workers, research personnel, and administrative support staff. Additionally, CTSCA provides clinical training and supervision to trainees, including child and adolescent psychiatry fellows, psychology interns, and clinical social work students. The program is an integral part of the Department of Psychiatry at Allegheny General Hospital and is affiliated with the Drexel University College of Medicine. Since its inception, CTSCA has received federally funded research grants to evaluate comparative treatment outcomes for sexually abused and other traumatized children.

The most recent research involved a multisite study conducted in collaboration with the Center for Children's Support (CCS) at the University of Medicine and Dentistry of New Jersey School of Osteopathic Medicine. Results are described below. The codirectors of CCS are a pediatrician and a clinical psychologist who have worked together to create a state-of-the-art multidisciplinary program serving the medical and mental health needs of children who have suffered abuse. CCS is a state-designated regional child abuse diagnostic and treatment center for southern New Jersey. In addition to serving as the primary referral source for suspected victims of child abuse in this region, CCS is committed to complementing its clinical services with related research, training, expert testimony, and community education efforts. Together, these two programs have conducted a substantial proportion of the empirical efficacy research on TF-CBT in the treatment of sexually abused children. The following description summarizes the methods from four research projects conducted by these two programs.

METHOD

Procedures

Because child sexual abuse is a criminal act and requires the involvement of Child Protective Services (CPS), screening procedures have included either a required independent forensic evaluation or abuse substantiation by CPS before a subject may enter the research protocols. The forensic evaluations have been conducted by specialized forensic programs in our respective communities. When an independent evaluation has failed to confirm that sexual abuse occurred, the child in question has not been included in the research program. Each of the studies described here required a threshold number of psychiatric symptoms for inclusion—for example, at least five PTSD symptoms, including at least one in each of the three PTSD symptom clusters (reexperiencing, avoidance, and hyperarousal). These symptoms were evaluated through the use of standardized instruments described in subsequent sections. In the three studies with children ages 8 to 14, subjects who met study inclusionary criteria were given verbal and written explanations of the study and they and their parents or legal guardians signed informed assents and consents to participate in the research. In the study of preschool children (ages 3–7), the parents or legal guardians received verbal and written explanations of the study and signed informed consents.

Assessments

The four research projects have used a variety of assessment instruments and have included both outcome measures and measures of potential mediating factors. The overall strategy for assessment at baseline has been to evaluate child, parent, and family functioning in a variety of domains thought to be affected by the child's sexual abuse. Consumer satisfaction with the treatment provided has also been assessed in these studies, typically at the end of the active treatment stage of the study. All four studies have included 6- and 12-month posttreatment follow-up assessments in addition to the pretreatment and posttreatment evaluations.

Study No. 1

Sixty-seven sexually abused children and their nonoffending parents completed treatment. The children's mean age was 4.68 years (range: 2 years, 11 months to 7 years, 1 month); 58% were female and 42% were male. Self-identified racial composition was 54% Caucasian, 42% African American, and 4% were of other ethnicity; mean socioeconomic status was Hollingshead IV. This study compared TF-CBT with Nondirective Supportive

Therapy (NST; Cohen & Mannarino, 1996a). Outcome measures included the Child Behavior Checklist (CBCL; Achenbach & Edelbrock, 1983); the Child Sexual Behavior Inventory (CSBI; Friedrich et al., 1992); and the Weekly Behavior Report (WBR; Cohen & Mannarino, 1996b), a measure of sexual abuse–related PTSD symptoms in preschoolers. Measures of potential mediating factors included the Beck Depression Inventory (BDI; with regard to the parent's depressive symptoms; Beck & Steer, 1993), the Family Adaptability and Cohesion Evaluation Scale (FACES–III; Olson, Portner, & Lavee, 1985), the Parent Emotion Reaction Questionnaire (PERQ) and the Parent Support Questionnaire (PSQ; Mannarino & Cohen, 1996; Cohen & Mannarino, 1996c), as well as two child developmental evaluation instruments. Parents also completed a Client Satisfaction Questionnaire (CSQ) at the end of treatment.

Study No. 2

Eighty-two sexually abused children between the ages of 8 and 15 and their nonoffending parents participated; 68% were female and 32% were male. Self-reported racial identity was 60% Caucasian, 37% African American, 2% Biracial, and 1% Hispanic. This study compared TF-CBT with NS (Cohen & Mannarino, 1998): Outcome measures included the Children's Depression Inventory (CDI; Kovacs, 1985); the CBCL, the CSBI, the Trauma Symptom Checklist for Children (TSC–C; Briere, 1995), and the State–Trait Anxiety Inventory for Children (STAIC; Spielberger, 1973). Measures of mediating factors included the Children's Attributions and Perceptions Scale (CAPS; Mannarino, Cohen, & Berman, 1994), which measures sexual abuse–related attributions and perceptions; FACES–III; the PERQ; and the PSQ.

Study No. 3

Ninety children between the ages of 7 and 13 and their nonoffending parents participated; 83% were female and 17% were male; 72% were Caucasian, 20% were African American, 6% were Hispanic, and 2% were of other ethnicity. This study compared TF-CBT (child only) with TF-CBT (parent only) with TF-CBT (child + parent) with Standard Community Care (Deblinger, Lippman, & Steer, 1996). Assessment instruments included the K-SADS–Epidemiologic; the STAIC, CDI, CBCL, and Parenting Practices Questionnaire (PPQ; Strayhorn & Weidman, 1988). Measures of mediating factors included the BDI and the Children's Report of Parenting Behavior Inventory (CRPBI; Kolko & Kazdin, 1980).

Study No. 4

Two hundred twenty-nine children between the ages of 8 and 14 and their nonoffending parents participated. This study was conducted jointly at both sites (CTSCA and CCS). Of 203 completers, 79% were female and 21% were male; 60% were Caucasian, 28% were African American, 4% were Hispanic, 7% were Biracial, and 1% were of other ethnicity. This was a multiply traumatized sample: 58% of these children also experienced domestic violence; 70% had experienced the sudden death of loved ones; 26% were victims of physical abuse; 37% had witnessed or been involved in a serious accident; 17% were victims or witnesses to community violence; 14% had experienced a fire or natural disaster; and 25% had experienced other PTSD-level traumatic events. These children experienced a mean of 3.6 different *types* of traumatic events. This study compared TF-CBT with Child Centered Therapy (CCT). Assessment instruments included the K-SADS–PL, CDI, STAIC, CAPS, CBCL, CSBI, BDI (for parental depressive symptoms), PERQ, PSQ, and PPQ.

TREATMENT PROCEDURES

The TF-CBT treatment protocols for the four studies have been quite similar but are not identical. In particular, the preschool study protocol was designed to be developmentally appropriate for that age group. A detailed description of that treatment model has been described elsewhere (Cohen & Mannarino, 1993). The treatment procedures for the other three studies are described below. Specific TF-CBT treatment manuals for each study are available from the authors.

In the three treatment studies that involved children ages 8 to 14, 12 parallel individual sessions were provided to the children and their parents or primary caretakers. In each session the children and parents addressed similar issues, with the exception of behavior management training, which was provided only to parents. The behavior management component was designed to assist parents in strengthening children's positive behaviors and minimize abuse-related behavioral difficulties. Thus, effective parenting practices based on cognitive–behavioral principles are taught and modeled by the therapist and practiced throughout treatment. The other major components in the TF-CBT protocol include identification of feelings, stress management, cognitive coping, gradual exposure, cognitive processing, and psychoeducation (including safety education). These were provided in the following manner.

Session 1: Identification of Feelings

Children were encouraged to identify as many feelings as possible and to discuss situations in which they experienced these feelings. The therapist then presented a variety of scenarios and asked the children to identify feelings they might have in such a situation. This request encouraged the children to accurately describe feelings and to believe that both positive, negative, and ambivalent feelings are acceptable. Children were asked to briefly describe their own sexual abuse experience and to identify feelings they experienced both during the abuse and while describing it during the treatment session. In the parallel parent sessions, parents were asked to describe what they knew about the child's abuse experience and to describe their own feelings about this, both at the time they first found out about it and when discussing it in the treatment session. Parenting skills were also introduced in this session, with an emphasis on providing positive parental attention and interactions and active ignoring of negative behaviors.

Session 2: Stress Management

Children were encouraged to learn and practice relaxation strategies tailored to their individual needs. Standard relaxation techniques such as focused breathing, progressive muscle relaxation, and thought interruption were utilized. Children were additionally encouraged to identify personal methods for relaxing such as listening to music, reading, sports, and so on. Parents were taught the above relaxation techniques and encouraged to develop personalized stress management strategies and to practice these skills with their children at home.

Session 3: Cognitive Processing

Children were introduced to the cognitive triangle of thought, feelings, and behaviors and the ways in which these three components are interrelated. Children were presented with a variety of scenarios in which they were asked to come up with alternative thoughts that they could have about the situation. Children were asked in each situation to explore the way their feelings and behaviors might change in response to changing their thoughts about a given scenario. In the parallel parent sessions, parents were introduced to the cognitive triangle and encouraged to examine the ways in which changing their thoughts in a given situation may lead to a change in feelings and behaviors. Parents' thoughts and feelings about their children's sexual abuse were explored in this manner, and cognitive distortions were identified and corrected. Further education about appropriate parenting was provided (e.g., how to effectively give the child time out), and interventions for any specific behavioral problems being displayed by the children were addressed and practiced with their parents.

Sessions 4 to 6: Gradual Exposure

In these sessions, children were introduced to psychoeducational material about child sexual abuse in general (e.g., what sexual abuse is, how many children are sexually abused, what kind of children are sexually abused, why perpetrators sexually abuse children, and common reactions to being sexually abused). The children read a book that was written and subsequently published by a child who herself had experienced sexual abuse. Children were then encouraged to write their own books about their own sexual abuse experience. Initially, the focus was on encouraging children to include the details of what occurred during the sexually abusive episode (children who experienced multiple episodes were encouraged to select one episode to start with and then include others as the book proceeded). In subsequent readings of the book in therapy sessions, children were encouraged to include more details about their feelings and thoughts during the abuse. With the children's permission, the children's books were shared with their parents in the parallel parent sessions. In other words, the therapist read and showed the children's books to their parents and discussed the parents' reaction to these books with them and their emotional and cognitive reactions to the children's writings. Parents were introduced to the need to educate children about healthy sexuality (because the sexual abuse had exposed them to unhealthy sexuality), and parents were provided with a variety of relevant psychoeducational materials to examine over the next week so that they might decide how much and what types of information they were comfortable sharing with their children at that point in time.

Session 7: Cognitive Processing of Abuse Experiences

Children's inaccurate and unhelpful thoughts about sexual abuse were identified, examined, and reframed using the cognitive triangle described above. Parents were also encouraged to examine and reframe inaccurate or unhelpful cognitions about their children's abusive experience and their own reactions to this experience.

Sessions 8 to 10: Joint Parent–Child Sessions

In these sessions, the therapist met individually with the children to generate questions about sexual abuse and healthy sexuality for later discussion with the parent in the joint meeting. The therapist then reviewed the children's books with the children again and prepared them to read the book directly to their parents. The therapist then met individually with the parents to determine what aspects of healthy sexuality the parents wanted to discuss with their children. The therapist reviewed with the parents the questions the children had generated for the joint meeting and encouraged the parents to become comfortable in answering these questions with their children present. The therapist then went over the children's books with the parents to prepare for the children's reading the books directly to their parents. Finally, the therapist met with both the children and parents together, and they discussed the children's questions about sexual abuse and healthy sexuality. The children then read their books to their parents, and the parents gave the children appropriate support and praise for doing so.

Sessions 11 and 12: Psychoeducation, Review, and Graduation

The children were presented with a variety of scenarios wherein decisions about the safest course of action were necessary. Problem-solving strategies were used to encourage the children to generate alternative behaviors and to select the best alternative to ensure safety. Information about sexual abuse and healthy sexuality was reviewed, and the children were given the opportunity to discuss their thoughts and feelings about the previous weeks' joint sessions. In the final session, the children's progress in therapy was reviewed and praised. In the parallel parent session, similar safety skills were addressed, with an emphasis on effective parental decision making (e.g., focusing on correcting parental overprotectiveness or overpermissiveness if these were factors in the parent's decision making). The children's and parents' progress in therapy was reviewed and praised. Table 28.1 provides a brief summary of the treatment sessions.

COMPARISON OF TREATMENT CONDITIONS

One of these studies utilized standard community care (SCC) as a comparison treatment condition (Deblinger et al., 1996). The other three studies have used various forms of nondirective supportive therapy (NST) or child-centered therapy (CCT) as the comparison treatment. As used in

TABLE 28.1
Treatment Sessions

Session	Child component	Parent component
1	Feeling identification	Parent skills
2	Stress management	Stress management
3	Cognitive processing	Cognitive processing
4–6	Gradual exposure	Gradual exposure, psychoeducation
7	Cognitive processing	Cognitive processing
	Healthy sexuality	Healthy sexuality
8–10	Joint parent-child exposure/ processing sessions	Joint parent-child exposure/ processing sessions
11	Psychoeducation, safety	Psychoeducation, safety
12	Review, graduation	Review, graduation

the completed studies (Cohen & Mannarino, 1996a, 1998; Cohen, Mannarino, & Knudsen, in press), NST was conceptualized as an active supportive counseling model, in which the collaborative, respectful, and trusting relationship between the therapist and patient or parent was paramount. In the preschool study, the individual sessions consisted of play therapy, in which children could raise issues about the sexual abuse when and in a manner in which they were most comfortable (in contrast to following the protocol schedule for these discussions in TF-CBT). In the study with children from ages 8 to 14, the individual child sessions included the use of expressive art techniques and encouragement of the children to discuss feelings and other issues that were most important to the children at the time of the session. The parent NST treatment in both of these studies consisted of the therapist encouraging the parents to discuss their feelings about whatever issues were most relevant to the parents at that time and assisting the parents in generating responses and solutions to these issues in ways that were most comfortable to the parent. This form of NST was based on the Rogerian therapy model (Rogers, 1957) and was selected in part because nondirective supportive therapies are widely used in treating sexually abused children in the community outside of academic centers (Conte, Fogarty, & Collins, 1991). It was also selected because the betrayal of trust and powerlessness are believed to be central psychological themes related to sexual abuse (Finkelhor, 1987), and the nondirective supportive therapeutic approach may optimally allow the child and parent to reestablish trust and a sense of control through the corrective emotional experience (Rogers, 1957).

In the recently completed multisite study, CCT was used (Cohen, Deblinger, Mannarino, & Steer, 2004). In addition to the NST interventions described above, CCT attempted to more closely resemble supportive child therapies provided in community settings. Specifically, in this CCT model the therapist is permitted to provide limited interpretations of therapeutic material and also prompts the children to focus on the sexual abuse experience at specified times (fourth and eighth sessions) during the course of therapy. Detailed NST manuals used in these studies are available from the authors upon request.

TREATMENT MEASURES

In all four studies, rigorous training and monitoring procedures have been used to ensure fidelity with the assigned treatment models and to minimize all potential sources of bias. Specifically, in the studies that used NST or CCT as a comparison treatment condition, hiring of therapists for the project was predicated on achieving a balance among therapists with regard to therapeutic model affiliation (i.e., equal numbers of therapists were hired who had primary affiliation to TF-CBT and to child-centered supportive treatment models). The studies required all therapists to be rigorously and repeatedly trained in both treatment models and to provide treatment to equal numbers of subjects in each model. Experienced faculty clinicians with an identified affiliation to the respective treatment model being provided offered intensive supervision. Weekly supervisory meetings were held, and supervisors listened to audiotapes of every treatment session to promptly identify and correct any violations of the assigned treatment protocol. In addition, 25% of the treatment audiotapes were randomly selected for blind, independent rating of adherence to the assigned treatment model; greater than 90% adherence was required for the subject to be included in the data analyses. (In the multisite study recently completed, content analyses are also being conducted on rated audiotapes to evaluate process variables.)

Clinical Vignette

After participating in a personal safety educational program in school, the patient, Dana, a 10-year-old female, disclosed episodes of sexual abuse perpetrated by her stepfather to her school guidance counselor. Dana reported that when her mother was hospitalized after giving birth prematurely to twins, her stepfather began inviting her to sleep in his bed and started touching and kissing her in her "private places." The guidance counselor reported the allegations, and the local child protection agency conducted a joint investigation with the county Prosecutor's Office. Although Dana's mother, Mrs. W., was stunned by the allegations and remained in a state of disbelief throughout the course of the investigation, she showed concern and support for her daughter after the allegations were substantiated and the stepfather was arrested. Mrs. W. was initially reluctant to bring her daughter to therapy because she was not working at the time of her husband's arrest and was overwhelmed by the parenting and financial demands that she would need to meet on her own. She did, however, agree to accompany her child to therapy after she, Dana, and her brothers temporarily moved in with Mrs. W.'s mother for assistance and support.

After completing a comprehensive assessment that included many of the standardized measures described in this chapter, the therapist presented the assessment findings and a proposed treatment plan to Dana and her mother. In the initial individual session with Mrs. W., the therapist explained that although Dana showed many strengths, such as maintaining good grades, establishing friendships in her new school, and exhibiting cooperative, prosocial behavior, Dana acknowledged numerous symptoms of PTSD and depression. Mrs. W. was particularly upset to learn of the severity of Dana's symptoms and feared that her initial disbelief may have contributed to Dana's anxious and depressed feelings. The therapist helped

Mrs. W. understand that both her and her daughter's emotional reactions to the sexual abuse were not unusual. Given the love and trust Mrs. W. felt for her husband, her initial inability to believe the allegations was not surprising. The therapist further acknowledged the distress that Mrs. W. had reported on her measures and encouraged her to elaborate on her feelings and reactions to the discovery that her husband had sexually abused her daughter. As Dana's mother tearfully expressed her thoughts and feelings, the therapist listened carefully for erroneous beliefs and dysfunctional thoughts that might underlie Mrs. W.'s fears and distress. Mrs. W. also indicated that she knew very little about what actually happened and felt that this lack of knowledge was one of the reasons she found it so hard to imagine that her mild-mannered, hard-working husband sexually abused her daughter. After listening and empathizing with Mrs. W.'s feelings and concerns, the therapist provided an overview of the treatment approach. The therapist explained that sessions would include 45 minutes with Mom and 45 minutes with Dana. Although they would be working on very similar issues, the time spent alone with Mom would allow the therapist to help Mrs. W. cope with her own emotional distress, thereby helping her to serve as an effective coping model for her daughter. This attention to Mrs. W.'s state of mind would be important because, as recent research indicates, support from a loving parent may be the most important factor influencing a child's recovery from the experience of sexual abuse.

Dana's initial therapy session provided an opportunity for the therapist to assess Dana's general ability to communicate about positive subjects such as friends, sports, and hobbies. Dana was easily engaged in discussion about favorite activities, but she became sullen and highly avoidant when the issue of sexual abuse was raised. She insisted that talking about it would only make her feel bad and might upset her mother. The therapist reassured Dana that she would not require her to talk about the sexual abuse but that educating Dana and her mom about child sexual abuse was important. She further indicated that although talking about the sexual abuse might be difficult now, therapy would help both Dana and her mom to cope with those upsetting feelings more effectively, and eventually they would both find it easier to talk about things. Still, Dana insisted that she would never talk to her mom about what happened because she feared her mother would become angry.

As the sessions proceeded, both Dana and her mother learned to use emotional expression skills and began effectively using the educational information to dispute some of their dysfunctional thoughts. Mrs. W., for example, was surprised to learn that most offenders were not dirty old men or strangers lurking in dark alleys but individuals who could be quite functional in some areas of their lives (e.g., work) and were often charming and engaging with children. Mrs. W. found it particularly helpful to remind herself that predicting her husband's behavior was impossible and that even the therapist could not identify a child molester by appearance or any particular behavioral profile.

With time, Dana became increasingly able to talk not only about child sexual abuse in the abstract but about her own personal experience of abuse. She was particularly enthusiastic about creating a book about her experience of sexual abuse that might help other children someday. During the course of one gradual exposure exercise, Dana reported that the very first time her stepfather sexually abused her, she had asked to sleep in his bed because she was worried about her mother being in the hospital. After that night, she never wanted to sleep in his bed, but night after night he would call her in and she would just do as he said as if she were, in her words, "sleepwalking." During the exposure sessions, Dana described how he would force her to put his penis in her mouth and how scared, helpless, and ashamed she felt. Moreover, she reported thinking that she was responsible because she had asked to go into his bed that very first time. She feared that her mother would be angry with her if she knew this and would conclude that Dana had initiated the abuse by going into her stepfather's bed wearing a frilly nightgown. After the exposure exercises, the therapist helped Dana process some of her thoughts and feelings. For example, the therapist asked Dana if she thought any of her friends wore frilly nightgowns. Dana replied that many of her friends had the same pink Barbie nightgown; in fact, they all wore them at a slumber party together. The therapist then asked if anyone had sexually abused any of the girls at the slumber party. When Dana said no, the therapist asked if Dana had worn that frilly nightgown around any other men. Dana indicated that she wore it all the time when she visited her biological father. After Dana acknowledged that her "real" Dad never touched her in a "not-okay" way, the therapist pointed out that maybe wearing a little girl's frilly nightgown doesn't cause sexual abuse to happen; maybe the sexual abuse happened not because of anything she wore or did but because her stepfather had a problem: He liked touching children in an inappropriate way, even though he knew it was wrong.

With time, Dana began to accept that the sexual abuse was not her fault and showed not only a willingness but an eagerness to share her book about the sexual abuse with her mother. With Dana's permission, the therapist shared the book with Mrs. W. in individual sessions so that she could work through the emotions it elicited and the therapist could prepare her for joint sessions when they would read the book with Dana. The joint parent–child sessions were particularly productive in helping Dana feel reassured that her mother did not blame her and in helping Mrs. W. to fully grasp the extent and impact of the sexual abuse. Mrs. W. also seemed to feel empowered by the active role she played in these sessions, particularly with respect to the practicing of personal-safety skills with her daughter.

By the final session, Dana had showed great improvement with respect to her distress levels (as measured by the PTSD interview and the CDI) and her ability to communicate with her mom. Aside from continuing to express some apprehension about the pending court proceedings, Dana, in fact, no longer met criteria for PTSD and reported no significant depressive symptoms. Dana's mother similarly reported less abuse-related distress (as measured by the PERQ) and a greater ability to be supportive to her daughter (as measured by the PSQ). Mrs. W. was still struggling with difficult financial circumstances, but she seemed much more optimistic about their future as a family and felt good about her role in helping her daughter recover. The therapist congratulated both mother and daughter for their therapy achievements and expressed confidence in their abilities to use the skills they learned to cope with stressful circumstances in the future. Mrs. W. seemed to appreciate the confidence the therapist had in their strength and ability to cope, but she indicated that she would be in touch if and when the criminal case was heard in court. The therapist indicated that she would be happy to offer additional support when the case was heard and would also look forward to hearing good news from them in the future.

OUTCOMES

Study No. 1

Within-group comparisons of pretreatment and posttreatment outcome measures indicated that whereas the NST group experienced significant improvement in the frequency of PTSD symptoms endorsed on the WBR ($p < .05$), the TF-CBT group experienced significant improvement on both the frequency and number of PTSD symptoms on the WBR ($p < .001$) and also demonstrated significant improvement on the CBCL internalizing, externalizing, and behavior problems total broadband factors ($p < .001$) as well as on the CSBI ($p < .001$). No significant pretreatment differences between the two treatment groups were noted on any measures, and pretreatment scores for both groups were in the clinical range on the four broadband CBCL factors. At posttreatment, there were significant between-group differences for the CBCL behavior problems total and internalizing scales on the CSBI and the total WBR score. Although all of the posttreatment CBCL broadband factor means were in the normal range for the TF-CBT group, two remained in the clinical range for the NST group. For means, standard deviations, and statistical tests on specific instruments, the reader is referred to Tables 1 through 3 in the original article (Cohen & Mannarino, 1996a). Repeated measures analyses also revealed significant group × time interactions on two of the four CBCL broad band factors ($p = .005$) (Cohen & Mannarino, 1996a). These differences were sustained at the 1-year follow-up assessment as well (Cohen & Mannarino, 1997). With regard to the hypothesized mediating factors, the strongest predictors of treatment outcome were treatment type and the parent's emotional distress related to the child's sexual abuse, as measured by the PERQ (Cohen & Mannarino, 1996b). At the 1-year follow-up, treatment group and parental support of the child as measured by the PSQ were the strongest predictors of outcome (Cohen & Mannarino, 1998b).

Study No. 2

Repeated measures analyses of treatment completers (20 TF-CBT, 19 NST) at posttreatment demonstrated significant group × time interactions on two measures, the CBCL Social Competence Scale and the CDI, with the TF-CBT group experiencing more improvement over time than the NST group on both instruments (Cohen & Mannarino, 1998a). At 6-month follow-up, treatment completers in the CBT group demonstrated significantly greater improvement in anxiety, depression, sexual problems, and dissociation. At the 12-month follow-up, the TF-CBT group demonstrated significantly greater improvement in PTSD and dissociation (Cohen, Mannarino, & Knudsen, in press). Because the NST group experienced higher rates of removal (for persistent dangerous behaviors) and dropout than the TF-CBT group, an intent-to-treat analysis was performed, using the conservative last-observation-carried-forward (LOCF) method. This analysis demonstrated significant group × time effects in favor of TF-CBT on measures of depression, anxiety, and sexual problems (Cohen, Mannarino, & Knudsen, in press). With regard to hypothesized mediating factors, children's abuse-related attributions and perceptions, as measured by the CAPS, and parental support, as measured by the PSQ, were the strongest predictors of treatment outcome (Cohen & Mannarino, 2000).

Study No. 3

Two-by-two least squares analyses of covariance indicated that in the conditions under which parents received TF-CBT, significantly greater improvement occurred in the children's externalizing behaviors, as measured by the CBCL externalizing scale, and in children's depression, as measured by the CDI; these parents also experienced greater improvement in their parenting skills as measured by the PPQ. Children assigned to the two conditions in which they received TF-CBT experienced significantly greater improvement in PTSD symptoms as measured by the K-SADS–E (Deblinger et al., 1996). (For means, standard deviations, and statistical tests on specific instruments, please refer to Table 1 of the original article.) These differences were sustained over the course of a 2-year follow-up (Deblinger, Steer, & Lippman, 1999a). This study also demonstrated that maternal depression, as measured by the BDI and the children's perception of their mother's parenting style being rejecting rather than accepting (as measured by the CRPBI), contributed to children's level of depression, whereas children's perceptions of maternal use of guilt and anxiety-provoking parenting methods, as measured by the CRPBI, predicted higher levels of child PTSD symptoms and externalized behavior problems (Deblinger, Steer, & Lippman, 1999b).

Study No. 4

Data analyses are completed for the posttreatment assessment and are currently under way for 6- and 12-month follow-ups. Initial data analyses indicate medium-to-large effect sizes in favor of TF-CBT with regard to all three PTSD symptom clusters and remission of PTSD diagnosis. TF-CBT was also superior to CCT in improving children's depression, anxiety, shame, behavior problems, and abuse-related perceptions, and in improving parental depression, emotional distress about the abuse, and positive parenting practices (Cohen, Deblinger, Mannarino, & Steer, 2004).

FUTURE DIRECTIONS

Treatment for Subpopulations of Sexually Abused Children: The Importance of Culture, Gender, and Developmental Factors

As knowledge accumulates about treatment response among sexually abused children in general, researchers must pay greater attention to the impact of culture, ethnicity, gender, and developmental factors on treatment response and the acceptability of different types of treatment. This issue is discussed in greater detail elsewhere (Cohen, Deblinger, Mannarino, & DeArellano, 2001). TF-CBT may need to be adapted for optimal use among cultural subgroups. For example, pilot studies are currently evaluating optimal TF-CBT adaptations for Hispanic and hearing-impaired children.

Out of the Ivory Tower

One of the legitimate concerns about treatment outcome studies with sexually abused children is whether findings are relevant to abused children in real-world settings. This concern arises from the fact that most treatment outcome studies have been conducted in traditional research settings (e.g., universities, medical centers) in which there is a major emphasis on research design and other methodological issues. Of particular importance here are the stringent inclusionary and exclusionary criteria that are typically used for subject populations. For example, in some studies of depressed children, potential subjects who fail to meet a cut-off score on a depression scale would not be included and children with comorbid diagnoses or those with parents with significant psychopathology would be specifically excluded.

In the treatment outcome studies that have been conducted by Deblinger and her colleagues and Cohen and Mannarino at their respective sites, as well as their past and current multisite collaboration, the researchers have made a concerted attempt to include representative samples of sexually abused children. Of course, all of these studies have had subject inclusionary and exclusionary criteria (e.g., normal intelligence, a specific number of PTSD symptoms). However, we have been consistently open to including a diverse array of sexually abused children so that our studies would not be perceived as overly academic. To illustrate, in addition to PTSD symptoms, many of our sexually abused subjects have had comorbid diagnoses, including other anxiety disorders, depression, and behavioral problems such as sexually reactive behaviors; children on stable psychotropic medication regimens have therefore been included in these studies. These comorbidities have sometimes made our treatment protocols more difficult to implement because we have, by clinical necessity, focused on other presenting problems, in addition to PTSD symptoms. In this respect, the sexually abused children in our treatment studies resemble sexually abused children who would be found in the real world.

Additionally, sexually abused children in our studies have been characterized by other features typically found in typical clinical settings. A significant minority of subjects, for example, have resided in foster homes; in some cases, they have experienced multiple home placements. We have also not excluded sexually abused children whose parents have experienced psychiatric problems, most notably depression, anxiety symptoms, and substance abuse. Moreover, our sexually abused subjects and their families have often been involved in legal proceedings, including criminal prosecutions and family court matters. As in other clinical settings, our patient records have occasionally been subpoenaed and our therapists asked to testify in court. Finally, our most recent multisite study documented that participants had experienced multiple trauma besides sexual abuse, with these children reporting a mean of 3.6 different *types* of PTSD-level traumas, as previously described. Thus, these families are representative of those typically seen in community settings, families with multiple problems and traumas.

Because our sexually abused subjects have closely resembled abused children treated in other clinical settings, we believe that our research studies have had real-world implications. Future research involving sexually abused children should continue to expand these broad subject selection procedures and move toward effectiveness studies performed in usual-care settings. Although this practice will invariably result in diagnostically complicated cases that require complex clinical decision making, research findings will be more easily generalized to other populations of sexually abused children.

Therapists' Discomfort With TF-CBT: The Need for Dismantling Studies

Although TF-CBT has been demonstrated to be clinically effective with sexually abused children, some therapists have communicated significant discomfort about using certain TF-CBT procedures—in particular, gradual exposure and cognitive restructuring, both of which encourage children to talk about the abusive experience or at least reprocess it in some way. However, sexually abused children frequently resist efforts to have them talk about the abuse, perhaps as a result of PTSD-related avoidance but also sometimes related to age-appropriate embarrassment or desire for privacy. Parents may also be reluctant to allow their children to undergo therapeutic procedures that are likely to cause some anxiety. Therapists themselves may experience some discomfort with gradual exposure and cognitive restructuring because they are hesitant to expose sexually abused children to additional trauma.

In addition to these clinical concerns, therapists may fear that by directly discussing the sexually abusive experience through techniques such as gradual exposure and cognitive processing, such procedures could have legal implications by potentially contaminating testimony that children may give in court. Therapists may also have personal concerns about being accused of planting false allegations in their young patients, a worry that is not unrealistic given the recent history of litigation in this area.

Thus, for clinical and legal reasons, clinicians may be reticent regarding therapeutic procedures that encourage sexually abused children to describe the abusive experience directly. An important empirical question, therefore, is whether these procedures (i.e., gradual exposure and cognitive processing) are necessary for TF-CBT to be clinically effective. To answer this question, we have recently initiated a dismantling study in which TF-CBT with gradual exposure and cognitive processing will be compared with TF-CBT that does not include these procedures. This study will also examine dosage effects (number of sessions needed for optimal response) and the effect of developmental level on treatment response.

Regardless of the outcome of such studies, they should have important clinical implications for therapists who treat sexually abused children. If it turns out that gradual exposure and cognitive processing are not necessary for a positive therapeutic outcome, then therapists can feel confident that they do not need to have their sexually abused patients undergo procedures that may be emotionally painful or cause transient anxiety. On the other hand, if gradual exposure and cognitive restructuring prove to be essential to the success of TF-CBT, therapists can at least be comforted by the fact that although these procedures may cause some anxiety in the short run, sexually abused children achieve significant benefits in the long run by receiving them. Also, comprehensive findings from dismantling studies may help inform clinicians as to which subgroups of sexually abused children may require gradual exposure and cognitive processing to achieve therapeutic success and which do not.

Fidelity of Treatment

In the studies conducted by Deblinger and her colleagues and Cohen and Mannarino, researchers have emphasized maintaining the fidelity of treatment through such methods as extensive therapist training before the treatment protocol being initiated, ongoing supervision of the therapists throughout the study, review of audiotaped treatment sessions by the principal investigators, and independent ratings of audiotaped sessions by trained observers. In real-world settings, however, therapists who use TF-CBT are unlikely to have access to such extensive training and supervision. The critical question, therefore, is whether such a high level of training and supervision is required for TF-CBT to be implemented successfully. We are currently conducting a study to address this question by comparing the treatment attitudes and efficacy of highly trained therapists with the treatment attitudes and efficacy of therapists who do not have this training but do have access to ongoing consultation and supervision. Such studies will help us to better understand whether TF-CBT can be transported to other clinical settings in which the fidelity of treatment could not be ensured.

Length of Treatment

In the studies by Deblinger and her colleagues and Cohen and Mannarino, treatment typically has comprised 12 sessions. Results from these studies suggest that 12 sessions may be sufficient to achieve symptom reduction. However, the goal of treatment should be return to preabuse functioning rather than simply symptom relief. No studies to date have adequately addressed improvement across broad areas of functioning. Additionally, subgroups of sexually abused children may need more extensive treatment because of the nature of their abuse history, comorbid diagnoses, family problems, and other factors. Also, therapists in other clinical settings may be reluctant to limit treatment to 12 sessions because of the nature of their previous training or other clinical reasons.

In contrast, managed care insurers have been placing severe restrictions on the length of treatment over the past several years. From the perspective of their care managers, 12 sessions may be too long in light of the overarching goal of reducing costs. Future investigations could shed some light on this issue by making length of treatment a significant focus. For example, TF-CBT could be offered in varying dosages. If the shorter length of treatment is not found to be adequate to achieve positive clinical outcomes, these data can be used with managed care companies to argue for longer courses of treatment. If the shorter length of treatment is sufficient, at least for some subgroups of sexually abused children, these data could be disseminated to therapists in other clinical settings to increase their comfort level with fewer sessions and to ultimately serve larger numbers of sexually abused children with limited therapeutic resources. In this case, offering training in ways to effectively conduct TF-CBT with fewer sessions is important if such shorter-term models are to gain widespread acceptance. As previously noted, we have recently begun a study that will evaluate the impact of varying dosages of TF-CBT on children's outcomes.

Findings from empirical studies proposed here would further refine our understanding of the critical elements in TF-CBT, the amount of training and supervision required to implement them successfully, and the appropriate length of treatment for different subgroups of sexually abused children. We hope that this information will encourage more clinicians in real-world settings to use TF-CBT interventions in the treatment of sexually abused children. Longer-term follow-up in treatment outcome studies with this population is also important. Currently, most studies have included a 1-year follow-up, but 2 to 5 years would be ideal. If positive clinical outcomes with TF-CBT can be sustained over these longer follow-up periods, this success would no doubt inspire therapists in other clinical settings to adopt this treatment model.

Testing TF-CBT for Children Traumatized by Events Other Than Sexual Abuse

As noted above, our recent study (Cohen et al., 2004) included a multiply traumatized cohort of sexually abused children and adolescents. We are currently beginning to conduct randomized controlled trials of TF-CBT for children with traumatic grief or domestic violence–related PTSD symptoms. In the future, we hope to compare TF-CBT to commonly used treatments in other populations of traumatized children and adolescents.

REFERENCES

Achenbach, T. M., & Edelbrock, C. S. (1983). *Manual for the Child Behavior Checklist and Revised Child Behavior Profile*. Burlington: University of Vermont, Department of Psychiatry.

Alter-Reid, K., Gibbs, M. S., Lachenmeyer, J. R., Sigal, J., & Massoth, N. A. (1986). Group therapy for women sexually abused as children. *Journal of Interpersonal Violence, 6*, 218–231.

American Academy of Child and Adolescent Psychiatry. (1998). Practice parameters for the diagnoses and treatment of posttraumatic stress disorder. *Journal of the American Academy of Child and Adolescent Psychiatry, 37*, 4S–26S.

American Psychiatric Association. (1980). *Diagnostic and statistical manual* (3rd ed.). Washington, DC: Author.

American Psychiatric Association. (2000). *Diagnostic and statistical manual* (4th ed., rev.). Washington, DC: Author.

Beck, A. T., & Steer, R. A. (1993). *Manual for Beck Depression Inventory*. San Antonio, TX: Psychological Corporation.

Briere, J. (1995). *The trauma symptom checklist for children manual*. Odessa, FL: Psychological Assessment Resources.

Cohen, J. A., Berliner, L., March, J. M. (2000). Treatment of children and adolescents. In E. B. Foa, T. M. Keane, & M. J. Friedman (Eds.), *Effective treatments for PTSD: Practice guidelines from the International Society for Traumatic Stress Studies* (pp. 106–138). New York: Guilford Press.

Cohen, J. A., Deblinger, E., Mannarino, A. P., & DeArellano, M. A. (2001). The importance of culture in treating abused and neglected children: An empirical review. *Child Maltreatment, 6*, 148–157.

Cohen, J. A., Deblinger, E., Mannarino, A. P., & Steer, R. A. (2004). A multi-site, randomized controlled trial for children with sexual abuse–related PTSD symptoms. *Journal of the American Academy of Child and Adolescent Psychiatry, 43*, 393–402.

Cohen, J. A., & Mannarino, A. P. (1993). A treatment model for sexually abused preschoolers. *Journal of Interpersonal Violence, 8*, 115–131.

Cohen, J. A., & Mannarino, A. P. (1996a). A treatment outcome study for sexually abused preschool children: Initial findings. *Journal of the American Academy of Child and Adolescent Psychiatry, 35*, 42–50.

Cohen, J. A., & Mannarino, A. P. (1996b). The weekly behavior report: A parent-report instrument for sexually abused preschoolers. *Child Maltreatment, 1*, 353–360.

Cohen, J. A., & Mannarino, A. P. (1996c). Factors that mediate treatment outcome in sexually abused preschool children. *Journal of the American Academy of Child and Adolescent Psychiatry, 35*, 1402–1410.

Cohen, J. A., & Mannarino, A. P. (1997). A treatment study of sexually abused preschool children: Outcome during one-year follow-up. *Journal of the American Academy of Child and Adolescent Psychiatry, 36*, 1228–1235.

Cohen, J. A., & Mannarino, A. P. (1998a). Interventions for sexually abused children: Initial treatment findings. *Child Maltreatment, 3*, 17–26.

Cohen, J. A., & Mannarino, A. P. (1998b). Factors that mediate treatment outcome of sexually abused preschoolers: Six- and twelve-month follow-ups. *Journal of the American Academy of Child and Adolescent Psychiatry, 37*, 44–51.

Cohen, J. A., & Mannarino, A. P. (2000). Predictors of treatment outcome in sexually abused children. *Child Abuse and Neglect, 24*, 983–994.

Cohen, J. A., Mannarino, A. P., & Deblinger, E. (2002). *Child and parent trauma-focused cognitive–behavioral therapy treatment manual*. Philadelphia: Drexel University College of Medicine.

Cohen, J. A., Mannarino, A. P., & Knudsen, K. (in press). Treating sexually abused children: One-year follow-up of a randomized controlled trial. *Child Abuse and Neglect.*

Conte, J. R., Fogarty, L., & Collins, M. E. (1991). National survey of professional practice in child sexual abuse. *Journal of Family Violence, 6,* 149–166.

Deblinger, E., & Heflin, A. H. (1996). *Cognitive–behavioral interventions for treating sexually abused children.* Thousand Oaks, CA: Sage.

Deblinger, E., Lippmann, J., & Steer, R. (1996). Sexually abused children suffering posttraumatic stress symptoms: Initial treatment outcome findings. *Child Maltreatment, 1,* 310–321.

Deblinger, E., McLeer, S. V., Atkins, M., Ralph, D., & Foa, E. (1989). Posttraumatic stress in sexually abused children: Physically abused and non-abused children. *International Journal of Child Abuse and Neglect, 13,* 403–408.

Deblinger, E., Steer, R. A., & Lippmann, J. (1999a). Maternal factors associated with sexually abused children's psychosocial adjustment. *Child Maltreatment, 4,* 13–20.

Deblinger, E., Steer, R. A., & Lippmann, J. (1999b). Two year follow-up study of CBT for sexually abused children suffering posttraumatic stress symptoms. *Child Abuse and Neglect, 23,* 1371–1378.

Einbender, A., & Friedrich, W. (1989). The psychological functioning and behavior of sexually abused girls. *Journal of Consulting and Clinical Psychology, 57,* 155–157.

Finkelhor, D. (1987). The trauma of child sexual abuse: Two models. *Journal of Interpersonal Violence, 2,* 348–366.

Finkelhor, D. (1998). A comparison of the responses of preadolescents and adolescents in a national victimization study. *Journal of Interpersonal Violence, 13,* 362–382.

Foa, E. B., Rothbaum, D. S., Riggs, B. O., & Murdock, T. (1991). Treatment of PTSD in rape victims: A comparison between cognitive–behavioral procedures and counseling. *Journal of Consulting and Clinical Psychology, 59,* 715–723.

Frank, E., Anderson, B., Stuart, B. D., Dancu, C., Hughes, C., & Wert, D. (1988). Efficacy of cognitive–behavioral therapy and systematic desensitization in the treatment of rape trauma. *Behavior Therapy 19,* 403–420.

Friedrich W. N., Grambsch, P., Damon, L., Hewitt, S. K., Koverola, C., Lang, R., et al. (1992). The Child Sexual Behavior Inventory: Normative and clinical comparisons. *Psychological Assessment, 4,* 303–311.

Kilpatrick, D. G., Saunders, B. E., & Veronen, L. J. (1987). Criminal victimization: Lifetime prevalence, reporting to police, and psychological impact. *Crime and Delinquency, 33,* 479–489.

Kolko, D. J., & Kazdin, A. E. (1980). Match play and firesetting in children: Relationship to parent, marital and family dysfunction. *Journal of Clinical Child Psychology, 19,* 229–238.

Kovacs, M. (1985). The Children's Depression Inventory (CDI). *Psychopharmacology Bulletin, 21,* 995–998.

MacFarland, K., Waterman, J., Conerly, S., Damon, L., Durfee, M., & Long, S. (1986). *Sexual abuse of young children.* New York: Guilford Press.

Mannarino, A. P., & Cohen, J. A. (1996). Family-related variables and psychological symptom formation in sexually abused girls. *Journal of Child Sexual Abuse,* *5*, 105–119.

Mannarino, A. P., Cohen, J. A., & Berman, S. R. (1994). The Children's Attributions and Perceptions Scale: A new measure of sexual abuse–related factors. *Journal of Clinical Child Psychology, 23,* 204–211

Mannarino, A. P., Cohen, J. A., & Gregor, M. (1989). Emotional and behavioral difficulties in sexually abused girls. *Journal of Interpersonal Violence, 4,* 437–451.

McLeer, S. V., Callaghan, M., Henry, D., & Wallen, J. (1994). Psychiatric disorders in sexually abused children. *Journal of the American Academy of Child and Adolescent Psychiatry, 33,* 313–319.

McLeer, S. V., Deblinger, E., Henry, D., & Orvashel, H. (1992). Sexually abused children at high risk for PTSD. *Journal of the American Academy of Child and Adolescent Psychiatry, 31,* 875–879.

Olson, D. H., Portner, J., & Lavee, Y. (1985). *Faces-III manual.* St Paul, MN: Family Social Science, University of Minnesota.

Resick, P. A., & Schnicke, M. K. (1992). Cognitive processing therapy for sexual assault victims. *Journal of Consulting and Clinical Psychology, 60,* 748–756.

Rogers, C. R. (1957). The necessary and sufficient conditions of therapeutic personality change. *Journal of Consulting Psychology, 21,* 95–103.

Rothbaum, B. O. C., & Foa, E. B. (1993). Subtypes of posttraumatic stress disorder and duration of symptoms. In J. R. T. Davidson & E. B. Foa (Eds.), *Posttraumatic stress disorder DSM–IV and beyond.* Washington, DC: American Psychiatric Press.

Sedlak, B., & Broadhurst, M. L. A. (1996). *Executive Summary of the Third National Incidence Study of Child Abuse and Neglect.* Washington, DC: U.S. Department of Health and Human Services, National Center of Child Abuse and Neglect.

Sgroi, S. M. (1982). *Handbook of clinical intervention in child sexual abuse.* Lexington, MA: Lexington Books.

Spielberger, C. D. (1973). *Manual for the State-Trait Anxiety Inventory for children.* Palo Alto, CA: Consulting Psychologists.

Steiner, H., Garcia, J. G., & Matthews, Z. (1997). Posttraumatic stress disorder in incarcerated juvenile delinquents. *Journal of the American Academy of Child and Adolescent Psychiatry, 36,* 357–365.

Strayhorn, J. M., & Weidman, C. S. (1988). A parent practices scale and its relation to parent and child mental health. *Journal of the American Academy of Child and Adolescent Psychiatry, 27,* 613–618.

Wozencroft, T., Wagner, W., & Pelligrin, A. (1991). Depression and suicidal ideation in sexually abused children. *Child Abuse and Neglect, 15,* 505–511.

Wyatt, G. E., & Peters, S. D. (1986). Methodological considerations in research on the prevalence of child sexual abuse. *Child Abuse and Neglect, 10,* 241–251.

VIII

EPILOGUE

29

GRADING THE PROGRESS IN CHILD AND ADOLESCENT PSYCHOTHERAPY RESEARCH: HOW ARE WE DOING?

PETER S. JENSEN AND EUTHYMIA D. HIBBS

Since the publication of the first edition of this volume, substantial progress has been made in the study of psychosocial treatments for child and adolescent disorders, as the many remarkable chapters in this volume prove. Empirical studies in this area have burgeoned since 1996, and the interest in evidence-based treatments has grown exponentially. Perhaps driven in part by managed care considerations and by increasing constraints on providers to provide only those treatments that are proven effective, researchers have conducted many reviews of the various treatment types for specific disorders, including attention-deficit/hyperactivity disorder (ADHD), conduct disorders (CDs), and oppositional disorders (ODs), anxiety, depression, and autism, as well as overall reviews that summarize the state of evidence in this field (e.g., Office of the Surgeon General, 1999; U.S. Public Health Service, 2000; Weisz & Jensen, 1999).

Some areas, such as cognitive–behavioral therapy (CBT), seem to have enjoyed particular growth, with new trials demonstrating their efficacy for various disorders; other areas, such as cognitive therapy, appear less successful and prevalent. Likewise, although a solid foundation of behavioral

This chapter was coauthored by an employee of the United States government as part of official duty and is considered to be in the public domain. Any views expressed herein do not necessarily represent the views of the United States government, and the author's participation in the work is not meant to serve as an official endorsement.

therapies demonstrates the efficacy of specific behavioral therapies for a range of childhood conditions, this area appears not to have grown substantially in the past 6 years, apart from its greater application to real-world settings. This apparent applicability might represent an important success, however, because the solid information base that now characterizes the behavioral–therapy research field may in fact demand more much *application than replication*. Perhaps the major challenge is not to develop yet another behavioral therapy but to apply those that we have already determined to be efficacious.

Studies of the application of treatments to somewhat different or nontraditional disorders or conditions have also begun to emerge, such as for child abuse, substance use, or subthreshold conditions that might not have merited full consideration for treatment in the past. Also, investigators are increasingly attempting to place various treatment components into more comprehensive packages so that an overall treatment program is applied to address a complex set of clinical needs. In some instances, we are witnessing attempts to tailor specific aspects of treatment to patients' and families' needs. In this chapter, we summarize some of the major new directions seen in the literature and characterized in this volume. We note several persisting problems that have not been fully addressed by the field, and we outline new strategies that are necessary to advance the child and adolescent psychotherapy research field.

MERGING DIRECTIONS IN THE LITERATURE

The Nature of Control Groups

Despite substantial progress in demonstrating the benefits of various forms of treatment over wait-list controls, surprisingly few studies have been conducted that show the benefits of a theory-based intervention or supposed active intervention over an attention control group, in which clinicians provide an educational or supportive intervention of similar intensity. Over the last half-dozen years, relatively few examples of this necessary but neglected strategy have been evident. Attention controls are necessary if researchers are to demonstrate that the presumed active ingredients of the intervention are the mechanisms for change, rather than general, nonspecific therapeutic processes or simple involvement in therapy. Although this area has been neglected, several good examples of studies employing attention controls have appeared in the last several years. For example, Beidel, Turner, and Morris (2000) tested three different therapies—social-effectiveness therapy versus an educational-support intervention versus a wait-list control—for the treatment of social phobia in children and adolescents. Their findings demonstrated that the social-effectiveness therapy was indeed superior to a similarly intense educational-support control. Similarly, Renaud et al. (1998) studied the effects of CBT versus a structured family therapy versus a supportive-educational intervention on youths with suicidal ideation. Their findings indicated relatively greater efficacy of CBT in terms of promoting earlier remission of symptoms than the other two forms of therapy. In the area of ADHD, Sonuga-Barke et al. (2001) studied three different approaches for the treatment of 3-year-old children with ADHD: parent behavioral training, similarly intensive educational support, and a wait-list control. The research showed that the parent behavioral training resulted in significantly greater clinical benefits to children's behavior than the other two forms of therapy. Lastly, in another example, Silverman et al. (1999a) studied the relative benefits of contingency management, self-control therapy, and educational support in children with phobic disorders. In contrast to the previously summarized findings by Beidel et al. (2000), these investigators found no difference between the contingency management and self-control methods.

By and large, these studies with attention control groups are the exception rather than the rule. Increasingly, however, as the empirical evidence base expands and treatments become increasingly well established as efficacious for children and adolescents, the institutional review boards (IRBs) and the investigators themselves seem less disposed to allow children to be assigned to wait-list controls when known and effective treatments are available. Different types of control groups are therefore necessary, such as those used in cancer studies in which different treatment combinations are compared. In the meantime, however, studies employing attention control groups are an important next step in advancing our understanding of the nature of the actual therapeutic ingredients in specific psychotherapies.

Combining Parent and Child Therapies

Concurrent with the growth in individual therapies for children, sensible investigators have aimed to maximize the effects of a given therapy on a child by treating both the parent and the child. Substantial data suggest that such combined approaches are sensible. For example, in a longitudinal study of more than a thousand children from childhood into adulthood, Lieb et al. (2000) reported that the children's likelihood of developing social phobic disorders was related to two factors: (a) parental family history of social phobic disorders and (b) given the family history of social phobia, the extent to which parents used overprotective and rejecting parenting approaches with the child. Perhaps surprisingly, overall family management strategies and family functioning levels were not related to the subsequent likelihood of youths to develop social phobia. Such considerations suggest that intervening with both the parent and child might mitigate the child's likelihood of subsequently developing a disorder and possibly even prevent it altogether.

A number of investigators have followed this line of reasoning to explore the individual and additive impact of parent and family treatments when children have specific disorders. For example, Cobham, Dadds, and Spence (1998) found that among children with an anxiety disorder whose parents were also anxious, treating both the child and the parent with CBT increased the impact on children's outcomes. Moreover, Mendlowitz et al. (1999) reported that a combination of parent and child therapy resulted in outcomes superior to therapy with either party alone, *regardless* of whether the parent had concurrent anxiety symptoms. Finally, in a study of children who had been traumatized by abuse, King et al. (2000) reported greater parental satisfaction with the combined parent-and-child therapy, even though in most instances no measurable differences in clinical outcomes were noted between the child-only and the combined child-and-parent treatment groups.

In contrast to these generally positive reports of the potential benefits of combining parent and child interventions to improve child outcomes, Spence, Donovan, and Brechman-Toussaint (2000) studied social-skills training interventions with children who had social phobia disorders. In this particular study, adding a parent component to the treatment made no difference in children's outcomes. And lastly, in a study of the effects of CBT on youths with depression, Clarke, Rohde, Lewinsohn, Hops, and Seeley (1999) reported that adding a concurrent parent intervention component did not make a difference in children's outcomes. It should be noted, however, that proving one active intervention to be more effective than another active intervention might require substantial sample sizes to achieve sufficient power, just as with cancer studies; any tentative conclusions that the addition of a parent component to a child intervention yields no incremental benefits would seem premature.

This area comparing two active treatments has constituted an important focus of research over the last several years, an emphasis that is likely to continue. However, substantially larger sample sizes are necessary to demonstrate meaningful and measurable effects, and the need for multisite studies to test such interventions is evident.

Combined Psychotherapeutic and Medication Therapies

Under what circumstances should one combine psychotherapy and medication? When might one treatment approach be preferred to another? Unfortunately, relatively few studies have addressed this very important question, although several sizeable investigations have been conducted and others are currently under way. For example, in the Multimodal Treatment Study of ADHD (MTA Cooperative Group 1999a, 1999b, 2004a, 2004b), investigators found that an intensive behavioral therapy delivered across multiple settings and modalities added little to a carefully crafted medication therapy after 14 months and at subsequent follow-up. Thus, although behavioral therapy itself was an effective approach, it offered few benefits to most children in the relief of ADHD symptoms. In other areas, however, such as anxiety, parent–child relations, academics, ODD and CD symptoms, and social skills, evidence showed modest additional advantages for the combined therapy approach over medication alone. As our studies become more sophisticated, we must carefully attend to the specific types of outcomes that are being assessed because different treatments may affect different types of outcomes. Similarly, children with different kinds of problems within the same disorder category might merit somewhat different treatment approaches on the basis of their particular constellation of problems and difficulties in functioning over and above their specific *DSM*–defined disorder (MTA Cooperative Group, 1999a, 1999b; Jensen et al., 2001). Thus, the child with ADHD with severe peer relationship problems may require a different treatment than the children with ADHD without peer relationship problems.

Several other large comparative studies are under way, such as the Treatment of Adolescents With Depression Study (TADS) and the Child and Adolescent Multimodal Anxiety Study (CAMS). Both of these studies are large comparative trials testing the relative benefits of CBT, a selective serotonin-reuptake inhibitor (SSRI), and a combination thereof. These studies will likely offer important new information about the circumstances under which one form or another (or a combination of treatments) should be considered.

In most instances, the combined approaches may very well offer the greatest advantages; in studies of adults, the combination therapies have often proved most effective. While the benefits of the combined treatment over medication management alone was modest within the MTA study, the combined form of therapy that included the behavioral therapies and medications were clearly preferred by parents to medications alone. In addition, the combination appears to have produced superior outcomes in a substantial subset of children compared with those treated only with medications (Jensen et al., 2001; Swanson et al., 2001).

Studies in other disorder areas suggest the merits of combined approaches. Thus, in the area of separation anxiety disorder, Bernstein et al. (2000) studied imipramine and CBT versus placebo and CBT in children with separation anxiety disorder. Their findings suggested that CBT was somewhat more effective with medication than with placebo. Such findings are not uniform, however. In the area of obsessive–compulsive disorder (OCD), De Haan, Hoogduin, Buitelaar, and Keijsers (1998) compared SSRI and behavioral therapies, with findings suggesting a slight superiority of the behavioral therapy over medications. Questions such as "which treatment works best?" and "when should we combine them?" will be important areas of study over the next decade because clinicians must rely on such comparative data to guide parents and families in their treatment choices.

Comparing Psychotherapy Treatments

One subject that has received increased attention and will certainly receive more in the future pertains to the actual comparisons of active psychotherapy treatments. For example, Eisler et al. (2000) compared conjoint family therapy and separated family therapy for adolescents with anorexia nervosa. Although this study appears superficially to be like the previously described studies that combined a parent therapy with a child therapy, this study was actually somewhat different in that the therapies themselves are not simply additive but actually different in the manner in which they are delivered. The researchers' findings suggested that, by and large, children receiving conjoint family therapy had somewhat superior overall outcomes than those receiving separated family therapy (76% and 47%, respectively). However, for a subset of families with high parental "expressed emotion" (expressed negative attributions about the child), the separated family therapy proved superior for those youngsters. In another comparative study of adolescents with anorexia nervosa, Robin et al. (1999) compared ego-oriented individual therapy and behavioral family–systems therapy. In this study, however, no advantage was found in either. Again, the comparison of potentially active treatments is a difficult and challenging process that will require substantially larger sample sizes and, most likely, multisite studies.

Comprehensive Treatment Programs

In the past decade, we have witnessed to an increasing degree the development of comprehensive and integrated treatment programs—programs that embed an array of efficacious ingredients into an overall package that considers the array of child and family needs and builds the ingredients into a particular delivery format. For example, in developing multisystemic therapy, Henggeler, Schoenwald, Borduin, Rowland, and Cunningham (1998) and Henggeler et al. (1999) applied proven principles of behavioral and family therapies but delivered them in an intensive, alternative format, relying on a home-based delivery system that emphasized the families' needs, values, and active involvement in treatment. Similarly, in the National Institute of Mental Health (NIMH) Multimodal Treatment of ADHD Study (the MTA Study), investigators developed a comprehensive package of treatments in each of the treatment arms, attempting to integrate them throughout to benefit all aspects of child and family functioning (MTA Cooperative Group 1999a, 1999b, 2004a, 2004b). As we move from attempting to demonstrate whether something is simply efficacious to determining whether it can actually be delivered and received by families in the real world, alternative delivery vehicles for interventions will be necessary. Standard clinic-based approaches, which might result in substantial patient and family attrition, or traditional approaches used in mental health settings are not likely to be adequate. Alternative methods, such as using other parents to be active components in the delivery of an evidence-based intervention (see Irvine, Biglan, Smolkowski, Metzler, & Ary, 1999), are likely to receive increasing emphasis.

Closing the Research–Practice Gap

In the last 5 to 7 years, we are seeing increased numbers of comparisons of real-world, or standard-care ("treatment as usual"), treatments and new, presumably more effective treatments. These studies allow us to examine the difference between the care that families typically receive in the community and the care that they receive under more optimal conditions, where the intensity and quality of service delivery and fidelity to the original treatment model can be better controlled. In effect, such studies have the potential to demonstrate the impact of quality and intensity of services, as well as the nature of specific therapeutic ingredients, and they offer an ethical alternative over a wait-list control.

Perhaps the best-known example of this approach is the MTA Study, wherein a community treatment-as-usual control group constituted a critical component of the study's overall findings: In this study, medication carefully delivered by the MTA investigator team proved superior to medication delivered under treatment-as-usual (TAU) conditions by community providers (MTA Cooperative Group, 1999a, 1999b, 2004a, 2004b). Other examples are increasingly available; however, in a study of the benefits of treatment as usual versus a higher-intensity therapeutic intervention, Chamberlain and Reid (1998) compared the benefits of an intensive therapeutic foster-care intervention on foster parents' behavior and outcomes and the benefits conferred under a tau condition. In a related study, members of the same investigative team also examined the benefits of an intervention on very young children whose foster parents had received the benefits of intensive assistance (Fisher, Gunnar, Chamberlain, & Reid, 2000); the team compared these children with other children in a foster parent tau condition. In other areas, such as autism, tau comparison groups have proved valuable, allowing investigators to show the benefits of a 12-week intensive intervention program in which parents learned skills, functional analysis, and behavior therapy over and above standard (inadequate) therapeutic child care (Jocelyn, Casiron, Beattie, Bow, & Kneisz, 1998).

PERSISTING PROBLEMS

Despite the promising trends noted above, significant difficulties remain in a number of areas. We commented on some of these problems in the previous volume, and although some progress has occurred since that time, much remains to be done.

Internal Versus External Validity

Perhaps because of the long time frame required by efficacy studies, investigators have historically paid a great deal of attention to ensuring that all aspects of their therapeutic experiments were as tightly controlled as possible. Such an approach places definite constraints on the potential applicability and generalizability of study findings to the problems, patients, or settings of the real world. A greater emphasis on studying treatments that are feasible, palatable, affordable, and sustainable is essential if our academic research efforts are to yield tangible benefits for patients and families. Since publication of our earlier volume, we are encouraged that investigators appear to be showing increased enthusiasm for this approach—that is, studying more complex real-world problems, even if it means, at times, sacrificing some of the simplicity of a tightly controlled (if potentially irrelevant or inapplicable) efficacy-style study.

Because efficacy studies have grown more prevalent and we now have an increased body of evidence relevant to treatments feasible in a variety of settings, attention to the problem of external validity has become increasingly important. The artificial dichotomy between efficacy and effectiveness studies has grown less pronounced, and many investigators commonly use the term *hybrid* to describe designs that incorporate characteristics of efficacy and effectiveness studies (Hoagwood, Hibbs, Brent, & Jensen, 1995).

Family Perspectives

Family and consumer perspectives are playing an increasingly greater role in our understanding and appreciation of treament benefits. Within the National Institutes of Health (NIH), consumers now have a central role on initial review groups and are charged with providing a consumer perspective as a part of the overall scientific review. Investigators are also applying a more comprehensive model of outcomes in their assessments, including consumer-related outcomes (Hoagwood, Jensen, Petti, & Burns, 1996). The satisfaction of patients, families, and consumers is an important goal in and of itself, and the patients' and families' values need to be carefully considered if adherence to and full participation in treatment is to be achieved and without this focus on consumer satisfaction, the health care provider is unlikely to be able to serve the patients' and families' perceived needs. Although this area has received some increasing attention over the last half-dozen years, we note that most research still fails to fully incorporate family and consumer perspectives into the research question, design, methods, analyses, and final reports (Jensen, Hoagwood, & Trickett, 1999).

Short-Term Versus Longer-Term Perspectives

As efficacy data have increased, investigators have turned to the important questions: not whether a treatment works but how long it works and how long it must be continued for it to achieve sustained effects. Just a few years ago, only a handful of treatment studies had examined children's outcomes 1 year after treatment. Now, in most NIMH-funded studies, as well as in industry pharmaceutical studies, a 1-year follow-up and examination of persistent gains and outcomes are expected rather than optional. Clearly, the shift from the short-term focus on symptoms to a longer-term perspective on overall child functioning and eventual outcomes is a much more sanguine perspective from both real-world clinicians' and families' viewpoints. Such an approach corresponds much more closely with the concerns found in daily practice. Although this shift is beginning to take place, many unnecessarily brief studies still fail to take this long-term perspective. Certainly, the long-term perspective will also be increasingly important to families, who do not want to risk exposing their children to short-term studies that could call for sporadic disruptions in their children's lives. For full family participation in research, investigators must take into account such considerations.

One Size Fits All

Very few studies have attempted to determine whether maximal gains are achieved by attempting to tailor a given treatment to a child's specific needs or by assuming that what works for one child will work equally well for another. In essence, the investigator who puts together a package of treatments without considering whether families in that group need all of the packaged components risks overburdening the family or discouraging participation in the various aspects of treatment. Furthermore, a one-size-fits-all treatment package is not exactly what real-world clinicians do as they attempt to apply specific treatments to specific problems. We note that some investigators are beginning to attempt to treat to a given criterion (i.e., stopping after six sessions if the child has become asymptomatic after 6 sessions rather than pursuing a full 12 sessions), and research designs have begun to consider such complexities. Although particularly challenging on an analytical level, such studies are, over time, likely to prove especially useful on a clinical level. Conceivably, researchers might compare a packaged, one-size-fits-all set of treatments to a tailored therapeutic program (i.e., one designed to fit the specific needs of the patient). Yet another design might compare a prepackaged, highly prescriptive set of treatments and one in which the patient's or family's preferences dictate the approach. Although they are still novel and unfamiliar to most investigators, these strategies offer a much closer approximation of the treatment practices common in effective clinical settings.

FUTURE CONSIDERATIONS

Public Health–Oriented Approaches

Additional intervention efforts will become increasingly necessary in public health arenas that have typically been neglected in most clinically oriented intervention efforts. A good example is the current interest in, and concern about, violence-prevention approaches (Cooper, Lutenbacher, & Faccia, 2000). Despite the abundance of promising strategies (e.g., peer mediation, direct family intervention, classroom-based methods), most have not been sufficiently evaluated. Such studies might not necessarily emphasize a behavioral or emotional disorder per se, instead targeting general behavioral constellations that characterize children in primary or secondary prevention settings. For example, Cunningham et al. (1998) developed a peer-mediation program using a multiple-baseline design, which showed impressive benefits in middle-school settings. Other secondary prevention efforts have been applied in other broad areas, such as child-focused divorce interventions with longer-term effects of children's outcomes (Emery, Laumann-Billings, Waldron, Sbarra, & Dillon, 2001; Wolchik et al., 2002), parent-focused programs with benefits on children's outcomes (Chernoff, Ireys, DeVet, & Kim, 2002; Huston et al., 2001; Toumbourou & Gregg, 2002), and studies of child abuse (Robinson, Wilde, Navracruz, Haydel, & Varady, 2001). The skills and therapeutic techniques of traditional clinical investigators are critical to understanding and maximizing the findings of such studies.

Studies of the effects of interventions on risk factors that fall outside the province of the standard clinical enterprise are likely to have a significant impact on the clinical outcomes of children, as well as on their healthy peers. For example, one recent controlled study of the effects of television watching and video games demonstrated that experimental reductions in television and video-game use resulted in decreased observations of playground verbal aggression and peer-nomination ratings of aggression. Other investigators have shown that a 12-session videotape–mass-media intervention focusing on parenting strategies has shown persisting benefits on parent behavior, with effects lasting over 2 years relative to control conditions (Spoth, Reyes, Redmond, & Shin, 1999). Yet another demonstrated the impact of a supportive intervention for families of children with chronic medical illnesses. Results indicated modest beneficial effects on parents' ratings of children's overall adjustment, with children who had low self-esteem most likely to benefit from the intervention (Chernoff, Ireys, DeVet, & Kim, 2002).

Increased Real-World Studies

As evidence of efficacious interventions mounts, it is essential to test the benefits of efficacious treatments in different, sometimes more difficult situations, such as applying interpersonal psychotherapy methods to the treatment of Hispanic youth (Rosselló & Bernal, 1999) or taking traditional individual therapies and moving them to group-based applications that might be more useful and affordable in the real world (e.g., Silverman et al., 1999b). Similarly, further efforts are required to determine whether treatments that have proved efficacious in longer formats can be shortened to more-affordable, yet still efficacious, briefer formats (e.g., Snyder, Kymissis, & Kessler, 1999). Treatments that have been applied in one setting might need to be adapted for children of different ethnic or socioeconomic backgrounds to ensure that the methods remain applicable (e.g., see Webster-Stratton, 1998).

Understanding Treatment Ingredients

As noted elsewhere (Jensen, 1999), most of the existing research fails to demonstrate the actual ingredients of efficacious treatments. What are the specific etiological or maintenance processes within given disorders? How do treatments exert their effects? A few investigators, most notably at the Oregon Social Learning Center, have tackled this challenging area. For example, Eddy and Chamberlain (2000) found within their therapeutic foster-care clinical trial that the key mediators of change involved the degree to which the therapy produced changes in parental supervision, increased positive parent–child relations, and decreased deviant peer associations. These were the actual processes targeted in the course of therapy, and the degree of change produced mirrored the extent to which these processes were also effectively altered. In the MTA Study, investigators found that the benefits of behavioral therapy were not related to parental attendance at the behavioral training sessions, per se; rather, benefits were related to the actual degree of improvement that parents manifested in their use of ineffective disciplinary strategies, the hypothesized mediating factor targeted by the behavioral therapies (Hinshaw et al., 2000; Wells et al., 2000).

Some of the emerging tools available from the neurosciences might also allow us to better understand therapeutic processes at the level of brain structure and function. For example, Richards et al. (2000) showed that theory-based treatments for dyslexia were linked to changes in the metabolic byproducts of brain functioning in those very brain regions hypothesized to be linked to the disorder itself. Nonetheless, far too little is known about the active ingredients of therapeutic change and the effective dose of therapy needed to produce optimal outcomes (Salzer, Bickman, & Lambert, 2000).

Persistence of Treatment Effects

Future studies must carefully examine when and why treatment effects persist over longer periods of time. For example, some studies have shown that although CBT produces earlier and more clinically significant changes than other forms of therapy at the conclusion of treatment, these differences have disappeared at later follow-up (Birmaher et al., 2000). A similar dissipation of effects at long-term follow-up has been reported in other studies (Dadds et al., 1999). There are exceptions to this general rule, however. Olds et al. (1998) showed that their early nurse-visitation intervention yielded persisting effects at 15-year follow-up. Similarly, Reynolds, Temple, Robertson, and Mann (2001) documented the benefits of an intensive early intervention on children's later functioning outcomes.

Although a number of studies have suggested that treatment effects wane 1 to 2 years after the end of treatment, such findings should not be taken to mean that these treatments do not work. Instead, given that many of the behavioral and emotional disorders of childhood are likely to be chronic conditions, ongoing or persistent *care* might be needed, and the hopes for *cure* after an abbreviated period of treatment may be overly optimistic—as fallacious as the notion that short-term treatments for asthma or diabetes should somehow result in persistent change, with ongoing interventions no longer needed. To illustrate, follow-up of the NIMH MTA study showed persisting effects of the medication interventions at 24 months (10 months poststudy endpoint), even after controlling for poststudy period medication use (MTA Cooperative Group, 2004a, 2004b). Although effect sizes were only about one-half of the original 14-month effect sizes, the lesson learned (one that will ideally be applied to future studies in other disorder areas) was that both initial and subsequent medication use appeared to contribute to long-term outcomes, much as one would expect with most chronic illnesses.

The following questions are likely to prove relevant to critical future research: Who needs only one or two relatively brief interventions before returning to normal functioning? And which children need persistent, ongoing care? These areas of great clinical complexity will only be understood with intensive additional research.

Matching Patients and Families to Treatment

What research has been done showing that a specific form of treatment applies to a specific kind of patient, apart from straightforward diagnosis? In other words, which depressed patient might need medication therapy and which might need CBT? Although children with ADHD clearly benefit from stimulants and not from SSRIs, determining which child with ADHD will benefit from stimulants and which might benefit from another ADHD-proven treatment, such as behavioral therapy, is considerably more difficult. In effect, this question regarding the correspondence of patients to treatment represents the holy grail, the ultimate quest of clinical trials. This pressing problem is also the clinician's most urgent priority once a correct diagnosis has been made.

Little progress has been made in this area, unfortunately. We note, however, that findings from the MTA study indicated that children with various patterns of comorbidity responded differentially to specific treatments in a pattern different from the overall sample's findings. For example, although the MTA's overall findings suggested a modest additional benefit of combined therapy over medication and a substantial advantage of both those treatments over behavioral therapy, an analysis of children's comorbid patterns indicated that children with ADHD with no comorbidity responded principally to medication only. In contrast, children who had ADHD and an internalizing disorder but no accompanying externalizing problems responded equally well to behavioral therapy only, medication only, and to the combination of therapies. Children with ADHD and an externalizing disorder only, such as ODD or CD, responded preferentially to treatments that included medication and not to behavioral therapy alone. And, lastly, children with ADHD and both an internalizing and an externalizing disorder (such as depression and CD) responded best to combined therapy (i.e., medication and behavior therapy; Jensen et al., 2001).

Such findings, which reflect the matching of specific patients to specific treatments, are urgently needed to guide future treatment activities. But such data only become possible when substantial numbers of subjects are available from a large or multisite clinical trial. Several of the current NIMH multisite studies (TADS, CAMS) offer the potential for findings in this area, given their fairly large sample sizes. Similarly, other NIMH-funded multisite studies now under way might also yield similarly helpful results.

Studies of the Treatment Delivery Process

Perhaps the most glaring omission among all of the previously noted research areas is the actual study of *how* therapies and other treatments should be delivered. Some investigators have chosen to redesign the therapy-delivery process to ensure that families actually get what they need. Simple reliance on families to come to a traditional outpatient clinic setting might not work for difficult-to-treat problems. Multisystemic therapy (MST; Henggeler et al., 1998, 1999) is perhaps the best-known example of this redesign of clinical-services delivery. Data from the MST studies show that this redesign process not only may yield robust clinical and functional outcomes but also may be cost-effective (Henggeler et al., 1998). Similar efforts to change the way services are delivered can be seen in the Olds et al. (1998) study, which relied principally on a home-based intervention to deliver therapeutic nursing services to teenage mothers. In another approach, Wright, Callum, Birks, and Jarvis (1998) revamped treatment for children who showed failure to thrive by delivering services in a home-visitation model. Compared with services that required the families to attend the clinic, the home-delivered services were significantly more effective in improving children's health outcomes.

SUMMARY

In spite of persistent gaps, the progress made in the last 6 years gives us cause for cautious optimism. We have compelling new evidence for the effectiveness of specific psychotherapies, alone and in combination with other forms of psychotherapy and medication. The term *evidence-based treatment* is now on almost everyone's lips, even when it is misapplied or not fully understood. Despite some misunderstandings, many parties—researchers, clinical practitioners, and family members—appear to want to join together to fill knowledge gaps where they exist and to close the gaps between what we know and what we do.

So, has there been progress? We would submit that there has been, to an impressive degree. But powerful forces for change are now afoot, ranging from new economic and health care system factors, to a sometimes impatient consumer base, to increased public awareness and appreciation of the importance of children's mental health (and illness)—not just in traditional clinical settings but also in larger public health contexts.

Given the current pace of change and revolutionary forces at play, assigning a "final grade" would clearly be premature. We will witness continued changes in our mental health care systems, its economic and reimbursement structures, and the contexts in which services are delivered. Families have become and will continue to be increasingly empowered, and whether we like it or not, they will and must exert a critical hand in shaping and participating in our shared future if we are to achieve optimal outcomes (Toumbourou & Gregg, 2002). Researchers, family members, and clinicians alike must work together to understand, accept, and embrace these changes, if we are to maximize the effectiveness of our therapies and play an effective role in addressing the problems of our future (Jensen, Hibbs, & Pilkonis, 1996; Jensen et al., 1999). As researchers and clinicians alike, we will be judged by how well we participate in and flexibly respond to this grand experiment over which we do not have much control.

REFERENCES

Beidel, D. C., Turner, S. M., & Morris, T. L. (2000). Behavioral treatment of childhood social phobia. *Journal of Consulting and Clinical Psychology, 68,* 1072–1080.

Bernstein, G. A., Borchardt, C. M., Perwien, A. R., Crosby, R. D., Kushner, M. G., Thuras, P. D., et al. (2000). Imipramine plus cognitive–behavioral therapy in the treatment of school refusal. *Journal of the American Academy of Child and Adolescent Psychiatry, 39*, 276–283.

Birmaher, B., Brent, D. A., Kolko, D., Baugher, M., Bridge, J., Holder, D., et al. (2000). Clinical outcome after short-term psychotherapy for adolescents with major depressive disorder. *Archives of General Psychiatry, 57*, 29–36.

Chamberlain, P., & Reid, J. B. (1998). Comparison of two community alternatives to incarceration for chronic juvenile offenders. *Journal of Consulting and Clinical Psychology, 66*, 624–633.

Chernoff, R. G., Ireys, H. T., DeVet, K. A., & Kim, Y. J. (2002). A randomized, controlled trial of a community-based support program for families of children with chronic illness: Pediatric outcomes. *Archives of Pediatric and Adolescent Medicine, 156*, 533–539.

Clarke, G. N., Rohde, P., Lewinsohn, P. M., Hops, H., & Seeley, J. R. (1999). Cognitive–behavioral treatment of adolescent depression: Efficacy of acute group treatment and booster sessions. *Journal of the American Academy of Child and Adolescent Psychiatry, 38*, 272–279.

Cobham, V. E., Dadds, M. R., & Spence, S. H. (1998). The role of parental anxiety in the treatment of childhood anxiety. *Journal of Consulting and Clinical Psychology, 66*, 893–905.

Cooper, W. O., Lutenbacher, M., & Faccia, K. (2000). Components of effective youth-violence prevention programs for seven- to fourteen-year-olds. *Archives of Pediatrics and Adolescent Medicine, 154*, 1134–1139.

Cunningham, C. E., Cunningham, L. J., Martorelli, V., Tran, A., Young, J., & Zacharias, R. (1998). The effects of primary division, student-mediated conflict resolution programs on playground aggression. *Journal of Child Psychology and Psychiatry, 39*, 653–662.

Dadds, M. R., Holland, D. E., Spence, S. H. Laurens, K. R., Mullins, M., & Barrett, P. M. (1999). Early intervention and prevention of anxiety disorders in children: Results at 2-year follow-up. *Journal of Clinical and Consulting Psychology, 67*, 145–150.

De Haan, E., Hoogduin, A. L., Buitelaar, J. K., & Keijsers, G. P. J. (1998). Behavior therapy versus clomipramine for the treatment of obsessive-compulsive disorder in children and adolescents. *Journal of the American Academy of Child and Adolescent Psychiatry, 37*, 1022–1029.

Eddy, J. M., & Chamberlain, P. (2000). Family management and deviant peer association as mediators of the impact of treatment condition on youth antisocial behavior. *Journal of Consulting and Clinical Psychology, 68*, 857–863.

Eisler, I., Dare, C., Hodes, M., Russell, G., Dodge, E., & Le Grange, D. (2000). Family therapy for adolescent anorexia nervosa: The results of a controlled comparison of two family interventions. *Journal of Child Psychology and Psychiatry and Allied Disciplines, 41*, 727–736.

Emery, R. E., Laumann-Billings, L., Waldron, M. C., Sbarra, D. A., & Dillon, P. (2001). Child-custody mediation and litigation: Custody contact and co-parenting twelve years after initial dispute resolution. *Journal of Consulting and Clinical Psychology, 69,* 323–332.

Fisher, P. A., Gunnar, M. R., Chamberlain, P., & Reid, J. B. (2000). Preventive intervention for maltreated preschool children: Impact on children's behavior, neuroendocrine activity, and foster-parent functioning. *Journal of the American Academy of Child and Adolescent Psychiatry, 39,* 1356–1364.

Henggeler, S. W., Rowland, M. D., Randall, J., Ward, D. M., Pickrel, S. G., Cunningham, P. B., et al. (1999). Home-based multi-systemic therapy as an alternative to the hospitalization of youths in psychiatric crisis: Clinical outcomes. *Journal of the American Academy of Child and Adolescent Psychiatry, 38,* 1331–1339.

Henggeler, S. W., Schoenwald, S. K., Borduin, C. M., Rowland, M. D., & Cunningham, P. B. (1998). *Multisystemic treatment for antisocial behavior in children and adolescents.* New York: Guilford Press.

Hinshaw, S. P., Owens, E. B., Wells, K. C., Kraemer, H. C., Abikoff, H. B., Arnold, L. E., et al. (2000). Family processes and treatment outcome in the MTA: Negative/ineffective parenting practices in relation to multimodal treatment. *Journal of Abnormal Child Psychology, 28,* 555–568.

Hoagwood, K., Hibbs, E., Brent, D., & Jensen, P. (1995). Efficacy and effectiveness in studies in child and adolescent psychotherapy. *Journal of Consulting and Clinical Psychology, 63,* 683–687.

Hoagwood, K., Jensen, P. S., Petti, T., & Burns, B. (1996). Outcomes of care for children and adolescents. I: A conceptual model. *Journal of the American Academy of Child and Adolescent Psychiatry, 35,* 1055–1063.

Huston, A. C., Duncan, G. J., Granger, R., Bos, J., McLoyd, V., Mistry, R., et al. (2001). Work-based antipoverty programs for parents can enhance the school performance and social behavior of children. *Child Development, 72,* 318–335.

Irvine, A. B., Biglan, A., Smolkowski, K., Metzler, C. W., & Ary, D. V. (1999). The effectiveness of a parenting-skills program for parents of middle-school students in small communities. *Journal of Consulting and Clinical Psychology, 67,* 811–825.

Jensen, P. S. (1999). Links among theory, research, and practice: Cornerstones of clinical scientific progress. *Journal of Clinical Child Psychology, 28,* 553–557.

Jensen, P., Hibbs, E., & Pilkonis, P. (1996). From ivory tower to clinical practice: Future directions for child and adolescent psychotherapy research. In E. D. Hibbs & P. Jensen (Eds.), *Psychosocial treatments for children and adolescent disorders: Empirically based strategies for clinical practice* (pp. 701–711). Washington, DC: American Psychological Association.

Jensen, P. S., Hinshaw, S. P., Kraemer, H. C., Lenora, N., Newcorn, J. H., Abikoff, H. B., et al. (2001). ADHD comorbidity findings from the MTA study: Comparing comorbid subgroups. *Journal of the American Academy of Child and Adolescent Psychiatry, 40,* 147–158.

Jensen, P. S., Hoagwood, K., & Trickett, E. (1999). Ivory towers or earthen trenches? Community collaborations to foster "real world" research. *Applied Developmental Science, 3,* 306–212.

Jocelyn, L. J., Casiro, O. G., Beattie, D., Bow, J., & Kneisz, J. (1998). Treatment of children with autism: A randomized controlled trial to evaluate a caregiver-based intervention program in community day-care centers. *Journal of Developmental and Behavioral Pediatrics, 19,* 326–334.

King, N. J., Tonge, B. J., Mullen, P., Myerson, N., Heyne, D., Rollings S, et al. (2000). Treating sexually abused children with posttraumatic-stress symptoms: A randomized clinical trial. *Journal of the American Academy of Child and Adolescent Psychiatry, 39,* 1347–1355.

Lieb, R., Wittchen, H. U., Höfler, M., Fuetsch, M., Stein, M. B., & Merikangas, K. R. (2000). Parental psychopathology, parenting styles, and the risk of social phobia in offspring: A prospective-longitudinal community study. *Archives of General Psychiatry, 57,* 859–866.

Mendlowitz, S. L., Manassis, K., Bradley, S., Scapillato, D., Miezitis, S., & Shaw, B. F. (1999). Cognitive behavioral group treatments in childhood anxiety disorders: The role of parental involvement. *The Journal of the American Academy of Child and Adolescent Psychiatry, 38,* 1223–1229.

MTA Cooperative Group. (1999a). A 14-month randomized clinical trial of treatment strategies for attention deficit hyperactivity disorder. *Archives of General Psychiatry, 56,* 1073–1086.

MTA Cooperative Group. (1999b). Moderators and mediators of treatment response for children with attention-deficit/hyperactivity disorder. *Archives of General Psychiatry, 56,* 1088–1096.

MTA Cooperative Group. (2004a). 24-month outcomes of treatment strategies for attention-deficit/hyperactivity disorder (ADHD): The NIMH MTA follow-up. *Pediatrics, 113,* 754–761.

MTA Cooperative Group. (2004b). Changes in effectiveness and growth during the follow-up phase of the NIMH-MTA study. *Pediatrics, 113,* 761–769.

Office of the Surgeon General. (1999). *Mental health: A report of the Surgeon General.* Washington, DC: U.S. Government Printing Office.

Olds, D., Henderson, C. R., Cole, R., Eckenrode, J., Kitzman, H., Luckey, D., et al. (1998). Long-term effects of nurse home visitation on children's criminal and antisocial behavior: 15-year follow-up of a randomized controlled trial. *Journal of the American Medical Association, 280,* 1238–1244.

Renaud, J., Brent, D. A., Baugher, M., Birmaher, B., Kolko, D. J., & Bridge, J. (1998). Rapid response to psychosocial treatment for adolescent depression: A two-year follow-up. *Journal of the American Academy of Child and Adolescent Psychiatry, 37,* 1184–1190.

Reynolds, A. J., Temple, J. A., Robertson, D. L., & Mann, E. A. (2001). Long-term effects of an early-childhood intervention on educational achievement and juvenile arrest. *Journal of the American Medical Association, 285,* 2339–2346.

Richards, T. L., Corina, D., Serafini, S., Steury, K., Echelard, D. R., & Dager, S. R., et al. (2000). Effects of phonologically driven treatment for dyslexia on lactate levels measured by proton MR spectroscopic imaging. *American Journal of Neuroradiology, 21*, 916–922.

Robin, A. R., Siegel, P. T., Moye, A. W., Gilroy, M., Dennis, A. B., & Sikand, A. (1999). A controlled comparison of family versus individual therapy for adolescents with anorexia nervosa. *Journal of the American Academy of Child and Adolescent Psychiatry, 38*, 1482–1489.

Robinson, T. N., Wilde, M. L., Navracruz, L. C., Haydel, K. F., & Varady, A. (2001). Effects of reducing children's television and video-game use on aggressive behavior. *Archives of Pediatrics and Adolescent Medicine, 155*, 17–23.

Rosselló, J., & Bernal, G. (1999). The efficacy of cognitive, behavioral, and interpersonal treatments for depression in Puerto Rican adolescents. *Journal of Consulting and Clinical Psychology, 67*, 734–745.

Salzer, M. S., Bickman, L., & Lambert, E. W. (1999). Dose-effect relationship in children's psychotherapy services. *Journal of Clinical and Consulting Psychology, 67*, 228–238.

Silverman, W. K., Kurtines, W. M., Ginsburg, G. S., Weems, C. F., Rabian, B., & Sarafini, L. T. (1999a). Contingency management, self-control, and education support in the treatment of childhood phobic disorders: A randomized clinical trial. *Journal of Consulting and Clinical Psychology, 67*, 675–687.

Silverman, W. K., Kurtines, W. M., Ginsburg, G. S., Weems, C. F., Lumpkin, P. W., & Carmichael, D. H. (1999b). Treating anxiety disorders in children with group cognitive–behavioral therapy: A randomized clinical trial. *Journal of Consulting and Clinical Psychology, 67*, 995–1003.

Snyder, K. V., Kymissis, P., & Kessler, K. (1999). Anger management for adolescents: Efficacy of brief group therapy. *Journal of the American Academy of Child and Adolescent Psychiatry, 38*, 1409–1416.

Sonuga-Barke, E. J. S., Daley, D., Thompson, M., Laver-Bradbury, C., & Weeks, A. (2001). Parent-based therapies for preschool attention-deficit/hyperactivity disorder: A randomized, controlled trial with a community sample. *Journal of the American Academy of Child and Adolescent Psychiatry, 40*, 402–408.

Spence, S. H., Donovan, C., & Brechman-Toussaint, M. (2000). The treatment of childhood social phobia: The effectiveness of a social-skills-training-based, cognitive–behavioral intervention, with and without parental involvement. *Journal of Child Psychology and Psychiatry and Allied Disciplines, 41*, 713–726.

Spoth, R., Reyes, M. L., Redmond, C., & Shin, C. (1999). Assessing a public health approach to delay onset and progression of adolescent substance use: Latent transition and log linear analyses of longitudinal family preventive intervention outcomes. *Journal of Consulting and Clinical Psychology, 67*, 619–630.

Swanson, J. M., Kraemer, H. C., Hinshaw, S. P., Arnold, L. E., Conners, C. K., Abikoff, H. B., et al. (2001). Clinical relevance of the primary findings of the MTA: Success rates based on severity of ADHD and ODD symptoms at the end of treatment. *Journal of the American Academy of Child and Adolescent Psychiatry, 40*, 168–179.

Toumbourou, J. W., & Gregg, M. E. (2002). Impact of an empowerment-based parent education program on the reduction of youth suicide risk factors. *Journal of Adolescent Health, 31*, 277–285.

U.S. Public Health Service. (2000). *Report of the Surgeon General's Conference on Children's Mental Health: A National Action Agenda.* Washington, DC: Department of Health and Human Services.

Webster-Stratton, C. (1998). Preventing conduct problems in Head Start children: Strengthening parenting competencies. *Journal of Consulting and Clinical Psychology, 5*, 715–730.

Weisz, J. R., & Jensen, P. S. (1999). Efficacy and effectiveness of psychotherapy and pharmacotherapy with children and adolescents. *Mental Health Services Research, 1*, 125–158.

Wells, K. C., Epstein, J. N., Hinshaw, S. P., Conners, C. K., Klaric, J., Abikoff, H. B, et al. (2000). Parenting and family stress treatment outcomes in attention deficit hyperactivity disorder (ADHD): An empirical analysis in the MTA study. *Journal of Abnormal Child Psychology, 28*, 543–553.

Wolchik, S. A., Sandler, I. N., Millsap, R. E., Plummer, B. A., Greene, S. M., Anderson, E. R., et al. (2002). Six-year follow-up of preventive interventions for children of divorce: a randomized controlled trial. *Journal of the American Medical Association, 288*, 1874–1881.

Wright, C. M., Callum, J., Birks, E., & Jarvis, S. (1998). Effect of community based management in failure to thrive: Randomised controlled trial. *British Medical Journal, 317*, 571–574.

AUTHOR INDEX

789

Marciano, P. L., 466, *474*
Mardekian, J., 133, *140*
Margolin, G., 491, *503*, 521, *551*
Marín, G., 192, *215*
Markham, M. R., *117*
Markman, A., 521, *551*
Markman, H. J., 509, *550*
Markowitz, J. C., 166, 168, *186*
Marks, I. M., 123–124, 134, *139*, *141*
Marlatt, G. A., 57, 68, *71*, 224, *236*
Marrs-Garcia, A., 51, 59, 63, 69–70
Marshall, A., 639–640, *656*
Marshall, P. T., 484, *505*
Marsteller, F., 718, *739*
Martin, D., 424, *434*
Martin, G., 383, 386, *405*
Martin, J., *185*
Martinez, O., 719, *740*
Martínez, S., 191, 207, *215*
Martinovich, Z., 112, *116*
Marton, P., 355, *373*
Martorelli, V., 778, *783*
Maser, J. D., *236*, 447, *476*
Mash, E. J., 426, *435*
Mason, E., 295, *318*
Mason, S. A., 664, *684*
Massetti, G., 390, *403*
Massoth, N. A., 743, *762*
Matarazzo, R. G., 591, *595*
Mathes, P. G., 387, *404*, *408*
Mathur, S. R., 694, *714*
Matkoski, K. M., 492, *502*
Matson, J. L., 242, 246, *262–263*
Matthews, Z., 744, *765*
Maughan, B., 447, *472*
Maultsby, L. T., 268, *290*
Maurer, R. G., 620, *625*
Mays, V. M., 188, *214*
Mazurick, J. L., 463, 465–466, *474*, 576, *596*
Mazza, J., *140*
McAlpine, D. D., 245, *261*
McAndrews, M. M., 492, *502*
McArthur, D., 613, *626*
McBurnett, K., 13, *38*, 352, 358, 371, *376*, 378, 386, *407–408*, 427, *437*, 699, *714*
McCarthy, D. A., 665, *684*
McCauley, E., 269, *289*
McClannahan, L. E., 661, *684*
McClaskey, C. L., 424, *434*
McClelland, G., 719, *742*

McClure, E., 150, *163*
McConnachie, G., 663, *681*
McConnell, S. R., 416, *437*, 680, *684*
McCord, J., 372, *373*
McCormick, M. E., 698–699, *714*
McDaniel, S., 207, *215*
McDonald, R., 520, *551*
McDougle, C. J., 131, *141*
McFayden-Ketchum, S. A., 381, 384, *405*
McGee, G. G., 637, 655, 661–662, 664, 670, *684*, *686*
McGee, R., 47, 68, 76, 94, 244, *261–262*
McGoldrick, M., 283, *292*
McGoldrick, N., 188, 190, *214*
McGonagle, K. A., 718, *740*
McGonigle, J. J., 609, *630*
McGrath, P., 484, *505*
McHale, J. P., 356, 365, *374*
McJunkin, J., 296, *317*
McKendree-Smith, N., 220, *234*
McKeon, R., 718, *739*
McLaughlin, P. M., 483, 494, *503*
McLeer, S. V., 743–744, *764–765*
McLeod, B. D., 36
Mcloughlin, C. S., 696, *714*
McLoyd, V., 778, *784*
McMahon, R. J., *435*, 459, 472, 513, 531, *551–552*, 576, 595–596
McNary, S. W., 22, 36
McNeil, C. B., 591, *595–596*
McNerney, E., 608, 617, 627, 638–640, 644, 646, *655*
McSwiggin-Hardin, M., *141*
McWade Paez, L., 300, *318*
Meece, D. W., 698, *713*
Mei, Z., 302, *318*
Meichenbaum, D. H., 355, *375*, 521, *552*
Meichenbaum, D. L., 386, *402*
Melisaratos, N., 104, *116*
Melnick, S. M., 354, 365, 371, *374–375*
Mendelson, M., 220, *234*
Mendlowitz, S. L., 61, *71*, 772, *785*
Menvielle, E., 298, *317*
Mericle, A., 719, *742*
Merikangas, K. R., 268, 293, 771, *785*
Merisca, R., 534, *551*
Metalsky, G. I., 240, *261*
Metzler, C. W., 775, *784*
Meucci, C., 735, *738*
Meyer, E. C., 481, 491, *505*
Meyer, J., 313, *318*
Michalek, J., 296, *317*

Pearce, J. K., 188, 190, *214*
Peck, C. A., 637, *656*, 670, *684*
Pekarik, E., 701, *713*
Pekarik, G., *476*
Pelham, W. E., 13–14, *37*, 328, *350*, 354–355, 359, 368, *375*, 378–379, 383–384, 386, 388–393, 395, 397, 400–401, *402–404*, *406–409*, 415, 429, *436*
Pelligrin, A., 743, *765*
Penman, D., 527, *553*
Pennington, R., 662, 675, *682*
Pepler, D., 527, *553*, 578, *597*
Perepletchikova, F., 465, *475*
Perez, M., 735, *738*
Pérez-Prado, E., 211, *211*
Perlman, T., 411, *437*
Perlmutter, S., *142*
Perrin, J. M., 398, *408*
Perrin, S., 76, *95*
Perry, D. G., 702, *713*
Perry, L. C., 702, *713*
Persinger, M., 299, 304–305, 312, 315, *317–318*
Perwien, A. R., 773, *783*
Peters, S. D., 743, *765*
Petersen, A. C., *215*, 245, *263*
Peterson, C., 269, *292*
Peterson, R. A., 98, *118*
Petti, T., 132, *139*, 242, *263*, 776, *784*
Pettit, G. S., 511, *550*, 698, 702, *711*, *713*
Pfeiffer, S. I., 558, *573*
Pfiffner, L. J., 331, *350*, 352, 358, 371, *376*, 386, *408*, 699, *714*
Philbrick, L. A., 663, *681*
Philips, V. A., 274, *292*
Phipps, P., 560, 567, *571*
Phung, T. M., *38*, 110, *119*
Piacentini, J., 429, *437*
Piaget, J., 669, *684*
Pickar, D., 128, *141*
Pickles, A., 273, *289*
Pickrel, S. G., 17, *35*, 774, 781, *784*
Pierce, K., 606, 608, 610, *624*, *629*, 662, *684*
Piers, E. V., 207, *215*, 426, *436*
Pilkonis, P., 782, *784*
Pillow, D. R., *407*
Pina, A. A., 98, 102–103, 112, *119*
Pincus, D., 578–579, *595*
Pine, D. S., 239, *263*

Pinsonneault, I., 502, *505–506*
Platt, J. J., 384, *408*
Platzek, D., 725, *741*
Plienis, A. J., 621–622, *629*
Pliner, P., 296, *319*
Plummer, B. A., 778, *787*
Polen, M. R., 231–232, *235*
Pollack Dorta, K., 167, 170, 172, 178, 182–183, *185*
Pope, A. W., 701, *714*
Portner, J., 747, *765*
Possell, L. E., 696, *714*
Postrado, L. T., 22, *36*
Potter, D., 606, *631*
Potts, M., *372*
Poulin, F., *372*, *373*
Powell, M. B., 520, *550*
Powell, T., 674, 679, *681*
Prata, G., 283, *292*
Press, G. A., 620, *625*
Preston, D., 484, 492, *502*
Price, G., 384, *406*
Price, J. M., 540, *550*, 697, 702, *711*, *713*
Price, L. H., 128, 131, *138*, *141*
Prien, R., 239, *262*
Prinstein, M. J., 698, *714*
Printz, B., 153, *163*
Prinz, R. J., *405*, 560, 572, 696, 701, *713*, *714*
Prior, K., 484, *505*
Prizant, B. M., 636–637, 653, *656–657*
Proffitt, V. D., 210, *217*, 242, *265*
Profilet, S., 698, *713*
Prupis, M. A., 718, *737*
Prusoff, B. A., 167, *184–185*, 268, *293*
Prutting, C. A., 638, *657*
Puig-Antich, J. H., 167, 178, *183*, *185*, 231, *236*, 246, *263*, 273, 290, *292*
Pumariega, A., 719, *741*
Putallaz, M., 702, *714*

Quay, H. C., 508, *551*
Querido, J. G., 577, 579, 581, *595–596*
Quinlan, D. M., 479, *505*
Quinn, M. M., 694, *714*
Quintero, J., 727, *737*
Quintero-Salinas, R., 719, *741*

Rabian, B., 48, 59–60, 65, *72*, 89, 96, 98, 100, 102–104, 110, 114–115, *118–119*, 779, *786*

Weinstein, M., 221, *236*

Weintraub, S., 701, *713*

Weiss, B., 10–11, 16, 22, *38–39,* 99,
110–111, *119,* 153, *164,* 210,
217, 241, *262,* 268, *293,* 378,
382, *409*

Weiss, G., 355, *376, 409,* 411, 423, *435,
437,* 699, *711*

Weiss, K., 423, *433*

Weissberg, R. P., 492, *506*

Weissman, A., 268, 273, *289*

Weissman, M. M., 75, 96, 150, 155, *163,*
166–167, 178, 182, *184–186,*
201, 210, *213–214,* 239, *262,*
268, *291, 293*

Weisz, J. R., 4, 10–12, 15–17, 22, 28, 36,
38–39, 48, 62, 65, 69, *73,* 99,
110–111, *119,* 210, *217,*
242–243, 262, 265, 268, *293,*
382, *409,* 448, 469, *475,*
719–720, 733, *739,* 769, *787*

Weizman, R., 61, *73*

Weller, E. B., 152, *164*

Weller, R. A., 152, *164*

Wells, K. C., 352, *374, 376,* 378, 390, 394,
400, *409,* 432, *434,* 558, *573,*
779, *784, 787*

Wells, R. C., 352, *373*

Wells, V., 189, *217*

Welner, Z., 708, *715*

Wenck, L., 665, *684*

Wener, A., 411, *437*

Wenzel, A., 88, *96*

Werba, B., 580, *597*

Wert, D., 744, *764*

Werts, M. G., 662, *686*

West, S. G., 509, *550,* 577, *594*

Westbrook, D., 124, *141*

Wetherby, A., 636, 638, 653, *656–657*

Wever, C., 129–130, *142*

Whalen, C. K., 353, 356–358, *362–364,*
366–369, 371, *373–374, 376,*
384, *404,* 416–417, *435, 437*

Wheeler, T., 13–14, *37,* 328, *350,* 378,
381, *408*

Wheeler, V. A., 82, *94*

Whidby, J. M., 448, *475*

Whitaker, A., *137*

White, M., 283, *293,* 721, *742*

White, R., 663, *681*

Whitehurst, G. J., 525, *555,* 635, *657*

Whitley, M. K., 463, 468, *475*

Whitney, W. M., 188, 192, *216*

Wickramaratne, P., 182, *185*

Wickstrom, S., 679, *682*

Wiebe, D. J., 125, *138*

Wierzbicki, M., *476*

Wigal, T., 13, *38,* 378, *408*

Wiger, D. E., 470, *476*

Wignall, A., 60, *72*

Wikler, L., 613, *626*

Wilcox, B. L., 670, *682*

Wilcox, D. K., 500, *505–506*

Wilde, M. L., 778, *786*

Williams, A., 386, 392, *402*

Williams, C. A., 520, *551*

Williams, E. C., *35*

Williams, J. A., 155, *162,* 229, *235,* 608,
614, *628*

Williams, J. B., *186,* 426, *437*

Williams, K. E., 296, *319*

Williams, R. A., *34*

Williams, S. E., 47, 68, 192, *216,* 244–245,
261

Williams, S. M., 76, *94*

Williamson, D. E., 167, *185,* 244, *261,*
268, *290*

Williard, J. C., 702, *713*

Wills, R. M., 304, 306, *319*

Wilson, D., 663, *681*

Wilson, G. T., 57, 68, 132, *139*

Wilson, J., 296, *318*

Winder, F., 273, *289*

Wineman, D., 558, *573*

Wing, L., 606–607, *631,* 708, *711*

Witmer, H. L., *39*

Wittchen, H. U., 771, *785*

Wolchik, S. A., 778, *787*

Wolery, M., 662, *686*

Wolfe, B., 180, *184*

Wolfe, D. A., 576–577, *594, 597*

Wolff, R., 124, *142*

Wolkow, R., 133, *140*

Wolmer, L., 61, *73*

Wolstenholme, F., 268, *291, 293*

Wood, A., 210, *217,* 220, *237,* 243, *265*

Wood, R., 384, *405*

Wood, V. M., 22, *35*

Wooden, W., 492, *506*

Woods-Cripe, J. J., 676, *680*

Wozencroft, T., 743, *765*

Wrate, R., 269, *293*

Wright, C. M., 782, *787*

Wright, S., 663, *681*

Adolescent Depression Empowerment
    Psychosocial Treatment
    Program
  assessments, 152
  clinical vignette of, 158–159
  future considerations, 161
  goals of, 150–151
  methods used by, 151–158
  outcomes, 159–161
  procedures, 151–152
  treatment used in
    family communication promoted
      by, 156–157
    measures for evaluating, 157–158
    meetings, 152–157
    procedures, 152–157
ADVANCE training program, for family
    training, 520–524, 529–530
Aggressive behavior, 448
Anger management training, for attention-
    deficit/hyperactivity disorder,
    362–363, 366–367
Anorexia, infantile
  assessments of, 300, 302–306
  clinical vignette of, 313–316
  description of, 297
  diagnostic criteria for, 297–298
  mother–infant conflict during feeding
    and, 298–299
  Multidisciplinary Feeding Disorders
    Clinic program for
    assessments, 300, 302–306
    clinical vignette of, 313–316
    malnutrition assessments, 305
    methods, 300–313
    overview of, 299–300
    procedures, 300–302
    treatment
      measures to assess, 312–313
      procedures used in, 306–312
  parental characteristics associated
    with, 298–299
  research regarding, 298–299
  transactional model of, 298
Anorexia nervosa, 14
Anticipatory anxiety, 124
Anxiety disorders
  assessment tools for
    behavioral observations, 52
    children's self-report measures,
      50–51
    parent reports, 52

parental measures, 51
structured diagnostic interviews
    and diagnostic ratings, 50
teacher report of child, 52
behavioral assessment test of, 83
Child and Adolescent Anxiety
    Disorders Clinic program for.
    See Child and Adolescent
    Anxiety Disorders Clinic
Childhood Anxiety and Phobia
    Program for. See Childhood
    Anxiety and Phobia Program
cognitive–behavioral treatment for
  active components of, 65–66
  benefits of, 62–65
  clinical significance of, 62–65
  comorbidity effects on, 64
  description of, 48
  developmental considerations, 57
  example of, 56
  factors that affect outcome of,
    63–65
  family-based, 58–62, 100
  goals of, 52–53
  group-based, 61, 99
  literature review regarding, 99
  long-term follow-up, 62, 66
  outcome of, 63–65
  outcomes studies of, 48
  parental involvement in, 58–62
  parental psychopathology effects,
    66
  practice, 55–56
  process variables, 66–67
  randomized clinical trials of,
    59–62
  relapse prevention, 57
  social-skills training-based, 61
  structure of, 52–53
  transfer of control in, 100
  transportability of, 67
contingency management for,
    106–107
definition of, 43
disorders secondary to, 47
family's role in, 58–59
prevalence of, 43
problem-solving skills for, 54–55
relapse of, 57
relaxation therapy for, 223
self-control strategies for, 106
social anxiety, 77

Deployment-focused model of
  intervention development and
  testing (*continued*)
  goals of, 27–28
  partial effectiveness tests, 30
  questions and answers about,
    32–33
  single-case pilot tests, 29
  steps involved in, 28–32
  sustainability tests, 30–31
Depression
  Adolescent Depression
    Empowerment Psychosocial
    Treatment Program for. *See*
    Adolescent Depression
    Empowerment Psychosocial
    Treatment Program
  in boys, 244–245
  clinical vignette of, 253–259
  cognition disturbances and, 240
  cognitive–behavioral therapy for
    clinical vignette of, 253–259
    description of, 150
    effectiveness studies, 243
    future considerations, 259–261
    outcome research for, 242–243
    parental involvement in, 251
    in Puerto Rican adolescents. *See*
      Depression, in Puerto Rican
      adolescents and children
    relaxation training vs., 243
    studies of, 246–261
    summary of, 245–246
  comorbidities associated with, 145,
    232
  Coping With Depression Course. *See*
    Adolescent Coping With
    Depression Course
  coping with stress and, 241
  emotion regulation and, 241,
    248–249
  family-oriented approaches for, 150
  in girls
    coping skills by, 249
    description of, 244–245
  incidence of, 239
  maternal, 306
  prevalence of, 145
  psychotherapies for
    description of, 166
    interpersonal. *See* Interpersonal
      psychotherapy

  in Puerto Rican adolescents and
    children
    cognitive–behavioral therapy for
      clinical trials of, 207–209
      clinical vignette of, 199–201
      cognitions sessions, 197–198
      concepts of, 193
      content issues, 192–193
      context used in, 194
      description of, 196–197
      developmental issues, 194–195
      efficacy of, 206–209
      goals of, 193
      language adaptations, 191
      manual used in, 191
      methods, 194
      outcome of, 206–209
      people contact sessions, 199
      pleasant activities sessions,
        198–199
      practical–technical issues,
        195–196
      sessions involved in, 196–199
      summary of, 209–211
    epidemiological study of, 189
    interpersonal psychotherapy for
      clinical trials of, 207–209
      clinical vignette of, 205–206
      concepts of, 193
      content issues, 192–193
      context used in, 194
      developmental issues, 195
      efficacy of, 206–209
      goals of, 193
      grief, 202
      initial phase of, 204
      intermediate phase of,
        204–205
      interpersonal deficits, 203
      interpersonal disputes,
        202–203
      language adaptations, 191
      manual used in, 191
      methods, 194
      outcome of, 206–209
      practical–technical issues, 196
      principles of, 201
      problem areas, 201–204
      role transitions, 203
      sessions, 204–205
      summary of, 209–211
      termination phase of, 205

Overstimulation myth, 662–663

Parent(s)
adolescent conflict with, 341–347
adolescent depression and, 268–269
anxiety management by, 60–61
of attention-deficit/hyperactivity
disorder child, 337–341,
381–382, 417–418
child therapies combined with
therapies for, 771–772
in children's friendships, 698–700
coercive behaviors by, 453, 511
cognitive–behavioral treatment
involvement by, 58–62, 251
of conduct disorder child, Incredible
Years Training Program for
BASIC program, 512–519,
527–530, 531–533
benefits of, 530–531
outcomes of, 527–530
prevention programs, 531–533
rationale for, 509–511
significance of, 533
summary of, 533
videotape modeling methods,
511–512
coping training for, 521
infantile anorexia, 298–299
negative affect by, 511
problem-solving skills training for,
521
self-care by, 521
self-control by, 521
social support for, 521
stress experienced by, 468, 622
Parent training
in attention-deficit/hyperactivity
disorder, 337–341, 381–382,
417–418
in autism
assessments, 610–613
clinical vignette of, 618–620
description of, 607
family characteristics effect on,
621–622
family measures, 612–613
future considerations for, 623–624
goals of, 607–610
interventions
delivery of, 617–618
generalizability of, 622–623

individualizing of, 622
motivation, 614–615
outcomes, 620–623
procedures, 614–617
responsivity to multiple cues,
615
self-management, 615–617
issues involved in, 607–610
overview of, 605–606
parent measures, 612–613
reasons for, 606
self-management, 609
studies of, 610–623
in behavioral management skills,
341–344
Incredible Years Training
BASIC program, 512–519,
527–530, 531–533
benefits of, 530–531
outcomes of, 527–530
prevention programs, 531–533
rationale for, 509–511
significance of, 533
summary of, 533
videotape modeling methods,
511–512
parent management training
basis for, 457–458
characteristics of, 454–457
clinical trials of, 459–462
core sessions of, 454–457
description of, 509–510
dropouts, 466
effectiveness of, 459–462
effects of, 462–463
implementation of, 457–459
measures to evaluate, 465
overview of, 453–454
problem-solving skills training
similarities with, 457–458
progress monitoring, 458
school performance addressed by,
457
studies of, 463
unresolved questions regarding,
463–464
Parent–child intervention therapy, for
disruptive behavior
assessments, 578–580
clinical vignette, 586–590
description of, 576
development of, 576–577

summary of, 209–211
treatments for
    adaptations of, 190–196
    cultural sensitivity of, 190
    ecological validity of, 190
    language used in, 191
    metaphors used in, 192
    persons used in, 191–192
    familism importance for, 192–193
Pupil Evaluation Inventory—Teacher, 701

Questionnaire on Resources and Stress, 613

Racial minorities
    demographics of, 187–188
    mental health services for, 188
    population growth of, 187–188
Real-world studies, 779
Reinforced practice, 13
Relaxation therapy
    for anxiety, 223
    for depression, 243
    for obsessive–compulsive disorder, 122–123
Research clinics, 110–112
Research–practice gap, 775
Revised Children's Manifest Anxiety Scale, 103
Revised Edition of the School Observation Coding System, 579–580
Revised Fear Survey Schedule for Children, 102
Role playing, 84
Role transitions
    definition of, 174
    interpersonal psychotherapy for, 174, 203
Running commands, 581

Schizotypy, 131
Selective mutism, 79–80
Selective serotonin reuptake inhibitors
    depression treated with, 166
    obsessive–compulsive disorder treated with, 135
    social phobia treated with, 93
Self-control, 106
Self-initiations, for autism, 638–641, 646–652
Self-schema
    depression and, 240

development of, 240–241
Self-talk, 54
Sense of self, 250–251
Separation anxiety disorder, 773
Sexual abuse
    incidence of, 743
    mental disorders secondary to, 743
    posttraumatic stress disorder caused by. *See* Posttraumatic stress disorder
Shaping, for obsessive–compulsive disorder, 124
Social adaptation, 611
Social Effectiveness Therapy for Adolescents, 92–93
Social Effectiveness Therapy for Children
    assessment, 81
    behavioral assessment test, 83
    comorbid disorders treated with, 80
    components and procedures of
        homework assignments, 88
        in vivo exposure, 86–88
        peer generalization, 86
        psychoeducation, 84
        social skills training, 84–85
    daily diary, 83–84
    development of, 78
    diagnostic interview, 81–82
    efficacy trials for, 92
    future directions for, 92–93
    goals of, 78–79
    lack of cognitive component in, 88–89
    parent ratings, 82–83
    patient considerations, 79–81
    self-report measures, 82
    social skills training, 79–80
    teacher ratings, 82–83
    treatment
        components of, 78–79
        measures of, 89–90
        outcome of, 90–91
Social phobia
    age of onset, 75
    behaviors associated with, 76
    contributing factors, 771–772
    definition of, 75
    emotional reactions associated with, 76
    future directions for, 92–93
    gender distribution of, 76
    major depression and, 80

ABOUT THE EDITORS

Euthymia D. Hibbs, PhD, worked for 25 years at the National Institute of Mental Health (NIMH) in the area of child and adolescent disorders research and psychosocial treatment research. She authored and coauthored a number of research articles, book chapters, and edited books on the topic of mental disorders in children and their families. She has received several professional and civic awards, including one from the American Psychological Association Division 53 (Society of Clinical Child and Adolescent Psychology), for her contributions to the field. She is a diplomate in psychotherapy of the American Psychotherapy Association. Since leaving NIMH, she maintains a private practice and does consulting work.

Peter S. Jensen, MD, is director of the Center for the Advancement of Children's Mental Health at Columbia University in New York and Ruane Professor of Child Psychiatry. Prior to his position at Columbia University, Dr. Jensen was associate director for child and adolescent research at the National Institute of Mental Health (NIMH), where he also served as the lead NIMH investigator on the Multimodal Treatment of ADHD study, as a collaborating investigator for other NIMH multisite studies, and as a member of the planning board for the landmark publication of *Mental Health: A Report of the Surgeon General* (1999). He is the author of over 200 scientific articles and book chapters and is currently president of the International Society for Research on Child and Adolescent Psychopathology.